Contents

Golfing Around Britain: 6
How to Use THE GOLF GUIDE   10
Golf Tours & Golfing Products 11-13
Golf Events 2007   14

Foreword:
Mike Harris (Golf Monthly)   4
Golf in the West Country
Peter Godsiff   17
Golf in the South
Peter Ward   61
Golf in the East
John H. Smith   120
Golf in the Midlands
Jennifer Prentice   162
Golf in the North
David Birtill   221
Golf in Scotland
Nick Rodger   301
Golf in Wales
Chris Smart   399
Golf in Ireland
Tony McGee   437

Holiday Golf in France
Michael Gedye   505
Holiday Golf in Portugal
Michael Gedye   520
Holiday Golf in Spain
Michael Gedye   531
Holiday Golf in the USA
Michael Gedye   540
Holiday Golf in Thailand
Michael Gedye   550

Clubs and Courses

ENGLAND
West   21
South   63
East   124
Midlands   164
North   225
SCOTLAND   308
WALES   402
IRELAND   447
THE ISLE OF MAN   502
CHANNEL ISLANDS   503
FRANCE   509
PORTUGAL   521
SPAIN and MAJORCA   534
CYPRUS   539
USA   544
SOUTH AFRICA   547
DUBAI   549
THAILAND   554
Driving Ranges   559
Index of Clubs and Courses   582
Index of Advertisers/Hotels   619

Foreword

by Mike Harris

Editor of

A YEAR AGO, when I sat down to write my foreword for the 2007 Golf Guide, I reminisced on Europe's momentous Ryder Cup win. I mused that, given such a resounding victory at the K Club, golf fans could look forward to the 2007 Open Championship at Carnoustie with genuine optimism that one of our 'home grown' heroes would emerge from the shadow of US Major Championship domination and lift the Claret Jug.

And so it was when, after four days of quite superb golf, Padraig Harrington emerged from a tense four-hole play-off with Sergio Garcia to be crowned the Champion Golfer for the year. A thoroughly deserved win that owed much to Harrington's dedication to practice and the mental strength that allowed him to bounce back from the potentially crushing blow of making double-bogey on the 72nd hole of regulation play.

Next year, at the 37th Ryder Cup matches, Harrington's grit and skill will be combined with not only Garcia's maverick genius, but also the assembled talents of a European team likely to include players such as Justin Rose, Luke Donald, Lee Westwood and Ian Poulter. Add in the possibility of the highly talented Rory McIlroy making his debut at Valhalla and the transatlantic tussle looks as mouth-watering as ever.

Not since the days of the famous five – Faldo, Lyle, Ballesteros, Woosnam and Langer – has the future looked quite so rosy for European golf.

Watching the game's greats in action always spurs me to get my clubs out from under the stairs and fix up a game. As British and Irish golfers, we are truly blessed with such a fantastic variety of courses to choose from on our doorstep. Be it one of our links layouts that are famed the world over or one of the great variety of inland tracks, there really is something to suit every ability and budget, and there is no better companion than the **The Golf Guide** to help you plan your next golfing away day or holiday.

Now in its 31st year of publication, **The Golf Guide** includes extensive details on almost 3000 courses, along with information on local accommodation, providing travelling golfers with all that is needed to know about where to play and and where to stay anywhere in the UK and Ireland. I hope, like me, you are inspired by the possibilities and that you will spend many happy hours planning your next golfing getaway.

2008
The
Golf Guide
Where to Play, Where to Stay in Britain & Ireland

Over 2800 courses, including a selection in holiday areas abroad, plus convenient accommodation

FHG
·K·U·P·E·R·A·R·D·

© FHG Guides Ltd, 2008
ISBN 978-1-85055-399-1

Maps: ©MAPS IN MINUTES™ / Collins Bartholmew 2007

Typeset by FHG Guides Ltd, Paisley.
Printed and bound in Malaysia by Imago.

Distribution. Book Trade: ORCA Book Services, Stanley House,
3 Fleets Lane, Poole, Dorset BH15 3AJ
(Tel: 01202 665432; Fax: 01202 666219)
e-mail: mail@orcabookservices.co.uk
Published by FHG Guides Ltd., Abbey Mill Business Centre,
Seedhill, Paisley PA1 ITJ (Tel: 0141-887 0428 Fax: 0141-889 7204).
e-mail: admin@fhguides.co.uk

The Golf Guide, Where to Play, Where to Stay is published by FHG Guides Ltd,
part of Kuperard Group.

Cover design: FHG Guides
Cover Pictures: Royal Dublin Golf Club, Adare Manor Golf Resort, courtesy of Fáilte Ireland.

Acknowledgements

The Publishers wish to acknowledge the assistance of Mike Harris of **Golf Monthly** and The Professional Golfers' Association regional golfing correspondents in the preparation of this 31st edition of
THE GOLF GUIDE Where To play, Where To stay.

Photographs
We wish to thank Mike Harris (p4), Peter Godsiff (p17, 18, 19, 20), Carl Markham (p61),
David Birtill (p221, 223), Northumberland National Park Authority (p222), Michael Gedye (p505, 506, 507, 508,
520, 521, 522, 523, 531, 532, 533, 540, 541, 542, 543, 550, 551, 552, 553)

plus all Golf Clubs for sending all photographs used.

We wish to thank all our advertisers and, finally, the Club Secretaries, Professionals and others who have
co-operated in the annual updating of the golf club directory entries which are the essential ingredients of
THE GOLF GUIDE Where To play, Where To stay.

Golfing around Britain and Abroad

Where to Play and Where to Stay around the Golfing Regions

2007 AT LAST PRODUCED a player from Europe capable of claiming the top prize in golf – The Open Championship. Not only did Europe provide the winner in the Irishman Padraig Harrington, it also had the runner-up, with Spaniard Sergio Garcia being narrowly beaten in a play-off.

It is well known that the coverage of tournaments on television encourages many casual golfers to brush off their clubs and to use *The Golf Guide, Where to Play, Where to Stay* to find courses where they can try to emulate the top players. When the contest proves as exciting as the 2007 Open Championship it is no wonder many are inspired.

Carnoustie was the venue again, and it was there in 1999 that the UK last had a winner of the most famous trophy in golf, with Paul Lawrie. On this occasion, Padraig Harrington brought back memories of Jean Van de Velde eight years previously, by not once, but twice, hitting into the Barry Burn on the last hole. Luckily for him Sergio Garcia failed to capitalise, and Harrington went on to win the 4-hole play-off by sinking a three foot putt on the 18th.

The game of golf and the development of golf courses continues to be as popular as ever as shown by the recent announcement by the US Billionaire Donald Trump that he would like to create the 'world's Greatest Golf Course' at Menie Estate in Aberdeenshire, to include a hotel, holiday homes and private housing. Whether such a development will manage to get past all the relevant planning problems is debateable, but it does show the interest and enthusiasm for this game is continuing unabated.

The fact that waiting lists for membership of many golf clubs are not as long as previously might give the impression that such developments might not be necessary. Anyone trying to book a space on a popular course would however disagree. What has changed is the increase in the popularity of 'Casual Golf', which shows up in the mix of players who use the courses.

It is believed that there are over thirty million golfers altogether, but in total there are just under 12 million club members, the remainder playing on a pay-per-play basis or only with friends, colleagues, on holiday, or simply when time permits.

The Golf Guide, Where to Play, Where to Stay caters for every type of golfer and includes details of every variety of course, including seaside links, parkland, moorland, hilly, flat etc, each with its own challenge, difficulties and enjoyments. Using this guide it is possible to plan a trip taking in a wide variety of courses, stopping off at the excellent accommodation recommended for golfers, as featured throughout the guide.

2007 was special for the world number one, Tiger Woods, but not just for his golf. His wife Elin gave birth to a daughter, Sam, and this gave other golfers a better chance of victory later in the year when Tiger took a two month break to concentrate on fatherly duties. Before that he did manage to win his 61st career PGA Tour title, making him only one short of Arnold Palmer's fourth spot in the all-time winners list (Sam Snead leads with 82 wins; Jack Nicklaus has 73 and Ben Hogan 64).

It may be a while until Lorena Ochoa from Mexico, the Ladies number one in the world, has to worry about a 'Woods', but she had a successful year in 2007. She not only achieved her first Major victory by winning the British Open at the Home of Golf in St Andrews, she also won the next two, the Canadian Open and the Safeway Classic, to be the first person since Annika Sorenstam in 2005 to win three straight tournaments.

Golf is not just about the Professionals, the future of the game seems fairly healthy. A large number of youngsters are attracted to the game, partly because of the media attention and partly through the activities of organisations such as the Golf Foundation, supported by people like Nick Faldo, with a programme of short course events for golfers aged 12 and under. Golf is a game to be enjoyed by all standards of player, male, female, young, old, serious or casual. *The Golf Guide, Where to Play, Where to Stay* gives everyone a chance to try some of the 3,000 courses spread throughout the UK, Ireland and selected holiday destinations.

We hope that we have laid out the guide in a manner which will make finding the courses you are interested in as easy as possible. We have worked with the PGA Regional Professionals, who have supplied articles about their regions summarising what is happening in the area and highlighting some of the accommodation and courses of particular interest to give you a brief idea of what is available. We have worked our way through the country starting in the South of the UK with the West Country and the South Region, travelling on to the East and then the Midlands, up to Northern England and following that with the countries of Wales, Scotland and Ireland. We finish with a selection of foreign courses in the most popular tourist destinations.

We have included detailed indexes at the back of the guide to make it as easy as possible to find any of the 3000 individual courses and

the hundreds of hotels featured in this, the most comprehensive of guides. If you make full use of the guide you will have a chance to get as much, if not more, enjoyment out of the game as any top professional, without the pressures they are constantly under.

If you do manage to visit a variety of new courses in 2008 please do remember a few basic rules to ensure that you are welcomed back. Basically, you should behave as you would like visitors to your own course to behave. We all know that we should rake bunkers (replacing the rake in its original position), repair pitch marks on greens and replace divots on fairways; but remember that the main thing that annoys most golfers is slow play – the holiday mood can cause even experienced golfers to walk more slowly, enjoying the scenery, talking more and forgetting about the job in hand. All this is fine if the course is quiet, but will not be appreciated if there are members behind looking to fit in a quick round.

All golfers, whether they play every day of the year or only on the occasional golfing holiday, can benefit from finding out the information about courses available in different areas, which ones will accept visitors and what the likely cost will be. Making full use of this guide can give all types of golfers the details they need to get the most enjoyment from the game.

One of the greatest pleasures is to enjoy a challenging game of golf and follow that by a relaxing evening spent in one of the many hotels featured in this guide. Comfort and good food is par for the course when seeking an overnight stay and remember that golfing out of season can have many advantages. Hotels are often willing to offer discount rates for short breaks in the winter months and there is something special about teeing off on a crisp winter morning with the sun sparkling on the grass.

No matter where you go in the UK or abroad, remember to take your copy of *The Golf Guide, Where to Play, Where to Stay* with you, and we would appreciate it if you could mention the guide when you contact Courses or Accommodation.

Golfing National Regions

England & Wales

North Region
Cheshire • Cumbria • Durham
Gt. Manchester • Lancashire
Merseyside • Northumberland
Tyne and Wear • Yorkshire

Isle of Man & Channel Islands
Isle of Man
Channel Islands

Midland Region
Derbyshire • Herefordshire
Leicestershire & Rutland
Lincolnshire • Northamptonshire
Nottinghamshire • Shropshire
Staffordshire • Warwickshire
West Midlands • Worcestershire

Wales
Anglesey & Gwynedd
North Wales • Ceredigion
Carmarthenshire
Pembrokeshire
Powys • South Wales

East Region
Bedfordshire
Cambridgeshire
Essex
Greater London
Hertfordshire
Norfolk
Suffolk

Some London clubs
are in **East Region**

West Region
Cornwall
Devon • Dorset
Gloucestershire
Somerset
Wiltshire

South Region
Berkshire • Buckinghamshire • Greater London
Hampshire and Isle of Wight
Kent • Oxfordshire • Surrey • Sussex

Scotland
Borders • Central • Dumfries and Galloway
Fife • Highland • Lothians
Orkney and Shetland
Strathclyde • Tayside
Western Isles

Northern Ireland
Antrim • Armagh • Co. Down
Fermanagh • Londonderry • Tyrone

Republic of Ireland
Carlow • Cavan
Clare • Cork
Donegal • Dublin
Galway • Kerry
Kildare • Kilkenny
Laois • Leitrim
Longford • Louth
Mayo • Meath
Monaghan
Offaly • Roscommon
Sligo • Tipperary
Waterford • Westmeath
Wexford • Wicklow

ENJOY PERFECT *Golf*

MACDONALD HOTELS & RESORTS OFFERS LUXURIOUS PROPERTIES WHERE YOU CAN ENJOY THE PERFECT ROUND OF GOLF

Experience impeccable courses then step inside and discover exceptional service, fine cuisine and first class accommodation.

MACDONALD PORTAL HOTEL, GOLF & SPA, TARPORLEY, CHESHIRE

The spectacular hotel is located within the rolling hills of Cheshire and is an established championship golf venue with three courses, golf academy and luxurious spa facilities.

MACDONALD LINDEN HOTEL, GOLF & COUNTRY CLUB, MORPETH, NORTHUMBERLAND

Built in 1812 and situated in 450 acres of beautiful countryside, the magnificent Linden Hall boasts a championship golf course, as well as exceptional service, hospitality and accommodation.

MACDONALD BOTLEY PARK HOTEL, GOLF AND COUNTRY CLUB, SOUTHAMPTON

Located amidst Hampshire's picturesque countryside and with a championship golf course and superb facilities, Botley Park is the ideal location for a round of golf.

MACDONALD HILL VALLEY HOTEL, GOLF & COUNTRY CLUB, WHITCHURCH, SHROPSHIRE

With stunning views over two impeccable golf courses and a luxury spa opening in January 2008, the hotel is the perfect place to stay, play and unwind.

"It's a privilege for me to be associated with Macdonald Golf Hotels & Resorts because their excellent golf courses offer enjoyment for serious and social golfers" **Sandy Lyle, Golf Ambassador, Macdonald Hotels & Resorts**.

 AA Hotel Group of the Year Winner 2007-8

MACDONALD
HOTELS & RESORTS

For our best available rates visit www.MacdonaldHotels.co.uk or call 0870 400 9090

How to use this Golf Guide

The Golf Guide, Where to play, Where to stay contains up to date basic information on every course (as far as we know) in Britain and Northern Ireland. Details are provided by the clubs themselves. You will also find sections on the Irish Republic plus holiday golf in Spain and Majorca, Portugal, France, the USA, South Africa, Dubai and Thailand.

The guide carries entries from hotels, guest houses and other accommodation convenient to specific courses or areas. These are generally 'paid' entries and usually follow a recommendation from a club.

The Golf Guide, Where to play, Where to stay in association with Golf Monthly, is usually available for sale in golf clubs through the Professional and/or the Secretary, as well as bookshops etc.

• Golf Course Information

For virtually every course you will find the following details, updated annually:

1. Name, address and telephone number.   2. Location.   3. Brief description.

4. Number of holes, length and Standard Scratch Score.   5. Green fees.

6. Details of facilities for visitors – individuals, groups and societies.

7. Name and telephone number of the Professional and the Secretary.

The accuracy of details published depends on the response of the clubs and to our best knowledge is correct at the time of going to press (October 2007). Where entry details have not been confirmed an asterisk (*) is shown.

• Choosing a Course

The golf clubs and courses are listed alphabetically by nearest town or village within the appropriate region and county section for England, Scotland, Wales, Ireland, the Isle of Man and the Channel Islands. Courses overseas are also listed by region. We have chosen to classify by place-name rather than club or course name since this seems more straightforward and recognisable to the majority.

If you want to find a club or course by its name, you should simply refer to the Index where you will see the page number of the listing. In each entry the name of the club or course is always shown in bold type after the place-name heading.

• Accommodation

Most of the accommodation advertised has been recommended by the local golf club, and the entries are placed as near a particular club or course as possible. A full index is provided.

The location details supplied with each entry should get you there and if you are in any doubt at all you should ask directions from the club itself.

Please mention *The Golf Guide, Where to play, Where to stay* when you make a hotel booking or play at courses after using our guide.

Golf Tours & Golfing Products

Golfing Tours

HeritageGolfToursScotland

Golf Tours customised to your own requirements.

We provide carefully selected Accommodation, Car Hire and Pre-Booked Tee Times.

Standard Tours also available

For further information visit our website:

www.golftours-scotland.co.uk

e-mail: hgolftours@aol.com
Tel: 01436 674630

Check our prices –
you will be pleasantly surprised

SCOTIA CHARTERS
FORT WILLIAM, SCOTLAND

Luxury charter vessel to be based in Corpach, Fort William, providing a very high standard of accommodation and facilities for 8-10 passengers as well as excellent traditional cuisine cooked onboard with overnight berthing along Scotland's coastline.

Cruises available primarily featuring golf tours, but will also incorporate trips including: other sporting activities, the famous Scottish historic and heritage sites and scenic trips along Scotland's coastline. The vessel will also be ideal for corporate/conference use and equipped with the necessary facilities.

Use of our private courtesy bus for transfers to and from airports and ferry terminals.
Individual golf itineraries arranged to suit your needs.
Available 2008, call for further information.

15 Skerry Drive, Peterhead, Aberdeenshire, Scotland AB24 2YH
Tel: 01779 479216   Fax: 01779 473416
Mobile: 07976 897332

skipper@scotiacharters.co.uk
www.scotiacharters.co.uk

Golf Tee-Time Service

Golf Tee-Time Service offers the complete range of golfing services. From tee-time bookings, Brittany Ferries golf breaks in France/Northern Spain, Golf breaks in Wales and Portugal, through to large corporate golf days. Please phone **01822 618181** for more information on any of our services or visit **www.golfteetimeservice.co.uk** (e-mail info@golfteetimeservice.co.uk).

- **Tournaments:** For competitive golf with a friendly atmosphere played on superb courses. We have a tournament programme.
- **Corporate Management:** A total solution-why waste time, money and precious resources organising your golf day.
- **Tee-Time Booking:** We specialise in organising pre-reserved tee-times in Portugal, Spain, France, Mallorca, UK and Ireland.
- **UK Specials:** Offering superb value for short breaks at some great locations.
- **World-Wide Golf:** Golf holidays in Madeira, Barbados, Bermuda, USA and other exotic locations.
- **Brittany Ferries Golf Desk** 0870-9021818. We manage the Brittany Ferries Golf Desk and can offer superb golf in France.
- **Greens of Southern Wales** 0870-600608. Golf breaks in Wales.
- **Golf in Portugal** 0870-8506124 Golf breaks in Portugal.

Golfing Products

ASHWORTH GOLF COMPANY | **NICK WATNEY** / PGA TOUR PRO

A selection of Golf Events in 2008

APRIL

Duncan Putter
Southerndown — *April 16-17*

Peter McEvoy Trophy
Copt Heath — *April 26-27*

Trubshaw Cup
Ashburnham/Tenby — *April 26-27*

MAY

Lytham Trophy
Royal Lytham & St Anne's — *May 2-4*

English Men's Stroke Play Championship (Brabazon Trophy)
Trevose Golf Club — *May 16-18*

English Ladies' Close Amateur Championship
Ganton Golf Club — *May 13-17*

Ladies Close Championship
Pyle & Kenfig — *May 18-21*

Welsh Open Stroke Play Championship
Conwy — *May 23-25*

JUNE

Welsh Open Youths' Championship
Vale of Llangollon — *May 31st - June 1*

English Seniors' Championship
Wildernesse & Knole Park — *June 4-6*

St Andrews Links Trophy
St Andrews — *June 6-8*

Welsh Seniors' Championship
Aberdovey — *June 10-12*

Ladies' British Amateur Championship
North Berwick — *June 11-15*

British Amateur Championship
Turnberry — *June 21-22*

Berkshire Trophy
Berkshire — *June 21-22*

Wales Seniors', Open
Newport — *June 24-26*

Aberconwy Trophy
Maesdu/Conwy — *June 28-29*

JULY

Open Championship
Royal Birkdale — *July 17-20*

Welsh Boys' Open Championship
Newport — *July 22-24*

Senior British Open Championship
Royal Troon — *July 24-27*

AUGUST

Welsh Amateur Championships
Royal Porthcawl — *July 29th – August 2*

Women's British Open
Sunningdale — *July 31st - August 3*

Boys' Home Internationals
Royal County Down — *August 5-7*

Girls' Home InternationalS
Panmuir (Barry) — *August 5-7*

British Seniors' Open Amateur Championship
Royal Cinque Port & Prince's Course — *August 6-8*

Girls' British Open Amateur Championship
Monifieth — *August 11-15*

Boys' Amateur Championship
Little Aston — *August 11-16*

Welsh Team Championship
Northop — *August 14-18*

Ladies' British Open Amateur Stroke Play Championship
Belvoir Park — *August 20-22*

English Mid-Amateur Championship
Shifnal — *August 22-24*

SEPTEMBER

Ladies' Home Internationals
Wrexham — *September 10-12*

Senior Ladies' British Open Amateur Championship
Hilton Templepatrick — *September 16-18*

Welsh Inter Counties Championship
Borth & Ynyslas — *September 21*

OCTOBER

Seniors Home Internationals
Tenby — *October 1-3*

LEGOLAND® WINDSOR SCORES A 'MOLE-IN-ONE'

A new 18-hole mini-golf attraction called 'Mole-In-One' has opened at LEGOLAND® Windsor. The woodland-themed course includes LEGO® brick models of squirrels, foxes, moles and otters as well as beautiful water features set in a stunning landscaped location.

Each hole has a different woodland animal theme and like all of the park's attractions, they focus on interactive, hands-on entertainment. There is even a special 'Heroes Hole' just for younger golfers so playing against an adult couldn't be more fun!

The new course is located in the DUPLO® Land area of the park and during the peak season 'Mole-In-One' can be separated into two nine hole courses to reduce waiting times. One of the nine hole courses is fully wheelchair accessible.

National leisure contractor, Western Log Group, was commissioned to build the £300,000 outdoor attraction and this latest addition to the Berkshire theme park is a joint venture project between two companies.

Vicky Brown, general manager of LEGOLAND® Windsor commented: "Our attractions are all about interacting and learning through play. The Mole-In-One mini-golf course allows children to practice new skills and have fun with their families at the same time so fits perfectly into a day here at the park."

www.legoland.co.uk

England and Wales • Counties

Unitary Authorities – England & Wales

1. Plymouth	12. Windsor & Maidenhead	23. Milton Keynes	34. Blackpool		**NORTH WALES**
2. Torbay	13. Bracknell Forest	24. Peterborough	35. N.E. Lincolnshire	a.	Denbighshire
3. Poole	14. Wokingham	25. Leicester	36. North Lincolnshire	b.	Flintshire
4. Bournemouth	15. Reading	26. Nottingham	37. Kingston-upon-Hull	c.	Wrexham
5. Southampton	16. West Berkshire	27. Derby	38. York		
6. Portsmouth	17. Swindon	28. Telford & Wrekin	39. Redcar & Cleveland		**SOUTH WALES**
7. Brighton & Hove	18. Bath & Northeast Somerset	29. Stoke-on-Trent	40. Middlesborough	d.	Swansea
8. Medway	19. North Somerset	30. Warrington	41. Stockton-on-Tees	e.	Neath & Port Talbot
9. Thurrock	20. Bristol	31. Halton	42. Darlington	f.	Bridgend
10. Southend	21. South Gloucestershire	32. Merseyside	43. Hartlepool	g.	Rhondda Cynon Taff
11. Slough	22. Luton	33. Blackburn with Darwen		h.	Merthyr Tydfil
				i.	Vale of Glamorgan
				j.	Cardiff
				k.	Caerphilly
				l.	Blaenau Gwent
				m.	Torfaen
				n.	Newport
				o.	Monmouthshire

Golf in the West

Peter Godsiff

Cornwall · Devon · Dorset
Gloucestershire · Somerset · Wiltshire

Saunton Golf Club, Braunton, Devon

MARK GORMAN, the new professional at South Devon club Bigbury, near Plymouth, reminded me the other day of the size of the county of Devon. He said: "I played in a Pro-Am at Royal North Devon and it was nearly 100 miles away."

The distance from north to south Cornwall is minimal in comparison but there are still many miles ahead of you when you enter the county from the North and head for Land's End.

This just shows what a vast area is covered by this flourishing golfing region, especially as Somerset, Dorset, Wiltshire and Gloucestershire

are included.

It is easy to list the great courses in the area – the championship links at St Enodoc, Saunton, Royal North Devon and Burnham and Berrow, where major English Golf Union championships visit on an almost annual basis.

Trevose Golf and Country Club, possibly my favourite complex in the whole region, joins its more illustrious neighbours on the EGU map by staging the 2008 Brabazon Trophy.

But there are so many links, parkland, heathland, downland and moorland layouts that it would take the best part of a year to play them all, even playing every day, and the green fees, all-important to the holiday traveller, vary enormously. There are marvellous courses costing less than £20 a round, and even a visit to the leading links can be less than £50.

Compare that with rates at courses in Spain, Portugal, Ireland and the elsewhere, and it is easy to understand the attractions of the West Country. Millions of tourists and golfers happily brave the M5 congestion every year because they are looking forward to what lies in store. The problem is choosing where to stop and where to play.

The gateway from the north is Gloucestershire. The Cotswolds provide a perfect stopover for a round of golf, as well as sightseeing, with stone-built towns and villages, and long, fascinating main streets dotted with antique shops, tea rooms, traditional pubs and hotels.

There are a number of play and stay hotel courses. Forest Hills and the nearby Bells Hotel Forest of Dean course staged a West Region Order of Merit tournament last year. The lavish

Hilton Puckrup Hall Hotel and nearby Tewkesbury Park and Gloucester Ramada Hotel also provide everything a golfer needs. Thornbury Golf Centre and the impressive 36-hole Tracy Park complex, now renamed The Park, are close to the Georgian city of Bath, and to Bristol. Here there are golf courses to satisfy every taste and level of play, while both cities claim some of the highest quality hotels in the country.

Bournemouth and Torquay are two popular holiday centres and both offer high standards of golf. The Dorset Golf and Country Club near Wareham boasts a hotel and pine lodges as well as a 27-hole course in the tranquil heart of the county.

Devon has several major hotel and golf complexes, the most exclusive and expensive being Bovey Castle on the fringe of Dartmoor, at Moretonhampstead. The revamped course glides through a magnificent rural setting with hidden streams. Others include Dartmouth Golf and Country Club, and the Ashbury holiday and golfing centre at Okehampton, where good golf

18th at Parkstone Golf Club, Poole, Dorset

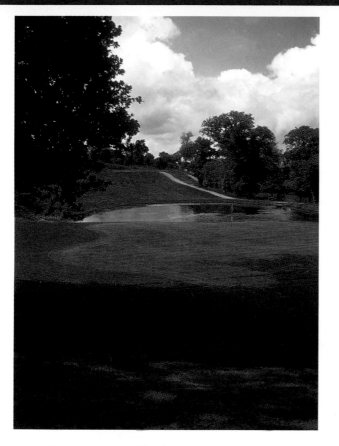

6th hole at Lanhydrock
Golf Club,
Bodmin, Cornwall

is supplemented by activities for the whole family. Nigel Mansell's Woodbury Park, with its new 55-bedroom hotel, is just a few minutes from the M5 motorway at Exeter.

Cornwall offers an alternative choice of residential golf packages. Brend Hotels own the Carlyon Bay Hotel, near St Austell, with an 18-hole clifftop course, as well as others in the region.

Crown Golf are the new owners of the Jack Nicklaus-designed championship course at St Mellion that once hosted the Benson and Hedges International on the European Tour. There are plans to project the club on to the European stage again, and having a hotel as well as many other properties on site is an obvious attraction.

The Treglos Hotel, just a wedge away from Trevose, also owns nearby Merlin golf course, where patrons enjoy playing at bargain rates.

Trethorne, near the historic town of Launceston, is another vastly improving course where accommodation is available.

If staying in a caravan in the middle of a golf course appeals to you, try the rolling links at Perranporth, or the Honiton course. Both have their own caravans on site.

Bowood Park is another emerging course with a hotel dedicated to golfers and golf packages, and Lostwithiel is also an affordable and delightful country hotel and golf course.

There is every conceivable activity in the West to cater for the needs of golfers and their families, with a wide variety of attractions as well as breathtaking landscapes, coastlines, beaches and all kinds of water-based sports.

There are simply so many places to stay and play in what is surely the country's favourite holiday area.

4th hole at Trevose Golf & Country Club, Padstow, Cornwall

Cornwall

BODMIN, **Lanhydrook Hotel & Golf Club,** Lostwithiel Road, Bodmin PL30 5AQ (01208 262570; Fax: 01208 262579). *Location:* 1½ miles outside Bodmin on B3269. Parkland with generous tees and greens, easy walking, with many natural water features. 18 holes, 6100 yards, 5600 metres, Par 70, S.S.S. 70. Practice range. *Green Fees:* on application. One week unlimited golf pass available. *Eating facilities:* full catering facilities available, Bistro restaurant, two bars. *Visitors:* welcome all week, booking advised. Pro shop, golf buggies available. 44-bedroom luxury hotel, conference facilities. *Society Meetings:* welcome by arrangement, private suite available. Professional: to be appointed. Manager: Graham Bond.
e-mail: info@lanhydrockhotel.com
website: www.lanhydrockhotel.com

BUDE. **Bude and North Cornwall Golf Club,** Burn View, Bude EX23 8DA (01288 352006; Fax: 01288 356855). *Location:* seaside links course situated in the centre of the town adjacent to beaches. 18 holes, 6006 yards. S.S.S. 70. Practice net and grounds. *Green Fees:* weekdays £27.00 per day; weekends £27.00 per round. *Eating facilities:* restaurant and bar snacks. *Visitors:* welcome without reservation. Snooker, billiards and pool. *Society Meetings:* catered for by bookings. Professional: John Yeo (01288 353635). Secretary: Mrs Pauline Ralph (01288 352006).

CAMBORNE. **Tehidy Park Golf Club,** Cot Road, Camborne TR14 0HH (Tel & Fax: 01209 842208). *Location:* A30 via Blackwater and Camborne by-passes to sign for Portreath. Parkland, wooded, 3 new lakes. 18 holes, 6241 yards. S.S.S. 71. *Green Fees:* weekdays £25.00, weekends £30.00. *Eating facilities:* bar snacks, à la carte restaurant except Mondays. *Visitors:* welcome with Handicap Certificate. *Society Meetings:* by arrangement; early booking essential. Catering Manager: M&K Hoyle (01209 842557). Professional: J. Lamb (01209 842914). Secretary/Manager Ian Veale (Tel & Fax: 01209 842208).
secretary-manager@tehidyparkgolfclub.co.uk
website: www.tehidyparkgolfclub.co.uk

The 4th hole at Trevose Golf & Country Club

CAMELFORD. **Bowood Park Hotel & Golf Course,** Lanteglos, Camelford PL32 9RF (01840 213017; Fax: 01840 212622). *Location:* M4, M5, A30, A39 through Camelford, turn right to Boscastle/Tintagel before BP garage, then left after Park Lane Motors. Well groomed, parkland course set in 230 acres of rolling hills and woodland with 26 ponds and lakes. 18 hole, par 72. Covered driving range and Golf School. *Green Fees:* price on application. *Eating facilities:* full restaurant and bar facilities. *Visitors:* welcome. Large, well-stocked Pro Shop. Buggies for hire. Hotel accommodation available in 31 spacious en suite rooms, most with golf views. *Society Meetings:* society and corporate days welcome by arrangement. Professional: Tony Nash. Hotel Manager: Tony Nash. •
e-mail: info@bowoodpark.org
website: www.bowoodpark.org

CARLYON BAY. **Carlyon Bay Hotel Golf Course,** Beach Road, Carlyon Bay, St Austell PL25 3RD (Hotel: 01726 812304; Golf Club: 01726 814250). *Location:* St Austell A390. Clifftop course running into parkland. 18 holes, 6597 yards. S.S.S. 71. Six acre practice ground. *Green Fees*: £25.00 to £42.00 depending on season. *Eating facilities*: bar open 11am to 11pm, food available during high season 10am to 9pm Tuesday to Friday, 10am to 6pm Saturday to Monday. *Visitors:* welcome, must phone Professional for starting times. Accommodation available in 4 star hotel. *Society Meetings:* catered for by arrangement. Professional: Mark Rowe (01726 814228). Director of Golf: Paul Martin (01726 814250). e-mail: golf@carlyonbay.com
website: www.carlyonbay.com

FALMOUTH. **Budock Vean Golf and Country House Hotel,** Near Mawnan Smith, Falmouth TR11 5LG (01326 250288; Fax: 01326 250892). *Location:* near Mawnan Smith, Falmouth – area of Helford River. 9 holes/18 tees, 5227 yards. Par 68. S.S.S. 65. *Green Fees:* weekdays £23.00, weekends and Bank Holidays £27.00. *Eating facilities:* two bars, two restaurants, lunchtime bar menu. *Visitors:* daily only for outside visitors who are most welcome, but must have Handicap Certificate and book start time. Hotel accommodation. Secretary: D. McFarlane (01326 252102). Golf Manager: A. Ramsden.

FALMOUTH. **Falmouth Golf Club,** Swanpool Road, Falmouth TR11 5BQ (01326 311262 / 314296; Fax: 01326 317783). *Location:* quarter of a mile west of Swanpool Beach, Falmouth, on the road to Maenporth. Magnificent course with stunning sea and coastal views. 18 holes, 6037 yards. S.S.S. 70, Par 71. Driving range. *Green Fees:* please ring for excellent rates. *Eating facilities:* excellent catering and bar all year round. *Visitors:* welcome at all times, except during major competitions. *Society Meetings:* always welcome. Professional: Nick Rogers. Director: Steve Burrows.

HELSTON. **Helston Golf,** Redruth Road, Wendron, Helston TR13 0LX (Golf: 01326 572228; Restaurant: 01326 565103). *Location:* one mile out of Helston on B3297 Redruth Road. Parkland course. 18 holes, 2000 yards. S.S.S. 54. Nets and practice green. *Green Fees:* £7.50 per 18 holes, day card £10.50. *Eating facilities:* licensed bar with meals and snacks. *Visitors:* welcome; family course, all ages welcome, pay and play; playable all weather. Club and ball hire £1.50. *Society Meetings:* all welcome, please book. Proprietor: J.M.Othen.

HELSTON. **Mullion Golf Club,** Cury, Helston TR12 7BP (01326 241176). *Location:* from Helston on the A3083 past Culdrose Air Station, take first right past roundabout; signposted three miles. Cliff top and links. Indoor Golf Teaching Academy. 18 holes, 6083 yards. S.S.S. 70. *Green Fees:* £25.00 per round, £30.00 per day weekdays, £30.00 per round, £35.00 per day weekends. *Eating facilities:* bar and catering available each day. Caterers: (01326 241231). *Visitors:* welcome, with Handicap only. *Society Meetings:* by prior arrangement. Professional: Ian Harris (01326 241176). Secretary/Treasurer: G. Fitter (01326 240685)

HELSTON. **RNAS Culdrose Golf Club,** Royal Naval Air Station, Helston TR12 7RH (01326 552413). *Location:* A3083 one mile from Helston towards Lizard. Flat parkland course built around part of the airfield. 18 holes, 6132 yards. S.S.S. 70. Large practice area. *Visitors:* members only. President: RNAS Culdrose.*

LAUNCESTON. **Launceston Golf Club,** St Stephen's, Launceston PL15 8HF (01566 773442). *Location:* one mile north of town on Bude road (B3254). Parkland. 18 holes, 6407 yards. S.S.S. 71. *Green Fees:* weekdays £28.00 per round, £35.00 per day. Subject to review. *Eating facilities:* available. *Visitors:* welcome. *Society Meetings:* catered for. Professional: J. Tozer (01566 775359). Secretary: P. M. Jones (01566 773442; Fax: 01566 777506). e-mail: secretary@tiscali.co.uk website: www.launcestongolfclub.co.uk

LAUNCESTON. **Trethorne Golf Club,** Kennards House, Launceston PL15 8QE (01566 86903). *Location:* 200 yards off A30. Set in a picturesque valley with mature trees and water. 18 holes, 6432 yards. S.S.S. 68/69/71. Driving range, putting green. *Green Fees:* from £24.00, early bird and twilight from £15.00. *Eating facilities:* bar, lounge bar and restaurant seating 150. *Visitors:* welcome, please ring for tee times. Accommodation available in 35 en suite bedrooms at the Club. Driving range available. *Society Meetings:* welcome, from £21.00. Groups of 12 or more. Professional: Bobby Moore. Proprietor: Jon Grainger. e-mail: reservations@trethornegolfclub.com website: www.trethornegolfclub.com

LOOE. **Looe Golf Club,** Bindown, Looe PL13 1PX (01503 240239; Fax: 01503 240864). *Location:* three miles east of Looe on A387. Downland/parkland, panoramic views over countryside to sea; designed by Harry Vardon. 18 holes, 5940 yards. S.S.S. 69. Large practice ground. *Green Fees:* on application. *Eating facilities:* catering available. *Visitors:* most welcome, phone for tee reservations. Clubs, buggies and electric trolleys for hire. Golf tuition available. *Society Meetings:* welcome by arrangement. Professional: Jason Bowen. Secretary: Tony Day. e-mail: enquiries@looegolfclub.co.uk website: www.looegolfclub.co.uk

LOSTWITHIEL. **Lostwithiel Hotel, Golf and Country Club,** Lower Polscoe, Lostwithiel PL22 0HQ (01208 873550; Fax: 01208 873479). *Location:* off A390, Lostwithiel. Parkland course. 18 holes, 5984 yards. S.S.S. 71. Driving range and practice area. *Green Fees:* information not available. *Eating facilities:* bar and restaurant. *Visitors:* welcome by prior arrangement. 21 bedroomed 3 Star Hotel. *Society Meetings:* welcome by prior arrangement. e-mail: reception@golf-hotel.co.uk website: www.golf-hotel.co.uk

NEWQUAY. **Merlin Golf Club and Driving Range,** St Eval Road, Mawgan Porth, Newquay TR8 4DN (01841 540222; Fax: 01841 541031). *Location:* on coast road between Newquay and Padstow, after Mawgan Porth take St Eval Road, golf course on right. Heathland, fairly flat course. 18 holes, 6210 yards. S.S.S. 71. Covered driving range. *Green Fees:* £15.00-£22.00 for 18 holes. *Eating facilities:* catering and bar all year round. *Visitors:* very welcome, some restrictions during club competitions. Buggies, carts and clubs for hire. Luxury self-catering apartments available all year. *Society Meetings:* very welcome. Secretary: Mr Richard Burrough.

NEWQUAY. **Newquay Golf Club,** Tower Road, Newquay TR7 1LT (01637 874354). *Location:* 400 yards from Newquay Town Centre. Gently undulating seaside course running parallel to the beach and open to wind. Breathtaking views. 18 holes, 6155 yards, S.S.S. 69. *Green Fees:* information not available. *Eating facilities:* lunches and bar snacks, evening meal by arrangement with the caterer on 01637 872091. *Visitors:* welcome at all times, please telephone. *Society Meetings:* catered for except Saturdays and Sundays. Professional: (01637 874830). Secretary: G. Binney (01637 874354; Fax: 01637 874066).

NEWQUAY. **Treloy Golf Club,** Newquay TR7 4JN (01637 878554). *Location:* five minutes' drive from Newquay on the A3059 Newquay to St. Columb Major road. Parkland. 9 hole Executive golf course. First of its kind in Cornwall – sculptured greens, American Pencross grass, extensive mouldings and bunkers. 9 holes, 2143 yards, 1955 metres. Par 32. Practice green. *Green Fees:* information not available. *Eating facilities:* available, bar. *Visitors:* welcome. *Society Meetings:* welcome. Changing facilities, golf shop, club hire and buggy hire. Secretary: Jane Paull.*

The 18th hole at Trethorne Golf Club

NEWQUAY near. **Carvynick Golf and Country Club,** Carvynick, Summercourt, Near Newquay (01872 510716; Fax: 01872 510172). *Location:* turn off the A30 at Summercourt then take B3058 towards Newquay. Half a mile on left. Parkland and wooded course. 9 holes, 1246 yards. S.S.S. 27. *Green Fees:* information not available. *Eating facilities:* at 16th century village inn and restaurant. *Visitors:* welcome all year. Sauna, gym, indoor swimming pool and badminton court. Luxury holiday cottages available.
e-mail: info@carvynick.co.uk
website: www.carvynick.co.uk*

NEWQUAY near. **Holywell Bay Golf Club,** Holywell Bay, Near Newquay TR8 5PW (01637 832916; Fax: 01637 831000). *Location:* take A3075 out of Newquay then follow signs to Holywell Bay and Cubert. Par 3 Links course. 18 holes, 2755 yards. Pitch and putt. "Best in Cornwall". Open 7 days a week, all year round. *Green Fees:* £15.00 (to include hire of half set of clubs); £11.50 (with own clubs). Fees under review. *Eating facilities:* bar and club house open April to October. *Visitors:* welcome at all times. Accommodation at Trevornick Holiday Park. *Society Meetings:* all welcome, ring for special prices. Secretary: R. Hartley (01637 832916).

PADSTOW. **Trevose Golf and Country Club,** Constantine Bay, Padstow PL28 8JB (01841 520208; Fax: 01841 521057). *Location:* M5 to A30 to A39 to B3274. At St Merryn turn right for golf club. Links course, superb test of golf in lovely coastal setting. H. Colt designed Championship course 18 holes,

6863 yards. S.S.S. 73. 9 hole full length course (Par 35) and one 9 hole short course (Par 29). *Green Fees:* information not available. *Eating facilities:* Club house with bar and restaurant providing à la carte catering facilities. *Visitors:* welcome if arranged by telephone beforehand; Handicap Certificate required. Accommodation, three tennis courts, heated swimming pool in summer. *Society Meetings:* welcome if arrangements have been made. Head Professional: Gary Lenaghan (01841 520261). Secretary: Nick Gammon (01841 520733).
e-mail: admin@trevose-gc.co.uk
website: www.trevose-gc.co.uk

PENZANCE. **Cape Cornwall Golf & Country Club,** Cape Cornwall, St Just, Penzance TR19 7NL (Tel & Fax: 01736 788611). *Location:* A30 to Land's End, A3071 from Penzance to St Just, turn left at clock tower to Cape Cornwall. Cliff top course with spectacular coastal views. 18 holes, 5650 yards. S.S.S. 68, Par 70. Practice putting green and golf area. *Green Fees:* Information not avaulable. *Eating facilities:* restaurant open daily; extensive à la carte evening menu Tues-Sat evenings incl. *Visitors:* welcome anytime. Accommodation available on site. Leisure facilities: gymnasium, indoor heated swimming pool, sauna, tanning suite. Golf shop now permanently on site. *Society Meetings:* welcome; prior booking advisable. PGA Professional: Scott Richards. Club Owners: E. Keddie, U. Handley.*
e-mail: info@capecornwall.com
website: www.capecornwall.com

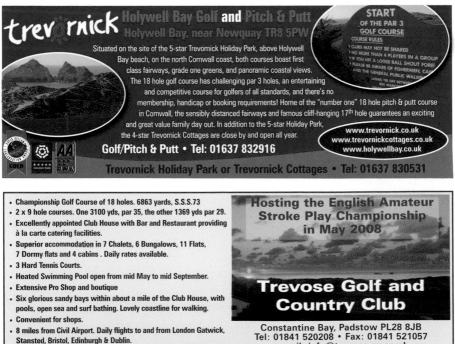

PENZANCE **Praa Sands Golf Club,** Germoe Crossroads, Near Penzance TR20 9TQ (01736 763445; Fax: 01736 763399). *Location:* midway between Helston and Penzance on A394. Parkland - beautiful sea views from all holes. 9 holes, 4122 yards. S.S.S. 60 men, 63 ladies, Par 62. Putting green and net. *Green Fees:* information not available. *Eating facilities:* restaurant, bar snacks. *Visitors:* welcome at all times without Handicap Certificate except Sunday mornings. Clubs and trolleys for hire. *Society Meetings:* catered for by arrangement. Secretary: Simon Edwards. Proprietors: Kate and David Phillips. e-mail:praasandsgolf@aol.com

PERRANPORTH. **Perranporth Golf Club,** Budnic Hill, Perranporth TR6 0AB. Seaside links course overlooking Perranporth and beach. 18 holes, 6272 yards. S.S.S. 72. Par 72. Practice green. *Green Fees*: £25.00 to £35.00. *Eating facilities*: lunch and dinner. *Visitors*: welcome without reservation. Accommodation and buggies available. *Society Meetings*: catered for with advance notice; concessionary rates. Professional: D. Michell (01872 572317). Secretary: David Mugford (01872 573701). website: www.perranporthgolfclub.com

REDRUTH. **Radnor Golf and Ski Centre,** Radnor Road, Treleigh, Redruth TR16 5EL (01209 211059). *Location*: two miles north east of Redruth, signposted from A3047 at Treleigh and North Country crossroads. Purpose-built Par 3 - interesting layout. 9 holes, 1312 yards. S.S.S. 52. Covered driving range. *Green Fees:* information not available. *Eating facilities:* coffee, tea etc, *Visitors:* welcome. Indoor ski training machine. Small touring caravan site. Professional: Gordon Wallbank*

ST AUSTELL. **St Austell Golf Club,** Tregongeeves, Tregongeeves Lane, St Austell PL26 7DS (01726 74756; Fax: 01726 71978). *Location:* one mile west of St Austell on A390 St Austell to Truro road. Parkland course. 18 holes, 6091 yards. S.S.S. 69. Floodlit driving range. *Green Fees:* information not available. *Eating facilities:* bar and restaurant – meals can be arranged. *Visitors:* welcome with reservation, must be club members and hold Handicap Certificate. *Society Meetings:* catered for weekdays by arrangement. Professional: Tony Pitts (01726 62681). Secretary: (01726 74756; Fax: 01726 71978).

ST IVES. **Tregenna Castle Hotel Golf and Country Club,** St Ives TR26 2DE (01736 797381). *Location:* on the main road between Carbis Bay and St Ives, half a mile from town centre. Parkland, 73 acres of grounds with beautiful sea views overlooking St Ives Harbour and Atlantic coast – a very tricky course. 14 holes, 1846 yards. Par 42. *Green Fees:* Information not available. *Visitors:* welcome. Accommodation available in the hotel if booked. *Society Meetings:* welcome. Golf Supervisor: Simon Davey.*

ST IVES. **West Cornwall Golf Club,** Church Lane, Lelant, St Ives TR26 3DZ (Tel & Fax: 01736 753401). *Location:* two miles from St Ives, in village of Lelant; take Church Road, course situated approximately quarter of a mile past Lelant Church. True links course - wonderful coastal views. 18 holes, 5884 yards. S.S.S. 69. Practice ground, putting green. *Green Fees:* weekdays £28.00 per day; weekends £33.00. Five Day ticket £100.00, Seven Day ticket £125.00. *Eating facilities:* bar with bar menus and à la carte dining room. *Visitors:* must be golf club members with Handicap Certificate. Trolleys for hire. Home of "Long" Jim Barnes, first American Professional Champ 1916, Open Champion USA 1921, British Open Champion 1925 and World Champion of Golf 1921–1925. *Society Meetings:* welcome, written application required. Professional: Jason Broadway (01736 753177). Secretary: Gareth Evans (01736 753401). e-mail: secretary@westcornwallgolfclub.co.uk website: www.westcornwallgolfclub.co.uk

SALTASH. **China Fleet Country Club,** Saltash PL12 6LJ (01752 848668). *Location*: one mile from Tamar Bridge. Parkland course with beautiful river views. 18 holes, 6551 yards, S.S.S. 72. 28 bay floodlit driving range. *Green Fees:* information on request. *Eating facilities:* bars and bar meals, full restaurant facilities, coffee shop. *Visitors:* welcome, Handicap Certificate required. Other facilities include large Pro Shop, full leisure facilities and 42 apartments. *Society Meetings:* welcome, minimum number 12 persons. Professional: Damien McEvoy (01752 854665; Fax: 01752 848456). Golf Manager: Linda Goddard (01752 854657; Fax: 01752 848456).

SALTASH. **St Mellion Hotel, Golf and Country Club,** Near Saltash PL12 6SD (01579 351351; Fax: 01579 350537). *Location*: A38 to Saltash, A388 from Saltash to Callington. Parkland. Nicklaus Course: 18 holes, 6651 yards, par 72, S.S.S. 72 - designer Jack Nicklaus. Venue of the Benson & Hedges International Open 1990-1995. Old Course: 18 holes, 5782 yards, par 68. S.S.S. 68 - designer J. Hamilton-Stutt. Practice range. *Green Fees:* information not available. *Eating facilities:* full restaurant (awarded AA Rosette) and The Gallery Brasserie. *Visitors:* welcome at all times. Leisure club includes two indoor swimming pools, gymnasium, dance studio, sauna, steam room, spa pool, sports hall, creche. Skincare and spa centre. Founder member of the Premier Golf Clubs of Great Britain. *Society Meetings:* welcome. Accommodation available in Hotel overlooking 18th fairway, and in Fairway Lodges in the grounds. Head Professional: David Moon (01579 352002).*
e-mail: info@stmelliongolfbreaks.co.uk
website: www.stmelliongolfbreaks.co.uk

TORPOINT. **Whitsand Bay Hotel Golf Club,** Portwrinkle, Torpoint PL11 3BU (01503 230276). *Location*: on coast six miles from Torpoint. Clifftop course. 18 holes, 5770 yards. S.S.S. 68. *Green Fees:* information not available. *Eating facilities:* hotel. *Visitors:* welcome at all times with Handicap Certificate. Swimming/leisure complex. *Society Meetings:* catered for and hotel accommodation arranged on application to hotel (01503 230276; Fax 01503 230329). Professional: S. Dougan (01503 230778). Secretary: J. M. Fisher (01752 814171).e-mail: whitsandbayhotel@btinternet.com*

TRURO. **Killiow Golf Club & Driving Range,** Kea, Near Truro TR3 6AG (01872 270246; Fax: 01872 240915). *Location*: take A39 Truro to Falmouth road, turn right into club at first Playing Place roundabout (2¼ miles). 18 holes, Par 72. All-weather floodlit driving range open 8am to 9pm weekdays (weekends until 6pm). *Green Fees:* information on request. *Eating facilities:* bar and restaurant. *Visitors:* only restricted by competitions; phone for availability. Secretary: John Crowson (01872 266876).*

TRURO. **Truro Golf Club,** Treliske, Truro TR1 3LG (01872 272640). *Location:* one mile west of Truro on A390 to Redruth. Undulating parkland with magnificent views. 18 holes, 5306 yards. S.S.S. 66. *Green Fees:* weekdays £25.00 per day or round, weekends and Bank Holidays £30.00 per day or round. *Eating facilities:* restaurant and bar snacks available. *Visitors:* welcome with Handicap Certificates. Buggies and carts available. *Society Meetings:* welcome – special rates on application. Professional: N. Bicknell (01872 276595). Secretary: H.W.D. Leicester (01872 278684; Fax: 01872 225972).

THE APPEARANCE OF AN ASTERISK (*) AT THE END OF A CLUB OR COURSE ENTRY INDICATES THAT UP-TO-DATE INFORMATION HAS NOT BEEN SUPPLIED

WADEBRIDGE. **Roserrow Golf and Country Club,** Roserrow, St Minver, Near Wadebridge PL27 6QT. *Location:* between Wadebridge and Polzeath off the B3314. Undulating wooded valley. 18 holes, 6507 yards, 5951 metres. S.S.S. 71. 15 bay driving range with indoor swing-analysis studio, practice putting green. *Green Fees:* £28.00 July and August, £20.00 rest of year. Discounts for groups of 8+. *Eating facilities:* restaurant, bar food available. *Visitors:* always welcome, phone for tee times. Luxury self-catering accommodation on site. Indoor swimming pool, fitness suite, sauna, jacuzzi, steam room, solarium, outdoor tennis courts. Buggies, electric trolleys, carts for hire. *Society Meetings:* welcome by arrangement. Club Manager: Simon Welch (01208 863000; Fax: 01208 863002).
e-mail: info@roserrow.co.uk
website: www.roserrow.co.uk

WADEBRIDGE. **St Enodoc Golf Club,** Rock, Wadebridge PL27 6LD (01208 863216; Fax: 01208 862976). *Location:* take the B3314 from Wadebridge, signposted Rock (three miles). Seaside links. Two courses: Church Course 18 holes, 6514 yards. S.S.S. 69; Holywell Course 18 holes, 4103 yards. S.S.S. 61. Practice range, putting greens, etc. *Green Fees:* Church £50.00 weekdays, £60.00 weekends and Bank Holidays. Holywell £17.00 weekdays, weekends and Bank Holidays. *Eating facilities:* restaurant and bar snacks. *Visitors:* Handicap Certificates (24 and below) required for Church Course; no restrictions for Holywell Course. *Society Meetings:* all welcome by arrangement with the General Manager. Professional: Nick Williams (01208 862402).
e-mail: enquiries@st-enodoc.co.uk
website: www.st-enodoc.co.uk

WADEBRIDGE. **St Kew Golf Club,** St Kew Highway, Near Wadebridge, Bodmin PL30 3EF (Tel & Fax: 01208 841500). *Location:* on the main A39, two-and-a-half miles from Wadebridge towards Camelford. Parkland course, 9 holes (18 tees), 4543 yards. S.S.S. 62. Covered driving range, practice chipping/bunker area. *Green Fees:* £11.00 9 holes, £15.00 18 holes. *Eating facilities:* coffee shop and restaurant; licensed bar. *Visitors:* welcome. No restrictions. *Society Meetings:* discounts for eight or more. Professional: Mike Derry (Tel & Fax: 01208 841500). Secretary: John Brown.

ISLES OF SCILLY

ST MARY'S. **Isles Of Scilly Golf Club,** St Mary's, Isles of Scilly (01720 422692). *Location*: one mile from Hugh Town, St Mary's. Heathland links course with magnificent views. 9 holes, 18 tees, 5898 yards. S.S.S. 69. Par 73. *Green Fees:* £22.00 per day (2006). *Eating facilities*: lunches and evening meals available. *Visitors*: welcome.

The 15th hole at Bowood Park Hotel & Golf Course

Devon

AXMOUTH. **Axe Cliff Golf Club,** Squires Lane, Axmouth, Seaton EX12 4AB (01297 21754; Fax: 01297 24371). *Location:* A35 from Sidmouth to Lyme Regis, turn right on to B3172 at junction with A358 Seaton. Clifftop course. 18 holes, 5969 yards, 5460 metres. S.S.S. 70. *Green Fees:* Inforamtion not available. *Eating facilities:* bar and small restaurant. *Visitors:* welcome without reservation, course closed until 11am on Sundays, Wednesdays till 10.30am and Fridays till 9.30am. Handicap Certificate not required. Electric cart hire, pull trolleys and clubs for hire. *Society Meetings:* societies very welcome, prices start from £18.00. More details on website. Secretary: (01297 21754).*
website: www.axecliff.co.uk

BARNSTAPLE. **Portmore Golf Park,** Landkey Road, Barnstaple EX32 9LB (01271 378378). *Location:* A361 just east of Barnstaple, turn right to Landkey 200 yards, turn right Newport, turn right again after a mile. Two parkland courses. The Landkey, Par 3. The Barum, Par 71. 24 bay floodlit golf range, chipping green, bunker, putting green. *Green Fees:* information not available. *Eating facilities:* full catering available. *Visitors:* welcome at all times, must telephone for tee times. Full dress code applies for Barum course. Tuition available. *Society Meetings:* welcome with prior booking, group rates available. Professionals: Steve Gould, Darren Everet.
website: www.portmoregolf.co.uk

BIDEFORD near. **Hartland Forest Golf Club,** Near Clovelly, Bideford EX39 5RA. *Location:* between Bideford and Bude A39, signposted from main A39 road. Parkland with water hazards. 18 holes, 6004 yards. S.S.S. 70. Par 71. *Green Fees:* £15.00 9 holes, £25.00 18 holes. *Visitors:* welcome at all times. Buggies for hire. *Society Meetings:* welcome. Secretary: A. Cartwright
e-mail: hfgolf@googlemail.com
website: www.hartlandforestgolf.co.uk

BIGBURY. **Bigbury Golf Club Ltd,** Bigbury-on-Sea, TQ7 4BB. *Location:* off main Plymouth to Kingsbridge road, turn right at Harraton Cross. Undulating cliff top course. 18 holes, 5896 yards. S.S.S. 68. *Green Fees:* currently under review; see website. *Eating facilities:* catering facilities available every day. *Visitors:* welcome, Handicap Certificate preferred. *Society Meetings:* catered for by prior arrangement. Professional: Mark Gorman (01548 810412). Secretary: Martin Lowry (01548 810557).
website: www.bigburygolfclub.com

BRIXHAM. **Churston Golf Club Ltd,** Dartmouth Road, Churston, Near Brixham TQ5 0LA (01803 842751; Fax: 01803 845738). *Location:* A379 from Torquay to Brixham. At Windy Corner take A3022 to Brixham. Club situated half-a-mile on. Downland/parkland course stretching westward along the cliffs towards Brixham. 18 holes, 6219 yards. S.S.S. 70. *Green Fees:* information not available. *Eating facilities:* restaurant, bar and separate function room. *Visitors:* welcome, must be members of recognised club. Conference facilities available. Handicap Certificate preferred. *Society Meetings:* catered for by arrangement. Mondays, Thursdays and Fridays only. Professional: Rob Butterworth (01803 843442; Fax: 01803 845738). Manager: S.R. Bawden (01803 842751; Fax: 01803 845738).*

BUDLEIGH SALTERTON. **East Devon Golf Club,** Links Road, Budleigh Salterton EX9 6DG (01395 445195). *Location:* exit M5 Junction 30; follow A376 and B3179 for Exmouth/Budleigh Salterton. Cliff top and heathland; special features: Superb greens, spectacular views over English Channel. 18 holes, 6239 yards. S.S.S. 70. *Green Fees:* information not available. *Eating facilities:* full bar and restaurant. *Visitors:* anytime by prior arrangement. Handicap Certificate required. Ladies' Day Tuesdays. *Society Meetings:* catered for Thursdays only by arrangement. Professional: T. Underwood (01395 445195). Secretary: Julian Reynolds (01395 443370).

CHITTLEHAMHOLT. **Highbullen Hotel Golf & Country Club,** Chittlehamholt, Umberleigh EX37 9HD (01769 540561; Fax: 01769 540492). *Location:* M5 Tiverton Exit 27, A361 to South Molton, B3226 five miles. Right uphill following tourist signs through Chittlehamholt. Undulating parkland setting amongst mature specimen trees and water hazards, spectacular views to Exmoor and Dartmoor. 18 holes, 5562 yards. S.S.S. 67. Practice ground, golf simulator, indoor putting green. *Green Fees:* weekdays £26.00, weekends £30.00. *Eating facilities:* restaurant, brasserie and bars. *Visitors:* welcome, check availability. Accommodation on site at Highbullen Hotel. New leisure complex and health spa with full shower and changing facilities. *Society Meetings:* golf societies welcome subject to availablilty. Professional: Paul Weston (01769 540530). Secretary: John Ayres (01769 540664).
e-mail: club@highbullen.co.uk
website: www.highbullen.co.uk

CHULMLEIGH. **Chulmleigh Golf Course,** Leigh Road, Chulmleigh EX18 7BL (Tel & Fax: 01769 580519). *Location:* approximately midway between Barnstaple and Crediton on A377. North Devon's only tailor-made short game course. Undulating parkland course. 18 holes, 1450 yards Summer, 2353 yards Winter for 18 holes. S.S.S. 54. *Green Fees:* from £7.50. *Eating facilities:* licensed bar, bar snacks. *Visitors:* welcome. No Handicap Certificate required. Suitable for experienced golfers to improve short game, ideal for beginners, Juniors and retired golfers. Teaching available for beginners, juniors and adults by arrangement. Holiday cottage available. *Society Meetings:* welcome by prior arrangement. Secretary: Roy Dow. Proprietors: Mr and Mrs R.W. Dow.
e-mail: chulmleighgolf@aol.com
website: www.chulmleighgolf.co.uk

CREDITON. **Downes Crediton Golf Club,** Hookway, Crediton EX17 3PT (01363 773025; Fax: 01363 775060). *Location:* off Crediton-Exeter road. Part flat, part hilly course featuring woods and water. 18 holes, 5951 yards. S.S.S. 69. *Green Fees:* £28.00 per day weekdays; £32.00 per day weekends. Special rates on application. *Eating facilities:* available from 11.30am to one hour before bar closes. *Visitors:* welcome, advisable to phone first and must produce Handicap Certificate. *Society Meetings:* by arrangement. Professional: Barry Austin (01363 774464). Managing Secretary: Philip Lee.

CREDITON near. **Waterbridge Golf Course,** Down St Mary, Near Crediton EX17 5LG (01363 85111). *Location:* on the A377 north of Crediton (one mile north of Copplestone). Attractive, gentle parkland course in a beautiful setting. 9 holes (18 tees), 3910 yards, S.S.S. 64. *Green Fees:* weekdays £7.50 9 holes, £12.50 18 holes; weekends £8.50 9 holes, £14.50 18 holes. 12.5% discount on parties of 10 and over. *Eating facilities:* café bar, lunches. *Visitors:* welcome. Club and trolley hire available. *Society Meetings:* welcome. Professional: David Ridyard. Secretary: Mrs A. Wren.

CULLOMPTON. **Padbrook Park Golf Club,** Padbrook Park, Cullompton EX15 1RU (01884 836100). *Location:* one mile from Junction 28 M5. Parkland. 9 holes (18 tees), 6108 yards. S.S.S. 70. Nets, 10 bay driving range. *Green Fees:* £14.00 9 holes, £19.00 18 holes. Juniors half price. *Eating facilities:* two bars and restaurant. *Visitors:* always welcome. Indoor bowls, fishing; full conference and meeting facilities. Health and Fitness studio. 40 bedroom hotel, crazy golf. *Society Packages:* welcome by prior arrangement. Golf Manager: Cary Rawlings. Directors: Susan and Garry Scargill (Fax: 01884 836101)
e-mail: info@padbrookpark.co.uk
website: www.padbrookpark.co.uk

DARTMOUTH. **Dartmouth Golf and Country Club,** Blackawton, Near Dartmouth TQ9 7DE (01803 712686; Fax: 01803 712628). *Location:* five miles from Dartmouth on the A3122. Undulating parkland course with lakes, rock faces and multiple tees. Dartmouth Course: 9 holes, 2583 yards. S.S.S. 33. Championship Course: 18 holes, 7191 yards. S.S.S. 74. 15-bay driving range. *Green Fees:* £38.00 weekdays, £48.00 weekends. *Eating facilities:* full restaurant and lounge bar. *Visitors:* welcome daily, Handicap Certificate not essential. 3 Star hotel accommodation in 35 en suite bedrooms. Leisure suite with pool, gym and beauty therapy etc. Buggies available £25.00 per round. *Society Meetings:* welcome daily. Professional: Rob Glazier (01803 712650). Secretary: Tony Chappell (01803 712016). e-mail: info@dgcc.co.uk
    golfoperations@dgcc.co.uk
website: www.dgcc.co.uk

DAWLISH. Warren Golf Club, Dawlish Warren EX7 0NF (01626 862255; Fax: 01626 888005). *Location:* 12 miles south of Exeter off A379. Links golf course lying on a spit of land between the sea and Exe Estuary. A challenging course situated in an internationally renowned conservation area. 18 holes, 5954 yards. S.S.S. 69. *Green Fees:* Information not available. *Eating facilities:* bar and full catering available. *Visitors:* members of other bona fide golf clubs welcome. *Society Meetings:* welcome by arrangement, Special Packages available. Professional: D. Prowse (01626 864002). Club Secretary: Tim Aggett (01626 862255).
e-mail: secretary@dwgc.co.uk
website: www.dwgc.co.uk*

EXETER. Exeter Golf and Country Club, Countess Wear, Exeter EX2 7AE (Tel & Fax: 01392 874139; Course Information: 01392 876413). *Location:* near M5, exit Junction 30, take main Plymouth/Torquay Road. Turn left Topsham, 300 yards left. Flat parkland course, many trees. 18 holes, 6023 yards. S.S.S. 69. Large practice ground. *Green Fees:* on application. *Eating facilities:* sports bar, lounge bar, diningroom. *Visitors:* welcome except Tuesdays (Ladies' Day) and Saturdays very busy course, booking sheet in operation, Bookings taken one week prior subject to availability. Booking number 01392 876303. Function suite. *Society Meetings:* catered for Thursdays only. Professional: Gary Milne (01392 875028; Fax: 01392 874914). Secretary: Keith Ham (01392 874639; Fax: 01392 874914).

EXETER. Woodbury Park Golf and Country Club, Woodbury Castle, Woodbury, Near Exeter EX5 1JJ (01395 233382; Fax: 01395 233384). *Location:* six miles east of Exeter between Sidmouth and Exmouth. Parkland with many water hazards. 18 hole championship course and 9 hole course. 18 holes, 7314 yards. S.S.S. 75. 16-bay driving range, practice green. *Green Fees:* on request. *Eating facilities:* two restaurants, two bars. *Visitors:* welcome at all times. Buggies for hire. Leisure Centre, Hydrotherapy Centre and conference facilities. Five chalet-style luxury lodges ideal for four/six golfers in each. 56-bedroom hotel. *Society Meetings:* welcome, Golf Packages available. Bookings please ring (01395 233500). Professional: Allan Perry. Golf Manager: Alan Richards.*
e-mail: golfbookings@woodburypark.co.uk

EXETER near. Fingle Glen Hotel, Golf and Country Club, Tedburn St. Mary, Near Exeter EX6 6AF (01647 61817; Fax: 01647 61135). *Location:* A30 five miles from Exeter on the Okehampton Road. Parkland with streams and lakes. 9 holes, 2475 yards. S.S.S. 63 (18 holes). Golf academy, 12 bay floodlit driving range. *Green Fees:* information not available. *Eating facilities:* restaurant, bar snacks, sun terrace. *Visitors:* welcome at all times. En suite accommodation available. *Society Meetings:* welcome at all times. Pro Shop: Mervyn Kemp. Teaching Professional: Stephen Gould. Secretary: Peter Miliffe. Manager: A. Bridgeman. *

EXETER near. Teign Valley Golf Club, Christow, Near Exeter EX6 7PA (01647 253026). *Location:* four miles off the A38 Devon Expressway between Exeter and Plymouth. Varied and interesting course set in beautiful valleys in the Dartmoor National Park. 18 holes, 6000 yards. *Green Fees:* information not available. *Eating facilities:* a welcoming spirit in the friendly clubhouse offering tasty bar snacks and a choice of real ales. *Visitors:* welcome. Clubhouse extension with 16 en suite double bedrooms, gymnasium and treatment rooms. *Society Meetings:* welcome. Conference facilities for 40 available.*
e-mail: reception@teignvalleygolf.co.uk
website: www.teignvalleygolf.co.uk

HOLSWORTHY. Holsworthy Golf Club, Killatree, Holsworthy EX22 6LP (Tel & Fax: 01409 253177). *Location:* leave Holsworthy on Bude road, A3072; one and a half miles on left. Parkland - gentle undulating hills. 18 holes, 6062 yards. S.S.S. 69. Practice area. *Green Fees:* Information not available. *Eating facilities:* bar, dining room. *Visitors:* welcome anytime. *Society Meetings:* welcome, special reductions for parties of 12 or more. Professional: Alan Johnston (01409 254771; Fax: 01409 253177). Secretary: (Tel & Fax: 01409 253177).
e-mail: secretary@holsworthygolfclub.co.uk
website: www.holsworthygolfclub.co.uk

HONITON. Honiton Golf Club, Middlehills, Honiton EX14 9TR (01404 44422). *Location:* one mile south of town proceed from A35 at Tower Cross to Farway. Flat parkland. 18 holes; 5897 yards, S.S.S. 73 (men); 5659 yards, S.S.S. 73 (ladies) . Small practice ground. *Green Fees:* weekdays £26.00 per day, weekends and

Bank Holidays £30.00. *Eating facilities:* bar and restaurant. *Visitors:* bona fide members of other clubs welcome, with restrictions on Wednesdays (Ladies' day) and weekends (club competitions). Facilities for 10 touring caravans during summer months with electrics. *Society Meetings:* by prior arrangement. Professional: Adrian Cave (01404 42943). Secretary: Brian Young (01404 44422; Fax: 01404 46383). website: www.honitongolfclub.co.uk

HONITON. **Otter Valley Golf Centre,** Upottery, Honiton EX14 9QP (Tel & Fax: 01404 861266). *Location:* Take the A303 from Honiton, continue one and a half miles, turn off left at Upottery and Rawridge. Rolling parkland course. 9 holes, 1500 yards. Par 29. Four indoor practice bays, large putting green, eight tees on the driving range, chipping green. *Green Fees:* information not available. *Eating facilities:* snacks and refreshments, hot and cold drinks. Lounge with TV. *Visitors:* welcome, no restrictions. Holiday cottages, video analysis, lessons. *Society Meetings:* Societies and Company Days very welcome. Please phone for information. Professional: Andrew Thompson. Manager: Ryan Eaton.*
e-mail: andrewthompson@otter-golf.co.uk
website: www.otter-golf.co.uk

ILFRACOMBE. **Ilfracombe Golf Club,** Hele Bay, Ilfracombe EX34 9RT. *Location:* on main coastal road between Ilfracombe and Combe Martin. Undulating parkland with spectacular views of sea and moors from every tee and green. 18 holes, 5893 yards. S.S.S. 68. 9 hole practice area and driving range. *Green Fees:* weekdays £25.00 per round,   £35.00 per day; weekends/Bank Holidays £30.00 per round, £40.00 per day. *Eating facilities:* catering available all day. *Visitors:* welcome, advance booking preferred. Members only before 10am weekends. *Society Meetings:* welcome, advance booking preferred. Bookings: (01271 863328). Catering: (01271 862675). Professional: Mark Davies (01271 863328). Club Secretary: Arnie Williams (01271 862176; Fax: 01271 867731).

ILFRACOMBE. **Ilfracombe and Woolacombe Golf Range,** Woolacombe Road, Ilfracombe EX34 7HF (01271 866222). *Location:* on main road between Ilfracombe and Woolacombe. Flat course. 9 holes, 695 yards. 300 yard driving range with covered bays, 18 hole putting course, golf shop. *Green Fees:* available on request. *Eating facilities:* pre-packed snacks, drinks and cream teas available. *Visitors:* everyone is welcome. Tennis court. Lessons and custom-built clubs provided. Secretary: David Crocker-White. Professional: Andrew Norman

IVYBRIDGE. **McCaulay's Fitness and Golf,** Dinnaton Golf Club, Ivybridge PL21 9HU (01752 892512; Fax: 01752 698334). *Location:* from the Ivybridge turn off on A38, we are just two minutes

drive, please follow the brown tourist signs. 9 holes, 2028 yards. Par 32. *Green Fees:* 9 holes from £8.00, 18 holes from £10.00. *Visitors:* always welcome. No Handicap Certificate required. Other facilities offered include gym, 25m heated swimming pool, aerobics studio, tennis, squash, sauna, solarium and steam room. Contact: Jamie Phillips.
website: www.mccaulays.com

MORETONHAMPSTEAD. **Bovey Castle,** Moretonhampstead TQ13 8RE (01647 445000; Fax: 01647 440961). *Location:* Junction 31 from M5, B3212 for two miles. Parkland with rivers and narrow fairways. 18 holes, 6303 yards, 5450 metres. S.S.S. 70. Golf academy. *Green Fees:* information not available. *Eating facilities:* brunch service, bar. *Visitors:* welcome. Please book in advance, golf shoes must be worn. Accommodation in 5 star Hotel, tennis courts; carts available. *Society Meetings:* by prior arrangement. Professional/ Secretary: Richard Lewis (01647 445009; Fax: 01647 440961).*
website: www.boveycastle.com

MORTEHOE. **Mortehoe and Woolacombe Golf Club,** Easewell Holiday Park, Mortehoe EX34 7EH (01271 870566). *Location:* just outside Mortehoe village. Parkland course with superb sea views. 9 holes (18 tees), 4729 yards, S.S.S. 63. Practice nets. *Green Fees:* information not available. *Eating facilities:* clubhouse; restaurant and bar snacks. *Visitors:* welcome at all times. Cafeteria and golf shop with extensive range of equipment. Touring campsite facilities. Indoor bowls, table tennis, indoor heated pool; trolleys available. *Society Meetings:* welcome by prior booking. Secretary: Malcolm Wilkinson (01271 870745).

NEWTON ABBOT. **Dainton Park Golf Club,** Totnes Road, Ipplepen, Newton Abbot TQ12 5TN (01803 815000). *Location:* on A381 between Newton Abbot and Totnes. Undulating parkland course. 18 holes, 6400 yards. S.S.S. 71. Driving range and practice area. *Green Fees:* £25.00. *Eating facilities:* full catering and licensed bar. *Visitors:* unrestricted. *Society Meetings:* welcome by arrangement. website: www.daintonparkgolf.co.uk

NEWTON ABBOT. **Hele Park Golf Club,** Ashburton Road, Newton Abbot TQ12 6JN (01626 336060; Fax: 01626 332661). *Location:* A383 on Newton Abbot to Ashburton road, one and a half miles from Newton Abbot town centre. Parkland course. 9 holes, 5168 yards. S.S.S. 65 (for 18 holes). Floodlit driving range. *Green Fees:* from £11.50 for 9 holes and £20.00 for 18 holes. *Eating facilities:* bar and restaurant. *Visitors:* welcome. Booking advised. Normal dress rules apply. Pay as you play and members' club. *Society Meetings:* welcome, special rates on application. Professionals: Duncan Arnold, Stuart Disney, Chris Gill, Malcolm Craig. Manager: Wendy Stanbury. e-mail: info@heleparkgolf.co.uk website: www.heleparkgolf.co.uk

NEWTON ABBOT. **Newton Abbot (Stover) Golf Club,** Bovey Road, Newton Abbot TQ12 6QQ (01626 352460; Fax: 01626 330210). *Location:* A382 three miles north of Newton Abbot. Tight wooded parkland course with river in play on 8 holes. 18 holes, 5764 yards, 5271 metres. S.S.S. 68. *Green Fees:* information not available. *Eating facilities:* full catering daily from 11am. *Visitors:* welcome on production of Handicap Certificate or membership card of county affiliated golf club. Must telephone in advance. *Society Meetings:* catered for on Thursdays. Professional: James Langmead (01626 362078). Secretary: Will Hendry (01626 352460).

OKEHAMPTON. **Okehampton Golf Club,** Off Tors Road, Okehampton EX20 1EF (01837 52113). *Location:* from A30 take turning from centre of Okehampton then follow the signposts. Parkland. 18 holes, 5294 yards. S.S.S. 66. *Green Fees:* £25.00. *Eating facilities:* bar and dining room. *Visitors:* welcome; contact by telephone or letter. *Society Meetings:* welcome by prior arrangement. Professional: Ashley Moon (01837 53541). Secretary: Clive Yeo. e-mail: okehamptongc@btconnect.com website: www.okehamptongc.co.uk

OKEHAMPTON near. **Ashbury Hotel,** Higher Maddaford, Ashbury, Near Okehampton EX20 4NL (01837 55453; Fax: 01837 55468). *Location:* signposted "Ashbury" off the B3079, three miles west of Okehampton. Hilly, wooded courses. Ashbury, three courses: Pines 18 holes, 5628 yards, Par 69; Beeches 18 holes, 5519 yards, Par 68; Willows 18 holes, Par 3. Oakwood Course 18 holes, 5400 yards, Par 68; Kigbeare 18 holes, 6379 yards, Par 72. Practice area, putting green and 8-bay covered driving range. *Green Fees:* information not available. *Eating facilities:* fully licensed bar, bar snacks 12 noon to 5pm. *Visitors:* welcome, after midday, please telephone to arrange a tee time. Buggies, clubs and trolleys for hire. Coaching available. Accommodation in 2 star hotel; tennis, bowls, snooker, swimming (01837 53053). Secretary: Ian Gill. website: www.ashburygolfhotel.co.uk

PLYMOUTH. **Elfordleigh Hotel, Golf and Leisure Club,** Colebrook, Plympton, Plymouth PL7 5EB (01752 336428; Fax: 01752 344581). *Location*: one mile from Plympton. Woodland course in picturesque countryside. 18 holes, S.S.S. 67. Practice area. *Green Fees:* information not available. *Eating facilities:* Churchill Restaurant; bar meals available from Brasserie. *Visitors:* welcome. Hotel accommodation available. *Society Meetings:* catered for, contact Golf Manager. Professional/Director of Golf: Dominik Naughton (01752 348425).* website: www.elfordleigh.co.uk

PLYMOUTH. **Sparkwell Golf Club,** Sparkwell, Plympton, Plymouth PL7 5DF (Tel & Fax: 01752 837219). *Location:* Sparkwell village centre. Parkland course. 9 holes, 5772 yards, S.S.S. 68. Practice area, pitch and putt. *Green Fees:* information not available. *Eating facilities:* restaurant and bar. *Visitors:* all welcome; pay-as-you-play course. *Society Meetings:* all welcome. Secretary: J. J. Sandiford.*

PLYMOUTH. **Staddon Heights Golf Club,** Staddon Heights, Plymstock, Plymouth PL9 9SP (01752 402475). *Location:* from A38/city centre follow signs to Kingsbridge (A379), then Turnchapel then Bovisand. Cliff top course with spectacular views over Plymouth Sound and the City. 18 holes, 6164 yards. S.S.S. 70. Practice range and short game area. *Green Fees:* weekdays £28.00, weekends and Bank Holidays £32.00; reductions for groups of eight or more; twilight golf available April - Oct. *Visitors:* welcome. *Eating facilities:* full bar and restaurant service available. *Society Meetings:* welcome. Secretary: Tim Aggett (01752 401475). website: www.staddon-heights.co.uk

SAUNTON. **Saunton Golf Club,** Saunton, Braunton EX33 1LG (01271 812436; Fax: 01271 814241). *Location:* eight miles west of Barnstaple. Two traditional links courses. East course 18 holes, 6779 yards. S.S.S. 72. West course 18 holes, 6403 yards. S.S.S. 71. Practice ground and covered practice range. *Green Fees:* (2008) £65.00 per 18 holes, £85.00 per day. *Eating facilities:* full catering available. *Visitors:* welcome, Handicap Certificate required. Prior booking recommended. *Society Meetings:* welcome with prior booking. Professional: A.T. MacKenzie (01271 812013; Fax: 01271 812126). General Manager: D. Cliffe (01271 812436; Fax: 01271 814241).
e-mail: di@sauntongolf.co.uk
website: www.sauntongolf.co.uk

SIDMOUTH. **Sidmouth Golf Club,** Cotmaton Road, Peak Hill, Sidmouth EX10 8SX (01395 513451; Fax: 01395 514661). *Location:* half a mile from town centre, 12 miles south east of M5 Junction 30. Parkland with breathtaking views over Sid Valley and Lyme Bay. 18 holes, 5068 yards. S.S.S. 65. *Green Fees:* £28.00. Summer and winter packages available. Society packages on request. *Eating facilities:* catering available everyday. *Visitors:* welcome anytime on tee reservations. *Society Meetings:* by arrangement with Professional: (01395 516407). Club Manager: Jonathan Lee (01395 513451; Fax: 01395 514661).
e-mail: secretary@sidmouthgolfclub.co.uk

SOUTH BRENT. **Wrangaton Golf Club,** Golf Links Road, Wrangaton, South Brent TQ10 9HJ (01364 73001). *Location:* A38 from Exeter (Wrangaton Cross turn off), from Plymouth A38 Ivybridge turn off via Bittaford. Parkland course, first 9 holes on Dartmoor. 18 holes, 6065 yards. S.S.S 69. Practice ground, putting green and net. *Green Fees:* weekdays £25.00; weekends and Bank Holidays £30.00. *Eating facilities:* full catering and bar facilities available. *Visitors:* welcome at all times but telephone first in case of club competition. *Society Meetings:* all welcome, written notice required. Professional: Glenn Richards (01364 72161). Secretary: Mike Daniels (Tel & Fax: 01364 73229).

TAVISTOCK. **Hurdwick Golf Club,** Tavistock Hamlets, Tavistock PL19 0LL (01822 612746). *Location:* one mile north of Tavistock on the Brentor Road. Parkland. 18 holes, 5300 yards. S.S.S. 66. *Green Fees:* £20.00 all day, including weekends. *Eating facilities:* fresh sandwiches, licensed bar. *Visitors:* welcome anytime. *Society Meetings:* (10 or more) 36 holes and buffet for £25.00 a head. Secretary: Roger Cullen and R. Hurle.

TAVISTOCK. **Tavistock Golf Club,** Down Road, Tavistock PL19 9AQ (Tel & Fax: 01822 612344). *Location:* Whitchurch Down one mile from Tavistock. Moorland course with spectacular views. 18 holes, 6546 yards. S.S.S. 71. Practice ground. *Green Fees:* weekdays £28.00 per day, weekends and Bank Holidays £36.00 per day. *Eating facilities:* all day catering and bar. *Visitors:* welcome, telephone first. *Society Meetings:* by prior arrangement, fees negotiable. Professional: D. Rehaag (01822 612316). Secretary: J. Coe (Tel & Fax: 01822 612344).
e-mail: tavygolf@hotmail.com
website: www.tavistockgolfclub.org.uk

TEIGNMOUTH. **Teignmouth Golf Club,** Haldon Moor, Teignmouth TQ14 9NY (01626 777070). *Location:* two miles north of Teignmouth on the Exeter Road - B3192. Level heathland course, designed by Dr Mackenzie (also designed Augusta National USA), with panoramic views. 18 holes, 6090 yards. S.S.S. 69. *Green Fees:* On application. *Eating facilities:* catering from 9 am to 6 pm. *Visitors:* welcome with reservation if members of another club with Handicap Certificate. *Society Meetings:* catered for Thursdays. Professional: Robert Selley (01626 772894). General Manager: Andy Stubbs (01626 777070; Fax: 01626 777304).

THURLESTONE. **Thurlestone Golf Club,** Thurlestone, Kingsbridge TQ7 3NZ (01548 560405). *Location:* turn off A379 near Kingsbridge. Undulating beside sandy beaches and over cliff tops, with superb coastal views. 18 holes, 6340 yards. S.S.S. 70. Practice area. *Green Fees:* £36.00 per day. Weekly and fortnightly tickets available. *Eating facilities:* catering available from 10.00am until 5.30pm daily. *Visitors:* must produce Handicap Certificate, please telephone in advance. *Society Meetings:* not catered for. Professional: Peter Laugher (Tel & Fax: 01548 560715). Secretary: Terry Gibbons (01548 560405; Fax: 01548 562149).

TIVERTON. **Tiverton Golf Club,** Post Hill, Tiverton EX16 4NE (01884 252187; Fax: 01884 251607). *Location:* three miles east of Tiverton, Junction 27 of M5, proceed through Sampford Peverell and Halberton. Parkland, tree-lined fairways. 18 holes, 6346 yards. S.S.S. 71. *Green Fees:* on application. *Eating facilities:* snacks, lunches, teas and evening meals. *Visitors:* welcome, must ring Pro Shop in advance. Handicap Certificate or introduction required. *Society Meetings:* by arrangement with General Manager. Professional: Mike Hawton (01884 254836). General Manager: Richard Jessop (01884 252187).

TORQUAY. **Torquay Golf Club,** Petitor Road, St Marychurch, Torquay TQ1 4QF (01803 314591; Fax: 01803 316116). *Location:* north east of Torquay at St. Marychurch. Parkland. 18 holes, 6192 yards. S.S.S. 69. *Green Fees:* £33.00 - £38.00. *Eating facilities:* lunches, teas and evening meals available. *Visitors:* welcome if members of a golf club with Handicap Certificate. *Society Meetings:* ring for rates. Professional: M. Ruth (01803 329113). Secretary: T.J. Fenson (01803 314591).
e-mail: info@torquaygolfclub.org.uk
website: www.torquaygolfclub.org.uk

TORRINGTON. **Great Torrington Golf Club,** Weare Trees, Torrington EX38 7EZ (01805 622229; Fax: 01805 623878). *Location:* one mile north of Torrington on Weare Giffard road. Heathland course with excellent views. 9 holes, 18 tees, 4419 yards. S.S.S. 62. Small practice area. *Green Fees:* £18.00 per day G.M.T., £18.00 per round (18 holes) or £23.00 per day B.S.T. Subject to review. *Eating facilities:* full meals and bar snacks available during bar hours. *Visitors:* welcome except on Tuesdays, Wednesdays, Saturdays and Sundays before noon and during club and open competitions. *Society Meetings:* catered for by arrangement. Secretary: Mrs J.M. Cudmore (01271 375927).

UMBERLEIGH. **Libbaton Golf Club,** High Bickington, Umberleigh EX37 9BS (01769 560269; Fax: 01769 560342). *Location:* A377 Exeter to Barnstaple, turn off on B3227 to Torrington, at Atherington, turn off B3217 to High Bickington. Parkland with many lakes. 18 holes, 6481 yards. S.S.S. 71. Driving range, teaching centre. *Green Fees:* weekdays £20.00; weekends £26.00. *Eating facilities:* bar, bar meals and first class restaurant. *Visitors:* always welcome, seven days a week. Dress code must be observed. *Society Meetings:* welcome by prior arrangement. Special Society Packages. Fully stocked golf shop. Secretary: Gerald Herniman (01769 560269).

WESTWARD HO!. **Royal North Devon Golf Club,** Golf Links Road, Westward Ho!, Bideford EX39 1HD (01237 473817). *Location:* two miles North Bideford. Oldest links course in England. 18 holes, 6653 yards. S.S.S. 72. Practice area. *Green Fees:* £40.00 per round weekdays; £46.00 per round weekends. Society discounts and winter rates available. *Eating facilities:* full catering available. *Visitors:* welcome with Handicap Certificate. Tee reservations should be made in advance. *Society Meetings:* catered for. Professional: Iain Parker (01237 477598; Fax: 01237 475347). Secretary: Bob Fowler (01237 473817; Fax: 01237 423456).
e-mail: info@royalnorthdevongolfclub.co.uk
website: www.royalnorthdevongolfclub.co.uk

YELVERTON. **Yelverton Golf Club,** Golf Links Road, Yelverton PL20 6BN (01822 852824). *Location:* eight miles north of Plymouth on A386 road. Testing moorland course with views across Dartmoor. 18 holes, 6353 yards. S.S.S. 71. Practice ground. *Green Fees:* weekdays £34.00 per day or part day; weekends and Bank Holidays £40.00 per day or part day. *Eating facilities:* full catering and bar facilities available. *Visitors:* welcome if member of a recognised golf club or golf society. Handicap Certificate required. Snooker. *Society Meetings:* catered for, welcome by arrangement with Secretary. Professional: T. McSherry (01822 853593). Secretary: S. M. J. Barnes (01822 852824; Fax: 01822 854869).
e-mail: secretary@yelvertongc.co.uk
website: www.yelvertongc.co.uk

Dorset

BLANDFORD. **The Ashley Wood Golf Club,** Wimborne Road, Blandford Forum DT11 9HN (01258 452253; Fax: 01258 450590). *Location:* half a mile south of Blandford on B3082. Downland with magnificent views over Tarrant and Stour valleys. 18 holes, 6284 yards. S.S.S. 70. Practice ground, putting green. *Green Fees:* weekdays £30.00; weekends £35.00 after 1pm. *Eating facilities:* hot and cold snacks all day. *Visitors:* welcome during week; after 12 noon Saturday and Sundays with Handicap Certificate or with member only. *Society Meetings:* welcome by arrangement. Professional: Jon Shimmons (01258 480379). Manager: Tim Salmon (01258 452253). e-mail: generalmanager@ashleywoodgolfclub.com website: www.ashleywoodgolfclub.com

BOURNEMOUTH. **Knighton Heath Golf Club,** Francis Avenue, Bournemouth BH11 8NX (01202 572633; Fax: 01202 590774). *Location:* A348 and A3049 roundabout exit Francis Avenue. Undulating heathland, 18 holes, 6094 yards. S.S.S. 69. *Green Fees:* weekdays £30.00 per round, £35.00 per day. *Eating facilities:* meals and bar snacks available daily. *Visitors:* welcome after 9.30am weekdays but please phone to check availability, Restrictions on competition days. Not at weekends unless with a member. Handicap Certificate required. *Society Meetings:* catered for if arranged in advance. Professional: Paul Brown (01202 578275). Club Secretary: S. Fletcher (01202 572633; Fax: 01202 590774). e-mail: khgc@btinternet.com website: www.khgc.co.uk

BOURNEMOUTH. **Meyrick Park Golf Club,** Central Drive, Bournemouth BH2 6LH (01202 786040). *Location:* one mile from Bournemouth town centre. Beautiful and challenging woodland course. 18 holes, 5802 yards. S.S.S. 68. Practice area. *Green Fees:* from £14.00. *Eating facilities:* Pulse Cafe Bar and Summer Terrace. *Visitors:* welcome. Lodge on site offering 17 en suite bedrooms – golf breaks available. *Society Meetings:* welcome by prior arrangement. Professional: Andrew Britton (01202 786040). website: www.theclubcompany.com

BOURNEMOUTH. **Queens Park (Bournemouth) Golf Club,** Queens Park West Drive, Bournemouth BH8 9BY (01202 437807). *Location:* off Wessex Way. Parkland course in centre of Bournemouth. 18 holes, 6090 yards. S.S.S. 69. Small practice area. *Green Fees:* weekdays £15.00; weekend £21.00. *Eating facilities:* restaurant and bar. *Visitors:* welcome anytime, last tee off times Sundays 12 noon. *Society Meetings:* welcome by prior arrangement. Secretary: Paul Greenwood (01202 302611).

BOURNEMOUTH. **Solent Meads Golf Centre,** Rolls Drive, Hengistbury Head, Bournemouth BH6 4NA (01202 420795). *Location:* south of Christchurch, 2 miles from Bournemouth town centre. Seaside course. 18 holes, 2159 yards. S.S.S. 54. Driving range, 9 hole `Snag' pitch and putt. Lessons available. *Green Fees:* £7.70 for 18 holes, concessions available. *Eating*

facilities: cafe. *Visitors:* no restrictions. Professional: Warren Butcher (01202 420795). e-mail: solentmeads@yahoo.co.uk website: www.solentmeads.co.uk www.golflessonsbournemouth.com

BOURTON. **Bullpits Golf Club,** Bourton, Near Gillingham SP8 5AX (01747 840091). *Location:* off the A303 at Bourton and follow sign in village. Wooded parkland with streams and water, and River Stour. 12 holes, 18 tees, 3362 yards. S.S.S. 55. Putting green. *Green Fees:* visitors £10.00. *Eating facilities:* light refreshments by prior arrangement. *Visitors:* welcome at all times except early Sunday mornings. *Society Meetings:* welcome by appointment. Owners: Richard & Cathy Price.

BRIDPORT. **Bridport and West Dorset Golf Club,** Burton Road, Bridport DT6 4PS (01308 421095). *Location:* one mile east of Bridport on B3157. Clifftop links course. 18 holes, 5729 yards. Par 70. Driving range and 9-hole pitch and putt course, 18 hole putting green May to September. *Green Fees:* (2007) £28.00, £22.00 after 2pm, £14.00 twilight time. *Eating facilities:* lounge and dining room, spikes bar. *Visitors:* welcome, but not before 9.30am Mondays, Wednesdays, Fridays and Saturdays, and after 1pm Tuesdays, Thursdays and Sundays. Members only 8am-9.30am daily and 11am-2pm weekends. Please check with Professional in advance. *Society Meetings:* catered for by prior arrangement. Clubhouse: (01308 422597). Caterer: (01308 421998). Professional: David Parsons (01308 421491). Secretary: Peter Ridler (Tel & Fax: 01308 421095). e-mail: secretary@bridportgolfclub.org.uk website: www.bridportgolfclub.org.uk

BROADSTONE. **Broadstone (Dorset) Golf Club,** Wentworth Drive, Broadstone BH18 8DQ (01202 692595). *Location:* off A349 to B3072 to Broadstone. Heathland. 18 holes, 6349 yards. S.S.S. 70. Practice area. *Green Fees:* weekdays £48.00 per round, £72.00 per day. Weekend/Bank Holidays one round £62.00 (very limited). *Eating facilities:* full catering service. *Visitors:* welcome weekdays, weekends by prior arrangement, current Handicap Certificate required. *Society Meetings:* welcome by arrangement except weekends. Professional: Nigel Tokely (Tel & Fax: 01202 692835). Secretary: Mathew Wilson (Tel & Fax: 01202 692595). e-mail: admin@broadstonegolfclub.com website: www.broadstonegolfclub.com

CHRISTCHURCH. **Dudmoor Farm Golf Course,** Dudmoor Farm Road, Christchurch BH23 6AQ. *Location:* off Fairmile road, near Christchurch Hospital. Wooded course. 9 holes. Longest hole 280 yards. *Green Fees:* 18 holes - £8.50 weekdays, £9.50 weekends and Bank Holidays. *Eating facilities:* tea, coffee, crisps, chocolate, ice cream. *Visitors:* welcome, no need to book. Riding instruction also available. (01202 473826; Fax: 01202 480207).

CHRISTCHURCH. **Highcliffe Castle Golf Club,** 107 Lymington Road, Highcliffe BH23 4LA (01425 272953). *Location:* on the coastal road linking Lymington and Christchurch. Flat, wooded course. 18 holes, 4776 yards, 4347 metres. S.S.S. 63. Two practice nets. *Green Fees:* weekdays £26.00; weekends £36.00. Reductions during winter months and after 4pm in summer. Must be in possession of Handicap Certificate. *Eating facilities:* full bar/catering facilities. *Visitors:* welcome after 9.30am if member of recognised golf club. Please phone to check tee reservations. *Society Meetings:* catered for by prior arrangement. Secretary: Graham Fisher (01425 272210).

CHRISTCHURCH. **Parley Court Golf Club,** Parley Green Lane, Hurn, Christchurch BH23 6BB (01202 591600). *Location:* opposite Bournemouth International Airport. Flat and challenging course. 9 holes (18 tees), 4938 yards (18 holes). S.S.S. 64, Par 68. Putting and chipping areas. *Green Fees:* Infomation not available. *Eating facilities:* licensed bar; catering available. *Visitors:* welcome. No booking or Handicap Certificate required. Membership available. *Society Meetings:* welcome. Professional: Richard Hill. Secretary: S.D. Mitchell (01202 591600).
e-mail: info@parleygolf.co.uk
website: www.parleygolf.com*

DORCHESTER. **Came Down Golf Club,** Came Down, Dorchester DT2 8NR (01305 813494). *Location:* two miles south of Dorchester. Downland course on chalk downs with excellent drainage and magnificent views. Birthplace of the Ryder Cup. Designed by Harry S. Colt. 18 holes, 6255 yards, 5720 metres. S.S.S. 70. Practice area and nets. *Green Fees:* information not available. *Eating facilities:* full catering facilities. *Visitors:* welcome without reservation except Sunday mornings - phone in advance. All visitors must have Handicap Certificate. Buggies for hire. Established in 1896. *Society Meetings:* Wednesdays only. Package (from £28.00) includes golf (36 holes), morning coffee,

lunch and evening meal. Professional: Nick Rodgers (01305 812670). Manager: (01305 813494)
e-mail: manager@camedowngolfclub.co.uk
website: www.camedowngolfclub.co.uk

DORCHESTER. **Charminster Golf Club,** Wolfedale Golf Course, Dorchester DT2 7SG (01305 260186; Fax: 01305 257074). *Location:* Dorchester. Parkland course. 18 holes, 5467 yards. S.S.S. 67. 6 hole practice area. *Green Fees:* information not available. *Eating facilities:* Caddy Shack bar and restaurant. *Visitors:* welcome anytime. Sundays mainly competition days. *Society Meetings:* welcome. Professional: Tim Lovegrove (01305 260186; Fax: 01305 833668). Secretary: R. Walker.

FERNDOWN. **Dudsbury Golf Club,** Christchurch Road, Ferndown BH22 8ST (01202 593499; Fax: 01202 594555). *Location:* Ferndown town centre. Follow signs for Poole on A348, turn left at first mini roundabout, turn left to Hurn Airport, 200 yards. Club on right hand side. Parkland course designed by Donald Steel, featuring six lakes in beautiful Dorset countryside rolling gently down to the River Stour. 18 holes, 6904 yards. S.S.S 73. 6 hole academy course, driving range. *Green Fees:* Information not available. *Eating facilities:* two bars, spike bar, food served all day. *Visitors:* welcome at all times. Buggies and trolleys available. *Society Meetings:* welcome, phone Secretary for details. Professional: Steve Pockneall (01202 594488). *

FERNDOWN. **Ferndown Golf Club,** 119 Golf Links Road, Ferndown BH22 8BU (01202 872022). *Location:* off A31. Wooded heathland. 18 holes, 6501 yards. S.S.S. 71. 9 holes, 5604 yards. S.S.S. 68. Practice ground. *Green Fees:* £60.00 per round, £80.00 per day weekdays. *Eating facilities:* available. *Visitors:* welcome but prior permission recommended. Handicap Certificate required from a recognised golf club. Professional: Neil Pike (01202 873825). Secretary: S. Malherbe (01202 874602; Fax: 01202 873926).

FERNDOWN. **Ferndown Forest Golf Club,** Forest Links Road, Ferndown BH22 9PH (01202 876096; Fax: 01202 894095). *Location:* off main A31 trunk road. Flat, wooded parkland. 18 holes, 5200 yards, Par 68. Covered, floodlit driving range; large practice putting green. *Green Fees:* £18.00/£16.00. *Eating facilities:* licensed bar and patio serving breakfast, lunch, dinner. *Visitors:* all welcome. *Society Meetings:* welcome. Professional: Graham Howell. Secretary: Chris Lawford.

HALSTOCK. **Halstock Golf Club,** Common Lane, Halstock BA22 9SF (01935 891689; Fax: 01935 891839). *Location:* six miles south of Yeovil near Sutton Bingham Reservoir, signposted in village. Flat parkland course, short, tight but challenging. 18 holes, 4481 yards. S.S.S. 63. 12 bay driving range. *Green Fees:* information not provided. *Eating facilities:* light refreshments available, bar, restaurant (01935 891747). *Visitors:* welcome at all times. Please telephone for booking. *Society Meetings:* catered for by prior arrangement. Secretary: John Page.

LYME REGIS. **Lyme Regis Golf Club,** Timber Hill, Lyme Regis DT7 3HQ (01297 442043). *Location:* between Lyme Regis and Charmouth (A35). Cliff top course (not hilly) with fine coastal views. 18 holes, 6283 yards. S.S.S. 70. Practice ground, chipping area and bunker. New Driving Range open, tokens from Pro Shop. *Green Fees:* £34 per round. *Eating facilities:* bars (normal hours) and catering every day. Visitors: welcome, but not before 9.30am weekdays and Saturdays, Thursdays after 2.15pm and Sundays after 12 noon. Best to check with Professional. Handicap Certificate or proof of membership of a golf club required. *Society Meetings:* Tuesdays and Wednesdays, minimum for Tee Booking 14. Professional: Duncan Driver (01297 442963 select option 1). Secretary: Miss Sue Davidge (01297 442963).
e-mail: secretary@lymeregisgolfclub.co.uk
website: www.lymeregisgolfclub.co.uk

POOLE. **Parkstone Golf Club,** 49a Links Road, Parkstone, Poole BH14 9QS (01202 707138). *Location:* off A35 Bournemouth to Poole. Wooded heathland. 18 holes, 6250 yards. S.S.S. 70. *Green Fees:* October to April: £50.00 per round, £75.00 per day weekdays; £60.00 per round, £85.00 per day weekends and Bank Holidays. May to September: £55.00 per round, £80.00 per day weekdays; £65.00 per round, £90.00 per day weekends and Bank Holidays. *Eating facilities:* comprehensive. *Visitors:* welcome with booking and Handicap Certificate. *Society Meetings:* catered for as above. Professional: Martyn Thompson (01202 708092). General Manager: Christine Radford (01202 707138; Fax: 01202 706027).

POOLE near. **Bulbury Woods Golf Club,** Bulbury Lane, Lytchett Minster, Poole BH16 6HR (01929 459574; Fax: 01929 459000). *Location:* just off A35 , one mile after the Bakers Arms roundabout, three miles from Poole centre. Excellent woodland course, superbly manicured, panoramic views across Poole harbour and the Purbeck Hills. 18 holes, 6000 yards, par 71. Practice ground. *Green Fees:* from £18.00. *Eating facilities:* fully licensed bar and restaurant. *Visitors:* welcome anytime subject to availability. *Society Meetings:* societies and corporate days by prior arrangement.

SHERBORNE. **Sherborne Golf Club,** Higher Clatcombe, Sherborne DT9 4RN (01935 814431; Fax: 01935 814218). *Location:* one mile north of Sherborne off the B3145 to Wincanton. Parkland with extensive views. 18 holes, 6414 yards. Par 72. S.S.S. 71. Practice ground. *Green Fees:* weekdays £25.00, weekends £35.00 *Eating facilities:* snacks, lunches, suppers, teas; dinners to order. *Visitors:* as commitment allows, telephone in advance. Handicap Certificates required. Thursday is Ladies' Day. *Society Meetings:* catered for Monday, Tuesday, Wednesday and Friday. Professional: Alistair Tresidder (Tel & Fax: 01935 812274). Managing Secretary: Geoff Scott (01935 814431; Fax: 01935 814218).
e-mail: secretary@sherbornegolfclub.co.uk
website: www.sherbornegolfclub.co.uk

SOUTH PERROTT. Chedington Court Golf Club, South Perrott DT8 3HU (01935 891413). *Location:* three miles south east of Crewkerne on A356. Parkland course surrounded by woods, very picturesque, several ponds. 18 holes, 5924 yards, S.S.S. 70. 5-acre practice area. *Green Fees:* information not available. *Eating facilities:* restaurant and bar open all day; new dining facility. *Visitors:* all welcome. Dress restrictions. Trolleys, buggies and clubs for hire. *Society Meetings:* all welcome, special rates available.
e-mail: info@chedingtoncourtgolfclub.co.uk
website: www.chedingtoncourtgolfclub.co.uk

STUDLAND. Isle of Purbeck Golf Club, Studland, Swanage BH19 3AB (01929 450361). *Location:* A351 towards Swanage, at Corfe Castle turn onto B3351 to Studland. Heathland courses with wonderful views. Purbeck - 18 holes, 6295 yards. S.S.S. 70. Dene - 9 holes, 2022 yards. S.S.S. 30. *Green Fees:* information not available. *Eating facilities:* bar and restaurant. *Visitors:* welcome. Buggies available. *Society Meetings:* catered for by arrangement, minimum 8. Professional: Ian Brake (01929 450354). Secretary: Mrs C. Robinson (01929 450361; Fax: 01929 450501).
e-mail: iop@purbeckgolf.co.uk
website: www.purbeckgolf.co.uk

VERWOOD. Crane Valley Golf Club, The Clubhouse, Verwood BH31 7LE (01202 814088; Fax: 01202 813407). *Location:* on B3081 Verwood to Cranborne Road. Parkland featuring lakes and River Crane. 18 holes, 6400 yards. S.S.S. 71. 9 hole woodland course, 2100 yards. Covered driving range. *Green Fees:* information not available. *Eating facilities:* restaurant and spikes bar. *Visitors:* welcome at all times. Accommodation adjoining course at West Farm. *Society Meetings:* by appointment. Secretary/ Manager: Andrew Blackwell.

WAREHAM. The Dorset Golf & Country Club, Bere Regis, Near Poole BH20 7NT (01929 472244; Fax: 01929 471294). *Location:* take A352 off Wareham by-pass, enter Puddletown Road, Worgret Heath or the Wool road from Bere Regis. After 4 miles, the Club is clearly signposted. A fantastic Golfing Complex. The courses have 27 holes with mixes of the three 9 holes. From 7027 yards Lakeland and Parkland, to 5901 yards Parkland and Woodland courses. Par 72 and Par 69. Driving range and Pro Shop. *Green Fees:* weekdays £38.00; weekends £42.00. *Eating facilities:* excellent bar and restaurant. *Visitors:* welcome anytime with prior tee reservation. *Society Meetings:* welcome by advance booking. The Dorset Golf Hotel overlooks course – 16 en suite bedrooms and luxury Scandinavian log homes for rent. Professional: Scott Porter (01929 472244). Secretary: Graham Packer (01929 472244; Fax: 01929 471294).
e-mail: admin@dorsetgolfresort.com
website: www.dorsetgolfresort.com

WAREHAM. Wareham Golf Club, Sandford Road, Wareham BH20 4DH (01929 554147; Fax: 01929 557993). *Location*: adjoining A351 north of Wareham. Partly wooded course with splendid views over Purbeck Hills and Poole Harbour. 18 holes, 5766 yards, S.S.S. 68. Practice ground, putting green. *Green Fees*: please telephone the Secretary for further information. *Eating facilities*: excellent bar and restaurant. *Visitors*: welcome, after 9.30am weekdays and after 1pm weekends. Handicap Certificate preferred. *Society Meetings*: very welcome, special packages available
e-mail:warehamgolf@tiscali.co.uk
website: www.warehamgolfclub.com

WEYMOUTH. Wessex Golf Centre, Radipole Lane, Weymouth DT4 9HX (01305 784737). *Location:* Wessex roundabout off Weymouth by pass, behind football stadium. Flat public course. 9 holes, 1432 yards. Par 3. Large driving range, putting green, practice bunker. *Green Fees:* information not available. *Visitors:* welcome; public course. Shop. Professional: Jon Bevan.*

WEYMOUTH. Weymouth Golf Club Ltd, Links Road, Weymouth DT4 0PF (01305 773981; Fax: 01305 788029). *Location:* A354 from Dorchester, take last exit at Manor roundabout then second left at Chafeys roundabout. Undulating parkland. 18 holes, 5996 yards. S.S.S. 69. Practice area. *Green Fees:* weekdays £32.00 per day, weekends and Bank Holidays £36.00. £19.00 after 4pm. Half price playing with a member. Juniors half price. Green fees are subject to review. *Eating facilities:* full restaurant and bar. *Visitors:* welcome, but only with EGU or Club Handicap Certificate. *Society Meetings:* welcome by prior arrangement except weekends. Special rates for Society, Company/ Corporate Days. Conference facilities and local transport arranged. Professional: Des Lochrie (01305 773997). Manager: Stuart Elliott (01305 773981; Fax: 01305 788029).
e-mail: weymouthgolfclub@aol.com
website: www.weymouthgolfclub.co.uk

WIMBORNE. **Canford Magna Golf Club,** Knighton Lane, Wimborne BH21 3AS (01202 592552; Fax: 01202 592550). *Location*: off A341, near Bear Cross roundabout on the main A348 Ringwood Road. Three courses: Parkland – 18 holes, 6519 yards; Riverside – 18 holes, 6173 yards; Knighton – 9 holes, 2754 yards, Par 3. 6-hole academy course and driving range, practice area. *Green Fees*: Knighton – 9 holes from £7.00; Riverside - 18 holes from £18.50; Parkland – 18 holes from £23.50. Under 18s £12.00. 2007 rates, subject to review. *Eating facilities*: two bars, meals served throughout day; restaurant. *Visitors*: welcome. Prior booking advisable (one week in advance). Club hire and lessons; Pro Shop. Handicap Certificate not required. Conference facilities. Professionals: 6 full-time professionals headed by PGA Pro Martin Cummins. General Manager: Stuart Hudson.
e-mail: admin@canfordmagnagc.co.uk
website: www.canfordmagnagc.co.uk

WIMBORNE. **Canford School Golf Club,** Canford School, Canford Magna. Wimborne BH21 3AD (01202 841254; Fax: 01202 881009). *Location*: close to Wimborne, Poole and Bournemouth. Flat Parkland course. 9 (x2) holes, 5934 yards, S.S.S. 69. *Green Fees*: £12.00 with member. *Society Meetings*: Contact Secretary. Secretary: Mark Burley (01202 841254; Fax: 01202 881009).

WIMBORNE. **Sturminster Marshall Golf Club,** Moor Lane, Sturminster Marshall, Wimborne BH21 4AH (01258 858444; Fax: 01258 858262). *Location:* Poole to Blandford Forum road, A350 signposted at village. Flat parkland course, suits golfers of all abilities. 9/18 holes, Par 64. Practice net. *Green Fees:* 9 holes £10.00, 18 holes £15.00. *Eating facilities:* fully licensed snack bar. *Visitors:* welcome, no restrictions. *Society Meetings:* welcome. Professional/Secretary: Mike Dodd.*

For full details of clubs and courses, plus convenient accommodation

www.uk-golfguide.com

Gloucestershire

BRISTOL. **Bristol and Clifton Golf Club,** Beggar Bush Lane, Failand, Bristol BS8 3TH (01275 393474). *Location:* M5 Junction 19 - A369 towards Clifton, turn right at A.T.S. into Beggar Bush Lane. Parkland course. 18 holes, 6294 yards. S.S.S. 70. Practice ground. *Green Fees:* weekdays £40.00; weekends £45.00. *Eating facilities:* full restaurant. *Visitors:* welcome weekdays without reservation, must have current golf club Handicap. *Society Meetings:* most welcome, Thursdays. Professional: Paul Mitchell (Tel & Fax: 01275 393031). Secretary: Charles Vane Percy (01275 393474; Fax: 01275 394611).
e-mail: mansec@bristolgolf.co.uk
website: www.bristolgolf.co.uk

BRISTOL. **Chipping Sodbury Golf Club,** Trinity Lane, Chipping Sodbury, Bristol BS37 6PU (01454 319042). *Location:* 12 miles north of Bristol, nine miles from Junction 14 on M5 and three miles from Junction 18 on M4. Parkland course. 6786 yards. *Green Fees:* 18-hole course weekdays £30.00; weekends £45.00. *Eating facilities:* full catering available. *Visitors:* welcome except Saturday/Sunday morning and Bank Holidays. Must have Handicap Certificate. *Society Meetings:* catered for by prior arrangement weekdays only. Professional: Mike Watts (01454 314087). Secretary: Bob Williams.
e-mail: info@chippingsodburygolfclub.co.uk
website: www.chippingsodburygolfclub.co.uk

BRISTOL. **Filton Golf Club,** Golf Course Lane, Filton, Bristol BS34 7QS (0117 969 4169; Fax: 0117 931 4359). *Location:* off A38 north of Bristol and only 3 miles from J15 of M5. Interesting, undulating and challenging mature parkland course on high ground to the north of the City. Established 1909 and regular host to County events. 18 holes, 6174 yards, Par 70, S.S.S 70. Excellent practice facilities. *Green Fees:* (2006) weekdays £32.00 per round, £40.00 per day. Weekends only as guest of member. Buggies and trolleys for hire. *Eating Facilities:* excellent menu of bar and main meals. *Visitors:* welcome weekdays with a Handicap Certificate or letter of competence. *Society Meetings:* welcome subject to programme of club events - usually available Monday, Wednesday and Friday - information pack on request. Advance booking essential. Professional: Daryl Kelley (0117 969 6968) Secretary: Trevor Atkinson (0117 969 4169; Fax: 0117 931 4359).
e-mail: thesecretary@filtongolfclub.co.uk
website:www,filtongolfclub.co.uk

BRISTOL **"The Gloucestershire",** Tracy Park Estate, Bath Road, Wick, Near Bristol BS30 5RN (0117 937 2251; Fax: 0117 937 4288). *Location:* M4 Junction 18, A46 towards Bath, A420 towards Bristol. Turn left at bottom of steep hill for Lansdown/Bath. Wooded parkland, 400-year-old trees with water hazards and magnificent views of surrounding countryside. Two courses: Crown Course - 18 holes, 6252 yards, Par 69; Cromwell Course - 18 holes, 6246 yards, Par 71. 13 bay driving range. *Green Fees:* information not available. *Eating facilities:* full catering available all day. *Visitors:* welcome – telephone ahead. *Society Meetings:* welcome. 18 en suite bedrooms. Professional: David Morgan. Tee reservations (0117 937 2251; Fax: 0117 937 4288). Secretary: David Knipe.*
e-mail: info@thegloucestershire.com
website: www.thegloucestershire.com

BRISTOL. **Henbury Golf Club,** Henbury Road, Westbury-on-Trym, Bristol BS10 7QB (0117 9500044). *Location:* north M5 Junction 17 A4018 to Westbury-on-Trym; right to Blaise Castle, top of hill turn left. Wooded parkland, very pretty; easily accessible from City Centre and M5. 18 holes, 6007 yards. S.S.S. 70. Practice ground. *Green Fees:* £30.00. *Eating facilities:* bars and dining room. *Visitors:* welcome weekdays, Handicap required. Clubs and trolleys for hire. *Society Meetings:* Tuesdays and Fridays only. Professional: Nick Riley (Tel & Fax: 0117 9502121) Secretary: John Keight (0117 9500044; Fax: 0117 9591928).
e-mail: thesecretary@henburygolfclub.co.uk

BRISTOL. **The Kendleshire Golf Club,** Henfield Road, Coalpit Heath, Bristol BS36 2TG (0117 956 7007; Fax: 0117 957 3433). *Location:* Henfield Road, off Westerleigh Road from New Avon Ring Road, five minutes from Junction 1 M32. Parkland with water features. 27 holes, from 6001 to 6507 yards. S.S.S. 71. Practice range. *Green Fees:* Monday £25.00, Tuesday - Thursday £35.00, Friday - Sunday £40.00. *Eating facilities:* two bars, restaurant, and function room. *Visitors:* welcome but prior booking essential. *Society Meetings:* welcome weekdays, packages available. Professional: Tony Mealing. Secretary: Patrick Murphy.
e-mail: info@kendleshire.com
website: www.kendleshire.com

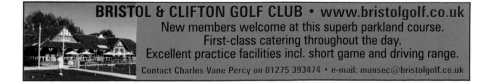

BRISTOL. **Knowle Bristol Golf Club,** Fairway, West Town Lane, Brislington, Bristol BS4 5DF (0117 977 0660). *Location:* three miles south of city centre, left off Wells Road. A4 – Bath. Parkland course. 18 holes, 6006 yards. S.S.S. 69. Practice field, putting green. *Green Fees:* weekdays £30.00 for 18 holes, £35.00 for 27 holes; weekends £40.00 for 18 holes, £40.00 for 27 holes. *Eating facilities:* bar/dining room, dinners by arrangement with Steward. *Visitors:* welcome with Handicap Certificate. *Society Meetings:* Thursdays only. Professional: Rob Hayward (0117 977 9193). Secretary: Terry Crane (0117 977 0660; Fax: 0117 972 0615). website: www.knowlegolfclub.co.uk

BRISTOL. **Long Ashton Golf Club,** Clarken Coombe, Long Ashton, Bristol BS41 9DW (01275 392229; Fax: 01275 394395). *Location:* three miles south-west of Bristol on the B3128 Clevedon/Bristol Road. Wooded parkland. 18 holes, 6193 yards. S.S.S. 70. Practice ground. *Green Fees:* weekdays £30.00 18 holes, £35.00 36 holes; weekends £35.00 18 holes. *Eating facilities:* full catering daily, bar open Monday to Sunday (11am to 10.30pm). *Visitors:* welcome, must have current Handicap Certificate. *Society Meetings:* by arrangement with Secretary. Professional: Mike Hart (01275 392229). Secretary: Colin Page (01275 392229). e-mail: secretary@longashtongolfclub.co.uk website: www.longashtongolfclub.co.uk

BRISTOL. **Shirehampton Park Golf Club,** Park Hill, Shirehampton, Bristol BS11 0UL (0117 982 2083). *Location:* two miles from Junction 18 on M5 on B4054 to Shirehampton. Parkland course with spectacular views across Avon Gorge. 18 holes, 5430 yards. S.S.S. 66. *Green Fees:* weekdays £22.00, weekends £20.00 only with member. *Eating facilities:* lunches, snacks, teas, etc available daily. *Visitors:* welcome. *Society Meetings:* catered for by prior arrangement. Professional: Jon Palmer (0117 316 7955). Club Secretary: Karen Rix (0117 982 2083).

BRISTOL. **Shortwood Lodge Golf Club,** Carsons Road, Mangotsfield, Bristol BS16 9LW (0117 9565501). *Location:* four miles M32 via Downend, one mile Warmley A420. Parkland, hilly course. 18 holes, 5337 yards, 4877 metres. S.S.S. 66. Small practice area. *Green Fees:* information not available. *Eating facilities:* no restriction on food and drink. *Visitors:* welcome anytime, no restrictions. *Society Meetings:* catered for weekdays only. Professional/Secretary:*

BRISTOL. **Thornbury Golf Centre,** Bristol Road, Thornbury, Bristol BS35 3XL (01454 281144; Fax: 01454 281177). *Location:* five miles A38 north from Junctions M4/M5 at Almondsbury. Parkland course overlooking River Severn. 18 holes, 6308 yards. S.S.S. 70. Par 3 course. 25 bay floodlit driving range. *Green Fees:* £19.95 weekdays; £24.00 weekends and Bank Holidays. Subject to review. *Eating facilities:* restaurant and licensed bar. *Visitors:* welcome seven days. Smart casual clothing desirable. Tuition. Golf Lodge available with 11 rooms. Stay and play packages. Conference and private function facilities. *Society Meetings:* welcome seven days. Professional: Mike Smedley. General Manager: Kevin Pickett. e-mail: info@thornburygc.co.uk website: www.thornburygc.co.uk

BRISTOL. **Woodlands Golf and Country Club,** Trench Lane, Almondsbury, Bristol BS32 4JZ (01454 619319). *Location:* Junction 16 M5 - A38 towards Bristol. Left off AZTEC roundabout, first left Woodlands Lane. Two magnificent parkland 18 hole courses with USGA greens. The Woodland Course 6237 yards. S.S.S. 70, with water in play on 8 holes. The Signature Course 6080 yards S.S.S. 69, water in play on 9 holes, drop hole with island green. Putting green. *Green Fees:* weekdays £16.00 per round, weekends £18.00 per round. *Eating facilities:* bar/lounge meals, snacks. *Visitors:* welcome, no restrictions and hire of clubs available. Trolleys and buggies available £12.00 per round. *Society Meetings:* bookable in advance. Well stocked Pro shop. Professional: Leigh Riddiford. Secretary: David Knipe (Fax: 01454 619397; Clubhouse: 01454 618121). website: www.woodlands-golf.com

BROADWAY. **Broadway Golf Club,** Willersey Hill, Broadway WR12 7LG (01386 853683; Fax: 01386 858643). *Location:* 1½-miles east Broadway (A44). 18 holes, 6211 yards. S.S.S. 70. *Green Fees:* weekdays £30.00, weekends £38.00. *Eating facilities:* available daily. *Visitors:* welcome; reservation advised. Handicap Certificates required. Saturdays (April/ September) with member only before 3pm. October/ March no restrictions. Affiliated to the "Gloucestershire Golf Union". *Society Meetings:* by arrangement (Wednesday, Thursday and Friday). Professional: Martyn Freeman (01386 853275). Secretary: Vic Tofts. Office: (01386 853683).

CHELTENHAM. **Cleeve Hill Golf Club,** Cleeve Hill, Near Cheltenham GL52 3PW (01242 672025). *Location:* three miles north of Cheltenham on B4632. Hilltop inland links with gorse and natural quarries. Outstanding views from the highest point in the Cotswolds. 18 holes, 6411 yards. S.S.S. 72. *Green Fees:* weekdays £15.00; weekends £20.00. *Eating facilities:* full restaurant and bar facilities. *Visitors:* welcome with prior booking. *Society Meetings:* welcome with prior booking (01242 672025). Professional: Dave Finch (01242 672592). Secretary: Hugh Fitzsimons (01242 672025).

CHELTENHAM. **Cotswold Hills Golf Club,** Ullenwood, Near Cheltenham GL53 9QT (01242 515264). *Location:* at Ullenwood, off the A436 south of Cheltenham (two miles from town). Undulating Cotswold country course, excellent drainage. 18 holes, 6557 yards. S.S.S. 71. Large practice ground. *Green Fees:* weekdays £36.00 18 holes; weekends £42.00 18 holes. *Eating facilities:* full restaurant and bars. *Visitors:* no restrictions as a rule, but it is wise to telephone. Handicap Certificate required. *Society Meetings:* catered for on Wednesdays and Fridays only by arrangement with Secretary. Professional: James Latham (01242 515263). Club Manager: Annie Hale (01242 515264).
e-mail: contact.us@cotswoldhills-golfclub.com
website: www.cotswoldhills-golfclub.com

CHELTENHAM. **Lilley Brook Golf Club,** Cirencester Road, Charlton Kings, Cheltenham GL53 8EG (01242 526785). *Location:* two miles south-east of Cheltenham on main Cirencester road (A435). Parkland, 18 holes, 6212 yards. S.S.S. 70. Practice field. *Green Fees:* weekdays £30.00 per round, £35.00 per day; weekends £35.00 per round. *Eating facilities:* full catering available. *Visitors:* welcome weekdays, weekends subject to availability. Handicap Certificate required, *Society Meetings:* by arrangement. Professional: Karl Hayler (01242 525201). Secretary: M.F. Jordan (01242 526785; Fax: 01242 256880)

CHELTENHAM. **Naunton Downs Golf Club Ltd,** Naunton, Cheltenham GL54 3AE (01451 850092; Fax: 01451 850091). Rolling Cotswold countryside with a valley running through course. 18 holes, 6135 yards. S.S.S. 70. Practice ground. *Green Fees:* Mondays £19.00, Tuesday - Friday £22.00, weekends and Bank Holidays £28.00. *Eating facilities:* available. *Visitors:* welcome, must book at all times. *Society Meetings:* welcome. Professional: Nick Ellis (01451 850092); Golf Manager: Nick Ellis (01451 850090); Club Steward: Steve Maddock-Lyon (01451 850093).

CHELTENHAM. **Ullenwood Manor Golf Course,** National Star College, Ullenwood, Cheltenham GL53 9QU (01242 527631). *Location:* turn off A436 past junction with A417. Parkland course, 18 holes (using 9 fairways). 2980 yards S.S.S. 54. Designed by Norm Allen, opened 1975. *Green Fees:* £10.00 all day. *Eating facilities:* catering available at Air Balloon pub half mile away. *Visitors:* welcome anytime. *Society Meetings:* welcome anytime. Secretary: Richard Greenwell.

CHURCHDOWN. **Brickhampton Court Golf Complex,** Cheltenham Road, Churchdown GL2 9QF (01452 859444; Fax: 01452 859333). *Location:* midway between Cheltenham and Gloucester on B4063; 5 minutes from Junction 11 of M5. Rolling parkland courses featuring lakes, streams, strategic white sand bunkers, tree plantations and no steep hills. Two courses: Spa Course – 18 holes, 6449 yards. S.S.S. 71; Glevum Course – 9 holes, 1859 yards. Par 31. 28 bay floodlit covered driving range with Ping custom fitting centre. *Green Fees:* Spa Course – Monday to Thursday £23.00 per round, Friday £26.00, weekends and Bank Holidays £30.00. Glevum Course – weekdays £8.50; weekends and Bank Holidays £10.50. *Eating facilities:* spike bar and restaurant offering varied menu and Sunday lunches. *Visitors:* welcome although pre-booking advised. Buggies and trolleys for hire. Two fully stocked Pro shops. Corporate and Society Golf days available, call for details. Professional: Bruce Wilson.
e-mail: info@brickhampton.co.uk
website: www.brickhampton.co.uk

CIRENCESTER. **Cirencester Golf Club,** Cheltenham Road, Bagendon, Cirencester GL7 7BH (01285 652465; Fax: 01285 650665). *Location:* two miles north of Cirencester on A435 Cheltenham road. Scenic and free-draining Cotswold course. 18 holes, 6030 yards. S.S.S. 69. Driving range, Par 3 course. *Green Fees:* weekdays £35.00, weekends £40.00. *Eating facilities:* bar and restaurant - snacks available 10am to 6pm. *Visitors:* welcome, dress code applies. Buggies for hire. *Society Meetings:* catered for Wednesday and Friday only. Professional: Ed Goodwin (01285 656124). Secretary/Manager: Jonathan Vickers (01285 652465). website: www.cirencestergolfclub.co.uk

COLEFORD. **Forest Hills Golf Club Ltd,** Mile End Road, Coleford GL16 7BY (01594 810620; Fax: 01594 810823). *Location:* 10 miles from Severn Bridge, six miles from Monmouth M5, M50. Coleford town centre on Gloucester Road. Parkland with panoramic views to Welsh hills. 18 holes, 6300 yards. Par 72. Practice ground, driving range. *Green Fees:* information not available. *Eating facilities:* bar, restaurant. *Visitors:* welcome, no restrictions. Buggies available. *Society Meetings:* very welcome. Professional: Richard Ballard. Secretary: Colin Revill.*

COLEFORD. **Forest of Dean Golf Club,** Lords Hill, Coleford GL16 8BD (01594 832583; Fax: 01594 832584). *Location:* quarter of a mile from Coleford town centre on B4431 Coleford to Parkend Road, 10 miles from Severn Bridge, M4, M5 and M50. Parkland course in Forest of Dean. 18 holes, 6033 yards. S.S.S. 69. Practice area. *Green Fees:* information not available. *Eating facilities:* food available all day - breakfast, coffee, lunches, teas and dinner. Table d'hôte restaurant, bar open all day. *Visitors:* always welcome, please book teeing-off times with Professional. Own 52 bedroom Hotel, golf shop on site, tennis court, bowling green, golf cars available. *Society Meetings:* welcome. Professional: Paul Davies (01594 833689). Secretary: Mrs J. Green (01594 832583).

DURSLEY. **Stinchcombe Hill Golf Club,** Stinchcombe Hill, Dursley GL11 6AQ (01453 542015; Fax: 01453 549545). *Location:* M5 between Junctions 13 and 14, A38 to Dursley. At traffic lights in centre of Dursley turn right to enter May Lane, continue to top of Hill and turn right onto Golf Course. A gently undulating course situated on a hilltop at the southern edge of the Cotswolds, spectacular views. 18 holes, 5734 yards. S.S.S. 68. Practice and teaching areas. *Green Fees:* £28.00 per round, £36.00 per day weekdays (£15.00 with member); £36.00 per round, £42.00 per day weekends and Bank Holidays (£20.00 with member). Under review for 2008. *Eating facilities:* full catering and bar service available. *Visitors:* welcome, please call the Professional in advance for availability. *Society Meetings:* Monday, Wednesday and Friday; other days by arrangement. Professional: Paul Bushell (01453 543878). Secretary: I. Crowther (01453 542015). e-mail: secretary@stinchcombehill.plus.com website: www.stinchcombehillgolfclub.com

GLOUCESTER. **Ramada Hotel and Golf Resort,** Matson Lane, Gloucester GL4 9EA (01452 411331; Fax: 01452 302212). *Location:* follow signs off B4073. Stunning 18 hole, par 72 championship golf course, with breathtaking views of the surrounding countryside, complemented by challenging Par 3, 9-hole course, ideal for beginners and improvers, but a test to better players. Floodlit covered 12 bay golf academy with Callaway custom fit centre open 9.00am to 9.00pm, 7 days a week. Grass practice area with putting, chipping, pitching and bunker areas. *Green Fees:* information not available. *Eating facilities:* full catering and bar services available. *Visitors:* very welcome, please call for availability. Well-stocked and priced golf shop with all the leading brands, including Callaway, Ping and Taylormade. Hotel with 107 rooms with 5 suites. Extensive leisure complex with indoor swimming pool, gymnasium, sauna and solarium, health and beauty centre. Gloucester Ski Centre with qualified ski instructors. Golf breaks available, golf school with 2, 3 or 5 day programmes. Gloucester Golf Academy with team of registered PGA Golf Professionals. Pro-shop: (01452 411331/01452 874807)* e-mail: gloucester@btopenworld.com website: www.gloucestergolf.com

GLOUCESTER. **Rodway Hill Golf Course,** Highnam, Gloucester GL2 8DN (01452 384222). 18 holes, 6040 yards. S.S.S. 69. Driving range. *Green Fees:* £15.00 weekdays, £17.00 weekends. *Eating facilities:* cosy bar and restaurant. *Visitors:* all welcome - pay as you play. *Society Meetings:* welcome, special rates available. website: www.rodway-hill-golf-course.co.uk

LYDNEY. **Lydney Golf Club,** The Links, off Lakeside Avenue, Lydney GL15 5QA (01594 842614). *Location:* between by-pass and the town, none - no access off by-pass, enter the town and take Hams Road off the main thoroughfare of Newerne Street. Lakeside Avenue is the 7th road on the left hand side. Flat meadowland with views over the River Severn. 9 holes, 5298 yards. S.S.S. 66. Small practice area. *Green Fees:* information not available. *Eating facilities:* snack meals only. *Visitors:* welcome weekdays, only with a member at weekends/Bank Holidays. *Society Meetings:* welcome by prior arrangement (maximum 36). Hon. Secretary: D.A. Barnard (01594 843940).*

MINCHINHAMPTON. **Minchinhampton Golf Club (Old Course),** Minchinhampton, Stroud GL6 9AQ (01453 832642). *Location:* three miles east of Stroud. Easy walking course. 18 holes, 6019 yards. S.S.S. 69. Practice area. *Green Fees:* weekdays £16.00, weekends and Bank Holidays £19.00. *Eating facilities:* bar and restaurant available. *Visitors:* welcome. *Society Meetings:* most welcome by arrangement. Admin Manager: A.P. Dangerfield (01453 832642). Shop: (01453 836382). e-mail: alan@mgcold.co.uk website: www.gcold.co.uk

www.uk-golfguide.com

FHG Guides
publish a large range of well-known accommodation guides.
We will be happy to send you details or you can use
the order form at the back of this book.

MINCHINHAMPTON. **Minchinhampton Golf Club (New Courses),** Minchinhampton, Stroud GL6 9BE (01453 833866; Fax: 01453 837360). *Location:* five miles east of Stroud. Reasonably level, set in typical Cotswold countryside. Avening is cleverly bunkered, Cherington has large undulating greens of superb quality. A members' club with two fine and challenging courses and a fine Cotswold stone clubhouse, all set in lovely countryside. Two courses: both 18 holes, Cherington 6434 yards S.S.S. 71, Avening 6263 yards. S.S.S. 70. Practice area. *Green Fees:* information not available. *Eating facilities:* dining room and bar. *Visitors:* welcome, telephone booking essential on 01453 833840. Handicap Certificate required. *Society Meetings:* welcome weekdays, details on application. Professional: Chris Steele (Tel & Fax: 01453 837351). Secretary: David Calvert (01453 833866; Fax: 01453 837360).*

PAINSWICK. **Painswick Golf Club,** Golf Course Road, Painswick, Near Stroud GL6 6TL (01452 812180). *Location:* one mile north of Painswick village on A46 turn left. Hilltop, wooded course. 18 holes, 4900 yards. S.S.S. 65. *Green Fees:* weekdays £19.00; Saturdays and Bank Holidays £22.00 but reduced if with a member and/or in the winter. *Eating facilities:* lunches at clubhouse bar Tuesday to Sunday, evening meals in restaurant Tuesday to Saturday subject to availability of tables. *Visitors:* welcome weekdays and Saturday mornings. Saturday afternoons, Sunday mornings and Public Holidays only with member. *Society Meetings:* welcome weekdays. Secretary: Ann Smith.

TETBURY. **Westonbirt Golf Course,** c/o Jack Doyle, Westonbirt School Ltd, Westonbirt, Near Tetbury GL8 8QG (01666 880 242). *Location:* three miles south from Tetbury on A433 to Bath. Parkland. 9 holes, 4504 yards. S.S.S. 61. Practice area and green. *Green Fees:* £10.00 weekdays; £12.00 weekends. *Eating facilities:* tea and refreshments from seasonal caravan. *Visitors:* welcome without reservation. *Society Meetings:* welcome.
e-mail: doyle@westonbirt.gloucs.sch.uk
website: www.westonbirt.gloucs.sch.uk

TEWKESBURY. **Sherdons Golf Centre,** Tredington, Tewkesbury GL20 7BP (01684 274782; Fax: 01684 275358). *Location:* follow brown sign directions from A38 two miles south of Tewkesbury or A46 two miles east. Countryside course with gentle slopes and new plantations. 9 holes, 5308 yards. S.S.S. 66. 26 bay floodlit driving range. *Green Fees:* Information not available. *Eating facilities:* bar, coffee and light snacks available. *Visitors:* welcome at all times. *Society Meetings:* by arrangement, weekdays only. Special weekday society deals. Professionals: Philip Clark and John Parker (01684 274782). Secretary: Richard Chatham (01684 274782; Fax: 01684 275358).*
website: www.sherdons.co.uk

THE APPEARANCE OF AN ASTERISK (*) AT THE END OF A CLUB OR COURSE ENTRY INDICATES THAT UP-TO-DATE INFORMATION HAS NOT BEEN SUPPLIED

TEWKESBURY. **Hilton Puckrup Hall,** Puckrup, Tewkesbury GL20 6EL (01684 296200; Fax: 01684 850788). *Location*: leave M5 at Junction 8. Take M50 one mile to Junction 1, leave and bear left taking A38 towards Tewkesbury, Puckrup is half a mile along on the right. Undulating parkland with water hazards, spectacular views of the Malverns. 18 holes, 6219 yards. S.S.S. 70. Practice ground. *Green Fees:* weekdays from £30.00 per round, £40.00 per day; weekends from £35.00 per round, £45.00 per day. *Eating facilities:* choice of bars and restaurants. *Visitors:* welcome, subject to golfing ability and course availability. Buggies available. 112 bedroomed hotel with full leisure facilities. Golfing Breaks available. *Society Meetings:* welcome, packages available from £25.00 (min. 16 players). Professional: Mark Fenning (01684 271591). Secretary: Russell Lazenby (01452 840133). website: www.tewkesbury.hilton.com

TEWKESBURY. **Tewkesbury Park Hotel Golf and Country Club,** Lincoln Green Lane, Tewkesbury GL20 7DN (01684 295405; Fax: 01684 292386). *Location:* off Junction 9 of M5 through Tewkesbury on A38 - signposted. Parkland. 18 holes, 6533 yards. S.S.S. 71. Golf range, and pitching and chipping greens. *Green Fees:* information not available. *Eating facilities:* full Hotel facilities. *Visitors:* welcome, reservation required. Valid Handicap Certificate required. 82-bedroom hotel plus leisure section. *Society Meetings:* all welcome by prior arrangement. Professional: Marc Cottrell (01684 272320; Fax: 01684 292386).
e-mail: tewkesburypark@foliohotels.com
website: www.tewkesburyparkgolfclub.co.uk

WOTTON-UNDER-EDGE. **Cotswold Edge Golf Club,** Upper Rushmire, Wotton-under-Edge GL12 7PT (01453 844167). *Location:* eight miles from Junction 14 M5, on B4058 Tetbury road. Fairly flat course with magnificent views. 18 holes, White Tees - 6170 yards. S.S.S. 71; Yellow Tees - 5816 yards. S.S.S. 69. *Green Fees:* information not provided. *Eating facilities:* good lunch time catering service, usual bar facilities. *Visitors:* welcome weekdays. Telephone call in advance advisable. *Society Meetings:* by arrangement with Secretary. Professional: Rod Hibbitt (01453 844398). Secretary: E. Johnson (01453 844167; Fax: 01453 845120).

The 5th hole at Tewkesbury Park Hotel Golf & Country Club

Somerset

BATH. **Bath Golf Club,** Sham Castle, North Road, Bath BA2 6JG (01225 425182). *Location:* off A36, one mile south-east of Bath City Centre. Hilltop, undulating downland course with views of Bath and the surrounding countryside. 18 holes, 6442 yards, 5891 metres. S.S.S. 71. *Green Fees:* information not available. *Eating facilities:* catering every day. *Visitors:* with bona fide Handicap welcome. *Society Meetings:* catered for Wednesday and Friday. Professional: Peter Hancox (Tel & Fax: 01225 466953). Managing Secretary: J. M. Galley (01225 463834; Fax: 01225 331027).*

BATH. **Entry Hill Golf Club,** Entry Hill, Bath BA2 5NA (01225 834248). *Location:* one mile south of city centre, off A367 road to Wells. Hilly parkland course with many young trees. 9 holes, 2103 yards, 1922 metres. S.S.S. 61 (18 holes). Practice net. *Green Fees:* information not available. *Visitors:* no restrictions but pre-booking up to one week in advance essential. Well equipped Pro Shop. *Society Meetings:* reduced green fees for pre-booked groups of 10 or more. Professional: T. Tapley (01225 834248). Secretary: J. Sercombe (01225 834248).*

BATH. **Fosseway Golf Club and Centurion Hotel,** Charlton Lane, Midsomer Norton, Bath BA3 4BD (01761 412214; Fax: 01761 418357). *Location:* off A367 Bath to Wells/Shepton Mallet. Flat parkland course on the edge of the Mendips. 9 holes, 2304 yards. S.S.S. 65. *Green Fees:* information not available. *Eating facilities:* full à la carte restaurant, five bars with bar meals. *Visitors:* welcome except Sunday mornings and Wednesday evenings. Accommodation available, gym, sauna, steam, Jacuzzi, swimming and bowls (outdoor). *Society Meetings:* welcome. Secretary: R D'Arcy (01761 417711).
e-mail: centurion@centurionhotel.co.uk
website: www.centurionhotel.com

BATH. **Lansdown Golf Club,** Lansdown, Bath BA1 9BT. *Location:* M4 Junction 18, A46 towards Bath, follow signs for Lansdown Park and Ride, adjacent Bath Racecourse. Flat parkland, 800ft above sea-level, panoramic views. 18 holes, 6428 yards. S.S.S. 71. Practice ground. *Green Fees:* weekdays £30.00, weekends £35.00. *Eating facilities:* dining room for 100, snacks, lunch or dinner. *Visitors:* welcome, must have Handicap Certificate. Trolleys and buggies for hire. *Society Meetings:* welcome weekdays. Professional: Terry Mercer (01225 420242; Fax: 01225 483597). Secretary: Erica Bacon (01225 422138; Fax: 01225 339252).
e-mail: admin@lansdowngolfclub.co.uk
website: www.lansdowngolfclub.co.uk

BATH/BRISTOL. Farrington Golf and Country Club, Marsh Lane, Farrington Gurney, Near Bristol BS39 6TS (01761 451596; Fax: 01761 451021). *Location:* 12 miles south of Bristol, 10 miles east of Bath (through Midsomer Norton) at the junction of the A37 and A362 roads. Wooded, undulating 27 hole complex, 6 lakes, USGA-spec greens (no temporaries), tees up to 800 square yards, irrigated. Championship Course - 18 holes, (Blue tees) 6716 yards, S.S.S. 72; (White tees) 6335 yards, S.S.S. 71; (Yellow tees) 5943 yards, S.S.S. 68; (Ladies' Red tees), 5595 yards, S.S.S 73 . Executive Course - 9 holes, 3002 yards, par 54, S.S.S. 53. Floodlit, covered driving range, 300 yard practice ground, two extensive putting greens, chipping green, one practice bunker, video professional teaching. *Green Fees:* Championship Course £17.50 weekdays, £25.00 weekends and holidays. Executive Course (9 holes): £6.00 weekdays, £7.50 weekends. (2007 fees, subject to review.) *Eating facilities:* Large clubhouse of character, full meals service, Sunday lunches, bars, dining room, patio and courtyard. Horizon Banqueting and Function Suite and King Charles Hall both licensed for civil weddings. *Visitors:* most welcome, 2 for 1 vouchers accepted, booking essential weekends. *Society Meetings:* special midweek packages available. PGA Professional: Jonathan Cowgill (01761 451046). Secretary: Stephen Cook. Owner: Paul Harwood. General Manager (for society and membership enquiries): Debbie Cole (01761 451596).
e-mail: info@farringtongolfclub.net
website: www.farringtongolfclub.net

BRIDGWATER. Cannington Golf Course, Cannington Centre For Land Based Studies, Cannington, Bridgwater TA5 2LS (01278 652394; Fax: 01278 652479). *Location:* M5 Junction 24, off A39 Bridgwater to Minehead road. Flat, with slight undulations, on parkland turf; exposed to sea breezes. 9 holes (18 tees to 9 greens), 6072 yards. S.S.S. 70. Small practice area. 10 bay floodlit driving range. *Green Fees:* information not available. *Eating facilities:* College restaurant. *Visitors:* pay and play course. *Society Meetings:* by arrangement with Professional/Course Manager. Professional/Course Manager: Ron Macrow (01278 655050; Fax: 01278 655055).*

BRIDGWATER. Enmore Park Golf Club, Enmore, Bridgwater TA5 2AN (01278 671481). *Location:* M5 Exit 23/24, left at lights in town to Spaxton, course signposted two miles on right. Wooded parkland course on Quantock foothills. 18 holes, 6411 yards. S.S.S. 71. Large practice ground. *Green Fees:* £32.00 per round, £48.00 per day weekdays; £48.00 per day weekends. *Eating facilities:* lunch and evening meal available. *Visitors:* welcome weekdays. Buggy available. *Society Meetings:* welcome by arrangement. Professional: Nigel Wixon (01278 672102; Fax: 01278 671740). Secretary: (01278 672100; Fax: 01278 671740).

THE APPEARANCE OF AN ASTERISK (*) AT THE END OF A CLUB OR COURSE ENTRY INDICATES THAT UP-TO-DATE INFORMATION HAS NOT BEEN SUPPLIED

BRISTOL. Mendip Spring Golf Club, Honeyhall Lane, Congresbury, Bristol BS49 5JT (01934 852322; Fax: 01934 853021). *Location:* between Congresbury and Churchill off B3133 (A370 and A38). Fairly flat courses with a lot of water hazards. Brinsea Course: 18 holes, 6412 yards. S.S.S. 70 men, 76 ladies; Lakeside Course: 9 holes, 2392 yards, S.S.S. 65 men and ladies. 15 bay floodlit driving range, putting green. *Green Fees:* Brinsea: weekdays £28.00 – £38.00 per day, weekends £35.00. Lakeside: £9.50 for 9 holes, £19.00 per day. *Eating facilities:* full restaurant and bar facilities. *Visitors:* welcome at any time. Tuition available. Buggies available April to September. *Society Meetings:* welcome, corporate days available by arrangement. Professionals: John Blackburn and Robert Moss. Secretary: A. Melhuish.

BRISTOL. Stockwood Vale Golf Club, Stockwood Lane, Keynsham, Bristol BS18 2ER (0117 9866505). *Location:* one mile from Hicks Gate - Bristol Ring Road. Testing parkland course set in beautiful surroundings. 18 holes, 6031 yards. S.S.S. 69. Driving range, practice green/bunker. *Green Fees:Information not available. Eating facilities:* licensed bar and restaurant. *Visitors:* welcome at all times, must reserve start times. *Society Meetings:* welcome weekdays, prior booking essential; packages available. Professional: Mr John Richards (0117 9866505). Secretary: Mr M. Edenborough (0117 9860509; Fax: 0117 9868974).*

BRISTOL. Tall Pines Golf Club, Cooks Bridle Path, Downside, Backwell, Bristol BS48 3DJ (01275 472076). *Location:* between A370 and A38 to Bristol Airport. Parkland. 18 holes, 6049 yards, 5420 metres. S.S.S. 70. Practice ground, putting green. *Green Fees:* £20.00. *Eating facilities:* fully licensed bar and restaurant. *Visitors:* welcome at all times, bookings at weekends. *Society Meetings:* welcome, weekends after 1.00pm. Professional: Alex Murray. Secretary: T. Murray (01275 472076; Fax: 01275 474869).

BRISTOL. Woodspring Golf & Country Club, Yanley Lane, Long Ashton, Bristol BS41 9LR (01275 394 378; Fax: 01275 394473). *Location:* located on the A38 4 miles south west of Bristol city centre. From M5 exit Junction 8 follow signs for Bristol Airport, from M4 exit Junction 19 onto M32 follow signs to Bristol Airport. Very attractive, 235 acre parkland course designed by Donald Steel, Peter Aliss and Clive Clark, with great views from high holes. Water on many holes. 27 holes, 3 x 9 hole loops giving a varying combination of yardage. 26 bay floodlit driving range, 15 automated. *Green Fees:* weekdays £30.00, weekends £34.00; fairway rate £15.00 weekday, £17.00 weekends. *Eating facilities:* food and drinks always available in large clubhouse. *Visitors:* always welcome. *Society Meetings:* always welcome, must book in advance. Tuition available from resident Professionals. Buggies for hire. Professionals: Kevin Pitts and David Morgan. Secretary: David Knipe.
e-mail: info@woodspring-golf.com
website: www.woodspring-golf.com

BURNHAM-ON-SEA. Brean Golf Club at Brean Leisure Park, Coast Road, Brean, TA8 2QY (Tel & Fax: 01278 752111). *Location:* leave M5 at Junction 22, follow signs to Brean Leisure Park (five miles). Flat moorland, easy access to five mile sandy beach (400 yards via path). 18 holes, 5715 yards. S.S.S. 67 (Par 69). Practice area, green and bunker. *Green Fees:* weekdays from £20.00 per round; weekends from £25.00 per round. Reduced rates with a member. *Eating facilities:* snacks at bar, meals in main restaurant. *Visitors:* welcome weekdays and after 11am weekends/Bank Holidays. Prior booking advised to Pro Shop (01278 752111). Buggy and trolleys for hire. *Society Meetings:* welcome by prior booking. Professional: David Haines. e-mail: golf@brean.com
website: www.breangolfclub.co.uk

BURNHAM-ON-SEA. Burnham and Berrow Golf Club, St Christopher's Way, Burnham-on-Sea TA8 2PE (01278 785760; Fax: 01278 795440). *Location:* one mile north of Burnham-on-Sea. Leave M5 at Exit 22. Seaside links. 18 holes, 6393 yards. S.S.S. 71; 9 holes, 5819 yards. S.S.S. 68. *Green Fees:* £50.00 weekdays, £63.00 weekends and Bank Holidays; 9 hole course £16.00 weekdays, £18.00 weekends and Bank Holidays. *Eating facilities:* catering available daily 11am to 6pm (other meals by arrangement). *Visitors:* welcome with reservation if members of a recognised golf club and with Handicap Certificate. Dormy House accommodation, sleeps up to 8. *Society Meetings:* catered for. Professional: M. Crowther-Smith (01278 785760). Managing Secretary: M. Blight (01278 785760). e-mail: secretary@burnhamandberrow.plus.com
website: www.burnhamandberrowgolfclub.co.uk

CHARD. Windwhistle Golf Club, Cricket St Thomas, Near Chard TA20 4DG (01460 30231; Fax: 01460 30055). Established 1932. *Location:* on A30 between Chard and Crewkerne, opposite Cricket St Thomas Wildlife Park and Warner's Hotel. Parkland course with breathtaking views. 18 holes, 6176 yards Par 72, S.S.S. 70. Driving range. Golf Shop. *Green Fees:* 18 holes; weekdays £21.00, weekends £26.00. *Eating facilities:* bar service, snacks and cooked meals daily. *Visitors:* welcome; starting time system in operation, bookings accepted up to seven days in advance. Squash courts available. *Society Meetings:* welcome. Professional: Paul Deeprose. Secretary: Ian Dodd.
website: www.windwhistlegolfclub.co.uk

CLEVEDON. Clevedon Golf Club, Castle Road, Walton, Clevedon BS21 7AA (01275 874057; Fax: 01275 341228). *Location:* M5 Junction 20, follow signs "Portishead", turn left into Holly Lane. Spectacular scenic parkland course overlooking Bristol Channel. 18 holes, 6557 yards. S.S.S. 72. Practice area. *Green Fees:* £32.00 weekdays, £40.00 weekends and Bank Holidays. *Eating facilities:* full catering every day. *Visitors:* welcome, please telephone Professional beforehand. Handicap Certificate essential. *Society Meetings:* welcome by prior arrangement. Professional: Robert Scanlan (01275 874704).
website: www.clevedongolfclub.co.uk

ENMORE. **Enmore Park Golf Club,** Enmore, Bridgwater TA5 2AN (01278 672100). *Location:* M5 Exit 23/24, left at lights in town to Spaxton, course signposted two miles on right. Wooded parkland course on Quantock foothills. 18 holes, 6406 yards, 5910 metres. S.S.S. 71. Large practice ground. *Green Fees:* Information not available. *Eating facilities:* lunch and evening meal available. *Visitors:* welcome weekdays. Buggy available. *Society Meetings:* welcome by arrangement. Professional: Nigel Wixon (01278 672102; Fax: 01278 672101). Secretary: Ian Wallace (01278 672100; Fax: 01278 672101).*

FROME. **Orchardleigh Golf Club,** Frome BA11 2PH (01373 454200; Fax: 01373 454202) *Location:* A362 Frome - Radstock. Parkland. 18 holes, 6824 yards. S.S.S. 73. Three practice greens, driving range. *Green Fees:* weekdays £35.00, weekends £37.50; member's guest £15.00 and £22.50. *Eating facilities:* bar menu; society and groups menu. *Visitors:* welcome anytime except before 11.00am Saturday and Sundays. *Society Meetings:* all very welcome, competitive rates. Professional: Ian Ridsdale (01373 454200). Club Secretary/Manager: Dave Forrest.

LANGPORT near. **Long Sutton Golf Club,** Long Sutton, Near Langport TA10 9JU (01458 241017; Fax: 01458 241022). *Location:* from Podimore roundabout on A303 towards Langport turn left for Long Sutton. Gently undulating course. 18 holes, 6368 yards. S.S.S. 71. Floodlit driving range. *Green Fees:* weekdays £20.00; weekends £25.00 for 18 holes. Weekdays £10.00; weekends £12.50 for 9 holes. *Eating facilities:* bar and food. *Visitors:* welcome at all times, phone for tee reservations at weekends. Golfing breaks available. *Society Meetings:* welcome. Professional: Andrew Hayes.

MINEHEAD. **Minehead and West Somerset Golf Club,** The Warren, Minehead TA24 5SJ (01643 702057). *Location:* beside the beach at eastern end of the town, three-quarters of a mile from town centre. Flat seaside links. 18 holes, 6153 yards. S.S.S. 69. *Green Fees:* weekdays – £35.00 daily, £25.00 off-peak, £17.50 twilight; weekends and Bank Holidays – £40.00 daily, £30.00 off-peak, £20.00 twilight. Weekly rate £130.00. *Eating facilities:* available at clubhouse, bar open every day. *Visitors:* welcome with tee reservation at Pro shop. *Society Meetings:* welcome with tee reservations. Special golf and meal deals available to groups of four or more. Wide wheel trolleys only. Trolley and equipment hire available. Professional: Ian Read. Secretary: Gerry Mason (01643 702057; Fax: 01643 705095).
e-mail: secretary@mineheadgolf.co.uk
website: www.minehead-golf-club.co.uk

SALTFORD. **Saltford Golf Club,** Golf Club Lane, Saltford, Bristol BS31 3AA (01225 873513; Fax: 01225 873525). *Location:* A4 between Bristol and Bath. Wooded parkland course. 18 holes, 6398 yards. S.S.S. 71. Practice area, chipping green. *Green Fees:* Monday - Friday £18.00, Weekends and Bank Holidays £22.00, restricted to one round per day at weekends. *Eating facilities:* restaurant, bar service. *Visitors:* welcome, restricted to one round of golf per day weekends and during Summer. *Society Meetings:* accepted by arrangement, please call the Club Secretary's office for further details. Professional: Darren Read (01225 872043). Club Secretary: Mike Penn (01225 873513).
e-mail: mike@saltfordgolfclub.co.uk

SHEPTON MALLET. **The Mendip Golf Club Ltd.,** Gurney Slade, Radstock, Shepton Mallett BA3 4UT (01749 840570; Fax: 01749 841439). *Location:* three miles north of Shepton Mallet (A37). Downland, undulating course. 18 holes, 6383 yards. S.S.S. 71. Practice ground. *Green Fees:* information not available. *Eating facilities:* bar and restaurant open seven days a week. *Visitors:* welcome every day, telephone Professional to check availability. *Society Meetings:* catered for Mondays to Fridays by arrangement. Professional: Adrian Marsh (01749 840793). Secretary: Jim Scott (01749 840570; Fax: 01749 841439).*
e-mail: mendipgolfclub@lineone.net
website: www.mendipgolfclub.co.uk

SOMERTON. **Wheathill Golf Club,** Wheathill, Somerton TA11 7HG (01963 240667; Fax: 01963 240230). *Location:* On B3153 three miles west of Castle Cary. Flat parkland. 18 holes, 5339 yards. S.S.S. 66. Large practice ground and 8 hole academy course. *Green Fees:* £20.00; £14.00 after 4pm. *Eating facilities:* bar and restaurant. *Visitors:* welcome. *Society Meetings:* welcome. Professional: Andrew England. Secretary: John Goymer.

STREET. **Kingweston Golf Club,** (Millfield School), Street TA11 6PP (01458 444320). *Location:* one mile south of Butleigh Village, near Street, Somerset. Flat course - trees. 9 holes, 2307 yards. S.S.S. 61. Practice area. *Green Fees:* information not available. *Eating facilities:* pub half a mile. *Visitors:* welcome only with a member. Secretary: G.L. Frisby (01458 832068).*

TAUNTON. **Oake Manor Golf Club,** Oake, Taunton TA4 1BA (01823 461993; Fax: 01823 461995). *Location:* seven minutes' drive from Junction 26 of the M5 - take A38 towards Taunton and follow signs to Oake. Enjoyable and challenging parkland course with water features on 10 of the 18 holes. Magnificent setting with views of the Blackdown and Quantock Hills. 18 holes, 6109 yards. S.S.S 69. Driving range,

practice holes. *Green Fees:* from £26.00 to £32.00. Phone (01823 461993) for Golf Reservations. *Eating facilities:* catering/bar snacks available all day. *Visitors:* welcome any day but booking tee time essential. Ideal course to play en route to, or returning from golf in Devon and Cornwall. Function rooms (seat up to 300). *Society Meetings:* by arrangement, contact Golf Manager. Golf Manager & Professional: Russell Gardner (01823 461993).
e-mail: russell@oakemanor.com
website: www.oakemanor.com

TAUNTON. **Taunton and Pickeridge Golf Club,** Corfe, Taunton TA3 7BY (01823 421240). *Location:* four miles south of Taunton on B3170. Undulating parkland. 18 holes, 6056 yards. S.S.S. 69. Practice ground, indoor shed. *Green Fees:* £26.00/£32.00 weekdays, £40.00 weekends. *Eating facilities:* restaurant and bar. *Visitors:* welcome. *Society Meetings:* by arrangement with the Secretary. Professional: Simon Stevenson (01823 421790). Secretary: M.P.D. Walls (01823 421537; Fax: 01823 421742).
e-mail: mail@tauntongolf.co.uk
website: www.tauntongolf.co.uk

TAUNTON. **Taunton Vale Golf Club,** Creech Heathfield, Taunton TA3 5EY (01823 412220; Fax: 01823 413583). *Location:* just off A361 at Junction with A38 between Junctions 24 and 25 of M5; easily accessible. Parkland. Two courses. 18 holes, 6234 yards. S.S.S. 70. 9 holes, 1943 yards. S.S.S. 32. 10 bay floodlit driving range. *Green Fees:* weekdays £23.00 for 18 holes, £10.00 for 9 holes; weekends £28.00 for 18 holes, £12.00 for 9 holes (subject to review). Special daily rates and Society rates available, please enquire. *Eating facilities:* two bars, dining room and conservatory. *Visitors:* welcome, telephone for bookings essential. *Society Meetings:* welcome by arrangement. For all the latest information see our website. Professional: Martin Keitch (01823 412880). Secretary: Joanne Wyatt (01823 412220; Fax: 01823 413583).
e-mail: tvgc@gotadsl.co.uk
website: www.tauntonvalegolf.co.uk

TAUNTON. **Vivary Golf Course,** Vivary Park, Taunton TA1 3JW (01823 289274). *Location:* turn into Wilton Road at side of police station. Turn left at Vivary Arms Inn. Flat parkland course with ponds and trees. 18 holes, 4533 yards. S.S.S. 63. Practice area. *Green Fees:* information not available. *Eating facilities:* licensed bar and restaurant. Available for private functions. *Visitors:* always welcome. Professional: James Smallacombe (01823 333875). Secretary: (01823 289274).

TICKENHAM. **Tickenham Golf Club,** Clevedon Road, Tickenham BS21 6RY (01275 856626). *Location:* M5 Junction 20, signposted Nailsea on left after Tickenham. Challenging championship style contoured greens. 9 holes, 2000 yards. S.S.S. 58, Par 60. 24 bay floodlit driving range, power tees, putting green, bunkers. *Green Fees:* off-peak - 9 holes £8.00, 18 holes £12.00; peak times - 9 holes £10.00, 18 holes £15.00. *Eating facilities:* 19th hole licensed bar, snacks. *Visitors:* welcome. *Society Meetings:* welcome, telephone for rates. Professionals: A. Sutcliffe, S. Jarrett, A. Smith, F. Amey.

WEDMORE. **Isle of Wedmore Golf Club,** Lineage, Wedmore BS28 4QT (01934 713649; Fax: 01934 713696). *Location:* from A38 Bristol/Bridgwater Road, take Wedmore Road from Lower Weare. Parkland, gently undulating fairways with magnificent views. Practice area. 18 holes, 6057 yards. S.S.S. 69. Small practice area, putting green. *Green Fees:* weekdays £22.00 per round (£24.00 in summer), £32.00 per day; weekends £22.00 per round, £32.00 per day; reduced rates with member. *Eating facilities:* full bar and restaurant, upstairs function/society room. *Visitors:* always welcome. Soft spikes only. *Society Meetings:* welcome. Professional: Nick Pope (01934 712452; Fax: 01934 713554). Manager: Andrew Edwards (01934 712222; Fax: 01934 713696).

WELLS. **Wells (Somerset) Golf Club Ltd,** Blackheath Lane, East Horrington, Wells BA5 3DS (01749 675005). *Location:* one mile east of city centre off B3139. Parkland, wooded. 18 holes, 6018 yards. S.S.S. 69. Practice area. 12 bay floodlit driving range open to the public. *Green Fees:* weekdays £30.00 per round, £40.00 per day; weekends and Bank Holidays £35.00 per round, £55.00 per day. *Eating facilities:* restaurant and bar. *Visitors:* welcome, no play before 9.30am weekends and Public Holidays. *Society Meetings:* full packages available at all times. Professional: Adrian Bishop (01749 679059). Secretary: Beverley New (01749 675005; Fax: 01749 683170).
e-mail:secretary@wellsgolfclub.co.uk
website: www.wellsgolfclub.co.uk

WESTON-SUPER-MARE. **Weston-Super-Mare Golf Club,** The Clubhouse, Uphill Road North, Weston-Super-Mare BS23 4NQ (01934 626968). *Location:* M5 Junction 21 - on the sea front. Flat links course with excellent greens. 18 holes, 6251 yards. S.S.S. 70. Practice area plus nets. *Green Fees:* information not available. *Eating facilities:* full bar and catering facilities. *Visitors:* welcome weekdays and weekends. Handicap Certificate required. *Society Meetings:* catered for weekdays. Professional: Mike LaBand (Tel & Fax: 01934 633360). Secretary: (01934 626968; Fax: 01934 621360).
e-mail: secretary@westonsupermaregolfclub.com
website: www.westonsupermaregolfclub.com

WESTON-SUPER-MARE. **Worlebury Golf Club,** Monks Hill, Worlebury, Weston-Super-Mare BS22 9SX (01934 625789). *Location:* from M5 (Junction 21) then A370 and first exit left onto old Bristol Road to town for two miles. Turn right into Baytree Road and continue to top of Milton Hill. Hill top with extensive views of the Severn Estuary and Wales. 18 holes, 5936 yards. S.S.S. 68. Practice ground and putting green. *Green Fees:* weekdays £30.00 per day, £15.00 with a member; weekends and Bank Holidays £35.00 per day, £20.00 with a member. *Eating facilities:* bar and restaurant. *Visitors:* welcome without reservation. *Society Meetings:* catered for by arrangement. Professional: Gary Marks (01934 418473). Secretary: Mike W. Wake (01934 625789; Fax: 01934 621935).
e-mail: secretary@worleburygc.co.uk

WINCANTON. **Wincanton Golf Club,** The Racecourse, Wincanton BA9 8BJ (01963 435850; Fax: 01963 34668). *Location:* middle of the racecourse, half a mile from the town centre. Very flat course, testing layout; large bunkers protecting very well maintained greens. 9 or 18 holes, 6182 yards. S.S.S. 69. Good practice facilities. Teaching/coaching on individual or group basis; hire of clubs/trolley/ buggy. *Green Fees:* on request. *Eating facilities:* licensed coffee shop. *Visitors:* welcome at all times. Overnight accommodation available. *Society Meetings:* can be catered for if booked in advance. Professionals: Andrew England and Tony Isaacs.

YEOVIL. **Yeovil Golf Club,** Sherborne Road, Yeovil BA21 5BW (01935 422965). *Location:* on A30, one mile from town centre towards Sherborne on right before Babylon Hill. Parkland. 18 holes, 6150 yards. S.S.S. 70. 9 holes, 4891 yards. S.S.S. 65. Putting green. 20-bay floodlit range. *Green Fees:* Old Course – winter (Nov - March incl.) £30.00 weekdays, £35.00 weekends and Bank Holidays; summer (April - Oct incl.) £35.00 weekdays, £45.00 weekends and Bank Holidays. 9 hole Newton course – £20.00 weekdays, £20.00 weekends and Bank Holidays. *Eating facilities:* bars and dining room with full menu every day. *Visitors:* welcome, Handicap Certificates required for 18 hole course, telephone Pro shop to check times. *Society Meetings:* welcome weekdays. Professional: G. Kite (01935 473763; Fax: 01935 478605). General Manager: M. Betteridge (01935 422965; Fax: 01935 411283).
website: www.yeovilgolfclub.com

Wiltshire

BRADFORD-ON-AVON. **Cumberwell Park Golf Club,** Bradford-on-Avon BA15 2PQ (01225 863322; Fax: 01225 868160). *Location*: on A363 between Bath and Bradford-on-Avon, close to J17 and J18 off M4. Recognised as one of the top courses in the west country, encompassing 315 acres of parkland, enhanced by nine lakes, 34 acres of forest and streams. 27 holes (3 x 9), 6723 yards (18 holes), S.S.S. 72. Practice greens, 10 acre driving range. *Green Fees*: information not available. *Eating facilities*: private dining rooms and spikes bar. *Visitors*: always welcome; accommodation can be arranged nearby. *Society Meetings*: packages including catering available from £24.00 winter, from £35.00 summer. Golf days tailored to individual requirements. Professional: John Jacobs.* e-mail: enquiries@cumberwellpark.com website: www.cumberwellpark.com

CALNE. **Bowood Golf and Country Club,** Derry Hill, Calne SN11 9PQ (01249 822228; Fax: 01249 822218). *Location*: A4 between Marlborough and Chippenham, signposted off M4 Junction 17. Grade I listed, Capability Brown landscaped, parkland. 18 holes, 7317, 6890, 6566: 6027 yards. S.S.S. 74, 73, 71: 75. Ladies 6015 yards, S.S.S. 75. Three academy holes, floodlit driving range, two putting greens. *Green Fees*: information not available. *Eating facilities*: public restaurant, private dining for up to 200. *Visitors*: welcome at all times except before 12 noon at weekends, bookings required. Four (double/twin) bedroomed house in centre of course, large clubhouse extension for banqueting, conferences, weddings, etc. Buggies, trolleys and clubs for hire; fully stocked Pro shop. *Society Meetings*: welcome, special packages available. Head Golf Professional: Max Taylor. Proprietor: The Marquis of Lansdowne.*

www.uk-golfguide.com

CASTLE COMBE. **The Manor House Hotel and Golf Club,** Castle Combe SN14 7JW (01249 782982; Fax: 01249 782992). *Location:* on the B4039 midway between M4 Junction 17 and 18. Parkland course situated in a series of wooded valleys in an Area of Outstanding Natural Beauty. 18 holes, 6500 yards. S.S.S. 71. Practice range. *Green Fees:* information not available. *Eating facilities:* full restaurant and bar facilities. *Visitors:* welcome by prior arrangement provided they have a club Handicap Certificate. The luxurious Manor House Hotel (four red stars) adjoins the course offering exceptional accommodation and an award-winning restaurant. *Society Meetings:* welcome by prior arrangement. Professional/Director of Golf: Steve Slinger (01249 782982; Fax: 01249 782992). General Manager: Paul Thompson (01249 782982; Fax: 01249 782992).*

CHIPPENHAM. **Chippenham Golf Club,** Malmesbury Road, Chippenham SN15 5LT (01249 652040). *Location:* A350 one mile from Chippenham, two miles from M4 (Junction 17). Parkland. 18 holes, 5570 yards. S.S.S. 67. *Green Fees:* Information not available. *Eating facilities:* snacks and evening à la carte (not Mondays). *Visitors:* welcome, prior arrangement necessary. *Society Meetings:* catered for Mondays, Tuesdays, Thursdays and Fridays only. Premier Travel Inn overlooking first fairway. Professional: Bill Creamer (01249 655519). Secretary: B. Cook (01249 652040).* website: www.chippenhamgolfclub.co.uk

CHIPPENHAM. **Monkton Park Golf Club,** Monkton Park, Chippenham SN15 3PE (01249 653928). *Location:* centre of Chippenham, two miles from M4 Junction 17. Parkland Par 3 course. Probably the best Par 3 course in the south west of England. 9 holes, 979 yards. S.S.S. 27. Crazy golf. *Green Fees:* from £5.50. *Eating facilities:* tearoom now open. *Visitors:* always welcome 364 days of the year! Golf clubs available. *Society Meetings:* welcome. Secretary: Mrs W. Claridge. website: www.pitchandputtgolf.com

CORSHAM. **Kingsdown Golf Club,** Corsham SN13 8BS (01225 743472). *Location:* five miles east of Bath. Heathland. 18 holes, 6445 yards, 5891 metres. S.S.S. 71. *Green Fees:* information not available. *Eating facilities:* lounge bar and diningroom. *Visitors:* welcome except at weekends and Bank Holidays and must have current Handicap Certificate. *Society Meetings:* catered for by arrangement. Professional: Andrew Butler (01225 742634). Secretary: Neil Newman (01225 743472).

CRICKLADE. **Cricklade Hotel & Country Club,** Common Hill, Cricklade SN6 6HA (01793 750751; Fax: 01793 751767). *Location:* A419 8 miles north of Swindon, B4040 out of Cricklade town by half a mile. Undulating course set around hotel. 9 holes, 1830 yards. S.S.S. 58 (18 holes). *Green Fees:* information upon request. *Eating facilities:* full à la carte restaurant and bar with snacks available. *Visitors:* guests of hotel welcome at all times, tee times must be booked at weekends. Weekends members and hotel guests only. 46-room hotel on site. *Society Meetings:* on application. Professional: Ian Bolt. Secretary: Colin Withers. Hotel General Manager: Paul Butler. e-mail: reception@crickladehotel.co.uk website: www.crickladehotel.co.uk

DEVIZES. **Erlestoke Golf Club,** Erlestoke, Near Devizes SN10 5UB. *Location:* six miles east of Westbury on B3098. Downland course, on two levels, spectacular 7th hole, 170 yards Par 3, with green 100ft below, one of the finest short holes in the West Country. 18 holes, 6406 yards. S.S.S. 71, Par 73. Large practice ground. *Green Fees:* available on request. *Eating facilities:* full catering service, lounge, bar and diningroom. *Visitors:* welcome (01380 831069). *Society Meetings:* welcome. Fabulous views and excellent food served from 11am.

DEVIZES. **North Wilts Golf Club,** Bishop's Cannings, Devizes SN10 2LP (01380 860257). *Location:* one and a half miles from A4 east of Calne. Four miles from Devizes. Downland, undulating course with spectacular views. 18 holes, 6414 yards. S.S.S. 71. Practice ground. *Green Fees:* Weekdays £32.00 per day, Weekends and Bank Holidays £37.00 per round. *Eating facilities:* full catering service. *Visitors:* welcome, except on medal days. *Society Meetings:* catered for by prior arrangement. Professional: Graham Laing (01380 860330; Fax: 01380 860061). Secretary: Mrs Trish Stephenson (01380 860627; Fax: 01380 860877).

HIGHWORTH. **Highworth Community Golf Centre,** Swindon Road, Highworth SN6 7SJ. *Location:* on A361 just south of the town. Undulating parkland. 9 holes, 3120 yards, 2851 metres. Par 35. 9 hole pitch and putt, 4 hole practice course. *Green Fees:* information not available. *Eating facilities:* vending machines. *Visitors:* municipal course, no restrictions. *Society Meetings:* welcome any day. Professional: Barry Sandry (01793 766014). Secretary: Steve Kearley.*

HIGHWORTH. **Wrag Barn Golf and Country Club,** Shrivenham Road, Highworth, Swindon SN6 7QQ (01793 861327; Fax: 01793 861325). *Location:* just six miles off the M4. Undulating, set in beautiful Wiltshire countryside, three lakes and moat around 17th green. 18 holes, 6633 yards. S.S.S. 72. 11 bay driving range, practice area. *Green Fees:* weekdays £32.00; weekends £40.00. *Eating facilities:* spike bar. restaurant, function rooms. *Visitors:* welcome weekdays and after 12 noon weekends. Buggies and trolleys for hire. *Society Meetings:* welcome any weekday. Professional: Danny White (01793 766027: Fax: 01793 861325). Secretary: Tracey Lee (01793 861327; Fax: 01793 861325).

MARLBOROUGH. **Marlborough Golf Club,** The Common, Marlborough SN8 1DU (01672 512147; Fax: 01672 513164). *Location:* about one mile north of Marlborough town centre on A346 towards Swindon. Seven miles south of J15 of the M4. Downland with panoramic views into the Og Valley and over the Marlborough Downs. 18 holes, 6514 yards, 5952 metres. S.S.S. 71, Par 72. Large practice ground and putting green. *Green Fees:* weekdays £30.00 per round, £42.00 per day; weekends £40.00 per round (after 4pm £19.00), £55.00 per day. *Eating facilities:* full restaurant facility, plus bar snacks open all day. *Visitors:* welcome generally, but it is best to telephone in advance; some restrictions at weekends. *Society Meetings:* discounted rates and packages available. Essential to book in advance. Professional: Simon Amor (01672 512493; Fax: 01672 513164). General Manager: J.A.D. Sullivan (01672 512147; Fax: 01672 513164). e-mail: contactus@marlboroughgolfclub.co.uk

SALISBURY. **Hamptworth Golf and Country Club,** Hamptworth Road, Hamptworth, Near Landford SP5 2DU (01794 390155; Fax: 01794 390022). *Location:* off A36 Salisbury to Southampton Road, turning off B3079. Parkland, wooded course with river running through. 18 holes, 6516 yards, 5957 metres. S.S.S. 71. Driving range, open to the public. *Green Fees:* information not available. *Eating facilities:* new clubhouse with full catering and bar. *Visitors:* welcome, must have tee reservation and Handicap Certificate. Buggies. *Society Meetings:* welcome. Professional: M. White.*

> **THE APPEARANCE OF AN ASTERISK (*) AT THE END OF A CLUB OR COURSE ENTRY INDICATES THAT UP-TO-DATE INFORMATION HAS NOT BEEN SUPPLIED**

SALISBURY. **High Post Golf Club Ltd,** Great Durnford, Salisbury SP4 6AT (01722 782356; Fax: 01722 782674). *Location:* midway between Salisbury and Amesbury on A345. Easy walking, classic chalk downland course. 18 holes, 6305 yards. S.S.S. 70. *Green Fees:* £32.00 per round, £50.00 per day midweek; £42.00 per round, £50.00 per day weekends. *Eating facilities:* full catering and bars available. *Visitors:* welcome weekdays no restrictions, weekends and Bank Holidays require Handicap Certificate. *Society Meetings:* catered for weekdays only. Professional: Tony Isaacs (01722 782219). Manager: Peter Hickling (01722 782356). e-mail: secretary@highpostgolfclub.co.uk website: www.highpostgolfclub.co.uk

SALISBURY. **Rushmore Golf Club,** Tollard Royal, Salisbury SP5 5QB (01725 516326). *Location:* off the B3081 between Tollard Royal and Sixpenny Handley. Parkland and wooded course. 18 holes, 6131 yards. S.S.S. 70. Covered driving range and large practice area. *Green Fees:* from £25.00. *Eating facilities:* Spike Bar plus restaurant, home cooked food seven days a week. *Visitors:* welcome any time. *Society Meetings:* welcome by prior arrangement. Professional: Phil Jenkins.

SALISBURY. **Salisbury and South Wilts Golf Club,** Netherhampton, Salisbury SP2 8PR (01722 742131). *Location:* on A3094, two miles from Salisbury, Wilton, opposite Netherhampton village. Parkland. 27 holes, 6528 yards. S.S.S. 71. Practice ground; 3-hole academy course. *Green Fees:* Information not available. *Eating facilities:* full catering service and bar. *Visitors:* welcome without reservation at all times, but preliminary phone call advised. *Society Meetings:* catered for by prior arrangement. Professional: Geraldine Teschner (Tel & Fax: 01722 742929). General Manager: Pat Clash (01722 742645; Fax: 01722 742676). e-mail: mail@salisburygolf.co.uk website: www.salisburygolf.co.uk*

SHRIVENHAM. **Shrivenham Park Golf Club,** Penny Hooks Lane, Near Swindon SN6 8EX (01793 783853/4). *Location:* M4 Exit 15. Follow signs to Shrivenham, go through village, golf club on left. A delightful parkland course in excellent condition. 18 holes, 5713 yards. S.S.S 69. Practice area. *Green Fees:* Monday to Thursday £17.00, Friday to Sunday (including Bank Holidays) £22.00. *Eating facilities:* restaurant and bar open seven days a week, families welcome. *Visitors:* open to all, Handicaps not required. *Society Meetings:* packages available. Professional: Richard Jefferies. Director of Golf: Stuart Ash (01793 783853).

SWINDON. **Broome Manor Golf Complex**, Pipers Way, Swindon SN3 1RG (01793 495761; Fax: 01793 433256) (Manager)). *Location:* two miles from Junction 15, M4 (follow signs to Swindon Town Centre then follow signs for "Golf Complex"). Wooded parkland. Two courses, 18 holes, 6283 yards, Par 71, S.S.S. 70. 9 holes, 5380 yards, Par 66, S.S.S. 66. 32 bay floodlit covered driving range. *Green Fees:* Information not available. *Eating facilities:* spike bar, conference facilities, restaurant. *Visitors:* welcome, no restrictions, booking essential for 18 hole course. *Society Meetings:* catered for weekdays. Professional: Barry Sandry (01793 491911; Fax 01793 433255). Manager: Dave Buckingham (01793 495761; Fax: 01793 4332553

SWINDON. **Ogbourne Downs Golf Club,** Ogbourne St. George, Marlborough SN8 1TB (01672 841287). *Location:* A346, four miles south of Junction 15 (M4), three miles north of Marlborough. Downland course with extensive views. 18 holes, 6422 yards. S.S.S. 71. Practice area, baskets of practice balls for hire. *Green Fees:* weekdays £30.00; weekends £35.00. *Eating facilities:* full catering and bar service. *Visitors:* welcome weekdays, phone Professional at weekends for starting times. Buggy hire. *Society Meetings:* welcome, packages available. Professional: Andrew Kirk (01672 841287). Office: (01672 841327).

SWINDON. **The Wiltshire Golf and Country Club**, Wootton Bassett, Swindon SN4 7PB (01793 849999). *Location*: through Wootton Bassett, head for Calne A3102, one mile on left hand side out of town. 27 holes designed by Peter Alliss and Howard Swann. 18 hole lake course with water features. 18 holes, 6782 yards. S.S.S. 72. 9 hole garden course 3214 yards. S.S.S. 71. Practice area, putting green. Driving range, chipping green. *Green Fees*: weekdays £28.00 per round, weekends £40.00 per round. *Eating facilities*: bars and restaurant. *Visitors*: welcome, booking advised. Club, buggy and trolley hire. Club repairs and fitting. Indoor pool with spa, sauna and steam room. Hotel with 58 en suite bedrooms. *Society Meetings*: conference and residential packages available. Professional: Richard Lawless. e-mail: reception@the-wiltshire.co.uk website: www.the-wiltshire.co.uk

TIDWORTH. **Tidworth Garrison Golf Club,** Bulford Road, Tidworth SP9 7AF (Tel & Fax: 01980 842301). *Location:* A338 Salisbury to Marlborough Road, golf course off Bulford Road. Undulating downland course. 18 holes, 6320 yards. S.S.S. 70. Practice driving area, chipping and putting greens. *Green Fees:* £47.00 per round/day, reductions when playing with member. *Eating facilities:* full bar and catering facilities. *Visitors:* welcome at all times, except Friday mornings and normally after 2pm at weekends and Bank Holidays. *Society Meetings:* catered for Tuesdays and Thursdays. Professional: Terry Gosden (Tel & Fax: 01980 842393). e-mail: tidworthgolfclub@btconnect.com website: www.tidworthgolfclub.co.uk

TROWBRIDGE. **Bradford-on-Avon Golf Course Ltd,** Avon Close, Trowbridge Road, Bradford-on-Avon, Trowbridge BA15 1JJ (Tel & Fax: 01225 752180). *Location*: M4, exit at Bath then take road to Bradford-on-Avon into centre, turn right on Trowbridge Road for half a mile, signpost for golf course on left. Parkland river bank course, mature trees, lakes. 9 holes Pay & Play course. *Green Fees*: information not available. *Visitors*: welcome. *Society Meetings*: welcome, please telephone for arrangements. Professional/Secretary: Richard Hussey (Tel & Fax: 01225 752180).*

UPAVON. **Upavon Golf Club,** Douglas Avenue, Upavon SN9 6BQ (01980 630787; Fax: 01980 635419). *Location:* off A342 Upavon to Andover Road, one-and-a-half miles out of Upavon. Undulating chalk downland course. 18 holes, 6402 yards. S.S.S. 71. Two practice areas. *Green Fees:* weekdays £30.00 per day, £80.00 four ball; weekends £36.00 per round, reductions when playing with a member. *Eating facilities:* bar and catering every day (restricted hours in winter). *Visitors:* visitors and societies welcome at Wiltshire's friendliest club. All County Cards and 2-fore-1 accepted. Daily course information line: 08712 300 800. Professional: Richard Blake (01980 630281). Secretary: Les Mitchell (01980 630787; Fax: 01980 635419). e-mail: play@upavongolfclub.co.uk website: www.upavongolfclub.co.uk

WARMINSTER. **West Wilts Golf Club, Elm Hill, Warminster BA12 0AU (Office: 01985 213133; Fax: 01985 219809; Bar: 01985 212702).** *Location*: **one mile off the A350 north of Warminster, signposted to the town centre. Established 1891, a chalk downland course 200 metres above sea level, designed by J.H. Taylor. 18 holes, 5754 yards. S.S.S. 68. Indoor and outdoor practice facilities available.** *Green Fees*: **weekdays £30.00 per round or day; Sundays £35.00 per round or day.** *Visitors*: **welcome except Saturdays.** *Society Meetings*: **welcome mainly Wednesday to Friday, contact Secretary. Professional: Rob Morris (Tel & Fax: 01985 212110). Secretary: Geoff Morgan. House Manager: Sandra Frankle.** e-mail: sec@westwiltsgolfclub.co.uk website: www.westwiltsgolfclub.co.uk

---

THE APPEARANCE OF AN ASTERISK (*) AT THE END OF A CLUB OR COURSE ENTRY INDICATES THAT UP-TO-DATE INFORMATION HAS NOT BEEN SUPPLIED

Golf in the South

Carl Markham

Berkshire • Buckinghamshire
Greater London • Hampshire & The Isle of Wight
Kent • Oxfordshire • Surrey • Sussex

A HIGHLIGHT for every golfer, whether a single-figure handicapper or an infrequent 'weekend warrior', is to follow in the footsteps of the world's greats. Very few get the chance to tread the same fairways as the legends, but for those determined to give it a go then any visit to the South of England has to incorporate at least one of the 'big name' venues.

Top of the list is Royal St George's in Sandwich, Kent - an Open Championship venue and a superb example of links golf. Scene of rookie American Ben Curtis' shock victory in 2003 and Greg Norman's brilliant defeat of

17th at Chart Hills Golf Club, Ashford, Kent

Nick Faldo 10 years earlier, St George's is as tough a test as you could expect to find anywhere. Only three Open winners, Curtis, Norman and Bill Rogers in 1981 have broken par in lifting the Claret Jug here, so the best advice is to head to Sandwich with the intention of enjoying the experience rather than playing your best golf.

But if the rarefied exclusivity of St George's is a little bit out of your range then try the next best thing next door – Prince's Golf Club, itself a former Open venue and now a regular for championship pre-qualifying. The club has 27 holes consisting of three loops of nine, known as the Shore, Dunes and Himalayas courses, each starting and finishing beside the clubhouse.

But links golf is not just restricted to Sandwich, as just down the road lies Royal Cinque Ports in Deal. It has an abundance of sand dunes and undulating fairways which make just standing up straight a challenge. Throw in the many steep bunkers and fast greens and this former Open venue provides another enjoyable seaside challenge - as does Littlestone further down the south-east coast near New Romney.

But if you prefer to play your golf among resplendent greenery then head further inland and be spoiled for choice. Continuing the celebrity golf feel, Sunningdale in Berkshire (venue for both Open and US Open qualifying) and Wentworth (BMW PGA Championship) in Surrey both offer high-quality, history-laden facilities at a premium.

But delve a little deeper and there are a number of hidden gems which are equally as pleasing to play at a fraction of the cost. The London Club, designed by Jack Nicklaus, to the south-west of London, just outside the M25, is an absolute delight and highly-regarded by professionals and amateurs alike. Nick Faldo's Chart Hills in Kent, picturesque venue for the Ladies' European Tour's English Open, has 200-year-old oaks, an island green and 138 bunkers for the more discerning golfer.

For uniqueness why not try Hampton Court Palace - the only golf club in the UK to be situated inside a Royal Park. Being a Grade I Listed Home Park means wandering fallow deer and untamed rough are just two of the challenges for the inland links course, redesigned by Willie Park and with USPGA specification greens.

There are more than 500 venues in the region, which means there are almost unlimited options for a golfing itinerary taking in the very best and most challenging and enjoyable courses in southern England, with a budget to suit everyone.

Some of those worthy of a visit include The Drift in Surrey, Sweetwoods Park on the Sussex-Kent border and, for something a little different, the testing par-three course at Burgess Hill Golf Centre in West Sussex which is used for one of the South Region's Order of Merit championship events. While in West Sussex the 9-hole, par-30 Effingham Park, situated in the ground of Copthorne Effingham Park Hotel, is also worth a visit.

Selsdon Park Golf Club, Croydon, Surrey

London (Central & Greater)

BEXLEYHEATH. **Barnehurst Public Pay and Play Golf Course,** Mayplace Road East, Bexleyheath, Kent DA7 6JU (01322 523746; Fax: 01322 523860). *Location:* 10 minutes from M25, follow signs for Erith. Mature inland course in traditional woodland setting. 9 holes, 2737 yards. S.S.S. 68 (for 18 holes). Designed by five times Open Champion James Braid in 1903. Practice ground. *Green Fees:* from £6.80 weekdays, £9.00 weekends. *Eating facilities:* fully licensed bar with catering facilities. *Visitors:* welcome, no restrictions. Newly refurbished club house. *Society Meetings:* catered for. Large function rooms. Golf Manager: Freda Sunley.

BROMLEY. **Bromley Golf Centre,** Magpie Hall Lane, Bromley, Kent BR2 8JF. *Location:* off A21 Bromley to Farnborough road. Open course with many trees and water. 9 holes, 2795 yards. S.S.S. 67. Putting green and teaching facilities. New 20 bay floodlit driving range. *Green Fees:* weekdays £8.50, weekends. £11.00. *Eating facilities:* food available. *Visitors:* no booking required as this is a public course. Professional: Peter Remy (0208 462 7014)

DULWICH. **Dulwich and Sydenham Hill Golf Club,** Grange Lane, College Road, London SE21 7LH (020 8693 3961). *Location:* off South Circular, Dulwich Common. 18 holes, 6079 yards. S.S.S. 69. *Green Fees:* Information not available. *Eating facilities:* lunch every day. *Visitors:* welcome, prior arrangement advised. *Society Meetings:* catered for. Professional: David Baillie. Secretary: Mark Hickson.*

ELTHAM. **Eltham Warren Golf Club,** Bexley Road, Eltham SE9 2PE (020 8850 1166). *Location:* off East Rochester Way (A2) at Falconwood, then onto A210 Bexley Road. Parkland course, narrow fairways. 9 holes, 5840 yards. S.S.S. 68. Practice ground. *Green Fees:* £28.00 per day; with member £14.00. *Eating facilities:* dining room and bar. *Visitors:* welcome weekdays only, weekends with member only. *Society Meetings:* welcome Thursdays only. Professional: Gary Brett (020 8859 7909). Secretary: D.J. Mabbott (020 8850 4477).

ELTHAM. **Royal Blackheath Golf Club,** The Clubhouse, Court Road, Eltham SE9 5AF. *Location:* M25, A20 exit London bound, second set of traffic lights turn right, 600 yards up hill on right. Parkland, wooded with water. 18 holes, 6219 yards. S.S.S. 70. Practice area. *Green Fees:* £50.00 per round, £70.00 per day. *Eating facilities:* excellent dining room and two bars. *Visitors:* welcome weekdays, weekends only if introduced by and playing with member. Museum. *Society Meetings:* catered for midweek, prior booking essential. Professional: Richard Harrison (020 8850 1763). Secretary: (020 8850 1795; Fax: 020 8859 0150).
e-mail: info@rbgc.com
website: www.royalblackheath.com

HAMPTON WICK. **Hampton Court Palace Golf Club,** Hampton Wick, Kingston-upon-Thames KT1 4AD (020 8977 2658). *Location:* between Hampton Court and Kingston Bridge, entrance at Kingston Bridge roundabout. An historic course, redesigned by Willy Park. Parkland and inland links. 18 holes, 6513 yards. S.S.S. 71. *Green Fees:* £40.00 weekdays. *Eating facilities:* New Clubhouse, full bar and dining facilities. *Visitors:* welcome; booking one week in advance through Pro Shop. *Society Meetings:* catered for by arrangement. Professional: Edward Litchfield (020 8977 2658). Contacts: (020 8977 2423) e-mail: hamptonwickpalace@crown-golf.co.uk

LONDON. **London Scottish Golf Club,** Windmill Enclosure, Wimbledon Common SW19 5NQ (020 8788 0135). *Location:* just off A3 – Tibbetts Corner – just south of Putney SW15. Wooded commonland. 18 holes, 5458 yards. S.S.S. 66. *Green Fees:* £15.00 Monday, £20.00 Tuesday - Friday. *Eating facilities:* bar and catering. *Visitors:* welcome weekdays only. Check with Professional recommended. Red top must be worn, no jeans or sweatshirts. *Society Meetings:* welcome. Professional/Secretary: Stephen Barr (020 8789 1207/7517).

LONDON. **Richmond Park Golf Club,** Roehampton Gate, Richmond Park, London SW15 5JR (020 8876 1795; Fax: 020 8878 1354). *Location:* set within parkland in Richmond. Two courses (36 holes), 6036 yards and 5868 yards. S.S.S. 68/68/67. Driving range. *Green Fees:* information not provided. *Visitors:* welcome every day. *Society Meetings:* all welcome. Secretary: Tony Gourvish (020 8876 3205).*

LONDON. **Thamesview Golf Centre,** Fairway Drive (off Summerton Way), Thamesmead North, London SE28 8PP (020 8310 7975; Fax: 020 8312 0546). Delightful, undulating Public Pay & Play Course, founded 1991. Water hazards and a mixture of new and mature trees. The 4th hole is a challenging 515 yards down a narrow fairway. 9 holes, 5414 yards, par 70. S.S.S. 66. Floodlit 30 bay driving range, putting green. *Green Fees:* information not provided. *Eating facilities:* restaurant, bars and function room. *Visitors:* no restriction. Fully stocked Pro Shop, club hire. *Society Meetings:* welcome, book by telephone or in writing. Professionals: Dean Vickerman and Richard Waugh. Site Manager: Steven Wooley
e-mail: golf@tvgc.co.uk
website: www.tvgc.co.uk

> # PLEASE NOTE
> Some London golf clubs are listed in the EAST REGION (see pages 124-129)

ROEHAMPTON. **Roehampton Club Ltd,** Roehampton Lane, London SW15 5LR (020 8480 4200; Fax: 020 8480 4265). *Location:* just off South Circular Road between Sheen and Putney. Parkland. 18 holes, 6065 yards. S.S.S. 69. *Green Fees:* information not provided. *Eating facilities:* restaurant, club café, juice bar. *Visitors:* welcome as members' guest only, Handicap Certificate required at weekends. *Society Meetings:* catered for by arrangement. Professional: Alan L. Scott (020 8876 3858). Chief Executive: Mark Wilson (020 8480 4205). Sports Manager: Alistair Cook (020 8480 4200).

SHOOTERS HILL. **Shooters Hill Golf Club Ltd,** "Lowood", Eaglesfield Road, Shooters Hill, London SE18 3DA (020 8854 6368; Fax: 020 8854 0469). *Location:* off A207 between Blackheath and Welling. Hilly wooded course with fine views. 18 holes, 5721 yards. S.S.S. 68. *Green Fees:* weekdays £28.00 per round, £35.00 per day; weekends with a member only, £16.00 per round or day. *Eating facilities:* bar and diningroom. *Visitors:* members of other clubs welcome weekdays on production of letter of introduction, or official Handicap Certificate. Buggies available. *Society Meetings:* catered for Tuesdays and Thursdays only. Professional: David Brotherton (020 8854 0073). Secretary: Tony Barclay (020 8854 6368).

SOUTHWARK. **Aquarius Golf Club,** Beachcroft Reservoir, Marmora Road, Honor Oak SE22 0RY (020 8693 1626). *Location:* nearest main road - Forest Hill Road. The course is situated on and around a reservoir, testing first and eighth holes. 9 holes, 5246 yards. S.S.S. 66. *Green Fees:* information not provided. *Eating facilities:* limited. *Visitors:* welcome with member only. Professional: F. Private. Secretary: Jim Halliday.
e-mail: aquariusgolfclub@btopenworld.com

SUNBURY ON THAMES. **Hazelwood Golf Club Ltd,** Croysdale Avenue, Sunbury on Thames TW16 6QU (01932 770932; Fax: 01932 770933). *Location:* Junction 1 of M3. Parkland course. 9 holes, 2785 yards. Practice putting green, 36 bay driving range, bunker and chipping practice. *Green Fees:* Midweek £9.50 9 holes, £15.00 18 holes; Weekend £13.00 9 holes, £20.00 18 holes. *Eating facilities:* bar/food. *Visitors:* welcome every day. *Society Meetings* welcome. Professional: Robert Catley-Smith.

WEST DRAYTON. **Heathpark Golf Club,** Stockley Road, West Drayton, Middlesex UB7 9NA (01895 444232). *Location:* in grounds of Crown Plaza Hotel, Junction 4 M40. Undulating parkland course. 9 holes, 2275 yards. S.S.S. 62. *Green Fees:* information not available. *Eating facilities:* catering and bars. *Visitors:* welcome, dress code. *Society Meetings:* welcome at all times. Contact: B. Sharma.

WIMBLEDON. **Royal Wimbledon Golf Club,** 29 Camp Road, Wimbledon SW19 4UW. *Location:* one mile west of War Memorial in Wimbledon Village. 18 holes, 6348 yards. S.S.S. 70. *Visitors:* weekdays by prior arrangement. *Society Meetings:* Wednesdays and Thursdays only, by arrangement. Professional: David Jones. Secretary: Norman Smith (020 8946 2125; Fax: 020 8944 8652).
e-mail: secretary@rwgc.co.uk
website: www.rwgc.co.uk

WIMBLEDON. **Wimbledon Common Golf Club,** 19 Camp Road, Wimbledon Common, Wimbledon SW19 4UW (020 8946 0294; Fax: 020 8947 8697). *Location:* Wimbledon Common. Wooded course. 18 holes, 5438 yards. S.S.S. 66. Par 68. *Green Fees:* Monday £15.00, Tuesday to Friday £20.00. *Eating facilities:* bar, full catering every day except Mondays. *Visitors:* welcome weekdays, only with a member at weekends. Dress code – pillar box red upper garment must be worn. *Society Meetings:* welcome, groups of up to 50 catered for. Professional: J.S. Jukes (020 8946 0294; Fax: 020 8947 8697). Secretary: Geoff Oakshett (020 8946 7571).

WIMBLEDON. **Wimbledon Park Golf Club,** Home Park Road, Wimbledon, London SW19 7HR (020 8946 1002; Fax: 020 8944 8688). *Location:* Church Road, Arthur Road and Home Park Road from Wimbledon High Street, or by District Line to Wimbledon Park Station where signposted. Parkland, wooded around a lake. 18 holes, 5492 yards. S.S.S. 66. *Green Fees:* £60.00. *Eating facilities:* dining room and bar snacks each day. *Visitors:* welcome on production of letter of introduction or Handicap Certificate. *Society Meetings:* welcome. Professional: Dean Wingrove (020 8946 4053). General Manager: Patrick Shanahan (020 8946 1250; 020 8944 8688).
e-mail: patrick@wpgc.co.uk
website: www.wpgc.co.uk

FHG Guides
publish a large range of well-known accommodation guides.
We will be happy to send you details or you can use
the order form at the back of this book.

Berkshire

ASCOT. **The Berkshire Golf Club,** Swinley Road, Ascot SL5 8AY (01344 621495). *Location:* on A332 between Bagshot and Ascot, Heathland (wooded) course. 36 holes. Blue Course: 6358 yards, S.S.S. 71, Par 71. Red Course: 6452 yards, S.S.S. 71, Par 72. Practice facilities. *Green Fees:* £90.00 per round, £120.00 per day. *Eating facilities:* dining room open daily except Monday, snack bar open daily; bar open every day. *Visitors:* welcome weekdays only by application to the Secretary. *Society Meetings:* catered for by prior bookings. Professional: P. Anderson (01344 622351). Secretary: Lt. Col. J.C.F. Hunt (01344 621496).

ASCOT. **Lavender Park Golf Centre,** Swinley Road, Ascot SL5 8BD (01344 893344). *Location:* Ascot to Bracknell Road, half a mile from racecourse. Very pleasant flat 9 hole, Executive course, 8 Par 3s and one Par 4. 9 holes, 1104 yards. S.S.S. 28. 23-bay driving range. *Green Fees:* information not available. *Eating facilities:* bar snacks. *Visitors:* welcome at all times; pay and play. 8 table snooker hall. *Society Meetings:* welcome. Director of Golf/Master Professional: David Johnson (01344 893344).

ASCOT. **Mill Ride Golf Club,** Mill Ride, Ascot SL5 8LT (01344 891494; Fax: 01344 886820). *Location:* off Junction 3 of M3 or Junction 6 of M4, one mile west Ascot Racecourse. Parkland, seven lakes in play on 11 holes; designed by Donald Steel. 18 holes, 6900 yards. S.S.S. 73. Driving range. *Green Fees:* information not provided. *Eating facilities:* bar food. *Visitors:* welcome on application. Accommodation available. *Society Meetings:* individual and corporate membership available. Professional: Terry Wild (01344 886777; Fax: 01344 886820). Manager: Wayne Sheffield (01344 891494; Fax: 01344 886820). e-mail: golf@mill-ride.com
website: www.mill-ride.com

ASCOT. **Royal Ascot Golf Club,** Winkfield Road, Ascot SL5 7LJ (01344 625228; Fax: 01344 872330). *Location:* Winkfield Road is off Ascot High Street (A329). Parkland; new 18-hole course. 18 holes, 6293 yards. S.S.S. 70. Par 70. *Green Fees:* weekdays £25.00 as member's guest; weekends £30.00 as member's guest, *Eating facilities:* full catering available. *Visitors:* welcome only as guests of members. *Society Meetings:* catered for by agreement, maximum 40. Professional: Alistair White (01344 624656). Secretary: Mrs Sheila Thompson (01344 625175). e-mail: secretaries@royalascotgolfclub.co.uk

ASCOT. **Swinley Forest Golf Club,** Coronation Road, Ascot SL5 9LE (01344 620197). *Location:* between Ascot and Bagshot. Wooded heathland course. 18 holes, 6001 yards. S.S.S. 69. *Green Fees:* information not provided. *Eating facilities:* lunches served. *Visitors:* welcome only with a member. *Society Meetings:* catered for. Professional: Stuart Hill (01344 874811). Secretary: Stewart Zuill (01344 874979; Fax: 01344 874733).

BINFIELD. **Blue Mountain Golf Centre,** Wood Lane, Binfield, Bracknell RG42 4EX (01344 300220; Fax: 01344 360960). *Location:* two miles from M4 near Bracknell/Wokingham. Parkland course with numerous lakes. 18 holes, 6097 yards. S.S.S 70. 33 bay covered floodlit range. *Green Fees:* information not available. *Eating facilities:* fully licensed restaurant/ bar, Blues Bar with live jazz and food. *Visitors:* welcome any time. *Society Meetings:* always welcome, please call for details. Professional: Chris Lilleystone (01344 300220).*

BURNHAM. **Huntswood Golf Club,** Taplow Common Road, Burnham SL1 8LS (01628 667144; Fax: 01628 663145). *Location:* Junction 7 of M4, at roundabout turn left onto A4, then at Sainsburys roundabout turn right. Go straight over next two roundabouts, Huntswood Golf Club is quarter of a mile on the left. 18 holes, Par 68. *Green Fees:* £16.00 weekdays, £20.50 weekends. *Eating facilities:* bar and dining facilities after 7am. All-day breakfast, Sunday lunch. All types of functions catered for. *Visitors:* very welcome, Pay and Play open to all. Smart golf attire required, strictly no jeans on course. Buggy, trolley, club hire available. *Society Meetings:* welcome, please phone for information. Professional: Graham Beynon.*
website: www.huntswoodgolf.com

CROWTHORNE. **East Berkshire Golf Club**, Ravenswood Avenue, Crowthorne RG45 6BD (01344 772041; Fax: 01344 777378). *Location*: M3 Junction 3 - Bracknell turn off, follow signs to Crowthorne, Ravenswood Avenue opposite Railway Station. Heathland course. 18 holes, 6344 yards. S.S.S. 70. *Green Fees*: information not available. *Eating facilities*: bar snacks. *Visitors*: welcome weekdays by prior notification. *Society Meetings*: Thursdays and Fridays only. Professional: Jason Brant (01344 774112). Secretary: Colin Day (01344 772041; Fax: 01344 777378).

MAIDENHEAD. **Maidenhead Golf Club,** Shoppenhangers Road, Maidenhead SL6 2PZ (01628 624693; Fax: 01628 780758). *Location*: adjacent to Maidenhead Station (south side), one mile from M4. Level parkland course with irrigated fairways. 18 holes, 6364 yards. S.S.S. 70. *Green Fees*: weekdays £36.00. *Eating facilities*: restaurant and bar meals Tuesday to Friday. *Visitors*: welcome weekdays, no visitors after 12 noon Fridays. Handicap Certificate required. *Society Meetings*: welcome Tuesday pm, Wednesday and Thursday. Professional: Steve Geary (01628 624067). Secretary: P.H. Jones.
e-mail: manager@maidenheadgolf.co.uk
website: www.maidenheadgolf.co.uk

MAIDENHEAD. **Temple Golf Club,** Henley Road, Hurley, Near Maidenhead SL6 5LH (01628 824248; Fax: 01628 828119). *Location*: exit M4 Junction 8/9 or M40 at Junction 4. From M4 or M40 take A404 then A4130 signposted Henley. Chalk Downland course - exceptional drainage. 18 holes, 6266 yards. S.S.S. 70. Excellent practice area, putting and chipping green. *Green Fees*: weekdays £44.00 per round, £56.00 per day; weekends and Public Holidays £55.00 per round, £60.00 per day. *Eating facilities*: bar and bar snacks available daily; lunch and dinner available by prior arrangement. *Visitors*: welcome by prior arrangement. Handicap Certificate required. *Society Meetings*: welcome weekdays by prior arrangement; booking accepted one year in advance; minimum number 12, maximum 40. Professional: James Whiteley (01628 824254; Fax: 01628 828119). Secretary: Keith G.M. Adderley (01628 824795; Fax: 01628 828119).
e-mail: templegolfclub@btconnect.com

MAIDENHEAD. **Winter Hill Golf Club,** Grange Lane, Cookham SL6 9RP (01628 527613). *Location*: M4 Junction 8/9, four miles from Maidenhead. Parkland with extensive views of the Thames. 18 holes, 6408 yards - white tees, 6228 yards - yellow tees. S.S.S. 71. Large practice area. *Green Fees*: information not available. *Eating facilities*: lunches and snacks available every day. *Visitors*: welcome weekdays; preliminary enquiries advisable, and with member at weekends. *Society Meetings*: may be accepted by application to the Secretary; minimum number 16, maximum 40. Dress rules: strictly no jeans, trainers on course or in clubhouse. PGA Club and Teaching Professional: Roger Frost (01628 527610). Secretary: Sue Bickle (01628 527613).*

MAIDENHEAD near. **Bird Hills (UK) Ltd.,** Drift Road, Hawthorn Hill, Near Maidenhead SL6 3ST (01628 771030; Fax: 01628 631023). *Location*: M4 Junction 8/9, take A308 then A330 to Bracknell. Flat parkland course. 18 holes, 6176 yards. S.S.S. 69. 36 bay driving range. *Green Fees*: see website. Juniors/Senior Citizens concessionary rates. *Eating facilities*: club bar, restaurant, members bar, barbecue, private function hall. *Visitors*: always welcome, open every day except Christmas Day. Large Pro shop, Conference facilities. *Society Meetings*: always welcome. Professional: Mr Nick Slimming. Secretary: Mrs Eve Lane.
website: www.birdhills.co.uk

NEWBURY. **Deanwood Park Golf Club,** Stockcross, Newbury RG20 8JP (Tel & Fax: 01635 48772). *Location*: 200 yards off the A4 west of Newbury towards Stockcross village. Two miles from Newbury town centre. Undulating parkland/wooded course. 9 holes, 2114 yards, 1932 metres. S.S.S. 60 (18 holes). 7 bay driving range, practice net, practice bunker and putting green. *Green Fees*: information not provided. *Eating facilities*: Lounge/ bar/restaurant facilities; food served all day. *Visitors*: welcome at all times but must book in advance. Standard golf dress code applies, no jeans allowed on the course. Trolley, club and buggy hire available. *Society Meetings*: Society/Company groups welcome at all times - mix and match price structuring for golf and catering. Professional: Claire Waite. Secretary: John Bowness (Tel & Fax: 01635 48772).
e-mail: info@deanwoodpark.co.uk
website: www.deanwoodpark.co.uk

NEWBURY. **Donnington Grove Country Club,** Grove Road, Newbury RG14 2LA (01635 581000; Fax: 01635 552259). *Location*: northwestern outskirts of Newbury 3 miles from M4 J13. From the A4 running through Newbury take the B4494 (signposted Wantage) at Waitrose roundabout. After 600 yards turn left at mini roundabout. Dave Thomas designed, USGA specification greens, championship standard course. Parkland with lakes and other features; 18 holes, 7108 yards. Practice range for members, guests and visitors only. *Green Fees*: contact Pro Shop for current rate. *Eating facilities*: hotel with bar snacks and restaurant. *Visitors*: welcome anytime weekdays, after 11am weekends. *Society Meetings*: catered for; several packages available - phone for information. Professional: Gareth Williams (01635 551975). Secretary: Elfed Davies (01635 581000).*
e-mail: enquiries@donnington-grove.com
website: www.donnington-grove.com

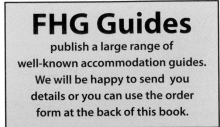

FHG Guides
publish a large range of well-known accommodation guides. We will be happy to send you details or you can use the order form at the back of this book.

NEWBURY. **Donnington Valley Hotel & Golf Club,** Snelsmore House, Snelsmore Common, Newbury RG14 3BG (01635 568140; Fax: 01635 568141). *Location:* Junction 13 of M4, then A34 towards Newbury. Take first exit off A34, follow signs to Donnington Castle, entrance on the right. 18 holes, 6353 metres. Practice net, computer analysis of swing. *Green Fees:* Information not available. *Eating facilities:* two bars and a restaurant. *Visitors:* welcome, must have own shoes. Accommodation in 4-star 111-bedroom hotel with a brand new Health Club and Spa. *Society Meetings:* welcome. Professional: Martin Balfour (01635 568142; Fax: 01635 568141). Secretary: Peter Smith (01635 568140; Fax: 01635 568141).*
e-mail: golf@donningtonvalley.co.uk
website: www.donningtonvalley.co.uk

NEWBURY. **Newbury and Crookham Golf Club Ltd,** Bury's Bank Road, Greenham, Newbury RG19 8BZ (01635 40035; Fax: 01635 40045). *Location:* on south side of Newbury; Junction 13 on M4. Varied and interesting with woods or trees on almost every hole. 18 holes, 5961 yards. S.S.S. 69. *Green Fees:* weekdays £40.00 per round, £50.00 per day. *Eating facilities:* restaurant/bar. *Visitors:* welcome, except weekends and Bank Holidays unless with a member. *Society Meetings:* welcome Wednesdays, Thursdays and Fridays. Buggies available. Professional: David Harris (01635 31201). Club Manager: Stephen Myers MBE (01635 40035).

NEWBURY. **Newbury Racecourse Golf Centre,** The Racecourse, Newbury RG14 7NZ (01635 551464; Fax: 01635 528354). *Location:* one mile south east of Newbury. Challenging flat links course for all standards. Good conditions throughout the year. 18 holes, 6500 yards. S.S.S. 71. Pro Shop, Driving range, practice area and green. *Green Fees:* information not available. *Eating facilities:* bar food. *Visitors:* welcome to pay and play. *Society Meetings:* all welcome. Professional: Nick Mitchell (01635 551464). Manager: N. Mitchell (01635 40015; Fax: 01635 528354).*

NEWBURY. **The West Berkshire Golf Course,** Chaddleworth, Newbury RG20 7DU (01488 638574). *Location:* M4 Junction 14. A338 towards Wantage, then follow signposts to RAF Welford. Downland. 18 holes, 7022 yards. S.S.S. 74. Two practice grounds, tuition available. *Green Fees:* information not provided. *Eating facilities:* full catering available. *Visitors:* welcome weekdays; restricted to afternoons weekends, reservation required. Trolleys and buggies available. *Society Meetings:* welcome by arrangement. Professional: Paul Simpson (01488 638851). Secretary: Mrs C.M. Clayton (01488 638574; Fax: 01488 638781).
website: www.thewbgc.co.uk

READING. **Calcot Park Golf Club,** Bath Road, Calcot, Reading RG31 7RN (0118 9427124; Fax: 0118 945 3373). *Location:* off Exit 12, M4 along A4 towards Reading, approximately one and a half miles. Undulating wooded parkland. 18 holes, 6216 yards. S.S.S. 70. Limited practice areas. *Green Fees:* weekdays £50.00 per day, £35.00 after 2pm. *Eating facilities:* fully licensed restaurant, snacks available, three bars. *Visitors:* welcome on provision of Handicap Certificate. Not weekends or Bank Holidays. Advisable to ring first to check availability. *Society Meetings:* catered for midweek. Professional: Mark Grieve (0118 942 7797; Fax: 0118 945 3373). Secretary: Kim Brake (0118 942 7124; Fax: 0118 945 3373).
e-mail: info@calcotpark.com
website: www.calcotpark.com

READING. **Castle Royle Golf and Country Club,** Knowl Hill, Reading RG10 9XA (01628 820700; Fax: 01628 829299). *Location:* alongside A4 between Maidenhead and Reading. Junction 8/9 M4. Parkland, links course. 18 holes, 6828 yards. S.S.S. 73. Practice ground. *Green Fees:* information not available. *Visitors:* members' guests only. Health and fitness club, 20x10m swimming pool, jacuzzi, sauna, gym, health and beauty and dance studio. *Eating facilities:* Full restaurant facilities and spike bar. Professional: Robert Watts. Golf Operations Manager: Nick Roberts. General Manager: Simon Jones.*

READING. **Hurst Golf Club,** Sandford Lane, Hurst, Reading RG10 0SU (01189 344355). *Location:* five miles Reading towards Wokingham. Parkland by the side of a large lake. 9 holes, 3154 yards. S.S.S. 70. *Green Fees:* Information not available. *Eating facilities:* bar and restaurant seating for 30, *Visitors:* unrestricted, bookings accepted. *Society Meetings:* welcome. Manager: Mr P. Priddle.*

READING. **Pincents Manor Golf,** Pincents Lane, Calcot, Reading RG31 4UQ (01734 323511; Fax: 01734 323503). *Location:* Junction 12 M4 behind Savacentre. Parkland. Two courses: Manor Course - 18 holes, 6028 yards. S.S.S. 69; Lodge Course - 9 holes, 2600 yards. S.S.S. 68. Par 3 course. *Green Fees:* Information not available. *Eating facilities:* Orchard Restaurant, Oak Bar, cruck barn. *Visitors:* welcome on Lodge Course, members only on Manor Course. Accommodation available in three bedrooms. *Society Meetings:* welcome. Professional: Alistair Thatcher.*

READING. **Reading Golf Club,** 17 Kidmore End Road, Emmer Green, Reading RG4 8SG (0118 947 2909). *Location:* two miles north of Reading off the Peppard Road (B481). Parkland. 18 holes, 6212 yards. S.S.S. 70. Practice facilities. *Green Fees:* Monday to Thursday £35.00 per round, £50.00 per day. *Eating facilities:* available. *Visitors:* welcome Monday to Thursday. Friday to Sunday with member only. *Society Meetings:* catered for by arrangement Tuesdays, Wednesdays and Thursdays. Buggies available. Professional: Scott Fotheringham (0118 947 6115). Secretary: Andrew Chaundy (0118 947 2909).
website: www.readinggolfclub.com

READING. **Sonning Golf Club,** Duffield Road, Sonning RG4 6GJ (01189 693332; Fax: 01189 448409). *Location*: left off A4 at Sonning Roundabout, then left again. Parkland. 18 holes, 6366 yards. S.S.S. 70. *Green Fees:* on application. *Eating facilities:* new restaurant - phone for booking 01189 272055. *Visitors:* welcome, must be member of a recognised golf club with an official handicap; weekends with members only. *Society Meetings:* catered for Wednesdays. Professional: R. McDougall (01189 692910). Secretary: A.J. Tanner.

READING. **Wokefield Park Golf Club,** Mortimer, Reading RG7 3AE (0118 9334018; Fax: 0118 9334031). *Location:* 10 minutes Junction 11 M4, 20 minutes Junction 5 M3. Championship parkland course with winding streams, 9 lakes and large bunkers. 18 holes, 6961 yards. S.S.S. 73. Practice facilities. *Green Fees:* Information not available. offers. *Eating facilities:* bar and two restaurants. *Visitors:* welcome at all times. Hotel with 322 en suite bedrooms; leisure facilities. *Society Meetings:* contact Golf Sales Team (0118 933 4018). Professional: Gary Smith (0118 9334078; Fax: 0118 9334162). Secretary: Norman West.*
website: www.verve-venues.com

SINDLESHAM. **Bearwood Golf Club,** Mole Road, Sindlesham RG41 5DB (0118 976 0060). *Location*: on B3030 from Winnersh to Arborfield. Flat, wooded course. 9 holes, 2802 yards. S.S.S. 68 (18 holes). Driving range 7.30am to 7.30pm every day. *Green Fees:* information not available. *Eating facilities:* food available all day. *Visitors:* welcome weekdays and weekends after 3pm. *Society Meetings:* maximum of 21 catered for. Thursday only. Professional: Bayley Tustin; Manager: Barry Tustin (0118 976 0060). Shop: 0118 976 0156.*

SLOUGH. **Datchet Golf Club,** Buccleuch Road, Datchet SL3 9BP (Tel & Fax: 01753 541872; Clubhouse: 01753 543887). *Location:* within two miles of both Windsor and Slough. 9 holes, 6087 yards. S.S.S. 69. *Green Fees:* £25.00 per round, £35.00 per day. Subject to review. *Visitors:* welcome weekdays and after 2.00pm weekends during BST. *Society Meetings:* welcome. Professional: Ian Godleman (01753 545222) Secretary/Manager: Keith Smith (Tel & Fax: 01753 541872).
e-mail: secretary@datchetgolfclub.co.uk
website: www.datchetgolfclub.co.uk

For full details of clubs and courses, plus convenient accommodation

www.uk-golfguide.com

STREATLEY ON THAMES. **Goring and Streatley Golf Club,** Rectory Road, Streatley on Thames RG8 9QA (01491 873229; Fax: 01491 875224). *Location:* 10 miles north west of Reading off A417 Wantage Road. Downland course on Berkshire Downs. 18 holes, 6355 yards. S.S.S. 70. *Green Fees:* £33.00 per round, £44.00 per day. *Eating facilities:* full restaurant and bar meals. Restaurant (01491 875122). *Visitors:* welcome on weekdays by telephone booking. *Society Meetings:* catered for. Professional: Jason Hadland (01491 873715). Secretary: A.B.W. James (01491 873229).
website: www.goringgc.org

SUNNINGDALE. **Sunningdale Ladies' Golf Club,** Cross Road, Sunningdale SL5 9RX (01344 620507). *Location:* second left going west on A30, past Sunningdale level crossing. Heathland. 18 holes, 3705 yards. (Designed for Ladies' Golf). S.S.S. 61, Men S.S.S. 58. *Green Fees:* £27.00 per round weekdays, £32.00 per round weekends/Bank Holidays (2008 rates, subject to review). *Eating facilities:* light lunches available except Sundays. *Visitors:* welcome, telephone first. Must have Handicap Certificate. *Society Meetings:* catered for. Secretary: Robin Mitchell.
e-mail: slgolfclub@tiscali.co.uk
website: www.sunningdaleladies.co.uk

WARGRAVE. **Hennerton Golf Club,** Crazies Hill Road, Wargrave RG10 8LT (0118 940 1000; Fax: 0118 940 1042). *Location:* halfway between Maidenhead and Reading off the A321 to Henley, follow "Golf Club" signs from Wargrave High Street. Challenging scenic course overlooking the Thames Valley. 18 holes, 4430 yards. Par 65. Driving range. *Green Fees:* on application. *Eating facilities:* clubhouse with full facilities. *Visitors:* welcome most times, phone Pro Shop. *Society Meetings:* telephone for details. Professional/Manager: William Farrow (0118 940 4778; Fax: 0118 940 1402).

WOKINGHAM. **Bearwood Lakes Golf Club,** Bearwood Road, near Sindlesham, Wokingham RG41 4SJ (0118 979 7900; Fax: 0118 979 2911). *Location:* just off M4 at Reading. Wooded 18 hole golf course. 6800 yards, S.S.S. 72. *Green Fees:* information not available. *Eating facilities:* restaurant, bar, function room, dining club. *Visitors:* must be the guest of a member. Practice ground available. Professional: Tim Waldron (0118 978 3030). General Manager: Scott Evans (0118 979 7900).*

WOKINGHAM. **Sand Martins Golf Club,** Finchampstead Road, Wokingham RG40 3RQ (0118 9792711; Fax: 0118 9770282). *Location:* off Nine Mile Ride, two miles from Wokingham town centre. Parkland, links/wooded course. 18 holes, 6204 yards. S.S.S. 70. Practice area including bunker/pitching area. *Green Fees:* £35.00. *Eating facilities:* bar food and restaurant. *Visitors:* welcome weekdays and at selected times at weekends. *Society Meetings:* welcome weekdays, except Friday afternoons. Professional: Andrew Hall (0118 9770265). Club Secretary: James McDonald (0118 9029965; Fax: 0118 9770282).

Buckinghamshire

AMERSHAM. **Harewood Downs Golf Club,** Cokes Lane, Chalfont St Giles HP8 4TA (01494 762184; Fax: 01494 766869). *Location:* off A413, two miles east of Amersham. Rolling, tree lined. 18 holes, 6028 yards. S.S.S. 69. Practice ground. *Green Fees:* weekdays £40.00 per round, £50.00 per day; weekends £45.00 per round, £50.00 per day. Special rates, winter golf. *Eating facilities:* full restaurant and bar. *Visitors:* welcome on weekdays with current Handicap, weekends by prior arrangement only. *Society Meetings:* welcome, mainly Thursdays and Fridays. Professional: G. Morris (01494 764102). Secretary: S.J. Thornton (01494 762184).

AYLESBURY. **Aylesbury Park Golf Club,** Oxford Road, Aylesbury HP17 8QQ (01296 399196; Fax: 01296 336830). *Location:* Just outside Aylesbury town centre off the A418. Historic parkland course. 18 holes, 6146 yards. S.S.S. 69. New 9 hole short course now open. *Green Fees:* information not available Numerous green fee special offers take place throughout the year - call for details. *Visitors:* welcome at all times. No Handicap Certificate required. *Society Meetings:* please call for details.

AYLESBURY. **Chiltern Forest Golf Club,** Aston Hill, Halton, Aylesbury HP22 5NQ (01296 631267; Fax: 01296 632709). *Location:* five miles south-east of Aylesbury, signposted St. Leonards. Wooded, hilly course. 18 holes, 5765 yards. S.S.S. 69. *Green Fees:* £34.00 weekdays; £17.00 with a member weekends. *Visitors:* weekdays unrestricted, weekends with a member. *Society Meetings:* welcome, preferably Wednesdays. Professional: Andy Lavers. Secretary: Bob Clift (01296 631267; Fax: 01296 632709).
e-mail: secretary@chilternforest.co.uk
website: www.chilternforest.co.uk.

www.uk-golfguide.com

AYLESBURY. **Ellesborough Golf Club,** Butlers Cross, Aylesbury HP17 0TZ (01296 622375). *Location:* on B4010 one-and-a-half miles from Wendover. Chiltern Hills course. Undulating links. 18 holes, 6360 yards, 5815 metres. S.S.S. 71. Practice net/ground. *Green Fees:* £35.00 per round, £55.00 per day. *Eating facilities:* full catering available. *Visitors:* welcome except Tuesday mornings and competition days, weekends with a member only. Must provide Handicap Certificate. *Society Meetings:* catered for Wednesdays and Thursdays only by arrangement. Professional: Mark Squire (Tel & Fax: 01296 623126). General Manager: (Tel & Fax: 01296 622114).

AYLESBURY. **Weston Turville Golf Club,** New Road, Weston Turville, Near Aylesbury HP22 5QT (01296 424084; Fax: 01296 395376). *Location:* two miles south east of Aylesbury off A41. Easy walking course at the foot of the Chiltern Hills. 18 holes, 6008 yards. S.S.S. 69. *Green Fees:* Information not available. *Eating facilities:* meals, snacks and visitors' bar. *Visitors:* truly welcome. *Society Meetings:* especially catered for. Professional: Gary George (01296 425949; Fax: 01296 395376). General Manager: David Allen (01296 424084; Fax: 01296 395376).*

BEACONSFIELD. **Beaconsfield Golf Club,** Seer Green, Near Beaconsfield HP9 2UR (01494 676545; Fax: 01494 681148). *Location:* from A40 at Beaconsfield, A355 Amersham Road, one mile turn right to Jordans, one mile signposted. Parkland course. 18 holes, 6508 yards, Par 72. Large practice ground, driving range. *Green Fees:* £50.00 per round, £60.00 per day. Subject to review. *Eating facilities:* dining room or bar menu; two bars. *Visitors:* welcome weekdays with accredited introduction – check with Pro. Handicap Certificate required. *Society Meetings:* catered for Tuesdays and Wednesdays. Professional: Mike Brothers (01494 676616). Secretary: K.R. Wilcox (01494 676545).
e-mail: secretary@beaconsfieldgolfclub.co.uk
website: www.beaconsfieldgolfclub.co.uk

BUCKINGHAM. **Buckingham Golf Club,** Tingewick Road, Buckingham MK18 4AE (01280 815566; Fax: 01280 821812). *Location*: two miles south west of Buckingham on A421. Undulating parkland - eight holes affected by river. 18 holes, 6162 yards. S.S.S. 70. Practice ground. *Green Fees:* weekdays £40.00; weekends as members' guests only. *Eating facilities:* seven day catering - bars, lunch and evening. (01280 813282) *Visitors:* welcome weekdays only. Pro shop (01280 815210). *Society Meetings:* pre-booked on Tuesdays or Thursdays. Secretary Manager: Gerald L. Pearce M. Inst. GCM (01280 815566; Fax: 01280 821812). Professional: Gregor Hannah (01280 815210). e-mail: admin@buckinghamgolfclub.co.uk website: www.buckinghamgolfclub.co.uk

BURNHAM. **Burnham Beeches Golf Club,** Green Lane, Burnham, Slough SL1 8EG (01628 661448; Fax: 01628 668968). *Location*: Junction 7 on M4. Parkland/wooded course. 18 holes, 6449 yards. S.S.S. 71. *Green Fees:* weekdays 18 holes £40.00, 36 holes £60.00. *Eating facilities:* bar and restaurant. *Visitors:* welcome weekdays, Handicap Certificate required. *Society Meetings:* welcome Wednesdays to Fridays April to October. Professional: R. Bolton (01628 661661). Secretary: T.P. Jackson (01628 661448).

BURNHAM. **The Lambourne Golf Club,** Dropmore Road, Burnham SL1 8NF (01628 666755; Fax: 01628 663301). *Location:* take M4 to Exit 7; take M40 to Exit 2. Parkland course, six lakes. 18 holes, 6798 yards. S.S.S. 73. Practice facilities available. *Green Fees:* Monday to Friday £60.00. *Eating facilities:* snack bar, half-way hatch, restaurant. *Visitors:* welcome. Handicap Certificate required. Golf Director: (01628 606717). Professional/General Manager: David Hart (01628 606717; Fax: 01628 663301).

CHALFONT ST GILES. **Oakland Park Golf Club,** Bowles Farm, Threehouseholds, Chalfont St Giles HP8 4LW (01494 871277 Office). *Location:* off main A413 towards Amersham, 10 minutes from J2, M40. Parkland course. 18 holes, 5246 yards. S.S.S. 66. Practice range, green and bunkers. *Green Fees:* Information not available. *Eating facilities:* clubhouse bar, full catering all week. *Visitors:* welcome 7 days (after midday at weekends and Bank Holidays). *Society Meetings:* welcome. Professional: Alistair Thatcher (01494 877333; Fax: 01494 874692). General Manager: Ian Donnelly.*

CHESHAM. **Chartridge Park Golf Club,** Chartridge, Chesham HP5 2TF (01494 791772). *Location*: M25 Junction 18, Amersham, Chesham, three miles from roundabout by pond. Flat parkland course with wooded areas, two water holes and views over the Chiltern Valley. 18 holes, 5409 yards, S.S.S. 66. Chipping and putting area, driving nets. *Green Fees*: £20 weekdays; £28 weekends. *Eating facilities*: snacks and cooked food available seven days a week; bar. *Visitors & Societies*: welcome, restrictions apply. Functions, Weddings, Corporate Events; Private, spacious suite available for hire. RGA Professional: Jeremy Reilly (07979 497465). General Manager: Eric Roca.

CHESHAM. **Chesham and Ley Hill Golf Club,** Ley Hill, Chesham HP5 1UZ (01494 784541). *Location:* off A41 on B4504 to Ley Hill, nearest town - Chesham. Wooded parkland. 9 holes, 5296 yards. S.S.S. 65. *Green Fees:* Information not available. *Eating facilities:* licensed bar, food available at certain times. *Visitors:* welcome Mondays and Thursdays all day; Wednesdays after 12 noon; Fridays up to 4pm. *Society Meetings:* Thursdays only by prior arrangement. Secretary: J. Short (01494 784541). website: www.cheshamgolf.co.uk*

DENHAM. **Buckinghamshire Golf Club,** Denham Court, Denham Court Drive, Denham UB9 5PG (01895 835777; Fax: 01895 835210). *Location:* Junction 1 M40 off Denham roundabout, follow signs to Denham Country Park. Gently undulating parkland, River Colne and River Misbourne run through course. 18 holes, 6880 yards. S.S.S. 73. Practice range with ball dispenser and collection. *Green Fees:* Information not available. *Eating facilities:* Heron Restaurant, spike bar; food served all day. *Visitors:* welcome Mondays to Thursdays; advance bookings only. *Society Meetings:* welcome, golf company days up to 80 – details on application. Professional: Paul Schunter. Golf Director: John O'Leary. Enquiries: Dubravka Barancek.* website: www.buckinghamshiregc.com

DENHAM. **Denham Golf Club,** Tilehouse Lane, Denham UB9 5DE (01895 832022; Fax: 01895 835340). *Location:* off A412 near Uxbridge. Parkland - undulating. 18 holes, 6462 yards, 5903 metres. S.S.S. 71. Practice ground. *Green Fees:* information not available. *Eating facilities:* diningroom, bar snacks. *Visitors:* welcome Monday to Thursday by prior arrangement only. Handicap Certificate. *Society Meetings:* catered for Tuesdays, Wednesdays and Thursdays. Professional: Stuart Campbell (01895 832801). Secretary: J. W. Tucker (01895 832022; Fax: 01895 835340). e-mail: club.secretary@denhamgolfclub.co.uk website: www.denhamgolfclub.co.uk

GERRARDS CROSS. **Gerrards Cross Golf Club,** Chalfont Park, Gerrards Cross SL9 0QA (01753 278500; Fax: 01753 883593). *Location:* alongside A413 (to Amersham) about three miles from junction with A40 (London to Oxford road). Wooded parkland course. 18 holes, 6295 yards. S.S.S. 70. Practice nets and putting green. *Green Fees:* weekdays £45.00 per round, £55.00 per day. Subject to review. *Eating facilities:* lunch, bar snacks, afternoon tea always available, evening meals to order. *Visitors:* welcome except at weekends and Public Holidays but must produce a letter of introduction or current Handicap Certificate. Tuesday is Ladies' Day. *Society Meetings:* catered for Thursdays and Fridays, maximum number 100. Professional: M. Barr (01753 885300). Secretary/Manager: (01753 883263).

THE APPEARANCE OF AN ASTERISK (*) AT THE END OF A CLUB OR COURSE ENTRY INDICATES THAT UP-TO-DATE INFORMATION HAS NOT BEEN SUPPLIED

HIGH WYCOMBE. **Flackwell Heath Golf Club Limited,** Treadaway Road, Flackwell Heath, High Wycombe HP10 9PE (01628 520929; Fax: 01628 530040). *Location:* M40 Exit 3 from London, Exit 4 from Oxford. 2 miles High Wycombe. Undulating heath and woodland. 18 holes, 6211 yards. S.S.S. 70. *Green Fees:* weekdays £36.00 per round, £50.00 per day; weekends with member only – £20.00. *Eating facilities:* restaurant and bars daily. *Visitors:* welcome weekdays with Handicap Certificate, weekends with member only. *Society Meetings:* catered for by arrangement Monday to Friday – contact the Secretary. Professional: Paul Watson (01628 523017). Secretary: I. R. Hulley (01628 520929).
e-mail: info@flackwellheathgolfclub.co.uk
website: www.flackwellheathgolfclub.co.uk

HIGH WYCOMBE. **Hazlemere Golf Club,** Penn Road, Hazlemere, Near High Wycombe HP15 7LR (01494 719300; Fax: 01494 713914). *Location:* from M40 North: Junction 2, via Beaconsfield and Penn on B474; from M40 South; Junction 4, through High Wycombe on A404. Undulating parkland course with a number of feature water holes. Practice area. 18 holes, 5833 yards. S.S.S. 69. *Green Fees:* weekdays £36.00; weekends £45.00. *Eating facilities:* coffee shop and bar. *Visitors:* welcome 7 days a week (after midday weekends). *Society Meetings:* welcome weekdays. Professional: Gavin Cousins (01494 719306). Secretary: (01494 719300).

HIGH WYCOMBE. **Wycombe Heights Golf Centre,** Rayners Avenue, Loudwater, High Wycombe HP10 9SZ (01494 816686; Fax: 01494 816728). *Location:* one mile south-east of High Wycombe off A40. Impressive tree-lined parkland course with panoramic views of Chilterns. Challenging final loop from 15th to 18th. 18 holes, 6265 yards, Par 70, S.S.S. 72. 18-hole, Par 3 course, practice green and bunker, 24-bay floodlit driving range. *Green Fees:* £18.00 weekdays, £25.00 weekends. Subject to review. *Eating facilties:* full clubhouse facilities. *Visitors:* welcome, booking in advance is essential. *Society Meetings:* welcome 7 days, telephone or write for details. In house Golfing Academy.

IVER. **Iver Golf Club,** Hollow Hill Lane, Off Langley Park Road, Iver SL0 0JJ (01753 655615; Fax: 01753 654225). *Location:* near Slough. Situated on the right off Langley Park Road leaving the town of Langley and heading towards Iver. Flat parkland, easy walking with natural ditches and ponds. 9 holes, 5628 yards. S.S.S. 67. 18 bay driving range, practice area, putting green, bunker area onto a green. Plus new 9 hole short course. *Green Fees:* weekdays £8.90 for 9 holes, £15.00 for 18; weekends £9.50 for 9 holes, £17.00 for

18. Veterans and Juniors: £6.30 for 9 holes, £10.00 for 18 holes. Special rates available Tues/Thurs, please enquire. *Eating facilities:* bar lunches 11:30am until 2:30pm seven days. *Visitors:* always welcome, best to phone on day of play for booking. We have a new Junior section, a Vet society every Tuesday and are willing to accommodate most requests. Senior Members' competitions Thursday mornings. *Society Meetings:* always welcome. Professional: Jim Lynch (01753 655615; Fax: 01753 654225).

IVER. **Richings Park Golf Club,** North Park, Iver SL0 9DL (01753 655370; Fax: 01753 655409). *Location:* M4 Junction 5. Flat parkland. 18 holes, 6209 yards. S.S.S. 70. Practice area, two putting greens, bunker and chipping area. *Green Fees:* information not provided. *Eating facilities:* bar, restaurant, and spike bar. *Visitors:* welcome with restrictions at weekend. *Society Meetings:* welcome, minimum 12. Professional/Secretary/General Manager: Steve Coles (01753 655352).

LITTLE CHALFONT. **Little Chalfont Golf Club,** Lodge Lane, Little Chalfont HP8 4AJ (01494 764877). *Location:* Junction 18 M25, two miles towards Amersham on A404, first left past garden centre. Undulating parkland. 9 holes, 5752 yards S.S.S. 68. *Green Fees:* weekdays £14.00, weekends £16.00. *Eating facilities:* full bar and restaurant. *Visitors:* always welcome. *Society Meetings:* welcome mid-week. Professional: J.M. Dunne (01494 762942). Secretary: Michael Dunne (01494 764877).

MARLOW. **Harleyford Golf Club,** Harleyford Estate, Henley Road, Marlow SL7 2SP (01628 816161; Fax: 01628 816160). *Location:* two miles from Marlow on the A4155 to Henley. Parkland course designed by Donald Steel. 18 holes, 6708 yards, S.S.S. 72. Excellent practice range and green available. Soft spikes only, no metal spikes allowed. *Green fees:* Information not available. *Eating facilities:* restaurant, lounge and bar. *Visitors:* book via Pro Shop. Handicap Certificate required. *Society Meetings:* welcome by arrangement Tuesday, Wednesday and Friday, contact Events Office (01628 816164). Professional: Mark Burroughes (01628 816162). General Manager: Gary Ivory (01628 816164).*
e-mail: info@harleyfordgolf.co.uk
website: www.harleyfordgolf.co.uk

MILTON KEYNES. Abbey Hill Golf Centre, Monks Way, Two Mile Ash, Milton Keynes MK8 8AA (01908 563845). *Location:* 2 miles west of town centre, just off the A5 on the H3. Undulating parkland course with mature trees and impressive backdrops. Water comes into play on seven holes. 18 holes, 6025 yards. S.S.S. 69, Par 71. Additional Par 3 course, putting green, 21 bay floodlit driving range. *Green Fees:* weekdays £17.00, weekends £23.00 *Eating facilities:* full clubhouse facilities. *Visitors:* welcome, booking in advance advisable. *Society Meetings:* welcome, telephone or write for details. Professional: Ricky Carvell PGA. Manager: Gordon Forster. website:www.abbeyhillgc.co.uk

MILTON KEYNES. Kingfisher Country Club, Buckingham Road, Deanshanger, Milton Keynes MK19 6DG (01908 560354; Fax: 01908 260857). *Location:* twixt Milton Keynes/Buckingham on A422. Mature course setting - wooded - lakes and ponds major feature. 9 holes, 5471 yards. S.S.S. 67. Full 9 hole floodlit. 10 bay covered range. *Green Fees:* information not available. *Eating facilities:* full club house overlooking lake. *Visitors:* welcome, some weekend restrictions on Sundays and Public Holidays. *Society Meetings:* welcome. Director: D.M. Barraclough. *

MILTON KEYNES. Three Locks Golf Club, Great Brickhill, Milton Keynes MK17 9BH (01525 270050 golf; Tel & Fax: 01525 270470). *Location:* A4146 Bletchley to Leighton Buzzard. Parkland with lakes and water hazards. 18 holes, 6400 yards. S.S.S. 71. Practice ground. *Green Fees:* weekdays £19.00 per round, £30.00 per day; weekends £26.00 per round. Twilight fees £13.00. *Eating facilities:* hot bar food. *Visitors:* welcome every day. Golf buggies for hire. *Society Meetings:* all welcome. Professional: Visiting Professional. Secretary: Julia Faid (01525 270470).

MILTON KEYNES. Wavendon Golf Centre, Lower End Road, Wavendon, Milton Keynes MK17 8DA (01908 281811; Fax: 01908 281257). *Location:* from Junction 13 M1, A421, follow signs to Woburn Sands. Parkland with six small lakes as hazards. Three courses: 18 holes, 5608 yards. S.S.S. 69. 9 holes, 1424 yards. S.S.S. 27, pitch and putt course, Par 26, 536 yards. 36 bay driving range, practice, information not available. *Eating facilities:* fully licensed bar and carvery restaurant. *Visitors:* always welcome. Buggies. *Society Meetings:* welcome. Professional/Secretary: Greg Iron (01908 281811).* e-mail: wavendon-jackbarker@btinternet.com

MILTON KEYNES. Windmill Hill Golf Centre, Tattenhoe Lane, Bletchley, Milton Keynes MK3 7RB (01908 630660; Fax: 01908 630034; Tee reservations 01908 631113. 7 days in advance). *Location:* M1 South Junction 14/M1 North Junction 13 A421 towards Buckingham. 32 bay covered floodlit driving range, seven grassed bays. Two putting greens; practice area. *Green Fees:* information not available. *Eating facilities:* restaurant, cafeteria, bars, function room; pool and games room. *Opening hours:* 7.30am till 11pm. *Society Meetings:* welcome (after 11am weekends and Bank Holidays); weekday and weekend packages. Three teaching Professionals, tuition, Pro shop. Professional: Colin Clingan (01908 378623). Secretary: Brian Smith (Tel & Fax: 01908 366457).*

MILTON KEYNES. Woburn Golf Club, Little Brickhill, Milton Keynes MK17 9LJ (01908 370756; Fax: 01908 378436). *Location:* four miles west of Junction 13 M1. Three courses, 54 holes: Duke's Course 6976 yards, S.S.S. 74; Duchess' Course 6651 yards, S.S.S. 72; Marquess Course 7214 yards, S.S.S. 74. Practice facilities. *Green Fees:* by request. *Eating facilities:* restaurant; breakfasts and lunches; dinner by prior arrangement. *Visitors:* welcome weekdays by prior arrangement. Weekends restricted to members and their guests only. *Society Meetings:* catered for, details on application. Secretary: Mrs G. Beasley (01908 370756). Professional: L. Blacklock (01908 626600). e-mail: enquiries@woburngolf.com website: www.discoverwoburn.co.uk

PRINCES RISBOROUGH. Princes Risborough Golf Club, Lee Road, Saunderton Lee, Princes Risborough HP27 9NX (01844 346989. Fax: 01844 274938). *Location:* A4010, Princes Risborough, turn off at Rose and Crown Inn, one mile on right. Parkland course, slightly undulating, water hazards and has beautiful views. 9 holes, 5552 yards. S.S.S. 67. Practice area and nets. *Green Fees:* 9 holes weekdays £12.00; weekends £14.00, 18 holes weekdays £17.00; weekends £22.00. *Eating facilities:* restaurant and bar. *Visitors:* always welcome properly attired. Memberships available. *Society Meetings:* welcome. Outside functions, wedding receptions, parties and Christmas dinners catered for. Professional: Simon Lowry (01844 274567). Secretary/Proprietor: J.F. Tubb. website: www.princesrisboroughgc.uwclub.net

www.uk-golfguide.com

PRINCES RISBOROUGH. **Whiteleaf Golf Club Ltd,** Upper Icknield Way, Whiteleaf HP27 0LY (01844 274058/343097). *Location:* A4010 from Princes Risborough turn off at signpost for Whiteleaf into Upper Icknield Way. Hilly course with beautiful Chiltern views. 9 holes, 5391 yards. S.S.S. 66. Practice area. *Green Fees:* £17.50 weekdays and weekends, weekends only with a member. *Eating facilities:* full catering facilities, except Mondays. *Visitors:* always welcome; probably better to phone Secretary in case of disappointment. *Society Meetings:* on Thursdays – apply to Secretary. Professional: Ken Ward (01844 345472). Secretary: Derek Hill (01844 274058).

SLOUGH. **Farnham Park Pay and Play Golf Course,** Park Road, Stoke Poges, Slough SL2 4PJ (Tel & Fax: 01753 643332). *Location:* just off A355, two miles north of A4. Challenging parkland course with water. 18 holes, 6172 yards. S.S.S. 71. Short game practice facilities. *Green Fees:* weekdays £15.00, weekends £21.00. Reductions for Juniors and Seniors. *Eating facilities:* hot and cold food always available. *Visitors:* welcome. Pro shop with hire facilities. *Society Meetings:* welcome, special packages available, from as little as £20.00 per person. Professional: Nigel Whitton (01753 643332). Operated by South Bucks District Council. Secretary: Mrs M. Brooker, M. Inst. GCM (01753 647065).

STOKE POGES. **Lanes Golfing Academy,** Stoke Road, Stoke Poges SL2 4NL (01753 554840). *Location:* half-a-mile from Slough Railway Station in direction of Stoke Poges. Parkland course ideal for the less experienced player. 9 holes. 2400 yds. S.S.S. 62 (18 holes). 18 bay driving range. *Green Fees:* information not available. *Eating facilities:* small lounge area with snack facilities. *Visitors:* open to the public seven days a week. Clubs for hire. Expert tuition available. The Tiger Club for under 12s with 12 monthly competitions held. *Society Meetings:* ideal for company tuition days. A Golf Foundation starter centre. Professional: Paul Warner (01753 554840). Operated by South Bucks District Council Contact: Mr K Simpkins (01753 533333).*

STOKE POGES. **Stoke Park Club,** North Drive, Park Road, Stoke Poges SL2 4PG (01753 717171; Fax: 01753 717181). *Location:* one mile north of Slough, eight miles from Heathrow. Parkland course. 27 holes, 6670 yards. S.S.S. 72. Practice ground (tokens available from Club Shop). *Green Fees:* weekdays £140.00, Saturdays and Sundays, members only. *Eating facilities:* Orangery, dining room, President's Bar and Park Restaurant. *Visitors:* welcome weekdays with Handicap Certificate or letter of introduction. 21 bedrooms now available, conference facilities. *Society Meetings:* catered for. Club Director: Mark Fagan (01753 717171; Fax: 01753 717181). Professional: Stuart Collier. Club Shop: 01753 717184. Secretary: Kelly Ford (01753 717116) . e-mail: info@stokeparkclub.com website: www.stokeparkclub.com

STOWE. **Silverstone Golf Club,** Silverstone Road, Stowe MK18 5LH (01280 850005; Fax: 01280 850156). *Location:* A43 half mile south of Silverstone Grand Prix Circuit. A parkland course with maturing copses bordered by woodland. 18 holes, Par 72. 6558 yards. S.S.S. 71. Putting area, covered driving range. *Green Fees:* information not provided. *Eating facilities:* meals at all times, licensed bar. *Visitors:* welcome, booking seven days in advance. Conference facilities. Corporate days. *Society Meetings:* welcome. Professional: Rodney Holt. Manager: Scott Barnes. e-mail: enquiries@silverstonegolfclub.co.uk website: www.silverstonegolfclub.co.uk

STOWE. **Stowe Golf Club,** Stowe, Buckingham MK18 5EH (01280 816264). *Location:* situated at Stowe School, four miles north of Buckingham. Parkland course with follies and lakes. 9 holes, 2189 yards. S.S.S. 63. *Green Fees:* information not available. *Visitors:* only as a guest of a member. *Society Meetings:* catered for by appointment. Secretary: Bill Kemp (01280 818282). *

WEXHAM. **Wexham Park Golf Course,** Wexham Street, Wexham, Slough SL3 6ND (01753 663271; Fax: 01753 663318). *Location:* M40 to Beaconsfield, A40 to Gerrards Cross, direction Fulmer on right hand side, near Wexham Park Hospital. Undulating parkland courses. 18 holes, 5251 yards. S.S.S. 66. Also 9 hole course, 2727 yards, par 34; and 9 hole course, 2219 yards, par 32. Driving range and short game practice area. *Green Fees:* information not available. *Eating facilities:* clubhouse bar and full kitchen facilities. *Visitors:* welcome, Pay and Play, open to all. *Society Meetings:* 7 days a week by prior arrangement. Professional: John Kennedy (01753 663271). Secretary: J. Dunne.

WOOBURN COMMON. **Hedsor Golf Course,** Pay & Play, Broad Lane, Wooburn Common HP10 0JW (01628 851285). *Location:* from Junction 2 of M40, take A355 to Slough, turn right at Hedsor Golf Course sign, then follow golf arrows to course. Easy walking course in mature parkland; many water hazards. 9 holes. Par 34. 18 holes S.S.S 64. *Green Fees:* special rates for senior citizens. *Eating facilities:* bar and catering available. Professional: Stuart Cannon.

Hampshire

ALDERSHOT. **Army Golf Club,** Laffan's Road, Aldershot GU 11 2HF (01252 337272). *Location:* access from Eelmoor Bridge off A323 Aldershot Fleet Road - second oldest course in Hampshire. 18 holes, 6550 yards. S.S.S. 71. *Green Fees:* from £37.00; special rates for military personnel. *Eating facilities:* bar snacks, restaurant/ dining room. *Visitors:* weekdays only, members' guests anytime. *Society Meetings:* catered for. Professional: G. Cowley (01252 336722). Manager: John Hiscock (01252 337272; Fax: 01252 337562).
e-mail: secretary@armygolfclub.com

ALRESFORD. **Alresford Golf Club**, Cheriton Road, Tichborne Down, Alresford SO24 0PN **(01962 733746; Fax: 01962 736040)**. *Location*: on B3046 south of A31, two miles north A272. Rolling downland, wooded. 18 holes, 5914 yards, 5408 metres. S.S.S. 69. Practice area. **Green Fees:** weekdays £30.00 per round; weekends and Bank Holidays £40.00 per round. *Eating facilities:* full catering. *Visitors*: welcome but not before 12 noon weekends/Bank Holidays. *Society Meetings*: welcome weekdays only, by arrangement. **Professional: Malcolm Scott (Tel & Fax: 01962 733998). Secretary: David Maskery (01962 733746; Fax: 01962 736040).**
e-mail: secretary@alresfordgolf.co.uk
website: www.alresfordgolf.co.uk

ALTON. **The Alton Golf Club,** Old Odiham Road, Alton GU34 4BU (01420 82042). *Location:* off B3349 (turn off at Golden Pot). Undulating meadowland, wooded course. 9 holes, 5744 yards. S.S.S. 68. Practice area, putting green. *Green Fees:* information not available. *Eating facilities:* bar, hot and cold snacks all day. *Visitors:* welcome any time without reservation. Buggies for hire. *Society Meetings:* welcome weekdays only.*

ALTON. **Blacknest Golf & Country Club,** Blacknest Road, Blacknest, Alton GU34 4QL (01420 22888). *Location*: Bently exit of A31, between Farnham and Alton. Parkland course with several water features. 18 holes, Par 69; also Par 3 course. *Green Fees:* weekdays £20.00 18 holes, weekends £25.00. *Eating facilities:* bar and dining available from 8am to 5pm. *Visitors:* welcome by arrangement. *Society Meetings:* welcome. Professional: Darren Burgess.

ALTON. **Worldham Golf Club,** Cakers Lane, Worldham, Alton GU34 3BF (01420 544606). *Location:* B3004 Alton to Bordon road, one mile from Alton. Parkland course with views of the Wey Valley. 18 holes, 6199 yards. S.S.S. 70. 14-bay driving range. *Green Fees:* weekdays £16.00, Fridays £18.00, weekends £20.00. *Eating facilities:* spike bar with hot and cold food, lounge area. *Visitors:* welcome - pay and play. Booking required at weekends. Professional shop. *Society Meetings:* welcome any day. Professional: Tony Cook (01420 543151). General Manager: Ian Yates (01420 544606).

AMPFIELD. **Ampfield Golf Club,** Winchester Road, Ampfield, Near Romsey SO51 9BQ (01794 368480). *Location:* A31 Winchester to Romsey road, next door to White Horse Public House. Parkland course designed by Sir Henry Cotton. Home of Short Course PGA Championships. 18 hole Par 3 course, 2478 yards. S.S.S. 53. Practice area. *Green Fees:* weekends £15.00, weekdays £13.00, £10.00 after 5pm. Special Junior rates. *Eating facilities:* excellent food served Tuesday to Sunday. Weddings and private parties up to 120 guests catered for. *Visitors:* welcome 7 days a week; golf shoes must be worn. Pro Shop. Disabled access. *Society Meetings:* welcome 7 days a week; excellent value packages. Managing Director: Mark Hazell. Events Manager: Julia Francis (01794 368750).
e-mail: juliafrancis@ampfieldgolf.com
website: www.ampfieldgolf.com

ANDOVER. **Andover Golf Club,** 51 Winchester Road, Andover SP10 2EF (01264 323980). *Location:* Stockbridge Exit from A303, left towards Andover, quarter of a mile on right. Gently sloping downland course with views over town and country. 9 holes, 6096 yards. S.S.S. 69. *Green Fees:* weekdays £22.00 per round, £12.00 with a member; £27.00 weekends and Bank Holidays, £17.00 with a member. *Eating facilities:* full catering available. *Visitors:* welcome, check tee reservations with Professional. *Society Meetings:* welcome, please phone for availability. Professional: A. Timms (01264 324151). Secretary: Guy Davis (01264 358040). Clubhouse Manager: (01264 323980).
e-mail: secretary@andovergolfclub.co.uk
website: www.andovergolfclub.co.uk

ANDOVER. **The Hampshire Golf Club,** Winchester Road, Goodworth Clatford, Andover SP11 7TB (01264 357555; Fax: 01264 356606). *Location:* one mile south of Andover on A3057 Stockbridge Road. Downland with new trees and lakes. 18 holes, 6145 yards. S.S.S. 71. 10 bay covered driving range. *Green Fees:* weekdays £20.00, weekends £27.00. 9 hole, par 3 course £5.00 weekdays, £6.00 weekends. *Eating facilities:* full catering facilities, bar seven days a week. *Visitors:* always welcome. *Society Meetings:* welcome weekdays only. 118Golf.co.uk shop(01264 357555). Professional: Rob Spurrier (01264 357555). Secretary: Jan Miles (01264 356462; Fax: 01264 356606).

BARTON-ON-SEA. **Barton-on-Sea Golf Club,** Milford Road, New Milton BH25 5PP (01425 615308; Fax: 01425 621457). *Location:* one mile from centre of New Milton on B3058 towards Milford-on-Sea. Cliff top links with easy walking; superb views of Isle of Wight and Christchurch Bay. 27 holes. S.S.S. 72 any 18 holes. *Green Fees:* £44.00 per day weekdays; £55.00 weekends and Bank Holidays. *Eating facilities:* lunch, snacks and teas daily, full bar service. *Visitors:* welcome after 8.30am weekdays; weekends and Bank Holidays after 8:45am; evening green fees after 5pm. Handicap Certificate required. Buggies for hire. *Society Meetings:* welcome by arrangement Mondays, Wednesdays and Fridays. Professional: P. Rodgers (01425 611210). Secretary/Manager: Gary Prince (01425 615308).
website: www.barton-on-sea-golf.co.uk

BASINGSTOKE. **Basingstoke Golf Club,** Kempshott Park, Basingstoke RG23 7LL (01256 465990; Fax: 01256 331793). *Location:* M3 Junction 7, A30 one mile from motorway on right. Parkland course – easy walking. 18 holes, 6350 yards. S.S.S. 70. Small practice ground. *Green Fees:* £40.00 per round, £50.00 per day. *Eating facilities:* dining room, lounge and back bar. *Visitors:* welcome weekdays. Buggies, trolleys for hire. *Society Meetings:* catered for Wednesdays, Thursdays and Fridays. Professional: R. Woolley (01256 351332). Secretary: S.E. Lawrence (01256 465990; Fax: 01256 331793).
e-mail: enquiries @basingstokegolfclub.co.uk

BASINGSTOKE. **Bishopswood Golf Club,** Bishopswood Lane, Tadley, Basingstoke RG26 4AT (0118-981 2200; Fax: 0118-940 8606). *Location:* six miles north of Basingstoke off the A340. Parkland/ wooded course. 9 holes, 6474 yards. S.S.S. 71. 12 bay floodlit driving range open seven days a week. *Green Fees:* 9 holes £13.50; 18 holes £19.50. *Eating facilities:* lounge and spike bars - snacks, bar meals and 50 seater restaurant facility. *Visitors:* welcome weekdays only by prior booking. *Society Meetings:* welcome by arrangement. Listed in the CAMRA *Good Beer Guide* 2007. Professional: S. Ward (Tel & Fax: 0118-981 5213; Fax: 0118-940 8602). Manager: D. Goss (0118-981 2200).
website: www.bishopswoodgolfcourse.co.uk

BASINGSTOKE. **Sandford Springs Golf Club,** Sandford Springs, Kingsclere, Hampshire. RG26 5RT (01635 296800; Fax: 01635 296801). *Location:* on north side of A339 Basingstoke to Newbury road at Kingsclere. Three scenic loops of 9 holes combines woodland, parkland and lakes quite beautifully. 27 holes. S.S.S. 69/70/71. Driving range and putting green. *Green Fees:* £40.00, 18 holes £50.00, daily rate. *Eating facilities:* available all day; also conference and banqueting facilities. *Visitors:* welcome every day, subject to availability. *Society Meetings:* welcome, subject to availability. Professional: Simon Plumb (01635 296808).

BASINGSTOKE. **Test Valley Golf Club,** Micheldever Road, Overton, Near Basingstoke RG25 3DS (01256 771737; Fax: 01256 771285). *Location:* on the C79, one mile north of A303 signposted Overton. Downland course; easy walking; beautiful countryside views; excellent drainage, playable all year. 18 holes, 6663 yards. S.S.S. 72. Full practice facilities, short game practice area and 10 bay covered driving range. *Green Fees:* weekdays £24.00, weekends £30.00 (under review). *Eating facilities:* spike bar; main bar, full dining facility. *Visitors:* welcome weekdays, or weekends after 12.00pm. *Society Meetings:* welcome weekdays. Professional/Manager: Alastair Briggs (01256 771737). Venue for Hampshire Open and Lombard Top Club Trophy.
website: www.testvalleygolf.com

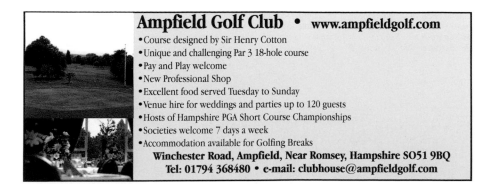

BASINGSTOKE. **Weybrook Park Golf Club,** Rooksdown Lane, Basingstoke RG24 9NT (01256 320347; Fax: 01256 812973). *Location:* two miles north west of Basingstoke town centre, A339 Newbury Road, turn at first crossroads on A339. Parkland course with magnificent views, pleasantly undulating and picturesque landscape, excellent chalk drainage ensures continuous play. 18 holes, 6468 yards, 5914 metres. S.S.S. 71. Driving range, practice area. *Green Fees:* information not available. *Eating facilities:* bar with restaurant and spike bar. *Visitors:* welcome, advisable to telephone in case of competitions. All players must have their own clubs, suitable casual/smart attire must be worn. *Society Meetings:* welcome, telephone for booking and costs. Professional: Mr Anthony Dillon (01256 333232; Fax: 01256 334242). Secretary: Mr P. M. Shearman (01256 320347; Fax: 01256 812973).

BASINGSTOKE near. **Dummer Golf Club,** Dummer Village, Near Basingstoke RG25 2AD (01256 397888; Fax: 01256 397889). *Location:* at Junction 7 of M3. A downland course designed by Peter Alliss – easy walking, panoramic views, free draining; genuine all-year-round course. Par 72, 6533 yards. S.S.S. 71. 10 bay covered driving range plus teaching studios and practice facilities. *Green Fees:* information not available. *Eating facilities:* Spike Bar, conservatory and dining room. *Visitors:* welcome weekdays and after midday at weekends, 25% off for a four ball. *Society Meetings:* welcome. Professionals: Andrew Fannon, Darren Lovegrove and David Holman. website: www.dummergolfclub.com

BORDON. **Blackmoor Golf Club,** Firgrove Road, Whitehill, Bordon GU35 9EH (01420 472775; Fax: 01420 487666). *Location:* lies midway between Petersfield and Farnham on A325. Parkland, wooded course. 18 holes, 6164 yards. S.S.S. 69. *Green Fees:* weekdays £37.00 per round, £49.00 36 holes. *Eating facilities:* dining room. *Visitors:* welcome weekdays, Handicaps necessary, Sat/Sun no visitors for golf but open for catering. Suitable dress code - no jeans in club or on course. Trolleys available. *Society Meetings:* catered for on weekdays. Morning coffee, lunch, evening meal. Golf Manager & Professional: Stephen Clay (01420 472345). Administration Manager: Mrs Jackie Dean (01420 472775; Fax: 01420 487666). e-mail: admin@blackmoorgolf.co.uk

BORDON near. **Kingsley Golf Club,** Main Road, Kingsley, Near Bordon GU35 9NG (01420 489478). *Location:* B3004 off A325 Farnham to Petersfield road. Ideal beginners' course. 9 holes. *Green Fees:* under review. Trolleys available. Professional/Acting Secretary: C. Howard.

BROCKENHURST. **Brokenhurst Manor Golf Club,** Sway Road, Brockenhurst SO42 7SG (01590 623332). *Location:* one mile from Brockenhurst. Beautiful New Forest forest course. 18 holes, 6222 yards. S.S.S. 70. Practice ground. *Green Fees:* information not provided. *Eating facilities:* restaurant and bar. *Visitors:* welcome by arrangement. Handicap Certificate required. *Society Meetings:* welcome Thursdays by arrangement. Professional: Bruce Parker (01590 623332). Secretary: Paul E. Clifford (01590 623332). e-mail: secretary@brokenhurst-manor.org.uk website: www.brokenhurst-manor.org.uk

CRONDALL. **Oak Park Golfing Complex,** Heath Lane, Crondall, Near Farnham, Surrey GU10 5PB (01252 850880; Fax: 01252 850851). *Location:* one and a half miles off A287 Farnham-Odiham road, five miles from Junctions 4, 4a and 5 of M3 motorway. Gently undulating parkland course. Woodland Course - 18 holes, 6247 yards. S.S.S. 70; Village Course - 9 holes, 3279 yards. Par 36. 16 bay covered driving range, putting green, chipping green and practice bunker. *Green Fees:* information not available. *Eating facilities:* Restaurant: available for private hire and special occasions. Bar snacks available. *Visitors:* welcome; must book through Professional; reserved tee system at all times. *Society Meetings:* by arrangement. Professional: Paul Archer (01252 850066; Fax: 01252 850851). Manager: Robert Brewer (01252 850850).

DENMEAD. **Furzeley Golf Club,** Furzeley Road, Denmead PO7 6TX (023 9223 1180). *Location:* A3(M) Exit for Waterlooville, follow the B2150 to Denmead. Parkland course. 18 holes, 4488 yards. S.S.S. 62. *Green Fees:* £8.50 weekdays, £9.00 weekends for 9 holes. £14.00 weekdays, £15.50 weekends for 18 holes. Concessions for Senior Citizens and Juniors. *Eating facilities:* restaurant. *Visitors:* welcome anytime - Pay and Play and membership available. *Society Meetings:* always welcome. Professional: Derek Brown (023 9223 1180). Secretary: Rosemary Brown.

DIBDEN. **Dibden Golf Centre,** Main Road, Dibden, Hythe, Southampton SO45 5TB Bookings: (023 8020 7508). *Location:* half-mile off A326 Totton to Fawley road, on the road to Hythe. Parkland course with views over Southampton Water. 18 holes, 5965 yards, 5455 metres. S.S.S. 69. 9 hole course, 24 bay floodlit driving range. *Green Fees:* information not available. *Eating facilities:* full catering facilities available. *Visitors:* welcome. *Society Meetings:* welcome by prior booking. Catering: Clare Flowers (02380 845060) Professionals: John Slade/ Paul Smith (023 8084 5596). *
website: www.nfdc.gov.uk/golf

EASTLEIGH. **Fleming Park Golf Course,** The New Club House, Passfield Avenue, Eastleigh SO50 9HL (023 8061 2797). *Location:* two miles off M27 Eastleigh Airport turning. Parkland. 18 holes, 4524 yards. S.S.S. 62. *Green Fees:* information not available. *Eating facilities:* bar. *Visitors:* welcome, book on day or one week in advance. *Society Meetings:* all welcome. Professional: I. Warwick (023 8061 2797). Secretary: A. Wheavil (023 8061 2797).*

FAREHAM. **Cams Hall Estate Golf Club,** Fareham PO16 8UP (01329 827732; Fax: 01329 827111). *Location:* Junction 11 M27 follow signs to Fareham/Portchester, take A27 to Portchester. 18 hole creek course links, 9 hole parkland course; five lakes, 99 bunkers, Fareham Creek. Creek course 18 holes, 6244 yards. S.S.S. 71; Park Course 9 holes, 3247 yards. S.S.S. 36. Practice ground, putting green, chipping green. *Green Fees:* information not available. *Eating facilities:* Bar food. *Visitors:* welcome. Luxurious clubhouse, spacious locker rooms, sauna. *Society Meetings:* Societies/Groups welcome. Professional: Jason Neve (01329 827732; Fax: 01329 827111). Sales Manager: Janet Bell (01329 827222; Fax: 01329 827111). General Manager: Robert Climas.*
e-mail: camshall@crown-golf.co.uk*

FAREHAM. **Southwick Park Golf Club,** Pinsley Drive, Southwick, Fareham PO17 6EL (023 9237 0683; Fax: 023 9221 0289). *Location:* near Southwick village (B2177). Parkland. 18 holes, 5884 yards. S.S.S. 69. Practice area, pitch and putt. *Green Fees:* Information not available. *Eating facilities:* bar and snacks available. *Visitors:* weekdays. *Society Meetings:* book through Manager. Professional: J. Green (023 9238 0442). Manager: N.W. Price (023 9238 0131).

FAREHAM. **Wickham Park Golf Club,** Titchfield Lane, Wickham, Fareham PO17 5PJ (01329 833342; Fax: 01329 834798). *Location:* 2 miles north of Fareham, J10 of M27. Undulating parkland course. 18 holes, 5733 yards. S.S.S. 67. 12-bay covered driving range and dedicated short game area. *Green Fees:* information not available. *Eating facilities:* full menu. *Visitors:* welcome at all times but must pre-book. *Society Meetings:* welcome Monday to Friday - please telephone to book in advance. Professional: James Pitcher. Manager: Rob Gumbrell.

FARNBOROUGH. **Southwood Golf Course,** Ively Road, Cove, Farnborough GU14 0LJ (01252 548700). *Location:* approximately half a mile west of A325. Flat parkland. 18 holes, 5738 yards. S.S.S. 68. Putting green. *Green Fees:* weekdays £18.20, Seniors £10.85; weekends £20.80, Seniors £20.00. *Eating facilities:* bar and diningroom available. *Visitors:* welcome, bookable at all times. *Society Meetings:* catered for by arrangement. Professional: Chris Hudson. Club Manager: Ian Attoe.

FLEET. **North Hants Golf Club,** Minley Road, Fleet GU51 1RF (01252 616443). *Location:* B3013 off A30, M3 Junction 4a. 400 yards from railway station. Heathland. 18 holes, 6472 yards. S.S.S. 72, Par 70. Practice ground. *Green Fees:* information not provided. *Eating facilities:* lunch daily, evening meals by prior arrangement. *Visitors:* welcome weekdays only by prior arrangement, Handicap Certificates required, Thursdays Ladies' Day. *Society Meetings:* Tuesdays and Wednesdays only. Professional: Steve Porter (01252 616655). Secretary: G. Hogg (01252 616443; Fax: 01252 811627)
e-mail: secretary@north-hants-fleetgc.co.uk
website: www.northhantsgolf.co.uk

FOUR MARKS. **Four Marks Golf Club,** Headmore Lane, Four Marks GU34 3ES (01420 587214; Fax: 01420 587313). *Location:* A31 to Four Marks, follow brown signs to golf course. Parkland course. 9 holes, 2300 yards, S.S.S 62. Practice nets. *Green Fees:* weekdays £7.95, weekends and Bank Holidays £8.95. *Eating facilities:* bar snacks and drinks available. *Visitors:* welcome at all times. Tuition by Professional available. *Society Meetings:* welcome at any time. Professional: Peter Chapman (01420 587214).

GOSPORT. **Fleetlands Golf Club,** DARA Fleetlands, Fareham Road, Gosport PO13 0AW (023 9254 4492). *Location:* two miles south of Fareham on Fareham/Gosport Road. Flat/wooded Course. 9 holes, 4852 yards. S.S.S. 64. *Green Fees:* information not available. *Eating facilities:* bar/clubhouse. *Visitors:* by appointment with member only. *Society Meetings:* by appointment with member only. Secretary: Mr R. Sheehan (023 9254 4903). *

GOSPORT. **Gosport and Stokes Golf Club,** off Fort Road, Haslar, Gosport PO12 2AT (023 9258 1625). *Location:* A32 to Gosport, course is one mile east of Stokes Bay, near Gilkicker Point. Water course, natural hazards. 9 holes, 5957 yards. S.S.S. 70. Nets and putting green. *Green Fees:* information not provided. *Eating facilities:* full catering service, fully licensed bar. *Visitors:* welcome all week, restricted Sundays and Thursdays. *Society Meetings:* by arrangement. Secretary/Manager: M. Chivers (Tel & Fax: 023 9252 7941). Tee Shop (023 9258 7423).

> **THE APPEARANCE OF AN ASTERISK (*) AT THE END OF A CLUB OR COURSE ENTRY INDICATES THAT UP-TO-DATE INFORMATION HAS NOT BEEN SUPPLIED**

HARTLEY WINTNEY. **Hartley Wintney Golf Club,** London Road, Hartley Wintney, Hook RG27 8PT (01252 844211; Fax: 01252 844211). *Location:* on A30 between Camberley and Basingstoke. Parkland, wooded. 18 holes, 6240 yards. S.S.S. 71. Practice area, indoor teaching studio. *Green Fees:* £30.00 per round, £45.00 per day. *Eating facilities:* full catering facilities available. *Visitors:* restricted Wednesdays (Ladies' Day). *Society Meetings:* catered for Mondays, Tuesdays, Thursdays and Fridays on application. Professional: Martin Smith (01252 844211). Secretary: Adrian Jackson (Tel & Fax: 01252 844211).

HAVANT. **Rowlands Castle Golf Club,** 31 Links Lane, Rowlands Castle PO9 6AE (023 9241 2216). *Location:* four miles north of Havant or Horndean/ Rowlands Castle Junction from A3M. Flat parkland, wooded course. 18 holes, 6639 yards White Tees, 6395 yards Yellow Tees. S.S.S. 72 (White), 70 (Yellow). *Green Fees:* weekdays £39.00 per round/day; weekends £42.00. Subject to review. *Eating facilities:* full catering and bar facilities. *Visitors:* welcome, except Saturdays unless playing with a member, maximum 12 visitors on a Sunday and Bank Holidays. *Society Meetings:* catered for Tuesdays and Thursdays, bookings through Secretary. Professional: Peter Klepacz (023 9241 2785). Secretary: K.D. Fisher (023 9241 2784).

HAYLING ISLAND. **The Hayling Golf Club,** Links Lane, Hayling Island PO11 0BX (023 9246 4491). *Location:* A3023 five miles south of Havant. Seaside links. 18 holes, 6531 yards, 5965 metres. S.S.S. 71. *Green Fees:* weekdays £47.00 per round; weekends £60.00 per round. Concessions for Juniors. Subject to review. *Eating facilities:* breakfasts, lunches and afternoon teas available and dinners by arrangement. *Visitors:* welcome with current Handicap Certificate and must be members of recognised clubs. *Society Meetings:* Tuesdays and Wednesdays only by arrangement with the Secretary. Professional: Ray Gadd (023 9246 4491). General Manager: Ian Walton (023 9246 4446; Fax: 02392 461119).
e-mail: generaloffice@haylinggolf.co.uk
website: www.haylinggolf.co.uk

HOOK. **Tylney Park,** Rotherwick, Hook RG27 9AY (01256 762079; Fax: 01256 763079). *Location:* two-and-a-half miles from M3 J5. Approx. 9 miles south of M4 J11 via A33. 18 holes, Par 72 scenic English Heritage registered parkland course with specimen mature trees including 5 lengths of tees from 5429 to 7017 yards. Championship course with USGA free draining sand based tees and greens, re-built in 2005 and designed by the leading duo Donald Steele and Tom Mackenzie. *Green Fees:* £55.00 per round including lunch. *Eating facilities:* catering and bar available. *Visitors:* weekdays unrestricted, weekends and Bank Holidays contact the Pro shop for availablility. *Society Meetings:* very competitive: £75 for all day golf, lunch and dinner. Hotel facilities adjoining with English Heritage Grade II listing, indoor and outdoor pools, gym and ladies' beauty treatments. PGA Professional: Chris de Bruin.
e-mail: contact@tylneypark.co.uk
website: www.tylneypark.co.uk

LEE-ON-THE-SOLENT. **Lee-On-The-Solent Golf Club,** Brune Lane, Lee-on-the-Solent PO13 9PB (023 9255 0207). *Location:* M27 Exit 9 eastbound, Exit 11 westbound, three miles south of Fareham. Flat parkland course. 18 holes, 5962 yards. S.S.S. 69. Practice range. *Green Fees:* Information not available. *Visitors:* welcome weekdays, Handicap Certificate required. *Society Meetings:* welcome weekdays, Handicap Certificate required. Professional: Rob Edwards (023 9255 1181). Manager: Rob Henderson (023 9255 1170; Fax: 023 9255 4233)*.
website: www.leegolf.co.uk

LIPHOOK. **Liphook Golf Club,** Wheatsheaf Enclosure, Liphook GU30 7EH (01428 723271; Fax: 01428 724853). *Location:* one mile south of Liphook on B2070 (old A3). Heathland. 18 holes, 6167 yards. S.S.S. 69. *Green Fees:* contact Club for details. *Eating facilities:* bar and restaurant. *Visitors:* welcome, Handicap Certificate required, check with Secretary. Buggy available for hire. *Society Meetings:* catered for Wednesdays to Fridays. Professional: Ian Mowbray (01428 723271). Secretary: (01428 723785; Fax: 01428 724853).
e-mail: secretary@liphookgolfclub.com
website: www.liphookgolfclub.com

LIPHOOK. **Old Thorns Golf & Country Estate,** Griggs Green, Liphook GU30 7PE (01428 724555). *Location:* A3 to Griggs Green then 500 yards on right. Parkland, wooded, with natural streams and lakes. 18 holes, 6529 yards. S.S.S. 72. Practice range, putting green, buggies, Pro shop. *Green Fees:* information not available. *Eating facilities:* choice of Greenview or award-winning Japanese Restaurant. *Visitors:* welcome at all times. *Society Meetings:* a range of golf days available for booking. Range of individual and corporate membership available. Facilities: 32 en suite bedrooms, indoor swimming pool, sauna, solarium, steam room, massage, fitness centre, treatment rooms, two tennis courts, conference and banqueting rooms. General Manager: Stephen Meakin.*
website: www.oldthorns.com

LYNDHURST. **Bramshaw Golf Club,** Brook, Lyndhurst SO43 7HE (023 8081 3433). *Location:* M27 (Interchange 1) one mile from M27 (north) at Brook. Two courses: one parkland, one woodland. Both 18 holes. Forest Course 5774 yards. S.S.S. 68. Manor Course 6527 yards. S.S.S. 71. Practice facilities. *Green Fees:* contact club or check website for current rates. *Eating facilities:* clubhouse and restaurant, also Bell Inn close by. *Visitors:* welcome. Accommodation in 22-bedroom hotel. *Society Meetings:* welcome by arrangement. Professional: Clive Bonner (023 8081 3434). General Manager: Ian Baker (023 8081 3433).
e-mail: golf@bramshaw.co.uk
website: www.bramshaw.co.uk

www.uk-golfguide.com

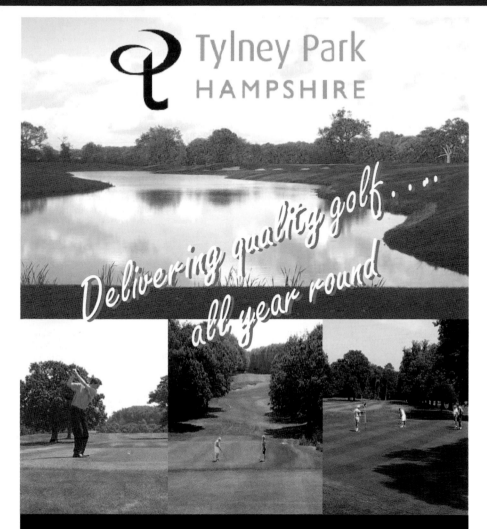

TyIney Park
HAMPSHIRE

*Delivering quality golf.....
all year round*

*Listed by English Heritage as a protected park and garden,
Tylney Park is an example of the very best inland golf available
in Britain. The championship course was redesigned in
2005 by Donald Steel/Tom Mackenzie with USGA free
draining sand based playing surfaces and five tee lengths
from 5429 to 7017 yards for all players.. Green Fees: £55
per round including lunch..*

Call us on: 01256 762079 or email us at:
contact@tylneypark.co.uk
Tylney Park Golf Club, Rotherwick, Hook

Tylney Park
HAMPSHIRE

LYNDHURST. **New Forest Golf Club Ltd,** Southampton Road, Lyndhurst SO43 7BU (023 8028 2752; Fax: 023 8028 4030). *Location:* on the A35 between Ashurst and Lyndhurst. Forest heathland course. 18 holes, 5772 yards. S.S.S. 67. Practice ground. *Green Fees:* please refer to our website. *Eating facilities:* bar, dining room. *Visitors:* welcome, restrictions may apply. Please telephone. *Society Meetings:* advance booking only. Professional: (023 8028 3094). Secretary: (023 8028 2484; Fax: 023 8028 4030).
e-mail: secretarynfgc@aol.com
website: www.newforestgolfclub.co.uk

PETERSFIELD. **Petersfield Golf Club,** Tankerdale Lane, Liss GU33 7QY. *Location:* from the north, first turning left past the Liss exit on the Petersfield by-pass; from the south, leave by-pass at the Liss turn off (B3006), join the Southern dual carriage way then take the first turning left. Members club in Area of Outstanding Natural Beauty, gently undulating and wooded. 18 holes. White, 6450 yards, S.S.S. 71, Par 72. Yellow, 6000 yards, S.S.S. 69, Par 69. Red, 5447 yards, S.S.S. 71, Par 72. Practice ground, nets and putting green. *Green Fees:* weekdays £28.00 per round, weekends £35.00. Booking required at weekends. *Eating facilities:* full bar and catering service. *Visitors:* welcome, Handicap Certificate or proof of club membership required. Booking required for weekends via Professional. *Society Meetings:* welcome, see our website for details of packages. Professional: Greg Hughes (01730 895216). General Manager: Peter Badger (01730 261675; Fax: 01730 894713).
website: www.petersfieldgolfclub.co.uk

PETERSFIELD. **Petersfield Golf Club (Pay & Play Course),** Sussex Road, Petersfield. *Location:* from Petersfield, take the B2146 (Sussex Road), the club is situated on the right hand side, just past the car park for Heath Lake. 12 hole pay & play course. Level wooded course. *Green Fees:* information not available. *Eating facilities:* limited, tea, coffee and cold drinks available. *Visitors:* welcome, booking advisable, especially at weekends (01730 267732). Equipment hire available.*
website: www.petersfieldgolfclub.co.uk

PORTSMOUTH. **Great Salterns Golf Course,** Burrfields Road, Portsmouth PO3 5HH (023 9266 4549). *Location:* public golf course and home of Southsea Golf Club. South on A2030 off M27 signposted "Southsea". Flat meadow-land course. 18 holes, 5620 yards. S.S.S. 67. Floodlit driving range. *Green Fees:* information not available. *Eating facilities:* full bar and catering service at Farmhouse Pub next door. *Visitors:* always welcome, tee time booking required one week ahead. Innlodge Hotel overlooks 18th green (73 bedrooms). *Society Meetings:* welcome, administered by Noreen Jefferies. Professional: Terry Healy (023 9266 4549; Fax: 023 9265 0525). Secretary (Southsea Golf Club): Roger Collinson (023 9269 9110)
e-mail: roger.collinson@ntlworld.com

PORTSMOUTH. **Portsmouth Golf Club (1926),** Crookhorn Lane, Widley, Waterlooville PO7 5QL (023 9237 2210). *Location:* two thirds of a mile from junction of B2177 and A3. Hilly course with views of harbour; outstanding 6th hole. 18 holes, 6139 yards. S.S.S. 70. Practice ground, putting green. *Green Fees:* Information not available. *Eating facilities:* full restaurant and bar. *Visitors:* welcome, tee bookings required. *Society Meetings:* welcome by prior arrangement with Pro Shop. Professional: (023 9237 2210 ext. 24). Secretary: S. Richard (023 9220 1827 ext. 21).*

PORTSMOUTH. **Waterlooville Golf Club,** Cherry Tree Avenue, Cowplain, Waterlooville PO8 8AP (023 9226 3388; Fax: 023 9224 2980). *Location:* off A3 or A3 (M), 10 miles north of Portsmouth. Parkland course. 18 holes, 6602 yards. S.S.S. 72. *Green Fees:* £34.00 per round, £44.00 per day, weekdays only. *Eating facilities:* full catering service available, bar facilities. *Visitors:* welcome weekdays, weekends as members' guests; some limited availability at weekend by prior arrangement with Professional. *Society Meetings:* Thursdays only by prior arrangement, limited availablility other days by prior arrangement. Professional: John Hay (Tel/Fax: 023 9225 6911). Secretary: David Nairne.

RINGWOOD. **Burley Golf Club,** Cott Lane, Burley, Ringwood BH24 4BB (01425 402431/403737; Fax: 01425 404168). *Location:* A31 from Ringwood and turn right at Picket Post and on through Burley Street. Open heathland course in the New Forest. 9 holes, 6151 yards. S.S.S. 69, Par 71. *Green Fees:* weekdays £16.00 per round (£10.00 with member), £20.00 per day; weekends and Bank Holidays £20.00 per round (£15.00 with member), £25.00 per day. Under 18s £8.00 per round weekdays, £9.00 per round weekends. Weekly ticket £75.00. *Eating facilities:* bar open, food available every day. *Visitors:* welcome, but not before 4pm Saturdays, 8am Sundays, and 1.45pm Wednesdays. Handicap Certificates preferred. *Society Meetings:* limited to 12 players Tuesdays or Fridays. Secretary: D.C. Gough (01425 402431; Fax: 01425 404168).
e-mail: secretary@burleygolfclub.co.uk
website: www.burleygolfclub.co.uk

RINGWOOD. **Moors Valley Golf Course,** Horton Road, Ashley Heath, Ringwood BH24 2ET (01425 479776). *Location:* signposted from A338/A31 roundabout. Heathland course set in the valley of the Moors River. Awarded Silver Medal by HSBC/Golf Monthly course rankings. 18 holes, 6337 yards. S.S.S. 70. 4 hole short course, full size pitching green and practice nets. *Green Fees:* £22.00. *Eating facilities:* spikes bar and bar. *Visitors:* welcome. *Society Meetings:* welcome by arrangement. Manager: Desmond Meharg (01425 479776).
e-mail: golf@eastdorset.gov.uk
website: www.moors-valley.co.uk/golf

THE APPEARANCE OF AN ASTERISK (*) AT THE END OF A CLUB OR COURSE ENTRY INDICATES THAT UP-TO-DATE INFORMATION HAS NOT BEEN SUPPLIED

ROMSEY. **Dunwood Manor Golf Club,** Danes Road, Awbridge, Near Romsey SO51 0GF (01794 340549; Fax: 01794 341215). *Location:* four miles from Romsey off A27. Undulating parkland. 18 holes, 5767 yards. S.S.S. 68. Practice area. *Green Fees:* £33.00 per round, £45.00 per day weekdays; £40.00 per round weekends. Society rates from £27.00. *Eating facilities:* full catering, all day bar. *Visitors:* welcome by prior arrangement. Self-catering accommodation for up to 32 people available. *Society Meetings:* welcome by prior arrangement. Professional: Heath Teschner (01794 340663; Fax: 01794 341215). Secretary: Hazel Johnson (01794 340549; Fax: 01794 341215).
e-mail: admin@dunwood-golf.co.uk

ROMSEY. **Paultons Golf Centre,** Old Salisbury Road, Ower, Near Romsey SO51 6AN (023 8081 3345; Fax: 023 8081 3993). *Location:* off M27 at Junction 2, A36 towards Salisbury, at first roundabout take first exit, then first right at the Vine Public House. Parkland/woodland laid out within the original grounds of Paulton House, landscaped by Capability Brown. 18 holes, 6200 yards, 5670 metres. S.S.S. 71. 9-hole academy course. 24-bay floodlit driving range. *Green Fees:* information not available. *Visitors:* welcome anytime. *Society Meetings:* welcome anytime with prior booking. Professional: M. Williamson.*

ROMSEY. **Wellow Golf Club,** Ryedown Lane, East Wellow, Romsey SO51 6BD (01794 322872; Fax: 01794 323832). *Location:* M27 Junction 2 - A36 Salisbury, one mile right to East Wellow, one mile right Ryedown Lane. Parkland. 27 holes (three loops of 9 holes). S.S.S. 69, 70, 68. Large practice ground. *Green Fees:* weekdays £20.00; weekends £26.00. *Eating facilities:* full catering and bar facilities available all day. *Visitors:* welcome – advise phone to confirm availability. Correct dress code must be observed. *Society Meetings:* all welcome. Professional: Neil Bratley (01794 323833). Secretary: Mrs C. Gurd.

SHEDFIELD. **Marriott Meon Valley Hotel and Country Club Resort,** Sandy Lane, Shedfield, Southampton SO32 2HQ (01329 833455; Fax: 01329 834411). *Location:* leave M27 at Exit 7, take A334 to Botley then towards Wickham. Sandy Lane is 2 miles on the left. Wooded course. 18 holes, 6520 yards. S.S.S. 71. 9 holes, 2714 yards. S.S.S. 34. Covered practice area. *Green Fees:* Information not available. *Eating facilities:* Treetops Restaurant, The Long Weekend Restaurant and three bars. *Visitors:* welcome, no restrictions. Handicap Certificates required to play. 113-bedroom 4 Star Hotel. *Society Meetings:* welcome, arranged in advance. Professional: Rod Cameron (01329 832184; Fax: 01329 834411). Director of Golf: George McMenemy (01329 833455; Fax: 01329 834411).*

SOUTHAMPTON. **Botley Park Golf Club,** Winchester Road, Botley, Southampton SO3 2UA (01489 780888; Fax: 01489 789242). *Location:* approximately two miles from Junction 7 on M27. Parkland. 18 holes, 6341 yards. S.S.S. 70. Driving range. *Green Fees:* information not available. *Eating facilities:* two bars, main restaurant and club lounge. *Visitors:* welcome by prior booking by phone. Handicap Certificate required. 100 bedroomed hotel on site; tennis, squash, swimming, sauna, solarium, steam room, fitness suite, beauty spa. Dance studio. *Society Meetings:* weekdays only. Professional: Kevin Caplehorn (01489 789771; Fax: 01489 789242). Secretary/Golf Manager: Phil Hanks (01489 796000).*

SOUTHAMPTON. **Chilworth Golf Club,** Main Road, Chilworth, Southampton SO16 7JP (02380 740544; Fax: 02380 733166). *Location:* situated off the A27. Parkland course. 18 holes, 5915 yards, S.S.S. 68. Covered driving range. *Green Fees:* weekdays 18 holes £12.00, weekends 18 holes £15.00. *Eating facilities:* bar. *Visitors:* welcome, must follow dress code, please telephone for details. Pro shop. Tuition available. Professional: Darren Newing. Secretary: Fred Bendal.

SOUTHAMPTON. **Corhampton Golf Club,** Shepherds Farm Lane, Corhampton, Southampton SO32 3GZ (01489 877279; Fax: 01489 877680). *Location:* one mile from Corhampton on Bishops Waltham–Corhampton road (B3135). Free draining downland course. 18 holes, 6444 yards. S.S.S. 71. Large practice ground. *Green Fees:* weekdays £35.00 per round, £50.00 per day; weekends £17.50 with a member only. *Eating facilities:* full catering. *Visitors:* welcome Monday to Friday; weekends and Bank Holidays with a member. Buggies and trolleys for hire. *Society Meetings:* Mondays and Thursdays. Professional: Ian Roper (01489 877638; Fax: 01489 877680). Secretary: Margaret Middleton (01489 877279).
e-mail: secretary@corhamptongc.co.uk

SOUTHAMPTON. **Romsey Golf Club Ltd,** Nursling, Southampton SO16 0XW (023 8073 4637; Fax: 023 8074 1036). *Location:* two miles south east of Romsey on A3057, M27/M271 Junction 3. Well wooded, undulating course with extremely good views. 18 holes, 5718 yards. S.S.S. 68. *Green Fees:* on application. *Eating facilities:* bar and restaurant. *Visitors:* welcome weekdays only. *Society Meetings:* welcome Mondays, Tuesdays or Thursdays only. Professional: James Pitcher (023 8073 6673). Secretary: Michael Batty.

SOUTHAMPTON. **Southampton Golf Club** (Play over the Municipal Golf Course), Golf Course Road, Bassett, Southampton SO16 7AY (023 8076 0546). *Location:* off Bassett Avenue. Parkland course. 18 holes, 6218 yards, S.S.S. 70. 9 hole Par 32. Practice area and putting greens. *Green Fees:* information not provided. *Eating facilities:* bar and full catering (023 8076 7996). *Visitors:* welcome but must book at weekends - three and four ball play only at weekends. Professional: Andy Gordon, (02380 760388). Secretary: E. Hemsley (023 8047 6582). Bookings: (023 8076 0546).

SOUTHAMPTON. **Stoneham Golf Club,** Monks Wood Close, Bassett, Southampton SO16 3TT (023 8076 9272). *Location:* A33/M27 north of Southampton find Chilworth roundabout, take road to Airport (A27), half mile on left. Undulating parkland course, used for Brabazon Trophy 1993, English County Finals 1998 and English Ladies' Championship 2001. 18 holes, 6387 yards. S.S.S. 70. *Green Fees:* weekdays £45.00 per round, £50.00 per day; weekends £50.00 per round, £60.00 per day. *Eating facilities:* full catering, bar open all day. *Visitors:* welcome, except competition days. *Society Meetings:* catered for Monday, Thursday and Friday by arrangement. Professional: Ian Young (023 8076 8397). Manager: Richard Penley-Martin (023 8076 9272; Fax: 023 8076 6320).

WINCHESTER. **Hockley Golf Club,** Twyford, Near Winchester SO21 1PL (01962 713165; Fax: 01962 713612). *Location:* 100 yards Junction 11 M3 motorway. Downland with excellent views of Winchester and surrounding areas. James Braid designed course, long vistas. 18 holes, 6506 yards. S.S.S. 71. Large practice ground. *Green Fees:* April to September £35.00 per 18 holes, £45.00 per day; October to March £38.00 per 18 holes, £48.00 per 36 holes. *Eating facilities:* full catering and bar facilities. *Visitors:* welcome. Handicap Certificate preferred. *Society Meetings:* welcome by prior arrangement. Professional: (01962 713678). Secretary: Mrs Lyn Dyer. e-mail: secretary@hockleygolfclub.com website: www.hockleygolfclub.com

WINCHESTER. **Otterbourne Golf Centre,** Poles Lane, Otterbourne, Winchester SO21 1DZ (Tel & Fax: 01962 775225). Parkland course. 9 holes, 1939 yards, S.S.S. 30. 10 bay uncovered driving range. *Green Fees:* information not available. *Visitors:* welcome, pay as you play. Tuition available. *Society Meetings:* open to discussion. Professional: Garry Stubbington.*

WINCHESTER. **The Park Golf Course,** Avington, Winchester SO21 1DA (01962 779945; Fax: 01962 779530). *Location:* 5 miles east of Winchester. Mature parkland course. 9 holes, 1907 yards, S.S.S. 58. *Green Fees:* information not available. *Visitors:* always welcome, please telephone to book.

WINCHESTER. **Royal Winchester Golf Club,** Sarum Road, Winchester SO22 5QE (01962 852462). *Location:* from Junction 11 M3 follow signs to Oliver's Battery. At Pitt roundabout follow signs to Winchester then left into Kilham Lane. At end turn right into Sarum Road. Traditional downland course. 18 holes, 6414 yards. S.S.S. 71. *Green Fees:* weekdays 18 holes £40.00, 36 holes £60.00; weekends with member only. *Eating facilities:* full catering and bar facilities available. *Visitors:* welcome weekdays, Handicap Certificate required. *Society Meetings:* by prior arrangement. Professional: Steven Hunter (01962 862473). Secretary: Andrew Buck (01962 852462; Fax: 01962 865048). e-mail: manager@royalwinchestergolfclub.com website: www.royalwinchestergolfclub.com

WINCHESTER. **South Winchester Golf Club,** Romsey Road, Pitt, Winchester SO22 5QX (01962 877800; Fax: 01962 877900). *Location:* situated between Winchester and Hursley in the village of Pitt. Championship links-style course - home of the Hampshire PGA. 18 holes, 7086 yards. S.S.S. 74. Driving range. Chipping green, practice bunker and practice green. *Green Fees:* information not available. *Eating facilities:* two bars, one dining room, one conservatory/dining room, food available all day. *Visitors:* visiting golfers welcome. Golf days for non members by arrangement with the Professional. Professional: Richard Adams (01962 840469). General Manager: Laurence Ross.* website: www.crown-golf.co.uk

Old Thorns Golf & Country Estate, Liphook

Isle of Wight

COWES. **Cowes Golf Club,** Crossfield Avenue, Cowes, Isle of Wight PO31 8HN (Tel & Fax: 01983 292303). *Location:* entrance adjacent Cowes High School. Parkland with sea views. 9 holes, 5934 yards. S.S.S. 68. *Green Fees:* weekdays £20.00; weekends £25.00. *Eating facilities:* snack meals available in bar in summer. Bar open 11am to 2pm summer months. *Visitors:* welcome except Sunday before 1pm and Thursday, Ladies' Day (11.30am to 3pm). *Society Meetings:* welcome Mondays to Wednesdays by arrangement with Secretary. Society rates by arrangement. Secretary: C.J. Laley (01983 292303) Steward (01983 280135)

EAST COWES. **Osborne Golf Club,** Osborne House Estate, East Cowes PO32 6JX (01983 295421). *Location:* off A3021 south-east of East Cowes. One mile from Southampton/East Cowes ferry terminal; 4 miles from Portsmouth/Fishbourne ferry terminal. Parkland. 9 holes, 6372 yards. S.S.S. 70. Practice area. *Green Fees:* weekdays £25.00; weekends and Bank Holidays £30.00. Subject to review. *Eating facilities:* catering available each day, bar facilities. *Visitors:* welcome except Tuesday, Saturday and Sunday before noon. Telephone for tee availability. *Society Meetings:* catered for (24 maximum). e-mail: osbornegolfclub@tiscall.co.uk website: www.osbornegolfclub.co.uk

FRESHWATER. **Freshwater Bay Golf Club,** Afton Down, Freshwater (Tel & Fax: 01983 752955). *Location:* western end of Island, approximately half-a-mile east of Freshwater Bay on coast road to Ventnor. Links type course on chalk uplands. 18 holes, 5725 yards. S.S.S. 68. *Green Fees:* information not available. *Eating facilities:* licensed bar, catering. *Visitors:* welcome. *Society Meetings:* welcome by arrangement. Secretary: Terry Riddett.* e-mail: tr.fbgc@btopenworld.com

NEWPORT. **Newport (Isle of Wight) Golf Club,** St Georges Down, Near Shide, Newport PO30 2JB Founded 1895. *Location:* one mile south east of Newport, taking Sandown road. Testing downland course. 9 holes, 5704 yards. S.S.S. 68. Driving range available to visitors. *Green Fees:* information not available. *Eating facilities:* full catering available-

breakfast, lunches, evening dinners. *Visitors:* welcome anytime except Wednesday 12pm-3pm, Saturday before 3pm and Sunday before noon. *Society Meetings:* groups of 12 plus welcome by arrangement weekdays except Wednesdays and not before 3pm on Saturdays or noon on Sundays. Secretary: Dave Boon (01983 525076).*

RYDE. **Ryde Golf Club,** Binstead Road, Ryde, Isle of Wight PO33 3NF. *Location:* on A3054 Ryde to Newport Road, just outside Ryde. Parkland course. 9 holes, extended June 2002 to 5772 yards. Par 70. S.S.S. 69. *Green Fees:* Information not available. *Eating facilities:* bar and catering available all day April to September; lunchtime only October to March. *Visitors:* welcome, restrictions Wednesdays and Sundays. *Society Meetings:* catered for. Limited Pro Shop on site. Secretary: Richard Dean (01983 614809; Fax: 01983 567418).* e-mail: ryde.golfclub@btinternet.com website: www.rydegolf.co.uk

SANDOWN. **Shanklin and Sandown Golf Club,** The Fairway, Lake, Sandown PO36 9PR (01983 404424/403217). *Location:* from Sandown travel towards Shanklin. Soon after Heights Leisure Centre turn right Into The Fairway. One mile to Club. A traditional, beautiful heathland County Championship course. The 13th hole is one of the best in Southern England. 18 holes, 6062 yards. S.S.S. 69. Practice ground. *Green Fees:* £32.00 weekdays; £40.00 weekends. Three day ticket weekdays £75.00. *Eating facilities:* full catering and bar facilities. *Visitors:* welcome. Handicap Certificate preferred. *Society Meetings:* welcome by arrangement. Professional: Peter Hammond (01983 404424). Secretary: A. Creed (01983 403217).

UPPER VENTNOR. **Ventnor Golf Club,** Steephill Down Road, Upper Ventnor PO38 1BP (01983 853326). *Location:* northwest boundary of Ventnor. Downland undulating with side slopes overlooking the sea. 12 holes, 5767 yards. S.S.S. 68. *Green Fees:* Information not available. *Eating facilities:* bar snacks only. *Visitors:* welcome, Sundays after 1pm, Ladies' Day Monday . Secretary: Stewart Blackmore.* website: www.ventnorgolfclub.co.uk

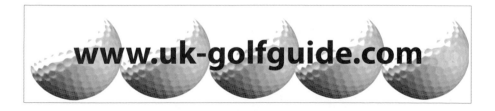

Kent

ASH. **The London Golf Club,** South Ash Manor Estate, Ash TN15 7EN (01474 879899; Fax: 01474 879912). *Location*: 1 mile east of Brands Hatch on A20, turn left after motorway underpass when leaving West Kingsdown. 36 holes Heritage Course: Nicklaus design 7208 yards, S.S.S. 74. International course: 7005 yards, S.S.S. 74. Practice range (350 yards), covered bays and grass tees; practice chipping and bunker facilities, 2x practice putting greens. *Green Fees*: Heritage Course: members guest only; International Course £90.00/£100.00. *Eating facilities*: restaurant, terrace bar, spike bar, plus private rooms, full changing facilities. *Visitors:* Heritage Course: members and guests only. International Course: visitors and corporate days by prior arrangement. General Manager: Mr Scott Evans. Director of Golf: Alasdair Robertson. Head Professional: Paul Stuart. Marketing: Heath Harvey. Golf Events: Gordon Frost. Events Co-ordinator: Nikki Evans. Membership Secretary: Steve Salter. e-mail: golf@londongolf.co.uk
website: www.londongolf.co.uk

ASH. **Redlibbets Golf Club,** Manor Lane, West Yoke, Ash TN15 7HT (01474 879190). Undulating woodland 18 hole course. Practice range, practice short game area, putting green and indoor net room. *Green Fees*: information not available. *Eating facilities*: Bar and restaurant. Secretary: J. Potter.*

ASHFORD. **Ashford Great Chart Golf & Leisure,** Great Chart, Ashford (01233 645858). *Location*: Junction 9 off M20; A28 to Great Chart, follow signs. 9 hole main course, family pitch and putt course. 26 bay floodlit covered driving range. *Green Fees*: weekdays - £9.50 for 9 holes, £13.50 for 18 holes. Reductions for Juniors/Seniors. *Eating facilities*: bar/cafe. Function room; weddings catered for. *Visitors*: welcome, juniors and families welcome. Video tuition, shop, practice bunkers. Volley ball/ beach soccer sand pitch; paintball. Professional: James Sheldrick. Secretary: Grant Kay/John Kay.

ASHFORD. **Ashford (Kent) Golf Club,** Sandyhurst Lane, Ashford TN25 4NT (01233 620180). *Location*: just off A20, one and a half miles west of Ashford. Parkland - stream cutting through course. 18 holes, 6261 yards. S.S.S. 70. *Green Fees:* information not available. *Eating facilities*: available every day. *Visitors*: welcome. Handicap Certificate required. *Society Meetings:* catered for Tuesdays and Thursdays by arrangement. Professional: Hugh Sherman (01233 629644). Secretary: A.H. Story (Tel & Fax: 01233 622655). *

ASHFORD. **Chart Hills Golf Club,** Weeks Lane, Biddenden, Ashford TN27 8JX (01580 292222; Fax: 01580 292233). *Location*: M25, M20 Leeds Castle turn off (B2163), A274 to Tenterden. Parkland course designed by Nick Faldo. 18 holes, 7119 yards. S.S.S. 74. Short game area, golf academy. *Green Fees:* weekdays £70.00 per person summer, weekends £80.00 per person summer. *Eating facilities:* restaurant,

bar snacks, bar, conference facilities. *Visitors:* welcome, after 1pm at weekends. Gymnasium, fitness centre. *Society Meetings:* Tuesday and Thursday only. e-mail: info@charthills.co.uk
website: www.charthills.co.uk

ASHFORD. **The Homelands Golf Centre,** Ashford Road, Kingsnorth, Ashford TN26 1NJ (01233 661620; Fax: 01233 720553). *Location:* take exit 10 off M20, follow A2070 course signposted from second roundabout to Kingsnorth. 9 hole parkland course. 2250 yards, S.S.S. 62. *Green Fees:* information not provided. *Visitors:* welcome at all times. Buggies, trolleys and clubs available for hire. *Society Meetings:* welcome with prior notice. Short breaks organised. Professional: Howard Bonaccorsi.

BECKENHAM. **Beckenham Place Park Golf Club,** Beckenham Hill Road, Beckenham. *Location:* on A222 north of Bromley. Parkland. 18 holes, 5722 yards. S.S.S. 68. Practice ground, nets, putting green. *Green Fees:* information not available. *Eating facilities:* bar and cafeteria. *Visitors:* welcome but must book in advance. *Society Meetings:* catered for. Other facilities include tennis courts and putting green. Professional: H. Davies-Thomas (020 8650-2292). Secretary: T. A. Moorcroft.*

BECKENHAM. **Braeside Golf Club,** Beckenham Place Park, Beckenham Hill, Beckenham (020 8650 2292). Parkland course. 18 holes, 5722 yards, 5230 metres. S.S.S. 69. Practice area, putting green and nets. *Green Fees:* information not available. *Eating facilities:* cafe and bar. *Visitors:* welcome, will need to book weekends. Secretary: Mr Nicholas Wilkins.*

BECKENHAM. **Langley Park Golf Club,** Barnfield Wood Road, Beckenham BR3 6SZ (020 8658 6849). *Location:* one mile from Bromley South station. Flat wooded parkland. 18 holes, 6469 yards, 5916 metres, S.S.S. 71. Practice areas and nets. *Green Fees:* information not provided. *Eating facilities:* bar snacks, restaurant/dining room. *Visitors:* welcome weekdays by arrangement with Pro Shop. Handicap Certificate required. *Society Meetings:* Wednesdays and Thursdays by arrangement with the Club Manager. Other days considered. Professional: Colin Staff (020 8650 1663). Club Manager: Rodger Pollard (020 8658 6849).

BEXLEYHEATH. **Bexley Heath Golf Club,** Mount Road, Bexley Heath DA6 8JS (020 8303 6951). *Location:* adjacent to A2. Hilly parkland. 9 holes, 5239 yards, 4788 metres. S.S.S. 66. *Green Fees:* £20.00 (approximately). Weekends with member only. *Eating facilities:* catering available. *Visitors:* weekdays only. Professional: To be appointed. Secretary: Mrs J. Smith.

BIGGIN HILL. **Cherry Lodge Golf Club,** Jail Lane, Biggin Hill TN16 3AX (01959 572250; Fax: 01959 540672). *Location:* A233 to M25 Junction 5, Bromley, eight miles. Undulating Parkland 600 ft. above sea level with panoramic views of surrounding countryside. 18

holes, 6652 yards, 6084 metres. S.S.S. 73. Extensive practice ground. *Green Fees:* £40.00. *Eating facilities:* bar snacks all day, Sunday lunches. *Visitors:* welcome weekdays except Bank Holidays. *Society Meetings:* welcome weekdays (except Bank Holidays) by arrangement. Professional: Craig Sutherland (01959 572989; Fax: 01959 540672), Secretary: Trevor Norman (01959 572250; Fax: 01959 540672). e-mail: info@cherrylodgegc.co.uk website: www.cherrylodgegc.co.uk

BRENCHLEY. **The Kent National Golf and Country Club,** Waterman's Lane, Brenchley, near Tonbridge TN12 6ND (01892 724400; Fax: 01892 723300). *Location:* from A21 take the B2160 to Matfield/Paddock Wood. Drive through Matfield ignoring the signpost to Brenchley, continue downhill through double bends until road flattens, turn right at post box into Chantlers Hill and then right into Watermans Lane. Parkland course built to an extremely high specification in the early 1990s. A 12-inch imported layer of sand across the course means it never has temporary greens, teeing mats or trolley bans, and remains open regardless of the weather. 18 holes, 6738 yards (white tees), 6260 yards (yellow tees), 5440 yards (red tees). S.S.S. 72. Full practice facilities. All golfers enjoy optional complimentary GPS buggy hire, subject to booking and availability. *Green Fees:* information available on request. *Eating facilities:* bars, lounge and private suites available. *Visitors:* welcome, but subject to availability of tee times. *Society Meetings:* welcome by arrangement. For up-to-date prices on all our products and services, call 01892 724400 or visit our website. e-mail: Info@kentnational.com website: www.kentnational.com

BROADSTAIRS. **North Foreland Golf Club,** The Clubhouse, Convent Road, Broadstairs CT10 3PU (01843 862140). *Location:* Broadstairs Station, A2, M2, A299, A253, A256, B2052. Cliff top, chalk based, free draining. 18 holes, 6382 yards. S.S.S. 71. Short Course: 18 holes, 1752 yards. Par 3. *Green Fees:* main course: weekdays £39.00 per round, £51.00 per day; weekends £51.00 per round. Par 3 course: weekdays £8.00 per day; weekends £9.50 per day. *Eating facilities:* bar, dining room and "Halfway House". *Visitors:* welcome weekdays and weekend afternoons with current Handicap Certificate. Tennis. *Society Meetings:* Wednesdays and Fridays by prior arrangement with Secretary. Professional: Darren Parris (01843 604471; Fax: 01843 862663). Secretary: Tony Adams (01843 862140). website: www.northforeland.co.uk

BROMLEY. **Magpie Hall Lane Municipal Golf Club,** Magpie Hall Lane, Bromley. *Location:* off Bromley Common on A21. 9 holes, 5590 yards, 5014 metres. S.S.S. 67. *Green Fees:*Information not available. *Eating facilities:* Food available. *Visitors:* welcome anytime without reservation.*

BROMLEY. **Shortlands Golf Club,** Meadow Road, Shortlands, Bromley BR2 0DX (020 8460 2471; Fax: 020 8460 8828). *Location:* car park and entrance in Ravensbourne Avenue, off the main Beckenham to Bromley Road, adjacent Shortlands B.R. Station. 9

holes, 5261 yards. S.S.S. 66. *Green Fees:* £15.00 for 18 holes, £10.00 for 9 holes. *Eating facilities:* available. *Visitors:* restricted to playing with a member. *Society Meetings:* only when member involved. Professional: (020 8464 6182). Manager: RS. May (020 8460 8828).

BROMLEY. **Sundridge Park Golf Club,** Garden Road, off Plaistow Lane, Bromley BR1 3NE (020 8460 0278). *Location:* five minutes' walk from Sundridge Park station. Wooded parkland. 36 holes. East 6493 yards. West 5973 yards. S.S.S. 71 and 69. Two practice grounds. *Green Fees:* £45.00 (West Course) & £60.00 (East Course) per round, £85.00 per day weekdays. *Eating facilities:* restaurant, spike bar, lounge bar, members' bar and snack bar. *Visitors:* welcome weekdays only, with Handicap Certificate. *Society Meetings:* catered for by arrangement. Professional: Stuart Dowsett (020 8460 5540). General Manager: Robert J. Walden (020 8460 0278; Fax: 020 8289 3050). e-mail: info@spgc.co.uk website: www.spgc.co.uk

CANTERBURY. **Broome Park Golf Club,** Broome Park Estate, Barham, Near Canterbury CT4 6QX (01227 830728; Fax: 01227 832591). *Location:* off the A2 at the A260 in the direction of Folkestone, half a mile on right. Undulating parkland, lake in front of 18th green. 18 holes, 6580 yards. S.S.S. 71. Driving range and practice ground. *Green Fees:* weekdays £40.00; weekends £50.00. *Eating facilities:* available all week. *Visitors:* welcome. Handicap Certificate required. *Society Meetings:* welcome weekdays by arrangement. Professional: Tienie Britz (01227 831126). Golf Manager: Graeme Robins (01227 830728; Fax: 01227 832591). e-mail: golf@broomepark.co.uk website: www.broomepark.co.uk

CANTERBURY. **Canterbury Golf Club,** Scotland Hills, Littlebourne Road, Canterbury CT1 1TW (01227 453532; Fax: 01227 784277). *Location:* one mile from centre of Canterbury on the A257 road to Sandwich. Parkland and wooded course. 18 holes, 6272 yards. S.S.S. 70. Practice ground. *Green Fees:* Information not available. *Eating facilities:* full bar and catering service (snacks, sandwiches, lunches, dinners). *Visitors:* welcome without reservation but Handicap Certificate necessary (or evidence that visitor is bona fide playing member of another club). *Society Meetings:* catered for Tuesday, Thursday and Friday. Professional: Paul Everard (01227 462865). Secretary: John Morgan (01227 453532).*

CHISLEHURST. **Chislehurst Golf Club,** Camden Park Road, Chislehurst BR7 5HJ (020 8467 3055). *Location:* between Bromley and junction of A222 and Sidcup bypass. Parkland. 18 holes, 5128 yards. S.S.S. 65. *Green Fees:* £30.00 per round. *Eating facilities:* catering available. Large parties by prior arrangement. *Visitors:* welcome but restricted to weekdays (except Wednesday mornings) and only with a member at weekends. *Society Meetings:* catered for by arrangement. Professional: (020 8467 6798). Secretary: Peter Foord (020 8467 2782; Fax: 020 8295 0874). Caterer: L. de Bruyn.

CHISLEHURST. **World of Golf,** A20 Sidcup Bypass, Chislehurst BR7 6RP (020 8309 0181). *Location:* six miles from Junction 3 on M25 heading towards London on A20. Parkland. Short game practice area, 54-bay driving range, adventure putting. *Eating facilities:* licensed cafe/bar. *Visitors:* welcome, no restrictions. Tennis courts. *Society Meetings:* welcome. Head Golf Professional: David Young.
e-mail: sc.worldofgolf@dsl.pipex.com
website: www.worldofgolf.biz

CRANBROOK. **Hemsted Forest Golf Club,** Golford Road, Cranbrook TN17 4AL (01580 712833; Fax: 01580 714274). *Location:* two miles south of Sissinghurst. Parkland, a beautiful tree lined course in superb condition. 18 holes, 6305 yards. S.S.S. 71. *Green Fees:* weekdays £28.00 per round, weekends £40.00 per round. *Eating facilities:* open all day, special menus catered for. *Visitors:* welcome weekdays after 8.30am and weekends after 11am. *Society Meetings:* available weekdays and weekends. Professional: Chris Weston (01580 712833; Fax: 01580 714274). Secretary: Karl Stevenson (01580 712833; Fax: 01580 714274).

DARTFORD. **Birchwood Park Golf Centre,** Birchwood Road, Wilmington, Dartford DA2 7HJ (01322 662038; Fax: 01322 667283). *Location:* from Junction 3 of M25, B2173 towards Sidcup. Turn right into Birchwood Road at Vauxhall Garage. Attractive undulating course surrounded by ancient woodland. Two courses - Main Course: 18 holes, 6364 yards, S.S.S. 70; Orchard Course: 9 holes, 1274 yards. 41 bay floodlit driving range. *Green Fees:* information not available. *Eating facilities:* snacks and bar food always available, dining/function room. *Visitors:* very welcome but advised to book tee times in advance. London Golf Centre Superstore, health and fitness facilities. *Society Meetings:* welcome, a variety of packages available. Teaching Professionals available. Manager: Scott Morley (01322 662038; Fax: 01322 667283).*

DARTFORD. **Dartford Golf Club Ltd.,** The Clubhouse, Heath Lane (Upper), Dartford DA1 2TN (01322 223616). *Location:* backing on to A2, one mile from Dartford Tunnel and M25. Flat parkland. 18 holes, 5914 yards. S.S.S. 69. *Green Fees:* weekdays £25.00 per round, £35.00 per day; weekends (accompanied by member): one round £16.00, two rounds £25.00. *Eating facilities:* catering available. *Visitors:* welcome on weekdays with reservation, must be member of another golf club. *Society Meetings:* welcome on Mondays and Fridays by prior arrangement with Secretary. Professional: John Gregory (01322 226409). Secretary: Amanda Malas (Tel & Fax: 01322 226455).
e-mail: dartfordgolf@hotmail.com

THE APPEARANCE OF AN ASTERISK (*) AT THE END OF A CLUB OR COURSE ENTRY INDICATES THAT UP-TO-DATE INFORMATION HAS NOT BEEN SUPPLIED

DARTFORD. **Fawkham Valley Golf Club,** Gay Dawn Farm, Valley Road, Fawkham, Longfield DA3 8LY (01474 707144). *Location:* off the A2 East of Dartford/off A20 North of Brands Hatch. Wooded course (tree lined), special feature being lakes in front of the 3rd and 6th greens. 9 holes, 6547 yards. S.S.S. 72. Practice area and putting green. *Green Fees:* information not available. *Eating facilities:* members' bar. *Visitors:* welcome anytime. *Society Meetings:* welcome Mondays, Wednesdays and Fridays. Professional: Nigel Willis. Secretary: Jo Marchant.
e-mail: info@fawkhamvalleygolf.co.uk
website: www.fawkhamvalleygolf.co.uk.

DEAL. **Royal Cinque Ports Golf Club,** Golf Road, Deal CT14 6RF (01304 374007; Fax: 01304 379530). *Location:* A258 from Sandwich. In Upper Deal leave for Middle Deal Road, left turn into Albert Road, Western Road, on to Golf Road (or from Dover, A258 via Sea front and Godwin Road). Championship 18 hole links course. 18 holes, 6942 yards. S.S.S. 73. Par 72. Large practice area. *Green Fees:* Information not available,*Eating facilities:* hot and cold comprehensive bar snack menu. *Visitors:* welcome, 4 ball rounds may be played on Tuesdays and Thursdays. Special packages available. Handicap Certificate required (max 22); times must be pre-booked. Buggies (with medical certificate); cart and caddies by arrangement. *Society Meetings:* by arrangement. Professional: Andrew Reynolds (01304 374170; Fax: 01304 379530). Secretary: Ian Symington (01304 374007; Fax: 01304 379530).*
e-mail: ian.symington@royalcinqueports.com
website: www.royalcinqueports.com

DEAL. **Walmer and Kingsdown Golf Club,** The Leas, Kingsdown, Deal CT14 8EP (01304 373256). *Location:* take A258 from Dover (A2) to Deal, Kingsdown club signposted at village of Ringwould. Downland course on the White Cliffs of Dover overlooking the English Channel. 18 holes, 6444 yards. S.S.S. 71. Practice ground. *Green Fees:* information not provided. *Eating facilities:* full catering and bar service. *Visitors:* welcome after 9.30am weekdays and 12 noon at weekends. *Society Meetings:* catered for by arrangement. Professional: Jude Read (01304 363017). Secretary: Reg Harrison (01304 373256; Fax: 01304 382336).
e-mail: info@kingsdowngolf.co.uk
website: www.kingsdowngolf.co.uk

DEANGATE. **Deangate Ridge Golf Club,** Duxcourt Road, Hoo, Rochester ME3 8RZ (01634 254481). *Location:* three miles from Rochester off A228 towards Isle of Grain. Municipal course – wooded. 18 holes, 6300 yards. S.S.S. 70. 11-bay driving range. *Green Fees:* information not provided. Special rates for Senior Citizens. *Eating facilities:* available. *Visitors:* welcome without reservation, bookings required for weekends. *Society Meetings:* catered for, book through Professional. Professional: Richard Fox (01634 251180). General Manager: Mike Smith (01634 254481). Club Members Secretary: Mrs C.J. Williams (01634 251950).

EDENBRIDGE. Kent and Surrey Golf and Country Club, Crouch House Road, Edenbridge TN8 5LQ (01732 867381; Fax: 01732 867167). *Location:* from M25 take A25, at Limpsfield take B2026 to Edenbridge, Parkland. Old Course 18 holes, 6577 yards. S.S.S. 72. 20-bay floodlit driving range. *Green Fees:* (2006) £27.00 weekdays, £32.00 weekends. Subject to review. *Eating facilities:* bar and restaurant. *Visitors:* welcome, call for start time. Buggies and carts available. Five tennis courts. *Society Meetings:* societies welcome weekdays and weekends. Conference facility seats up to 65.
e-mail: info@thekentandsurrey.com
website: www.thekentandsurrey.com

ETCHINGHILL. Etchinghill Golf Club, Canterbury Road, Etchinghill CT18 8FA (01303 863863; Fax: 01303 863210). *Location:* one mile north of M20 Junction 12 on B2065. 27 holes, 6121 yards. S.S.S. 69. 9 hole Par 3 course. Covered and floodlit driving range. *Green Fees:* information not available. *Eating facilities:* full range of catering facilities available. *Visitors:* welcome. Professional: Roger Dowle (01303 863966). website: www.pentlandgolf.co.uk

EYNSFORD. Austin Lodge Golf Club, Upper Austin Lodge Road, Eynsford DA4 0HU (01322 863000; Fax: 01322 862406). *Location:* Eynsford - 10 minutes' drive from Junction 3 of M25, M20, A20. Secluded rolling countryside with lakes, 18 holes, 6575 yards Yellow Tees, 7118 yards White Tees. S.S.S. 73. Practice ground. *Green Fees:* information not available. *Eating facilities:* bar, restaurant with light meals all day. *Visitors:* welcome weekdays, and after 12noon weekends. Buggies available. *Society Meetings:* welcome, telephone booking only. Professional/Manager: Greg Haenan.*

FARNBOROUGH. High Elms Golf Club, High Elms Road, Downe BR6 7SL (01689 853232). *Location:* two miles from Farnborough Hospital on A21, turn right at Shire Lane, second on left. Beautiful parkland. 18 holes, 6210 metres. S.S.S. 70. *Green Fees:* weekdays £17.50; weekends £25.00. Subject to review. *Eating facilities:* food available every day. *Visitors:* welcome, no restriction but should phone in advance. *Society Meetings:* apply to Catering Manager - Chris Crabtree. Professional: Peter Remy (01689 858175). Secretary: Mrs P. O'Keeffe.

FAVERSHAM. Boughton Golf Club, Brickfield Lane, Boughton, Faversham ME13 9AJ (01227 752277; Fax: 01227 7523610. *Location:* north-east of Boughton, near M2/A2 interchange; six miles west of Canterbury. 18 holes, 6452 yards. S.S.S. 71. Driving range. *Green Fees:* information not provided. *Eating facilities:* available. *Visitors:* welcome. Manager: G. Haenen.

FAVERSHAM. Faversham Golf Club Ltd., Belmont Park, Faversham ME13 0HB (01795 890561). *Location:* M2 Faversham Exit (A251) to A2 junction, left to Brogdale Road, left to Belmont. Long established (1902) very attractive parkland course in rural surroundings. 18 holes, 5965 yards. S.S.S. 69. *Green Fees:* £35.00 per round, £45.00 per day. *Eating facilities:* full catering. *Visitors:* welcome weekdays (Handicap Certificate required); weekends with member only. *Society Meetings:* catered for Mondays, Wednesdays and Fridays only. Professional: S. Rokes (01795 890275). Secretary: J. Edgington (01795 890561; Fax: 01795 890760).

FOLKESTONE. Sene Valley Golf Club, Sene, Folkestone CT18 8BL (01303 268513). *Location:* M20 Junction 12, take A20 to Ashford turn left at first roundabout. Downland course with magnificent views over English Channel. 18 holes, 6271 yards. S.S.S. 70. Practice area. *Green Fees:* weekdays £30.00; weekends (after 11am) £45.00. *Eating facilities:* snacks, meals on request. *Visitors:* welcome, Handicap Certificate required. Preferable to book in advance. *Society Meetings:* welcome by prior arrangements. Professional: Nick Watson (Tel & Fax: 01303 268514). Manager: John Hemphrey.
e-mail: senevalleygolf@btconnect.com
website: www.senevalleygolfclub.co.uk

GILLINGHAM. Gillingham Golf Club Ltd., Woodlands Road, Gillingham ME7 2AP (01634 850999). *Location:* on old A2 Gillingham. Flat parkland. 18 holes, 5514 yards, 5042 metres. Par 67. Practice nets. *Green Fees:* available weekdays, rates on application. *Eating facilities:* available. *Visitors:* welcome at all times except weekends. Must have proof of Handicap or membership of another club. *Society Meetings:* welcome by prior arrangement. Professional: (01634 855862). Office (01634 853017; Fax: 01634 574749).

GRAVESEND. **Mid-Kent Golf Club,** Singlewell Road, Gravesend DA11 7RB (01474 352387). *Location:* A227 off A2. Parkland. 18 holes, 6106 yards. S.S.S. 70. *Green Fees:* weekdays £35.00 per round, £50.00 per day; weekends with member only. *Eating facilities:* breakfast, dinner by arrangement, lunch every day, bar 11am to 11pm. *Visitors:* welcome weekdays except competition days with Handicap Certificate. *Society Meetings:* catered for Tuesdays only. Professional: Mark Foreman (01474 332810). Secretary: P. Gleeson (01474 568035; Fax: 01474 564218).
e-mail: secretary@mkgc.co.uk
website: www.mkgc.co.uk

GRAVESEND. **Southern Valley Golf Course,** Thong Lane, Shorne, Gravesend DA12 4LF (01474 568568; Fax: 01474 360366). *Location:* take J4 off A2 (not M2), signposted "Inn on the Lake/Thong", at top of slip road turn left into Thong Lane at T-junction. Golf course is approx. one mile along on right-hand side. Undulating greens and rolling fairways. 18 holes, 6100 yards. Par 69. *Green Fees:* Monday to Thursday £16.50, weekends £22.00. *Eating facilities:* fully licensed bar and restaurant. *Visitors:* all welcome. No jeans or tracksuits; golf shoes must be worn. Tuition available; golf shop; buggies for hire April to October. *Society Meetings:* welcome, telephone in advance. Professional: Larry Batchelor. Club Administrator: Mrs Anne Green (01474 740026).
e-mail: info@southernvalley.co.uk

HALSTEAD. **Broke Hill Golf Club,** Sevenoaks Road, Halstead, Kent TN14 7HR (01959 533225; Fax: 01959 532680). *Location:* four minutes from M25 Junction 4, A21, four miles from Bromley and two miles from Orpington. Parkland course, with strategically placed bunkers and 5 holes where water comes into play. 18 holes, 6415 yards. S.S.S. 71.Two practice grounds. *Green Fees:* phone for prices. *Eating facilities:* lounge bar, restaurant and banqueting facilities. *Visitors:* welcome weekdays only, strict dress code applies. Soft spikes. Golf buggies and carts available. *Society Meetings:* weekdays only. Professional: Iain Naylor (01959 533810; Fax: 01959 532680). General Manager: Jon Pleydell (01959 533225; Fax: 01959 532680).

HAWKHURST. **Hawkhurst Golf Club,** High Street, Hawkhurst TN18 4JS (01580 754074/752396; Fax: 01580 754074). *Location:* on A268 from Flimwell to Hawkhurst. Undulating parkland. 9 holes, 5751 yards. S.S.S. 68. Practice ground. *Green Fees:* £22.00 per round weekdays; £26.00 weekends. *Eating facilities:* bar, spike bar, dining room. *Visitors:* welcome weekdays, weekends with member only. Handicap Certificate recommended. Squash courts. Trolleys and buggies are available for hire. *Society Meetings:* welcome. Professional: Peter Chandler (Tel & Fax: 01580 752396). Secretary: (Tel & Fax: 01580 754074).

HEADCORN. **Weald of Kent Golf Course,** Maidstone Road, Headcorn TN27 9PT (01622 890866; Fax: 01622 890070). *Location:* Junction 8 M20, five miles south of Maidstone on A274. Scenic undulating parkland course featuring a range of natural hazards, including waterways, lakes and ditches. 18 holes, 6310 yards. S.S.S. 70. *Green Fees:* information not available. *Eating facilities:* spacious architect designed clubhouse, extensive bar menu available 7.00am till 9.30pm. Banqueting and conference facilities also available (30 to 200 delegates). *Visitors:* welcome anytime, bookings available seven days in advance (01622 890866). Hotel accommodation. Golf Breaks available (01622 890866). *Society Meetings:* welcome midweek and generally after 12pm, weekends subject to availability; booking required in advance, minimum 12. Director of Golf: Rob Golding.

HERNE BAY. **Herne Bay Golf Club,** Eddington, Herne Bay CT6 7PG (01227 373964). *Location:* off the New Thanet Way. Parkland/links course. 18 holes, 5567 yards. S.S.S. 68. Practice ground. *Green Fees:* information not available. *Eating facilities:* bar meals, restaurant by arrangement. *Visitors:* welcome weekdays unrestricted, weekends and Bank Holidays after 12 noon only. Handicap Certificate required. *Society Meetings:* welcome by prior arrangement. Professional: D. Ledingham (01227 374727).*

HEVER. **Hever Castle Golf Club,** Hever, Edenbridge TN8 7NP (01732 700771; Fax: 01732 700775). *Location:* from M25 Junction 5 or 6 follow signs to Hever Castle. The golf club is one mile east of the castle on the same lane. Parkland, wooded. 27 holes. Kings and Queens course: 18 holes, 7002 yards. S.S.S. 74. Princes course: 9 holes, 2784 yards. S.S.S. 67 (for 18 holes). Large practice range, chipping and pitching areas, practice bunker, putting green. *Green Fees:* £38.50 Monday to Thursday, £41.50 Friday, £47.00 Weekend. *Eating facilities:* restaurant and bars. *Visitors:* welcome by appointment. *Society Meetings:* welcome by prior arrangement; competitive rates available. Head PGA Professional: Peter Parks. General Manager: Jon Wittenberg.

HYTHE. **Hythe Imperial Golf Club,** Princes Parade, Hythe CT21 6AE (01303 267441). *Location:* come off M20 Junction 11, directions for Hythe A261. Flat seaside course. 9 holes, 5533 yards. S.S.S. 67. Practice ground. *Green Fees:* information not provided. *Eating facilities:* available at the hotel. *Visitors:* welcome weekdays, no green fees weekends up to 1pm. *Society Meetings:* welcome weekdays only. Professional: J. Leaver (01303 233745). Professional Shop: (01303 233745) Secretary: R. Duncan (Tel & Fax: 01303 267554).

LYDD. **Lydd Golf Club and Driving Range,** Romney Road, Lydd, Romney Marsh TN29 9LS (01797 320808; Fax: 01797 321482). *Location:* B2075 within half a mile of Lydd Airport. Traditional links course with added water hazards. 18 holes, 6517 yards. S.S.S. 71. 24 bay floodlit driving range. *Green Fees:* information not available. *Eating facilities:* bar and restaurant. *Visitors:* no restrictions. Pull trolleys, electric trolleys and golf carts. *Society Meetings:* welcome, discount rates available. Professional: Richard Perkins (01797 321201). Secretary: Brian Evans (01797 320808; Fax: 01797 321482). *

MAIDSTONE. **Bearsted Golf Club,** Ware Street, Bearsted ME14 4PQ (01622 738389). *Location:* Junction 7 off M20, turn right to Bearsted and follow signs. Undulating parkland course with view of North Downs. 18 holes, 6320 yards, 5739 metres. S.S.S. 70. Practice area, putting green, net. *Green Fees:* £32.00/£42.00 weekdays; weekends with a member. *Eating facilities:* bar/restaurant, open all day. *Visitors:* welcome weekdays, weekends must be with members. Current Handicap Certificates required. *Society Meetings:* catered for Mondays to Fridays by prior arrangement. Professional: Tim Simpson (01622 738024). Secretary: Mr R. Adcock (01622 738198; Fax: 01622 735608).

MAIDSTONE. **Cobtree Manor Park Golf Club,** Chatham Road, Sandling, Maidstone ME14 3AZ (01622 753276). *Location:* M20, A229 Chatham (not Maidstone). Undulating course with trees, and interesting 12th hole over lake. 18 holes, 5611 yards. S.S.S. 69. Tuition, practice, putting. *Green Fees:* information not available. *Eating facilities:* restaurant and bar. *Visitors:* welcome, book four days in advance through Professional. *Society Meetings:* welcome phone (01622 751881). Professional: Paul Foston (01622 753276).

MAIDSTONE. **Leeds Castle Golf Course,** Leeds Castle, Near Maidstone ME17 1PL (01622 767828). *Location:* M20 Junction 8, A20 near Maidstone. Situated in the grounds of Leeds Castle, parkland. 9 holes, 2681 yards. S.S.S. 33. Putting green and practice nets. *Green Fees:* Information not available. *Eating facilities:* Leeds Castle Restaurant on Leeds Castle Estate. *Visitors:* welcome anytime, bookings taken from six days in advance. Correct dress must be worn - no denim jeans allowed, golf shoes preferred. *Society Meetings:* welcome weekdays. Professional: Steve Purves. Secretary: Ann Bishop.*

MAIDSTONE. **Marriott Tudor Park Hotel and Country Club,** Ashford Road, Bearsted, Maidstone ME14 4NQ (01622 734334). *Location:* east of Maidstone, on A20 at Bearsted. Off Junction 8 of M20. Parkland. 18 holes, 6085 yards. S.S.S. 69. Practice area. *Green Fees:* weekdays £35.00; weekends £40.00. *Eating facilities:* restaurants and bars. *Visitors:* Hotel with 120 bedrooms, leisure and conference facilities. *Society Meetings:* Societies and Company Days catered for. Professional: Andrew Brooks (01622 739412). Secretary: John Ladbrooke (01622 737119). Golf Director: Jason King.

MAIDSTONE. **The Ridge Golf Club,** Chartway Street, East Sutton, Maidstone ME17 3JB (01622 844243; Fax: 01622 844168). *Location:* Junction 8 M20, past Leeds Castle on Sutton Valence Road to A274 turn left and first turning on left. 18 holes, 6254 yards. S.S.S. 71. Driving range. *Green Fees:* on request. *Eating facilities:* bar snack menu and full menu. *Visitors:* welcome. *Society Meetings:* welcome Monday to Sunday. (01622 844243).

MAIDSTONE. **West Malling Golf Club,** London Road, Addington, West Malling ME19 5AR (01732 844785; Fax: 01732 844795). *Location:* M20, A228 turn off. Parkland/wooded course. Spitfire Course - 18 holes, 6142 yards. S.S.S. 70. Hurricane Course - 18 holes, 6300 yards. S.S.S 70. Practice ground. *Green Fees:* Information not available. *Visitors:* welcome weekdays anytime, weekends after 12 noon. Conference/function facilities available. Buggies available. *Society Meetings:* catered for by prior arrangement. Professional: Duncan Lambert (01732 844022). Secretary: Mike Ellis (01732 844785; Fax: 01732 844795).

NEW ROMNEY. **Littlestone Golf Club,** St Andrews Road, Littlestone, New Romney TN28 8RB (01797 362231; Fax: 01797 362740). *Location:* M20 Junction 10 (Ashford), B2070 to Brenzett - New Romney, one mile from New Romney. Seaside Championship links course. 18 holes, Blue tees 6676 yards, S.S.S. 73, White tees 6486 yards, S.S.S 72. Practice range, practice ground, chipping and putting greens. *Green Fees:* £45.00 per round, £65.00 per day weekdays; £65.00 per round, £80.00 per day weekends. *Eating facilities:* full dining room and bar. *Visitors:* Handicap Certificate required. Visitors restricted at weekends. Singles and foursomes only. Caddie cars available. *Society Meetings:* welcome. Professional: Andrew Jones (01797 362231). Secretary: Col. Charles Moorhouse (01797 363355; Fax: 01797 362740). e-mail: secretary@littlestonegolfclub.org.uk website: www.littlestonegolfclub.org.uk

NEW ROMNEY. **Romney Warren Golf Club,** St Andrews Road, Littlestone, New Romney TN28 8RB (01797 362231; Fax: 01797 362740). *Location:* one mile from New Romney off A259, down B2070; 20 minutes from J10 on M20. Undulating seaside links crisscrossed with dykes. 18 holes, 5126 yards. S.S.S. 67. Practice range. *Green Fees:* weekdays £19.00 per round, £30.00 per day; weekends £23.00 per round, £36.00 per day. *Eating facilities:* bar and restaurant. *Visitors:* welcome. *Society Meetings:* welcome by arrangement. Professional: Andrew Jones. Hon. Secretary: J. Purkiss (01797 362768). website: www.romneywarrengolfclub.org

1st Augustine's Golf Club

**Cottington Road, Cliffsend,
Ramsgate, Kent CT12 5JN**

SOCIETY PACKAGES AVAILABLE

◆

18 HOLE COURSE • 5129 yards

◆

Weekdays £24 per round, £34 per day
Weekends £30 per round, £40 per day
To book golf, phone Pro Shop on
01843 590222

◆

Catering facilities available. Licensed bar

**Secretary: 01843 590333
Professional: 01843 590222
Fax: 01843 590444
e-mail: sagc.@ic24.net**

ORPINGTON. **Chelsfield Lakes Golf Centre,** Court Road, Orpington BR6 9BX (01689 896266; Fax: 01689 824577). *Location:* M25 Junction 4, A224 Court Road. Gently undulating course with hazards and sandtraps; played through some orchards. 18 holes, 6077 yards. S.S.S. 69. 9 holes, 1188 yards. Par 3. 40 bay floodlit driving range, practice area. *Green Fees:* information not available. *Eating facilities:* bar and restaurant. *Visitors:* welcome, pay as you play facility, non members can book 7 days in advance. Pro shop. *Society Meetings:* welcome. Professionals: Nigel Lee, Bill Hodkin.*

ORPINGTON. **Cray Valley Golf Club,** Sandy Lane, St. Paul's Cray, Orpington BR5 3HY. *Location:* Ruxley roundabout A20; turn off into Sandy Lane, half a mile on left. Parkland. 18 holes, 5624 yards. S.S.S. 67. Also 9 hole course. *Green Fees:* information not available. *Eating facilities:* hot meals available lunchtimes, also bar. *Visitors:* welcome all week. *Society Meetings:* welcome. Professional: Gary Stewart (01689 837909). General Manager: Tom Ashman (01689 839677). *

ORPINGTON. **Lullingstone Park Golf Club,** Park Gate Road, Chelsfield, Near Orpington, Kent BR6 7PX (01959 533794). *Location:* two miles from Junction 4 off M25, fifth exit on left (signposted). Undulating parkland. 18 holes, 6734 yards. S.S.S. 72. 9 holes, 2379 yards. Par 33. 22 bay driving range, pitch and putt course, putting green. *Green Fees:* information

not available. *Eating facilities:* cafeteria and bar. *Visitors:* bookings welcome. *Society Meetings:* very welcome, telephone Professional for package details. Professional: Mark Watt (01959 533793; Fax: 01959 534129). Secretary: Chris Pocock.

ORPINGTON. **Orpington Golf Centre,** Sandy Lane, St. Pauls Cray, Orpington BR5 3HY (01689 871490; Fax: 01689 891428). *Location:* off old A20 at Ruxley Corner. 53 holes, Par 71, 71, 32 and Academy course. 28 bays, covered, floodlit, grassed. *Green Fees:* information not available. *Eating facilities:* breakfast, lunch available, bar open all day. *Society Meetings:* welcome all week. Head Professional: Brad McLean. General Manager: Russell Mayne.

ORPINGTON. **West Kent Golf Club,** Milking Lane, Downe, Near Orpington BR6 7LD (01689 851323). *Location:* from Downe village south along Luxted Lane, 600 yards turn right into West Hill. 18 holes, 6426 yards. S.S.S. 70. *Green Fees:* £40.00 per round, £50.00 per day. *Eating facilities:* meals by arrangement. *Visitors:* welcome weekdays only with recognised Handicap. Casual golfers should phone at least 24 hours in advance. *Society Meetings:* catered for. Professional: C.W. Forsyth (Tel & Fax: 01689 856863). Secretary: Sean Trussell (01689 851323).

RAMSGATE. **Manston Golf Centre,** Manston Road, Manston, Ramsgate CT12 5BE (01843 590005). *Location:* a quarter mile east of Manston village on the B2050. Flat seaside course with superb views across the English Channel. 9 holes, 4958 yards. Par 66. *Green Fees:* weekdays £7.00 9 holes; weekends £9.50 for 9 holes. 20 bay floodlit covered driving range. Grass tees and shortgame area with bunkers and two putting greens. Six "Positive Impact" PGA qualified coaches. *Eating facilities:* snacks and drinks. *Visitors:* unrestricted. *Society Meetings:* groups of 8 or more. Secretary. Professional: Philip Sparks (01843 590005).
website:www.manstongolf.co.uk

RAMSGATE. **St Augustine's Golf Club,** Cottington Road, Cliffsend, Ramsgate CT12 5JN (01843 590333; Fax: 01843 590444). *Location:* two miles south-west of Ramsgate – approaching from A253 or A256 follow signs to St Augustine's Cross. Entrance 75 yards beyond Cross by railway bridge. Mainly parkland, flat - tight and challenging course. 18 holes, 5129 yards. S.S.S. 65. *Green Fees:* weekdays £24.00 per round, £34.00 per day; weekends and Bank Holidays £30.00 per round, £40.00 per day. *Eating facilities:* usual bar facilities; catering available 9am to 3.30pm daily; Fridays also 6.30pm to 10.30pm. *Visitors:* welcome, advisable to ring Professional the day before to check periods booked for matches; booking necessary Saturdays and Sundays (Sundays visitors only after 1pm). To book golf phone Professional shop (01843 590222). *Society Meetings:* catered for, book through Secretary. Dormy flat available for 7 nights stay - ring Secretary. Professional: D. Scott (01843 590222). Secretary: R. F. Tranckle (01843 590333). e-mail: sagc@ic24.net

RAMSGATE. **Stonelees Golf Centre,** Ebbsfleet Lane, Near Ramsgate CT12 5DJ (01843 823133; Fax: 01843 850569). *Location:* near junction of A256 and B2048 (Ebbsfleet Lane). Undulating seaside/ parkland courses. Three 9 hole courses. The Executive, 1471 yards, S.S.S. 29; The Par 3, 1159 yards, S.S.S. 27; The Heights , a full length 9-hole course, 2857 yards, Par 34. Excellent teaching facilities, 20 bay driving range, Smart Golf simulator, practice putting green, chipping area, miniature putting course. Fully stocked golf shop. *Green Fees:* Executive weekdays £6.30 9 holes, £9.60 18 holes; weekends £6.90 9 holes, £10.30 18 holes. Par 3 - weekdays £4.80 9 holes, £7.90 18 holes; weekends £5.70 9 holes, £9.00 18 holes. Heights weekdays £9.00 9 holes, £14.00 18 holes, weekends £12.00 9 holes, £18.00 18 holes. Prices subject to review. Junior rates and membership discounts available. *Eating facilities:* licensed bar, restaurant. *Visitors:* always welcome, no restrictions. *Society Meetings:* small societies/groups welcome. Professional: David Bonthron. Manager: R.J. Chapman.
e-mail: stonelees@stonelees.com
website: www.stonelees.co.uk

ROCHESTER. **Rochester and Cobham Park Golf Club,** Park Pale, by Rochester ME2 3UL (01474 823411; Fax: 01474 824446). *Location:* on A2, two miles east of Gravesend East turn-off. Open championship regional qualifying course. Undulating parkland. 18 holes, 6597 yards. S.S.S. 72. Extensive practice facilities. *Green Fees:* weekdays £37.50 per round, £47.50 per day. *Eating facilities:* morning coffee, lunch, tea, dinner available, two bars. *Visitors:* welcome midweek only with Handicap Certificate. *Society Meetings:* welcome Tuesdays and Thursdays, must be pre-booked. Professional: Iain Higgins (01474 823658). Manager: David Smith (01474 823411; Fax: 01474 824446).

SANDWICH. **Royal St. George's Golf Club,** Sandwich CT13 9PB (01304 613090; Fax: 01304 611245). *Location:* one mile from Sandwich on the road to Sandwich Bay. From Canterbury A257, from Dover A258. Links. 18 holes, Championship 7102 yards, Medal 6607 yards. S.S.S. Championship 74, Medal 72. Practice ground. *Green Fees:* £120.00 for one round, £150.00 for two rounds weekdays. Subject to review. *Eating facilities:* snack bar and dining room. *Visitors:* welcome weekdays only, must be pre-booked. No visitors at weekends or on Public Holidays. Must have Handicap Certificate (under 18) and be member of club affiliated to EGU. Caddies to be booked in advance, trolleys available. *Society Meetings:* catered for by arrangement. All players must meet requirements for visitors. Professional: A. Brooks (01304 615236). Secretary: H.C.G. Gabbey (01304 613090; Fax: 01304 611245). Caddiemaster: (01304 626931).

SANDWICH BAY. **Prince's Golf Club,** Prince's Drive, Sandwich Bay, Sandwich CT13 9QB (01304 611118; Fax: 01304 612000). *Location:* four miles from Sandwich through the Sandwich Bay Estate. Seaside links. 27 holes arranged as 3 loops of 9 holes named "Dunes", "Himalayas", "Shore". D & H 6262 - 6776 yards, Par 71, S.S.S. 70-73. H & S 6238 - 6813 yards, Par 71, S.S.S. 70-73. S & D 6466-7204 yards, Par 72, S.S.S. 71-73. Championship 7204 yards. Driving range, full practice facilities. *Green Fees:* information not available. *Eating facilities:* breakfast, lunch, available every day; bar; light snacks throughout the day. Dinner by arrangement. *Visitors & Societies:* welcome without restriction, Company days and private parties catered for. Brochure available on request. Professional: Rob McGuirk (01304 613797). Information & Bookings: Richard Kimber (01304 611118). General Manager: Bill Howie (01304 626909; Fax: 01304 612000).
e-mail: office@princesgolfclub.co.uk
website: www.princesgolfclub.co.uk

SEVENOAKS. **Darenth Valley Golf Course Ltd,** Station Road, Shoreham, Near Sevenoaks TN14 7SA (01959 522944; Fax: 01959 525089). *Location:* A225 between Otford and Eynsford, approximately four miles north of Sevenoaks. Pay and play parkland course. 18 holes, 6258 yards. S.S.S. 72. Practice area, putting green. *Green Fees:* weekdays £20.00; weekends £27.00, four-ball £100.00 (subject to review). *Eating facilities:* bar snacks and meals; diningroom, functions up to 150 covers. *Visitors:* welcome with reservation through Pro shop. *Society Meetings:* welcome by arrangement. Professionals Shop: (01959 522922). General Manager: Jonathan Cooper (01959 522944; Fax: 01959 525089).
website: www.dvgc.co.uk

SEVENOAKS. **Knole Park Golf Club,** Seal Hollow Road, Sevenoaks TN15 0HJ (01732 452150; Fax: 01732 463159). *Location:* one mile north-east of Sevenoaks town centre. Deer Park; beautiful, natural course. Second to none in the South East. 18 holes, 6246 yards. S.S.S. 70. Practice ground and nets. *Green Fees:* weekdays only, £39.00 per round, £50.00 per day. Subject to review. *Eating facilities:* full bar and catering. *Visitors:* welcome by appointment, Handicap Certificate required. Squash courts. Society Meetings: catered for by arrangement only. Professional: (01732 451740). Secretary: Peter Mitchell (01732 452150; Fax: 01732 463159).
website: www.knoleparkgolfclub.co.uk

SEVENOAKS. **Wildernesse Club,** Park Lane, Seal, Sevenoaks TN15 0JE (01732 761199). Location: A25 between Sevenoaks and Borough Green. Park and woodland. 18 holes, 6532 yards. S.S.S. 71. Large practice ground. *Green Fees:* £50.00 per round. *Eating facilities:* by arrangement. *Visitors:* welcome weekdays only by prior arrangement; Handicap Certificate required. *Society Meetings:* catered for Mondays, Thursdays and Fridays. Professional: Craig Walker (01732 761527). Secretary: Major (Retd) K.P. Loosemore (01732 761199).

SEVENOAKS. **Woodlands Manor Golf Club,** Tinkerpot Lane, Woodlands, Near Otford, Sevenoaks TN15 6AB (01959 523806). Location: Junction 3, M25 take "Brands Hatch" sign on A20, seven miles. Parkland, designated Area of Outstanding Natural Beauty. 18 holes, 6100 yards. S.S.S. 69. Six acre practice ground. *Green Fees:* information not provided. *Eating facilities:* bar daily. *Visitors:* welcome weekdays, weekends after 1pm. Buggies for hire. *Society Meetings:* welcome by arrangement Monday to Friday. On-line booking system. Professional: Philip Womack. Secretary: C.G. Robins (01959 523806). website: www.woodlandsmanorgolf.co.uk

SEVENOAKS. **Wrotham Heath Golf Club,** Seven Mile Lane, Comp, Sevenoaks TN15 8QZ (01732 884800). Location: on B2016 half-a-mile south of junction with A20. Woodland/heathland. 18 holes, 5994 yards. S.S.S. 70. *Green Fees:* £35.00. *Eating facilities:* bar and snacks, meals by arrangement, except Mondays. *Visitors:* welcome on weekdays with Handicap Certificate, but not Bank Holidays. *Society Meetings:* catered for Thursdays and Fridays only, no more than 30 people. Professional: H. Dearden (01732 883854). Secretary: A. Watts (01732 884800).

SHEERNESS. **Sheerness Golf Club,** Power Station Road, Sheerness ME12 3AE (01795 662585). Location: follow A249 then A250 towards Sheerness. Flat marshland/meadowland; numerous water hazards. 18 holes, 6390 yards. S.S.S. 71. Practice area. *Green Fees:* weekdays £22.00 per round, £31.00 per day; weekends £28.00 per round (by appointment only). *Eating facilities:* available. *Visitors:* weekdays only except with member. *Society Meetings:* catered for weekdays, except Mondays, by previous arrangement. Secretary: D. Nehra. e-mail: thesecretary@sheernessgc.freeserve.co.uk

SIDCUP. **Sidcup Golf Club,** Hurst Road, Sidcup DA15 9AW (020 8300 2864). Location: A222 near Sidcup Station. Parkland. 9 holes, 5571 yards. S.S.S. 68. *Green Fees:* on application *Eating facilities:* restaurant and bar. *Visitors:* welcome Monday to Thursday except Bank Holidays. *Society Meetings:* not catered for. Secretary: John Aughterlony (020 8300 2150). e-mail: sidcupgolfclub@tiscali.co.uk

SITTINGBOURNE. **The Oast Golf Centre Ltd,** Church Road, Tonge, Sittingbourne ME9 9AR (01795 473527). *Location*: one mile north A2 between Faversham and Sittingbourne, take the turning to Tonge at Bapchild. 9-hole par 3 course. 17 bay covered floodlit driving range. *Green Fees*: 9 holes £5.50, 18 holes £7.50. *Eating facilities*: sandwiches, rolls. *Visitors*: welcome. Tuition available, golf shop. Two short mat bowls facility. *Society Meetings*: welcome. Professional: David Chambers. Secretary: Sally Chambers. e-mail: mail@oastgolf.co.uk

SITTINGBOURNE. **Sittingbourne and Milton Regis,** Wormdale, Newington, Sittingbourne ME9 7PX (01795 842261; Fax: 01795 844117). *Location*: Junction 5 M2, follow signs to Danaway Chestnut Street, three quarters of a mile, first left over Bridge to Wormdale. Gently undulating tree-lined course. 18 holes, 6291 yards, 5771 metres. S.S.S. 70. *Green Fees*: 18 holes £32.00, 36 holes £40.00. No visitors weekends. *Eating facilities*: available. *Visitors*: welcome weekdays. *Society Meetings*: catered for Tuesdays and Thursdays by arrangement. Professional: J. Hearn (01795 842775). Manager: Charles Maxted.

SITTINGBOURNE near. **Upchurch River Valley Golf Courses,** Oak Lane, Upchurch, near Sittingbourne ME9 7AY (01634 360626; Fax: 01634 387784). *Location:* M2, Junction 4 (A278) or Junction 5 (A249) onto A2 between Rainham and Newington, Oak Lane (opposite Little Chef). Undulating parkland with ponds and panoramic views. 18 holes, 6237 yards, 5701 metres. S.S.S. 70. 9 holes, 1596 yards, Par 30. Driving range. *Green Fees:* information not available. *Eating facilities:* 120 seater à la carte restaurant, all day food and drinks lounge. *Visitors:* unrestricted. Swimming pool. *Society Meetings:* welcome weekdays. Professional: Roger Cornwell (01634 379592). Secretary: (Members only) D. Candy (01634 260594). Course Controller: URVGC Ltd.*

SNODLAND. **Oastpark Golf Course,** Sandhole, Malling Road, Snodland ME6 5LG (01634 242661). *Location*: half a mile from M20, two miles from M2; five miles from Maidstone. Easy walking, good test of golf, lots of water/sand/trees. 9 holes, 3150 yards. S.S.S. 70. Extensive practice facilities. Floodlit driving range. *Green Fees:* information not provided. *Eating facilities:* full bar and catering service. *Visitors:* welcome, no restrictions. No jeans, tracksuits; golf shoes must be worn. *Society Meetings:* all welcome weekdays, and weekends after 11am. Professional: David Porthouse (01634 242661). Secretary: Mrs Lesley Murrock (01634 242818; Fax: 01634 240744)

SWANLEY. **Pedham Place Golf Centre,** London Road, Swanley BR8 8PP (01322 867000; Fax: 01322 861646). *Location:* 300 yards east of Junction 3 M25, on A20 towards Brands Hatch. Two elevated links-style courses. 18 holes, 6444 yards. S.S.S. 71, Par 72; 9 holes, 1165 yards, Par 3. 40-bay floodlit driving range, putting green, practice facilities. *Green Fees:* information not provided. *Eating facilities:* bar snacks to full meals; licensed bar. Modern marquee for larger groups. *Visitors:* all welcome. Thursday morning Ladies' day, Wednesday morning Veterans. Appropriate clothing/footwear must be worn. Buggy hire available. *Societies:* welcome, special rates available. Sales: Beverley Smith. Head Professional: John Woodroffe.
e-mail: golf@ppgc.co.uk
website: www.ppgc.co.uk

TATSFIELD. **Park Wood Golf Club,** Chestnut Avenue, Tatsfield, Near Westerham TN16 2EG (01959 577744). *Location:* on B2024 Croydon road which becomes Clarks Lane. At Church Hill junction join Chestnut Avenue. In an area of natural beauty, flanked by an ancient woodland, with superb views across Kent and Surrey. Undulating course, tree-lined and with some interesting water features. Playable in all weather. 18 holes, 6835 yards. Par 72. S.S.S. 72. Course record 66. *Green Fees:* on application. *Visitors:* telephone in advance. May not play on Bank Holidays. *Societies:* apply in writing/telephone (01959 577744). Professional: Nick Terry.
e-mail: mail@parkwoodgolf.co.uk
website: www.parkwoodgolf.co.uk

TENTERDEN. **Tenterden Golf Club,** Woodchurch Road, Tenterden TN30 7DR (Tel & Fax: 01580 763987). *Location:* 30 minutes from Channel Tunnel and west of Ashford International Station, on B2067 Woodchurch Road, Tenterden. Parkland course set in beautiful undulating Wealden countryside. 18 holes, 6152 yards. S.S.S. 70. Practice ground. *Green Fees:* All day £34.00; 18 holes am £22.00. 18 holes pm £15.00; 9 holes (evening) £9.00. *Eating facilities:* available, breakfast on request, lunch, snacks and dinner, all day bar. *Society Meetings:* dedicated society days Tuesday to Friday. Professional: (01580 762409). Secretary: Duncan J. McDowall (01580 763987).
website: www.tenterdengolfclub.co.uk.

TENTERDEN. **London Beach Golf Club**, Ashford Road, Tenterden TN30 6HX (01580 766279; Fax: 01580 763884). *Location:* A28 Tenterden. Parkland course. 9 holes, 3018 yards. S.S.S. 71 (18 holes). Putting, pitch and putt, driving range (members only). *Green Fees:* weekdays !8 holes £20.00; weekends 18 holes £25. *Eating facilities:* restaurant and bar. Visitors: welcome; restrictions Tuesday, Wednesday and Sunday before midday. Tuition available, book in advance. Hotel accommodation; golf breaks catered for. *Society Meetings:* welcome by arrangement. Professional: Mark Chilcott. Secretary: Pierre Edmonds.*
e-mail: enquiries@londonbeach.com
website: www.londonbeach.com

TONBRIDGE. **Hilden Golf Centre,** Hilden Park, Rings Hill, Hildenborough, Tonbridge TN11 8LX (01732 833607; Fax: 01732 834484). *Location*: take exit off A21 for Tonbridge North/Hildenborough; take second turning right (Watts Cross Road), follow road past station to bottom of the hill, golf centre is on the left. 36 bay covered, floodlit driving range with PowerTee. *Green Fees:* weekdays 9 holes £7.50, 18 holes £11.25; weekends 9 holes £10.00, 18 holes £15.00. *Eating facilities:* fully licensed cafe bar open 8am to 10pm. all year round. Opening hours: Monday to Thursday 8am to 10pm, Friday to Sunday 7.30am to 9pm. Five PGA professionals (tuition available), large golf shop, 9 hole golf course and putting green. Leisure centre and crèche. Teaching academy and large golf discount store stocking all the top brands at discount prices. Professionals: Nick McNally, Karl Steptoe, Oliver Brown, Nicky Way and Rupert Hunter. Secretary: Jan Parfett (01732 834404; Fax: 01732 834484).

TONBRIDGE. **Nizels Golf Club,** Nizels Lane, Hildenborough, Near Tonbridge TN11 8NU (01732 833833; Fax: 01732 833492). *Location:* M25 B245 off A21. Take signs to Tonbridge North, club one mile, Nizels Lane. Undulating parkland, several holes where water comes into play, many mature trees. 18 holes, 6361 yards off white tees. S.S.S. 71. Par 72. Limited practice area. *Green Fees:* £30.00 weekday only. *Eating facilities:* bar snacks and fine dining available. *Visitors:* welcome weekdays after 9.30am. Pro shop. *Society Meetings:* weekdays only after 9.30am. Professional: Ashley Weller (01732 838926). General Manager: Patrick Ferguson.
website: www.theclubcompany.com

TONBRIDGE. **Poult Wood Public Golf Centre,** Higham Lane, Tonbridge TN11 9QR (01732 364039). *Location:* signposted from the A26 between Hadlow and Tonbridge. Parkland, very wooded. 18 holes, 5569 yards. S.S.S. 67. 9 hole course, practice ground. *Green Fees:* information not available. *Eating facilities:* restaurant, bar, snack bar. *Visitors:* welcome every day. *Society Meetings:* welcome by booking only (01732 366180). Squash court. Professional: Bill Hodkin (01732 364039).

TUNBRIDGE WELLS. **Lamberhurst Golf Club,** Church Road, Lamberhurst TN3 8DT (01892 890241; Fax: 01892 891140). *Location:* A21 from Tunbridge Wells to Hastings, take 3rd exit on roundabout towards Lamberhurst village, turn left prior to descending hill to Lamberhurst and golf club is on the right. Attractive parkland course. 18 holes, 6423 yards. S.S.S. 71. Small practice ground. *Green Fees:* available from website. *Eating facilities:* full catering by arrangement. *Visitors:* welcome after 8am weekdays, 12 noon weekends and Bank Holidays. Handicap Certificate required. *Society Meetings:* catered for Tuesdays, Wednesdays and Thursdays by arrangement. Professional: Brian Impett (01892 890552). Secretary: Mrs S. Deadman (01892 890591; Fax: 01892 891140).
e-mail: secretary@lamberhurstgolfclub.com
website: www.lamberhurstgolfclub.com

TUNBRIDGE WELLS. **Nevill Golf Club,** Benhall Mill Road, Tunbridge Wells TN2 5JW (01892 527820; Fax: 01892 517861). *Location:* off Forest Road, south of Tunbridge Wells. Parkland course with trees. 18 holes, 6349 yards. S.S.S. 70. Practice ground. *Green Fees:* weekdays £35.00 per round, £60.00 per day; weekends and Bank Holidays £50.00. *Eating facilities:* lunches at club by prior arrangement. *Visitors:* welcome with 48 hours notice. Handicap Certificate required. Trolley hire. *Society Meetings:* welcome with previous booking. Professional: Paul Huggett (01892 532941). Secretary: Mr F. Prescott (01892 525818; Fax: 01892 517861).
e-mail: manager@nevillgolfclub.co.uk
website: www.nevillgolfclub.co.uk

www.uk-golfguide.com

TUNBRIDGE WELLS. **Tunbridge Wells Golf Club,** Langton Road, Tunbridge Wells TN4 8XH (01892 523034). *Location:* adjoining Spa Hotel on A264. Parkland. 9 holes, 4725 yards. S.S.S. 62. *Green Fees:* information not available. *Eating facilities:* menu choices available daily but best to check requirements in advance. *Visitors:* welcome anytime subject to availability. *Society Meetings:* welcome, contact the Secretary for details. Secretary: Ray Akerman (01892 536918).

WESTERHAM. **Westerham Golf Club,** Valence Park, Brasted Road, Westerham TN16 1LJ (01959 567100; Fax: 01959 567101). *Location*: midway between Westerham and Brasted on the A25. Mainly wooded with some parkland. 18 holes, 6270 yards. S.S.S. 72. Driving range and short game area. *Green Fees*: Monday to Thursday £34.00 per round, £50.00 per day; Friday £37.00 per round, £55.00 per day; weekends and Bank Holidays £40.00 after 12 noon; £25.00 after 3pm. *Eating facilities*: bar and catering facilities available. *Visitors*: welcome weekdays and weekends (at restricted times). Buggies and carts available for hire. *Society Meetings*: welcome weekdays only. Professional: James Marshall. General Manager: Rob Sturgeon.
e-mail:tom.terry@westerhamgc.co.uk
website: www. westerhamgc.co.uk

WESTGATE ON SEA. **Westgate and Birchington Golf Club,** 176 Canterbury Road, Westgate on Sea CT8 8LT. *Location:* seaside course between Westgate on Sea and Birchington (A28). Seaside links course. 18 holes, 4926 yards, 4547 metres. S.S.S. 64. *Green Fees:* weekdays £17.00, weekends and Bank Holidays £20.00 (includes £1.00 compulsory insurance). *Eating facilities:* available by prior arrangement with Steward. *Visitors:* welcome after 10am. *Society Meetings:* by arrangement with Secretary. Professional: R. Game (01843 831115). Secretary: T.J. Sharp (01843 831115).

WEST MALLING. **King's Hill Golf Club,** Discovery Drive, King's Hill, West Malling ME19 4AG (01732 875040; Fax: 01732 875019). *Location*: Junction 4 of M20. Heathland course. 18 holes, 6622 yards. S.S.S. 72. *Green Fees*: information not provided. *Eating facilities*: restaurant and bar open all day. *Visitors*: welcome Monday to Friday. Tuition available. *Society Meetings*: welcome Monday to Friday. Professional: David Hudspith (01732 842121). Secretary: Margaret Gilbert (01732 875040; Fax: 01732 875019).
e-mail: khatkhgolf@aol.com
website: www.kingshillgolf.co.uk

WHITSTABLE. **Chestfield (Whitstable) Golf Club,** 103 Chestfield Road, Chestfield, Whitstable CT5 3LU (01227 794411). *Location:* half a mile south of Old Thanet Way (A2990). Parkland with sea views. 18 holes, 6208 yards. S.S.S. 70. *Green Fees:* £36.00 midweek, £40.00 weekends. *Eating facilities:* lunchtime snacks, bar 11am to 11pm. Halfway House open for hot/cold snacks 7 days a week. *Visitors:* welcome. *Society Meetings:* welcome and catered for weekdays. Professional: John Brotherton (01227 793563).
e-mail: secretary@chestfield-golfclub.co.uk
website: www.chestfield-golfclub.co.uk

WHITSTABLE. **Whitstable and Seasalter Golf Club,** Collingwood Road, Whitstable CT5 1EB (01227 272020). *Location:* course adjoins town centre, take Nelson Road turning off main street. Flat seaside links. 9 holes, 5357 yards. S.S.S. 65. Practice net. *Green Fees:* information not available. *Eating facilities:* bar snacks. Secretary: M.D. Moore.*

THE APPEARANCE OF AN ASTERISK (*) AT THE END OF A CLUB OR COURSE ENTRY INDICATES THAT UP-TO-DATE INFORMATION HAS NOT BEEN SUPPLIED

Pedham Place Golf Cente, Swanley

Oxfordshire

ABINGDON. **Frilford Heath Golf Club,** Abingdon OX13 5NW (01865 390864; Fax: 01865 390823). *Location:* on A338 Oxford/Wantage Road seven miles south-west of Oxford, four miles west of Abingdon. Flat, wooded heathland. Red course: 18 holes, 6617 yards yellow tees, 6884 white tees. S.S.S. 71/73; Green course: 18 holes, 5763 yards yellow tees, 6006 white tees. S.S.S. 69; Blue course: 18 holes, 6379 yards yellow tees, 6728 white tees. S.S.S 71/72. Three practice areas. *Green Fees:* weekdays £65.00; weekends and Bank Holidays £80.00. *Eating facilities:* first class restaurant and bars. *Visitors:* welcome weekdays with Handicap Certificate, phone ahead for weekends and Bank Holidays. *Society Meetings:* welcome weekdays, enquire at office. Professional: D.C. Craik (01865 390887). Secretary/Manager: S. Styles (01865 390864). e-mail: reservations@frilfordheath.co.uk

BANBURY. **Banbury Golf Club,** Aynho Road, Adderbury, Banbury OX17 3NT (01295 810419; Fax: 01295 810056). *Location:* 6 miles south of Banbury on B4100. M40 junction 10 or 11. Undulating wooded course with water features. Three 9 hole courses, can be played in various combinations. Red & Yellow Course, 18 holes, 6553 yards, S.S.S. 71. Yellow & Blue Course, 6599 yards, S.S.S. 71. Red & Blue course, 6706 yards, S.S.S. 72. *Green Fees:* £23.00 weekdays, £29.00 weekends and Bank Holidays. *Eating facilities:* bar menu and three-course meals available. *Visitors:* welcome at all times. Tuition available. *Society Meetings:* welcome at all times. Professional: (01295 812880; Fax: 01295 810056). Secretary: B. Fowler. e-mail: office@banburygolfclub.co.uk website: www.banburygolfclub.co.uk

BANBURY. **Cherwell Edge Golf Club,** c/o Cherwell Edge Course, Chacombe, Banbury OX17 2EN (01295 711591). *Location:* half-a-mile off M40 at Banbury. Parkland. 18 holes, 6085 yards. S.S.S. 69 men, 69 ladies. Practice area. *Green Fees:* information on request. *Eating facilities:* restaurant and bar. *Visitors:* welcome, some time restrictions. *Society Meetings:* welcome, some time restrictions. Professional: Jason Newman (01295 711591). Manager: David Newman (01295 711591). e-mail: enquiries@cherwelledgegolfclub.co.uk website: www.cherwelledgegolfclub.co.uk

BANBURY. **Rye Hill Golf Club,** Milcombe, Banbury OX15 4RU (01295 721818; Fax: 01295 720089). *Location:* six miles from Junction 11 M40 at Banbury, turn off A361 and follow signs through to Milcombe. Naturally free draining course. 18 holes, 6919 yards. S.S.S 73. Practice ground and Junior Trigolf Course. *Green Fees:* weekdays £25.00, weekends £32.00 (subject to review for 2008). 9-hole and 5-hole rates. *Eating facilities:* spike bar and restaurant, conference venue for up to 300. *Visitors:* welcome, no restrictions. Booking advisable at weekends. Trolleys can always be used. *Society Meetings:* welcome; various packages available. Professional: T. Pennock. website: www.ryehill.co.uk

BANBURY. **Tadmarton Heath Golf Club,** Wigginton, Banbury OX15 5HL (01608 737278; Fax: 01608 730548). *Location:* off M40 Junction 11, off A422, off B4035, five miles west of Banbury. Flat links; heathland. 18 holes, 5936 yards. S.S.S. 69. Practice area. *Green Fees:* weekdays £45.00; weekends £25.00 with a member only. *Eating facilities:* full catering and bars. *Visitors:* welcome weekdays (restrictions Thursdays); weekends with member only. Must be member of another golf club with Handicap Certificate. Hand carts available. *Society Meetings:* welcome weekdays by prior arrangement. Professional: Tom Jones (01608 730047). Secretary: J. R. Cox (01608 737278; Fax: 01608 730548). e-mail: thgc@btinternet.com website: www.thgc.btinternet.co.uk

BICESTER. **Bicester Golf & Country Club,** Chesterton, Near Bicester OX6 8TE (01869 241204). *Location:* five minutes from Junction 9 M40, one mile off A421, Bicester/Oxford. Two miles south-west of Bicester. Flat parkland course. 18 holes, 6013 yards. S.S.S. 70. Practice ground and putting green. *Green Fees:* information not available. *Eating facilities:* restaurant and bar meals available daily. *Visitors:* welcome at all times, telephone bookings up to four days ahead. *Society Meetings:* welcome by prior arrangement. Manager: Paul Fox (01869 241204).*

BURFORD. **Burford Golf Club,** Burford OX18 4JG (01993 822149). *Location:* A40 - Burford roundabout. Flat parkland with superb greens. 18 holes, 6401 yards. S.S.S. 71. *Green Fees:* £40.00 per day weekdays. *Eating facilities:* full catering. *Visitors:* welcome weekdays and weekends by arrangement with the Secretary. *Society Meetings:* catered for on application. Professional: Michael Ridge (01993 822344). Secretary: Robin Thompson (01993 822583; Fax: 01993 822801).

CHIPPING NORTON. **Chipping Norton Golf Club,** Southcombe, Chipping Norton OX7 5QH (01608 642383; Fax: 01608 645422). *Location:* Junction of A3400 and A44, 18 miles from Oxford, 20 miles from Stratford-on-Avon. Downland with lakes and trees and four Par 3s. 18 holes, 6316 yards, 5830 metres. S.S.S. 70. Practice ground and putting green. *Green Fees:* £32.00 per day. *Eating facilities:* diningroom and bars – new clubhouse. *Visitors:* welcome Monday to Friday but not Bank Holidays. *Society Meetings:* welcome Mondays to Fridays by arrangement. Professional: Neil Rowlands (01608 643356; Fax: 01608 645422). Secretary/Manager: Neil Clayton (01608 642383; Fax: 01608 645422). website: www.chippingnortongolfclub.com

CHIPPING NORTON. **The Wychwood Golf Club,** Lyneham, Chipping Norton OX7 6QQ (01993 831841; Fax: 01993 831775). *Location:* six miles from Burford off the A361 Burford to Chipping Norton Road. Parkland, several interesting water holes. 18 holes, 6844 yards, 6099 metres. S.S.S. 72. Practice range (15 bays). *Green*

Fees: £25.00 weekdays; £30.00 weekends. *Eating facilities:* bar, dining room, lounge. *Visitors:* always welcome, can book start time three days in advance. *Society Meetings:* welcome, various packages available, assistance available for starting, score cards, notice board, etc. Licensed for Civil Ceremonies and available for private parties and receptions. Professional: David Griffin. Hon. Secretary: Cyril Howkins. General Managers: Susan Lakin/Phil Garner

DIDCOT. **Hadden Hill Golf Club,** Wallingford Road, Didcot OX11 9BJ (01235 510410). *Location:* on A4130, half-a-mile east of Didcot on the Wallingford road. Well drained parkland with superb greens - never closed for rain! 18 holes, 6563 yards. S.S.S. 71. 20-bay floodlit driving range. *Green Fees:* Information not available. *Eating facilities:* good food all day, every day. *Visitors:* telephone bookings for tee times. *Society Meetings:* very welcome weekdays only. Professional: Ian Mitchell (01235 510410). Secretary: Adrian Smith (01235 510410; Fax: 01235 511260).*
website: www.haddenhillgolf.co.uk

DRAYTON. **Drayton Park Golf Course,** Steventon Road, Drayton, near Abingdon OX14 4LA (01235 528989; Fax: 01235 525731). *Location:* A34 Didcot turn off, through Steventon to Drayton (south of Oxford). 18 hole Par 70 golf course, 9 hole Par 3 course. Driving range. Tuition from PGA qualified professionals. *Green Fees:* weekdays £20.00; weekends £26.00. *Eating facilities:* full catering and bar facilities. Clubhouse open to visitors. *Visitors:* welcome. Clubhouse available for conferences and weddings; large function room. *Society Meetings:* welcome. Professional: M. Morbey (01235 550607). Secretary: I. Rhead (01235 528989).
e-mail: draytonpark@btclick.com.

FARINGDON. **Carswell Golf and Country Club,** Carswell Home Farm, Carswell, Faringdon SN7 8PU (01367 870422). *Location:* just off A420 between Oxford and Swindon, near Faringdon. Parkland course with many trees and water hazards. 18 holes, 6200 yards. S.S.S. 72. 19-bay floodlit driving range, practice area with putting green. *Green Fees:* weekdays £20.00, weekends £28.00. Twilight fees available, telephone for more details and prices. *Eating facilities:* clubhouse bar serving varied menu. *Visitors:* welcome, soft spikes preferred. Golf shop; club, cart and buggy hire. Clubhouse accommodation

- four en suite rooms. *Society Meetings:* all welcome weekdays, please telephone for information on packages. Health Club on site, call for details. Secretary: Sarah Sample (01367 870422).
e-mail: info@carswellgolfandcountryclub.co.uk
website: www.carswellgolfandcountryclub.co.uk

HENLEY-ON-THAMES. **Badgemore Park Golf Club,** Badgemore, Henley-on-Thames RG9 4NR (01491 637300). *Location:* one mile from Henley town centre on road to Rotherfield Greys. Mature parkland course. 18 holes, 6129 yards. S.S.S. 69. Chipping green, two putting greens, practice net, bunker practice. *Green Fees:* information not available. *Visitors:* always welcome, weekends during summer after 12 noon, winter after 11am. Professional lessons available. Large car park. *Society Meetings:* welcome Wednesdays, Thursdays, Fridays. Professional: Jonathan Dunn (01491 574175). Secretary: Mr J. Connell (01491 637300; Fax: 01491 576899). *

HENLEY-ON-THAMES. **Henley Golf Club,** Harpsden, Henley-on-Thames RG9 4HG (01491 575781). Centenary Year 2007. *Location:* from centre of Henley-Reading, one mile from Harpsden Way to clubhouse. Parkland with many trees. 18 holes, 6264 yards. S.S.S. 70. *Green Fees:* weekdays £45.00; weekends with member only £20.00. *Eating facilities:* bar snacks at all times, meals by arrangement. *Visitors:* welcome weekdays, weekends and Bank Holidays with a member only. Handicap Certificate required. *Society Meetings:* catered for Wednesdays and Thursdays. Professional: Mark Howell (01491 575710). Manager: Gary Oatham (01491 575742; Fax: 01491 412179).
e-mail: manager@henleygc.com
website: www.henleygc.com

HENLEY-ON-THAMES. **Huntercombe Golf Club,** Nuffield, Henley-on-Thames RG9 5SL (01491 641207). *Location:* A4130, six miles west of Henley-on-Thames. Downland wooded course. 18 holes, 6271 yards. S.S.S. 70. Practice ground. *Green Fees:* information not available. *Eating facilities:* catering and bar facilities. *Visitors:* welcome by prior arrangement only. *Society Meetings:* Tuesdays and Thursdays by arrangement. Professional: Ian Roberts (01491 641241). Secretary: Ken McCrea (Fax: 01491 642060).
e-mail: office@huntercombegolfclub.co.uk
website: www.huntercombegolfclub.co.uk

HORTON-CUM-STUDLEY. **Studley Wood Golf Club,** The Straight Mile, Horton cum Studley, Oxford OX33 1BF (01865 351144; Fax: 01865 351166). *Location*: 4 miles east of Oxford. Gently undulating mature woodland course. 18 holes, 6722 yards, S.S.S. 72. 15 bay covered driving range, Callaway Custom Fit Centre, short game academy. *Green Fees*: weekdays £43.50; weekends £52.50 after midday only. *Eating facilities*: function room, restaurant and bar. *Visitors*: welcome at all times weekdays, afternoons only at weekends, must play to Handicap standard. Tee time bookings taken four days in advance. Buggies available. *Society Meetings*: welcome any time Mondays to Thursdays, and Friday mornings. Packages from £30.00 per person. Professional: Tony Williams (01865 351122). Secretary: Annie Anderson.
e-mail: admin@swgc.co.uk
website: www.studleywoodgolf.co.uk

KIRTLINGTON. **Kirtlington Golf Club,** Lince Lane, Kirtlington OX5 3JY (01869 351133; Fax: 01869 351143). *Location*: A4095, Witney/Bicester, half a mile outside Kirtlington. Undulating, dry, open parkland course with well contoured greens. 18 holes, 6107 yards. S.S.S. 69. Covered and grassed driving range, pitching/putting. Academy 9-hole course and new fully equipped clubhouse. Conference/corporate days available. *Green Fees:* weekdays £25.00; weekends £30.00. Special rates on application. *Eating facilities:* available. *Visitors:* very welcome. *Society Meetings:* welcome. Secretary: Pamela Smith.
e-mail: info@kirtlingtongolfclub.com
website: www.kirtlingtongolfclub.com

MAPLEDURHAM. **The Club at Mapledurham,** Chazey Heath, Mapledurham, Reading RG4 7UD (01189 463353; Fax: 01189 463363). *Location:* leave Reading on A4074 towards Mapledurham, Woodcote and Wallingford, club is on the right immediately after leaving built up area. Parkland. 18 holes, 5700 yards. Par 69. Academy area. *Green Fees:* Information not available. *Eating facilities:* bar/lounge, food available. *Visitors:* welcome, no restrictions. Facilities include fully equipped gym, sauna, steam room, spa and swimming pool. *Society Meetings:* welcome. Professional: Tim Gilpin. Manager: Rob Davies.*

OXFORD. **Hinksey Heights Golf Course,** South Hinksey OX1 5AB (01865 327775; Fax: 01865 736930). Location On the Southern bypass, 4km west of Oxford. Undulating course. 18 holes, 6936 yards, 6342 metres. S.S.S. 73, 9 hole course. Driving range; outdoor practice areas. 9 hole par 3 course. *Green Fees:* information not available. *Eating facilities:* Spike Bar, bar and restaurant. *Visitors:* welcome including weekends. Contact General Manager or Professional. *Society Meetings and Company Days:* welcome including weekends with forward booking. Contact General Manager or Professional. Professional: Dean Davis. Club Secretary: K. McCallum.*
e-mail: play@oxford-golf.co.uk
website: www.oxford-golf.co.uk

OXFORD. **North Oxford Golf Club,** Banbury Road, Oxford OX2 8EZ (01865 554415; Fax: 01865 515921). *Location:* just north of Oxford on the Banbury Road to Kidlington. Flat parkland course with tree-lined fairways - six Par 3 holes. 18 holes, 5689 yards, S.S.S. 67. Indoor driving bay in Pro shop. *Green Fees:* £33.00 per day, £28.00 per round weekdays; £42.00 per day, £33.00 per round weekends. Twilight £16.00 midweek after 5pm and £20.00 weekends after 4pm. *Eating facilities:* dining room, lounge and stud bar. *Visitors:* welcome weekdays and after 12 noon weekends and Bank Holidays. *Society Meetings:* welcome, details on request. Professional: R.J. Harris (01865 553977). Manager: C.Smith (01865 554924; Fax: 0845 2805262).
e-mail: adminmanager@nogc.co.uk
website: www.nogc.co.uk

OXFORD. **Southfield Golf Club,** (home of Oxford City Golf Club, Oxford Ladies Golf Club, Oxford University Golf Club), Hill Top Road, Oxford OX4 1PF. *Location:* one mile from BMW Works, along Cowley Road, turn right into Southfield Road, then right at end of road. Hilly parkland. 18 holes, 6328 yards. S.S.S. 70. Practice ground available. *Green Fees:* £40.00 per day. *Eating facilities:* restaurant facilities available, bar open seven days. *Visitors:* welcome. *Society Meetings:* welcome by arrangement (not weekends or Bank Holidays). Professional: Tony Rees (01865 244258). Admin. Secretary: Michael Blight (01865 242158).

OXFORD. **Waterstock Golf Club & Driving Range,** Thame Road, Waterstock, Oxford OX33 1HT (01844 338093; Fax: 01844 338036). *Location:* on Junction 8 and 8A, M40, at the Wheatley Service Station, five minutes from Thame and Oxford, 30 minutes from London and Birmingham. Rolling parkland with 15,500 trees. 18 holes, 6535 yards, Par 72, S.S.S 71. Practice bunkers and putting facilities, 22 bay driving range. *Green Fees:* 9 holes weekdays £12.50, weekends £15.00; 18 holes weekdays £23.00, weekends £28.00; twilight weekdays £16.50, weekends £19.00; per day £40.50 weekdays, £48.00 weekends. *Eating facilities:* full bar and restaurant. *Visitors:* no restrictions, welcome at all times. Changing rooms. *Society Meetings:* fully catered for, packages available on request. Head Professional: Paul Bryant. Secretary: Andrew Wyatt.
e-mail: wgc_oxfordgolf@btinternet.com
website: www.waterstockgolf.co.uk

OXON/BUCKINGHAMSHIRE. **Magnolia Park Golf & Country Club,** Arncott Road, Boarstall, Bucks HP18 9XX (01844 239700). *Location:* B4011 south from Bicester or north from Thame; two miles north of Oakley turn to Boarstall. Parkland and landscaped terrain with seven lakes. 18 holes. Par 72. Excellent practice facilities. *Green Fees:* weekdays £40.00, weekends £50.00. *Eating facilities:* Bar and dining 8am to 8pm (to 6pm during winter), function room available. *Society Meetings:* societies and corporate days welcome. Professional: Dusan Gavrilovic. General Manager: (01844 239700; Fax: 01844 238991) e-mail: info@magnoliapark.co.uk
website: www.magnoliapark.co.uk

THAME. **The Oxfordshire Golf Club,** Rycote Lane, Milton Common, Thame OX9 2PU (01844 278300; Fax: 01844 278003). *Location:* from south Junction 7 M40, A329 to Thame. From north Junction 8 M40, A418 to Thame then A329. A combination of mounded fairways and lakes offers American-style target golf. 18 holes, 6856 yards. S.S.S. 74. 28-bay driving range, practice area. *Green Fees:* on application. *Eating facilities:* spike bar, Lakes Lounge and Oaks Restaurant offering light snacks to

Continental and Japanese cuisine. Private rooms available for conferences, weddings and private dining. Luxurious changing facilities with Japanese ofuro baths. *Visitors:* welcome subject to availability, call reservations 01844 278300. Electric trolleys, pull trolleys and caddies (reserved in advance) available from well stocked Pro shop. *Society Meetings:* on application. PGA Professional: Stephen Gibson (01844 278505).
e-mail: info@theoxfordshiregolfclub.com
website: theoxfordshiregolfclub.com

WALLINGFORD. **The Springs Hotel and Golf Club,** Wallingford Road, North Stoke, Wallingford OX10 6BE (01491 836687; Fax: 01491 836877). *Location:* two miles south-west of Wallingford on the B4009. M40 Junction 6. 18 holes, 6470 yards. par 72. *Green Fees:* weekdays £29.00, weekends £35.00. *Eating facilities:* restaurant and clubhouse. *Visitors:* by arrangement. Professional: David Boyce (01491 827310; Fax: 01491 827312).
e-mail: info@thespringshotel.com
    proshop@thespringshotel.com
website: www.thespringshotel.com

WITNEY. **Witney Lakes Golf Club,** Witney Lakes Resort, Downs Road, Witney OX29 0SY (01993 893011; Fax: 01993 778866). *Location:* two miles west of Witney town centre, turn into Downs Road. From B4095. Parkland with five large lakes. 18 holes, 6500 yards. S.S.S. 71. 22-bay floodlit covered driving range, practice area. *Green Fees:* £20.00 midweek, £28.00 weekends. *Eating facilities:* Greens Sports Bar and Greens Restaurant. *Visitors:* no restrictions. Rawles - Hairdressers. Retreat Spa and Beauty Salon. Function/conference room; health and fitness club includes swimming pool, gymnasium and sauna. 86 bedroom hotel opening March 2008. Large well-stocked golf shop, two teaching Professionals. *Society Meetings:* all welcome. Professional: (01993 893011; Fax: 01993 778866). Secretary (01993 893005; Fax: 01993 778866).
e-mail: golf@witney-lakes.co.uk
website:www.witney-lakes.co.uk

Surrey

BAGSHOT. **Pennyhill Park Hotel and Country Club,** London Road, Bagshot GU19 5EU (01276 471774; Fax: 01276 473217). *Location*: just off A30 at Bagshot. Wooded, hilly course. 9 holes, 2000 yards. S.S.S. 64. *Green Fees*: information not available. *Eating facilities*: Ascot Bar, St James Brasserie restaurant, Latymer à la carte restaurant, five star hotel with 123 luxury bedrooms; tennis court, outdoor heated swimming pool, clay pigeon shooting, gym etc. *Visitors*: prior booking must be made in advance. *Society Meetings*: welcome anytime. Country Club Manager: Claire Williams.*

BAGSHOT. **Windlesham Golf Club,** Grove End, Bagshot GU19 5HY. *Location:* A30 west from Sunningdale at Junction of A30 and A332 or Junction 3 from M3 and take the A322 to Bracknell then junction of A30/A332. Challenging parkland course designed by Tommy Horton - USPGA, greens and tees of highest specification. 18 holes, 6650 yards. S.S.S. 72. Practice range with three covered bays, practice green. *Green Fees:* call for details. *Visitors:* welcome, please ring first on weekdays, weekends, Bank Holidays after 12 noon. Teaching Academy School; carts available. Professional Lee Mucklow (01276 472323). Secretary: Richard Griffiths (01276 452220; Fax: 01276 452290). website: www.windleshamgolf.com

BANSTEAD. **Cuddington (Banstead) Golf Club Ltd,** Banstead Road, Banstead SM7 1RD (020 8393 0952; Fax: 020 8786 7025). *Location*: 200 yards from Banstead Railway Station. 18 holes, 6614 yards. S.S.S. 71. *Green Fees*: information not available. *Visitors*: welcome with reservation. *Society Meetings*: catered for on Thursdays and some Tuesdays pm. Professional: M. Warner. Secretary: S. P. Davis. e-mail:secretary@cuddingtongc.co.uk website: www.cuddingtongc.co.uk

BLETCHINGLEY. **Bletchingley Golf Club,** Church Lane, Bletchingley RH1 4LP (01883 744666; Fax: 01883 744284). *Location:* off A25, three miles west from Junction 6 M25. Parkland course, sand based. 18 holes, 6513 yards. S.S.S. 71. Practice ground. *Green Fees:*weekdays £35.00, weekends £48.00. *Eating facilities:* lounge/dining room, large function room, bar. *Visitors:* welcome. Carts available. *Society Meetings:* welcome. Professional: A. Dyer (01883 744848; Fax; 01883 744284). Manager: M. Hazelden (01883 744666; Fax: 01883 744284).* website: www.bletchingleygolf.co.uk

For full details of clubs and courses, plus convenient accommodation

www.uk-golfguide.com

CAMBERLEY. **Camberley Heath Golf Club**, Golf Drive, Portsmouth Road, Camberley GU15 1JG (01276 23258; Fax: 01276 692505). *Location*: south of the M3 on the A325 Portsmouth Road, near Frimley. Heathland and pine, designed by Harry Colt - his best, established 1913. 18 holes, 6326 yards, 5780 metres. S.S.S. 71. Practice ground. *Green Fees*: £60.00. *Eating facilities:* restaurants and Teppan Yaki (Japanese Steak Bar). *Visitors*: welcome weekdays only by prior arrangement. *Society Meetings*: welcome by prior arrangement weekdays only; various packages available. Professional: Glenn Ralph (01276 27905). Managing Director/Secretary: C.M. Kennedy (01276 23258). e-mail: info@camberleyheathgolfclub.co.uk website: www.camberleyheathgolfclub.co.uk

CARSHALTON. **Oaks Sports Centre Ltd,** Woodmansterne Road, Carshalton SM5 4AN (020 8643 8363; Fax: 020 8770 7303). *Location:* on the B2032 past Carshalton Beeches Station, Oaks Sports Centre signposted north of A2022, half way between A217 and A237. Open 6am, 7 days, 364 days per year. Meadowland course. 18 holes, 6054 yards. S.S.S 69. 9 holes, 1497 yards. S.S.S 28. 18 bay golf range. *Green Fees:* information not available. *Eating facilities*: bar lounge and cafeteria. *Visitors:* public course, everyone welcome. *Society Meetings:* by arrangement. Professionals: Mr M. Pilkington. Mr C. Mitchell. Secretary: Mr D.J. Capper. e-mail: golf@oaks.sagehost.co.uk website: www.oakssportscentre.co.uk

CATERHAM. **Surrey National Golf Club,** Rook Lane, Chaldon, Caterham CR3 5AA (01883 344555). *Location*: M25, Junction 7 (M23) towards Croydon. After two miles turn right into Dean Lane and then left into Rook Lane, entrance on the left. Mature landscape with stunning views of South Downs. 18 holes. 6850 yards. Par 72. *Green Fees*: call club. *Eating facilities*: bar and catering facilities available. *Visitors*: welcome weekdays at anytime and weekends after 11am. Buggies and carts available for hire. *Society Meetings*: welcome weekdays at anytime and weekends at restricted times. Professional: Matthew Stock. General Manager: Simon Hodsdon. e-mail: caroline@surreynational.co.uk website: www.surreynational.co.uk

CATERHAM near. **Woldingham Golf Club,** Halliloo Valley Road, Woldingham, near Caterham CR3 7HA (01883 653501; Fax: 01883 653502). *Location:* Caterham, Junction 6 M25, 3 miles. Downland course. 18 holes. 6393 yards. S.S.S. 71. Putting greens, practice ground. *Green Fees:* £30.00 per round, £15.00 juniors; £40.00 per day. *Eating facilities:* Function suite, Spike bar. *Visitors:* welcome after 10.30am at weekends. *Society Meetings:* welcome Monday to Sunday (after 10.30am on weekends). Buggy hire (18 holes) £24.00. "ASTAR" video studio on site. Professional: Ian Hayward (01883 653501). website: www.woldingham-golfclub.co.uk

CHERTSEY. **Barrow Hills Golf Club,** Longcross, Chertsey KT16 0DS (01344 635770). *Location:* four miles west of Chertsey, adjacent to M3 at Longcross. 18 holes, 3090 yards. S.S.S. 53. *Green Fees:* information not provided. *Visitors:* only with a member. Secretary: R. Hammond (01483 234807 home).

CHERTSEY. **Laleham Golf Club,** Laleham Reach, Mixnams Lane, Chertsey KT16 8RP (01932 562188; Fax: 01932 564448). *Location:* M25 to Junction 11, follow directions to Thorpe Park, entrance opposite roundabout. Flat but interesting parkland course with water features. 18 holes, 6291 yards. S.S.S. 70. *Green Fees:* weekdays £35.00 per day, £30.00 per round; weekends £32.00 per round. *Eating facilities:* full restaurant and bar facilities. *Visitors:* welcome weekdays; weekends after 2pm in summer and 12.30pm in winter. Please phone to ensure no tee reservations. *Society Meetings:* catered for at competitive rates. Professional: Hogan Stott (01932 562877). Club Manager: Ross McCue (01932 564211; Fax: 01932 564448).
e-mail: manager@laleham-golf.co.uk
website: www.laleham-golf.co.uk

CHESSINGTON. **Chessington Golf Centre,** Garrison Lane, Chessington KT9 2LW (020 8391 0948). *Location:* off A243, 500 yards from Chessington World of Adventure. Opposite Chessington South Station, Junction 9 M25. Parkland course. 9 holes, 1679 yards. S.S.S. 28. Covered floodlit driving range. *Green Fees:* weekdays £9.00, weekends £11.00. *Eating facilities:* bar, coffee, catering available. *Visitors:* welcome. Facilities open to public 8.00am until 10.00pm (8.00pm Saturday and Sunday). *Society Meetings:* welcome. Professional: Mark Janes (020 8391 0948; Fax: 020 8397 2068). Secretary: Martin Bedford (020 8391 0948; Fax: 020 8397 2068).

CHESSINGTON. **Surbiton Golf Club,** Woodstock Lane, Chessington KT9 1UG (020 8398 3101; Fax: 020 8339 0992). *Location:* two miles east of Esher, off A3 at Ace of Spades roundabout. Undulating parkland. 18 holes, 6055 yards. S.S.S. 69, Par 70. Practice area. *Green Fees:* information not available. *Eating facilities:* snacks and lunches to order by reservation weekdays. *Visitors:* at weekends play with member only. *Society Meetings:* catered for Monday and Friday only. Professional: Paul Milton (020 8398 6619). Secretary: Chris Cornish (020 8398 3101).*
e-mail: surbitongolfclub@hotmail.com

CHIDDINGFOLD. **Chiddingfold Golf Club,** Petworth Road, Chiddingfold GU8 4SL (01428 685888). *Location:* Exit 10 off M25, A3 towards Portsmouth, take A283 turn off, golf course quarter-of-a-mile past Chiddingfold village. Parkland. 18 holes, 5500 yards. Par 70 S.S.S. 67. *Green Fees:* information not available. *Visitors:* welcome seven days, including Bank Holidays. *Society Meetings:* welcome seven days, including Bank Holidays. Professionals: Jon Wells. Manager/Secretary: Moreno Pascolini.*
e-mail: chiddingfoldgolf@btconnect.com
website: www.chiddingfoldgc.co.uk

CHIPSTEAD. **Chipstead Golf Club Ltd,** How Lane, Coulsdon CR5 3LN (01737 555881; Fax: 01737 555404). *Location:* by Chipstead Station (Chipstead Valley Road). Parkland. 18 holes, 5504 yards, 5332 metres. S.S.S. 67. *Green Fees:* information not provided. *Eating facilities:* full catering 7 days a week, bar. *Visitors:* welcome weekdays except Tuesday mornings. *Society Meetings:* welcome full or half days. Director of Golf: Gary Torbett (01737 554939).

COBHAM. **Silvermere Golf and Leisure Complex,** Redhill Road, Cobham KT11 1EF (01932 584300). *Location:* half a mile from Junction 10 of M25 at A3. Wooded, parkland course with water on two holes. 34 bay driving range. *Green Fees:* £20.00-£24.00 midweek, £37.50 weekend. *Eating facilities:* half-million pound new lakeside clubhouse serving food all day from 7am to 9pm, bar meals, snacks and lunches. *Visitors:* welcome every day but not early weekend mornings. *Society Meetings:* welcome, contact Secretary for details. Professional: Doug McClelland PGA (01932 584348). Secretary: Pauline Devereux (01932 584306; Fax: 01932 584301).

COULSDON. **Coulsdon Manor Hotel and Golf Centre,** Coulsdon Court Road, Coulsdon CR5 2LL (020 8668 0414; Fax: 020 8668 0342). *Location:* off J7 of M25 through Coulsdon towards Caterham B2030 turning left via Stoneyfield Road and left in Coulsdon Court Road. Parkland. 18 holes, 6037 yards. Par 70. S.S.S. 68. *Green Fees:*Information not available. *Eating facilities:* Terrace Bar/Orangery and Manor House Restaurant. *Visitors:* welcome, subject to availability. *Society Meetings:* welcome Mondays, Tuesdays, Thursdays and Fridays. Extensive banquet and conference facilities, 35 luxurious bedrooms, all en suite. Professional: Matt Asbury (020 8660 6083; Fax: 020 8668 3118). General Manager: Tom Hindle.*

COULSDON. **Woodcote Park Golf Club,** Meadow Hill, Bridle Way, Coulsdon CR5 2QQ. *Location:* south of Croydon, off A237. Parkland course. 18 holes, 6720 yards. S.S.S. 72. *Green Fees:* £50.00 per round/day. *Eating facilities:* meals at all times. *Visitors:* welcome with reservation. *Society Meetings:* up to 90 catered for, by arrangement. Professional: Wraith Grant. Secretary: A. Dawson (020 8668 2788; Fax: 020 8660 0918).
e-mail: info@woodcotepgc.com
website: www.woodcotepgc.com

CRANLEIGH. **The Cranleigh Golf and Leisure Club,** Barhatch Lane, Cranleigh GU6 7NG (01483 268855; Fax: 01483 267251). *Location:* Guildford A281 Horsham take Cranleigh turn-off. Interesting parkland course. 18 holes, 5644 yards. S.S.S. 67. Covered driving range, practice ground. *Green Fees:* information not provided. *Eating facilities:* bar, bar snacks, banqueting facilities available. *Visitors:* welcome weekdays and weekends except Thursday before 11am. Weekends subject to availability. *Society Meetings:* welcome weekdays and weekends after 11.30am. Professional: Trevor Longmuir (01483 277188). Secretary: Mike Kateley (01483 268855; Fax: 01483 267251).

CRANLEIGH. **Wildwood Country Club,** Horsham Road, Alfold, Cranleigh GU6 8JE (01403 753255; Fax: 01403 752005). *Location:* 10 miles from Guildford on the A281 to Horsham, near Cranleigh. Only 40 minutes from London on the A3. Championship parkland course with mature woodland and water hazards. An exhilarating challenge to all golfers. 27 holes, 6655 yards. S.S.S. 72. All-weather practice range and 9 hole course. *Green Fees:* weekdays 18 holes £40.00, weekends 18 holes £60.00. Discounted rates in winter. *Eating facilities:* two bars/restaurant. *Visitors:* welcome. Gymnasium. *Society Meetings:* welcome, corporate days organised. Accommodation available locally. Director of Golf: Phil Harrison.

CRONDALL. **Bowenhurst Golf Centre Ltd,** Mill Lane, Crondall, Near Farnham GU10 5RP (01252 851695). *Location:* public golf course, south of M3, 5 miles from exit 5 Farnham side on A287 (behind garage). Parkland course with mature trees and lakes. 3658 yards S.S.S. 60. 20 bay floodlit driving range, two practice putting greens, practice bunker. *Green Fees:* information not available. *Visitors:* welcome at any time. Pro shop. *Society Meetings:* welcome, rates on application. Professional: Alaister Hardaway (01252 851344). Secretary: Geoffrey Corbey.

CRONDALL. **Oak Park Golfing Complex,** Heath Lane, Crondall, Near Farnham, Surrey GU10 5PB (01252 850880; Fax: 01252 850851). *Location:* one and a half miles off A287 Farnham-Odiham road, five miles from Junctions 4, 4a and 5 of M3 motorway. Gently undulating parkland course. Woodland Course - 18 holes, 6247 yards. S.S.S. 70; Village Course - 9 holes, 3279 yards. Par 36. 16 bay covered driving range, putting green, chipping green and practice bunker. *Green Fees:* information not available. *Eating facilities:* Restaurant: available for private hire and special occasions. Bar snacks available. V*isitors:* welcome; must book through Professional; reserved tee system at all times. *Society Meetings:* by arrangement. Professional: Paul Archer (01252 850066; Fax: 01252 850851). Manager: Mr. Robert Brewer (01252 850850).*

CROYDON. **Addington Court Golf Ltd,** Featherbed Lane, Addington, Croydon CR0 9AA (020 8657 0281; Fax: 020 8651 0282). *Location*: two miles east of Croydon. Leave B281 at Addington Village. Dry, well-drained, wooded parkland course. Four courses: Championship 5755 yards, S.S.S. 67. Falconwood 5513 yards, S.S.S. 67. Lower 9 hole course S.S.S 62. 18 hole, Par 3 course. 32-bay floodlit driving range. *Green Fees:* information not available. *Eating facilities:* restaurant, bar. *Visitors:* welcome anytime, no restrictions, public courses. *Society Meetings:* welcome. Professional: Tony Healy (020 8657 0281).*

CROYDON. **The Addington Golf Club,** 205 Shirley Church Road, Croydon CR0 5AB (020 8777 1055; Fax: 020 8777 6661). *Location:* Croydon, Surrey, 30 minutes from centre of London. Heath and woodland as set out by the famous J.F. Abercromby with the world renowned 13th Par 3. 18 holes, 6338 yards. S.S.S. 71. *Green Fees:* Prices on application. *Eating facilities:* bar and restaurant with full snack menu. *Visitors:* welcome, weekends restricted. *Society Meetings:* by prior arrangement. Assistant Manager: Oliver Peel. Secretary: Bob Hill (020 8777 1055). e-mail: info@addingtongolf.com website: www.addingtongolf.com

CROYDON. **Addington Palace Golf Club,** Gravel Hill, Addington, Croydon CR0 5BB (020 8654 3061). *Location:* two miles east of Croydon Station. Undulating parkland course. 18 holes, 6339 yards. S.S.S. 70. *Green Fees:* information not provided. *Eating facilities:* bar all day, catering 10am to 6.30pm. *Visitors:* welcome weekdays; at weekends and Bank Holidays must be accompanied by a member. Buggies available. *Society Meetings:* welcome on Mondays, Tuesdays, Wednesdays and Fridays. Professional: Roger Williams (020 8654 1786). Secretary: John Bowen. e-mail: johnb@addingtonpalacegolf.co.uk website: www.addingtonpalacegolf.co.uk

CROYDON. **Croham Hurst Golf Club,** Croham Road, South Croydon CR2 7HJ (020 8657 5581; Fax: 020 8657 3229). *Location:* midway between Croydon and Selsdon. Parkland. 18 holes, 6290 yards. S.S.S. 70. *Green Fees:* information not available. *Eating facilities:* lunches, teas, snacks. *Visitors:* welcome with reservation on weekdays. *Society Meetings:* catered for booked one year ahead. Director of Golf: David Green (020 8657 7705). Prefessional Shop: (020 8657 5581). e-mail: secretary@chgc.co.uk website: www.chgc.co.uk

CROYDON. **Selsdon Park Hotel & Golf Club,** Addington Road, Sanderstead, South Croydon CR2 8YA (020 8657 8811; Fax: 020 8651 6171). *Location:* three miles south of Croydon on A2022 Purley-West Wickham road. Parkland course, designed by J.H. Taylor. 18 holes, 6473 yards. S.S.S. 71. Practice ground. *Green Fees:* Information not available. *Eating facilities:* hotel bars, restaurant and grill. *Visitors:* welcome all week with pre-bookable tee-off times. Buggies. *Society Meetings:* welcome by prior arrangement. P.G.A. Professional: Gary Wallis (020 8657 4129) Ext 3116. Golf Office: (020 8657 8811) Ext. 3073. website: www.principal-hotels.com*

CROYDON. **Shirley Park Golf Club Ltd,** 194 Addiscombe Road, Croydon CR0 7LB (020 8654 1143; Fax: 020 8654 6733). *Location:* on A232 one and a half miles from East Croydon Station. Parkland. 18 holes, 6210 yards. S.S.S. 69. Practice area. *Green Fees:* £40.00 weekdays; Saturday with a member only. Winter rate £30.00. Subject to review. *Eating facilities:* seven day catering, two bars. *Visitors:* welcome weekdays and Sunday afternoons. Trolleys and buggies available. Reduced accommodation charges available from Croydon Park Hotel if booked through the Secretary. *Society Meetings:* welcome Mondays, Tuesdays, Thursdays and Fridays. Professional: Michael Taylor (020 8654 8767; Fax: 020 8654 6733). Secretary: Steve Murphy (020 8654 1143; Fax: 020 8654 6733).
e-mail: secretary@shirleyparkgolfclub.co.uk
website: www.shirleyparkgolfclub.co.uk

DORKING. **Betchworth Park Golf Club,** Reigate Road, Dorking RH4 1NZ (01306 882052). *Location:* on A25 one mile east of Dorking on Reigate Road. Established parkland course. 18 holes, 6307 yards, Par 69,. S.S.S 70. *Green Fees:* £40.00 Monday to Friday. *Eating facilities:* snacks available daily. *Visitors:* welcome, by arrangement. *Society Meetings:* welcome Mondays and Thursdays. Professional: A. Tocher (01306 884334). Manager: John Holton (01306 882052; Fax: 01306 877462).

DORKING. **Dorking Golf Club,** Deepdene Avenue, Dorking RH5 4BX (01306 886917). *Location:* on A24 half-a-mile south of junction with A25. Parkland/downland. 9 holes, alternative tees second 9, 5158 yards. S.S.S. 65. *Green Fees:* information not available. *Eating facilities:* full catering. *Visitors:* weekdays only without reservation. *Society Meetings:* catered for up to 48. Professional/Manager: A. Smeal.*

DORKING. **Gatton Manor,** Standon Lane, Ockley, Near Dorking RH5 5PQ (01306 627555; Fax: 01306 627713). *Location:* to the west of the village of Ockley on the A29 between Dorking and Horsham, easy access from M25 Junction 9. 18 hole championship length course in parkland, makes good use of the many rivers and lakes to make it a picturesque but challenging course. 18 holes, 6653 yards. S.S.S. 72. Additional practice facilities. *Green Fees:* information not available. *Eating facilities:* full à la carte restaurant and bar with bar meals. *Visitors:* a warm and friendly welcome anytime except Sunday mornings. Refurbished changing rooms.

Hotel with 18 bedrooms all en suite, conference suites and, gym. Fishing and tennis available. *Society Meetings:* welcome weekdays only. Ideal society/corporate day venue. 7 and 5 day memberships available. Golf bookings: (01306 627555). Secretary: Patrick Kiely (01306 627555; Fax: 01306 627713.* e-mail: golf@gattonmanor.co.uk*

EAST HORSLEY. **Drift Golf Club,** The Drift, East Horsley KT24 5HD (01483 284641). *Location:* the club is located just off the Drift Road which runs between Ockham Road (B2039) and Forest Road, East Horsley. Picturesque woodland course set in the heart of Surrey countryside. 18 holes, 6425 yards, 5877 metres. S.S.S. 72. Golf Academy, driving range and putting green. *Green Fees:* information not provided. *Eating facilities:* full bar, lounge, restaurant and bar snacks. *Visitors:* welcome Monday to Friday, and after midday at weekends. Bookings accepted up to seven days in advance. *Society Meetings:* catered for weekdays. (01483 284641).

EFFINGHAM. **Effingham Golf Club,** Guildford Road, Effingham KT24 5PZ (01372 452203; Fax: 01372 459959). *Location:* A246 between Guildford and Leatherhead. Downland course with magnificent views towards London. 18 holes, 6542 yards. S.S.S. 71. Large practice ground. *Green Fees:* information not available. *Eating facilities:* full bar and catering facilities. *Visitors:* welcome Monday-Friday. Handicap Certificate required. *Society Meetings:* welcome Wednesdays, Thursdays, Fridays. Professional: Steve Hoatson (01372 452606). Secretary: Robin Easton (01372 452203).

EPSOM. **Epsom Golf Club,** Longdown Lane South, Epsom KT17 4JR (01372 721666; Fax: 01372 817183). *Location:* off A240 into B288, 200 yards south of Epsom Downs Station. Downland, links-type course with fast, undulating greens. 18 holes, 5656 yards. S.S.S. 67. Par 69. Practice nets, putting green and chipping area. *Green Fees:* Information not available. *Eating facilities:* bar snacks available from two bars; dining room. *Visitors:* welcome anytime except am on Tuesday, Saturday and Sunday. *Society Meetings:* always welcome with similar exceptions to visitors. Professional and Tee Reservations: R. Goudie (01372 741867). e-mail: enquiries@epsomgolfclub.co.uk website: www.epsomgolfclub.co.uk*

EPSOM. **Horton Park Golf & Country Club,** Hook Road, Epsom KT19 8QG (020 8393 8400; Fax: 020 8394 1369). *Location:* Junction 9 of M25 four miles. Epsom Town and station five minutes car or taxi. Attractive parkland course situated within a picturesque country park with water hazards and lakes. 18 holes, 5728 yards. S.S.S. 68. *Eating facilities:* bar food, restaurant and function room. *Visitors:* welcome. *Society Meetings:* welcome weekdays and weekend afternoons. Pro shop (020 8394 2626). Professional: John Terrell. General Manager: Mike Cooper.

ESHER. **Cranfield Golf at Sandown,** More Lane, Esher KT10 8AN. *Location:* signposted from A3, centre of Sandown Park Racecourse. Three golf courses; floodlit 33-bay driving range, plus grassed area. Cranfield Golf Academy. *Green Fees:* information not available. *Eating facilities:* bar and snacks. *Visitors:* welcome. *Society Meetings:* welcome. General Manager: David Parr (01372 461234; Fax: 01372 461203).*

ESHER. **Moore Place Golf Club,** Portsmouth Road, Esher KT10 9LN (01372 463533). *Location:* half a mile from Esher town centre on Portsmouth Road. Undulating parkland course with featured trees - recently lengthened. 9 holes, 2148 yards. S.S.S. 62. *Green Fees:* information not available. *Eating facilities:* bar and restaurant. *Visitors:* welcome, unrestricted. Smart casual dress; golf shoes required, hire available. *Society Meetings:* welcome anytime, 10% reduction for groups of 10 or more. Professional: Nick Gadd (01372 463533). Hon. Secretary: Reg Egan (07860 133606). website: www.moore-place.co.uk*

ESHER. **Thames Ditton and Esher Golf Club,** Portsmouth Road, Esher KT10 9AL (020 8398 1551). *Location:* "Scilly Isles" roundabout(s), Junction Kingston by-pass, A3. Wooded commonland. 9 holes played twice from different tees, 5149 yards. S.S.S. 65. Practice nets. *Green Fees:* information not available. *Eating facilities:* bar snacks, meals by arrangement. *Visitors:* welcome except Sunday mornings. Trolleys. *Society Meetings:* always welcome, phone the Professional. Professional: Rob Jones. Secretary: Allan Barry.*

FARNHAM. **Farnham Golf Club Ltd,** The Sands, Farnham GU10 1PX (01252 782109; Fax: 01252 781185). *Location:* off A31 at Seale or Runfold slip roads. Follow signs to The Sands club situated at junction of Sands Road and Blighton Lane. Mixture of wooded parkland and heathland. 18 holes, 6447 yards. S.S.S. 71. Large practice ground. *Green Fees:* weekdays £45.00 round, £50.00 day; weekends with a member £20.00 per day. May to August twilight rate £25.00 inclusive, after 5.30pm. *Eating facilities:* two bars and diningroom, full high standard catering. *Visitors:* welcome weekdays with Handicap Certificate. *Society Meetings:* welcome Wednesday to Friday by prior booking. Professional: Grahame Cowlishaw (01252 782198; Fax: 01252 781185). Secretary: Mrs J. Elliott (01252 782109; Fax: 01252 781185).

FARNHAM. **Hankley Common Golf Club,** Tilford Road, Tilford, Farnham GU10 2DD (01252 792493; Fax: 01252 795699). *Location:* off A3, right at lights at Hindhead. Off A31 (Farnham by-pass) left at lights, three miles beyond level crossing. Heathland, dry and sandy links-type course. 18 holes, 6702 yards. S.S.S. 72. Practice ground. *Green Fees:* weekdays £65.00 per round, £80.00 per day; weekends £80.00 per round after 2pm. *Eating facilities:* full range available, restaurant and two bars. *Visitors:* welcome by appointment with Secretary. Handicap Certificate required. *Society Meetings:* catered for on Tuesdays and Wednesdays. Professional: Peter Stow (01252 793761). Secretary: (01252 792493).

GODALMING near. **Hurtmore Golf Club,** Hurtmore Road, Near Godalming GU7 2RN (01483 426492; Fax: 01483 426121). *Location:* A3 Guildford, M25 (15 minutes) A3 exit Guildford to Portsmouth. Undulating parkland with seven large lakes. 18 holes, 5530yards. S.S.S. 67 men, 68 ladies. Practice nets and putting green. *Green Fees:* weekdays £14.50, weekends £20.50. Twilight available from £11.00. *Eating facilities:* bar, restaurant. *Visitors:* welcome at all times, pay and play course with 200 members. Bookings taken by telephone. *Society Meetings:* welcome by prior booking. Professional and General Manager: Maxine Burton.

GODALMING. **West Surrey Golf Club,** Enton Green, Godalming GU8 5AF (01483 421275). *Location:* off the A3 south of Guildford, half mile past Milford Station/crossing. Wooded parkland. 18 holes, 6482 yards. S.S.S. 71. Practice ground. *Green Fees:* on application. *Eating facilities:* bar, diningroom. *Visitors:* welcome, must be member of recognised golf club and have current Handicap Certificate. *Society Meetings:* catered for by prior arrangement. Professional: A. Tawse (01483 417278). Secretary: A. Gravestock (01483 421275) e-mail: office@wsgc.co.uk website: www.wsgc.co.uk

GUILDFORD. **Bramley Golf Club,** Bramley, Near Guildford GU5 0AL (01483 892696; Fax: 01483 894673). *Location:* three miles south of Guildford on the Horsham road, A281. Parkland. 18 holes, 5930 yards. S.S.S. 69. Practice area, driving range. *Green Fees:* £38.00; weekends with member only. *Eating facilities:* catering from 7:30am to 9pm, bar from 11am to 10pm. *Visitors:* welcome Monday to Friday. *Society Meetings:* by prior arrangement with the Club. Professional Shop: 01483 893685. General Manager/Director of Golf: Gary Peddie (01483 892696). e-mail: secretary@bramleygolfclub.co.uk website: www.bramleygolfclub.co.uk

GUILDFORD. **Guildford Golf Club,** High Path Road, Merrow, Guildford GU1 2HL (01483 563941). Steward: (01483 5631842). *Location:* from Guildford take Epsom Road (A246) turn right at the third set of traffic lights. Downland course. 18 holes, 6090 yards. S.S.S. 70. Practice area. *Green Fees:* £44.00 per round, £50.00 per day weekdays; weekends with a member only. Subject to review. *Eating facilities:* snacks and restaurant service. *Visitors:* welcome weekdays, with member weekends. *Society Meetings:* catered for Tuesday to Friday. Professional: P. G. Hollington (01483 566765). Secretary: B.J. Green (01483 563941; Fax: 01483 453228). e-mail: secretary@guildfordgolfclub.co.uk website: www.guildfordgolfclub.co.uk

GUILDFORD. **Merrist Wood Golf Club,** Holly Lane, Worplesdon, Guildford GU3 3PB (01483 238890; Fax: 01483 238896). *Location:* three miles from Guildford, off A323 to Aldershot. 18 holes, 6909 yards. S.S.S. 73. *Green Fees:* information not available. *Visitors:* welcome; after 11.30am at weekends. Please call for up to date specials. *Society Meetings:* welcome. Professional: Greg Brodie (01483 238897). Golf Manager: Ben Beagley.*

GUILDFORD. **Puttenham Golf Club,** Heath Road, Puttenham, Guildford GU3 1AL (01483 810498; Fax: 01483 810988). *Location:* On B3000 between Farnham and Guildford, signposted off Hog's Back (A31). Wooded/heathland course. 18 holes, 6211 yards. S.S.S. 70. Practice ground. *Green Fees:* on application. *Eating facilities:* dining room, bar and 19th. *Visitors:* welcome weekdays only by prior arrangement. (Weekends playing with a member). *Society Meetings:* catered for Wednesdays, Thursdays and some Fridays. Secretary and Professional: Gary Simmons.
e-mail: enquiries@puttenhamgolfclub.co.uk
website: www.puttenhamgolfclub.co.uk

GUILDFORD. **Roker Park Golf Club,** Fairlands Farm, Aldershot Road, Guildford GU3 3PB (01483 236677 Fax: 01483 232324). *Location:* from A3 Guildford take A323 to Aldershot, course two miles on right. Flat parkland course. 9 holes, 3037 yards. S.S.S.72. Driving range. *Green Fees:* information not available. *Eating facilities:* restaurant and bar. *Visitors:* welcome, pay and play course. *Society Meetings:* welcome weekdays only, reductions for parties over 12. Professional: Adrian Carter. Secretary: Mr. G. Barnett (Tel & Fax: 01438 232324).*

GUILDFORD near. **Sutton Green Golf Club,** New Lane, Sutton Green, Near Guildford GU4 7QF (01483 766849). *Location:* midway between Guildford and Woking, just off A3. Easy walking parkland course, co-designed by Laura Davies, water features on nine holes. 18 holes, 6300 yards. S.S.S. 70. Practice ground. *Green Fees:* weekdays £50.00; weekends £60.00. *Eating facilities:* fully air conditioned bar and restaurant. *Visitors:* welcome midweek, weekends after 2pm. Golf buggies and carts available; changing room. *Society Meetings:* welcome midweek. Professional: Paul Tedder (01483 766849; Fax: 01483 750289). Secretary: John Buchanan (01483 747898; Fax: 01483 750289).*
e-mail: admin@suttongreengc.co.uk
website: www.suttongreengc.co.uk

HINDHEAD. **The Hindhead Golf Club,** Churt Road, Hindhead GU26 6HX (01428 604614; Fax: 01428 608508). *Location:* one and a half miles north of Hindhead on A287 to Farnham. The course is played over heathland and wooded valleys. Open Championship regional qualifying venue 2000-2005. 18 holes, White Tees 6356 yards, S.S.S. 70; Yellow Tees 6106 yards, S.S.S. 69. *Green Fees:* weekdays £50.00 per round, £60.00 per day. *Eating facilities:* restaurant, snack bar, summer bar and members' bar. *Visitors:* welcome with Handicap Certificate, weekends by appointment. *Society Meetings:* Wednesdays and Thursdays only. Professional: Ian Benson (01428 604458). Secretary: N. Hallam Jones.
e-mail: secretary@the-hindhead-golf-club.co.uk
website: www.the-hindhead-golf-club.co.uk

KINGSTON-UPON-THAMES. **Coombe Hill Golf Club,** Golf Club Drive, off Coombe Lane West, Kingston KT2 7DF (020 8336 7600; Fax: 020 8336 7601). *Location:* from A3 take A238 to Kingston. Heathland/Parkland mix, highly manicured course with quick greens. 18 holes, 6401 yards. S.S.S. 71. *Green Fees:* information not available. *Eating facilities:* dining room 8am to 3.30pm weekdays, bar (varying hours). *Visitors:* weekdays only, with a member at weekends. *Society Meetings:* please contact Secretary. Professional: Andy Dunn (020 8336 7615). Secretary: David Cromie.

KINGSTON-UPON-THAMES. **Coombe Wood Golf Club,** George Road, Kingston Hill KT2 7NS (020-8942 0388). *Location:* from A3 take A308(east) or A238(west). Wooded course. 18 holes, 5312 yards. S.S.S. 65. *Green Fees:* weekdays £35.00, £25.00 after 5pm; weekends £45.00 afternoons after 2.30pm. *Eating facilities:* catering all week. *Visitors:* welcome; weekends afternoons only. *Society Meetings:* by arrangement Monday, Wednesday, Thursday and Friday. Professional: P. Wright (020-8942 6764). Office: G. McKay (020-8942 0388: Fax: 020 8942 5665).
e-mail: info@coombewoodgolf.com
website: www.coombewoodgolf.com

KINGSWOOD. **Kingswood Golf and Country Club Ltd,** Sandy Lane, Kingswood, Tadworth KT20 6NE (01737 832188: Fax: 01737 833920). *Location:* five miles south of Sutton just off A217/Junction 8 M25. 18 holes, 6904 yards. S.S.S. 73. Large practice area. *Green Fees:* information not available. *Eating facilities:* table d'hôte Monday to Friday (reservations only) and bar snacks. *Visitors:* welcome anytime, restricted times at weekends. Squash court, snooker tables. *Society Meetings:* Corporate Golf Days catered for. Professional: Terry Sims (01737 832334). Administration: Elaine Labbett/Jackie Dunne (01737 832188).

LEATHERHEAD. **Leatherhead Golf Club,** Kingston Road, Leatherhead KT22 0EE (01372 843966; Fax: 01372 842241). *Location:* off Junction 9 of M25, onto A243 to Kingston. Parkland, many mature trees. 18 holes, 6203 yards. S.S.S. 70. Practice ground, putting green. *Green Fees:* Monday to Friday £38.00 18 holes, £57.00 36 holes; Saturday and Sunday £40.00 18 holes. *Eating facilities:* à la carte restaurant, cafe/ brasserie and lounge bar. *Visitors:* welcome, no visitors Saturday or Sunday mornings. *Society Meetings:* welcome, from 16 to 100 by reservation. Head Professional: Timothy Lowe (01372 849413). e-mail: sales@lgc-golf.co.uk
website: www.lgc-golf.co.uk

LEATHERHEAD. **Pachesham Park Golf Centre,** Oaklawn Road, Leatherhead KT22 0BT (01372 843453). *Location:* half a mile outside Leatherhead just off A244, quarter of a mile off Junction 9 M25. Undulating parkland course. 9 holes, 2806 yards. S.S.S. 67. 33 bay floodlit driving range, putting green, chipping area. *Green Fees:* weekdays £10.00 9 holes; weekends £14.00 9 holes. *Eating facilities:* fully licensed bar, restaurant. *Visitors:* welcome, bookings taken two days in advance. *Society Meetings:* welcome. Professional/Secretary: Phil Taylor. e-mail: enquiries@pacheshamgolf.co.uk

LEATHERHEAD. **Tyrrells Wood Golf Club Ltd,** Leatherhead KT22 8QP (01372 376025). *Location:* south-east on A24 Leatherhead by-pass, half a mile left to Headley, then 200 yards right. Hillside, wooded course with glorious views. 18 holes, 6234 yards. S.S.S. 70. Small practice ground. *Green Fees:* information not available. *Eating facilities:* catering by arrangement with Manager. *Visitors:* no visitors Saturday or Sunday mornings. *Society Meetings:* catered for by arrangement with Manager. Professional: Simon Defoy (01372 375200). Secretary: Luke Edgcumbe (01372 376025).*

LINGFIELD. **Lingfield Park Golf Club,** Racecourse Road, Lingfield Park, Lingfield RH7 6PQ (01342 834602; Fax: 01342 836077). *Location:* A22 turn off at Blindley Heath, six miles from M25 Junction 6. Parkland/wooded course with streams. 18 holes, 6472 yards. S.S.S. 72. Driving range and practice ground. *Green Fees:* information not available. *Eating facilities:* lounge, dining room, spike bar. *Visitors:* welcome midweek only by arrangement. Changing rooms. *Society Meetings:* catered for. Professional/ Secretary: C.K. Morley (01342 832659; Fax: 01342 836077). *

MILFORD. **Milford Golf Club,** Station Lane, Milford, Near Godalming GU8 5HS (01483 419200; Fax: 01483 419199). *Location:* five minutes from Guildford on the A3, follow signs to Milford train station, just this side of it. Parkland course which plays like a links in the wind, mixture of attractive water holes. 18 holes, 5960 yards. S.S.S. 68. Excellent practice facilities. *Green Fees:* information not available. *Eating facilities:* restaurant and pleasant bar area. *Visitors:* welcome at most times, must phone for reservations. *Society Meetings:* all welcome, packages available, please phone Sales Manager (01483 419200). Professional: Paul Creamer (01483 416291). General Manager: Robert Brewer.*

MITCHAM. **Mitcham Golf Club,** Carshalton Road, Mitcham Junction CR4 4HN (020 8648 1508; Fax: 020 8648 4197). *Location:* Carshalton Road, aim for Mitcham Junction Station. Flat course. 18 holes, 6022 yards. S.S.S. 68. *Green Fees:* information not available. *Eating facilities:* meals and snacks available. *Visitors:* welcome, book times via Professional. *Society Meetings:* catered for, book through Secretary. Professional: P. Burton (020 8640 4280). Secretary: D. Tilley (Tel & Fax: 020 8648 4197). e-mail: mitchamgc@hotmail.co.uk
website: www.mitchamgolfclub.co.uk

NEWDIGATE. **Rusper Golf Club,** Rusper Road, Newdigate RH5 5BX (Tel & Fax: 01293 871456). *Location:* Dorking-Horsham A24. Beare Green roundabout left to Newdigate, through Newdigate, right to Rusper, course on right. Parkland course with mature woodland and natural water features.18 holes, 6724 yards. S.S.S. 72. Driving range. *Green Fees:* please contact the club for details. *Eating facilities:* fresh food and daily specials available every day. Full bar. *Visitors:* welcome every day, times bookable in advance. No Handicaps required. Golf Shop (01293 871871). *Society Meetings:* welcome, groups up to 50, various packages. Professional: Janice Arnold. Secretary: Mrs Jill Thornhill. e-mail: jill@ruspergolfclub.co.uk
website: www.ruspergolfclub.co.uk

NEW MALDEN. **Malden Golf Club,** Traps Lane, New Malden KT3 4RS (020 8942 0654; Fax: 020 8336 2219). *Location:* half a mile from Malden Station - near A3, between Wimbledon and Kingston. Fairly flat parkland. 18 holes, 6295 yards. S.S.S. 70. *Green Fees:* information not provided. *Eating facilities:* restaurant and bar. *Visitors:* welcome weekdays, restricted weekends and Bank Holidays. Advisable to telephone Professional. Buggies and trolleys for hire. *Society Meetings:* catered for Wednesday and Thursdays. Professional: Robert Hunter (020 8942 6009). Secretary: Mrs Angela Besant (020 8942 0654; Fax: 020 8336 2219).

OTTERSHAW. **Foxhills,** Stonehill Road, Ottershaw KT16 0EL (01932 872050; Fax: 01932 874762). *Location:* Exit 11 M25, follow signs to Woking, right at roundabout, left at next roundabout, left at junction into Stonehill Road. Parkland course (Bernard Hunt) 18 holes, 6734 yards, S.S.S. 72. Wooded course (Longcross) 18 holes, 6417 yards, S.S.S. 71. Par 3 course (9 holes). *Green Fees:* midweek £75.00 Summer, £35.00 Winter; weekends £95.00 Summer, £45.00 Winter. Twilight £35.00 Summer. *Eating facilities:* Bar XIX open from 7am - midnight serving everything from boiled eggs to three course à la carte menu. Manor House restaurant for breakfast, lunch and fine dining in the evening. Summerhouse brasserie from 11am. *Visitors:* welcome from 7.30am weekdays and after 12 noon at weekends. 70 rooms; health spa, 11 tennis courts, 3 squash courts, 4 swimming pools, 6 conference rooms and a large function room. *Society Meetings:* bookings for weekdays only. Head Professional: Richard Summerscales; Professionals: Bernard Hunt MBE, Scott Patience (01932 704465). Golf Operations Manager: Roger Hyder PGA (01932 704466).

OXTED. **Limpsfield Chart Golf Club,** Westerham Road, Limpsfield, Oxted RH8 0SL (01883 722106). *Location:* on A25 between Westerham and Oxted. Heathland, now well wooded plus heather, gorse. Second/eleventh is played over an old gravel pit, a carry of 140 yards. 9 holes – alternate tees for 18 holes, 5718 yards. S.S.S. 68. Small practice area, practice net, putting green. *Green Fees:* weekdays £20.00, evenings £13.00; weekends £22.00 with a member only. *Eating facilities:* snacks always available 11.30am to 6pm; breakfast, lunch, dinner by prior arrangement. *Visitors:* welcome weekdays, Thursdays after 3pm, weekends by appointment. *Society Meetings:* catered for by prior arrangement. Secretary: R. Smitherman (01883 723405).

OXTED. **Tandridge Golf Club,** Oxted RH8 9NQ (01883 712274; Fax: 01883 730537). *Location:* from M25 Junction 6 take A22 south to A25 east, two miles. Parkland with flat first nine and undulating second nine. 18 holes, 6250 yards. S.S.S. 70. *Green Fees:* information not available. *Eating facilities:* full catering facilities. *Visitors:* welcome Monday, Wednesday and Thursday only. *Society Meetings:* catered for Mondays, Wednesdays and Thursdays. Professional: Chris Evans (01883 713701). Secretary: Lt. Cdr. S.E. Kennard.* e-mail: secretary@tandridgegolfclub.com website: www.tandridgegolfclub.com

PIRBRIGHT. **Goal Farm Golf Course,** Gole Road, Pirbright, Woking GU24 0PZ (01483 473183). *Location:* public course between Woking and Guildford, off A322. Challenging, picturesque course. 9 holes, 1273 yards. S.S.S. 48. Practice net, putting green, bunker. *Green Fees:* Information not provided. *Eating facilities:* licensed bar and cafe. *Visitors:* welcome, restrictions Saturday and Thursday mornings (Club Competitions). Lessons available from Professional. Clubs available for hire. Professional: Peter Fuller. Secretary: Graham Williams (01483 473182).

PURLEY. **Purley Downs Golf Club,** 106 Purley Downs Road, South Croydon CR2 0RB (020 8657 8347). *Location:* three miles south of Croydon, one mile east of A235. Undulating downland course. 18 holes, 6308 yards. S.S.S. 70. Practice area, nets. *Green Fees:* information not available. *Eating facilities:* dining room, bar snacks, two bars. *Visitors:* welcome weekdays. *Society Meetings:* catered for all days except Tuesday mornings and Fridays. Professional: S. Illife (020 8651 0819). Secretary/ Manager: Mrs S.J. Burr (020 8657 8347; Fax: 020 8651 5044). e-mail: info@purleydowns.co.uk website: www.purleydownsgolfclub.co.uk

REDHILL. **Redhill Golf Centre,** Canada Avenue, Redhill RH1 5BF (01737 770204). *Location:* in the grounds of East Surrey Hospital. Parkland. 9 holes, 1632 yards. S.S.S. 58 (18 holes); 29 (9 holes). 37 bay floodlit driving range. *Green Fees:* information not available. *Eating facilities:* available at Causeway Pub. Open 8am to 10pm; weekends 9pm. *Visitors:* welcome no restrictions. Sponsored by Golf Foundation to give free junior coaching. *Society Meetings:* welcome. Professional: Mike Lovegrove. Secretary: Steven Furlonger.

REDHILL. **Redhill and Reigate Golf Club,** Clarence Lodge, Pendleton Road, Redhill RH1 6LB (01737 244626; Fax: 01737 242117). *Location:* one mile south of Reigate between A23 and A25 – Junction 8 M25. Flat well wooded parkland course. 18 holes, 5272 yards, 4978 metres. S.S.S. 68. Small practice area. *Green Fees:* weekdays £21.00, weekends £21.00. *Eating facilities:* available seven days a week. *Visitors:* welcome weekdays, Saturdays with booking 11am to 12.30pm, Sundays please telephone. *Society Meetings:* catered for by arrangement with Manager. Professional: Warren Pike (01737 244433). Secretary: Dot Simpson (01737 240777; Fax: 01737 242117). Clubhouse Manager: Mark Wileman. e-mail: dot@rrgc.net website: www.rrgc.net

REIGATE. **Reigate Heath Golf Club,** The Clubhouse, Reigate Heath, Reigate RH2 8QR (01737 242610). *Location:* south of A25 on western boundary of Reigate. Heathland. 9 holes, 5658 yards. S.S.S. 68. *Green Fees:* on application. *Eating facilities:* lunches and snacks available. *Visitors:* welcome weekdays, advisable to telephone before coming. *Society Meetings:* catered for on Thursdays. Manager: Mr Richard Arnold (01737 226793; Fax: 01737 249226). e-mail: reigateheath@surreygolf.co.uk website: www.reigateheathgolfclub.co.uk

REIGATE. **Reigate Hill Golf Club,** Gatton Bottom, Reigate RH2 0TU (01737 645577; Fax: 01737 642650). *Location:* J8, M25 (two minutes). Parkland. 18 holes, 6175 yards. S.S.S. 70. Practice range, practice bunker and putting green. *Green Fees:* information not available. *Eating facilities:* Extensive bar menu, spike bar, lounge bar. *Visitors:* Monday - Friday no restrictions, weekends and Bank Holidays after 12.00pm. *Society Meetings:* welcome. Professional: Stephen Dundas (01737 646070). Operations Manager: John Holmes.* website: www.reigatehillgolfclub.co.uk

RICHMOND. **The Richmond Golf Club,** Sudbrook Park, Petersham, Richmond TW10 7AS (020 8940 4351; Fax: 020 8332 7914). *Location:* off A307 two miles south of Richmond, end of Sudbrook Lane. Parkland. 18 holes, 6100 yards. S.S.S. 70. Practice driving range. *Green Fees:* weekdays £45.00; weekends £50.00 after 3.30 pm. *Eating facilities:* lunches available Monday to Friday. *Visitors:* welcome weekdays without reservation. *Society Meetings:* welcome Tuesdays, Thursdays and Friday mornings only by arrangement with General Manager. Professional: Steve Burridge (020 8940 7792; Fax: 020 8332 6694). General Manager: J.M. Maguire (020 8940 4351; Fax: 020 8332 7914).

RICHMOND. **Royal Mid-Surrey Golf Club,** Old Deer Park, Richmond TW9 2SB (020 8940 1894; Fax: 020 8939 0150). *Location:* entrance on A316, five minutes from Richmond station. Parkland links designed by J.H. Taylor. Two 18 hole courses, Inner: 5544 yards, S.S.S. 67 men, 71 ladies; Outer: 6385 yards, S.S.S. 71. Practice ground, putting green, pitching green. *Green Fees:* weekdays £75.00 and £60.00 (inner) (£50.00 after 1pm and in winter). *Eating facilities:* bars and dining areas. *Visitors:* welcome weekdays only. *Society Meetings:* corporate and society golf days welcome. Professional: Matthew Paget (020 8939 0148). Secretary: Marc Newey (020 8940 1894).

SUNNINGDALE. **Sunningdale Golf Club,** Ridgemount Road, Sunningdale, Ascot SL5 9RR (01344 621681; Fax: 01344 624154). *Location:* 350 yards west of station, off A30, 25 miles from London. Heathland, 36 holes, 2 courses. *Green Fees:* Information not available. *Eating facilities:* diningroom and three bars. *Visitors:* require introduction from Secretary of own club plus Handicap Certificate on weekdays. Fridays and weekends with member only. *Society Meetings:* accepted Tuesdays, Wednesdays and Thursdays only, by arrangement. Professional: Keith Maxwell (01344 620128). Secretary: Stephen Toon. Golf Operations for bookings (01344 298006). *

SUTTON. **Banstead Downs Golf Club,** Burdon Lane, Belmont, Sutton SM2 7DD (020 8642 2284; Fax: 020 8642 5252). *Location:* A217 (10 minutes from Belmont Station). 18 holes, 6192 yards. S.S.S. 69. *Green Fees:* information not available. *Eating facilities:* lunches served at Club every day. *Visitors:* welcome Monday, Tuesday, Wednesday, Thursday with letter of introduction; on Friday, Saturday, Sunday with member. *Society Meetings:* catered for all day Thursdays. Professional: Ian Golding (020 8642 6884). General Manager: Mrs Karen Cote

TADWORTH. **Walton Heath Golf Club,** Deans Lane, Walton-on-the-Hill, Tadworth KT20 7TP (01737 812060). *Location:* Junction 8 M25, A217 towards London, B2032 towards Dorking, turning right hand side Deans Lane. Two 18 hole heathland courses. Old: 7462 yards, S.S.S. 72. New: 7171 yards, S.S.S. 74. Large putting green; indoor nets and small outdoor practice facilities. *Green Fees:* information not available. *Eating facilities:* restaurant and two bars. *Visitors:* welcome by previous arrangement, Handicap Certificate or letter of introduction required; limited play weekends. *Society Meetings:* catered for by arrangement. A variety of packages available for both summer and winter. Professional: Ken MacPherson (01737 812152). Secretary: Mike Bawden.

VIRGINIA WATER. **Wentworth Club Ltd,** Wentworth Drive, Virginia Water GU25 4LS (01344 842201; Fax: 01344 842804). *Location:* 21 miles south-west of London, just off the A30 at junction with A329 to Ascot. M25 and M3 three miles. Wooded heathland. West course - 18 holes, 7308 yards, S.S.S. 74; East course - 18 holes, 6201 yards, S.S.S. 70; Edinburgh course - 18 holes, 7004 yards, S.S.S. 74; Executive course - 9 holes. Driving range. *Green Fees:*

information not available. *Eating facilities:* dining room, ballroom, private rooms, bar. *Visitors:* welcome weekdays only by appointment. Handicap Certificates required: Ladies 32, Men 24. Accommodation available. *Society Meetings:* welcome by prior arrangement. Director of Golf: Stephen Gibson (01344 846306). Managing Director: Julian Small (01344 842201). Director of Operations: Stuart Christie (01344 846313).

WALTON-ON-THAMES. **Burhill Golf Club,** Burwood Road, Walton-on-Thames KT12 4BL. *Location:* M25 Junction 10, take A3 London turn off, A245 Weybridge, right into Seven Hills Road and again into Burwood Road. Two 18 hole parkland courses both differing in character, Old Course 6479 yards. S.S.S. 71, New Course 6940 yards, S.S.S. 72 - opened May 2001. Full irrigation on both courses. Practice area, driving range, putting green and short game practice area. *Green Fees:* weekdays £65.00 per round, £85.00 per day. Special rates November to March. *Eating facilities:* Orangery Restaurant, Captains Bar, Honours Bar, Iveagh Lounge, Barnes Wallis suite for private dining and special occasions. *Visitors:* welcome Monday to Friday. *Society Meetings:* catered for Monday to Friday. Golf Days organised to suit your particular requirements. Professional: (01932 221729; Fax: 01932 252533). General Manager: David Cook (01932 227345; Fax: 01932 267159). Sales Manager: Gill Fee (01932 227345; Fax: 01932 267159).
e-mail: info@burhillgolf-club.co.uk

WARLINGHAM near. **Farleigh Court Golf Club,** Old Farleigh Road, Farleigh CR6 9PX (01883 627711; Fax: 01883 627722). *Location:* south of Croydon. Exciting course utilising two landscaped valleys with many natural features. 27 holes (18 holes members, 9 hole pay and play). 9155 yards, 8368 metres. Practice bunker, chipping green, putting green and 285 yard practice range. *Green Fees:* information not available. *Eating facilities:* full catering facilities available (seven days). *Visitors:* welcome anytime after 10am weekdays or weekends on members course and anytime on 9 hole pay and play. *Society Meetings:* welcome anytime. Professional/Secretary: Scott Graham.*

WEST BYFLEET. **West Byfleet Golf Club,** Sheerwater Road, West Byfleet KT14 6AA (01932 343433). *Location:* Junction 10 M25 onto A245 – half a mile west of West Byfleet. Easy walking, woodland course. 18 holes, 6211 yards. S.S.S. 70. *Green Fees:* weekdays £50.00 per round, £75.00 per day. *Eating facilities:* lunches, bar snacks, teas and evening meals available. Catering: (01932 353525). Bar: (01932 343433). *Visitors:* welcome weekdays with reservation, weekends with member only. *Society Meetings:* catered for, advance bookings, minimum group size 20. Professional: David Regan (01932 343433). Secretary: D. Lee (01932 343433).

www.uk-golfguide.com

WEST CLANDON. **Clandon Regis Golf Club Ltd,** Epsom Road, West Clandon GU4 7TT (01483 224888; Fax: 01483 211781). *Location:* between Guildford and Leatherhead on A246. Parkland setting, fairly mature for new course, four areas of water. Course designed by David Williams. 18 holes, 6419 yards. S.S.S. 71/69. Indoor practice nets, full length driving area, putting green, chipping area. *Green Fees:* weekdays £37.50; weekends £45.00 (limited). *Eating facilities:* bar meals, restaurant available for booking. *Visitors:* welcome weekdays, weekends depending on club bookings. *Society Meetings:* welcome weekdays only. Professional: Steve Lloyd (01483 223922). General Manager: Mr Paul Napier.

WEYBRIDGE. **New Zealand Golf Club,** Woodham Lane, Woodham, Addlestone KT15 3QD (01932 345049). *Location:* junction Woodham Lane and Sheerwater Road on A245. Traditional club with secluded heathland course in heather and woodland setting. 18 holes, 6075 yards. S.S.S. 69. *Green Fees:* information not available. *Eating facilities:* lunch available Tuesdays to Fridays. *Visitors:* welcome by prior arrangement. *Society Meetings:* catered for Tuesday, Wednesday, Thursday, Friday. Professional: V.R. Elvidge. Secretary: R.A. Marrett Esq.*

WEYBRIDGE. **St George's Hill Golf Club,** Golf Club Road, St. George's Hill, Weybridge KT13 0NL (01932 847758; Fax: 01932 821564). *Location:* M25, Junction 10 take A3 towards London, turn off towards Byfleet (A245) then B374 Brooklands Road, entrance to St. George's Hill estate one mile on right. Hilly, Surrey heathland - well wooded with plentiful heather and rhododendron. 27 holes, 6513 yards. S.S.S. 71. *Green Fees:* Information not available. *Eating facilities:* dining room, two bars. *Visitors:* welcome Wednesdays, Thursdays. Fridays only by prior arrangement with Secretary's office. *Society Meetings:* catered for on Wednesdays, Thursdays and Fridays by prior arrangement. Professional: A.C. Rattue (01932 843523). Secretary: J. Robinson (01932 847758). *

WOKING. **Chobham Golf Club,** Chobham Road, Knaphill, Woking GU21 2TZ (01276 855584; Fax: 01276 855663). *Location:* on A3046 one mile outside Chobham village, ten minutes from M3 Junction 3. Wooded parkland course. 18 holes, 5959 yards. S.S.S. 69. Practice area, putting green. *Green Fees:* information not available. *Eating facilities:* bar snacks

and restaurant. *Visitors:* welcome, handicap required. Must pre-book teetime with Pro shop. *Society Meetings:* welcome. Professional: Tim Coombes (01276 855748).
e-mail: info@chobhamgolfclub.co.uk
website: www.chobhamgolfclub.co.uk

WOKING. **Hoebridge Golf Centre,** Old Woking Road, Old Woking GU22 8JH (01483 722611; Fax: 01483 740369). *Location*: Undulating parkland on well-draining sand, well established wooded location. Three courses: Hoebridge Course - 18 holes, Back Tees 6536 yards, Par 72, Yellow Tees 6178 yards, Par 71, Ladies 5842 yards, Par 73; Maybury Course – 18 holes, 2181 yards, Par 54; Shey Copse – 9 holes, 2294 yards, Par 33. 36 bay covered, floodlit driving range. *Green Fees:* Information not available. *Eating facilities*: full catering and bar facilities open all day. *Visitors*: welcome. Pay-and-Play facility. Clubs for hire. *Society Meetings*: welcome weekdays by prior arrangement, various packages available. Professional: Russell Covey. Men's Secretary: Steve Royston. Ladies' Secretary: Elaine Watts. Centre Manager: Mike O'Connell.
e-mail: sales@hoebridgegc.co.uk
website: www.hoebridgegc.co.uk

WOKING. **Traditions Golf Course 1999,** Pyrford Road, Pyrford, Woking GU22 8UE (01932 350355; Fax: 01932 350234). *Location:* into West Byfleet and turn at traffic lights into Pyrford Road. Peter Alliss design with tree-lined holes, lakes and many streams. 18 holes. Par 71. *Green Fees:* information not available. *Eating facilities:* from 7am to 10pm (to 6pm in winter). Professional: Adam Whatford.*

WOKING. **West Hill Golf Club,** Bagshot Road, Brookwood GU24 0BH (01483 474365). *Location:* M3, Junction 3, A322 entrance adjacent railway bridge Brookwood. Heathland, wooded course. Golf World "Top 100 courses in UK" listed. 18 holes, 6368 yards. S.S.S. 70. Practice range and net. *Green Fees:* contact the club. *Eating facilities:* bar snacks available, meals including dinner by prior arrangement. *Visitors:* members' guests only at weekends. Buggies, caddies by arrangement. *Society Meetings:* catered for by arrangement through the Secretary. Professional: Guy Shoesmith (01483 473172). Secretary: I.M. McColl (01483 474365; Fax: 01483 474252).
e-mail: secretary@westhill-golfclub.co.uk
website: www.westhill-golfclub.co.uk

WOKING. **Windlemere Golf Club,** Windlesham Road, West End, Near Woking GU24 9QL (01276 858727). *Location:* off A322. Well designed parkland course. 9 holes, 2673 yards. S.S.S. 33. Floodlit 12-bay driving range. *Green Fees:* Information not available. *Eating facilities:* bar with light menu, normal clubhouse facilities. *Visitors:* always welcome, may book up to one week in advance. Snooker, pool facilities. *Society Meetings:* welcome to book. Professional: Dave Thomas. Secretary: M. Walsh (01276 858727).*

WOKING. **Woking Golf Club,** Pond Road, Hook Heath, Woking GU22 0JZ (01483 760053; Fax: 01483 772441). *Location:* via Hollybank Road and Golf Club Road or Hook Heath Road and Pond Road. Traditional heathland course. 18 holes, 6340 yards. S.S.S. 70. Practice ground. *Green Fees:* information not provided. *Eating facilities:* lunches and snacks available. *Visitors:* welcome but only by prior arrangement, Handicap Certificate required. *Society Meetings:* welcome by prior arrangement. Professional: C.I. Bianco (01483 769582). Secretary: G.T. Ritchie.
website: www.wokinggolfclub.co.uk

WOKING. **Worplesdon Golf Club,** Heath House Road, Woking. *Location:* off A322, six miles from Guildford and six miles from Junction 3 (M3). Wooded heathland course. 18 holes, 6431 yards. S.S.S. 71. *Green Fees:* £60.00 per round, £80.00 per day. *Eating facilities:* lunches served at club. *Visitors:* weekdays only. *Society meetings:* by arrangement. Professional: Jim Christine (01483 473287) Secretary: C.K. Symington (01483 472277; Fax: 01483 473303).

WOKING near. **Pyrford Golf Club 1993,** Warren Lane, Pyrford, Near Woking, GU22 8XR (01483 723555; Fax: 01483 729777). *Location:* A3 - Ripley turn off, turn next to Mitsubishi garage, continue for approximately two miles, on the right Warren Lane. Inland water links, 23 acres of water. 18 holes, 6230 yards. Par 72. Practice range, putting green. *Green Fees:* information not available. *Eating facilities:* bar snack menu available all day. *Visitors:* welcome anytime Monday to Friday and after 12 noon at weekends, tee times MUST be booked. *Society Meetings:* welcome weekdays only. Professional: Andrew Blackman (01483 751070). Secretary: Bradley Chard.
e-mail: pyrford@crown-golf.co.uk*

WOLDINGHAM. **North Downs Golf Club,** Northdown Road, Woldingham, Caterham CR3 7AA (01883 652057). *Location:* Wapses Lodge roundabout at Caterham. Two miles Woldingham Road. 18 holes, 5857 yards, S.S.S. 68. *Green Fees:* £35.00 per round, £46.00 per day. *Eating facilities:* full restaurant facilities. *Visitors:* welcome with Handicap Certificate Monday to Friday (Thursdays after 12 noon only). *Society Meetings:* catered for. Professional: M. Homewood (01883 653004). Secretary/Manager: D. Sinden (01883 652057).

YATELEY. **Blackwater Valley Golf Course,** Chandlers Lane, Yateley GU46 7SZ (01252 874725). *Location:* Junction 4 of M3. Into Yateley to White Lion pub roundabout, into Vicarage Road, then Vicarage Lane. Parkland course with lakes and mature trees. 9 holes. Par 34. Driving range. *Green Fees:* information not available. *Eating facilities:* From 11am to 10pm (to 8pm during winter). Professional: James Rodger.*

Hoebridge Golf Centre, Woking

East Sussex

BATTLE. **Battle Golf Club,** Netherfield Hill, Battle TN37 7QU (Tel & Fax: 01424 775677). *Location*: A2100, just 1½ miles outside historic town of Battle. Parkland, woodland course. Panoramic views, gently undulating. 9 holes, 18 tees, 5941 yards. S.S.S 68. Practice ground. *Green Fees*: weekdays 9 holes £13.00, 18 holes £20.00; weekends 9 holes £15.00, 18 holes £22.00. Special offer Mondays and Wednesdays - play 18 and pay for 9. Senior Citizens and Juniors welcome, special rates. *Eating facilities:* large bars, 3-course meals and bar snacks available. 3-course Sunday roast + 9 holes of golf for just £17.50. *Visitors:* welcome daily from 7am. Strict dress code. En suite B&B in rooms overlooking the course available throughout the year. Accommodation available plus 2, 3 or 5 days of golf with tuition. Special midweek offers available; for more information phone or view website. Tuition available for individuals and groups. *Society Meetings:* welcome, special rates, please telephone for details. PGA Professional: Mike Barton. Club Secretary: Clare Lyons (01424 775677). e-mail: clare@battlegolfclub.com website: www.battlegolfclub.com

BEXHILL-ON-SEA. **Cooden Beach Golf Club,** Cooden Sea Road, Bexhill-on-Sea TN39 4TR (Tel & Fax: 01424 842040). *Location:* A259 Eastbourne to Hastings road, follow `Cooden Beach' sign at Little Common roundabout (one mile). Seaside course, slightly undulating. 18 holes, 6500 yards. S.S.S. 72. Practice facilities. *Green Fees:* weekdays £37.00; weekends and Bank Holidays £46.00. *Eating facilities:* catering and bar every day. *Visitors:* welcome, preferably by prior arrangement. Buggies for hire. *Society Meetings:* prior booking necessary. Professional: Jeffrey Sim (01424 843938; Fax: 01424 842040). Secretary: Keith Wiley (Tel & Fax: 01424 842040). Caterers: Steve Ede (01424 843936). e-mail: enquiries@coodenbeachgc.com website: www.coodenbeachgc.com

BEXHILL-ON-SEA. **Highwoods Golf Club,** Ellerslie Lane, Bexhill-on-Sea TN39 4LJ (01424 212625). *Location:* off A259 north west of town. Parkland, wooded course. 18 holes, 6218 yards. S.S.S. 70. *Green Fees:* £32.00 all day, £20.00 with member. *Eating facilities:* snacks, lunches and teas always available. *Visitors:* welcome Monday to Saturday. Sunday mornings with member only. *Society Meetings:* welcome Thursdays by arrangement. Professional: M. Andrews (01424 212770). Office: (01424 212625; Fax: 01424 216866). e-mail: highwoods@btconnect.com website: www.highwoodsgolfclub.co.uk

BRIGHTON. **Brighton and Hove Golf Club,** Devil's Dyke Road, Brighton BN1 8YJ (01273 507861). *Location:* A27 Brighton bypass exit for Devil's Dyke, club 1½ miles north of A27. Downland course with sea views. 9 holes, 5704 yards. S.S.S. 68. Practice area. *Green Fees:* (18 holes) weekdays £24.00; weekends and Bank Holidays £30.00. *Eating facilities:* bar and restaurant daily, limited on Mondays. *Visitors:* welcome, phone call advisable Wednesday after 12 noon, Friday after 11am, Saturday and Sunday after 12 noon. *Society Meetings:* catered for; up to 30, eating 60. Director of Golf: Phil Bonsall (01273 556482). Shop (01273 556686).

BRIGHTON. **Brighton and Hove Golf Club,** Devil's Dyke Road, Brighton BN1 8YJ (01273 507861). *Location:* A27 Brighton bypass exit for Devil's Dyke, club 1½ miles north of A27. Downland course with sea views. 9 holes, 5704 yards. S.S.S. 68. Practice area. *Green Fees:* (18 holes) weekdays £24.00; weekends and Bank Holidays £30.00. *Eating facilities:* bar and restaurant daily, limited on Mondays. *Visitors:* welcome, phone call advisable Wednesday after 12 noon, Friday after 11am, Saturday and Sunday after 12 noon. *Society Meetings:* catered for; up to 30, eating 60. Director of Golf: Phil Bonsall (01273 556482). Shop (01273 556686).

BRIGHTON. **The Dyke Golf Club, Devil's Dyke, Devil's Dyke Road, Brighton BN1 8YJ (01273 857296; Fax: 01273 857078). *Location:* A23 onto A27 (New Brighton By-pass) heading west to Worthing, turn off for Devil's Dyke and follow signs for same. Brighton's premier downland course. 18 holes, 6627 yards. S.S.S. 72. Practice fairway and putting green. *Green Fees:* weekdays £35.00 per round, £45.00 per day; weekends £45.00 per round. Twilight round £18.00 weekdays, £26.00 weekends. *Eating facilities:* full restaurant and bar available. *Visitors:* welcome with reservation, not before 12 noon Sundays. *Society Meetings:* catered for by appointment, from £60.00 for full day inclusive of snack lunch and evening meal (other meal arrrangements can be made). Professional: Mark Stuart-William (01273 857260; Fax: 01273 857564). Secretary: (01273 857296; Fax: 01273 857078). e-mail: office@dykegolfclub.co.uk**

BRIGHTON. **East Brighton Golf Club,** Roedean Road, Brighton BN2 5RA (01273 604838). *Location:* one and a half miles east of Palace Pier, just off A259, behind the Marina. Undulating downland course offering superb views over the Channel. 18 holes, 6346 yards. S.S.S. 71 (white tees). Putting green. *Green Fees:* information not available. *Eating facilities:* restaurant, diningroom, bars. *Visitors:* welcome from 9am weekdays, after 11am weekends and Bank Holidays. Handicap Certificate not required. Buggy hire available. *Society Meetings:* welcome, full days golf and catering from £40.00 per person. General Manager: George Mckay (01273 604838; Fax: 01273 680277).

BRIGHTON. **Hollingbury Park Golf Club,** Ditchling Road, Brighton BN1 7HS (01273 552010). *Location:* between A23 and A27. 18 holes, 6429 yards. S.S.S. 71. *Green Fees:* weekdays £17.00 per round, £26.00 per day; weekends £23.00 per round. *Visitors:* welcome. All bookings through Professional. *Society Meetings:* catered for weekdays only. Professional: Graeme Crompton (01273 500086). Secretary: (Tel & Fax: 01273 552010)

BRIGHTON. **Waterhall Golf Club,** Saddlescombe Road, Brighton BN1 8YN (01273 508658). *Location:* off A27 Brighton bypass, take Devil's Dyke turn off, course on the right. Downland course. 18 holes, 5773 yards, 5328 metres. S.S.S. 68. Practice area. *Green Fees:* information not available. *Visitors:* welcome except weekends. *Society Meetings:* catered for except weekends or Bank Holidays by prior arrangement with Secretary. Professional: Graeme Crompton (01273 555529). Secretary: L.B. Allen.*

CROWBOROUGH. **Crowborough Beacon Golf Club,** Beacon Road, Crowborough TN6 1UJ (01892 661511). *Location:* nine miles south of Tunbridge Wells on the A26. Heathland, superb views to the sea and South Downs (on clear days). 18 holes, 6273 yards. S.S.S. 70. *Green Fees:* £50.00 per round, £60.00 per day weekdays. *Eating facilities:* restaurant available. *Visitors:* welcome weekdays, Handicap Certificate or letter of introduction essential. Please contact either the Professional or Secretary. *Society Meetings:* bookings welcome through the Secretary's office. Professional: D.C Newnham (01892 653877). Secretary: Mrs V. Harwood (01892 661511).
e-mail: secretary@cbgc.co.uk
website: www.cbgc.co.uk

DITCHLING. **Mid-Sussex Golf Club,** Spatham Lane, Ditchling BN6 8XJ (01273 846567; Fax: 01273 847815). *Location:* five minutes from A23, one mile east of Ditchling. Mature parkland course with superbly contoured greens and strategic bunkers. 18 holes, 6431 yards. S.S.S. 71. Practice ground, driving range and short game areas. *Green Fees:* £30.00. Twilight rates available. *Eating facilities:* full bar/restaurant facilities. *Visitors:* welcome weekdays, weekends restricted. Buggies available. *Society Meetings:* welcome weekdays only. Professional: Neil Plimmer. General Manager: Andy McNiven.
website: www.midsussexgolfclub.co.uk

EASTBOURNE. **Eastbourne Downs Golf Club,** East Dean Road, Eastbourne BN20 8ES (01323 720827; Fax: 01323 412506). *Location:* half a mile west of Eastbourne on A259. Downland course with spectacular views to the South Downs and over the sea. 18 holes, 6601 yards. S.S.S. 72. Practice area. *Green Fees:* Weekdays: £20 per round; weekends: £28.00 per round. *Eating facilities:* two bars; restaurant open seven days a week 7.30am to 8.30pm. *Visitors:* welcome unrestricted after 9am weekdays and 11.15am weekends. Trolleys for hire. *Society Meetings:* welcome – full day with coffee, lunch and four-course dinner. Professional: Terry Marshall (01323 732264). Secretary: Tony Reeves (01323 720827; Fax: 01323 412506).

EASTBOURNE. **Eastbourne Golfing Park,** Lottbridge Drove, Eastbourne BN23 6QJ (Tel & Fax: 01323 520400). *Location:* end of A22; half a mile south of Hampden Park and one mile north of the sea. Pleasant easy walk, a fairly short flat course but with water on seven of the nine holes it tests the accuracy of any golfer. 9 holes, 5046 yards. S.S.S. 66. 21-bay floodlit driving range. *Green Fees:* weekdays 9 holes £11.00, 18 holes £17.00, weekends 9 holes £12.00, 18 holes £19.00. Senior Citizens and Juniors reduced rates. *Eating facilities:* full bar and restaurant open to all. *Visitors:* welcome at all times. Equipment hire available. *Society Meetings:* all welcome, please ring to book. Professionals: Rob Lowe, Barry Finch, Ian Pearson and Keith Robson. Secretary: Maggie Garbutt (Tel & Fax: 01323 520400).

EASTBOURNE. **Royal Eastbourne Golf Club,** Paradise Drive, Eastbourne BN20 8BP (01323 744045). *Location:* one mile from town centre via Meads Road and Compton Place Road. Undulating downland and parkland. Devonshire course:18 holes, 6077 yards. S.S.S. 69. Hartington course: 9 holes, 2147 yards. S.S.S. 61. *Green Fees:* (2006) Devonshire weekday £33.00, weekend £39.00; Hartington £19.00. *Eating facilities:* full catering. *Visitors:* welcome. Handicap Certificate required Long Course only. Cottage accommodation for four people. *Society Meetings:* catered for. Professional: Alan Harrison (Tel & Fax: 01323 736986). Secretary: (01323 744045).

EASTBOURNE. **Willingdon Golf Club,** Southdown Road, Willingdon, Eastbourne BN20 9AA (01323 410983). *Location:* north of Eastbourne, one mile from station, just off A22 at traffic lights (signposted). Downland course of particular beauty. 18 holes, 6158 yards. S.S.S. 69. Practice ground and nets. *Green Fees:* weekdays £18.00 per round winter, £24.00 per round summer. *Eating facilities:* diningroom, lounge and casual bar. *Visitors:* welcome weekdays after 9am. Buggies and trolleys available. *Society Meetings:* welcome, book well in advance. Professional: Troy Moore (01323 410984; Fax: 01323 411510). Secretary: Mrs Jacqueline Packham (01323 410981; Fax: 01323 411510).

EAST GRINSTEAD. **Sweetwoods Park Golf Club,** Cowden, Edenbridge TN8 7JN (01342 850729; Fax: 01342 850866). *Location:* directly off the A264 at Holtye, 5 miles east of East Grinstead. Wooded, parkland course with many water features. 18 holes, 5339-6617 yards, S.S.S. 69-73, Par 72. Practice ground, driving range and carts provided. *Green Fees:* (2007) £30.00 weekdays, £36.00 weekends (subject to review for 2008). *Visitors:* welcome anytime, no restrictions, can book up to 7 days in advance. *Society Meetings:* welcome Monday to Friday and Saturday pm. Professional: Paul Lyons (01342 850729). Secretary: Louise Palmer (01342 850729).
website: www.sweetwoodspark.com

**THE APPEARANCE OF AN ASTERISK (*)
AT THE END OF A CLUB OR COURSE ENTRY
INDICATES THAT UP-TO-DATE INFORMATION
HAS NOT BEEN SUPPLIED**

FOREST ROW. **Royal Ashdown Forest Golf Club (Old Course)** Chapel Lane, Forest Row, Near East Grinstead RH18 5LR (01342 822018; Fax: 01342 825211). *Location:* three miles south of East Grinstead to Forest Row. Take B2110 to Tunbridge Wells in the middle of village (left at second mini-roundabout) then take fourth turning on right into Chapel Lane, turn sharp left at top of Chapel Lane then bear right through golf course to Clubhouse. Undulating heathland. 18 holes, 6502 yards. S.S.S. 71. Selected to host regional qualifier until 2008 Open Championship. *Green Fees:* weekdays £55.00 per round, £70.00 per day; weekends £75.00 per round. *Eating facilities:* lunch and tea, bar snacks. *Visitors:* welcome by prior arrangement. *Society Meetings:* welcome on Wednesday, Thursday and Friday; prior reservation essential. Steward: (01342 823014). Professional: M. Landsborough (01342 822247) Secretary: D. Neave (01342 822018; Fax: 01342 825211).
e-mail: office@royalashdown.co.uk
website: www.royalashdown.co.uk

FOREST ROW. **Royal Ashdown Forest Golf Club (West Course)** Chapel Lane, Forest Row, East Sussex RH18 5LR (01342 824866; Fax: 01342 825211). *Location:* four miles south of East Grinstead to Forest Row. Take B2110 to Tunbridge Wells in the middle of village (left at second mini-roundabout) then take fourth turning on right into Chapel Lane, turn sharp left at top of Chapel Lane then bear right through golf course to Clubhouse. 5606 yards, S.S.S. 67, a shorter, but not easier, version of the Old Course with, according to the late Henry Longhurst, "one of the finest par fours in the South of England" as its closing hole. *Green Fees:* weekdays £28.00 per round, £38.00 per day; weekends £33.00 per round, £45.00 per day. *Eating facilities:* Full dining facilities and bar snacks available all day. *Visitors and Societies:* welcome 7 days a week by prior arrangement. Professional: M. Landsborough (01342 822247).

HAILSHAM near. **Wellshurst Golf and Country Club,** North Street, Hellingly, Near Hailsham BN27 4EE (01435 813636; Fax: 01435 812444). *Location:* two miles from the A22 roundabout at Hailsham on the A267. Parkland course. 18 holes, 6084 yards, S.S.S. 68. 16 bay driving range with two bunker bays. *Green Fees:* 18 holes weekdays £24.00, weekends £28.00. *Eating facilities:* bar and restaurant open 7 days a week. *Visitors:* no restrictions, pay as you play course; advisable to book at weekends. Conference/wedding suite. *Society Meetings:* all welcome at any time, good rates. Professional: Richard Hollands (01435 813456). Secretary: M. Adams.

HASTINGS. **Beauport Park Golf Course Ltd,** Battle Road, St. Leonards-on-Sea TN37 7BP (01424 854245; Clubhouse functions 01424 851165). *Location:* A2100 between Hastings and Battle, in the heart of 1066 Country in an Area of Outstanding Natural Beauty. Scenic, tree-lined undulating parkland course said to be among the best in Southern England and a very good test for all handicaps. 18 holes, 6180 yards. S.S.S. 70. 9 hole Par 3 short course, 14-bay driving range. *Green Fees:* weekdays £15.00, weekends £20.00. *Eating facilities:* clubhouse, restaurant and bar. *Visitors:* unrestricted, but booking advised at weekends. Professional coaching, beginners and Junior coaching groups. Adjacent riding stables and leisure centre. Other facilities and accommodation available at Beauport Park Hotel. *Society Meetings:* welcome; special rates available on request for societies/Corporate Days. Course Manager: Charles Giddins.
e-mail: beauport.park@foremostgolf.com
website: www.beauportparkgc.co.uk

www.uk-golfguide.com

PLEASE MENTION **THE GOLF GUIDE** WHEN YOU WRITE
OR PHONE TO ENQUIRE ABOUT CLUBS OR ACCOMMODATION

West Sussex

ALBOURNE. **Singing Hills Golf Course Ltd,** Albourne BN6 9EB (01273 835353; Fax: 01273 835444). *Location:* on the B2117 just off the A23. Gently undulating parkland course with spectacular views of the South Downs. 3 x 9 hole courses. S.S.S. 70. 15 bay driving range, putting green. *Green Fees:* information not available. *Eating facilities:* Pavilion Restaurant, large bar. *Visitors:* welcome, no restrictions. *Society Meetings:* welcome, variety of golf and food packages for minimum 12 players. Professional: Wallace Street. Secretary: Nicholas Hughes.*
e-mail: info@singinghills.co.uk
website: www.singinghills.co.uk

ANGMERING. **Ham Manor Golf Club Ltd,** Angmering BN16 4JE (01903 775653). *Location:* on A259 between Worthing and Littlehampton. Flat parkland course. 18 holes, 6216 yards. S.S.S. 70. *Green Fees:* information not available. *Eating facilities:* lunches served at club except on Mondays. *Visitors:* welcome. Handicap Certificate required. *Society Meetings:* catered for thursdays only. Professional: Simon Buckley (01903 783732). Secretary: Roy Brown (01903 783288).

BILLINGSHURST. **Foxbridge Golf Club,** Foxbridge Lane, Plaistow Road, Kirdford, Billingshurst RH14 0LB (Tel & Fax: 01403 753303). *Location:* B2133, A281 Guildford to Horsham Road. Parkland course with eight lakes. 9 holes, 6236 yards. S.S.S. 70. Practice ground. *Green Fees:* midweek 9 holes £12.50, 18 holees £17.00; weekends 9 holes £13.50, 18 holes £19.50. *Eating facilities:* restaurant and bar. *Visitors:* welcome. Buggies and carts available. *Society Meetings:* welcome. Professional: Neil Burke. Secretary: Elaine Purton (01403 753303; Fax: 01403 751975).

BOGNOR REGIS. **Bognor Regis Golf Club,** Downview Road, Felpham, Bognor Regis PO22 8JD (01243 865867; Fax: 01243 860719). *Location:* turn north at traffic lights on A259 at Felpham village. Flat parkland, many dogleg holes and water hazards. 18 holes, 6238 yards. S.S.S. 69, Par 70. Practice area. *Green Fees:* information not available. *Eating facilities:* bar open every day; hot and cold snacks available weekdays, light snacks available weekends. *Visitors:* welcome weekdays (Ladies' Day Tuesday), weekends only with a member. Handicap Certificate required. *Society Meetings:* welcome by arrangement (minimum 16). Professional: (01243 865209). Secretary: (01243 821929; Fax: 01243 860719).*
e-mail: sec@bognorgolfclub.co.uk
website: www.bognorgolfclub.co.uk

BRIGHTON. **Pyecombe Golf Club,** Clayton Hill, Pyecombe, Brighton BN45 7FF (01273 845372; Fax: 01273 843338). *Location:* four miles north of Brighton on A273 Burgess Hill Road. Downland with magnificent views. 18 holes, 6251 yards, 5716 metres. S.S.S. 70. Two practice areas. *Green Fees:* £28.00 weekdays. *Eating facilities:* catering/bars from 11am daily. *Visitors:* welcome, after 9.15am weekdays. *Society Meetings:* welcome weekdays by prior arrangement. Professional: C. White (01273 845398; Fax: 01273 843338). Secretary: J.M. Wilkinson (01273 845372; Fax: 01273 843338).

BURGESS HILL. **The Burgess Hill Golf Centre,** Cuckfield Road, Burgess Hill RH15 8RE (01444 258585; Fax: 01444 247318). *Location:* the B2036 north of Burgess Hill, on the Burgess Hill to Cuckfield road. An excellent short course in undulating wooded, parkland setting. 9 holes, 1250 yards. Par 3. 28 bay floodlit driving range, practice area, PGA teaching academy, Pro shop. *Green Fees:* information not provided. *Eating facilities:* bar and restaurant. *Visitors:* welcome, open from 8am to 9pm. Professional/Secretary: Mark Collins (01444 258585; Fax: 01444 247318).
website: www.burgesshillgolfcentre.co.uk

CHICHESTER. **Chichester Golf Club,** Hunston Village, Chichester PO20 1AX (01243 533833). *Location:* take B2145 south of Chichester, on left hand side after Hunston Village. 45 hole golf complex. Cathedral Course 18 holes, 6442 yards, Par 72; Tower Course 18 holes, 6109 yards, Par 69. Separate family golf centre: Par 3, 829 yards short course, mini golf, Golf Academy with video analysis and 27-bay floodlit driving range including automated power tee system. *Green Fees:* weekdays Tower £17.50, Cathedral £21.00; weekends Tower £21.50, Cathedral £30.00. *Eating facilities:* fully licensed non-smoking bar and restaurant. *Visitors:* welcome anytime. *Society Meetings:* welcome. Well stocked golf shops. Head Professional: James Willmott (01243 528999). Proprietor: Sally Haygarth (01243 536666; Fax: 01243 539922).
e-mail: enquiries@chichestergolf.com
website: www.chichestergolf.com

CHICHESTER. **Golf at Goodwood,** The Kennels, Goodwood, Chichester PO18 0PN. *Location:* one mile north of Chichester at east end of Chichester Bypass (A27). Architect James Braid (1914), renovated Howard Swan (2005). Undulating downland. 18 holes, 7104 yards. S.S.S. 74. Practice ground, nets, putting greens. *Green Fees:* members only (Membership Sales 01243 755144). *Eating facilities:* full catering and bar. *Visitors:* members only. *Society Meetings:* members only. Professional: Damon Allard (01243 755135). Secretary: (01243 755130; Fax: 01243 755135).*
e-mail: golf@goodwood.co.uk
website: www.goodwood.co.uk/golf

> **THE APPEARANCE OF AN ASTERISK (*) AT THE END OF A CLUB OR COURSE ENTRY INDICATES THAT UP-TO-DATE INFORMATION HAS NOT BEEN SUPPLIED**

CHICHESTER. **Selsey Golf Club,** Golf Links Lane, Selsey, Chichester PO20 9DR (01243 602203). *Location:* B2145, seven miles south of Chichester. Flat course. 9 holes playing 18, 5532 yards. S.S.S. 68. *Green Fees:* information not provided. *Eating facilities:* lunches and snacks served in club. *Visitors:* welcome with bona fide Handicap Certificate or playing with a member. *Society Meetings:* small societies catered for weekdays only. Professional: P. Grindley (01243 608936). Secretary: B. Rogers (01243 608935; Fax: 01243 607101).
e-mail: secretary@selseygolfclub.com
website: www.selseygolfclub.co.uk

COWDRAY PARK **Cowdray Park Golf Club,** Petworth Road, Midhurst GU29 0BB (01730 813599; Fax: 01730 815900). *Location:* one mile east of Midhurst on A272 between Midhurst and Petworth. A testing parkland course with scenic views of the Downs and polo fields and Cowdray ruins. 18 holes, 6265 yards. S.S.S. 70. Driving range and Par 3 Academy. *Green Fees:* from £45.00 weekdays and weekends. *Eating facilities:* restaurant and bar snacks. *Visitors:* welcome. Dormy house. *Society Meetings:* catered for. Professional: Scott Brown. Secretary: Malcolm Upfield.
e-mail: enquiries@cowdraygolf.co.uk
website: www.cowdraygolf.co.uk

CRAWLEY. **Copthorne Golf Club,** Borers Arms Road, Copthorne, Crawley RH10 3LL (01342 712033). *Location:* off Exit 10 M23, one mile on A264 towards East Grinstead. Flat wooded course. 18 holes, 6505 yards. S.S.S. 71. Practice area. *Green Fees:* weekdays £38.00 per round, £45.00 per day. Half fees if playing with member. *Eating facilities:* catering all day, bar. *Visitors:* welcome weekdays without reservation, after 3pm weekends. *Society Meetings:* welcome with advance bookings. Professional: Joe Burrell (01342 712405). Secretary: J. Pyne (01342 712508; Fax: 01342 717682).

CRAWLEY. **Cottesmore Golf and Country Club,** Buchan Hill, Pease Pottage, Crawley RH11 9AT (01293 528256; Fax: 01293 522819). *Location:* one mile west of Junction 11 off M23 on road through Pease Pottage. Two mature golf courses set in 247 acres of rolling Sussex countryside. The fairways are lined with rhododendrons, silver birch, oak and chestnut trees. Four holes over lakes. Griffin Course 18 holes, 6248 yards. S.S.S. 70, par 71. Phoenix Course 18 holes, 5514 yards. S.S.S. 66, par 69. Practice ground, putting greens. *Green Fees:* information on request. *Eating facilities:* restaurant, coffee shop, two bars. *Visitors:* welcome. Health Club including indoor heated pool, tennis courts and gymnasium; en suite accommodation (21 rooms) also available. Trolleys and buggies available. *Society Meetings:* welcome, advance bookings required. Professional: Calum Callan (01293 861777; Fax: 01293 522819). General Manager: (01293 528256).

CRAWLEY. **Ifield Golf and Country Club,** Rusper Road, Ifield, Crawley RH11 0LN (01293 520222). *Location:* outskirts of Crawley near A23 to Gossops Green. Undulating parkland. 18 holes, 6314 yards. S.S.S. 70. Practice ground. *Green Fees:* £35.00 per round, £45.00 per day weekdays; weekends with a member only. *Eating facilities:* fully licensed bar, à la carte restaurant. *Visitors:* welcome, please telephone. Trolley and buggies for hire. *Society Meetings:* welcome. Professional: Jon Earl (01293 523088; Fax: 01293 612973). Golf Manager: George Fielding (01293 520222).

CRAWLEY. **Pease Pottage Golf Centre,** Horsham Road, Pease Pottage, Crawley (01293 521706; Fax: 01293 521706). *Location:* M23 Junction 11, Pease Pottage, Black Swan. Wooded areas surrounding golf course. 9 holes, 1864 yards. S.S.S. 60, Par 4/3. 22 bay floodlit driving range, open from dawn 'till dusk. *Green Fees:* weekdays £8.50; weekends £11.00 for 18 holes. Senior Citizens £5.00. *Eating facilities:* restaurant, coffee shop. *Visitors:* welcome, no restrictions. Two PGA Professionals available for tuition. New Golf Superstore. Full on site repair service. *Society Meetings:* welcome. Professional: David Blair (01293 521706). Secretary: Natalie Leszczar.

CRAWLEY. **Tilgate Forest Golf Centre,** Titmus Drive, Tilgate, Crawley RH10 5EU (01293 530103). *Location:* Crawley, five minutes from Junction 11 M23. Wooded parkland. 18 holes, 6167 yards, 5643 metres. Par 72. 35 bay floodlit driving range. Par 3 course. *Green Fees:* weekdays £18.00; weekends £24.00. *Eating facilities:* restaurant and bar. *Visitors:* welcome at all times but there is a booking system in operation. *Society Meetings:* welcome, phone for details. Professional: William Easdale (01293 530103; Fax: 01293 523478).

CUCKFIELD. **Cuckfield Golf Centre,** Staplefield Road, Cuckfield RH17 5HY (01444 459999). *Location:* one mile north west of Cuckfield village. Undulating open parkland course with outstanding views in an Area of Outstanding Natural Beauty. 9 holes, 18 tees. 5066 yards. Par 71. Putting green. *Green Fees:* 9 holes weekdays £9.00; weekends £10.00; 18 holes weekdays £13.00; weekends £14.50; £1.00 discount Juniors and Senior Citizens. *Eating facilities:* new clubhouse with fully licensed cafe bar. *Visitors:* always welcome. Pay and play; no Handicap Certificate required. Hire clubs and trolleys, please phone for availability. New teaching academy and practice facilities available. *Society Meetings:* always welcome. Professional: R. Dickman. Secretary: Mrs L. Dickman.
e-mail: lucy@cuckfieldgolf.co.uk
website: www.cuckfieldgolf.co.uk

EAST GRINSTEAD. **Chartham Park,** Felcourt Road, Felcourt, East Grinstead RH19 2JT (01342 870340; Fax: 01342 870719). *Location:* Felcourt Road off A22 on north side of East Grinstead. Parkland. 18 holes, 6680 yards. S.S.S. 72. Driving range, putting green. *Green Fees:* information not available. *Eating facilities:* restaurant, light snacks and bar all day. *Visitors:* pre-booking required. Golf carts and trolleys can be hired. *Society Meetings:* by prior arrangement. Professional: David Hobbs. General Manager: David Reeves.*

EAST GRINSTEAD. **Holtye Golf Club,** Holtye Common, Cowden, Near Edenbridge TN8 7ED (01342 850635). *Location:* four miles east of East Grinstead on A264, seven miles west of Tunbridge Wells. Undulating forest course; alternate tees. 9 holes, 5325 yards. S.S.S. 66. Large practice ground. *Green Fees:* weekdays £16.00; weekends £20.00. *Eating facilities:* available every lunchtime, some evenings in summer season. *Visitors:* welcome, restrictions Wednesday, Thursday and weekend mornings. *Society Meetings:* catered for. Professional: Kevin Hinton (01342 850635). Secretary: Mrs D. M. Botham (01342 850635).

EFFINGHAM. **Effingham Park Golf Club,** West Park Road, Copthorne RH10 8AL (01342 716528). *Location:* Junction 10 M23, two miles east on A264. Parkland (wooded), large lake in play over four holes. 9 holes, 1815 yards. S.S.S. 57 (18 holes). *Green Fees:* information not available. *Eating facilities:* club bar and restaurant. *Visitors:* welcome, restricted Tuesday evenings, Wednesday and Thursday mornings. Five star Hotel on site and leisure club. *Society Meetings:* catered for anytime weekdays, weekends after 12 noon. Club Professional: Mark Root. Secretary: Ian McRobbie.*

HASSOCKS. **Hassocks Golf Club,** London Road, Hassocks BN6 9NA . *Location:* on the A273 between Burgess Hill and Hassocks. Gently undulating pay and play course. 18 holes, 5703 yards, 5215 metres. S.S.S. 67. Driving range, irons only. *Green Fees:* weekdays £20.00; weekends £25.00, twilight rates available on application. *Eating facilities:* restaurant, bar, stud bar. *Visitors:* welcome anytime. Buggy for hire, £20.00. *Society Meetings:* welcome. Professional: Charles Ledger (01273 846990). Manager: Jaki Brown (01273 846630; Fax: 01273 846070).
e-mail: hassocksgolfclub@btconnect.com
website: www.hassocksgolfclub.co.uk

HAYWARDS HEATH. **Haywards Heath Golf Club,** High Beech Lane, Haywards Heath RH16 1SL (01444 414457). *Location:* two miles north of Haywards Heath. Parkland. 18 holes, 6216 yards. S.S.S. 70. Practice areas. *Green Fees:* weekdays £30.00 per round, £45.00 for 36 holes; weekends and Bank Holidays £40.00 for 18 holes, £50.00 for over 18 holes. Subject to review. Packages for societies. *Eating facilities:* bar and catering both available. *Visitors:* welcome, by arrangement, phone Professional; Handicap Certificate required. *Society Meetings:* catered for Wednesdays and Thursdays by arrangement with the Secretary. Professional: M.P. Henning (01444 414866). Secretary: G.K. Honeysett.

HORSHAM. **Horsham Golf and Fitness,** Worthing Road, Horsham RH13 0AX (01403 271525; Fax: 01403 274528). *Location*: A24 Horsham bypass (southwest roundabout), 200 yards towards Horsham. Parkland with several water features. 9 holes, 4122 yards. S.S.S. 60. Driving range. *Green Fees*: information not available. *Eating facilities*: restaurant/bar open all day. *Visitors*: welcome at all times. Large well stocked shop, fitness suite on site. *Society Meetings*: welcome with booking. Professional/Secretary: Warren Pritchard.

HORSHAM. **Mannings Heath Golf Club,** "Fullers", Hammerpond Road, Mannings Heath, Near Horsham RH13 6PG (01403 210228; Fax: 01403 270974). *Location*: off J11 M23, three miles south of Horsham off A281. Undulating wooded course with featured streams. Waterfall: 18 holes, 6683 yards (Gold tees). S.S.S. 70; Kingfisher Course: 18 holes, 6217 yards. S.S.S. 70. Driving range, two practice putting greens, chipping green. *Green Fees*: Waterfall Course members and residents only; Kingfisher Course £30.00 weekdays. 36 hole day package £45.00pp. *Eating facilities*: luxurious clubhouse "Fullers", full bar, restaurant and spike bar facilities. *Visitors*: welcome, may book 21 days in advance (by phone). Conference/meeting facilities. *Society Meetings*: welcome at all times, full/half day. Professional: Clive Tucker. General Manager: Steve Slinger.
e-mail: enquiries@manningsheath.com
website: www.manningsheath.com

HORSHAM near. **Slinfold Park Golf and Country Club,** Stane Street (A29), Slinfold, Near Horsham RG13 7RE (01403 791154; Fax: 01403 791465). *Location:* situated on the A29, four miles west of Horsham with good road links to the M23 and East/West on the A272. A gently undulating parkland course with many interesting water features and mature trees. 18 Hole Championship Course, 6418 yards. 9 Hole course. S.S.S. 71. 19 bay floodlit driving range. *Green Fees:* information not available. *Eating facilities:* purpose built clubhouse with restaurant and bar. *Visitors:* welcome subject to tee time availability. Reservations can be made up to seven days in advance. No handicap required. *Society Meetings:* welcome weekdays, minimum group size 10; call for society pack. Professional: Alistair Cardwell (01403 791555). Secretary: Stewart Judd (01403 791154).*

LINDFIELD. **Lindfield Golf Club,** East Mascalls Lane, Lindfield RH16 2QN (01444 484467; Fax: 01444 482709). *Location*: take Lewes Road out of Lindfield village one mile then left. Downland with water and River Ouse. 18 holes, 5957 yards. S.S.S. 68. Practice ground, putting green. *Green Fees*: weekdays £18.00, weekends £23.00. *Eating facilities*: restaurant and bar. *Visitors*: welcome daily. Trolleys. *Society Meetings*: welcome every day. Professional: Paul Lyons. General Manager: Louise Marks.
website: www.thegolfcollege.com

LITTLEHAMPTON. **Littlehampton Golf Club,** 170 Rope Walk, Riverside West, Littlehampton BN17 5DL (01903 717170; Fax: 01903 726629). *Location:* leave A259 one mile west of Littlehampton at sign. Seaside links. 18 holes, 6244 yards. S.S.S. 70. *Green Fees:* information not provided. *Eating facilities:* restaurant and two bars. *Visitors:* welcome weekdays, weekends after 1pm, but phone prior to arrival. *Society Meetings:* societies only, minimum number 12. Professional: Stuart Fallow (01903 717170 ext 225). Secretary: Steven Graham.
e-mail: lgc@talk21.com
website: www.littlehamptongolf.co.uk

PETWORTH. **Petworth Golf Course,** "Osiers Farm", London Road, Petworth GU28 9LX (Tel & Fax: 01798 344097; mobile: 07932 163941). Open all year round. *Location*: 2 miles north of Petworth on A283, heading northbound towards Guildford. Undulating natural farmland course, plenty of hedges and ditches. 18 holes, 6191 yards, S.S.S. 71. Nets and course practice holes. *Green Fees*: £15.00 per round, £25.00 per day. *Eating Facilities*: clubhouse catering for up to 80 people. *Visitors*: welcome anytime, B&B on site. Tuition available. *Society Meetings*: welcome, rates from £17.50 to £45.00. Professional: Steve Hall (01798 873487). Manager: Andy Long (01798 344097). Secretary: Matt Harrison (01798 343518).
e-mail: info@petworthgolfcourse.co.uk
website: www.petworthgolfcourse.co.uk

PULBOROUGH. **West Sussex Golf Club,** Golf Club Lane, Wiggonholt, Pulborough RH20 2EN (01798 872563). *Location:* between Storrington and Pulborough on the A283. Heathland. 18 holes, 6264 yards. S.S.S. 70. *Green Fees:* £75.00 per day (or part of). Subject to review. Driving range. *Eating facilities:* lunch and tea daily, bars. *Visitors:* welcome by prior arrangement (not Fridays and weekends). No three or four balls. *Society Meetings:* catered for Wednesdays and Thursdays. Professional: T. Packham (01798 872426). Secretary: C.P. Simpson (01798 872563; Fax: 01798 872033).
e-mail: secretary@westsussexgolf.co.uk
website: www.westsussexgolf.co.uk

RUSTINGTON. **Rustington Golf Centre,** Golfers Lane, Angmering BN16 4NB (01903 850790; Fax: 01903 850982). *Location:* on A259 at Rustington, near Littlehampton. 18 holes, 5735 yards, S.S.S. 70. 9 hole Par 3 course, three hole academy course, putting green, 30 bay floodlit driving range (15 automated). *Green Fees:* information not available. *Eating facilities:* coffee shop and licensed bar. *Visitors:* welcome at all times. Scott Cranfield Golf Academy available for tuition of all standards. Large 3000 foot square Golf Store. *Society Meetings:* societies and corporate days welcome by appointment. Centre Manager/ Secretary: Gary Salt (01903 850790; Fax: 01903 850982).*

WEST CHILTINGTON. **West Chiltington Golf Club,** Broadford Bridge Road, West Chiltington RH20 2YA (01798 813574; Fax: 01798 812631). *Location:* A29 Bognor to London Road, right at Adversane village B2132 then signposted. Gently undulating parkland with spectacular views of South Downs. 18 holes, 5967 yards. S.S.S. 69. 9 holes, 1360 yard short course ideal for beginners. 13-bay driving range. *Green Fees:* Information not available. *Visitors:* always welcome, smart dress. Tee times may be booked through Pro Shop (01798 812115). *Society Meetings:* welcome, apply to Secretary. Secretary: Debbie Haines. General Manager: Richard Gough.*
website: www.westchiltgolf.co.uk

WORTHING. **Hill Barn Golf Club,** Hill Barn Lane, Worthing BN14 9QF (01903 237301). *Location:* signposted on the roundabout at the top of Broadwater, Worthing on the A27. Downland course with a few trees but generally fairly open. 18 holes, 6229 yards. S.S.S. 70. Small practice area (balls not provided) and putting green. *Green Fees:* Information not available. *Eating facilities:* clubhouse and bar. *Visitors:* welcome, no restrictions or Handicap required. *Society Meetings:* welcome. Manager: James Martin (01903 237301).*
e-mail: info@hillbarngolf.com

WORTHING. **Worthing Golf Club,** Links Road, Worthing BN14 9QZ (01903 260801; Fax: 01903 694664). *Location:* on A27 250 yards east of junction with A24 (Offington Roundabout). Two downland courses. Lower course: 18 holes, 6530 yards. S.S.S. 71. Upper course: 5243 yards. S.S.S. 65. *Green Fees:* weekdays £45.00 per day; weekends and Bank Holidays £40.00/£30.00 per round. *Eating facilities:* dining room, lounge and bar. *Visitors:* welcome, check in advance with Secretary. No visitors at weekends (for golf) during G.M.T. *Society Meetings:* catered for by arrangement. Professional: Stephen Rolley (01903 260718; Fax: 01903 694613). Secretary: Ian Evans (01903 260801; Fax: 01903 694664).

Golf in the East

John Smith • Regional Secretary, PGA East

Bedfordshire • Cambridgeshire • Essex
Greater London • Hertfordshire • Norfolk • Suffolk

Barnham Broom Hotel & Golf Club, Norwich

THE COUNTIES of the PGA East Region provide many attractive golfing opportunities, from those well established coastal clubs in Norfolk to an assortment of lesser-known gems to be found in Suffolk, Bedfordshire, Cambridgeshire, Essex, Hertfordshire, Middlesex and Greater London. Clubs established some 25 years ago are now maturing so fast that they are on a par with many long-established clubs whose centenaries have long since gone by. There are superb links courses, traditional heathland courses and scenic parkland courses in the region, all ready to offer an enjoyable golfing experience.

Sheringham, Royal Cromer and Hunstanton are famous clubs on The Wash with special charm and wonderful views. The hospitality and catering at these famous clubs is second to none. They provide ideal venues for a short break.

Not far away is King's Lynn, set among pine trees at Castle Rising. It has been called

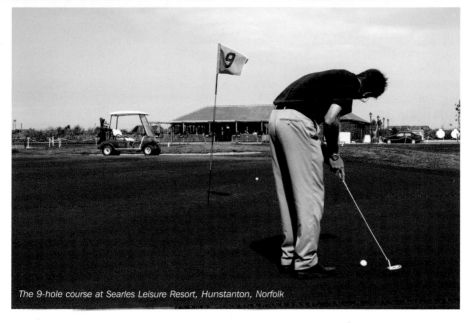

The 9-hole course at Searles Leisure Resort, Hunstanton, Norfolk

the "Augusta of the East" and is, in many ways, like Woburn. The opportunity to play there on a course designed by Dave Thomas and Peter Allis should not be missed.

On the Suffolk coast there are a couple of wonderful courses within three of miles of one another. Aldeburgh, which hosted the 2007 Varsity match, has no par fives, but the length of some of the par fours has been extended. The fairways and greens are top class, while the gorse on either side of most fairways can appear daunting, especially on a windy day. This is a venue to enjoy in early spring when many other clubs are below their best.

Thorpeness's heathland course was designed by James Braid. The same visitors tend to return year after year, but despite its popularity it always seems in pristine condition.

Rushmere, also a heathland course on the outskirts of Ipswich, provides quality greens, especially in winter when there are regular visits from golfers further south, frustrated by the wet clay at their own clubs.

Felixstowe Ferry, founded in 1880, is one of the oldest courses in the country, and has stood the test of time. Two holes have been altered in recent years for safety purposes but the new Hawtree designs have proved popular.

In Essex the new Blakes Golf Club at North Weald has surprised everyone with the speed with which it has settled down. They call it an "inland links", which is an apt description. It has sand-based tees and greens that drain well and will provide welcome winter golf without temporary greens. Designed by Howard Swan, it has sleepered bunkers and, with a bit of imagination, you could think it was a seaside course.

Some parkland courses, like East Herts Golf Club at Hamels Park, Weston Park near Norwich, and Braintree Golf Club at Stisted Park and Hadley Wood, have been laid out in the grounds of mansions where mature trees are in abundance. These provide a perfect setting.

Colchester, now 100 years old, and Chelmsford, are splendid courses, while many of the newer clubs are maturing fast.

Nazeing, with its deep ponds, offers an intriguing test, while Stock Brook Golf and Country Club near Billericay is 6905 yards long and has former amateur champion Craig Laurence as its professional.

Woolston Manor, with the River Roding meandering through the course, has 12 holes featuring water. It is par 72 and 6408 yards in length. Gary Player has described it as the "best young course he has ever played", which is praise indeed. A variety of freshwater fish can be seen as players cross bridges while playing the first seven holes.

Those who seek a golfing oasis in London should look no further than Hendon, while it's not to far to locate Canons Brook or West Essex Golf Club where Walker Cup player Oliver Fisher, now a teenage professional, started his career. Crews Hill, a parkland course 6230 yards long, and the scenic Bush Hill Park, shorter still, but memorable because of its attractive location, are both close to Enfield.

It is amazing how many courses there are in and around London. Highgate, Ilford, Wanstead, Upminster, Northwood, Chigwell, Grim's Dyke, Fulwell, Romford, Hampstead all spring readily to mind.

Bishop's Stortford, the headquarters of the PGA East Region, provides a true test of golf. If the par five third hole offers an encouraging birdie opportunity, some of those that follow will cut players of all standards down to size. A friendly welcome for that well earned post match glass is assured here.

The Grove, near Watford, is another new star in the East so far as golf is concerned. The 7125 yard course designed by American Kyle Philips hosted the World Golf Championship won by Tiger Woods.

Bedfordshire's John O'Gaunt Golf Club, which also has the shorter Carthagena course, is another massive test, while a visit to Brocket Hall near Welwyn is an experience. There are two courses, both named after Prime Ministers who used to live in the mansion, the Melbourne course designed by Peter Allis and Clive Clark and the 7000-yard plus Palmerston Course designed by Donald Steel.

Leighton Buzzard, where Ian Poulter played his golf before he became an established star, is another course with charm which earned great praise from Henry Longhurst. Opened in 1925, it is described as a "thinking man's course", built in woodland and sandy grazing land that is the site of Iron Age earth works.

A good day out for racing enthusiasts can be to play golf at The Links at Newmarket in the morning and then visit the Rowley Mile or July Course to follow the horses in the afternoon. The Links, built on a former steeplechase course and polo ground owned by the Jockey Club, was the idea of Colonel Henry McCalmont, a local Member of Parliament, in 1893.

There is such a wide variety on offer for golfers of all standards. At Hunstanton, for example, Searles Resort Golf and Country Club offers a par 34 nine-hole layout for those who want to warm up or perhaps feel they may not be quite ready for a Championship challenge. Happy golfing in the PGA East Region!

Looking for Holiday Accommodation?

for details of hundreds of properties throughout the UK, visit our website

www.holidayguides.com

London (Central & Greater)

ASHFORD. **Ashford Manor Golf Club,** Fordbridge Road, Ashford, Middlesex TW15 3RT (01784 424644; Fax: 01784 424649). Parkland course, flat with narrow fairways. 18 holes, 6351 yards. S.S.S. 71. *Green Fees:* weekdays £40.00 per round, £50.00 per day. *Eating facilities:* dining room and snacks. *Visitors:* welcome weekdays; it is advisable to ring in advance, Handicap Certificate required. May not play at weekends other than with a member. *Society Meetings:* welcome. Professional: (01784 255940). Manager: Gina Rivett (01784 424644; Fax: 01784 424649). e-mail: secretary@amgc.co.uk

BARNET. **North Middlesex Golf Club,** The Manor House, Friern Barnet Lane, Whetstone N20 0NL (020 8445 1604; Fax: 020 8445 5023). *Location:* five miles south of Junction 23 of M25. 18 holes, 5594 yards. S.S.S. 67. *Green Fees:* information not available. *Eating facilities:* luncheons, snacks and dining facilities. *Visitors:* welcome (with Official Handicap), weekends after 12 noon. Advisable to telephone Professional to book time. *Society Meetings:* catered for. Professional: Freddy George (020 8445 3060). General Manager: Mrs Janet Underhill (020 8445 1604; Fax: 020 8445 5023).

BARNET. **Old Fold Manor Golf Club,** Old Fold Lane, Hadley Green, Barnet, Herts EN5 4QN (020 8449 1650). *Location:* Junction 23 M25 - A1000 one mile north of Barnet. Heathland course. 18 holes, 6447 yards. S.S.S. 71. Practice ground and putting green. *Green Fees:* information not provided. *Eating facilities:* restaurant and bar. *Visitors:* welcome weekdays, discount Green Fee days Monday/Wednesday; special visitors' concessions at weekends by arrangement. *Society Meetings:* catered for Monday-Friday. Professional: Peter McEvoy (020 8440 7488). Manager: Brian Cullen (020 8440 9185; Fax: 020 8441 4863). website: www.oldfoldmanor.co.uk

CHINGFORD. **Chingford Golf Club,** 158 Station Road, Chingford E4 (020 8529 2107). 18 holes, 6342 yards. S.S.S. 70. *Green Fees:* information not available. *Visitors:* welcome weekdays only, an article of red must be worn. Pro shop: 020 8529 5708. Professional: Andy Traynor. Secretary: Bryan Sinden.*

PLEASE NOTE
Some London golf clubs are listed in the SOUTH REGION (see pages 63-64)

CHINGFORD. **Royal Epping Forest Golf Club,** Forest Approach, Chingford, London E4 7AZ (020 8529 2195). *Location:* 200 yards east of Chingford (BR) Station. A private club on a public course. Wooded. 18 holes, 6342 yards. S.S.S. 71. *Green Fees:* weekdays £16.00; weekends £20.00. *Eating facilities:* public snack bar. *Visitors:* may play course but may not use clubhouse. Must wear red garment (trousers or shirt/sweater). Professional: Andy Traynor (020 8529 5708). Secretary: D. Bright-Thomas (020 8529 2195).

CHINGFORD. **West Essex Golf Club,** Bury Road, Sewardstonebury, Chingford, London E4 7QL (020 8529 7558; Fax: 020 8524 7870). *Location:* two miles north of Chingford BR Station. M25 (Junction 26) and Waltham Abbey follow directions to Chingford (Daws Hill on left). Parkland, wooded, hilly. 18 holes, 6289 yards. S.S.S. 70. Driving range (for members, members' guests and societies). *Green Fees:* weekdays £40.00 per round, £45.00 per day; weekends with member only. *Eating facilities:* restaurant and bar facilities. *Visitors:* welcome weekdays except Tuesday mornings. Phone first. *Society Meetings:* catered for by arrangement Mondays, Wednesdays and Fridays. Professional: Robert Joyce (Tel & Fax: 020 8529 4367). Secretary: (020 8529 7558; Fax: 020 8524 7870). e-mail: sec@westessexgolfclub.co.uk website: www.westessexgolfclub.co.uk

EDMONTON. **Leaside Golf Club,** Lee Valley Leisure Centre, Pickett's Lock Lane, Edmonton N9 0AS (020 8803 3611; Fax: 020 8884 4975). *Location:* M25 Juntion 25, nearest town Enfield. Flat parkland course, lake on first 9 holes, good drainage; short but challenging course. 18 holes, 4811 yards (yellow). S.S.S. 64 (yellow). 20 bay driving range, practice ground. *Green Fees:* information not available. *Eating facilities:* cafe and bar. *Visitors:* welcome everyday. Trolleys available. Professional: Richard Gerken (020 8803 3611). Membership/Secretary: David Campbell (020 8364 7782)*

EDMONTON. **Lee Valley Leisure Golf Course,** Picketts Lock Lane, Edmonton N9 0AS. (020 8803 3611). *Location:* off Meridian Way between north Circular Road and Ponders End. Flat parkland course with lake and River Lea as water hazards. Short but challenging. 18 holes, 5204 yards. S.S.S. 65. *Green Fees:* please phone for details (020 8803 3611). Senior Citizens/Junior weekday concessions. *Visitors:* welcome, pay and play everyday. *Society Meetings:* small societies welcome, prior booking. Professional: R.G. Gerken (020 8803 3611).

ENFIELD. **Crews Hill Golf Club (1920) Ltd,** Cattlegate Road, Crews Hill, Enfield EN2 8AZ (020 8363 6674). *Location:* off Junction 24 M25, follow directions to Enfield. H.S. Colt designed parkland course. 18 holes, 6281 yards. S.S.S. 70. *Green Fees:* on application. *Eating facilities:* full bar and snacks available, restaurant by arrangement. No catering Mondays. *Visitors:* welcome weekdays. Handicap Certificate required. Weekends by prior booking. *Society Meetings:* by arrangement. Professional: N. Wichelow (020 8366 7422). Club Manager: Bob Hill (020 8363 6674; Fax: 020 8363 2343).

ENFIELD. **Enfield Golf Club,** Old Park Road South, Enfield, Middlesex EN2 7DA (020 8363 3970; Fax: 020 8342 0381). *Location:* off Junction 24, M25; follow directions to Enfield. Parkland; designed by James Braid. 18 holes, 6154 yards. S.S.S. 70. *Green Fees:* on request. *Eating facilities:* full bar and catering facilities. *Visitors:* welcome weekdays, limited availability at weekends. Please telephone Professional Shop before travelling. *Society Meetings:* welcome weekdays by prior arrangement. Professional: Martin Porter (020 8366 4492). Secretary: Peter Monument (020 8363 3970; Fax: 020 8342 0381).
e-mail: secretary@enfieldgolfclub.co.uk
website: www.enfieldgolfclub.co.uk

ENFIELD. **Whitewebbs Golf Club,** Clay Hill, Beggars Hollow, Enfield EN2 9JN (020 8363 2951). *Location:* A10 off M25, north of Enfield. Parkland course. 18 holes, 5863 yards. S.S.S. 68. Practice area, separate 9 hole pitch and putt. *Green Fees:* information not available. *Eating facilities:* public cafe on site. *Visitors:* welcome, public course, no restrictions. *Society Meetings:* contact the Secretary. Professional: Gary Sherrif (020 8363 4454). Secretary: Stephen Pyke (020 8363 2951). *

FINCHLEY. **Finchley Golf Club,** Nether Court, Frith Lane, Mill Hill NW7 1PU (020 8346 2436; Fax: 020 8343 4205). *Location:* close A1/M1, near Mill Hill East underground station. Parkland course, tree lined, designed by James Braid. 18 holes, 6411 yards. S.S.S. 71. *Green Fees:* weekdays £35.00 per round, £45.00 per day; weekends £45.00 per round. *Eating facilities:* two bars and catering. *Visitors:* welcome weekdays except Tuesdays, Thursdays and weekend mornings. Clubs, shoes, trolleys and carts for hire. Excellent 19th century Manor House. *Society Meetings:* catered for Mondays, Wednesdays and Fridays. Professional: David Brown (020 8346 5086). Secretary: M. Gottlieb (020 8346 2436).
e-mail: secretary@finchleygolfclub.co.uk

GREENFORD. **Ealing Golf Club,** Perivale Lane, Greenford, Middlesex UB6 8TS. *Location:* on Western Avenue A40 half a mile from Hanger Lane Gyratory System. Parkland. 18 holes, 6216 yards. S.S.S. 70. *Green Fees:* £35.00 Monday to Friday. *Eating facilities:* spike bar, mixed lounge, restaurant - lunch, dinner and bar snacks. Conference room. *Visitors:* welcome weekdays with reservation through Professional Shop. *Society Meetings:* catered for Monday to Friday. Professional: Ricky Willison (020 8997 3959). General Manager: Guy Stacey (020 8997 0937).
e-mail: ealinggolfoffice@aol.com

GREENFORD. **Horsenden Hill Golf Club,** Greenford, Middlesex UB6 0RD. *Location:* two miles from A40; off Whitton Avenue East, next door to Sudbury Golf Course. Situated on Horsenden Hill Conservation Area. Undulating parkland course, eight Par 3, one Par 4. 9 holes, 1632 yards. S.S.S. 28. Practice area, nets and putting green. *Green Fees:* £4.80 for 9 holes weekdays, £7.50 weekends. *Eating facilities:* bar/cafe. *Visitors:* welcome at all times, public course. Membership available. Trolley hire. *Society Meetings:* welcome. Professional: Jeff Quarshie (020 8902 4555). Golf Course Manager: Ray Peters (07989 243219).

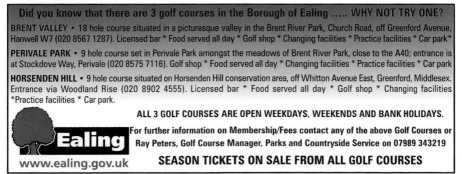

GREENFORD. **Perivale Park Golf Club,** Stockdove Way, Argyle Road, Greenford, Middlesex. *Location:* A40, turn off at sign for Ealing and Perivale. Entrance to golf club is at Stockdove Way, Perivale. Flat, riverside course set amongst the meadows of Brent River Park. Internal out of bounds areas. 9 holes (18 holes), 2733 yards (white tees). S.S.S. 65. Practice area. *Green Fees:* weekdays £8.00, weekends and Public Holidays £9.00. *Eating facilities:* cafeteria. *Visitors:* welcome at all times. Public course. Membership available. Professional: P. Bryant (020 8575 7116). Golf Course Manager: Ray Peters: (07989 243219).

HAMPTON. **The Fulwell Golf Club,** Wellington Road, Hampton Hill, Middlesex TW12 1JY. *Location:* opposite Fulwell Railway Station and bus garage. Stunning parkland course. 18 holes, 6544 yards. S.S.S. 71. Practice ground. *Green Fees:* weekdays £40.00 per round, £50.00 per day; weekends £55.00, £20.00 with member. *Eating facilities:* bar lunches and teas. *Visitors:* welcome weekdays, weekends by prior arrangement. *Society Meetings:* welcome Monday, Thursday and Friday. Professional: Nigel Turner (Tel & Fax: 020 8977 3844). Secretary: Mark Walden (020 8977 2733; Fax: 020 8977 7732). e-mail: secretary@fulwellgolfclub.co.uk website: www.fulwellgolfclub.co.uk

HAMPSTEAD. **Hampstead Golf Club,** Winnington Road, London N2 0TU (020 8455 6420). *Location:* off Hampstead Lane adjacent to Spaniards Inn. Undulating parkland with mature trees. 9 holes, 5812 yards. S.S.S. 68. *Green Fees:* information not available. *Eating facilities:* bar meals/snacks and afternoon teas. *Visitors:* welcome weekdays (not Tuesdays); limited at weekends, telephone Professional. Professional: P J. Brown (020 8455 7089). Secretary: (020 8455 0203); *

HANWELL. **Brent Valley Golf Club,** Church Road, Hanwell, London W7. *Location*: one mile from Uxbridge Road, off Greenford Avenue, entrance at Church Road. Situated in a picturesque valley in the Brent River Park, 18 holes, 5446 yards. S.S.S. 67. Pay and Play. Nets and practice area. *Green Fees*: information not available. *Eating facilities*: bar/cafe. *Visitors* :welcome at all times. Membership available Public course. *Society Meetings*: welcome. Professional: V. Santos (020 8567 1287). Golf Course Manager: Ray Peters (07989 243219).*

HENDON. **Hendon Golf Club,** Ashley Walk, Devonshire Road, Mill Hill, London NW7 1DG (020 8346 6023) *Location:* leave M1 southbound at Junction 2. Turn off A1 into Holders Hill Road, first circle , take first left into Devonshire Road, golf club approx. 50 metres on the left. 10 miles north of London. Parkland, wooded, well bunkered. 18 holes, 6289 yards. S.S.S. 70. *Green Fees:* weekdays £35.00 per round, £45.00 per day; weekends £45.00 per round. *Eating facilities:* full bar and catering facilities. *Visitors:* welcome weekdays (limited at weekends and Bank Holidays), book through Pro Shop. *Society Meetings:* catered for by arrangement Tuesdays to Fridays, book through Secretary's office. Professional: Matt Deal (020 8346 8990). Secretary: Clive Bailey (020 8346 6023; Fax: 020 8343 1974). e-mail: hendongolfclub@globalnet.co.uk website: www.hendongolfclub.co.uk

HIGHGATE. **Highgate Golf Club,** Denewood Road, Highgate, London N6 4AH (020 8340 1906). Founded 1904. *Location:* near A1, turn down Sheldon Avenue, opposite Kenwood House and first left. Parkland. 18 holes, 5985 yards. S.S.S. 69. *Green Fees:* £35.00. *Eating facilities:* bar, restaurant. *Visitors:* welcome weekdays except Wednesdays. Telephone Pro Shop before travelling. *Society Meetings:* catered for Tuesdays, Thursdays (pm only), and all day Friday Book through Secretary's office. Professional: Robin Turner (020 8340 5467). Secretary: Nick Higginson (020 8340 3745). website: www.highgategc.co.uk

HILLINGDON. **Hillingdon Golf Club,** 18 Dorset Way, Hillingdon, Uxbridge, Middlesex UB10 0JR (01895 239810). *Location:* near A40, adjacent to RAF Uxbridge. Gently undulating wooded parkland course sloping down to river. 9 holes, 5490 yards, 5068 metres. S.S.S. 67. *Green Fees:* information not available. *Eating facilities:* bar meals available Tuesday to Friday. *Visitors:* welcome Mondays, Tuesdays and Fridays; Thursdays - Ladies' Day. *Society Meetings:* catered for by special arrangement only with Committee through Club Secretary. Professional: Phil Smith (01895 460035). Secretary: B.L. Russell (01895 233956).*

HOUNSLOW. **Airlinks Golf Club,** Southall Lane, Hounslow, Middlesex TW5 9PE (020 8561 1418; Fax: 020 8813 6284). *Location:* Junction 3 on M4, A312 to Hayes. Same entrance as D. Lloyd Tennis Centre. Parkland course with water holes and doglegs. 18 holes, 6000 yards. S.S.S. 68. Floodlit driving range. *Green Fees:* information not available. *Eating facilities:* full catering and bar facilities/restaurant area. *Visitors:* weekdays no restrictions, some restrictions weekends, bookings advised seven days in advance. Membership, including 5 and 7 day, now open. *Society Meetings:* catered for all week. Professional: Tony Martin. Secretary: Stefan Brewster.*

HOUNSLOW. **Hounslow Heath Golf Centre,** Staines Road, Hounslow TW4 5DS (020 8570 5271). *Location:* Staines Road A315 between Hounslow and Bedfont. Heathland course with water hazards, tight fairways. 18 holes, 5901 yards. S.S.S. 68. Practice area. *Green Fees:* information not provided. *Eating facilities:* snacks; teas and coffee. *Visitors:* welcome at all times, bookings seven days in advance for weekends and Bank Holidays. *Society Meetings:* by arrangement.

ISLEWORTH. **Wyke Green Golf Club,** Syon Lane, Osterley, Isleworth, Middlesex TW7 5PT (020 8560 8777). *Location:* situated half-a-mile north of A4 near Gillettes Corner. Fairly flat parkland. 18 holes, 6182 yards. S.S.S. 70. *Green Fees:* Monday £20.00 (£15.00 with member), Tuesday - Friday £30.00 (£18.00 with member). £40.00 per day. Monday - Thursday "early bird" 8am - 9am £15.00, twilight £20.00 after 4pm (Monday - Tuesday only) *Eating facilities:* full catering restaurant and halfway house. *Visitors:* welcome; weekends only with member until after 4pm. *Society Meetings:* catered for by arrangement, minimum 12. Professional: Neil Smith (020 8847 0685) Secretary: David Pearson (020 8560 8777; Fax: 020 8569 8392).
e-mail: office@wykegreengolfclub.co.uk
website: www.wykegreengolfclub.co.uk

LONDON. **Dukes Meadows Golf Club,** Dukes Meadows, Dan Mason Drive, London W4 2SH (020 8995 0537 Fax: 020 8995 5326). *Location:* next to Chiswick Bridge on the A316, one mile south Hogarth roundabout. Parkland course, greens to USGA standard. 50 bay floodlit driving range.6 hole Academy Course for young players accompanied by adult golfers. *Green Fees:* information not available. *Eating facilities:* bar/restaurant area available. *Visitors:* welcome, tee times up to 48 hours advance booking. 12 teaching PGA professionals, trolleys available. *Society Meetings:* welcome by arrangement. Professional: Malcolm Henbery (020 8995 0537). General Manager/PGA Professional: Scott Margetts. (020 8994 3314).

LONDON. **Mill Hill Golf Club,** 100 Barnet Way, Mill Hill, London NW7 3AL (020 8959 2339). Est. 1925. *Location:* A1, south half a mile before Apex Corner left into clubhouse car park – signposted. Wooded parkland. 18 holes, 6247 yards, 5697 metres. S.S.S. 70. Practice ground. *Green Fees:* (2006) weekdays £30.00, weekends £37.00 (subject to review). *Eating facilities:* restaurant and bar. *Visitors:* welcome Monday to Friday; weekends and Bank Holidays prior bookings recommended. Two snooker tables. *Society Meetings:* welcome weekdays with prior

booking. For green fees ring the Pro Shop (020 8959 7261); for society and membership enquiries ring Club Office (020 8959 2339). Professional: D. Beal. Secretary: R. Bauser.

LONDON. **Trent Park Public Golf Course,** Bramley Road, Southgate, London N14 (020 8367 4653). *Location:* opposite Oakwood Tube Station. Undulating parkland. 18 holes, 6176 yards. S.S.S. 69. Modern heated, floodlit 36 bay driving range. *Green Fees:* information not available. *Eating facilities:* restaurant and snacks. *Visitors:* open to public at all times. Bookings advised on weekdays and necessary at weekends. Golf superstore. *Society Meetings:* welcome any day. Professional: Ray Stocker. Secretary: Richard Flint.*

MUSWELL HILL. **Muswell Hill Golf Club,** Rhodes Avenue, London N22 7UT (020 8888 2044; Fax: 020 8889 9380). *Location:* North Circular/Bounds Green tube station one mile. Mature parkland. 18 holes, 6438 yards. S.S.S. 71. *Green Fees:* enquire for details. *Eating facilities:* restaurant open seven days. *Visitors:* welcome weekdays, weekends pre-booked with Professional. *Society Meetings:* welcome weekdays; terms on request. Professional: D. Wilton (020 8888 8046). Manager: J. Pascoe (020 8888 1764).

NORTHWOOD. **Northwood Golf Club Ltd,** Rickmansworth Road, Northwood, Middlesex HA6 2QW (01923 821384; 01923 840150). *Location:* on A404 between Pinner and Rickmansworth. Parkland/wooded course. 18 holes, 6535 yards. S.S.S. 71. *Green Fees:* information not available. *Eating facilities:* restaurant and bar snacks, lounge bar. *Visitors:* welcome weekdays, except Tuesdays; with members only at weekends. *Society Meetings:* by arrangement, details from the Secretary. Professional: C.J. Holdsworth (01923 820112). Secretary: T. N. Collingwood (01923 821384).

NORTHWOOD. **Sandy Lodge Golf Club,** Sandy Lodge Lane, Northwood, Middlesex HA6 2JD. *Location:* adjacent to Moor Park Underground Station. Sandy Lodge Golf Club is a member of the Hertfordshire Golf Union and situated on the Moor Park Estate close to Moor Park, Batchworth Park. Chorleywood and Rickmansworth. Inland links. 18 holes, 6328 yards. S.S.S. 71 (white). *Green Fees:* on application. *Eating facilities:* full catering and bar service available. *Visitors:* weekdays only, please telephone in advance. Handicap Certificate required. *Society Meetings:* by prior written arrangement. Professional: Jeff Pinsent (01923 825321). Secretary: John C. Coombes (01923 825429; Fax: 01923 824319).

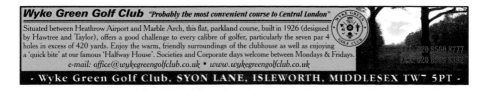

PINNER. **Grim's Dyke Golf Club,** Oxhey Lane, Hatch End, Pinner, Middlesex HA5 4AL (020 8428 4539). *Location:* on A4008 Watford to Harrow (2 miles north of Harrow). Undulating parkland, tree-lined, testing greens. 18 holes, 5600 yards. S.S.S. 67. Practice area. *Green Fees:* £30.00 weekday, £15.00 on Monday (subject to review). *Eating facilities:* bar snacks, lunches available on request. *Visitors:* must produce Certificate of Handicap. Buggies available. Phone Pro shop for tee times. *Society Meetings:* catered for Mondays to Fridays. Professional: Lee Curling. Office & Pro: (020 8428 4539; Fax: 020 8421 5494).

PINNER. **Pinner Hill Golf Club,** Southview Road, Pinner Hill HA5 3YA (020 8866 0963; Fax: 020 8868 4817). *Location:* one mile west Pinner Green. Parkland course with magnificent views over London. 18 holes, 6392 yards. S.S.S. 71. *Green Fees:* Monday, Tuesday and Friday £35.00; Wednesday and Thursday £18.50. *Eating facilities:* bar and catering available at all times; parties by prior arrangement please. *Visitors:* welcome with Handicap Certificate. *Society Meetings:* weekdays. Professional: Mr Chris Duck (020 8866 2109). General Manager: Craig Anderson (020 8866 0963). e-mail: phgc@pinnerhillgc.com website: www.pinnerhillgc.com

RUISLIP. **Ruislip Golf Club,** King's End, Ickenham Road, Ruislip, Middlesex HA4 7OQ (01895 638081). *Location:* two and a half miles from Junction 1, M40, first left after M40/A40 merge, onto B467, then left at T-Junction onto B466. Parkland course. 18 holes, 5571 yards. S.S.S. 67. Driving range (40 bays). *Green Fees:* information not available. *Eating facilities:* full restaurant facilities. *Visitors:* welcome, booking system at all times. *Society Meetings:* welcome by arrangement. Professional: Paul Glozier (01895 638835). Secretary: P.C. Thornton (01895 638081).*

SHEPPERTON. **Sunbury Golf Centre,** Charlton Lane, Shepperton TW17 8QA (01932 772898). *Location:* two miles south-west of M3 Junction 1; south-east of Queen Mary Reservoir between villages of Charlton and Upper Halliford. Two parkland courses. 18 holes, 5103 yards. S.S.S. 65, Par 68. 9 holes, 2444 yards, Par 33. 32 bay floodlit driving range (8am to 10pm), practice puttting green. *Green Fees:* 18 hole course £23.00 weekends, £18.50 weekdays; 9 hole course £11.00 weekends, £9.00 weekdays. *Eating facilities:* snacks, meals and bar. *Visitors:* welcome, no restrictions. Booking up to one week in advance essential. Buggies and trolleys for hire. *Society Meetings:* welcome at all times; advance booking required; special packages available. Professional: Adrian McColgan. General Manager: Patrick Dawson (01932 771414; Fax: 01932 789300).

SOUTHALL. **West Middlesex Golf Club,** Greenford Road, Southall, Middlesex UB1 3EE (020 8574 3450). *Location:* junction of Uxbridge Road (A4020) and Greenford Road. 18 holes, 6119 yards. S.S.S. 69. *Green Fees:* please telephone the Pro Shop on 020 8574 1800. *Visitors:* welcome weekdays and at weekends after 2.00pm, except on competition days. *Society Meetings:* catered for by prior arrangement. Professional: T. Talbot. Secretary: Miss R. Khanna (020 8574 3450; Fax: 020 8574 2383).

STANMORE. **Brockley Hill Golf Park,** Brockley Hill, Stanmore HA7 4LR (020 8420 6222; Fax: 020 8420 6333). *Location:* Junction 4 M1, A41. Parkland course. 9 holes, 1102 yards, 1007 metres. S.S.S. 27. Covered and floodlit 2 tier driving range. *Green Fees:* information not available. *Visitors:* welcome anytime - pay as you play. *Society Meetings:* welcome on application. Professionals: Cranfield Golf Academy.*

STANMORE. **Stanmore Golf Club,** 29 Gordon Avenue, Stanmore, Middlesex HA7 2RL (Tel & Fax: 020 8954 2599). *Location:* turn off A410 by church to Old Church Lane, Gordon Avenue is to the right. Wooded, parkland course. 18 holes, 5879 yards. S.S.S. 68. Practice and putting areas. *Green Fees:* from £17.00. *Eating facilities:* restaurant facilities available *Visitors:* welcome. No jeans or trainers. Jacket and tie after 7pm. *Society Meetings:* catered for by prior booking only. Professional: James Reynolds. Secretary: Allan Knott. Caterer: (020 8954 4661). e-mail: secretary@stanmoregolfclub.co.uk website: www.stanmoregolfclub.co.uk

TOTTERIDGE. **South Herts Golf Club,** Links Drive, Totteridge N20 8QU (020 8445 2035). *Location:* off Totteridge Lane N20, one mile from Whetstone, nearest underground station Totteridge & Whetstone. Parkland. 18 holes, 6432 yards. S.S.S. 71. *Green Fees:* Information not available. *Eating facilities:* lunch, high tea (breakfast and dinner by arrangement). *Visitors:* welcome with reservation Monday to Friday and Sunday pm. *Society & Corporate Meetings:* welcome Monday to Friday. Professional: R.Y. Mitchell (020 8445 4633). Secretary: B. Weeds (020 8445 2035; Fax: 020 8445 7569).* website: www.southhertsgolfclub.co.uk

TWICKENHAM. **Amida Golf Course and Teaching Academy,** Staines Road, Twickenham TW2 5JD (020 8783 1698; Fax: 020 8941 9134). *Location*: at end of M3, on A305 near its junction with 35. Golf teaching academy. *Green Fees*: information not available. *Eating facilities:* Golfers' Bar and Indoor Virtual Golf. *Visitors:* welcome, play and pay. Function room available. *Society Meetings*: welcome. Professional: Suzy Watt (020 8783 1698; Fax: 020 8941 9134)* website: www.amidaclubs.com

PLEASE NOTE
Some London golf clubs are listed in the SOUTH REGION
(see pages 63-64)

TWICKENHAM. **Strawberry Hill Golf Club,** Wellesley Road, Strawberry Hill, Twickenham TW2 5SD (020 8894 1246). *Location:* near Twickenham Green, 200 yards Strawberry Hill Station. Flat parkland. 9 holes, 4762 yards. S.S.S. 63. *Green Fees:* 18 holes £20.00; with a member £13.00. 9 holes £15.00, with a member £10.00. *Eating facilities:* restaurant and bar. *Visitors:* welcome, restrictions weekends and competition days. *Society Meetings:* welcome weekdays, small parties only. Professional: Peter Buchan (020 8898 2082). Secretary: Paul Astbury (020 8894 0165). e-mail: secretary@shgc.net

UXBRIDGE. **Stockley Park Golf Club,** Stockley Park, Uxbridge UB11 1AQ (020 8813 5700; Fax: 020 8813 5655). *Location:* Junction 4 M4, Heathrow Airport turnoff, A408 to Uxbridge. Parkland course, designed by Robert Trent Jones Snr. 18 holes, 6754 yards. S.S.S. 71. Practice nets, chipping and putting greens. *Green Fees:* Information not available. *Eating facilities:* balcony restaurant and bar. *Visitors:* all welcome. Trolleys available all year round. *Society Meetings:* welcome. Professional: Stuart Birch. Adminstration: Jackie Hickey.*
website: www.stockleyparkgolf.com

UXBRIDGE. **Uxbridge Golf Course,** The Drive, Harefield Place, Uxbridge UB10 8AQ (01895 237287; Fax: 01895 810262). *Location*: off Swalkelys Junction - M40. Undulating parkland. 18 holes, 5753 yards. S.S.S. 68. *Green Fees*: information not available. *Eating facilities*: bars, carvery restaurant. *Visitors*: welcome anytime, booking required at weekends. Function suite. *Society Meetings*: welcome. Professional: Phil Howard (01895 237287). Secretary: Tom Atkins (01895 272457).*

WANDSWORTH. **Central London Golf Centre,** Burntwood Lane, Wandsworth SW17 0AT (020 8871 2468; Fax: 020 8874 7447). *Location:* turn right through the Wandsworth town centre into Garrat Lane, Burntwood Lane is off Garrat Lane. Short course with three good Par 3s and several good Par 4s. 9 holes, 2223 yards. S.S.S. 31. Large practice putting green. 14 bay driving range. *Green Fees:* information not available. *Eating facilities:* full bar and restaurant;

function room. *Visitors:* welcome, no restrictions. Special disabled putting green. Trolleys for hire. *Society Meetings:* welcome, special terms on request. Professional: Jeremy Robson (020 8871 2468).*
e-mail: golf@clgc.co.uk
website: www.clgc.co.uk

WANSTEAD. **Wanstead Golf Club,** Overton Drive, Wanstead E11 2LW (020 8989 3938; Fax: 020 8532 9138). *Location:* one mile from junction of A12 and A406. Parkland bordering Epping Forest with featured lake. 18 holes, 6109 yards. S.S.S. 69. *Green Fees:* information not available. *Eating facilities:* dining room and bars. *Visitors:* welcome weekdays by prior arrangement with the General Manager. Handicap Certificate required. Weekends with member only. *Society Meetings:* welcome, apply General Manager. Professional: David Hawkins (020 8989 9876). General Manager: Keith Jones (020 8989 3938; Fax: 020 8532 9138).

WEMBLEY. **Sudbury Golf Club Ltd,** Bridgewater Road, Wembley, Middlesex HA0 1AL (020 8902 3713). *Location:* junction of A4005 (Bridgewater Road) and A4090 (Whitton Ave East). Undulating parkland. 18 holes, 6282 yards. S.S.S. 70. *Green Fees:* information not provided. *Eating facilities:* dining room and bars. *Visitors:* welcome weekdays with Handicap Certificate. *Society Meetings:* catered for. Professional: Neil Jordan (020 8902 7910). General Manager: Neil Cropley.

WINCHMORE HILL. **Bush Hill Park Golf Club,** Bush Hill, Winchmore Hill, London N21 2BU (020 8360 5738; Fax: 020 8360 5583). *Location:* half a mile south of Enfield town (off London Road). Parkland. 18 holes, 5825 yards. S.S.S. 68. Practice ground and nets. *Green Fees:* weekdays £29.50 per round, weekends only with member. *Eating facilities:* restaurant, bar, bar snacks. *Visitors:* welcome weekdays, Handicap Certificate required. *Society Meetings:* catered for Mondays, Tuesdays, Thursdays and Fridays. Professional: Lee Fickling (020 8360 4103). Manager: Tony Hutchinson (020 8360 5738; Fax: 020 8360 5583).

The 13th hole at Crews Hill Golf Club, Enfield

Bedfordshire

AMPTHILL. **The Millbrook Golf Club,** Millbrook, Ampthill MK45 2JB (01525 840252; Fax: 01525 406249). *Location:* just off A507 Ampthill to Woburn Road, near Junction 13 of M1. Rolling links situated on the Greensand Ridge overlooking Bedfordshire. 18 holes, 6966 yards. Par 73. S.S.S. 73. Two practice areas. *Green Fees:* weekdays £25.00 18 holes; weekends only after 12 noon £35.00. *Eating facilities:* bar/restaurant, breakfasts, lunches, dinners. *Visitors:* welcome midweek. *Society Meetings:* welcome. Professional & Tee Time bookings: Rob Brightman (01525 402269). Manager: Derek Cooke (01525 840252; Fax: 01525 406249).
e-mail: info@themillbrook.com
website: www.themillbrook.com

ASPLEY GUISE. **Aspley Guise and Woburn Sands Golf Club,** West Hill, Aspley Guise MK17 8DX (Tel & Fax: 01908 583596). *Location:* two miles west of Junction 13 M1, between Aspley Guise and Woburn Sands. Undulating parkland, 18 holes, 6079 yards. S.S.S. 70. *Green Fees:* weekdays £34.00 per round, £44.00 per day; weekends by prior arrangement. *Eating facilities:* catering service, bar. *Visitors:* welcome weekdays with bona fide handicaps - check with Secretary. *Society Meetings:* Wednesdays and Fridays. Professional: Colin Clingan (01908 582974). Secretary: Richard Norris (Tel & Fax: 01908 583596).

BEADLOW. **Beadlow Manor Hotel, Golf and Country Club,** Beadlow, Near Shefford SG17 5PH (01525 860800). *Location:* from M1 (J12) take A5120 east to Ampthill, then A507 to Shefford. From A1 (J10) take A507 west to Ampthill. Challenging, rolling parkland with water hazards. Two courses (Baron and Baroness): 18 holes, 6819 yards. S.S.S. 72; 18 holes, 6072 yards. S.S.S 69. Covered 25 bay floodlit driving range, practice area. *Green Fees:* information not available. *Eating facilities:* restaurant, three bars, snacks, refreshments, two function rooms. *Visitors:* welcome at all times. Residential Golf Breaks available. Professional academy and shop. Special mid-week and weekend Breaks for Society and Company Groups. All reservations through Sales and Marketing Office. General Manager: Graham Wilson.

BEDFORD. **The Bedford Golf Club,** Great Denham Golf Village, Biddenham, Bedford MK40 4FF (01234 320022; Fax: 01234 320023). *Location:* two miles west of Bedford on A428. American-style course with 90 bunkers and eight water features, built on free-draining sandy soil. 18 holes, 6478 yards. S.S.S. 72. Practice range and putting green. *Green Fees:* midweek £40.00, weekends £60.00. *Eating facilities:* restaurant and bar meals; course refreshments. *Visitors:* always welcome - excellent rates. Buggies for hire. Part of the Kolven Golf Group. *Society Meetings:* welcome midweek and weekend. Group Manager: Simon Pepper.
e-mail: thebedford@btopenworld.com
website: www.kolvengolf.com

BEDFORD. **Bedford and County Golf Club,** Green Lane, Clapham, Bedford MK41 6ET (01234 354010). *Location:* off the old A6 road north of Bedford just before the village of Clapham. Parkland. 18 holes, 6420 yards. S.S.S. 70. *Green Fees:* midweek only £34.00 per round, £42.00 per day; twilight after 4pm £22.00 (2007). *Eating facilities:* full catering facilities and bar. *Visitors:* welcome without reservation except weekends. *Society Meetings:* catered for Mondays, Tuesdays, Thursdays and Fridays. Professional: R. Tattersall (01234 359189). Manager: R. Walker (01234 352617; Fax: 01234 357195). website: www.bedfordandcountygolfclub.co.uk

BEDFORD. **Bedfordshire Golf Club,** Spring Lane, Stagsden, Bedford MK43 8SR (01234 822555; Fax: 01234 825052). *Location:* one mile west of Bedford town centre on the A422. Wooded parkland, flat. 18 holes, 6565 yards. S.S.S. 71. 9-hole course. 24-bay driving range. *Green Fees:* information not available. *Eating facilities:* bar and catering; evening meals by arrangement. *Visitors:* welcome on weekdays, must be with members at weekends. *Society Meetings:* catered for weekdays. Professional: Geraint Dixon (01234 826100). Manager: Ross Ellens (01234 822555).
e-mail: office@bedfordshiregolf.com
website: www.bedfordshiregolf.com

BEDFORD. **Mowsbury Golf Club,** Cleat Hill, Kimbolton Road, Bedford MK41 8BJ (01234 771493). *Location:* on B660 at northern limit of city boundary. 18 holes, 6451 yards. S.S.S. 71. Driving range. *Green Fees:* on request. *Eating facilities:* meals and bar snacks until 3pm; evening meals if booked in advance. *Visitors:* welcome. Squash courts. *Society Meetings:* by arrangement with the Professional. Professional: Malcolm Summers (01234 772700), for tee reservations and fees. Secretary: T.W. Gardner (01234 771041).

BEDFORD. **Pavenham Park Golf Club,** Pavenham, Bedford MK43 7PE (01234 822202; Fax: 01234 826602). *Location:* take the A6 out of North Bedford, from Clapham follow signs to Pavenham. Parkland course with fast and contoured greens. 18 holes, 6400 yards. S.S.S. 71. Practice ground. *Green Fees:* weekdays £40.00, weekends £60.00. *Eating facilities:* bar and catering available. *Visitors:* welcome midweek only, must adhere to dress code. Buggies and carts available. Part of the Kolven Golf Group. *Society Meetings:* welcome, excellent rates. Professional: Zac Thompson. Secretary: Lee Pepper.
e-mail: kolvengolf@ukonline.co.uk
website: www.kolvengolf.com

www.uk-golfguide.com

CADDINGTON. **Caddington Golf Club,** Chaul End Road, Caddington LU1 4AX (01582 415573 Fax: 01582 415314). *Location:* Ten minutes from Junctions 9 or 11 M1. Gently undulating parkland. 18 holes, 6240 yards. S.S.S.70. *Green Fees:* information not available. *Eating facilities:* bar with catering available. *Visitors:* welcome anytime midweek; weekends by arrangement. *Society Meetings:* welcome, special deals available. Secretary: David Isger.
e-mail: info@caddingtongolfclub.co.uk

COLMWORTH. **Colmworth and North Bedfordshire Golf Club,** New Road, Colmworth MK44 2NN (01234 378181; Fax: 01234 376678). *Location:* north of Bedford just off B660 and only 10 minutes from the A1 at Wyboston. Fast maturing, well drained course in its 17th year offering easy walking yet challenging golf all year round. 18 holes, 6459 yards. S.S.S. 71. 9-hole Par 3 course. 8 bay driving range. *Green Fees;* weekdays £16.00; weekends and Bank Holidays £25.00. *Eating facilities:* licensed clubhouse with bar. *Visitors:* no restrictions. Mix-and-match Golf Breaks available in one of our spacious, well equipped self-catering cottages; includes reduced green fees and buggy hire.

DUNSTABLE. **Dunstable Downs Golf Club,** Whipsnade Road, Dunstable LU6 2NB (01582 604472; Fax: 01582 478700). *Location:* on B4541; one and a half miles from town centre. Downland course with exceptional views. 18 holes, 5903 yards. S.S.S. 70. Practice ground. *Green Fees:* information not provided. *Eating facilities:* bar and restaurant. *Visitors:* welcome weekdays, weekends with member only. Handicap Certificate required. Carts for hire. *Society Meetings:* Mondays, Tuesdays and Thursdays, limited availability on Fridays. Professional: Darren Charlton (01582 662806). Secretary/Manager: Alan Sigee (01582 604472; Fax: 01582 478700).

DUNSTABLE. **Tilsworth Golf Centre,** Dunstable Road, Tilsworth, Leighton Buzzard LU7 9PU (01525 210721; Fax: 01525 210465). *Location:* two miles north of Dunstable off A5, Tilsworth turn-off. Parkland course, water hazards on three holes! 18 holes, 5306 yards. S.S.S. 67, Par 69. 30 bay floodlit driving range. *Green Fees:* information not provided. *Eating facilities:* bar snacks and restaurant available. *Visitors:* welcome any time except Sundays before 10am. Bookings taken up to seven days in advance. *Society Meetings:* welcome by prior arrangement. Professional: Nick Webb.

HENLOW. **Mount Pleasant Golf Course,** Station Road, Lower Stondon, Henlow SG16 6JL (01462 850999). *Location:* three-quarters of a mile west of A600 (Hitchin to Bedford) at Henlow Camp roundabout. Undulating meadowland. 9 holes (alternative tees for second 9 holes), 6185 yards, 5656 metres. S.S.S. 70. Practice chipping, putting and nets. *Green Fees:* weekdays £10.00 for 9 holes, £17.50 for 18 holes; weekends and Bank Holidays £12.50 for 9 holes, £21.50 for 18 holes. Reductions for Senior Citizens and Juniors. *Eating facilities:* spike bar, dining room. Group catering by prior arrangement. *Visitors:* welcome anytime, booking

required for weekends and summer evenings. *Society Meetings:* welcome on weekdays and weekend afternoons. Professional: Glen Kemble. Proprietor: David Simkins.
website: www.mountpleasantgolfclub.co.uk

LEIGHTON BUZZARD. **Aylesbury Vale Golf Club,** Stewkley Road, Wing, Leighton Buzzard LU7 0UJ (01525 240196). *Location:* four miles west of Leighton Buzzard on Stewkley to Wing road. Gently undulating course with water hazards. 18 holes, 6622 yards, S.S.S. 72. 9-bay driving range. *Green Fees:* weekdays £21.00; weekends £30.00 up to 11am, £22.00 after 11am. Please telephone for availability. Senior Citizens £10.00 Tuesdays. *Eating facilities:* first floor bar and balcony, ground floor bar and restaurant. *Visitors:* welcome any time, no restrictions apart from correct dress. Telephone in advance. Individual lessons from £15.00. *Society Meetings:* welcome, competitive rates, Monday to Friday only. Professional: Terry Bunyan (07731 966749). Secretary: Chris Wright (01525 240196).

LEIGHTON BUZZARD. **Leighton Buzzard Golf Club,** Plantation Road, Leighton Buzzard LU7 3JF (01525 244800). *Location:* off A5 between Dunstable and Milton Keynes at village of Heath and Reach. Wooded parkland course. 18 holes, 6101 yards. S.S.S. 70. Practice ground. *Green Fees:* weekdays, please call for current prices; weekends with members only. *Eating facilities:* available - dining room and three bars. *Visitors:* welcome weekdays. (Tuesday Ladies' Day). Weekends and Bank Holidays with member only. *Society Meetings:* catered for weekdays only, except Tuesdays. Professional: M. Campbell (01525 244815). Secretary: D. Mutton (01525 244800; Fax: 01525 244801).
e-mail: secretary@leightonbuzzardgolf.net
website: www.leightonbuzzardgolf.net

LEIGHTON BUZZARD near. **Ivinghoe Golf Club,** Wellcroft, Ivinghoe, Near Leighton Buzzard LU7 9EF (01296 668696; Fax: 01296 662755). *Location:* leave A41 at Tring and take B488 to Ivinghoe. When approaching the village, the church is on the left, and Vicarage Lane is on the right. Go down the lane to the Rose & Crown pub and turn right up to the club. Gently rolling parkland course in lee of Ivinghoe Beacon. 9 holes, 4508 yards. S.S.S. 62. Pro shop, tuition available. *Green Fees:* 9 holes £6.00, 18 holes £10.00. *Eating facilities:* bar meals anytime. *Visitors:* welcome except before 8am Monday to Saturday and 9am Sundays; dress code in operation. *Society Meetings:* catered for. Professional: Mark Flitney (01296 668696). Secretary: Mrs S.E. Garrad (01296 668696). Steward: Mr B. Burton (01296 661186).

THE APPEARANCE OF AN ASTERISK (*) AT THE END OF A CLUB OR COURSE ENTRY INDICATES THAT UP-TO-DATE INFORMATION HAS NOT BEEN SUPPLIED

LEIGHTON BUZZARD near. **Mentmore Golf and Country Club,** Mentmore, Near Leighton Buzzard LU7 0UA (01296 662020; Fax: 01296 662592). *Location:* between Leighton Buzzard and Aylesbury in village of Mentmore. Rolling parkland, mature trees and with many water features. Two courses - Rothschild and Rosebery. 36 holes, 6777 and 6763 yards. S.S.S. 72. Driving range. *Green Fees:* information not available. *Eating facilities:* restaurant, two bars, spike bar; function room. *Visitors:* welcome. Also available swimming pool, sauna, jacuzzi and steam room, two tennis courts, full gymnasium and aerobics studio. *Society Meetings:* welcome everyday, please telephone for details. General Manager: Kevin Whitehouse. Sales Manager: Matthew Darley. Professional: Robert Davies.*

LUTON. **South Beds Golf Club,** Warden Hill Road, Luton LU2 7AE (01582 591500). *Location:* on east side A6, two and a half miles north of Luton. Undulating downland course. 18 holes, 6438 yards. S.S.S. 71. Also 9 holes, 4784 yards. S.S.S. 63. Practice fairway and chipping area. *Green Fees:* weekdays 9 hole course £10.00 for 18 holes, 18 hole course £23.00; weekends 9 hole course £13.00 for 18 holes, 18 hole course £32.00. *Eating facilities:* three-course meals (must be booked), snacks at all times. *Visitors:* welcome anytime on 9-hole course, weekdays and limited weekends on 18-hole course. Handicap Certificate essential for 18-hole course. Tuesday is Ladies' Day. *Society Meetings:* catered for by arrangement on Mondays, Wednesdays and Thursdays. Professional: Eddie Cogle (01582 591209). Secretary: Ray Wright (01582 591500; Fax: 01582 495381).

LUTON. **Stockwood Park Golf Club,** London Road, Luton LU1 4LX (01582 431788). *Location:* adjacent Exit 10/10A of M1 exit for Luton Airport. Parkland. 18 holes, 6049 yards. S.S.S. 69. Driving range, par 3 nine hole course. *Green Fees:* contact 01582 413704. *Eating facilities:* two bars and restaurant. *Visitors:* always welcome, municipal Golf Centre run by Active Luton Trust. Changing rooms. *Society Meetings:* catered for by prior arrangement. Professional: Matt Green. Club Administrator: Brian E. Clark (01582 413708).
e-mail: spgc@hotmail.com

SANDY. **John O'Gaunt Golf Club,** Sutton Park, Sandy SG19 2LY (01767 260360; Fax: 01767 262834). *Location:* on B1040 off A1 two miles north of Biggleswade. Parkland courses. Two 18 hole courses: John O'Gaunt Course 6513 yards S.S.S. 71 and Carthagena Course 5869 yards S.S.S. 69. Small practice area. *Green Fees:* weekdays £35.00 per round, £50.00 per day; weekends £60.00 (subject to review). *Eating facilities:* restaurant and bar. *Visitors:* welcome weekdays, Handicap Certificate required. *Society Meetings:* welcome weekdays. Professional: Lee Scarbrow (01767 260094). Secretary: Stephen Anthony (01767 260360).

SHARNBROOK. **Colworth Golf Club,** Colworth House, Sharnbrook MK44 1LQ (01933 353269). *Location:* off A6 between Bedford and Rushden through Sharnbrook village. Parkland course, narrow fairways, tree lined. 9 holes, 5210 yards. S.S.S. 66. *Green Fees:* information not available. *Eating facilities:* none. *Visitors:* with members only. Secretary: E.W. Thompson (01933 353269).

TODDINGTON. **Chalgrave Manor Golf Club,** Dunstable Road, Toddington, Near Dunstable LU5 6JN (01525 876556). *Location:* two minutes from Junction 12 M1 (Toddington Services), on main A5120 between Toddington and Houghton Regis. Rolling, open course with many natural undulations; four holes with water features. 18 holes, 6417 yards, 5892 metres. S.S.S. 71. Practice areas. *Green Fees:* weekdays £20.00 per round, weekends and Bank Holidays £30.00 per round. Day tickets available. *Eating facilities:* meals available every day, licensed bar. *Visitors:* booking not required. No starting times before 1pm weekends and Bank Holidays, no restrictions midweek. *Society Meetings:* welcome weekdays by prior arrangement. Secretary: Steve Rumball (01525 876554).
e-mail: steve@chalgravegolf.co.uk
website: www.chalgravegolf.co.uk

WYBOSTON. **Wyboston Lakes Golf Course,** Great North Road, Wyboston Lakes, Wyboston MK44 3AL (01480 223004). *Location:* one mile south of St Neots at the junction of the A1 and the A428 east. Flat parkland with five lakes. 18 holes, 5955 yards. S.S.S. 69. Driving range. Putting green. *Green Fees:* phone for details. *Eating facilities:* available. *Visitors:* welcome, bookings required for weekends and Bank Holidays. Motel on site. *Society Meetings:* catered for seven days. Professional: P.G. Ashwell (01480 223004; Fax: 01480 407330). Secretary: D. Little (01480 212625; Fax: 01480 223000).

For full details of clubs and courses, plus convenient accommodation
www.uk-golfguide.com

Cambridgeshire

CAMBRIDGE. **Cambridge Golf Club,** Station Road, Longstanton, Cambridge CB24 3DS (01954 789388). *Location:* 10 minutes from city, off A14 at Bar Hill, turn right to Longstanton B1050. Parkland course. 18 holes, 6736 yards, S.S.S. 73. 9 bay floodlit grassed driving range, 9 holes pitch and putt. *Green Fees:* information not provided. *Eating facilities:* clubhouse; 50-seat function room available for hire. *Visitors:* welcome, may need to book on competition days. Coaching by appointment. *Society Meetings:* catered for. Professional: Geoff Hugget.

CAMBRIDGE. **Cambridge National Golf (Home of Cambridge Meridian Golf Club),** Comberton Road, Toft, Cambridge CB23 2RY (01223 264702; Fax: 01223 264701). *Location:* 5 minutes from Junction 12 of M11 onto B1046. Heavily landscaped championship design set in 250 acres with six lakes and 108 bunkers. 18 holes, 6707 yards. S.S.S. 72. Practice ground and putting green. *Green Fees:* weekdays £28.00 round, £45.00 day; weekends £35.00 round, £55.00 day. Subject to review. *Eating facilities:* available all day. *Visitors:* welcome at all times (subject to availability). Buggies and trolleys for hire. *Society Meetings:* corporate and society golf days catered for. Professional: Craig Watson (01223 264702). Golf Administrator: Steve Creighton. e-mail: meridian@golfsocieties.com

CAMBRIDGE. **Girton Golf Club,** Dodford Lane, Girton, Cambridge CB3 0QE (01223 276169; Fax: 01223 277150). *Location:* two miles north of Cambridge. Flat parkland. 18 holes, 6012 yards. S.S.S. 69. Large practice area. *Green Fees:* Monday to Friday £25.00. *Eating facilities:* diningroom, lounge and bar. *Visitors:* weekdays only. *Society Meetings:* welcome Tuesdays to Fridays. Professional: S. Thomson (01223 276991). Secretary: Miss V. Webb (01223 276169; Fax: 01223 277150). website: www.girtongolf.co.uk

CAMBRIDGE. **Gog Magog Golf Club,** Shelford Bottom, Cambridge CB22 3AB (01223 247626; Fax: 01223 414990). *Location:* Two miles from the A11-A1307 roundabout, Colchester - Cambridge Road A604. Open, undulating chalkland hill course. Old Course - 18 holes, 6400 yards, S.S.S. 70. Wandlebury Course - 18 holes, 6750 yards, S.S.S. 72. Large driving range and practice areas, with ball hire available. *Green Fees:* weekdays £45.00 per round. *Eating facilities:* diningroom, bar meals, large bar area with lounge and spike bar. *Visitors:* welcome, only with members at weekends and Bank Holidays, Handicap Certificate required. *Society Meetings:* catered for Tuesdays and Thursdays. Professional: I. Bamborough (01223 246058). Secretary: Mrs C. A. Davison (01223 247626). e-mail: secretary@gogmagog.co.uk website: www.gogmagog.co.uk

CAMBRIDGE. **Menzies Cambridge Hotel & Golf Club,** Bar Hill, Cambridge CB3 8EU (01954 249988). *Location:* five miles north from Cambridge on A14 Huntingdon Road, Junction 29. Well established Championship parkland course with many mature trees. 18 holes, 6750 yards. Par 72. S.S.S. 73. Practice facilities. *Green Fees:* prices on application. *Eating facilities:* two restaurants and three bars. *Visitors:* welcome anytime by prior phone call. 135 Bedroom 4 star Hotel with excellent conference facilities. Full leisure facilities including gym, heated pool, sauna, solarium, steam rooms and tennis courts. *Society Meetings:* Society and Corporate days welcome. Golf Manager: Tom Turner (01954 780098; Fax: 01954 780010). e-mail: cambridge.golfpro@menzies-hotels.co.uk website: www.bookmenzies.com

ELY. **Ely City Golf Course Ltd,** 107 Cambridge Road, Ely CB7 4HX (01353 662751). *Location:* on southern outskirts of city on A10 if heading towards Cambridge. Parkland course, undulating, magnificent views of the 12th century cathedral. 18 holes, 6627 yards. S.S.S. 72. Practice area. *Green Fees:* weekdays £34.00, weekends £40.00. *Eating facilities:* full bar, catering and restaurant facilities. *Visitors:* welcome anytime with a member or if in possession of a valid Handicap Certificate. Jeans, T-shirts and trainers not allowed. Well equipped Pro Shop. Snooker. *Society Meetings:* welcome Tuesday to Friday inclusive by arrangement. Professional: Andrew George (01353 663317). General Manager: Michael Hoare (01353 662751; Fax:01353 668636) e-mail: elygolf@lineone.net website: www.elygolf.co.uk

---

ELY CITY GOLF CLUB, 107 Cambridge Road, Ely CB7 4HX

18 hole 'family' course used extensively for County Competitions and Regional Finals.
Practice ground and putting green. Pleasant Clubhouse.
Full bar and restaurant service. Well-stocked Professional's shop.
For lessons, coaching and equipment contact: Andrew George (Head Professional) on 01353 663317.
Tel: 01353 662751 • Fax: 01353 668636 • e-mail: elygolf@lineone.net • www.elygolf.co.uk

---

THE APPEARANCE OF AN ASTERISK (*) AT THE END OF A CLUB OR COURSE ENTRY INDICATES THAT UP-TO-DATE INFORMATION HAS NOT BEEN SUPPLIED

HUNTINGDON. **Brampton Park Golf Club,** Buckden Road, Brampton, Huntingdon PE28 4NF (01480 434705). *Location*: three-quarters of a mile off A1, travelling north take first Huntingdon turn, south take second sign for "RAF Brampton". Picturesque with many water hazards, wooded areas and prolific wildlife – swans, badgers, muntjac deer, Canada geese, water fowl, etc. 18 holes, 6300 yards. S.S.S. 72. 10 bay driving range. *Green Fees*: Information not available. *Eating facilities*: bar snacks, restaurant, two bars. *Visitors*: welcome at all times, no restrictions save telephone for tee reservations prior to arrival. Accommodation and business conference facilities and banqueting for up to 120 available. Buggies now available. *Society Meetings*: welcome. Professional: Alisdair Currie (Tel & Fax: 01480 434705). Secretary: Richard Oakes (01480 434700; Fax: 01480 411145).*

HUNTINGDON. **Hemingford Abbots Golf Club,** Cambridge Road, Hemingford Abbots, Huntingdon PE28 9HQ (01480 495000; Fax: 01480 496000). *Location:* two miles south of Huntingdon on the A14. Gently undulating parkland with trees. 9 holes, 2680 yards. S.S.S.68. *Green Fees:* weekdays £10.00 for 9 holes, £15.00 for 18 holes; weekends £12.00 for 9 holes, £18.00 for 18 holes. *Visitors:* welcome, no restrictions. Comfortable clubhouse with bar. *Society Meetings:* welcome. 'The Friendly One', all standards welcome. Alternative tee positions on back nine. Secretary: Dennis Brown. Proprietor: R. D. Paton.

HUNTINGDON. **Lakeside Lodge Golf Centre,** Fen Road, Pidley, Huntingdon PE28 3DF (01487 740540; Fax: 01487 740852). *Location*: on the B1040 St Ives to Warboys Road. Course has 8 lakes and considerable landscaping. Three courses - Lodge Course: 18 holes, 6437 yards. S.S.S. 73; Manor Course: 9 holes, 2601 yards; Church Course: 6 holes, 1645 yards. Driving range and Teaching Academy. *Green Fees:* weekdays £17.00 for 18 holes, £10.00 for 9 holes; weekends £27.00 for 18 holes, £14.00 for 9 holes. After 12 noon weekends £18.00. *Eating facilities:* full bar serving all day snacks and meals. *Visitors:* welcome but best to book. Ten Pin Bowling. Accommodation available in 64 twin en suite bedrooms adjoining the course. *Society Meetings:* all welcome. Professional: Scott Waterman

PGA (01487 741541). Secretary: Mrs Jane Hopkins (01487 740540; Fax: 01487 740852). e-mail: info@lakeside-lodge.co.uk website: www.lakeside-lodge.co.uk

HUNTINGDON. **Ramsey Golf and Bowls Club,** 4 Abbey Terrace, Ramsey, Huntingdon PE26 1DD (01487 812600: Fax: 01487 815746). *Location:* 20 minutes from A1, 12 miles south of Peterborough, 10 miles north of Huntingdon. Flat parkland with a river running full length which comes into play on many holes. 18 holes, 6163 yards. S.S.S. 70. Two practice grounds, chipping area. *Green Fees:* information not available. *Eating facilities:* bar and full catering service available. *Visitors:* welcome weekdays, with member weekends. Six rink county standard bowling green. *Society Meetings:* welcome by prior arrangement. Professional: Stuart Scott (01487 813022). Secretary/Administrator: M. Kjenstad (01487 812600; Fax: 01487 815746). e-mail: admin@ramseyclub.co.uk website: www.ramseyclub.co.uk

MARCH. **March Golf Club Ltd,** Frogs Abbey, Grange Road, March PE15 0YH (01354 652364). *Location:* quarter of a mile west of March bypass (A141). Flat parkland. 9 holes, 6204 yards. S.S.S. 70. Six acre practice area. *Green Fees:* £21.00 per day weekdays, £25.00 weekends. *Eating facilities:* bar, bar meals (Saturday). *Visitors:* welcome. *Society Meetings:* welcome mid week only. Professional: Alex Oldham. Secretary: Mrs M.A. Simpson. website: www.marchgolfclub.co.uk

PETERBOROUGH. **Elton Furze Golf Club,** Bullock Road, Haddon, Peterborough PE7 3TT (01832 280189; Fax: 01832 280299). *Location*: four miles west of Peterborough on old A605 Oundle to Peterborough road. Opened April 1993. Scenic parkland, wooded. 18 holes, 6279 yards, 5715 metres. S.S.S. 70. Driving range. *Green Fees:* weekdays £33.00 per round; weekends £37.00 per round. Subject to review. *Eating facilities:* new spacious bar and restaurant (holds 120). *Visitors:* welcome any time. Buggies available for hire £14.50 for 18 holes, £25.00 all day. *Society Meetings:* welcome Monday to Friday - small groups only on Friday - need to pre-book. Contact: Secretary. Professional: Glyn Krause (01832 280614).

PETERBOROUGH. **Orton Meadows Golf Course,** Ham Lane, Orton Waterville, Peterborough PE2 5UU (01733 237478). *Location*: three miles west of Peterborough on A605, at entrance to Nene Park. Parkland, lakes. 18 holes, 5613 yards. S.S.S. 68. with 12 hole pitch and putt course adjoining. *Green Fees*: weekdays £14.20, Juniors £5.30; weekends and Bank Holidays £19.00. Pitch and Putt weekends £3.60, Juniors £2.70. *Visitors*: welcome; unrestricted – Pay as you Play course. Catering at adjoining pub/restaurant. Bookings taken seven days in advance. *Society Meetings*: Golf Societies welcome, contact Pro Shop (01733 237478). Head Professional: Stuart Brown. Director of Golf: Roger Fitton.
e-mail: enquiries@ortonmeadowsgolfcourse.co.uk
website: www.ortonmeadowsgolfcourse.co.uk

PETERBOROUGH. **Peterborough Milton Golf Club,** Milton Ferry, Peterborough PE6 7AG. *Location*: on A47 west of Peterborough, three miles east of A1. Parkland. 18 holes, 6541 yards. S.S.S. 72. *Green Fees:* £35.00 per round, £45.00 per day. Societies £40.00 per day. *Eating facilities:* available daily except Mondays. *Society Meetings:* available by arrangement with Secretary. Professional: Jasen Barker (01733 380793). Secretary: Andy Izod (01733 380489).

PETERBOROUGH. **Thorney Golf Centre,** English Drove, Thorney, Peterborough PE6 0TJ (01733 270570). *Location:* approximately two miles off the middle roundabout, just off the Thorney Bypass; Thorney Golf Centre is one mile on the left. Fen Course - flat, ideal for beginners; Lakes Course - challenging links with lakes. 36 holes: Fen 18 holes, 6104 yards, S.S.S. 69; Lakes 18 holes, 6399 yards, S.S.S. 71. Driving range. *Green Fees:* weekdays Fen £9.75, Lakes £16.50; weekends Fen £11.75, Lakes £25.00. *Eating facilities:* three bars and restaurant. *Visitors:* welcome, no restrictions on Fen Course, Lakes Course contact in advance at weekends. *Society Meetings:* all welcome. Professional: Mark Templeman. Secretary: Jane Hind.

PETERBOROUGH. **Thorpe Wood Golf Course,** Thorpe Wood, Peterborough PE3 6SE (01733 267701). *Location:* two miles west of Peterborough on A47. Parkland. 18 holes, 7086 yards. S.S.S. 74. Practice ground. *Green Fees:* weekdays £13.80; Concessions; £8.40; Juniors £5.50. Weekends and Bank Holidays £18.50, no concessions, Juniors £5.50. *Visitors:* welcome, unrestricted - Pay-as-you-Play course. Catering at adjoining pub/restaurant. Bookings taken 7 days in advance. *Society Meetings:* Golf Societies welcome – contact Jenny Walters (01733 267701). Head Coach: Gary Casey (01733 267701). Director of Golf: Roger Fitton.*
e-mail: enquiries@thorpewoodgolfcourse.co.uk
website: www.thorpewoodgolfcourse.co.uk

RAMSEY. **Old Nene Golf Club,** Muchwood Lane, Bodsey, Ramsey PE26 2XQ (01487 813519 or 815622). *Location:* three-quarters of a mile north of Ramsey towards Peterborough, halfway between Ramsey and Ramsey Mereside and half mile from Rainbow Superstore. Easy walking course with water hazards, quiet with wildlife – herons, swans, pheasants, partridges. 1996 Eastern Area Environmental Winner. 9 holes, 5605 yards, S.S.S. 68. Edrich driving range on site. *Green Fees:* information not available. *Eating facilities:* in clubhouse, open to all, fully licensed bar; bar snacks always available, meals to order.. *Visitors:* welcome, telephone to avoid club tee closures. *Society Meetings:* welcome. Professional: Adrian Perkins. Secretary: G. Stoneman (01487 815622).

ST IVES. **St Ives (Hunts) Golf Club,** Westwood Road, St Ives PE27 6DH (01480 464459). *Location:* B1040 off A14. 9 holes, 6180 yards. S.S.S. 70. *Green Fees:* information not available. *Eating facilities:* full catering. *Visitors:* welcome weekdays. *Society Meetings:* welcome. Professional: Mark Pond (Tel & Fax: 01480 466067). Manager: Mark Simpson (Tel & Fax: 01480 468392).
e-mail: stivesgolfclub@zoom.co.uk

ST NEOTS. **Abbotsley Golf Club and Hotel,** Eynesbury Hardwicke, St Neots PE19 6XN (01480 474000; Fax: 01480 471018). *Location:* A428 St Neots bypass, turn towards St. Neots at Tesco's follow signs to Eynesbury Hardwicke and Abbotsley. Pleasantly undulating, parkland course with several water features. Two courses, 36 holes - Abbotsley 6311 yards, S.S.S. 72; Cromwell 6087 yards, S.S.S. 69. Floodlit covered driving range, 300 yard grass practice area. 9 hole Par 3 course. *Green Fees:* information not available. *Eating facilities:* 80 cover restaurant, three bars. *Visitors:* always welcome. 42 bedroom hotel. *Society Meetings:* welcome. General Manager: Nicky Briggs. Professional: Steve Connolly. Sales: (01480 474000; Fax: 01480 471018).

ST NEOTS. **St Neots Golf Club,** Crosshall Road, St Neots PE19 7GE (01480 472363). *Location:* just off the A1, Junction B1048 heading for St Neots. Picturesque, undulating parkland course with water hazards and challenging greens. 18 holes, 6033 yards. S.S.S. 69. Practice ground, putting green. *Green Fees:* weekdays £35.00. *Eating facilities:* full catering and bar. *Visitors:* welcome, with Handicap Certificates; weekends with a member only. *Society Meetings:* welcome weekdays. Club Secretary: (01480 472363; Pro Shop: 01480 476513). e-mail: office@stneots-golfclub.co.uk website: www.stneots-golfclub.co.uk

WISBECH. **Tydd St Giles Golf & Country Club,** Kirkgate, Tydd St Giles, Wisbech PE13 5NZ (01945 871007; Fax: 01945 870566). *Location:* A1101 from Wisbech to Long Sutton to Tydd Gate and follow the river to Tydd St Giles, one mile from this junction on right hand side. Slightly undulating course, fenland Grade 1 silt/loam free draining. Course always open. 18 holes, 6264 yards, S.S.S. 70. Indoor/outdoor floodlit driving range. *Green Fees*: Midweek £17.00, weekends £20.00, prices for all day golf. Twilight £10.00 after 1pm (Mon - Sun) all year. *Eating facilities*: all day snacks/grills. Full Pub licence - everyone welcome. *Visitors*: welcome, please ring for a tee off time, dress code applies. Tuition available daily. *Society Meetings*: welcome, packages available. AA Professional: Ashley Howard (07812081838). e-mail: enquiries@tyddgolf.co.uk website: www.tyddgolf.co.uk

FHG Guides

publish a large range of well-known accommodation guides. We will be happy to send you details or you can use the order form at the back of this book.

Cambridge National Golf (Cambridge Meridian Golf Club)

Essex

BASILDON. **Basildon Golf Club,** Clay Hill Lane, Basildon SS16 5JP (01268 533297). *Location:* off A13 or A127 on A176 – Kingswood Roundabout. Undulating woodland. 18 holes, 6236 yards. S.S.S. 70. Practice area. *Green Fees:* information not available. *Eating facilities:* snacks, full meals, bar. *Visitors:* welcome anytime, booking system at weekends and Bank Holidays. *Society Meetings:* welcome, booking through Professional. Professional: Mike Oliver (01268 533532). Secretary: A.M. Merrington (01268 533297; Fax: 01268 284163).

BILLERICAY. **Stock Brook Golf & Country Club,** Queens Park Avenue, Stock, Near Billericay CM12 0SP (01277 653616; Fax: 01277 633063). *Location:* nearest main roads A12 and A127, Billericay. Parkland - gently undulating with featured lakes. 18 hole championship course, 6905 yards. S.S.S. 72. Manor - 9 holes, 2997 yards. Driving range, putting green and three par 3 practice holes. *Green Fees:* weekdays £30.00. weekends (after 12 noon) £35.00. *Eating facilities:* bar meals available. *Visitors:* welcome weekdays, and Saturday/Sunday after 12 noon. Extensive conference and banqueting facilities. Country club, swimming pool, tennis courts, gym. *Society Meetings:* welcome. Professional: Craig Laurence (01277 658181). Membership, Corporate and Society enquiries: Caron Morton.

BRAINTREE. **Braintree Golf Club,** Kings Lane, Stisted, Braintree CM77 8DD (01376 346079; Fax: 01376 348677). *Location:* A120 to Colchester, 300 yards east of Braintree by-pass, signposted Stisted and Golf Club. Parkland, with slopes down to the river, many specimen trees. 18 holes, 6228 yards, S.S.S. 70. Practice ground, pitching area. *Green Fees:* weekdays £45.00 per day, £35.00 per round; weekends £65.00 per day, £50.00 per round. *Eating facilities:* available. *Visitors:* welcome Monday to Fridays (weekends must have Handicap Certificate). *Society Meetings:* catered for Wednesdays, Thursdays and Friday pm. Professional: A.K. Parcell (01376 343465). Secretary: Mrs N. Wells (01376 346079; Fax: 01376 348677).

BRAINTREE. **Towerlands Golf Club,** Panfield Road, Braintree CM7 5BJ (01376 326802; Fax: 01376 552487). *Location:* off A120 into Braintree, then B1053. Undulating course. 9 holes, 2749 yards. S.S.S. 66. Practice area. *Green Fees:* information not available. *Eating facilities:* bars and restaurants. *Visitors:* welcome. We have equestrian facilities, no accommodation. *Society Meetings:* by arrangement. Secretary: B. Clark (01376 326802; Fax: 01376 552487).

BRENTWOOD. **Bentley Golf Club,** Ongar Road, Brentwood CM15 9SS (01277 373179). *Location:* situated on A128 approximately five miles from Junction 28 of M25. Undulating parkland course, a great test of golf. 18 holes, 6709 yards, 6136 metres.

S.S.S. 72. Practice field. *Green Fees:* 18 holes £27.50. *Eating facilities:* food and bar available all day. *Visitors:* welcome weekdays; Bank Holidays after 11am. *Society Meetings:* welcome by prior arrangement. Professional: Nick Garrett (01277 372933). Secretary: Andy Hall (01277 373179).

BRENTWOOD. **Hartswood Golf Club,** (Play on Brentwood Municipal), King George's Playing Fields, Ingrave Road, Brentwood CM15 8AY (01277 218850). *Location:* one mile south of Brentwood on A128. Parkland, 18 holes, 6238 yards. S.S.S. 70. *Green Fees:* information not provided. *Eating facilities:* full catering available. *Visitors:* welcome without reservation. Tee Reservation – 01277 214830. *Society Meetings:* unlimited weekdays. Professional: Stephen Cole (01277 218714). Secretary:J Gander (01277 218850)

BRENTWOOD. **South Essex Golf and Country Club,** Brentwood Road, Herongate, Brentwood CM13 3LW (01277 811006; Fax: 01277 811304). *Location:* Halfway House Exit (A128) from A127 (Junction 29 - M25). Gently rolling countryside incorporating established woodland. 27 holes, 6851 yards. S.S.S. 73. Covered 14 bay driving range. *Green Fees:* information not available. *Eating facilities:* restaurant and fully licensed bar. *Visitors:* welcome with appropriate dress. Buggies available. *Society Meetings:* welcome, including weekends. General Manager: Olly Wooster (01277 811289; Fax: 01277 811304).*

BRENTWOOD. **Thorndon Park Golf Club Ltd,** Thorndon Park, Ingrave, Brentwood CM13 3RH (01277 811666). *Location:* three miles south of Brentwood on A128. 18 holes, 6512 yards. S.S.S. 71. *Green Fees:* £60.00 per day, £45.00 per round weekdays, £50.00 per round after 1pm Sundays. Saturday and Sunday morning with members only. Subject to review. *Eating facilities:* lunches served at club. *Visitors:* welcome with reservation, weekdays subject to prior permission. *Society Meetings:* catered for. Professional: Brian White (01277 810736). Secretary: Lt Col R.M. Estcourt (01277 810345). website: www.thorndonparkgolfclub.com

BRENTWOOD. **The Warley Park Golf Club,** Magpie Lane, Little Warley, Brentwood CM13 3DX (01277 224891). *Location:* leave M25 at Intersection 29. A127 towards Southend. Turn left three-quarters-of-a-mile Little Warley, Hall Lane. Turn left into Magpie Lane. Parkland, 3 Courses, (27 holes). S.S.S. 70-70-69. Large practice area, putting greens. *Green Fees:* information not available. *Eating facilities:* lounge bar and restaurant/spike bar. *Visitors:* welcome Monday to Friday, must produce club Handicap Certificate. *Society Meetings:* catered for. Professional: K. Smith (01277 200441). Golf Manager: S. Young (01277 224891).*

BRENTWOOD. **Weald Park Golf Club,** Coxtie Green Road, South Weald, Brentwood CM14 5RJ (01277 375101). *Location:* M25 and A12 junction (map available). Parkland course surrounded by countryside. 18 holes, 6612 yards. S.S.S. 72/70. *Green Fees:* information not available. *Eating facilities:* bar and restaurant. *Visitors:* welcome. *Society Meetings:* welcome Monday to Friday. Professional: Dean Vickerman (01277 375101; Fax: 01277 374888). General Manager: Darcy Tallon (01277 375101; Fax: 01277 374888).*

BULPHAN. **The Langdon Hills Golf & Country Club,** Lower Dunton Road, Bulphan RM14 3TY (01268 548444; Fax: 01268 490084). *Location:* eight miles from M25, Dartford River crossing, Basildon three miles between A127 and A13. Gently undulating parkland. Three loops of 9 holes – 27 holes: 6760 yards S.S.S. 72, 6537 yards S.S.S. 72, 6279 yards S.S.S. 71. Two putting greens. *Green Fees:* information not available. *Eating facilities:* restaurant, Function Suite available. *Visitors:* welcome at all times (except Saturday and Sunday morning), subject to availablity. Hotel accommodaton and function suite available. *Society Meetings:* welcome. Professional: Terry Moncur (01268 544300; Fax: 01268 490084). Secretary: Keith Thompson (01268 548444; Fax: 01268 490084). website: www.golflangdon.co.uk

BURNHAM-ON-CROUCH. **Burnham-on-Crouch Golf Club Ltd,** Ferry Road, Creaksea CM0 8PQ (01621 782282). *Location:* Burnham-on-Crouch, one and a half miles before Burnham town. Undulating meadowland rolling alongside River Crouch. 18 holes, 6056 yards. S.S.S. 69. Par 70. Practice ground. *Green Fees:* information not provided. *Eating facilities:* bar, full catering. *Visitors:* welcome weekdays, and weekend afternoons, with Handicap Certificate. *Society Meetings:* welcome Mondays, Tuesdays, Wednesdays and Fridays. Secretary: Claire Rumble (01621 782282; Fax: 01621 784489). Private members club.
e-mail: burnhamgolf@hotmail.com
website: www.burnhamgolfclub.co.uk

CANVEY ISLAND. **Castle Point Golf Club,** Somnes Avenue, Canvey Island SS8 9FG (01268 696298). *Location:* A13 towards Southend, A130 to Canvey Island, opposite sports centre. Links course, with views of Hadleigh Downs and Castle. 18 holes, 6176 yards. S.S.S. 69. Floodlit driving range. *Green Fees:* information not available. *Eating facilities:* clubhouse open to public – full catering. *Visitors:* welcome anytime, booking required at weekends. Changing room and showers; buggies available. Pro Shop (01268 510830). *Society Meetings:* welcome. Professional: Steve Richardson (01268 510830). Secretary: Belinda de Kuster (01268 692899).*

CHELMSFORD. **Channels Golf Club,** Belsteads Farm Lane, Little Waltham, Chelmsford CM3 3PT (01245 440005). *Location:* three miles north east of Chelmsford on A130. Reclaimed gravel workings, many lakes, hazards and an abundance of wild life. Two courses – Channels 6402 yards, S.S.S. 71; Belsteads 4779 yards, S.S.S. 63. *Green Fees:* Channels Course – weekdays only £40.00 per 18 holes; members and guests only at weekends. Belsteads Course – £15.00 9 holes, £20.00 18 holes, no restrictions weekends. *Eating facilities:* excellent restaurant in 13th century clubhouse. *Visitors:* welcome. 'Channels' 6-bedroom lodge opens April 2006. *Society Meetings:* catered for weekdays. Professional: I.B. Sinclair (01245 441056). Secretary: Mrs S. Stubbings-Larner (01245 440005; Fax: 01245 442032).
e-mail: info@channelsgolf.co.uk
website: www.channelsgolf.co.uk

CHELMSFORD. **Chelmsford Golf Club,** Widford Road, Chelmsford CM2 9AP (Tel & Fax: 01245 256483). *Location:* A12–A414 to Chelmsford, first roundabout turn right. Parkland course. 18 holes, 5996 yards. S.S.S. 69. *Green Fees:* weekdays £40.00. *Eating facilities:* dining room and bar. *Visitors:* welcome Monday to Friday with reservation. *Society Meetings:* welcome, discounts available. Professional: Mark Welch (01245 257079). Secretary: G. Winckless.
e-mail: office@chelmsfordgc.co.uk
website: www.chelmsfordgc.co.uk

CHELMSFORD. **The Regiment Way Golf Centre,** Pratts Farm Lane, Little Waltham, Chelmsford CM3 3PR (01245 361100). *Location:* three miles north east of Chelmsford off A130. Flat parkland, ideal novice course. 9 holes, 2500 yards. S.S.S. 64. 22 bay floodlit driving range. *Green Fees:* weekdays £11.00 9 holes, £15.00 18 holes; weekends £12.00 9 holes, £17.00 18 holes. Student and Senior discount £2.00 9 holes, £3.00 18 holes. Subject to review. *Visitors:* pay as you play. *Society Meetings:* welcome. Professional: David March. Secretary: Roger Pamphilon.

CHELMSFORD. **Three Rivers Golf and Country Club,** Stow Road, Cold Norton, Purleigh, Near Chelmsford CM3 6RR (01621 828631; Fax: 01621 828060). *Location:* four miles from South Woodham Ferrers, six miles from Maldon. Parkland with lakes and wooded copses; spectacular views. Two courses: 36 holes, 6403 yards Kings Course, 4501 Jubilee Course. Kings par 72/Jubilee par 64. *Green Fees:* Information not available. *Eating facilities:* bar meals available all day, carvery available Sunday lunchtime. *Visitors:* welcome. Function suites available. Buggies available. *Society meetings:* very welcome. Specialists in looking after companies and groups. Professional: Kevin Clark, individual and group lessons available. (01621 829781).*

THE APPEARANCE OF AN ASTERISK (*) AT THE END OF A CLUB OR COURSE ENTRY INDICATES THAT UP-TO-DATE INFORMATION HAS NOT BEEN SUPPLIED

CHIGWELL. **Chigwell Golf Club,** The Clubhouse, High Road, Chigwell IG7 5BH (020 8500 2059; Fax: 020 8501 3410). *Location:* on A113, 14 miles from London, seven miles from Exit 26 on the M25. Testing undulating parkland course. 18 holes, 6296 yards. S.S.S. 70. Practice bays and ground. *Green Fees:* weekdays £35.00 per round (£25.00 after 2.30pm), £55.00 per day; weekends with introduction by member only. *Eating facilities:* restaurant and bars available. *Visitors:* weekdays by prior arrangement, Handicap Certificate required and membership of authorised Golf Club. *Society Meetings:* weekdays by arrangement. Professional: J. Fuller (020 8500 2384). General Manager: Chris Bishop (020 8500 2059; Fax: 020 8501 3410). e-mail: info@chigwellgolfclub.co.uk website: www.chigwellgolfclub.co.uk

CHIGWELL. **Hainault Forest Golf Club,** Romford Road, Chigwell IG7 4QW (020 8500 2097). *Location:* off A12 towards Hainault/Chigwell. Undulating parkland with tree-lined fairways. 36 holes: Lower 6545 yards. S.S.S. 72; Upper 5886 yards. S.S.S. 69. Driving range, practice hole and putting green. *Green Fees:* information not available. *Eating facilities:* fully licensed bar and restaurant, cafe. *Visitors:* welcome any time, all week. *Society Meetings:* welcome all week, enquiries welcome. Head Professional: Chris Hope. Secretary: Ben Jones.*

CHIGWELL. **Woolston Manor Golf Club,** Woolston Manor, Abridge Road, Chigwell IG7 6BX (020 8500 2549; Fax: 020 8501 5452). Private exclusive members' club - for membership enquiries call membership secretary on 020 8500 2549. *Location:* Junction 5, M11 one mile. Parkland, Neil Coles Championship design, 18 holes, 6435 yards. S.S.S. 71. Top golf driving range. *Green Fees:* information not available. *Eating facilities:* full catering available. *Visitors:* welcome weekdays after 10.30am and after 11.30am weekends. Handicap Certificate required. *Society Meetings:* welcome weekdays only. Professional: Paul Eady (020 8559 8272; Fax: 020 8501 5452). Secretary: Peter Spargo.*

CLACTON-ON-SEA. **Clacton-on-Sea Golf Club,** West Road, Clacton-on-Sea CO15 1AJ (01255 421919). *Location:* A12 then A120 and A133 to Clacton-on-Sea, follow signs for promenade/pier then turn right along promenade to sharp right hand bend. 250 metres on left. Seaside course. 18 holes, 6448 yards. S.S.S. 71. *Green Fees:* weekdays £30.00 per round, £40.00 per day; weekends £35.00 per round, £50.00 per day. *Eating facilities:* full bar and catering facilities available from 11am. *Visitors:* welcome with reservation and current Handicap Certificate. Please check with Pro Shop prior to visit. *Society Meetings:* Monday to Friday catered for by arrangement. Professional: Stuart Levermore (01255 426304). e-mail: secretary@clactongolfclub.com website: www.clactongolfclub.com

COLCHESTER. **Birch Grove Golf Club,** Layer Road, Colchester CO2 0HS (01206 734276). *Location:* on B1026, two miles south of town. Parkland - small but challenging. 9 holes, 4500 yards. Par 66. *Green Fees:* £10.00 per 9 holes, £15.00 per 18 holes. *Eating facilities:* hot meals and snacks are available during opening hours. *Visitors:* welcome without reservation Monday to Saturday and after 1pm Sundays. *Society Meetings:* catered for weekdays. Secretary: Mrs M. Marston.

COLCHESTER. **Colchester Golf Club,** Braiswick, Colchester CO4 5AU (01206 853396). *Location:* one mile north-west of Colchester North Station, on B1508. Parkland course with wooded areas. 18 holes, 6347 yards. S.S.S. 70. *Green Fees:* information not provided. *Eating facilities:* catering available all day. *Visitors:* welcome except Saturday and Sunday mornings, must have Handicap Certificates. *Society Meetings:* catered for by prior arrangement. Professional: Mark Angel (01206 853920). Secretary: J. H. Wiggam (01206 853396; Fax: 01206 852698). e-mail: colchester.golf@btinternet.com

COLCHESTER. **Colne Valley Golf Club,** Station Road, Earls Colne, Colchester CO6 2LT (01787 224343; Fax: 01787 224126). *Location:* off the A1124, 10 miles from Colchester. Parkland course in the Valley of the River Colne. 18 holes, 6286 yards. S.S.S. 71. Practice ground. *Green Fees:* weekdays £30.00 per round; weekends £35.00 per round. *Eating facilities:* two bars and restaurant facilities open all day. *Visitors:* welcome anytime but weekends only after 11am and please phone in advance to confirm. Carts for rental. *Society Meetings:* midweek anytime, weekends after 11am, packages available. Head Professional: Peter Garlick.

FHG Guides
publish a large range of well-known accommodation guides. We will be happy to send you details or you can use the order form at the back of this book.

COLCHESTER. **The Essex Golf and Country Club,** Earls Colne, Colchester CO6 2NS (01787 224466; Fax: 01787 224410). *Location:* B1024 off the A120 opposite Coggeshall. Flat parkland 18 hole/9 hole courses. 18 holes, 7090 yards. S.S.S. 73. Floodlit driving range. *Green Fees:* information not available. *Eating facilities:* Poolside Grill, sports brasserie, restaurant. *Visitors:* all welcome, no restrictions. Buggies and trolleys available. Full leisure facilities, indoor pool, sauna, steam room, gym, tennis courts. Full day nursery facilities available, conference and entertainment facilities. On site 42 bedroom hotel including two suites. *Society Meetings:* welcome.*
e-mail: essex.golfops@theclubcompany.com
website: www.theclubcompany.com

COLCHESTER. **Lexden Wood Golf Club,** Colchester and Lexden Golf Centre, Bakers Lane, Colchester CO3 4AU (01206 843333; Fax: 01206 854775). *Location:* one mile north west of Colchester, two minutes on the A12 northbound on A133. Undulating parkland with many water features. 27 holes –18 hole Par 70 5895 yards and 9 hole short course. *Green Fees:* £22.00 weekday, £30.00 weekend. *Eating facilities:* home cooked food always available during opening hours. *Visitors:* always welcome, please phone to book tee time. Floodlit covered driving range/putting green. *Society Meetings:* always welcome by prior arrangement. Professional: Phil Grice (01206 843333; Fax: 01206 854775).

ELSENHAM. **Elsenham Golf Centre,** Hall Road, Elsenham CM22 6DH (01279 812865). *Location:* A120 Takley, turn towards Elsenham. Just past the "Jam Factory". Parkland, part wooded course. Dual 9 hole course, 5919 yards. Par 70. 18 bay driving range, 3 hole Academy Course. *Green Fees:* Monday to Friday 9 holes £13.00, 18 holes £18.00; weekends 9 holes £15.00, 18 holes £20.00. *Eating facilities:* bar, food. Open to non-members, children welcome. *Visitors:* always welcome. Changing facilities. Pro Shop. Teaching facility. *Society Meetings:* all welcome. Professional: Owen McKenna (01279 812865).

EPPING. **North Weald Golf Club,** Rayley Lane, North Weald, Epping CM16 6AR (01992 522118; Fax: 01992 522881). *Location:* from M11 Junction 7 take A414 to Chelmsford, two miles to first roundabout, turn right. Club is 200 yards on left. Parkland and lakes. 18 holes, 6377 yards. S.S.S. 71. Driving range, putting green, chipping green and practice bunker. *Green Fees:* weekdays £20.00; weekends £30.00. *Eating facilities:* available. *Visitors:* welcome. *Society Meetings:* welcome by arrangement. Tee bookings (01992 525737). Club Manager: Stacey Smith (01992 522118; Fax: 01992 522881).
website: www.northwealdgolfclub.co.uk

EPPING. **Theydon Bois Golf Club,** Theydon Road, Epping CM16 4EH. *Location:* M25 Waltham Abbey/ Epping A121 London to Cambridge, turn right at Bell Motel. Wooded course. 18 holes, 5480 yards. S.S.S. 68. Practice area. *Green Fees:* £30.00 per round, £20.00 after 5pm weekdays. *Eating facilities:* restaurant and bar. *Visitors:* welcome except Wednesday and Thursday morning. *Society Meetings:* Monday, Tuesday and Friday. Professional: R. Hall (01992 812460). Manager: M.C. Slatter (01992 813054).

FRINTON-ON-SEA. **Frinton Golf Club,** 1 Esplanade, Frinton-on-Sea CO13 9EP. *Location:* 17 miles east of Colchester, A12-A133, B1033. Flat seaside links-type course, strength of wind always a feature. Main Course: 18 holes, 6265 yards. Par 71. Kirby Course 3062 yards. Indoor practice facilities. *Green Fees:* Information not available. *Visitors:* welcome, check with Pro Shop. Handicap Certificate required for Main Course. *Society Meetings:* catering by arrangement. Professional: Peter Taggart (Tel & Fax: 01255 671618). Office: 01255 674618.*
e-mail: secretary@frintongolfclub.com
website: www.frintongolfclub.com

HALSTEAD. **Gosfield Lake Golf Club,** The Manor House, Gosfield, Halstead CO9 1SE. *Location:* off the A1017 four miles north of Braintree. Gently undulating parkland course with lakes and woods; designed by Sir Henry Cotton. Two courses: Lakes Course 18 holes, 6615 yards. S.S.S. 72; Meadows Course 9 holes (double teed to 18), 4990 yards S.S.S. 64. Practice facilities including putting, chipping, bunkers. *Green Fees:* please contact Pro Shop for information (01787 474488). *Eating facilities:* bar and catering facilities from 11am; bar menu. *Visitors:* welcome. Weekdays booking advisable, weekends from 12 noon (booking necessary). Handicap Certificate required for Lakes Course, Meadows Course ideal for beginners/ improvers. Trolley hire. Buggy hire (summer only). *Society Meetings:* welcome by prior arrangement. Professional: Richard Wheeler (01787 474488) Secretary: J.A. O'Shea (01787 474747; Fax: 01787 476044).
e-mail: gosfieldlakegc@btconnect.com.
website: www.gosfield-lake-golf-club.co.uk

HARLOW. **Canons Brook Golf Club,** Elizabeth Way, Harlow CM19 5BE (01279 425142). *Location:* Turn onto Elizabeth Way at Harlow Town Station on A414 from M11. Parkland course. 18 holes, 6745 yards. S.S.S. 73. *Green Fees:* information not available. *Eating facilities:* available, open all day. *Visitors:* welcome weekdays, weekends with a member. *Society Meetings:* catered for Mondays, Wednesdays and Fridays. Professional: Alan McGinn (01279 418357). Secretary: Mrs S. Langton (01279 421482; Fax: 01279 626393). *

HARWICH. **Harwich and Dovercourt Golf Club,** Station Road, Parkeston, Harwich CO12 4NZ (01255 503616; Fax: 01255 503323). *Location:* A120 then to Parkeston Quay, course marked on left hand side of Station Road. Flat course. 9 holes, 5742 yards. S.S.S. 68. *Green Fees:* £20.00 (2006 rates, subject to review). *Eating facilities:* licensed clubhouse, catering available to order (not Thursdays). *Visitors:* welcome with Handicap Certificates. Saturdays, Sundays and Bank Holidays after 11am. *Society Meetings:* small groups welcome by arrangement. Hon. Secretary: Mr P. J.Cole (01255 503616).

ILFORD. **Fairlop Waters,** Forest Road, Barkingside, Ilford IG6 3JA (020 8500 9911). *Location:* two miles north of Ilford, half a mile from A12, one and a half miles from southern end of M11. Covered, floodlit range, 36 bays. 18 hole golf course, 9 hole Par 3 course. Individual or group tuition available. *Green Fees:* information not available. Opening hours: 9am to 10pm. *Eating facilities:* bars and diner. Banqueting facilities and conferences. 38 acre sailing lake, 25 acre country park, children's play area. Professional: Paul Davies (020 8501 1881). General Manager: Mr F. Taylor.*

ILFORD. **Ilford Golf Club,** 291 Wanstead Park Road, Ilford IG1 3TR (020 8554 2930). *Location:* at end of M11, off A406. Parkland with winding river. 18 holes, 5299 yards. S.S.S. 66. *Green Fees:* weekdays £19.00 plus special offers, weekends £24.00. *Eating facilities:* restaurant and bar. *Visitors:* welcome weekdays, restricted times at weekends. *Society Meetings:* welcome. Professional: S. Jackson (020 8554 0094). General Manager (020 8554 2930; Fax: 020 8554 0822).

INGATESTONE. **Hylands Golf Complex,** Main Road, Margaretting, Ingatestone CM4 0ET (01277 356016; Fax: 01277 356056). *Location:* off A12. Parkland course. 9 holes 2445 yards, 18 holes 6604 yards, Driving range, practice bunker. *Green Fees:* information not available. *Eating facilities:* coffee and soft drinks available. *Visitors:* all welcome. New complex, pay and play only; no membership. Accommodation at Ivy Hill Hotel, Margaretting. Professional: Lee Porter (01277 356016; Fax: 01277 356056).*

LEIGH-ON-SEA. **Belfairs Golf Club,** Eastwood Road North, Leigh-on-Sea SS9 4LR (01702 526911). Park front 9, heavy woodland back 9; easy walking but challenging golf. Play over Belfairs Municipal course, 18 holes, 5857 yards. S.S.S. 68. *Green Fees:* information not provided. *Visitors:* unrestricted on the course but no clubhouse facilities available. Bookings required (01702 525345). Secretary: B. J. Harvey (01702 714567).

LITTLE BURSTEAD. **The Burstead Golf Club,** Tye Common Road, Little Burstead CM12 9ST (01277 631171; Fax: 01277 632766). Parkland course. 18 holes, 6275 yards, S.S.S. 70. Practice field, chipping area, putting green. *Green Fees:* information not available. *Eating facilities:* restaurant, bar and spike bar. *Visitors:* welcome Monday to Friday except Bank Holidays, weekends after 1pm. Tuition available. *Society Meetings:* welcome Monday to Friday, except Bank Holidays. Professional: Keith Bridges. Secretary: Lee Mence.*

LOUGHTON. **Loughton Golf Club,** Clay's Lane, Debden Green, Loughton IG10 2RZ (020 8502 2923). *Location:* just north of Loughton, on edge of Epping Forest. Parkland, wooded. 9 holes, 4700 yards. S.S.S. 63. Practice range. *Green Fees:* weekdays £8.50 9 holes, £14.00 18 holes; weekends £9.50 for 9 holes, £16.00 for 18 holes. *Eating facilities:* bar, snacks available. *Visitors:* welcome, telephone to book. *Society Meetings:* welcome. Manager: Alan Day.

MALDON. **Bunsay Downs Golf Club,** Little Baddow Road, Woodham Walter, Maldon CM9 6RW (01245 222648; Fax: 01245 223989). *Location:* 7 miles east of Chelmsford off A414 at Woodham Walter, left onto Little Baddow Road. Undulating landscape partly wooded course. 9 holes, 2932 yards. S.S.S. 68. Par 3 course. *Green Fees:* Information not available. *Eating facilities:* bar/grill restaurant. *Visitors:* welcome at all times. Gift shop. *Society Meetings:* small societies welcome. Professional: Mickey Walker. Secretary: Mr M. Durham (01245 223258).

Essex Golf & Country Club, Colchester

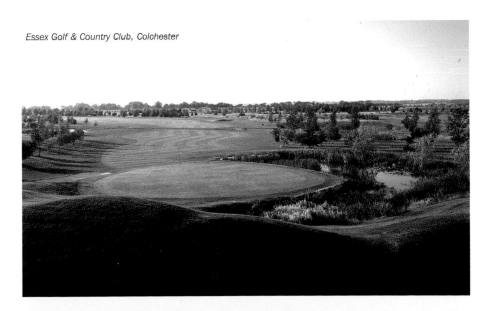

MALDON. **Five Lakes Resort,** Colchester Road, Tolleshunt Knights, Maldon CM9 8HX (01621 868888; Fax: 01621 869696). *Location*: seven miles from A12 on B1026 north of Maldon and south of Colchester. Parkland. Two courses: Links Course - 18 holes, 6181 yards, S.S.S. 70; Lakes Course - 18 holes, 6751 yards, S.S.S. 72. Driving range, three putting greens. *Green Fees*: information not available. *Eating facilities:* three restaurants and two bars. *Visitors:* welcome at most times except before 10am weekend mornings. 194 en suite bedrooms, conference and banqueting facilities, indoor pool, air conditioned gym, health club, sauna, steam room and spa bath, tennis, squash and badminton. *Society Meetings:* catered for by appointment. Professional: Gary Carter (01621 862326; Fax: 01621 862320). Golf Consultant: James Taylor (01621 862307; Fax: 01621 862320).

MALDON. **Forrester Park Golf and Tennis Club,** Beckingham Road, Great Totham, Near Maldon CM9 8EA (Tel & Fax: 01621 891406). *Location:* three miles off A12 Rivenhall turn-off, on B1022 in Great Totham, near Maldon between Compasses and Bull. Parkland course. 18 holes, 6073 yards. S.S.S. 69. Practice ground. *Green Fees:* weekdays £23.00 per round, £26.00 per day; weekends £24.00 after 12 noon only (under review). *Eating facilities:* full catering and bar facilities. *Visitors:* welcome subject to prior booking, but not before 12 noon Tuesdays, Wednesdays and weekends. Trolley hire. Buggy hire. *Society Meetings:* welcome subject to prior booking. Professional: Gary Pike (01621 893456). Manager: Tim Forrester-Muir (Tel & Fax: 01621 891406). e-mail: info@forresterparkltd.com

MALDON. **Maldon Golf Club,** Beeleigh, Langford, Maldon CM9 6LL (01621 853212). *Location:* B1019 two miles northwest of Maldon, turn off by the Museum of Power. Flat parkland. 9 holes, 6253 yards, 5718 metres. S.S.S. 70. *Green Fees:* Information not available. *Eating facilities:* full catering service, bar. *Visitors:* welcome weekdays. *Society Meetings:* catered for by arrangement. Secretary: D. Allen. *

MALDON. **Warren Golf Club,** Woodham Walter, Maldon CM9 6RW (01245 223198/223258; Fax: 01245 223989). *Location:* close to Chelmsford. A414 turn off to Maldon. Undulating wooded course. 18 holes, 6263 yards. S.S.S. 70. Large practice area. *Green Fees:* information not provided. *Eating facilities:* restaurant, bar, bar snack menu. *Visitors:* welcome with reservation weekdays except Wednesday mornings. Handicap Certificate required. Golf Academy. *Society Meetings:* catered for weekdays - up to 40 players. Professional: David Brooks (01245 224662). Managing Director: M.F.L. Durham.

NAZEING. **Nazeing Golf Club,** Middle Street, Nazeing EN9 2LW (01992 893915; Fax: 01992 893882). *Location:* from Waltham Abbey Town Centre – signposted. Parkland course, American design (sand based greens and tees). 18 holes, 6617 yards. S.S.S. 72. Continental style driving range. *Green Fees:* information not available. *Eating facilities:* available. *Visitors:* welcome anytime except weekend mornings, must ring and book through Pro shop. Buggies, trolleys available. *Society Meetings:* welcome. Professional: Robert Green (01992 893798; Fax: 01992 893882).*

OCKENDON. **Belhus Park Golf Club,** Belhus Park, Aveley By-Pass, South Ockendon RM15 4QR (01708 852248 complex, 01708 854748 office). *Location:* on A13 London - Southend Road, approximately one mile from Dartford Tunnel. Parkland. 18 holes, 5350 yards. S.S.S. 69. Driving range. *Green Fees:* information not available. *Eating facilities:* cafe and bar. *Visitors:* welcome anytime (municipal course), but booking essential weekends and Bank Holidays. Swimming pool. *Society Meetings:* by arrangement, telephone complex. Professional: Jamie Gowan (01708 854260). Secretary: J. Cleary (01708 865645).*

ONGAR. **Toot Hill Golf Club,** School Road, Toot Hill, Near Ongar CM5 9PU (01277 365523; Fax: 01277 364509). *Location:* A128 to Ongar, A414 to Harlow, two miles left at Blake Hall Road. Parkland course, lakes and brook. 18 holes, 6197 yards, Par 70, S.S.S. 69. Practice range, putting and chipping green. *Green Fees:* midweek £25.00 per round, £35.00 per day. *Eating facilities:* available, clubhouse and spike bar. *Visitors:* welcome. *Society Meetings:* welcome Tuesdays and Thursdays, various packages. Professional: Mark Bishop (01277 365747). Secretary: Mrs C. Cameron.

ORSETT. **Orsett Golf Club,** Brentwood Road, Orsett RM16 3DS (01375 892471). *Location:* A13 Junction roundabout with A128. South towards Chadwell St Mary on A128. Heathland course. 18 holes, 6682 yards. S.S.S. 72. *Green Fees:* weekdays £40.00 per round, £55.00 all day. *Eating facilities:* full catering available. *Visitors:* welcome on weekdays only by arrangement. Must be members of a club and have Handicap. Proof must be produced. *Society Meetings:* welcome all day Mondays and Tuesdays; afternoons only Wednesdays and Thursdays. Professional: R. Herring (01375 891797). Secretary: Office (01375 891352; Fax: 01375 892471).

RAYLEIGH. **Hanover Golf and Country Club,** Hullbridge Road, Rayleigh SS6 9QS (01702 232377; Fax: 01702 231811). *Location:* A130, A127 Rayleigh. Parkland, gently undulating, with featured lakes. Spectacular views. 36 holes. Georgian Course 6669 yards. Par 73. Regency Course Par 68. Floodlit driving range. *Green Fees:* on application. *Eating facilities:* bar meals available all day; Sunday carvery; function suites and restaurant. *Visitors:* welcome, Handicap Certificate required for Georgian Course. *Society Meetings:* welcome. Professional: A. Blackburn. Secretary: J. Court.*

ROCHFORD. **Rochford Hundred Golf Club,** Hall Road, Rochford SS4 1NW (01702 544302; Fax: 01702 541343). *Location:* A127 towards Southend on Sea, turning for Rochford. Flat parkland course, ancient clubhouse, course surrounds church. 18 holes, 6176 yards (white boxes). S.S.S. 71. *Green Fees:* information not available. *Eating facilities:* full restaurant and snack facilities; bars. *Visitors:* welcome, Tuesday mornings ladies only. Handicap Certificate necessary. *Society Meetings:* catered for except Tuesday mornings, Fridays and weekends. Professional: G. Hill (01702 548968). Secretary: M.A. Boon.*

ROCHFORD near. **Ballards Gore Golf and Country Club,** Gore Road, Canewdon, Near Rochford SS4 2DA (01702 258917). *Location*: Southend Airport three miles, London via A127, club two miles from Rochford. Parkland with lakes. 18 holes, 6845 yards. S.S.S. 73. Practice area. *Green Fees:* £35.00 per round or day. *Eating facilities:* diningroom (100 covers). Daily special menu available from £4.95. *Visitors:* welcome weekdays, except Tuesday mornings. *Society Meetings:* catered for by arrangement. Professional: Gary McCarthy (01702 258924; Fax: 01702 258924). Secretary: Iain Evans (01702 258917; Fax: 01702 258571).

ROMFORD. **Maylands Golf and Country Club,** Harold Park, Romford RM3 0AZ (01708 341777). *Location:* turn off Junction 28 M25, directly on A12 between Romford and Brentwood. 18 holes, 6182 yards. S.S.S. 70. Driving range and putting green. *Green Fees:* weekdays £40.00. *Eating facilities:* bar, spike bar, restaurant and bar snacks. *Visitors:* welcome midweek. *Society Meetings:* catered for Mondays, Wednesdays and Fridays. Professional: Darren Parker (01708 346466). Secretary/Proprietor: B. Bosworth (Tel & Fax: 01708 341777). website: www.maylandsgolf.com

ROMFORD. **Risebridge Golf Centre,** Risebridge Chase, Romford RM1 4DG (01708 741429). Location: off Lower Bedfords Road, between Collier Row and Harold Hill, signposted from Gallows Corner (A12). Mature parkland course with some long tough holes. 18 holes, 6342 yards. S.S.S. 70. 9 hole Par 3 course, driving range, practice green. *Green Fees:* information not available. *Eating facilities:* cafe and spike bar. *Visitors:* welcome at all times. *Society Meetings:* all welcome, for details contact the Professional. Professional/Manager: Mr P. Jennings (Tel & Fax: 01708 741429). *

SAFFRON WALDEN. **Saffron Walden Golf Club,** Windmill Hill, Saffron Walden CB10 1BX (01799 522786). *Location:* end of town on B184 to Cambridge. 18 holes, 6632 yards. S.S.S. 72. *Green Fees:* on application. *Eating facilities:* snacks, lunches and evening meals (by prior arrangement). *Visitors:* welcome with current Handicap Certificate Monday to Friday. *Society Meetings:* on application. Professional: Philip Davis. General Manager: Chris Charlton.
e-mail: office@swgc.com
website: www.swgc.com

SOUTH BENFLEET. **Boyce Hill Golf Club Ltd,** Vicarage Hill, South Benfleet SS7 1PD (01268 793625). *Location*: one-and-a-half-miles south of A13/A127. Hilly course, 18 holes, 6003 yards, 5489 metres. S.S.S. 69. *Green Fees*: £35.00 18 holes, £45.00 36 holes. *Eating facilities*: full bar and dining facilities daily. *Visitors*: welcome, except Tuesday mornings and weekends. 24 hours notice of booking and Handicap Certificate required. *Society Meetings*: catered for Thursdays only. Professional: G. Burroughs (01268 752565). Secretary: D. Kelly (01268 793625; Fax: 01268 750497).

SOUTHEND-ON-SEA. **Southend-on-Sea Golf Club,** Belfairs Lodge, Belfairs Park, Leigh-on-Sea SS9 4LR (01702 524836). *Location*: A127 London to Southend Road. Parkland/wooded course (Belfairs Municipal course). 18 holes, 5877 yards. S.S.S. 68. *Green Fees:* information not available. *Eating facilities:* restaurant in the park near Starter's Hut. *Visitors:* welcome, unrestricted, but bookings required by phone to Starter's Hut (01702 525345). Professional: Martin Foreman (01702 520202). Secretary: Alan Wood (01702 474737).*

SOUTHEND-ON-SEA. **Thorpe Hall Golf Club,** Thorpe Hall Avenue, Thorpe Bay, Southend-on-Sea SS1 3AT (Tel & Fax: 01702 582205). *Location:* one mile east of Southend-on-Sea. Parkland. 18 holes, 6290 yards. S.S.S. 70. *Green Fees:* information not available. *Eating facilities:* Two restaurants and bars. *Visitors:* welcome weekdays with Handicap Certificate, weekends with members only. Squash, snooker and sauna available. *Society Meetings:* welcome Fridays only. Professional: Bill McColl (01702 588195). Secretary: J. Hetherington (01702 582205; Fax: 01702 584498).

STANFORD LE HOPE. **St. Cleres Hall Golf Club,** St. Cleres Hall, London Road, Stanford le Hope SS17 0LX (Tel & Fax: 01375 361565). *Location:* from M25, A13 Stanford turnoff, Linford exit on roundabout, course half mile on left. Parkland course with Thames Estuary views, sand based, year round play. 18 holes, 6474 yards. S.S.S. 71. 19 bay floodlit driving range, chipping and putting greens. 9 hole Par 3 course. *Green Fees:* information not provided. *Eating facilities:* bar; restaurant. *Visitors:* welcome, enquire about tee closures. *Society Meetings:* welcome anytime weekdays; weekends afternoons only. Please telephone for details. Professional/Secretary: David Wood.

STAPLEFORD ABBOTTS. **Stapleford Abbotts Golf Club,** Horseman's Side, Tysea Hill, Stapleford Abbotts, Romford RM4 1JU (01708 381108; Fax: 01708 386345). *Location:* three miles from Junctions 28 and 29 of the M25, off main Ongar Road B175 at Stapleford Abbotts. Parkland course with many mature trees, large bunkers and water hazards. 18 holes, 6501 yards, S.S.S. 72. Par 3 9-hole course. Two practice grounds and practice nets. Also The Priors 18 hole pay-and-play course, 5878 yards, S.S.S 70. *Green Fees:* information not available. *Eating facilities:* fully licensed bar, extensive menu. *Visitors:* welcome weekdays, weekends after 12 noon; welcome all week on 9-hole course. Correct golfing attire must be worn. *Society Meetings:* welcome, call 01708 381108 for more information. Pro Shop: 01708 381278 .*

THE APPEARANCE OF AN ASTERISK (*) AT THE END OF A CLUB OR COURSE ENTRY INDICATES THAT UP-TO-DATE INFORMATION HAS NOT BEEN SUPPLIED

STAPLEFORD TAWNEY. Abridge Golf and Country Club, Epping Lane, Stapleford Tawney RM4 1ST (01708 688396). *Location:* A113 from London through Chigwell to Abridge, left at The Rodings, right after 300 yards. Two miles on. Parkland. 18 holes, 6704 yards. S.S.S. 72. *Green Fees:* information not available. *Eating facilities:* bar lunches, drinks, snacks available all week. *Visitors:* welcome but must be a member of a recognised golf club and produce evidence of current Handicap, weekdays and weekend afternoons. *Society Meetings:* catered for on Mondays, Wednesdays and Fridays only by arrangement. Professional: Stuart Layton (01708 688333). Secretary: Mr M Gottlieb (Fax: 01708 688550)*.
e-mail:info@abridgegolf.com
website: www.abridgegolf.com

STOCK. Crondon Park Golf Club, Stock Road, Stock CM4 9DP (01277 841115; Fax: 01277 841356). *Location:* off the A12, on to B1007 towards Billericay. Set in parkland valley with trees, lakes and magnificent greens, longest hole in the country (18th 655yds). 18 holes, 6250 yards (Club). S.S.S. 70. 9-hole Par 3 course. Driving range and putting green. Academy Lessons. *Green Fees:* information not available. *Eating facilities:* bar, restaurant. *Visitors:* welcome weekdays; weekend afternoons only. Modern changing rooms, showers, etc. *Society Meetings:* welcome weekdays, Saturday and Sunday (pm). Professional: Fred Sunderland (Head Pro), Chris Woods (01277 841887). Secretary: Paul Cranwell (01277 841115).*

STOKE BY NAYLAND. Stoke by Nayland Golf & Spa, Keepers Lane, Leavenheath, Colchester CO6 4PZ (01206 262836; Fax: 01206 263356). *Location:* just off A134 Colchester to Sudbury on B1068 towards Stoke by Nayland. Host venue to PGA Seniors' Championship 2006. Undulating parkland with water hazards. Two courses (1) Gainsborough - 18 holes, 6516 yards. S.S.S. 71. (2) Constable - 18 holes, 6544 yards. S.S.S. 71. 20 bay covered range, practice area. *Green Fees:* Information not available. *Eating facilities:* full catering and bars. *Visitors:* welcome, please ring for availability and tee bookings. *Society Meetings:* welcome weekdays, book well in advance. Seasonal packages offered. Excellent golf and spa breaks. Extensive Health and Leisure Facility including gymnasium, pool, sauna, jacuzzi and spa; modern, spacious, en suite hotel rooms overlooking lake and fairways. Professional: Kevin Lovelock (01206 262769). Golf Secretary: Peter Barfield (01206 265815).*
e-mail: mary.saward@stokebynayland.com
website: www.stokebynaylandclub.co.uk

UPMINSTER. Top Meadow Golf Club and Hotel, Fen Lane, North Ockendon, Upminster RM14 3PR (01708 852239; Fax: 01708 852598) *Location:* M25, A127, B186 towards North Ockendon - Fen Lane. Parkland course with panoramic views of Essex countryside. 18 holes, 6227 yards. S.S.S. 72. Practice range. On site hotel. *Green Fees:* information not available. *Eating facilities:* fully licensed bar and à la carte restaurant. *Visitors:* Visitors and Societies welcome Monday to Friday. Golfing holidays available midweek and weekends. Professional: Roy Porter (01708 859545). Secretary: Daniel Stock (01708 852239). *

UPMINSTER. Upminster Golf Club, 114 Hall Lane, Upminster RM14 1AU (01708 222788). *Location:* one mile (north) Upminster Station, one and a half miles west M25/A127 junction. Parkland/wooded – River Ingrebourne runs through the course. Beautiful Grade II Listed Clubhouse, rebuilt in 1654, with an official ghost – listed in the British Book of Ghosts. 18 holes, 6076 yards. S.S.S. 69. *Green Fees:* information not available. *Eating facilities:* full catering service every day. *Visitors:* welcome weekdays by arrangement except Tuesday mornings. *Society Meetings:* catered for Wednesdays, Thursdays and Fridays (max 60). Professional: Steven Cipa (01708 220000). Secretary: Russell Winmill (01708 222788; Fax: 01708 222484).
e-mail: secretary@upminstergolfclub.co.uk
website: www.upminstergolfclub.co.uk*

WITHAM. Benton Hall Golf Club, Wickham Hill, Witham CM8 3LH (01376 502454 Fax: 01376 521050). *Location:* one mile from A12 between Chelmsford and Colchester. Wooded course with natural lakes. 18 holes 6495 yards. S.S.S. 72. 9 hole executive par three course. *Green Fees:* information not available. *Eating facilities:* Blackwater Suite function room, Waterside Bar and Restaurant. *Visitors:* welcome, not before 12 noon at weekends. *Society Meetings:* welcome. Director of Golf: Colin Fairweather. General Manager: James Gathercole.*

WITHAM. Braxted Park Golf Club, Braxted Park, Witham CM8 3EN (01376 572372; Fax: 01376 572372). *Location:* A12 south of Witham; from Chelmsford take Rivenhall turn-off, if travelling from Colchester take Silver End turn-off. Established 54 years, set in 18th century parkland. 9 holes, 5880 yards. Par 35, S.S.S. 34. Practice ground. *Green Fees:* information not available. *Eating facilities:* clubhouse (licensed), snacks. *Visitors:* welcome. Corporate entertainment available, activity days, wedding receptions. *Society Meetings:* welcome.*

WOODFORD GREEN. Woodford Golf Club, Sunset Avenue, Woodford Green (020 8504 3330). *Location:* near The Harvester (formerly The Castle Public House), Woodford High Road. Forest land. 9 holes, 5867 yards. S.S.S. 68. *Green Fees:* £15.00 per 18 holes. Subject to review. *Eating facilities:* bar. *Visitors:* no green fees Tuesday mornings, Tee Times available on Saturdays by arrangement, Sundays between 8.50am - 9.30am. and after 11.30 am. Red (scarlet) clothing must be worn - trousers or top. *Society Meetings:* welcome. Professional: Jon Robson (020 8504 4254). Secretary: P. Willett (020 8504 3330; Fax: 020 8559 0504).
e-mail: office@woodfordgolfclub.fsnet.co.uk

Hertfordshire

BARKWAY. **Barkway Park Golf Club,** Nuthampstead Road, Barkway SG8 8EN (01763 849070). *Location:* A10 north from M25 for 15 miles, B1368 to Barkway 8 miles. Inland links. 18 holes, 6997 yards. S.S.S. 74. Practice areas. *Green Fees:* information not available. *Eating facilities:* bar, restaurant. *Visitors:* welcome at all times. *Society Meetings:* always welcome. Professional: Jamie Bates. Secretary: Val Sadler. *

BARNET. **Arkley Golf Club,** Rowley Green Road, Barnet EN5 3HL (Fax: 020 8440 5214). *Location:* follow A411 from A1 Stirling Corner towards Barnet, left into Rowley Lane. Wooded parkland. 9 holes, 18 tees, 6046 yards. S.S.S. 69. Practice ground. *Green Fees:* weekdays £25.00 per round, £32.00 per day; weekends with a member only £20.00. *Eating facilities:* available. *Visitors:* welcome weekdays, please phone Professional. *Society Meetings:* catered for Wednesdays and Fridays; special rates available. Professional: Andrew Hurley (020 8440 8473). Secretary: R. Campbell (020 8449 0394). website: www.arkleygolfclub.co.uk

BARNET. **Hadley Wood Golf Club,** Beech Hill, Near Barnet EN4 0JJ (020 8449 4328). *Location:* off the exit from M25 at Junction 24 on to A111 Cockfosters. Down hill, third turning on the right. Very attractive undulating parkland with lakes. Regional Open qualifying venue 2000 - 2005. 18 holes, 6514 yards. S.S.S. 71. Practice range open to members and green fees only. Chipping and putting areas. *Green Fees:* £50.00 weekdays, £70.00 weekends. *Eating facilities:* available weekdays. *Visitors:* welcome weekdays, (not Tuesday a.m.), with club Handicap Certificate or letter of introduction. *Society Meetings:* corporate and society days catered for weekdays except Tuesday mornings and Wednesdays. Professional: Peter Jones (020 8449 3285). General Manager: Bill Beckett (020 8449 4328; Fax: 020 8364 8633). e-mail: gm@hadleywoodgc.com website: www.hadleywoodgc.com

BERKHAMSTED. **Ashridge Golf Club,** Little Gaddesden, Berkhamsted HP4 1LY (01442 842244). *Location:* on B4506, five miles north west of Berkhamsted. Parkland. 18 holes, 6625 yards. Par 72. Practice area, putting green. *Green Fees:* on application. *Eating facilities:* dining room and spike bar, two lounges. *Visitors:* welcome with reservation weekdays only. *Society Meetings:* catered for. Professional: Peter Cherry (01442 842307). Secretary: Martin S. Silver (01442 842244; Fax: 01442 843770). e-mail: info@ashridgegolfclub.ltd.uk website: www.ashridgegolfclub.ltd.uk

BERKHAMSTED. **Berkhamsted Golf Club,** The Common, Berkhamsted HP4 2QB (01442 865832; Fax: 01442 863730). *Location:* A41 to Berkhamsted, up past the castle to the common. Heathland, wooded, grass bunkers. 18 holes, 6605 yards. S.S.S. 72. Two practice grounds. *Green Fees:* weekdays £40.00 per round, £55.00 per day; weekends £55.00 per round after 11.30am. (2006 prices subject to review). *Eating facilities:* bar and restaurant. *Visitors:* welcome, best to phone first. Handicap Certificate required. *Society Meetings:* catered for Mondays, Wednesdays and Fridays. Professional: John Clarke (01442 865851). General Manager: Barry Hill (01442 865832) e-mail: barryh@berkhamstedgc.co.uk website: www.berkhamstedgolfclub.co.uk

BISHOP'S STORTFORD. **Bishop's Stortford Golf Club,** Dunmow Road, Bishop's Stortford CM23 5HP (01279 654715). *Location:* M11 Junction 8, follow signs for Bishop's Stortford, entrance quarter of a mile on left. Undulating parkland, fairly flat: well-established course and a true test of golf. 18 holes, 6404 yards. S.S.S. 71. *Green Fees:* weekdays £40.00 per round, £50.00 per day, weekends as guest of member. *Eating facilities:* restaurant and bar service. *Visitors:* welcome weekdays; weekends with member only. Valid Handicap Certificate required. *Society Meetings:* catered for weekdays except Tuesdays (minimum 12). Special rates available. Professional: Simon Sheppard (01279 651324). Secretary: Judy Barker (01279 654715; Fax: 01279 655215). e-mail: office@bsgc.co.uk website: www.bsgc.co.uk

BISHOP'S STORTFORD. **Great Hadham Golf and Country Club,** Great Hadham Road, Much Hadham, Near Bishop's Stortford SG10 6JE (01279 843558; Fax: 01279 842122). *Location:* two miles west of Bishop's Stortford on the B1004, four miles west of Junction 8 M11 motorway. Rolling meadowland course. 18 holes, 6854 yards. S.S.S. 73. Three Par 3 practice holes, practice bunker, 18 bay driving range. *Green Fees:* information not provided. *Eating facilities:* well stocked bar, comfortable lounge and dining room/spike bar. *Visitors:* welcome weekdays (Ladies' Day Wednesday mornings), weekends after 12 noon. Health Club with fitness centre facilities. *Society Meetings:* welcome weekdays. Professional: Kevin Lunt. Secretary: Ian Bailey.

WARE. **Briggens House Golf Club,** Briggens Park, Stanstead Road, Stanstead Abbotts, Ware SG12 8LD (01279 793742; Fax: 01279 793685). *Location:* A414 near Harlow, Essex. Parkland course. 9 holes, 5582 yards. S.S.S. 69. Practice area. *Green Fees:* information not available. *Eating facilities:* hotel restaurant and coffee shop with snacks, both with bars. *Visitors:* welcome anytime except Sunday mornings. *Society Meetings:* very welcome. Professional: Alan McGinn. Secretary: Alan Battle.*

WARE. **Chadwell Springs Golf Club,** Hertford Road, Ware SG12 9LE (01920 461447). *Location:* just off A10 Hertford to Ware. Heathland. 9 holes, 6418 yards, S.S.S. 71. Practice ground. *Green Fees:* Information not available. *Eating facilities:* bar, bar meals; function room. *Visitors:* welcome weekdays except Tuesday and Thursday mornings; weekends with member only. Carts available. *Society Meetings:* welcome weekdays by arrangement. Professional: David Smith. Secretary: David Robertson (01920 462075).*

WARE. **Hanbury Manor Golf and Country Club,** Ware SG12 0SD (01920 487722; Fax: 01920 487692). *Location:* leave the M25 at Junction 25 and take the A10 towards Hertford, continue for 12 miles and Hanbury Manor is located on the left. Parkland and Championship course designed by Jack Nicklaus II. Host to 1997, 1998 and 1999 English Open. 18 holes, 7052 yards. S.S.S. 74 (blue tees). Putting green, practice ground. *Green Fees:* information not available. *Eating facilities:* two award-winning restaurants in five star Marriott Hotel which overlooks course. *Visitors:* golf available only to Club members or hotel guests. Club and buggy hire, golf shop. *Society Meetings:* Corporate Golf Days are available. Director of Golf: Simon Clough. website: www.hanbury-manor.com

WARE. **Whitehill Golf Club,** Whitehill Golf Centre, Dane End, Ware SG12 0JS (01920 438495; Fax: 01920 438891). *Location:* turn off A10 at Raj Villa, High Cross. Undulating course. 18 holes, 6618 yards. S.S.S 72. 25 bay floodlit driving range. *Green Fees:* information not available. *Eating facilities:* bar, restaurants and function room. *Visitors:* welcome. Snooker room. *Society Meetings:* welcome, groups of 12 or more. Professional: Matt Belsham. Secretary: Andrew Smith.
e-mail: whitehillgolfcentre@btconnect.com

WATFORD. **Aldenham Golf and Country Club,** Church Lane, Aldenham, Watford WD25 8NN (01923 853929; Fax: 01923 858472). *Location:* three minutes from M1 Junction 5, off B462 to Radlett. Flat parkland course. 18 holes, 6500 yards. S.S.S. 71. 9 holes, 2350 yards. Practice area. *Green Fees:* weekdays £30.00, weekends £40.00. *Eating facilities:* full catering and bar facilities. *Visitors:* welcome, weekends after 1pm. Buggy cars for hire. *Society Meetings:* welcome by prior arrangement. Professional: Tim Dunstan (01923 857889). Secretary: (01923 853929).
e-mail: info@aldenhamgolfclub.co.uk
website: www.aldenhamgolfclub.co.uk

WATFORD. **West Herts Golf Club,** Cassiobury Park, Watford WD3 3GG (01923 236484). *Location:* off Rousebarn Lane from Links Way, A412 at Croxley Green. Parkland. 18 holes, 6612 yards. S.S.S. 72. *Green Fees:* weekdays £40.00 per round; weekends £50.00. *Eating facilities:* catering (including breakfast) available seven days a week. *Visitors:* welcome. *Society Meetings:* catered for. Professional: Charles Gough (01923 220352). General Manager: Clive Dodman (01923 236484; Fax: 01923 222300).

WELWYN GARDEN CITY. **Brocket Hall Golf Club,** Welwyn Garden City AL8 7XG (01707 335241; Fax: 01707 390052). *Location:* A1(M) two minutes from Junction 4. 36 holes Melbourne Course, parkland course, 6616 yards, S.S.S. 72; Palmerston Course, woodland, 18 holes, 7080 yards, S.S.S. 73. Par 3 course, Faldo Golf Institute. *Eating facilities:* available all day. *Visitors:* must be a member's guest. Packages for Play and Stay available. *Society Meetings:* corporate days welcome. Professional: Keith Wood.
e-mail: info@brocket-hall.co.uk
website: www.brocket-hall.co.uk

WELWYN GARDEN CITY. **Mill Green Golf Club,** Gypsy Lane, Welwyn Garden City AL7 4TY (01707 276900; Fax: 01707 276898). *Location:* from A1 North exit 4 (Hatfield) A414 to Hertford, take first slip road on left to A1000, left at lights, second right Ascots Lane, mini roundabout turn right into Gypsy Lane. Parkland course. Peter Alliss and Clive Clarke designed. 18 holes, 6615 yards. S.S.S. 72. Two contrasting loops of 9 holes. Front 9 open and elevated, back 9 long narrow fairways through woodland. Par 3 course, driving range, putting green. *Green Fees:* Information not available. *Eating facilities:* full bar menu available and extensive conference and banqueting facilities. *Visitors:* Monday to Friday all day, after midday at weekends. *Society Meetings:* welcome Monday to Friday. Professional: Ian Parker. General Manager: Tim Hudson.*
e-mail: millgreen@crown-golf.co.uk

WELWYN GARDEN CITY. **Panshanger Golf Complex,** Old Herns Lane, Panshanger, Welwyn Garden City AL7 2ED (01707 333350; Fax: 01707 390010). *Location*: just off Junction 6 A1(M), 10 minutes from M25. Parkland set in the Mimram Valley. 18 holes, 6347 yards. S.S.S. 70. Practice ground, 9 hole pitch and putt. *Green Fees:* information not available. *Eating facilities:* Fairway Tavern and cafe. *Visitors:* municipal course, pay as you play, all welcome, dress conditions. *Society Meetings:* welcome weekdays. Professionals: Bryan Lewis and Michael Corlass (01707 333350; Fax: 01707 339507). Secretary: Trish Skinner (01707 332837). General Manager: Michael Corlass.

WELWYN GARDEN CITY. **Welwyn Garden City Golf Club Ltd,** Mannicotts, High Oaks Road, Welwyn Garden City AL8 7BP (01707 325243). *Location*: from north Junction 5 on A1M and take B197 to Valley Road. From south Junction 4 on A1M to Lemsford Lane and Valley Road. Undulating parkland. 18 holes, 6200 yards. S.S.S. 69. Practice ground. *Green Fees:* £35.00 weekdays. *Eating facilities*: by order for lunches; sandwiches available. *Visitors*: welcome weekdays with Handicap Certificate; weekends with member only. *Society Meetings*: Mondays, Wednesdays and Thursdays only (£60.00 per person per day). Professional: R. May (01707 325525). General Manager: (01707 325243; Fax: 01707 393213)
website: www.welwyngardencitygolfclub.co.uk

WHEATHAMPSTEAD. **Lamerwood Country Club,** Codicote Road, Wheathampstead AL4 8GB (01582 833013; Fax: 01582 832604). *Location:* from London take A1(M) exit at Junction 4. After Hatfield Tunnel take B653 towards Wheathampstead. Set in 240 acres of mature wood and parkland. 18 holes, 6953 yards. S.S.S. 73. 9 hole short course and practice facilities available. *Green Fees:* information not available. *Eating facilities:* full bar and restaurant, private function rooms. *Visitors:* always welcome. *Society Meetings:* always welcome. Accommodation available at Sopwellhouse Hotel and Country Club, St. Albans (01727 864477; Fax: 01727 844741). Professional: Matthew Masters (01582 833013). Director: Mr. S. Takabatake. *

WHIPSNADE. **Whipsnade Park Golf Club,** Studham Lane, Dagnall HP4 1RH (0144-284 2330/2331; Fax: 0144-284 2090). *Location:* between Dagnall and Studham. Junction 11 M1 (from north), Junction 9 (from south). Parkland. 18 holes, 6800 yards. S.S.S. 72. Large practice area. *Green Fees:* £29.00 per round, £40.00 two rounds weekdays, weekends after 1pm visitors welcome, (without member) £35.00. *Eating facilities:* restaurant open daily, two bars. *Visitors:* welcome weekdays with reservation. *Society Meetings:* welcome with reservation. Professional: Mark Day (0144-284 2310). Secretary: Ruth Whalley (0144-284 2330).
e-mail: whipsnadeparkgolfc@btopenworld.com
website: www.whipsnadeparkgolf.co.uk

www.uk-golfguide.com

Norfolk

CROMER. **Links Country Park Hotel and Golf Club,** Sandy Lane, West Runton, Cromer NR27 9QH (01263 838383). *Location:* midway between Cromer and Sheringham on the A149, turn left opposite the village inn. Undulating parkland with narrow fairways and tricky greens. 9 holes, 4814 yards, S.S.S. 64. *Green Fees:* £25.00 per day, £15.00 after 3pm. *Eating facilities:* grill room, snacks, hotel restaurant table d'hôte and à la carte. *Visitors:* welcome weekdays, restrictions weekends. Adjoining Hotel offers free golf to residents; gym, sauna, solarium, swimming pool etc. *Society Meetings:* welcome. Professional/Manager: Gary Potter (01263 838675; Fax: 01263 838264).
e-mail: sales@links-hotel.co.uk
website: www.links-hotel.co.uk

CROMER. **Royal Cromer Golf Club,** 145 Overstrand Road, Cromer NR27 0JH (01263 512884; Fax: 01263 512430). *Location:* one mile east of Cromer on B1159 Coast Road. Undulating cliff top course. 18 holes, 6280 yards. S.S.S. 72. Practice ground. *Green Fees:* £45.00 weekdays, £55.00 weekends; weekly tickets available (fees under review for 2008). *Eating facilities:* full catering and bar snacks. *Visitors:* welcome, booking essential from 1st April to 31st October, Handicap Certificates required. *Society Meetings:* welcome. Professsional: Lee Patterson (Tel & Fax: 01263 512267). Secretary/Manager: G. A. Richardson (01263 512884).

DEREHAM. **Dereham Golf Club,** Quebec Road, Dereham NR19 2DS (01362 695900; Fax: 01362 695904). *Location:* three-quarters of a mile from town centre on B1110. Wooded parkland. 9 holes (double tees), 6225 yards. S.S.S. 70, Par 71. Practice nets, practice ground. *Green Fees:* Information not available. *Visitors:* welcome with prior notice. Handicap Certificates required. *Society Meetings:* catered for with advance booking. Professional: Neil Allsebrook (01362 695631). Secretary: D. A. Mayers (01362 695900; Fax: 01362 695904).*

DISS. **Diss Golf Club,** Stuston Common, Diss IP21 4AA (01379 641025). *Location:* close to the town of Diss on the Suffolk/Norfolk border. Links-type course with natural hazards abounding, and 30 bunkers to avoid. A good test of golf for every standard of player. 18 holes, 6206 yards. S.S.S. 70, Par 70. Good practice facilities; driving range one mile. *Green Fees:* £28.00 per round, £36.00 per day. Summer and Winter Green Fee deals are available, phone for details. *Eating facilities:* good dining and bar facilities at the clubhouse. *Visitors:* always welcome, membership available. Lessons available; golf shop. *Society Meetings:* societies and groups always welcome. For all enquiries contact the Secretary Manager. Professional: (01379 644399). Secretary Manager: (01379 640125). Club Bar and Catering Manager: (01379 642847) after 11am.
e-mail: sec.dissgolf@virgin.net
website: www.club-noticeboard.co.uk/diss

DOWNHAM MARKET. **Ryston Park Golf Club,** Ely Road, Denver, Downham Market PE38 0HH (01366 382133; Fax: 01366 383834). *Location:* one mile south Downham Market on A10. 36 miles north Cambridge. Parkland with mature trees and water on three holes. 9 holes, 6310 yards, 5774 metres. S.S.S. 70. Practice ground, practice putting green, practice bunker. *Green Fees:* weekdays £20.00, weekends restricted – contact Club. *Eating facilities:* restaurant and bar. *Visitors:* welcome weekdays, weekends by prior arrangement. *Society Meetings:* welcome (up to 50 members). Secretary: Joe Flogdell (01366 382133).

FAKENHAM. **Fakenham Golf Club,** Gallow Sports Centre, Hempton Road, Fakenham NR21 7LA (01328 862867). *Location:* half-a-mile town centre on Swaffham Road. Parkland. 9 holes, 6245 yards. S.S.S. 70. Large practice area. *Green Fees:* information not available. *Eating facilities:* available in Sports Centre. *Visitors:* welcome by appointment. *Society Meetings:* welcome, reduced rates. Professional: Colin Williams (01328 863534). Secretary: G.G. Cocker (01328 855678).

GREAT YARMOUTH. **Caldecott Hall Golf Club and Hotel,** Beccles Road, Fritton, Great Yarmouth NR31 9EY (01493 488488; Fax: 01493 488561). *Location:* on the A143 just north of the village of Fritton. Parkland. 18 holes, 6685 yards, S.S.S. 73. 18-hole short course. Floodlit driving range, putting and pitching practice area. *Green Fees:* information not avcailable. *Eating facilities:* bar, restaurant. *Visitors:* welcome at all times, starting sheets weekends and Bank Holidays. Luxury en suite rooms. Packages available. The Barnworks Leisure Spa; massage treatments. *Society Meetings:* welcome by arrangement. Professional: (01493 488488; Fax: 01493 488561).* website: www.caldecotthall.co.uk

GREAT YARMOUTH. **Gorleston Golf Club,** Warren Road, Gorleston, Great Yarmouth NR31 6JT (01493 661082). *Location:* A12 Lowestoft to Great Yarmouth. Seaslde Ilnks, seventh green is the most easterly green in the British Isles. 18 holes, 6400 yards. S.S.S. 71. *Green Fees:* weekdays £25.00 per person, weekends £30.00 per person. *Eating facilities:* restaurant/bars open seven days. *Visitors:* welcome, advisable to check in advance for details of restrictions. *Society Meetings:* catered for by prior arrangement (membership of recognised club required). Professional: Nick Brown (01493 662103). Secretary: J.E. Woodhouse (01493 661911).

www.uk-golfguide.com

GREAT YARMOUTH. **Great Yarmouth and Caister Golf Club,** Beach House, Caister-on-Sea, Great Yarmouth NR30 5TD (01493 728699). *Location:* A149 coast road, two miles north of Great Yarmouth. Links. 18 holes, 6330 yards. S.S.S. 70. Practice ground. *Green Fees:* £35.00 per day, £25.00 after 12 noon weekdays; £45.00 per day, £35.00 after 12 noon weekends. (2005/6) Members' guests 50%. *Eating facilities:* full range of oatering; bar. *Visitors:* welcome, not before 11.30am Saturdays, Sundays and Bank Holidays. *Society Meetings:* catered for. Clubhouse Catering (01493 720214). Professional: Martyn Clarke (01493 720421). Secretary: R. Peck. e-mail: office@caistergolf.co.uk website: www.caistergolf.co.uk

HUNSTANTON. **Hunstanton Golf Club,** Golf Course Road, Old Hunstanton PE36 6JQ (01485 532811; Fax: 01485 532319). *Location:* off A149. Adjoins Old Hunstanton village, approximately half a mile north east of Hunstanton. Championship links course with excellent fast greens. 18 holes, 6735 yards. S.S.S. 72. Practice ground. *Green Fees:* (2005) weekdays £65.00 per day; weekends £75.00 per day. Special rates in winter, also after 4pm all year. Subject to review. *Eating facilities:* catering and bar facilities. *Visitors:* welcome but limited times available at weekends. Prior booking advisable. Visitors must be member of recognised golf club and hold a current Handicap. Play in two-ball format only. *Society Meetings:* welcome. Professional: Jim Dodds (01485 532751). Secretary: Derek Thomson (01485 532811).*

HUNSTANTON. Searles Resort Golf Course, Searles Leisure Resort, South Beach Road, Hunstanton PE36 5BB (01485 536010; Fax: 01485 533815). *Location:* A149 from King's Lynn to Hunstanton; at roundabout on hill at Hunstanton take 2nd left down Oasis Way; at mini-roundabout straight over and immediate left into Leisure Resort; follow signs. Seaside links-style course. 9 holes, 2850 yards. S.S.S. 34. 10-bay covered driving range. Putting. *Green Fees:* £10.00 adults, £6.50 under-18s (add £1.00 for weekends). *Eating facilities:* new clubhouse with bar, restaurant, shop, changing facilities etc. *Visitors:* welcome at all times. Lodges and cabin on site available for hire. Club hire. Fishing lake and bowling green. *Society Meetings:* all welcome. Secretary/Manager: Paul Searle.
e-mail: golf@searles.co.uk

KING'S LYNN. Eagles Golf Club, 39 School Road, Tilney All Saints, King's Lynn PE34 4RS (01553 827147). *Location:* off A47 between King's Lynn and Wisbech. Parkland. 9 holes, 4284 yards. S.S.S. 61. Par 3 course, driving range, practice bunkers and putting green. *Green Fees:* weekdays £11.00 9 holes, £16.00 18 holes; weekends and Bank Holidays £12.00 9 holes, £18.50 18 holes. Weekday special Seniors/Juniors £7.00 9 holes, £12.00 18 holes. *Eating facilities:* bar/restaurant. *Visitors:* welcome, restrictions at weekends; no visitors before 10am. Dress code must be adhered to at all times. *Society Meetings:* apply to Secretary. Professional: Nigel Pickerell. Secretary: R. K. Shipman (Tel & Fax: 01553 829777).

KING'S LYNN. King's Lynn Golf Club, Castle Rising, King's Lynn PE31 6BD (01553 631654; Fax: 01553 631036). *Location:* four miles north-east of King's Lynn. Undulating wooded course. 18 holes, 6609 yards. Par 72, S.S.S. 73. Practice areas. *Green Fees:* information not available. *Eating facilities:* snacks, lunches, teas available; dinners by arrangement; two bars. *Visitors:* welcome on production of Handicap Certificate. *Society Meetings:* catered for by prior arrangement. Professional: J. Reynolds (01553 631655). General Manager: A.H. Mackenzie.

KING'S LYNN. Middleton Hall Golf Club, Middleton, King's Lynn PE32 1RH (Tel & Fax: 01553 841800). *Location:* on A47 King's Lynn to Norwich, 3 miles from King's Lynn. Undulating parkland. 18 holes, 6004 yards. Par 71. Floodlit driving range, practice greens. *Green Fees:* weekdays £25.00, weekends £30.00. *Eating facilities:* full restaurant services. *Visitors:* welcome. *Society Meetings:* welcome, special rates available. Professional: Steve White (01553 841801). Secretary: J. Holland (Tel & Fax: 01553 841800).

KING'S LYNN. Royal West Norfolk Golf Club, Brancaster, Near King's Lynn PE31 8AX (01485 210223). *Location:* one mile off A149, Beach Road junction, seven miles east of Hunstanton. Seaside links. 18 holes, 6458 yards. S.S.S. 71. *Green Fees:* weekdays £70.00 per day; weekends £85.00 per day. *Eating facilities:* available. *Visitors:* all visitors must be members of a recognised Golf Club, hold an official Handicap and must make prior arrangements with the Secretary to play. No visitors prior to 10am Sundays and no visitors in August. Maximum numbers in party 24. Professional: S. Rayner (01485 210616). Secretary: Major N.I Symington (Tel & Fax: 01485 210087).

MATTISHALL. Mattishall Golf Club, South Green, Mattishall, Dereham NR20 3JZ (01362 850111). *Location:* Signposted from Mattishall Church. 9 hole (18 tees), flat course, 6170 yards, SSS 69. *Green Fees:* £10.00 for 9 holes. *Eating facilities:* small bar only. *Visitors:* welcome seven days, no restrictions. Secretary: Mrs Bridgette Hall.

NORWICH. Barnham Broom Hotel & Golf Club, Barnham Broom, Norwich NR9 4DD (01603 759393 (Hotel); 01603 757505 (Golf Shop); Fax: 01603 758224). *Location:* situated 10 miles west of Norwich off A47 and A11 trunk routes; follow brown tourist signs. Two 18 hole courses in 250 acres of the beautiful River Yare Valley. The Valley Course: 6483 yards, S.S.S. 71; The Hill Course: 6495 yards, S.S.S. 71. Exceptional practice facilities including 5-acre practice ground and three full length academy holes. GPS buggies available. Group and individual tuition at the Barnham Broom Golf School. *Green Fees:* information not available. *Eating facilities:* Flints Restaurant, Sports Bar and Cafe (serving light meals and drinks throughout the day). Conference and private dining for up to 200 people. *Visitors:* welcome anytime. Hotel with 52 en suite bedrooms. Leisure Club. *Society Meetings:* welcome all year; corporate Golf Events. PGA Professional: Ian Rollett, PGA Golf Manager: Alan Battle (01603 757504).
e-mail: golfschool@barnham-broom.co.uk
      alan@barnham-broom.co.uk
website: www.barnham-broom.co.uk

NORWICH. Bawburgh Golf Club, Glen Lodge, Marlingford Road, Bawburgh, Norwich NR9 3LU (01603 740404; Fax: 01603 740403). *Location:* directly off Norwich Southern Bypass – exit follow Royal Norfolk Showground/Bawburgh. Rolling landscape mixture of heath and parkland. 18 holes, 6231 yards. S.S.S. 70. Driving range covered and floodlit, group tuition. *Green Fees:* (2007) weekdays £27.00; weekends £30.00 on application. *Eating facilities:* restaurant and bar, snacks. *Visitors:* welcome, advisable to ring in advance. *Society Meetings:* welcome on application, Corporate Days arranged. Professional: Chris Potter (01603 742323). General Manager: Ian Ladbrooke.
e-mail: info@bawburgh.com
website: www.bawburgh.com

THE APPEARANCE OF AN ASTERISK (*) AT THE END OF A CLUB OR COURSE ENTRY INDICATES THAT UP-TO-DATE INFORMATION HAS NOT BEEN SUPPLIED

NORWICH. **Costessey Park Golf Course,** Old Costessey, Norwich NR8 5AL (01603 746333). *Location:* off the A47 Norwich to King's Lynn road, in the village of Old Costessey (adjacent to Norwich). Set in river valley with some parkland. 18 holes, 5900 yards. S.S.S. 69. Par 71. Practice area. *Green Fees:* information not available. *Eating facilities:* bar and bar snacks; set meals available. *Visitors:* welcome anytime except weekends when visitors allowed only after 11am. Handicap Certificates required weekends only. Golf carts available for hire. *Society Meetings:* catered for by arrangement. Professional: Andrew Young (01603 747085).*

NORWICH. **De Vere Dunston Hall,** Ipswich Road, Norwich NR14 8PQ (Hotel: 01508 470444; Fax: 01508 470689; Shop: 01508 470178). *Location:* on A140 Ipswich Road. Parkland, wooded, with many water features. USGA spec. greens. 18 holes, 6319 yards. Par 71. 22 bay covered driving range, putting green. *Green Fees:* information not available. *Eating facilities:* three restaurants, two bars. *Visitors:* pay and play course, all welcome at any time. Golfing weekends; accommodation available in 130-bedroom Hotel; tennis courts; leisure centre with indoor pool, sauna, steam room and jacuzzi. *Society Meetings:* special packages available. Professional: Peter Briggs.*

NORWICH. **Eaton (Norwich) Golf Club,** Newmarket Road, Norwich NR4 6SF (01603 451686; Fax: 01603 457539). *Location:* off A11, one and a half miles from city centre. Parkland course – "the hidden gem". 18 holes, 6114 yards. S.S.S. 70. Practice areas available. *Green Fees:* information not available. *Eating facilities:* full bar, snacks, lunches, dinners by arrangement. *Visitors:* welcome; only after 11.30am weekends. Handicap Certificate required. *Society Meetings:* welcome, fees by arrangement. Professional: Mark Allen (01603 251 394). Club Manager: Kieron Tuck (01603 451686; Fax: 01603 457539).
e-mail: admin@eatongc.co.uk
website: www.eatongc.co.uk

NORWICH. **Marriott Sprowston Manor Hotel and Country Club,** Wroxham Road, Norwich NR7 8RP (0870 400 7229; Fax: 0870 400 7329). *Location:* off A1151 Norwich to Wroxham. £1.6 million Championship course set in mature parkland. Host to Sky Televised PGA Europro Tour 2004 & 2005. Full USGA specification greens and tees. Designed by Ross McMurray (European Golf Design), who has also designed the Marquess at Woburn and improvements at Celtic Manor for 2010 Ryder Cup. 18 holes, 6547 yards. S.S.S. 71. Putting green, chipping and bunker practice area. 27 bay floodlit driving range, PGA tuition including Explanar and GASP video analysis. *Green Fees:* weekdays £40.00 per round; weekends £50.00 per round. *Eating facilities:* Zest café bar and grill. Four-star hotel on site. *Visitors:* always welcome. Bookings 10 days in advance. *Society Meetings:* special packages available - must be pre-booked. Preferential green fee rates and group packages available for residents. Professional: Guy Ireson (0870 400 7229). Secretary: Mr A. Moule (0870 400 7229).
website: www.marriott.co.uk/nwigs

NORWICH. **Mundesley Golf Club,** Links Road, Mundesley, Norwich NR11 8ES (01263 720279; Fax: 01263 722849). *Location:* one mile from village centre. Undulating, testing downland course with fine panoramic views. 9 holes, 5377 yards. S.S.S. 66. Covered driving range, small practice area. *Green Fees:* £28.00 per round weekdays, £30.00 per round weekends. *Eating facilities:* full catering facilities. *Visitors:* welcome, but course reserved for members until 11.30am at weekends and Bank Holidays and 10.30am to 2.30pm Wednesdays. *Society Meetings:* catered for, restrictions as for visitors. Professional: T.G. Symmons (01263 720279). Manager: T.E. Duke (01263 720095; Fax: 01263 722849).
website: www.mundesleygolfclub.co.uk

NORWICH. **Royal Norwich Golf Club,** Drayton High Road, Hellesdon, Norwich NR6 5AH (01603 429928; Fax: 01603 417945). *Location:* centre of city and thence by A1067 Fakenham or via Ring Road, then 500 yards along A1067. Mature parkland. 18 holes, 6506 yards. S.S.S. 72. Large practice ground. *Green Fees:* weekdays and weekends £40.00 per day, £25.00 per round. Discounted rates for groups of 12 and over £30.00 per day, £22.00 per round. Reduction if playing with a member, special winter rates available on request. *Eating facilities:* two bars, restaurant plus bar menu. Prior booking required for evening meals. *Visitors:* welcome weekdays after 9am, weekends by prior booking only. Handicap Certificate required. *Society Meetings:* welcome weekdays except Wednesday by prior arrangement. Golf Manager: Simon Youd (01603 408459). General Manager: John Meggy.
e-mail: mail@royalnorwichgolf.co.uk
website: www.royalnorwichgolf.co.uk

NORWICH. **Wensum Valley Hotel, Golf and Country Club,** Beech Avenue, Taverham, Norwich NR8 6HP (01603 261012; Fax: 01603 261664). *Location:* five miles out of Norwich on the A1067 to Fakenham. Two courses. Parkland and very picturesque set in the valley. Wensum Course: 18 holes, 6922 yards S.S.S. 73. Valley Course: 18 holes, 6223 yards. S.S.S. 70. Covered, floodlit driving range. *Green Fees:* please call 01603 261012. *Eating facilities:* full catering and bar facilities. *Visitors:* always welcome. Hotel on site with en suite twin and double bedrooms. Special golf, fishing and leisure breaks available. *Society Meetings:* all welcome; package available. Professional: James Blake. Secretary: Bridgette Hall (01603 261012).
e-mail: enqs@wensumvalleyhotel.co.uk
website: www.wensumvalleyhotel.co.uk

NORWICH. **Weston Park Golf Club,** Weston Longville, Norwich (01603 872998; Fax: 01603 873040). *Location:* nine miles north west of Norwich off the A1067 Norwich to Fakenham road. Parkland, wooded course. 18 holes, 6606 yards. S.S.S. 72. Practice ground and net. *Green Fees:* weekdays £37.00; weekends £47.00 (subject to review). *Eating facilities:* available. *Visitors:* welcome. Must book teeing off times. Handicap Certificate required. Two tennis courts and croquet lawn. *Society Meetings:* welcome. Professional: Michael Few (01603 872998). Sales Manager: C. E. Ashmore (01603 872363).
e-mail: info@weston-park.co.uk

REYMERSTON. **The Norfolk Golf and Country Club,** Hingham Road, Reymerston NR9 4QQ (01362 850297; Fax: 01362 850614). *Location:* Dereham B1135 five miles, Wymondham 10 miles. Parkland course. 18 holes, 6609 yards. S.S.S. 72. *Green Fees:* information not available. *Eating facilities:* clubhouse, bar, function room. *Visitors:* welcome subject to availability. Advisable to check in advance. Full Leisure facilities in Leisure Centre; swimming pool, sauna, gym, spa bath. *Society Meetings:* society and conference packages available. Professional: Tony Varney (01362 850297; Fax: 01362 850614). Secretary: Mike de Boltz.
e-mail: norfolkgolfsec@ukonline.co.uk
website: www.the-norfolk.co.uk

SHERINGHAM. **Sheringham Golf Club,** Weybourne Road, Sheringham NR26 8HG (01263 823488). *Location:* one mile west of town on Weybourne Road (A149). Clifftop course. 18 holes, 6456 yards. S.S.S. 71. Large practice area. *Green Fees:* Sunday to Friday per day £50.00 (April to Oct), £35.00 (Nov to March). Saturday per day £60.00 (April to Oct), £45.00 (Nov to March). Subject to review. Twilight and 3-day tickets available. *Eating facilities:* full catering to order. *Visitors:* welcome, telephone first, with reservation for members of other clubs, Handicap Certificate required. *Society Meetings:* catered for by prior arrangement with Secretary. Professional: M.W. Jubb (01263 822980). Secretary: P.J. Mounfield (01263 823488).

SWAFFHAM. **Dunham Golf Club,** Canister Hall, Little Dunham near Swaffham PE32 2DF (Tel. & Fax: 01328 701906). *Location:* off A47 four miles from Swaffham at Necton Q8 garage. Follow Tourist Board golf flags. Parkland with lakes. 9 holes, 4986 yards. S.S.S. 64. *Green Fees:* information not available. *Eating facilities:* restaurant and bar. *Visitors:* welcome with dress restrictions. Accommodation and swimming pool. *Society Meetings:* welcome, telephone for details. Professional: Gary Potter (01328 701906). Secretary: F. Reid (01328 701718).*

SWAFFHAM. **Swaffham Golf Club,** Cley Road, Swaffham PE37 8AE (01760 721611/721621). *Location:* two miles south-west of Swaffham Market Place (signposted) on Cley Road. Heathland course.

18 holes, 6533 yards. S.S.S. 71. Practice ground. *Green Fees:* Please call (01760 721621 option 2) for Summer/Winter deals. *Eating facilities:* full catering now available every day. *Visitors:* welcome without reservation weekdays, weekends only if playing with member. *Society Meetings:* catered for subject to prior notice being given. Professional: Peter Field. Secretary: M. Rust.

THETFORD. **Feltwell Golf Club,** Thor Avenue, off Wilton Road, Feltwell, Thetford IP26 4AY (01842 827644). *Location:* take the B1386 off the A10 at Southery (five miles south of Downham Market). Inland links – can be windy! 9 holes, 6488 yards, 6197 metres. S.S.S. 71. Practice range and nets. *Green Fees:* weekdays £16.00 per day, £10.00 with a member; weekends £25.00, per day, £16.00 with a member. *Eating facilities:* bar, hot and cold food available Tuesday through Sunday from noon. *Visitors:* welcome at all times but check with Secretary. *Society Meetings:* welcome, packages available. Secretary: David Rodwell (01842 827644). e-mail: secretary@feltwellgolfclub.F9.co.uk

THETFORD. **Richmond Park Golf Club,** Saham Road, Watton, Thetford IP25 6EA (01953 881803; Fax: 01953 881817). **Location:** half a mile north west of Watton town centre. Parkland. 18 holes, 6289 yards. S.S.S. 71. Driving range. **Green Fees:** weekdays £25.00 per round, weekends £35.00 per round. **Eating facilities:** bar, bar food, restaurant. **Visitors:** welcome. Accommodation available on site. **Society Meetings:** welcome, excellent facilities available. Professional/Secretary: Alan Hemsley.

THETFORD. **Thetford Golf Club,** Brandon Road, Thetford IP24 3NE (01842 752258). *Location:* one mile west of Thetford on B1107 Brandon Road. Wooded breckland course. 18 holes, 6849 yards. S.S.S. 73. Practice ground. *Green Fees:* £32.00 per round, £43.00 per day weekdays and after 1pm weekends. *Eating facilities:* catering and bar service. *Visitors:* welcome weekdays. *Society Meetings:* catered for Mondays, Wednesdays, Thursdays and Fridays – Handicap Certificate needed. Professional: Gary Kitley (01842 752662). Secretary: Mrs Diane Hopkins (01842 752169; Fax: 01842 766212 e-mail: thetfordgolfclub@btconnect.com

Great Yarmouth & Caister Golf Club

Suffolk

ALDEBURGH. **Aldeburgh Golf Club,** Saxmundham Road, Aldeburgh IP15 5PE (01728 452890). *Location:* A12 north from Ipswich; turn right on A1094 to Aldeburgh. Heathland course, abundance of dense gorse, many challenging Par 4s, no Par 5s. 18 holes, 6349 yards. S.S.S. 71; also 9 holes, 2114 yards. S.S.S. 32. *Green Fees:* weekdays £55.00 per day, £45.00 after 12 noon; weekends £60.00 per day, £50.00 after 12 noon. *Eating facilities:* lunches by arrangement. *Visitors:* welcome by arrangement, to play on 18-hole course must have club Handicap Certificate. No three or four balls allowed. *Society Meetings:* by arrangement. Professional: K.R. Preston (01728 453309). Secretary: 01728 452890; Fax: 01728 452937).

BECCLES. **Beccles Golf Club,** The Common, Beccles NR34 9BX (01502 712244). *Location:* A146 Beccles by-pass, to town centre at Safeway roundabout, left over level crossing. Flat commonland. 9 holes, 5558 yards, 5084 metres. S.S.S. 67. *Green Fees:* Information not available. *Eating facilities:* bar snacks available. *Visitors:* welcome anytime. *Society Meetings:* catered for by prior arrangement. Secretary: Alan Ereira (01502 712244).*

BUNGAY. **Bungay and Waveney Valley Golf Club,** Outney Common, Bungay NR35 1DS (01986 892337; Fax: 01986 892222). *Location:* a quarter mile from town centre and alongside A143. Flat, heath-type course. 18 holes, 6050 yards. S.S.S. 69. *Green Fees:* Information not available. *Eating facilities:* available everyday. *Visitors:* welcome weekdays, weekends with member only. Must telephone (01986 892337) prior to a visit to book a tee time. *Society Meetings:* by arrangement with Secretary. Professional: Andrew Collison (01986 892337; Fax: 01986 892222). Secretary: John Lunniss (01986 892337; Fax: 01986 892222). *

BURY ST EDMUNDS. **Bury St Edmunds Golf Club,** Tut Hill, Bury St Edmunds IP28 6LG. *Location:* B1106 just off A14. Flat parkland. 18 holes, 6675 yards. S.S.S. 72; 9 holes, 2217 yards. S.S.S. 31. Practice facilities. *Green Fees:* weekdays £35.00 per round, £45.00 per day on 18-hole course; two rounds on 9 hole course £14.00 weekdays, £17.00 weekends. *Eating facilities:* available. *Visitors:* welcome Monday to Friday on both courses; weekends on 9-hole course only. *Society Meetings:* catered for. Professional: Mark Jillings (01284 755978). Secretary: John Taylor (01284 755979; Fax: 01284 763288). e-mail: info@burygolf.co.uk

BURY ST EDMUNDS. **Flempton Golf Club,** Flempton, Bury St Edmunds IP28 6EQ (01284 728291). *Location:* follow A1101 from Bury St Edmunds towards Mildenhall for about four miles, course on right. 9 holes, 6240 yards. S.S.S. 70. *Green Fees:* £30.00 per round, £35.00 per day. *Eating facilities:* by arrangement. *Visitors:* welcome, except Bank Holidays. By prior arrangement and must produce Handicap Certificate. Professional: Chris Aldred (01284 728291). Secretary: M.S. Clark.

BURY ST EDMUNDS. **The Suffolk Hotel Golf and Country Club,** Fornham St Genevieve, Bury St Edmunds IP28 6JQ (01284 706777; Fax: 01284 706721). *Location:* Exit A14 at Bury St Edmunds West and travel north on B1106 for approx. 2 miles. Mature parkland, testing water hazards. Putting green and practice ground. 18 hole Genevieve course 6350 yards. S.S.S. 71. *Green Fees:* information not available. *Eating facilities:* Bars and restaurant; residential packages available. *Visitors:* welcome, booking advised. Club, buggy and trolley hire. Indoor pool, with spa sauna and steam room. 41 bedroom en suite hotel. Conference facilities. *Society Meetings:* society packages available. Professional/Director of Golf: Stephen Hall. e-mail: proshop.suffolkgolf@ohiml.com website: www.oxfordhotelsandinns.com

DISS. **Diss Golf Club**, Stuston Common, Diss IP21 4AA (01379 641025). *Location:* close to the town of Diss on the Suffolk/Norfolk border. Links-type course with natural hazards abounding, and 30 bunkers to avoid. A good test of golf for every standard of player. 18 holes, 6206 yards. S.S.S. 70, Par 70. Good practice facilities; driving range one mile. *Green Fees:* £28.00 per round, £36.00 per day. Summer and Winter Green Fee deals are available, phone for details. *Eating facilities:* good dining and bar facilities at the clubhouse. *Visitors:* always welcome, membership available. Lessons available; golf shop. *Society Meetings:* societies and groups always welcome. For all enquiries contact the Secretary Manager. Professional: (01379 644399). Secretary Manager: (01379 640125). Club Bar and Catering Manager: (01379 642847) after 11am. e-mail: sec.dissgolf@virgin.net website: www.club-noticeboard.co.uk/diss

FELIXSTOWE. **Felixstowe Ferry Golf Club,** Ferry Road, Felixstowe IP11 9RY (01394 286834). *Location:* one mile from town centre, follow signs to Golf Club. Seaside links course. 18 holes, 6269 yards. S.S.S. 70. Also a 9 hole course, 2986 yards. S.S.S. 69. Practice area. *Green Fees:* weekdays £37.50 per day; £27.50 per round. *Eating facilities:* diningroom and bar. *Visitors:* welcome weekdays, but advisable to check first; weekends must play with member before 14.30 hours. Handicap Certificates required. Two self catering flats available, free golf included in charges. *Society Meetings:* catered for weekdays only. Professional: Ian MacPherson (01394 283975). Secretary: Richard Tibbs (01394 286834).

FRAMLINGHAM. **Cretingham Golf Club,** Swans Lane, Cretingham, Woodbridge IP13 7BA (01728 685275). *Location:* off A1120, signposted to Cretingham, 10 miles north of Ipswich. Wooded inland course, challenging water holes. 18 holes, 5278 yards. Par 68. Practice 9 hole course. *Green Fees:* weekdays 9 holes £10.00, 18 holes £18.00; weekends and Bank Holidays 9 holes £12.00, 18 holes £20.00. *Eating facilities:* restaurant and fully licensed bar. *Visitors:* always welcome, no restrictions. Please book in advance. Tennis available. Outdoor swimming pool. Caravans welcome. Log cabins available to let. *Society Meetings:* welcome. Professional: Neil Jackson (01728 685275). Secretary: Kate Jackson.

HALESWORTH. **Halesworth Golf Club,** Bramfield Road, Halesworth IP19 9XA (01986 875567). *Location:* on A144 between Halesworth and Bramfield. 18 hole Blyth course, 6506 yards, par 72. 9 hole Valley course, 2280 yards, par 33. Practice area, putting green, 10 bay floodlit driving range. *Green Fees:* Blyth weekdays £20.00 per round £25.00 per day, Valley £5.00 9 holes, £10.00 18 holes; weekends and Bank Holidays Blyth £25.00 per round, £30.00 per day, Valley £6.00 9 holes, £11.00 18 holes. *Eating facilities:* bar and restaurant. *Visitors:* welcome. *Society Meetings:* welcome. Buggies available.
e-mail: info@halesworthgc.co.uk

HAVERHILL. **Haverhill Golf Club Ltd,** Coupals Road, Haverhill CB9 7UW (Tel & Fax: 01440 761951). *Location:* Sturmer Road turn into Chalkestone Way, right into Coupals Road. Club is one mile on right. Undulating parkland with river. 18 holes, 5967 yards. S.S.S. 69. Practice ground. *Green Fees:* weekdays £30.00 per day, weekends and Bank Holidays £35.00. Half price if playing with a member. *Eating facilities:* clubhouse, snacks, hot meals, bar. *Visitors:* welcome at all times except when first tee booked for matches and societies. *Society Meetings:* welcome. Professional: Nick Duc (01440 712628; Fax: 01440 712628). Secretary: Linda Farrant (Tel & Fax: 01440 761951).

IPSWICH. **Fynn Valley Golf Club,** Witnesham, Ipswich IP6 9JA (01473 785267; Fax: 01473 785632). *Location:* two miles north of Ipswich on B1077. Attractive, undulating parkland along the Fynn Valley. 18 holes, 6371 yards. S.S.S. 71. 9 hole Par 3 course, 23 bay floodlit golf range (10 undercover), practice bunker and putting greens. *Green Fees:* £26.00 per round weekdays; £32.00 per round weekends (twilight discounts). *Eating facilities:* bar, terrace, gourmet restaurant. *Visitors:* welcome, members only Sunday mornings, Ladies priority Wednesday mornings. Special rates for parties of 12 or more. Two golf shops. Teaching facilities, golf buggies, trolley hire. *Society Meetings:* welcome by prior arrangement. Professionals: Paul Wilby, Simon Dainty, Danny Barton (01473 785463). Secretary: A.R. Tyrrell (01473 785267; Fax: 01473 785632).
e-mail: enquiries@fynn-valley.co.uk
website: www.fynn-valley.co.uk

IPSWICH. **Hintlesham Golf Club,** Hintlesham, Ipswich IP8 3JG (01473 652761; Fax: 01473 652750). *Location:* four miles west of Ipswich on the A1071 to Sudbury. Parkland, championship standard - Architect: Martin Hawtree. 18 holes, 6638 yards. S.S.S. 72. Full practice facilities. *Green Fees:* information not available. *Eating facilities:* full catering facilities. *Visitors:* please telephone for tee off times. Accommodation available at Hintlesham Hall Hotel. *Society Meetings:* telephone enquiries welcome. We have a growing national reputation for the organisation of golf days. Professional: Henry Roblin.
e-mail: sales@hintleshamgolfclub.com
website: www.hintleshamgolfclub.com

IPSWICH. **Ipswich Golf Club,** Purdis Heath, Bucklesham Road, Ipswich IP3 8UQ. *Location:* three miles east of Ipswich on Bucklesham Road. Heathland. 18 holes, 6439 yards. S.S.S. 71. 9 holes, 1930 yards. S.S.S. 59. *Green Fees:* weekdays £35.00 per round, £45.00 per day; weekends and Bank Holidays £40.00 per round, £50.00 per day. 9-hole course: weekdays £10.00 per day, weekends and Bank Holidays £12.50 per day (subject to review). *Eating facilities:* full catering facilities available for visitors. *Visitors:* by prior arrangement for 18 hole course, and must produce Handicap Certificate or letter of introduction. No restriction for 9 hole course. *Society Meetings:* by special reservation only and on Society terms. Professional: (01473 724017). Secretary: N.M. Ellice (01473 728941).
e-mail: neill@ipswichgolfclub.com
website: www.ipswichgolfclub.com

IPSWICH. **Rushmere Golf Club,** Rushmere Heath, Woodbridge Road, Ipswich IP4 5QQ (01473 727109). *Location:* off A1214 north from Ipswich, 300 yards signposted. Heathland course. 18 holes, 6265 yards. S.S.S. 70. Practice facilities. *Green Fees:* £25.00 per round, £40.00 per day. *Eating facilities:* full catering available. *Visitors:* welcome except 4.30-5.30pm, weekends after 2.30pm. Handicap Certificate required. *Society Meetings:* welcome. Professional: Kelvin Vince (01473 728076). Secretary: R.W.G. Tawell (01473 725648).
e-mail: rushmeregolfclub@btconnect.com
website: www.club-notlceboard.co.uk/rushmere

IPSWICH/WOODBRIDGE. **Best Western Ufford Park Hotel, Golf and Spa,** Yarmouth Road, Melton, Woodbridge, Near Ipswich IP12 1QW (01394 383555; Fax: 01394 383582). *Location:* A12 northwards to A1152 to Melton. In Melton turn left at traffic lights, one mile on the right hand side. Challenging 120-acre parkland course. A "Top 10 Inland British Winter Course" for the last 3 years. 18 holes, 6312 yards. S.S.S. 71. 32 bay (2 storey) floodlit driving range: 'American Golf and the Doctorgolf Academy'. *Green Fees:* weekdays £30.00; weekends £40.00. Special Golf Breaks available. *Eating facilities:* bar snacks, children's menu and restaurant. *Visitors:* welcome anytime, need to book tee time in advance. 87 en suite bedroom hotel. Ideal for groups; full leisure centre with pool and gym, new Thermal Suite for spa experiences. Buggies for hire, tuition breaks available. *Society Meetings:* welcome, competitive rates, details on request. PGA Head Professional. Stuart Robertson (01394 383480 (The Doctorgolf Academy)). Secretary: Ray Baines (01394 382836; Fax: 01394 383582).
website: www.uffordpark.co.uk
    www.doctorgolf.co.uk

LOWESTOFT. **Rookery Park Golf Club,** Beccles Road, Carlton Colville, Lowestoft NR33 8HJ (01502 509190; Fax: 01502 509191)). *Location:* A146 Beccles to Lowestoft road. Parkland. 18 holes, 6729 yards. S.S.S. 72. 9 hole Par 3 course. Practice ground. New driving range. *Green Fees:* weekdays £29.50, with a member £18.50; weekends £35.00, with a member £21.50. *Eating facilities:* bar, restaurant. *Visitors:* welcome weekdays (Saturdays and Bank Holidays after 11am). Handicap Cards must be produced. *Society Meetings:* welcome. Professional: M. Elsworthy (01502 515103). Secretary/Manager: R.F. Jones (01502 509190; Fax: 01502 509191).

MILDENHALL. **Royal Worlington and Newmarket Golf Club,** Golf Links Road, Worlington, Bury St. Edmunds IP28 8SD (01638 712216; Fax: 01638 717787). *Location:* seven miles north east of Newmarket, signposted off A11 just south of Barton Mills roundabout. Inland links type course. 9 holes, 3105 yards. S.S.S. 70 (18 holes). Practice ground. *Green Fees:* weekdays £60.00 per day, £45.00 after 2pm (12 noon in winter). *Eating facilities:* lunch and tea available with prior notice; no evening meals. *Visitors:* welcome weekdays only, Handicap Certificate or letter of introduction from home club required. Trolleys for hire. Professional: (01638 715224). Secretary: Scott Ballentine (Tel & Fax: 01638 717787).

NEWMARKET. **Links Golf Club,** Cambridge Road, Newmarket CB8 0TG (01638 663000; Fax: 01638 661476). *Location:* one mile south-west of Newmarket, opposite racecourse. Relatively flat parkland. 18 holes, 6582 yards. S.S.S. 72. Two practice grounds. *Green Fees:* midweek £26.00 per round, £34.00 per day; weekends and Bank Holidays £30.00 per round, £38.00 per day. Subject to review. *Eating facilities:* restaurant and bar. *Visitors:* welcome, not before 11.30am Sundays. Handicap Certificate required. *Society Meetings:* by arrangement. Professional: John Sharkey (01638 662395). Secretary: M.L. Hartley (01638 663000; Fax: 01638 661476). website: www.club-noticeboard.co.uk/newmarket

RAYDON. **Brett Vale Golf Club,** Noakes Road, Raydon, Ipswich IP7 5LR (01473 310718). *Location:* midway between Colchester and Ipswich, just off A12 on B1070 to Hadleigh, head for Raydon Water Tower. Undulating countryside parkland course within Dedham Vale in natural valley setting. 18 holes, 5864 yards. S.S.S. 69. 5 bay outdoor Golf Academy, practice ground, putting green. *Green Fees:* weekdays £22.50, day ticket £35.00; weekends £28.00. *Eating facilities:* clubroom bar and restaurant; society/function room and bar. *Visitors:* welcome anytime. Pro shop; buggies and power trolley hire. *Society Meetings:* welcome anytime, various packages available. Secretary: John Reid (01473 310718).

SOUTHWOLD. **Southwold Golf Club,** The Common, Southwold IP18 6TB (01502 723234). *Location:* from A12 Blythburgh turn off on A1095 to Southwold. Flat common land with sea views. 9 holes, 6052 yards. S.S.S. 69. *Green Fees:* information not available. *Visitors:* welcome, phone for availability. *Society Meetings:* welcome, Fridays only. Professional: B.G. Allen (01502 723790). Hon. Secretary: P. Obern (01502 723248).*

STOKE-BY-NAYLAND. **Stoke-by-Nayland Golf & Spa,** Keepers Lane, Leavenheath, Colchester CO6 4PZ (01206 262836; Fax: 01206 263356). *Location:* just off A134 Colchester to Sudbury on B1068 towards Stoke-by-Nayland. Host venue to PGA Seniors' Championship 2006. Undulating parkland with water hazards. Two courses (1) Gainsborough - 18 holes, 6516 yards. S.S.S. 71. (2) Constable - 18 holes, 6544 yards. S.S.S. 71. 20 bay covered range, practice area. *Green Fees:* information not available. *Eating facilities:* full catering and bars. *Visitors:* welcome, please ring for availability and tee bookings. *Society Meetings:* welcome weekdays, book well in advance. Seasonal packages offered. Extensive Health and Leisure Facility including gymnasium, pool, sauna, jacuzzi and spa; modern, spacious, en suite hotel rooms overlooking lake and fairways. Professional: Kevin Lovelock (01206 262769). Secretary: Peter Barfield (01206 265815). e-mail: mary.saward@stokebynayland.com website: www.stokebynaylandclub.co.uk

STOWMARKET. **Stowmarket Golf Club Ltd,** Lower Road, Onehouse, Stowmarket IP14 3DA (01449 736473; Fax: 01449 736826). *Location:* on B1508 from Stowmarket to Onehouse. Parkland. 18 holes, 6101 yards. S.S.S. 69. Driving range. *Green Fees:* Information not available. *Eating facilities:* lunches, snacks all week. *Visitors:* welcome, avoid Wednesdays. Handicap Certificate required. *Society Meetings:* catered for Thursdays and Fridays only. Professional: D. Burl (01449 736392). Secretary: G.R. West (01449 736473).

SUDBURY. **Newton Green Golf Club,** Newton Green, Sudbury CO10 0QN. *Location:* on A134 three miles east of Sudbury. Flat course. 18 holes, 5947 yards. Par 69. Practice ground. *Green Fees:* Information not available. *Eating facilities:* fully licensed bar, full catering facilities, separate dining room available. *Visitors:* welcome (except Sundays and Tuesdays before 12.30pm); trolleys for hire. *Society Meetings:* welcome by arrangement. PGA Professional: Tim Cooper (01787 313215). Secretary/Manager: Carole List (01787 377217). e-mail: info@newtongreengolfclub.co.uk website: www.newtongreengolfclub.co.uk

THORPENESS. **Thorpeness Golf Club and Hotel,** Thorpeness, Leiston IP16 4NH (01728 452176; Fax: 01728 453868). *Location:* leave A12 at Aldeburgh turnoff. Heathland coastal course. 18 holes, 6271 yards. S.S.S. 71. *Green Fees:* information not available. *Eating facilities:* bar, restaurant, terrace and garden. *Visitors:* welcome on application, telephone Pro shop for times. Handicap Cetificate required. Accommodation available – 30 bedrooms. Snooker room, seven tennis courts. *Society Meetings:* welcome. Professional: Frank Hill (01728 454926). Golf Manager: Charlie Langlands (01728 452176). website: www.thorpeness.co.uk

WOODBRIDGE. **Seckford Golf Club,** Seckford Hall Road, Great Bealings, Near Woodbridge IP13 6NT (01394 388000; Fax: 01394 382818). *Location:* between Martlesham and Woodbridge just off A12. Undulating parkland course maintained in excellent condition. 18 holes, 4881 yards. Par 67. Full length driving range and putting green. *Green Fees:* Please call for rates and specials. *Eating facilities:* fully licensed bar and restaurant. *Visitors:* always welcome, telephone to book your place. Buggies, trolleys, clubs and shoes available for hire. *Society Meetings:* Welcome by prior arrangement, packages available. PGA Professional: Simon Jay (Tel: 01394 388000) GASP Video analysis. e-mail: info@seckfordgolf.co.uk website: www.seckfordgolf.co.uk

WOODBRIDGE. **Waldringfield Golf Club,** Newbourne Road, Waldringfield, Woodbridge IP12 4PT (01473 736768). *Location:* five miles north of Ipswich, off the old A12. Easy walking, picturesque heathland course with attractive water features. 18 holes, 6079 yards. S.S.S. 69. Limited practice area available. *Green Fees:* weekdays £24.00, weekends £28.00. Special rates available for societies by arrangement. *Eating facilities:* full service. *Visitors:* welcome weekdays and weekends. *Society Meetings:* welcome weekdays and weekends by arrangement. Course Administrator: (01473 736417). Manager: Pat Whitham (01473 736768. Fax: 01473 736793)

WOODBRIDGE. **Woodbridge Golf Club,** Bromeswell Heath, Woodbridge IP12 2PF (01394 382038; Fax: 01394 382392). *Location:* leave A12 at Melton Roundabout. After traffic lights, follow A1152 over level crossing, fork left at roundabout. Club is 400 yards on right. Heathland. 18 holes, 6299 yards. S.S.S. 70. 9 holes, 3191 yards. S.S.S. 70. Large practice ground. *Green Fees:* £42.00 18 hole course, £18.00 9 hole course. *Eating facilities:* main bar, casual bar and restaurant. *Visitors:* not before 9.30am, not at weekends. Handicap Certificates mandatory on 18 hole course, no restriction on 9 hole course. Telephone call advisable. *Society Meetings:* by prior arrangement, maximum number 36. Professional: T. Johnson (01394 383213). Secretary: J. Cross (01394 382038; 01394 382392).

Golf in the Midlands

Jennifer Prentice

Derbyshire • Herefordshire • Leicestershire
& Rutland • Lincolnshire • Northamptonshire
Nottinghamshire • Shropshire • Staffordshire
Warwickshire • West Midlands • Worcestershire

The Abbey Hotel, Golf & Country Club, Warwickshire

IT IS ALWAYS said that a change is as good as a rest – whether for a weekend break, a few days away midweek, or a longer period of time. This applies as much to golf as to any other sport or interest or, indeed, other facets of our increasingly busy lives.

Golf offers a huge diversity of challenges, all within a wide choice of settings.

Certainly, golfers of all abilities can find a vast range of choices to satisfy their personal playing preferences in the Midlands. This is the perfect 'getaway' region, with good transport links stretching across a wide and varied area.

If you normally play inland, you may choose to golf on an established seaside links. Alternatively, you may decide to leave the coast for the rich choice of traditional courses, or for one of the more modern ones which present enticing contemporary challenges. These have opened as the Royal and Ancient game has become even more popular.

Golfers, like other travellers, make their decisions based on a number of factors, and within the Midlands there is good golf to be found within easy reach of other attractions – ancient houses, museums, high class entertainment and shopping - suiting all ages and demands. Personal recommendations from family or friends carry weight, but a look around some of the tournament venues in the region may also provide inspiration.

In 2007 professional tour tournaments, including regional PGA events, were held over a good range of locations, with some of the same courses also hosting leading amateur championships.

The Belfry has long been a jewel in the Midlands crown, having staged several Ryder Cup matches between Europe and the USA, as well as major European Tour events. In September 2007 the Quinn Direct British Masters was contested there, attracting a strong field of Europe's leading golfers to the famous Brabazon course, now 30 years old. In addition to the Brabazon, the PGA National and the Derby provide good challenges. Off-course facilities match the high standards of the three courses. There is even a popular nightclub on site here, as well as sophisticated health and relaxation amenities.

Also in the autumn, the Marriott Forest of Arden was the venue for the EuroPro Tour, and, in the spring, the English Amateur Stroke Play Championship for the Brabazon Trophy drew an international field to sample its delights. Yet again, facilities on and off the course are of the highest order.

A little earlier, the EuroPro Tour was at Whittlebury Park, close to Silverstone racing circuit, with a top class hotel, huge clubhouse, academy, and three 9-hole 'loops'. Another EuroPro tournament in Northamptonshire was played in early summer at Collingtree Park, with a number of hotels close by providing accommodation.

PGA Midland fixtures took professionals to a variety of hotel venues too. Among these were Morley Hayes in Derbyshire; to Stapleford Park Country House Hotel and Sporting Estate near Melton Mowbray in rural Leicestershire; and to two in Lincolnshire – Forest Pines and Belton woods, where there are challlenging courses and other superb leisure facilities for families of all ages.

The centuries-old Nailcote Hall Hotel in Warwickshire provided a tough test for professionals over its 9-hole Cromwell course for the British Par 3 Championship. This has been its home since its revival a few years ago, after a long absence from the fixture list, and attracted a star-studded field. There was a major change there in 2007 – the 1st hole is now modelled on the world-famous 17th island green at Sawgrass, Florida. It has been extended, and is virtually surrounded by a new water feature joining the existing lake, to present an even greater challenge.

Pro/Am competitions took golfers to other hotel/course complexes too. Among them were The Welcombe on the fringe of Shakespeare's Stratford-upon-Avon, and Moor Hall, close to Birmingham, with its many and varied delights, as well as other competitive courses, such as Little Aston, near to Moor Hall, Woodhall Spa – headquarters of the English Golf Union, and Kedleston Park in Derbyshire – all with a wide choice of accommodation in the vicinity.

Derbyshire

ALFRETON. **Alfreton Golf Club,** Wingfield Road, Alfreton DE55 7LH (01773 832070). *Location:* B6024 (Matlock Road) one mile from Alfreton. Parkland course. 11holes, 5121 yards. S.S.S. 66. *Green Fees:* £20.00 per round, £28.00 per day. *Eating facilities:* bar snacks and fully licensed restaurant every day 10am - 9pm. *Visitors:* welcome Monday to Friday with reservation. *Society Meetings:* catered for. Lessons available from teaching professional by prior arrangement. Professional: (01773 831901). Secretary: S. Bradley.

ASHBOURNE. **Ashbourne Golf Club Ltd,** Off Wyaston Road, Ashbourne DE6 1NB (01335 342078; Fax: 01335 347937). *Location:* Wyaston Road, Ashbourne, one and a half miles out of Ashbourne. Undulating parkland. 18 holes, 6402 yards. S.S.S. 71. Practice area. *Green Fees:* £28.00 weekdays, £35.00 weekends and Bank Holidays. *Eating facilities:* available daily; parties must make prior arrangement. *Visitors:* welcome by arrangement with Professional. *Society Meetings:* welcome weekdays. Professional: Andrew Smith (01335 347960). Secretary: J.W. Hammond (01335 342078).
website: www.ashbournegolfclub.co.uk

BAKEWELL. **Bakewell Golf Club,** Station Road, Bakewell DE45 1GB (01629 812307). *Location:* Sheffield Road out of Bakewell, turn right after the river bridge. Parkland, scenic hillside course. 9 holes, 5240 yards. S.S.S. 68. *Green Fees:* £16.00 weekdays, £21.00 weekends. *Eating facilities:* bar meals, formal catering except Mondays. *Visitors:* welcome weekdays, occasional weekends by prior arrangement. *Society Meetings:* welcome by arrangement. Secretary: Mrs P. Moody.
website: bakewellgolfclub.co.uk

BRAILSFORD. **Brailsford Golf Club,** Pools Head Lane, Brailsford, Near Ashbourne DE6 3BU (01335 360096). *Location:* on the main A52 Derby to Ashbourne road, Derby 6 miles, Ashbourne 5 miles. Parkland course. 9 holes, planning permission granted for a further 6 holes 5758 yards (18 hole), S.S.S. 68. Practice facilities and 15 bay covered,floodlit, driving range. *Green Fees:* weekdays 9 holes £12.00, 18 holes £17.00; weekends 9 holes £14.00, 18 holes £22.00. Special rates for Juniors, Senior Citizens (weekdays only). *Eating facilities:* available. *Visitors:* welcome at any time except Sunday mornings. Tuition available - two teaching Professionals. *Society Meetings:* welcome except Sunday mornings. Special rates available. Professional: David McCarthy (01335 360096). Secretary: K. Wilson (01332 553703).

BURTON-ON-TRENT. **Burton-on-Trent Golf Club,** 43 Ashby Road East, Burton-on-Trent DE15 0PS *Location:* three miles east of Burton-on-Trent on the A511 towards Ashby de la Zouch. Undulating parkland course with many trees, testing finishing hole. 18 holes, 6579 yards. S.S.S. 71. Practice ground. *Green Fees:* weekdays £38.00 per round, £50.00 per day; weekends and Bank Holidays £44.00 per round, £57.00 per day. 2007 rates, subject to review. Special rates by arrangement. *Eating facilities:* dining room, lounge bar. *Visitors:* welcome weekdays, restrictions at weekends and Bank Holidays. *Society Meetings:* welcome, apply in writing for terms. Professional: Gary Stafford (01283 562240). Secretary: Martin Leggett (Tel & Fax: 01283 544551).
e-mail: TheSecretary@BurtonGolfClub.co.uk
website: www.burtongolfclub.co.uk

BUXTON. **Buxton and High Peak Golf Club,** Town End, Waterswallows Road, Buxton SK17 7EN (01298 23453; Fax: 01298 26333; Office: 01298 26263). *Location:* A6 one mile north of Buxton. Parkland, good positional play required. 18 holes, 5966 yards. S.S.S. 69. Practice facilities. *Green Fees:* weekdays £24.00 per round, £30.00 per day; weekends £30.00 per round, £36.00 per day. *Eating facilities:* full catering facilities. *Visitors:* welcome without reservation, ring at weekends. *Society Meetings:* welcome. Professional: John Lines (01298 23112). Secretary: John Harris.
e-mail: sec@bhpgc.co.uk
website: www.bhpgc.co.uk

BUXTON. **The Cavendish Golf Club Ltd,** Gadley Lane, Buxton SK17 6XD (01298 79708). *Location:* three quarters of a mile from town centre, on Leek Road A53, signposted. Parkland/moorland course, designed by Dr Alister Mackenzie who designed Augusta. Parkland/moorland course. 18 holes, 5833 yards. S.S.S. 68. Practice ground. *Green Fees:* £30.00 per round weekdays; £40.00 per round weekends. Juniors half price and visitors £15.00 if playing with a member. Visiting parties £28.00. *Eating facilities:* restaurant, usual bar hours, snacks, meals available at all times. *Visitors:* apply to Professional. Snooker. *Society Meetings:* catered for weekdays only, apply to the Secretary for booking arrangements. Professional: Simon Townend (01298 79708). Secretary: G. Nicholls (Tel & Fax: 01298 79708).

CHAPEL-EN-LE-FRITH. **Chapel-en-le-Frith Golf Club,** The Cockyard, Manchester Road, Chapel-en-le-Frith SK23 9UH (01298 812118). *Location:* midway between Sheffield and Manchester, 25 miles from each on the B5470. Parkland, scenic. 18 holes, 6434 yards. S.S.S. 71. Practice ground. *Green Fees:* weekdays £32.00 per round, weekends £42.00 per round (subject to review for 2008). *Eating facilities:* all meals daily. *Visitors:* welcome, small numbers without reservation. *Society Meetings:* catered for by arrangement. Professional: D. Cullen (01298 812118). Secretary: D. Goldfinch (01298 813943; Fax: 01298 814990).
e-mail: info@chapelgolf.co.uk

CHESTERFIELD. **Birch Hall Golf Club,** Sheffield Road, Unstone, Near Chesterfield S18 5DH (01246 291979). *Location:* off A61 between Sheffield and Chesterfield. Moorland course with outstanding views. 18 holes, 6409 yards, 5860 metres. S.S.S. 71. Practice area. *Green Fees:* information not provided. *Eating facilities:* bar with meals available. *Visitors:* welcome but prior booking essential. *Society Meetings:* welcome but prior booking essential. Hon. Gen. Secretary: E. Gallagher.

CHESTERFIELD. **Chesterfield Golf Club Ltd,** Matlock Road, Walton, Chesterfield S42 7LA (01246 279256; Fax: 01246 276622). *Location:* two miles from Chesterfield town centre on Matlock road (A632); Junction 29 M1. Parkland with natural hazards. 18 holes, 6281 yards. S.S.S. 70. Practice ground, putting green. *Green Fees:* weekdays £32.00 per round, £40.00 per day; Sundays £40.00 per round after 1.30pm. *Eating facilities:* full catering (dining room), two bars. *Visitors:* welcome weekdays, and Sundays after 1.30pm; other times at weekend as members' guests only. Trolleys. Snooker. *Society Meetings:* catered for on application. Professional: Michael McLean (01246 276297). Secretary: Trevor Marshall.

CHESTERFIELD. **Grassmoor Golf Centre,** North Wingfield Road, Grassmoor, Chesterfield S42 5EA (01246 856044; Fax: 01246 853486). *Location:* 4 miles M1 Junction 29 or A61 near Chesterfield. Heathland course incorporating water hazards, testing greens, testing par 3's for distance. 18 holes, 5723 yards, S.S.S. 68. 25 bay covered, floodlit range. 9 hole practice putting area and a practice area. *Green Fees:* weekdays £12.00, weekends £15.00. County Cards reduction. *Eating facilities:* Excellent bar and restaurant facilities available 8am to 10pm. *Visitors:* welcome, weekends included, 6 days' advance booking system by phone. *Society Meetings:* group bookings and societies welcome, including at weekends. Lessons available with Senior PGA Professional. Open daily 8am to 10pm, everyone welcome. Professional: Gary Hagues. Club Manager: Helen Hagues (01246 856044). website: www.grassmoorgolf.co.uk

CHESTERFIELD. **Stanedge Golf Club,** Walton Hay Farm, Chesterfield S45 0LW (01246 566156). *Location:* five miles south-west of Chesterfield, off B5057 near "Red Lion" public house. Course 1000ft above sea level, views of four counties. 9 holes, 5786 Information not available. *Visitors:* welcome. Must book in by 2pm Monday to Fridays. No visitors on Sundays until 4pm and they must be with member. *Society Meetings:* catered for by prior arrangement. Secretary: W.C. Tyzack (01246 276568)*

CHESTERFIELD. **Tapton Park Golf & Leisure Centre,** Crow Lane, Chesterfield S41 0EQ (01246 239500; Fax: 01246 555140). *Location:* behind railway station. Wooded parkland course. 18 hole course, 9 hole course and pitch and putt course. 18 hole course - 6025 yards. S.S.S. 69; 9 hole course - 2595 yards, Par 34. Putting and pitching greens. *Green Fees:* information not available. *Eating facilities:* bar and restaurant open to the public. *Visitors:* welcome at all times, booking for 18 hole course taken six days in advance. Club/Trolley/Locker hire. *Society Meetings:* welcome on written application. Professional: Andrew Carnall. Secretary: (01246 273887; Fax: 01246 558024). *

CODNOR. **Ormonde Fields Golf Club,** Nottingham Road, Codnor, Ripley DE5 9RG (01773 744157). *Location:* five miles M1 Junction 26 towards Ripley on A610. Parkland. 18 holes, 6504 yards. S.S.S. 72. Practice area, putting green. *Green Fees:* information not provided. *Eating facilities:* full restaurant available. *Visitors:* unrestricted. *Society Meetings:* catered for; book through Secretary. Professional: M. Myford (01773 742987). Secretary: Mr K. Constable (01773 570043).

DERBY. **Allestree Park Golf Club,** Allestree Hall, Duffield Road, Allestree, Derby DE22 2EU (01332 552971). Location: 3 miles north of Derby city centre on A6. Municipal undulating parkland course with outstanding views. 18 holes, 5728 yards. Par 68, S.S.S. 68. Practice ground and putting green. *Green Fees:* weekdays £11.50, weekends £13.50. Off peak rates and discounts available. *Eating facilities:* full bar, catering available. *Visitors:* always welcome, call Pro Shop for booking a time. *Society Meetings:* available any time weekdays after 1pm, weekends – details on request. Professional: Leigh Woodward (01332 550616. Secretary: Clive Barker (01332 552971). e-mail: Leigh.woodward@derby.gov.uk

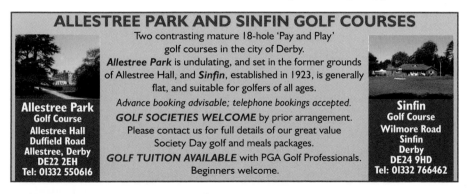

DERBY. **Derby Golf Club,** Wilmore Road, Sinfin, Derby DE24 9HD (01332 766323). *Location:* two miles city centre. Parkland. 18 holes, 6185 yards, 5653 metres. S.S.S. 70. Practice area. *Green Fees:* £13.50. *Eating facilities:* bar and catering available. *Visitors:* welcome at any time (Saturdays until 1pm reserved for club members). Phone Pro Shop for tee times. *Society Meetings:* welcome at any time (except Saturdays until 1pm). Professional: Dan Delaney (01332 766462; Fax: 01332 769004). Secretary: D.P. Anderson (01332 766323).

DERBY. **Marriott Breadsall Priory Hotel and Country Club,** Moor Road, Morley DE7 6DL (01332 836080; Fax: 01332 836036). *Location:* turn off the A61 towards Breadsall, proceed on Croft Lane, turn left into Rectory Lane, then bear right onto Moor Road, continue past the Church for approximately one mile. Two courses - Priory is a parkland course and Moorland is a contrast of open moorland. Priory - 18 holes, 5871 yards. S.S.S. 68 off yellow tees; Moorland - 18 holes, 5820 yards. S.S.S. 68 off yellow tees. Practice area and putting green; floodlit driving range. *Green Fees:* Information not available. *Visitors:* welcome any time subject to availability. *Society Meetings:* welcome at any time subject to availability. Hotel has 112 bedrooms, leisure club and conference facilities. GPS golf buggies. Professional: Darren Steels.*

DUFFIELD. **Chevin Golf Club,** Golf Lane, Duffield Belper DE56 4ES (01332 841864). *Location:* five miles north of Derby on A6 at Duffield village. Hilly course, part parkland, part moorland with superb views. 18 holes, 6057 yards, 5451 metres. S.S.S. 69. Two practice areas. *Green Fees:* information not provided. *Eating facilities:* bar snacks and diningroom. *Visitors:* always welcome Handicap Certificates required. Snooker. *Society Meetings:* welcome weekdays, but never weekends. Professional: W. Bird (01332 841112). Secretary: J.A. Milner (Tel: 01332 841864; Fax: 01332 844028).

GLOSSOP. **Glossop and District Golf Club,** Sheffield Road, Glossop SK13 7PU (01457 865247). *Location:* off A57, one mile from town centre. Moorland course. 11 holes, 5800 yards. S.S.S. 68. *Green Fees:* information not available. *Eating facilities:* full catering facilities available. *Visitors:* welcome with reservation through Professional, except Saturdays during playing season. *Society Meetings:* welcome, same restrictions as visitors. Professional: Daniel Marsh (01457 853117). Secretary: R. Hargreaves (01457 861977). *

HORSLEY. **Horsley Lodge Golf Club and Hotel,** Smalley Mill Road, Horsley DE21 5BL (01332 780838; Fax: 01332 781118). *Location:* north of Derby on A61, past Little Eaton, right turn to Horsley – signposted. Parkland. 18 holes, 6381 yards. S.S.S. 70. Par 71. Driving range. *Green Fees:* £30.00, £20.00 as members' guests, weekends by arrangement. *Eating facilities:* two bars, bar meals, à la carte restaurant; function room seats 140. *Visitors:* welcome weekdays and some weekends but not on competition days. Four-star accommodation available. *Society Meetings:* by appointment. Professional: Mark Whithorn (01332 780838; Fax: 01332 781118). Company Secretary: Richard Salt. Hon. Secretary (club): Dennis Wake (01332 780838). website: www. horsleylodge.co.uk

ILKESTON. **Erewash Valley Golf Club Ltd,** Stanton-by-Dale, Near Ilkeston DE7 4QR (0115 932 3258). *Location:* Junction 25 of the M1, Stanton-by-Dale village. Parkland with two holes in an old quarry. 18 holes, 6557 yards, 5996 metres. S.S.S. 71. Driving, pitching and putting practice area. *Green Fees:* weekdays £35.00 per round, £45.00 per day; weekends and Bank Holidays £45.00 per round. DUGC Card reduced rate. *Eating facilities:* bar snacks available at all times, diningroom service on request. *Visitors:* welcome at all times subject to club events and society bookings. *Society Meetings:* welcome Monday, Wednesday and Friday only. Professional: Darren Bartlett (0115 932 4667). Secretary: Neil Cockbill (0115 932 2984). e-mail: secretary@erewashvalley.co.uk website: www.erewashvalley.co.uk

ILKESTON. **Ilkeston Borough Golf Club,** Peewit Municipal Golf Course, West End Drive, Ilkeston DE7 5GH (01602 304550). *Location:* one mile west of Ilkeston market place. Slightly hilly meadowland. 9 holes, 4116 yards. S.S.S. 60. *Green Fees:* information not available. *Eating facilities:* not available. *Visitors:* welcome, no restrictions. Secretary: B. Smith (01602 302114).*

ILKESTON. **Morley Hayes Golf Club,** Main Road, Morley, Ilkeston (01332 782000). *Location:* just north of Junction 25 of M1, on A608 between Derby and Heanor. Championship parkland course with water features and established trees, surrounded by mature woodland and deer park. Manor course, 18 holes, 6891 yards. Par 72. Tower course, 9 holes, 1614 yards, Par 30. 17 bay driving range. Pay and Play course. *Green Fees:* Manor course weekdays: £19.50, weekends/Bank Holidays: £27.00. Tower course weekdays: £9.00, weekends/Bank Holidays £11.00. *Eating facilities:* two bars, bar meals, à la carte restaurant, function suites. Hotel, 32 bedrooms, golf breaks available. *Society Meetings:* company and society days welcome seven days a week. Professional: James Whatley. Golf Manager: Debby Hollis (01332 782000). e-mail: golf@morleyhayes.com website: www.morleyhayes.com

MATLOCK. **Matlock Golf Club,** Chesterfield Road, Matlock Moor, Matlock DE4 5LZ (01629 582191). *Location*: Matlock-Chesterfield road, A632, one mile out of Matlock, left hand side main road. Moorland with extensive views. 18 holes, yellow tees, 5808 yards. S.S.S. 68. *Green Fees:* £28.00 per round, £35.00 per day. *Eating facilities:* snacks available, luncheons and evening meals by arrangement (except on Mondays). *Visitors:* welcome weekdays. *Society Meetings:* catered for Tuesday to Friday. Professional: C.J. Goodman (01629 584934). Secretary: M. Wain.

MICKLEOVER. **Mickleover Golf Club,** Uttoxeter Road, Mickleover, Derby DE3 9AD (Tel & Fax: 01332 516011). *Location:* three miles west of Derby on the A516/B5020 to Uttoxeter. Undulating course. 18 holes, 5702 yards, 5222 metres. S.S.S. 68. *Green Fees:* £30.00 per round, £40.00 per day Monday - Sunday. Societies £25.00 (no restriction on holes to be played). *Eating facilities:* full restaurant facilities. *Visitors:* welcome, no restrictions; telephone Professional before arrival. *Society Meetings:* Tuesdays and Thursdays. Company days Fridays. Professional: Tim Coxon (01332 518662). Secretary: Graham Finney (Tel & Fax: 01332 516011).

MICKLEOVER. **Pastures Golf Club,** Social Centre, Off Merlin Way, Mickleover DE3 0DQ (01332 516700). *Location:* four miles west of Derby, A516, half a mile past Mickleover Court Hotel. Undulating meadowland. 9 holes, 5014 yards. S.S.S. 64. Practice area, putting area. *Green Fees:* information not available. *Eating facilities:* snacks; bar/lounge bar. *Visitors:* welcome, DUGC Card holders welcome. *Society Meetings:* welcome any weekday by arrangement, catering available. Secretary: S. McWilliams (01332 516700). *

QUARNDON. **Kedleston Park Golf Club,** Kedleston, Quarndon, Derby DE22 5JD (01332 840035). *Location:* Derby, follow signs to Kedleston Hall. Parkland with lakes. 18 holes, 6731 yards. S.S.S. 72. *Green Fees:* weekdays £45.00 per round, £55.00 per day. *Eating facilities:* full catering, bars. *Visitors:* welcome Monday and Friday; weekends with member. Carts available. *Society Meetings:* welcome Monday and Friday. Professional: Paul Wesselingh. Secretary: G. Duckmanton (01332 840035). e-mail: secretary@kedleston-park-golf-club.co.uk website: www.kedlestonparkgolf.co.uk

RISLEY. **Maywood Golf Club,** Off Rushy Lane, Risley, Draycott DE72 3SW (0115 939 2306). *Location:* between Derby and Nottingham at Risley, two minutes from Junction 25 M1. Parkland course. 18 holes, 6424 yards. Practice area. *Green Fees:* information not available. *Eating facilities:* licensed bar and bar meals. *Visitors:* welcome, please phone to check availability. *Society Meetings:* rates on request. Professional: Simon Purcell-Jackson (0115 949 0043). Manager: Miss Tory Moon. Proprietors: Miss Tory Moon and Brian Tucker.*

SHEFFIELD. **Renishaw Park Golf Club,** Golf House, Mill Lane, Renishaw, Sheffield S21 3UZ (01246 432044). *Location:* A6135 Barlborough (Junction 30 M1) to Sheffield. Parkland/meadowland. 18 holes, 6262 yards. S.S.S. 70. Practice area. *Green Fees:* weekdays £28.00 per round, £38.00 per day; weekends £42.00 per round/day. *Eating facilities:* bar meals, full restaurant. *Visitors:* welcome without reservation (advisable to ring Pro prior to arrival). *Society Meetings:* by prior arrangement. Full day package available. Professional: N. Parkinson (01246 435484). Secretary: T.J. Childs (01246 432044).

SHEFFIELD. **Sickleholme Golf Club,** Bamford, Hope Valley S33 0BN (01433 651306). *Location:* 3A625 west of Sheffield, right at Marquis of Granby, Bamford. Scenic wooded course in the Peak District. 18 holes, 6064 yards. S.S.S. 69. Practice ground, putting green. *Green Fees:* information not available. *Eating facilities:* bar snacks and restaurants. *Visitors:* no visitors Wednesday mornings; must be members of a recognised Golf Club; advance booking required. *Society Meetings:* welcome by prior arrangement. Professional/ Secretary: P. H. Taylor (01433 651306).*

SHIRLAND. **Shirland Golf Club,** Lower Delves, Shirland, Alfreton DE55 6AU (01773 834935). *Location:* one mile north of Alfreton off A61, three miles from M1 Junction 28 via A38. Tree-lined rolling parkland, 18 holes, 6072 yards. S.S.S. 69. Par 71. Practice ground. *Green Fees:* £15.00 per round weekdays, £18.00 per round weekends. 2-Fore-1 vouchers accepted throughout the week and after 1pm at weekends. *Eating facilities:* bar meals. Conference and banquet rooms. *Visitors:* unrestricted weekdays, but must book through Manager at weekends. *Society Meetings:* welcome. Manager: Mr A. Colton (01773 834935). Secretary: G. A. Towle (01773 874224).

STOCKPORT. **The New Mills Golf Club,** Shaw Marsh, New Mills, High Peak SK22 4QE (01663 743485). *Location:* signposted off the B6101 from Marple to New Mills, between Buxton and Stockport. Relatively flat upland course, magnificent views, excellent greens. 18 holes, 5604 yards. S.S.S. 69. Large practice area and driving range. New members accepted. *Green Fees:*Information not available. *Eating facilities:* full catering, very good value; wide range of food. *Visitors:* welcome any day but not competition days, contact the Professional for these dates. *Society Meetings:* welcome. Professional: Carl Cross (01663 746161). Secretary: Philip Jenkinson (07919 818225).*

Herefordshire

BELMONT. **Belmont Lodge and Golf,** Belmont, Hereford HR2 9SA (01432 352666; Fax: 01432 358090). *Location:* one and a half miles south of Hereford, off A465 to Abergavenny. Parkland running alongside the River Wye offering tremendous views. 18 holes, 6511 yards. S.S.S. 72. *Green Fees:* please ring for information. *Eating facilities:* restaurant meals and bar snacks. *Visitors:* welcome at all times, advisable to check availability first. Other facilities available include a 30 bedroom hotel, tennis, fishing and walking; buggies and trolleys for hire. *Society Meetings:* catered for, special packages available. Professional: (01432 352717). Reception/ Reservations: (01432 352666; Fax: 01432 358090). General Manager: Christopher T. Smith.
e-mail: info@belmont-hereford.co.uk
website: www.belmont-hereford.co.uk

HAY-ON-WYE. **Summerhill Golf Course,** Clifford, Near Hay-on-Wye HR3 5EW (01497 820451). *Location:* half a mile out of Hay on B4350 for Clifford and Whitney Toll Bridge and Hereford Road A438. Parkland. 9 holes 2929 yards (18 holes, 5858 off white Information not available. *Eating facilities:* restaurant, two bars and large function room. *Visitors:* welcome, not on Thursday evening or Sunday mornings. *Society Meetings:* welcome Monday, Wednesday and Friday. Professional: Will Dowd. Secretary: Mike Tom. website: www.summerhillgolfcourse.co.uk*

HEREFORD. **Burghill Valley Golf Club,** Tillington Road, Burghill, Hereford HR4 7RW (01432 760456; Fax: 01432 761654). *Location:* three miles north-west of Hereford. From Worcester and North (avoiding Hereford city), take A4103 for two miles, first right after traffic lights. From south (via Hereford city) take A4110, turn left at traffic lights after Three Elms Inn and then first right. Follow signs to club. Pleasantly undulating parkland including two lakes, and easy walking with some interesting holes through mature cider orchards. 18 holes, 6204 yards. S.S.S. 70. Large practice area. *Green Fees:* on application. *Eating facilities:* bar and dining room with full catering available every day. *Visitors:* welcome at any time, must book tee time with Professional. *Society Meetings:* by prior arrangement with the Manager. Special rates available, please enquire. Professionals: Keith Preece PGA, Andy Cameron PGA (01432 760808; Fax: 01432 761654). General Manager: Keith Smith.
e-mail: info@bvgc.co.uk
website: www.bvgc.co.uk

HEREFORD. **Hereford Municipal Golf Club,** Hereford Leisure Centre, Holmer Road, Hereford HR4 9UD (01432 344376; Fax: 01432 266281). *Location:* follow A49 Leominster to Hereford road; north of city centre next to Leisure Centre. Flat parkland course with excellent greens all year round. 9 holes, 3060 yards. S.S.S. 68 for 18 holes. Large practice area, bunker and practice green. *Green Fees:* please ring for details. *Eating facilities:* full catering and bar in Leisure Centre. *Visitors:* welcome at all times. *Society Meetings:* welcome, prices on application. Professional: Gary Morgan (01432 344376; Fax: 01432 266281).

HEREFORD. **The Herefordshire Golf Club,** Raven's Causeway, Wormsley, Hereford HR4 8LY (01432 830219). *Location:* six miles north-west of Hereford on a B road to Weobley. Undulating parkland course. 18 holes, 6031 yards. S.S.S. 69. *Green Fees:* information available on request. *Eating facilities:* catering available at all times. *Visitors:* welcome. *Society Meetings:* welcome, packages arranged through Secretary (01432 830219).
e-mail: herefordshire.golf@breathe.com
website: www.herefordshiregolfclub.co.uk

KINGTON. **Kington Golf Club,** Bradnor Hill, Kington HR5 3RE (01544 230340). *Location:* one mile out of Kington, on B4355 to Presteigne. Easy walking hill course with superb greens and views over seven counties. Highest 18 hole course in England. 18 holes, 5966 yards. S.S.S. 69. *Green Fees:* weekdays £20.00 per round, £24.00 per day; weekends and Bank Holidays £26.00 per round, £30.00 per day. *Eating facilities:* full catering and bar facilities. *Visitors:* welcome. Please contact Professional to ensure course is available. *Society Meetings:* by arrangement with the Professional. Professional: Andy Gealy (01544 231320). Secretary: Glyn R. Wictome (Tel & Fax: 01544 340270).

LEOMINSTER. **Grove Golf Centre,** Fordbridge, Leominster HR6 0LE (01568 610602). *Location:* three miles south of Leominster on A49. Challenging wooded course with many water features, U.S.G.A. spec greens. 9 holes, 1780 yards. S.S.S. 60. New 9 holes opening 2004, S.S.S.72. Floodlit, covered driving range. Golf shop. *Green Fees:* information not available. *Eating facilities:* full catering and bar. *Visitors:* welcome anytime. Professional: Phil Brookes (01568 615333).*

LEOMINSTER. **Leominster Golf Club,** Ford Bridge, Leominster HR6 0LE (01568 610055). *Location:* three miles south of Leominster on A49 bypass, clearly signed. Undulating parkland with some holes alongside River Lugg and extensive views over Herefordshire countryside. 18 holes, 6026 yards. S.S.S. 69. *Green Fees:* weekdays £16.00 per round, £20.00 per day; Mondays and Fridays £10.00 after 9.30am; weekends £25.00 per round, £30.00 per day.

Eating facilities: bar open daily, full catering daily. *Visitors:* welcome every day; please telephone to check availability. Trolley and buggy hire available. *Society Meetings:* most welcome. From £25.00 weekdays, £32.00 weekends, golf and catering. Professional: Nigel Clarke (01568 611402). Secretary: Les Green (Tel & Fax: 01568 610055). Manager: Jessica Kingswood.
e-mail: contact@leominstergolfclub.co.uk
website: www.leominstergolfclub.co.uk

ROSS-ON-WYE. **The Ross-on-Wye Golf Club,** Gorsley, Ross-on-Wye HR9 7UT (01989 720267; Fax: 01989 720212). *Location:* adjacent Junction 3 M50, five miles east of Ross-on-Wye. Tree lined, undulating parkland course. 18 holes, 6451 yards. S.S.S. 71. Driving range, practice area. *Green Fees:* information not available. *Eating facilities:* full restaurant catering, excluding Mondays. *Visitors:* welcome any day if prior arrangement made with Professional or Secretary. Buggies and trolleys available. Snooker tables (2). *Society Meetings:* welcome, minimum 16. Tee reservations Wednesdays to Fridays. Professional: P. Middleton (01989 720439). Secretary: P.H. Plumb (01989 720267; Fax: 01989 720212).
e-mail: secretary@therossonwyegolfclub.co.uk
website: www.therossonwyegolfclub.co.uk

ROSS-ON-WYE. **South Herefordshire Golf Club,** Twin Lakes, Upton Bishop, Ross-on-Wye HR9 7UA (01989 780535; Fax: 01989 740611). *Location:* end roundabout of M50 at Ross take B4221 to Upton Bishop, in Upton Bishop turn right, club half a mile. Good test of golf for all standards with variety of holes. Superb views. Rarely on temporary greens in Winter. 18 holes S.S.S. 72. 16 bay covered, floodlit driving range. *Green Fees:* weekdays £22.00 per round; weekends £26.00 per round. *Eating facilities:* fully licensed bar serving snacks and full meals. *Visitors:* always welcome, no restrictions. Ring to reserve tee time. Buggies and trolleys available. Fully qualified PGA Professional, club fitting centre, Pro shop. Free junior training Saturday mornings, group lessons available. *Society Meetings:* always welcome; weekend prices from £20.00 for day's golf. Director of Golf: James Leaver.
e-mail: info@herefordshiregolf.co.uk
website: www.herefordshiregolf.co.uk

FHG Guides
publish a large range of well-known accommodation guides. We will be happy to send you details or you can use the order form at the back of this book.

Leicestershire & Rutland

ASHBY DE LA ZOUCH. **Willesley Park Golf Club,** Measham Road, Ashby de la Zouch LE65 2PF (01530 411532). *Location:* on B5006 towards Tamworth, one mile from centre of Ashby. Wooded parkland, semi-heathland. 18 holes, 6314 yards. S.S.S. 70. *Green Fees:* weekdays £35.00, weekends £40.00. *Eating facilities:* dining room and bar, no catering Mondays. *Visitors:* welcome with reservation. *Society Meetings:* catered for Wednesday, Thursday and Friday. Professional: B.J. Hill (01530 414820). Secretary: Mrs T. Harlow (01530 414596).
e-mail: info@willesleypark.com
website: www.willesleypark.com

BLABY. **Blaby Golf Centre,** Lutterworth Road, Blaby LE8 4DP (0116 278 4804). Flat parkland. 9 holes, S.S.S. 68. Par 4 9-hole pitch and putt. *Green Fees:* £7.00 per 9 holes, £10.00 for 18 holes. Pitch & Putt £3.00 9 holes. New 18 hole Adventure putting course open for all the family. *Eating facilities:* snacks available. *Visitors:* welcome.
website: www.blabygolfcourse.com

BOTCHESTON. **Forest Hill Golf Club,** Markfield Lane, Near Botcheston LE9 9FJ (01455 824800; Fax: 01455 828522). *Location:* M1 junction 22, take Leicester exit on A50, at first roundabout turn right towards Desford, golf course 3 miles on left. Parkland course with trees, easy walking. 18 holes, 6550 yards. S.S.S. 72, Par 72. 28 Bay floodlit driving range, par 3 Academy Course. *Green Fees:* Information not available. *Eating facilities:* available. *Visitors:* welcome Monday to Thursday. Professional tuition available. Conference facilities. *Society Meetings:* welcome by prior arrangement Monday to Thursday. Professional: Glyn Quilter (01455 824800). Secretary: Gerry Hyde (01455 824800).*
e-mail: gerry@hyde14.fsnet.co.uk

COSBY. **Cosby Golf Club,** Chapel Lane, off Broughton Road, Cosby, Leicester LE9 1RG (0116 2864759; Fax: 0116 2864484). *Location:* eight miles south of Leicester, four miles from Junction 21 M1. Undulating parkland. 18 holes, 6410 yards. S.S.S. 71. *Green Fees:* Information not available. *Eating facilities:* wide range of snacks and meals always available. *Visitors:* most welcome before 4pm weekdays. Handicap Certificates may be required for all visitors. *Society Meetings:* welcome, prior booking essential. Professional: Martin Wing (0116 2848275). Secretary/Manager: T. Sanders (0116 2864759; Fax: 0116 2864484).
e-mail: secretary@cosbygolfclub.co.uk
website: www.cosbygolfclub.co.uk

EAST GOSCOTE. **Beedles Lake Golf Centre,** 170 Broome Lane, East Goscote LE7 3WQ (0116 2607086). *Location:* off A46 just north of Leicester, through village of Ratcliffe on the Wreake. Fairly flat course in river valley, adjoining lake. 18 holes, 6641 yards, 6156 metres. S.S.S. 72. 17-bay floodlit driving range. *Green Fees:* weekdays £15.00, weekends £22.00. Twilight fees £12.00. (under review for 2008). *Eating facilities:* restaurant and bar always. *Visitors:* always very welcome. *Society Meetings:* welcome but with restricted tee-times at weekends. Steward: (0116 260 7086). Professional: Sean Byrne (0116 260 6759). Manager: Ian Needham (0116 260 4414).

ENDERBY. **Enderby Golf Course,** Mill Lane, Enderby (0116 2849388) *Location:* two miles from M1/M69 Junction 21 roundabout. Gently undulating course with lakes and ditches. 9 holes. 2856/5712 yards. S.S.S. 61. Par 36/72. *Green Fees:* information not available. *Eating facilities:* two bars, restaurants, open 9.30am to 10.30pm. *Visitors:* welcome at all times, no booking required. Leisure centre, bowls, squash, badminton, sauna, solarium, fitness suite, etc. Professional/Secretary: Chris d'Araujo.

HINCKLEY. **Hinckley Golf Club,** Leicester Road, Hinckley LE10 3DR (01455 615124; Fax: 01455 890841). *Location:* situated one mile from Hinckley, just off Hinckley's A47 perimeter road. Parkland with lakeside features. 18 holes, 6517 yards, 5959 metres. S.S.S. 71. Practice area for members. *Green Fees:* weekdays £33.00 per round, £43.00 per day; weekends £40.00 per round. *Eating facilities:* bar meals daily except Sundays. *Visitors:* welcome except Tuesdays and weekends. *Society Meetings:* Mondays and Wednesdays by appointment. Professional: R. Jones (01455 615014). Finance and Administration Manager: Y. Watts (01455 615124). e-mail: rjones@hinckleygolfclub.com website: www.hinckleygolfclub.com

KIRBY MUXLOE. **Kirby Muxloe Golf Club,** Station Road, Kirby Muxloe LE9 2EP (0116 2393457). *Location:* Junction 21a M1, just off A47 heading to Hinckley, towards Kirby Muxloe village. Parkland, fourth tee is set outside the course. 18 holes, 6351 yards. S.S.S. 71. Driving range, practice area and tuition from Professional. *Green Fees:* information not available. *Eating facilities:* full restaurant and bar. *Visitors:* welcome weekdays except Monday and Tuesday. Advisable to phone in advance. Snooker room. *Society Meetings:* by arrangement with Manager. Professional: B. Whipham (Tel & Fax: 0116 2392813). Club Manager: P. Jelly (0116 2393457; Fax: 0116 2388891). e-mail: kirbymuxloegolf@btconnect.com

LEICESTER. **Humberstone Heights Golf Club,** Gipsy Lane, Leicester LE5 0TB (0116 276 1905). *Location:* A563 ring road, Uppingham side of Leicester. Parkland. 18 holes, 6343 yards. S.S.S. 70. 30 bay driving range, 9 hole pitch and putt course. *Green Fees:* weekdays £12.50 per round; weekends £15.50. 9 holes £9.50. Twilight £9.50. Subject to review. *Eating facilities:* bar, snacks; clubhouse closed Mondays. *Visitors:* welcome (Municipal Golf Course). Green Fee ticket gains entry to Clubhouse. *Society Meetings:* welcome. Professional: P. Highfield (0116 299 5570). Secretary: Margaret Weston (0116 288 2998).

LEICESTER. **Kibworth Golf Club,** Weir Road, Kibworth Beauchamp, Leicester LE8 0LP (0116 2792301). *Location:* A6, four miles Market Harborough, 12 miles Leicester. Flat wooded course. 18 holes, 6354 yards. S.S.S. 71. 8 bay golf range. *Green Fees:* information not available. *Eating facilities:* Contact Catering (0116 2796560). *Visitors:* welcome, Handicap Certificate required or introduction from club member. *Society Meetings:* welcome, prior booking essential; reductions for large societies. Professional: Mike Herbert (0116 2792283). Secretary: J. Noble (0116 2792301; Fax: 0116 2796434). e-mail: secretary@kibworthgolfclub.freeserve.co.uk

LEICESTER. **The Leicestershire Golf Club,** Evington Lane, Leicester LE5 6DJ (Tel & Fax: 0116 2738825). *Location:* Evington Village, two miles from city centre off A6 road. Parkland. 18 holes, 6329 yards. S.S.S. 71. Practice area. *Green Fees:* information not available. *Eating facilities:* available. *Visitors:* welcome but not normally weekends or Tuesdays. Handicap Certificate required. *Society Meetings:* welcome. Professional: D. Jones (Tel & Fax: 0116 2736730) Secretary: C.R. Chapman (0116 2738825; Fax: 0116 2498799).* e-mail: secretary@leicestershiregolfclub.co.uk

LEICESTER. **Scraptoft Golf Club,** Beeby Road, Scraptoft, Leicester LE7 9SJ (0116 241 9000). *Location:* off A47 Scraptoft. Undulating. 18 holes, 6235 yards. S.S.S. 70. *Green Fees:* information not available. *Eating facilities:* full restaurant service seven days a week from April to October. *Visitors:* welcome, proof of Handicap required. *Society Meetings:* catered for on application weekdays only (contact Secretary). Professional: Simon Wood (0116 2419138).*

LEICESTER. **Western Park Golf Club,** Scudamore Road, Braunstone Frith, Leicester LE3 1UQ. *Location:* four miles west of Junction 21 (M1) and M69. Flat, wooded course. 18 holes, 6518 yards. S.S.S. 71. Practice area. *Green Fees:* Information not available. *Eating facilities:* full catering facilities. *Visitors:* welcome, book weekends - Tuesdays at 8am for Saturdays and Wednesdays at 8am for Sundays. Indoor school; carts for hire. *Society Meetings:* all welcome, contact Professional. Professional: Mr Dave Butler (01162 995566; Fax: 01162 995567). Secretary: Lee Preston (0116 291 3644).*

LEICESTER. **Whetstone Golf Club and Driving Range,** Cambridge Road, Cosby LE9 5SH (Tel & Fax: 0116 286 1424). *Location:* 10 minutes off Junction 21 M1, between Cosby and Whetstone. Flat parkland. 18 holes, 5795 yards. S.S.S. 68. Driving range, putting green. *Green Fees:* information not available. *Eating facilities:* bar/lounge serving full range of meals. Smart casual dress please. *Visitors:* Handicap not required. Welcome by prior arrangement. Dress code to be observed. *Society Meetings:* welcome by prior arrangement. Professional: D. Raitt. Secretary: J. Fisher..

LOUGHBOROUGH. **Charnwood Forest Golf Club,** Breakback Road, Woodhouse Eaves, Near Loughborough LE12 8TA (Tel & Fax: 01509 890259). Steward: 01509 890925. *Location:* A6 to B591 or M1 Junction 23–A512–Snells Nook Lane. Heather, gorse and bracken, no bunkers. Oldest golf club in Leicestershire played around volcanic rocks. 9 holes, 5960 yards. S.S.S. 69. *Green Fees:* weekdays £25.00 per 18 holes, £30.00 per 36 holes; weekends £30.00 per 18 holes. *Eating facilities:* full catering. *Visitors:* welcome except Tuesdays (Ladies' Day). *Society Meetings:* welcome by prior arrangement. Secretary: P.K. Field (01509 890259).
e-mail: secretary@charnwoodforestgc.co.uk
website: www.charnwoodforestgc.co.uk

LOUGHBOROUGH. **Longcliffe Golf Club,** Snell's Nook Lane, Nanpantan, Loughborough LE11 3YA (01509 239129; Fax: 01509 231286). *Location:* M1 Junction 23 – A512 Loughborough, first right, Snells Nook Lane. Wooded heathland, EGU Championship course. 18 holes, 6625 yards. S.S.S. 73. Practice ground. *Green Fees:* weekdays £30.00 per round, £40.00 per day. *Eating facilities:* bar and restaurant. *Visitors:* welcome weekdays. Handicap Certificate required. *Society Meetings:* welcome by arrangement Mondays, Tuesdays, Wednesdays, Thursdays and Fridays. Professional: D.C. Mee (01509 231450). Manager: (vacant) (01509 239129; Fax: 01509 231286).
e-mail: longcliffe@btconnect.com
website: www.longcliffegolf.co.uk

LOUGHBOROUGH. **Park Hill Golf Club,** Park Hill, Seagrave, Loughborough LE12 7NG (01509 815454; Fax: 01509 816062). *Location:* 5 miles from J21a of M1 northbound. Just off the A46 northbound. Undulating parkland course with rolling tree-lined fairways and excellent views – the closing hole is a challenging par 5 with water protecting both sides of the green. Excellent playing conditions all year round! 18 holes, 7219 yards. S.S.S. 74. Large practice area and putting green. 20 bay fully covered floodlit driving range, including grass bays. *Green Fees:* weekdays £26.00, with a member £15.00; weekends and Bank Holidays £32.00, with a member £18.00. Seniors (55 years and over) Monday to Wednesday. Students £16.00. weekdays, £22.00 weekends. *Eating facilities:* lunch/dinner/ bar snacks, fully licensed bar. *Visitors:* welcome at all times Monday to Friday, after 9am at weekends. Conference room for up to 120 people (function room). *Society Meetings:* all welcome by prior arrangement. Special rates for societies over 12 people. Professional: Matt Ulyett (01509 815775; Fax: 01509 816062). Secretary: Jonathan Hutson (01509 815454; Fax: 01509 816062).
e-mail: mail@parkhillgolf.co.uk
website: www.parkhillgolf.co.uk

LUTTERWORTH. **Lutterworth Golf Club,** Rugby Road, Lutterworth LE17 4HN. *Location:* Junction 20 M1; Junction 1 M6. Parkland course. 18 holes, 6226 yards. S.S.S. 70. Practice area, computerised indoor teaching academy. *Green Fees:* £28.00 per round, £36.00 per day. *Eating facilities:* catering available and bar facilities. *Visitors:* welcome all day Monday to Thursday, and Friday till noon. *Society Meetings:* welcome Monday to Thursday all day, and Friday mornings. Secretary: John Faulks (01455 552532). Professional: Lee Challinor (01455 557199). Bar/Catering (01455 557141).

LUTTERWORTH near. **Ullesthorpe Court Golf Club,** Frolesworth Road, Ullesthorpe, Near Lutterworth LE17 5BZ. *Location:* 10 minutes M1, M6, M69, A5; near Lutterworth between Leicester and Coventry. Open parkland course, with interesting greens, a fair test for all abilities; lakes on three holes. 18 holes, 6662 yards. S.S.S. 72. *Green Fees:* visitors £22.00. *Eating facilities:* à la carte restaurant, bar meals, club bar. *Visitors:* welcome weekdays, except Bank Holidays, and must book in advance. Hotel with 72 en suite bedrooms and full leisure centre. *Society Meetings:* five packages available, bookable in advance. Tel: Golf Office 01455 209023. Professional: Jonathan Salter (01455 209150; Fax: 01455 202537).
e-mail: bookings@ullesthorpecourt.co.uk

MARKET HARBOROUGH. **Market Harborough Golf Club,** Great Oxendon Road, Market Harborough LE16 9HB (01858 463684). *Location:* one mile south of Market Harborough on A508. Parkland. An excellent testing course, lovely views and lakes a feature of the course. 18 holes, 6070 yards. S.S.S. 69. Practice ground. *Green Fees:* information not available. *Eating facilities:* bar snacks and full meals available. *Visitors:* welcome weekdays; weekends only with a member. *Society Meetings:* welcome on application. Professional: F. Baxter. Secretary: P. Weston (01858 463684).*

MELTON MOWBRAY. **Melton Mowbray Golf Club**, Thorpe Arnold, Melton Mowbray LE13 1TZ (Tel & Fax: 01664 562118). *Location:* approximately 11/2 miles east of Melton Mowbray on A607 towards Grantham. Parkland, easy walking but challenging. 18 holes, 6243 yards, S.S.S. 70 (men), 71 (ladies). Practice area including mid iron, practice chipping and bunker play. Practice putting green. 7-bay driving range. Golf lessons available. *Green Fees:* weekdays £25.00 per round, £35.00 per day; weekends £30.00 per round. *Eating facilities:* bar and restaurant. *Visitors:* welcome, contact Pro Shop to book. *Society Meetings:* packages available. No societies on Saturdays. Professional: Neil Curtis (01664 569629; Fax: 01664 562118). Secretaries: Sue Millward and Marilyn Connelly (Tel & Fax: 01664 562118). e-mail: meltonmowbraygc@btconnect.com website: www.mmgc.org

MELTON MOWBRAY. **Six Hills Golf Club,** Six Hills, Melton Mowbray LE14 3PR (01509 881225). *Location:* on B676, half way between Melton Mowbray and Loughborough. Flat course. 18 holes, 5758 yards, S.S.S. 69. Practice green and ground. Driving range. *Green Fees*: £15.00 weekdays, £19.00 weekends. *Eating facilities:* cafe style; restaurant and bar. *Visitors*: no restrictions. Professional: James Hawley. Secretary: Mrs J. Showler.

NORTH KILWORTH. **Kilworth Springs Golf Club,** South Kilworth Road, North Kilworth LE17 6HJ (Clubhouse/office: 01858 575082; Pro-shop: 01858 575974; Fax: 01858 575078). *Location*: six miles from Junction 20, four miles M6 - A14 Junction. Links type, parkland course. 18 holes, 6718 yards. S.S.S. 72. Driving range. *Green Fees*: weekdays £16.00 9 holes, £25.00 18 holes; weekends £18.00 9 holes, £28.00 18 holes. Day rate £42.00. Special society rates for 12 people or over. *Eating facilities*: restaurant, bar, bar snacks. *Visitors*: welcome at all times subject to tee times being available. Buggies available. *Society Meetings*: welcome. Professional: Anders Mankert. Secretary: Ann Vicary.

OADBY. **Glen Gorse Golf Club,** Glen Road, Oadby LE2 4RF (0116 271 4159). *Location:* on A6, four and a half miles south of Leicester between Oadby and Great Glen. Fairly flat parkland course, some ridge and furrow. 18 holes, 6648 yards, 6079 metres. S.S.S. 72. *Green Fees:* weekdays £30.00 per round, £35.00 per day (£15.00 with member); weekends £15.00 with member only. *Eating facilities:* bar and meals/snacks. *Visitors:* welcome weekdays, weekends with members only. Snooker room. *Society Meetings:* welcome Monday to Friday by prior arrangement. Professional: Dominic Fitzpatrick (0116 271 3748). Secretary: Mrs J. James (Tel & Fax: 0116 271 4159). e-mail: secretary@gggc.org website: www.gggc.org

OADBY. **Oadby Golf Course,** Leicester Road, Oadby, Leicester LE2 4AJ (0116 270 0215). *Location:* on A6 south of Leicester, one mile from City boundary, at Leicester Racecourse. Parkland. 18 holes, 6376 yards, 5827 metres. S.S.S. 70. Practice ground, coaching, driving bays. *Green Fees:* (2007) weekdays £12.00, weekends £15.00. Subject to review. *Eating facilities:* snacks always available, bar with meals on prior notice. *Visitors:* welcome, booking is advised at weekends and Bank Holidays. Please contact Professional. *Society Meetings:* welcome, bookings taken through Golf Shop (0116 270 9052).Caterers (0116 270 0215).

ROTHLEY. **Rothley Park Golf Club,** Westfield Lane, Rothley, Leicester LE7 7LH (0116 2302809). *Location:* off A6, north of Leicester. Parkland. 18 holes, 6481 yards. S.S.S. 71. *Green Fees:* £40.00 per day (midweek). *Eating facilities:* available daily. *Visitors:* welcome except Tuesdays, weekends and Bank Holidays, must be members of recognised golf club with Handicap. *Society Meetings:* As visitors' restrictions and by prior arrangement only. Professional: Danny Spillane (Tel & Fax: 0116 2302809). Secretary: S.G. Winterton (Tel & Fax: 0116 2302809). e-mail: secretary@rothleypark.co.uk website: www.rothleypark.com

RUTLAND. **Greetham Valley Hotel, Golf and Conference Centre**, Wood Lane, Greetham, Near Oakham, Rutland LE15 7NP (01780 460444; Fax: 01780 460623). *Location:* one mile off A1 between Stamford and Grantham on the B668. Four miles from Rutland Water. Parkland, gently undulating with many water features. Many holes playing over natural valley. 45 holes. "The Lakes" 6736 yards, S.S.S 72; "The Valley" 5595 yards, S.S.S. 68; Academy Course 9 holes, 1263 yards, S.S.S. 27. 14 bay floodlit driving range. *Green Fees:* please contact for seasonal rates. *Eating facilities:* excellent clubhouse, lounge, bar and restaurants. *Visitors:* welcome, please phone first for tee availability. Conference rooms, banqueting suite, pool table, quad biking, 4x4 off-roading, mud buggies, fishing and bowls. Buggies and electric trolleys for hire. Hotel with 35 en-suite bedrooms, hair, beauty and health massage suite. Golf breaks welcome all year. *Society Meetings:* welcome except weekends and Bank Holidays. Professional: Neil Evans (01780 460666; Fax: 01780 460623). Secretary: Dee Hinch (01780 460444; Fax: 01780 460623).
e-mail: info@greethamvalley.co.uk
website: www.greethamvalley.co.uk

THE APPEARANCE OF AN ASTERISK (*) AT THE END OF A CLUB OR COURSE ENTRY INDICATES THAT UP-TO-DATE INFORMATION HAS NOT BEEN SUPPLIED

STAMFORD. **Luffenham Heath Golf Club,** South Luffenham Road, Ketton, Stamford, Lincolnshire PE9 3UU (01780 720205; Fax: 01780 722146). *Location:* 6 miles from Stamford and 1½ miles south-west of Ketton on the A6121. Undulating heathland, in conservation area for flora and fauna. 18 holes, 6563 yards. S.S.S. 72. Practice ground. *Green Fees:* £45.00 per round, £55.00 per day. Subject to review. *Eating facilities:* snacks available daily, full meals by arrangement. *Visitors:* Monday to Friday excluding Tuesdays. Weekends and Bank Holidays 10.30am-12 noon and after 2pm. Handicap Certificate required. *Society Meetings:* welcome, except Tuesdays and weekends/Bank Holidays. Details of packages on request. Professional: Ian Burnett (Tel & Fax: 01780 720298). Secretary: John R. Ingleby (01780 720205; Fax: 01780 722146).
e-mail: jringleby@theluffenhamheathgc.co.uk
website: www.luffenhamheath.co.uk

WOODHOUSE EAVES. **Lingdale Golf Club,** Joe Moore's Lane, Woodhouse Eaves, Near Loughborough LE12 8TF (01509 890703). *Location:* on B5300, Anstey – Shepshed road, three miles from Exit 23 on M1. Woodland and parkland – set in Charnwood Forest. 18 holes, 6545 yards. S.S.S. 71. Practice ground. *Green Fees:* weekdays £28.00 per round, £33.00 per day; weekends £35.00 per round, £46.00 per day. *Eating facilities:* full catering available. *Visitors:* welcome, but please telephone first. *Society Meetings:* welcome. Details and booking form available from Secretary. Professional: P. Sellears (01509 890684). Managing Secretary: Tim Stephens (01509 890703).

Lincolnshire

ALFORD. **Woodthorpe Hall Golf Club,** Woodthorpe, Alford LN13 0DD (01507 450294). *Location:* on the B1373, 3 miles north of Alford, 8 miles SE of Louth. Undulating parkland. 18 holes, 5067 yards. S.S.S. 64. *Green Fees:* information not available. *Eating facilities:* at Woodthorpe Country Inn on site; conference rooms also available (01507 450079). *Visitors:* welcome, unrestricted. *Society Meetings:* by prior arrangement (01507 450294). Secretary: Mrs J. Smith. (Tel & Fax: 01507 450000).

BLANKNEY. **Blankney Golf Club,** near Metheringham, Lincoln LN4 3AZ (01526 320202). *Location:* near Metheringham on B1188 Lincoln to Sleaford Road. Parkland, slightly undulating. 18 holes, 6638 yards. Par 72. Centenary Year 2004, host to Midland PGA Tournament. Practice area, putting green and snooker. *Green Fees:* weekdays £28.00; weekends £34.00. Special rates available Tuesday/Thursday. *Eating facilities:* dining room and bar meals. *Visitors:* welcome except Wednesday mornings, limited numbers at weekends. *Society Meetings:* welcome with prior booking. Professional/Club Manager: G. Bradley (01526 320202). Admin Office (01526 320263; Fax: 01526 322521).
e-mail: grahambradley5@btconnect.com
website: www.blankneygolf.co.uk

BOSTON. **Boston Golf Club,** Cowbridge, Horncastle Road, Boston PE22 7EL (01205 350589; Fax: 01205 367526). *Location:* two miles north of Boston on B1183. Look for sign to right if travelling north. Parkland with featured water. 18 holes, 6415 yards, 5885 metres. S.S.S. 71. *Green Fees:* midweek and weekends £30.00 round and day. *Eating facilities:* daily by arrangement with resident Steward (01205 352533). *Visitors:* welcome without reservation. *Society Meetings:* groups catered for Wednesday, Thursday and Friday. Professional: N. Hiom (01205 362306). Secretary: S.P. Shaw (Tel & Fax: 01205 350589).

BOSTON. **Boston West Golf Club,** Hubberts Bridge, Boston PE20 3QX (01205 290670; Fax: 01205 290725). *Location:* Junction of A1121 and B1392, one-and-a-half miles west of Boston. Parkland course with 25,000 trees and shrubs planted, with water in play on five holes. 18 holes, 6411 yards. S.S.S. 71. 6 hole short course, putting greens, practice bunker. 20 bay floodlit driving range. *Green Fees:* weekdays £20.00; weekends £25.00. *Eating facilities:* catering available all day in newly extended Clubhouse, with restaurant overlooking the course. *Visitors:* no restrictions but must book in advance. Lessons available from Nigel Bark. VI Digital Coaching System available. Large discount store with custom fitting on site. Buggies available. New 24-bedroom hotel opened June 2006. *Society Meetings:* welcome at all times, including weekends. Special rates on request. Secretary: Mike Couture (01205 290670).
e-mail: info@bostonwestgolfclub.co.uk
website: www.bostonwestgolfclub.co.uk

BOSTON. **Kirton Holme Golf Club,** Holme Road, Kirton Holme, Boston PE20 1SY (01205 290669). *Location:* four miles west of Boston, signposted off A52. Flat parkland. 9 holes, 2884 yards. S.S.S. 34. Small practice area includes net. *Green Fees:* weekdays £7.00 per 9 holes, £11.00 per day; weekends and Bank Holidays £8.00 per 9 holes, £12.00 per day. *Eating facilities:* bar open 11am to dusk, snack meals available. *Visitors:* always welcome, smart dress required. *Society Meetings:* by arrangement. Secretary: T. Welberry (01205 290669)

BOURNE. **The Toft Hotel Golf Club,** Toft, Near Bourne PE10 0JT (01778 590614; Fax: 01778 590264). *Location:* in Toft village on A6121 Stamford to Bourne road. Undulating course with natural lake, 18 holes, 6486 yards. S.S.S. 71. Practice area. *Green Fees:* information not available. *Eating facilities:* bar open all day; bar snacks and restaurant. *Visitors:* welcome at all times, prior booking essential. Hotel has 22 bedrooms. *Society Meetings:* welcome, prior booking essential. Professional: Mark Jackson (01778 590616). Secretary: Robin Morris (01778 590616).*
website: www.thetofthotelgolfclub.com

BRIGG. **Elsham Golf Club,** Barton Road, Elsham, Brigg DN20 0LS (01652 680291; Fax: 01652 680308). *Location:* off M180 at J5 or A15 through Brigg to Barton. Wooded parkland course. 18 holes, 6428 yards. S.S.S. 71. Outdoor practice ground. *Green Fees:* weekdays only £27.00 for 18 holes, £37.00 for 36 holes. £13.50 (18 holes) with a member both during the week and at weekends. Special rates for societies of 12 or more. *Eating facilities:* full catering. *Visitors:* welcome weekdays. *Society Meetings:* catered for on weekdays. Steward (01652 688382). Professional: Stuart Brewer (01652 680432). Secretary: T. Hartley (01652 680291).
e-mail: manager@elshamgolfclub.co.uk
website: www.elshamgolfclub.co.uk

BRIGG. **Forest Pines Golf Club,** The Forest Pines Hotel, Ermine Street, Broughton, Near Brigg DN20 0AQ (01652 650770; Fax: 01652 650495). *Location:* 200 yards from Junction 4 M180 towards Scunthorpe. Three 9 hole courses – Forest, Pines, Beeches. Forest/Pines Championship Course: 6882 yards, S.S.S. 73. Pines/Beeches: 6693 yards, S.S.S. 72. Forest/Beeches: 6393 yards, S.S.S. 70. Practice range, practice green, bunkers. *Green Fees:* information not available. *Eating facilities:* clubhouse. *Visitors:* welcome; telephone in advance. Compulsory 'soft spikes' or dimples, no steel spikes. All facilities of The Forest Pines Hotel, golf course and spa available - 188 bedrooms. Buggies and carts for hire; residential golf schools, leisure club (swimming, gym, sauna and jacuzzi). *Society Meetings:* welcome. Various packages available from £29.95, residential Golfing Breaks available. Please call the golf events team for details (01652 650777).
e-mail: forestpinesgolf@qhotels.co.uk
website: www.qhotels.co.uk

CLEETHORPES. **Cleethorpes Golf Club (1894) Ltd,** Golf House, Kings Road, Cleethorpes DN35 0PN (01472 816110). *Location:* approximately one mile south of Cleethorpes Leisure Centre. Mature coastal course, slight undulations give variation but local topography makes for easy walking. Presented to the highest standards the course provides a challenge to all level of players. 18 holes, 6272 yards. S.S.S. 71. Large and small practice areas. *Green Fees:* weekdays £25.00, £12.00 with member, weekends £30.00, £15.00 with member. Handicap Certificate preferred. *Eating facilities:* bar lunches, evening meals. *Visitors:* welcome anytime except Wednesdays. *Society Meetings:* welcome by arrangement with the Secretary. Attractive packages available Monday, Thursday, Friday and Sunday. Professional: P. Davies (01472 814060). Secretary: Andrew Thompson (01472 816110).
e-mail: secretary@cleethorpesgolfclub.co.uk
website: www.cleethorpesgolfclub.co.uk

GAINSBOROUGH. **Gainsborough Golf Club,** Thonock, Gainsborough DN21 1PZ (01427 613088; Fax: 01427 810172). *Location:* signposted from A631 Gainsborough to Grimsby Road. Thonock Park Course is a parkland course with many deciduous trees, Karsten Lakes Course is a Championship Course designed by Neil Coles (opened 1.4.97). Thonock Park Course - 18 holes, 6620 yards. Par 70, S.S.S. 70. Karsten Lakes Course - 18 holes, 6724 yards. Par 72, S.S.S. 72. 20 bay floodlit driving range. *Green Fees:* Thonock Park Course - weekdays £30.00 per round, £40.00 per day; Karsten Lakes Course - £30.00 per round, £40.00 per day. *Eating facilities:* restaurant and coffee shop, two bars. *Visitors:* welcome, seven days on both courses (tee time bookings available). *Society Meetings:* welcome (booking in advance necessary). Professional: Stephen Cooper. Secretary: J.D. Bowers.

GRANTHAM. **Belton Park Golf Club,** Belton Lane, Londonthorpe Road, Grantham NG31 9SH (01476 567399; Fax: 01476 592078). *Location:* two miles from Grantham. 250 acre Deer Park adjacent to the historical Belton House. Three loops of 9 holes each beginning and ending at the clubhouse: Brownlow Course 6472 yards (Championship). S.S.S. 71. Ancaster Course 6325 yards. S.S.S. 70. Belmont Course 6075 yards. S.S.S. 69. Two large practice areas. *Green Fees:* weekdays £30.00 per round, £36.00 per day; weekends and Bank Holidays £36.00 per round, £42.00 per day. Special winter rates November to March. *Eating facilities:* full restaurant facilities every day. *Visitors:* welcome without reservation. *Society Meetings:* catered for by arrangement weekdays only (except Tuesday). Special day package. Professional: S. Williams. General Manager: S Rowley.
e-mail: greatgolf@beltonpark.co.uk

GRANTHAM. **Stoke Rochford Golf Club,** Stoke Rochford, Near Grantham NG33 5EW (01476 530275). *Location:* five miles south of Grantham on A1. Entrance at BP petrol station. Parkland. 18 holes, 6313 yards. S.S.S. 70. Small practice ground. *Green Fees:* £30.00 per round, £37.00 per day. *Eating facilities:* meals available daily, to be booked before playing. *Visitors:* cannot commence play before 10.30am at weekends or on Public Holidays. No visitors on Sundays November, December and January. Buggies and numerous trolleys for hire. Snooker room. *Society Meetings:* by prior arrangement. Professional: A.E. Dow (01476 530218). Secretary: J.Martindale (01572 756305).

GRANTHAM. **Sudbrook Moor Golf Club,** Charity Street, Carlton Scroop, Grantham NG32 3AT (01400 250796). *Location:* A607 Lincoln to Grantham, six miles north-east of Grantham. Private course in picturesque valley; easy walking parkland/meadowland. 9 holes, 4827 yards. S.S.S. 63/64/65. Covered driving range bays. *Green Fees:* under review. *Eating facilities:* Spike Bar and dining room. Bistro menu, Monday-Saturday, closed Sunday Catering (01400 250876). *Visitors:* welcome by appointment, no Society groups. All enquiries via Club Secretary's office. Professionals: Tim Hutton/Ben Hutton. Club Secretary: Judith M. Hutton (01400 250796).

GRANTHAM near. **De Vere Belton Woods Hotel,** Belton, Near Grantham NG32 2LN (01476 593200; Fax: 01476 574547). *Location:* three miles from Grantham, two miles from the A1. Belton Woods Hotel offers a golfers' paradise with three very challenging golf courses. The Lakes Course- 6831 yards, Par 73; The Woodside Course- 6623 yards, Par 72; The Red Arrows Academy Course, 9 holes par 3 course, 1116 yards. Practice facilities include a floodlit undercover 20 bay driving range, a practice chipping and bunker and a putting green. Tuition available from the five golf professionals on site. *Green Fees:* information not available. *Eating facilities:* three eating experiences, Tapps Cafe Bar, an informal restaurant which serves food all day, Stantons Restaurant, an informal brasserie style menu and The Manor Restaurant, offers a fine dining menu. *Visitors:* welcome, please call to book to avoid disappointment. Accommodation in Hotel – 136 luxurious bedrooms and suites, with extensive leisure and conference facilities. Golf holidays, society and corporate events are our speciality. Please ring the hotel for any special offers on golfing breaks (01476 514335/4308). Golf and Leisure Manager: Andrew Cameron. Head Golf Professional: Steve Sayers. Golf Sales: Tracey Orsmond (01476 514335), Oliver Williams (01476 514308)*

GRIMSBY. **Grimsby Golf Club Ltd,** Littlecoates Road, Grimsby DN34 4LU (01472 342823). *Location:* two miles west of town centre, one mile from A180 and A46. Undulating parkland course. 18 holes, 6098 yards. S.S.S. 69. Practice ground, chipping area. *Green Fees:* information not available. *Eating facilities:* quality food available at all times and bar facilities. *Visitors:* welcome weekdays, must be members of golf clubs. *Society Meetings:* catered for Mondays and Fridays by arrangement with Secretary (Club Ladies' Day Tuesday, club ladies have priority in the afternoons). Professional: Richard Smith (01472 356981). Secretary: Mr K. Skingle (Tel & Fax: 01472 342630).*

GRIMSBY. **Manor Golf Club,** Laceby Manor, Laceby, Grimsby DN37 7EA (01472 873468; Fax: 01472 871266). *Location:* A18, half a mile on left hand side from Oaklands Hotel, situated at Laceby roundabout. Parkland - tree lined fairways, many water features including green surrounded by water. 18 holes, 6343 yards. S.S.S. 70. Netted driving area, putting green, chipping area. *Green Fees:* £20.00 weekdays, £24.00 weekends. Twilight £12.00 (not feasible to complete 18 holes at this time). Subject to review. *Eating facilities:* bar, lounge bar, dining area. *Visitors:* welcome any day. Booked tee system operated all days, non-members may book up to six days in advance. *Society Meetings:* welcome by prior arrangement. Professional: Neil Laybourne (01472 873468). Secretary: Judith MacKay (01472 873468).
e-mail: judith@manorgolfclub.wanadoo.co.uk

www.uk-golfguide.com

GRIMSBY. **Waltham Windmill Golf Club**, Cheapside, Waltham, Grimsby DN37 0HT (01472 824109). *Location:* off A16 main Louth to Grimsby road. Parkland course incorporating seven lakes. 18 holes, 6442 yards. S.S.S. 71. Practice ground. *Green Fees:* weekdays £25.00, with member £14.00; weekends £30.00, with member £20.00. Reductions for societies; minimum 12. *Eating facilities:* bar and restaurant. *Visitors:* welcome, telephone booking. *Society Meetings:* welcome, contact the Secretary. Professional: Stephen Bennett (01472 823963). Secretary: Ivor Williams (01472 824109; Fax: 01472 828391).

HORNCASTLE near. **Horncastle Golf Club**, West Ashby, Near Horncastle LN9 5PP (01507 526800). *Location:* just off A158 between Horncastle and Baumber. Parkland course - water features on 14 holes. 18 holes, 5800 yards. S.S.S. 70. *Green Fees:* information not available. *Eating facilities:* bars, restaurant. *Visitors:* welcome anytime but helpful to phone. Special package available golf range, golf course, food and drink. Ballroom and conference facilities. Accommodation available, caravan site. Carts. Fishing lakes. *Society Meetings:* please phone in advance. Professional: Alison Johns. Secretary: Chris Redfearn.*

IMMINGHAM. **Immingham Golf Club**, St Andrew's Lane, Church Lane, Immingham DN40 2EU (01469 575298; Fax: 01469 577636). *Location:* two miles off A180, behind St Andrew's Church, Immingham. Undulating parkland with water hazards. Drainage dyke comes into play for over half the holes. Excellent greens. 18 holes, 6215 yards, 5682 metres. S.S.S. 70. Small practice area. *Green Fees:* £24.00 7 days, £12 with member 7 days. Subject to review for 2008. *Eating facilities:* snacks; full catering (book in advance). *Visitors:* welcome anytime except Thursday pm, Saturday pm and Sunday am. Handicap Certificate preferred. *Society Meetings:* welcome midweek during the day, limited availability at weekends. Professional: Nick Harding (01469 575493). Manager: C. Todd (01469 575298).
e-mail: immgc@btconnect.com
website: www.immgc.com

LINCOLN. **Carholme Golf Club**, Carholme Road, Lincoln LN1 1SE (01522 523725). *Location:* one mile from city centre on A57 to Worksop. Flat parkland. 18 holes, 6215 yards. S.S.S. 70. *Green Fees:* £20.00 per round, £24.00 per day. *Eating facilities:* full service. *Visitors:* welcome most days subject to restrictions regarding starting times, information available on request. *Society Meetings:* by prior arrangement only. Office: Tel/Fax: 01522 533733. Secretary: J. Lammin (01522 523725).
e-mail: info@carholme-golf-club.co.uk
website: www.carholme-golf-club.co.uk

THE APPEARANCE OF AN ASTERISK (*) AT THE END OF A CLUB OR COURSE ENTRY INDICATES THAT UP-TO-DATE INFORMATION HAS NOT BEEN SUPPLIED

LINCOLN. **Canwick Park Golf Club**, Canwick Park, Washingborough Road, Lincoln LN4 1EF (01522 522166). *Location:* two miles east of Lincoln on B1190. Parkland, wooded course - two testing Par 3s (5th & 13th). 18 holes, 6148 yards, 5600 metres, S.S.S. 69. Practice ground. *Green Fees:* £23.00, Special rate 10am-noon and 2pm-4pm, £16.00. £215.00 weekends. *Eating facilities:* bar snacks and meals to order. *Visitors:* welcome weekdays; weekends after 2:30pm without a member. Locker rooms. *Society Meetings:* welcome by prior arrangement. Manager: N. Porteus (01522 542912; Fax: 01522 526997).
e-mail: manager@canwickpark.org
website: www.canwickpark.org

LINCOLN. **Lincoln Golf Club**, Torksey, Lincoln LN1 2EG (Tel/Fax: 01427 718721). *Location:* A156 approx. 6 miles south of Gainsborough. Mature, testing championship standard course built on sandy subsoil. 18 holes, 6438 yards. S.S.S. 71. *Green Fees:* £35.00 per round, £45.00 per day. Subject to review. Winter packages available. *Eating facilities:* full facilities available. *Visitors:* welcome anytime except Tuesday mornings (Ladies' Day). *Society Meetings:* welcome by prior arrangement (not weekends). Professional: Ashley Carter (Tel/Fax: 01427 718273). Manager: Derek B. Linton (Tel/Fax: 01427 718721).
e-mail: info@lincolngc.co.uk
website: www.lincolngc.co.uk

LINCOLN. **Martin Moor Golf Club**, Martin Road, Blankney LN4 3BE (01526 378243). *Location:* B1189 between Martin and Metheringham. Flat wooded course. 9 holes, 18 tees including three Par 5s, 6345 yards. Par 72. Large practice area. *Green Fees:* 9 holes £7.00, 18 holes £10.00. *Eating facilities:* new clubhouse, bar and restaurant opened June 2006; meals available. *Visitors:* welcome. Lessons by arrangement. *Society Meetings:* welcome. Rates negotiable. Catering on request. Secretary: Mrs C. Roberts (01526 378243).
e-mail: martinmoorgc@freenet.co.uk

LINCOLN. **Pottergate Golf Club**, Moor Lane, Branston, Lincoln (01522 794867). *Location:* south of Lincoln on B1188 to Branston. Turn left at Moor Lodge Hotel into Moor Lane. Parkland course. 9 holes. Par 34. Indoor golf simulator with 17 golf courses and driving range. Putting green. *Green Fees:* £8.50 weekdays 9/18 holes (under review), weekends and Bank Holidays £10.00 (under review). *Eating facilities:* bar open 11am to 10pm (light snacks available 10.30am-3pm), closed Tuesdays. Food by prior arrangement. *Society Meetings:* welcome. Professional: Lee Tasker. Proprietor: Robert Mawer

LINCOLN. **RAF Coningsby Golf Club**, Coningsby, Lincoln LN4 4SY (01526 342581). *Location:* on the B1192 halfway between Tattershall Thorpe and Woodhall Spa, signposted RAF Woodhall. Parkland course. 9 holes (18 tees), 5354 yards, S.S.S. 66. *Green Fees:* £8.00, with member £6.00, Juniors £4.00. Day ticket £10.00, Juniors £4.00. *Visitors:* welcome weekdays except Monday am (Ladies). *Society Meetings:* welcome weekdays by appointment. Secretary: Nick Parsons (01526 347946; Fax: 01526 347413).

LINCOLN. **Welton Manor Golf Centre,** Hackthorn Road, Welton, Lincoln LN2 3PA (01673 862827). *Location:* six miles north of Lincoln. Off A46 to Welton village, through Welton, turn left at mini roundabout signposted Spridlington, entrance half-a-mile on left. Gently undulating parkland with streams, ponds and tree-lined fairways. 10-bay floodlit driving range. *Green Fees:* under review. *Eating facilities:* bar meals and The Falcon Restaurant, from 8am to 11pm. Licensed patio area. Caravan club site, fishing lake. *Visitors:* welcome, phone for tee closures, buggies available. Professional: Gary Leslie.
e-mail: enquiries@weltonmanorgolfcentre.co.uk
website:www.weltonmanorgolfcentre.co.uk

LOUTH. **Kenwick Park Golf Club,** Kenwick Park, Louth LN11 8NY (01507 605134; Fax: 01507 606556). *Location:* one mile south of Louth. Undulating parkland, wooded course. 18 holes, 6872 yards (white tees), 6244 yards (yellow tees). S.S.S. 73. Driving range, teaching facilities. *Green Fees:* £35.00 weekdays, £45.00 weekends. *Eating facilities:* contact 01507 608210. *Visitors:* welcome but please telephone in advance. Buggies available. Hotel (01507 608806). *Society Meetings:* welcome, contact Secretary. Professionals: Paul Spence & Michael Langford (Tel & Fax: 01507 607161). Director of Golf: Eric Sharp (01507 605134; Fax: 01507 606556).
e-mail: secretary@kenwickparkgolf.co.uk
website: www.kenwickparkgolf.co.uk

LOUTH. Louth Golf Club, 59 Crowtree Lane, Louth LN11 9LJ (01507 603681; Fax: 01507 608501). *Location:* western outskirts of Louth. Undulating parkland course in an Area of Outstanding Natural Beauty. 18 holes, 6411 yards. S.S.S. 71. Practice ground, putting green. *Green Fees:* weekdays £25.00 per round, £30.00 per day; Sundays £30.00 per round, £36.00 per day. *Eating facilities:* full catering 11am to 9pm (earlier to order). *Visitors:* welcome without reservation other than notification and dress rules. Squash court. *Society Meetings:* catered for. Professional: Nick Taylor (01507 604648). General Manager: Simon Moody (01507 603681; Fax: 01507 608501). website: www.louthgolfclub.com

MABLETHORPE. Sandilands Golf Club, Roman Bank, Sandilands, Sutton-on-Sea LN12 2RJ (01507 441432). *Location:* A52 one mile south of Sutton-on-Sea. Seaside links adjacent to sea and sand. 18 holes, 6021 yards. S.S.S. 69. 40 acre practice area. *Green Fees:* information not available. *Eating facilities:* Bar and restaurant. *Visitors:* welcome. *Society Meetings:* welcome with reductions for numbers, catered for weekdays. Professional: Andrew Myers. Secretary: Philip Ross (01507 441432).

MARKET RASEN. Market Rasen and District Golf Club, Legsby Road, Market Rasen LN8 3DZ (01673 842319). *Location:* A46 to Market Rasen - one mile east of town. Wooded heathland course. 18 holes, 6239 yards. S.S.S. 70. Practice ground. *Green Fees:* weekdays £35.00 per day, £25.00 per round; weekends only with member. Under review for 2008. *Eating facilities:* available every day. *Visitors:* welcome weekdays with prior booking, must be members of a bona fide golf club, weekends with members only. *Society Meetings:* welcome weekdays with prior booking. Professional: A.M. Chester (01673 842416). Secretary: J.P. Smith (01673 842319). e-mail: sleafordgolfclub@btinternet.com website: www.sleafordgolfclub.co.uk

MARKET RASEN. Market Rasen Racecourse 9-Hole Pay and Play Course, Legsby Road, Market Rasen LN8 3EA (01673 843434; Fax: 01673 844532). *Location:* on A631 Market Rasen to Louth road, midway between Lincoln and Grimsby. Course is in centre of picturesque National Hunt racecourse. 9 holes, 2532 yards. S.S.S. 33. *Green Fees:* information not available. *Eating facilities:* hot and cold drinks

and sweet shop available April to October. *Visitors:* no restrictions. Golf course is closed on race days. *Society Meetings:* welcome on application to Secretary. Secretary: Pip Adams*

SCUNTHORPE. Ashby Decoy Golf Club, Burringham Road, Scunthorpe, North Lincolnshire DN17 2AB (01724 866561; Fax: 01724 271708). *Location:* leave M181 Scunthorpe South, turn right, right again, third right by ASDA Superstore. Flat wooded, parkland course. 18 holes, 6281 yards. S.S.S. 70. Large practice area. *Green Fees:* information not available. *Eating facilities:* full catering and bar available. *Visitors:* welcome weekdays only, not Tuesdays. *Society Meetings:* by arrangement weekdays, except Tuesdays. Professional: Andrew Miller (01724 868972). Secretary: Mrs J.A. Harrison (01724 866561; Fax: 01724 271708). e-mail: info@ashbydecoygolfclub.co.uk website: www.ashbydecoy.co.uk

SCUNTHORPE. Grange Park Golf Club, Butterwick Road, Messingham, Scunthorpe DN17 3PP (01724 762945). *Location:* five miles south of Scunthorpe between Messingham and East Butterwick, four miles south of Junction 3 of M180. New parkland course with interesting water features. 18 holes, 6146 yards. S.S.S. 69. Second 9 hole course – flat parkland course, 1300 yards. S.S.S 27. Floodlit driving range. Clubhouse offering full facilities. New Pine Lodges available for golf holidays, societies/groups welcome. *Green Fees:* weekdays £16.00, weekends £18.00, Juniors 50% reduction. Memberships available. *Eating facilities:* full catering facilities available. *Visitors:* welcome at all times. Pro shop. Caravan site also available. *Society Meetings:* welcome, ring for details. Golf Professional: Jonathan Drury. Manager: Ian Cannon.

SCUNTHORPE. Holme Hall Golf Club, Holme Lane, Bottesford, Scunthorpe DN16 3RF (Tel & Fax: 01724 862078). *Location:* M180 Exit 4 (Scunthorpe East). Heathland with sandy subsoil. 18 holes, 6413 yards. S.S.S. 71. *Green Fees:* £25.00 per round, £35.00 per day (under review). *Eating facilities:* full catering and restaurant facilities available. *Visitors:* welcome Monday to Friday. *Society Meetings:* society and corporate packages available by arrangement. Professional: R. McKiernan (01724 851816). Secretary/ Manager: Roger.B. Bickley (01724 862078; Fax: 01724 862081). e-mail: secretary@holmehallgolf.co.uk website: www.holmehallgolf.co.uk

SCUNTHORPE. **The Lincolnshire Golf Course,** Crowle, Scunthorpe DN17 4BU (01724 711619). *Location:* M180 Junction 2, A161 to Crowle Goole, course 800 yards on left. Flat parkland. 18 holes, 6430 yards. S.S.S.70. Practice green. *Green Fees:* information not available. *Eating facilities:* bar and restaurant. *Visitors:* welcome, no restrictions. *Society Meetings:* welcome, no restrictions. Proprietor: A. York. Secretary: J. Middlehurst.*

SCUNTHORPE. **Normanby Hall Golf Club,** Normanby Park, Near Scunthorpe DN15 9HU (01724 720226). *Location:* five miles north of Scunthorpe on B1130. Follow signs for Normanby Hall Country Park. Parkland. 18 holes, 6561 yards. S.S.S. 71. Practice area. *Green Fees:* information not available. *Eating facilities:* fully licensed Clubhouse, restaurant; meals most times. *Visitors:* welcome, check times in advance with Professional. *Society Meetings:* bookings taken for weekdays. Professional: Dean Worral (01724 720226). Manager: Susan Hopkinson (01724 720588).

SKEGNESS. **North Shore Hotel and Golf Club,** North Shore Road, Skegness PE25 1DN (01754 763298; Fax: 01754 761902). *Location:* north of town one mile. Part links, part parkland, challenging course situated overlooking the sea. 18 holes, 6134 yards. S.S.S. 71. Putting green. *Green Fees:* information on request. *Eating facilities:* formal restaurant, spike bar serving home cooked bar food 10am to 9 pm. Hotel accommodation on course 36 en suite bedroomed hotel. Special winter deals available. *Visitors:* welcome, prior notice required. Golf schools and instruction provided by professional; juniors welcome. *Society Meetings:* welcome, catering from between 4 and 200. Professional: John Cornelius (01754 764822). General Manager: N. Wardle e-mail: golf@northshorehotel.co.uk

SKEGNESS. **Seacroft Golf Club,** Drummond Road, Seacroft, Skegness PE25 3AU (Tel & Fax: 01754 763020). *Location:* towards Gibraltar Nature Reserve. Seaside links course. 18 holes, 6492 yards. S.S.S. 71. *Green Fees:* weekdays £40.00 per round, £50.00 per day; weekends and Bank Holidays £45.00 per round, £55.00 per day. *Eating facilities:* available all day/evenings. *Visitors:* welcome after 9.30am if members of recognised club or society, Handicap Certificate required. *Society Meetings:* societies/company golf days and groups catered for. Professional: R. Lawie (01754 769624). Secretary: Richard England (Tel & Fax: 01754 763020). e-mail: richard@seacroft-golfclub.co.uk website: www.seacroft-golfclub.co.uk

SKEGNESS. **Southview Golf Club,** Southview Leisure Park, Burgh Road, Skegness PE25 2LA (01754 760589; Fax: 01754 768455). *Location:* half a mile from Skegness towards Burgh Le Marsh A158. Flat parkland. 9/18 holes, 5126 yards. S.S.S. *Green Fees:* information not available. *Eating facilities:* full bar and meals service. *Visitors:* welcome. *Society Meetings:* welcome weekdays. Golf Manager: P. Cole.*

SLEAFORD. **Sleaford Golf Club,** Willoughby Road, Greylees, Sleaford NG34 8PL (01529 488273). *Location:* off A153, two miles west of Sleaford. Inland links-type course, fairly flat and lightly wooded. 18 holes, 6503 yards. S.S.S. 71. Practice field, 6 hole pitch and putt. *Green Fees:* weekdays £27.00 per round, £34.00 per day, £14.00 with a member, Juniors £9.00 per round or day; weekends £36.00 per round or day. Subject to review. *Eating facilities:* full catering. Bar open seven days. *Visitors:* welcome without reservation, except winter weekends. Handicap Certificate required and must be members of a recognised club. *Society Meetings:* catered for weekdays only by prior arrangement. Professional: (01529 488644). Secretary: Ms E.N. Downey (01529 488273). e-mail: sleafordgolfclub@btinternet.com website: www.sleafordgolfclub.co.uk

SOUTH KYME. **South Kyme Golf Club,** Skinners Lane, South Kyme LN4 4AT (01526 861113; Fax: 01526 861080). *Location:* approximately four miles off A153 road from Sleaford to Horncastle, turn right before North Kyme. Four miles off A17 from Sleaford to Boston, turn left before East Heckington. An interesting "inland links" with excellent greens all year round. 18 holes, 6556 yards White, 6194 yards Yellow, 5389 yards Red. S.S.S. White 71, Yellow 69, Red 70. 6 hole Par 3 course, practice ground. *Green Fees:* from £16.00 per round. Check for seasonal 'special offers'. Society discount for 8 players or more. Expert golf instruction available, send for brochure. *Eating facilities:* bar and restaurant. Snacks available all day. Lunch menu available. *Visitors:* no restrictions at present but advisable to check at weekends in case of competitions. *Society Meetings:* welcome with prior booking. PGA Director of Golf/Secretary: Peter Chamberlain. e-mail: southkymegc@hotmail.com website: www.skgc.co.uk

SPALDING. **The Spalding Golf Club,** Surfleet, Spalding PE11 4EA (01775 680474). *Location:* four miles from Spalding on A16 to Boston. Parkland course, water features on many of the holes with the drive on the second over the River Glen. 18 holes, 6433 yards. S.S.S. 71. Driving range and practice area. *Green Fees:* weekdays £30.00 per round, £35.00 per day, half rate with a member; weekends £40.00, £20.00 with a member. *Eating facilities:* full catering and bar facilities except Tuesdays when there is a bar and filled rolls only. *Visitors:* welcome, advisable to telephone in advance. Handicap Certificates required. *Society Meetings:* large groups on Thursdays, smaller groups of up to 16, any weekday April to October. Professional: John Spencer (01778 680474). Secretary: Barrie Walker (01778 680386). e-mail: secretary@spaldinggolfclub.co.uk website: www.spaldinggolfclub.co.uk

www.uk-golfguide.com

SPALDING. **Sutton Bridge Golf Club,** New Road, Sutton Bridge, Spalding PE12 9RQ (01406 350323). *Location:* off A17 between Long Sutton and King's Lynn, New Road leads off Sutton Bridge main street (Bridge Road), almost opposite church. Parkland course built around former Victorian dock basin. 9 holes. Small practice ground, new driving range from June 2002. *Green Fees:* April to September £25.00; October to March £15.00. £15.00 with a member. *Eating facilities:* bar and catering open Tuesday to Sunday. *Visitors:* welcome weekdays except Tuesday after 3pm, and Wednesday mornings. *Society Meetings:* welcome weekdays by arrangement; some restrictions, contact club for details. Special concessions for groups of 8 or more; package available. Professional: Antony Lowther (01406 351422). Secretary: P. L. Land.

SPALDING near. **Gedney Hill Golf Course,** West Drove, Gedney Hill, Near Spalding PE12 0NT (01406 330183). *Location:* six miles from Radar Tower near Crowland, off B1073 follow signs or follow 1066 off A47. Testing interesting course, Guinness Book of Records for longest hole in Britain (671 yards). 18 holes, 5357 yards. S.S.S. 66. Practice/putting area. *Green Fees:* weekdays £9.50 per round, £15.00 per day, £7.00 Seniors; weekends £13.50 per round, £20.00 per day. *Eating facilities:* two bars (one casual spike bar), Chinese restaurant (70 seater). *Visitors:* welcome, no restrictions. Full snooker room/snookerette table, new restaurant conservatory. *Society Meetings:* all very welcome. Discount Golf shop: Neil Venters (01406 330922). Secretary: R. Newns.

STAMFORD. **Burghley Park (Stamford) Golf Club,** St. Martins Without, Stamford PE9 3JX (Tel & Fax: 01780 753789). *Location:* leave A1 at roundabout on B1081 south of Stamford, club one mile on right. Flat parkland. 18 holes, 6236 yards. S.S.S. 70. *Green Fees:* weekdays £30.00, weekends as members' guests only. Half price after 5pm May to September. *Eating facilities:* restaurant and bar. *Visitors:* welcome weekdays. Handicap Certificates required. Visit Burghley House, the greatest of Elizabethan mansions. *Society Meetings:* Tuesdays, Wednesdays and Thursdays only. Professional: (Tel & Fax: 01780 762100). Secretary: (Tel & Fax: 01780 753789). e-mail: burghley.golf@lineone.net website: www.burghley.golf.org

STAMFORD. **Rutland County Golf Club,** Great Casterton, Stamford PE9 4AQ (Tel & Fax: 01780 460330). *Location:* head north on A1 from Stamford roundabout, take Pickworth turn, follow golf signs. Inland links, easy walking. 18 holes, 6401 yards. S.S.S. 71. 9 holes short course. 20 bay driving range, practice bunker, chipping green, putting green. *Green Fees:* weekdays £25.00 to £30.00 per day; weekends £30.00 to £35.00 per day. *Eating facilities:* bar meals, lounge bar, dining room. *Visitors:* welcome. *Society Meetings:* welcome on application. Professional: ian Melville (01780 460239). Secretary: Steve Lowe. e-mail: info@rutlandcountygolf.co.uk website: www.rutlandcountygolf.co.uk

WOODHALL SPA. **The National Golf Centre,** The Broadway, Woodhall Spa LN10 6PU (01526 352511). Fax: 01526 351817). *Location:* 19 miles from Lincoln, Boston, Sleaford; 23 miles from Skegness; 50 miles from Nottingham. The Hotchkin is a flat heathland course rated 47th in the world; The Bracken is a parkland course opened in 1998. Hotchkin Course: 18 holes, 7080 yards. S.S.S. 75; Bracken Course: 18 holes, 6735 yards S.S.S. 74. Driving range, short game academy, grass tees, putting greens and 9-hole pitch and putt. *Green Fees:* Hotchkin – £80.00 per round (£65.00 EGU/ELGA members); Bracken – £50.00 per round, (£40.00 EGU/ELGA members). Daily rates and reduced rates for Juniors available. *Eating facilities:* clubhouse with restaurant and bar with all facilities. *Visitors:* welcome at all times, all tee times to be booked in advance. Handicap Certificates required. *Society Meetings:* welcome and catered for, but must book in advance. Please contact Golf Reservations (01526 352511). e-mail: bookings@englishgolfunion.org website: www. woodhallspagolf.com

Northamptonshire

CORBY near. **Priors Hall Golf Club,** Stamford Road, Weldon, Near Corby NN17 3JH (01536 260756). *Location:* on the A43, four miles from Corby on the Stamford Road. Parkland course. 18 holes, 6631 yards, 6063 metres. S.S.S. 72. Practice nets and ground. *Green Fees:* weekdays £15.00; weekends £18.00. Certain concessions apply to local residents. *Eating facilities:* bar meals. *Visitors:* welcome at all times; pre-booking advisable; starting sheet in operation. *Society Meetings:* welcome by prior arrangement. Professional: Jeff Bradbrook. Secretary: Phill Ackroyd (01536 263722).

DAVENTRY. **Daventry and District Golf Club,** Norton Road, Daventry NN11 5LS (01327 702829). *Location:* on Borough Hill, site of Iron Age Fort and Roman Camp. 9 holes, 5812 yards. S.S.S. 68. *Green Fees:* £15.00 weekdays, £20.00 weekends *Visitors:* welcome weekdays and weekends except Sunday before 11.30am. *Society Meetings:* welcome with prior booking. Hon. Secretary: M. Sheppard.

DAVENTRY. **Staverton Park Golf Club,** Daventry Road, Staverton, Near Daventry NN11 6JT (01327 302000; Fax: 01327 311428). *Location:* one mile from Daventry on A425 to Leamington Spa. Easy access from M1 Junctions 16 or 18. Undulating parkland. Championship course – 18 holes, 6609 yards. S.S.S. 73. Practice range, two putting greens. *Green Fees:* information not available. *Eating facilities:* full catering available at all times. *Visitors:* always welcome. Handicap Certificate required at weekends. Advance Tee Time (visitors) booking (01327 705506). 245 bedroomed hotel with leisure and conference facilities. Residential golf packages available. Buggies, trolleys and clubs for hire. *Society Meetings:* welcome, for details please contact Lindi Rawden (01327 302000). Professional: Richard Mudge (01327 311119; Fax: 01327 312787). Secretary: Roy Patrick (01327 876020).*
e-mail: staverton@initialstyle.co.uk
website: www.verve-venues.com*

HELLIDON. **Hellidon Lakes Golf Club,** Hellidon Lakes Hotel, Hellidon, Daventry NN11 6GG (01327 262550; Fax: 01327 262559). *Location:* one and a half miles from A361, six miles from Daventry, 12 miles from Banbury. Parkland. 27 hole championship course, putting green. *Green Fees;* information not available. *Eating facilities:* themed 100 seater casual bar and restaurant. AA rosette restaurant. *Visitors:* always welcome. 110 en suite bedrooms, leisure centre, tennis, health and beauty centre with salon, gym, sunbed, steam room, whirlpool bath and heated indoor swimming pool. Indoor golf simulator, 4-lane tenpin bowling. *Society Meetings:* all welcome. Professional: Joe Kingston (01327 262551).*
e-mail: hellidon@marstonhotels.com
website: www.hellidon@marstonhotels.com*

KETTERING. **Kettering Golf Club,** Headlands, Kettering NN15 6XA (01536 511104). *Location:* off A14 (Junction 8) A43 to Kettering, right at 1st roundabout and follow signs for golf club. Flat parkland. 18 holes, 6035 yards, 5515 metres. S.S.S. 69. *Green Fees:* information not provided. *Eating facilities:* by prior arrangement. *Visitors:* welcome weekdays only. *Society Meetings:* catered for Wednesdays and Fridays only by arrangement. Professional: K. Theobald (01536 481014). Secretary: J. Gilding (01536 511104; Fax: 01536 523788).

MARKET HARBOROUGH near. **Stoke Albany Golf Club,** Ashley Road, Stoke Albany, Market Harborough LE16 8PL (01858 535208; Fax: 01858 535505). *Location:* A427, A14 five minutes away, Market Harborough 10 minutes. Undulating parkland. 18 holes, 6175 yards. S.S.S. 70. Practice area, putting green. *Green Fees:* weekdays £17.00; weekends £21.00 per round. *Eating facilities:* restaurant, bar and spike bar. *Visitors:* welcome, no restrictions. *Society Meetings:* all welcome, but booking is essential. Professional: Adrian Clifford. Secretary: R. Want. e-mail: info@stokealbanygolfclub.co.uk
website: www.stoygolfclub.co.uk

NORTHAMPTON. **Brampton Heath Golf Centre,** Sandy Lane, Church Brampton, Northampton NN6 8AX (01604 843939; Fax: 01604 843885). *Location:* signposted off A5099 five miles north of Northampton town centre. Undulating heathland course, very dry winter conditions. 18 holes, 6533 yards. S.S.S 71, par 72. 18 bay covered, floodlit driving range, PGA Short Course British Championships Par 3 course. *Green Fees:* information not available. *Eating facilities:* full facilities available from 7.30am. *Visitors:* welcome, no restrictions, advisable to book. Buggies and carts available all year round. Short course available - ideal for beginners. Golf superstore. *Society Meetings:* welcome seven days. Professional: Alan Wright. Manager: Kate Brett.
website: www.bhgc.co.uk

NORTHAMPTON. **Cold Ashby Golf Club,** Stanford Road, Cold Ashby, Northampton NN6 6EP (Tel & Fax: 01604 740548). *Location:* midway between Rugby, Leicester and Northampton, close to Junction 1 A14 and Junction 18 M1. Undulating parkland. 27 holes, 6308 yards. S.S.S. 71. Short game practice area. Driving range. *Green Fees:* midweek £18.00 per round, £28.00 per day; weekends £23.00 per round, £35.00 per day. *Eating facilities:* meals and bar snacks available daily. *Visitors:* welcome midweek anytime, weekends must reserve a starting time. *Society Meetings:* catered for weekdays and weekends. Professional: Shane Rose (01604 740099; Fax: 01604 740548). Secretary: David Croxton (01604 740548). e-mail: info@coldashbygolfclub.com
website: www.coldashbygolfclub.com

NORTHAMPTON. **Collingtree Park Golf Course Ltd,** Windingbrook Lane, Northampton NN4 0XN (01604 700000; Fax: 01604 702600). *Location:* 2 minutes from Junction 15 off M1-A508. Johnny Miller design Championship Course with its signature 18th hole set on a stunning island green. Host to The British Masters 1995/96 and Europro Challenge Tour, and Mobile Cup Seniors Tournament 2005. 18 holes, 6692 yards. S.S.S. 72. Floodlit, covered 16 bay driving range. *Green Fees:* information not provided. *Eating facilities:* members bar, Greens restaurant open to the public. *Visitors:* welcome, advised to book in advance. Handicap Certificates required. Indoor teaching facilities. *Society Meetings:* welcome, advisable to book in advance; discount for group bookings. Professionals: Geoff Pook and Brian Mudge (01604 701202/700000). Club Secretary: Les Pullan (01604 700000).
e-mail: kmundy@collingtreeparkgolf.com

NORTHAMPTON. **Delapre Golf Centre,** Eagle Drive, Nene Valley Way, Northampton NN4 7DU (01604 764036; Fax: 01604 706378). *Location:* two miles from Junction 15 M1 on A45 towards Wellingborough. Parkland. Five courses: 18 hole main course; 9 holes course; two Par 3 courses; pitch and putt course and putting greens. 40 bay covered floodlit range. *Green Fees:* please visit website for information. *Eating facilities:* licensed bar and restaurant, coffee shop. Opening hours: 7am to 10pm daily. Digicards and meal deals available. *Visitors:* PGA qualified coaches available for private or group tuition; golf schools, video etc. Buggies for hire. *Society Meetings:* welcome. Professional: Greg Iron. Centre Manager: Andrew Coleman (01604 764036).
website: www.jackbarker.com

NORTHAMPTON. **Kingsthorpe Golf Club,** Kingsley Road, Northampton NN2 7BU. *Location:* off M1 and A43. Undulating parkland. 18 holes, 5903 yards. S.S.S. 69. *Green Fees:* weekdays £30.00 per round, £40.00 per day April-October; £20.00 per round, £30.00 per day November-March; weekends members and guests only. *Eating facilities:* full catering. *Visitors:* welcome weekdays; weekends must be guest of member. *Society Meetings:* catered for by arrangement normally Thursdays and Fridays only; brochure available. Professional: Paul Armstrong (01604 719602). Secretary: John Harris (Tel & Fax: 01604 710610).
e-mail: secretary@kingsthorpe-golf.co.uk
website: www.kingsthorpe-golf.co.uk

NORTHAMPTON. **Northampton Golf Club,** Harlestone, Northampton NN7 4EF (01604 845102; Fax: 01604 820262). *Location:* on A428 north-west of Northampton in the village of Harlestone. Parkland with a lake coming into play 16th and 18th holes. 18 holes, 6615 yards. S.S.S. 72. Practice ground. *Green Fees:* £40.00 weekdays, weekends must play with a member. *Eating facilities:* restaurant and bar snacks. *Visitors:* welcome weekdays but must have a Certificate of Handicap. *Society Meetings:* weekdays except Wednesdays. Inclusive packages available. Professional: Barry Randall (01604 845167). Secretary/Manager: Gavin Reed (01604 845155; Fax: 01604 820262).
e-mail: golf@northamptongolfclub.co.uk
website: www.northamptongolfclub.co.uk

NORTHAMPTON. **Northamptonshire County Golf Club,** Sandy Lane, Church Brampton, Northampton NN6 8AZ (01604 842951). *Location:* four miles north west of Northampton between A50 and A428. Heathland with woods, gorse and stream. 18 holes, 6505 yards, 5948 metres. S.S.S. 72. Practice ground. *Green Fees:* (summer)18 holes £45.00, 27/36 holes £55.00 (under review for 2008). *Eating facilities:* restaurant and bar. *Visitors:* by prior arrangement, must have Club Handicap. *Society Meetings:* catered for Wednesdays, small groups on Thursdays. Professional: T. Rouse (Tel & Fax: 01604 842226). Secretary: (01604 843025; Fax: 01604 843463).

NORTHAMPTON. **Overstone Park Golf and Country Club,** Billing Lane, Northampton NN6 0AP (01604 647666; Fax: 01604 642635). *Location:* seven miles from Junction 15 M1 A508 merges with A45. Follow signs for Overstone from Billing turn off. Undulating parkland with some water features. 18 holes, 6602 yards. S.S.S. 72. Practice ground. *Green Fees:* telephone for up to date prices. *Eating facilities:* bar, brasserie/restaurant and spike bar. *Visitors:* welcome seven days - must pre book at weekends. *Society Meetings:* welcome Monday to Friday, special packages available. Accommodation available in 30 en suite rooms. Leisure Club. Professional: Stuart Kier (01604 643555). General Manager: Allan McLundie.
e-mail: enquiries@overstonepark.com
website: www.overstonepark.com

OUNDLE. **Oundle Golf Club,** Benefield Road, Oundle, Peterborough PE8 4EZ (01832 273267). *Location:* one mile from Oundle on Corby Road A447. Parkland course. Home of "The Oundle Putter".18 holes, 6265 yards. Par 72 S.S.S. 70. *Green Fees:* weekdays £26.50 per round, £35.50 per day; weekends £30.50 per round. *Eating facilities:* bar meals/restaurant. *Visitors:* welcome, check with Professional. No visitors before 10.30am at weekends. *Society Meetings:* welcome by arrangement. Professional: R. Keys (01832 273267 Ext. 2). Secretary: D. Foley (01832 273267 Ext. 1; Fax: 01832 273008). GKInfoline: (01832 274882).
e-mail: office@oundlegolfclub.com
website: www.oundlegolfclub.com

RUSHDEN. **Rushden Golf Club,** Kimbolton Road, Chelveston, Wellingborough NN9 6AN (01933 418511). *Location:* on B645 two miles east of Higham Ferrers. Undulating meadowland. 10 holes, 6249 yards. S.S.S. 70. Small practice area. *Green Fees:* weekdays £20.00, weekends restricted. *Eating facilities:* bar and dining area - no catering Mondays. *Visitors:* welcome except Wednesday afternoons, weekends must play with member. *Society Meetings:* small societies catered for weekdays. Secretary: Miss E.J. Williams (01933 418511).

TOWCESTER near. **Farthingstone Golf Club and Hotel,** Farthingstone, Near Towcester NN12 8NA (01327 361291; Fax: 01327 361645). *Location:* just a few minutes from Junction 16 of the M1, close to A5 and A45. Major towns within easy reach include Milton Keynes, Banbury, Oxford, Rugby and Northampton. Undulating wooded countryside. 18 holes, 6299 yards. S.S.S. 70 (Par). Practice area. *Green Fees:* information not available. *Eating facilities:* bar snacks and restaurant. *Visitors:* welcome, advance bookings available. Rental of golf buggies. Hotel, squash court. *Society Meetings:* bookings welcome. Professional: Luke Brockway (01327 361533). Secretary: Christian Donaldson.
website: www.farthingstone.co.uk

TOWCESTER near. **Whittlebury Park Golf and Country Club,** Whittlebury, Near Towcester NN12 8WP (01327 850000; Fax: 01327 850001). *Location*: on A413 south of Whittlebury village, 10 minutes from M1, J 15a (Northampton), 15 minutes from M1, J14 (Milton Keynes), 20 minutes M40, J10 (Banbury/ Oxford). 36 hole Championship course in 4 loops of 9, each with its own distinctive character. Two tier driving range with extensive practice facilities. *Green Fees*: from £20.00. *Eating facilities*: bar/bistro within clubhouse plus special function suites. *Visitors*: individual golfers, societies and corporate guests welcome seven days. Other sports and activities offered. Indoor Golf Centre with astro turfed putting green and private teaching bays. *Society Meetings*: welcome seven days, by arrangement. Bookings: please contact Golf Shop on (01327 858588).
e-mail: enquiries@whittlebury.com
website: www.whittlebury.com

WELLINGBOROUGH. **Wellingborough Golf Club**, Harrowden Hall, Great Harrowden, Wellingborough NN9 5AD (01933 677234; Fax: 01933 679379). *Location*: one mile out of Wellingborough on A509, turn right at crossroads by Great Harrowden Church. Undulating parkland. 18 holes, 6651yards, 6079 metres. S.S.S. 72. Practice ground. *Green Fees*: information not provided. *Eating facilities*: bar with casual lunch or dinner menu, restaurant. *Visitors*: weekdays only. Buggies available. *Society Meetings*: welcome by appointment. Conference facilities available. Professional: David Clifford (01933 678752). General Manager: David Waite (01933 677234; Fax: 01933 679379).
e-mail: info@wellingboroughgolfclub.com
website: www.wellingboroughgolfclub.com

Nottinghamshire

BRAMCOTE. Bramcote Hills Golf Course, Thoresby Road, off Derby Road, Bramcote NG9 3EP (0115 928 1880). *Location:* A52 Nottingham to Derby road, close to Bramcote Leisure Centre, turn off A52 at Bramcote into Thoresby Road, half a mile on left hand side. Mainly flat parkland but some slightly hilly areas. 18 holes, 1500 yards. Par 3. *Green Fees:* information not available. *Eating facilities:* refreshments available. *Visitors:* always welcome anytime, pay and play course. *Society Meetings:* welcome.* website: www.bramcotehillsgolf.com

BULWELL. Bulwell Forest Golf Club, Hucknall Road, Bulwell NG6 9LQ. *Location:* A610 north of Nottingham, M1 Junction 26, three miles from course. Heathland or links type course. 18 holes, 5726 yards. S.S.S. 68. *Green Fees:* £13.00 per round weekdays; £16.00 per round weekends. Offers often available and twilight reductions. *Eating facilities:* bar snacks available, societies or parties catered to order. *Visitors:* welcome weekdays except Tuesday mornings (Ladies' Day) and Saturday morning. Flat green bowls, hard tennis court and children's play ground all on site. *Society Meetings:* catered for every day, but book well in advance. Professional: Barry Hurt (0115 9763172). Secretary: John Bush (0115 9770576). e-mail: barryhurt@hotmail.co.uk

CALVERTON. Ramsdale Park Golf Centre, Oxton Road, Calverton NG14 6NU (0115 965 5600; Fax: 0115 965 4105). *Location:* take the A60 Mansfield road from Nottingham to Redhill roundabout, take Doncaster turn off. Seely, scenic parkland course; Lee, par 3 short course. 18 holes, 6541 yards. S.S.S. 72. 26-bay driving range. *Green Fees:* weekdays Seely £20.50, Lee £10.50; weekends Seely £26.00, Lee £12.50. *Eating facilities:* bar, restaurant, banqueting suites. *Visitors:* welcome any time, Juniors, OAP and student rates available. Eight Professionals on duty. *Society Meetings:* welcome, packages to suit all societies. Professional: Robert Macey. Secretary: Nick Birch (0115 965 5600; Fax: 0115 965 4105). e-mail: info@ramsdaleparkgc.co.uk website: www.ramsdaleparkgc.co.uk

CALVERTON. Springwater Golf Club, Moor Lane, Calverton, Nottingham NG14 6FZ (0115 965 2129). *Location:* off A6097. Moor Lane is one mile south east of Oxton roundabout, course one mile south east of Calverton. Parkland course set in an orchard with new and mature trees, four ponds, well drained. 18 holes, 6262 yards. S.S.S. 71. Floodlit driving range. *Green Fees:* £22.00 weekdays, £27 weekends. *Eating facilities:* fully licensed, bar food, and function rooms available every day. *Visitors:* welcome, weekdays and weekends off peak, seven day booking in advance for non-members. Dress code in operation. *Society Meetings:* weekdays and off peak weekends. Professional: Paul Drew (0115 965 2129). Secretary: Eddie Brady (0115 952 3956).

EAST LEAKE. Rushcliffe Golf Club, Stocking Lane, East Leake, Near Loughborough LE12 5RL (01509 852959). *Location:* on A60 signposted eight miles south of Nottingham. Wooded hills on edge of the Wolds. 18 holes, 6013 yards, 5800 metres. S.S.S. 70. Practice ground. *Green Fees:* information not provided. *Eating facilities*: full catering except Mondays when bar snacks only. *Visitors:* welcome with reservation, weekends without a member between 9.30am to 11am and 3pm to 4.30pm. *Society Meetings:* catered for Mondays, Wednesdays, Thursdays and Fridays strictly by prior booking. Professional: Chris Hall (01509 852701). Secretary: C. Bee (01509 852959). e-mail: secretary@rushcliffegolfclub.com website: www.rushcliffegolfclub.com

EDWALTON. Edwalton Golf Courses, Wellin Lane, Edwalton, Nottingham NG12 4AS (0115 923 4775). *Location:* follow Nottingham ring road, course signposted from roundabout on ring road. Gently sloping parkland. 9 holes, 3342 yards. S.S.S. 72. Also 9 hole par 3 course. Driving range (seasonal). *Green Fees:* prices on application. *Eating facilities:* first class catering, bar open all day. *Visitors:* welcome, book in advance. Professional: Lee Rawlings (0115 923 4775). Secretary: Debbie (0115 923 5473 Mon-Fri 8.30am-12.30pm).

HUCKNALL. Hucknall Golf Centre, Wigwam Lane, Hucknall, Nottingham NG15 7TA (0115 9642037; Fax: 0115 9642724). *Location:* 300 yards from Hucknall Railway Station (signposted). Parkland course. 18 holes, 6001 yards. S.S.S. 70. Driving range, putting green and chipping green. *Green Fees:* weekdays £10.00, weekends £13.00. *Eating facilities:* "Swan" bar and restaurant. *Visitors:* always welcome. Handicap certificates not required. *Society Meetings:* always welcome. Manager: Richard Hanson.

KIRKBY-IN-ASHFIELD. Notts. Golf Club Ltd, Hollinwell, Kirkby-in-Ashfield, Nottingham NG17 7QR (01623 753225; Fax: 01623 753655). *Location:* three miles from Exit 27 on M1, turn off M1 then left on A611. Testing heathland championship course. 18 holes, 7213 yards. S.S.S. 75. *Green Fees:* £66.00 per round, £99.00 per day. *Visitors:* welcome on production of Handicap Certificate (weekends and Bank Holidays on application only). Advisable to book beforehand. *Society Meetings:* welcome weekdays. Professional: Mike Bradley. Secretary: Brian Noble.

LENTON LANE. Riverside Golf Centre, Trentside, Lenton Lane NG7 2SA. *Location:* A52 Nottingham to Grantham, two miles from Nottingham city centre, near Clifton Bridge. Flat course, easy to walk. 9 holes, 2000 yards. S.S.S. 31. Par 3 course. *Green Fees:* information not available. *Eating facilities:* licensed restaurant/bar. Excellent facilities. *Visitors:* welcome all week. Pay and play course, booking required. *Society Meetings:* very welcome. Professionals: Neil Thacker, Russell Meek (0115 9862179; Fax: 01159 865989). Secretary: G. Meek (0115 9862220; Fax: 01159 865989).*

LONG EATON. Trent Lock Golf Centre, Lock Lane, Sawley, Long Eaton, Nottingham NG10 2FY (0115 9464398; Fax: 0115 9461183). *Location:* Sawley/ Long Eaton, two miles from M1 Junctions 24 and 25. Set in rural countryside with six lakes and River Trent. 18 holes, 6000 yards, Par 69. 9 hole Pay and Play, 2990 yards, Par 36. 23 bay floodlit driving range. *Green Fees:* information not provided. *Eating facilities:* à la carte restaurant (0115 9461184), bar food, 200 seater function room. *Visitors:* welcome anytime. *Society Meetings:* all welcome. Professional: Mark Taylor. Director of Golf: E.W. McCausland (0115 9464398).

MANSFIELD. Coxmoor Golf Club, Coxmoor Road, Sutton in Ashfield, Mansfield NG17 5LF (01623 559878). *Location:* exit Junction 27 M1, A611 for three miles. Testing heathland championship course. 18 holes, 6577 yards. S.S.S. 72. Practice area and nets. *Green Fees:* weekdays £40.00 per round, £55.00 per day. Golf/food packages available. *Eating facilities:* restaurant and bars. *Visitors:* welcome except weekends and Bank Holidays, pre-book through Professional. (Tuesday Ladies' Day). *Society Meetings:* catered for by prior application to Secretary. Professional: Craig Wright (01623 559906). Secretary: P. Snow (01623 557359; Fax: 01623 557435). e-mail: coxmoorgc@btconnect.com website: www.coxmoor.freeuk.com

MANSFIELD. Mansfield Woodhouse Golf Club, Leeming Lane North, Mansfield Woodhouse NG19 9EU (01623 23521). *Location:* Junction 27 of M1, A60 Mansfield – Warsop. Flat parkland. 9 holes, 2446 yards. S.S.S. 64. *Green Fees:* information not available. *Eating facilities:* bar snacks. *Visitors:* welcome, unrestricted – pay and play. Professional: L. Highfield Jnr. (01623 23521). Manager/Secretary: S.L. Highfield (01623 623521).*

MANSFIELD. Sherwood Forest Golf Club, Eakring Road, Mansfield NG18 3EW (01623 626689). *Location:* leave M1 at Exit 27, take signs for Mansfield, proceed via Southwell Road and Oak Tree Lane - course is located one mile east on Eakring Road. Traditional heathland course with an abundance of heather, pines and silver birch. 18 holes, 6849 yards. S.S.S. 74. Two practice grounds. *Green Fees:* £50.00 per round, £70.00 per day. *Eating facilities:* bar with snooker table, lounge and dining room; full catering service every day. *Visitors:* welcome by arrangement and must be member of a recognised golf club with a Handicap. *Society Meetings:* catered for by arrangement. Professional: K. Hall (01623 627403; Fax: 01623 420412). e-mail: sherwood@forest43.freeserve.co.uk

www.uk-golfguide.com

MAPPERLEY. **Mapperley Golf Club,** Central Avenue, Plains Road, Mapperley NG3 6RH (0115 9556672). *Location:* B684, four miles north east of centre of Nottingham. Hilly picturesque course. 18 holes, 6335 yards. S.S.S. 70. Practice ground. *Green Fees:* weekdays £22.50 per round; weekends £27.50 per round. *Eating facilities:* bar and food all day. *Visitors:* welcome except Saturdays and Ladies' Day (Tuesdays). *Society Meetings:* catered for, please ring Professional for price. Ass. Professional: John Newham (0115 9556673). Secretary: Michael Mulhearn (0115 9556672).

NEWARK. **Newark Golf Club,** Coddington, Newark NG24 2QX (01636 626282; Fax: 01636 626497). *Location:* off the A17 Sleaford road four miles east of Newark. Parkland, wooded course. 18 holes, 6444 yards. S.S.S. 71. Practice ground. *Green Fees:* £28.00 weekdays; weekends £34.00. *Eating facilities:* full catering, bar all day. *Visitors:* welcome with reservation. Handicap Certificates will be required. Restriction at peak times Saturday and Sunday, Ladies' Day Tuesday. Snooker. Professional tuition and computer/video analysis. *Society Meetings:* welcome except Tuesdays, weekends. Professional: Peter Lockley. Secretary: David Collingwood.

NOTTINGHAM. **Beeston Fields Golf Club,** Old Drive, Wollaton Road, Beeston NG9 3DD (0115 925 7062). *Location:* Wollaton road off A52 Derby road, M1, Exit 25. Parkland. 18 holes, 6430 yards. S.S.S. 71. Practice ground and net available. *Green Fees:* weekdays £33.00, weekends £39.00. *Eating facilities:* available daily. *Visitors:* welcome with reservation, Tuesday not until 2.30pm. *Society Meetings:* catered for Mondays and Wednesdays and Fridays. Professional: Alun Wardle (0115 925 7062). Secretary: J. Lewis (0115 925 7062).
e-mail: beestonfields@btconnect.com
website: www.beestonfields.co.uk

NOTTINGHAM. **Chilwell Manor Golf Club,** Meadow Lane, Chilwell, Nottingham NG9 5AE (0115 925 8958; Fax: 0115 922 0575). *Location:* four miles from Nottingham on main Nottingham to Birmingham road. Flat parkland course. 18 holes, 6379 yards. S.S.S. 70. *Green Fees:* Winter (Nov-March) £30.00 per round; Summer (Apr-Oct) £35.00 per round. *Eating facilities:* available. *Visitors:* welcome weekdays with reservation, restricted at certain busy times. *Society Meetings:* societies catered for by appointment (minimum 16). Professional: P. Wilson. Hon. Secretary: D. Shakespeare.
e-mail: chilwellmanorgolfclub@barbox.net

NOTTINGHAM. **Cotgrave Place Golf and Country Club,** Stragglethorpe, Nottingham NG12 3HB (0115 9333344; Fax: 0115 9334567). *Location:* ten minutes east of Nottingham on the A52 towards Radcliffe-on-Trent, 20 miles from M1. Lakeside and parkland course. Two courses: Open Course 18 holes, 6302 yards; Masters Course 18 holes, 5933 yards. 9 bay floodlit driving range, practice net, short game area, putting green. *Green Fees:* from £24.00 *Eating facilities:* newly refurbished restaurant and snack bar. *Visitors:* welcome at all times, subject to reservation. Conference facilities for up to 200 people. *Society Meetings:* welcome, please telephone for packages. Professional: Robert Smith. General Manager: Nick Leuty.
e-mail: cotgrave@crown-golf.co.uk

NOTTINGHAM. **Nottingham City Golf Club,** Lawton Drive, Bulwell, Nottingham NG6 8LF. *Location:* Exit 26 M1, at first roundabout follow signs for Bulwell. Parkland. 18 holes, 6218 yards. S.S.S. 69. Secretary: David Buxton (0115 927 6916).

NOTTINGHAM. **Oakmere Park Golf Club,** Oaks Lane, Oxton, Near Nottingham NG25 0RH (0115 965 3545; Fax: 0115 965 5628). *Location:* eight miles north east of Nottingham on A614. Parkland course. Admirals Course: 18 holes, 6612 yards, S.S.S. 72. Commanders Course: 9 holes, 6573 yards. S.S.S. 72. 20 bay floodlit driving range. *Green Fees:* from £22.00 weekdays, £32.00 weekends (Admiral's); from £7.00 for 9 holes weekdays (Commander's). *Eating facilities:* clubhouse bar, spike bar, restaurant and resident chef. *Visitors:* welcome at all times, phone to book. *Society Meetings:* welcome, weekends after 2.00pm require maximum notice possible. Professional/ Director of Golf: Daryl St. John Jones.
e-mail: enquiries@oakmerepark.co.uk
website: www.oakmerepark.co.uk

NOTTINGHAM. **Ruddington Grange Golf Club,** Wilford Road, Ruddington, Nottingham NG11 6NB (0115 9214139). *Location:* M1 Junction 24 Nottingham road, A52 to Nottingham Knight island, right to Ruddington, half a mile outside Ruddington. Parkland. 18 holes, 6515 yards. Par 72. S.S.S. 72. *Green Fees:* Information not available. *Eating facilities:* full restaurant. *Visitors:* welcome all the time but at weekends members have priority. Tee times must be booked, *Society Meetings:* welcome Monday to Friday. Professional: R. Simpson (0115 9211951). Secretary: Paul Deacon.*
e-mail: info@ruddingtongrange.co.uk
website: www.ruddingtongrange.co.uk

NOTTINGHAM. **Wollaton Park Golf Club,** Lime Tree Avenue, Wollaton Park, Nottingham NG8 1BT (0115 978 7574; Fax: 0115 970 0736). *Location:* entrance off slip road from A52 Derby Road at junction A614 Nottingham Ringroad. Traditional parkland course with many mature trees; two deer herds roam the course. 18 holes, 6445 yards. S.S.S. 71. Two practice areas and pitch and putt course. *Green Fees:* weekdays £35.00/£48.00; weekends £40.00/£55.00 (2007 rates, subject to review). Special rates on application for visiting societies. *Eating facilities:* full restaurant and snack bar. *Visitors:* welcome at all times except Wednesday which is Ladies' Day. *Society Meetings:* catered for Tuesdays and Fridays. Professional: John Lower (0115 978 4834). Secretary: Avril Jamieson (0115 978 7574).
e-mail: wollatonparkgc@aol.com

RADCLIFFE-ON-TRENT. **Radcliffe-on-Trent Golf Club,** Dewberry Lane, Cropwell Road, Radcliffe-on-Trent NG12 2JH (0115 9333000). *Location:* A52 from Nottingham turn right at traffic lights on Cropwell Road; 400 yards along on left hand side. Flat, wooded parkland. 18 holes, 6374 yards. S.S.S. 71. Two large practice areas. *Green Fees:* weekdays £26.00 per round, £36.00 per day; weekends £33.00 per round, £41.00 per day (reductions for members' guests). *Eating facilities:* snacks, meals and bar. *Visitors:* welcome, confirm course availability with Professional or Secretary. *Society Meetings:* catered for on Wednesdays. Professional: Craig George (l0115 9333000). Secretary: Les Wake (0115 9333000; Fax: 0115 9116991).
e-mail: les.wake@radcliffeontrentgc.co.uk
website: www.radcliffeontrentgc.com

RETFORD. **Retford Golf Club Ltd,** Brecks Road, Ordsall, Retford DN22 7UA (01777 711188). *Location:* one mile south off A620 midway between Worksop and Gainsborough. Wooded parkland. 18 holes, 6409 yards. S.S.S. 72, Par 72. Practice ground. *Green Fees:* information not provided. *Eating facilities:* meals available and licensed bar. *Visitors:* welcome, except Tuesday mornings. *Society Meetings:* welcome by prior arrangement. Professional: C. Morris (01777 703733). Secretary (01777 711188; Fax: 01777 710412).

RUFFORD. **Rufford Park Golf & Country Club,** Rufford Lane, Rufford, Newark NG22 9DG (01623 825253; Fax: 01623 825254). *Location:* 400 yards off A614, two miles south of Ollerton roundabout. Map available on request. Scenic parkland course. 18 holes, 6368 yards. S.S.S. 71. 16-bay floodlit driving range, practice facilities. *Green Fees:* weekday £22.00, weekend £28.00 (subject to review for 2008). *Eating facilities:* clubhouse and restaurant with spectacular views. Large function suite and meeting rooms for up to 200 people. *Visitors:* always welcome; buggies for hire. *Society Meetings:* corporate hospitality and society days catered for. *Professionals:* James Thompson and John Vaughan. Secretary: Kay Whitehead.
website: www.ruffordpark.co.uk

SOUTHWELL. **Norwood Park Golf Course Ltd,** Norwood Park, Southwell NG25 0PF (01636 816626). *Location:* half-a-mile west of Southwell, off the road to Kirklington. American-style layout parkland course in beautiful grounds of stately home. Natural water features and large undulating greens. 18-acre grass practice ground. 18 holes, 6805 yards from the back tees. Par 72. *Green Fees:* from £20.00. *Eating facilities:* available. *Visitors:* always welcome. 2-Fore-1 welcome any day. *Society Meetings:* always welcome. Conference facilities in stately home available. Professional: Paul Thornton. Secretary: Ron Beckett. Manager: Henry Starkey.
e-mail: golf@norwoodpark.co.uk
website: www.norwoodpark.co.uk

SOUTHWELL. **Southwell Golf Club,** Southwell Racecourse, Rolleston, Newark NG25 0TS (01636 816501/813706). Flat parkland course with water features. 18 holes, 5767 yards, S.S.S. 68. Driving nets, pitching, putting green, practice area. *Green Fees:* weekdays £18.00, with member £10.00; weekends £21.00, with member £12.00. *Eating facilities:* full service all day. *Visitors:* welcome, please book in advance. 12 bedroomed Motel on site. Professional: Chris White (01636 813706). Secretary: Mike Harness (01636 821651).
e-mail: misylharness@btinternet.com

STANTON-ON-THE-WOLDS. **Stanton-on-the-Wolds Golf Club,** Golf Course Road, Stanton-on-the-Wolds NG12 5BH (0115 937 4885). *Location:* seven miles south of Nottingham, one mile west of main Nottingham-Melton road. Meadow land. 18 holes, 6184 yards, 5708 metres. S.S.S. 70 (yellow tees). Practice ground. *Green Fees:* information not available. *Eating facilities:* restaurant and bar. *Visitors:* welcome by prior arrangement with Secretary, weekends with member only. *Society Meetings:* catered for by arrangement with Secretary. Professional: Nick Hernon (0115 937 2390). Secretary: Michael J. Price (0115 937 4885).
e-mail: info@stantongc.co.uk
website: www.stantongc.co.uk

THE APPEARANCE OF AN ASTERISK (*) AT THE END OF A CLUB OR COURSE ENTRY INDICATES THAT UP-TO-DATE INFORMATION HAS NOT BEEN SUPPLIED

WORKSOP. **Bondhay Golf Club,** Bondhay Lane, Whitwell, Worksop S80 3EH (01909 723608 Fax: 01909 720226. *Location:* from Junction 30 M1, A619 signposted after three-and-a-half miles. Turn left onto Bondhay lane. Flat with bordering woodland. 18 holes, 6839 yards. S.S.S.72. Par 3 family course, floodlit driving range, putting green, buggies for hire. *Green Fees:* information not provided. *Eating facilities:* full catering service available. *Visitors:* welcome. *Society Meetings:* welcome, phone for brochure. Golf Professional: M. Ramsden. Director: Helen Hardisty.

WORKSOP. **College Pines Golf Club,** Worksop College Drive, Worksop S80 3AL (Clubhouse 01909 488785; Pro Shop: 01909 501431; Fax: 01909 481227). *Location:* situated on outskirts of town on B6034, Edwinstowe road adjacent to Worksop College. Heathland course surrounded by woodland; very well drained, with Winter play a speciality. 18 holes, 6801 yards. S.S.S. 73. Driving range and short game practice area. *Green Fees:* weekdays £15.00 per round, £10.00 with a member; weekends £22.00 per round, £13.00 with a member. Subject to review. *Eating facilities:* full facilities. *Visitors:* welcome by appointment; phone for starting times. *Society Meetings:* welcome by appointment. Golf Director/Professional: Charles Snell (01909 501431). website: www.collegepinesgolfclub.co.uk

WORKSOP. **Kilton Forest Golf Club,** Blyth Road, Worksop S81 0TL (01909 479199). *Location:* main Worksop to Blyth road, right hand side. Undulating parkland. 18 holes, 6424 yards. S.S.S. 71, Par 72. Practice and putting areas. *Green Fees:* information not available. *Eating facilities:* bar meals and restaurant area. *Visitors:* welcome, club competitions most Sundays – check with Professional. *Society Meetings:* by arrangement with Professional. Professional: Stuart Betteridge (01909 486563). Secretary: Alan Mansbridge.*

WORKSOP. **Lindrick Golf Club,** Lindrick Common, Worksop S81 8BH (01909 485802). *Location:* on A57 four miles west of Worksop. M1 Junction 31 on to A57 Worksop. Heathland. 18 holes, 6612 yards, 6046 metres. S.S.S. 71. Two practice areas. *Green Fees:* summer £50.00 per round, £65.00 per day; winter (1 Nov–31 Mar) £35.00 per round, £45.00 Sundays. *Eating facilities:* dining room and Ryder Cup Room. *Visitors:* welcome weekdays, except Tuesday mornings. Enquire re Sunday availability. Prior booking required. *Society Meetings:* catered for weekdays. Professional: John King (01909 475820). Secretary: John Armitage (01909 475282; Fax: 01909 488685).
website: www.lindrickgolfclub.co.uk

WORKSOP. **Worksop Golf Club,** Windmill Lane, Worksop S80 2SQ (01909 477731; Fax: 01909 477732). *Location:* just off Worksop bypass (A57), take B6034 Edwinstowe immediately left; clubhouse 400 yards. Heathland with gorse, broom, birch and oak; easy walking. 18 holes, 6660 yards. S.S.S. 72. Practice ground. *Green Fees:* weekdays 18 holes £40.00 per day weekends £55.00 (18 holes only). *Eating facilities:* dining room and bar. *Visitors:* welcome Mondays, Wednesdays and Fridays. Advise preliminary phone call to Professional. Snooker table. *Society Meetings:* weekdays only by arrangement with Professional. Not Bank Holidays. Professional: K. Crossland (01909 477731). Secretary: D.A. Dufall 01909 477731; Fax: 01909 530917).

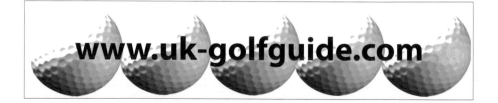

Shropshire

BRIDGNORTH. **Bridgnorth Golf Club,** Stanley Lane, Bridgnorth WV16 4SF (01746 763315; Fax: 01746 763315). *Location:* one mile from town centre on Broseley road. Parkland, alongside River Severn. 18 holes, 6582 yards. S.S.S. 73. Practice ground. *Green Fees:* weekdays £25.00, weekends £35.00. *Eating facilities:* full catering available except Mondays. *Visitors:* welcome weekdays except Wednesday. Handicap Certificate or bona fide club membership required. *Society Meetings:* catered for Monday, Tuesday, Thursday, Friday only. Professional: Paul Hinton. Secretary: G.C. Kelsall.

BRIDGNORTH. **Chesterton Valley Golf Club,** Chesterton, Near Worfield, Bridgnorth WV15 5NX (01746 783682). *Location:* B4176 Dudley/Telford road. 18 holes, Par 71. *Green Fees:* £16.00. *Visitors:* no restrictions but can book 24 hours in advance. Professional/Secretary: Philip Hinton.

BRIDGNORTH. **Severn Meadows Golf Club,** Highley, Bridgnorth (01746 862212). *Location:* seven miles from Bridgnorth on B4555. Eight miles from Bewdley on B4194, then on to B4555. Signposted from village. Undulating woodland course. Severn Valley Steam Railway runs through the middle of the course, on the banks of the River Severn. 18 holes, 6388 yards. S.S.S. 70. *Green Fees:* £15.00 weekdays, £20.00 weekends and Bank Holidays. *Eating facilities:* by arrangement. *Visitors:* welcome anytime weekdays but must book tee times at weekends. *Society Meetings:* by arrangement only, contact Ann Jones (01746 861046). Secretary: Colin Harrison (01746 861296).

CHURCH STRETTON. **Church Stretton Golf Club,** Trevor Hill, Church Stretton SY6 6JH (01694 722281). *Location*: one mile west of A49, adjacent to Carding Mill Valley. Set on the lower slopes of the Longmynd Hills, with wonderful springy turf and panoramic views of the surrounding country. No winter greens. 18 holes, 5020 yards. S.S.S. 65. *Green Fees*: information not available. *Eating facilities*: meals and snacks available daily, full bar facilities. *Visitors*: welcome, Saturdays not between 9am and 10.30am and 1pm to 2.30pm (Winter 12noon to 1.30pm), Sundays not before 10.30am or between 1pm and 2.30pm (Winter 12noon to 1.30pm). *Society Meetings*: welcome. Contact Hon. Secretary or Professional to pre-book. Professional: James Townsend (01694 722281; mobile: 07973 762510). Hon. Secretary John Povall (01743 860679; mobile: 07817 538080).*
e-mail: secretary@churchstrettongolfclub.co.uk
website: www.churchstrettongolfclub.co.uk

CLEOBURY MORTIMER. **Cleobury Mortimer Golf Club,** Wyre Common, Cleobury Mortimer, Near Kidderminster DY14 8HQ (01299 271112). *Location:* two miles out of Cleobury on B4201. 27 hole course comprising three loops of nine holes. Badgers Sett 3271 yards, Foxes Run 2960 yards, Deer Park 3167 yards, giving three 18 hole courses with S.S.S. 71, 70, 69. *Green Fees:* weekdays £24.00 per round (£14.00 with member), £30.00 per day; weekends £32.00 per round (£16.00 with member), £36.00 per day. *Eating facilities:* restaurant and Spike Bar. *Visitors:* welcome midweek; weekends by arrangement. Snooker room. Golf Buggies for hire £17.00 per round, trolleys £3.00 per round bookable in advance. *Society Meetings:* welcome by prior arrangement, ring for details. PGA Professional: Martin Payne (01299 271112). Director of Golf: Jon Jones. Secretary/Manager: Graham Pain (01299 271112; Fax: 01299 271468).
e-mail: enquiries@cleoburygolfclub.com
website: www.cleoburygolfclub.com

LUDLOW. **Elm Lodge Golf Course,** Elm Lodge, Fishmore, Ludlow SY8 3DP (01584 872308; Fax: 01584 877397). *Location:* from the A49 Ludlow bypass turn towards Ludlow town centre at the roundabout junction A4117 Kidderminster road; after 1/3 mile turn right. Various types of terrain. 9 holes, 1051 yards, Par 3, S.S.S. 27. *Green Fees:* adults £5.00, under 16s £4.00. Discounts for groups of 10 or more. *Visitors:* welcome, pay-and play course. Accommodation available in Elm Lodge.
e-mail: info@elm-lodge.org.uk
website: www.elm-lodge.org.uk

LUDLOW. **Ludlow Golf Club,** Bromfield, Ludlow SY8 2BT (01584 856285; Fax: 01584 856366). *Location:* A49 one mile north of Ludlow bypass, turn right onto the Bridgnorth road. Well signposted. Heathland course based on sandy soil providing springy fairways and superb greens. 18 holes, 6277 yards. S.S.S. 70. Practice ground. *Green Fees:* weekdays £28.00 per round, £35.00 a day; weekends £35.00 per round (reductions with member). Subject to review. *Eating facilities:* full catering and bar service during normal hours. *Visitors:* welcome weekdays and weekends with prior booking. *Society Meetings:* call for details. Professional/Administrator: R. Price (Pro Shop: 01584 856366; Admin: 01584 856285).

MARKET DRAYTON. **Market Drayton Golf Club,** Sutton, Market Drayton TF9 2HX (01630 652266). *Location:* A41 south towards Newport, turn left at crossroads just past Tern Hill Barracks. Parkland with exceptional views. 18 holes, 6214 yards, 5702 metres. S.S.S. 71. *Green Fees:* £28.00. *Eating facilities:* bar and high class catering open all day. *Visitors:* welcome weekdays only; first tee closed daily until 9.30am and from 12.30pm to 1.30pm. Tuesday Ladies' Day. On-course bungalow (sleeps 6) available from £650.00 weekly including FREE golf. *Society Meetings:* catered for weekdays by prior arrangement. Professional: Russell Clewes (01630 656237). Secretary: Chris Stubbs (01630 652266). Stewardess: Helen Crocket (01630 658083).
e-mail: marketdraytongc@btconnect.com

NEWPORT. **Aqualate Golf Centre,** Stafford Road, Newport TF10 9DB (01952 811699). *Location:* two miles east of Newport town centre; 400 yards from the junction with A41. Parkland course with gentle gradients and water hazards. 18 holes, 5659 yards. S.S.S. 67. 20 bay floodlit driving range, practice putting green. *Green Fees:* weekdays 9 holes £8.00, 18 holes £13.00; weekends 9 holes £10.00, 18 holes £16.00. *Eating facilities:* coffee bar. *Visitors:* welcome at all times (pay and play), but advance booking advisable. No handicap restrictions. PGA Professional tuition available by appointment - group and/or personal lessons. Golf Club Memberships available. *Society Meetings:* welcome by prior arrangement. Hire clubs and trolleys available. Opening hours: weekdays 9.00am to 10.00pm, weekends and Bank Holidays 7.30am to 9.00pm. Professional: Kevin Short (01952 811699). Director: H. Brian Dawes (01952 811699).

NEWPORT. **Lilleshall Hall Golf Club,** Lilleshall, Near Newport TF10 9AS (01952 604776; Fax: 01952 604272). *Location:* at Lillyhurst turn north off Abbey Road, which joins Wellington Road near Lilleshall and the B4379 near Sheriffhales. Wooded parkland. 18 holes, 5813 yards. S.S.S. 68. Practice ground. *Green Fees:* £30.00 midweek, £40.00 weekends (with approval). *Eating facilities:* meals served 10am to 5.30pm, order in advance. *Visitors:* welcome on weekdays, check with Professional for tee restrictions. *Society Meetings:* catered for by prior arrangement with Secretary. Professional: R. Bluck. Secretary: A. Marklew.
e-mail: honsec@lhgc.entadsl.com
website: www.lillieshallgolfclub.co.uk

OSWESTRY. **Llanymynech Golf Club,** Pant, Near Oswestry SY10 8LB (01691 830542). *Location:* six miles south of Oswestry on A483, turn at Cross Guns Inn, Pant. Undulating lush hilltop course with extensive views, 15 holes in Wales, three in England. 18 holes, 6047 yards. S.S.S. 69. Practice area and putting green. *Green Fees:* (2006) weekdays £25.00 per round, £35.00 per day; weekends £30.00 per round. Under review. Half price with member. Reductions for Juniors. *Eating facilities:* restaurant and bar. *Visitors:* welcome weekdays; some weekends by prior arrangement; prior enquiry advisable. *Society Meetings:* weekdays by arrangement with Secretary. Professional: A.P. Griffiths (01691 830879). Secretary: Howard Jones (01691 830983).
website: www.llanymynechgolfclub.co.uk

OSWESTRY. **Mile End Golf Club,** Mile End, Oswestry SY11 4JF (01691 671246 (bookings); Fax: 01691 670580). *Location:* signposted off A5, one mile south-east of Oswestry. Gently undulating course with water features. 18 holes, 6292 yards. S.S.S. 70. Driving range. *Green Fees:* weekdays £18.00 per round, £27.00 per day; weekends £26.00 per round, £39.00 per day. *Eating facilities:* full bar/catering available. *Visitors:* welcome at all times subject to course availability. Extensively stocked quality golf shop with all top name brands. *Society Meetings:* welcome weekdays by prior arrangement. Professional: Scott Carpenter (01691 671246). Secretary: Richard Thompson (01691 671246; Fax: 01691 670580)
e-mail: info@mileendgolfclub.co.uk
website: www.mileendgolfclub.co.uk

27 unique holes set in 200 acres of Shropshire's most beautiful countryside

At Cleobury Mortimer Golf Club we believe that a really enjoyable game of golf takes more than just a great golf course. We make sure that your whole experience – from the friendly welcome in the golf shop to your drinks and meal in our relaxed clubhouse – is all part of a day that you'll remember.

27 holes set out in three individual 9-hole loops, covering 200 acres of Shropshire's most beautiful countryside. Each hole is designed to a very high specification, with its own character and challenge.

A Clubhouse with excellent facilities, from a full-sized antique snooker table and spike bar, – to everything a modern club must have. Choice of refreshment and dining areas to suit all tastes – open 7 days. Golf Shop with wide range of stock from all the leading brands.

Cleobury Mortimer Golf Club
Wyre Common, Cleobury Mortimer, Shropshire DY14 8HQ
Enquiries: 01299 271112 • Fax: 01299 271468
e-mail: enquiries@cleoburygolfclub.com
www.cleoburygolfclub.com

Self Catering Holiday Cottages **available on site**

Once described as the Pine Valley of England, quietly tucked away in rolling Shropshire countryside, this picturesque, relatively flat and easy walking course is a popular favourite with visiting golfers. A 5813 yard course set in 165 acres, with tight fairways cutting through mature trees with undulating greens.

Lilleshall Hall Golf Club, Lilleshall, Newport, Shropshire TF10 9AS
Tel: 01952 604776 Fax: 01952 604372
e-mail: honsec@lhgc.entadsl.com • www.lilleshallhallgolfclub.co.uk

The Shropshire, Telford, Shropshire

OSWESTRY. **Oswestry Golf Club,** Aston Park, Queen's Head, Oswestry SY11 4JJ. *Location:* a friendly members' club four miles south-east of Oswestry on A5. Mature parkland course with many feature trees, laid out by James Braid in rolling Shropshire countryside. Well drained soils ensure excellent year-round play. 18 holes, 6038 yards. S.S.S. 69. Practice ground. *Green Fees:* Sunday–Friday £28.00, Saturdays £32.00, Twilight £15.00. *Eating facilities:* dining room and bar. *Visitors:* welcome; must be member of another club with a recognised Handicap Certificate or playing with a member. Snooker table. *Society Meetings:* societies of 16 plus welcomed Wednesdays and Fridays by arrangement with the Secretary. Smaller groups catered for by arrangement with the Professional. Professional: David Skelton (01691 610448). Secretary: Peter Turner (Tel & Fax: 01691 610535).
e-mail: secretary@oswestrygolfclub.co.uk
website: www.oswestrygolfclub.co.uk

SHIFNAL. **Shifnal Golf Club,** Decker Hill, Shifnal TF11 8QL (Tel & Fax: 01952 460330). *Location:* one mile north east of Shifnal, one mile from A5, Junction 4 M54. Parkland course. 18 holes, 6504 yards. S.S.S. 71. *Green Fees:* £30.00 per round, £40.00 per day; weekends with member only. *Eating facilities:* full catering service. *Visitors:* welcome, phone first, not Thursdays, weekends or Bank Holidays. *Society Meetings:* catered for by arrangement with Secretary. Professional: D. Ashton (01952 461560). Secretary: N.R. Milton (Tel & Fax: 01952 460330).
e-mail: secretary@shifnalgolfclub.co.uk
website: www.shifnalgolfclub.co.uk

SHREWSBURY. **Arscott Golf Club,** Arscott, Pontesbury, Shrewsbury SY5 0XP (Tel & Fax: 01743 860114). *Location:* 10 minutes from Shrewsbury off the A488 Bishops Castle road. Set in mature parkland with stunning views of South Shropshire and Welsh Borders. 18 holes, 6158 yards. S.S.S. 69. Practice area, putting green and driving net. *Green Fees:* £20.00 weekdays; £25.00 weekends. *Eating facilities:* food and beverages available from 10.30am daily. *Visitors:* welcome at all times. Please telephone Shop to book tees. Self-catering cottage available. *Society Meetings:* by arrangement, please telephone. Secretary: Miss Sian Cadwallader (01743 860114 or 01743 860881).

SHREWSBURY. **Hawkstone Park,** Weston-under-Redcastle, Shrewsbury SY4 5UY (01939 200611; Fax: 01939 200311). *Location:* 14 miles north of Shrewsbury off A49. Hawkstone Course – parkland, 18 holes, 6491 yards (white). S.S.S. 71; Windmill Course – parkland (designed by Brian Huggett), 18 holes, 6476 yards (white). S.S.S. 71; Academy Par 3 Course – 6 holes, 741 yards. Par 18, S.S.S. 18. Target practice ground, putting green and short game area. Open all year. *Green Fees:* information not available. Eating facilities: Terrace Room, all day bar and restaurant. *Visitors:* welcome. 66 room Hotel and Historic park. *Society Meetings:* welcome. Reservations for bookings: 01939 200611. Professional: Stuart Leech (01939 200611).*
e-mail: bookings@hawkstone.co.uk
website: www.hawkstone.co.uk

SHREWSBURY. **Shrewsbury Golf Club,** Condover, Shrewsbury SY5 7BL (Tel & Fax: 01743 872977). *Location:* A49 two miles south west of Shrewsbury. Parkland first 9 holes, undulating back 9 holes with fine views of Longmynd. 18 holes, 6207 yards. S.S.S. 70. Large practice ground. *Green Fees:* £28.00 per round, £34.00 per day weekdays; £32.00 per round, £39.00 per day weekends and Bank Holidays. *Eating facilities:* full facilities available seven days. *Visitors:* welcome at all times except Wednesday mornings and weekends before 10am. *Society Meetings:* welcome by arrangement. Professional: Peter Seal (01743 872977). Secretary: Mrs S.M. Kenny (01743 872977).
e-mail: info@shrewsbury-golf-club.co.uk

TELFORD. **The Shropshire,** Muxton, Telford TF2 8PQ (01952 677800; Fax: 01952 677622). *Location:* off Junction 4 of M54, follow signs for Muxton (signposted). Parkland course featuring many water hazards, wide, American-type fairways, and undulating well-bunkered greens. Three loops of 9 holes (Blue, Silver, Gold): 27 holes, 3286 yards, 3303 yards, 3334 yards, S.S.S. 71, 72, 72. 30 bay floodlit driving range, 12 hole short course, 18 hole putting green. *Green Fees:* information not available. *Eating facilities:* Greenkeeper Bar and Grill, Conservatory Restaurant. *Visitors:* welcome, no restrictions. Pay as you Play. 15 buggies, golf school. *Society Meetings:* very welcome, packages available. Professional: Rob Grier.

TELFORD. **Telford Golf & Spa Hotel,** Great Hay Drive, Sutton Heights, Telford TF7 4DT (01952 429977; Fax: 01952 586602). *Location:* turn off A442 between Bridgnorth and Telford, only two miles to M54 Junction 4. Hotel overlooks Ironbridge Gorge - a World Heritage site. Rolling parkland course with water features, suspended water table greens as at Augusta. 18 holes, 6741 yards (whites). S.S.S. 72. All-weather driving range, two putting greens. *Green Fees:* information on request. *Eating facilities:* bar and refreshments adjacent 18th green. 114 bedrooms, restaurant, leisure and spa suite and indoor heated pool (half Olympic size). *Visitors:* welcome, but advance booking essential. Handicap Certificates or membership of bona fide golf club essential. *Society Meetings:* by arrangement. Private room available. Professional: George Boden (01952 586052). Secretary: Ian Lucas (01952 429977).
e-mail: telford@qhotels.co.uk

TELFORD. **Wrekin Golf Club,** Ercall Woods, Golf Links Lane, Wellington, Telford TF6 5BX (01952 244032; Fax: 01952 252906). *Location:* from M54 Junction 7 to Wellington, turn back along Holyhead road towards Wellington for three-quarters-of-a-mile. Golf Links Lane on right hand side. Undulating parkland. 18 holes, 5570 yards. S.S.S. 67. Small practice ground. *Green Fees:* midweek £22.00 per round, £30.00 per day, weekends £30.00 per round. *Eating facilities:* restaurant and bar facilities by arrangement with Stewardess. *Visitors:* welcome except weekends and Bank Holidays when limited. *Society Meetings:* by arrangement with the Secretary. Professional: K. Housden (01952 223101). Secretary: D. Briscoe (01952 244032; Fax: 01952 252906).

WHITCHURCH. **Macdonald Hill Valley Hotel Golf and Country Club,** Terrick Road, Whitchurch SY13 4JZ (01948 667788; Fax: 01948 667373). *Location:* signposted from Whitchurch Bypass. Magnificent Alliss/Thomas Emerald Championship Course. 18 holes, 6628 yards. Par 73. Sapphire Course 4801 yards, Par 66. *Green Fees:* information not available. *Eating facilities:* full restaurant/bars, snacks available. *Visitors:* welcome without reservation. Luxury 90 bedroom 4-star hotel; leisure facilities also available. *Society Meetings:* please contact for details. Professional: Graeme Bagnall (01948 663032). Secretary: John Pickering (01948 860425).*
e-mail: general.hillvalley@macdonald-hotels.co.uk
website: www.hillvalleygolfclub.co.uk

WOLVERHAMPTON. **Patshull Park Hotel, Golf and Country Club,** Patshull Park, Pattingham, Near Wolverhampton WV6 7HR (01902 700100; Fax: 01902 700874). *Location:* take Junction 3 off M54, turn left on A41 back towards Wolverhampton and fork right into Albrighton. From main crossroads turn right along Cross Road, taking T-junction with A464 Wolverhampton/Shifnal Road and turning right towards Shifnal. Signposted Patshull Park Golf Course. Glorious parkland course set in landscapes by Capability Brown; John Jacobs designed course. 18 holes, 6345 yards. S.S.S. 69. Large practice area. *Green Fees:* £40.00 per 18 holes. Please pre-book. Handicap Certificates required. *Eating facilities:* Lakeside Restaurant and two bars. Earl's Bar. *Visitors:* welcome on application. 49 bedroom hotel, country club and swimming pool, fishing lakes (80 acres). Residential Breaks. Buggies available. *Society Meetings:* corporate and society meetings welcome; special group rates and facilities. Professional: Richard Bissell (01902 700342).
website: www.patshull-park.co.uk

WORFIELD. **Worfield Golf Club,** Roughton, Worfield, Near Bridgnorth WV15 5HE (01746 716541; Fax:01746 716302). *Location:* A454 Wolverhampton to Bridgnorth Road, three miles from Bridgnorth. Parkland course set on rolling countryside. 18 holes, 6440 yards. S.S.S. 71. Chipping area, practice area, putting greens. *Green Fees:* weekdays £20.00. weekends after 1pm £25.00. *Eating facilities:* restaurant and bar meals all day. *Visitors:* welcome. Buggies available. *Society meetings:* all welcome. Professional: Stephen Russell (01746 716541). Secretary: William Weaver (01746 716372; Fax: 01746 716302).

Staffordshire

BARLASTON. **Barlaston Golf Club,** Meaford Road, Stone ST15 8UX (Tel & Fax: 01782 372795). *Location:* one mile south of Barlaston off A34; between Stoke and Stone. 18 holes, 5801 yards. S.S.S. 68. *Green Fees:* weekdays £35.00 per day, £23.00 for 18 holes. weekend £40.00 per day, £35.00 for 18 holes. *Eating facilities:* dining room and bar snacks with lounge bar. *Visitors:* welcome anytime. *Society Meetings:* welcome weekdays. Professional: Ian Rogers. Secretary: M. Emberton (01782 372867; Fax: 01782 373648). e-mail: barlaston.gc@virgin.net
website: www.bgc.evelplay.net

BURTON UPON TRENT. **The Branston Golf and Country Club,** Burton Road, Branston, Burton upon Trent DE14 3DP (01283 512211; Fax: 01283 566984). *Location:* A38 Junction A5121. Flat parkland adjacent to the River Trent, spectacular 18th hole, water on 13 holes (flowing). 18 holes, 6697 yards. S.S.S. 72. 9 holes 1856 yards. S.S.S. 58. Driving range. *Green Fees:* information not available. *Eating facilities:* restaurant, bar, spikes bar, private rooms. *Visitors:* welcome, two week advance booking system in operation, restrictions weekends. Buggy hire, trolleys available. Country Club has extensive leisure facilities. *Society Meetings:* welcome midweek, special rates. Professional: Iain Ross (01283 512211; Fax: 01283 566984). Golf and Estates Manager: Graham Pyle (01283 512211; Fax: 01283 566984).*

BURTON UPON TRENT. **The Craythorne,** Craythorne Road, Rolleston on Dove, Burton upon Trent DE13 0AZ (01283 564329; Fax: 01283 511908). *Location:* A38 first turning to Burton from Derby, A5121 signposted Stretton. Parkland. 18 holes, 5602 yards. S.S.S. 68. Floodlit driving range, pitch and putt course. *Green Fees:* £22.00 per round, twilight price varies. *Eating facilities:* bars and restaurant open daily; function room. *Visitors:* welcome at all times, booking required at weekends. Special society and golfing packages. *Society Meetings:* welcome, prices from £28.50 for parties of 12 and over. Professional: Steve Hadfield (01283 533745). Managing Director: Tony Wright. e-mail: admin@craythorne.co.uk
website: www.craythorne.co.uk

CANNOCK. **Beau Desert Golf Club,** Rugeley Road, Hazel Slade, Cannock WS12 0PJ (01543 422626; Fax: 01543 451137). *Location:* A460 Hednesford, signposted. Fowler-designed heathland course. 18 holes, 6310 yards. S.S.S. 71. Driving range, practice ground. *Green Fees:* £45.00 weekdays; £55.00 weekends. *Eating facilities:* full catering and bar. *Visitors:* welcome anytime subject to availability. *Society Meetings:* catered for Monday to Thursday.

Professional: Barrie Stevens (01543 422492). Secretary: John Bradbury.
website: www.bdgc.co.uk

CANNOCK. **Cannock Park Golf Club,** Stafford Road, Cannock WS11 2AL (01543 578850). *Location:* on the A34 Stafford Road, quarter of a mile from Cannock town centre. Parkland course, playing alongside Cannock Chase. 18 holes, 5149 yards. S.S.S. 65. *Green Fees:* £11.50 weekdays; £14.50 weekends (am), £11.50 weekends (pm). Phone bookings up to two weeks in advance. Reductions for Juniors. *Eating facilities:* available. *Visitors:* welcome every day. Golf shop, inside leisure centre. *Society Meetings:* welcome weekdays. Pro-shop (01543 578850). Secretary: Chris Milne (01543 571091).

CHEADLE near. **Whiston Hall Golf Club and Mansion Court Hotel,** Whiston, Near Cheadle ST10 2HZ (01538 266260). *Location:* A52 Stoke to Ashbourne road, three miles from Alton Towers. Scenic course set in beautiful countryside. 18 holes, 5784 yards. S.S.S. 69. *Green Fees:* £10.00 per round. *Eating facilities:* extensive Clubhouse Bar Menu available from 8.00am onwards. *Visitors:* welcome at any time. Golfing theme rooms for all types of golfing breaks. Snooker, fly fishing. *Society Meetings:* all welcome 7 days a week. 27 hole package and lunch, three course evening meal from £29.95 per person. Golf breaks also available from £49.95 per person. Secretary: R. Cliff.

LEEK. **Leek Golf Club,** Cheddleton Road, Birchall, Leek ST13 5RE (01538 384779). *Location:* one mile south of Leek on A520. Undulating parkland. 18 holes, 6218 yards. S.S.S. 70. *Green Fees:* weekdays £26.00; weekends and Bank Holidays £32.00. *Eating facilities:* full catering facilities 11.30am-11pm. Light refreshments from 10am. *Visitors:* welcome most times by prior arrangement. *Society Meetings:* catered for by arrangement Wednesdays (limited availability on Mondays and Fridays). Catering (01538 384779). PGA Professional: Fred Fearn. Secretary: David T. Brookhouse (Tel & Fax: 01538 384779).

LEEK. **Leek Westwood Golf Club,** Newcastle Road, Leek ST13 7AA (01538 398385). *Location:* A53 one and a half miles south of Leek. Moorland/ parkland. 18 holes, 6207 yards. S.S.S. 70. Practice area, nets, chipping green. *Green Fees:* information not available. *Eating facilities:* full facilities. *Visitors:* welcome weekdays. *Society Meetings:* weekdays by arrangement. Professional: Darren Squire (01538 398897). Secretary: A.J. Horton (Tel & Fax: 01538 398385; Fax: 01538 382485). Club Administrator: Carol Povey.

LICHFIELD. **The Seedy Mill Golf Club,** Elmhurst, Near Lichfield WS13 8HE (01543 417333; Fax: 01543 418098). *Location:* just off A51 north of Lichfield. Parkland with lakes, ponds and streams. The Mill: 18 holes, 6305 yards. S.S.S. 70; The Spires: 9 holes, Par 3. 26 bay floodlit driving range. *Green Fees:* information not available. *Eating facilities:* full clubhouse facilities open 7.30am to 11pm. *Visitors:* welcome at all times. *Society Meetings:* welcome weekdays and weekends. Professional: Simon Joyce. Secretary: Abi Burns. General Manager: Richard Gee.*

LICHFIELD. **Whittington Heath Golf Club,** Tamworth Road, Lichfield WS14 9PW (01543 432317). *Location:* on A51 Tamworth-Lichfield Road. Wooded heathland. 18 holes, 6490 yards. S.S.S. 71. Practice ground. *Green Fees:* weekdays £40.00 per round, £50.00 36 holes. *Eating facilities:* meals available at all times. *Visitors:* welcome weekdays only. Handicap Certificate or letter of introduction required. *Society Meetings:* catered for Wednesdays and Thursdays by arrangement. Professional: Adrian Sadler (01543 432261). Secretary: Mrs J.A. Burton (01543 432317; Fax: 01543 433962). Steward: 01543 432212. e-mail: info@whittingtonheathgc.co.uk website: www.whittingtonheathgc.co.uk

NEWCASTLE-UNDER-LYME. **Jack Barkers Keele Golf Centre,** Keele Road, Newcastle-under-Lyme ST5 5AB (01782 627596). *Location:* A525 Newcastle to Whitchurch, opposite University of Keele. Undulating parkland. 18 holes, 6396 yards, 5822 metres. S.S.S. 70. Driving range. *Green Fees:* information not available. *Eating facilities:* available. *Visitors:* welcome at all times. Hire: Buggies £10.00 per round; Clubs £6.00 per round; Trolleys £2.50 per round. *Society Meetings:* welcome by arrangement. Manager: Mr N. Worrall.*

NEWCASTLE-UNDER-LYME. **Newcastle-under-Lyme Golf Club,** Whitmore Road, Newcastle-under-Lyme ST5 2QB (01782 616583). *Location:* M6 Junction 15, one mile from Newcastle-under-Lyme. Parkland. 18 holes, 6395 yards white, 6276 yards yellow. S.S.S. 71 white, 70 yellow. *Green Fees:* £25.00 for 18 holes, £35.00 for 36 holes. *Eating facilities:* restaurant and bar meals. *Visitors:* welcome. Restrictions at weekends. *Society Meetings:* welcome most week days except Tuesdays by arrangement. Contact Secretary/Manager for details. Professional: Ashley Salt (01782 618526). Secretary/Manager: Vicki Wiseman (01782 617006).

PENKRIDGE. **The Chase Golf Club,** Pottal Pool Road, Penkridge ST19 5RN (01785 712191). *Location:* M6 Junction 13, take the A449 to Wolverhampton, then left onto B5012 towards Cannock then onto Rugeley Road. Flat parkland with Links characteristics. 18 holes, 6613 yards. S.S.S. 71. 20 bay floodlit driving range and teaching academy. Putting green, bunker, and chip and run facility. *Green Fees:* information not provided. *Eating facilities:* excellent clubhouse facilities. *Visitors:* please ring to book, members have priority. Fully stocked pro shop. *Society Meetings:* welcome at reduced rates. Professional: Michael Beaumont. General Manager: Sean Hall.*

RUGELEY. **Lakeside Golf Club,** Rugeley Power Station, Armitage Road, Rugeley WS15 1PR (01889 575667). *Location:* nearest town Rugeley (between Lichfield and Stafford), course over power station grounds. Flat parkland adjacent River Trent. 18 holes, 5765 yards. S.S.S. 68. *Green Fees:* £10.00 with member. *Eating facilities:* bar, lunchtime weekends and every evening. *Visitors:* must be accompanied by member. *Society Meetings:* welcome if arranged in advance. Secretary: T.A. Yates (01889 575667).

RUGELEY near. **St Thomas's Priory,** Armitage Lane, Armitage, Near Rugeley WS15 1ED (Tel & Fax: 01543 492096). *Location:* one mile south-east of Rugeley on A513, opposite Ash Tree Inn. Undulating parkland. 18 holes, 5969 yards. S.S.S. 70. Practice area available. *Green Fees:* weekdays £15.00, weekends £20.00. *Eating facilities:* full restaurant and bar facilities. *Visitors:* welcome weekdays, weekends, Handicap Certificates required. *Society Meetings:* by arrangement. Professional: Phillip Cary (Tel & Fax: 01543 492096).

STAFFORD. **Brocton Hall Golf Club,** Brocton, Stafford ST17 0TH (01785 661901; Fax: 01785 661591). *Location:* off A34 Stafford to Cannock four miles south east of Stafford. Undulating parkland. 18 holes, 6095 yards. S.S.S. 69. *Green Fees:* (2007) weekdays £38.00, weekends £45.00. *Society Meetings:* by arrangement Tuesdays and Thursdays. Professional: Nevil Bland (01785 661485). Secretary: Jeremy Duffy (01785 661901).

STAFFORD. **Ingestre Park Golf Club,** Ingestre, Near Stafford ST18 0RE (01889 270845; Fax: 01889 271434). *Location:* six miles east of Stafford, between Tixall and Great Haywood. Parkland. 18 holes, 6352 yards. S.S.S. 70. Extensive practice ground. *Green Fees:* 18 holes £27.00, £32.50 more than 18 holes weekdays (under review). *Eating facilities:* lunch and dinner menu. *Visitors:* welcome weekdays before 3.30pm. Handicap Certificate required. Buggies available. *Society Meetings:* welcome with reservation except Wednesday. £45.00 all inclusive 27 holes package for Societies. Special winter rates on application. Rates subject to review. Professional: Danny Scullion (01889 270304). Manager: D. Warrilow (01889 270845).

STAFFORD. **Stafford Castle Golf Club,** Newport Road, Stafford ST16 1BP (01785 223821). *Location:* M6 Junction 13 or 14, two miles from club. Parkland course. 9 holes, (18 tees). 6383 yards. S.S.S. 70, Par 71. *Green Fees:* weekdays £18.00 per day; weekends £22.00 per day. Subject to review. *Eating* facilities: snacks and full catering available except Mondays. *Visitors:* welcome except Sunday mornings. Handicap Certificate required. Society Meetings: catered for by arrangement. Administrator: S. Calvert.*

THE APPEARANCE OF AN ASTERISK (*) AT THE END OF A CLUB OR COURSE ENTRY INDICATES THAT UP-TO-DATE INFORMATION HAS NOT BEEN SUPPLIED

STOKE-ON-TRENT. **Burslem Golf Club Ltd,** Wood Farm, High Lane, Tunstall, Stoke-on-Trent ST6 7JT (01782 837006). *Location:* leave Burslem centre by Hamil Road, turn left at High Lane junction, one mile on right. Parkland. 9 holes, 5360 yards. S.S.S. 66. *Green Fees:* weekdays £10.00 per round, £16.00 per day. *Eating facilities:* meals and refreshments by arrangement except Wednesday and Sunday. *Visitors:* welcome weekdays with reservation. Bona fide golf club members only. *Society Meetings:* catered for.

STOKE-ON-TRENT. **Goldenhill Golf Course,** Mobberley Road, Goldenhill, Stoke-on-Trent ST6 5SS (01782 784715). *Location:* on A34 between Tunstall and Kidsgrove, north of Stoke city centre. Rolling parkland course, panoramic views of Mow Cop and Newchapple. 18 holes, 5957 yards, 5447 metres. S.S.S. 69. *Green Fees:* information not available. *Eating facilities:* fully licensed bar and cafeteria. *Visitors:* municipal course with small membership, visitors and societies always welcome.*

STOKE-ON-TRENT. **Jack Barker's Greenway Hall,** Stanley Road, Stockton Brook, Stoke-on-Trent ST9 9LJ (01782 503158). *Location:* M6 (Junction15) – A500 - A53 to Leek, right at crossroads in Stockton Brook. Countryside course with wooded areas and some beautiful scenic views. 18 holes, 5681 yards, 5194 metres. S.S.S. 67. *Green Fees:* weekdays £10.00, weekends £15.00. *Eating facilities:* meals available from 10am to 11pm. *Visitors:* welcome. *Society Meetings:* welcome, packages available on request. Manager: Jonathan Latham.

STOKE-ON-TRENT. **Parkhall Golf Course,** Hulme Lane, Weston Coyney, Stoke-on-Trent ST3 5BH (01782 599584). *Location:* one mile east of Longton. Tight unforgiving heathland course, great character, ideal for new golfers looking to improve their game. 18 holes, 2335 yards, 2136 metres. S.S.S. 54. Par 3. *Green Fees:* information not provided. *Eating facilities:* chocolate, crisps, pop, tea and coffee. *Visitors:* all welcome. Golf clubs and trolley hire available. Seven days advance booking for weekends and Bank Holidays. *Society Meetings:* welcome. Professional: Joe Mortimore.

STOKE-ON-TRENT. **Trentham Golf Club,** 14 Barlaston Old Road, Trentham, Stoke-on-Trent ST4 8HB (01782 658109). *Location*: off A34 travelling south of Newcastle (Staffs.). Left at Trentham Gardens onto Longton Road (A5035); right at National Westminster Bank. Open Championship Regional Qualifying course. 18 holes, 6632 yards. S.S.S. 72. Practice ground. *Green Fees*: weekdays £50.00, weekends £50.00 (Sundays after 2.30pm). Playing with member first guest £15.00, second guest £20.00. *Eating facilities*: lunches and dinners available. *Visitors*: welcome weekdays, and Sundays after 2.30pm. Handicap Certificate required. *Society Meetings*: welcome by prior arrangement. Professional: S. Wilson (01782 657309). Secretary: R.N. Portas (01782 658109).

STOKE-ON-TRENT. **Trentham Park Golf Club,** Trentham Park, Trentham, Stoke-on-Trent ST4 8AE *Location:* off A34 adjoining Trentham Gardens near Junction 15 on M6. 18 holes, 6425 yards. S.S.S. 71. *Green Fees:* information not available. Visitors: welcome weekdays with reservation. *Society Meetings:* catered for Wednesdays and Fridays only. Professional: Simon Lynn (01782 642125; Fax: 01782 658800). Secretary: John Adams (Tel & Fax: 01782 658800).
e-mail: admin@trenthamparkgolfclub.com
website: www.trenthamparkgolfclub.com

STONE. **Izaak Walton Golf Club,** Eccleshall Road, Cold Norton, Stone ST15 0NS (01785 760900). *Location:* on the B5026 linking Stone and Eccleshall. Testing course with many water features. 18 holes, 6370 yards. S.S.S. 72. Driving range. *Green Fees:* available. *Visitors:* welcome with some restrictions. *Society Meetings:* welcome with some restrictions. Contact the Secretary for information. Professional: Paul Brunt (01785 760808). Secretary: Mr T. T. Tyler. e-mail: secretary@izaakwaltongolfclub.co.uk
website: www.izaakwaltongolfclub.co.uk

www.uk-golfguide.com

Trentham
Golf Club

Recognised by the R& A in 1894, Trentham Golf Club is regarded today as one of the finest in the Midlands, and has hosted the Open Championship regional qualifying rounds in the years 2002-2007. Visitors welcome weekdays and after 2.30pm on Sundays. Lunches and dinners available at the clubhouse. Handicap certificate required. Societies are welcome by prior arrangement.

Barlaston Old Road • Trentham • Stoke-on-Trent ST4 8HB
Tel: 01782 658109 • www.trenthamgolf.org.

TRENTHAM GOLF CLUB

STONE. **Stone Golf Club,** The Fillybrooks, Stone ST15 0NB (01785 813103). *Location:* one mile north west of Stone on the A34 adjacent to the Walton Inn. Parkland. 9 holes, 6299 yards. S.S.S. 70. *Green Fees:* weekdays £20.00. *Eating facilities:* full meals to order, snacks always available, bar. *Visitors:* welcome weekdays only, not Bank Holidays. Snooker table. *Society Meetings:* catered for by arrangement. Secretary: P.R. Farley (01630 672275).

STOURBRIDGE. **Enville Golf Club Ltd,** Highgate Common, Enville, Stourbridge DY7 5BN (01384 872074). *Location:* leave A449 at Stewpony Hotel taking Bridgnorth Road A458, fork right after Fox Inn following signs for Halfpenny Green Airport. Two flat wooded heathland courses. Highgate Course: 18 holes, 6556 yards. S.S.S 72; Lodge Course: 18 holes, 6217 yards. S.S.S. 70. *Green Fees:* 18 holes £40.00, 36 holes £50.00. *Eating facilities:* meals available. *Visitors:* welcome weekdays, advisable to phone prior to visit. Ladies' Day Thursday; weekends with members only. *Society Meetings:* welcome except Thursdays and weekends. Party of 30 or more receives a 10% discount. Professional: S. Power (01384 872585). Secretary/Manager: J.J. Bishop (01384 872074; Fax: 01384 873996).
e-mail: secretary@envillegolfclub.com
website: www.envillegolfclub.com

STREETLY. **Little Aston Golf Club,** Roman Road, Streetly, Sutton Coldfield B74 3AN (0121-353 2066). *Location:* off A454. Parkland course. 18 holes, 6670 yards. S.S.S. 73. *Green Fees:* £75.00. *Eating facilities:* dining room and bars, lunch and dinner. *Visitors:* welcome on weekdays by prior arrangement, weekends with a member. *Society Meetings:* welcome Monday, Tuesday, Wednesday and Friday. Professional: Brian Rimmer (0121-353 0330), Manager: Glyn Ridey (0121-353 2942; Fax: 0121-580 8387).
e-mail: manager@littleastongolf.co.uk
website: littleastongolf.co.uk

TAMWORTH. **Drayton Park Golf Club,** Drayton Park, Fazeley, Tamworth B78 3TN (01827 251139; Fax: 01827 284035). *Location:* follow signs for Drayton Pleasure Park, adjacent drive at the top. Parkland with well defined wooded holes. 18 holes, 6473 yards. S.S.S. 71. Practice ground. *Green Fees:* Information not available. *Eating facilities:* full catering facilities. *Visitors:* welcome weekdays except Wednesday mornings. *Society Meetings:* catered for Tuesdays and Thursdays, booked through Secretary. Professional: M.W. Passmore (01827 251478). Secretary: D.O. Winter (01827 251139; Fax: 01827 284035).*
website: www.drayton

TAMWORTH. **Tamworth Golf Centre Limited,** Eagle Drive, Amington, Tamworth B77 4EG (01827 709303; Fax: 01827 709305). *Location:* Junction 10 M42 Tamworth, A5, towards Amington. Parkland course used by NAPGC for Juniors' and Ladies' Championships. 18 holes, 6488 yards. Par 73 S.S.S. 72. Practice area, putting green. *Green Fees:* £16.00 weekdays, £18.00 weekends (as at October 2007). *Eating facilities:* lounge bar with catering. *Visitors:* welcome. *Society Meetings:* function room available for meetings, parties, etc.

UTTOXETER. **Manor Golf Club,** Leese Hill, Kingstone, Uttoxeter ST14 8QT (01889 563234). *Location:* A518, Uttoxeter to Stafford road, 3 miles from Uttoxeter. Grassland course. 18 holes, 6008 yards. S.S.S. 69. Practice range and putting green. *Green Fees:* weekdays £19.00; weekends £29.00. *Eating facilities:* bar meals available Monday to Friday from 12pm till 4pm, Saturday and Sunday from 11am to 4pm. *Visitors:* welcome every day, please book in advance for Saturdays and Sundays. Tuition available. *Society Meetings:* welcome Monday to Friday, please call for rates. Course Manager: Ant Foulds.
e-mail: manorgc@btinternet.com
website: www.manorgolfclub.org.uk

> **THE APPEARANCE OF AN ASTERISK (*) AT THE END OF A CLUB OR COURSE ENTRY INDICATES THAT UP-TO-DATE INFORMATION HAS NOT BEEN SUPPLIED**

UTTOXETER. **Uttoxeter Golf Club,** Wood Lane, Uttoxeter ST14 8JR (01889 566552; Fax: 01889 567501). **Location:** approximately half a mile past the main entrance to the racecourse. Undulating parkland, very picturesque scenery. 18 holes, 5801 yards. S.S.S. 69. Practice area and putting green. **Green Fees:** weekdays £28.00 per day, weekends and Bank Holidays £30.00 per day. **Eating Facilities:** bar, clubhouse dining room. **Visitors:** welcome except on days of "major" competitions. A starting sheet operates at weekends. Buggies and trolleys available for hire. **Society Meetings:** welcome by arrangement (maximum 60), but not at weekends or on Bank Holidays. Professional: Mr Adam McCandless (01889 564884; Fax: 01889 556552). Secretary: Roger Harvey (Tel & Fax: 01889 566552).

WOLSTANTON. **Wolstanton Golf Club,** Dimsdale Old Hall, Hassam Parade, Wolstanton, Newcastle ST5 9DR (01782 622413; Fax: 01782 622718). *Location:* one mile north of Newcastle, turn right off A34 (Dimsdale Parade), first right (Hassam Parade) then right again 75 yards. Flat parkland. 18 holes, 5533 yards. S.S.S. 68. *Green Fees:* information not provided. *Eating facilities:* full catering service and bar. *Visitors:* welcome weekdays; weekends only as member's guest. Trolleys available. *Society Meetings:* catered for by arrangement. Professional: Simon Arnold (Tel & Fax: 01782 622718). Secretary: Valerie Keenan (01782 622413; Fax: 01782 622413).

Warwickshire

ATHERSTONE. **Atherstone Golf Club,** The Outwoods, Coleshill Road, Atherstone CV9 2RL (01827 713110). *Location:* off Coleshill Road, Atherstone, five miles north of Nuneaton and seven miles south of Tamworth. Undulating parkland. 18 holes, 6006 yards. S.S.S. 71. *Green Fees:* £25.00 per day/round Tuesday to Friday, £12.00 with a member; Saturdays with member only. *Eating facilities:* bar and dining room. *Visitors:* welcome weekdays without reservation, Saturdays with member only, not Sundays. Ladies' Day Wednesday. *Society Meetings:* 12 and above by prior arrangement with Secretary. Secretary: D. Bond (01827 704948).

BERKSWELL. **Nailcote Hall Golf Club,** Nailcote Lane, Berkswell CV7 7DE (02476 466174; Fax: 02476 470720). Parkland setting. Cromwell Course - 9 holes, 1037 yards. *Green Fees:* £10.00 adults, £5.00 children; under 12 unlimited play.. *Eating facilities*: two restaurants and two bars. *Visitors:* welcome. Host venue to the "British Par 3 Championship". Mark Mouland Short Game and Junior Academy available for lessons. Accommodation in hotel and leisure club facilities. Professional: Mark McKay. website: www.nailcotehall.co.uk

BIDFORD. **Bidford Grange Golf Club,** Stratford Road, Bidford B50 4LY (01789 490319; Fax: 01789 490998). *Location:* 6 miles west of Stratford-upon-Avon on the B439. American links course with a variety of water holes. 18 holes, 7233 yards. S.S.S. 74. Driving range and putting green. *Green Fees:* information not available. *Eating facilities:* Spikes Bar and restaurant. *Visitors:* welcome any day, after 9am. On-site Hotel. *Society Meetings:* please call for details or view website. Secretary: Daniel Broadhurst.* e-mail: enquiries@bidfordgrange.com website: www.bidfordgrange.com

---

THE APPEARANCE OF AN ASTERISK (*) AT THE END OF A CLUB OR COURSE ENTRY INDICATES THAT UP-TO-DATE INFORMATION HAS NOT BEEN SUPPLIED

BRAILES. **Brailes Golf Club Ltd,** Sutton Lane, Lower Brailes, Banbury OX15 5BB (01608 685633; Fax: 01608 685205). *Location:* M40 Exit 11 Banbury, 10 miles west on B4035; A3400 Shipston on Stour, four miles east on B4035. Parkland/meadowland course. 18 holes, 6311 yards. S.S.S. 70. Practice ground. *Green Fees:* weekdays £25.00 per round, £35.00 per day, twilight (times vary) £10.00 per round; weekends £35.00 per round, twilight (times vary) £15.00 per round. *Eating facilities:* modern clubhouse; bar (11am to 11pm) and restaurant (8am to 9pm) facilities. *Visitors:* welcome subject to availability. Tuition; buggies and trolleys for hire. *Society Meetings:* welcome subject to availability; from £23.50pp. Professional: Mark McGeehan (01608 685633). General Manager: Philip Gibbs (01608 685336). e-mail: office@brailesgolfclub.co.uk website: www.brailesgolfclub.co.uk

COVENTRY. **City of Coventry Brandon Wood Golf Course,** Brandon Lane, Wolston, Near Coventry CV8 3GQ (024 7654 3141). *Location:* six miles south of Coventry off southbound carriageway A45. Parkland on banks of River Avon. 18 holes, 6521 yards. S.S.S. 71. Floodlit driving range. *Green Fees:* £15.75 weekdays; £21.00 weekends and Bank Holidays. Subject to review. *Eating facilities:* bar and restaurant. *Visitors:* welcome anytime, unrestricted, bookings available up to seven days in advance, telephone Pro Shop. *Society Meetings:* phone Pro Shop for details. Professional/Secretary: Chris Gledhill (024 7654 3141). Stewardess: Paula Howson (024 7654 3133). website: www.brandonwoodgolfclub.co.uk

COVENTRY. **Marriott Forest of Arden Hotel & Country Club,** Maxstoke Lane, Meriden, Coventry CV7 7HR (0870 400 7272; Fax: 0870 400 7372). *Location:* take Junction 6 from M42, follow A45 to Coventry. After one mile turn left into Shepherds Lane, hotel is one and a half miles on left. Parkland and greenside water hazards. Home to 13 consecutive European Tour events. Two courses. The Arden - 7213 yards. S.S.S. 73; The Aylesford - 5801 yards. S.S.S. 68. Floodlit golf academy. *Green Fees:* from £25.00 to £110.00. *Eating facilities:* bars and restaurants available. *Visitors:* welcome seven days subject to tee-time availability. 214-bedroom four star hotel with extensive conference and luxurious leisure facilities. *Society Meetings:* enquiries welcome. Professional: Philip Hoye (0958 632170). Director of Golf: Iain Burns.

FHG Guides

publish a large range of well-known accommodation guides. We will be happy to send you details or you can use the order form at the back of this book.

HENLEY-IN-ARDEN. **Henley Golf and Country Club,** Birmingham Road, Henley-in-Arden B95 5QA (01564 793715; Fax: 01564 795754). *Location:* two miles from M40 Junction 16; 20 minutes from Birmingham, Solihull, Stratford-upon-Avon and Warwick. Parkland, with lovely countryside views. 18 holes, 6933 yards. S.S.S. 73. 9-hole Par 3 course. Practice range. *Green Fees:* information not available. *Eating facilities:* bar lounge menu, Brasserie. *Visitors:* no restrictions, but must book in advance. Smart casual dress required, no denim. *Society Meetings:* very welcome. Professional: Neale Hyde.*
e-mail: enquiries@henleygcc.co.uk

KENILWORTH. **Kenilworth Golf Club Ltd,** Crewe Lane, Kenilworth CV8 2EA (01926 854296; Fax: 01926 864453). *Location:* A429 Coventry to Kenilworth adjacent to A46 Coventry to Warwick Road. Parkland and wooded course. 18 holes, 6400 yards. S.S.S. 71. *Green Fees:* £35.00 weekdays; £45.00 weekends and Bank Holidays. *Eating facilities:* diningroom, bar snacks, bar. *Visitors:* must be members of another club with official Handicap Certificate. *Society Meetings:* groups (under 20 in number) weekdays, Societies (over 20) Wednesday only. Professional: S. Yates (01926 512732). Secretary: J.H. McTavish (01926 858517; Fax: 01926 864453).

LEAMINGTON SPA. **Leamington and County Golf Club,** Golf Lane, Whitnash, Leamington Spa (01926 420298). *Location:* three and a half miles from M40 south of town centre of Royal Leamington Spa. 18 holes, 6418 yards, 5869 metres. S.S.S. 72. *Green Fees:* weekdays £35.00 per round, £45.00 per day; weekends £40.00 per round. *Eating facilities:* luncheons, teas, evening meals and snacks. *Visitors:* welcome without reservation. *Society Meetings:* catered for. Professional: J. Mellor (01926 428014). Secretary: David M. Beck (01926 425961).

LEAMINGTON SPA. **Newbold Comyn Golf Club,** Newbold Terrace East, Leamington Spa CV32 4EW (01926 421157). *Location:* signposted off Willes Road. Parkland, front 9 hilly, back 9 flat. 18 holes, 6315 yards. S.S.S. 70. Practice area. *Green Fees:* weekdays £11.50 per 18 holes; weekends £14.50 per 18 holes. *Eating facilities:* Newbold Arms on site. *Visitors:* welcome, unrestricted, but please book. Leisure centre on site. *Society Meetings:* catered for, book through Professional. Professional: David Playdon (01926 421157). Secretaries: L. Ryan (01926 429458) I. Shepherd (01926 313825).

MERIDEN. **Stonebridge,** Somers Road, Meriden CV7 7PL (01676 522442; Fax: 01676 522447). *Location:* two minutes from NEC, M42 Junction 6, just off the A45. Parkland. 18 holes, 6240 yards. S.S.S. 70. 21 bay floodlit driving range. *Green Fees:* weekdays £20.00, weekends £30.00. *Eating facilities:* Spike Bar 8am to 8pm, restaurant Wednesday to Saturday evenings, Sunday lunch. *Visitors:* welcome, seven day advance booking facility for tee-times. Conference and private function suites available. *Society Meetings:* welcome weekdays, packages available. Professional: Spencer Edwards (01676 522442; Fax: 01676 522447).

NORTH WARWICKSHIRE. **Purley Chase Golf Club,** Ridge Lane, Near Nuneaton CV10 0RB (024 7639 3118; Fax: 024 7639 8015). *Location:* three miles off A5 between Atherstone and Nuneaton. Slightly undulating parkland. 18 holes, 6772 yards. S.S.S. 72. Conference and corporate. *Green Fees:* information not available. *Eating facilities:* restaurant. *Visitors:* welcome. *Society Meetings:* welcome, weekdays only. Special rates. Secretary: Linda Jackson (024 7639 3118; Fax: 024 7639 8015).*

NUNEATON. **Bramcote Waters Golf Course,** Bazzard Road, Bramcote, Nuneaton CV11 6QJ (01455 220807). *Location:* approximately five miles from Nuneaton, off B4114. Undulating parkland. 9 holes, 2491 yards. S.S.S. 64. *Green Fees:* weekdays £9.00 9 holes, £16.00 18 holes; weekends £10.00 9 holes, £17.00 18 holes. Reductions for Juniors. *Visitors:* always welcome, pay and play or book up to one week in advance. *Society Meetings:* welcome. Professional: Nic Gilks. Secretary: S. Britain.

NUNEATON. **Nuneaton Golf Club,** Golf Drive, Whitestone, Nuneaton CV11 6QF (024 7638 3281). *Location:* Nuneaton Road, B4112 cross with two small roundabouts, Lutterworth Road. Wooded course. 18 holes, 6429 yards. S.S.S. 71. Practice ground. *Green Fees:* information not available. *Eating facilities:* catering available except Mondays; bar open usual hours. *Visitors:* welcome weekdays. *Society Meetings:* welcome - special days Wednesdays. Professional: Mr John Salter (024 7634 0201). Secretary: Mr P. Smith (024 7634 7810; Fax: 024 7632 7563).*

NUNEATON. **Oakridge Golf Club,** Arley Lane, Ansley Village, Nuneaton CV10 9PH (01676 541389; Fax: 01676 542709). *Location:* on outskirts of Nuneaton, approximately 15 minutes from town centre, 20 minutes from Coventry and 25 minutes from Tamworth. Woodland; undulating fairways with many water hazards. 18 holes, 6242 yards. S.S.S. 70. Practice area, Pro shop, putting green. *Green Fees:* information not available. *Eating facilities:* à la carte restaurant, bar meals, lounge bar. *Visitors:* welcome. Snooker room. *Society Meetings:* welcome weekdays (Monday - Friday). Golf Shop: Tony Harper Golf (01676 540542). Secretary (Admin. and Society Bookings): Mrs S. Lovric; Mr K. Clegg (Golf Section Secretary).

RUGBY. **Rugby Golf Club,** Clifton Road, Rugby CV21 3RD (01788 544637). *Location:* one mile from Rugby town centre on the Clifton road. Parkland course. 18 holes, 5457 yards. S.S.S. 67. Practice ground. *Green Fees:* Information not available. *Eating facilities:* bar open daily, dining - contact Steward (01788 544637). *Visitors:* welcome weekdays; weekends and Bank Holidays only with a member. Ladies' Day Wednesday. Snooker room. Carts for hire. *Society Meetings:* welcome if pre-booked. Professional: David Quinn (01788 575134). Secretary: Ken Clark (Tel & Fax: 01788 542306).*

RUGBY near. **Whitefields Golf Club and Draycote Hotel,** London Road, Thurlaston, Near Rugby CV23 9LF (01788 815555; Fax: 01788 521695). *Location:* A45 near Rugby where it meets the M45. Undulating parkland course, with water feature; not hilly. Backdrops onto Draycote Water to the south. 18 holes, 6223 yards. S.S.S. 70, Par 71. 16-bay floodlit driving range. *Green Fees:* from £15.00. *Eating facilities:* restaurant, spike bar, 19th hole. *Visitors:* welcome. Accommodation available in 50 en suite bedrooms all with Sky TV. Five conference rooms available. Golf Shop (01788 815555; Fax: 01788 817777). *Society Meetings:* welcome. Special rates and packages available. Secretary: Brian Coleman (01788 815555; Fax: 01788 817777).

STONELEIGH. **Stoneleigh Deer Park Golf Club,** The Old Deer Park, Coventry Road, Stoneleigh CV8 3DR (024 7663 9991; Fax: 024 7651 1533). *Location:* A46 Stoneleigh Village, close to N.A.C. Stoneleigh. Parkland. 18 holes, 6056 yards. S.S.S. 69. 9 hole par 3 course; putting green and practice area. *Green Fees:* Monday to Thursday £20.00, Friday £22.00, weekends and Bank Holidays £30.00. *Eating facilities:* bar and restaurant with full catering. *Visitors:* welcome midweek, restrictions at weekends. *Society Meetings:* welcome midweek, restrictions at weekend. Professional: Matt McGuire (024 7663 9912). Secretary: Cherry Reay.

STRATFORD-UPON-AVON. **Ingon Manor Hotel & Golf Club,** Ingon Lane, Snitterfield, Stratford-upon-Avon CV37 0QE (01789 731938). *Location:* Junction 15 of M40, A46 to Stratford, then signposted 'Ingon Manor'. Undulating greens with stunning views across Welcombe Hills. 18 holes, 6554 yards. Par 72. Large practice area, putting green, driving range. *Green Fees:* information not available. *Eating facilities:* available daily. Professional: Neil Evans.*
e-mail: info@ingonmanor.co.uk
website: www.ingonmanor.co.uk

STRATFORD-UPON-AVON. **Stratford-on-Avon Golf Club,** Tiddington Road, Stratford-upon-Avon CV37 7BA (01789 205749). *Location:* half a mile from town on B4086. Flat parkland. 18 holes, 6374 yards. S.S.S. 71. *Green Fees:* information not available. *Eating facilities:* full catering/bar service. *Visitors:* welcome any time subject to domestic commitments. *Society Meetings:* catered for Tuesdays and Thursdays. Professional: D. Sutherland (01789 205677). Secretary: C.J. Hughes (01789 205749). *

STRATFORD-UPON-AVON. **Menzies Welcombe Hotel and Golf Course,** Warwick Road, Stratford-upon-Avon CV37 0NR (01789 295252; Fax: 01789 414666). *Location:* exit M40 at Junction 15, follow signs to Stratford. Club is on A439 after five miles. Or take A439 out of town and club is on left after one mile. Undulating parkland with mature trees, lakes and waterfall. 18 holes, 6288 yards. S.S.S. 70. Practice area and putting green. *Green Fees:* information not available. *Eating facilities:* clubhouse with Atrium Brasserie and private function suites *Visitors:* welcome, please telephone for starting times. Hotel on site, four star facilities. *Society Meetings:* welcome. Please contact Corporate Golf Office (01789 295252; Fax: 01789 266336) *

SUTTON COLDFIELD. **Marston Lakes Golf Club,** Lea Marston Hotel & Leisure Complex, Haunch Lane, Lea Marston, Sutton Coldfield B76 0BY (01675 470707; Fax 01675 470871). *Location:* from junction 9, M42 take A4097 signposted Kingsbury (KGBY) for one mile. Take second right hand turning into Haunch Lane, hotel and golf course 150 yards on right hand side. Beautifully laid out lake and parkland course built to USGA standards. 9 holes, 2059 yards (white tees), S.S.S. 61; 1840 yards (yellow tees), S.S.S. 59; 1695 yards (red tees), S.S.S.59 (over 18 holes). Putting green, 30 bay floodlit driving range. *Green Fees:* weekdays 18 holes £14.50, 9 holes £8.95; weekends and bank holidays 18 holes £18.50, 9 holes £14.50. Golf Packages available. *Eating facilities:* Hathaways Bar/Restaurant serving snacks, hot beverages, lunches, dinners, also fully licensed restaurant in hotel. *Visitors:* welcome any time. 88 bedroom, four star hotel on site. Tuition, golf simulater, fully stocked golf shop. *Society Meetings:* welcome. Professional: Darren Lewis (01675 470707; Fax: 01675 470871). Secretary: Katya Townsend (01675 470468; Fax: 01675 470707).
e-mail: info@leamarstonhotel.co.uk
membership@leamarstonhotel.co.uk
website: www.leamarstonhotel.co.uk

WARWICK. **Warwick Golf Club,** Warwick Golf Centre, Racecourse, Warwick CV34 6HW (01926 494316). *Location:* off M40, from A41/A46 junction, travel half a mile towards Warwick, turn right into racecourse. Flat parkland course. 9 holes, 2682 yards. S.S.S. 66. Driving range (floodlit). *Green Fees:* information not available. *Eating facilities:* bar open 7 to 10.30pm weekdays, no catering. *Visitors:* welcome any time except Sunday mornings. *Society Meetings:* accepted, must book in advance. Professional: P. Sharp (01926 491284). Secretary: R. Dunkley.

WARWICK. **The Warwickshire,** Leek Wootton, Near Warwick CV35 7QT (01926 409409; Fax: 01926 497911). *Location:* on B4115, just off A46, five minutes from M40 Junction 15. Parkland and woodland courses with many attractive holes over water. North/West Course: 18 holes, 7407 yards. S.S.S. 74. South/East Course: 18 holes, 7157 yards. S.S.S. 74. 9-hole Par 3 course, driving range, practice and putting greens. *Green Fees:* information not available. *Eating facilities:* bar and restaurant. *Visitors:* welcome at all times. Conference facilities available. *Society Meetings:* Golf Days arranged for groups from 12 to 300. Professional: M. Dulson (01926 409409). General Manager: Steve Dixon (01926 409409; Fax: 01926 408409). *

Marston Lakes Golf Course is a beautifully laid out 9-hole lake and parkland course built to USGA specification, providing an enjoyable test for golfers of all abilities. Other facilities include a Par 3 Academy course, 30-bay floodlit driving range with power tees, targets and teaching bays, a fully stocked Pro shop, computerised golf simulator and tuition by our golf professionals. Our partnership with Wishaw golf club offers residential golfers the option of playing an 18-hole course situated only 6 minutes' drive from the hotel. Societies also welcome.

Haunch Lane, Lea Marston,
Warwickshire B76 0BY (off Junction 9, M42)
Tel: 01675 470468 • www.leamarstonhotel.co.uk

www.uk-golfguide.com

West Midlands

BIRMINGHAM. **Brandhall Golf Club,** Heron Road, Oldbury, Warley B68 8AQ (0121-552 2195). *Location:* Wolverhampton Road A4123 off Junction 2 M5; right at Hen and Chickens Junction. Wooded course, elevated tees. 18 holes, 5833 yards. S.S.S. 68. *Green Fees:* information not available. Senior Citizens cards. *Visitors:* welcome, ring course for details. Tuition available, buggies (summer only) for hire. *Society Meetings:* welcome by prior arrangement. Professional: Carl Yates.*

BIRMINGHAM. **Cocks Moors Woods Golf Club,** Alcester Road South, Kings Heath, Birmingham B14 4ER (0121-464 3584; Fax: 0121 441 1305). *Location:* A435 Alcester Road, three and a half miles from M42 Junction 3. Undulating woodland course, many meandering streams. 18 holes, 5769 yards, Par 69. S.S.S. 68. *Green Fees:* information not available. *Eating facilities:* adjacent to leisure centre offering excellent bar and catering facilities. *Visitors:* welcome at all times. Full range of leisure facilities within complex. *Society Meetings:* welcome during quiet times, please telephone. Professional: Steve Ellis. Secretary: D. W. Wincott (0121-777 7837).*

BIRMINGHAM. **Edgbaston Golf Club Ltd,** Church Road, Edgbaston, Birmingham B15 3TB (0121-454 1736; Fax: 0121-454 2395). *Location*: from Birmingham City Centre take A38 (Bristol Road). After one mile and at third set of traffic lights turn right into Priory Road, at end of which turn into Church Road; the club entrance is 80m on the left. Undulating parkland course set in the grounds of historic Edgbaston Hall, which is now the club house. Course designed by H.S. Colt in 1935. Ancient trees, sloping fairways and a large lake contribute to the challenge and enjoyment of the course which is also a conservation area. 18 holes, 6106 yards. S.S.S. 69, Par 69. Practice area. *Green Fees*: weekdays £47.00, weekends £57.00 (summer); weekdays £30.00 (winter). *Eating facilities*: fully licensed, lunches, teas daily and bar meals daily; other meals by prior arrangement. *Visitors*: welcome subject to some restrictions on starting times, and the production of Handicap Certificate. Facilities for business meetings/seminars; snooker rooms; fully stocked shop, offering tuition, organisation of competitions, prizes, clinics. *Society Meetings*: welcome by arrangement with General Manager. Professional: Jamie Cundy (0121-454 3226; Fax: 0121-454 2395). General Manager: Adam Grint (0121-454 1736). e-mail: secretary@edgbastongc.co.uk website: www.edgbastongc.co.uk

BIRMINGHAM. **Fulford Heath Golf Club Ltd,** Tanners Green Lane, Wythall, Birmingham B47 6BH (01564 822806). *Location:* one mile from Alcester Road, via Tanners Green Lane. Parkland with two lakes and River Cole. 18 holes, 6179 yards. S.S.S. 70. Practice ground. *Green Fees:* weekdays £36.00 (Societies £30.00). Subject to review. *Eating facilities:* available. *Visitors:* welcome weekdays, not at weekends and Bank Holidays. Buggies for hire. *Society Meetings:* catered for on application. Professional: R. Dunbar (01564 822930). Secretary: Mrs M. Tuckett (01564 824758; Fax: 01564 822629)

BIRMINGHAM. **Gay Hill Golf Club,** Hollywood Lane, Hollywood, Birmingham B47 5PP (0121-430 8544; Fax: 0121 436 7796). *Location:* M42 Junction 3, three miles. Parkland course. 18 holes, 6406 yards. S.S.S. 72. Practice area. *Green Fees:* £35.00 (18 holes). *Eating facilities:* available. *Visitors:* welcome all week. *Society Meetings:* catered for by arrangement Thursdays. Professional: Chris Harrison (0121-474 6001). Secretary: Mrs Julie Morris (0121-430 8544).

BIRMINGHAM. **Great Barr Golf Club,** Chapel Lane, Great Barr, Birmingham B43 7BA (0121-357 1232). *Location:* six miles north-west of Birmingham M6 Junction 7. Parkland. 18 holes, 6523 yards. S.S.S. 72. *Green Fees:* information not available. *Eating facilities:* meals served, order in advance. *Visitors:* welcome weekdays, restricted at weekends. Weekends maximum handicap 18. Handicap Certificate required. *Society Meetings:* Packages available. Professional: R. Spragg (0121-357 5270). Secretary: D. Smith (0121-358 4376).*

BIRMINGHAM. **Handsworth Golf Club,** 11 Sunningdale Close, Handsworth Wood, Birmingham B20 1NP (0121-554 0599). *Location:* M5 Junction 1. A41 left at first lights, left at next set of lights, second left, second left/M6 Junction 7. A34 Birmingham Road, Old Walsall Road, Vernon Avenue, Westover Road, Craythorne Avenue. Parkland course. 18 holes, 6272 yards, 5733 metres. S.S.S. 70. Large practice area and putting green. *Green Fees:* information not available. *Eating facilities*: bar snacks to à la carte menu in restaurant. *Visitors:* welcome weekdays with Handicap Certificate. *Society Meetings:* catered for by arrangement with Secretary. Special packages available. Professional: L. Bashford (0121-523 3594). Secretary: P.S. Hodnett (0121-554 3387; Fax: 0121-554 6144). e-mail: info@handsworthgolfclub.net

BIRMINGHAM. **Harborne Golf Club,** 40 Tennal Road, Harborne, Birmingham B32 2JE (0121-427 3058). *Location:* A4123, A456, B4124 three miles west Birmingham city centre. Undulating parkland/moorland. 18 holes, 6210 yards. S.S.S. 70. *Green Fees:* weekdays £30.00. *Eating facilities:* bar and dining area daily. *Visitors:* welcome except weekends and Bank Holidays. Trolleys for hire. *Society Meetings:* welcome with pre-booking. Special rates for parties comprising over 20 players. Professional: Stuart Mathews (0121-427 3512). General Manager: Adrian Cooper (0121-427 3058).

BIRMINGHAM. **Harborne (Church Farm) Golf Club,** Vicarage Road, Harborne, Birmingham B17 0SN (0121-427 1204; Fax: 0121-428 3126). *Location:* signposted from Harborne Centre. Parkland, brooks a special feature on five holes. 9 holes, 2441 yards. S.S.S. 64. *Green Fees:* information not available. *Eating facilities:* canteen serves hot and cold snacks. *Visitors:* welcome anytime - phone call required as a booking system is in operation. *Society Meetings:* by arrangement with the Professional. Professional: Paul Johnson. Secretary: William Flanagan (0121-427 1204; Fax: 0121-428 3126).*

BIRMINGHAM. **Hatchford Brook Golf Club,** Coventry Road, Sheldon, Birmingham B26 3PY (0121-743 9821; Fax: 0121 743 3420). *Location:* on A45 3 miles from Junction 6 M42, next to Birmingham International Airport. Parkland course with wide fairways and large greens. 18 holes, 6137 yards. S.S.S. 69. Large practice area. *Green Fees:* £14.00 (subject to review); special rates for Senior Citizens, unemployed and Link Card holders. *Eating facilities:* restaurant and bar in clubhouse. *Visitors:* welcome with some restrictions. *Society Meetings:* contact Professional. Professional: Mark Hampton (0121 743 9821). Secretary: Ian Thomson (0121 742 6643).

BIRMINGHAM. **Hilltop Public Golf Course,** Park Lane, Handsworth, Birmingham B21 8LJ (0121-554 4463; Fax: 0121-515 2842). *Location:* Two miles from M5 J1, turn into Park Lane opposite West Bromwich Albion football ground. Wide fairways. 18 holes, 6254 yards. S.S.S. 70. *Green Fees:* 18 holes weekdays £11.00; 18 holes weekends £13.00. *Eating facilities:* café serving drinks and hot meals. Licensed bar. *Visitors:* welcome, phone to book a starting time. Municipal course. *Society Meetings:* bookings available through Professional. Professional/ Secretary: Kevin Highfield.

BIRMINGHAM. **Kings Norton Golf Club Ltd.,** Brockhill Lane, Weatheroak, Alvechurch, Birmingham B48 7ED (01564 826706; Fax: 01564 826955). *Location:* M42 Junction 3, A435 to Birmingham, sign on left to Weatheroak, follow for one mile, over first crossroads. Club on right hand side. Parkland course. 27 holes, 7000 yards. S.S.S. 72, plus 12 hole par 3 course and 22 acre practice field. *Green Fees:* information not available. *Eating facilities:* excellent restaurant and bar snacks available. *Visitors:* welcome weekdays only, weekends with member. *Society Meetings:* catered for weekdays only; minimum number 20. Buggies available. Professional: Kevin Hayward (01564 822635). Manager: Terry Webb (01564 826789). e-mail: info@kingsnortongolfclub.co.uk website: www.kingsnortongolfclub.co.uk

BIRMINGHAM. **Maxstoke Park Golf Club,** Castle Lane, Coleshill, Birmingham B46 2RD (01675 462158). *Location:* three miles north east of Coleshill on B4114, turn right for Maxstoke. Parkland with trees and lakes. Water-filled moat surrounding Maxstoke Castle. 18 holes, 6442 yards, S.S.S. 71. Two practice areas. *Green Fees:* £30.00 per round, £40.00 per day. *Eating facilities:* restaurant and bar. *Visitors:* welcome weekdays only, weekends with member. Handicap Certificate required. *Society Meetings:* catered for Tuesdays/Thursdays. Professional: N. McEwan (01675 464915). Secretary: A. J. Brown (01675 466743; Fax: 01675 466185).

BIRMINGHAM. **Moseley Golf Club,** Springfield Road, Kings Heath, Birmingham B14 7DX (0121-444 2115). *Location:* from M42 take A435 north to Kings Heath, turn right into Wheelers Lane (A4040), left into Barn Lane crossing Addison Road into Springfield Road where the club is on the right hand side. Rolling parkland course with major water feature. 18 holes, 6300 yards. S.S.S. 70. Practice area. *Green Fees:* information not available. *Eating facilities:* dining room and bar. *Visitors:* welcome midweek only by prior arrangement. Handicap Certificates required. *Society Meetings:* welcome Wednesdays and Fridays, minimum of 12 players. Professional: Martin Griffin (0121-444 2063). General Manager: Janet Hey (0121-444 4957; Fax: 0121-441 4662).

BIRMINGHAM. **North Worcestershire Golf Club,** Frankley Beeches Road, Northfield, Birmingham B31 5LP (0121-475 1026). *Location:* A38 from Birmingham City Centre. Parkland, established inland course. 18 holes, 5959 yards. S.S.S. 68. *Green Fees:* information not available. *Eating facilities:* catering facilities on request, normal bar opening hours. *Visitors:* welcome weekdays. *Society Meetings:* catered for Tuesdays and Thursdays. Professional: D. Cummins (0121-475 5721). Secretary: D. Wilson (0121-475 1047; Fax: 0121-476 8681).*

BIRMINGHAM near. **Rose Hill Golf Club,** Rose Hill, Rednal, Near Birmingham B45 8RR. *Location:* Lickey Hills Country Park, Junction 1 M42, Junction 4 M5. Established 1921, parkland, semi flat course. 18 holes, 5890 yards. S.S.S. 68. *Green Fees:* information not available. *Eating facilities:* no bars, restaurant all day. *Visitors:* welcome with prior bookings only via Professional. Old Rose and Crown Hotel on course. *Society Meetings:* welcome with prior booking via Professional. Professional: Mark Toombs (0121-453 3159). Secretary: A Cushing (07976 793698; Fax: 0121-250 1719).*

COVENTRY. **Ansty Golf Centre,** Brinklow Road, Ansty, Coventry CV7 9JH (024 7662 1341; Fax: 024 7660 2568). *Location:* half a mile from Junction 2 M6 and parallel to the M69 is the B4065 signposted to Ansty. Parkland. 18 holes, 6150 yards. S.S.S. 69, Par 71. 9 hole par 3 course, Driving range. *Green Fees:* weekdays £10.00, weekends £16.00. Golf day package £12.00 weekdays, £18.00 weekends. *Eating facilities:* available 7 days a week; fully licensed restaurant with family room. *Visitors:* always welcome. Fully stocked Golf Shop, teaching academy, open 7 days regardless of weather, driving range, putting green, practice area. *Society Meetings:* welcome. Individual parties, corporate golf days and society golf days tailored to individual requirements. Professional: Mark Goodwin (024 7662 1341; Fax: 024 7660 2568). Secretary: K. Smith (Tel & Fax: 024 7660 2671).

COVENTRY. **Copsewood Grange Golf Club,** Copsewood Sports Ground, Allard Way, Coventry CV3 1JP (024 7663 5452). *Location:* three miles from centre of Coventry on A4082 off the A428 road to Rugby, Lutterworth. 9 holes, 6048 yards. S.S.S. 71. *Green Fees:* weekdays guests £8.00 per round, £15.00 per day; visitors £16.00 per round, £20.00 per day. Sundays guests £10.00 per round, visitors £20.00 per round. *Visitors:* welcome except Saturdays, weekdays after 2.30pm Tuesday and Friday or Sunday mornings. Secretary: R.E.C. Jones (07794 143840).

COVENTRY. **Coventry Golf Club,** St. Martins Road, Finham Park, Coventry CV3 6RJ (024 7641 4152; Fax: 024 7669 0131). *Location:* south Coventry off A45, one mile along B4113. Gently undulating parkland course designed by Vardon/Hawtree, an exciting challenge to all golfers. 18 holes, 6601 yards. S.S.S. 73. Practice ground. *Green Fees:* information not available. *Eating facilities:* full catering in lounge bar, restaurant (maximum 120). *Visitors:* welcome weekdays. Fully stocked shop. *Society Meetings:* welcome Wednesdays and Thursdays by prior arrangement with Secretary's Office. Handicap Certificates required. Group bookings accepted two years in advance. Professional: P. Weaver (024 7641 1298). Secretary: Anne Smith (024 7641 4152).*

COVENTRY. **Coventry Hearsall Golf Club,** Beechwood Avenue, Coventry CV5 6DF (024 7671 3470; Fax: 024 7669 1534). *Location:* off A45 south of Coventry, one mile south of city centre. Flat parkland, easy walking. 18 holes, 6005 yards. S.S.S. 69, Par 70. *Green Fees:* weekdays £35.00, weekends £40.00. *Eating facilities:* restaurant open six days a week; closed Mondays but snack meals offered.

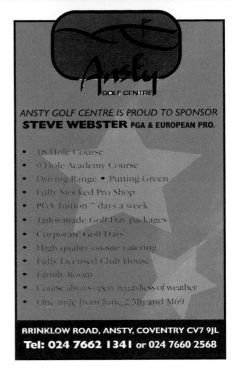
Visitors: welcome weekdays, special request at weekends. Pull carts for hire. *Society Meetings:* welcome, must book in advance with Secretary. Professional: Michael Tarn (024 7671 3156). Secretary: Rachael Meade (024 7671 3470; Fax: 024 7669 1534).
e-mail: secretary@hearsallgolfclub.co.uk
website: www.hearsallgolfclub.co.uk

COVENTRY. **Marriott Forest of Arden Hotel & Country Club,** Maxstoke Lane, Meriden, Coventry CV7 7HR (0870 400 7272; Fax: 0870 400 7372). *Location:* take Junction 6 from M42, follow A45 to Coventry. After one mile turn left into Shepherds Lane, hotel is one and a half miles on left. Parkland and greenside water hazards. Home to the British Masters 2003. Two courses. The Arden - 7213 yards. S.S.S. 73; The Aylesford - 5801 yards. S.S.S. 68. Floodlit golf academy. *Green Fees:* information not available. *Eating facilities:* bars and restaurants available. *Visitors:* welcome seven days subject to tee-time availability. 214-bedroom four star hotel with extensive conference and luxurious leisure facilities. *Society Meetings:* enquiries welcome. Professional: Philip Hoye (0958 632170). Director of Golf: Iain Burns.*

COVENTRY. **North Warwickshire Golf Club Ltd,** Hampton Lane, Meriden, Warwickshire CV7 7LL (01676 522915; Fax: 01676 523004). *Location:* on B4102, one mile from Stonebridge on A45, approximately midway between Birmingham and Coventry. Heathland. 9 holes, 6352 yards. S.S.S. 71. Small practice ground. *Green Fees:* £25.00 weekdays; weekends with member only. *Eating facilities:* snack lunch, meals by prior arrangement. *Visitors:* welcome weekdays without reservation except Thursdays, weekends by invitation. *Society Meetings:* catered for by prior arrangement, limited numbers. Professional: Andrew Bownes (01676 522259). Secretary: Mr I. W. Ford (01676 522915; Fax: 01676 523004).
e-mail: nwgcltd@btconnect.com

COVENTRY. **Windmill Village Hotel and Golf Club,** Birmingham Road, Allesley, Coventry CV5 9AL (024 7640 4041; Fax: 024 7640 4042). *Location:* A45 westbound, west of Coventry. Rolling parkland with water features. 18 holes, 5213 yards. S.S.S. 66. Course record 63 Pro, 66 Amateur. *Green Fees:* Monday to Thursday and Friday before 11.30am £18.95; Friday after 11.30am and Saturday/Sunday £22.50. 2-Fore-1 vouchers Mon-Fri £22.50. Twilight golf available. *Eating facilities:* food and drinks available all day. *Visitors:* welcome with booking. 4-star standard 100-bedroom hotel with leisure centre; conferences, weddings catered for. *Society Meetings:* welcome, special rates available. Professional: Robert Hunter. Managers: Marci Hartland and Brian Brodie.

DUDLEY. **Dudley Golf Club Ltd,** Turners Hill, Rowley Regis, Warley B65 9BD (01384 233877). *Location:* one mile south of Dudley town centre on Oakham Road. 18 holes, 5730 yards. S.S.S. 68. *Green Fees:* weekdays £25.00 per day. Weekends only with member. *Eating facilities:* full catering facilities available. *Visitors:* welcome but only with a member at weekends. *Society Meetings:* by prior arrangement. Professional: Gary Kilmister (01384 254020). Secretary: B.M. Clee (01384 233877).
e-mail: secretary@dudleygolfclub.com

DUDLEY. **Himley Hall Golf Centre,** Log Cabin, Himley Park, Himley Road, Dudley DY3 4DF (01902 895207). *Location:* just off A449 at Himley near Dudley. Parkland. Pay and Play course. 9 holes, 3145 yards. S.S.S. 35 for 9 holes. Practice ground, pitch and putt. *Green Fees:* Information not available. *Eating facilities:* hot and cold snacks. *Visitors:* welcome weekdays, weekends with booking. *Society Meetings:* midweek only. Professional: Mark Sparrow (01902 895207). Secretary: Margaret Hurley (01902 895207

DUDLEY. **Sedgley Golf Centre,** Sandyfields Road, Sedgley, Dudley DY3 3DL (01902 880503). *Location:* half a mile from Sedgley town centre near Cotwall End Valley Nature Reserve, just off the A463. Undulating contours and mature trees with extensive views over surrounding countryside. 9 holes, 3147 yards. S.S.S. 71 (18 holes). Covered and floodlit golf range. *Green Fees:* £7.50 9 holes, £10.00 18 holes. Reductions weekdays for Juniors and Senior Citizens. *Eating facilities:* hot and cold snacks available on request. *Visitors:* pay and play course throughout the week, booking advisable at weekends. *Society Meetings:* weekdays preferred by prior arrangement. Professional: Garry Mercer (01902 880503). Secretary: J.A. Cox (01902 672452

DUDLEY near. **Swindon Golf Club,** Bridgnorth Road, Swindon, Near Dudley DY3 4PU (01902 897031). *Location:* B4176 Dudley/Bridgnorth Road, three miles from A449 at Himley. Woodland and parkland course with exceptional views. 18 holes - 6121 yards. S.S.S. (18) 70. *Green Fees:* Information not available. *Eating facilities:* fully licensed bar and restaurant. *Visitors:* always welcome, booking required. Buggies available. Fishing. *Society Meetings:* by arrangement weekdays only. General Manager: S.T. Edwin (01902 897031; Fax: 01902 326219).
e-mail: admin@swindongolfclub.co.uk
website: www.swindongolfclub.co.uk

HALESOWEN. **Halesowen Golf Club,** The Leasowes, Leasowes Lane, Halesowen B62 8QF (Tel & Fax: 0121-501 3606). *Location:* exit Junction 3 M5, A456 (Kidderminster) two miles, Halesowen town centre one mile. Parkland course in the Midlands with a Grade I Listed clubhouse and park. 18 holes, 5754 yards. S.S.S. 69. *Green Fees:* (2006) weekdays £28.00 per round, £34.00 per day; weekends by special arrangement. Subject to review. *Eating facilities:* available every day. *Visitors:* welcome weekdays. *Society Meetings:* by arrangement with Secretary. Professional: Jon Nicholas (Tel & Fax: 0121-503 0593). Secretary: Peter Crumpton (Tel & Fax: 0121-501 3606).

REDNAL. **Lickey Hills Golf Club,** Rose Hill, Rednal, Birmingham B45 8RR (0121-453 3159; 0121-457 8779). *Location:* Three miles from M42 J1 or M5 J4 at the bottom of Rose Hill on Lickey Hills Country Park. Picturesque course with dramatic slopes and banks of pine trees. 18 holes, 5866 yards. S.S.S. 68. *Green Fees:* information not available. *Eating facilities:* cafe at clubhouse. *Visitors:* welcome. Professional: Mark Toombs.*

SOLIHULL. **Copt Heath Golf Club,** 1220 Warwick Road, Knowle, Solihull B93 9LN (01564 772650). *Location:* on A4141 half-a-mile south of Junction 5 with M42. Flat parkland. 18 holes, 6528 yards. S.S.S. 71. Full practice facilities available. *Green Fees:* weekdays £40.00. Weekends and Public Holidays must be introduced by a member. *Eating facilities:* lunch and evening meal available except Mondays. *Visitors:* no restrictions weekdays. *Society Meetings:* by arrangement with Secretary. Professional: Brian Barton. Secretary: Clive Hadley.
e-mail: golf@copt-heath.co.uk
website: www.coptheathgolf.co.uk

SOLIHULL. **Ladbrook Park Golf Club Ltd,** Poolhead Lane, Tanworth-in-Arden, Solihull B94 5ED (01564 742220). *Location:* south from Junction 3 M42. Parkland, gently undulating. 18 holes, 6427 yards. S.S.S. 71. Practice ground. *Green Fees:* weekdays £35.00 18 holes, £45.00 36 holes; weekends with a member only. *Eating facilities:* excellent dining. *Visitors:* welcome weekdays, prior telephone call suggested. Weekends with member only. *Society Meetings:* catered for by prior arrangement with the Secretary. Professional: Richard Mountford (01564 742581). Secretary: M.R. Newman (01564 742264; Fax: 01564 742909).

A Course Played By Champions
SWINDON GOLF CLUB

near Dudley in the West Midlands provides golfers with the one thing that makes the sport so great – a challenge. For at Swindon the course is littered with holes, bunkers and obstacles to test the talents of the greatest players. Almost all holes are surrounded by ferns, pines and firs. The feature hole is the 5th, a boomerang of a Par 5 flanked on both sides by towering firs. Swindon is a wonderful course to play, where accuracy, not length, is required. The clubhouse has a friendly and relaxed atmosphere and you will find a selection of great food to satisfy any appetite, a snooker table and a great atmosphere.

For more information telephone or visit the course.

SWINDON GOLF CLUB, BRIDGNORTH ROAD, SWINDON, DUDLEY, WEST MIDLANDS DY3 4PU
TEL: 01902 897031 • FAX: 01902 326219
e-mail: admin@swindongolfclub.co.uk
www.swindongolfclub.co.uk

Halesowen Golf Club, The Leasowes, Halesowen B62 8QF

The Club, which has been established for over 100 years, has an 18 hole course set in the only Grade 1 Listed Park in the Midlands, with excellent panoramic views of Worcestershire, and is always in excellent condition. Playing membership of over 500 but visitors and new members are always welcome. Places available with special rates.
Arrangements with the Secretary on 0121 501 3606, or Professional 0121 503 0593

Looking for holiday accommodation?
search for details of properties close to golf courses
www.holidayguides.com

www.uk-golfguide.com

SOLIHULL. **Olton Golf Club Ltd,** Mirfield Road, Solihull B91 1JH (0121-705 1083; Fax: 0121-711 2010). *Location:* approximately two miles off Junction 5 (M42), A41 - Birmingham. Parkland. 18 holes, 6229 yards, 5694 metres. S.S.S. 71. *Green Fees:* from £35.00 weekdays. Discounts for large groups. *Eating facilities:* by arrangement. *Visitors:* welcome weekdays only except Wednesdays. *Society Meetings:* catered for by arrangement. Professional: C. Haynes (0121-705 7296). Hon. Secretary: Bob Gay (0121-704 1936; Fax: 0121-711 2010).

SOLIHULL. **Robin Hood Golf Club,** St. Bernards Road, Solihull B92 7DJ (0121-706 0159). *Location:* eight miles south of Birmingham, off A41 Birmingham to Warwick road. Flat parkland. 18 holes, 6635 yards, 6067 metres. S.S.S. 72. *Green Fees:* £30.00 weekdays. *Eating facilities:* by prior arrangement with Steward (0121-706 5010). *Visitors:* welcome weekdays only subject to limitations. Arrange with Secretary or Professional. *Society Meetings:* catered for by prior booking. Professional: A.R. Harvey (0121-706 0806). Secretary: Miss J.S. Evans (0121 706 0061; Fax: 0121-700 7502).
e-mail: robin.hood.golf.club@dial.pipex.com

SOLIHULL. **Shirley Golf Club,** Stratford Road, Monkspath, Solihull B90 4EW (0121-744 6001; Fax: Fax: 0121-746 5645). *Location:* (A3400), Junction 4 M42, towards Birmingham. Parkland. 18 holes, 6507 yards. S.S.S. 71. Practice ground, putting area. *Green Fees:* £35.00 per day. *Eating facilities:* bar and restaurant. *Visitors:* welcome weekdays without reservation, must have Handicap. Trolleys available. *Society Meetings:* welcome by arrangement. Professional: Stuart Bottrill (Tel & Fax: 0121-746 5646). General Manager: Steve Wilkins (0121-744 6001; Fax: 0121-746 5645)
e-mail: shirleygolfclub@btclick.com

SOLIHULL. **Tidbury Green Golf Club,** Tilehouse Lane, Shirley, Solihull B90 1HP (01564 824460). *Location:* two miles from Shirley and three miles off the M42. To play over numerous ponds, lakes and the River Coal. 18 holes, 4792 yards, 4382 metres. S.S.S. 64. 15 bay driving range, 9 hole pitch 'n' putt.. *Green Fees:* information not available. *Eating facilities:* excellent bar and restaurant facilities. *Visitors:* welcome, no restrictions. Facilities for fishing. *Society Meetings:* catered for. Secretary: L.M. Broadhurst.*

SOLIHULL. **West Midlands Golf Club,** Marsh House Farm Lane, Barston, Solihull B92 0LB (01675 444 890). *Location:* located between Birmingham and Coventry, five minutes from National Exhibition Centre, Junction 4 of M6, Junction 6 of M42. Take A452 towards Leamington and Warwick (Balsall Common) and look for signs to club. USGA Golf Course over rolling parkland with island green. Putting green, open driving range, practice green. 18 holes, 6624 yards. S.S.S. 72. *Green Fees:* Information not available. *Eating facilities:* spike bar serving light meals and à la carte restaurant. *Visitors:* welcome. *Society Meetings:* please call for information, we will tailor a package to suit your needs. Secretary: Ron Guthrie.*
website: www.wmgc.co.uk

SOLIHULL. **Widney Manor Golf Club,** Saintbury Drive (off Widney Lane), Widney Manor, Solihull B91 3SZ (0121-704 0704; Fax: 0121-704 7999). *Location:* exit M42 Junction 4 and follow signs for Shirley, then Monkspath. A challenging course for golfers of all abilities, set in parkland with mature oaks and water hazards. 18 holes, 5500 yards. 14-bay covered driving range. *Green Fees:* Information not available. *Eating facilities:* normal bar hours, catering facilities available all day. *Visitors:* welcome at all times with advance booking available. Casual but smart dress code. *Society Meetings:* welcome any day. Tailor-made to suit the customer. Professional Tim Atkinson. Secretary: Ron Guthrie.*
website: www.wmgc.co.uk

STOURBRIDGE. **Stourbridge Golf Club,** Worcester Lane, Pedmore, Stourbridge DY8 2RB (01384 395566). *Location:* situated between Hagley and Stourbridge on Worcester road. Parkland. 18 holes, 6231 yards. S.S.S. 70. Small practice ground. *Green Fees:* weekdays £30.00; weekends with a member only £14.00. *Eating facilities:* bar meals available, lunch, dinner. *Visitors:* welcome weekdays, weekends with member. *Society Meetings:* catered for. Professional: Mark Male (01384 393129). Secretary: Miss M. Kite (01384 395566; Fax: 01384 444660).
e-mail: secretary@stourbridge-golf-club.co.uk
website: www.stourbridge-golf-club.co.uk

SUTTON COLDFIELD. **Aston Wood Golf Club,** Blake Street, Little Aston, Sutton Coldfield B74 4EU (0121-580 7803; Fax: 0121-353 0354). *Location:* situated on Blake Street off A5127 Lichfield to Sutton Coldfield Road. Gently rolling Allis-Clark designed course with many water hazards.18 holes, 6480 yards. S.S.S. 71. Practice area, bunker and green. *Green Fees:* information not available. *Eating facilities:* superb restaurant and bars open daily 7.30am-11pm. *Visitors:* weekdays only. Buggies. *Society Meetings:* corporate and societies welcome. Excellent packages available. Superb functions and conference facilities. Professional: Simon Smith (0121-580 7800). General Manager: Ken Heathcote (0121-580 7803).*

SUTTON COLDFIELD. **Boldmere Golf Club,** Monmouth Drive, Sutton Coldfield B73 6JL (0121-354 3379; Fax: 0121-355 4534). *Location:* off A452 (Chester road North), next to Sutton Park on Monmouth Drive. Flat parkland, wooded. 18 holes, 4463 yards. S.S.S. 62. Practice net and putting area. Shorter, lush course ideal for those who prefer a less exhaustive round of golf. *Green Fees:* information not available. *Eating facilities:* cafe in clubhouse. *Visitors:* welcome, Link Card system in operation. *Society Meetings:* welcome at quiet times, to be arranged with the Professional. Professional: Trevor Short (0121-354 3379). Secretary: Roy Leeson (0121-354 3379; Fax: 0121-354 4534).
e-mail: boldmeregolfclub@hotmail.com
website: www.boldmeregolfclub.co.uk

www.uk-golfguide.com

West Midlands Golf Club
Marsh House Farm Lane, Barston, Solihull, West Midlands B92 0LB

Located just 5 minutes from the NEC, between Meriden and Balsall Common, this superb new course (6624 yards, par 72) has been built to the highest specification with USGA tees and greens. Several holes demand tee shots and approach shots over water, including the signature 18th hole, par 3 with an island green.

www.wmgc.co.uk   01675 444890

ASTON WOOD GOLF CLUB

For GOLF
FOR LEISURE
FOR BUSINESS
FOR YOU

Aston Wood Golf Club has everything you would wish for in a first class facility, combining high standards of service with a friendly, comfortable atmosphere. Lying in the heart of England, Aston Wood is easily accessible from Birmingham and the rest of the country (M6, M6 Toll, M40 and M42). Visitors welcome weekdays.

This 18-hole championship course, designed by Peter Alliss and Clive Clarke, is constructed to USPGA standards, with many water features and undulating greens, presenting a good test of golf to all players.

Aston Wood has excellent restaurant, bar and lounge facilities, offering breakfast, bar snacks and a full à la carte menu, and is the perfect facility in which to hold your next business conference or private function.

For full details see our website: **www.astonwoodgolfclub.co.uk**

Blake Street, Little Aston, Sutton Coldfield B74 4EU

Tel: 0121 580 7800 • Tee Bookings: 0121 580 7801 • Fax: 0121 353 0354
Administration: 0121 580 7803 • enquiries@astonwoodgolfclub.co.uk

Visit the FHG website
www.holidayguides.com
for details of the wide choice of accommodation featured in the full range of FHG titles

SUTTON COLDFIELD. **Moor Hall Golf Club Ltd,** Moor Hall Drive, Sutton Coldfield B75 6LN (0121-308 6130). *Location:* one mile east of Sutton Coldfield, A446. Parkland. 18 holes, 6293 yards. S.S.S. 70. Practice area. *Green Fees:* £45.00 per round, £60.00 per day. Subject to review. *Eating facilities:* available weekdays. *Visitors:* welcome weekdays only (not Thursday mornings). 4-star Moor Hall Hotel on golf estate (independently owned). *Society Meetings:* catered for. Professional: Cameron Clark (0121-308 5106). Secretary: D.J. Etheridge (0121-308 6130).

SUTTON COLDFIELD. **Pype Hayes Golf Club,** Eachelhurst Road, Walmley, Sutton Coldfield B76 8EP (0121-351 1014). *Location:* off the A38 Kingsbury Road, one and a half miles from Junction 9 M42. Flat wooded course with small greens, four demanding Par 3's. 18 holes, 5996 yards. S.S.S. 69. *Green Fees:* Information not available. *Eating facilities:* cafeteria. *Visitors:* welcome but must book via telephone. *Society Meetings:* welcome but must book via telephone. Professional: Joe Kelly. Secretary: C.R. Marson (0121-788 3450).*

SUTTON COLDFIELD. **Sutton Coldfield Golf Club,** Thornhill Road, Streetly, Sutton Coldfield B74 3ER (0121-353 9633; Fax: 0121-353 5503). *Location:* situated in Sutton Park, one mile off A452, seven miles from centre of Birmingham. Natural heathland. 18 holes, 6549 yards. S.S.S. 71. *Green Fees:* weekdays £33.00 per round, £44.00 all day; weekends £44.00 per round. *Eating facilities:* by arrangement with Chef (0121-353 2014). *Visitors:* welcome without reservation but please ring Professional to check availability. Handicap Certificate required. *Society Meetings:* Special arrangements for societies by arrangement with Secretary. Professional: J.K. Hayes (0121-580 7878). Secretary: R.G. Mitchell (0121-353 9633; Fax: 0121-353 5503). website: www.suttoncoldfieldgc.com

SUTTON COLDFIELD. **Walmley Golf Club,** Brooks Road, Wylde Green, Sutton Coldfield B72 1HR (0121-373 0029; Fax: 0121-377 7272). *Location:* Birmingham/Sutton Coldfield main road, turn right at Green Hill Road. Parkland. 18 holes, 6585 yards. S.S.S. 72. Practice ground. *Green Fees:* Information not available. *Eating facilities:* lunch and evening meals available. *Visitors:* welcome weekdays only. *Society Meetings:* catered for Wednesdays, Thursdays and some Fridays only. Professional: Chris Wicketts (0121-373 0029 Ext.3). e-mail: walmleygolfclub@aol.com

WALSALL. **Bloxwich Golf Club (1988) Ltd,** 136 Stafford Road, Bloxwich, Walsall WS3 3PQ (01922 476593; Fax: 01922 493449). *Location:* off main Walsall-Cannock road (A34). Semi parkland. 18 holes, 6257 yards. S.S.S. 71. *Green Fees:* information not available. *Eating facilities:* available. *Visitors:* welcome with or without reservation except weekends and Bank Holidays. *Society Meetings:* catered for midweek, reduced rates for 20 or more. Professional: R.J. Dance (01922 476889; Fax: 01922 493449). Secretary/Manager: R.J. Wormstone (01922 476593; Fax: 01922 493449).

WALSALL. **Calderfields Golf Club,** Aldridge Road, Walsall WS4 2JS (01922 632243; Fax: 01922 640540). *Location:* A454 between Aldridge and Walsall, Junction 10 M6. Parkland, water hazards. 18 holes, 6509 yards, S.S.S. 73. 27 bay floodlit driving range, practice bunkers, putting green. *Green Fees:* weekdays £18.00, weekends and Bank Holidays £20.00 (subject to review). *Eating facilities:* Lake View restaurant and bar. New function suite for all occasions, seating for 150. *Visitors:* welcome at all times. *Society Meetings:* packages available 7 days a week, subject to availability. Booking Tee Time (01922 632243). website: www.calderfieldsgolf.com

WALSALL. **Druids Heath Golf Club,** Stonnall Road, Aldridge, Walsall WS9 8JZ (01922 455595; Fax: 01922 452887). *Location*: off A452 near Little Aston – Aldridge. Testing undulating heathland course. 18 holes, 6665 yards. S.S.S. 73. Practice ground and net. *Green Fees*: £34.00 weekdays; £42.00 weekends after 2pm. *Eating facilities*: dining room and bar snacks. *Visitors*: welcome by prior arrangement. *Society Meetings*: catered for by prior arrangement. Professional: Glenn Williams (01922 459523). Secretary: K.I Taylor. e-mail: dhgcadmin@uku.co.uk website: www.druidsheathgc.co.uk

WALSALL. **Walsall Golf Club,** The Broadway, Walsall WS1 3EY (01922 613512; Fax: 01922 616460). *Location:* one and a half miles from M6/M5 junction. Wooded course. 18 holes, 6259 yards. S.S.S. 71. *Green Fees:* on application. *Eating facilities:* all facilities available. *Visitors:* welcome weekdays only. *Society Meetings:* catered for. Professional: R. Lambert (01922 626766). Secretary: H. J. Durkin (01922 613512).

WARLEY. **Warley Woods Golf Club,** The Pavillion, Lightwoods Hill, Smethwick B67 5EO (0121-429 2440; Fax: 0121-434 4430). *Location:* Hagley Road. Adjacent to Warley Woods. Warley water tower at top of course. Parkland course. 9 holes, 2686 yards. S.S.S. 66. *Green Fees:* information not available. *Eating facilities:* cafe. *Visitors:* welcome, advised to book in advance as this is a very busy club. *Society Meetings:* welcome during quiet times, telephone Course Manager for details. Course Manager: H. Hardman (0121-429 2440; Fax: 0121-434 4430). Secretary: Ron Simcox (0121-686 2619; Fax: 0121-241 3451).

WEST BROMWICH. **Dartmouth Golf Club,** Vale Street, West Bromwich B71 4DW (0121-588 5746). *Location:* one mile from West Bromwich town centre. All Saints Way A4031, turn right at McDonalds and follow signposts. Part flat, part undulating course, a good test for all categories. 9 holes, 6036 yards. S.S.S. 70. Practice area, putting green. *Green Fees:* weekdays 18 holes £20.00, 9 holes £12.00; with a member 18 holes £12.00, 9 holes £8.00, weekends 18 holes £25.00, with a member 18 holes £20.00, subject to review. *Eating facilities:* bar snacks always available, meals by prior arrangement. *Visitors:* welcome weekdays, weekends with a member only. *Society Meetings:* welcome by prior arrangement. Secretary: C.F. Wade (0121-532 4070).

WEST BROMWICH. **Sandwell Park Golf Club Ltd,** Birmingham Road, West Bromwich B71 4JJ (0121-553 4637; Fax: 0121-525 1651). *Location*: on A41 to Birmingham 200 yards from Junction 1 M5, turn left under footbridge. Wooded, heathland course. 18 holes, 6468 yards. S.S.S. 73. Two practice areas, chipping green. *Green Fees*: 18 holes £40.00, 27 or 36 holes £50.00. Societies from £35.00 per person. *Eating facilities*: full restaurant facilities and two bars. *Visitors*: welcome weekdays, weekend and Bank Holidays with a member only. Handicap Certificate required. *Society Meetings*: by prior arrangement with the Manager. Manager: A. Turner. Professional: Nigel Wylie (0121-553 4384). Secretary: D.A. Paterson (0121-553 4637).
website: www.sandwellparkgolfclub.co.uk

WISHAW. **The Belfry,** Wishaw, Sutton Coldfield B76 9PR (01675 470301; Fax: 01675 470178). *Location:* leave M42 at Junction 9 and follow signs for Lichfield, The Belfry is on A446. Parkland courses. The Brabazon - 18 holes, 7153 yards. S.S.S. 74. PGA National - 18 holes, 7053 yards. S.S.S. 71. The Derby - 18 holes, 6057 yards. S.S.S. 69. PGA National Golf Academy, 34 bay driving range, putting green. National club fitting centre, 10 brands to be fitted with. Over 20 professionals. *Green Fees:* information not available. *Eating facilities:* use of hotel facilities including a selection of bars and restaurants. *Visitors:* welcome. 324 bedroomed four-star hotel, 21 conference rooms, leisure club, indoor heated pool, sauna, solarium, hairdressing salon, beauty rooms, Aqua Spa, gymnasium; two squash courts, snooker room, pool tables, outdoor tennis courts and jogging trail. Bel Air Night Club situated within hotel grounds. Buggies, carts and caddies available. *Society Meetings:* always welcome subject to availablity. Director of Golf: Gary Silcock. Professional: Gary Alliss (Golf Monthly Top 25 coach) (01675 470301).
e-mail: enquiries@thebelfry.com
website: www.thebelfry.com

WOLVERHAMPTON. **Oxley Park Golf Club Ltd,** Stafford Road, Bushbury, Wolverhampton WV10 6DE. *Location:* 1½ miles M54/A449 junction, 1½ miles Wolverhampton town centre. Undulating parkland. 18 holes, 6226 yards. S.S.S. 71. *Green Fees:* £34.00 per round, £40.00 per day. *Eating facilities:* available daily except Monday. *Visitors:* welcome weekdays, weekends by arrangement with Professional. *Society Meetings:* preferred day Wednesday; for alternatives please contact Secretary. Professional: Leslie Burlison (01902 425445). Secretary: (01902 773989; Fax: 01902 773981).*

WOLVERHAMPTON. **Penn Golf Club Ltd,** Penn Common, Penn, Wolverhampton WV4 5JN (01902 341142). *Location:* two miles south west of Wolverhampton, off A449. Heathland. 18 holes, 6487 yards. S.S.S. 72. *Green Fees:* £35.00 per round, £30.00 per day. *Eating facilities:* full catering and bar facilities. *Visitors:* welcome weekdays. *Society Meetings:* catered for. Professional: G. Dean (01902 330472). Club Administrator: Mrs A Rafferty (01902 341142).
e-mail: secretary@penn-golf.freeserve.co.uk

WOLVERHAMPTON. **Wergs Golf Club,** Keepers Lane, Tettenhall, Wolverhampton WV6 8UA (01902 742225). *Location:* from centre of Wolverhampton, take A41 (to Newport), after two and a half miles turn right, half a mile on right. Open parkland. 18 holes, 6949 yards. S.S.S. 73. 20 acre practice area. *Green Fees:* weekdays £17.00; weekends and Bank Holidays £22.00. Senior Citizens and Juniors £14.50 weekdays, £19.00 weekends and Bank Holidays. *Eating facilities:* full catering and bar facilities. *Visitors:* always welcome. Membership available. *Society Meetings:* welcome anytime during week, after 10am at weekends. Secretary: Mrs G. Parsons. e-mail: wergs.golfclub@btinternet.com

PLEASE MENTION THE GOLF GUIDE WHEN YOU WRITE OR PHONE TO ENQUIRE ABOUT CLUBS OR ACCOMMODATION

BROMSGROVE. **Bromsgrove Golf Centre,** Stratford Road, Bromsgrove B60 1LD (01527 575886; Course Reception 01527 570505; Conference and Restaurant 01527 579179). *Location:* easily located on the junction of the A38 and A448, one mile from Bromsgrove town centre. Just five minutes' drive from juctions 4 and 5 of the M5 and Junction 1 of the M42 (exit west bound only). Course: Gently undulating parkland course, large contoured greens with superb views over Worcestershire. 18 holes, 5969 yards. S.S.S. 68. *Visitors:* most welcome. Tee times bookable up to seven days in advance. Golf shoes or similar, with socks, collared shirts, tailored trousers/shorts. *Society Meetings:* welcome by prior arrangement, packages available on request. *Green Fees:* available on request. *Facilities include:* 35 bay floodlit driving range, large multilevel putting green. Conference and function rooms, Golf Shop, Golf Academy. Wide range of tuition available with resident PGA Professionals (Tuition Fees list available). New "Teaching Studio" complete with state of the art computerised video systems. *Eating facilities:* friendly clubhouse with full bar and restaurant facilities available to non members. Head Professional: Graeme Long . Assistant Professional: Danny Wall. Secretary: David Went.
e-mail: enquiries@bromsgrovegolfcentre.com
website: www.bromsgrovegolfcentre.com

BROMYARD. **Sapey Golf Club,** Upper Sapey, Worcester WR6 6XT (01886 853288). *Location:* situated six miles north of Bromyard on B4203. Parkland course with water features, outstanding views over Malvern Hills. The Rowan: 18 holes, 5935 yards. S.S.S. 68. The Oaks: 9-holes, 1203 yards. Practice, putting green. *Green Fees:* The Rowan – weekdays £27.00; weekends £32.00. The Oaks – weekdays £7.00. weekends £9.00. *Eating facilities:* bar and restaurant meals available seven days a week. *Visitors:* always welcome. Buggies, power trolleys, trolleys for hire. Fully stocked Pro Shop with PGA tuition available for all, including Junior coaching under the Golf Foundation Scheme. *Society Meetings:* always welcome. Professional: Chris Knowles (01886 853288). Secretary: Lynn Stevenson (01886 853506; Fax: 01886 853485).
e-mail: anybody@sapeygolf.co.uk
website: www.sapeygolf.co.uk

DROITWICH. **Droitwich Golf and Country Club Ltd,** Westford House, Ford Lane, Droitwich WR9 0BQ. Location: between Junction 5 of M5 and Droitwich just off A38. Parkland, undulating, wooded. 18 holes, 5976 yards. S.S.S. 69. Practice area. *Green Fees:* information not available. *Eating facilities:* full catering and bar facilities available. *Visitors:* welcome without reservation Mondays to Fridays (Ladies Day Tuesday, tee closed to 12 noon), weekends with member only. *Society Meetings:* catered for Wednesdays or Fridays, £30.00 per player. Professional: P. Cundy (01905 770207). Secretary: C.S. Thompson (01905 774344; Fax: 01905 797290).

DROITWICH near. **Ombersley Golf Club,** Bishops Wood Road, Linholt, Ombersley, Near Droitwich WR9 0LE (01905 620747; Fax: 01905 620047). *Location:* from A449, two and a half miles north of Ombersley, take A4025 then first left. High, though gently undulating course enjoying panoramic views over Severn Valley. 18 holes, 6139 yards. S.S.S. 69. Covered driving range, chipping green and bunker, putting green. *Green Fees:* off peak £19.70, peak £27.95. *Eating facilities:* bar facilities, snacks and meals available. *Visitors:* all visitors welcome, bookable seven days in advance. Seventeen buggies, cart rental available. *Society Meetings:* welcome by arrangement – we specialise in corporate golf. Professional/General Manager: Graham Glenister.

DROITWICH SPA. **Gaudet Luce Golf Club,** Middle Lane, Hadzor, Droitwich Spa WR9 7JR (Tel: 01905 796375; Fax: 01905 797245). *Location:* Junction 5 or 6 off M5, Droitwich Spa, located just off Tagwell Road. Undulating parkland course with a mixture of long and short holes offering a demanding challenge for all golfers. 18 holes, 5887 yards. S.S.S. 69. Par 3, 9 hole Academy Course, 12 bay Driving Range. *Green Fees:* Monday - Thursday £20.00, Friday, Saturday & Sunday £25.00. *Eating facilities:* full clubhouse facilities including restaurant, lounge and bar. *Visitors:* welcome most days (essential to phone the Pro Shop before visit). Fully stocked Pro Shop with PGA tuition available for all, including Junior coaching under the Young Masters Golf. *Society Meetings:* welcome most weekdays by prior arrangement with Pro Shop. Professional: Russell Adams.
e-mail: info@gaudet-luce.co.uk
website: www.gaudet-luce.co.uk

EVESHAM. **Evesham Golf Club,** Craycombe Links, Fladbury Cross, Pershore WR10 2QS (01386 860395). *Location:* M5 at Junction 6, A4538 and A44 to Evesham approximately 10 miles then towards Worcester for about three miles. Meadowland, tree-lined fairways. 9 holes (18 tees), 6415 yards, 5866 metres. S.S.S. 71. Practice area. *Green Fees:* information not available. *Eating facilities:* diningroom and bar. *Visitors:* must be members of a recognised club and have a certified Handicap. Tuesday Ladies' Day. *Society Meetings:* catered for by prior arrangement. Professional: Dan Clee (01386 861011). Secretary: John Dale.*

HAGLEY. **Hagley Golf and Country Club,** Wassell Grove Lane, Hagley DY9 9JW (01562 883701; Fax: 01562 887518). *Location:* A456 Birmingham to Kidderminster Road. Wooded undulating course with many testing holes. 18 holes, 6553 yards. S.S.S. 72. Practice ground. *Green Fees:* Information not available. *Eating facilities:* full à la carte restaurant and bars. *Visitors:* welcome to play Monday to Friday, weekends with a member only. Buggies available. *Society Meetings:* welcome weekdays by prior arrangement. Professional: Iain Clark (01562 883852). Secretary: Graham F. Yardley.*

THE APPEARANCE OF AN ASTERISK (*) AT THE END OF A CLUB OR COURSE ENTRY INDICATES THAT UP-TO-DATE INFORMATION HAS NOT BEEN SUPPLIED

KIDDERMINSTER. **Habberley Golf Club,** Habberley, Kidderminster DY11 5RF. *Location*: north west side of Kidderminster. Undulating parkland course. 9 holes, 5401 yards. S.S.S. 68. *Green Fees:* Information not available. Twilight golf available at reduced rates, after 4pm, including weekends. *Eating facilities:* food and bar available. *Visitors:* welcome weekdays, without reservation; weekends afternoons only. *Society Meetings:* welcome, on application. Group rate £10.00 per person. Secretary: D.S.McDermott (01562 745756).*

KIDDERMINSTER. **Kidderminster Golf Club,** Russell Road, Kidderminster DY10 3HT (01562 822303; Fax: 01562 827866). *Location:* signposted off A449 Worcester–Wolverhampton Road. Wooded parkland course. 18 holes, 6422 yards. S.S.S. 71. Practice ground. *Green Fees:* Information not available. *Eating facilities:* bar and restaurant available. *Visitors:* welcome weekdays only if bona fide member of another club, weekends if guest of member. Snooker room with bar. *Society Meetings:* Thursdays; small parties catered for other weekdays. Professional: (01562 740090). Secretary: (01562 822303; Fax: 01562 827866).
e-mail: info@kidderminstergolfclub.com
website: www.kidderminstergolfclub.com

KIDDERMINSTER. **Wyre Forest Golf Club,** Zortech Avenue, Kidderminster DY11 7EX (01299 822682; Fax: 01299 879433). *Location*: from Kidderminster to Stourport-on-Severn on the A451. Flat inland links type course. Full practice facilities. 18 holes, 57901 yards. S.S.S. 68. *Green Fees*: information not available. *Eating facilities*: clubhouse bar open until 9pm daily. *Visitors*: can book 6 days in advance. Must book at weekends. *Society Meetings*: catered for. Packages start from £18.50 including golf and two-course meal. Professional/General Manager: C. Botterill.*
e-mail: c.botterill@wyreforestgolf.com

MALVERN WELLS. **The Worcestershire Golf Club,** Wood Farm, Malvern Wells WR14 4PP (01684 575992; Fax: 01684 893334). *Location*: two miles south of Great Malvern, near junction of A449 and B4209. Exceptionally scenic - Malvern Hills and Vale of Evesham. 18 holes, 6500 yards. S.S.S. 72. *Green Fees*: weekdays £38.00 per day; weekends £42.00 per day. *Eating facilities*: available. *Visitors*: visitors unaccompanied by a member must provide a current Handicap Certificate. Weekends after 10am. *Society Meetings*: catered for Mondays, Thursdays and Fridays only on application. Professional: R. Lewis (Tel & Fax: 01684 564428). Secretary/Manager: David Wilson (01684 575992; Fax: 01684 893334).
e-mail: secretary@worcsgolfclub.co.uk

PERSHORE. **The Vale Golf Club,** Hill Furze Road, Bishampton, Near Pershore WR10 2LZ (01386 462781; Fax: 01386 462597). *Location:* off the A44 road, between Evesham and Pershore at Fladbury crossroads. Feature lakes and wooded surrounds. Two courses: The Lenches, 9 holes, 2628 to 2918 yards. S.S.S 66 to 68; The International Championship Course, 18 holes, 6663 to 7174 yards. S.S.S. 72/74. Driving range. *Green Fees:* The International per round Mon - Thur £28.00, Friday £32.00, Weekends £40.00; The Lenches, 9 holes Mon - Fri £11.00, Weekends £12.00; 18 holes Mon - Fri £15.00, Weekends £18.00. Reductions for Juniors and members' guest. *Eating facilities:* Vale restaurant, spike bar, Sir William Lyons Suite. *Visitors:* welcome. *Society Meetings:* corporate and society days welcome. Professional: Richard Jenkins (01386 462520; Fax: 01386 462660). General Manager: Melanie Drake.
e-mail: vale-sales@crown-golf.co.uk

REDDITCH. **Pitcheroak Golf Course,** Plymouth Road, Redditch B97 4PB (01527 541043). *Location*: 500 yards from bus/train stations. Hilly parkland course very tricky, lots of trees and bunker. 9 holes (18 tees), 4561 yards. S.S.S. 62. Practice grounds, nets, putting green. *Green Fees:* Information not available. *Eating facilities:* bar and cafeteria facilities open all day. *Visitors:* welcome any time, municipal course. Changing rooms (ladies and gents). *Society Meetings:* welcome. Professional: D. Stewart (01527 541054). Secretary: Ray Barnett (01386 793370). *

REDDITCH. **Redditch Golf Club,** Lower Grinsty, Green Lane, Callow Hill, Redditch B97 5PJ (01527 543079; Fax: 01527 547413). *Location:* three miles west of Redditch town centre, off Redditch to Bromsgrove road (A448), or Astwood Bank to Redditch (A441), take Windmill Drive, look for Callow Hill signs. First 9 holes parkland, second 9 holes wooded. White - 18 holes, 6671 yards. S.S.S. 72; Yellow - 18 holes, 6285 yards. S.S.S. 70. Two practice areas. *Green Fees:* Information not available. *Eating facilities:* restaurant and bar with bar snacks except Mondays. *Visitors:* welcome, weekends with member. *Society Meetings:* catered for by arrangement. Professional: David Down (01527 546372). Secretary: T.J. Sheldon (01527 543079; Fax 01527 547413).*
website: www.redditchgolfclub.com*

THE APPEARANCE OF AN ASTERISK (*) AT THE END OF A CLUB OR COURSE ENTRY INDICATES THAT UP-TO-DATE INFORMATION HAS NOT BEEN SUPPLIED

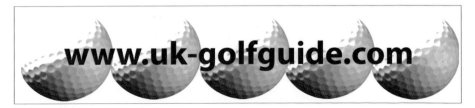

www.uk-golfguide.com

REDDITCH. **Redditch Kingfisher Golf Club,** Pitcheroak Golf Course, Plymouth Road, Redditch B97 4PB. *Location:* just up from the station. Hilly parkland course. 9 holes, 4561 yards. S.S.S. 62. Practice, nets, putting green. *Green Fees:* Information not available. *Eating facilities:* full catering and bar facilities. *Visitors:* welcome at all times. Showers/ changing rooms. *Society Meetings:* welcome at all times. Professional: David Stewart (01527 541054). Secretary: Ray Barnett (01386 793370).*

REDDITCH. **The Abbey Hotel & Country Club,** Hither Green Lane, Dagnell End Road, Redditch B98 9BE (01527 406500; Fax: 01527 406514). *Location:* on the northern boundary of Redditch town, between the villages of Bedley and Bordesley. From M42, junction 2, take A441 towards Redditch, signposted Redditch, turn left at first traffic lights, signposted Bedley, B4101. Turn right after approximately 500 metres into Hither Green Lane. The golf course is immediately on the left. Donald Steel designed parkland course. 18 holes, 6691 yards (white tees), S.S.S. 72, 6405 yards (yellow tees) S.S.S. 71, 5729 yards (red tees), S.S.S. 72. Golf range, putting green. *Green Fees:* £30.00. Golf Packages available. *Eating facilities:* Tawnys Bar serving bar snacks, hot beverages, lunches and dinners. Fully licensed restaurant in the hotel. *Visitors:* welcome alll week; bookings to be made 4 days or less in advance. Golf tuition, trolley and buggy hire, golf shop. 100 room, 4 star hotel on site. *Society Meetings:* welcome. Professional: Rob Davies (01527 406500; Fax: 01527 406514). Secretary: Mrs P. Williamson (01527 406538; Fax 01527 406514).
e-mail: info@theabbeyhotel.co.uk
      membership@theabbeyhotel.co.uk
      golfshop@theabbeyhotel.co.uk
website: www.theabbeyhotel.co.uk

TENBURY WELLS. **Cadmore Lodge Golf and Country Club,** Berrington Green, Tenbury Wells WR15 8TQ (01584 810044). *Location:* two miles south of Tenbury Wells, just off A4112 to Leominster. Parkland with lake and streams in constant play. *Green Fees:* information not available. *Eating facilities:* hotel bar and restaurant. *Visitors:* welcome, no restrictions. Hotel with AA Rosette restaurant and 14 en suite bedrooms. *Society Meetings:* welcome. Secretary: R.V. Farr (01584 810306 home).

WORCESTER. **Perdiswell Park Golf Club,** Bilford Road, Worcester WR3 8DX (01905 754668). *Location:* 600 yards from A38, north of the city centre. A testing 18 hole parkland course with many natural features. *Green Fees:* information not available. *Eating facilities:* food available. *Visitors:* welcome at any time, but advised to phone first. *Society Meetings:* welcome. PGA Professional: Mark Woodward (01905 754668). Secretary: Richard Gardner (01905 452399; Fax: 01905 453133).*

WORCESTER. **Ravenmeadow Golf Club,** Hindlip Lane, Claines, Worcester WR3 8SA (01905 757525; Fax: 01905 458876). *Location:* Junction 6 (M5 motorway) A449, leave at Blackpole exit; at main road turn right then first left into Hindlip Lane, entrance is half-mile on the left. Gently undulating course, with greens and tees to USGA standards; Barbourne Brook meanders through the course. 10 holes (18 tees). 5352 yards, S.S.S. 66. Excellent practice facilities: driving range, 9 hole pitch and putt, adults' and children's practice greens, chipping green. *Green Fees:* weekdays 9 holes £10.00, 18 holes £14.00; weekends 9 holes £12.00, 18 holes £17.00. Over 55s weekdays 9 holes £7.50, 18 holes £9.50. Wednesday Ladies' Day 9 holes £5.00, 18 holes £7.00. *Eating facilities:* Bar open 7 days, food available from 11am. *Visitors:* always welcome, telephone to reserve tee times. *Society Meetings:* welcome every day. Telephone (01905 458876) for special rates. Professional: Leo Tarrant (PGA) (01905 756665). Manager: Tony Senter (Tel & Fax: 01905 458876).

WORCESTER. **Worcester Golf and Country Club,** Boughton Park, Worcester WR2 4EZ (01905 422555). *Location:* one-and-a-quarter miles west of city on A4103 (to Hereford). Parkland with lakes and specimen trees. 18 holes, 6251 yards. S.S.S. 70. Practice areas. *Green Fees:* information not available. *Eating facilities:* full catering available. *Visitors:* welcome weekdays, telephone Professional. Handicap Certificate required. *Society Meetings:* welcome, telephone Secretary. Professional: Graham Farr (01905 422044). Secretary: P. Tredwell (01905 422555).
e-mail: worcestergcc@btinternet.com
website: www.worcestergcc.co.uk

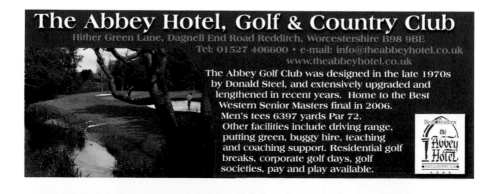

Golf in the North

David Birtill

Cheshire · Cumbria · Durham
Greater Manchester · Lancashire · Merseyside
Northumberland · Tyne & Wear · Yorkshire

HOW TIME FLIES when you're enjoying yourself!

It does not seem more than a few months since the Open made a triumphant return to Royal Liverpool after an absence of 39 years.

Thank heavens we won't have to wait so long again, with Hoylake back firmly on the roster after staging what many considered to be the best Championship in modern times. And that was not just down to Tiger Woods adroitly plotting his way round scorched fairways to an inevitable victory.

The overall organisation was truly superb, but would you expect anything less from the friendly North West?

Well, here we are again – back on Merseyside and at Royal Birkdale for golf's greatest showpiece in July. The appropriately dubbed

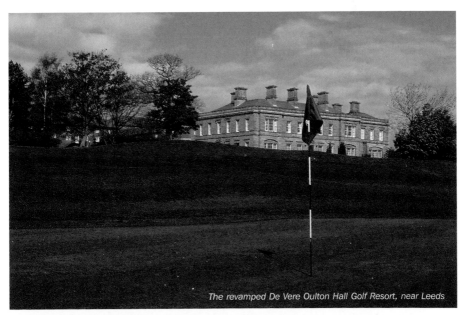

The revamped De Vere Oulton Hall Golf Resort, near Leeds

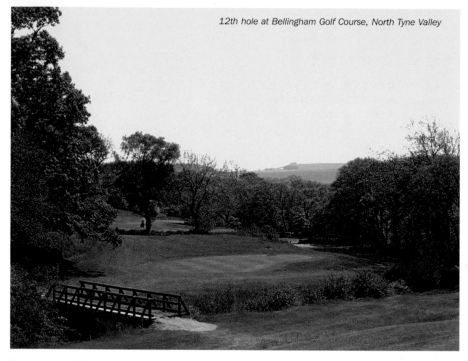

12th hole at Bellingham Golf Course, North Tyne Valley

England's Golf Coast certainly gets its share of the big occasions and rightly so. It stretches from Blackpool down to the Wirral and contains unquestionably some of the most spectacular and testing links in the country, with a combination of sea, sand and the forces of nature offering an irresistible challenge for players of all levels.

The three Royals – Birkdale, Lytham St Annes and Liverpool – have all hosted the Championship on several occasions, and the former two the British Women's Open, not forgetting Formby, which staged the Curtis Cup in 2004.

A record 230,000 attended Hoylake in 2006 and don't be surprised if that figure is beaten this year because Birkdale had the previous best attendance of 200,000.

While only the privileged few can hope to kick a ball at Wembley or hit a six at Lord's, anyone irrespective of handicap can follow in the spike marks of the greats such as Tiger Woods, Ernie Els and Jack Nicklaus. And there's plenty of 'em in this region!

Hillside, which butts on to Birkdale, is almost as great a challenge, and it's easy to see why its next door neighbour on the other side of the fence, Southport and Ainsdale, is a former Ryder Cup venue.

But if you really want to sample links golf in the raw try pegging up at West Lancs when the prevailing wind whistles across the Mersey estuary; or Wallasey, which has been home for many major international events.

Stand on Southport promenade and you can't fail to spot Blackpool and its famous tower just across the water. That's where you'll find Royal Lytham, which needs no introduction. In addition to major Pro tournaments many other important competitions are staged there, including, at the start of May, its own Lytham Trophy, one of the county's top amateur events. A short flight or leisurely ferry crossing will take you to the Isle of Man where, despite its tiny population, there are nine courses to savour.

Castletown, home of the PGA North Region's Manx Classic, remains the jewel in the crown – especially after the links underwent a few

changes last year, with bunkers appearing in strategic places. But they did not bother Paul Eales, who won the 54-hole event!

Back over the Irish Sea and moving inland, De Vere Mottram Hall, near Macclesfield, bears all the hallmarks of the worthy skills of former Ryder Cup player Dave Thomas. He has blended the relatively flat front nine with the contrasting, more demanding inward holes, making it a fitting venue for the Manchester Evening News Manchester Open. De Vere have also recently acquired the former public course which surrounds their five star Oulton Hall. They've wasted no time in upgrading the 27-hole lay-out, and the multi-million pound investment also includes a splendid new clubhouse.

Staying in Yorkshire, there's a vast array of courses, but few can rival Ganton, near Scarborough, one of the country's greatest inland links and a former Walker Cup venue.

Alwoodley, Fulford, Sand Moor, Moor Allerton, Pannal, Lindrick, Catterick are all well established clubs, complementing a host of new ones which have sprung up, including the

The testing 5th hole at Castletown Golf Links, Isle of Man

excellent Aldwark Manor and Rudding Park, both not a million miles away from the beautiful spa town of Harrogate.

But if you're visiting the area, Leeds Golf Club at Cobble Hall is a must for your itinerary. The Leeds Cup, professional golf's oldest trophy, returned to its spiritual home in 2006 and the beautiful parkland course exceeded all expectations.

Further north, Matfen Hall and Ramside are among fairly recent developments which sit comfortably with well established clubs such as Newbiggin, Whitley Bay, Prudhoe in Northumberland, and Seaton Carew, South Shields, Bishop Auckland and Barnard Castle in Durham. Matfen Hall, where another North Region tournament, The Rock, has become

established, has added another nine holes which blend in perfectly with the original classic parkland lay-out, opened in 1995.

Burgham Park, another new venture, has proved the ideal home for the PGA North Region Championship.

Back over the Pennines – try the Military Road to Carlisle if you're travelling from the North East – you'll be spoiled for choice for somewhere to play and stay.

Drop into Penrith for a round, then wend your way to magnificent Silloth-on-Solway and see how you cope with the wind-swept dunes.

For more gentle alternatives there are Windermere, and Carus Green, a delightful new course in Kendal.

Cheshire

ADLINGTON. **Adlington Golf Centre,** Sandy Hey Farm, Adlington, Macclesfield SK10 4NG (01625 850660). *Location*: 2 miles south of Poynton off A523. 9 hole Par 3 course plus 9 hole Academy Course. 24 bay covered, floodlit driving range. *Fees*: information not available. *Eating facilities:* tea and coffee available. Reductions for Senior Citizens/Juniors. Tuition available all the time. Proprietor: David Moss (01625 850660).*

ALDERLEY EDGE. **Alderley Edge Golf Club,** Brook Lane, Alderley Edge SK9 7RU (01625 586200). *Location:* off A34. 9 holes, 5836 yards. S.S.S. 68. *Green Fees:* Information not available. *Eating facilities:* meals served in clubhouse. *Visitors:* subject to restrictions on Tuesday mornings, Wednesday afternoons and weekends. *Society Meetings:* welcome on Thursdays. Professional: P. Bowring (01625 584493). Secretary: R.C. Harrison.*

ALSAGER. **Alsager Golf and Country Club,** Audley Road, Alsager, Stoke-on-Trent ST7 2UR (01270 875700; Fax: 01270 882207). *Location:* off M6 at Junction 16 onto A500 to Stoke, first left to Alsager, course is one and a half miles on right. Parkland. 18 holes, 6225 yards. S.S.S. 70. *Green Fees:* information not available. *Eating facilities:* restaurant and bar snacks. *Visitors:* welcome Mondays, to Thursdays and Fridays 8am to 12pm, without reservation. Wedding, conference and banqueting facilities, Bowls. *Society Meetings:* welcome Mondays, Wednesdays and Thursdays, packages arranged. Professional: Richard Brown (01270 877432; Fax: 01270 882207). Administration Manager: Margaret Davenport (01270 875700).
e-mail: business@alsagergolfclub.com
website: www.alsagergolfclub.com

APPLETON. **Warrington Golf Club,** Hill Warren, London Road, Appleton, Near Warrington WA4 5HR (01925 261620). *Location:* M56 Junction 10, A49 Warrington one and a half miles on left. Parkland course. 18 holes, 6210 yards. S.S.S. 70. Practice ground. *Green Fees:* information not available. *Eating facilities:* available every day. *Visitors:* welcome with booking through Professional. *Society Meetings:* Wednesdays only, booked through Secretary. Professional: R. MacKay (01925 265431). Secretary: S. Higham (01925 261775; Fax: 01925 265933)*.
e-mail: secretary@warrington-golf-club.co.uk

CHEADLE. **Cheadle Golf Club,** Cheadle Road, Cheadle SK8 1HW (0161-428 2160). *Location:* one-and-a-half miles Junction 11 M63. Parkland. 9 holes, 5006 yards. S.S.S. 65. *Green Fees:* on application. *Eating facilities:* by arrangement with the Steward. *Visitors:* welcome, must be members of a bona fide golf club; current Handicap Certificate to be produced; no visitors on Tuesdays or Saturdays. *Society Meetings:* catered for by arrangement with the Secretary. Professional: Sam Dunford (0161-428 9878). Secretary: C.T. Openshaw (0161-491 4452).

CHEADLE. **Gatley Golf Club Ltd,** Waterfall Farm, Styal Road, Heald Green, Cheadle SK8 3TW (0161-437 2091). *Location:* from Gatley village to South down Styal Road and follow directions into Yew Tree Grove, then Motcombe Grove to Club entrance. Parkland course. 9 holes, 5934 yards. S.S.S. 68. *Green Fees:* information not available. Special rates by arrangement. *Eating facilities:* available except Monday, bar. *Visitors:* welcome Mondays, Wednesdays and Thursdays. *Society Meetings:* welcome Thursdays. Professional: James Matterson (0161-436 2830). Secretary: A. Poole (0161-437 2091)*.

CHESTER. **Aldersey Green Golf Club,** Aldersey, Near Chester CH3 9EH (01829 782157). *Location:* on A41 Chester to Whitchurch road five minutes from Broxton roundabout. Flat wooded parkland. 18 holes, 6159 yards. S.S.S. 69. Practice area. *Green Fees:* Information not available. *Eating facilities:* bar with meals available. *Visitors:* welcome. *Society meetings:* welcome. Professional and Secretary: Stephen Bradbury. *

CHESTER. **Carden Park Hotel Golf Resort & Spa,** Carden, near Chester CH3 9DQ (01829 731000; Fax: 01829 731032). *Location:* take A41 from Chester to Broxton roundabout, turn right onto A534 (Wrexham). Parkland courses with trees and superb views over the Cheshire countryside. Cheshire Course, 18 holes, 6824 yards. Par 72. Nicklaus Course, 18 holes, 7045 yards, Par 72. Par 3 Azalea Course. Driving range. *Green Fees:* information not available. *Eating facilities:* Clubhouse; brasserie within hotel. *Visitors:* welcome, some restriction on certain competition and members' days. No metal spikes allowed. Accommodation in 192 bedroom hotel. *Society Meetings:* welcome. Professional: Paul Hodgson.*
e-mail: enquiries.carden@devere-hotels.com

CHESTER. **Chester Golf Club,** Curzon Park, Chester CH4 8AR (01244 675130). *Location:* one mile south west of city centre. From Chester Castle take A483 (Wrexham) to first roundabout over Grovesnor Bridge. Turn right into Curzon Park North and follow signs. Parkland on two levels overlooking the River Dee. 18 holes, 6508 yards. S.S.S. 71. *Green Fees:* Information not available. *Eating facilities:* full restaurant and bar facilities. *Visitors:* welcome most days but advisable to telephone first. *Society Meetings:* catered for by prior arrangement. Professional: Scott Booth (01244 671185). Secretary: V.F.C. Wood (01244 677760).*

CHESTER. **Eaton Golf Club,** Guy Lane, Waverton, Chester CH3 7PH (01244 335885). *Location*: three miles south east of Chester off A41. 18 holes, 6580 yards. S.S.S. 72. Substantial practice area. *Green Fees:* weekdays £35.00, weekends £40.00. Subject to review. *Eating facilities:* catering available seven days. *Visitors:* welcome at all times but with Handicap Certificate and prior checking with either Secretary or Professional. *Society Meetings:* welcome except Wednesdays. Society rates available on request. Professional: Bill Tye (01244 335826). Secretary: Kerry Brown (01244 335885; Fax: 01244 335782).
e-mail: office@eatongolfclub.co.uk
website: www.eatongolfclub.co.uk

CHESTER. **Mollington Grange Golf Club,** Townfield Lane, Mollington, Chester CH1 6NJ (01244 851185; Fax: 01244 851349). *Location:* A 540, 5 minutes from end of M56 and two miles from Chester City. A superb undulating course with five lakes, 16 ponds and a Par 3 island green, providing a challenge for the advanced player while remaining friendly to the average player or beginner. 18 holes, 6400 yards. Par 71. Driving range. *Green Fees:* information not available. *Eating facilities:* club house with warm and friendly atmosphere, lounge and bar area, restaurant

and sports lounge/bar situated on the first floor. *Visitors:* welcome. Membership open, details on request. Fully stocked golf shop and comfortable changing facilities. *Society Meetings:* welcome. Corporate days and corporate membership catered for. Details available on request. Director of Golf: Ben Keegan. Secretary: Gail Matthews.*

CHESTER. **Pryors Hayes Golf Club,** Willington Road, Oscroft, Near Tarvin CH3 8NL (01829 741250; Fax: 01829 749077). *Location:* signposted; situated just off A54 between Kelsall and Tarvin. Flat, parkland course. 18 holes, 6054 yards. S.S.S. 69. Practice area. *Green Fees:* £30.00 weekdays, £40.00 weekends. *Eating facilities:* restaurant and bar. *Visitors:* welcome every day subject to availability. *Society Meetings:* Societies/Companies/Groups all welcome. Professional: Martin Redrup (01829 740140; Fax: 01829 749077). Secretary: Joan Quinn (01829 741250; Fax: 01829 749077)

CHESTER. **Upton-by-Chester Golf Club,** Upton Lane, Chester CH2 1EE (01244 381183; Fax: 01244 376955). *Location:* off A41, near Zoo turn-off traffic lights. Flat parkland course. 18 holes, 5807 yards. S.S.S. 68. *Green Fees:* £35.00 per day, £25.00 per round. *Eating facilities:* large restaurant and bar. *Visitors:* no restrictions except Competition Days. *Society Meetings:* welcome except Mondays, Tuesdays and weekends. Minimum number 16. All day packages £44.00. Professional: Stephen Dewhurst (01244 381183). Secretary: Fred Hopley (01244 381183; Fax: 01244 376955).

CHESTER. **Vicars Cross Golf Club,** Tarvin Road, Great Barrow, Chester CH3 7HN (01244 335174; Fax: 01244 335686). *Location:* four miles east of Chester on the A51. Undulating parkland course, wooded. 18 holes, 6446 yards. S.S.S. 71. Practice grounds/ covered bays. *Green Fees:* £30.00 weekdays, £35.00 weekends and Bank Holidays, £20.00 after 3pm every day. Subject to review. *Eating facilities:* restaurant and bar snacks. *Visitors:* welcome every day except competition days - phone Secretary or Professional beforehand. *Society Meetings:* welcome Tuesday/Thursday. Conference facilities, lounge/dining rooms available for hire. Professional: John Forsythe (01244 335595). Secretary: Mrs Katrina Hunt.
e-mail: manager@vicarscrossgolf.co.uk

CONGLETON. **Astbury Golf Club,** Peel Lane, Astbury, Near Congleton CW12 4RE (01260 272772). *Location:* on outskirts south of Congleton, leave A34 Congleton to Newcastle Road at Astbury Village. Parkland/meadowland, water feature on four holes. 18 holes, 6178 yards. S.S.S. 69. Large practice area. *Green Fees:* information not provided. *Eating facilities:*

dining room and bar. *Visitors:* welcome weekdays, weekend with a member only. Must be members of recognised golf club with bona fide Handicap. Smart casual dress in clubhouse, jackets expected when meal/presentation held. *Society Meetings:* Thursdays only April to November. Professional: Neil Dawson (01260 272772). Secretary: Fred Reed (01260 272772). Caterer: (01260 272772).

CONGLETON. **Congleton Golf Club,** Biddulph Road, Congleton CW12 3LZ (01260 273540). *Location:* one mile south of Congleton Railway Station on Biddulph Road. Parkland. 9 holes, 5119 yards. S.S.S. 65. *Green Fees:* Information not available. *Eating facilities:* lunches and evening meals served if ordered in advance. Snacks available. *Visitors:* welcome. *Society Meetings:* welcome Mondays and Thursdays by prior arrangement. Professional: Andrew Preston (07796 444321). Secretary: D. Lancake (01260 273540).*

CREWE. **Crewe Golf Club Ltd,** Fields Road, Haslington, Crewe CW1 5TB (01270 584099). *Location:* off A534 between Crewe and Sandbach in the village of Haslington. Parkland course. 18 holes, 6424 yards. S.S.S. 71. *Green Fees:* available on request. *Eating facilities:* bar, diningroom. *Visitors:* welcome weekdays only, not Bank Holidays. Snooker room. *Society Meetings:* Tuesdays only. Catering (01270 584227). Professional: David Wheeler (01270 585032). Secretary: Janet Stubbs (01270 584099; Fax: 01270 256482).
e-mail: secretary@crewegolfclub.co.uk
website: www.crewegolfclub.co.uk

CREWE. **Onneley Golf Club,** Barr Hill Road, Onneley, Near Crewe CW3 5QF (01782 750577). *Location:* one mile from Woore on A525, 12 miles from Stoke-on-Trent. Parkland on gentle slope. 18 holes, 5728 yards. S.S.S. 68. Par 70. *Green Fees:* weekdays £20.00 per day, Saturday £25.00 per round. *Eating facilities:* dining room and bar snacks. *Visitors:* welcome weekdays unrestricted. *Society Meetings:* welcome (weekdays £22.50 per round including meal, Saturdays £27.50 per round including meal). Secretary: Peter Ball (01782 846759).
website: www.onneleygolfclub.co.uk

CREWE. **Queens Park Golf Course,** Queens Park Drive, Crewe CW2 7SB (01270 662378). *Location:* next to Queens Park, one mile from Crewe Station. Parkland. 9 holes x 2, 4920 yards. S.S.S. 64. *Green Fees:* information not available. *Eating facilities:* bar with excellent bar snacks. *Visitors:* welcome, restrictions Sunday mornings to 11am. *Society Meetings:* welcome. Professional: Jamie Lowe (01270 666724). Secretary: Tom Weston (01270 662887).*

DISLEY. **Disley Golf Club Ltd,** Stanley Hall Lane, Disley, Stockport SK12 2JX (01663 764001). *Location:* off A6 at Disley Village. Open hillside/parkland course. 18 holes, 6015 yards, 5832 metres. S.S.S. 69. *Green Fees:* £28.00 weekdays, £40.00 weekends. *Eating facilities:* available. *Visitors:* welcome. *Society Meetings:* catered for by arrangement. Professional: A.G. Esplin (01663 764001). Secretary: Paul Smallwood (01663 764001

FRODSHAM. **Frodsham Golf Club,** Simons Lane, Frodsham WA6 6HE (01928 732159; Fax: 01928 734070). *Location:* 10 minutes from Junction 12 M56. Parkland with views over Mersey estuary. 18 holes, 6328 yards. S.S.S. 70 (gents), 70 (ladies). Two practice areas, putting green, bunker and net. *Green Fees:Information not available.* *Eating facilities:* clubhouse: dining room, lounge bar, spike bar, snooker room. *Visitors:* welcome weekdays only, guests of members only at weekends. *Society Meetings:* welcome weekdays. Professional: Graham Tonge (01928 739442; Fax: 01928 739037). Secretary: A. Webb (01928 732159; Fax: 01928 734070).*
e-mail: alastair@frodshamgc.co.uk
website: www.frodshamgolfclub.co.uk

HELSBY. **Helsby Golf Club,** Towers Lane, Helsby WA6 0JB (01928 722021; Fax: 01928 725384). *Location:* 7 miles south of Chester. M56 Junction 14 take B5117 to Helsby. Through traffic lights one mile, first right into Primrose Lane, then first right into Towers Lane (400 yards). James Braid designed parkland course. 18 holes, 6229 yards. S.S.S. 70. Practice area available. *Green Fees:* £27.50 weekdays; £17.00 with a member weekends. Subject to review. *Eating facilities:* full restaurant facilities. *Visitors:* welcome weekdays, weekends must play with a member. Snooker facilities. *Society Meetings:* welcome Tuesdays and Thursdays by arrangement. Professional: M. Jones (Tel & Fax: 01928 725457). Secretary: L.J. Norbury (01928 722021).

KNUTSFORD. **Heyrose Golf Club,** Budworth Road, Tabley, Knutsford WA16 0HZ (Tel & Fax: 01565 733664). *Location:* Junction 19 on M6 right at Windmill Pub to Pickmere, three-quarters of a mile right fork, half a mile further on right. Undulating parkland, wooded course. 18 holes, 6513 yards. S.S.S. 71. New 12 bay driving range, net and bunker, putting green, indoor teaching room. *Green Fees:* Information not available. *Eating facilities:* bar and restaurant. *Visitors:* no visitors on Saturdays before 3.30pm, Ladies priority Wednesdays, Seniors priority Thursdays. *Society Meetings:* welcome weekdays. Professional: Philip Bills (Tel & Fax: 01565 734267). General Manager: Mrs Elizabeth Bridge (Tel & Fax: 01565 733664).*
e-mail: info@heyrosegolfclub.com
website: www.heyrosegolfclub.com

KNUTSFORD. **Knutsford Golf Club,** Mereheath Lane, Knutsford WA16 6HS (01565 633355). *Location:* quarter of a mile from town centre. 9 holes, 6200 yards. S.S.S. 70. *Green Fees:* information not provided. *Eating facilities:* bar snacks, other meals by prior arrangement. *Visitors:* welcome with reservation except Wednesdays and Saturdays and Sundays before 10:00am. *Society Meetings:* catered for by prior arrangement. Professional: Tim Maxwell. Secretary: Danny Burgess.

KNUTSFORD. **Mere Golf and Country Club,** Chester Road, Mere, Knutsford WA16 6LJ (01565 830155; Fax: 01565 830713). *Location*: one mile east of Junction 19 M6 and two miles west of Junction 7 M56. Parkland Championship course. 18 holes, 6817 yards. S.S.S. 73. Short game practice area, one 18 hole putting green, driving range (April to October). *Green Fees:Information not* available . *Eating facilities:* informal atrium spike bar and brasserie. *Visitors:* welcome by prior arrangement only. *Society Meetings:* Mondays, Tuesdays and Thursdays only by arrangement. Professional: Peter Eyre (01565 830219). Golf Bookings: James Leeman (01565 830155). Secretary: Peter Whitehead.*
e-mail: honsec@meregolf.co.uk

KNUTSFORD. **Mobberley Golf Club,** Burleyhurst Lane, Mobberley, Knutsford WA16 7JZ (01565 880188; Fax: 01565 880178). *Location*: exit 6 M56 to A538 Wilmslow, turn right at Mobberley Road. 9 hole course set in rolling Cheshire countryside. 5542 yards, S.S.S. 67. *Green Fees*: information not available. *Eating facilities*: fully licensed facilities available. *Visitors*: welcome at all times. Dress code must be adhered to. No denims, tracksuits, collarless shirts. Golf shoes must be worn. *Society Meetings*: welcome at all times. Professional: John Cheetham. Secretary: Nicholas Donaghy (Tel & Fax: 01565 880178).*

KNUTSFORD. **The Wilmslow Golf Club,** Great Warford, Mobberley, Knutsford WA16 7AY (01565 872148). *Location:* two miles from Wilmslow off the Knutsford Road. Parkland course. 18 holes, 6635 yards. S.S.S. 72. Practice facility. *Green Fees:* weekdays £45.00 per round, £55.00 per day; weekends £55.00 per round, £65.00 per day. Subject to review. *Eating facilities:* full catering, two bars. *Visitors:* welcome, Ladies' Day Wednesday. *Society Meetings:* Tuesdays, Thursdays, and occasionally Fridays. Professional: L. J. Nowicki (01565 873620). Secretary: Mrs M. I. Padfield (01565 872148; Fax: 01565 872172).
e-mail: info@wilmslowgolfclub.co.uk
website: www.wilmslowgolfclub.co.uk

KNUTSFORD near. **Peover Golf Club,** Plumley Moor Road, Lower Peover, Near Knutsford WA16 9SE (01565 723337; Fax: 01565 723311). *Location:* Junction 19 of M6, A556, Knutsford. Parkland course, 18 holes, 6702 yards. S.S.S. 72. Practice area, putting green. *Green Fees:* £25.00 weekdays, £30.00 weekends. Subject to change. *Eating facilities:* bar food and function room. *Visitors:* always welcome. Please ring for a tee time. Buggy and trolley hire. *Society Meetings:* welcome.
e-mail: mail@peovergolfclub.co.uk
website: www.peovergolfclub.co.uk

LYMM. **Lymm Golf Club,** Whitbarrow Road, Lymm WA13 9AN (Tel & Fax: 01925 755020). *Location:* five miles south east of Warrington, two and a half miles from Junction 20 on M6 and Junction 9 on M56. Parkland. 18 holes, 6304 yards. S.S.S. 70. Practice ground. *Green Fees:* weekdays £32.00. *Eating facilities:* coffee, bar snacks, lunches and dinner, bar. *Visitors:* welcome with Handicap Certificates, no visitors at weekends, Bank Holidays or Thursdays until 2.30pm. *Society Meetings:* catered for with reservation. Professional: Steve McCarthy (01925 755054). Secretary: T.H.Glover (Tel & Fax: 01925 755020). Clubhouse (01925 752177).
website: www.lymm-golf-club.co.uk

MACCLESFIELD. **Macclesfield Golf Club,** The Hollins, Macclesfield SK11 7EA (01625 423227). *Location:* turn off A523 Leek Road into Windmill Street, half a mile fork right. Hillside course with extensive views. 18 holes, 5714 yards. S.S.S. 68. *Green Fees:* £30.00 weekdays; £40.00 weekends and Bank Holidays. *Eating facilities:* full catering and bars. *Visitors:* welcome by arrangement. *Society Meetings:* welcome weekdays except Thursdays. Professional: Tony Taylor (01625 423227). Secretary: Bob Littlewood (01625 423227; Fax: 01625 260061).
e-mail: secretary@Maccgolfclub.co.uk
website: www.Maccgolfclub.co.uk

MACCLESFIELD. **The Tytherington Club,** Dorchester Way, Tytherington, Macclesfield SK10 2JP (01625 506000; Fax: 01625 506040). *Location:* one mile north of Macclesfield off A523. Undulating parkland with numerous water features and ample woodland. 18 holes, 6765 yards. S.S.S. 74. Driving range, short game area. *Green Fees:* information not available. *Eating facilities:* bar with brasserie-style food and private function rooms available. *Visitors:* welcome, by prior arrangement. Buggies available. *Society Meetings:* welcome weekdays only. Highly competitive packages available. Professional: Gavin Beddow (01625 506013). General Manager: Ian Barthorpe.
e-mail: tytherington.events@theclubcompany.com

NANTWICH. **Alvaston Hall Golf Club,** Alvaston Hall Hotel, Middlewich Road, Nantwich CW5 6PD (01270 628473; Fax: 01270 623395). *Location:* A530 Middlewich Road. Parkland course. 9 holes. S.S.S. 59. *Green Fees*: 9 holes £8.00; £10.00 per day. Professional: Kevin Valentine. Secretary: John Walkington.*

Mere Golf & Country Club

From the welcoming yet peaceful grounds, the friendly service, the five star food and wines and the fact that you are spoilt for choice when it comes to an unusually large venue with superb leisure facilities, including a fitness studio, swimming pools and tennis court, a golfing experience at Mere will be a memorable occasion.

For an exhilarating round of golf, it's hard to beat the 6,817 yard, par 71 course created out of 150 acres of Cheshire parkland in 1934 by none other than Open Champions James Braid and George Duncan.

It would be hard to find a more picturesque course than Mere, with its parkland setting alongside the beautiful lake which gives the course its name. Mere offers cleverly sited hazards and some of the best greens in Britain.

Over the years Mere has hosted several major events, including the 2001 Dan Technology Seniors and the Tournament of Champions, and is a regional qualifying course for the 2009 Open at Turnberry.

- Individual and Corporate Golfing Packages.
- Clubs, Trolleys and Buggies for hire. Caddies available.
- Unique Floating Golf Ball Range.
- Extensively stocked Professional Shop. • Resident Professional.
- First class Restaurant and Conference & Banqueting facilities

One of the most exclusive leisure and sporting facilities in the North West.

**Mere Golf
& Country Club**
Chester Road, Mere
Knutsford, Cheshire WA16 6LJ
Telephone: 01565 830 155
Fax: 01565 830 713
e-mail: enquiries@meregolf.co.uk
www.meregolf.co.uk

NANTWICH. **Reaseheath Golf Club,** Reaseheath College, Nantwich CW5 6DF. *Location:* B5074 just north of Nantwich. Flat parkland. 9 holes, 1866 yards. S.S.S. 58. Short challenging course (4 par 4s, 5 par 3s) with narrow fairways and well guarded greens. Two tee positions for most holes. Also used for training greenkeepers. *Green Fees:* October to March £8.00, April to September £10.00. *Visitors:* with a member or by prior approval. *Society Meetings:* subject to approval. Secretary: Chris Bishop (01270 625131; Fax: 01270 625665).

NORTHWICH. **Antrobus Golf Club,** Foggs Lane, Antrobus, Northwich CW9 6JQ (01925 730890; Fax: 01925 730100). *Location:* two minutes from Junction 10 of M56 between Northwich and Warrington. Parkland course with lakes. 18 holes, 6220 yards. S.S.S. 72. Putting green and driving range. *Green Fees:* Monday to Friday £25.00, Sundays £28.00. *Eating facilities:* available. *Visitors:* welcome every day, except Saturdays. *Society Meetings:* welcome any day except Saturday. Ring for discounted rates. Professional: Paul Farrance (01925 730900). Secretary: Celia Axford (01925 730890; Fax: 01925 730100).

NORTHWICH. **Delamere Forest Golf Club,** Station Road, Delamere, Northwich CW8 2JE (01606 883264). *Location:* opposite Delamere Station on the B5152 Tarporley to Frodsham road. Undulating heathland course suitable for play winter or summer. 18 holes, 6348 yards. S.S.S. 71. Two practice grounds. *Green Fees:* weekdays £40.00 18 holes; £60.00 per day, weekends £55.00 *Eating facilities:* bar meals, diningroom. *Visitors:* welcome most weekdays if no large parties booked. Some restrictions on four balls on Sundays. Prior booking with Pro advisable. *Society Meetings:* societies, corporate days, parties and small groups catered for. Professional: E.B. Jones (01606 883307). Secretary: J.J Mulder (01606 883800; Fax: 01606 889444). e-mail: info@delameregolf.co.uk
website: www.delameregolf.co.uk

NORTHWICH. **Hartford Golf Club,** Burrows Hill, Hartford, Northwich CW8 3AP (01606 871162; Fax: 01606 872182). *Location:* Just off A49 and A556 near ICI at Winnington. Undulating parkland course with numerous water hazards. 9 holes, 2780 yards, Par 35. 26 bay driving range with automatic tees. *Green Fees:* weekdays £7.50, weekends £9.50. *Eating facilities:* available. Large golf shop, tuition available. *Society Meetings:* welcome. Professional: L. Percival (01606 871162; Fax: 01606 872182). Secretary: C. Maddock.

NORTHWICH. **Sandiway Golf Club,** Chester Road, Sandiway, Northwich CW8 2DJ (01606 883247). *Location:* off A556, Northwich by-pass. Undulating heavily wooded parkland. 18 holes, 6404 yards. S.S.S. 71. *Green Fees:* information not available. *Eating facilities:* lunches and teas served daily, full restaurant facilities. *Visitors:* welcome on weekdays with Handicap Certificate from home club. *Society Meetings:* restricted to Tuesdays, parties up to 90; Wednesday and Friday; parties up to 20. Professional: William Laird (01606 883180). Secretary: R.H. Owens (01606 883247; Fax: 01606 888548). Caterer: (01606 882606).*

NORTHWICH. **Vale Royal Abbey Golf Club,** Whitegate, Northwich CW8 2BA (01606 301291; Fax: 01606 301414). Parkland championship course. 18 holes, 6463 yards, S.S.S. 71. Short game practice area, putting green, chipping green, practice range. *Green Fees:* information not available. *Eating facilities:* informal spike bar. *Society Meetings:* welcome by arrangement. Professional: David Ingman.*

POYNTON. **Davenport Golf Club,** Worth Hall, Middlewood Road, Poynton SK12 1TS (01625 876951; Fax: 01625 877489). *Location:* A6 from Stockport, Macclesfield Road at Hazel Grove, left at Poynton Church. Undulating parkland course. 18 holes, 6034 yards. S.S.S. 69. Putting green and practice ground. *Green Fees:* weekdays £30.00 (£12.50 with member), weekends £40.00 (£15.00 with a member). *Eating facilities:* bar snacks daily except Mondays, full meals by arrangement. *Visitors:* welcome, advisable to check with the Professional for availability of first tee. *Society Meetings:* catered for Tuesdays and Thursdays only. Professional: Tony Stevens (01625 877319). Secretary: Chris Souter (01625 876951; Fax: 01625 877489). website: www.davenportgolf.co.uk

POYNTON. **Shrigley Hall Hotel, Golf & Country Club,** Shrigley Park, Pott Shrigley, Near Macclesfield SK10 5SB (01625 575757; Fax: 01625 575437). *Location:* easily accessible from the M56, M62,M60, M6,A523 and A6, only 10 minutes from Manchester Airport. Parkland course with magnificent views. 18 holes, 6305 yards. S.S.S 71. *Green Fees:* information not provided. *Eating facilities:* private rooms catering for 16-250 people, plus hotel Orangery Restaurant. *Visitors:* corporate, society and resident golfers welcome. 156-bedroom Four Star hotel. Secretary: Alex Brannigan (01625 576681).*

PRESTBURY. **De Vere Mottram Hall Golf Course,** Wilmslow Road, Mottram St. Andrew, Prestbury SK10 4QT (01625 820064). *Location*: M56 and M6. Flat parkland/woodland course. 18 holes, 7006 yards, 6250 metres. S.S.S. 72. Practice area. *Green Fees*: information not available. *Eating facilities*: Golf Brasserie. *Visitors*: no restrictions. Accommodation in 132 bedrooms. *Society Meetings*: no restrictions except at weekends. Professional: Matthew Turnock. Head of Golf Operations: Tim Hudspith.

PRESTBURY. **Prestbury Golf Club,** Macclesfield Road, Prestbury, SK10 4BJ (01625 828241). *Location*: between Wilmslow and Macclesfield. 18 holes, 6371 yards, 5825 metres. S.S.S. 71. Practice ground. *Green Fees:* £50.00 per day, (2008). *Eating facilities:* snacks, lunches, teas and dinners. *Visitors:* welcome on weekdays 9.30am to 11.30am and after 2.30pm; Tuesdays Ladies' Day until 2.30pm. Wednesdays Gentlemen members only until 2pm. Bank Holidays and weekends only with a member. *Society Meetings:* Thursdays only. Professional: Nick Summerfield (01625 828242). Secretary: N. Young (Tel & Fax: 01625 828241). e-mail: office@prestburygolfclub.com website: www.prestburygolfclub.com

RUNCORN. **Runcorn Golf Club,** Clifton Road, Runcorn WA7 4SU (01928 572093). *Location:* signposted The Heath, A557; M56 Junction 12. High parkland, easy walking course. 18 holes, 6035 yards, 5514 metres. S.S.S. 69. *Green Fees:* information not provided. *Eating facilities:* bar snacks, lunches; dinner by arrangement. *Visitors:* welcome weekdays, Tuesday is Ladies' Day. No visitors weekends or Bank Holidays except with a member. Handicap Certificate required. *Society Meetings:* by arrangement Mondays and Fridays. Professional: K.Hartley (01928 564791). Secretary: B.R. Griffiths (Tel & Fax: 01928 574214).

SANDBACH. **Malkins Bank Municipal Golf Course,** Betchton Road, Malkins Bank, Sandbach CW11 4XN (01270 765931). *Location:* M6, Junction 17 west on A534 for one mile, south on A533 for 400 metres, turn into Hassall Road (signposted). Parkland course. 18 holes, 5971 yards, S.S.S. 69. Practice area. *Green Fees:* information not provided. All rates subject to review. *Eating facilities:* bar and food available. *Visitors:* welcome at all times, please pre-book (01270 765931). *Society Meetings:* welcome, please pre-book (01270 765931). Professional: Davron Hackney (01270 765931; Fax: 01270 764730)

SANDBACH. **Sandbach Golf Club,** 117 Middlewich Road, Sandbach CW11 1FH (01270 762117). *Location:* two miles from Junction 17 of M6 on Middlewich Road. Meadowland course. 9 holes, 5397 yards. S.S.S. 69. Practice field. *Green Fees:* information not available. *Eating facilities:* available except Mondays and Thursdays. *Visitors:* welcome weekdays, weekends by invitation only. *Society Meetings:* catered for only by advance arrangement with Hon. Secretary. Secretary: H. Buckley.*

SOUTH WIRRAL. **Ellesmere Port Golf Centre,** Chester Road, Childer, Thornton, South Wirral CH66 1QF (0151-339 7689). *Location:* approximately six miles north of Chester on main A41 trunk road to Birkenhead. Wooded parkland with a lot of ponds. 18 holes, 6296 yards. S.S.S. 70. Practice ground with green and Smart Golf Simulator. *Green fees:* information not available. Eating facilities: bar and catering facilities. *Visitors:* welcome anytime. *Society Meetings:* by arrangement with Professional. Professional: Danny Youd (0151-339 7689). Secretary: Colin Craggs (0151-334 6579).*

STALYBRIDGE. **Stamford Golf Club,** Oakfield House, Huddersfield Road, Carrbrook, Stalybridge SK15 3PY (01457 832126). *Location:* off B6175 off A6018. Moorland course. 18 holes, 5701 yards. S.S.S. 68. *Green Fees:* weekdays and weekends £25.00. Special rates for golf societies. *Eating facilities:* full meals except Monday (bar available). *Visitors:* welcome without restrictions. *Society Meetings:* catered for by appointment only. Golf Shop: (01457 832126). Secretary: J. Kitchen (01457 766937) e-mail: stamford.golfclub@totalise.co.uk

STYAL. **Styal Golf Club,** Station Road, Styal SK9 4JN. (01625 530063). *Location:* Station Road, Styal, five minutes from Manchester Airport, Junction 5 M56, five minutes from Wilmslow. Flat, parkland course with many water hazards and interesting features. 18 holes, 6238 yards, 5704 metres. S.S.S. 70. 9 hole, par 3 course, 1242 yards, Par 27. 24 bay deluxe driving range and short game academy. New 12 bay outdoor range. *Green Fees:* £23.00 midweek, £29.00 weekends. *Eating facilities:* fully equipped restaurant and bar. *Visitors:* welcome. *Society Meetings:* welcome; packages available. Professional: Simon Forrest (01625 528910). Director of Golf: Glynn Traynor (01625 530063 ext. 214). Golf booking line (01625 531359).
e-mail: gtraynor@styalgolf.co.uk
website: www.styalgolf.co.uk

SUTTON WEAVER (NEAR RUNCORN). **Sutton Hall Golf Club,** Aston Lane, Sutton Weaver WA7 3ED (01928 790747; Fax: 01928 759174). *Location:* M56, Junction 12 signposted Frodsham. Wooded, parkland course, 18 holes, 6642 yards. S.S.S. 71. Full practice ground, putting green. *Green Fees:* weekdays £20, weekends £25 (subject to review). *Eating facilities:* Club catering available all day. *Visitors:* welcome weekdays; by arrangement only at weekends. *Society Meetings:* welcome. Professional: Jamie Hope (01928 714872; Fax: 01928 759174). Secretary: Maxwell Faulkner.

TARPORLEY. **Portal Golf and Country Club,** The Championship Course, Cobblers Cross Lane, Tarporley CW6 0DJ (01829 733933; Fax: 01829 733928). *Location:* half-a-mile from Tarporley on A49. Near Oulton Park. Donald Steel Championship course set in scenic parkland in the heartland of Cheshire with breathtaking panoramic views – lots of water! 18 holes, 7037 yards. S.S.S. 74. Practice facilities, putting green. Indoor golf academy. *Green Fees:* information not available. *Eating facilities:* excellent facilities with large banquet suite and bar area. *Visitors:* all visitors are required to book tee times in advance - seven day availability. Golf Shop, locker rooms, buggies. *Society Meetings:* welcome. Professional: Adrian Hill. Director of Golf: David Wills.*.

TARPORLEY. **Portal, The Premier Course,** Forest Road, Tarporley CW6 0JA (01829 733884). *Location:* half a mile from Tarporley on A49. Undulating parkland with scenic views of Cheshire Plains. 18 holes, 6600 yards. S.S.S. 71. Putting green. *Green Fees:* information not available. *Eating facilities:* bar and restaurant. *Visitors:* welcome. *Society Meetings:* welcome, except weekends. Professional: Judy Statham (01829 733703). Director of Golf: David Wills.*

WARRINGTON. **Alder Root Golf Club,** Alder Root Lane, Winwick, Warrington WA2 8RZ (Tel & Fax: 01925 291919). *Location:* M62 Junction 9, A49 2 miles north of Warrington. Flat, parkland course. 10 holes, 6017 yards. S.S.S. 69. Putting green. Practice ground. Lessons available. *Green Fees:* mid-week 18 holes £15.00, 9 holes £10.00; weekends 18 holes £20.00, 9 holes £12.00. Two "Fore" one rates available. *Eating facilities:* available. *Visitors:* some restrictions, ring for details. *Society Meetings:* welcome. Professional: C. McKevitt (Tel & Fax: 01925 291932). Secretary: Mr E. Lander (Tel & Fax: 01925 291919).

WARRINGTON. **Birchwood Golf Club,** Kelvin Close, Science Park North, Birchwood, Warrington WA3 7PB (01925 818819; Fax: 01925 822403). *Location:* Junction 11 off M62, follow A574 signs for Risley then Science Park North signs. Flat parkland course with numerous natural ponds and streams. 18 holes, 6727 yards. S.S.S. 72. Practice ground, putting green. *Green Fees:* information not available. *Eating facilities:* bar snacks throughout the day; restaurant facilities on request. *Visitors:* welcome on weekdays. Conference and banqueting facilities. Trolleys for hire. *Society Meetings:* Societies, companies and groups are welcome Mondays, Wednesdays and Thursdays if booked in advance. Professional: Paul McEwan (01925 825216; Fax: 01925 822403). Secretary: Barrie Wickens (01925 818819; Fax: 01925 822403).

WARRINGTON. **Leigh Golf Club,** Kenyon Hall, **Broseley Lane, Culcheth, Warrington WA3 4BG (01925 762943). *Location:* off A580 East Lancs Road to Culcheth Village. Parkland with tree-lined fairways. 18 holes, 5876 yards. S.S.S. 69. Three practice areas, practice nets. *Green Fees:* £30.00. *Eating facilities:* two bars and restaurant. *Visitors:* check with Professional. *Society Meetings:* catered for Mondays, Tuesdays and Fridays. Professional: Andrew Baguley (01925 762013). Secretary: D.A. Taylor. See website for special offers.** website: www.leighgolf.co.uk

WARRINGTON. **Poulton Park Golf Club Ltd,** Dig Lane, Cinnamon Brow, Warrington WA2 0SH (01925 812034). *Location:* M6 (Junction 21), off A574 (Warrington/Leigh) Crab Lane. 9 holes, 5651 yards. S.S.S. 69. Practice ground. *Green Fees:* £20.00 weekdays. *Eating facilities:* available except Mondays. *Visitors:* welcome most days, restricted at weekends. *Society Meetings:* catered for at any time if possible. Golf plus two-course meal £28.00; Winter Warmer (golf plus hotpot) £15.00. PGA Professional: Ian Orrell (01925 825220). Secretary: D. N. Owen(01925 822802).

WARRINGTON. **Walton Hall Golf Club,** Warrington Road, Higher Walton, Warrington WA4 5LU (01925 266775). *Location:* two miles south of Warrington off A56. Wooded parkland. 18 holes, 6801 yards. S.S.S. 73, Par 72. Practice ground. *Green Fees:* information not provided. *Eating facilities:* licensed clubhouse, meals and bar snacks. *Visitors:* unrestricted. *Society Meetings:* welcome, weekends after 1pm. Professional: J. Jackson (01925 263061). Secretary: Dave Johnson (01925 266775 or 01925 230860). e-mail: theclub@waltonhallgolfclub.co.uk website: www.waltonhallgolfclub.co.uk

WESTON. **Wychwood Park Golf Club,** Weston Crewe, CW2 5GP (01270 829200; Fax: 01270 829201). Location: 5 minutes from Junction 16 of M6 towards Nantwich. European PGA tour-standard course opened in 2002. 7191 yards off the championship tees. Water features throughout with a number of protected wildlife areas. Practice range, chipping and putting green. *Green Fees:* contact the Professional Shop (01270 820955). *Eating facilities:* superb modern clubhouse facility to cater for up to 150 people. *Visitors:* always welcome, handicap certificate requested. 108 en suite twin and double bedrooms, fitness suite. Meeting rooms for up to 160. *Society Meetings:* society and corporate welcome. Professional: Frank Kiddie (01270 820955). Golf Club Manager: Jon Cann (01270 820787). website: www.verve-venues.com

WIDNES. **Mersey Valley Golf & Country Club,** Warrington Road, Bold Heath, Widnes WA8 3XL (0151-424 6060; Fax: 0151 257 9097). *Location:* two miles from Junction 7 off M62, on the A57 towards Warrington. Flat parkland course. 18 holes, 6511 yards. S.S.S. 71, Par 72. *Green Fees:* Information not available. *Eating facilities:* full facilities available. *Visitors:* welcome at all times. Tuition available. Non-members welcome. Buggies available. *Society Meetings:* very welcome, special rates apply. Contact General Manager. Professional: Andy Stevenson PGA. General Manager: Chris Gerrard. *

WIDNES. **St Michaels Jubilee Golf Club,** Dundalk Road, Widnes WA8 8BS (0151-424 6230). Parkland course. 18 holes, 5638 yards. S.S.S. 67, Par 69. *Visitors:* unrestricted. Professional: D.Chapman (0151-424 6230). Secretary: A.J. Woodall (01695 726953).*

WIDNES. **Widnes Golf Club,** Highfield Road, Widnes WA8 7DT (0151-424 2440; Fax: 0151-495 2849). *Location:* near town centre, five miles from M56 and M62. Parkland course. 18 holes, 5729 yards. S.S.S. 68 White, 69 Ladies. *Green Fees:* information not available. *Eating facilities:* two bars and full catering service. *Visitors:* welcome weekdays; weekends by arrangement. *Society Meetings:* very welcome, special rates apply, contact Secretary (0151-424 2995). Professional: Jason O'Brien (0151-420 7647).

WINSFORD. **Knights Grange Sports Complex,** Grange Lane, Winsford CW7 2PT (01606 552780). *Location:* signposted "Knights Grange Sports Complex" from traffic lights Winsford Town Centre. 6 miles from M6, 16 miles from Chester. Set in beautiful Cheshire countryside on the outskirts of Winsford. A challenging course for golfers of all abilities. 18 holes - front 9 mainly flat but with water, ditches and other hazards. Back 9 take players deep into the countryside with many tees giving panoramic views of the course. There is also a lake and many mature woodland areas. Red Tees 5137 yards, S.S.S. 70; yellow tees 5270 yards, S.S.S. 66; white tees 5921 yards, S.S.S. 70. *Green Fees:* information not available. *Eating facilities:* snacks and hot drinks available from Complex. Public house adjacent. *Visitors:* unrestricted, advance booking (01606 552780). Tennis, football, athletics. *Society Meetings:* welcomed - booking in writing in advance to Manager. Manager: Mrs P. Littler (01606 552780*

Cumbria

ALSTON. **Alston Moor Golf Club,** The Hermitage, Middleton in Teesdale Road, Alston CA9 3DB (Tel & Fax: 01434 381675; Fax: 01434 381675). *Location:* one and three quarter miles from Alston on B6277 to Barnard Castle. Penrith, Hexham, Carlisle all within 30 miles. Parkland with panoramic views (highest golf course in England). 18 holes, 5456 yards. S.S.S. 66. Practice ground. *Green Fees:* information not available. *Eating facilities:* 19th Hole bar, May to October. *Visitors:* welcome anytime, prior notice required for groups. Competitions most Sundays, tee reserved 9am to 10am and 1pm to 2.30pm. *Society Meetings:* welcome by arrangement. Secretary: Paul Parkin (01434 381354).*

APPLEBY. **Appleby Golf Club,** Brackenber Moor, Appleby-in-Westmorland CA16 6LP (017683 51432). *Location:* off A66 at Coupland Beck, two miles east of Appleby. Moorland course. 18 holes, 5901 yards. S.S.S. 68. *Green Fees:* weekdays £22.00 per round, £28.00 per day; weekends and Bank Holidays £27.00 per round, £34.00 per day. *Eating facilities:* meals available each day. *Visitors:* welcome with Handicap Certificate without reservation. *Society Meetings:* catered for by prior arrangement. Handicap Certificate required. Secretary: J.M.F. Doig.

ASKAM-IN-FURNESS. **Dunnerholme Golf Club,** Duddon Road, Askam-in-Furness LA16 7AW (01229 462675/467421). *Location:* A595 Askam-in-Furness, over level crossing. Seaside links with stream on four holes, spectacular views from elevated 6th green. 10 holes (18 tees) 6154 yards. S.S.S. 70 White, 70 Red, 69 Yellow. Practice ground. *Green Fees:* £15.00 per day. *Eating facilities:* bar in evenings; meals not available. *Visitors:* welcome without reservation, excluding competition days. Competitions Saturday mornings and Sundays May to October. *Society Meetings:* catered for by prior arrangement. Secretary: A. Haines (01229 462675 day, 01229 826198 evenings).

ASPATRIA. **Brayton Park Golf Club,** Lakeside Inn, Brayton, Aspatria CA7 3TD (016973 20840). *Location:* one mile east of Aspatria. Parkland course. 9 holes. S.S.S. 65 (18 holes). *Green Fees:* 9 holes £6.00. 18 holes £10.00. *Eating facilities:* available at Lakeside Inn. *Visitors:* always welcome. *Society Meetings:* welcome. Coarse fishing pond. Secretary: Mr J. Gibson (01697 322517).

BARROW-IN-FURNESS. **Barrow Golf Club,** Rakesmoor Lane, Hawcoat, Barrow-in-Furness LA14 4QB (01229 825444). *Location:* one mile from Barrow town centre, approach via Dalton bypass, turn left at Bank Lane opposite "Kimberley Clarke" paper mill. Clubhouse at top of hill on left hand side. 18 holes, 6184 yards, 5679 metres. S.S.S. 70. *Green Fees:* Monday to Friday £28.00; Saturdays, Sundays and Bank Holidays £35.00. County Cards/2 for 1 (weekdays only) accepted. Ladies' Day Fridays. *Eating facilities:* catering available by prior arrangement. *Visitors:* welcome without formal reservation. *Society Meetings:* welcome by prior arrangement, call Club Administrator or Secretary. Club Administrator: E. Payne (01229 825444). Secretary: S.G. Warbrick (01229 831358). e-mail: barrowgolf@supanet.com

BARROW-IN-FURNESS. **Furness Golf Club,** Central Drive, Walney Island, Barrow-in-Furness LA14 3LN (01229 471232). *Location:* A590 into Barrow via Dalton by-pass, follow sign to Walney Island, over bridge, straight on at lights. Clubhouse half-a-mile on right hand side. Seaside links. 18 holes, 6363 yards. S.S.S. 71. Practice area. *Green Fees:* please see website. *Eating facilities:* full catering (except Mondays), licensed bar. *Visitors:* parties by prior arrangement, others without reservation; must hold current Handicap Certificate. Ladies' Day Wednesdays; Competition Days - Saturdays or Sundays in summer. *Society Meetings:* welcome (tee reservation by prior arrangement). Secretary: W.T. French. e-mail: furnessgolfclub@chessbroadband.co.uk website: www.furnessgolfclub.co.uk

Sedbergh Golf Club

BRAMPTON. **Brampton Golf Club,** Tarn Road, Brampton CA8 1HN (016977 2255). *Location*: situated on the Brampton-Castle Carrock road (B6413), approximately one and a half miles from Brampton. Rolling fell countryside, excellent views. 18 holes, 6407 yards. S.S.S. 71. Driving range/practice facilities available plus snooker and pool tables. *Green Fees*: weekdays £30.00 per round, £38.00 per day; weekends and Bank Holidays £36.00 per round, £45.00 per day. *Eating facilities:* catering available every day during playing season and on most days during winter period. *Visitors:* welcome without reservation but pre-booking is advisable. *Society Meetings:* very much catered for, limited numbers at weekends. Secretary and contact for visiting societies/party bookings: I.J. Meldrum (016977 2255). Professional: S. Wilkinson (016977 2000; Fax: 016977 41487).
e-mail: secretary@bramptongolfclub.com
website: www.bramptongolfclub.com

CARLISLE. **Carlisle Golf Club,** Aglionby, Carlisle CA4 8AG (01228 513029). *Location*: on A69 Newcastle Road, half a mile from Junction 43 of M6. Parkland course with wide variety of trees, strategic hazards, etc. 18 holes, 6278 yards. S.S.S. 70. Practice area. *Green Fees*: weekdays £35.00 per round, £50.00 per day; £50.00 per round Sundays only; Saturdays with member only. Subject to review. Package deals for parties of 20 or more. *Eating facilities*: bar meals, restaurant, two bars, etc. *Visitors*: welcome except on a Saturday (unless with a member), unless tee is reserved; visitor bookings (01228 513029). Trolley hire. *Society Meetings*: catered for Mondays, Wednesdays, Thursdays and Fridays. Professional: G. Lisle (01228 513241). Secretary: Roger Johnson (01228 513029; Fax: 01228 513303).
website: www.carlislegolfclub.org

CARLISLE. **Dalston Hall Golf Club & Holiday Park,** (aka Caldew Golf Club) Dalston Hall, Dalston, Carlisle CA5 7JX (01228 710165). *Location:* leave M6 at Exit 42, take road to Dalston; at Dalston take B5299, Carlisle road, course on the right after one mile. Scenic parkland course. 10 holes, (18 Tees) 5294 yards. S.S.S. 67. Practice area. *Green Fees:* £18.00 to £20.00 for 18 holes. *Eating facilities:* full catering and bar facilities *Visitors:* welcome, tee reservation is required at Bank Holidays and weekends and after 4pm during the week. Pool table. *Society Meetings:* welcome by prior arrangement. Secretary: Paul Holder (01228 710165). website: www.dalstonhall.co.uk

CARLISLE. **The Eden Golf Course,** Crosby-on-Eden, Carlisle CA6 4RA (01228 573003). *Location*: M6 Junction 44, A689 to Low Crosby. Parkland course incorporating lakes, streams and River Eden. 18 holes, 6368 yards. S.S.S. 72. 9-hole Hadrian's Course, par 71, S.S.S. 71. *Green Fees*: Information not available. *Eating facilities*: full restaurant and bar meals. *Visitors*: welcome at all times, telephone booking requested. *Society Meetings*: welcome at all times, telephone booking requested. 16 bay floodlit driving range and practice facilities. Professional: Steven Harrison.
e-mail: edengolf1@aol.com
website: www.edengolf.co.uk*

CARLISLE. **Stoney Holme Municipal Golf Course,** St Aidans Road, Carlisle (01228 33208). *Location:* off A69 between M6 Junction 42 and town. Parkland course, 18 holes, 6000 yards. S.S.S. 68. Large practice area, changing rooms. *Green Fees:* information not available. *Eating facilities:* bar and restaurant. *Visitors:* welcome without reservation, but booking advisable weekends and Bank Holidays. *Society Meetings:* welcome by prior arrangement. Professional: Stephen Ling (01228 625511).

EMBLETON. **Cockermouth Golf Club,** The Clubhouse, Embleton, Near Cockermouth CA13 9SG (017687 76223/76941; Fax: 017687 76941). *Location:* three miles east of Cockermouth. Scenic fell land course. 18 holes, 5496 yards, S.S.S. 67. *Green Fees:* weekdays £20.00; weekends and Bank Holidays £25.00. Concessionary rates parties of 10 or more (includes food):negotiable. *Eating facilities:* bar, meals by arrangement with Secretary. *Visitors:* welcome except Wednesdays between 3.30pm and 6pm, some restrictions at weekends. Some trolleys for hire. *Society Meetings:* welcome as per visitors. Secretary: R.S.Wimpress (Tel & Fax: 017687 76941 mornings only weekdays).
e-mail: secretary@cockermouthgolf.co.uk
website: www.cockermouthgolf.co.uk

GRANGE-OVER-SANDS. **Grange Fell Golf Club,** Fell Road, Grange-over-Sands LA11 6HB (015395 32536). *Location:* Cartmel Road from Grange one mile. Hillside course with panoramic views. 9 holes, 4840 metres. S.S.S. 66. *Green Fees:* weekdays £15.00, weekends and Bank Holidays £20.00. *Eating facilities:* bar. *Visitors:* welcome without reservation, closed most Sundays until 4pm during season. *Society Meetings:* not catered for. Secretary: Mr J. G. Park (015395 58513).

GRANGE-OVER-SANDS. **Grange-over-Sands Golf Club,** Meathop Road, Grange-over-Sands LA11 6QX (015395 33180; Fax: 015395 33754). *Location:* leave the A590 at roundabout signposted Grange, take the B5277 for approximately three miles. Flat parkland. 18 holes, 6065 yards. S.S.S. 69. Practice area, bunker, green. *Green Fees:* £28.00 per round, £35.00 per day. *Eating facilities:* dining room open every day; bar snacks and bar every day. *Visitors:* welcome without reservation weekdays and most weekends. *Society Meetings:* by arrangement with Secretary. Professional: Nick Lowe (015395 35937). Secretary: S.D. Wright (015395 33754).

KENDAL. **Carus Green Golf Club,** Burneside Road, Kendal LA9 6EB (Tel & Fax: 01539 721097). *Location:* one mile north-east of Kendal on Burneside Road. Flat riverside parkland location. 18 holes, 5800 yards, Par 70. 160 yard practice ground, 300 yard automated driving range, putting green, net. *Green Fees:* Information not available. *Eating facilities:* Full catering facilities and bar. *Visitors:* welcome anytime, restrictions on competition days. Tuition available from 2 PGA teaching professionals. Buggy hire. *Society Meetings:* packages available, please call for details. Large golf super-shop. Professional: David Turner and Nick Barron (Tel & Fax: 01539 721097). Secretary: Bryan Lumsden.*

KENDAL. **Kendal Golf Club,** The Heights, Kendal LA9 4PQ (01539 733708). *Location:* off A6 at Town Hall, signposted. Undulating parkland course with magnificent views in all directions. 18 holes, 5769 yards. S.S.S. 68. *Green Fees:* weekdays £28.00 per round, £36.00 per day; weekends £34.00 per round, £44.00 per day. *Eating facilities:* meals available all day; bar. *Visitors:* welcome with reservation. Buggy hire available. Professional: Peter Scott (01539 723499). website: www.kendalgolfclub.co.uk

KESWICK. **Keswick Golf Club,** Threlkeld Hall, Threlkeld, Keswick CA12 4SX (017687 79324; Fax: 017687 79861). *Location:* four miles from Keswick on A66 road to Penrith. Scenic fell and parkland course. 18 holes, 6225 yards. S.S.S. 70, Par 71. Extensive practice area. *Green Fees:* weekdays £28.00; weekends and Bank Holidays £34.00. Subject to review. *Eating facilities:* bar and restaurant. *Visitors:* welcome, Ladies' Day Thursdays 11am to 2pm. *Society Meetings:* welcome by arrangement. Professional: Gary Watson. Administration Manager: May Lloyd.

KIRKBY LONSDALE. **Kirkby Lonsdale Golf Club,** Scaleber Lane, Barbon, Kirkby Lonsdale, Carnforth, Lancs LA6 2LJ (015242 76365). *Location:* three and a half miles from Kirkby Lonsdale on the A683 Sedbergh Road. Parkland course in Lune Valley crossing Barbon Beck and along the banks of the River Lune. 18 holes, 6542 yards. S.S.S. 72. Par 72. Practice area, lessons. *Green Fees:* weekdays £30.00; weekends £35.00. Subject to review. *Eating facilities:* full facilities. *Visitors:* welcome, no restrictions except on competition days. Handicap Certificate required or certificate of competence. *Society Meetings:* welcome by arrangement. Package deals available for groups of eight or more. Professional: Chris Barrett (015242 76366). Secretary: Geoffrey Hall (015242 76365). e-mail: klgolf@dial.pipex.com website: www.klgolf.dial.pipex.com

KIRKBY LONSDALE near. **Casterton Golf Course,** Sedbergh Road, Casterton, Near Kirkby Lonsdale, Cumbria LA6 2LA (015242 71592; Fax: 015242 74387). *Location:* from Junction 36 of M6 take A65 to Skipton, five miles to Kirkby Lonsdale, one mile north on A683. Undulating parkland course, scenic with wonderful views. 9 holes, 5726 yards. S.S.S. 68. Practice area and driving net. *Green Fees:* weekdays £14.00; weekends and Bank Holidays £17.00. *Eating facilities:* light refreshments and shop in clubhouse (licensed). *Visitors:* always welcome. Booking advisable. Clubhouse has well-stocked Pro Shop, changing facilities and toilets. Clubs and trolleys available for hire. Two holiday flats sleeping four/five. *Society Meetings:* parties of under 32 persons only. Professional: Roy Williamson. Secretary: Elizabeth Makinson. Course Manager: John Makinson. e-mail: castertongc@hotmail.com website: www.castertongolf.co.uk

MARYPORT. **Maryport Golf Club Ltd,** Bankend, Maryport CA15 6PA (01900 812605). *Location:* approximately one mile north of Maryport on B5300 towards Silloth. 9 holes links extended to 18 with new holes parkland type, exposed. 18 holes, 5982 yards. S.S.S. 69. *Green Fees:* Information not available. *Eating facilities:* available. *Visitors:* welcome, no restrictions. *Society Meetings:* catered for by prior arrangement. Secretary: Mrs L. Hayton.*

PENRITH. **Penrith Golf Club,** Salkeld Road, Penrith CA11 8SG (01768 891919). *Location:* off Junction 41 M6 motorway, towards Penrith, golf course signposted. Parkland course. 18 holes, 6026 yards. S.S.S. 69. Range facilities. *Green Fees:* weekdays £28.00/£33.00; weekends £33.00/£38.00. *Eating facilities:* all day catering seven days a week. *Visitors:* welcome, book through Professional shop, tee times required at weekends. *Society Meetings:* by appointment with Secretary. Professional: Garry Key (Tel & Fax: 01768 891919). Secretary: David Noble (Tel & Fax: 01768 891919).

ST BEES. **St Bees Golf Club,** Peckmill, Beach Road, St Bees (01946 824300). *Location:* four miles south of Whitehaven off A595. Hilly, seaside course. 9 holes, 5307 yards. S.S.S. 66. *Green Fees:* information not available. *Visitors:* welcome weekdays (except after 4pm Wednesdays). Only after 3pm weekends. Bar available April to September between 12 noon and 8pm. Secretary: B. G. Ritson.*

SEASCALE. **Seascale Golf Club,** Seascale CA20 1QL (Tel & Fax: 019467 28202). *Location:* B5344 off A595 to north of village. Links. 18 holes, 6495 yards. S.S.S. 71. 16-acre practice ground. *Green Fees:* information not available. *Eating facilities:* catering available every day. *Visitors:* welcome when no tee reservations in force. *Society Meetings:* catered for by arrangement with Secretary. Secretary: David Stobart (019467 28202).
website: www.seascalegolfclub.co.uk

SEDBERGH. **Sedbergh Golf Club,** Sedbergh LA10 5SS (015396 21551). *Location:* five miles J37, M6, one mile out of Sedbergh on road to Dent, well signposted. Superbly scenic course in Yorkshire Dales National Park. 9 holes, 5588 yards. S.S.S. 69. *Green Fees:* Information not available. *Eating facilities:* full bar and catering facilities. *Visitors:* welcome, but prior booking advisable (essential at weekends). Various packages available. Golf shop; hire trolleys. *Society Meetings:* very welcome by prior arrangement. Manager: Craig Gardner (015396 21551).*

THE APPEARANCE OF AN ASTERISK (*) AT THE END OF A CLUB OR COURSE ENTRY INDICATES THAT UP-TO-DATE INFORMATION HAS NOT BEEN SUPPLIED

SILECROFT. **Silecroft Golf Club,** Silecroft, Near Millom LA18 4NX (01229 774250). *Location:* three miles north of Millom on the coast. Near junction of A595 and A5093, eight miles west of Broughton-in-Furness. Seaside links course with good greens. 9 holes (18 tees), 5877 yards. S.S.S. 68 (67 off Yellow tees). *Green Fees:* £15.00 per day Monday to Friday, £20.00 per day weekends and Bank Holidays. Winter green fees £10.00 per day. (subject to review). *Eating facilities:* catering available at nearby public house (Silecroft Miners Arms), bar at club. *Visitors:* welcome, although access to the course may be restricted on Bank Holidays or on competition days. Secretary: Mr Keith Newton (01229 770467). e-mail: silecroftgcsec@aol.com

SILLOTH. **Silloth on Solway Golf Club,** The Clubhouse, Silloth, Wigton CA7 4BL (016973 31304), *Location:* from south - M6 Junction 41 B5305 Wigton, B5302 Silloth. From north and east - M6 Junction 43 A69 Carlisle, A595/596 Wigton, B5302 Silloth. Seaside links, rated in the best five links courses in England. 18 holes, 6600 yards. S.S.S. 71. Practice facilities. *Green Fees:* weekdays £38.00 per day, weekends and Bank Holidays £50.00 per round. Subject to review. Restriction, only one round allowed per day at weekends. *Eating facilities:* full bar and catering. *Visitors:* welcome without reservation. *Society Meetings:* welcome midweek, weekend times available on request. Professional: J. Graham (016973 32404; Fax: 016973 31782). Secretary: John Hill (016973 31304; Fax: 016973 31782).

SILVERDALE. **Silverdale Golf Club, Redbridge Lane, Silverdale, Carnforth LA5 0SP** (01524 701300). *Location*: Exit 35 off M6 to Carnforth, then two miles west, adjacent to railway station and RSPB nature reserve. Testing heathland course with rock outcrops and excellent views. 18 holes, 5535 yards. S.S.S. 67. **Green Fees**: weekdays from £25.00, weekends and Bank Holidays from £30.00. *Eating facilities*: full catering and bar facilities. *Visitors*: welcome except Sundays a.m. in the summer unless with a member. *Society Meetings*: welcome by arrangement with Secretary. Secretary: K. Smith (Tel & Fax: 01524 702074).
website: www.silverdalegolfclub.co.uk

ULVERSTON. **Ulverston Golf Club Ltd,** Bardsea Park, Ulverston LA12 9QJ (01229 582824). *Location*: Exit 36, M6. A590 to Barrow then A5087 to Bardsea village. Wooded parkland. 18 holes, 6191 yards. S.S.S. 70. *Green Fees*: weekdays £30.00 per round, weekends £35.00 per round. *Eating facilities*: lunch and bar snacks. *Visitors*: welcome except Saturdays (competition day), and Tuesdays (Ladies' Day). Must be members of accredited golf club and have a Handicap. *Society Meetings*: welcome, write with reservation to the Secretary. Professional: P.A. Stoller (01229 582806). Secretary: R. Rushforth.

WHITEHAVEN. **Whitehaven Golf Club,** Red Lonning, Whitehaven CA28 8UD (01946 591177). *Location*: set in parkland above Whitehaven. Parkland course with spectacular views of the Lakeland fells. 18 holes, 6289 yards, Par 70. 16-bay floodlit driving range plus golf super store. *Green Fees*: £21.00 midweek, £26.00 weekends (subject to review). *Eating facilities*: clubhouse and bar. *Visitors*: always welcome. Tees can be booked all year round, phone 01946 591144. 7 golf buggies available. Professional: Craig Hamilton.
e-mail: craighamilton@whitehavengolfclub.com
website: www.whitehavengolf.com

WINDERMERE. **Windermere Golf Club,** Cleabarrow, Windermere LA23 3NB (015394 43123). *Location*: one mile from Bowness-on-Windermere on Crook road, B5284. Idyllic National Park setting. 18 holes, 5122 yards, S.S.S. 65. Practice ground. *Green Fees*: Monday to Friday £30.00 per round, weekends and Bank Holidays £37.00 per round. Subject to review. *Eating facilities*: Restaurant. *Visitors*: made most welcome. *Society Meetings*: catered for by prior arrangement with the Secretary, numbers from 12 to 50, corporate days by arrangement. Professional: W.S.M. Rooke (015394 43550). Secretary: B. Grundy (015394 43123).
e-mail: office@windermeregc.demon.co.uk
website: www.windermeregolfclub.net

WORKINGTON. **Workington Golf Club Ltd,** Branthwaite Road, Workington CA14 4SS (01900 603460). *Location*: on A596, two miles east of town. Meadowland. 18 holes, 6252 yards. S.S.S. 70. *Green Fees*: information not available. *Eating facilities*: available seven days a week. *Visitors*: welcome without reservation; must have own insurance and must be members of recognised golf club. Buggies only by prior arrangement with Pro. *Society Meetings*: welcome by prior arrangement. Professional: A. Drabble (01900 67828). Secretary: R. Vaughan (01900 603460).

> **THE APPEARANCE OF AN ASTERISK (*) AT THE END OF A CLUB OR COURSE ENTRY INDICATES THAT UP-TO-DATE INFORMATION HAS NOT BEEN SUPPLIED**

Durham

BARNARD CASTLE. **Barnard Castle Golf Club,** Harmire Road, Barnard Castle DL12 8QN (01833 638355 or 637237). *Location:* one mile north of Barnard Castle Town Centre on the B6278. Open parkland with a number of streams to be crossed and with maturing copses. 18 holes, 6406 yards. S.S.S. 71. Practice area. *Green Fees:* weekdays £20.00 per round, £24.00 per 27 holes; weekends and Bank Holidays £30.00 per round, £35.00 27 holes. Reduced rates playing with member. *Eating facilities:* full catering. *Visitors:* welcome, but formal booking system applies at weekends and Bank Holidays. *Society Meetings:* catered for by prior arrangement. Professional: Darren Pearce (01833 631980). Secretary: J. Kilgarriff (01833 638355).

BEAMISH. **Beamish Park Golf Club,** Beamish, Stanley DH9 0RH (0191-370 1382; Fax: 0191-370 2937). *Location:* follow directions to Beamish Museum. Parkland, 18 holes, 6183 yards (white markers). S.S.S. 70. 5963 yards (yellow markers). S.S.S. 69. Two practice areas. *Green Fees:* information not available. *Eating facilities:* bar and à la carte menu. *Visitors:* welcome weekdays. Carts for hire. *Society Meetings:* welcome. Professional: Chris Cole (0191-370 1984). Hon. Secretary: Les Pickering.*

BILLINGHAM. **Billingham Golf Club,** Sandy Lane, Billingham TS22 5NA (01642 554494). *Location:* off A19 trunk road, one mile west of Billingham town centre. Undulating parkland. 18 holes, 6346 yards. S.S.S. 70. Practice area including pitching green and putting greens. *Green Fees:* weekdays £28.00, £16.00 with member; weekends £40.00, £20.00 with member. *Eating facilities:* full catering. *Visitors:* welcome weekdays, prior booking advised. Buggies available. *Society Meetings:* catered for by prior arrangement with Secretary. Caterer (01642 554494). Professional: M. Ure (01642 557060). Secretary: P. B. Hodgson (Tel & Fax: 01642 533816).
e-mail: billinghamgc@onetel.com
website: www.billinghamgolfclub.com

BISHOP AUCKLAND. **Bishop Auckland Golf Club,** High Plains, Durham Road, Bishop Auckland DL14 8DL (01388 661618). *Location:* leave Bishop Auckland Market Place on route to Spennymoor/ Durham, half a mile on left. Parkland, 18 holes, 6379 yards. S.S.S. 71 (Par 72). Practice fairways. *Green Fees:* weekdays £30.00 per round, £35.00 per day; weekends £35.00 per round, £40.00 per day. *Eating facilities:* bar, full catering facilities. *Visitors:* welcome mid-week only. Ladies' Day Tuesday. Two snooker tables. *Society Meetings:* catered for on application, official Handicap required. Special package start from £33.95 for parties

of 4 or more, includes catering. Professional: D. Skiffington (01388 661618). Secretary: M.S. Metcalf (01388 661618).
e-mail: enquiries@bagc.co.uk
website: www.bagc.co.uk

BRANCEPETH. **Brancepeth Castle Golf Club,** The Clubhouse, Brancepeth DH7 8EA (0191-378 0075; Fax: 0191-378 3835). *Location:* A690 Durham to Crook, turn left at crossroads in Brancepeth village, take immediate left at the castle gates, 200 yards down lane. Parkland course undulating in parts. 18 holes, 6400 yards, S.S.S. 70, Practice field, putting green. *Green Fees:* weekdays £35.00, weekends £50.00. *Eating facilities:* full bar and restaurant facilities. *Visitors:* parties welcome weekdays, individuals only at weekends. Changing rooms and showers, lessons by arrangement. *Society Meetings:* welcome weekdays, good rates available. Tee available 9.30am and 1.30pm. Professional: D. Howdon (0191-378 0183). Manager: D. Young (0191-378 0075; Fax: 0191-378 3835)

CHESTER-LE-STREET. **Chester-le-Street Golf Club,** Lumley Park, Chester-le-Street DH3 4NS (0191 3883218). *Location:* half a mile east of Chester-le-Street adjacent to Lumley Castle. Fairly flat parkland. 18 holes, 6457 yards, 5535 metres. S.S.S. 71. Practice area. *Green Fees:* midweek £25.00 per round, £30.00 per day; weekends and public holidays £30.00 per round, £35.00 per day. *Eating facilities:* snacks, lunches, dinners. *Visitors:* welcome 9.30am to 12 noon, 1.30pm to 4.30pm weekdays; 10.30am to 12 noon, 2pm onwards weekends. Must be members of a golf club and have a Handicap. Hotel adjacent. *Society Meetings:* welcome except weekends and Public Holidays. Professional: D. Fletcher (0191 3890157; Fax: 0191 3881220). Secretary: Bill Routledge (0191 3883218).
e-mail: clsgcoffice@tiscali.co.uk
website: www.clsgolfclub.co.uk

CHESTER-LE-STREET. **Roseberry Grange Golf Club,** Grange Villa, Chester-le-Street DH2 3NF (0191-370 0670). *Location:* three miles west of Chester-le-Street on A693. Parkland course. 18 holes, 5809 yards. S.S.S. 68. Driving range. *Green Fees:* weekdays £16.00; weekends £22.00; visiting party packages. *Eating facilities:* bar meals 12 noon to 2pm and 7pm to 9.30pm. *Visitors:* welcome, no restrictions weekdays, Saturdays 7am to 10.30am, Sundays 7am to 11.30am. Professional: C. Jones (0191-370 0660). Secretary: Raymond McDermott (0191-370 2047).

CONSETT. **Consett and District Golf Club Ltd,** Elmfield Road, Consett DH8 5NN (01207 502186; Fax: 01207 505060). *Location:* 14 miles north of Durham on A691 (hidden turning on steep hill). 18 holes, 6019 yards. S.S.S. 69. Parkland, undulating, excellent views over Derwent Valley. *Green Fees:* weekdays £25.00, weekends £30.00; reduced fees with member. *Eating facilities:* full catering available (limited on Mondays). *Visitors:* welcome most times, phone Secretary. *Society Meetings:* catered for by arrangement, enquiries welcomed through Secretary. Secretary: P. Crinnion (01207 505060 Fax/ Answer machine)

CROOK. **Crook Golf Club,** Low Jobs Hill, Crook DL15 9AA (01388 762429). *Location:* eleven miles west of Durham City on A690. Scenic views; excellently conditioned course. 18 holes, 6102 yards, 5902 metres. S.S.S. 69. Practice area. *Green Fees:* available on request. *Eating facilities:* available, book in advance. *Visitors:* welcome but limited times at weekends. *Society Meetings:* welcome by arrangement with Secretary. Special packages available. Hon Secretary: Les Shaw (01388 762429).

DARLINGTON. **Blackwell Grange Golf Club,** Briar Close, Blackwell, Darlington DL3 8QX (01325 464464). *Location:* one mile south of Darlington on A66 turn into Blackwell. Signposts to Club. Parkland course. 18 holes, 5621 yards. S.S.S. 68. *Green Fees:* weekdays £25.00 per round, £35.00 per day; weekends and Bank Holidays £35.00 per round. *Eating facilities:* full menu except Sundays and Mondays. *Visitors:* welcome without reservation except weekends. *Society Meetings:* catered for except Wednesdays and weekends. Professional: Joanne Furby (01325 462088). Secretary: Phil Wraith (Tel & Fax: 01325 464458).

DARLINGTON. **The Darlington Golf Club (Members) Ltd,** Haughton Grange, Darlington DL1 3JD (01325 355324; Fax: 01325 366086). *Location:* northern outskirts of town, A1150 off A167, easy access from A1(M) or A19. Flat wooded parkland course designed by Dr Alister Mackenzie. 18 holes, 6209 yards. S.S.S. 70. 10 acre practice ground, Information not available *Eating facilities:* dining room, lounge and bar. *Visitors:* welcome weekdays and selected weekends with reservation. Must be members of recognised golf club. Buggies available for hire. *Society Meetings:* package deals by arrangement weekdays. Professional: Craig Dilley (01325 484198). Secretary: Arthur R. Ellis (01325 355324 Ext.1or2.)*
e-mail: mdilley@darlington-gc.co.uk
website: www.darlington-gc.co.uk

DARLINGTON. **Dinsdale Spa Golf Club,** Neasham Road, Middleton-St-George, Darlington DL2 1DW (01325 332222). *Location:* near Teesside Airport. Parkland. 18 holes, 6462 yards, S.S.S. 71 (white); 6107 yards, S.S.S. 69 (yellow). Large practice ground. New course layout (3 holes) in May 2006. *Green Fees:* £28.00 per day. Playing with a member £15.00 weekdays, £20.00 weekends. *Eating facilities:* bar, catering. *Visitors:* welcome weekdays, weekends with a member only. *Society Meetings:* catered for Wednesday, Thursday and Friday by advance booking. Professional: Martyn Stubbings (Tel & Fax: 01325 332515). Secretary: P. Davison (01325 332297)

DARLINGTON. **Hall Garth Golf and Country Club Hotel,** Coatham, Mundeville, Darlington DL1 3LU (01325 300400; Fax: 01325 310083). *Location:* A1 J59, follow the A167 toward Darlington, after 300 yards turn left at Brafferton, entrance after 200 yards on right. Parkland course. 9 holes, 6621 yards. S.S.S. 72. *Green Fees:* information not available. *Eating facilities:* Stables Country Pub. *Visitors:* always welcome. *Society Meetings:* welcome; prices on request.*

DARLINGTON. **Stressholme Golf Club,** Snipe Lane, Darlington DL2 2SA (01325 461002; Fax: 01325 461002). *Location:* signposted off the A66 Teesside to Scotch Corner outside of Darlington. Parkland course with water features. 18 holes, 6431 yards. S.S.S. 71. 25 bay driving range with nets, chipping greens, distance markers, etc. *Green Fees:* information not provided. *Eating facilities:* bar in clubhouse with extensive catering facilities. *Visitors:* welcome all week. Professional/Secretary: Ralph Givens (Tel & Fax: 01325 461002).

DURHAM. **Durham City Golf Club,** Littleburn, Langley Moor, Durham DH7 8HL (0191-378 0806). *Location:* from Durham City take A690 to Crook - course signposted in Langley Moor. Parkland, bordered by the River Browney. 18 holes, 6326 yards. S.S.S. 70. Large practice area. *Green Fees:* Information not available. *Eating facilities:* no catering Mondays or Thursday evenings. *Visitors:* welcome at all times, only restrictions when club competitions are being held – ring Professional for details. *Society Meetings:* welcome, but restricted to weekdays. Professional: S. Corbally (0191-378 0029). Hon. Secretary: Ian Wilson (0191-386 4434).*

DURHAM. **Mount Oswald Manor and Golf Course,** South Road, Durham DH1 3TQ (0191-386 7527; Fax: 0191-386 0975; *Location:* A1(M) Junction marked Bowburn, A177 Durham City follow signs for Darlington. Parkland, partially wooded. 18 holes, 5991 yards. S.S.S. 69. *Green Fees:* Summer; weekdays £15.25, weekends £17.50, Winter; weekdays £11.50, weekends £15.75 (under review). *Eating facilities:* bar meals, Sunday lunches, set meals, etc. *Visitors:* welcome except Sunday mornings before 10am (members only). Bookings only at weekends and Bank Holidays. *Society Meetings:* welcome, same restrictions as visitors. Must order food. General Manager: Mr N. P. Galvin (0191-386 7527).
e-mail: information@mountoswald.co.uk
website: www.mountoswald.co.uk

DURHAM. **Ramside Hall Hotel and Golf Club,** Carrville DH1 1TD (0191-386 9514; Fax: 0191- 386 9519). *Location:* two miles north-east of Durham on A690. A1 (M) Junction 62. 27 holes, 6217/6851 yards. S.S.S. 70/73. Driving range and golf academy. *Green Fees:* information not available. *Eating facilities:* choice of three eating areas. *Visitors:* welcome. Professional: K. Jackson (0191-386 9514). Golf Operations Manager/Secretary: K. Jackson.

EAGLESCLIFFE. **Eaglescliffe Golf Club Ltd,** Yarm Road, Eaglescliffe, Stockton-on-Tees TS16 0DQ (01642 780098; Office: 01642 780238). *Location:* on A135 one mile north of Yarm and three miles south of Stockton. Hilly parkland course, sloping to River Tees. 18 holes, 6245 yards. S.S.S. 70. Practice area and putting green.

Green Fees: weekdays £32.00 per round, £40.00 per day.; weekends and Bank Holidays £40.00 per round, £55.00 per day. *Eating facilities:* two bars, meals available, separate diningroom. *Visitors:* welcome weekdays, restriction on Tuesdays and Fridays. *Society Meetings:* societies and visiting parties catered for weekdays, some restrictions Tuesdays and Fridays. Professional: Graeme Bell (01642 790122). Secretary: M.R. Sample (01642 780238).

HARTLEPOOL. **Castle Eden Golf Club,** Castle Eden, Hartlepool TS27 4SS (01429 836510). *Location:* two miles south of Peterlee, use exits from A19. Picturesque parkland course. 18 holes, 6262 yards. S.S.S. 70. Practice ground. *Green Fees:* weekdays £28.00, weekends and Bank Holidays £36.00. *Eating facilities:* restaurant, lounge and bar and snooker room. *Visitors:* welcome weekdays 9.30am-11.30am, 1.45pm-3.30pm. Tuesday Ladies' day. No visiting parties weekends or Bank Holidays. *Society Meetings:* weekdays only with reservation. Professional: Peter Jackson (01429 836510). Secretary: Derek Livingston (01429 836510).

HARTLEPOOL. **Hartlepool Golf Club Ltd,** Hart Warren, Hartlepool TS24 9QF (01429 274398; Fax: 01429 274129). *Location:* turn right off A1086 at Hart Station – north of town, signposted. Seaside links course. 18 holes, 6125 yards. S.S.S. 70. *Green Fees:* midweek £34.00, weekends £44.00. *Eating facilities:* full catering available except Mondays. *Visitors:* welcome (excluding Sunday) without reservation. Caddy carts. *Society Meetings:* catered for by prior arrangement. Professional: G. Laidlaw (01429 267473). Hon. Secretary: L.G. Gordon (01429 274398).
website: www.hartlepoolgolfclub.co.uk

HARTLEPOOL. **High Throston Golf Club,** Hart Lane, Hartlepool TS26 0UG (01429 275325). *Location:* two miles from A19. Course designed by Jonathan Gaunt (USGA specification) with natural banks, rolling countryside with sea views - 7000 trees planted. 18 holes, 6247 yards, S.S.S. 71. Practice nets, putting green. *Green Fees:* information not available. *Eating facilities:* only light refreshments available at present. *Visitors:* welcome usually at all times. Secretary: Mrs J. Sturrock (01429 268071). *

HARTLEPOOL. **Seaton Carew Golf Club,** Tees Road, Seaton Carew, Hartlepool TS25 1DE (01429 266249). *Location:* two miles south of Hartlepool on A178. Championship seaside links. 22 holes. Old Course: 6658 yards. S.S.S. 72. Brabazon Course: 6900 yards. S.S.S. 73. Micklem Course: 6574 yards. S.S.S. 71. *Green Fees:* on application. *Eating facilities:* bar snacks, full catering to order. *Visitors:* welcome midweek and some weekends. Advance booking recommended. Buggies for hire. *Society Meetings:* catered for by arrangement. Professional: Mark Rogers (01429 890660). Secretary: J. Hall (01429 296496; Fax: 01429 296496).
e-mail: seatoncarewgolf@btconnect.com
website: www.seatoncarewgolf.co.uk

NEWTON AYCLIFFE. **Oak Leaf Golf Complex,** School Aycliffe Lane, Newton Aycliffe DL5 6QZ (01325 310820). Location: three miles from A1(M) and A68 on the outskirts of Newton Aycliffe. Rolling parkland. 18 holes, 5568 yards. S.S.S. 67. Driving range (floodlit), chipping and bunker practice. *Green Fees:* information not provided. *Eating facilities:* bar and catering available at Oakleaf Golf Complex. Contact (01325 300600). *Visitors:* public course. Visiting parties by appointment. Showers/toilets/changing facilities. Squash/Indoor Bowls at Oakleaf Golf Complex. *Society Meetings:* all welcome by prior arrangement. Professional: Ernie Wilson (01325 310820) Secretary: Mr B. Oliver (Club) (01325 316040).

NEWTON AYCLIFFE. **Woodham Golf and Country Club,** Burnhill Way, Newton Aycliffe DL5 4PN (01325 320574; Fax: 01325 315254). *Location:* A167, one mile north of Newton Aycliffe on the Shildon road. Parkland, wooded with lakes. 18 holes, 6771 yards. S.S.S. 72. Practice grounds, putting green. *Green Fees:* weekdays £22.00, weekends £35.00. *Eating facilities:* bar/restaurant. *Visitors:* welcome anytime, must book though on Friday, Saturday and Sunday. Buggies, trolleys available. *Society Meetings:* all welcome. Professional: Peter Kelly (01325 315257; Fax: 01325 315254). Secretary: John D. Jenkinson. Steward: (01325 301551).

SEAHAM. **Seaham Golf Club,** Shrewsbury Street, Seaham SR7 7RD (0191-581 2354). *Location:* Dawdon, two miles north east of A19 leave for Murton/Seaham. Heathland. 18 holes, 6017 yards. S.S.S. 69. Practice area. *Green Fees:* weekdays £25.00 (£15.00 playing with a member); weekends and Bank Holidays £28.00 (£18.00 playing with a member). *Eating facilities:* snacks available, meals on request. *Visitors:* welcome, unrestricted weekdays, booking for weekends. *Society Meetings:* welcome on application. Professional: Andrew Blunt (0191-513 0837). Secretary: Terry Johnson (0191-581 1268). website: www.seahamgolfclub.co.uk

STANLEY. **South Moor Golf Club,** The Middles, Craghead, Stanley DH9 6AG (01207 232848; Fax: 01207 284616). *Location:* eight miles north-west of Durham, seven miles west of A1 (M) from Chester-le-Street. Parkland and moorland. 18 holes, 6273 yards. S.S.S. 70. *Green Fees:* Information not available. *Eating facilities:* available. *Visitors:* visiting parties between 10am and 11.30am and 2pm to 3.30pm. *Society Meetings:* catered for except Sundays. Professional: Shaun Cowell (01207 283525). Secretary: B. Davison (01207 232848).*
e-mail: bryandavison@southmoorgc.freeserve.co.uk

STOCKTON-ON-TEES. **Knotty Hill Golf Centre,** Sedgefield, Stockton-on-Tees TS21 2BB (01740 620320; Fax: 01740 622227). *Location:* A1 (M) Junction 60, one mile north of Sedgefield A177. Princes Course set in rolling parkland with many holes routed through shallow valleys. Bishops Course, a developing course with varied water features laid out within attractive rolling terrain. Princes Course – 18 holes, 6433 yards, 5882 metres, S.S.S. 71, par 72; Bishops Course – 18 holes, 5915 yards, 5406 metres, par 70. Academy Course - 9 holes, 2494 yards, Par 32. Indoor Golf Academy, video and tuition range, high quality floodlit driving range, open grass tee area, chipping and putting greens, practice bunker. *Green Fees:* 9 holes £8.00, 18 holes £13.00. *Eating facilities:* restaurant, coffee shop. *Visitors:* welcome at all times. Buggy and cart hire. *Society Meetings:* welcome, information on request. Secretary: Mrs J. Reynolds (01740 620320).

STOCKTON-ON-TEES. **Norton Golf Course,** Blakeston Lane, Norton, Stockton-on-Tees TS20 2SU (01642 676385; Fax: 01642 608467). *Location:* turn into Junction Road to Norton from A177 at Horse and Jockey, two miles north of Stockton roundabout. Slightly hilly course with five lakes. 18 holes, 5393 yards. S.S.S. 70. *Green Fees:* weekdays £12.00 for 18 holes, weekends and Bank Holidays £14.00. Subject to review. *Visitors:* must have golf shoes and own clubs; no jeans. Parties welcome weekdays. *Society Meetings:* rates on application. Contact (01642 676385).

STOCKTON-ON-TEES. **Teesside Golf Club,** Acklam Road, Thornaby, Stockton-on-Tees TS17 7JS (01642 676249; Fax: 01642 676252). *Location:* A19 - A1130 to Thornaby, 0.7 miles on right hand side. Flat parkland. 18 holes, 6535 yards. S.S.S. 71. Practice ground, putting green. *Green Fees:* weekdays £26.00, weekends £30.00. *Eating facilities:* catering except Mondays, bar 11am to 11pm. *Visitors:* welcome midweek up to 4.30pm, weekends after 11am by arrangement. *Society Meetings:* Monday - Friday. Special rates and conditions for parties and guests. Professional: S. Pilgrim (01642 673822). Secretary: M. Fleming (01642 616516).
e-mail: teessidegolfclub@btconnect.com
website: www.teessidegolfclub.com

Lancashire

ACCRINGTON. **Accrington and District Golf Club,** Devon Avenue, Oswaldtwistle, Accrington BB5 4LS (01254 231091). *Location*: on A679, 2 miles from Blackburn. 18 holes, 6060 yards. S.S.S. 69. *Green Fees*: Monday to Thursday £30.00, Friday to Sunday £35.00. *Eating facilities*: lunches and evening meals. *Visitors*: welcome by prior arrangement. *Society Meetings*: prior bookings catered for. Professional: Mark Harling (01254 231091). Secretary: S. Padbury (01254 350112). e-mail: info@accringtongolfclub.com

ACUP. **Bacup Golf Club,** Bankside Lane, Bacup OL13 1HY (01706 873170; Fax: 01706 87726). *Location:* one mile from Bacup centre. Moorland. 9 holes, 6018 yards. S.S.S. 69. *Green Fees:* information not available. *Eating facilities:* by arrangement except Mondays. *Visitors:* welcome without reservation except Mondays and Saturdays. Secretary: T. Leyland (01706 879644).*

BAXENDEN. **Baxenden and District Golf Club,** Wooley Lane, Baxenden BB5 2EA (01254 234555). *Location*: towards Accrington from M65, past Hollands Pies right, signposted. Golf course has fantastic views as far as the Fylde Coast and Ingleborough. 9 holes, 5702 yards. S.S.S. 68. *Green Fees*: information not provided. *Eating facilities*: available. *Visitors*: welcome weekdays only. *Society Meetings*: welcome by arrangement with Secretary. Secretary: N. Turner (01254 234555).* e-mail: baxgolf@hotmail.com website: www.baxendengolf.co.uk

BLACKBURN. **Blackburn Golf Club,** Beardwood Brow, Blackburn BB2 7AX (01254 51122; Fax: 01254 665578). *Location:* off A677 within easy reach of M6 (Junction 31), M61 and M65; west end of Blackburn. Parkland with superb views of Lancashire coast and Pennine Hills. 18 holes, 6144 yards. S.S.S. 70. Par 71. Practice area. *Green Fees:* weekdays £26.00 (£12.00 with a member); weekends and Bank Holidays £30.00 (£12.00 with a member). *Eating facilities:* full catering and bar facilities (restricted Mondays). *Visitors:* welcome without reservation except on competition days. *Society Meetings:* catered for by arrangement. Professional: Alan Rodwell (01254 55942). Hon. Secretary: G. Readett (01254 51122; Fax: 01254 665578).

BLACKBURN. **Great Harwood Golf Club,** Harwood Bar, Whalley Road, Great Harwood, Blackburn BB6 7TE (01254 884391). Flat wooded course. 9 holes, 6404 yards, 5856 metres. S.S.S. 71. Practice area. *Green Fees:* £20.00 weekdays, £26.00 weekends. *Eating facilities:* all meals catered for, bar hours 12-2pm, 4-11pm. *Visitors:* welcome Wednesday - Friday. *Society Meetings:* catered for by advance bookings. Secretary: J. Spibey (01254 884391).

BLACKBURN. **Mytton Fold Hotel & Golf Complex,** Whalley Road, Langho, Blackburn BB6 8AB (01254 245392/240662). *Location:* from Junction 31 of M6, follow A59 towards Whalley/Clitheroe for 10 miles. At second roundabout follow Whalley sign, entrance 500 yards on right. Undulating parkland with panoramic views over the Ribble Valley. 18 holes. Par 70. *Green Fees:* Monday to Friday £21.00, weekend £22.00 (subject to review for 2008). *Eating facilities:* bar open all day, food till 9.30pm. *Visitors:* prior booking essential. Buggies available. *Society Meetings:* welcome, from £19.00 per person. Professional: Mike Bardi. e-mail: info@myttonfold.co.uk

BLACKBURN. **Pleasington Golf Club,** Pleasington, Near Blackburn BB2 5JF (01254 202177). *Location:* five minutes from Junction 3 of the M65. Undulating woodland. 18 holes, 6402 yards. S.S.S. 71. *Green Fees:* weekdays £45.00, weekends and Bank Holidays £50.00. *Eating facilities:* full catering available. *Visitors:* welcome by prior arrangement. *Society Meetings:* Mondays, Wednesdays, Thursdays and Fridays by arrangement. Professional: G.J. Furey (01254 201630). Secretary/General Manager: T. Ashton (01254 202177). Caterer: D. Whittam (01254 207346). e-mail: secretary-manager@pleasington-golf.co.uk website: www.pleasington-golf.co.uk

BLACKBURN. **Rishton Golf Club,** Eachill Links, Rishton BB1 4HG (01254 884442; Fax: 01254 887701). *Location:* between Junctions 6 and 7 M65 signposted from Rishton village centre. Moorland course. 9 holes, 6094 yards. S.S.S. 69. *Green Fees:* information not available. *Eating facilities:* full catering by prior arrangement. *Visitors:* welcome on weekdays and with a member at weekends and on Bank Holidays. *Society Meetings:* visiting parties welcome by prior arrangement, special rates can be obtained. Secretary: T. Charnock (0771 0371118).*

BLACKBURN. **Wilpshire Golf Club Ltd,** 72 Whalley Road, Wilpshire, Blackburn BB1 9LF (01254 248260; Fax: 01254 246745). *Location:* A666 three miles north of Blackburn on Blackburn to Whalley road. Parkland/moorland. 18 holes, 5961 yards. S.S.S. 69. Practice ground. *Green Fees:* information not available. *Eating facilities:* lunch, high tea, dinner except Mondays. *Visitors:* welcome, no restrictions except competition days. Clubs and trolley hire. *Society Meetings:* catered for by prior booking through Secretary. Professional: Walter Slaven (01254 249558; Fax: 01254 246745). Secretary: S.H. Tart. e-mail: admin@wilpshiregolfclub.co.uk website: www.wilpshiregolfclub.co.uk

BLACKPOOL. **Blackpool North Shore Golf Club,** Devonshire Road, Blackpool FY2 0RD (01253 352054; Fax: 01253 591240). *Location:* north Blackpool on A587 behind North Prom. Undulating parkland. 18 holes, 6431 yards. S.S.S. 71. *Green Fees:* weekdays £37.00 day; weekends £44.00 day. Society Package £46.00, *Eating facilities:* full catering and bar facilities. *Visitors:* welcome except Thursdays and Saturdays. Professional: Andrew Richardson (01253 352054). Secretary: John Morris (01253 352054).
e-mail: office@bnsgc.com
website: www.bnsgc.com

BLACKPOOL. **Blackpool Park Golf Club,** North Park Drive, Blackpool FY3 8LS (Tel & Fax: 01253 397916). *Location:* one mile east of Tower. Mackenzie-designed course. 18 holes, 6089 yards. S.S.S. 70. *Green Fees:* information not available. *Eating facilities:* full restaurant facilities. *Visitors:* welcome (bookings for tee reservations must be made on 01253 478176). *Society Meetings:* Apply to Blackpool Borough Council in writing. Professional: B. Purdie (01253 391004). Secretary: David Stones (Tel & Fax: 01253 397916).

BLACKPOOL. **De Vere Herons' Reach Golf & Leisure Resort,** East Park Drive, Blackpool FY3 8LL (01253 766156; Fax: 01253 798800). *Location:* leave M55 at Junction 4, follow signs for Stanley Park and Victoria Hospital. Designed by Peter Alliss & Clive Clark. Testing championship course with 10 man-made lakes- all year round play course. Heron's Reach Course -18 holes, 6461 yards, S.S.S. 70. 17 bay floodlit driving range, putting and chipping green. *Green Fees:* information not available. *Eating facilities:* Nineteen Bar serving from 7am daily, leisure bar and Brasserie open seven days. *Visitors:* welcome. 172 bedroomed hotel with extensive conference and banqueting facilities for up to 600 plus leisure complex. *Society Meetings:* welcome. Golf Centre: (01253 766156; Fax: 01253 798800).*

BLACKPOOL. **Knott End Golf Club Ltd,** Wyre Side, Knott End-on-Sea, Poulton-le-Fylde FY6 0AA (01253 810576). *Location:* M55 Exit 3, A585 Fleetwood Road then A588 to Knott End. Scenic riverside course, slight undulations. 18 holes, 5843 yards. S.S.S. 68. Practice ground. *Green Fees:* £31.00 18 holes weekdays, weekends £39.00. *Eating facilities:* full catering and bar. *Visitors:* welcome, time sheet in use, contact Professional with 24 hours notice. Buggies for hire. *Society Meetings:* by arrangement weekdays. Professional: Paul Walker (01253 811365). Manager: Louise Freeman (01253 810576; Fax: 01253 813446).
e-mail: louise@knottendgolfclub.com
website: www.knottendgolfclub.com

BLACKPOOL. **Poulton-le-Fylde Golf Club,** Myrtle Farm, Breck Road, Poulton-le-Fylde, Blackpool FY6 7HJ (Tel & Fax: 01253 892444). *Location:* from M55 follow Poulton/Thornton/Cleveleys, roundabout with River Wyre pub on left, turn left and follow signs. Parkland/wooded course. 9 holes, 3260 yards. Par 36. Practice and putting facilities. *Green Fees:* Information not available. *Eating facilities:* breakfast and lunch served, all day bar in summer. *Visitors:* welcome anytime, bookings taken up to one week in advance (01253 892444). Snooker. *Society Meetings:* welcome by prior booking. Professional: John Greenwood (Tel & Fax: 01253 892444). Secretary: John Greenwood (Tel & Fax: 01253 892444).*
website: www.poultonlefyldegolfclub.com

BOLTON. **Bolton Open Golf Course,** Longsight Park, Longsight Lane, Harwood, Bolton BL2 4JX (01204 597659). *Location:* one and a half miles from Bolton town centre. Parkland, mature wooded, superb layout. 18 holes, 6000 yards. S.S.S. 68. 20 bay floodlit driving range. *Green Fees:* £10.00 weekdays, £14.00 weekend.. *Eating facilities:* one bar, all day catering. *Visitors:* no restrictions, everyone welcome at all times. *Society Meetings:* welcome anytime, discounts available.

BOLTON. **Douglas Valley Golf Club,** A6 Blackrod By-Pass, Blackrod, Bolton BL6 5HX. *Location:* M61 Junction 6, off A6. Parkland greens. 9 holes, 2190 yards, 2004 metres. 22-bay floodlit driving range. *Green Fees:* weekdays - 9 holes £8.00, 18 holes £10.00, weekends - 9 holes £9.00, 18 holes £12.00. Subject to review. *Visitors:* welcome anytime. Bookings two days in advance. Fully stocked Pro Shop and Teaching Academy. *Eating facilities:* Portofino Italian Restaurant and Function Suite available, ring for details (01257 476012) or see website below. *Society Meetings:* society and corporate days available, ring for details. Head Professional: Andrew Green. Company Secretary: Julie Downes (01257 474844).
website: www.golfdealstoday.co.uk
　　　　www.portofinoristorante.co.uk

BURNLEY. **Burnley Golf Club,** Glen View, Burnley BB11 3RW (0870 330 6655; Fax: 01282 451281). *Location:* 300 yards from junction of A56 and A646. Moorland. 18 holes, 5939 yards, 5430 metres. S.S.S. 69. *Green Fees:* weekdays £25.00; weekends and Bank Holidays £30.00. *Eating facilities:* generally available, please telephone to check. *Visitors:* welcome except Saturdays. *Society Meetings:* catered for. Director of Golf: Matthew Baker (0870 330 6655). Secretary/Manager: R. D. M. Wills (0870 330 6655).
e-mail: burnleygolfclub@onthegreen.co.uk
website: www.burnleygolfclub.sitenet.pl

BURNLEY. **Towneley Golf Club,** Towneley Park, Todmorden Road, Burnley BB11 3ED (01282 415636). *Location:* Todmorden Road, Burnley, Top Gates to Towneley Park. Guarded greens (ie. bunkered) and internal O.B.B. 18 holes, 5811 yards. S.S.S. 68. Practice ground. *Green Fees:* information not provided. *Eating facilities:* full licensed bar and catering (full meals). *Visitors:* welcome but make tee reservations in advance. *Society Meetings:* welcome, apply to course booking shop. Professional: James Major (01282 438473) Secretary: Chris Gilbert (01282 415636).

CHORLEY. **Charnock Richard Golf Club,** Preston Road, Charnock Richard, Chorley PR7 5LE (01257 470707). *Location:* on A49 between M6 turn-offs for Standish and Leyland, five minutes from Camelot Theme Park. Parkland with water features. 18 holes. Par 71. Buggy hire. *Green Fees:* Information not available. *Eating facilities:* Italian restaurant on site. Director of Golf: Alan Lunt.*

CHORLEY. **Chorley Golf Club,** Hall o' the Hill, Heath Charnock, Chorley PR6 9HX (01257 480263; Fax: 01257 480722). *Location:* south of Chorley, just off the A673 at the junction with the A6. Scenic course with some of the finest views in Lancashire. 18 holes, 6269 yards. S.S.S. 70. *Green Fees:* weekdays £34.00 (under review). *Eating facilities:* restaurant and lounge bar. *Visitors:* welcome by prior arrangement except Bank Holidays or weekends. Two buggies and carts for hire. *Society Meetings:* catered for by arrangement. Professional: M.N. Bradley (01257 481245). Secretary: Mrs A. Green (01257 480263). Catering: (01257 474664).

CHORLEY. **Duxbury Park Golf Club (Municipal),** Duxbury Hall Road, Duxbury Park, Chorley PR7 4AS (01257 265380, 01257 241634). *Location:* one mile south of town centre off A6. Wooded parkland with water hazards on several holes. 18 holes, 6390 yards, 5843 metres. S.S.S. 70. Practice area. *Green Fees:* information not available. *Eating facilities:* Golf Cafe open 7 days a week, very reasonable prices. For details contact Paul (01257 277049). *Visitors:* welcome, book seven days in advance. *Society Meetings:* book in advance. Professional: (01257 265380). Secretary: F. Holding (01257 262209). Membership available, contact Secretary.*

CHORLEY. **Euxton Park Golf Centre,** Euxton Lane, Chorley PR7 6DL (01257 261601; Fax: 01257 261601). *Location:* Euxton Lane, between A6 and A49, next to Royal Ordnance factory. A short, yet challenging Par 3 course, ideal for beginners. 9 holes, Par 3. 40 bay driving range, practice bunkers. *Green Fees:* information not available. *Eating facilities:* fully licensed bar. *Visitors:* welcome every day, no need to book, pay and play course. *Society Meetings:* welcome, professionally catered for. Professional: Jon Halnes (01257 233500). Secretary: T.R. Evans (Tel & Fax: 01257 261601).*

CHORLEY. **Shaw Hill Hotel Golf and Country Club,** Preston Road, Whittle-le-Woods, Chorley PR6 7PP (01257 269221; Fax: 01257 261223). *Location:* A6 between Chorley and Preston. (Near M6 J28 & M61 J8) Parkland course with many water hazards. 18 holes, 6283 yards. S.S.S. 71 yellow. Practice area. *Green Fees:* on request. *Eating facilities:* spike bar and formal bar, à la carte restaurant. *Visitors:* welcome weekdays only, must hold current Handicap Certificate. Hotel with 30 bedrooms available. Golf trolleys and buggies also available. *Society Meetings:* catered for midweek only. Professional: D. Clarke (01257 279222). General Manager: Mrs K. Tyrer. Secretary: L. Bateson.

CLITHEROE. **Clitheroe Golf Club,** Whalley Road, Pendleton, Clitheroe BB7 1PP (Tel & Fax: 01200 422292). *Location:* A59, junction A671 (south of Clitheroe); 300m turn left (signposted Barrow) clubhouse 100m on right. Parkland with extensive countryside views. 18 holes, 6326 yards, 5785 metres. S.S.S. 71. Practice ground and range. *Green Fees:* weekdays from £35.00; weekends and Bank Holidays £45.00. With a member £12.00. Subject to review. *Eating facilities:* full service available. *Visitors:* welcome but restricted to times available. No jeans, trainers, track/shell suits. *Society Meetings:* catered for, maximum 48 Friday; maximum 24 Thursday. No parties weekends. Professional: Paul McEvoy (01200 424242). Secretary: (01200 422292). e-mail: secretary@clitheroegolfclub.com website: www.clitheroegolfclub.com

CLITHEROE. **Whalley Golf Club,** Long Lease Barn, Clerk Hill Rd, Whalley, Clitheroe BB7 9DR (01254 822236). *Location:* seven miles east of Blackburn on A59. Parkland. 9 holes, 6258 yards, 5727 metres. S.S.S. 71. *Green Fees:* weekdays £25.00, weeknds/Bank Holidays £30.00. *Eating facilities:* full catering and bar facilities. *Visitors:* welcome except Thursday afternoons and Saturdays April to September. *Society Meetings:* welcome by appointment. Professional: Jamie Hunt (01254 824766).

COLNE. **Colne Golf Club,** Law Farm, Skipton Old Road, Colne BB8 7EB (01282 863391). *Location:* come off eastern end of M65. Carry on one mile to next roundabout and take first exit on left, signposted Lothersdale, Goup Hill. Flat scenic moorland course with trees. 9 holes, 6053 yards, 5535 metres. S.S.S. 69. Full practice facilities. *Green Fees:* £20.00 weekdays, £25.00 weekends and Bank Holidays (subject to review). Parties of 12 or more £19.00 per person (not weekends, Thursdays or competition days). *Eating facilities:* available daily except Mondays. *Visitors:* welcome except on competition days; two-balls only on Thursdays. *Society Meetings:* welcome except weekends, Thursdays and competition days. Secretary: A. Turpin.

DARWEN. **Darwen Golf Club,** Winter Hill, Darwen BB3 0LB (01254 704367). *Location:* one-and-a-half miles from Darwen centre. Moorland. 18 holes, 6354 yards. S.S.S. 71. Large practice area. *Green Fees:* £25.00 per round. *Eating facilities:* full catering. *Visitors:* welcome, not Tuesdays (Ladies' Day) or Saturdays. *Society Meetings:* welcome, except Saturdays. Professional: W. Lennon (01254 776370). Secretary: H. J. Catterall (01254 704367).

FLEETWOOD. **Fleetwood Golf Club Ltd.,** The Golf House, Princes Way, Fleetwood FY7 8AF (Tel & Fax: 01253 773573). *Location:* on Fylde Coast, eight miles from Blackpool, Coast Road Blackpool to Fleetwood, two miles west of Fleetwood Centre. Seaside, true links. White course 18 holes, 6557 yards, S.S.S. 71; Yellow course 18 holes, 6308 yards, S.S.S. 70. *Green Fees:* per round weekdays £35.00, weekends £45.00; per day weekdays £45.00, weekends £50.00. Special rates available on request. *Eating facilities:* full catering and bar service. *Visitors:* welcome weekdays, certain Saturdays and Sundays. *Society Meetings:* welcome by arrangement. Professional: Ian Taylor (01253 873661). Office Secretary: Ernie Longford (01253 773573; Fax: 01253 877643).
e-mail: secretary@fleetwoodgolf.co.uk
website: www.fleetwoodgolf.co.uk

HEYSHAM. **Heysham Golf Club,** Trumacar Park, Middleton Road, Heysham LA3 3JH (01524 851011; Fax: 01524 853030). *Location:* five miles from M6 via Lancaster and Morecambe. Parkland, flat, part-wooded. 18 holes, 6338 yards. S.S.S. 70. Driving range and chipping green. *Green Fees:* weekdays £30.00 per round, £35.00 per day; weekends/Bank Holidays £40.00. Subject to review. Special rates for parties. *Eating facilities:* full catering seven days, closed Mondays October to March. *Visitors:* welcome with Handicap Certificates. Tee reserved for members 1pm to 1.45pm. Buggy hire available. *Society Meetings:* catered for by arrangement. Professional: R. Done (01524 852000). Secretary: F.A. Bland (01524 851011).

LANCASTER. **Lancaster Golf Club Ltd,** Ashton Hall, Ashton-with-Stodday, Lancaster LA2 0AJ (01524 752090). *Location:* three miles south of Lancaster on A588. Parkland. 18 holes, 6512 yards. S.S.S. 71. *Green Fees:* £40.00 per round, £47.00 per day (subject to review for 2008). *Eating facilities:* available (Caterer: 01524 751105). *Visitors:* welcome weekdays only unless staying in the Dormy House. Club has a Dormy House (part of Ashton Hall), single and double rooms with en suite facilities, two nights minimum stay. Professional: David Sutcliffe (01524 751802). Secretary: E. Burrow (01524 751247; Fax: 01524 752742).
e-mail: secretary@lancastergc.co.uk

LANCASTER. **Lansil Golf Club,** Caton Road, Lancaster LA1 3PE (01524 39269/61233). *Location:* A683, towards Lancaster from Junction 34 M6. Parkland. 9 holes, 5608 yards. S.S.S. 67. *Green Fees:* information not available. *Eating facilities:* bar meals available - contact Steward. *Visitors:* welcome weekdays, not before 1pm Sundays. *Society Meetings:* groups of 12 plus welcome weekdays by prior arrangement. Steward: 01524 39269. *

LEYLAND. **Leyland Golf Club Ltd.,** Wigan Road, Leyland, Preston PR25 5UD (01772 436457). *Location:* leave M6 at Exit 28, turn right to traffic lights, (200 yards) turn right onto the A49, course located one mile on left. Flat parkland. 18 holes, 6298 yards. S.S.S. 70. *Green Fees:* £25.00 weekdays. *Eating facilities:* full catering except Mondays in winter. *Visitors:* welcome weekdays; weekends only with a member. *Society Meetings:* welcome by arrangement. Professional: C. Burgess (01772 423425). Admin. Manager: Stephanie Drinkall (01772 436457).
e-mail: manager@leylandgolfclub.co.uk
website: www.leylandgolfclub.co.uk

LYTHAM ST ANNES. **Fairhaven Golf Club,** Oakwood Avenue, Lytham St Annes FY8 4JU (01253 736741). *Location:* on B5261, two miles from Lytham, eight miles from Blackpool. A final qualifying Open Championship course. 18 holes, 6883 yards. S.S.S. 73. Par 74. Practice ground, chipping and putting greens, and nets. *Green Fees:* information on request from office, or visit website. *Eating facilities:* full catering service seven days a week. *Visitors:* welcome, advisable to reserve tee time. Handicap Certificate required. Well stocked Pro Shop; lessons available. *Society Meetings:* various packages can be arranged on Mondays, Tuesdays, Wednesdays and Fridays. Professional: B. Plucknett (01253 736976). Secretary: Bob Thompson (Tel & Fax:01253 736741).
e-mail: secretary@fairhavengolfclub.co.uk
website: www.fairhavengolfclub.co.uk

LYTHAM ST ANNES. **Lytham Green Drive Golf Club,** Ballam Road, Lytham St Annes FY8 4LE (01253 737390; Fax: 01253 731350). *Location:* one mile from town centre. Flat parkland course. 18 holes, 6363 yards. S.S.S. 70. *Green Fees:* from £32.00 per person, depending on group numbers. *Eating facilities:* catering available daily. *Visitors:* welcome. *Society Meetings:* welcome by prior arrangement. Professional: A. Lancaster (01253 737379). Secretary: I. Stewart (01253 737390; Fax: 01253 731350).
e-mail: secretary@lythamgreendrive.co.uk
website: www.lythamgreendrive.co.uk

LYTHAM ST ANNES. **Royal Lytham and St Annes Golf Club,** Links Gate, Lytham St Annes FY8 3LQ (01253 724206; Fax: 01253 780946). *Location:* within one mile of the centre of St Annes on Sea. Seaside Championship links course. 18 holes, 6334 yards. S.S.S. 71. Practice ground. *Green Fees:* Mondays and Thursdays £120.00 including lunch, limited availability on Sundays £180.00 including lunch. Subject to review. *Eating facilities:* restaurant and bar. *Visitors:* welcome, times by arrangement. Dormy House accommodation available. *Society Meetings:* by arrangement. Professional: Eddie Birchenough (01253 720094). Secretary: R.J.G Cochrane.
e-mail: bookings@royallytham.org

LYTHAM ST ANNES. **St Annes Old Links Golf Club,** Highbury Road, Lytham St Annes FY8 2LD (01253 723597). *Location:* M55 via Blackpool South Shore, following airport signs. Past airport down to coast road, turn left and first left at next real traffic lights. The only true links course in Lancashire. 18 holes, 6684 yards. S.S.S. 72. Practice ground, putting and chipping greens. *Green Fees:* weekdays from £55.00 per day, from £40.00 for 18 holes after 1.30pm. *Eating facilities:* restaurant and snack facilities, bar. *Visitors:* welcome, not Saturdays, restricted Sundays. Tuesday is Ladies' Day. *Society Meetings:* restricted to those with Handicaps and membership of other clubs. Professional: D. Webster (01253 722432). Secretary: J. Donohoe (01253 723597; Fax: 01253 781506).
e-mail: secretary@stannesoldlinks.com
website: www.stannesoldlinks.com

www.uk-golfguide.com

MORECAMBE. **Morecambe Golf Club Ltd.,** The Club House, Bare, Morecambe LA4 6AJ (01524 418050). *Location:* on A589 leaving Morecambe towards Carnforth. Parkland course affected by sea breezes and offering superb views. 18 holes, 5770 yards. S.S.S. 69. *Green Fees:* available on request. *Eating facilities:* diningroom and bar snacks. *Visitors:* welcome at all times, tee reserved for members up to 9.30am and from 12 noon to 1.30pm, *Society Meetings:* welcome at all times. Professional: Simon Fletcher (Tel & Fax: 01524 415596). Secretary: Mrs Judith Atkinson (01524 412841; Fax: 01524 400088). e-mail: secretary@morecambegolfclub.com website: www.morecambegolfclub.com

NELSON. **Nelson Golf Club,** King's Causeway, Brierfield, Nelson BB9 0EU (01282 611834). *Location:* leave M65 at Junction 12, take A682 for Brierfield, turn left at Brierfield centre traffic lights, course on the right at top of the hill. Wooded moorland, good views of the surrounding Pendle Area. 18 holes, 6007 yards. S.S.S. 69. Large practice area. *Green Fees:* weekdays £30.00, weekends and Bank Holidays £35.00. *Eating facilities:* lunches, dinners by arrangement except Mondays. *Visitors:* weekdays except Thursdays (Ladies' Day), or Saturdays during Competition season. Carts. *Society Meetings:* daily except Monday, Thursday and Saturday. Professional: Neil Reeves (01282 617000). Secretary: B.R. Thomason (01282 611834).

ORMSKIRK. **Mossock Hall Golf Club,** Liverpool Road, Bickerstaffe, Ormskirk L39 0EE (01695 421717). *Location:* one mile from Junction 3 of M58 or two miles from Junction 1 of M57, between Kirby and Ormskirk. Parkland course; USGA greens with water in play on four holes. 18 holes. Par 71. *Green Fees:* information available on (01695 421717). *Eating facilities:* licensed bar and restaurant. *Society Meetings:* catered for - advance bookings only, contact manager Jackie Fray (01695 421717). Professional: Brad Millar.

ORMSKIRK. **Ormskirk Golf Club,** Cranes Lane, Lathom L40 5UJ (01695 572112). *Location:* two miles east of Ormskirk. Parkland course. 18 holes, 6358 yards. S.S.S. 70. *Green Fees:* weekdays £40.00 per round, £50.00 per day, weekends £50.00 per round, £60.00 per day. *Eating facilities:* available except Monday. *Visitors:* welcome, Handicap Certificates required, notice advised with reservation. *Society Meetings:* catered for, book in advance. Professional: J. Hammond (01695 572074). Secretary: R.D.J. Lawrence (01695 572227).

PRESTON. **Ashton and Lea Golf Club Ltd,** Tudor Avenue, off Blackpool Road, Lea, Preston PR4 0XA (01772 735282; Fax: 01772 735762). *Location:* on A5085, three miles west of Preston, turn opposite Toby Carvery. Parkland with water features. 18 holes, 6334 yards. S.S.S. 70. Practice ground. *Green Fees:* weekdays £30.00; weekends and Bank Holidays £35.00. *Eating facilities:* full catering every day. *Visitors:* welcome but please telephone the Professional to reserve tee time. Conference and function facilities available. Reduced rates for groups of 12 or more. *Society Meetings:* catered for weekdays only, contact the Secretary. Professional: Mike Greenough (01772 720374). Secretary: Mark Caunce (01772 735282). e-mail: secretary@ashtonleagolfclub.co.uk website: www.ashtonleagolfclub.co.uk

PRESTON. **Fishwick Hall Golf Club,** Glenluce Drive, Farringdon Park, Preston PR1 5TD (01772 798300). *Location:* two minutes from Junction 31 M6, off A59 Blackburn to Preston Road. Parkland, part wooded, bounded by river. 18 holes, 6084 yards. S.S.S. 69. Small practice area. *Green Fees:* weekdays £28.00; weekends and Public Holidays £32.00. Reductions if playing with members. *Eating facilities:* bar, full catering available except Mondays. *Visitors:* welcome unless club competition on. *Society Meetings:* welcome weekdays and Sundays. Professional: M. Watson (01772 795870). Secretary: R. E. Stamp (01772 798300; Fax: 01772 704600).

PRESTON. **Ingol Golf Club,** Tanterton Hall Road, Ingol, Preston PR2 7BY (01772 734556; Fax: 01772 729815). *Location:* two miles from Junction 32 M6 (joins M55). Parkland. 18 holes, 6294 yards, Par 72. Chipping and putting practice areas. *Green Fees:* information not available. *Eating facilities:* bar/restaurant. *Visitors:* welcome anytime, please telephone to check tee reservations. Buggies and trolleys available. Squash courts. Meeting room available. Stay and play packages. *Society Meetings:* welcome by arrangement. Professional: Ryan Grimshaw (01772 769646). Secretary: Marjorie Kenny (01772 734556; Fax: 01772 729815).* website: www.ingolgolfclub.co.uk

PRESTON. **Longridge Golf Club,** Fell Barn, Jeffrey Hill, Longridge, Preston PR3 2TU (01772 783291; Fax: 01772 783022). **Location: eight miles north-east of Preston off B6243. Moorland with extensive spectacular views. One of the oldest clubs in England (Est. 1877). 18 holes, 5975 yards. S.S.S. 69. Green Fees: weekdays £30.00 per day, £20.00 per round; weekends £35.00. (under review). Eating facilities: full catering and bars. Visitors: welcome. Society Meetings: welcome by prior arrangement. Professional: Stephen Taylor. Secretary: David Simpson. e-mail: secretary@longridgegolfclub.fsnet.co.uk website: www.longridgegolfclub.com**

PRESTON. **Penwortham Golf Club Ltd.,** Blundell Lane, Penwortham, Preston PR1 0AX (01772 744630; Fax: 01772 740172). *Location:* one mile west of Preston on main Southport to Liverpool road. Parkland. 18 holes, 5877 yards. S.S.S. 69. *Green Fees:* £25.00 weekdays; £33.00 weekends. *Eating facilities:* lunches and dinners served at Club. *Visitors:* welcome. *Society Meetings:* by arrangement Monday, Wednesday, Thursday, Friday only. Professional: Darren Hopwood (01772 742345). Secretary: Neil Annandale (01772 744630; Fax: 01772 740172).

THE APPEARANCE OF AN ASTERISK (*) AT THE END OF A CLUB OR COURSE ENTRY INDICATES THAT UP-TO-DATE INFORMATION HAS NOT BEEN SUPPLIED

Greater Manchester

ALTRINCHAM. **Altrincham Golf Club,** Stockport Road, Timperley, Altrincham, Cheshire WA15 7LP (0161-928 0761). *Location:* one mile east of Altrincham on A560. Parkland. 18 holes, 6190 yards, 5659 metres. S.S.S. 69. Driving range. *Green Fees:* information not available. *Eating facilities:* Old Hall Hotel attached to course. *Visitors:* welcome any time, book one week in advance. Public course. Professional: Scott Partington Secretary: C. Golding.*

ALTRINCHAM. **Dunham Forest Golf and Country Club,** Oldfield Lane, Altrincham WA14 4TY (0161-928 2605; Fax: 0161-929 8975). *Location:* approximately 9 miles south of Manchester off A56. Wooded parkland. 18 holes, 6772 yards. S.S.S. 72. *Green Fees:* weekdays £56.00, weekends £62.00. *Eating facilities:* clubhouse restaurant and bar open daily. *Visitors:* welcome, but should telephone to check availability. *Society Meetings:* welcome by prior arrangement. Professional: I. Wrigley (0161-928 2727). Secretary: Mrs A. Woolf (0161-928 2605).

ALTRINCHAM. **Hale Golf Club,** Rappax Road, Hale, Altrincham WA15 0NU (0161-980 4225). *Location:* off Bankhall Lane near Altrincham Priory Hospital. Undulating parkland with River Bollin featuring on 3 holes. 9 hole course (played twice for a round), 5780 yards, S.S.S. 68. Practice ground. *Green Fees:* £30.00 per day. *Eating facilities:* by arrangement with Steward; lunches available, dinner; two bars. *Visitors:* welcome weekdays (except Thursday), weekends with a member only. Meetings: by arrangement with Hon. Secretary. Professional: Alec Bickerdike (0161-904 0835). Hon. Secretary: John Savin (0161-980 4225).

ALTRINCHAM. **The Ringway Golf Club Ltd,** Hale Road, Hale Barns, Altrincham WA15 8SW (0161-980 2630). *Location:* Junction 6, M56 then A538 signposted Hale and Altrincham, one mile. Parkland. 18 holes, 6482 yards. S.S.S. 71. Putting green, short game area and practice ground. *Green Fees:* weekdays £40.00, weekends and Bank Holidays £50.00. Subject to review. *Eating facilities:* full service except Mondays (snacks only). *Visitors:* generally not on Tuesdays, Fridays or Saturdays. *Society Meetings:* catered for by arrangement. Professional: Nick Ryan (0161-980 2630). Secretary: A. Scully (0161-980 2630; Fax: 0161-980 4414).

ASHTON-IN-MAKERFIELD. **Ashton-in-Makerfield Golf Club Ltd,** Garswood Park, Liverpool Road, Ashton-in-Makerfield, Wigan WN4 0YT (01942 727267). *Location:* M6, Junction 23 from south, Junction 24 from north. Parkland course. 18 holes, 6205 yards. S.S.S. 70. *Green Fees:* £30.00 to £35.00. *Eating facilities:* available. *Visitors:* welcome midweek (except Wednesday) with reservation but not before 9.45am. *Society Meetings:* catered for Mondays, Tuesdays, Thursdays and Fridays by prior appointment. Professional: P. Allan (01942 724229). Secretary: H. G. Williams (01942 719330)

ASHTON-UNDER-LYNE. **Ashton-under-Lyne Golf Club,** Gorsey Way, Ashton-under-Lyne OL6 9HT (0161-330 1537; Fax: 0161-330 6673). *Location:* three miles from town centre, Mossley Road, left at Queens Road, right at Nook Lane, Clubhouse top of St. Christopher's Road. Wooded course. 18 holes, 6209 yards. S.S.S. 70. Practice ground. *Green Fees:* £27.00; weekends £27.00 with member only. *Eating facilities:* full catering except Mondays. *Visitors:* welcome weekdays except Wednesdays; members of recognised golf clubs welcome without reservation. *Society Meetings:* catered for on application: special daily rates. Professional: Mr Colin Boyle (0161-308 2095). Secretary: Mr A.H. Jackson.
e-mail: info@ashtongolfclub.co.uk
website: www.ashtongolfclub.co.uk.

BOLTON. **Bolton Golf Club Ltd,** Lostock Park, Chorley New Road, Bolton BL6 4AJ (01204 843067). *Location:* off main road half-way between Bolton and Horwich. 18 holes, 6237 yards. S.S.S. 70. *Green Fees:* winter: (1 Nov-4 April) £22.50, summer (5 April -31 Oct) £30.00. Fourball £110.00. *Eating facilities:* luncheons and evening meals. *Visitors:* welcome. *Society Meetings:* catered for weekdays except Tuesdays. Professional: R. Longworth (01204 843073). Secretary: S. Higham (Tel & Fax: 01204 843067)

BOLTON. **Bolton Old Links Golf Club Ltd,** Chorley Old Road, Montserrat, Bolton BL1 5SU (01204 840050). *Location:* on B6226, 400 yards north of roundabout on ring road. Championship course, moorland. 18 holes, 6469 yards. S.S.S. 71. Practice facilities, indoor net. *Green Fees:* £35.00 weekdays, £45.00 weekends. *Eating facilities:* available. *Visitors:* welcome except weekends. *Society Meetings:* catered for weekdays. Professional: P. Horridge (01204 843089). Secretary: Mrs J. Boardman (01204 842307).

BOLTON. **Breightmet Golf Club,** Red Bridge, Ainsworth, Bolton BL2 5PA (01204 399275). *Location*: leave Bolton on main road to Bury, turn left two miles on Milnthorpe road for the bridge. 18 holes, 6405 yards. S.S.S. 71. *Green Fees*: weekdays £20.00, weekends £25.00. *Eating facilities*: lunches and light refreshments. *Visitors:* welcome, preliminary phone call advisable. *Society Meetings*: catered for on application. Secretary: I.D. Cooke.

BOLTON. **Deane Golf Club,** Broadford Road, Deane, Bolton (01204 61944). *Location:* one mile east of Junction 5 of M61 towards Bolton Centre. Rolling parkland with number of small ravines to cross. 18 holes, 5652 yards, 5168 metres. S.S.S. 67. *Green Fees:* weekdays £25.00; weekends £30.00. *Eating facilities:* lunches and evening meals by arrangement. *Visitors:* welcome. *Society Meetings:* Tuesdays, Thursdays and Fridays only. Professional: David Martindale. Secretary: P. Parry (01204 651808; Fax: 01204 652047).
e-mail: secretary@deanegolfclub.com

BOLTON. **Dunscar Golf Club Ltd,** Longworth Lane, Bromley Cross, Bolton BL7 9QY (01204 598228). *Location:* one and a half miles north of Bolton on A666. Parkland, moorland course. 18 holes, 5995 yards. S.S.S. 69. Practice ground available. *Green Fees:* weekdays £30.00, weekends £36.00. *Eating facilities:* available. *Visitors:* welcome, on Sunday by arrangement. Carts available. *Society Meetings:* catered for by arrangement with the Secretary. Professional: Gary Treadgold (01204 592992). Secretary: Alison Jennings (01204 303321).
e-mail: dunscargolfclub@uk2.net

BOLTON. **Great Lever and Farnworth Golf Club Ltd,** Plodder Lane, Farnworth, Bolton BL4 0LQ (01204 656650; Fax: 01204 656137). *Location:* A666 or M61 (Junction 4), two miles from Bolton town centre. Parkland. 18 holes, 5745 yards. S.S.S. 68. Practice ground. *Green Fees:* weekdays £25.00; weekends £30.00. *Eating facilities:* restaurant and bar every day except Monday. *Visitors:* welcome, preferably by appointment. *Society Meetings:* welcome weekdays. Professional: Tony Howarth (01204 656650). Secretary: Mrs J. Ivill (Tel & Fax: 01204 656137).

THE APPEARANCE OF AN ASTERISK (*) AT THE END OF A CLUB OR COURSE ENTRY INDICATES THAT UP-TO-DATE INFORMATION HAS NOT BEEN SUPPLIED

BOLTON. **Harwood Golf Club,** Roading Brook Road, Harwood, Bolton BL2 4JD (01204 522878). *Location:* situated just off the B6196 three miles east of Bolton between Harwood and Ainsworth. Parkland/meadowland course. 18 holes, 5915 yards. S.S.S. 69. Par 70. Large practice area. *Green Fees:* with a member £12.00 weekdays and weekends, without a member £25.00 weekdays only. *Eating facilities:* catering available Tuesday to Sunday (Monday by arrangement). *Visitors:* welcome weekdays only, weekends only with a member. Should be members of recognised golf club or society. Carts allowed. *Society Meetings:* welcome Monday, Tuesday, Thursday and Friday by arrangement with the Secretary. Professional: Colin Maroney (01204 362834). Secretary: Ian W. Lund (01204 524233).
e-mail: secretary@harwoodgolfclub.co.uk
website: www.harwoodgolfclub.co.uk

BOLTON. **Regent Park Golf Club Ltd,** Links Road, off Chorley New Road, Lostock, Bolton BL6 4AF (01204 495421). *Location:* midway between Bolton and Horwich, A763. Parkland, stream and ditches cross five fairways, par 5 start, out of bounds to the left; 18 holes, 6217 yards. S.S.S. 69. Driving range and practice chipping to green; floodlit, automated golf driving range. *Green Fees:* £11.00 weekdays, £14.00 weekends and Bank Holidays. *Eating facilities:* meals/bar available. *Visitors:* welcome seven days, telephone Professional to book time slot. Buggies and club hire. *Society Meetings:* welcome every day. Book in advance. Professional: Neil Brazzel (01204 842336/495421). Secretary: K. J. Taylor (01204 652882).

BOLTON. **Turton Golf Club,** Wood End Farm, Hospital Road, Bromley Cross, Bolton BL7 9QD (01204 852235). *Location:* three miles north of Bolton off the A666; follow signs for Last Drop Village, literally a few hundred yards up the hill from the Last Drop. Host to Bolton Championship 2003. An interesting and challenging 18 hole moorland golf course with stunning views across seven counties. 6124 yards. S.S.S. 69. Practice area. *Green Fees:* April-October: midweek £26.00 per round, £39.00 per day; weekend/Bank Holidays £33.00 per round £49.00 per day. November-March: midweek/weekends £20.00 per round £30.00 per day. *Eating facilities:* Bar and restaurant. *Visitors:* welcome, Monday, Tuesday, Thursday, Friday and Sunday. Please call for availability on any day. *Societies:* welcome by arrangement. Changing facilities; lockers, pro shop, buggies and trolley hire. General Manager: Simon Kay (01204 852235).
e-mail: info@turtongolfclub.com
website: www.turtongolfclub.com

BURY. **Bury Golf Club,** Unsworth Hall, Blackford Bridge, Bury BL9 9TJ (0161-766 4897; Fax: 0161-766 3480). *Location:* A56 between Whitefield and Bury. Semi-moorland course, tight fairways, good greens. 18 holes, 5927 yards. S.S.S. 69. Small practice area. *Green Fees:* weekdays £30.00, with a member £15.00; weekends £35.00, with a member £18.00. *Eating facilities:* restaurant and bar. *Visitors:* welcome, Tuesday is Ladies' Day. Handicap Certificate will be required prior to play. *Society Meetings:* welcome except weekends (£40.00 per person including meal). Professional: Mr G. Coope (0161-766 2213). Secretary: Mr R. Adams.

BURY. **Greenmount Golf Club,** Greenhalgh Fold Farm, Greenmount, Bury BL8 4LH (01204 883712). *Location:* three miles north of Bury. Undulating parkland. 9 holes, 6214 yards. S.S.S. 70. *Green Fees:* £20.00, £10.00 with member. *Eating facilities:* available, clubhouse closed all day Monday. *Visitors:* welcome, weekends with members only, Tuesday – Ladies' Day. *Society Meetings:* welcome, £20.00 per player. Secretary: Martin Barron (Tel & Fax: 01204 882576).

BURY. **Lowes Park Golf Club Ltd,** Hill Top, Lowes Road, Bury BL9 6SU (0161-764 1231). *Location:* take A56 north from Bury, turn right at Sundial Inn into Lowes Road. Moorland course, exposed, easy walking. 9 holes, 6009 yards. S.S.S. 69. Small practice area. *Green Fees:* £15.00, £10.00 with member. *Eating facilities:* full catering except Mondays. *Visitors:* welcome weekdays except Wednesdays (Ladies' Day); weekends, Sunday by appointment. *Society Meetings:* catered for by appointment. Secretary: Alan Taylor (0161-764 1231; Fax: 0161-763 9503).
e-mail: lowesparkgc@btconnect.com

BURY. **Pike Fold Golf Club,** Hills Lane, Unsworth, Bury BL9 8QP (0161-766 3561). *Location:* just off the Whitfield turn off on the M60. New course with an abundance of water and USA specification greens. 9 holes, 6312 yards. S.S.S. 72. 18 holes as of spring 2008, 6462 yards *Green Fees:* weekdays £22 per round; weekends £25 per round (subject to review for 2008). *Eating facilities:* restaurant and bar facilities available at all times. *Visitors:* welcome weekdays without reservation. *Society Meetings:* catered for Tuesday to Friday. Professional: Grant Hamerton.
e-mail: info@pikefold.co.uk
website: www.pikefold.co.uk

BURY. **Walmersley Golf Club,** Garretts Close, Walmersley, Bury BL9 6TE (0161-764 1429). *Location:* leave A56 approximately two miles north of Bury at Walmersley Post Office into Old Road, right at Masons Arms Inn. Moorland course. 18 holes, 5385 yards, 4925 metres. S.S.S. 67. *Green Fees:* £30 per day, £15 with a member (subject to review for 2008). *Eating facilities:* lunches and evening meals served except Mondays. *Visitors:* welcome weekdays except Tuesday afternoon. *Society Meetings:* weekdays. Professional: S. Halsall (0161-763 9050). Secretary: D.L. Thomas (0161-764 7770).

DAVYHULME. **Davyhulme Park Golf Club,** Gleneagles Road, Davyhulme, Urmston M41 8SA (0161-748 2260). *Location:* one mile from M60/M62. Wooded parkland, flat course. 18 holes, 6237 yards. S.S.S. 70. *Green Fees:* information not available. *Eating facilities:* lunches and dinners. *Visitors:* welcome Tuesdays and Thursdays. *Society Meetings:* catered for Tuesdays and Thursdays. Professional: Dean Butler (0161-748 3931). Secretary: G.R. Swarbrick (0161-748 2260).*

DENTON. **Denton Golf Club,** Manchester Road, Denton M34 2GG (0161-336 3218; Fax: 0161-336 4751). *Location:* M60 Junction 24 to Manchester (A57), after quarter of a mile turn right at traffic lights. Parkland. 18 holes, 6443 yards, 5891 metres. S.S.S. 71. Practice area and putting green. *Green Fees:* weekdays £28.00; weekends and Bank Holidays £35.00. Subject to review. *Eating facilities:* catering by arrangement. *Visitors:* welcome with Club Handicap. *Society Meetings:* catered for on Wednesday to Friday. Professional: Michael Hollingworth (0161-336 2070; Fax: 0161-336 4751). Secretary (0161-336 3218; Fax: 0161-336 4751).
e-mail: dentongolfclub@btinternet.com
website: dentongolfclub.com

DUKINFIELD. **Dukinfield Golf Club,** Lyne Edge, Yew Tree Lane, Dukinfield SK16 5DB (0161-338 2340). Location: six miles east of Manchester via Ashton-under-Lyne. Parkland. 18 holes, 5303 yards. S.S.S. 66. *Green Fees:* information not available. *Eating facilities:* full catering and bar facilities. *Visitors:* welcome except Wednesdays noon to 2pm and 4pm to 6pm and weekends. Times may be booked in advance by phoning Pro Shop. *Society Meetings:* catered for by prior arrangement; special package rates available. Professional: Mr David Green. Secretary: Mr Pat O'Keeffe (0161-338 5032).*

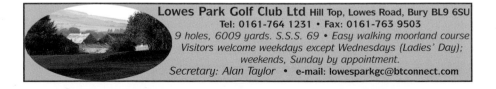

ECCLES. **Worsley Golf Club,** Stableford Avenue, Monton, Eccles M30 8AP (0161-789 4202). *Location:* A580 East Lancs Road, one mile from Junction 13 M62. Parkland. 18 holes, 6200 yards. S.S.S. 70. *Green Fees:* information not provided. *Eating facilities:* snacks, lunches and evening meals. *Visitors:* welcome, if past or present members of recognised golf clubs. *Society Meetings:* catered for Mondays, Wednesdays and Thursdays. Professional: Andrew Cory. Hon. Secretary: M. Heath.
e-mail: secretary@worsleygolfclub.co.uk
website: www.worsleygolfclub.co.uk

FLIXTON. **Acre Gate Golf Club,** Pennybridge Lane, Flixton, Manchester M41 5XD (0161 748 1226 (Sat/Sun). *Location:* off Flixton Road downside of Bird in the Hand public house. Flat parkland course. 18 holes, Par 64. Chipping area, putting green, practice net and bunkers. *Green Fees:* information not available. *Eating facilities:* food and drink available at clubhouse by prior arrangement. *Visitors:* course is Municipal (William Wroe Golf Course) and bookings, in advance, with Golf Shop.   William Wroe Golf Course Shop/Professional: (0161-748 8680).

HORWICH. **Horwich Golf Club,** Victoria Road, Horwich, Bolton BL6 5PH (01204 696980). *Location:* Junction 6 M61 - Chorley New Road - Victoria Road, Horwich. Tight tricky course, hilly with fast greens. 9 holes, 5286 yards, 4832 metres. S.S.S. 66. *Green Fees:* information not available. *Eating facilities:* dining and bar. *Visitors:* Wednesday Ladies' Day but tee times still available. Snooker room. *Society Meetings:* by arrangement. Professional: B. Sharrock. Secretary: R. Swift.*

HYDE. **Werneth Low Golf Club Ltd,** Werneth Low Road, Hyde, Cheshire SK14 3AF (0161-368 2503). *Location:* M67 to Hyde, through town to Gee Cross turn left to NLQC. Scenic, hilly course with excellent views, postage stamp greens, terrific test of golf. 18 holes,(7,4,7) 6550 yards. S.S.S. 70. *Green Fees:* information not available. *Eating facilities:* bar snacks daily, à la carte by arrangement. *Visitors:* welcome any time except Sunday before 4pm and Tuesday mornings and after 4pm. *Society Meetings:* catered for by prior arrangement. Professional: Tony Bacchus (0161-367 9376). Secretary: M. Gregg (0161-336 9496; Fax: 0161-320 0053).*
e-mail: mel.gregg@btinternet.com

LEIGH. **Pennington Golf Club (Municipal),** Pennington Golf Course, Pennington Country Park, off St Helens Road, Leigh WN7 3PA. *Location:* Junction 23 on M6 follow A580 towards Manchester, then follow signs for Pennington Flash. Flat parkland with water coursing through. 9 holes, 5516 yards. S.S.S. 68. *Green Fees:* 9 holes: weekdays £4.70, weekends and Bank Holidays £6.00 (subject to review). *Eating facilities:* snack facilities. *Visitors:* welcome, no restrictions. Bookings: (01942 682852). Secretary: Mrs A. Lythgoe (01942 741873).

LITTLEBOROUGH. **Whittaker Golf Club,** Whittaker Lane, Littleborough OL15 0LH (01706 378310). *Location:* one mile from town centre along Blackstone Edge Old Road. Moorland course. 9 holes, 5632 yards. S.S.S. 67. *Green Fees:* information not provided. *Eating facilities:* bar only. *Visitors:* welcome without reservation, except Tuesday afternoons and Sundays. *Society Meetings:* weekdays and Saturdays only by prior arrangement with Secretary. Secretary: S. Noblett (01706 842541).

MANCHESTER. **Blackley Golf Club,** Victoria Avenue East, Blackley, Manchester M9 7HW (0161-643 2980). *Location:* five miles north from City Centre. Parkland. 18 holes, 5473 yards, 5708 metres. S.S.S. 69. *Green Fees:* £24.00. *Eating facilities:* diningroom/bar. *Visitors:* welcome, Thursdays and weekends with member only. *Society Meetings:* catered for. Professional: Craig Gould (0161-643 3912). Secretary: Brenda Beddoes (0161-654 7770; Fax: 0161 653 8300).

MANCHESTER. **Brookdale Golf Club Ltd,** Medlock Road, Woodhouses, Failsworth, Manchester M35 9WQ (Tel & Fax: 0161-681 4534). *Location:* five miles north of Manchester. Parkland course, hilly with river running through. 18 holes, 5874 yards. S.S.S. 68. Small practice ground. *Green Fees:* information not provided. *Eating facilities:* bar snacks available; evening meal by prior arrangement. *Visitors:* welcome, only with a member weekends. *Society Meetings:* welcome except Tuesdays (Ladies' Day). Package Deal £35.00 by arrangement. Professional: Tony Cuppello (0161-681 2655). Secretary: F. Woodworth (Tel & Fax: 0161-681 4534).
website: www.brookdalegolfclub.co.uk

MANCHESTER. **Chorlton-cum-Hardy Golf Club,** Barlow Hall Road, Chorlton-cum-Hardy M21 7JJ (0161-881 3139; Fax: 0161-881 4532). *Location:* near junction of A5145 and A5103 (M60) Barlow Moor Road, South Cemetery. Meadowland. 18 holes, 5980 yards. S.S.S. 69. *Green Fees:* weekdays £27.00, weekends £32.00. *Eating facilities:* catering provided 7 days a week. *Visitors:* welcome without reservation, except on Competition days, must provide proof of recognised Handicap. *Society Meetings:* catered for Thursdays and Fridays by arrangement with Secretary. Professional: D.R. Valentine (0161-881 9911). Secretary: I.R. Booth (0161-881 5830).

MANCHESTER. **Didsbury Golf Club Ltd,** Ford Lane, Northenden, Manchester M22 4NQ (0161-998 2743). *Location:* Junction 5 on M60 to Palatine Road, to Church Road, to Ford Lane. Riverside parkland. 18 holes, 6276 yards. S.S.S. 70. Good practice facilities. *Green Fees:* information not available. *Eating facilities:* fully equipped bar and restaurant. *Visitors:* welcome 10am to 12 noon and 1.30pm to 4pm except competition times and match days. *Society Meetings:* catered for Thursdays and Fridays. Professional: P. Barber (Tel & Fax: 0161-998 2811). Manager: A.L. Watson (0161-998 9278; Fax: 0161-902 3060).*
e-mail: golf@didsburygolfclub.com
website: www.didsburygolfclub.com

www.uk-golfguide.com

MANCHESTER. **Ellesmere Golf Club,** Old Clough Lane, Worsley, Manchester M28 7HZ (0161-790 2122; Fax: 0161-790 7322). *Location:* off A580 East Lancs Road, adjacent to M60 (clockwise) northbound, (eastbound) access. Wooded parkland. 18 holes, 6247 yards. S.S.S. 70. *Green Fees:* information not available. *Eating facilities:* bar; catering available, with or without reservation. *Visitors:* members of recognised golf clubs welcome, but not during club competitions or Bank Holidays, contact Professional for restrictions. *Society Meetings:* catered for by appointment. Professional: Simon Wakefield (0161-790 8591). Secretary: M. J. Farrington (0161-799 0554). e-mail: honsec@ellesmeregolf.fsnet.co.uk

MANCHESTER. **Fairfield Golf and Sailing Club,** "Boothdale", Booth Road, Audenshaw, Manchester M34 5QA *Location:* off A635, five miles east of Manchester. Parkland bounded in part by reservoir. 18 holes, 5276 yards. S.S.S. 68. *Green Fees:* information not available. *Eating facilities:* available. *Visitors:* welcome, restrictions Wednesdays and weekends. *Society Meetings:* catered for by prior arrangement midweek. Professional: Steven Pownell (0161-370 2292). Manager: M. Jones (0161-301 4528; Fax: 0161 301 4254). e-mail: fairfield.golf@btconnect.com website: www.fairfieldgolfclub.co.uk

MANCHESTER. **Flixton Golf Club,** Church Road, Flixton, Urmston M41 6EP (Tel & Fax: 0161-748 2116). *Location:* five miles from Manchester on B5213. Parkland. 9 holes, 6410 yards. S.S.S. 71. *Green Fees:* £9.00 weekdays, Bank Holidays and Christmas and New Year holiday period - playing with a member. £18.00 weekdays without a member. *Eating facilities:* daily. *Visitors:* welcome, please contact Professional. Hand pulled golf carts for hire from Professional. *Society Meetings:* catered for by arrangement. Professional: G. Coope (Tel & Fax: 0161-746 7160). Hon. Secretary: F. Baker (Tel & Fax: 0161-748 2116). Catering: (0161-749 8834).

> **THE APPEARANCE OF AN ASTERISK (*) AT THE END OF A CLUB OR COURSE ENTRY INDICATES THAT UP-TO-DATE INFORMATION HAS NOT BEEN SUPPLIED**

MANCHESTER. **Heaton Park Golf Centre,** Middleton Road, Prestwich, Manchester M25 2SW (0161-654 9899; Fax: 0161-653 2003). *Location:* Junction 19 M60. Undulating mature parkland, J.H. Taylor designed. 18 holes, 5755 yards. S.S.S. 68. Also 18-hole Par 3 pitch and putt course. *Green Fees:* Main Course - adults weekdays £12.00 (Seniors/Juniors half price); adults weekends £15.00 (concessions from 2pm). Par 3 course weekdays £5.00, weekends £6.00 (concessions available). *Eating facilities:* spike bar and dining/function room; range of meals and snacks available. *Visitors:* welcome 7 days a week. Pro Shop, Teaching Academy and tuition available. *Society Meetings:* Society packages a speciality. Professional: Gary Dermot. General Manager: Brian Dique. e-mail: heatonpark@btconnect.com www.manchester.gov.uk/leisure/parks/heaton/golf

MANCHESTER. **Houldsworth Golf Club Ltd,** Houldsworth Street, Reddish, Stockport SK5 6BN (0161-442 1712). *Location:* off A6 between Manchester and Stockport, close to M60. Flat parkland with water hazards. 18 holes, 6209 yards. S.S.S. 70, Par 71. Practice area. *Green Fees:* weekdays £32.00 per day; weekends £38.00 per day. Half price with member. (2007 rates). *Eating facilities:* bar snacks, or full restaurant service. *Visitors:* must be pre-arranged with Professional or Office Manager. *Society Meetings:* Monday, Thursday and Friday, catered for on application (0161-442 1712). Professional: Danial Marsh (0161-442 1714). Honorary Secretary: G. Foy (0161-442 1712). e-mail: secretary@houldsworthgolfclub.co.uk website: www.houldsworthgolfclub.co.uk

MANCHESTER. **The Manchester Golf Club Ltd.,** Hopwood Cottage, Rochdale Road, Middleton, Manchester M24 6QP (0161-643 3202; Fax: 0161-643 9174). *Location:* M62 Junction 20 to Middleton. Moorland/parkland. 18 holes, 6491 yards, 5935 metres. S.S.S. 72. Large practice ground. Driving range. *Green Fees:* weekdays £35.00 per round, £45.00 per day; weekends £50.00 per round. *Eating facilities:* two bars; restaurant booking by arrangement. *Visitors:* welcome weekdays. *Society Meetings:* parties up to 120 catered for by arrangement. Professional: B. Connor (0161-643 2638). Secretary: S. Armstead (0161-643 3202; Fax: 0161-643 9174).

MANCHESTER. **New North Manchester Golf Club Ltd,** Rhodes House, Manchester Old Road, Middleton, Manchester M24 4PE (0161-643 2941). *Location:* A576, less than one mile from Junction 19 on M60. Rolling parkland including lakes. 18 holes, 6436 yards. S.S.S. 71. Large practice area. *Green Fees:* £32.00 per day. Weekends £37.00. *Eating facilities:* catering every day except Tuesdays. *Visitors:* welcome most days, please telephone for course availability. *Society Meetings:* welcome, contact Professional for details. Reductions available for societies over 12. Professional: J. Peel (0161-643 7094). Secretary: D. Parkinson (0161-643 9033; Fax: 0161-643 7775).
e-mail: tee@nmgc.co.uk
website: www.northmanchestergolfclub.co.uk

MANCHESTER. **Northenden Golf Club,** Palatine Road, Northenden, Manchester M22 4FR (0161-998 4738; Fax: 0161-945 5592). *Location:* half a mile off Junction 2 M56, half a mile off Junction 5 M60. Parkland with plenty of trees, first six tees on bank of river. 18 holes, 6432 yards. S.S.S. 71. Practice net. *Green Fees:* available on request. *Eating facilities:* available (0161-998 4079). *Visitors:* welcome most days, preferably with reservation. Restrictions 11.30am to 1.30pm Monday to Friday, Thursday Ladies Day. Carts available. *Society Meetings:* catered for Tuesdays and Fridays only. Professional: James Curtis (0161-945 3386; Fax: 0161-945 5592). Manager: P. Powell (0161-998 4738; Fax: 0161-945 5592). Steward: R. Singleton (0161-998 4079).

MANCHESTER. **Prestwich Golf Club,** Hilton Lane, Prestwich, Manchester M25 9XB (0161-772 0700). *Location:* 1 mile from Junction 17 of the M60 on the A6044. Parkland, 18 holes, 4819 yards. S.S.S. 64. *Green Fees:* £18.00 midweek, £20.00 weekends and Bank Holidays. *Eating facilities:* available Tuesday to Sunday (no catering on Mondays). *Visitors:* welcome weekdays. *Society Meetings:* catered for weekdays, special rates for parties of 16 and over. Professional: Mark Pearson (0161-773 1404). Exec. Member for Administration Ron Mason (0161-772 0700). website: www.prestwichgolf.co.uk

MANCHESTER. **Stand Golf Club,** The Dales, Ashbourne Grove, Whitefield, Bury, Manchester M25 7GX (0161-766 2388). *Location:* M62 Exit 17, A56/A665 one mile. Undulating parkland with sandy subsoil, playable all year round. 18 holes, 6426 yards. S.S.S. 71. *Green Fees:* weekdays £35.00; weekends £40.00. Various Society packages; information on request. *Eating facilities:* meals served daily and bar except Mondays, order in advance. *Visitors:* welcome Monday to Friday; weekends by prior arrangement. *Society Meetings:* welcome Wednesday/Friday by prior arrangement. Professional: Mark Dance (0161-766 2214). Hon. Secretary: Trevor E. Thacker (0161-766 3197; Fax: 0161-796 3234).

MANCHESTER. **Swinton Park Golf Club,** East Lancashire Road, Swinton, Manchester M27 5LX (0161-794 1785). *Location:* on the A580 Manchester to Liverpool Road, five miles from Manchester centre. Parkland course. 18 holes. White tees 6726 yards – Yellow tees 6519 yards. Practice area. *Green Fees:* on application. *Eating facilities:* full catering facilities available. *Society meetings:* welcome, please ring for details. Conferencing, meetings and banqueting facilities. Private hire also available Corporate golf days catered for. Professional: J. Wilson (0161-793 8077). General Manager: Barbara Wood (0161-794 0861; Fax: 0161-281 0698).

MANCHESTER. **Withington Golf Club,** 243 Palatine Road, West Didsbury, Manchester M20 2UE (0161-445 3912). *Location:* three miles from Manchester city centre, adjacent M56 and M63. Flat parkland. 18 holes, 6410 yards. S.S.S. 70. *Green Fees:* weekdays only (except Thursdays) £28.50 per round, £32.50 per day; weekends by prior arrangement only (£32.50 per round, £36.50 per day). *Eating facilities:* lunches and evening meals to order. Snacks available at all times. *Visitors:* welcome except Thursdays, and weekends which are by prior arrangement. Ring Professional for times. *Society Meetings:* catered for by arrangement with the Secretary. Professional: S. Marr (0161-445 4861). Secretary/Manager: Patrick Keane (0161-445 9544).

MARPLE. **Marple Golf Club,** Barnsfold Road, Marple, Stockport SK6 7EL (0161-427 2311). *Location:* off A6 at Hawk Green sign. Parkland. 18 holes, 5554yards. S.S.S. 67. Practice area. *Green Fees:* (including liability insurance) Mon to Fri £30.00 per day, if playing with a member £12.50. Sat, Sun and Bank Holidays £40.00 per day, £15.00 if playing with a member. *Eating facilities:* full meals available every day along with bar snacks. *Visitors:* welcome, not competition days or Tuesdays between 10am and midday or Thursdays between 11am and 3.30pm. *Society Meetings:* all welcome by arrangement with Professional. Professional: D. Myers (0161-427 1195). Secretary: R. Hough (Tel & Fax: 0161-427 2311). e-mail: marple.golfclub@virgin.net

OLDHAM. **Crompton and Royton Golf Club Ltd,** High Barn, Royton, Oldham OL2 6RW (0161-624 0986; Fax: 0161-652 4711). *Location:* near Junction 20 follow signs to Oldham/Royton. Heathland. 18 holes, 6186 yards. S.S.S. 70. Nets. *Green Fees:* information not provided. *Eating facilities:* lunches and meals served, except Mondays. *Visitors:* welcome without reservation, not at weekends. *Society Meetings:* catered for by arrangement with Steward. Professional: D.A. Melling (0161-624 2154). Hon. Secretary (0161-624 0986). Steward: (0161-624 9867).*

OLDHAM. **Oldham Golf Club,** Lees New Road, Oldham OL4 5PN (0161-624 4986). *Location:* B6194 between Ashton-under-Lyne and Oldham. Moorland course. 18 holes, 5122 yards. S.S.S. 65. *Green Fees:* information not available. *Eating facilities:* full catering. *Visitors:* welcome, telephone to check for competitions, especially weekends. *Society Meetings:* catered for by prior arrangement with Secretary. Professional: R. Heginbotham (0161-626 8346). Secretary: J. Brooks (0161-624 4986).*

OLDHAM. **Saddleworth Golf Club,** Mountain Ash, Ladcastle Road, Uppermill, Near Oldham OL3 6LT (01457 873653). *Location:* five miles from Oldham – M62. A moorland course with superb views of the Pennines. 18 holes, 6118 yards. S.S.S. 69. Practice area. *Green Fees:* weekdays £25.00 per day (£10.00 per day with member), weekends and Bank Holidays £35.00 per day (£15.00 per day with member); weekends after 4.30pm with member £8.00. *Eating facilities:* snacks and meals available. *Visitors:* welcome weekdays. Ladies' Day Thursdays. Buggies available. *Society Meetings:* groups of 12 or more catered for except weekends. Professional: R.I. Johnson (01457 810412; Fax: 01457 820647). Secretary: Paul Green (01457 873653).

OLDHAM. **Werneth Golf Club,** 124 Green Lane, Garden Suburb, Oldham OL8 3AZ (0161-624 1190). Semi moorland. 18 holes, 5363 yards. S.S.S. 66. Practice ground. *Green Fees:* £18.00 weekdays only. *Eating facilities:* full catering service available. *Visitors:* welcome, ring for details. *Society Meetings:* catered for, ring for details. Professional: James Mattenson (Tel & Fax: 0161-628 7136). Secretary: John Barlow.

ROCHDALE. **Castle Hawk Golf Club,** Chadwick Lane, Castleton, Rochdale OL11 3BY (01706 640841; Fax: 01706 860587). *Location:* five minutes from exit 20 M62. Parkland course. 18 holes, 2699 yards. S.S.S. 55. 9 holes, 5398 yards, S.S.S. 66. Driving range. *Green Fees:* information not available. *Eating facilities:* fully licensed bar and restaurant. *Visitors:* welcome. Trolley and equipment hire. Tuition available, fully stocked Pro shop. *Society Meetings:* welcome. Professional: Andy Duncan. Secretary: Louise Entwistle.*
e-mail: teeoff@castlehawk.co.uk
website: www.castlehawk.co.uk

ROCHDALE. **Lobden Golf Club,** Whitworth, Near Rochdale OL12 8XJ (Tel & Fax: 01706 343228). *Location:* take A671 from Rochdale, turn right at Dog and Partridge Pub in Whitworth. Moorland. 9 holes, 5697 yards, 5212 metres. S.S.S. 68. *Green Fees:* weekdays £12.00; weekends £15.00, £10.00 at all times with a member. Subject to review. *Eating facilities:* by prior arrangement with Secretary. *Visitors:* welcome all week except Saturday. *Society Meetings:* catered for by arrangement. Secretary: B. Harrison (01706 852752).

ROCHDALE. **Rochdale Golf Club,** The Clubhouse, Edenfield Road, Rochdale OL11 5YR (01706 643818; Fax: 01706 861113). *Location:* three miles from M62, Junction 20, on A680. Parkland. 18 holes, 6034 yards. S.S.S. 69. Practice ground, putting green. *Green Fees:* per round or day – weekdays £22.00, £15.00 with a member; weekends £29.00, £17.00 with a member. *Eating facilities:* meals and bar snacks available. *Visitors:* welcome, please check for tee closures. *Society Meetings:* catered for by prior arrangement Mondays, and Wednesdays. Professional: A. Laverty (01706 522104). General Manager: Phil Kershaw (01706 643818).
e-mail: rochdale.golfclub@zen.co.uk

ROCHDALE. **Springfield Park Golf Club,** Springfield Park, Bolton Road, Marland, Rochdale OL11 4RE (01706 56401 weekends only). *Location:* A58 out of Rochdale, along Bolton Road on right. Parkland. 18 holes, 5237 yards. S.S.S. 66. *Green Fees:* information not available. *Visitors:* welcome, no restrictions weekdays, booking in advance weekends. Professional: Mr D. Wills (01706 49801). Secretary: Mr J. Wallis (01706 623570).*

SALE. **Ashton-on-Mersey Golf Club,** Church Lane, Ashton-on-Mersey, Sale M33 5QQ (0161-973 3220). *Location:* M60 Junction 7; 1½ miles, off Glebelands Road. Parkland course. 9 holes, 6242 yards. S.S.S. 69. *Green Fees:* £25.50 weekdays, £10.00 with a member. *Eating facilities:* available weekdays except Mondays. *Visitors:* welcome on weekdays. Saturdays, Sundays and Bank Holidays only with member. *Society Meetings:* Thursdays. Professional: K. Andrews (0161 962 3727). Secretary: R. Coppock (0161 976 4390).

SALE. **Sale Golf Club,** Sale Lodge, Golf Road, Sale M33 2XU (0161-973 1638; Fax: 0161-962 4217). *Location:* M60 Junction 6, A6144. Flat parkland course. 18 holes, 6301 yards. S.S.S. 70. Practice ground. *Green Fees:* weekdays £32.00, weekends £35.00. *Eating facilities:* catering and bar facilities 7 days. *Visitors:* welcome Mondays, Tuesdays, Wednesdays, Fridays and Sundays. Carts and buggies available for hire. *Society Meetings:* welcome by arrangement with Professional. Professional: Mike Stewart (0161-973 1730). Hon. Secretary: C.J. Boyes (0161-973 1638; Fax: 0161-962 4217).

THE APPEARANCE OF AN ASTERISK (*) AT THE END OF A CLUB OR COURSE ENTRY INDICATES THAT UP-TO-DATE INFORMATION HAS NOT BEEN SUPPLIED

SALFORD. **Brackley Golf Club,** Bullows Road, Little Hulton, Worsley M38 9TR (0161-790 6076). *Location:* off Captain Fold Lane. M61 to Junction 4 onto A6, left at roundabout onto A6 (Walkden), half a mile turn left at White Lion pub. Flat parkland course. 9 holes, 3003 yards, 2747 metres. S.S.S. 69. *Green Fees:* information not provided. *Visitors:* welcome anytime. *Society Meetings:* welcome. Secretary: Gary Jones (0161-790 6076).

STOCKPORT. **Bramall Park Golf Club,** 20 Manor Road, Bramhall, Stockport SK7 3LY (0161-485 3119). *Location*: 10 miles south of Manchester, one mile from Cheadle Hulme. Parkland. 18 holes, 6247 yards. S.S.S. 70. *Green Fees*: weekdays £34.00; weekends and Bank Holidays £40.00. *Eating facilities:* full eating facilities except Mondays. *Visitors:* welcome, apply to Professional. *Society Meetings:* welcome, please contact Secretary's office. Professional: M. Proffitt (0161-485 2205). Secretary: C.J. Shallcross (Tel & Fax: 0161-485 7101).

STOCKPORT. **Bramhall Golf Club,** The Clubhouse, Ladythorn Road, Bramhall, Stockport SK7 2EY (0161-439 6092). *Location:* half-a-mile from Bramhall Railway Station off Bramhall Lane South. Parkland with views of Pennines and Lyme Park. 18 holes, 6347 yards, 5801 metres. S.S.S 70. Practice ground. *Green Fees*: information available on request. *Eating facilities:* full bar and dining facilities and bar snacks. *Visitors*: welcome except Thursdays, weekends and Competition Days. *Society Meetings*: catered for Wednesdays, minimum 30; Fridays maximum 30. Professional: R. Green (0161-439 1171; Fax: 0161-439 0789). Secretary: (0161-439 6092). e-mail: office@bramhallgolfclub.com website: www.bramhallgolfclub.com

STOCKPORT. **Hazel Grove Golf Club,** Buxton Road, Hazel Grove, Stockport SK7 6LU (0161-483 3978 clubhouse). *Location:* A6 to Buxton out of Hazel Grove, three miles south of Stockport. Parkland with tree-lined fairways. 18 holes, 6310 yards. S.S.S. 71. *Green Fees:* weekdays £35.00 per round; weekends and Public Holidays £40.00 per round. Subject to review. Society booking £38.00 for parties of 12 or more. *Eating facilities*: available daily. *Visitors:* welcome, ring Professional for booking of tee times. *Society Meetings:* catered for on Mondays, Thursdays and Fridays. Professional: James Hopley (0161-483 7272). Secretary: David J. Billington (0161-483 3978).

STOCKPORT. **Heaton Moor Golf Club,** Mauldeth Road, Heaton Mersey, Stockport SK4 3NX (0161-432 2134). *Location:* M56 to A34 or M60 Junction 1; near Glass Pyramid – Didsbury Road. Flat parkland course, tree lined fairways. 18 holes, 5970 yards. S.S.S. 69. Practice ground. *Green Fees:* weekdays £30.00 per day, £27.00 per round; weekends £40.00 per day, £35.00 per round; winter: £30.00 per day, £22.00 per round weekdays, £38.00 per day, £30.00 per round weekends. Subject to review. *Eating facilities:* lunches and evening meals available; bar. *Visitors:* welcome all times. Trolley hire. *Society Meetings:* catered for by arrangement. Professional: Simon Marsh (0161 432 0846). Secretary: J. Whiston (0161 432 2134).

STOCKPORT. **Mellor and Townscliffe Golf Club Ltd,** Gibb Lane, Mellor, Tarden, Stockport SK6 5NA (0161-427 9700 – Clubhouse/Steward). *Location:* seven miles south-east of Stockport off A626. Parkland with trees/moorland. 18 holes, 5925 yards. S.S.S. 69. *Green Fees:* weekdays £24.00 per day, £11.00 with a member; weekends and Bank Holidays £32.00, with a member £13.00. *Eating facilities:* available daily except Tuesdays. *Visitors:* welcome weekdays, no casual visitors weekends. *Society Meetings:* catered for by prior arrangement. Professional: Gary R. Broadley (0161-427 5759). Secretary: J. Dixon (0161-427 2208). website: www.mellorgolf.co.uk

STOCKPORT. **Reddish Vale Golf Club,** Southcliffe Road, Reddish, Stockport SK5 7EE (0161-480 2359). *Location:* one mile north east of M60 in central Stockport. Varied undulating heathland course, designed by Dr Alister MacKenzie. 18 holes, 6086 yards. S.S.S. 69. *Green Fees:* Monday £20.00 per round, Tuesday-Friday £28.00 per round, weekdays £32.00 per day, weekends £40.00 per round. *Eating facilities:* bar and catering. *Visitors:* welcome on weekdays (not 12.30-1.30pm). Buggies available. *ociety Meetings:* catered for by arrangement, groups of eight or more. Professional: Bob Freeman (0161-480 3824). Secretary: G. Lee (0161-480 2359).

STOCKPORT. **Romiley Golf Club Ltd,** Goosehouse Green, Romiley, Stockport SK6 4LJ (0161-430 2392). *Location:* B6104 off A560, signposted from Romiley village. Parkland. 18 holes, 6454 yards. S.S.S. 71. *Green Fees:* information not available. *Eating facilities:* full catering by arrangement. *Visitors:* welcome all week except Saturdays. *Society Meetings:* catered for by prior arrangement with Secretary. Professional: Matt Ellis (0161-430 7122). Secretary: D.H. Mason (0161-430 2392).

STOCKPORT. **Stockport Golf Club Ltd,** Offerton Road, Offerton, Stockport, Cheshire SK2 5HL (Tel & Fax: 0161 427 8369). *Location:* one mile from lights at Hazel Grove, along Torkington Road. Parkland. 18 holes, 6326 yards. S.S.S. 71. *Green Fees:* weekdays £40.00 per round, weekends £50.00 per round. *Eating facilities:* available, excellent. *Visitors:* welcome weekdays, contact Professional at weekends. *Society Meetings:* catered for. Professional: M. Peel (0161 427 8369). Secretary: D.R.G. Mitchell (0161 427 8369).

TRAFFORD. **William Wroe Municipal Golf Course,** Pennybridge Lane, off Flixton Road, Flixton, Trafford M41 5DC (0161-748 8680). Course and shop managed by Trafford Borough Council, Acre Gate Golf Club play over the course. *Location:* from M60 follow Urmston, Flixton Road to Bird i'th Hand pub. Flat parkland course. 18 holes, 4395 yards. S.S.S. 61. Driving range two miles from course. *Green Fees:* information not available. *Eating facilities:* at Bird i'th Hand Public House. *Visitors:* public course - book seven days in advance, weekend mornings some restrictions. *Society Meetings:* booking accepted in writing. Professional: Scott Partington (0161-928 0761).*

WESTHOUGHTON. **Westhoughton Golf Club,** Long Island, School Street, Westhoughton, Bolton BL5 2BR (01942 811085). *Location:* four miles south west of Bolton on A58. Parkland.   18 holes, 5918 yards. S.S.S. 69. *Green Fees:* information not available. *Eating facilities:* bar meals and home cooking. *Visitors:* welcome weekdays except Tuesdays. Snooker room. *Society Meetings:* welcome weekdays except Tuesdays and Saturdays, maximum 32. Secretary: D. Moores (01942 811085).

WHITEFIELD. **Whitefield Golf Club, Higher Lane,** Whitefield, Manchester M45 7EZ (0161-351 2700; Fax: 0161-351 2712).*Location*: Exit 17, off M60 then take road to Radcliffe for half a mile. 18 holes, 6063 yards. S.S.S. 69. *Green Fees*: on application.*Eating facilities*: restaurant facilities every day. *Visitors*: welcome. **Society Meetings**: catered for. Professional: R. Penney (0161-351 2709). Secretary: Mrs M. Rothwell (0161-351 2700; Fax: 0161-351 2712). e-mail: enquiries@whitefieldgolfclub.com

WIGAN. **Gathurst Golf Club,** Miles Lane, Shevington, Wigan WN6 8EW (01257 252861). *Location:* one mile south of Junction 27 M6. Parkland course.   18 holes, 6016 yards (from men's tee). S.S.S.69. *Green Fees:* £30.00; weekends with a member only. *Eating facilities:* available bar hours daily. *Visitors:* welcome Monday, Tuesday, Thursday and Friday with reservation. *Society Meetings:* catered for by appointment with Secretary. Professional: David Clarke (01257 255882). Secretary: Mrs. I. Fyffe (01257 255235).

WIGAN. **Haigh Hall Golf Club,** Haigh Country Park, Aspull, Near Wigan WN2 1PE (01942 831107). *Location:* well signposted from M6, Junction 27 and M61, Junction 5. Balcarres 18 hole course, 6358 yards. Par 70. Crawford course 9 holes, 1446 yards. Par 28. 18 hole Himalayan putting green and golf academy practice facilities. All U.S.G.A specification greens and tees. Brand new golf complex in the superb surroundings of Haigh Country Park. *Green Fees:* information not available. *Eating facilities:* full catering available, bar facilities and function rooms in The Stables Golf & Visitor Centre. *Visitors:* welcome at all times. *Society Meetings:* welcome at all times - packages available. Professional: Ian Lee (01942 831107). Members' Secretary: Steve Eyres (01942 833337).* e-mail: secretary@haighhall-golfclub.co.uk website: www.haighhall-golfclub.co.uk

WIGAN. **Hindley Hall Golf Club,** Hall Lane, Hindley, Wigan WN2 2SQ (01942 525020). *Location:* two miles east of Wigan, Junction 6 M61, or A58 to Ladies Lane/Hall Lane. 18 holes, 5913 yards. S.S.S. 68. *Green Fees:* weekdays £25.00, weekends and Bank Holidays £30.00. *Eating facilities:* book before playing. *Visitors:* welcome without reservation if members of a recognised golf club. *Society Meetings:* catered for by arrangement with the Secretary. Professional: D. Clarke (01942 255991). Secretary: S. Tyrer (01942 255131). website: www.hindleyhallgolfclub.co.uk

WORSLEY. **Marriott Worsley Park Hotel & Country Club,** Worsley Park, Worsley, Manchester (0161 975 2043). *Location:* Junction 13 off M60, follow A575 to Worsley. Challenging new parkland course. 18 holes. Par 71. *Green Fees:* information not available. *Eating facilities:* bar and dining facilities 8am to 10pm. *Visitors:* welcome. Handicap Certificate is required. *Society Meetings:* details of golf and leisure breaks on request. Conference and banqueting facilities available. Superbly equipped country club, including 20-metre pool, spa bath, sauna, steam room and health and beauty salons. Professional: David Screeton.* website: www.marriott.com/marriot/mangs

For full details of clubs and courses, plus convenient accommodation www.uk-golfguide.com

Merseyside

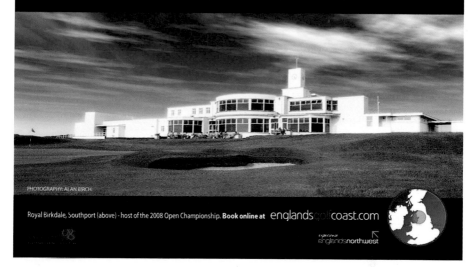

BIDSTON. **Bidston Golf Club Ltd,** Bidston Link Road, Wallasey, Wirral CH44 2HR (0151-638 3412). *Location:* M53 Junction 1 (from Chester direction) turn right at roundabout, course entrance 200 yards on dual carriageway. Parkland. 18 holes, 6140 yards. S.S.S. 70. Practice ground and nets. *Green Fees:* information not available. *Eating facilities:* restaurant, snacks, lounge bar. *Visitors:* welcomed weekdays and weekends. *Society Meetings:* welcome weekdays and weekends. Professional: Alan Norwood (0151-638 3412). Administrator: L. Letts. e-mail: linda@bidstongolf.co.uk website: www.bidstongolf.co.uk

BIRKENHEAD. **Arrowe Park Golf Course,** Arrowe Park, Birkenhead CH49 5LW. *Location:* Mersey Tunnel into Brough Road, then Woodchurch Road, head for Arrowe Park roundabout, bear left approximately 400 yards, turn right into Arrowe Park. Flat tree-lined parkland. 18 holes, 6396 yards, 5885 metres. S.S.S. 71. 9 hole pitch and putt, putting green. *Green Fees:* information not available. *Eating facilities:* restaurant/cafe - bar. *Visitors:* welcome except weekends before noon. *Society Meetings:* by arrangement through Professional. Professional: Colin Disbury (0151-677 1527). Secretary: P. Hickey (0151-678 3296).*

BIRKENHEAD. **Prenton Golf Club,** Golf Links Road, Prenton, Birkenhead CH42 8LW (0151-609 3426). *Location:* M53 Junction 3, off A552 towards Birkenhead. Parkland course. 18 holes, 6411 yards. S.S.S. 71. *Green Fees:* prices on application. *Eating facilities:* full catering facilities available. *Visitors:* welcome, reservation advisable. *Society Meetings:* catered for Mondays, Wednesdays and Fridays. Professional: Robin Thompson (0151-608 1636). Secretary: N. Brown.

BIRKENHEAD. **The Wirral Ladies' Golf Club Ltd,** 93 Bidston Road, Oxton, Birkenhead CH43 6TS (0151-652 5797). *Location:* off the M53 Junction 1 or 3. Acid heath/gorse and heather course. 18 holes, 4948 yards (Ladies), 5182 yards (Men). S.S.S. 69 (Ladies), S.S.S. 65 (Men). Practice ground. *Green Fees:* £30.00 per round, £40.00 per day. *Eating facilities:* dining room, meals during day to order. *Visitors:* welcome weekdays; weekends after 11am Club Competitions permitting. Trolleys. *Society Meetings:* welcome weekdays only. Professional: Angus Law (0151-652 2468). Secretary: S.A. Headford (0151-652 1255; Fax: 0151-653 4323).

BLUNDELLSANDS. **West Lancashire Golf Club,** Hall Road West, Blundellsands, Merseyside L23 8SZ (0151-924 1076; Fax: 0151-931 4448). *Location:* A565 Liverpool - Southport to Crosby, follow signs to West Lancashire Golf Club from Crosby. Links Course. 18 holes, 6767 yards. S.S.S. 73. Substantial practice ground. *Green Fees:* weekdays £65.00 per round, £80.00 per day; weekends £85.00 per round. *Eating facilities:* full bar and catering available. *Visitors:* welcome on weekdays except Tuesdays. All subject to availability. *Society Meetings:* booking in advance with Secretary. Professional: Gary Edge (0151-924 5662). Secretary: Stewart King (0151-924 1076; Fax: 0151-931 4448).
e-mail: golf@westlancashiregolf.co.uk
website: www.westlancashiregolf.co.uk

BOOTLE. **Bootle Golf Club,** 3 Dunnings Bridge Road, Bootle L30 2PP (0151-928 6196). *Location:* five miles north of Liverpool, one mile from M57 and M58. Links course. 18 holes, 6362 yards. S.S.S. 70. *Green Fees:* information not available. *Eating facilities:* full catering as required by arrangement. *Visitors:* welcome weekdays and by arrangement at weekends. *Society Meetings:* by arrangement. Professional: Alan Bradshaw (0151-928 1371). Secretary: John Morgan (07966 208972).*

BROMBOROUGH. **Bromborough Golf Club,** Raby Hall Road, Bromborough, Wirral, Merseyside CH63 0NW(0151-334 2155). *Location:* Exit 4 Wirral Motorway M53. Parkland. 18 holes, 6547 yards. S.S.S. 72. *Green Fees:* information not provided. *Eating facilities:* bar and full catering facilities. *Visitors:* welcome weekdays, but essential to ring in advance for weekends and Bank Holidays. *Society Meetings:* catered for by prior arrangement. Professional: G. Berry (0151-334 4499). Secretary: P. McMullen (0151-334 2155; Fax: 0151-334 7300).

CALDY. **The Caldy Golf Club Ltd,** Links Hey Road, Caldy, Wirral CH48 1NB (0151 625 5515). *Location:* one mile south of West Kirby on the River Dee, 10 miles from Chester. Undulating heathland with cliff top, links, open aspect with views across the Dee to the North Wales hills. 18 holes, 6707 yards, 6133 metres. S.S.S. 72. Practice ground and putting green. *Green Fees:* weekdays £60.00 per round, £70.00 per day; weekends with member only. *Eating facilities:* bars and restaurant throughout the day. *Visitors:* welcome weekdays with advance booking and Handicap Certificate. Restrictions Tuesdays and Wednesdays. Jeans not allowed on course or in Clubhouse. *Society Meetings:* Thursdays by prior arrangement. Professional: Alan Gibbons (Tel & Fax: 0151-625 1818). Secretary/ Manager: G.M. Copple (0151-625 5660; Fax: 0151-625 7394).
e-mail: secretarycaldygc@btconnect.com
website: www.caldygolfclub.co.uk

EASTHAM. **Eastham Lodge Golf Club,** 117 Ferry Road, Eastham, Wirral CH62 0AP (0151-327 3003). *Location:* exit Junction 5 M53 into Eastham village from A41, follow signs for Eastham Country Park. Flat pleasant parkland course with many trees. 18 holes, 5706 yards. S.S.S. 68. *Green Fees:* weekdays £24.50; weekends with a member only, £12.50. *Eating*

facilities: bar snacks, full restaurant (book in advance). *Visitors:* welcome weekdays, with member weekends. *Society Meetings:* welcome by special arrangement; £24.50 per day, £19.50 per round. Professional: Nick Sargent (0151-327 3008). Secretary: Mrs J.L. Lyon (0151-327 3003).
e-mail: easthamlodge.g.c@btinternet.com

FORMBY. **Formby Golf Club,** Golf Road, Formby, Liverpool L37 1LQ (01704 872164). *Location:* one mile west of A565 by Freshfield Station. Seaside links, wooded. 18 holes, 6698 yards. S.S.S. 73. *Green Fees:* weekdays £95.00 per day, weekends £105.00 per day. Subject to review. *Eating facilities:* available. *Visitors:* welcome by arrangement with the Secretary, except before 10am Wednesdays, 3.30pm weekends or Bank Holidays. Handicap Certificate/ introduction required. "Dormy" accommodation available. *Society Meetings:* catered for Tuesdays, Thursdays and Fridays. Professional: G.H Butler (01704 873090). Secretary: (01704 872164; Fax: 01704 833028).
e-mail: info@formbygolfclub.co.uk

FORMBY. **Formby Ladies' Golf Club,** Golf Road, Formby, Liverpool L37 1YH (01704 873493; Fax: 01704 834654). *Location:* A565 (Southport Bypass) to Formby. Seaside links. 18 holes, 5374 yards, 4914 metres. S.S.S. 72. Practice area. *Green Fees:* £47.00 weekday, £52.00 weekend. *Eating facilities:* light lunches, afternoon teas. *Visitors:* by prior reservation. *Society Meetings:* catered for with prior reservation. Professional: Gary Butler (01704 873090). Secretary: Mrs A. Bromley (Tel: 01704 873493; Fax: 01704 834654).

HESWALL. **Heswall Golf Club,** Cottage Lane, Gayton, Wirral CH60 8PB (0151-342 1237). *Location:* off A540, eight miles north-west of Chester. Parkland on the banks of River Dee estuary overlooking Welsh coast and hills. 18 holes, 6556 yards, 5993 metres. S.S.S. 72. Large practice area. *Green Fees:* Information not available. *Eating facilities:* bar snacks, full meals by arrangement. *Visitors:* welcome, subject to availability. Must have accredited Handicaps. *Society Meetings:* catered for fully on Wednesdays and Fridays only. Winter packages available October/March. Professional: Alan Thompson (0151-342 7431). Secretary: (0151-342 1237).*
e-mail: dawn@heswallgolfclub.com

HOYLAKE. **Royal Liverpool Golf Club,** Meols Drive, Hoylake, Wirral, Merseyside CH47 4AL (0151-632 3101 *Location:* 10 miles south-west of Liverpool on Wirral Peninsula. Approach from M6, M56 and M53 Junction 2. Championship links. Host to The Open Championship in 2006. 18 holes, 6847 yards. S.S.S. 74. Large practice area. **Green Fees:** on application. **Eating facilities:** buffet lunch included in green fee. **Visitors:** welcome weekdays except Thursday mornings (Ladies' Day). No visitor play at weekends. Proof of Handicap required (max 21). Caddies available. **Society Meetings:** catered for Wednesdays and Fridays. Professional: John Heggarty (0151-632 5868). Secretary: Group Captain C.T. Moore CBE (0151-632 3101).
e-mail: secretary@royal-liverpool-golf.com
website: www.royal-liverpool-golf.com

HUYTON. **Bowring Municipal,** Bowring Park, Roby Road, Knowsley L36 4HD (0151-489 1901). *Location:* Junction 5, M62 signposted. 200 metres. Parkland. 18 holes, S.S.S. 73. *Green Fees:* information not available. *Eating facilities:* limited. Private club facilities on site, bar. *Visitors:* no restrictions. *Society Meetings:* bookings required.*

HUYTON. **Huyton and Prescot Golf Club Ltd,** Hurst Park, Huyton Lane, Huyton, Liverpool L36 1UA (0151-489 3948). *Location:* from M57 Junction 2 follow B5199 signposted Huyton. Parkland. 18 holes, 5779 yards. S.S.S. 68 white, 67 yellow. *Green Fees:* information not available. *Eating facilities:* bar snacks and restaurant area 9am-5pm; normal bar hours. *Visitors:* welcome, midweek days 9.30am to 12.00pm, 2pm to 4pm, except Tuesdays. Snooker table. *Society Meetings:* catered for Mondays, Wednesdays, Thursdays and Fridays. Summer and Winter packages available. Professional: John Fisher (0151-489 2022). Secretary: David Hughes (0151-489 3948; Fax: 0151-489 0797).*

LIVERPOOL. **Allerton Park Golf Club,** Allerton Municipal Golf Course, Allerton Road, Liverpool L18 3JT (0151-428 8510). *Location:* end of M62, two miles to Allerton Road, one and a half miles along Allerton Road. Undulating parkland course. 18 holes, 5494 yards, 5023 metres. S.S.S. 67. 9 hole course 1685 metres. S.S.S. 34. *Green Fees:* information not available. *Eating facilities:* in clubhouse, (bar snacks only), licensed bar. *Visitors:* welcome anytime, booking system for all games. *Society Meetings:* welcome by prior arrangement with the Professional. Professional: Barry Large (0151-428 7490). Secretary: H. O'Neill.*

LIVERPOOL. **The Childwall Golf Club Ltd.,** Naylors Road, Gateacre, Liverpool L27 2YB (0151-487 9982). *Location:* Exit 6 M62 to Liverpool, follow Huyton A5080 to second set of traffic lights, turn left into Wheathill Road. Parkland, flat, designed by James Braid. 18 holes, 6547 yards. S.S.S. 72. Practice area. *Green Fees:* information not provided. *Eating facilities:* bar, snacks and restaurant. *Visitors:* no visitors weekends and Tuesdays. *Society Meetings:* catered for on weekdays, contact the Manager. Professional: N.M. Parr (0151-487 9871). Manager: P. Bowen (0151-487 0654; Fax: 0151-487 0882). website: www.childwallgolfclub.co.uk

LIVERPOOL. **Dudley Golf Club,** Allerton Municipal Golf Course, Menlove Avenue, Allerton, Liverpool L18 3EE (0151-428 8510). *Location:* end of M62, then two miles on Allerton road, five miles from city centre. Wooded parkland. Two courses. (1) 18 holes, 5459 metres. S.S.S. 67. (2) 9 holes, 1685 metres. S.S.S. 34. *Green Fees:* information not provided. *Eating facilities:* licensed bar, bar snacks. *Visitors:* welcome at any time, please book in advance. *Society Meetings:* welcome by advance booking. Professional: Barry Large (0151-428 1046). Secretary: Brian L. Harris (01244 661511).

LIVERPOOL. **Lee Park Golf Club,** Childwall Valley Road, Liverpool L27 3YA (0151-487 3882; Fax: 0151-498 4666). *Location:* M62 J6, A5080 to Huyton, turn left at second set of lights (Wheathill Road), turn left at next lights (one mile), club on right 200 yards. Easy walking parkland course, a challenging test of golf with 6 doglegs and well protected raised greens. 18 holes, 5959 yards. Medal tees: 5721 yards. Front tees: S.S.S. 69. Ladies' tees: 5543 yards. S.S.S. 72. Driving nets, chipping/bunker practice green, practice area. *Green Fees:* weekdays £30.00, weekends £40.00. 2-fore-1/Open Fairways - 50% discount one 4-ball per weekday. *Eating facilities:* informal Spike Bar for bar snacks, restaurant, formal main lounge for larger parties. *Visitors:* welcome Monday, Wednesday, Thursday, Friday, Saturday (12-2.15pm members and guests only). *Society Meetings:* catered for mainly Monday, Thursday, Friday only. Professional: Chris Crowder (07984 253821). Manager: Steve Settle (0151-487 3882; Fax: 0151-498 4666). e-mail: lee.park@virgin.net website: www.leepark.co.uk

LIVERPOOL. **West Derby Golf Club,** Yew Tree Lane, West Derby, Liverpool L12 9HQ (0151-254 1034). Flat parkland course. 18 holes, 6275 yards. S.S.S. 70. *Green Fees:* weekdays £35.00 per round; weekends £40.00 after 2pm. *Eating facilities:* soup and sandwiches, light meals available at lunch. Evening meals by prior arrangement. *Visitors:* welcome if members of a recognised golf club. *Society Meetings:* catered for only by arrangement with Secretary. Professional: Andrew Witherup (0151-254 1034). Secretary: A.P. Milne (0151-254 1034; Fax: 0151-259 0505).

LIVERPOOL. **Woolton Golf Club,** Doe Park, Speke Road, Woolton, Liverpool L25 7TZ (0151 486 2298). *Location:* South Liverpool, one mile from Woolton Village. Parkland, rolling terrain, excellent springy fairways affording inviting lies. 18 holes, 5747 yards. S.S.S. 68. *Green Fees:* Information not available. *Eating facilities:* bar snacks daily, evening dining by arrangement. *Visitors:* welcome; very few restrictions. *Society Meetings:* catered for by arrangement with the Secretary; various packages - information pack on request. Professional: D. Thompson (0151-486 1298). Secretary: K. Hamilton (0151-486 2298; Fax: 0151-486 1664). *

MORETON. **Leasowe Golf Club,** Leasowe Road, Moreton, Wirral, Merseyside CH46 3RD (0151-677 5852; Fax: 0151-641 8519). *Location:* Exit 1 from M53, one mile towards Hoylake. Flat seaside links. 18 holes, 6263 yards, S.S.S. 71. Practice area. *Green Fees:* information not provided. *Eating facilities:* dining room and bar snacks. *Visitors:* welcome anytime except Saturdays and Sunday mornings. Phone first. *Society Meetings:* available at discount, catered for except Saturdays , must book in advance. Professional: Andrew Ayre (0151-678 5460). Secretary/ Manager: L. Jukes (0151-677 5852).

NEWTON-LE-WILLOWS. **Haydock Park Golf Club,** Newton Lane, Newton-le-Willows WA12 0HX (01925 228525). *Location:* off East Lancs Road (A580) and M6, three quarters of a mile from Newton-le-Willows High Street. Flat, wooded parkland course in beautiful setting. 18 holes, 6058 yards. S.S.S. 69. Large practice ground. *Green Fees:* weekdays £35.00; weekends £12.00 with member only. *Eating facilities:* restaurant and two bars. *Visitors:* welcome weekdays except Tuesdays, identification (club membership card) or letter of introduction required. *Society Meetings:* catered for by arrangement. Professional: P. Kenwright (01925 226944). Secretary: Mr S. Dale (01925 228525).

RAINHILL. **Blundells Hill Golf Club,** Blundells Lane, Rainhill L35 6NA (0151-426 9040; Fax: 0151-426 5256). *Location:* three minutes from Junction 7 of M62, course lies adjacent to eastbound M62. Built on a gently sloping hill, created from some 120 acres of parkland surroundings with wide fairways, big bunkers and large undulating greens, several ponds, ditches and a beautifully landscaped lake. 18 holes, 6256 yards. S.S.S. 71. Practice ground, putting green. *Green Fees:* information not available. *Eating facilities:* licensed bar, restaurant, snooker room, function room, Sky TV. *Visitors:* all welcome, call 0151-430 0100 to pre-book tee times. No jeans, tracksuits, tee shirts, trainers, short socks, etc. Expert tuition. *Society Meetings:* welcome, packages available; call 0151-430 9551 for brochure. Professional: Richard Burbidge (0151-430 0100). Hon. Secretary: Andy Roberts (0151-430 9551; Fax: 0151-426 5256). *

RAINHILL. **Eccleston Park Golf Club,** Rainhill Road, Rainhill, Prescot L35 4PG (0151 493 0033). *Location:* Junction 7 of M62, follow A57 towards Prescot; at traffic lights after humpback bridge, turn right into Rainhill. Gently undulating open parkland layout. 18 holes. Par 70. *Green Fees:* information not available. *Eating facilities:* bar and dining from 8am to 11pm (9am to 6pm during winter). *Visitors:* Handicap Certificate required at weekends.*
e-mail: eccleston-sales@crown-golf.co.uk

ST HELENS. **Grange Park Golf Club,** Prescot Road, St. Helens WA10 3AD (Tel & Fax: 01744 26318). *Location:* one and a half miles south west of St. Helens on A58. Wooded parkland. 18 holes, 6422 yards. S.S.S. 71. Practice area. *Green Fees:* weekdays £30.00, weekends £35.00 (subject to review for 2008). *Eating facilities:* full catering and bar facilities. *Visitors:* welcome anytime except Tuesdays and times are often not available at weekends/Bank Holidays; reservation through Professional recommended. *Society Meetings:* welcome except Tuesdays, Bank Holidays and weekends. Professional: Paul Roberts (01744 28785; Fax: 01744 26318). Secretary: Gavin R Brown (Tel & Fax: 01744 26318).
e-mail: secretary@grangeparkgolfclub.co.uk
website: www.grangeparkgolfclub.co.uk

ST HELENS. **Sherdley Park Municipal Golf Course and Driving Range,** Off Eltonhead Road, Sutton, St Helens WA9 5DE (01744 813149). *Location:* Exit 7 off M62, follow St Helens Linkway to second island, turn right for 300 yards, course on left hand side. Undulating parkland course. 18 holes, 5974 yards. S.S.S. 71. Driving range. *Green Fees:* for information and bookings phone (01744 813149). *Eating facilities:* Licensed bar and Cafe in the Park open most times, phone (01744 815518) for more information. *Visitors/Society Meetings:* welcome mid-week and weekends (book early). Booking system operates up to six days in advance. Golf Professional: Danny Jones. Manager: Jeff Barston (01744 817967).

www.uk-golfguide.com

SOUTHPORT. **Hesketh Golf Club,** Cockle Dick's Lane, Cambridge Road, Southport PR9 9QQ (01704 536897). *Location:* one mile north of town centre. Seaside links Championship course. 18 holes, 6655 yards. S.S.S. 72. Practice ground. *Green Fees:* weekdays £55.00 per round, £70.00 per day; weekends and Bank Holidays £70.00 per round. *Eating facilities:* bar snacks and dining room; three bars. *Visitors:* welcome by prior arrangement with Secretary. *Society Meetings:* catered for by arrangement with Secretary; special rates for parties over 12 in number. Professional: Scott Astin (01704 530050). Secretary: Martyn G. Senior (01704 536897; Fax: 01704 539250).
e-mail: secretary@heskethgolfclub.co.uk
website: www.heskethgolfclub.co.uk

SOUTHPORT. **Hillside Golf Club,** Hastings Road, Hillside, Southport PR8 2LU (01704 567169; Fax: 01704 563192). *Location:* three miles south of town centre on A565, Hillside station one mile. Championship links course. 18 holes, 6850 yards. S.S.S. 74. Practice ground. *Green Fees:* Monday to Friday £75.00 per round, £95.00 per day; Saturday and Sunday £95.00 per round (2007). *Eating facilities:* bar and restaurant. *Visitors:* welcome, book through Office. Tuesday up to 2pm Ladies' Day; no visitors Saturdays, limited Sundays. Buggies and carts for hire. *Society Meetings:* welcome with prior reservations. Professional: B. Seddon (01704 568360). Secretary: Simon H. Newland (01704 567169; Fax: 01704 563192).

SOUTHPORT. **Southport and Ainsdale Golf Club,** Bradshaw's Lane, Off Liverpool Road, Ainsdale, Southport PR8 3LG (01704 578000; Fax: 01704 570896). *Location:* south of Southport on A565. Links course. 18 holes, 6749 yards. S.S.S. 73. *Green Fees:* weekdays £65.00 per round, £90.00 per day; weekends £90.00 per round (under review). *Eating facilities:* full catering available. *Visitors:* welcome at all times; by arrangement at weekends. *Society Meetings:* catered for by arrangement. Professional: J. Payne (01704 577316). Secretary: (01704 578000; Fax: 01704 570896).
e-mail: secretary@sandagolfclub.co.uk
website: www.sandagolfclub.co.uk

The Royal Clifton Hotel & Spa
★ ★ ★
Southport

The Royal Clifton Hotel has become the major hospitality hotel for golfing celebrities from around the world, winning critical acclaim for sensible rates, quality and service.

A choice of bedrooms and suites, all tastefully furnished with modern facilities. Two spacious lounge bars, a choice of restaurants for snacks or superb dinner specialities. Our on-site Leisure Club offers a superb heated indoor swimming pool, poolside sauna and steam room, bubbling jacuzzi, air-conditioned gymnasium, and a fantastic health and beauty salon.

* Special rates for golfing parties
* Golfing Breaks to suit your individual needs can be arranged.

The Royal Clifton Hotel & Spa
The Promenade, Southport PR8 1RB
Tel: 01704 533771 • Fax: 01704 500657
www.royalclifton.co.uk • sales@royalclifton.co.uk

SOUTHPORT. **Royal Birkdale Golf Club,** Waterloo Road, Birkdale, Southport PR8 2LX (01704 567920; Fax: 01704 562327). *Location:* one mile south of Southport town centre. Classic Links on the Open Championship rota. 18 holes, 6708 yards. S.S.S. 73. *Green Fees:* Information not available. *Visitors:* welcome but it is essential to make prior arrangements with the Secretary's office, official golf Handicap required. *Society Meetings:* catered for, dining room facilities. Professional: Brian Hodgkinson (01704 568857). Secretary: M.C. Gilyeat (01704 567920).
e-mail: secretary@royalbirkdale.com
website: www.royalbirkdale.com*

SOUTHPORT. **Southport Municipal Golf Club,** Park Road West, Southport PR9 0JR (01704 55130). *Location:* Park Road West, north end of Promenade, near Marine Lake, Southport. Flat seaside links. 18 holes, 6139 yards. S.S.S. 70. *Green Fees:* information not available. *Eating facilities:* licensed cafe. *Visitors:* booking system operates up to seven days in advance (visitors unrestricted). *Society Meetings:* welcome, book in advance. Professional: William Fletcher (01704 35286)*

SOUTHPORT. **Southport Old Links Golf Club,** Moss Lane, Churchtown, Southport PR9 7QS (01704 228207). *Location:* end of Roe Lane, Churchtown, at the rear of Meols Hall. Tree lined links course. 9 holes, (x2), 6450 yards. S.S.S. 71. *Green Fees:* information not provided. *Eating facilities:* available daily except Mondays. *Visitors:* welcome except Wednesdays, Sundays and Bank Holidays. *Society Meetings:* catered for by arrangement, letter of application required. Secretary: B. Kenyon (01704 228207; Fax: 01704 505353).

WALLASEY. **Wallasey Golf Club,** Bayswater Road, Wallasey CH45 8LA (0151-691 1024; Fax: 0151-638 8988). *Location:* via M53 through Wirral or 15 minutes from Liverpool centre via Wallasey Tunnel. Championship seaside links. 18 holes, 6503 yards. S.S.S. 72. *Green Fees:* weekdays £70.00 per round, £80.00 per day; weekends and Bank Holidays £75.00 per round, £85.00 per day. *Eating facilities:* snacks and full catering facilities. *Visitors:* welcome with reservation. *Society Meetings:* catered for by arrangement. Professional: Mike Adams (0151-638 3888). Secretary: Trevor Barraclough (0151-691 1024)

WALLASEY. **Warren Golf Club,** The Grange, Grove Road, Wallasey CH45 0JA (0151-639 8323). *Location:* 300 yards Grove Road Station. Seaside links course, wonderful view over Mersey. 9 holes, 5914 yards. S.S.S. 68. *Green Fees:* information not available. *Visitors:* welcome Mondays to Saturdays. Course closed to public Sundays 7am to 11am. *Society Meetings:* welcome. Professional: Mark Eagles (0151-639 5730). Secretary: Kevin McCormack (0151-678 0330-).
e-mail: golfer@warrengc.freeserve.co.uk

WIRRAL. **Brackenwood Golf Club,** Bracken Lane, Bebington, Wirral L63 2LY (0151-608 5394). *Location:* M53 Clatterbridge roundabout Junction 4. Flat parkland. 18 holes, 6200 yards. S.S.S. 70. *Green Fees:* £12.00 per round. *Visitors:* welcome, weekends must be booked through Professional one week in advance. *Society Meetings:* welcome, book through Professional for tee times and Secretary for bar/catering. Professional: Ken Lamb (0151-608 3093). Secretary: G.W. Brogan (0151-339 9817).

WIRRAL. **Hoylake Golf Club,** Carr Lane, Hoylake, Wirral CH47 4BG (0151 632 2956). *Location:* turn at roundabout Hoylake town centre, over railway. Part flat semi links. 18 holes, 6313 yards, 5780 metres. S.S.S. 70. *Green Fees:* information not available. *Eating facilities:* cafe and bar. Phone in advance (0151 632 4883). *Visitors:* welcome, booking fee required in advance. *Society Meetings:* society bookings weekdays and after 1.30pm Saturday; after 12 midday Sunday. Professional: S.N. Hooton (0151-632 2956). Secretary: Peter Davies (0151 632 0523)

THE APPEARANCE OF AN ASTERISK (*) AT THE END OF A CLUB OR COURSE ENTRY INDICATES THAT UP-TO-DATE INFORMATION HAS NOT BEEN SUPPLIED

Northumberland

ALLENDALE. **Allendale Golf Club,** High Studdon, Allenheads Road, Allendale, Hexham NE47 9DH (0700 5808246). *Location:* B6295 Allendale to Allenheads Road, 10 miles south of Hexham. Parkland course, hilly but not too severe. 9 holes, 16 tees. 4501 yards. S.S.S. 64. Driving net and putting green. *Green Fees:* £12.00 weekdays, £15.00 weekends. £2.00 reduction if playing with a member. Special rates after 6pm weekdays, and for visiting parties. *Eating facilities:* new clubhouse with licensed bar, catering by arrangement. *Visitors:* welcome anytime other than August Bank Holiday Monday before 3pm. Secretary: Norman Harris (01434 683115). e-mail: norman@harris8484.freeserve.co.uk website: www.allendale-golf.org

ALNMOUTH. **Alnmouth Golf Club Ltd,** Foxton Hall, Lesbury, Alnwick NE66 3BE (01665 830231). *Location:* four miles east of Alnwick. 18 holes, 6414 yards, 5855 metres. S.S.S. 71. *Green Fees:* Information not available. *Eating facilities:* diningroom and bars. *Visitors:* welcome Monday to Thursday and Sundays. Packages available. Handicap Certificate required. Dormy House accommodation available. *Society Meetings:* welcome Monday to Thursday and Sundays. Secretary: Ian Wort (01665 830231; Fax: 01665 830922).* e-mail: secretary@alnmouthgolfclub.com website: www.alnmouthgolfclub.com*

ALNMOUTH. **Alnmouth Village Golf Club,** Marine Road, Alnmouth NE66 2RZ (01665 830370). *Location:* leave A1 from Alnwick to Alnmouth. Seaside links course. 9 holes, 6090 yards, 5572 metres. Par 71. S.S.S. 70. *Green Fees:* weekdays £16.00 per 18 holes; weekends and Bank Holidays £20.00 per 18 holes, weekly ticket £60.00. *Eating facilities:* available. *Visitors:* welcome, restrictions on club competition days. *Society Meetings:* must book in advance and only with official Golf Club Handicaps. Secretary: J. E. Clark (01665 603797).

ALNWICK. **Alnwick Golf Club,** Swansfield Park, Alnwick NE66 2AB (01665 602632). *Location:* signposted from the south A1 slip road. A friendly welcome awaits you at Alnwick Golf Club. Established in 1907, extended to 18 holes in 1995. Superb layout set in mature parkland, open grassland and gorse with panoramic views out to sea. 18 holes, 6250 yards. S.S.S. 70. *Green Fees:* weekdays £20.00 per round, £30.00 per day; weekends and Bank Holidays £22.00 per round, £30.00 per day. *Eating facilities:* catering and bar facilities available most times. *Visitors:* welcome most times, part restrictions during

competitions. Buggies available. Packages available. *Society Meetings:* welcome by prior arrangement with the Secretary. Secretary: Lawrie E. Stewart (01665 602499). e-mail: edd41uk@yahoo.co.uk website: www.alnwickgolfclub.co.uk

BAMBURGH. **Bamburgh Castle Golf Club,** The Club House, Bamburgh NE69 7DE (01668 214378). *Location:* midway between Alnwick and Berwick upon Tweed on A1, take B1341 or B1342 to Bamburgh village. Seaside course with outstanding views of Farne Islands, Holy Island and magnificent coastal area. 18 holes, 5621 yards, 5132 metres. S.S.S. 67. Practice area. *Green Fees:* weekdays £33.00 per round, £45.00 per day; weekends and Bank Holidays £38.00 per round, £50.00 per day. Five-day weekday ticket £95.00. Juniors £20.00. Restricted play at weekends. *Eating facilities:* bar snacks, lunch, high tea, beverages, etc. *Visitors:* welcome except on competition days and Bank Holidays. Buggy hire. *Society Meetings:* welcome, by written application. Secretary: M. N. D. Robinson (01668 214321).

BEDLINGTON. **Bedlingtonshire Golf Club,** Acorn Bank, Bedlington NE22 6AA (01670 822457). *Location:* one mile south west of Bedlington on A1068. Parkland. 18 holes, 6813 yards, 6230 metres. S.S.S. 73. Practice ground and putting green. *Green Fees:* £25.00 per round midweek; £32.00 per round weekends and Bank Holidays. *Eating facilities:* catering, bar services, open all day. *Visitors:* welcome, but not before 9.00am weekdays and 10.00am weekends. *Society Meetings:* welcome, contact the Secretary. Professional: Marcus Webb (01670 822457). Secretary: (01670 822457). e-mail: secretary@bedlingtongolfclub.com website: www.bedlingtongolfclub.com

BELFORD. **The Belford,** South Road, Belford NE70 7DP (01668 213232; Fax: 01668 213282). *Location:* turn off A1 sign-posted Belford, first turning on right. Parkland course. 9 holes, 18 tee box, 6225 yards. S.S.S. 70, Par 72. Floodlit driving range. *Green Fees:* weekdays £12.00 for 9 holes, £18.00 for 18 holes; weekends £14.00 for 9 holes, £20.00 for 18 holes. *Eating facilities:* catering available 9am - 9pm, 7 days a week. *Visitors:* welcome all year. Buggies available. *Society Meetings:* open all year round to non-members, visitors and societies. Secretary: A.M. Gilhome (01668 213433).* website: www.thebelford.com

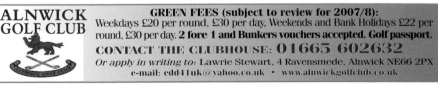

BELLINGHAM. **Bellingham Golf Club,** Boggle Hole, Bellingham, Hexham NE48 2DT (01434 220530). *Location:* 17 miles north of Hexham on B6320, in the picturesque North Tyne Valley between Hadrian's Wall and the Scottish Border. Rolling parkland course with an abundance of natural hazards. 18 holes, 6077 yards, 5557 metres. S.S.S. 70. Driving range. *Green Fees:* weekdays £24.00; weekends £30.00. *Eating facilities:* full bar and catering available throughout the year. *Visitors:* welcome at all times, daily starting sheet. Buggies for hire. *Society Meetings:* welcome by advance booking. Secretary: Jaimie Self (01434 220530). e-mail: admin@bellinghamgolfclub.com website: www.bellinghamgolfclub.com

BERWICK-UPON-TWEED. **Berwick-upon-Tweed (Goswick) Golf Club,** Goswick, Berwick-upon-Tweed TD15 2RW (01289 387256; Fax: 01289 387392). *Location:* signposted off A1, five miles south of Berwick-upon-Tweed. Seaside links, undulating fairways, elevated tees. 18 holes, 6686 yards. S.S.S. 72. Driving range, practice ground. *Green Fees:* weekdays £33.00 per round, £42.00 per day; weekends £38.00 per round, £48.00 per day. *Eating facilities:* full catering available. *Visitors:* welcome, restricted at weekends. Buggies and carts for hire. *Society Meetings:* welcome midweek and weekends. Professional: Paul Terras (01289 387380). Secretary: (01289 387256; Fax: 01289 387392). e-mail: goswickgc@btconnect.com website: www.goswicklinksgc.co.uk

BERWICK-UPON-TWEED. **Magdalene Fields Golf Club,** Magdalene Fields, Berwick-upon-Tweed TD15 1NE (01289 306130). *Location*: five minutes' walk from town centre and railway station. Seaside, parkland course with stunning scenic views. 18 holes, 6407 yards. S.S.S. 71. Practice area and putting area. *Green Fees*: weekdays £22.00 per round; weekends £24.00 per round. Reductions for Senior Citizens, Ladies, Juniors, parties. Fees subject to review. *Eating facilities*: bar and dining area - first class meals. *Visitors*: welcome Monday to Saturday, restrictions on Sundays. Member of Parsport to Scenic Northumberland. *Society Meetings*: all welcome. Club Manager: M. Lynch (01289 306130). Secretary: M.J. Lynch (01289 306130). website: www.magdalene-fields.co.uk

BLYTH. **Blyth Golf Club Ltd,** New Delaval, Blyth NE24 4DB. *Location:* 12 miles north of Newcastle near the coast. Flat parkland, water hazards. 18 holes, 6424 yards. S.S.S. 71. Large practice area and putting green. Host to Northumberland County Championships 2005. *Green Fees:* weekdays £23.50 per round, £33.00 per day; weekends £26.00 per round. *Eating facilities:* full catering and bar. *Visitors:* welcome weekdays up to 4pm and weekends after 2pm. Starting times available three days in advance; please ring Professional. *Society Meetings:* welcome, packages available. Professional: Andrew Brown (01670 356514). Manager: Jim Wright (01670 540110). e-mail: clubmanager@blythgolf.co.uk website: www.blythgolf.co.uk

CARLISLE. **Haltwhistle Golf Course,** Wallend Farm, Gilsland, Greenhead, Via Carlisle CA8 7HN (016977 47367). *Location*: off the A69 at the village of Greenhead on Gilsland Road, two and a half miles west of Haltwhistle. Undulating parkland course with wooded areas. 18 holes, 5532 yards. S.S.S. 67. Practice area. *Green Fees*: information not provided. *Eating facilities*: clubhouse bar, catering by prior arrangement. *Visitors*: welcome, no restrictions except Sundays 8am to 11am competition days. *Society Meetings*: welcome by prior arrangement. Secretary: Mr K.L. Dickinson (01434 320708).

EMBLETON. **Dunstanburgh Castle Golf Club,** Embleton NE66 3XQ (01665 576562). *Location:* seven miles off A1, to the north-east of Alnwick. Seaside links course in area of outstanding natural beauty. Designed by James Braid. 18 holes, 6298 yards. S.S.S. 70. *Green Fees:* weekdays £24.00 per day; weekends £28.00 per round, £35.00 per day. *Eating facilities:* snacks, lunches, high teas; bar. *Visitors:* welcome without reservation. *Society Meetings:* welcome anytime. Secretary: P.F.C. Gilbert. e-mail: enquiries@dunstanburgh.com website: www.dunstanburgh.com

HEXHAM. **Hexham Golf Club,** Spital Park, Hexham NE46 3RZ (01434 603072; Fax: 01434 601865). *Location:* 20 miles west of Newcastle upon Tyne, one mile west of Hexham town centre. An undulating parkland course, one of the driest in the area, with superb views of the north and south Tyne valleys. 18 holes, 6294 yards. S.S.S. 70. *Green Fees:* weekdays £30.00 per round, £40.00 per day; weekends and Bank Holidays £40.00 per round only. Special packages available. *Eating facilities:* lunches and evening meals. *Visitors:* welcome without reservation. Preliminary booking advisable. *Society Meetings:* catered for Monday to Friday by arrangement. Professional: Ben West(01434603072). Secretary: Dawn Wylie (01434 603072; Fax: 01434 601865).

HEXHAM. **Tynedale Golf Club,** Tynegreen, Hexham NE46 3HQ (01434 608154). *Location:* off A69 towards Hexham over Tyne Bridge, first roundabout turn right - golf course at the end of road. Flat, parkland course along the banks of the river. 9 holes, 5403 yards. S.S.S. 67. *Green Fees:* information not provided. *Eating facilities:* full catering available. *Visitors:* welcome, restricted Sunday mornings 11.30am members only. *Society Meetings:* welcome, discounts for parties over 10 people. Secretary: Trevor Hodge.*

MATFEN. **Matfen Hall Golf Club,** Matfen, Newcastle-upon-Tyne NE20 0RH (01661 886400; Fax: 01661 886055). *Location:* 15 miles west of Newcastle, five miles north of Corbridge, off B6318 (Military Road). Lovely parkland setting directly in front of Matfen Hall, with natural and added water hazards. 27 holes, 6700 yards. S.S.S. 72. New Dewlaw course: full 9 hole course, approx 3400 yards. Old front 9 called Douglas, back 9 called Standing Stone. Covered driving range. *Green Fees:* £35.00 Mon-Fri, £40.00 Sat-Sun. *Eating facilities:* bar, dining room. *Visitors:* very welcome any day; after 11am weekends. Good locker room facilities. 'Stay and Play' packages available at Matfen Hall Country House Hotel. *Society Meetings:* very welcome. Professional: John Harrison; Director of Golf: Craig Parkinson.

MORPETH. **Burgham Park Golf and Leisure Club,** Near Felton, Morpeth NE65 9QP (01670 787898; Fax: 01670 787164). *Location:* 5½ miles north of Morpeth, one mile west of A1 on Longhorsley Road. 18 holes; 7065 yards championship tees, 6804 yards medal tees, 6403 leisure tees. S.S.S. 72. Practice area. *Green Fees:* £26.00 weekdays, £32.00 weekends and Bank Holidays. *Eating facilities:* catering and bar available daily. *Visitors:* welcome; special rates for parties by arrangement. Professional: David Mather. Secretary/ Golf Manager: Terry Minett.
e-mail: info@burghampark.co.uk
website: www.burghampark.co.uk

MORPETH. **Longhirst Hall Golf Course,** Longhirst, Morpeth NE61 3LL (Tee Reservations: Tel & Fax: 01670 791562). *Location:* on A1 3 miles north from Morpeth take B1337 Hebron road. Florida-style course with two 18-hole layouts during the summer, and one layout in winter, with water featuring on many holes. Greens built to USGA specifications. Astro Turf driving range. Full spec chipping and putting green. *Green Fees:* £30.00, £20.00 and £15.00 twilight rate depending on time of day. All prices subject to change without notice. *Eating facilities:* bar and restaurant. *Visitors:* welcome (advisable to pre-book). *Society Meetings:* welcome any day of the week. 75 bedroom hotel on site with sports village. Clubhouse Manager: Ian Brodie (01670 791562).
e-mail: enquiries@longhirstgolf.co.uk
website: www.longhirstgolf.co.uk

MORPETH. **Macdonald Linden Hall,** Longhorsley, Morpeth NE65 8XF (01670 500011; Fax: 01670 500001). *Location:* A697 from A1, half a mile from Longhorsley. Mature woodland parkland and rolling countryside with many water features. 18 holes, 6846 yards. S.S.S. 73. Driving range, pitching green, putting green. *Green Fees:* weekdays £30.00, weekends £35.00. Handicap Certificate required. *Eating facilities:* Linden Tree (traditional country pub), Dobson Restaurant, function suites. *Visitors:* welcome, prior booking essential, packages available. *Society Meetings:* welcome, telephone for enquiries. Director of Golf/Professional: David Curry.
website: www.macdonald-hotels.co.uk

MORPETH. **The Morpeth Golf Club Ltd.,** The Clubhouse, Morpeth NE61 2BT (01670 515675). *Location:* turn off A1 for Morpeth, A167 south side of town. Easy walking parkland. 18 holes, 6206 yards. S.S.S. 69. Practice area. *Green Fees:* information not available. *Eating facilities:* restaurant/bar meals/snacks etc. *Visitors:* welcome, weekdays after 9.30am, Handicap Certificates may be asked for. Venue for 1997 County Strokeplay and 2000 County Matchplay Championships. *Society Meetings:* catered for weekdays by prior arrangement; discounts available for large parties. Professional: M.R. Jackson (01670 515675). Secretary: B.Flower (01670 504942; Fax: 01670 504918).

NEWBIGGIN-BY-THE-SEA. **Newbiggin-by-the-Sea Golf Club,** Clubhouse, Prospect Place, Newbiggin-by-the-Sea NE64 6DW (01670 817344; Fax: 01670 520236). *Location:* take signpost for Newbiggin off A189 (spine road from Tyne Tunnel). Clubhouse at most easterly point of village, adjacent to Church Point Caravan Park. Links course. 18 holes, 6452 yards, 5900 metres. S.S.S. 71. Practice area. *Green Fees:* information not available. *Eating facilities:* restaurant, bar and lounge. *Visitors:* welcome, not before 10am or on competition days. *Society Meetings:* catered for by prior arrangement with Secretary. Secretary: George Beattie (01670 817344).

> **THE APPEARANCE OF AN ASTERISK (*) AT THE END OF A CLUB OR COURSE ENTRY INDICATES THAT UP-TO-DATE INFORMATION HAS NOT BEEN SUPPLIED**

NEWCASTLE UPON TYNE. **Arcot Hall Golf Club Ltd,** Arcot Hall, Dudley, Cramlington NE23 7QP (0191-236 2794). *Location:* seven miles north of Newcastle. Turn off A1 for Cramlington and then signposted. Flat, parkland – mostly tree lined. 18 holes, 6329 yards, 5788 metres. S.S.S. 70. Practice ground, chipping area, putting green. *Green Fees:* weekdays £28.00 (£23.00); weekends £32.00. *Eating facilities:* good restaurant, bar. *Visitors:* welcome, booking is essential due to popularity of the course. *Society Meetings:* catered for on application to Secretary. Professional: (0191-236 2794). Secretary: Frank Elliott (0191-236 2794).

NEWCASTLE UPON TYNE. **De Vere Slaley Hall Hotel, Golf Resort and Spa,** Hexham NE47 0BX (01434 673350; Fax: 01434 673152). *Location:* 20 miles west of Newcastle upon Tyne, seven miles south of Corbridge, signposted off A68. Set in parkland and moorland with an abundance of lakes and streams, woodland and heather. PGA European Tour Venue. Hunting Course:- Championship Standard, home of the Compaq European Grand Prix: 18 holes, 7088 yards (5903 yards - ladies). S.S.S. 74, 72. Priestman Course: Championship Standard, 18 holes, 6951 yards (5755 yards - ladies). S.S.S 72, 73. Golf academy and driving Range. *Green Fees:* Information not available. *Eating facilities:* clubhouse bar and restaurant; hotel bar and restaurant. *Visitors:* welcome, prior booking essential. 4-star hotel. *Society Meetings:* welcome anytime, book through Golf Co-ordinator. Golf Reservations (01434 673154) Manager: Mark Stancer (01434 673350; Fax: 01434 673152).*
e-mail: slaley@dircon.co.uk

NEWCASTLE UPON TYNE. **Ponteland Golf Club,** Bell Villas, Ponteland, Newcastle upon Tyne NE20 9BD (01661 822689). *Location:* A696, one and a half miles north of Newcastle Airport. Parkland. 18 holes, 6524 yards. S.S.S. 71. Large practice area. *Green Fees:* £30.00 per day or round (inclusive VAT). *Eating facilities:* full menu in restaurant and bar. *Visitors:* welcome Monday to Thursday, must be member's guest Friday, weekends and Bank Holidays. Handicap Certificate required. *Society Meetings:* Tuesdays or Thursdays, catered for with pre-booking agreed by Secretary. Professional: Alan Robson-Crosby (01661 822689). Secretary: Mrs P.M. Spong (01661 822689). e-mail: secretary@thepontelandgolfclub.co.uk
website: www.thepontelandgolfclub.co.uk

PRUDHOE. **Prudhoe Golf Club,** Eastwood Park, Prudhoe NE42 5DX (01661 832466; Fax: 01661 830710). *Location:* 10 miles west of Newcastle upon Tyne, off A695 to Hexham. Wooded parkland with scenic views of the Tyne Valley. 18 holes, 5839 yards. S.S.S. 69. Practice area. *Green Fees:* £24.00 weekdays; £32.00 weekends. £11.00 with a member, parties £20.00. *Eating facilities:* bar facilities and bar meals available. *Visitors:* welcome midweek and after 4pm weekends. *Society Meetings:* welcome. Professional: John Crawford (01661 836188). Secretary: Ian Pauw (01661 835168).

ROTHBURY. **Rothbury Golf Club**, Whitton Bank Road, Rothbury, Morpeth, Northumberland NE65 7RX (01669 621271). *Location:* 15 miles north of Morpeth, take A697 turn off at Weldon Bridge for Rothbury. On entering village turn left, cross river and turn immediately right. Club entrance few hundred yards on right, just past hospital. 18 holes, 6100 yards.S.S.S. 70. Undulating course adjacent to River Coquet. Practice ground. *Green Fees:* weekday £20.00, weekends £25.00. *Eating facilities*: catering and bar facilities available. *Visitors:* welcome by arrangement. New Clubhouse with function room, showers etc. *Society Meetings:* welcome by arrangement. Secretary: F. Brown (01669 621271 or 0191 2150268). website: www.rothburygolfclub.com

SEAHOUSES. **Seahouses Golf Club,** Beadnell Road, Seahouses NE68 7XT (01665 720794; Fax: 01665 721994). *Location:* 15 miles north of Alnwick, turn off A1 for B1340. Flat seaside links with water hazards. 18 holes, 5542 yards. S.S.S. 67. Practice ground. *Green Fees:* weekdays £24.00 per round, £32.00 per day; weekends £32.00 per round, £40.00 per day. *Eating facilities:* full catering and bar. *Visitors:* welcome with no restrictions, please telephone clubhouse. *Society Meetings:* by arrangement. Secretary: John A. Gray (01665 720794; Fax: 01665 721994). e-mail: secretary@seahousesgolf.co.uk website: www.seahousesgolf.co.uk*

STOCKSFIELD. **Stocksfield Golf Club,** New Ridley, Stocksfield NE43 7RE (01661 843041; Fax: 01661 843046). *Location:* 15 miles west of Newcastle on A69, and three miles east of A68. Half woodland, half parkland, slight hillside. 18 holes, 5991 yards. S.S.S. 69. Small practice areas. *Green Fees:* weekdays £20.00 per round, £25.00 per day; weekends and Bank Holidays £25.00 per round. Subject to review. 2-Fore-1 tickets accepted weekdays only. *Eating facilities:* available, also bar. *Visitors:* welcome except Wednesday mornings. Full size snooker table. Buggies, trolleys and clubs for hire. *Society Meetings:* catered for by prior arrangement. Professional: S. Harrison. Secretary: B. Garrow.

SWARLAND. **Percy Wood Golf & Country Retreat,** Coast View, Swarland, Morpeth NE65 9JG (01670 787940). *Location:* approximately one mile west of A1 trunk road, eight miles south of Alnwick. Undulating parkland course within mature woodland. 18 holes, 6628 yards, 6060 metres. S.S.S. 72. *Green Fees:* weekdays £18.00 per round, weekends £24.00 per round. *Eating facilities:* full dining facilities, bar meals, licensed bar. *Visitors:* welcome any day, but suggest telephoning to avoid club competitions on Sundays. Accommodation available on site. *Society Meetings:* welcome. Golf shop. Professional: Peter Ritchie (01670 787010).

WARKWORTH. **Warkworth Golf Club,** The Links, Warkworth, Morpeth NE65 0SW (01665 711596). *Location:* off A1068 at Warkworth. Seaside links orginally designed by "Old Tom Morris" in 1891. 9 holes, 5986 yards, S.S.S. 69. Practice area. *Green Fees:* weekdays £15.00 per day, weekends £20.00 per day. *Eating facilities:* bar open 11.30am to 2.30pm and from 7.30pm to 11pm during season. *Visitors:* welcome except Tuesdays and Saturdays. *Society Meetings:* welcome by arrangement. Secretary: M. Rowe (01665 711596).

WOOLER. **Wooler Golf Club,** Dod Law, Doddington, Wooler NE71 6EA. *Location:* situated on the high ground named Dod Law to the east of the B6525 Wooler–Berwick road. The route is signposted from Doddington village. Hillside course with exceptional panoramic views. 9 holes (18 tees), 6411 yards. S.S.S. 71. Limited practice area. *Green Fees:* weekdays £15.00 per day, weekends and Bank Holidays £20.00 per day. *Eating facilities:* bar open evenings (operated voluntarily). *Visitors:* always welcome except during all day competitions, check with Secretary. Buggies available. *Society Meetings:* welcome by arrangement with Secretary. Secretary: S. Lowrey (01668 281631).

Tyne & Wear

BIRTLEY. **Birtley Golf Club,** Birtley Lane, Birtley DH3 2LR (0191-410-2207). *Location:* just off old Durham road and main A1. Parkland. 9 holes, 5740 yards. S.S.S. 67. *Green Fees:* £15.00 per round. *Eating facilities:* bar open after 7.15pm each evening and 11.45am to 5pm Saturday, 11.45 to 4pm Sunday; snacks available. *Visitors:* welcome weekdays; weekends and Bank Holidays with a member only. *Society Meetings:* welcome, must be pre-booked. Catering available. Secretary: G. Barras (0191 410 2207).
e-mail: birtleygolfclub@aol.com
website: www.birtleyportobellogolfclub.co.uk

CHOPWELL. **Garesfield Golf Club,** Chopwell NE17 7AP (Tel & Fax: 01207 561309; Bar/Catering 01207 561278). *Location:* leave A694 at Rowlands Gill, follow signposts for Chopwell, approximately three miles. Turn left at Bute Arms; golf course is one mile up road on left. Undulating wooded parkland 18 holes, 6403 yards. par 72. Practice ground, nets and putting green. *Green Fees:* weekdays £28.00 per day, £22.00 per round; weekends: details on request. *Eating facilities:* full catering except Mondays. *Visitors:* welcome weekdays; weekends and Bank Holidays after 4.30pm. Buggies available £16.00 per round. *Society Meetings:* welcome. Group rates (min. 12, max. 24 on Sundays at 10.30am): £30.00 per round. Professional: S. Cowell (01207 563082). Secretary: (Tel & Fax: 01207 561309).

EAST BOLDON. **Boldon Golf Club Ltd,** Dipe Lane, East Boldon NE36 0PQ (0191-536 5360). *Location:* near Sunderland, approximately one mile from roundabout at junction of A19 and A184 highways. Fairly flat parkland. 18 holes, 6348 yards. S.S.S. 70. *Green Fees:* weekdays £20.00, with a member £15.00; weekends £23.00, with a member £17.50. *Eating facilities:* bar snacks and restaurant. *Visitors:* welcome, not between 9am and 10am, 12.30pm and 1.30pm or 4.30pm and 6pm. Not before 2pm at weekends. *Society Meetings:* catered for. Professional: Phipps Golf (0191-536 5835; Fax: 0191-537 2270). Secretary: D.A. Greenfield (0191-536 5360; Fax: 0191-537 2270).
e-mail: info@boldongolfclub.co.uk
website: www.boldongolfclub.co.uk

GATESHEAD. **Heworth Golf Club,** Gingling Gate, Heworth, Gateshead. *Location:* A1 (M) south east boundary of Gateshead. Flat wooded course. 18 holes, 6422 yards. S.S.S. 71. Practice area. *Green Fees:* Infprmation not available. *Eating facilities:* diningroom, two bars. *Visitors:* weekdays up to 4pm, no visitors Saturdays; but after 10am on Sundays. *Society Meetings:* welcome mid-week only up to 4pm. Professional: A. Marshall (0191-438 4223). Secretary: C. J. Watson (0191-469 9832).*

GATESHEAD. **Ravensworth Golf Club Ltd,** 'Angel View', Longbank, Gateshead NE9 7NE (0191-487 6014). *Location:* two miles south of Gateshead town centre, near A1 (Angel of the North). Parkland course. 18 holes, 5825 yards. S.S.S. 69. *Green Fees:* Information not available. *Eating facilities:* meals served with reasonable notice (not Mondays). *Visitors:* welcome, weekends very restricted. *Society Meetings:* catered for. General Manager: (0191-487 6014).*

HEDDON ON THE WALL. **Close House Country Club,** Heddon on the Wall, Newcastle upon Tyne NE15 0HT (01661 852255). *Location:* 10 miles west of Newcastle off A69 to Wylam. A picturesque parkland/part wooded course set in the Tyne Valley. 18 holes, 6100 yards. S.S.S. 70. Golf packages available for visiting parties. *Green Fees:* available on request. *Eating facilities:* catering facilities available for visiting parties and also casual visitors.. *Visitors:* Visiting parties and casual visitors welcome with restricted times on weekends, preliminary phone calls advisable. Golf Operations Manager: John Glendinning (01661 852953; Fax: 01661 853322). e-mail: john.glendinning@closehouse.co.uk
website: www.closehouse.co.uk

HETTON-LE-HOLE. **Elemore Golf Course,** Elemore Lane, Hetton-Le-Hole (0191-517 3057; Fax: 0191 517 3054). *Location:* follow signs to Easington Lane, located off A1068, following signs to Elemore/Pittington. Flat meadowland Public Pay & Play golf course. 18 holes, 5947 yards. S.S.S. 69. Practice area. *Green Fees:* information not available. *Eating facilities:* clubhouse with bar/lounge serving snacks and meals. *Visitors:* welcome, no restrictions. Buggy Hire £12.00 per round. *Society Meetings:* welcome throughout the year. Contact Course Manager for advance bookings (14 days' notice required). Professional: To be arranged. Course Manager: Barbara Blenkinsop. *

HOUGHTON-LE-SPRING. **Houghton-le-Spring Golf Club,** Copt Hill, Houghton-le-Spring DH5 8LU (0191 5841198). *Location:* off A690 Durham road take Seaham road, course is situated at the top of Copt Hill Bank. Testing hillside course. 18 holes, 6120 yards, S.S.S. 71, Par 72. *Green Fees:* Information not available. *Eating facilities:* excellent food available (not Mondays), bar open every day. *Visitors:*

welcome every day except competition days (Sundays). Buggies available. *Society Meetings:* catered for by arrangement with Professional. Professional: K. Gow (0191 5847421). Secretary: G. Ferguson (0191 5840048).*
e-mail: houghton.golf@ntlworld.com
website: www.houghtongolfclub.co.uk

NEWCASTLE UPON TYNE. **City of Newcastle Golf Club,** Three Mile Bridge, Gosforth, Newcastle upon Tyne NE3 2DR (0191-285 1775; Fax: 0191-284 0700). *Location:* B1318 three miles north of city. Flat parkland. 18 holes, 6528 yards. S.S.S. 71. *Green Fees:* Monday to Saturday £28.00, £34.00 per day; Sunday £25.00. Discount for parties over 12. *Eating facilities:* bar, meals. *Visitors:* welcome without reservation, restricted times Fridays. *Society Meetings:* very welcome. Professional: S. McKenna (0191-285 5481; Fax: 0191-284 0700). Club Manager: A.J. Matthew (0191-285 1775; Fax: 0191-284 0700).
e-mail: info@cityofnewcastlegolfclub.com
website: www.cityofnewcastlegolfclub.com

NEWCASTLE UPON TYNE. **Gosforth Golf Club,** Broadway East, Gosforth, Newcastle upon Tyne NE3 5ER (0191-285 0553). *Location:* three miles north of Newcastle near Great North Road, B1318. Parkland with stream. 18 holes, 6024 yards. S.S.S. 69. *Green Fees:* weekdays £25.00 per round, £30.00 per day; weekends £28.00 per round, £32.00 per day.Reduced fees for Juniors. *Visitors:* welcome weekdays and weekends. *Society Meetings:* catered for by arrangement with the Secretary, including some weekends and Bank Holidays. Professional: G. Garland (0191-285 0553). Secretary: Greg Waugh (0191-285 3495; Fax: 0191-284 6274).
e-mail: gosforth.golf@virgin.net
website: www.gosforthgolfclub.com

NEWCASTLE UPON TYNE. **Hobson Golf Club,** Hobson, Burnopfield, Newcastle upon Tyne NE16 6BZ (01207 271605). *Location:* on Newcastle to Consett road. Fairly flat, well designed course. 18 holes, 6403 yards, 5854 metres. S.S.S. 71. Practice area. *Green Fees:* information not provided. *Eating facilities:* bar, lounge and restaurant. *Visitors:* no restrictions; booking system at weekends. Strict dress code in operation. *Society Meetings:* by prior arrangement with Professional (all bookings). Professional: J.W. Ord (01207 271605). Secretary: P. Taylor.

NEWCASTLE UPON TYNE. **Newcastle United Golf Club,** 60 Ponteland Road, Cowgate, Newcastle upon Tyne NE3 3JW (0191-286 9998). *Location:* two miles west of city centre in direction of airport. Moorland. 18 holes, 6617 yards, 6048 metres. S.S.S. 72. Practice area. *Green Fees:* information not available. *Eating facilities:* bar meals available.

Visitors: no restrictions midweek, welcome weekends if no competitions. Book through the golf shop or see our website. *Society Meetings:* welcome, book through Secretary. Golf Shop: (0191-286 9998). Secretary: S. Darbyshire.*
website: www.nugc.co.uk

NEWCASTLE UPON TYNE. **The Northumberland Golf Club Ltd,** High Gosforth Park, Newcastle upon Tyne NE3 5HT (0191-236 2498). *Location:* off A1. 18 holes, 6680 yards. S.S.S. 72. *Green Fees:* £40.00 per round weekdays, £50.00 weekends. *Visitors:* club members are most welcome but should contact Secretary to avoid disappointment. *Society Meetings:* small groups can now be catered for on Mondays and at weekends. Secretary: Jamie Forteath (0191-236 2498; Fax: 0191-236 2036).
e-mail: sec@thengc.co.uk
website: www.thengc.co.uk

NEWCASTLE UPON TYNE. **Parklands Golf Club,** High Gosforth Park, Newcastle upon Tyne NE3 5HQ (0191-236 4480). *Location:* three miles north of centre of Newcastle, off the A1 follow signs for Gosforth Park. Parkland. 18 holes, 6013 yards, 5742 metres. S.S.S. 69. 18 hole mini golf course, 28 bay floodlit driving range. *Green Fees:* weekdays £20.00; weekends £25.00. *Eating facilities:* restaurant and bar. *Visitors:* welcome, no restrictions. *Society Meetings:* catered for. Complex Manager: David King (0191-236 3322). Secretary: Geoff Brown (0191-236 4480).

NEWCASTLE UPON TYNE. **Tyneside Golf Club Ltd,** Westfield Lane, Ryton NE40 3QE (0191-413 2742; Fax: 0191-413 0199). *Location:* seven miles west of Newcastle upon Tyne, off B6317 in Ryton Village. Parkland, hilly with water hazards. Large practice area. 18 holes, 6009 yards, 5477 metres. S.S.S. 69. Practice field. *Green Fees:* weekdays £25.00; weekends negotiable. *Eating facilities:* full catering. *Visitors:* bona fide golfers welcome by arrangement with the Secretary. *Society Meetings:* weekdays by arrangement with Secretary; possibly Sunday afternoons. Professional: Geoff Dixon (0191-413 1600). Secretary: Ed Stephenson (0191-413 2742).

NEWCASTLE UPON TYNE. **Westerhope Golf Club,** Whorlton Grange, Westerhope, Newcastle-upon-Tyne NE5 1PP (0191-286 9125). *Location:* Stamfordham Road, Westerhope, near Jingling Gate Public House. Parkland/wooded. 18 holes, 6444 yards. S.S.S. 71. Two practice areas. *Green Fees:* £26.00 per round. *Eating facilities:* lunches and high teas. *Visitors:* welcome weekdays, weekends and Bank Holidays with a member only. *Society Meetings:* welcome weekdays. Professional: M. Nesbit (0191-286 0594). Secretary: B. Bell (0191-286 7636).

COTTINGHAM. **Hessle Golf Club,** Westfield Road, Raywell, Cottingham HU16 5YL (01482 306844). *Location:* three miles south west of Cottingham. Parkland. 18 holes, 6608 yards, S.S.S. 72. Two practice areas. *Green Fees:* (2007 rates) weekdays £28.00 per round, £38.00 per day; weekends £40.00 per round. *Eating facilities:* snack lunches Tuesday to Sunday, set lunches by arrangement. *Visitors:* mid-week unrestricted except Tuesdays 9am - 1pm. Weekend visitors may play after 12.00 noon at Professional's discretion. *Society Meetings:* catered for weekdays and weekends after 1.30pm only by arrangement. Professional: G. Fieldsend (01482 306842). Secretary: Derrick Pettit (01482 306840; Fax: 01482 652679).

DRIFFIELD. **Driffield Golf Club,** Sunderlandwick, Beverley Road, Driffield YO25 9AD (01377 253116; Fax: 01377 240599). *Location:* from Driffield A164 to Beverley 300 yards from main roundabout on right. Mature parkland course within the attractive Sunderlandwick Estate. 18 holes, 6215 yards. S.S.S. 70. Two practice areas, practice green and two practice putting greens. *Green Fees:* Summer (1st April to 31st October): weekdays £26.00 per round, £35.00 per day; weekends £35.00 per round, £45.00 per day. Winter: weekdays £18.00 per round, weekends £24.00 per round. *Eating facilities:* full catering and bar service. *Visitors:* welcome by arrangement with the manager. Limited numbers on weekends and Bank Holidays,18 holes only. *Society Meetings:* welcome by prior arrangement. Professional: Kenton Wright (01377 241224). Manager: Simon Collingwood.

HORNSEA. **Hainsworth Park Golf Club,** Brandesburton, Near Driffield YO25 8RT (01964 542362). *Location:* eight miles north east of Beverley, just off A165 road to Bridlington, at the Brandesburton roundabout. Easy going, well drained parkland course with mature trees. 18 holes, 6362 yards. S.S.S. 71, Par 71. Practice area. *Green Fees:* weekdays £20.00 - £24.00; weekends £24.00 - £29.00, subject to confirmation. *Eating facilities:* bar and full catering. *Visitors:* welcome anytime, please phone. Hotel accommodation. *Society Meetings:* welcome. Professional: P. Myers (01964 542362). Secretary: R. Hounsfield (01964 542362).

HORNSEA. **Hornsea Golf Club,** Rolston Road, Hornsea HU18 1XG (Tel & Fax: 01964 532020). *Location:* follow signs for Hornsea Freeport – Golf Course 200 yards past Freeport. Flat parkland. 18 holes, 6661 yards. S.S.S. 72. Practice area. *Green*

Fees: £30.00 per round, £36.00 per day. *Eating facilities:* available every day. *Visitors:* welcome, please ring Professional for a time. Ladies' Day Tuesdays. Snooker room. *Society Meetings:* welcome by prior arrangement with the Secretary. Professional: S. Wright (01964 534989). Secretary: Mr Geoff Drewery (Tel & Fax: 01964 532020). e-mail: hornseagolfclub@aol.com website: www.hornseagolfclub.co.uk

HOWDEN. **Boothferry Golf Club,** Spaldington Lane, Howden, Near Goole DN14 7NG (01430 430364). *Location:* two and a half miles from Junction 37 of the M62 on the B1228 road between Howden and Bubwith. Flat meadowland, with natural dykes and ponds. 18 holes, 6651 yards. S.S.S. 72. Large practice area. *Green Fees:* weekdays £16.00, weekends £20.00. *Eating facilities:* restaurant and bar facilities available. *Visitors:* welcome at all times. No jeans, trainers or collarless shirts. *Society Meetings:* all Golf Societies and individual parties receive group discounts and are welcome with prior booking through the Professional. Professional: Matthew Rumble (01430 430364; Fax: 01430 430567).

HULL. **Cottingham Parks Golf & Country Club,** Woodhill Way, Cottingham HU16 5RZ (01482 846030; Fax: 01482 845932). *Location:* from the Humber Bridge to Beverley road, take the B1233 turnoff at the Skidby roundabout to Cottingham Golf Club turnoff. Mature parkland with several water hazards. 18 holes, 6459 yards. S.S.S. 71. Two tier driving range. *Green Fees:* weekdays £20.00 (with introduction £14.00); weekends £30.00 (with introduction £20.00). *Eating facilities:* bar snacks and full dining room menu available. *Visitors:* welcome. *Society Meetings:* welcome with restrictions at weekends. Special packages available. Conference and social functions catered for; full leisure facilities including gym, 20 metre pool, steam room and jacuzzi. Professional: Chris Gray (01482 842394). Administrative Office: 01482 846030; Fax: 01482 845932. website: www.cottinghamparks.co.uk

HULL. **Hull Golf Club (1921) Ltd,** The Hall, 27 Packman Lane, Kirk Ella, Hull HU10 7TJ. *Location:* five miles west of Hull. Parkland and wooded. 18 holes, 6262 yards. S.S.S. 70. *Green Fees:* £27.50 per round, £35.00 per day. *Eating facilities:* available. *Visitors:* welcome weekdays except Wednesday. *Society Meetings:* by prior arrangement. Professional: David Jagger (01482 653074). General Manager: David Crossley (Tel & Fax: 01482 658919). website: www.hullgolfclub.com

HULL. **Springhead Park Golf Club,** Willerby Road, Hull HU5 5JE (01482 614968 - Ticket Office). *Location:* off the M62/M18 onto the A63. Parkland surrounded by many trees, some undulating fairways, three ponds and many ditches around course. 18 holes, 6102 yards, 5680 metres. S.S.S. 71. Two practice areas. *Green Fees:* £13.00 per day. *Eating facilities:* mobile sandwich bar on course, restaurant and basket meals for club members and societies. *Visitors:* welcome. Tuition and club hire available. *Society Meetings:* welcome. Secretary: Mr P. Smith (01482 654334 - Home, or phone clubhouse number 01482 656309).

HULL. **Sutton Park Golf Club,** Saltshouse Road, Hull HU8 9HF (01482 374242). *Location:* A63, north ring road, Sutton Road, Leads Road, Robson Way. Flat parkland course. 18 holes, 6251 yards. S.S.S. 70. Practice area and nearby driving range. *Green Fees:* information not available. *Eating facilities:* restaurant/bar. *Visitors:* welcome, no restrictions. *Society Meetings:* welcome, bookings via Secretary. Professional: To be appointed. Secretary: Philip Webster (Tel & Fax: 01482 701428).*

www.uk-golfguide.com

KILNWICK PERCY. **Kilnwick Percy Golf Club,** Kilnwick Percy, Pocklington YO42 1UF (01759 303090). *Location:* one mile east of Pocklington off B1246. Scenic, undulating parkland course on the edge of the wolds above Pocklington. New clubhouse opening in October 2007. Major course improvements including added drainage, new and refurbished bunkers. 18 individually designed holes, 6218 yards. S.S.S. 70. *Green Fees:* weekdays £20.00 per round, £30.00 per day; weekends and Bank Holidays £25.00 per round, £35.00 per day. *Eating facilities:* bar snacks available all day; evening meals by prior arrangement for 10 or more golfers. *Visitors:* welcome. Buggy, trolley and club hire; professional tuition available. Accommodation locally at discounted rates for golf club visitors. *Society Meetings:* special packages, tailored to your requirements. Manager: Jonathan Dixon (01759 303090).

WITHERNSEA. **Withernsea Golf Club,** Chestnut Avenue, Withernsea HU19 2PG (01964 612078 or 612258). *Location:* 25 miles north-east of Hull on main road into Withernsea (signposted). Flat course. 9 holes, 6207 yards. S.S.S. 70. *Green Fees:* £15.00 per 18 hole round. *Eating facilities:* bar and meals available (except Monday). *Visitors:* welcome weekdays, weekends after 1.00pm Sunday. *Society Meetings:* by arrangement. Special rates available. Administrator: John Boasman (01964 612078). e-mail: golf@withernseagolfclub.fsnet.co.uk

North Yorkshire

ALDWARK. **Aldwark Manor Golf Club,** Aldwark, Alne, York YO61 1UF (01347 838353; Fax: 01347 833991). *Location:* in village of Aldwark, five miles south-east of Boroughbridge off A1 and12 miles north-west of York off A19. Easy walking parkland with water hazards. 18 holes, 6187 yards. S.S.S. 70. Practice ground, putting green, practice bunker. *Green Fees:* weekdays £35.00 per round, weekends and Bank Holidays £40.00. *Eating facilities:* two restaurants and two bars. *Visitors:* always welcome weekdays, restricted weekends. 60 bedroomed hotel on the course. *Society Meetings:* societies and corporate meetings always welcome, restricted weekends. PGA Professional Alastair Grindlay (01347 838353; Fax: 01347 833991).

BARNOLDSWICK. **Ghyll Golf Club,** Ghyll Brow, Barnoldswick, Colne, Lancs BB8 6JH (01282 842466). *Location:* M65 to Colne. A56 towards Skipton. 1 mile past Earby B6252 to Barnoldswick. Parkland course. 9 holes, 5706 yards, 5213 metres. S.S.S. 68. *Green Fees:* weekdays £15.00 per day (£10.00 with a member), weekends £20.00 per day (£15 with a member). *Eating facilities:* bar, evening only. *Visitors:* welcome except Sundays and some Saturdays. *Society Meetings:* catered for by arrangement. Secretary: John L. Gill (01524 412958).

BEDALE. **Bedale Golf Club,** Leyburn Road, Bedale DL8 1EZ. *Location:* from A1 take A684 at Leeming Bar to Bedale; club is situated 400 yards out of town on the Leyburn Road. Undulating parkland with tree-lined fairways and water hazards. 18 holes, 6610 yards. S.S.S. 72. Practice facilities, fully stocked golf shop, lessons available. *Green Fees:* weekdays 18 holes £27.00, 27 holes £33.00; weekends 18 holes £36.00, 27 holes £41.00 (subject to review). *Eating facilities:* bar and catering always available. *Visitors:* welcome weekdays and weekends. *Society Meetings:* catered for weekdays by prior arrangement, limited availability on some Saturday afternoons; tailor-made packages and discounts available. Professional: Tony Johnson (01677 422443). Manager: Kevin Rhodes (01677 422451; Fax: 01677 427143).
e-mail: bedalegolfclub@aol.com
website: www.bedalegolfclub.com

BENTHAM. **Bentham Golf Club,** Robin Lane, Bentham, Near Lancaster LA2 7AG (01524 262455). *Location:* B6480 north-east of Lancaster towards Settle. Parkland with magnificent views. 18 holes, 6075 yards. *Green Fees:* £30.00. *Eating facilities:* hot and cold snacks and meals available. *Visitors:* welcome all week. *Society Meetings:* welcome–contact Secretary. Secretary: John Mann (01524 262470).

BROTTON. **Hunley Hall Golf Club & Hotel,** Brotton, Saltburn TS12 2QQ (01287 676216; Fax: 01287 678250). *Location:* off A174 at St. Margarets Way in Brotton. Signposted through housing estate, approximately half-a-mile to club. Picturesque 27 hole coastal courses adjacent to Heritage Coast. Morgan's Course 18 holes, 6918 yards, 6320 metres. S.S.S. 73. Millennium Course, 18 holes, 6510 yards, S.S.S. 68. Floodlit driving range, large practice and chipping area. *Green Fees:* weekdays £25.00 per day, weekends and Bank Holidays £35.00 per day. Discounts for parties and guests staying at the hotel. *Eating facilities:* excellent facilities including two restaurants, lounge bar, spike bar, golfers' bar; quality food served daily 8am to 9.30pm. *Visitors:* always welcome. Three Star Hotel offering en suite rooms, etc. Club hire, buggy hire and tuition available. *Society Meetings:* welcome Monday to Saturday, packages available. Golfing Holidays and golf schools available. Professional: Andrew Brook (Tel & Fax: 01287 677444). Secretary: Liz Lillie (01287 676216; Fax: 01287 678250).
e-mail: reservations@hunleyhall.co.uk
website: www.hunleyhall.co.uk

CATTERICK. **Catterick Golf Club,** Leyburn Road, Catterick Garrison, Catterick DL9 3QE (01748 833268). *Location:* six miles south-west Scotch Corner, A1 turn off to Catterick Garrison. Undulating parkland/ moorland with spectacular views. 18 holes, 6329 yards, S.S.S. 71. Practice ground. *Green Fees:* information not available. E*ating facilities:* bar and restaurant. *Visitors:* welcome without reservation. *Society Meetings:* catered for by appointment only. Professional: Andy Marshall (01748 833671). Secretary: Mairi Young (Tel & Fax: 01748 833268).

EASINGWOLD. **Easingwold Golf Club,** Stillington Road, Easingwold, York YO61 3ET (01347 821486; Fax: 01347 822474). *Location:* 12 miles north of York, course one mile along Stillington Road. Flat, wooded parkland established 1930. 18 holes, 6717 yards, 6142 metres, S.S.S. 73. Practice ground. *Green Fees:* weekdays £28.00 per round, £35.00 per day; weekends and Bank Holidays £35.00., with a member £17.00; £15.00 1st November to 31st March. *Eating facilities:* available. *Visitors:* welcome weekdays only, prior booking essential, contact Secretary. *Society Meetings:* weekdays only, prior booking essential, contact Secretary. Professional: John Hughes (01347 821964). Secretary: D.B. Stockley (Tel & Fax: 01347 822474). e-mail: brian@easingwold-golf-club.fsnet.co.uk website: www.easingwold-golf-club.co.uk

FILEY. **Filey Golf Club, The Clubhouse,** West Avenue, Filey YO14 9BQ (01723 513293; Fax: 01723 514952). *Location:* one mile south of town centre. Links, parkland course. 18 holes, 6112 yards. S.S.S. 69. 9 holes, 1570 yards. Par 30. Two practice grounds. *Green Fees:* information not available. *Eating facilities:* full dining and bar facilities. Visitors: welcome, no restrictions. *Society Meetings:* welcome by arrangement with the Secretary. Professional: Darren Squire (01723 513134). Secretary: Davina Willis (01723 513293; Fax: 01723 514952). website: www.fileygolfclub.com

HARROGATE. **Crimple Valley Golf Club,** Hookstone Wood Road, Harrogate HG2 8PN (01423 883485; Fax: 01423 881018). *Location:* one mile south from town centre. Turn off A61 at Nidd Vale Garage on to Hookstone Road, signposted to right. Gently sloping fairways in rural setting. 9 holes, 2500 yards. S.S.S. 33. *Green Fees:* Information not available. *Eating facilities:* licensed bar, no eating facilities Monday or Sunday; breakfasts available Tuesday to Sunday. *Visitors:* welcome at all times. *Society Meetings:* special rates available. Club Proprietor: Kate Johnson.*

HARROGATE. **Harrogate Golf Club Ltd,** Forest Lane Head, Harrogate HG2 7TF (01423 863158). *Location:* nine miles from Harrogate on the A59 Harrogate/Knaresborough Road. Parkland, wooded. 18 holes, 6241 yards, 5706 metres. S.S.S. 70. Large practice ground, covered net. *Green Fees:* weekdays £35.00 per round, £40.00 per day, weekends £45.00 per round/per day. *Eating facilities:* chef catering and bar menu, lounge and casual spike bars. *Visitors:* welcome subject to club events. *Society Meetings:* catered for weekdays except Tuesdays. Parties of 12 or more welcome. Professionals: G. Stothard/ S. Everson (01423 862547). Secretary: Peter Banks (01423 862999). Caterer: (01423 860278). e-mail: secretary@harrogate-gc.co.uk website: www.harrogate-gc.co.uk

HARROGATE. **Oakdale Golf Club,** Oakdale Glen, Harrogate HG1 2LN (01423 567162). *Location:* five minutes from Harrogate town centre, off Ripon road into Kent Road, follow signs. Parkland, with featured stream. 18 holes, 6456 yards. S.S.S. 71. Practice ground. *Green Fees:* weekdays £39.00 per round, £45.00 per day; weekends £55.00 per round. *Eating facilities:* first class restaurant, bar. *Visitors:* welcome at all times, Tuesday Ladies' Day. *Society Meetings:* welcome weekdays by arrangement. Professional: Clive Dell (01423 560510). Secretary: (01423 567162; Fax: 01423 536030).

HARROGATE. **Pannal Golf Club,** Follifoot Road, Pannal, Harrogate HG3 1ES (01423 872628; Fax: 01423 870043). *Location*: two miles south of Harrogate A61 (Leeds Road). 18 holes, 6622 yards. S.S.S. 72. Large practice ground with driving range facility. *Green Fees*: weekdays £45.00 per round, £55.00 per day; weekends and Bank Holidays £60.00 per round (under review). *Eating facilities*: lunch available daily, dinner by arrangement. *Visitors:* welcome Monday to Friday, enquiry advised. *Society Meetings*: catered for Monday, Tuesday (pm only), Wednesday, Thursday and Friday. Professional: D. Padgett (01423 872628). Secretary: N.G. Douglas (01423 872628; Fax: 01423 870043). e-mail: secretary@pannalgc.co.uk website: www.pannalgc.co.uk

THE APPEARANCE OF AN ASTERISK (*) AT THE END OF A CLUB OR COURSE ENTRY INDICATES THAT UP-TO-DATE INFORMATION HAS NOT BEEN SUPPLIED

HARROGATE. **Rudding Park Golf,** Harrogate HG3 1JH (01423 872100; Fax: 01423 873011). *Location*: lies just off the A658 linking the A61 from Leeds to the A59 York Road. Parkland course designed to USGA specifications. 18 holes, 6883 yards, Par 72. Six hole Par 3 short course opens April 2008. 18 bay floodlit driving range with four Professionals. *Green Fees:* Winter (November 1st until March 31st: Mondays to Thursdays £23.00, Fridays to Sundays £27.00. Summer (April 1st until October 31st): Mondays to Thursdays £35.00, Fridays to Sundays £39.50. *Eating facilities*: clubhouse bar open all day, every day. *Visitors*: welcome at all times, must have a Handicap Certificate. Shop and buggies available all year round, with all-year-weather buggy tracks; caddies on request. Hotel on site with 4 Red Stars and AA 2 Rosette restaurant. *Society Meetings*: society and corporate days welcome. Professional: Mark Moore (01423 873400).
e-mail: golf.admin@ruddingpark.com
website: www.ruddingpark.com

KIRKBYMOORSIDE. **Kirkbymoorside Golf Club,** Manor Vale, Kirkbymoorside, York YO62 6EG (01751 431525). *Location:* on A170 through Kirkbymoorside. Undulating parkland. 18 holes, 6207 yards, 5676 metres. S.S.S. 69. Practice area, putting green. *Green Fees:* weekdays £22.00 per round, £28.00 per day; weekends and Bank Holidays £32.00 . Reduced fees in winter. *Eating facilities:* available every day. *Visitors:* welcome after 9am, not during weekend

Medal competitions. *Society Meetings:* catered for by arrangement with Rose Rivis, Club Administrator. Professional: J. Hinchliffe (01751 430402).

KNARESBOROUGH. **Knaresborough Golf Club,** Boroughbridge Road, Knaresborough HG5 0QQ (01423 863219). *Location:* one-and-a-half miles from town centre, direction A1 Boroughbridge. Wooded parkland. 18 holes, 6780 yards. Par 72. Large practice area. *Green Fees:* 2007 under review. Please contact Secretary for further details. *Eating facilities:* full catering. *Visitors:* welcome but not before 9.30am weekdays and 2pm weekends and Bank Holidays. *Society Meetings:* welcome by prior arrangement. Professional: Darren Tear (01423 864865). Secretary: C. Hill. (01423 862690).

MALTON. **Malton and Norton Golf Club,** Welham Park, Malton YO17 9QE (01653 697912). *Location:* off A64 to Malton between York and Scarborough. One mile south on Welham road turn right at Norton level crossing. 27 holes – Longest 18: 6488 yards. S.S.S. 71. Medal Course: 6147 yards. S.S.S. 69 (Club). *Green Fees:* weekdays £27.00; weekends and Bank Holidays £32.00. *Eating facilities:* full bar and catering available. *Visitors:* welcome without reservation except club match days, and Saturdays unless with member. *Society Meetings:* catered for by arrangement with Secretary. Professional: S. Robinson (01653 693882). Secretary: L. Gurnell (01653 697912).
e-mail: maltonandnorton@btconnect.com

MIDDLESBROUGH. **Middlesbrough Golf Club,** Brass Castle Lane, Marton, Middlesbrough TS8 9EE (01642 311515; Fax: 01642 319607). *Location:* five miles south of Middlesbrough west of the A172. Parkland course. 18 holes, 6255 yards. S.S.S./Par 70. Practice facilities available. *Green Fees:* weekdays £18.00/£37.00 per day; weekends £22.00/£42.00 per day. *Eating facilities:* lunches, teas and dinners. *Visitors:* welcome when tee not booked. Venue of the North of England Open Amateur Youth Golf Championship. Conference facilities. *Society Meetings:* welcome Mondays, Wednesdays, Thursdays and Fridays. Professional: Don Jones (01642 311766). Secretary: P. M. Jackson (01642 311515).

MIDDLESBROUGH. **Middlesbrough Municipal Golf Centre,** Ladgate Lane, Middlesbrough TS5 7YZ (01642 315533; Fax: 01642 300726). *Location:* three miles south of Middlesbrough on A174. Parkland course with featured streams. 18 holes, 6333 yards. S.S.S. 71. Floodlit driving range, practice area and putting green. *Green Fees:* Information not available. *Eating facilities:* lunches available seven days, snacks at all other times. *Visitors:* welcome anytime, but starting times must be booked in advance through Manager. *Society Meetings:* must be booked through Manager, special golf packages available. Professional: Alan Hope (01642 300720). Manager: M. Gormley (01642 315533). Hon. Secretary: J. Brannagan (01642 886706).*

NORTHALLERTON. **Romanby Golf Course,** Yafforth Road, Northallerton DL7 0PE. *Location:* west of Northallerton on the B6271 Richmond Road. Parkland course with formidable "Great Lake Complex" on the 2nd, 11th and 12th. 18 holes, 6663 yards. 12 bay floodlit driving range. *Green Fees:* information not available. *Visitors:* always welcome, best to telephone for tee times. *Society Meetings:* golf parties a speciality. Bookings telephone (01609 778855; Fax: 01609 779084).*
e-mail: mark@romanby.com
website: www.romanbygolf.com

REDCAR. **Cleveland Golf Club,** Majuba Road, Redcar TS10 5BJ. *Location:* on entering town via A1042 or A1085 follow signs to Esplanade, course runs adjacent to beach on north side of town. Flat seaside links course, easy walking. Championship course: 18 holes, 6696 yards. S.S.S. 72. Oldest golf course in Yorkshire, founded 1887. *Green Fees:* information not available. *Eating facilities:* full catering at all times. *Visitors:* welcome anytime subject to availability. *Society Meetings:* welcome by prior arrangement, special rates available. Professional: Craig Donaldson (01642 483462). Secretary: W. E. Pattison (Tel & Fax: 01642 471798)*
e-mail: secretary@clevelandgolfclub.co.uk
website: www.clevelandgolfclub.co.uk

REDCAR. **Wilton Golf Club,** Wilton, Redcar TS10 4QY (01642 465265). *Location:* eight miles east of Middlesbrough (A174), four miles west of Redcar. Parkland course, partly wooded. 18 holes, 6276 yards. S.S.S. 69. Small practice area. *Green Fees:* weekdays £26.00 per day; Sundays and Bank Holidays £32.00 per day. *Eating facilities:* lunches, including Sundays; evening meals by arrangement, lounge bar and 19th bar. *Visitors:* welcome except Saturdays; weekdays and Sundays not before 10am. Tuesdays ladies playing in competitions have priority on 1st tee. *Society Meetings:* welcome by arrangement, except Saturdays. Please contact the Club Secretary. Special rates for parties over 20. Professional: Miss P.D. Smillie (01642 452730). Secretary: Ray Douglas (01642 465265).
e-mail: secretary@wiltongolfclub.co.uk
website: www.wiltongolfclub.co.uk

RICHMOND. **Richmond (Yorkshire) Golf Club,** Bend Hagg, Richmond DL10 5EX (01748 825319). *Location:* Scotch Corner (A1). Wooded, parkland, some hills. 18 holes, 6073 yards. S.S.S. 69. Par 71. *Green Fees:* midweek £30.00 per day, £23.00 per round; weekends £35.00 per day, £28.00 per round. *Eating facilities:* bar and catering. *Visitors:* welcome but not before 3.30pm Sundays. Pro Shop. *Society Meetings:* catered for, book with Professional. Professional: James Cousins (01748 822457). Secretary: Mrs A. Lancaster (01748 823231).

RIPON. **Masham Golf Club,** Burnholme, Swinton Road, Masham, Ripon HG4 4HT (01765 689379). *Location:* nine miles north of Ripon just off A6108. Parkland, River Burn flows through course and is featured in several holes. 9 holes, 6068 yards. S.S.S. 69. *Green Fees:* 18 holes £17.00, £20.00 per day. (under review). *Eating facilities:* mainly midday catering, bar all day. *Visitors:* welcome Mon-Fri, not weekends or Bank Holidays. *Society Meetings:* by arrangement with Secretary. Office: 01765 688054

RIPON. **Ripon City Golf Club,** Palace Road, Ripon HG4 3HH (01765 603640). *Location:* one mile north of Ripon on A6108 (Masham). Undulating parkland with magnificent views over Ure Valley, city of Ripon, Hambleton Hills. 18 holes, 6084 yards. S.S.S. White 69, Yellow 68. Nearby golf range. *Green Fees:* information not available. *Eating facilities:* available every day. *Visitors:* welcome (not Saturdays). *Society Meetings:* welcome. Professional: S.T. Davis (01765 600411). Secretary: M.J. Doig MBE (01765 603640).
e-mail: secretary@riponcitygolfclub.com
website: www.riponcitygolfclub.com

www.uk-golfguide.com

THE APPEARANCE OF AN ASTERISK (*) AT THE END OF A CLUB OR COURSE ENTRY INDICATES THAT UP-TO-DATE INFORMATION HAS NOT BEEN SUPPLIED

SALTBURN BY THE SEA. **Saltburn by the Sea Golf Club Ltd,** Hob Hill, Saltburn by the Sea TS12 1NJ (01287 622812). *Location:* east on A174, right at Quarry Lane roundabout, left at traffic lights; club one mile on right. Parkland course. 18 holes, 5846 yards. S.S.S. 68. *Green Fees:* information not available. *Eating facilities:* available. *Visitors:* welcome, limited Sundays and Thursdays and no visitors Saturdays. *Society Meetings:* catered for by arrangement. Professional: (01287 624653). Secretary: Mike Murtha (01287 622812).
e-mail: info@saltburngolf.co.uk
website: www.saltburngolf.co.uk

SCARBOROUGH. **Ganton Golf Club Ltd,** Ganton, Near Scarborough YO12 4PA (01944 710329; Fax: 01944 710922). *Location:* on A64, nine miles west of Scarborough. Heathland/links Championship course, host to Ryder Cup (1949), Walker Cup (2003), Curtis Cup (2000). 18 holes, 6734 yards. S.S.S. 73. *Green Fees:* weekdays £73.00 per round or day; weekends and Bank Holidays £83.00 per round or day. 2007 rates, subject to review. *Eating facilities:* available. *Visitors:* welcome by prior arrangement. *Society Meetings:* catered for with reservation. Professional: Gary Brown. Secretary: Major R.G. Woolsey (01944 710329).
e-mail: secretary@gantongolfclub.com
website: www.gantongolfclub.com

SCARBOROUGH. **Scarborough North Cliff Golf Club,** North Cliff Avenue, Scarborough YO12 6PP (01723 355397; Fax: 01723 362134). *Location:* two miles north of Scarborough on coastal road to Whitby. Mainly parkland course with a cliff top start and finish; views of North Bay and Castle. 18 holes, 6425 yards. S.S.S. 71. Practice ground, chipping green, putting green. *Green Fees:* on application. *Eating facilities:* available. *Visitors:* welcome (restrictions on competition days, not allowed Sundays before 10.30am.). Must be members of golf club. Electric trolleys, carts available. *Society Meetings:* catered for, parties from 8 to 40. Prior booking through Secretary. Professional: S.N. Deller (01723 365920). Secretary: Mrs J H Lloyd (01723 355397).
e-mail: info@northcliffgolfclub.co.uk

SCARBOROUGH. **Scarborough South Cliff Golf Club Ltd,** Deepdale Avenue, Scarborough YO11 2UE (01723 360522). *Location:* one mile south of Scarborough off Filey road. Parkland and clifftop with panoramic sea views. 18 holes, 6432 yards. S.S.S. 71 (white tees), 69 (yellow tees). Practice ground. *Green Fees:* £35.00 Monday to Thursday, £40.00 Friday to Sunday. *Eating facilities:* dining room, bar; full catering facilities. *Visitors:* welcome when course available. *Society Meetings:* catered for by prior arrangement. Professional: T. Skingle (01723 365150). Secretary: David Roberts (Tel & Fax: 01723 374737).

SELBY. **Selby Golf Club,** Mill Lane, Brayton Barff, Selby YO8 9LD (01757 228622). *Location:* off A64 Selby bypass. Links-type course, very well drained. 18 holes, 6374 yards. S.S.S. 71. *Green Fees:* information not available. *Eating facilities:* restaurant and bar. *Visitors:* welcome weekdays. Snooker tables. *Society Meetings:* welcome Wednesday to Friday. Professional: Nick Ludwell (01757 228785). Secretary: Neil Proctor.*

SETTLE. **Settle Golf Club,** Buck Haw Brow, Giggleswick, Settle BD24 0DH (Tel & Fax: 01729 825288). *Location:* one mile north of Settle on B6480. Moorland. 9 holes, 6200 yards. S.S.S. 72. *Green Fees:* Information not available. *Eating facilities:* bar only on Sundays. *Visitors:* welcome, restrictions Sundays. *Society Meetings:* welcome with prior notice. Secretary: J. Ketchell (01729 841140).*

SKIPTON. **Skipton Golf Club Ltd,** Short Lee Lane, Skipton BD23 3LF (01756 793922). *Location:* one and a half miles northwest of Skipton town centre on A65. Undulating, with panoramic views, some water hazards. 18 holes, 6090 yards. S.S.S. 69. Practice ground. *Green Fees:* weekdays £26.00; weekends £30.00. *Eating facilities:* full bar and catering daily. *Visitors:* welcome at all times, some restrictions weekends and Tuesdays. *Society Meetings:* welcome by prior arrangement. Special package rates. Professional: P. Robinson (01756 793257). Business Manager: Karen Chapman (01756 795657; Fax: 01756 796665).

Visit the FHG website
www.holidayguides.com
for details of the wide choice of accommodation featured
in the full range of FHG titles

STOCKTON-ON-TEES. **Teesside Golf Club,** Acklam Road, Thornaby, Stockton-on-Tees TS17 7JS (01642 676249; Fax: 01642 676252). *Location*: A19 - A1130 to Thornaby, 0.7 miles on right hand side. Flat parkland. 18 holes, 6535 yards. S.S.S. 71. Practice ground, putting green. *Green Fees:* information not available. *Eating facilities:* catering except Mondays, bar 11am to 11pm. *Visitors:* welcome midweek up to 4.30pm, weekends after 11am by arrangement. *Society Meetings:* Monday - Friday. Special rates and conditions for parties and guests. Professional: K.W. Hall (01642 673822). Secretary: M. Fleming (01642 616516).*
e-mail: teessidegolfclub@btconnect.com
website: www.teessidegolfclub.com

TADCASTER. **Scarthingwell Golf Course,** Scarthingwell. Tadcaster LS24 9PF (01937 557878; Fax: 01937 557909). *Location*: 4 miles south of Tadcaster on the A162 Tadcaster/Ferrybridge Road approximately 3 miles from A1. Parkland Course. 18 holes, 6642 yards. S.S.S.72. *Green Fees*: information not provided. *Eating facilities*: licensed clubhouse facilities and snooker table, restaurant. *Visitors*: welcome every day except before 2pm on Saturdays. *Society Meetings*: welcome, packages and special rates available. Professional: Simon Danby (01937 557864). Secretary: Kathryn Pick (01937 557878).
website: www.scarthingwellgolfcourse.co.uk

THIRSK. **Thirsk and Northallerton Golf Club,** Thornton-le-Street, Thirsk YO7 4AB (01845 522170). *Location:* on Northallerton Road (A168), two miles from Thirsk. Flat parkland with excellent views of Hambleton Hills. 18 holes, 6495 yards. S.S.S. 71. Practice ground. *Green Fees:* on application. *Eating facilities:* catering and bar. *Visitors:* welcome, phone before arrival. Trolleys, buggies for hire. *Society Meetings:* welcome. Handicaps required. Professional: Robert Garner (01845 526216). Manager: S. C. Owram (01845 525115).
e-mail: secretary@tngc.co.uk
website: www.tngc.co.uk

WHITBY. **Whitby Golf Club,** Sandsend Road, Low Straggleton, Whitby YO21 3SR (Tel & Fax: 01947 600660). *Location:* on the A174, one mile from Whitby. Picturesque coastal course on cliff tops,

three holes over ravines. 18 holes, 6003 yards. S.S.S. 69. *Green Fees:* £32.00 weekends, £26.00 midweek. *Eating facilities:* dining room and bar. *Visitors:* welcome, parties by prior reservation. *Society Meetings:* catered for by prior arrangement. Professional: Tony Mason (01947 602719). Office: (Tel & Fax: 01947 600660).

YORK. **Forest of Galtres Golf Club,** Moorlands Road, Skelton, York YO32 2RF (01904 766198; Fax: 01904 769400). *Location:* two miles from the northern section of the ring road around the historic city of York. Parkland course, designed by Simon Gidman. 18 holes, 6534 yards. S.S.S. 71. Covered driving range and practice ground. *Green Fees:* weekdays £25.00 per round, £30.00 all day; weekends and Bank Holidays £30.00 per round, £40.00 all day. Midweek Specials starting from £30.00 including food. Sunday Specials after 12 noon from £40.00. *Eating facilities:* full facilities available. *Visitors:* welcome any day. *Society Meetings:* welcome but must be pre-booked with Secretary, No Societies on Saturdays. Professional: Phil Bradley PGA (Tel & Fax: 01904 766198). Secretary: Mrs Sue Procter (Tel & Fax: 01904 769400).
e-mail: secretary@forestofgaltres.co.uk
website: www.forestofgaltres.co.uk

YORK. **Forest Park Golf Club,** Stockton on Forest, York YO32 9UW (01904 400425). *Location:* one and a half miles from east end of York bypass, follow signs for Stockton on Forest. Flat parkland course with trees and stream running through. 18 holes, 6673 yards. S.S.S. 71; 9 holes, 3186 yards. S.S.S 70 (twice round). Open air driving range and 8 bay driving range, practice area. *Green Fees:* weekdays £10.00 for 9 holes, £25.00 per round, £32.00 per day; weekends £12.00 for 9 holes, £30.00 per round, £40.00 per day. Subject to annual review. Special party and package rates; quotation on request. *Eating facilities:* full bar and golf club catering facilities. *Visitors:* welcome mid week, limited availability weekends. *Society Meetings:* welcome by prior arrangement. Professional: Mark Winterburn (01904 400425). Secretary: Sally Crossley (01904 400688).
e-mail: admin@forestparkgolfclub.co.uk
website: www.forestparkgolfclub.co.uk

YORK. **Fulford (York) Golf Club Ltd,** Heslington Lane, York YO10 5DY *Location:* A19 (Selby) from city, turn left to Heslington (signposted to University). Heathland. 18 holes, 6775 yards. S.S.S. 72. Practice ground. *Green Fees:* weekdays from £42.50 per round, £65.00 per day; weekends £65.00. *Eating facilities:* lounge, diningroom and bar. *Visitors:* welcome Monday to Friday, prior reservation recommended. Snooker table. *Society Meetings:* Monday to Friday by arrangement with Manager. Professional: Guy Wills (01904 412882). General Manager: Gary Pearce (01904 413579; Fax: 01904 416918).
e-mail: info@fulfordgolfclub.co.uk
website: www.fulfordgolfclub.co.uk

YORK. **Heworth Golf Club,** Muncaster House, Muncastergate, York YO31 9JY (01904 426156). *Location:* one and a half miles east of City Centre on A1036 Malton/Scarborough road. Parkland, easy walking. 12 holes, 6105 yards, 5635 metres. S.S.S. 69. Practice ground. *Green Fees:* Information not available. *Eating facilities:* bar (snacks), dining room. *Visitors:* generally welcome, advisable to telephone Professional in advance. Carts for hire. *Society Meetings:* by written arrangement with Professional. Professional: Stephen Burdett (Tel & Fax: 01904 422389). Secretary: Joe Baxter (Tel & Fax: 01904 426156).*

PLEASE NOTE

All the information regarding Golf Clubs in this guide is given in good faith in the belief that it is correct. However, the publishers cannot guarantee the facts given in these pages, neither are they responsible for changes in ownership or facilities, such as green fees, that may take place after the date of going to press. Readers should always satisfy themselves that the facilities they require are available and that the terms, if quoted, still apply.

YORK. **The Oaks Golf Club,** Aughton Common, Aughton, York YO42 4PW (01757 288577; Fax: 01757 288232). *Location:* on the B1228 one mile north of Bubwith village. Wooded course with seven lakes that come into play. 18 holes, 6743 yards, 6035 metres. S.S.S. 72. Practice ground. *Green Fees:* Information not available. *Eating facilities:* lounge bar, normal meals, à la carte restaurant. *Visitors:* welcome weekdays. Accommodation available, for details telephone (01757 288577). *Society Meetings:* on application. Head Professional: Graham Walker. Senior Professional: Lysa Jones. Secretary: Sheila Nutt.*
e-mail: sheila@theoaksgolfclub.co.uk
website: www.theoaksgolfclub.co.uk

YORK. **Pike Hills Golf Club,** Tadcaster Road, Askham Bryan, York YO23 3UW (01904 706566). *Location:* four miles from York on Tadcaster Road (A64), left hand side going east. Flat parkland surrounding wildlife reserve. 18 holes, 6146 yards. S.S.S. 70. *Green Fees:* £26.00 per round, £32.00 per day. *Eating facilities:* restaurant and bar facilities. *Visitors:* welcome except weekends or Bank Holidays. *Society Meetings:* welcome by arrangement. Professional: Ian Gradwell (01904 708756). Secretary: Garry Dunn (Tel & Fax: 01904 700797).

YORK. **The York Golf Club,** Lords Moor Lane, Strensall, York YO32 5XF (01904 490304). *Location:* two miles north of York ring road (A1237). Wooded heathland. 18 holes, 6301 yards. S.S.S. 70. Practice ground; Professional shop. *Green Fees:* information not available. *Eating facilities:* full catering. *Visitors:* welcome weekdays, but advisable to ring before visiting. *Society Meetings:* catered for weekdays and Sundays. Professional: A.P. Hoyles (01904 490304). Secretary: Mike Wells (01904 491840; Fax: 01904 491852).

Forest of Galtres Golf Club, Skelton, York

South Yorkshire

BARNSLEY. **Barnsley Golf Club,** Wakefield Road, Staincross, Barnsley S75 6JZ (01226 382856). *Location:* A61 three miles north of Barnsley, five miles south of Wakefield. Parkland course. 18 holes, 6048 yards, 5529 metres. S.S.S. 69. *Green Fees:* information not provided. *Eating facilities:* full catering and licensing facilities every day except Monday and Tuesday. *Visitors:* welcome, no restrictions; booking through Professional. Professional: S. Wyke (01226 380358). Secretary: Mr T. Jones (01226 382856).

BARNSLEY. **Sandhill Golf Club,** Middlecliffe Lane, Little Houghton, Barnsley S72 0HW (Tel & Fax: 01226 753444). *Location:* 6 miles east of Barnsley, off A635. 18 holes, 6273 yards. S.S.S. 70. *Green Fees:* on request. *Eating facilities:* licensed bar providing tea, coffee and meals at various prices. *Visitors:* welcome. Buggies available. *Society Meetings:* welcome with various packages on request. Winter Society Specials available. Secretary: Mrs V. Wistow. e-mail: vwistow@sandhillgolfclub.co.uk website: www.sandhillgolfclub.co.uk

BARNSLEY. **Silkstone Golf Club,** Field Head, Elmhirst Lane, Silkstone, Barnsley S75 4LD (01226 790328). *Location:* one mile from Junction 37 (M1) along A628 (the road to Manchester). Parkland/downland course. 18 holes, 6674 yards, Par 72. Practice ground. *Green Fees:* on application. *Eating facilities:* full catering facilities and bar. *Visitors:* welcome weekdays, Ladies' Day Tuesdays, with a member only at weekends and Bank Holidays. Caddie cart and buggy hire. *Society Meetings:* by arrangement. Professional: Kevin Guy (01226 790128). Secretary: A. Butcher (01226 790328).

> THE APPEARANCE OF AN ASTERISK (*) AT THE END OF A CLUB OR COURSE ENTRY INDICATES THAT UP-TO-DATE INFORMATION HAS NOT BEEN SUPPLIED

DONCASTER. **Bawtry Golf Club,** Cross Lane, Austerfield, Doncaster DN10 6RF (Tel & Fax: 01302 710841). *Location:* two miles from Bawtry on the A614. Parkland. 18 holes, 6900 yards. S.S.S. 73. 10 bay floodlit golf range, practice ground. *Green Fees:* Midweek £20.00, Weekends and Bank Holidays £28.00. *Eating facilities:* bar snacks and full restaurant. *Visitors:* welcome without reservation. Trolley and cart hire; buggies. *Society Meetings:* welcome, special package rates. Professional: Daniel Gregory (01302 710841). Office: (01302 711409). Catering: 01302 711755).

DONCASTER. **Crookhill Park (Municipal) Golf Club,** Carr Lane, Conisborough, Doncaster DN12 2AH (01709 862979). *Location:* off A630 Doncaster–Rotherham Road turn on A6094 (opposite castle) then one mile. 18 holes, 5846 yards. Parkland, special feature hole 11 (index 1) – approach to green over small wall to elevated green. S.S.S. 68. Practice area. *Green Fees:* information not provided. *Eating facilities:* buffet lunches at club. *Visitors:* welcome pre-book with Professional if specific time is required. Professional: Richard Swaine (01709 862979). Hon. Secretary: M. Belk (07870 417467).

DONCASTER. **Doncaster Golf Club,** Bawtry Road, Doncaster DN4 7PD (01302 868316). *Location:* four miles south of Doncaster town centre on the A638. Wooded, heathland course. 18 holes, 6244 yards. S.S.S. 70. Practice area, putting green. *Green Fees:* Information not available. *Eating facilities:* all day catering Monday to Saturday, up to 4pm Sundays. *Visitors:* welcome weekdays, Wednesday Ladies' Day; restricted tee times at weekends and Bank Holidays. *Society Meetings:* by arrangement, contact Secretary. Professional: G. Bailey (01302 868404). Secretary: G.J. Needham (01302 865632; Fax: 01302 865994).*
e-mail: doncastergolf@aol.com
website: www.doncastergolfclub.org.uk

DONCASTER. **Doncaster Town Moor Golf Club,** Bawtry Road, Belle Vue, Doncaster DN4 5HU (01302 533778; Bar: 01302 533167). *Location:* clubhouse approximately 300 yards from racecourse roundabout travelling south towards Bawtry, same entrance as Doncaster Rovers Football Club. Flat parkland/lowland heath, centre of Doncaster racecourse. 18 holes, 5650 yards, S.S.S. 69. *Green Fees:* weekdays £14.00, with a member, £22.00 without a member; weekends £16.00 with a member, £24.00 without a member. 2006 rates, subject to review. Special rates for societies. *Eating facilities:* restaurant and bar meals. *Visitors:* welcome by arrangement. *Society Meetings:* catered for by arrangement with Professional. Discount package available. Professional: Steve Shaw (01302 535286). Secretary: R. Smith (01302 533778).

DONCASTER. **Hickleton Golf Club,** Lidgett Lane, Hickleton, Near Doncaster DN5 7BE (01709 896081; Fax: 01709 896083). *Location:* from Junction 37 A1(M) six miles on A635 to Barnsley, in Hickleton village turn right to Thurnscoe, 500 yards on right. Undulating parkland. 18 holes, 6434 yards. S.S.S. 71. Practice ground. *Green Fees:* weekdays £32.00; weekends and Bank Holidays £35.00. Winter and Summer packages available. *Eating facilities:* available seven days a week. *Visitors:* welcome by arrangement, restricted times at weekends. Buggies by arrangement with Professional. *Society Meetings:* welcome by arrangement. Professional: Paul Audsley (Tel & Fax: 01709 888436). Manager: John Little (01709 896081; Fax: 01709 896083).
e-mail: john@hickletongolfclub.co.uk
website: www.hickletongolfclub.co.uk

DONCASTER. **Owston Hall**, Owston, Askern, Doncaster DN6 9JF (01302 722231; Fax: 01302 728885). *Location:* 7 miles north of Doncaster on the A19 from Doncaster to Askern, take the B1220 and turn right through the stone gates. Championship venue on the PGA Euro Pro Tour schedule. Parkland with mature trees. 18 holes, 6937 yards. S.S.S. 72. Putting Green, practice ground. *Green Fees:* weekdays £22.00; weekends £30.00. *Eating facilities:* bar lunches and full evening menu. *Visitors:* welcome, booking at weekends recommended. Function and conference rooms. Hotel with 49 de luxe bedrooms; gym. *Society Meetings:* packages available – please phone for brochure. Dress code applies – locker changing and shower facilities. PGA Instruction available. Professional: Jason Laszkowicz (01302 722231; Fax: 01302 728885). Secretary: Gerry Briggs (01302 722800).
e-mail: reservations@owstonhall.com
proshop@owstonhall.com
website: www.owstonhall.com

DONCASTER. **Serlby Park Golf Club,** Serlby, Doncaster DN10 6BA (01777 818268). *Location:* between Bawtry and Blyth. Parkland, wooded course. 9 holes, 5300 yards. S.S.S. 66. *Green Fees:* with a member–£10.00 weekdays, £20.00 weekends and Bank Holidays. Societies £20.00 weekdays, £25.00 weekends and Bank Holidays. *Eating facilities:* catering and bar. *Visitors:* limited to playing

with a member. *Society Meetings:* parties of 4 or more welcome any time if booked through Secretary. Secretary: K.J. Crook (01302 742280).

DONCASTER. **Thorne Golf Club,** Kirton Lane, Thorne, Near Doncaster DN8 5RJ (01405 812084; Fax: 01405 741899). *Location:* M18 Junction 5, onto M180, take first junction onto A614 Thorne, follow signposts. Flat parkland with three ponds. 18 holes, 5366 yards. S.S.S. 66. Practice ground and putting green. *Green Fees*: weekdays £12.00 for 18 holes, weekends £13.00 for 18 holes. *Eating facilities*: snacks and meals available. *Visitors*: welcome, no restrictions. *Society Meetings*: welcome, please book in advance. Secretary/ Professional: Edward Highfield. Proprietor: Richard Highfield.
e-mail: edwardhighfield@hotmail.co.uk
website: www.thornegolf.co.uk

DONCASTER. **Thornhurst Park Golf Course,** Holme Lane, Owston, Doncaster DN5 0LR (01302 337799). *Location:* 10 minutes from centre of Doncaster through Bentley on A19 to Selby. Flat, parkland course with excellent countryside views. 18 holes, 6490 yards. S.S.S. 71. Practice area, putting green. *Green Fees:* weekdays 18 holes £12.00; weekends 18 holes £14.00. 9 holes: weekdays £7.00, weekends £8.00. Subject to review. *Eating facilities:* restaurant, lounge bar, function room. *Visitors:* welcome every day, members have priority between 8am and 9am. *Society Meetings:* welcome any day. Professional: Kevin M. Pearce.

DONCASTER. **Wheatley Golf Club,** Armthorpe Road, Doncaster DN2 5QB (01302 831655). *Location:* follow East Coast route alongside Racecourse boundary to water tower at first crossroads. Flat parkland, water hazards between 10th and 18th holes. 18 holes, 6209 yards, S.S.S. 70 (yellow markers); 6405 yards, S.S.S. 71 (white markers). Practice area and putting green. *Green Fees:* weekdays £30.00 per round, £37.00 per day; weekends £40.00 per round. *Eating facilities:* restaurant and bars. *Visitors:* welcome if member of another club. *Society Meetings:* catered for weekdays only on written application. Professional: S. Fox (01302 834085). Secretary: T. Roberts (01302 831655).

ROTHERHAM. **Grange Park Golf Club,** Upper Wortley Road, Kimberworth Park, Rotherham S61 2SJ (01709 558884). Municipal golf course, private clubhouse. *Location:* A629 from Rotherham, easy access from M1. Parkland. 18 holes, 6353 yards. S.S.S. 71. Practice ground, driving range. *Green Fees:* information not available. *Eating facilities:* licensed bar and full catering. *Visitors:* welcome without restriction. *Society Meetings:* contact Professional in first instance. Professional: Eric Clark (01709 559497). Secretary: Roy Charity (01709 583400 home, 01709 558884 club). *

www.uk-golfguide.com

ROTHERHAM. **Phoenix Golf Club,** Phoenix Sports and Social Club, Pavilion Lane, Brinsworth, Rotherham S60 5PA (Tel & Fax: 01709 363788). *Location:* M1 (J34) Tinsley roundabout, Bawtry Road, Pavilion Lane one mile on left. 18 holes, 6181 yards. S.S.S. 70. Practice area, 20 bay driving range. *Green Fees:* information not available. *Eating facilities:* snacks or full meals. *Visitors:* welcome anytime. *Society Meetings:* welcome weekdays, limited availability on Sundays. Professional: M. Roberts (01709 382624). Secretary: I. Gregory (Tel & Fax: 01709 363788).*

ROTHERHAM. **Rotherham Golf Club Ltd,** Thrybergh Park, Doncaster Road, Thrybergh, Rotherham S65 4NU (01709 850466). *Location:* three and a half miles east of Rotherham on A630. Wooded parkland. 18 holes, 6327 yards. S.S.S. 70. Practice ground. *Green Fees:* available on request. *Eating facilities:* full catering, bar and restaurant. *Visitors:* welcome all day with limitations. *Society Meetings:* welcome weekdays and weekends (after 1400 hrs). Professional: Mr Simon Thornhill (01709 850480). Manager: (01709 859500; Fax: 01709 859517). e-mail: manager@rotherhamgolfclub.com website: www.rotherhamgolfclub.com

ROTHERHAM. **Roundwood Golf Club,** Green Lane, Rawmarsh, Rotherham S62 6LA (01709 826134). *Location:* half a mile from the A633. Flat course, easy walking. 18 holes, 5568 yards, S.S.S. 67. *Green Fees:* information not available. *Eating facilities:* bar open seven days a week, food available Fridays and Saturdays. *Visitors:* welcome midweek and Sunday afternoons. *Society Meetings:* welcome weekdays and Sunday afternoons. Secretary: G. Billups (01709 525208).*

ROTHERHAM. **Sitwell Park Golf Club,** Shrogswood Road, Rotherham S60 4BY (01709 541046; Fax: 01709 703637). *Location:* A631 off M18, Bramley turn off to Rotherham thence to Sheffield, Exit 33 off M1, follow A631 to Bawtry. Undulating parkland. 18 holes, 6229 yards. Par 71. Practice ground. *Green Fees:* weekdays £26.00 per round, £34.00 per day; Sundays and Bank Holidays £32.00 per round, £40.00 per day. Parties of 30 or more players 10% discount. *Eating facilities:* restaurant and bar. *Visitors:* welcome with reservation, Saturdays only with member, Sundays after 11.30am. Buggies and carts available. *Society Meetings:* catered for if pre-arranged with Secretary. Not Saturdays; Sundays after 11.30am only. Professional: N. Taylor (01709 540961). Secretary: Geoff Hardy (01709 541046; Fax: 01709 703637). e-mail: secretary@sitwellgolf.co.uk website: www.sitwellgolf.co.uk

ROTHERHAM. **Wath Golf Club,** Abdy, Rawmarsh, Rotherham S62 7SJ (01709 872149). *Location:* A633 from Rotherham, through Rawmarsh, taking B6090 towards Wentworth, right along B6089 taking signed road to Clubhouse 300 yards on right. Flat parkland course with small greens, dykes and two ponds. 18 holes, 6086 yards. S.S.S. 70. Limited practice area. *Green Fees:* £26.00 per round, £31.00 per day. Golf/meal package £33.00/£38.00. *Eating facilities:* lounge bar and dining area with seating for up to 100 people. *Visitors:* weekdays only. *Society Meetings:* welcome weekdays only by prior arrangement. Professional: Chris Bassett. Secretary: M. Godfrey (01709 878609; Fax: 01709 877097).

SHEFFIELD. **Abbeydale Golf Club,** Twentywell Rise off, Twentywell Lane, Dore, Sheffield S17 4QA (0114 2360763; Fax: 0114 2360762). *Location:* A621 five miles south of Sheffield. Parkland. 18 holes, 6241 yards. S.S.S. 70. Practice ground. *Green Fees:* weekdays £35.00; weekends and Bank Holidays £45.00. *Eating facilities:* restaurant and bar meals. *Visitors:* welcome by arrangement. Starting time restrictions April-October. *Society Meetings:* catered for by arrangement. Golf Manager/Professional: N. Perry (0114 2365633). Office Manager: Mrs J. Wing (0114 2360763; Fax: 0114 2360762).

SHEFFIELD. **Beauchief Golf Club,** Abbey Lane, Beauchief, Sheffield S8 0DB (0114 236 7274). *Location:* near the junction with A621 Abbeydale Road 5 miles SW of Sheffield. Access from J33 or J29 via outer ring road. 'Pay and Play' parkland course with some hilly holes. 18 holes, 5452 yards,. S.S.S. 66. Practice area. *Green Fees:* Mondays to Thursdays £12.00; Fridays to Sundays £14.00. *Eating facilities:* cafe/bar, open daily from 11am to dusk. *Visitors:* welcome weekdays and after 10am at weekend. *Society Meetings:* welcome weekdays and after 10am weekend, contact M. Trippett. Professional: M. Trippett (01142 367274). Secretary: Mrs B. Fryer (0114 236 5628).

SHEFFIELD. **Birley Wood Golf Club,** Birley Lane, Sheffield S12 3BP (0114 264 7262). *Location:* Junction 30 M1 then A616 to Sheffield. Undulating meadowland course with good views. Fairway Course: 18 holes, 5734 yards. Par 69, S.S.S. 68. Short Birley Course: 18 holes, 4906 yards. Par 66. S.S.S. 65. Practice field near course. Membership available. *Green Fees:* information not available. *Eating facilities:* restaurant and bar meals at adjacent Fairway Inn. *Visitors:* welcome anytime. *Society Meetings:* contact Mr N. Luety (0114 279 7451). Secretary: P. Renshaw (0114 265 3784).*

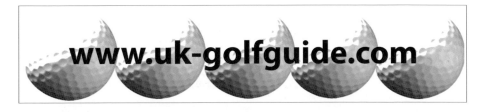

SHEFFIELD. **Concord Park Municipal Golf Course,** Shiregreen Lane, Shiregreen, Sheffield S5 6AE (0114 2577378). *Location:* M1 Junctions 34/35, one and a half miles north of junctions. Parkland, hilly, good views. 18 holes, 4872 yards, S.S.S. 64, Par 67. Driving range; buggies available. *Green Fees:* weekday £10.00, weekends and Bank Holidays £11.00. *Eating facilities:* available in new clubhouse. *Visitors:* welcome any time; busy Saturday and Sunday mornings. *Society Meetings:* welcome. Professional: W. Allcroft (0114 2577378). Secretary: A. Martin (01709 877287).

SHEFFIELD. **Dore and Totley Golf Club,** The Clubhouse, Bradway Road, Bradway, Sheffield S17 4QR (0114 236 0492; Fax: 0114 235 3436). *Location:* leave M1 at Junction 33. Flat, easy walking parkland course. 18 holes, 6256 yards. S.S.S. 70. *Green Fees:* information not available. *Eating facilities:* bar catering facilities available except Mondays. *Visitors:* welcome. After 10am Tuesdays and Thursday; afternoons only Wednesdays and Sundays. No visitors on Saturdays. Handicap Certificates may be requested. *Society Meetings:* welcome by arrangement. Special all day price; catering by arrangement with Stewardess. Professional: Gregg Roberts (Tel & Fax: 0114 236 6844). Secretary: J. Johnson (0114 2369872).*

SHEFFIELD. **Hallamshire Golf Club Ltd,** Sandygate, Sheffield S10 4LA (0114 230 1007; Fax: 0114 230 2153). *Location:* A57 out of Sheffield, four miles out of city then fork left for Lodge Moor. Undulating moorland course, not suitable for beginners. 18 holes, 6359 yards, 5815 metres. S.S.S. 71. *Green Fees:* information not available. *Eating facilities:* dining room/verandah, two bars. *Visitors:* welcome weekdays by arrangement, some weekends. Dress code. Snooker table. *Society Meetings:* catered for by arrangement with Secretary. Professional: Geoffrey Tickell (0114 230 5222). Secretary: Bob Hill (0114 230 2153; Fax: 0114 230 5413).

SHEFFIELD. **Hallowes Golf Club,** Hallowes Lane, Dronfield, Near Sheffield S18 1UR (01246 411196; Fax: 01246 413753). *Location:* six miles south of Sheffield on old A61 (not bypass to Chesterfield). Moorland/parkland. 18 holes, 6342 yards. S.S.S. 71. Large practice area and short game facility. *Green Fees:* weekdays £35.00 per round, £40.00 per day. *Eating facilities:* bars, dining room. *Visitors:* weekdays only, no visitors at weekends and Bank Holidays except with members. *Society Meetings:* EGU registered societies welcome. special reduced packages available. Professional: John Oates (01246 411196). Manager: Dr Nigel Ogden (01246 413734).

SHEFFIELD. **Hillsborough Golf Club Ltd,** Worrall Road, Sheffield S6 4BE (0114 234 9151 – Office; 0114 229 4103 – Steward). *Location:* three miles from city centre. Worrall Road via Middlewood Road, Dykes Hall Road. Undulating wooded parkland and heath. 18 holes, 6035 yards. S.S.S. 70. Practice field. *Green Fees:* weekdays £30.00, weekends and Bank Holidays £35.00. *Eating facilities:* snacks available; lunches, teas, evening meals by arrangement (not Fridays). *Visitors:* welcome weekdays, weekends with a member only. *Society Meetings:* catered for by arrangement with Professional. Professional: Lewis Horsman (0114 229 4100). Secretary: G.F. Smalley (0114 234 9151).

SHEFFIELD. **Lees Hall Golf Club Ltd,** Hemsworth Road, Norton, Sheffield S8 8LL (0114 255 4402). *Location:* three miles south of Sheffield, between A61 and A6102 ring road. Undulating parkland with extensive views over Sheffield. 18 holes, 6171 yards. S.S.S. 70. *Green Fees:* information not available. *Eating facilities:* available daily. *Visitors:* welcome, except Saturday and Sunday before 10.30am. *Society Meetings:* by arrangement only. Professional: Simon Berry (0114-250 7868). Secretary: R.W. Balloch (0114 255 2900). e-mail: secretary@leeshallgolfclub.co.uk*

SHEFFIELD. **Rother Valley Golf Centre,** Mansfield Road, Wales Bar, Sheffield S26 5PQ (0114 2473000; Fax: 0114 2476000). *Location:* centrally situated between Sheffield, Rotherham, and Chesterfield. Two miles from Junction 31 of M1, signposted. Parkland with water features. Island green at 7th hole and monster par 5 18th hole. Floodlit driving range and 9 hole pitch and putt course. Jack Barker golf school. 18 holes, 6602 yards. S.S.S. 72. *Green Fees:* Monday to Thursday £15.00; Fridays: £17.00; weekends £19.50. *Eating facilities:* bar open 9am to 10.30pm. *Visitors:* welcome. *Society Meetings:* welcome including weekends. Phone for special offers. General Manager: Maureen Goodman.

SHEFFIELD. **Stocksbridge and District Golf Club Ltd,** 30 Royd Lane, Deepcar, Sheffield S36 2RZ (0114 2882003). *Location:* 10 miles from Sheffield on A616 heading towards Manchester. Moorland course. 18 holes, 5200 yards. S.S.S. 65. Practice ground. *Green Fees:* weekdays £17.00 per round (unaccompanied), £25.00 per day (unaccompanied); weekends £37.00 per day (unaccompanied). Visiting parties £25.00 – 18 holes, soup and sandwiches, 18 holes, dinner. *Eating facilities:* dining room and bars available. *Visitors:* welcome weekdays, restrictions weekends. *Society Meetings:* catered for during the week. Professional: Roger Broad (0114 2882779). Secretary: Dennis Haley (0114 2882003).

SHEFFIELD. **Tankersley Park Golf Club Ltd,** High Green, Sheffield S30 4LG (0114 2468247; Fax: 0114 2457818). *Location:* M1 north to Junction 35a, A616, golf club on right. M1 south Junction 36, A61 Sheffield, left on A616, golf club on left. Parkland/wooded. 18 holes, 6212 yards. S.S.S. 70. Practice area and practice green. *Green Fees:* £27.00 per round, £36.00 per day. 10% discount for parties of 20 or more players. *Eating facilities:* sandwiches, bar and evening meals. *Visitors:* welcome weekdays without reservation but not before 3pm weekends. *Society Meetings:* catered for by prior arrangement with Secretary. Professional: I. Kirk (Tel & Fax: 0114 2455583). Secretary: A. Brownhill (0114 2468247).

SHEFFIELD. **Tinsley Park Golf Club (Municipal),** High Hazels Park, Darnall, Sheffield S9 4PE (0114 2448974). *Location:* three miles from Junction 33 M1, exit – A6102. Wooded course. 18 holes, 6096 yards. S.S.S. 69. Practice facilities. *Green Fees:* Monday to Thursday £12.00, Friday - Sunday £15.00. *Eating facilities:* 2007/8 limited facilities due to refurbishment of the clubhouse. *Visitors:* welcome without restriction, times booked through Professional up to 8 days in advance. *Society Meetings:* bookings through Professional. Professional: Wayne Yellott (0114 244 8974).

SHEFFIELD. **Wortley Golf Club,** Hermit Hill Lane, Wortley, Sheffield S35 7DF (0114 288 8469; Fax: 0114 288 8488). *Location:* leave M1 Junction 36 or 35A - A616 or A61 to A629 leading to Wortley Village, through village turn right. Parkland. 18 holes, 6035 yards, 5520 metres. S.S.S. 69. Practice ground. *Green Fees:* weekdays £30.00 per round, weekends £35.00 per round. *Eating facilities:* order in advance, limited on Mondays. *Visitors:* welcome, no restrictions. Golf buggy, trolley and club hire available. *Society Meetings:* welcome, must pre-book. Professional: Ian Kirk (0114 288 6490). Office: (0114 288 8469).
e-mail: wortley.golfclub@btconnect.com
website: www.wortleygolfclub.co.uk

WORKSOP. **Lindrick Golf Club,** Lindrick Common, Worksop S81 8BH (01909 485802). *Location:* on A57 four miles west of Worksop. M1 Junction 31 on to A57 Worksop. Heathland. 18 holes, 6612 yards, 6046 metres. S.S.S. 71. Two practice areas. *Green Fees:* Information not available. *Eating facilities:* dining room. *Visitors:* welcome weekdays, except Tuesday mornings. Enquire for Sunday availability. Prior booking required. *Society Meetings:* catered for weekdays. Professional: John King (01909 475820). Secretary: John Armitage (01909 475282; Fax: 01909 488685).*
website: www.lindrickgolfclub.co.uk

THE APPEARANCE OF AN ASTERISK (*) AT THE END OF A CLUB OR COURSE ENTRY INDICATES THAT UP-TO-DATE INFORMATION HAS NOT BEEN SUPPLIED

West Yorkshire

BINGLEY. **Bingley (St Ives) Golf Club,** The Golf Clubhouse, Harden, Bingley BD16 1AT (01274 562436; Fax: 01274 511788). *Location:* A650 Keighley/Bradford Road. Parkland/moorland. 18 holes, 6480 yards. S.S.S. 71. Practice ground. *Green Fees:* information not available. *Eating facilities:* daily. *Visitors:* welcome weekdays, limited availability weekends. *Society Meetings:* welcome, book through Professional. Professional: Nigel Barber (01274 562436). Manager: Ray Adams (01274 562436; Tel & Fax: 01274 511788).
e-mail: secretary@bingleystivesgc.co.uk
website: www.bingleystivesgc.co.uk

BRADFORD. **Baildon Golf Club,** Moorgate, Baildon, Shipley BD17 5PP (01274 584266). *Location:* five miles north-west of Bradford via Shipley. Hilly, moorland course. 18 holes, 6225 yards. S.S.S. 70. *Green Fees:* information not available. *Eating facilities:* catering except Mondays. Bar and separate dining room. *Visitors:* welcome, restricted at weekends and Tuesdays. *Society Meetings:* welcome weekdays only, by written application. Professional: R. Masters (01274 595162). Secretary: Hetley C. Burnham.
website: www.baildongolfclub.com

BRADFORD. **Bradford Moor Golf Club,** Scarr Hall, Pollard Lane, Bradford BD2 4RW (01274 771716). *Location:* A658 two miles from top of M606. Moorland, undulating course. 9 holes, 5854 yards.

S.S.S. 68. *Green Fees:* Information not available. *Eating facilities:* available by appointment only. *Visitors:* welcome weekdays. *Society Meetings:* welcome weekdays. Secretary: Geoff Lee (01274 771693).*

BRADFORD. **Clayton Golf Club,** Thornton View Road, Clayton, Bradford BD14 6JX (01274 880047). *Location:* two miles south west of Bradford, via Thornton Road, then Listerhills Road. Parkland course. 9 holes, 6200 yards. S.S.S. 72. *Green Fees:* Information not available. *Eating facilities:* diningroom – meals and snacks daily; evening meals by arrangement; two bars. *Visitors:* welcome at all times except before 4.00pm on Sundays. Snooker room. *Society Meetings:* catered for by arrangement. Secretary: D.A. Smith (01274 572311)*.

BRADFORD. **East Bierley Golf Club,** South View Road, East Bierley, Bradford BD4 6PP (01274 683666). *Location:* situated about three miles east of Bradford on the Wakefield/Heckmondwike Road. Turn off at Bierley Bar and down South View Road. Parkland course. 9 holes, 4308 metres. S.S.S. 63. *Green Fees*: information not available. *Eating facilities*: lunchtime and evening catering (except Tuesdays). *Visitors*: welcome, not Sundays or Mondays after 4pm. Secretary: Mr R.J. Welch (01274 683666). Hon. Secretary: R.J. Welch. Steward: (01274 680450).

BRADFORD. **Headley Golf Club,** Headley Lane, Thornton, Bradford BD13 3LX (01274 833481). *Location:* five miles west of Bradford. Undulating parkland, excellent views. 9 holes, 4914 yards. S.S.S. 65. *Green Fees:* information not provided. *Eating facilities:* dining room and bar. *Visitors:* weekdays only. *Society Meetings:* welcome weekdays, special packages available. Hon. Secretary: D. Britton (01274 833481).

BRADFORD. **The Manor Golf Club,** Bradford Road, Drighlington, Bradford BD11 1AB (0113 2852644). *Location:* between Leeds and Bradford, just off M62 Junction 27. Undulating parkland/meadowland, features six lakes. 18 holes, 6564 yards. S.S.S 71, Par 72. 20 bay floodlit driving range, 6 hole Par 3 course. *Green Fees:* midweek £16.00 per round, weekend £20.00 per round - after 3.30pm £12.50. *Eating facilities:* clubhouse. *Visitors:* welcome at all times but prior enquiry advised. *Society Meetings:* welcome with reservation. Director of Golf/Professional: Graham Thompson.

BRADFORD. **Northcliffe Golf Club,** High Bank Lane, Shipley BD18 4LJ (01274 584085). *Location:* three miles west of Bradford on A650; turn left at roundabout Junction of A650/A657. Undulating woodland parkland with feature holes. 18 holes, 6104 yards. S.S.S. 70. *Green Fees:* weekdays £25.00; weekends and Bank Holidays £30.00. *Eating facilities:* bars 11am to 11pm, food 11.30am to 9.00pm summer months. No catering or bar facilities Mondays, except Bank Holidays. *Visitors:* Monday to Friday, Saturday after 4.30pm, Sunday all day. Wide wheel/electric trolleys for hire. *Society Meetings:* welcome, packages available. Professional: M. Hillas (01274 587193). Hon. Secretary: I. Collins (01274 596731; Fax: 01274 584148).

BRADFORD. **Queensbury Golf Club,** Brighouse Road, Queensbury, Bradford BD13 1QF (01274 882155). *Location:* M62 Junction 25, A644 to Brighouse, Hipperholme and Queensbury. Wooded course. 9 holes, 5024 yards. S.S.S. 66. *Green Fees:* weekdays £15.00, weekends and Bank Holidays £30.00. *Eating facilities:* lunches, teas except Monday. Bar available. *Visitors:* welcome any day, must have Handicap. No parties at weekends. *Society Meetings:* by arrangement. Professional: N. Stead (01274 816864). Secretary: M . H . Heptinstall (01274 882155).

BRADFORD. **Shipley Golf Club,** Beckfoot Lane, Cottingley Bridge, Bingley BD16 1LX (01274 568652; Fax: 01274 567739). *Location:* off A650 at Cottingley Bridge, Bradford six miles, Bingley one mile. Flat parkland. 18 holes, 6235 yards. S.S.S. 70. Practice area and net putting green. *Green Fees:* weekdays £35.00 per round, £42.00 per day; weekends and Bank Holidays £40.00 per round, £49.00 per day. Subject to change. Winter rates by arrangement. *Eating facilities:* available. *Visitors:* welcome by arrangement with Golf Manager; not Tuesdays or Saturdays. *Society Meetings:* catered for by arrangement with Golf Manager. Packages available. Professional/Golf Manager: R. Parry (01274 563674; Fax: 01274 567739). Manager/Secretary: Mrs M.J. Bryan (01274 568652; Fax: 01274 567739).

BRADFORD. **South Bradford Golf Club,** Pearson Road, Odsal, Bradford BD6 1BH (01274 679195 Club; 01274 690643 Office). *Location:* follow signs for Odsal Stadium, roundabout at Stadium turn left and first left again, road leads down to clubhouse. Parkland type course with some hilly sections. 9 holes, 6004 yards. S.S.S. 69. Practice ground. *Green Fees:* information not provided. *Eating facilities:* bar meals available except Mondays. *Visitors:* welcome; not before 3.30pm on weekends and Bank Holidays. *Society Meetings:* welcome – must apply in writing. Professional: Paul Cooke (01274 673346). Secretary: B. Broadbent (01274 679195).

BRADFORD. **West Bradford Golf Club Ltd,** Chellow Grange Road, Haworth Road, Bradford BD9 6NP. *Location:* 3 miles west of city centre off B6144 Haworth Road. Easy walking, undulating, wooded parkland course. 18 holes, 5723 yards. S.S.S. 68, Par 69. *Green Fees:* £31.00. Package deals for parties and societies from £16.00 (unlimited golf). Happy hour weekends after 4pm – reduced green fee. *Eating facilities:* available every day except Monday. *Visitors:* welcome, except Saturdays before 4pm. *Society Meetings:* welcome by arrangement. Professional: Warren Kemp (01274 542102). Secretary: N.S. Bey (01274 542767; Fax: 01274 482079).

BRIGHOUSE. **Castlefields Golf Club,** Rastrick Common, Rastrick, Brighouse HD6 3HL. *Location:* one mile out of Brighouse on A643. Parkland course, founded 1903. 6 holes, 2406 yards. S.S.S. 50, Par 54. *Green Fees:* information not available. *Eating facilities:* Globe Inn 200 yards away. *Visitors:* welcome at all times but must be accompanied by a member. *Society Meetings:* contact Secretary for details at above address.

BRIGHOUSE. **Crow Nest Park Golf Club,** Coach Road, Hove Edge, Brighouse HD6 2LN (01484 401121). *Location:* Bradford Road out of Brighouse, left at Ritz Ballroom, right after one mile. Gently undulating parkland. 9 holes, 6020 yards. S.S.S. 69. Floodlit driving range with power tees and swingcam. *Green Fees:* 9 holes £14.00, 18 holes £24.00. *Eating facilities:* food available from 11.30am till 2.30pm and then from 5.30pm till 9.30pm, bar open from 11am until 11pm. *Visitors:* welcome but tees must be booked in advance with Professional. *Society Meetings:* welcome by prior arrangement. Professional: Paul Everitt. Secretary: (01484 401121). Clubhouse: (01484 401152). e-mail: info@crownestgolf.co.uk website: www.crownestgolf.co.uk

BRIGHOUSE. **Willow Valley Golf and Country Club,** Highmoor Lane, off Walton Lane, Clifton, Brighouse HD6 4JB (01274 878624). *Location:* Junction 25 off M62 to Brighouse A644, right at roundabout A643, two miles on right. American-style island greens, undulating fairway, water. Willow Valley course: 18 holes, 7025 yards. S.S.S. 72. Fountain Ridge 9 hole course. New 18 hole Pine Valley course. 18-bay covered range. *Green Fees:* Willow Valley - weekdays £25.00; weekends £35.00. Pine Valley - weekdays £14.50, weekends £16.50. 9-hole Fountain Ridge course from £7.50. *Eating facilities:* fully licensed bar and catering. *Visitors:* always welcome. *Society meetings:* welcome, please contact the Sales Manager Helen Butterfield. website: www.wvgc.co.uk

CLECKHEATON. **Cleckheaton and District Golf Club Ltd,** Bradford Road, Cleckheaton BD19 6BU (01274 851266; Fax: 01274 871382). *Location:* four miles south of Bradford on A638, 200 yards from Junction 26 M62. Dr Alister MacKenzie designed parkland course. 18 holes, 5706 yards. Par 70, S.S.S. 68. Practice area. *Green Fees:* weekdays (May–October) £30.00 per round, £35.00 per day; weekends and Bank Holidays £39.00. *Eating facilities:* available except Mondays. *Visitors:* welcome except Saturdays, suggest prior enquiry. *Society Meetings:* catered for by prior arrangement with Secretary except Saturdays. Professional: Mike Ingham. Manager: Andrew Callaway. e-mail: info@cleckheatongolfclub.co.uk

DEWSBURY. **Hanging Heaton Golf Club,** White Cross Road, Dewsbury WF12 7DT (01924 461606; Fax; 01924 430100). *Location:* one mile from town centre on main A653 Dewsbury to Leeds road. 9 holes, 5836 yards (for 18 holes). S.S.S. 68. *Green Fees:* Information not available). *Eating facilities:* available. *Visitors:* welcome without reservation, except weekends. *Society Meetings:* catered for by arrangement with Secretary. Professional: G. Moore (01924 467077). Secretary: Derek Atkinson (01924 430100). *

ELLAND. **Elland Golf Club,** Hammerstone Leach Lane, Elland HX5 0TA (01422 372505). *Location:* M62 Junction 24 exit off roundabout for Blackley, one mile. Parkland. 9 holes, 5498 yards. S.S.S. 67. *Green Fees:* weekdays £18.00; weekends £30.00. *Eating facilities:* meals/bar snacks except Mondays. *Visitors:* welcome

weekdays except Thursdays. *Society Meetings:* by arrangement. Professional: N. Krzywicki (01422 374886). Secretary: P. A. Green (01422 251431).

GUISELEY. **Bradford Golf Club,** Hawksworth Lane, Guiseley, Leeds LS20 8NP (01943 875570). *Location:* Shipley to Ilkley road, left at top of Hollins Hill, one mile up Hawksworth Lane. Moorland/parkland. 18 holes, 6259 yards. S.S.S. 71. *Green Fees:* £36.00 per round or day. Discounts available for parties over 20. *Eating facilities:* every day, preferably by prior arrangement. *Visitors:* welcome, phone Professional for availability, not on weekends without prior arrangement. *Society Meetings:* catered for on weekdays (except Tuesdays) by prior arrangement. Professional: Andrew Hall (01943 873719). Secretary: T. Eagle (01943 875570).

HALIFAX. **Halifax Bradley Hall Golf Club,** Holywell Green, Halifax HX4 9AN (01422 374108). *Location:* three miles south of Halifax on B6112. Undulating moorland. 18 holes, 6138 yards. S.S.S. 70. Practice ground. *Green Fees:* information not available. *Visitors:* welcome. Snooker. *Society Meetings:* welcome with prior reservation weekdays. Handicap Certificate. Professional: P. Wood (01422 370231). Secretary: M. Dredge (01422 374108).*

HALIFAX. **The Halifax Golf Club Ltd,** Union Lane, Ogden, Halifax HX2 8XR (01422 244171). *Location:* four miles out of Halifax, A629 towards Keighley. Moorland. 18 holes, 6037 yards. S.S.S. 70. *Green Fees:* £30.00 per round, £35.00 per day. *Eating facilities:* luncheons and dinners served. Good restaurant facilities. *Visitors:* welcome most days by arrangement (not Saturdays). *Society Meetings:* catered for by arrangement: £20.00 - £40.00. Professional: David Delaney (01422 240047).

HALIFAX. **Lightcliffe Golf Club,** Knowle Top Road, Lightcliffe, Halifax HX3 8RG (01422 202459). *Location:* three miles east of Halifax on A58 (main Halifax to Leeds road). Parkland. 9 holes, 5388 metres. S.S.S. 68. *Green Fees:* information not available. *Eating facilities:* bar snacks and meals (except Mondays). *Visitors:* welcome without reservation but must confirm with Professional. Not Wednesdays. *Society Meetings:* catered for. Professional: Ron Tickle (01422 202459). Secretary: Rod Crampton (01484 384066).

HALIFAX. **Ryburn Golf Club,** The Shaw, Norland, Sowerby Bridge, Near Halifax HX6 3QP (01422 831355). *Location:* Halifax to Sowerby Bridge, turn left on station road, turn right up hill, right towards Hobbit Inn (signposted), left after cottages. Demanding, hilly, windy course. 9 holes, 5127 yards. S.S.S. 65. *Green Fees:* information not provided. *Eating facilities:* good catering facilities and bar. *Visitors:* welcome weekdays, weekends by prior arrangement. *Society Meetings:* welcome by prior arrangement. Secretary: Jack Hoyle (01422 843070 home).

HALIFAX. **West End Golf Club (Halifax) Ltd,** Paddock Lane, Highroad Well, Halifax HX2 0NT (01422 341878). *Location:* two miles west of town centre. Parkland. 18 holes, 5937 yards. S.S.S. 68 (White markers). *Green Fees:* weekdays £30.00 per round, £35.00 per day; weekends and Bank Holidays £35.00 per round, £40.00 per day. Subject to review. *Eating facilities:* full bar and catering except Mondays. *Visitors:* welcome except Saturdays - please check with Professional. No visiting parties on Saturdays. *Society Meetings:* catered for by arrangement with Secretary. Professional: David Rishworth (01422 341878). Secretary: G. Gower (Tel & Fax: 01422 341878). e-mail: westendgc@btinternet.com

HEBDEN BRIDGE. **Hebden Bridge Golf Club,** Wadsworth, Hebden Bridge HX7 8PH (01422 842896). *Location:* one mile upwards past Birchcliffe Centre. Moorland with superb Pennine views. 9 holes, 5242 yards. S.S.S. 67. *Green Fees:* weekdays £12.00; weekends £15.00. 50% reduction for Juniors or if playing with member. Subject to review. *Eating facilities:* bar and dining room facilities, private functions catered for. *Visitors:* welcome, please check first at weekends. *Society Meetings:* welcome midweek only except by special arrangement. Co-ordinator: Alan Platten (01422 842896; Mobile: 07932394836).

HUDDERSFIELD. **Bradley Park Municipal Golf Course,** Off Bradley Road, Huddersfield HD2 1PZ (01484 223772). *Location:* M62 Junction 25, follow Huddersfield signs then A6107. Parkland course, rolling hills with panoramic views. 18 holes, 6220 yards. S.S.S. 70. Floodlit driving range, 9 hole Par 3 course. *Green Fees:* information not available. *Eating facilities:* full catering. *Visitors:* welcome, no restrictions. No block bookings for parties at weekends, only telephone bookings to the Professional for individuals. *Society Meetings:* all welcome, book through Professional. Professional: P.E. Reilly. Secretary: K. Blackwell (01484 223772; Fax: 01484 451613).*

HUDDERSFIELD. **Crosland Heath Golf Club Ltd,** Felks Stile Road, Crosland Heath, Huddersfield HD4 7AF (01484 653216). *Location:* 3 miles from town centre off A62 Oldham road. Flat heathland with extensive views. 18 holes, 6087 yards. Par 71. Practice facilities. *Green Fees:* £37.00 to £42.00. *Eating facilities:* full catering except Mondays. *Visitors:* welcome, suggest prior enquiry. *Society Meetings:* Tuesdays and Thursdays. Professional: (01484 653877). General Manager: (01484 653216; Fax: 01484 461079). website: www.croslandheath.co.uk

HUDDERSFIELD. **Huddersfield Golf Club,** Fixby Hall, Lightridge Road, Fixby, Huddersfield HD2 2EP (01484 426203; Fax: 01484 424623). *Location:* M62 Junction 24; A643 from Cedar Court Hotel; turn right first traffic lights by Sun Inn. Parkland course. 18 holes, 6466 yards. S.S.S. 71. Practice ground. *Green Fees:* weekdays £45.00 for 18 holes, £55.00 for 27/36 holes; weekends and Public Holidays £55.00 for 18 holes, £65.00 for 27/36 holes. £15.00 playing with a member. *Eating facilities:* available. *Visitors:* always welcome, reservation essential. Tuesday Ladies' Day; no visitors Saturdays. Snooker. *Society and Company Days:* catered for except weekends, well appointed private rooms. Catering to suit all occasions. Professional: P. Carman (01484 426463). Office Manager: Mrs D. Lockett (01484 426203). General Manager: Mrs S. Dennis (01484 426203). e-mail: secretary@huddersfield-golf.co.uk website: www.huddersfield-golf.co.uk

HUDDERSFIELD. **Longley Park Golf Club,** Maple Street (off Somerset Road), Aspley, Huddersfield HD5 9AX (01484 426932). *Location:* one mile town centre, Wakefield side. 9 holes, 5212 yards. S.S.S. 66. *Green Fees:* £17.00 weekdays; £21.00 weekends and Bank Holidays. *Eating facilities:* available. *Visitors:* welcome Mondays, Tuesdays and Fridays, other times by previous arrangement only. *Society Meetings:* welcome by previous arrangement with Secretary. Professional: Nick Leeming (01484 422304). Secretary: D. Palliser.

HUDDERSFIELD. **Marsden Golf Club,** Hemplow, Marsden, Huddersfield HD7 6NN (01484 844253). *Location:* eight miles west of Huddersfield off A62 from Huddersfield to Manchester. Moorland. 9 holes, 5702 yards. S.S.S. 68. *Green Fees:* weekdays £15.00, weekends £20.00. *Eating facilities:* lunches and snacks available except Tuesdays. *Visitors:* welcome weekdays, with a member only weekends. *Society Meetings:* catered for by arrangement. Society package from £20.00 for day golf and evening meal. Professional: James Crompton (01484 844253). Secretary: S. J. Boustead (01457 874158).

HUDDERSFIELD. **Meltham Golf Club,** Thick Hollins Hall, Meltham, Huddersfield HD9 4DQ (Tel & Fax: 01484 850227). *Location:* half mile east of Meltham, six miles south west of Huddersfield (B6107). Gently sloping course in wooded valley. 18 holes, 6390 yards, 5832 metres. S.S.S. 70. Restricted practice area. *Green Fees:* weekdays £28.00 per round, £33.00 per day; weekends and Bank Holidays £33.00 per round, £38.00 per day. 2005 rates, subject to review. *Eating facilities:* lunches, dinners (with reservation), bar meals available. *Visitors:* welcome weekdays and Sundays without reservation, not Saturdays. *Society Meetings:* catered for by arrangement. Professional: P. Davies (01484 851521). Secretary: G.W. Hopwood. website: www.meltham-golf.co.uk

HUDDERSFIELD. **Woodsome Hall Golf Club,** Woodsome Hall, Fenay Bridge, Huddersfield HD8 0LQ (01484 602739). *Location:* A629 five miles from Huddersfield. Parkland and wooded course. 18 holes, 6096 yards. S.S.S. 69. Practice ground. *Green Fees:* information not available. *Eating facilities:* bar snacks and dining available; new casual bar open. *Visitors:* welcome Mondays, Wednesdays, Thursdays and Fridays, limited on Sundays by application. *Society Meetings:* welcome by arrangement, jacket and tie in public rooms. Professional: M. Higginbottom (01484 602034). Hon Secretary: R.B. Shaw (01484 602739; Fax: 01484 608260). General Manager: Mrs T.J. Mee (01484 602739).

ILKLEY. **Ben Rhydding Golf Club,** High Wood, Ben Rhydding, Ilkley LS29 8SB (01943 608759). *Location:* one mile south-east of Ilkley town centre via Ben Rhydding Road or Wheatley Lane. Turn up Wheatley Grove and keep going up and left.Moorside parkland course with fine panoramic views over Wharfedale and surrounding moors. 9 holes, 4611 yards (18 holes). S.S.S. 63. *Green Fees:* weekdays £15.00, with member £7.50; weekends £20.00, with member £10.00. *Society Meetings:* by prior arrangement. Secretary: John Hartley (01943 865749).

ILKLEY. **Bracken Ghyll Golf Club,** Skipton Road, Addingham, Ilkley LS29 0SL (01943 831207; Fax: 01943 839453). *Location:* situated between Ilkley and Skipton on the A65, signposted just after roundabout indicating Silsden and Keighley. Parkland course in rolling dales countryside. 18 holes, 5600 yards, S.S.S. 67. Indoor nets, practice fairway and putting green. *Green Fees:* weekdays £20.00, weekends £24.00. *Eating facilities:* fully licensed bar, lunches served seven days a week in season. *Visitors:* welcome at all times outside competitions weekends and Tuesday and Thursday mornings. Telephone bookings accepted. *Society Meetings:* welcome, brochure on application. Secretary: Trevor Newman.*
e-mail: office@brackenghyll.co.uk
website: www.brackenghyll.co.uk

ILKLEY. **Ilkley Golf Club,** Nesfield Road, Ilkley LS29 0BE (01943 607277). *Location:* 15 miles north of Bradford. Flat course. 18 holes, 6262 yards. S.S.S. 70. *Green Fees:* 1st April to 31st October - weekdays £47.00, weekends £55.00; 1st November to 31st March - £30.00. Subject to review. *Eating facilities:* by

arrangement. *Visitors:* welcome by arrangement. *Society Meetings:* catered for by arrangement. Professional: J.L. Hammond (01943 607463). Secretary: Norman Hudson (01943 600214; Fax: 01943 816130). e-mail: honsec@ilkleygolfclub.co.uk
website: www.ilkleygolfclub.co.uk

KEIGHLEY. **Branshaw Golf Club,** Branshaw Moor, Oakworth, Keighley BD22 7ES (01535 643235). *Location:* on B6143, two miles from town centre. Moorland with extensive views. 5888 yards. S.S.S. 68. *Green Fees:* £20.00 midweek, £25.00 weekend, twilight green fees available. *Eating facilities:* full catering except Mondays. *Visitors:* welcome anytime by prior arrangement. *Society Meetings:* catered for weekdays and weekends. Professional: Mr Simon Jowitt (01535 647441). Secretary: Mr Simon Jowitt (01535 643235). e-mail: simonjowitt@tiscali.co.uk
website: www.branshawgolfclub.co.uk

KEIGHLEY. **Keighley Golf Club,** Howden Park, Utley, Keighley BD20 6DH (01535 604778). *Location:* one mile west of Keighley towards Utley on B6143. Parkland. 18 holes, 6141 yards. S.S.S. 70. Practice ground and green. *Green Fees:* weekdays 18 holes £35.00, 27 holes £43.00; weekends and Bank Holidays 18 holes £39.00, 27 holes £47.00. Full package for 9 or over, from £45.00. *Eating facilities:* full catering and bar facilities available. *Visitors:* welcome by prior arrangement. Tuesday Ladies' Day. *Society Meetings:* catered for by arrangement. Professional: Andy Rhodes. Secretary: Cameron Dawson (Fax: 01535 604778). e-mail: manager@keighleygolfclub.com
website: www.keighleygolfclub.com

KEIGHLEY. **Riddlesden Golf Club,** Howden Rough, Riddlesden, Keighley BD20 5QN (01535 602148). *Location:* A650 Keighley-Bradford road, left into Bar Lane, left on Scott Lane, which leads on to Scott Lane West and Elam Wood Road, approximately two miles. Moorland, with spectacular 3 par 3s in "Best Extraordinary Golf Holes Book". 18 holes, 4295 yards. S.S.S. 61. *Green Fees:* weekdays £15.00; weekends £20.00. *Eating facilities:* catering available during bar hours. *Visitors:* welcome except between 10am–2pm Saturdays and before 2pm Sundays. *Society Meetings:* catered for by prior arrangement. Secretary: S. Morton (01535 604450).

KEIGHLEY. **Silsden Golf Club,** Brunthwaite Lane, Brunthwaite, Silsden, Near Keighley BD20 0ND (01535 652998). *Location:* five miles north of Keighley. Undulating downland with extensive views. 18 holes, 5062 yards. S.S.S. 64. Practice area and putting green. *Green Fees:* £15.00 Sunday to Friday, £25.00 Saturday. *Eating facilities:* licensed bar, full catering available except Mondays. *Visitors & Society Meetings:* Welcome anytime by prior arrangement with the office (01535 652998).

KNOTTINGLEY. **Ferrybridge Golf Club,** PO Box 39, Stranglands Lane, Knottingley WF11 8SQ. *Location:* off the A1 at Ferrybridge and quarter of a mile towards Castleford on the B6136. Undulating land. 9 holes, 6047/6076 yards. S.S.S. 69. Architect: George Barton. Practice ground. *Green Fees:* information not available. *Visitors:* welcome by prior booking. *Society Meetings:* by prior arrangement with Secretary. Secretary: T.D. Ellis (01977 884165).

LEEDS. **Alwoodley Golf Club,** Wigton Lane, Alwoodley, Leeds LS17 8SA (0113 2681680). *Location:* five miles north of Leeds on A61 (Leeds to Harrogate). 18 holes, 6666 yards. S.S.S. 72. *Green Fees:* (2007) £70.00 weekdays (summer), £55.00 weekdays (winter); £85.00 weekends, £40.00 Summer twilight. *Eating facilities:* available. *Visitors:* welcome by arrangement. *Society Meetings:* catered for by arrangement. Professional: J.R. Green (0113 2689603). Secretary: Mrs J. Slater. website: www.alwoodley.co.uk

LEEDS. **Calverley Golf Club,** Woodhall Lane, Pudsey, Leeds LS28 5QY (0113 256 9244; Fax: 0113 256 4362). *Location:* off Leeds outer ring road, signposted Pudsey. Bradford turn off, turn right at next roundabout onto Woodhall Lane. Parkland course. 18 holes, 5590 yards. S.S.S. 67. Brand new 9 holes opened Summer 2007 completes 27 holes of fabulous golf. Practice ground, putting green. *Green Fees:* weekdays £14.00, with a member £10.00; weekends £17.00, with a member £13.00. Juniors £7.00. *Eating facilities:* full bar and catering facilities available. *Visitors:* very welcome, booking advisable. Members only weekends till 1pm. Buggies. Tuition available. *Society Meetings:* welcome by prior arrangement. Professional: Neil Wendel-Jones (0113 256 9244; Fax: 0113 256 4362). Hon. Secretary: Phil Dyson (0113 256 9244; Fax: 0113 256 4362).

LEEDS. **Cookridge Hall Golf Club,** Cookridge Lane, Leeds LS16 7NL (0113 2300641; Fax: 0113 2030198). *Location:* five miles to north of Leeds, two miles from Leeds and Bradford Airport on Cookridge Lane. Heavily mounded American parkland course. Designed by Karl Litten who designed The Emirates Golf Course in Dubai and The Warwickshire in the West Midlands. 18 holes, 6779 yards, 6000 metres. S.S.S. 72. 22-bay driving range with floodlights. *Green Fees:* from £25.00. *Eating facilities:* clubhouse with full bar and restaurant. *Visitors:* very welcome, weekends after 12 noon; tee times can be reserved 7 days in advance, subject to availability. Academy and lessons. *Society Meetings:* all welcome with appropriate advance booking. For information please contact Sales Office. e-mail: info@cookridgehall.co.uk website: www.cookridgehall.co.uk

LEEDS. **Garforth Golf Club Ltd,** Long Lane, Garforth, Leeds LS25 2DS (0113 286 3308). *Location:* six miles east of Leeds on A63, then turn left on to A642. Flat parkland. 18 holes, 6376 yards. S.S.S. 70. Practice area. *Green Fees:* weekdays £36.00 per round, £42.00 per day. *Eating facilities:* available. *Visitors:* welcome, but not before 9.30am or between 12 noon and 2pm (1.30pm Tuesdays and Thursdays). Weekend as member's guest only. *Society Meetings:* catered for. Professional: K. Findlater (0113 286 2063). Managing Secretary: Richard Green (Tel & Fax: 0113 286 3308).

LEEDS. **Gotts Park Municipal Golf Club,** Gotts House, Gotts Park, Armley Ridge Road, Leeds LS12 2QX (0113 231 0492). *Location:* two miles west of city centre off A647 Stanningley Road. Undulating parkland. 18 holes, 4319 yards. S.S.S. 64. Putting green and practice area. *Green Fees:* information not provided. *Eating facilities:* cafe, bar facilities evenings/weekends only. *Visitors:* welcome, tee reserved Sundays 7am to 10am for members. Secretary: Clive Walton (0113 368 5500; Mobile: 07843 689377).

LEEDS. **Headingley Golf Club,** Back Church Lane, Adel, Leeds LS16 8DW (0113 2679573). *Location:* leave Leeds/Otley road (A660) at Church Lane, Adel about five miles from city centre. 18 holes, 6608 yards. S.S.S. 72. *Green Fees:* £36.00 per round, £45.00 per day weekdays; £45.00 per round or day weekends and Bank Holidays. *Eating facilities:* full catering and bar facilities. *Visitors:* members of other golf clubs welcome, preferably with prior reservation. Two snooker tables. *Society Meetings:* catered for by arrangement. Professional: N.M. Harvey (0113 2675100; Fax: 0113 2817334). Manager: M. Seaton (0113 2679573).

LEEDS. **Horsforth Golf Club Ltd,** Layton Rise, Horsforth, Leeds LS18 5EX (0113 258 6819; Fax: 0113 258 9336). *Location:* midway between Leeds and Bradford, close to the Leeds and Bradford Airport. Easily accessible from the Leeds outer ring road and the main Bradford to Harrogate road. White tees 6258 yards, Yellow tees 5976, Ladies' tees 5563 yards. Par 71. *Green Fees:* weekdays £30.00 per round, £36.00 per day (2-Fore-1 valid); weekends £40.00 per day, £20.00 afer 2pm on Sundays. *Eating facilities:* Bar sevice available from 11.30am to 11pm. Catering ranges from coffees, breakfast, light or full lunches; buffet and formal evening meals. No smoking in dining room or lounge bar. *Visitors:* welcome, must comply with dress code. *Society Meetings:* welcome. Professionals: Dean Stokes & Simon Booth (0113 258 5200) Steward: C. Taylor (0113 258 1703). Secretary: Mrs L. Harrison (0113 258 6819).
e-mail: secretary@horsforthgolfclubltd.co.uk
          hosforthgolfclub@tiscali.co.uk
website: www.horsforthgolfclubltd.co.uk

LEEDS. **Howley Hall Golf Club,** Scotchman Lane, Morley, Leeds LS27 0NX (01924 350107; Fax: 01924 350104). *Location:* turn off the A650 Bradford/Wakefield road at the Halfway House Public House, take the B6123 towards Batley – the course is on the left. Parkland. 18 holes, 6454 yards. S.S.S. 71.

Practice ground. *Green Fees:* weekdays £30.00 per round, £36.00 per day; weekends £40.00. *Eating facilities:* dining room and bar snacks available. *Visitors:* welcome. *Society Meetings:* welcome by reservation. Professional: Gary Watkinson (01924 350102). Secretary/ Manager: David Jones (01924 350100; Fax: 01924 350104).
e-mail: office@howleyhall.co.uk

LEEDS. **Leeds Golf Centre,** Wike Ridge Lane, Shadwell, Leeds LS17 9JW (0113 288 6000; Fax: 0113 288 6185). *Location:* two miles north of Leeds between A61 and A58 at the village of Wike. Set in magnificent rolling Yorkshire countryside. Leeds Golf Centre is open to the public and members all year round. Wike Ridge course: 18 hole Championship Course. 18 holes, 6482 yards, Par 71. Oaks course: 12 holes, 1610 yards. Par 36. The centre offers the best practice facilities in the area which include 20-bay fully floodlit and covered driving range, chipping green, putting green and bunker facilities. *Green Fees:* available on request. *Eating facilities:* restaurant, bar and function room. *Visitors:* welcome any time. Resident teaching Professionals–tuition for individuals and groups. *Society Meetings:* welcome any time; society packages and special offers available throughout the year. General Manager: Andrew Levine.
e-mail: info@leedsgolfcentre.com
website: www.leedsgolfcentre.com

LEEDS. **Leeds Golf Club,** Cobble Hall, Elmete Lane, Leeds LS8 2LJ (0113 2658775). *Location:* Leeds ring road to A58, turn left if from east, right if from west, fork right at dual carriageway, turn right after 250 yards, 18 holes, 6078 yards. S.S.S. 69. *Green Fees:* £36.00 per day; £32.00 per round weekdays only; weekends only with a member. Subject to review. Golf packages available with restrictions. *Eating facilities:* full catering, all day bar. *Visitors:* welcome. *Society Meetings:* very welcome. Some limited society days available on Sundays. Professional: Simon Longster (0113 2658786). Secretary: Stephen Clarkson (0113 2659203; Fax: 0113 2323369).
e-mail: secretary@leedsgolfclub.co.uk
website: www.leedsgolfclub.co.uk

LEEDS. **Middleton Park (Municipal) Golf Club,** Ring Road, Beeston, Middleton, Leeds LS10 3TN (0113 270 9506). *Location:* ring road to Middleton off A653 (Water Tower). Parkland, wooded course. 18 holes, 5036 yards. S.S.S. 66. Practice ground. *Green Fees:* information not available.*Visitors:* welcome any time, contact the Pro Shop for bookings. *Society Meetings:* contact the Pro Shop. Professional: (0113 270 9506). *

LEEDS. **Moor Allerton Golf Club,** Coal Road, Wike, Leeds LS17 9NH (0113 2661154; Fax: 0113 2371124). *Location:* off the A61, 6 miles from Leeds city centre. Undulating parkland, PGA European Tour championship course designed by Robert Trent Jones Senior. 27 holes - three loops of 9 holes. Any combination playable. 6 bay driving range, practice ground. *Green Fees:* information not available. *Eating facilities:* full restaurant facilities plus snack bar. *Visitors:* welcome but must pre-book via Professional Shop. No visitors Sundays. Banqueting facilities for 200 people; conference/room hire for

groups of all sizes. *Society Meetings:* welcome by prior arrangement via club office. Professional: Richard Lane (0113 2665209) Office: (0113 2661154; Fax: 0113 2371124).*
e-mail: info@magc.co.uk
website: www.magc.co.uk

LEEDS. **Moortown Golf Club,** Harrogate Road, Alwoodley, Leeds LS17 7DB (0113 2686521; Fax: 0113 2680986). *Location:* five miles north of Leeds centre, A61 Leeds to Harrogate road. 18 holes, 6453 yards. S.S.S. 72. Large practice field. *Green Fees:* £65.00 per round, £75.00 per day. *Eating facilities:* lunches every day, evening meals Tuesday to Saturday. *Visitors:* welcome weekdays, some tee-off time restrictions. *Society Meetings:* catered for. Professional:M. Heggie (0113 2683636). Secretary: (0113 2686521).

LEEDS. **Oulton Park,** Rothwell Lane, Rothwell, Leeds LS26 8EX (0113 282 3152; Fax: 0113 282 6290). *Location:* M62 - Rothwell turn off, Junction 30; left at second roundabout. Parkland course built by Dave Thomas, many bunkers. 27 holes, 22 bay driving range, putting green. *Green Fees:* information not available. *Eating facilities:* restaurant and bar. *Visitors:* welcome, no restrictions; advance booking (five days) available. Dress code on course. *Society Meetings:* welcome except weekends. Professional: Steve Gromett. Manager: Allan Cooper.*

LEEDS. **Rawdon Golf and Lawn Tennis Club,** Buckstone Drive, Micklefield Lane, Rawdon, Leeds LS19 6BD (0113-250 6040). *Location:* eight miles north of Leeds on A65, left at Rawdon traffic lights on to Micklefield Lane. Undulating parkland, with trees a special feature. 9 holes (18 tees), 5842 yards. S.S.S. 68. *Green Fees:* Information not available. *Eating facilities:* meals and bar snacks except Mondays. *Visitors:* welcome. Facilities for tennis, visitors welcome. *Society Meetings:* catered for on application to Secretary. Secretary: John Lawson (01943 872430).*

LEEDS. **Roundhay Golf Club,** Park Lane, Leeds LS8 2EJ (0113 2662695). *Location:* four miles north of Leeds city centre, leave A58 to Wetherby at Oakwood. Wooded parkland. 9 holes, 5322 yards. S.S.S. 65. Practice ground. *Green Fees:* on application. *Eating facilities:* bar for members, guests, and anyone purchasing a green fee, restaurant in evenings. *Visitors:* welcome without reservation. *Society Meetings:* arrangements with Leeds City Council. Professional: J. Pape (0113 2661686). Hon. Secretary: R.H. McLauchlan (0113 2664225).

LEEDS. **Sand Moor Golf Club,** Alwoodley Lane, Leeds LS17 7DJ (0113 2681685). *Location:* five miles north of Leeds off A61. Moorland, overlooking picturesque Wharfedale. 18 holes, 6414 yards, 5862 metres. S.S.S. 71. *Green Fees:* information on request. *Eating facilities:* lunches daily, evening meals by arrangement. *Visitors:* welcome most weekdays and Sundays by arrangement. *Society Meetings:* catered for by arrangement. Professional: Frank Houlgate (0113 2683925). Secretary: Ian Kerr (0113 2685180; Fax: 0113 2661105).

LEEDS. **Scarcroft Golf Club,** Syke Lane, Leeds LS14 3BQ (0113 289 2311). *Location:* A58 Wetherby road; turn left at Bracken Fox Public House, Scarcroft village seven miles north of Leeds. Undulating parkland. 18 holes, 6426 yards. S.S.S. 71. Practice ground. *Green Fees:* information not provided. *Eating facilities:* bar and restaurant. *Visitors:* casuals after 9.30am. *Society Meetings:* accepted Mondays to Fridays April to October. Must have official Handicaps. Party rates for groups of 5 or more. Professional: David Hughes (0113 289 2780). General Manager: Mike Gallagher (0113 289 2311).

LEEDS. **South Leeds Golf Club,** Parkside Links, Gipsy Lane, Leeds LS11 5TU (0113 277 1676). *Location:* M62 and M1 within five minutes' drive, Leeds City Centre 5 minutes' drive. Parkland course with undulating fairways. 18 holes, 5865 yards. S.S.S. 69. Practice ground and net. *Green Fees:* £21.00 weekdays; £28.00 weekends and Bank Holidays (rates may change). *Eating facilities:* full catering except Mondays; bar. *Visitors:* welcome weekdays. *Society Meetings:* catered for by prior arrangement. Professional: Nick Sheard (0113 272 3757). Secretary: B. Clayton (0113 277 1676).

LEEDS. **Temple Newsam Golf Club,** Temple Newsam, Leeds LS15 0LN (0113 264 5624). *Location:* easily reached by public transport from City (to Temple Newsam or Halton). Two 18 hole courses. No. 1 Course 6448 yards. S.S.S. 71. No. 2 Course 5731 yards. S.S.S. 70. *Green Fees:* weekdays £9.50, twilight (after 5pm) £6.50; weekends £12.50, after 2pm £8.50, after 5pm £6.50. *Eating facilities:* cafe open six days a week 7.30am till 4.00pm weekends, 10.00am till 4.00pm midweek. *Visitors:* welcome without reservation, except that parties must book in advance. *Society Meetings:* catered for. Professional: Adrian Newbould (0113 264 1464). Secretary: Christine Wood.
e-mail: secretary@tngolfclub.co.uk
website: www.tngolfclub.co.uk

MIRFIELD. **Dewsbury District Golf Club,** The Pinnacle, Sands Lane, Mirfield WF14 8HJ (01924 491928). *Location:* turn off A644 opposite Swan Inn, two miles west of Dewsbury. Undulating moorland/parkland with panoramic views over surrounding countryside. 18 holes, 6360 yards. S.S.S. 71. Practice field, putting green. *Green Fees:* weekdays £22.00 per round, £28.00 per day; weekends £17.50 after 3pm. Subject to review. *Eating facilities:* bar and restaurant (catering every day). *Visitors:* welcome without reservation weekdays, weekends with member only before 3pm. *Society Meetings:* welcome by prior arrangement. Parties over 12: day £25.25 per person. Professional: N.P. Hirst (01924 496030). General Manager: Ray Dando (01924 492399).
e-mail: dewsbury.golf@btopenworld.com
website: www.dewsburygolf.co.uk

OTLEY. **Otley Golf Club,** West Busk Lane, Otley LS21 3NG (01943 465329). *Location:* off main Bradford to Otley road. Parkland with magnificent views across Wharfedale. 18 holes, 6211 yards. S.S.S. 70. Large practice ground. *Green Fees:* weekdays £34.00 for 18 or 27 holes, £40.00 for two rounds; weekends £40.00 for 18 or 27 holes, £47.00 for two rounds. *Eating facilities:* large dining rooms. *Visitors:* welcome except Tuesday mornings and Saturdays. Trolleys and clubs for hire. *Society Meetings:* catered for by arrangement; special facilities for company days. Professional: Steven Tomkinson (01943 465329 ext. 203; Fax: 01943 463403). Secretary/Manager: Peter J. Clarke (01943 465329 ext 202; Fax: 01943 850387).

OUTLANE. **Outlane Golf Club,** Slack Lane, off New Hey Road, Outlane, Near Huddersfield HD3 3FQ (01422 374762; Fax: 01422 311789). *Location:* from Huddersfield (A640) through Outlane Village, entrance on left just after bus terminus. Semi-moorland course, part wooded. Offers panoramic views and is challenge to the amateur. 18 holes, 6100 yards. S.S.S. 69. Practice areas and nets available. *Green Fees:* £22.00 midweek; £32.00 weekends and Bank Holidays. Reduced rates playing with member and after 1pm Sundays. *Eating facilities:* full catering available except Mondays. *Visitors:* welcome except Saturdays; Sundays by arrangement. Carts available. *Society Meetings:* welcome with reservation. Professional: D.M. Chapman (01422 374762; Fax: 01422 311789). Secretary: P. Jackson (Tel & Fax: 01422 311789). Stewardess: Mrs C.E. Hirst (01422 374762).

PONTEFRACT. **Mid Yorkshire Golf Club,** Havercroft Lane, Darrington, Pontefract (01977 704522; Fax: 01977 600823). *Location:* 300 yards from A1 at Darrington half-mile south of A1/M62 interchange. Undulating with established woodland and lakes. 18 holes, 6308 yards. Par 70. Covered floodlit driving range, tee to green irrigation, 18 greens played all year round. *Green Fees:* £21.00 weekdays, £31.00 weekends. *Eating facilities:* two bars; private functions catered for. *Visitors:* welcome weekdays, afternoons only at weekends. Buggies available. *Society Meetings:* welcome weekdays, afternoons only at weekends. Professional: Mike Hessay (01977 600844).
website: www.midyorkshiregolfclub.com

PONTEFRACT. **Pontefract and District Golf Club,** Park Lane, Pontefract WF8 4QS (01977 792241). *Location:* M62 Exit 32, one mile from Pontefract on B6134. Parkland. 18 holes, 6455 yards. S.S.S. 71. Practice ground. *Green Fees:* weekdays £30.00 per round, £35.00 per day; weekends £35.00. *Eating facilities:* available all week. *Visitors:* welcome. *Society Meetings:* catered for Mondays, Tuesdays, Thursdays and Fridays by arrangement. Professional: Nick J. Newman (01977 706806). Manager: (01977 792241).
e-mail: manager@pdgc.co.uk
website: www.pdgc.co.uk

PUDSEY. **Fulneck Golf Club Ltd,** Fulneck, Pudsey LS28 8NT (0113 2565191). *Location:* between Leeds and Bradford. Undulating wooded parkland course. 9 holes, 5456 yards. S.S.S. 67. *Green Fees:* information not available. *Society Meetings:* catered for by arrangement. Secretary: Mr S. Tempest.
e-mail: fulneckgolf@aol.com

PLEASE

NOTE

All the information regarding Golf Clubs in this guide is given in good faith in the belief that it is correct. However, the publishers cannot guarantee the facts given in these pages, neither are they responsible for changes in ownership or facilities, such as green fees, that may take place after the date of going to press. Readers should always satisfy themselves that the facilities they require are available and that the terms, if quoted, still apply.

PUDSEY. **Woodhall Hills Golf Club Ltd,** Woodhall Road, Calverley, Pudsey, Leeds LS28 5UN (0113 256 4771). *Location:* signposted Calverley from A647 Leeds to Bradford Road, quarter of a mile beyond Calverley Golf Club. Parkland course. 18 holes, 6184 yards. S.S.S. 70. *Green Fees:* Information not available. *Eating facilities:* available daily except Mondays. *Visitors:* welcome without reservation. *Society Meetings:* catered for by previous arrangement. Golf Manager/Professional: W. Lockett (0113 256 2857). Club Office: (0113 255 4594)*

SHIPLEY. **Marriott Hollins Hall Hotel & Country Club,** Hollins Hill, Baildon, Shipley BD17 7QW (01274 534212). Home to the PGA European Professional Tour. *Location:* North/South Leeds Ring Road, take A65 Skipton Road, then A6038 (towards Shipley), entrance on right. Superb championship heathland course in the beautiful Yorkshire Dales. 18 holes. Par 71. *Green Fees:* information not available. *Eating facilities:* available all day. *Visitors:* welcome. Trolley, buggy and shoe hire.*

TODMORDEN. **Todmorden Golf Club,** Rive Rocks, Cross Stone Road, Todmorden OL14 8RD (01706 812986). *Location:* A646 Halifax Road, half a mile from centre, turn into Cross Stone Road, half a mile, bear left at top. Moorland. 9 holes, 5902 yards. S.S.S. 68. *Green Fees:* weekdays £15.00; weekends and Bank Holidays £20.00. Packages (18 or 27 holes from £25.00) available Monday, Tuesday, Wednesday and Sunday, includes coffee and biscuits on arrival, soup and sandwiches, evening meal. *Eating facilities:* available, order in advance. *Visitors:* welcome without reservation, but advisable to phone beforehand. Thursday is Ladies' Day. *Society Meetings:* welcome, please phone for course availability.

WAKEFIELD. **City of Wakefield Golf Club,** Lupset Park, Horbury Road, Wakefield WF2 8QS (01924 360282). *Location:* one mile from city centre, two miles from M1 Junctions 39/40. Undulating partially wooded parkland. 18 holes, 6319 yards, 5760 metres. S.S.S. 70. *Green Fees:* information not provided. *Eating facilities:* full or snack catering, bar available. *Visitors:* booked times only. *Society Meetings:* by arrangement with Stewardess (07971 554548). Secretary: (01924 367442).

WAKEFIELD. **Lofthouse Hill Golf Club,** Leeds Road, Wakefield WF3 3LR (Tel & Fax: 01924 823703). *Location:* A61 between Leeds and Wakefield. Parkland course. 18 holes, 5933 yards, S.S.S. 68. *Green Fees:* £12.00. Buggies £12.00. *Eating facilities:* food available all day in bar. *Visitors:* welcome, please telephone. Teaching professional. *Society Meetings:* welcome, see website. Professional: Derek Johnson (Tel & Fax: 01924 823703). Secretary: David Nicklin. website: www.lofthousehillgolfclub.co.uk

WAKEFIELD. **Low Laithes Golf Club Ltd,** Parkmill Lane, Flushdyke, Ossett, Wakefield WF5 9AP (01924 266067). *Location:* one mile from Junction 40 M1, or along A638 Dewsbury to Wakefield road. Parkland, undulating. 18 holes, 6456 yards. S.S.S. 71. Practice area. *Green Fees:* Monday - Friday £25.00 per round, £30.00 per day. *Eating facilities:* bar and catering.

Visitors: welcome weekdays after 9.30am to 12.30 and after 1.30pm. *Society Meetings:* by arrangement, not weekends or Bank Holidays - 27 holes and catering £37.00. Professional: Paul Browning (01924 274667). Secretary: Paul Browning (Tel 01924 266067; Fax: 01924 266266).

WAKEFIELD. **Normanton Golf Club,** Hatfeild Hall. Aberford Road, Stanley WF3 4JP (01924 377943; Fax: 01924 200777). *Location:* M62 Junction 30, A642 toward Wakefield. Parkland course. Practice area. 18 holes, 6191 yards, 5662 metres. S.S.S. 70. *Green Fees:* information not available. *Society Meetings:* welcome during the week. Restricted at weekend. Professional: Gary Pritchard (01924 200900). General Manager (01924 377943).*

WAKEFIELD. **Wakefield Golf Club,** Woodthorpe Lane, Sandal, Wakefield WF2 6JH (01924 258778; Fax: 01924 242752). *Location:* leave M1 at Junction 39, golf club off Barnsley Road. Parkland. 18 holes, 6653 yards. S.S.S. 72. *Green Fees:* weekdays £32.00 per round, £37.00 per day, with a member £15.00 per day; weekends and Bank Holidays £40.00, with a member £20.00. *Eating facilities:* full catering available. *Visitors:* visiting parties by arrangement Mondays, Wednesdays, Thursdays, Fridays and Sunday (pm only). *Society Meetings:* welcome, catered for by arrangement. Professional: I.M. Wright. Secretary: Mrs E. Newton (01924 258778).

WAKEFIELD. **Woolley Park Golf Club,** Mount Farm, Abbot Lane, Woolley, Wakefield WF4 2JJ (01226 380144; Fax: 01226 390295). *Location:* half a mile from A61 half way between Barnsley and Wakefield. Parkland course. 18 holes, 6636 yards (white tees), S.S.S. 72. Practice area, putting green. *Green Fees:* weekdays £20.00; weekends £27.50 (under review). *Eating facilities:* food available all day every day, bar. *Visitors:* welcome all week, weekend bookings from Thursday only. Tuition available. *Society Meetings:* welcome, please telephone for details. Professional: Jon Baldwin (01226 380144; Fax: 01226 390295). Secretary: David Rowbottom (01226 380144; Fax: 01226 390295). website: www.woolleyparkgolfclub.co.uk

WETHERBY. **Wetherby Golf Club,** Linton Lane, Linton, Wetherby LS22 4JF (01937 580089; Fax: 01937 581915). *Location:* three quarters of a mile west of A1 roundabout. Parkland course adjoining River Wharfe. 18 holes, 6213 yards. S.S.S. 70. Practice ground. *Green Fees:* Information not available. *Eating facilities:* available seven days a week. *Visitors:* welcome, advisable to phone first. *Society Meetings:* catered for weekdays except Tuesday mornings. Professional: Mark Daubney (01937 580089 ext. 22). Golf Club Manager: Matthew Streets (01937 580089 ext. 20).*

THE APPEARANCE OF AN ASTERISK (*) AT THE END OF A CLUB OR COURSE ENTRY INDICATES THAT UP-TO-DATE INFORMATION HAS NOT BEEN SUPPLIED

Golf in Scotland

Nick Rodger

Aberdeen, Banff & Moray • Angus & Dundee
Argyll & Bute • Ayrshire & Arran • Borders • Dumfries &
Galloway • Dunbartonshire • Edinburgh & Lothians • Fife
Glasgow & District • Highlands •Lanarkshire • Perth & Kinross
Renfrewshire • Stirling & The Trossachs •Scottish Islands

The clubhouse from the 9th, Scotscraig Golf Club, Tayport, Fife

AFTER THE GREAT SUMMER of Scottish golf last year, which saw four open championships held north of the Border in the space of four weeks, one could be forgiven for thinking that 2008 would be relatively quiet in comparison. Make no mistake however, the cradle of the game will still be the place to be this season for those followers of the sport who are keen to sample top-level action at some of the world's finest courses.

During a month-long golfing festival in 2007, comprising the Barclays Scottish Open, the Open Championship, the Senior British Open and the Ricoh Women's British Open, almost 330,000 paying customers were drawn to the respective venues of Loch Lomond, Carnoustie, Muirfield and St Andrews as the soggy summer failed to dampen the spirits of the legions behind the ropes. Record attendances were achieved at both the Scottish Open and the Seniors' event and all indications are that these two championships will continue to prosper this year when they headline another bumper year

of competition in the Home of Golf.

Now firmly established as one of the European Tour's most eagerly anticipated events, the Barclays Scottish Open always conjures up drama, and the 2007 contest was no different as Frenchman Gregory Havret staved off the challenge of Phil Mickelson in a play-off to seize the £500,000 top prize on the Bonnie Banks.

Like the Scottish Open, the Seniors' championship has become a firm fixture on the calendar and, in 2008, the over-50s showpiece will be held in Scotland for the fourth consecutive year when it makes the trip to the venerable links of Royal Troon.

With Major-winning Ryder Cup captains, Bernhard Langer, Hal Sutton and Ian Woosnam, as well as Scotland's very own Sandy Lyle, all eligible to play in this July's event, title holder Tom Watson will face stern competition as he launches the defence of his crown.

In a notable career gilded with 13 Major wins on both the main and Senior tours, Watson

Blackloch, Blairgowrie Golf Club, Perth & Kinross

8th hole, Aboyne Golf Club, Aberdeenshire

has a fondness for the great golfing heartland of Ayrshire, having lifted two Claret Jugs in the region, at Turnberry in 1977 and Troon in 1982. With such an impressive track record on Scottish soil, it's no wonder the popular American said after his Seniors' win at Muirfield last year: "I wish I could play every tournament in Scotland."

While the Scottish Open and the Seniors' Open will provide the highlights of the professional season, the amateur scene continues to blossom in this country and, thanks to the successes enjoyed by the likes of Richie Ramsay and Lloyd Saltman on the world stage, the profile of the Scottish game has never been higher.

With a mouth-watering programme of national and international events scheduled for some of the country's leading venues, the coming months will provide bountiful opportunities to witness the next generation of golfing stars.

The traditional curtain-raiser to the domestic campaign, the Scottish Boys' championship, heads south in April to the exacting links of Southerness on the Galloway coast, while the Scottish Open Strokeplay championship, with

an impressive roll of honour which includes Bernard Gallacher, Colin Montgomerie and Andrew Coltart, will take place at the Duke's Course near St Andrews in May. The world's finest amateurs will then make the trip to Ayrshire in June for the Amateur championship at Turnberry while Carnoustie, which provided the stage for an enthralling Open Championship in 2007, will return to the spotlight in late July when it plays host to the SGU's flagship event, the Scottish Amateur championship, for the first time since 1997. Team competition is very much to the fore in Scotland this year, and after Great Britain and Ireland take on their European rivals in the St Andrews Trophy at Kingsbarns in August, the leading lights from the home nations will cross swords in the Home Internationals over the redoubtable links of Muirfield a month later. With such a vast array of professional and amateur events taking place across the length and breadth of the country in 2008, this year's golfing calendar will guarantee that, wherever you may be in Scotland, you'll never be too far away from the cut and thrust of first class competition.

Looking for Holiday Accommodation?

for details of hundreds of properties
throughout the UK, visit our website
www.holidayguides.com

Aberdeen, Banff & Moray

ABERDEEN. **Aberdeen City Golf, Auchmill Golf Club,** Bonnyview Road, Aberdeen AB2 7FQ (01224 714577). *Location:* approximately four miles from city centre, beside Bucksburn area. Parkland, wooded course. 18 holes, 5391 metres. Practice area. Putting area. *Green Fees:* information not available. *Visitors:* welcome anytime. Starter: (01224 714577).*
website: www.aberdeencity.gov.uk

ABERDEEN. **Aberdeen City Golf, Balnagask Golf Course,** St Fitticks Road, Aberdeen. (01224 876407). *Location:* on coast beside Girdleness Lighthouse between Aberdeen Harbour and Nigg Bay, south side of city. Seaside links. 18 holes, 5541 metres. 9-hole pitch and putt. *Green Fees:* information not available. *Visitors:* welcome. Starter: (01224 876407).*
website: www.aberdeencity.gov.uk

ABERDEEN. **Aberdeen City Golf, Hazlehead Golf Course,** Hazlehead Avenue, Aberdeen AB9 1XJ (01224 321830). *Location:* situated on west edge of city, four miles from city centre. From A944 into Aberdeen turn off into Groats Road. Two courses - 18 holes, 5690 metres; 18 holes, 5270 metres. 9 hole course, 2531 metres. *Green Fees:* information not available. *Eating facilities:* restaurant adjoining park. *Visitors:* welcome. Professional: (01224 317336). Starter: (01224 321830).*
website: www.aberdeencity.gov.uk

ABERDEEN. **Aberdeen City Golf, King's Links Golf Course,** Golf Road, Aberdeen (01224 632269). *Location:* behind the Pittodrie Stadium, on the King's Links, by the beach. Seaside links. 6-hole, 1273 yards. 18-hole, 6296 yards, S.S.S 71. *Green Fees:* information not available. *Visitors:* welcome at all times. Starter: (01224 632269).*
website: www.aberdeencity.gov.uk

ABERDEEN. **Bon Accord Golf Club,** 19 Golf Road, Aberdeen AB24 5QB (01224 633464). *Location:* next to Pittodrie Stadium at Aberdeen beach. Seaside links. 18 holes, 6300 yards. S.S.S. 69. *Green Fees:* information not available. *Eating facilities:* meals on request. *Visitors:* welcome; please call starters box (01224 632269) for information regarding booking of tee times and green fees. *Society Meetings:* bookings in advance. Secretary: J. A. Morrison.*

ABERDEEN. **Caledonian Golf Club,** 20 Golf Road, Aberdeen AB24 5QB (01224 632443). *Location:* 50 yards to right of Richard Donald Stand/Pittodrie Football Club. Seaside links. 18 holes, 6437 yards. S.S.S. 69. 6 hole course; driving range nearby. *Green Fees:* information not available. *Eating facilities:* clubhouse snacks and meals. *Visitors:* welcome. Entertainment is provided in clubrooms on Saturdays for members and their guests. Secretary: R. Petrie.*

ABERDEEN. **Deeside Golf Club,** Golf Road, Bieldside, Aberdeen AB15 9DL (01224 869457). *Location:* A93 from Aberdeen to Braemar. Wooded parkland. 18 holes, 6264 yards. S.S.S. 70. Also 9 hole course, 5042 yards. S.S.S. 68. Practice ground. *Green Fees:* information not provided. *Eating facilities:* full catering and bar facilities. *Visitors:* welcome weekdays up to 4pm, weekends after 4pm. *Society Meetings:* by arrangement. Professional: F.J. Coutts (01224 861041). Managing Secretary: D. P. Pern (Tel & Fax: 01224 869457).
e-mail: admin@deesidegolfclub.com
website: www.deesidegolfclub.com

ABERDEEN. **Murcar Links Golf Club,** Bridge of Don, Aberdeen AB23 8BD (01224 704354). *Location:* A90 Aberdeen - Fraserburgh Road, 5 miles north of Aberdeen city centre. Championship seaside links. 18 holes, 6314 yards. S.S.S. 72; Strabathie 9-hole course, 5369 yards. S.S.S 66. Practice ground, driving range. *Green Fees:* Murcar, weekdays £70.00 per round, £95.00 per day; weekends £90.00 per round. Strabathie, weekdays £15.00 per 9 holes, £38.00 per day; weekends £22.50 per 9 holes, £45.00 per 18 holes. *Eating facilities:* dining room/bars. *Visitors:* welcome by advance booking. Hand trolleys for hire. *Society Meetings:* catered for by advance booking. Secretaries: Joanne Mitchell/ Karen McKechnie (Tel & Fax: 01224 704354). Professional: Gary Forbes (Tel & Fax: 01224 704370).
e-mail: golf@murcarlinks.com
website: www.murcarlinks.com

ABERDEEN. **Nigg Bay Golf Club,** St Fitticks Road, Torry, Aberdeen AB1 3QT (01224 871286; Fax: 01224 873418). *Location:* junction of Victoria Road and St Fitticks Road. Seaside links, hills and hidden holes. 18 holes, 5986 yards, 5472 metres. S.S.S. 69. 9 hole pitch and putt. *Green Fees:* information not available. *Eating facilities:* full catering. *Visitors:* welcome anytime (Municipal course); golfers welcome in clubhouse after playing. Secretary: Alan Fraser.*

ABERDEEN. **Northern Golf Club** 22 Golf Road, Aberdeen AB24 5QB (01224 636440; Fax: 01224 622679). *Location:* Golf Road, opposite Pittodrie Stadium. 18 holes, 5731 metres. S.S.S. 70. 6 hole course, 1251 metres; driving range next door. *Green Fees:* information not available. *Visitors:* welcome, book in person on the day of play. Public bookings restricted on Saturdays for club matches. *Society Meetings:* all welcome by writing to Aberdeen District Council (14 days notice). Professional: Mr B. Davidson (01224 641577). Secretary: Denis Sangster (Tel & Fax: 01224 622679). Steward: (01224 636440).

www.uk-golfguide.com

"A Century in the making and a venue used by the PGA European Tours"

Par 71 - SS 73 - USGA Rating 72.6 - USGA Slope 138

ABERDEEN. **Royal Aberdeen Golf Club,** Links Road, Balgownie, Bridge of Don AB23 8AT (01224 702571; Fax: 01224 826591). *Location:* on A92 Aberdeen/Fraserburgh Road, cross Bridge of Don, second right. Seaside links. Two Courses - Championship (Balgownie): 18 holes, 6900 yards, 6309 metres. S.S.S. 72; Silverburn: 18 holes, 4021 yards, 3717 metres. S.S.S. 61. Practice putting green. *Green Fees:* weekdays £100.00 per person per round, £150.00 per day; weekends £120.00 per person per round. *Eating facilities:* Old Bar, main lounge and dining room - jacket and tie. *Visitors:* welcome weekdays 10am to 11.30am and 2pm to 3.30pm, weekends after 3.30pm. Letter of introduction or Handicap Certificate required. Hire carts. *Society Meetings:* welcome. Professional/ Director of Golf: Ronnie MacAskill (01224 702221; Fax: 01224 826591). Exe. Secretary: Sandra Nicolson. e-mail: admin@royalaberdeengolf.om

ABERDEEN. **Tarland Golf Club,** Aberdeen Road, Tarland, Aboyne AB34 4TB (Tel & Fax: 013398 81000). *Location:* six miles north of Aboyne on A93, 30 miles west of Aberdeen on B9119. Difficult upland Tom Morris course in picturesque scenery. 9 holes, 5816 yards for 18 holes, S.S.S. 68. Small practice area. *Green Fees:* weekdays £18.00 per day; weekends £24.00. Weekly tickets £90.00, fortnightly tickets £150.00. Subject to review. *Eating facilities:* catering available, bar 11am to midnight. *Visitors:* welcome without reservation but phone call advisable due to club competitions at weekends. *Society Meetings:* catered for with prior reservation at all times. Secretary: Mrs J. Joseph (013398 81000) Apr-Oct.

ABOYNE. **Aboyne Golf Club,** Formaston Park, Aboyne AB34 5HP (013398 86328). *Location:* A93, 30 miles west of Aberdeen. Part parkland, part hilly with lovely views. 18 holes, 6009 yards. S.S.S. 69. Practice ground. *Green Fees:* weekdays £25.00 per round, £32.00 per day; weekends £28.00 per round, £38.00 per day. *Eating facilities:* full restaurant and bar facilities. *Visitors:* welcome without reservation. *Society Meetings:* by arrangement with Secretary. Professional: Steven Moir. (013398 86328). Secretary: (013398 87078; Fax: 013398 87592). e-mail: aboynegolfclub@btconnect.com website: www.aboynegolfclub.co.uk

ABOYNE. **Aboyne Loch Golf Centre,** The Lodge on the Loch of Aboyne, Aboyne, AB34 5BR (013398 86444 reservations). *Location:* 30 minutes' drive from Aberdeen. A scenic 9 hole course beside the Loch of Aboyne, with a combination of Par 3, 4 and 5s, together with water hazards, offering a challenge to golfers of any ability. *Green Fees:* adults £10.00 per round, £14.00 per days weekdays; £12.00 per round, £16.00 per day weekends. Weekly ticket £45.00. Juniors £6.00 per round, £10.00 per day weekdays; £8.00 per round, £12.00 per day weekends. Weekly ticket £25.00. *Eating facilities:* restaurant and bar. *Visitors:* always welcome. Clubs, carts and golf car hire. Health and Beauty Spa. *Society meetings:* golf outings, corporate and family fun days catered for. e-mail: info@thelodgeontheloch.com website: www.thelodgeontheloch.com

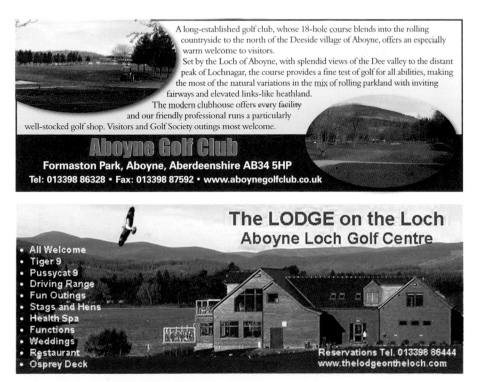

ALFORD. **Alford Golf Club,** Montgarrie Road, Alford AB33 8AE (Tel & Fax: 019755 62178; Fax: 019755 64910). *Location:* A944, 26 miles west of Aberdeen. Flat, parkland course. 18 holes, 5483 yards. S.S.S. 66. Practice area. *Green Fees:* £20.00 per round, £25.00 per day weekdays; £25.00 per round, £30.00 per day weekends. Subject to review. *Eating facilities:* catering 9am-9pm; bar services. *Visitors:* always welcome; call club to book tee, weekends very busy. Changing rooms and showers. Buggy Hire available. *Society Meetings:* welcome by prior arrangement. Secretary: Irene Currie.
e-mail: info@alford-golf-club.co.uk
website: www.alford-golf-club.co.uk

AUCHENBLAE. **Auchenblae Golf Course,** Auchenblae Parks Committee, Linwood, Auchenblae AB30 1WQ. *Location:* nine miles south of Stonehaven, off A90, two miles west of Fordoun. Parkland. 9 holes, 4434 yards SSS 61. *Green Fees:* £15.00 (concessions) subject to review for 2007. *Eating facilities:* shop open April to October. *Visitors:* welcome. Telephone Pavilion (01561 320002) for details of club nights and current information. Trolleys for hire. *Society Meetings:* welcome. Treasurer/Secretary: J.M. Thomson (01561 320245). website: www.auchenblae.org

BALLATER. **Ballater Golf Club,** Victoria Road, Ballater AB35 5QX (013397 55567). *Location:* A93, 42 miles west of Aberdeen and 62 miles from Perth. Flat picturesque parkland course close to Balmoral Castle. 18 holes, 5638 yards. S.S.S. 67. Practice ground, putting. *Green Fees:* information not provided. *Eating facilities:* full catering and refreshments April to October. *Visitors:* all welcome, booking well in advance is advisable. Tennis, bowling. *Society Meetings:* all welcome, book well in advance. Professional: Bill Yule (013397 55658). Secretary: Mrs Jennifer Smith (013397 55567).
e-mail: sec@ballatergolfclub.co.uk
website: www.ballatergolfclub.co.uk

BALMEDIE. **East Aberdeenshire Golf Centre,** Millden, Balmedie AB23 8YY (01358 742111; Fax: 01358 742123). *Location:* 3 miles from the Aberdeen Exhibition Centre, on left side of road before you reach Balmedie, on the Peterhead/Fraserburgh road. Parkland course. 18 holes, 6276 yards, S.S.S. 71. 16 bay floodlit driving range, practice chipping green, 5 hole Par 3 course. *Green Fees:* information not provided. *Eating facilities:* bar, restaurant, function room, all with public house licence. *Visitors:* welcome any time, no jeans on course please. *Society Meetings:* welcome, midweek rate includes tea/coffee, bacon roll, 18 holes, two-course meal. Professional: David McCormack (01358 742111). Secretary: Sandra or David Watson (01358 742111).
e-mail: info@eagolf.com
website: www.eagolf.com

BANCHORY. **Inchmarlo Golf Club,** Glassel Road, Inchmarlo AB31 4BQ (01330 826424). *Location:* half a mile from A93 Aberdeen-Braemar road, 25 minutes from Aberdeen city centre. 9-hole course: beautiful but tricky parkland course, 4300 yards, S.S.S. 62, Par 64. 18 hole championship Laird's Course, 6218 yards, Par 71, S.S.S. 71. 30-bay floodlit driving range. *Green Fees:* weekdays – 9-hole course £11.00, £16.00 for 2x9 holes; Laird's Course £32.00. Weekends – 9-hole course £12.00, £18.00 for 2x9 holes; Laird's Course £37.00. *Eating facilities:* Gillie's Restaurant, function/conference room, choice of bars. *Visitors:* very welcome any time, advisable to book in advance. *Society Meetings:* welcome all year by prior arrangement. Luxury serviced apartments and villas on site. Secretary: Andrew Shinie (01330 826427).
e-mail: secretary@inchmarlo.com
website: www.inchmarlo.com
    www.inchmarlogolf.com

THE APPEARANCE OF AN ASTERISK (*) AT THE END OF A CLUB OR COURSE ENTRY INDICATES THAT UP-TO-DATE INFORMATION HAS NOT BEEN SUPPLIED

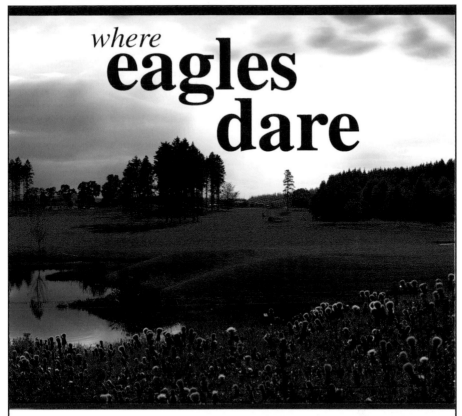

where **eagles dare**

At the heart of Royal Deeside there is a special place where buzzards soar with eagles and the land rises and falls gracefully.

In the foothills of the Scottish Highlands near Aberdeen, Inchmarlo's spectacular 18-hole Laird's course follows the natural twists and turns of the undulating countryside creating a truly breath-taking golfing experience.

- **Stunning Laird's 18-hole championship course**
- **Challenging Queen's 9-hole course**
- **Floodlit 30-bay driving range**
- **Fully stocked golf shop**
- **Professional tuition**
- **Corporate event management**
- **Accommodation available nightly/weekly etc**
- **Gillies Restaurant - Open to the public**
- **Golf Societies welcome Monday - Friday (prior booking essential)**

INCHMARLO
GOLF CLUB
ROYAL DEESIDE

Inchmarlo • Banchory • Royal Deeside • AB31 4BQ • Scotland
Tel: 01330 826424 • www.inchmarlo.com • info@inchmarlo.com

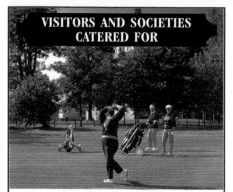

VISITORS AND SOCIETIES
CATERED FOR

DUFF HOUSE ROYAL
GOLF CLUB

THE BARNYARDS, BANFF AB45 3SX

OFFICE: 01261 812062 • PRO SHOP: 01261 812075

e-mail: duff_house_royal@btinternet.com

18-HOLE PARKLAND COURSE

PRACTICE PUTTING AREA • GOLF SHOP

PGA PROFESSIONAL • PUTTING GREEN

LOUNGE BAR • CATERING FACILITIES

OPEN DAYS • CHANGING FACILITIES

BANCHORY. **Banchory Golf Club,** Kinneskie Road, Banchory AB31 5TA (01330 822365; Fax: 01330 822491). *Location:* 100 yards off the A93 Aberdeen to Braemar Road. Flat parkland course, several holes on the banks of the River Dee. 18 holes, 5801 yards. S.S.S. 68. Practice ground and putting green. *Green Fees:* £26.00 per round, £35.00 per day. 7 month season ticket £310.00, 12 monthly season ticket £350.00. *Eating facilities:* attractive lounge and dining room. *Visitors:* welcome any time, restrictions on Tuesdays and weekends. *Society Meetings:* welcome but restrictions on Tuesdays and at weekends. Professional: David Naylor (Tel & Fax: 01330 822447). Secretary: William Crighton (01330 822365; Fax: 01330 822491).
e-mail: info@banchorygolfclub.co.uk
website: www.banchorygolfclub.co.uk

BANCHORY. **Lumphanan Golf Club,** Main Road, Lumphanan, Banchory AB31 4PW (01339 883480). *Location*: on the road between Torphins and Lumphanan about 10 miles from Banchory. Hilly, quiet, village course. 9 holes, 3718 yards, S.S.S 62. Course re-designed in 2000. *Green Fees*: information not available. *Eating facilities*: clubhouse/bar open weekends and some evenings; food weekends only. *Visitors*: welcome - no need to book. *Society Meetings*: outings welcome by arrangement with Secretary. Secretary: Pamela Thorn (01339 883589).*
e-mail: lumphanan.golf.club@lineone.net
website: www.lineone.net/~lumphanan.golf.club

BANFF. **Duff House Royal Golf Club,** The Barnyards, Banff AB45 3SX (01261 812062; Fax: 01261 812224). *Location:* two minutes from town centre, A97, A98. Level parkland. 18 holes, 6161 yards. S.S.S. 70. Practice putting area. *Green Fees:* information not available. *Eating facilities:* lounge bar and full catering service. *Visitors:* welcome weekdays after 9.30am, restrictions at weekends but times available. Pro shop. *Society Meetings:* catered for by prior arrangement. Professional: G. Holland (01261 812075). Secretary: G. MacKenzie (01261 812062).
e-mail: duff_house_royal@btinternet.com

BRAEMAR. **Braemar Golf Club,** Cluniebank Road, Braemar AB35 5XX (013397 41618). *Location:* about one mile from centre of the village, signposted opposite Fife Arms Hotel. Flat parkland, highest 18 hole course in Scotland, course split in two by River Clunie. 18 holes, 5030 yards. S.S.S. 64. *Green Fees:* weekdays £20.00 per round, £25.00 per day; weekends £25.00 per round, £30.00 per day. Weekly ticket £90.00. Special rates for parties of more than 10. *Eating facilities:* full bar and catering facilities. *Visitors:* No restrictions on visitors but advisable to phone in advance for weekends. *Society Meetings:* welcome - book through Secretary. Secretary: Colin McIntosh (013397 41595).
e-mail: info@braemargolfclub.co.uk
website: www.braemargolfclub.co.uk

BUCKIE. **Buckpool Golf Club (Buckie),** Barhill Road, Buckie AB56 1DU (Tel & Fax: 01542 832236). *Location:* turn off A98 signposted Buckpool. Links course with superlative view over Moray Firth. 18 holes, 6097 yards. S.S.S. 69. Putting green and net area. *Green Fees:* weekdays £20.00 per round, £25.00 per day, Senior Citizens £17.00 per round, £20.00 per day; weekends £25.00 per round, £30.00 per day, Senior Citizens £22.00 per round, £27.00 per day. (2007 rates). Reductions during winter months and for Juniors, discounts for parties. *Eating facilities:* full catering daily (pre-arranged bookings), normal bar hours. *Visitors:* no restrictions except when there are scheduled competitions and visiting parties; advisable to telephone first. Two changing rooms with showers, etc; snooker, pool and squash. *Society Meetings:* welcome by prior arrangement. Club Administrator: Mrs Moira Robertson. (Tel & Fax: 01542 832236).

BUCKIE. **Strathlene Golf Club,** Portessie, Buckie AB56 2DJ (01542 831798). *Location:* equidistant between Aberdeen and Inverness. Raised links course which follows the natural contours of the land. 18 holes, 5996 yards. S.S.S 69. Practice facilities. 3-hole pitch and putt, driving range. *Green Fees:* weekdays £18.00 per round, £22.00 per day; weekends £21.00 per round, £30.00 per day (2007 fees, subject to review). *Eating facilities:* summer catering and all-day bar. *Visitors:* prior booking advised; avoid Saturday and Sunday mornings. Locker room. *Society Meetings:* booking required. Secretary: George Jappy (01542 831798).

BUCKSBURN. **Craibstone Golf Centre,** Craibstone Estate, Bucksburn AB21 9YA (01224 716777; Fax: 01224 711298). *Location*: on A96 5 miles north of Aberdeen turn left at Craibstone Roundabout (private access) through Estate to T-junction, left then first right. Parkland course. 18 holes S.S.S. 67. *Green Fees*: information not available. *Eating facilities*: available, also bar. *Visitors*: welcome. *Society Meetings*: welcome - please telephone for details. Professional: Iain Buchan (01224 716777) Secretary: Susan May (01224 711195).*
e-mail: ballumbie2000@yahoo.com

CRUDEN BAY. **Cruden Bay Golf Club,** Aulton Road, Cruden Bay, Peterhead AB42 0NN (01779 812285). *Location:* seven miles south of Peterhead, 23 miles north east of Aberdeen, just off A92. Traditional seaside links with magnificent views near Bay of Cruden. 18 holes, 6291 yards. S.S.S. 72; 9 holes, 2463 yards. S.S.S. 64. Covered driving range. *Green Fees:* weekdays - £60.00 per round, £80.00 per day; weekends £70.00 per round. *Eating facilities:* full bar and catering facilities. *Visitors:* welcome but restricted at weekends, telephone for details. *Society Meetings:* welcome weekdays only. Professional: Robbie Stewart (Tel & Fax: 01779 812414). Secretary: Mrs Rosemary Pittendrigh (01779 812285; Fax: 01779 812945).

www.uk-golfguide.com

THE APPEARANCE OF AN ASTERISK (*) AT THE END OF A CLUB OR COURSE ENTRY INDICATES THAT UP-TO-DATE INFORMATION HAS NOT BEEN SUPPLIED

CULLEN. **Cullen Golf Club,** The Links, Cullen AB56 4WB (01542 840685). *Location:* off A98 midway between Aberdeen and Inverness, on Moray Firth coast. Seaside links course designed by Old Tom Morris, with elevated section, natural rock landscaping and sandy beach coming into play at several holes. 18 holes, 4597 yards. S.S.S. 62. Putting green and net area. *Green Fees:* weekdays £20.00 per round, £28.00 per day; weekends £25.00 per round, £28.00 per day. Winter Greens £8.00. Juniors all year £8.00 per round. Weekly 5-day (Mon-Fri) and 7-day rates available, prices on request. All prices subject to review. *Eating facilities:* catering and bar facilities. *Visitors:* welcome, check for club competitions. *Society Meetings:* welcome.
e-mail: cullengolfclub@btinternet.com
website: www.cullengolfclub.co.uk

DUFFTOWN. **Dufftown Golf Club,** Tomintoul Road, Dufftown AB55 4BS (Tel & Fax: 01340 820325). *Location:* on B9009 Dufftown to Tomintoul Road, one mile from Dufftown. Moorland/ Parkland course, partially hilly. 18 holes, 5308 yards. S.S.S. 67. Practice and putting facilities. *Green Fees:* £15.00 per round. Weekly (five day) ticket £60.00. Reductions for parties of 12 or more. Juniors half price. *Eating facilities:* available by arrangement. *Visitors:* welcome at all times. Tee reserved at some times Tuesdays, Wednesdays and Sundays . Please phone for details. Trolleys, clubs and buggies for hire, advance notice. *Society Meetings:* welcome by arrangement.
e-mail: admin@dufftowngolfclub.com

ELGIN. **Elgin Golf Club,** Hardhillock, Birnie Road, Elgin IV30 8SX (01343 542338; Fax: 01343 542341). *Location:* half a mile south of Elgin town centre just off A941 Rothes Road; on Birnie Road. Undulating parkland on sandy subsoil, many tree-lined fairways. 18 holes, 6411 yards. S.S.S. 71. Driving range, practice ground and net. *Green Fees:* £35.00 per round, £45.00 per day. *Eating facilities:* bar and catering every day. *Visitors:* welcome, arrangement through Professional is advisable. *Society Meetings:* by arrangement with Professional. Professional: Kevin Stables (Tel & Fax: 01343 542884). Secretary: James S. Macpherson (01343 542338).
e-mail: secretary@elgingolfclub.com
website: www.elgingolfclub.com

ELGIN. **Hopeman Golf Club,** Hopeman, Elgin IV30 5YA (01343 830578). *Location:* 7 miles north-east of Elgin on B9012. Seaside links, with spectacular 12th hole. 18 holes, 5624 yards. S.S.S. 68. *Green Fees:* weekdays £22.00 per round, £28.00 per day; Saturdays £28.00 per round, £34.00 per day; Sundays £20 per round, £26.00 per day. Juniors half price. Senior Citizens reduced rates. Generous discounts for parties of ten or more. 2007 rates, subject to review. *Eating facilities:* bar, catering. *Visitors:* welcome, some restrictions on tee times at weekends. Trolleys and golf buggies for hire. *Society Meetings:* welcome by arrangement. Secretary: Jim Fraser (01343 835068; Fax: 01343 830152).
e-mail: hopemangc@aol.com
website: www.hopemangc.co.uk

ELLON. **McDonald-Ellon Golf Club,** Hospital Road, Ellon AB41 9AW (01358 720576). *Location:* A90 from Aberdeen to Ellon. One mile down A948, on left. Flat parkland with trees and stream. 18 holes, 6012 yards. S.S.S. 70. Putting green and practice nets. *Green Fees:* on application. *Eating facilities:* full catering and bar facilities all week. *Visitors:* welcome at all times weekdays, after 10am and booking advisable at weekends. *Society Meetings:* must book in advance. Professional: Ronnie Urquhart (01358 722891). Secretary: George Ironside (01358 720576).
e-mail: mcdonald.golf@virgin.net

FOCHABERS. **Garmouth & Kingston Golf Club,** Spey Street, Garmouth, Fochabers IV32 7NJ (Tel & Fax: 01343 870388). *Location:* three miles north from A96 at Mosstodloch crossroads. Flat parkland/part links. 18 holes, 5957 yards. S.S.S. 69. Practice net. *Green Fees:* weekdays £25.00 per round, £28.00 per day, half price for Senior Citizens; weekends £25.00 per round or day. Reductions for parties over 10. Subject to review for 2008. *Eating facilities:* catering available on request. *Visitors:* very welcome except 4pm to 7pm Tuesdays (Ladies) and during club competitions (evenings). *Society Meetings:* welcome by arrangement with Admin. Assistant: I. Fraser (01343 870388).

FORRES. **Forres Golf Club,** Muiryshade, Forres IV36 2RD (Tel & Fax: 01309 672250). *Location:* one mile south from clock tower in town centre; 26 miles east of Inverness on A96. Parkland - feature hole 16th. 18 holes, 6236 yards. S.S.S. 70. Practice ground and putting green. *Green Fees:* £30.00 per round, £40.00 per day. *Eating facilities:* bar and catering all day every day. *Visitors:* welcome - booking system in operation by Professional. Buggies/Trolleys for hire. *Society Meetings:* welcome. Professional: S. Aird (Tel & Fax: 01309 672250). Secretary: (01309 672949; Fax: 01309 672261).

FORRES. **Kinloss Country Golf Course,** Kinloss, Forres IV36 2UB (01343 850585). *Location*: 4 miles east of Forres on B9089. Parkland courses. Two 9 hole courses, Course 1 - 2535 yards, Course 2 - 2939 yards. Practice area, driving range. *Green Fees*: information not available. *Eating facilities*: cafe, bar. *Visitors*: welcome everyday, pay-as-you-play. Trolleys, clubs and buggies for hire. *Society Meetings*: discounts for large parties. Corporate outings catered for. Contact Karen or Tommy (01343 850585).*

FRASERBURGH. **Fraserburgh Golf Club,** Philorth Links, Fraserburgh AB43 8TL (01346 516616). *Location:* turn right at roundabout on entry to town from Aberdeen then first right. Splendid true seaside links, reputedly the 7th oldest in the world, founded 1777. 18 holes, 6308 yards. S.S.S. 71. Additional 9 hole Rosehill Family Course 2400 yards. Practice area. *Green Fees:* to be arranged, single round, day tickets, weekly and monthly tickets available. *Eating facilities:* full bar and catering facilities. *Visitors:* welcome, some restrictions weekends. *Society Meetings:* welcome, book in advance. Tel (01346 516616).

GRANTOWN-ON-SPEY. **Craggan Golf Club,** Grantown-on-Spey PH26 3NT (01479 873283; Fax: 01479 872325). *Location*: situated beside the A95, one mile south of Grantown-on-Spey. Parkland course. 18 holes, 2005 yards. *Green Fees*: adults £15.00 per round, £20.00 per day; under 16s £7.00. *Eating facilities*: snacks and soft drinks available; bar in Clubhouse. *Visitors*: welcome at all times. Secretary: Fergus Laing (01479 873283). e-mail: fhglaing@btopenworld.com website: www.cragganforleisure.co.uk

HUNTLY. **Huntly Golf Club,** Cooper Park, Huntly AB54 4SH (01466 792643). *Location*: north side of Huntly, 38 miles from Aberdeen on A96. Open parkland course between the Rivers Deveron and Bogie. 18 holes, 5399 yards. S.S.S. 66. Practice area. *Green Fees*: information not available. *Eating facilities*: full catering by arrangement, lounge bar. *Visitors*: welcome, no restriction except Wednesday and Thursday evenings. Carts for hire. *Society Meetings*: by arrangement with Secretary, maximum of 40. Special package deal Mon - Fri. Administrator: Alan Donald (01466 792643).

INSCH. **Insch Golf Club,** Golf Terrace, Insch AB52 6JY (Tel & Fax: 01464 820363). *Location:* A96 27 miles from Aberdeen. Parkland - trees, water hazards. 18 holes, 5350 yards. S.S.S. 67. *Green Fees:* £16.00 per round/day, all week (Monday to Friday), £22.00 (Saturday and Sunday). Subject to review for 2008. *Eating facilities:* bar and catering available. *Visitors:* welcome except Mondays from 4.30pm, Tuesdays from 5pm and Wednesdays from 3.30pm. *Society Meetings:* welcome. Administrator: Jill Townsend.

INVERALLOCHY. **Inverallochy Golf Club,** Whitelink, Inverallochy, Fraserburgh AB43 8XY (01346 582000). *Location:* three miles south of Fraserburgh. Seaside links course. 18 holes, 5431 yards. S.S.S. 66. *Green Fees:* weekdays £17.00 per round, £26.00 per day; weekends £20.00 per round, £30.00 per day. *Eating facilities:* full catering/ fully licensed, advance booking required. *Visitors:* welcome, apply in writing. *Society Meetings:* welcome, apply in writing. Secretary: George Young.

INVERURIE. **Inverurie Golf Club,** Davah Wood, Inverurie AB51 5JB (01467 624080; Fax: 01467 672869). *Location*: off A96 Blackhall roundabout, at next roundabout, approx. 300 yards, turn right. Parkland with three tree-lined (wood holes). 18 holes, 5483 yards. S.S.S. 67. Practice ground. *Green Fees*: information not available. *Eating facilities*: full catering, bar and lounge area. *Visitors*: welcome, phone 01467 672863. *Society Meetings*: catered for. Professional: John Logue (01467 672863). Secretary: Arthur Angus (01467 672860; Fax: 01467 672869).*

KEITH. **Keith Golf Club,** Mar Court, Fife Keith, Keith AB55 5DF (01542 882469). *Location:* leave A96 on B9014 take first right. Parkland, open, panoramic views. 18 holes, 5800 yards, 5300 metres. S.S.S. 68. Small practice area and putting green. *Green Fees:* £15.00 per round, £20.00 per day. *Eating facilities:* catering available by arrangement, normal bar hours. *Visitors:* welcome anytime, advisable to telephone in advance during playing season. *Society Meetings:* all welcome, applications to Outings Convener J. Mackay. e-mail: Secretary@keithgolfclub.org.uk website: www.keithgolfclub.org.uk

KEMNAY. **Kemnay Golf Club,** Monymusk Road, Kemnay AB51 5RA (01467 642225). *Location:* from A96 main Aberdeen/Inverness road. Take B994 signposted Kemnay and pass through village of Kemnay to find golf course on left hand side on leaving village. Flat wooded parkland. 18 holes, 6342 yards, 5398 metres. S.S.S. 71. *Green Fees:* weekdays £20.00 per round, £26.00 per day; weekends £24.00 per round, £30.00 per day. *Eating facilities:* bar and full catering. *Visitors:* welcome at all times except during club competitions/matches; phone club shop to book tee time. *Society Meetings:* welcome by arrangement. Professional: R. McDonald (01467 642225). Secretary: S. Taylor (Tel & Fax: 01467 643746). Club Shop: (01467 642225). Administrator: (Tel & Fax: 01467 643746).

www.uk-golfguide.com

KINTORE. **Kintore Golf Club,** Balbithan Road, Kintore, Inverurie AB51 0UR (01467 632631). *Location:* off A96 12 miles north of Aberdeen. Undulating moorland course. 18 holes, 5323 yards. S.S.S. 66. *Green Fees:* weekdays £20.00 per round; weekends £25.00 per round. *Eating facilities:* available all day during the season, by arrangement at other times. *Visitors:* welcome daily except Tuesdays, Wednesdays and Fridays between 4pm and 7pm. Trolleys and buggies for hire during season. *Society Meetings:* welcome by appointment. Secretary: C. Lindsay.
e-mail: info@kintoregolfclub.net
website: www.kintoregolfclub.net

LOSSIEMOUTH. **Moray Golf Club,** Stotfield Road, Lossiemouth IV31 6QS (01343 812018; Fax: 01343 815102). Location: five miles from Elgin on A941, 40 miles from Inverness A96 Links course. Old Course 18 holes, 6697 yards. S.S.S. 73. New Course 18 holes, 6008 yards. S.S.S. 69. Practice ground, putting green. Green Fees: information not available. Discounts through local hotel and for parties of 12 or more. Eating facilities: bar plus full catering. Visitors: welcome every day. Secretary will advise on availability. Buggies, carts, caddies. Society Meetings: welcome by arrangement with Secretary. Professional: Alastair Thomson (01343 813330). Secretary: S. Crane (01343 812018 Ext 2; Fax: 01343 815102).*
e-mail:secretary@moraygolf.co.uk
website: www.moraygolf.co.uk

MACDUFF. **Royal Tarlair Golf Club,** Buchan Street, Macduff AB44 1SQ (01261 832897). *Location:* A98 Fraserburgh to Inverness road. Seaside cliff top course, beautiful seascapes, 13th feature hole. 18 holes, 5866 yards, 5373 metres. S.S.S. 68. *Green Fees:* £20.00 per round weekdays, day ticket £25.00; £20.00 per round weekends and public holidays, £22.00 per day ticket. *Eating facilities:* full catering and bar available. *Visitors:* very welcome. *Society Meetings:* welcome, bookings through Secretary. Treasurer/Secretary: Mrs M. McMurray
e-mail: info@royaltarlair.co.uk
website: www.royaltarlair.co.uk

NAIRN. **The Nairn Golf Club,** Seabank Road, Nairn IV12 4HB (01667 453208; Fax: 01667 456328). *Location:* Nairn West Shore, on the southern shore of the Moray Firth, 16 miles east of Inverness on A96. Hosted "Amateur" Championship in 1994. Traditional Scottish links championship course, hosted 37th Walker Cup in 1999. Championship Course - 18 holes, 6705 yards. S.S.S. 73 (blue tees); Medal Course 18 holes, 6430 yards. S.S.S 72 (white tees); 9 holes (Newton Course), 1918 yards. Practice area. *Green Fees:* information not available. *Eating facilities:* full catering facilities and two bars available. *Visitors:* welcome subject to availability, restrictions at weekends - 8am to 11.00am and from 12 noon to 2.30pm for members only. Full size snooker table. *Society Meetings:* welcome subject to availability. Professional: Robin P. Fyfe (01667 452787). Secretary: David Corstorphine (01667 453208; Fax: 01667 456328). Catering Manager: (01667 452103).*
e-mail: bookings@nairngolfclub.co.uk
website: www.nairngolfclub.co.uk

NEWBURGH. **Newburgh-on-Ythan Golf Club,** Beach Road, Newburgh AB51 6BY(01358 789058). *Location:* 10 miles north of Aberdeen. Championship links course, founded 1888. Home of Paul Lawrie Golf Classic, only 2 miles from Trump International. 18 holes, 6373 yards. S.S.S. 71. 6 hole practice course. Driving range. *Green Fees:* weekdays £25.00 per round, weekends £30.00 per round. *Eating facilities:* bar/restaurant. *Visitors:* welcome at all times. Tennis courts, wireless access, indoor swing studio. Contact Professional Ian Bratton (01358 789058).
e-mail: secretary@newburghgolfclub.co.uk
website: www.newburghgolfclub.co.uk

NEWMACHAR. **Newmachar Golf Club,** Swailend, Newmachar AB21 7UU (01651 863002). *Location:* two and a half miles north of Dyce on A947. Two courses – Hawkshill: Championship standard wooded parkland course with ponds being main feature. 18 holes, 6700 yards. S.S.S. 74; Swailend: undulating parkland course. 18 holes, 6388 yards. S.S.S. 71. 12 bay driving range, practice bunker and putting green. *Green Fees:* information not provided. *Eating facilities:* fully licensed clubhouse with restaurant. *Visitors:* welcome by prior arrangement. Handicap Certificate required. *Society Meetings:* welcome by prior arrangement. Head Professional: Andrew Cooper (01651 863222). Secretary: Sam Wade (01651 863002; Fax: 01651 863055).

OLDMELDRUM. **Oldmeldrum Golf Club,** Kirk Brae, Oldmeldrum, Inverurie AB51 0DJ (01651 872648). *Location:* 17 miles north-west of Aberdeen on A947 to Banff. First on right entering from Aberdeen direction. Undulating parkland with tree-lined fairways and water features. 18 holes, 5988 yards, 5479 metres. S.S.S. 69. Practice area. *Green Fees:* information not provided. *Eating facilities:* fully licensed bar, full catering. *Visitors:* welcome, advisable to phone first. Professional's Shop: (01651 873555) for tee reservations. *Society Meetings:* catered for by arrangement. Professional: Hamish Love (01651 873555). Administrator: Eva Beech-Campbell (01651 872648).

PETERCULTER. **Peterculter Golf Club,** Oldtown, Burnside Road, Peterculter, Aberdeen AB14 0LN (01224 735245; Fax: 01224 735580). *Location:* from North Deeside Road (A93) at west end of Peterculter travel southwards, following signs for club. Scenic, undulating course, bounded by River Dee, excellent views of hills to west. 18 holes, Medal 6219 yards, Forward Tees 6000 yards, S.S.S. Medal 69, Forward Tees 68. Small practice/teaching area. *Green Fees:* weekdays £25.00, weekends £30.00. *Eating facilities:* dining room, lounge bar. *Visitors:* welcome except weekdays 3.30pm to 6pm. *Society Meetings:* welcome Tuesdays to Fridays. Not Public/local holidays. Professional: Dean Vannet (01224 734994).
e-mail: info@petercultergolfclub.co.uk
website: www.petercultergolfclub.co.uk

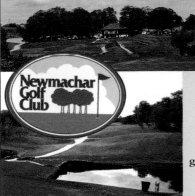

PETERHEAD. **Longside Golf Club,** West End, Longside, Peterhead AB42 4XJ (01779 821558; Fax: 01779 821564). *Location*: take A950 west from Peterhead towards Mintlaw. Wooded course with river. 18 holes, 5225 yards, S.S.S 66. *Green Fees*: £13.00 Monday to Saturday, £19.00 sunday. *Eating facilities*: full bar and catering facilities. *Visitors*: always welcome - no visitors before 10.30am on Sunday. *Society Meetings*: welcome, £32.00 for two rounds including catering. £21.00 for one round including catering, booking forms available from club. Secretary: Mrs Kathleen Allan (01771 622424).

PETERHEAD. **Peterhead Golf Club,** Riverside Drive, Peterhead AB42 1LT (01779 472149; Fax: 01779 480725). *Location:* north end of town off Blackhouse Terrace at mouth of River Ugie. Seaside links – can be affected by variable wind conditions. Old Course – 18 holes, 6173 yards. S.S.S. 71; New Course – 9 holes, 2228 yards. Par 62 for 4456 yards. Practice area. *Green Fees:* weekdays £35.00 per round, day ticket £45.00, 9 holes £14.00; weekends £45.00 per round, £55.00 per day. 9 holes course £16.00. *Eating facilities:* snacks, meals, full bar facilities. *Visitors:* welcome anytime except some restrictions on a Saturday. Phone call advised. *Society Meetings:* welcome by arrangement. Handicap Certificate may be asked for. Secretary: D.G. Wood (Fax: 01779 480725).

PORTLETHEN. **Portlethen Golf Club,** Badentoy Road, Portlethen, Aberdeen AB12 4YA (01224 781090). *Location:* five miles south of Aberdeen on main Stonehaven Road. Rolling parkland. 18 holes, 6670 yards. S.S.S. 72. Large practice area. *Green Fees:* information not available. *Eating facilities:* bar and restaurant. *Visitors:* welcome, no visitors Saturdays, Sundays also difficult in summer. Golf buggies for hire. Snooker. *Society Meetings:* welcome weekdays by arrangement. Professional: Muriel Thomson (01224 782571). Bar/catering: 01224 782575.*

> **THE APPEARANCE OF AN ASTERISK (*) AT THE END OF A CLUB OR COURSE ENTRY INDICATES THAT UP-TO-DATE INFORMATION HAS NOT BEEN SUPPLIED**

ROSEHEARTY. **Rosehearty Golf Club,** C/o Masons Arms Hotel, 1 Castle Street, Rosehearty, Fraserburgh AB43 4JP (01346 571250). *Location:* east of Rosehearty on Fraserburgh Road. Seaside links. 9 holes, 2197 yards. S.S.S. 62. Driving range and golf shop. *Green Fees:* information not available. *Eating facilities:* Masons Arms Hotel adjacent to course. *Visitors:* always welcome. *Society Meetings:* welcome by prior arrangement. Lessons available. Teaching facilities across road from Masons Arms Hotel. Professional: Scott Hornal. Secretary: Alan Watt (01346 571250).*

ROTHES. **Rothes Golf Club,** Blackhall, Rothes, Aberlour AB38 7AN (01340 831443). *Location:* south west of Rothes, off A941 Elgin to Craigellachie road. A parkland course with fine views over the River Spey. 9 holes, 2486 yards (4972 yards), 2273 metres (4546 metres). S.S.S. 64. Practice net. *Green Fees:* Weekdays 9 holes £10.00, Juniors £5.00. 18 holes £15.00, Juniors £7.50; Weekends 9 holes £12.00, Juniors £6.00. 18 holes £20.00, Juniors £10.00. *Eating facilities:* licensed bar open summer evenings and weekends, catering for parties by arrangement. *Visitors:* always welcome, tee reserved for Ladies 5pm to 7.30pm Tuesdays, and 5pm to 6.30pm Mondays for Juniors. *Society Meetings:* welcome, contact Secretary. Secretary: K.J. MacPhee (01340 831676).

SPEY BAY. **Golf Spey Bay,** Spey Bay Hotel, Spey Bay, Fochabers IV32 7PJ (01343 820424 all enquiries). *Location:* halfway between Inverness and Aberdeen, at the mouth of River Spey. Traditional 18-hole championship links. Special characteristics being small greens and tight, gorse-lined fairways with superb scenic views over the Moray Firth. 6230 yards. S.S.S. 70. Driving range, practice area. *Green Fees:* £20.00 (group discounts). Buggy and trolley hire available. *Eating facilities:* snacks. *Visitors:* all visitors welcome all year round. *Society Meetings:* catered for by prior arrangement. Special golf breaks tailor-made to suit individual requirements. All enquiries contact The Spey Bay Hotel. e-mail: spaybaygolf@hotmail.co.uk

STONEHAVEN. **Stonehaven Golf Club,** Cowie, Stonehaven AB39 3RH (01569 762124; Fax: 01569 765973). *Location:* A92, one mile north of town signposted at mini roundabout near Leisure Centre. Parkland course on cliffs overlooking North Sea with some challenging holes over natural gullies. 18 holes, 5128 yards. S.S.S. 65. Limited practice area. *Green Fees:* weekdays: £19.00 per round, £25.00 per day; weekends: £25.00 per round, £30.00 per day. *Eating facilities:* full catering including bar lunches. *Visitors:* welcome, but advised to reserve tee time in advance, restricted Saturdays after 4pm. *Society Meetings:* catered for except for Saturday. Secretary/ Manager: W.A. Donald.
e-mail: stonehaven.golfclub@virgin.net

TORPHINS. **Torphins Golf Club,** Bog Road, Torphins, Banchory AB31 4JU (013398 82115). *Location:* through village towards Lumphanan, club signposted to right. Parkland with lovely views to Highlands. 9 holes, 4738 yards (18 holes). S.S.S. 64. *Green Fees:* £13.00 weekdays; £15.00 weekends. £8.00 for 9 holes. Juniors half price. *Eating facilities:* light refreshments at weekends, unlicensed. *Visitors:* welcome at weekends; on medal days by arrangement. *Society Meetings:* welcome; at weekends by arrangement. Secretary: Stuart MacGregor (013398 82402).
e-mail: stuartmacgregor5@btinternet.com

TURRIFF. **Turriff Golf Club,** Rosehall, Turriff AB53 4HD (01888 562982; Fax: 01888 568050). *Location:* A947 signposted on south side of Turriff. Wooded parkland course. 18 holes, 6118 yards. S.S.S. 70. Practice area, putting green. *Green Fees:* weekdays £22.00 per round, £26.00 per day; weekends £26.00 per round, £32.00 per day. *Eating facilities:* bar and restaurant. *Visitors:* no visitors before 10am weekends, selected times on Medal days. Tee reservation by contacting Professional – during the week up to four days in advance, weekends up to two days in advance. Buggy and electric trolley hire. *Society Meetings:* by arrangement with Secretary. Professional: James Mooney (Tel & Fax: 01888 563025). Secretary: G.A. Robertson (01888 562982; Fax: 01888 568050). Administrator: Grace Stephen e-mail: grace@turriffgolf.sol.co.uk
website: www.turriffgolfclub.com

WESTHILL. **Westhill Golf Club,** Westhill Heights, Westhill, Aberdeenshire AB32 6RY (01224 742567; Fax: 01224 749124). *Location:* six miles from Aberdeen on A944. Parkland course. 18 holes, 5849 yards. S.S.S. 69. Practice ground. *Green Fees:* weekdays £20.00 per round, £25.00 per day; weekends and Public Holidays £25.00 per round, £30.00 per day (subject to review). Special packages available on request. *Eating facilities:* lounge bar and dining area. *Visitors:* welcome any time. *Society Meetings:* welcome per visitors' times by arrangement. Professional: George Bruce (01224 740159).

www.uk-golfguide.com

Angus & Dundee

ARBROATH. **Arbroath Golf Course,** Elliot, By Arbroath DD11 2PE (Tel & Fax: 01241 875837). *Location*: off Dundee Road. Seaside links course. 18 holes, 6185 yards. S.S.S. 70. Practice area, new putting green. *Green Fees*: information not available. *Eating facilities*: full catering and bar facility. *Visitors*: welcome. *Society Meetings:* all welcome. Professional: L. Ewart (Tel & Fax: 01241 875837). Secretary: Scott Milne (01382 229111).*

ARBROATH near. **Letham Grange Golf Course,** Colliston, By Arbroath DD11 4RL (01241 890373; Fax: 01241 890725). *Location:* follow brown Scottish Tourist Board signs for Letham Grange from Arbroath. Two courses – Old Course is a blend of tree-lined parkland and open rolling fairways; water plays a major role which makes the course both scenic and dramatic. Glens Course is slightly shorter and without water hazards, offers golfers a more relaxed and less arduous round; however, it could be deceptive! 36 holes, Old 6968 yards, Glen's 5528 yards. S.S.S. Old 73, Glen's 68. Very large practice area, practice putting green, practice chipping green. *Green Fees:* £45.00 and £50.00; Glens Course £27.00 and £32.00. *Eating facilities:* golfers' bar and restaurant. *Visitors:* welcome. Hotel on site. Trolley, club and buggy hire, PGA Professional group tuition available. *Society Meetings:* all most welcome. Golf shop (01241 890377 or 01241 890373).

BARRY. **Panmure Golf Club,** Burnside Road, Barry, By Carnoustie DD7 7RT (01241 855120). *Location:* two miles west of Carnoustie on A930, signposted from the Barry village bypass. Championship links. 18 holes, 6330 yards. S.S.S. 70. Driving range, practice area. *Green Fees:* £65.00 per round, £85.00 per day. *Eating facilities:* full catering seven days a week. *Visitors:* welcome daily except Tuesday and Saturday mornings. Buggy hire. Putting Simulator. *Society Meetings:* restricted but welcome. Professional: Neil Mackintosh. Managing Secretary: Charles Philip (01241 855120).
e-mail: secretary@panmuregolfclub.co.uk
website: www.panmuregolfclub.co.uk

BRECHIN. **Brechin Golf and Squash Club,** Trinity, By Brechin DD9 7PD (01356 622383). *Location*: Trinity Village, one mile north of Brechin just off A90. Rolling parkland course with glorious views of Grampian Mountains. 18 holes, 6096 yards. S.S.S. 70. Practice ground. *Green Fees*: weekdays £28.00 per round, weekends £30.00. Parties of 8 or more £40.00. *Eating facilities*: excellent catering available at all times;

large bar. *Visitors*: very welcome seven days. Buggies, carts, club hire. Two squash courts. *Society Meetings*: catered for, reservations in advance. Professional: Stephen Rennie (01356 625270).
e-mail: brechingolfclub@tiscali.co.uk
website: www.brechingolfclub.co.uk

CARNOUSTIE. **Carnoustie Golf Links,** Links Parade, Carnoustie DD7 7JE (01241 853789; Fax: 01241 852720). *Location:* 12 miles east of Dundee. Three 18-hole courses. Championship Course 6941 yards. S.S.S. 75; Burnside Course 6028 yards. S.S.S. 70; Buddon Links 5420 yards. S.S.S. 66. Golf trolleys permitted. *Green Fees:* Championship Course £125.00 per round; Burnside Course £34.00 per round; Buddon Links Course £29.00 per round. Subject to review. Juvenile rates available. Three course combination ticket £145.00. *Eating facilities:* catering facilities can be arranged with the local golf clubs. *Visitors:* welcome, times must be booked. Handicap Certificates required for play on Championship Course. *Society Meetings:* catered for by arrangement. Professional: Colin Sinclair. Course Manager: John Philp. General Manager: G.Duncan. Golf Services Manager: Colin McLeod.

DUNDEE. **Ballumbie Castle Golf Club,** 3 Old Quarry Road, Off Ballumbie Road, Dundee DD4 0SY (01382 770028). *Location*: one and a half miles north of Claypotts Junction, less than 2 miles from Dundee city centre. Parkland/heathland course. 18 holes, 6127 yards, S.S.S. 70. 22 bay driving range, putting green, chipping green. *Green Fees*: information not available. *Eating facilities*: clubhouse facilities with menu and full bar. Public house licence. *Visitors*: welcome. Tuition available at driving range. *Society Meetings*: welcome, please telephone for details. Professional: Lee Sutherland (01382 770028).*
e-mail: ballumbie2000@yahoo.com
website: www.ballumbiecastlegolfclub.com

DUNDEE. **Caird Park Golf Club,** Mains Loan, Dundee DD4 9BX (01382 453606). *Location:* northern edge of city, off Kingsway. Wooded parkland. 18 holes, 6273 yards, 5740 metres. S.S.S. 70. Practice range on course. *Green Fees:* information available from Starter 01382 438871. *Eating facilities:* at clubhouse. *Visitors:* welcome, must book in advance to ensure game. *Society Meetings:* see Dundee District Council, Parks Department. Professional: Jackie Black (01382 459438). Secretary: Greg Martin (01382 461460).

DUNDEE. **Camperdown Golf Club,** Camperdown House, Camperdown Park, Dundee DD2 4TF (01382 623398). *Location:* two miles north-west of city, enter at Kingsway/Coupar Angus road junction. Wooded parkland. 18 holes, 6561 yards. S.S.S. 72, Par 71. *Green Fees:* information not available. *Eating facilities:* must be booked in advance. *Visitors:* welcome, bookable all week. Contact: Leisure and Communities Department, Dundee City Council, Tayside House. *Society Meetings:* by arrangement, with above and Camperdown Golf Club for date and times. Professional: Roddy Brown (01382 623398). Secretary: John S. Clinton (01382 884741).
e-mail: jack.clinton@blueyonder.co.uk
          jack.clinton@dundeecity.gov.uk

DUNDEE. **Downfield Golf Club,** Turnberry Avenue, Dundee DD2 3QP (01382 825595; Fax: 01382 813111). *Location:* follow tourist signs from the main A90 Kingsway for Downfield Golf Course. Wooded, parkland course. 18 holes, 6802 yards, 6266 metres. S.S.S. 73. Large practice area. *Green Fees:* information not provided. *Eating facilities:* full catering and bar seven days. *Visitors:* welcome weekdays 9.30am to 11.15am and 2.15pm to 3.30pm, Sunday after 2pm only, pre-booking essential. Carts for hire. Professional: Kenny Hutton (01382 889246). Secretary: Margaret Stewart (01382 825595; Fax: 01382 813111).

DUNDEE. **Piperdam Golf and Leisure Resort,** Foulis, Dundee DD2 5LP (01382 581374; Fax: 01382 581102). *Location:* off A923 Coupar Angus road. Parkland course, 18 holes, 6500 yards. S.S.S. 72.12 bay driving range. *Green Fees:* information not available. *Eating facilities:* restaurant and bar. *Visitors:* welcome. No restrictions. Leisure Centre and Spa. Two and three bedroom lodges. *Society Meetings:* welcome. Packages available. Director: Murdie Smith.*
e-mail: enquiries@piperdam.com
website: www.piperdam.com

EDZELL. **Edzell Golf Club,** High Street, Edzell DD9 7TF (01356 647283; Fax: 01356 648094). *Location:* travelling north from Dundee on A90, take B966 north of Brechin by-pass, continue 3.5 miles to village of Edzell. Parkland course with tree-lined fairways at the entrance to the Angus Glens and in the foothills of the Grampians. "Golfers who are visiting the Angus area cannot afford to miss what is one of Scotland's true hidden gems" Golf Monthly, 1999. 18 holes, 6427 yards. S.S.S. 71. 9-hole West Water Course 4114 yards, S.S.S. 61. 300 yard driving range, chipping area and putting green. *Green Fees:* weekdays £33.00 per round, £45.00 per day; weekends £40.00 per round, £56.00 per day. West Water Course; Monday to Sunday £12.00 per 9 holes, £16.00 per 18 holes. *Eating facilities:* dining room, lounge and bar. *Visitors:* welcome, apply to Secretary. *Society Meetings:* welcome apply to Secretary. Professional: Alistair J. Webster (01356 648462). Secretary: Ian G. Farquhar (01356 647283). Caterer: Neil Jack (01356 648235).
e-mail: awebsterpro@aol.com
          secretary@edzellgolfclub.net
website: www.edzellgolfclub.net

FORFAR. **Forfar Golf Club,** Cunninghill, Arbroath Road, Forfar DD8 2RL (01307 463773). *Location:* one mile from Forfar on A932 to Arbroath. Undulating wooded heathland Tom Morris/James Braid designed course. 18 holes, 6066 yards. S.S.S. 69. *Green Fees:* information not available. *Eating facilities:* available. *Visitors:* welcome. *Society Meetings:* catered for. Professional: Peter McNiven (01307 465683). Secretary: Stuart Wilson (01307 463773; Fax: 01307 468495).*

KIRRIEMUIR. **Kirriemuir Golf Club Ltd,** Northmuir, Kirriemuir DD8 4LN (01575 573317; Fax: 01575 574608). *Location:* 20 miles north-west of Carnoustie and six miles north-west of Forfar on A926 and A928, just on edge of Kirriemuir, north of town centre. Parkland and heathland course with stunning views of Angus Glens. 18 holes, 5510 yards, 5038 metres. S.S.S. 67. Putting green, practice ground. *Green Fees:* information not available. *Eating facilities:* full catering and bar facilities. *Visitors:* welcome weekdays; at weekends by arrangement. *Society Meetings:* by prior arrangement. Special golf/catering packages available. Professional: Karyn Dallas (01575 573317; Fax: 01575 574608).*

> THE APPEARANCE OF AN ASTERISK (*) AT
> THE END OF A CLUB OR COURSE ENTRY
> INDICATES THAT UP-TO-DATE
> INFORMATION HAS NOT BEEN SUPPLIED

MONIFIETH. **Broughty Golf Club,** 6 Princes Street, Monifieth, Dundee DD5 4AW (01382 532147). Starter (01382 532767). *Location:* eight miles east of Dundee, in village of Monifieth. Seaside links, some fairways fringed with trees. Medal Course: 18 holes, 6655 yards. S.S.S. 72. Ashludie Course: 18 holes, 5123 yards. S.S.S. 65. Practice area. *Green Fees:* information not available. *Eating facilities:* full catering; no catering Tuesdays or Thursdays. *Visitors:* no visitors before 2pm on Saturdays or before 10am Sundays. All tee times must be booked through Starter's Box. *Society Meetings:* by arrangement. Professional: Mr I. McLeod. Secretary: Peter Flynn.*

MONIFIETH. **Monifieth Golf Links,** Princes Street, Monifieth, Angus DD5 4AW (01382 532767). *Location:* seven miles east of Dundee, Monifieth High Street. Seaside links. Medal Course 18 holes, 6657 yards. S.S.S. 72; Ashludie Course 18 holes, 5123 yards. S.S.S. 64. Practice facilities. *Green Fees:* Medal Course: £45.00 weekdays, £55.00 weekends. Ashludie Course: £22.00 weekdays, £26.00 weekends. *Eating facilities:* clubs and Hotel. *Visitors:* welcome after 9.30am Monday to Friday; Saturdays after 2pm; Sundays after 10am. *Society Meetings:* parties over 12, must provide club Handicap Certificates. Buggies for hire. Packages available £65.00. Professional: Ian McLeod (01382 532945). Managing Secretary: J. Brodie (01382 535553; Fax: 01382 535816).
e-mail: monifiethgolf@freeuk.com
website: www.monifiethgolf.co.uk

MONTROSE. **Montrose Golf Links Ltd,** Traill Drive, Montrose DD10 8SW (01674 672932). *Location*: A92 runs from Dundee to Aberdeen, through Montrose. Links Medal Course 6544 yards. Par 71. S.S.S. 72. Broomfield Course 4830 yards. Par 66. S.S.S. 63. *Green Fees*: Medal: weekdays £45.00 per round, £57.00 per day, Juniors £20.00 per round, £32.00 per day; weekends £50.00 per round, £65.00 per day, Juniors £22.00 per round, £34.00 per day. Broomfield: Monday to Friday £18.00 per round, Juniors £6.00 per round; weekends £20.00 per round, Juniors £6.00. Composite day fees and special rates on request. Group discounts available. Green fees subject to review. *Eating facilities*: catering facilities available by arrangement in golf clubs. *Visitors*: very welcome; no restrictions midweek, visitors allowed on Medal Course between 2.44pm and 3.38pm on Saturdays and after 10am on Sundays. Handicap Certificates required on Medal Course. *Society Meetings*: welcome by arrangement. Temporary membership available at the following clubs: Caledonia Golf Club (01674 672313); Mercantile Golf Club (01674 672408); Royal Montrose (01674 672376). Professional: Jason J. Boyd. Secretary: Mrs Margaret Stewart (01674 672932; Fax: 01674 671800).
e-mail: secretary@montroselinks.co.uk
website: www.montroselinks.co.uk

MONTROSE. **Royal Montrose Golf Club,** Dorward Road, Montrose DD10 8SW (01674 672376). *Location:* A92 north from Dundee. Private club playing over the Montrose courses. 18 holes, 6533 yards. S.S.S. 72. *Green Fees:* information not available. *Eating facilities:* available. *Visitors:* apply Montrose Golf Links Ltd. *Society Meetings:* apply Montrose Golf Links Ltd. Professional: Jason Boyd. Secretary: M.J. Cummins (01674 672376).*

MONTROSE GOLF LINKS LTD

Medal Course (Par 71, SSS 72)
Broomfield Course (Par 66, SSS 63)
Medal course ranked fifth oldest in the world.
Open Championship Final Qualifying Course 1999 & 2007

Individual Round and Day Tickets available on both courses: All Visitors and Parties Welcome. Group Discounts offered. Special Packages available including catering and in conjunction with local hotels.

Enquiries to: **Mrs M. Stewart, Secretary, Montrose Golf Links Ltd , Traill Drive, Montrose, Angus DD10 8SW**

Telephone: (01674) 672932 • Fax: (01674) 671800
e-mail: Secretary@montroselinks.co.uk • www.montroselinks.co.uk

The 15th hole at Edzell Golf Club

Argyll & Bute

Ballachulish House
& GOLF COURSE
Accommodation • Lunch & Dinner
Golf Packages & Memberships
Featuring Head Chef, Darin Campbell, formerly
of Andrew Fairlie's restaurant at Gleneagles.

Challenging 5038 yard par 66
course, with spectacular views to
Loch Linnhe and the Munros to the
north. Home to several local golf clubs.

Special packages available, call
01855 811266 or
www.ballachulishhouse.com

BALLACHULISH. **Ballachulish House Golf Course**, Ballachulish PH49 4JX (01885 811695). *Location*: near the village of Glencoe, two hours north of Glasgow and Edinburgh, 13 miles south of Fort William. Challenging course with spectacular views. 9 holes (18 tees), 5038 yards. Par 68/65. *Green Fees:* £14.00 for 9 holes; £20.00 for 18 holes. E*ating facilities:* clubhouse with bar and grill. *Visitors:* welcome. Golf packages available.
website: www.ballachulishhouse.com

CAMPBELTOWN. **Machrihanish Golf Club**, Machrihanish, by Campbeltown PA28 6PT (01586 810213). *Location:* five miles west of Campbeltown on B843 road. Championship standard natural links course. 18 holes, 6225 yards. S.S.S. 71. Also 9 holes, 2395 yards. Practice area. *Green Fees:* Sunday to Fridays £40.00 per round, £60.00 per day; Saturdays £50.00 per round, £75.00 per day. Advance booking necessary. Subject to review. *Eating facilities:* full catering and bar facilities. *Visitors:* welcome, some restrictions on competition days. Open competitions in summer. Special Flight/Golf packages available through Loganair, Glasgow Airport, Paisley. *Society Meetings:* as visitors. Professional: Ken Campbell (01586 810277; Fax: 01586 810221). Secretary: Mrs Anna Anderson (01586 810213).
e-mail: secretary@machgolf.com
website: www.machgolf.com

CARRADALE. **Carradale Golf Club,** Carradale, By Campbeltown PA28 6RY. *Location:* 15 miles north of Campbeltown on B842. Seaside course, short but demanding, unbelievable views. 9 holes. Medal Tees – 2358 yards out, 2336 yards in; Yellow Tees – 1999 yards. S.S.S. 64 (18 holes). *Green Fees:* £15.00 per day; £60.00 per week. Country Membership £98.00 per annum (may take part in competitions). *Eating facilities:* Carradale Hotel at first tee, Ashbank Hotel 100 yards. Dunvalanree close by. Network centre one mile (open Easter to October for midday meals and snacks). Glen Bar and Restaurant one-and-a-half miles. *Visitors:* all welcome, no restrictions. *Society Meetings:* welcome, would be advisable to book tee-off times. Secretary: Dr R.J. Abernethy (01583 431321).

DALMALLY. **Dalmally Golf Club,** C/o Old Sawmill, Dalmally PA33 1AE (01866 822708). *Location:* alongside the A85, two miles west of Dalmally. Flat parkland course bounded by the River Orchy and surrounded by mountains. 9 holes, 2264 yards. S.S.S. 63. *Green Fees:* information not available. *Eating facilities:* bar and snacks by arrangement. *Visitors:* welcome at all times. Clubs and carts by arrangement. *Society Meetings:* all welcome by arrangement. Secretary: Ms C. Brown (01866 822708).*

DUNOON. **Blairmore and Strone Golf Club,** High Road, Strone, by Dunoon PA23 8TH (01369 840676). *Location:* take A880, five miles north of Dunoon and first left after leaving Kilmun. A Braid designed course set above the Clyde with spectacular views, mixture of hill and flatter parkland. 9 holes, 2112 yards, 1933 metres. S.S.S. 62. *Green Fees:* weekdays and weekends, £10.00. *Eating facilities:* bar facilities Saturdays. *Visitors:* welcome but some restrictions on competition days. *Society Meetings:* welcome, apply through Secretary. Secretary: Mrs J.C. Fleming (01369 860307).

DUNOON. **Cowal Golf Club,** Ardenslate Road, Kirn, Dunoon PA23 8LT (01369 705673). *Location:* quarter mile off A815 at Kirn (north-east boundary of Dunoon). Rising wooded parkland with superb views over Firth of Clyde. 18 holes, 6063 yards. S.S.S. 70. Practice area. *Green Fees:* information not available. *Eating facilities:* full service available. *Visitors:* welcome weekdays, possible restrictions weekends. Separate visitor changing/shower facilities. Local hotels offer golf holidays – apply to Secretary for details. *Society Meetings:* welcome, special rates available. Professional: R.D. Weir (01369 702395). Secretary: Alan Douglas (Tel & Fax: 01369 705673).*
e-mail: secretary@cowalgolfclub.com
website: www.cowalgolfclub.com

DUNOON. **Innellan Golf Club,** Knockamillie Road, Innellan, By Dunoon PA23 7SG (01369 830242). *Location:* south of Dunoon to Innellan Pierhead, then follow signposts. Parkland course in elevated position overlooking Firth of Clyde. 9 holes, 2343 yards. S.S.S. 64. *Green Fees:* £10.00 per 9 holes, £13.00 per day; weekends £15.00 per day. 25% discount for parties. *Eating facilities:* snack/bar; food by arrangement. *Visitors:* welcome, except Monday evenings, ladies welcome Thursday evenings. *Society Meetings:* welcome by arrangement. Secretary: Andrew Wilson (01369 702573).

INVERARAY. **Inveraray Golf Club,** North Cromalt, Inveraray PA32 8XT. *Location:* on the A83 Campbeltown road, one mile west of Inveraray, signposted. Testing course, wooded with natural trees, oak, birch, etc. Flat, some water hazards. 9 holes, 2814 yards. S.S.S. 69. *Green Fees:* weekdays and weekends £15.00 per day/round; Juniors £5.00. *Eating facilities:* none at course but good choice locally. *Visitors:* very few restrictions weekdays, occasionally at weekends. *Society Meetings:* welcome by prior arrangement through George Morrison (01499 302116).

ISLE OF BUTE. **Bute Golf Club,** c/o St. Ninians, 32 Marine Place, Ardbeg, Rothesay PA20 0LF (01700 502158). *Location:* six miles from Rothesay on the A845, situated on shores of Stravanan Bay. Flat seaside links in beautiful setting. 9 holes, 2497 yards, 2284 metres. S.S.S. 64 (18 holes). *Green Fees:* £10.00 adults, £5.00 Juniors. *Visitors:* welcome any day, Saturdays after 11.30am. *Society Meetings:* catered by arrangement. Secretary: Frazer Robinson (01700 502158).
e-mail: Info@butegolfclub.com
website: www.butegolfclub.com

LOCHGILPHEAD. **Lochgilphead Golf Club,** Blarbuie Road, Lochgilphead PA31 8LE (01546 602340). *Location:* close to Argyll and Bute Hospital, Lochgilphead. Signposted from town centre. Parkland. 9 holes, 4518 yards. S.S.S. 63. *Green Fees:* £15.00. *Eating facilities:* limited snacks available at weekends. *Visitors:* welcome but some restriction on competition days. *Society Meetings:* welcome by arrangement. Secretary: Mr R. Foyle (01546 510383).

OBAN. **Glencruitten Golf Club,** Glencruitten Road, Oban PA34 4PU (01631 562868). *Location:* one mile from town centre. Hilly parkland. 18 holes, 4452 yards. S.S.S. 63. Practice area. Putting green. *Green Fees:* weekdays £25.00, weekends £30.00 per day. *Eating facilities:* full catering and bar facilities. *Visitors:* very welcome. *Society Meetings:* welcome. Shop: (01631 564115). Secretary: A.G. Brown (01631 564604).
e-mail: enquiries@obangolf.com
website: www.obangolf.com

OBAN. **Isle of Seil Golf Club,** Balvicar, Isle of Seil. *Location:* turn off the A816 Oban-Lochgilphead Road at Kilninver onto the B844, follow B844, cross the Atlantic Bridge onto Seil, then on to Balvicar. Partly on shore of Balvicar Bay, partly on reclaimed quarry land. 9 holes, 2141 yards, Par 31. *Green Fees:* £12.00 per day; Juniors £5.00. *Visitors:* welcome all day, every day. *Society Meetings:* by arrangement. Secretary: B.R. Mitchell (01852 300348).

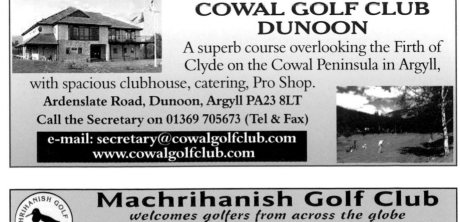

ROTHESAY. **Port Bannatyne Golf Club,** Bannatyne Mains Road, Port Bannatyne (01700 504544). *Location:* two miles north of Rothesay (ferry terminal). Hill course overlooking bays and sea lochs. 13 holes, 5085 yards, S.S.S. 65. *Green Fees:* weekdays £12.00 per round, £17.00 per day; weekends £18.00 per round, £22.00 per day. *Eating facilities:* can be arranged in new clubhouse. *Visitors:* welcome – almost unrestricted. *Society Meetings:* very welcome. Secretary: J. Bicker (01700 504270).

ROTHESAY. **Rothesay Golf Club,** Canada Hill, Rothesay PA20 9HN. *Location:* Beautiful island in the Firth of Clyde, frequent ferries from Wemyss Bay, 35 miles south-west of Glasgow, and from Colintraive in mainland Argyll. One of Scotland's most scenic island courses, designed by James Braid and Ben Sayers. 18 holes, 5456 yards. S.S.S. 67. Practice area. *Green Fees:* information not provided. *Eating facilities:* full catering and bar facilities. *Visitors:* welcome, but prior booking at weekends through Professional. *Society Meetings:* welcome by arrangement. PGA Professional: James M. Dougal (Tel & Fax: 01700 503554). website: www.rothesaygolfclub.com

SOUTHEND. **Dunaverty Golf Club,** Southend, Campbeltown PA28 6RW (Tel & Fax: 01586 830677). *Location:* about 10 miles south of Campbeltown on B842. Scenic seaside course with great views to Ireland and Mull of Kintyre. 18 holes, 4799 yards. S.S.S. 63. Small practice ground. *Green Fees:* £20.00 per round, £28.00 per day. 2007 fees, subject to review. *Eating facilities:* snacks, teas/coffees, meals by arrangement; no bar. *Visitors:* welcome, phone if visiting at weekends. Limited equipment hire. *Society Meetings:* welcome, phone or write to N. Hind for bookings. Steward: N. Hind. website: www.dunavertygolfclub.com

TARBERT. **Tarbert Golf Club,** Kilberry Road, Tarbert PA29 6XX (01880 820565). *Location:* approximately one mile south of Tarbert on B8024. Hilly wooded parkland. 9 holes, 4460 yards. S.S.S. 63. *Green Fees:* £20.00 per day. *Eating facilities:* licensed clubhouse, open weekends. *Visitors:* welcome at all times. *Society Meetings:* by arrangement. Secretary: Peter Cupples (01546 606896).

TAYNUILT. **Taynuilt Golf Club,** Taynuilt PA35 1JE (01866 822429). *Location:* 12 miles from Oban on A85, quarter of a mile, through the village from the main road. Situated in a scenic and majestic location, surrounded by mountains and overlooking picturesque Loch Etive. The challenging 9 hole course of undulating parkland is dominated by Ben Cruachan. 9 Holes, 4510 yards. S.S.S.63 (men), 67 (ladies). *Green Fees:* £15.00. *Eating facilities:* not available - two hotels and a tearoom nearby. *Visitors:* welcome most days, some restrictions Tuesdays and Sundays for club competitions. Toilet facilities available. *Society Meetings:* welcome. Secretary: Michael J.P. Urwin (01866 833341). e-mail: michaelurwin152@btinternet.com website: www.taynuiltgolfclub.co.uk

TIGHNABRUAICH. **Kyles Of Bute Golf Club,** Ravenswood, Kames, Tighnabruaich PA21 2AB. *Location:* access from Dunoon and Strachur. Clubhouse by Kames Farm, turn south off B8000 Kames to Millhouse road. Hillside course with magnificent views. 9 holes, 4778 yards. S.S.S. 64. *Green Fees:* weekdays £10.00 per day; weekends £10.00. *Eating facilities:* no bar. *Visitors:* welcome, except Sunday mornings. *Society Meetings:* by special arrangement. Secretary: Dr Jeremy Thomson (01700 811603).

Ayrshire & Arran

AYR. **Belleisle Golf Course,** Doonfoot Road, Ayr KA7 4DU (01292 441258). *Location:* follow main road south through Ayr. Gently sloping parkland course with fine mature trees. 18 holes, 6477 yards. S.S.S. 72. Practice area. *Green Fees:* information not available. *Eating facilities:* hotel and bars with catering. *Visitors:* no restrictions but booking in advance advisable. Juniors under 17 must have handicap of 12 or under. *Society Meetings:* catered for, groups up to 40; groups over 40 by special application. Professional: David Gemmell (Tel & Fax: 01292 441314). Starter: Alan Thomson (01292 441258; Fax: 01292 442632).*

AYR. **Dalmilling Golf Course,** Westwood Avenue, Ayr KA8 0QR (01292 263893; Fax: 01292 610543). *Location:* A77, on north-east boundary, one mile from town centre. Parkland. 18 holes, 5724 yards. S.S.S. 68. Putting green. *Green Fees:* weekdays £14.00 per round, £22.00 per day; weekends £17.50 per round, £27.00 per day. *Eating facilities:* snacks/lunches/high teas, table licence. *Visitors:* welcome, not before 9.30am weekends, telephone to ensure availability. *Society Meetings:* welcome by arrangement. Professional: Philip Cheyney. Secretary: Raymond Smith (01292 289206).

AYR. **Seafield Golf Course,** Doonfoot Road, Ayr KA7 4DU (01292 441258). *Location:* follow main road south through Ayr. Parkland and links, gently sloping. 18 holes, 5498 yards. S.S.S. 66. *Green Fees:* information not available. *Eating facilities:* hotel and bars with catering. *Visitors:* welcome, no restrictions but booking in advance advisable. *Society Meetings:* catered for, groups up to 40; groups over 40 by special application. Professional: David Gemmell (Tel & Fax: 01292 441314). Starter: Alan Thomson (01292 441258; Fax: 01292 442632).*

BEITH. **Beith Golf Club,** Threepwood Road, Beith KA15 2JR (01505 503166). *Location:* first left off Beith bypass road travelling south. Hilly parkland course with trees and gorse. 18 holes, 5616 yards. S.S.S. 68. *Green Fees:* available on request. *Eating facilities:* snacks and meals available, bar open 9am to 11pm. *Visitors:* welcome. Restrictions as follows; Tuesday 4.30pm to 6.30pm. Saturday 7am to 2pm. Sunday 1pm to 2.30pm. *Society Meetings:* welcome by prior arrangement. Secretary: Margaret Murphy (Tel & Fax: 01505 506814).

DAILLY. **Brunston Castle Golf Course,** Dailly, Girvan KA26 9GD (01465 811471). *Location:* 18 hole championship course in most scenic part of Ayrshire, five miles north of Girvan on B471, five miles from Turnberry. *Green Fees:* on application. Open 8am to 11pm (summer). Driving range. Full PGA tuition by Professional, full practice facilities. *Eating facilities:* full bar and restaurant facilities. *Visitors:* welcome. 16-seater minibus and trailer available. On-line booking available.
e-mail: golf@brunstoncastle.co.uk
website: www.brunstoncastle.co.uk

GALSTON. **Loudoun Gowf Club,** Galston KA4 8PA (01563 820551). *Location:* five miles east of Kilmarnock on A71. Fairly flat parkland. 18 holes, 6005 yards. S.S.S. 69. Green Fees: £25.00 per round, £35.00 per day weekdays. *Eating facilities:* full catering and bar. *Visitors:* welcome weekdays only. Trolleys and buggies available for hire. *Society Meetings:* welcome by arrangement. Secretary: (01563 821993; Fax: 01563 820011).

GIRVAN. **Girvan Golf Course,** 40 Golf Course Road, Girvan, KA26 9HW (01465 714346). *Location:* A77 from Glasgow, through Ayr, on coast road to Stranraer, off A77 north of Harbour. 8 holes seaside, 10 holes parkland. 18 holes, 5064 yards. S.S.S. 64. Practice area. *Green Fees:* information not provided. *Eating facilities:* full catering available in clubhouse. *Visitors:* welcome, no restrictions except when course closed for local competitions (approximately 4 per year). *Society Meetings:* welcome, book through Starter. Secretary: W.B. Tait.

IRVINE. **Glasgow Golf Club,** Gailes Links, Irvine KA11 5AE (01294 311258; Fax: 01294 279366). *Location:* eight miles from Kilmarnock, two miles south of Irvine, four miles north of Troon. Championship links course with heather lined fairways. 18 holes, 6535 yards. S.S.S. 72, Par 71. Practice ground. *Green Fees:* weekdays £60.00 per round, £75.00 per day; Saturday and Sunday afternoons £70.00. Subject to review. *Eating facilities:* full catering and bar facilities. *Visitors:* welcome weekdays 8.30am-4.30pm, weekend afternoons. Prior booking recommended through the Secretary. Caddy cars/buggies for hire, caddies by arrangement. *Society Meetings:* by application to Managing Secretary. Professional: John Greaves (01294 311561). Managing Secretary: P. G. McMillan (0141-942 2011; Fax: 0141-942 0770).
e-mail: secretary@glasgow-golf.com
website: www.glasgowgailes-golf.com

IRVINE. **The Irvine Golf Club,** Bogside, Irvine KA12 8SN (01294 275979). *Location:* through Irvine going towards Kilwinning, turn left at Ravenspark Academy. Flat links course. 18 holes, 6408 yards. S.S.S. 72. Practice ground. *Green Fees:* information not provided. *Eating facilities:* dining room and bars. *Visitors:* welcome, after 3pm weekends. *Society Meetings:* welcome. Professional: J. McKinnon (01294 275626). Secretary: W.J. McMahon (01294 275979).

THE APPEARANCE OF AN ASTERISK (*) AT THE END OF A CLUB OR COURSE ENTRY INDICATES THAT UP-TO-DATE INFORMATION HAS NOT BEEN SUPPLIED

IRVINE. **Irvine Ravenspark Golf Club,** 13 Kidsneuk Lane, Irvine KA12 8SR (01294 271293). *Location:* on A78 between Irvine and Kilwinning at Irvine Royal Academy. Flat parkland course. 18 holes, 6453 yards. S.S.S. 71. *Green Fees:* information not available. *Eating facilities:* diningroom, bar. *Visitors:* welcome, except on Saturdays before 2.30pm March to October. No jeans or training shoes allowed in the clubhouse. *Society Meetings:* welcome, by arrangement weekends. Professional: P. Bond (01294 276467). Secretary: S. Howie (01294 553904). Steward: J. McVay (01294 271293).*
e-mail: secretary@irgc.co.uk
website: www.irgc.co.uk

IRVINE. **Thistle Hotel, Roseholm Golf Course,** 46 Annick Road, Irvine KA11 4LD (Hotel Tel: 0870 3339156; Fax: 0870 3339256). *Location:* course is situated on the grounds of the Thistle Hotel, Irvine. Flat parkland. 9-holes, 1277 yards. *Green Fees:* information not available. Golf free to hotel guests. Club hire for hotel guests. *Eating facilities:* lunches, snacks, tea and coffee served in the hotel bar. *Visitors:* welcome all year.*
e-mail: irvine@thistle.co.uk
website: www.thistlehotels.com/irvine

IRVINE. **Western Gailes Golf Club,** Gailes, By Irvine KA11 5AE (01294 311649; Fax: 01294 312312). *Location:* three miles north of Troon. Seaside links. 18 holes, 6639 yards, 6179 (yellow tees). S.S.S. 74. Par 71. Limited practice facilities. *Green Fees:* (2007) weekdays £110.00 per round, £160.00 per day, both include lunch; Sunday after 2.00pm £120.00 per round (lunch not included), subject to review. *Eating facilities:* full bar and catering facilities. *Visitors:* welcome Mondays, Wednesdays and Fridays and Sunday afternoons, advance booking required, telephone Reservations Department, Lyn or Vicky (01294 311649). Caddies and trollies available for hire. *Society Meetings:* welcome by arrangement with Secretary. Secretary: Barry J. Knowles.
e-mail: enquiries@westerngailes.com

KILBIRNIE. **Kilbirnie Place Golf Club,** Largs Road, Kilbirnie KA25 7AT (01505 683398). *Location:* on main Kilbirnie to Largs Road, left hand side just outside town boundary. Parkland. 18 holes, 5116 yards. S.S.S. 67. *Green Fees:* information not

provided. *Eating facilities:* catering and bar. *Visitors:* welcome weekdays and Sundays only, no visiting parties Saturdays. Secretary: C. McGurk (01505 684444/683398).

KILMARNOCK. **Annanhill Golf Club,** Irvine Road, Kilmarnock KA3 2RT (01563 521644). *Location:* between Kilmarnock and Crosshouse on road to Irvine. Parkland course with excellent views and tree-lined fairways. 18 holes, 6285 yards. S.S.S. 70. Practice area. *Green Fees:* prices on request to Starter on (01563 521512). *Eating facilities:* full catering available on application. *Visitors:* no parties Saturdays, but welcome Sundays and weekdays by reservation. *Society Meetings:* catered for. Secretary: Thomas C. Denham (01563 521644).

KILMARNOCK. **Caprington Golf Club,** Ayr Road, Kilmarnock (01563 523702). Parkland/wooded course. 18 holes, 5810 yards. S.S.S. 68. *Green Fees:* information not available. *Eating facilities:* available. *Visitors:* welcome except Saturdays. *Society Meetings:* all welcome. Secretary: Gordon Bray (01563 520566).*

LARGS. **Largs Golf Club,** Irvine Road, Largs KA30 8EU (01475 673594). *Location:* A78, south end of Largs town (opposite Marina). Parkland/woodland with scenic views over Cumbraes and Isle of Arran. 18 holes, 6140 yards. S.S.S. 71. *Green Fees:* on request. *Eating facilities:* full catering and bar. *Visitors:* welcome, tee can be reserved one day ahead of play. Carts, caddies by arrangement. *Society Meetings:* catered for by prior arrangement Tuesdays and Thursdays, Fridays between 9.30am and 11am and 2.30pm and 4pm. Professional: Kenneth Docherty PGA (01475 686192). Secretary: Ms Jan Duncker (Tel & Fax: 01475 673594).
e-mail: secretary@largsgolfclub.co.uk
website: www.largsgolfclub.co.uk

LARGS. **Routenburn Golf Club,** Routenburn Road, Largs KA30 8SQ (01475 673230). Hilly moorland course. 18 holes, 5765 yards. S.S.S. 67. *Green Fees:* information available from Professional. *Eating facilities:* lunches at club except Thursdays, order in advance. *Visitors:* welcome. Parties welcome, contact Professional. Professional: Greig McQueen (01475 687240). Secretary: Mr R.B. Connal.

LARGS. **sportscotland National Centre: Inverclyde, Golf Training Facility,** Burnside Road, Largs KA30 8RW (01475 674666). *Location:* 40 minutes from Glasgow and Prestwick airports. Parkland, links, training bunkers. 6 hole practice area plus driving bays. *Green Fees:* information not available. *Eating facilities:* cafeteria, dining room, accommodation and bar. *Visitors:* one and two day ladies' and mixed beginners' courses, booking essential. Professionals: Kenny Docherty, Greg McQueen, Gordon Sherry, Campbell Donaldson. Assistant Pro: Derek Watters. Admin. Co-ordinator: Sandra Samuel. Manager: Angela Liddel.*

MAUCHLINE. **Ballochmyle Golf Club,** Mauchline KA5 6LE (01290 550469; Fax: 01290 553657). *Location:* on B705 off A76, one mile south of Mauchline. Wooded parkland course. 18 holes, 5990 yards. S.S.S. 69. *Green Fees:* £32.50 per day weekdays; £35.00 per day weekends. *Eating facilities:* all day bar opening from 1st April until 30th September, snacks and meals available during bar hours. *Visitors:* welcome every day except Saturdays. Dress regulations both on and off the course must be adhered to. Two full size snooker tables. *Society Meetings:* all welcome to a total of 30 per party. Secretary: R. Leslie Crawford (01290 550469). e-mail: secretary@ballochmylegolf.wanadoo.co.uk

MAYBOLE. **Maybole Golf Course,** Memorial Park, Kirkoswald Road, Maybole KA19 7DX (01292 612000). *Location:* A77 from Glasgow, on main Girvan road at Maybole. Hilly parkland. 9 holes, 2635 yards. S.S.S. 33. *Green Fees:* information not available. *Visitors:* welcome. *Society Meetings:* welcome. Secretary: A. Ferguson. Starter (01655 889770).*

MUIRKIRK. **Muirkirk Golf Club,** "Southside", Furnace Road, Mulrklrk KA18 3RE. *Location:* 10 miles off A74 on A70 to Ayr. Picturesque country scenery, the course nestles amongst heather clad hills. 9 holes, 5380 yards. S.S.S. 67. *Green Fees:* information not available. *Eating facilities:* can be accommodated. Secretary: Robert Bradford (01290 660184).*

NEW CUMNOCK. **New Cumnock Golf Club,** 55 Pathhead, New Cumnock KA18 4DQ (01290 338000). *Location:* A76, one mile west of New Cummock. Parkland, protected area for wildlife birds, next to loch. 9 holes, 5176 yards (18). S.S.S. 66. *Green Fees:* information not available. *Eating facilities:*

Lochside House Hotel sits on the edge of the course. *Visitors:* welcome at all times except Sunday up to 4pm for competitions. Clubhouse. *Society Meetings:* welcome. Secretary: John McGinn (01290 338041).

PATNA. **Doon Valley Golf Club,** Hillside, Patna KA6 7JT (01292 531607). *Location:* 10 miles south of Ayr on the A713 Ayr to Castle Douglas road. Undulating hillside parkland course. 9 holes, 5859 yards, 5402 metres. S.S.S. 70. *Green Fees:* £12.00 per round, £16.00 per day. *Eating facilities:* bar open weekdays 7pm to 11pm, weekends 12 noon to 12 midnight. *Visitors:* welcome anytime weekdays, weekends by arrangement. *Society Meetings:* welcome, groups of more than six must apply for tee off times. Secretary: Hugh Johnstone MBE (01292 550411).

PRESTWICK. **Prestwick St Nicholas Golf Club,** Grangemulr Road, Prestwlck KA9 1SN (01292 477608; Fax: 01292 473900). *Location:* Grangemuir Road is half a mile from town centre on Prestwick to Ayr Road. Traditional links course enjoying wonderful panoramic views across Firth of Clyde to island of Arran. 18 holes, 5952 yards, 5441 metres. S.S.S. 69. *Green Fees:* weekdays £55.00 per round, weekend £60.00 per round. Weekday day ticket £75.00. Subject to review. *Eating facilities:* full service. *Visitors:* welcome most weekdays and Sunday afternoons. *Society Meetings:* welcome by arrangement. Secretary: T.D.M. Hepburn (01292 477608; Fax: 01292 473900). e-mail: secretary@prestwickstnicholas.com website: www.prestwickstnicholas.com

PRESTWICK. **Prestwick Golf Club,** Links Road, Prestwick KA9 1QG (01292 477404). *Location:* one mile from Prestwick airport, 40 minutes by car from Turnberry Hotel, 10 minutes from Troon, 15 minutes from Ayr. 18 holes, 6544 yards. S.S.S. 73. *Green Fees:* weekdays £110.00 per round, £165.00 per day; Sundays (limited times) £140.00 per round. Subject to review for 2008. *Eating facilities:* dining room (male only: prior booking required) open from 12.30pm to 2.30pm. Cardinal Room (light lunches) open to ladies and gentlemen from 10.00am until 3.30pm. *Visitors:* welcome with reservation. *Society Meetings:* catered for. Professional: D. A. Fleming. Secretary: I.T. Bunch (01292 477404; Fax: 01292 477255). e-mail: secretary@prestwickgc.co.uk website: www.prestwickgc.co.uk

PRESTWICK. **Prestwick St Cuthbert Golf Club,** East Road, Prestwick KA9 2SX (01292 477101; Fax: 01292 671730). *Location:* south-east area of Prestwick near A77 Whitletts roundabout, follow signs for Heathfield and Prestwick Airport. Flat parkland. 18 holes, 6470 yards, 6063 metres. S.S.S. 71. Limited practice area. *Green Fees:* £30.00 per round, £45.00 day ticket. *Eating facilities:* bar and restaurant. *Visitors:* welcome except weekends unless introduced by and playing with member. *Society Meetings:* catered for. Secretary: Jim Jess (01292 477101).

SKELMORLIE. **Skelmorlie Golf Club,** Beithglass Road, Skelmorlie PA17 5ES (01475 520152). *Location:* two miles from Wemyss Bay Pier. Hillside, moorland course. 18 holes, 5030 yards. S.S.S. 65. *Green Fees:* (2007) weekdays £22.00 per round, £27.00 per day; weekends £27.00 per round, £32.00 per day. *Eating facilities:* bar 11am to 10 pm, catering by arrangement. *Visitors:* welcome except Saturdays before 3pm. *Society Meetings:* welcome by arrangement. Parties at discounted "all-in" rate. Secretary: Mrs E. Linton (01475 520152).

STEVENSTON. **Ardeer Golf Club,** Greenhead, Stevenston KA20 4JX (01294 464542). *Location:* north of Ayr, six miles from Irvine New Town, off A78. Parkland course lined with trees incorporating water on several holes. 18 holes, 6409 yards. S.S.S. 71. *Green Fees:* on application. *Eating facilities:* restaurant and bars. *Visitors:* welcome except Saturdays before 3pm, check for availability. *Society Meetings:* special rates available for groups of 12 or more. Secretary: Peter Watson (Tel & Fax: 01294 464542).

STEVENSTON. **Moorpark Golf Club,** Auchenharvie Golf Complex, Moorpark Road West, Stevenston KA20 3HU. *Location:* on the A738 Stevenston/ Saltcoats; five miles from Irvine, 20 miles from Glasgow. Flat parkland course with water feature incorporated into two holes. 18 holes, 5203 yards. S.S.S. 66. 18 bay floodlit driving range. *Green Fees:* information not available. *Eating facilities:* privately owned lounge bar within complex

open to public, bar meals, functions, snacks available (01294 469051). *Visitors:* welcome, restrictions when there are club competitions. *Society Meetings:* all welcome. The course is situated right next door to Sandylands Caravan Park and there are plenty of other golf courses to play all within easy reach. Secretary: R. Paterson (01294 602493).*

TROON. **Kilmarnock (Barassie) Golf Club,** 29 Hillhouse Road, Barassie, Troon KA10 6SY (01292 313920; Fax: 01292 318300). *Location:* two miles north of Troon. Links course. 27 holes: Barassie Links 18 holes, 6484 yards. S.S.S. 74; Hillhouse 9 holes, 2888 yards, par 34. Practice ground. *Green Fees:* £65.00 per day Monday to Friday, £75.00 per round Sunday only from 2.30pm (under review). *Eating facilities:* coffee, lunches, snacks, high teas. *Visitors:* welcome Mondays, Tuesdays, Thursdays and Friday afternoons; limited visitors Wednesdays; Sundays after 2.30pm. All visitors must adhere to club dress code – no denim, trainers, etc. *Society Meetings:* catered for Tuesdays and Thursdays. Professional: Gregor Howie (Tel & Fax: 01292 311322). Secretary: Donald D. Wilson (01292 313920/311077). e-mail: golfkbgc@lineone.net website: www.kbgc.co.uk

TROON. **Troon Municipal Golf Courses,** Harling Drive, Troon (01292 312464). *Location:* adjacent to railway station, one mile off the Ayr-Glasgow road. Three 18 hole courses. Lochgreen 6820 yards. S.S.S. 73. Darley 6360 yards. S.S.S. 72. Fullarton 4870 yards. S.S.S. 63. *Green Fees:* information not available. *Eating facilities:* hot snacks, 8am - 6pm. Bar snacks and lunches, evening meals bookings only. *Visitors:* catered for. Broad wheeled trolleys only. *Society Meetings:* catered for. Caterer: John Darge. Professional: Gordon McKinley. Advance booking should be made in writing to Starter's Office, Troon Municipal Golf Courses, Harling Drive, Troon, Ayrshire (Fax: 01292 312578). Special short breaks and day tickets available, for details telephone 01292 616270.*

TROON. **Royal Troon Golf Club,** Craigend Road, Troon KA10 6EP (01292 311555; Fax: 01292 318204). *Location:* three miles from A77 (Glasgow/Ayr trunk road). Old Course (Championship) 18 holes, 6493 metres, 7101 yards. S.S.S. 74. Portland Course 18 holes, 5751 metres, 6289 yards. S.S.S. 71. *Green Fees:* on request. *Eating facilities:* full restaurant service available, including bar snacks. *Visitors:* Mondays, Tuesdays and Thursdays between 9.30 and 11.00am and 14.30 and 16.00pm. Letter of introduction from own club and Handicap Certificate required (maximum; male 20; Ladies 30). Golfers under 16 years play on the Portland Course. *Society Meetings:* parties in excess of 24 by special arrangement. Professional: Brian Anderson (01292 313281). Secretary/Manager: J.W. Chandler (01292 311555; Fax: 01292 318204).
e-mail: bookings@royaltroon.com
website: www.royaltroon.com

TURNBERRY. **The Westin Turnberry Resort,** Maidens Road, Turnberry KA26 9LT (01655 331000; Fax: 01655 331706). *Location:* on main A77 between Maybole and Girvan. Two Championship Links Courses, Ailsa (host to British Open) 18 holes, 6976 yards. S.S.S. 72; The Kintyre, 6827 yards. S.S.S. 72, and The Arran (9 holes). The Colin Montgomerie Links Golf Academy, putting greens. *Green Fees:* information not available. *Eating facilities:* clubhouse, restaurant and bar. *Visitors:* written requests only. Accommodation at The Westin Turnberry Resort, 219 Bedrooms. *Society Meetings:* written requests only. Director of Golf: Paul Burley (01655 334000; Fax: 01655 331069). Golf Sales Manager: E.C. Bowman (01655 334198).*

WEST KILBRIDE. **The West Kilbride Golf Club,** 33-35 Fullerton Drive, Seamill, West Kilbride KA23 9HT (01294 823911; Fax: 01294 829573). *Location:* mid-way between Largs (to north) and Ardrossan (south) on A78. Seaside links course with magnificent views to Isle of Arran and Cumbraes across Firth of Clyde. 18 holes, 6452 yards, 5898 metres. S.S.S. 71. Practice area, putting greens. *Green Fees:* on application. *Eating facilities:* bar, lounge, dining room. *Visitors:* welcome weekdays only. Caddy cars for hire. *Society Meetings:* catered for Tuesdays and Thursdays. Handicap Certificates required. Professional: Graham Ross (01294 823042). Secretary: Hamish Armour (01294 823911).

THE ISLAND OF ARRAN

BLACKWATERFOOT. **Shiskine Golf and Tennis Club,** Blackwaterfoot, Shiskine, Isle of Arran KA27 8HA (Tel: 01770 860226. Fax: 01770 860205). *Location:* off B880 at Blackwaterfoot. Seaside links with outstanding views. 12 holes, 2990 yards. S.S.S. 42. Putting green, nets. *Green Fees:* weekdays £18.00 per round, £30.00 per day; weekends £22.00 per round, £3500 per day. Special rates: Week £110.00, Fortnight £160.00. Subject to review. Maximum of two rounds per day. *Eating facilities:* tearoom, snacks, lunches, high teas, dinner. *Visitors:* welcome, preferably with Club Handicap. July and August are very busy so prefer visitors September to June. Tennis and bowls. Shop open Easter–October. Pro Shop and lessons, all year. *Society Meetings:* only if pre-booked with Match Secretary. Proof of Handicap required. Club Manager/PGA Professional: Douglas Bell.
e-mail: info@shiskinegolf.com
website: www.shiskinegolf.com

BRODICK. **Brodick Golf Club,** Brodick KA27 8DL (Tel & Fax: 01770 302349). *Location:* one mile north of pier. Flat seaside course. 18 holes, 4736 yards. S.S.S. 64. Practice area. *Green Fees:* information not available. *Eating facilities:* bar snacks available. *Visitors:* welcome without restriction. *Society Meetings:* welcome with reservation by letter. Professional: P.S. McCalla (01770 302513). Secretary: Douglas Robertson (Tel & Fax: 01770 302349).*

CORRIE. **Corrie Golf Club,** Sannox, Corrie KA27 8JD (01770 810223). *Location:* seven miles north of Brodick. Short 9 hole course, full of character and very picturesque with some magnificent views. 9 holes, 1948 yards. S.S.S. 61. *Green Fees:* £15.00 per day ticket; twilight ticket £7.00. *Eating facilities:* meals available 9am to 6pm April to October. *Visitors:* welcome, course closed Saturday afternoons, Ladies' medal first Thursday of every month. *Society Meetings:* catered for by arrangement (maximum number 12). Secretary: J. Milesi (01770 850247).

LAMLASH. **Lamlash Golf Club,** Lamlash KA27 8JU (Tel & Fax: 01770 600296). *Location:* A841, three miles south of Brodick Pier ferry terminal. Undulating heathland course. 18 holes, 4640 yards. S.S.S. 64. *Green Fees:* weekdays £22.00 per day; weekends £28.00. After 4pm any day £15.00 per round. Reductions for Senior Citizens. Rates subject to review. *Eating facilities:* catering, lounge bar. *Visitors:* welcome, no restrictions. Pro shop: (01770 600196). Carts/buggies for hire. *Society Meetings:* welcome, book in advance by letter. Secretary: J. Henderson (01770 600272). Starter: (01779 600196).
website: www.lamlashgolfclub.co.uk

LOCHRANZA. **Lochranza Golf,** Isle of Arran KA27 8HL (01770 830273). *Location:* Lochranza village. A special 'pay & play' golf course in spectacular setting with extensive wildlife. Very interesting challenging layout, fun for everyone. All handicaps may play medal tees. 18 holes from 18 tees to 12 greens (six double, six single), 5470 yards, 5033 metres. Par 70. *Green Fees:* £18.00 per round every day. *Visitors:* welcome daily May to October inclusive. Proprietor: Iain M. Robertson.
e-mail: office@lochgolf.demon.co.uk
website: www.lochranzagolf.com

MACHRIE. **Machrie Bay Golf Course,** Machrie, Near Brodick KA27 8DZ (01770 840329). *Location:* on A841, three and a half miles north of Blackwaterfoot. Flat seaside course. 9 holes, 2200 yards. S.S.S. 32. Putting green and small practice area. *Green Fees:* information not available. *Eating facilities:* tea room, snacks/meals; no licence. *Visitors:* welcome anytime. *Society Meetings:* by arrangement. Secretary: R. Waine (01770 860380).*

WHITING BAY. **Whiting Bay Golf Club,** Golf Course Road, Whiting Bay, Brodick KA27 8QT (01770 700487). *Location:* eight miles south of Brodick. Undulating parkland. 18 holes, 4405 yards. S.S.S. 63. Practice net. *Green Fees:* information not provided. *Eating facilities:* catering and bar. *Visitors:* welcome anytime. Clubhouse, shower, snooker and pool rooms; buggies and caddy cars for hire. *Society Meetings:* by prior booking. Secretary: Margaret Auld (01770 820208).

Borders

ASHKIRK. **Woll Golf Course,** New Woll Estate, Selkirk TD7 4PE (01750 32711). *Location:* through the village of Ashkirk, just off the A7 and only an hour from Edinburgh, Newcastle and Carlisle. Challenging course In natural parkland setting of outstanding beauty incorporating the Woll Burn and other water features. Flat course. 18 holes, 6051 yards, S.S.S. 69. *Green Fees:* £28.00 (subject to review). *Eating facilities:* full clubhouse facilities available; bar, restaurant and function suite all year round. *Visitors:* most welcome at all times. Luxury self-catering accommodation available on the course.
e-mail: wollgolf@btinternet.com
website: www.wollgolf.co.uk

COLDSTREAM. **Hirsel Golf Club,** Kelso Road, Coldstream TD12 4NJ (01890 882678; Fax: 01890 882233). *Location:* A697 west end of Coldstream. Parkland. 18 holes, 6024 yards, 5570 metres. S.S.S. 70. Practice ground. *Green Fees:* information not provided. *Eating facilities:* full catering all year. Snack catering November to mid-March. *Visitors:* welcome, no restrictions; groups of over 10 players must book in advance. Two person golf carts for hire (6). *Society Meetings:* catered for by arrangement.

DUNS. **Duns Golf Club,** Hardens Road, Duns TD11 3NR (01361 882194). *Location:* about one mile west of Duns just off A6105, signposted Longformacus. Upland, undulating course with view south to Cheviot Hills. A burn runs through the course and is the main hazard. 18 holes, 6298 yards. S.S.S. 70. Practice ground. New driving range 2 miles from golf course. *Green Fees:* weekdays £25.00 per round, £32.00 per day; weekends £30.00 per round, £38.00 per day. Children £7.00 per round. Reductions 1st November to 15th March. *Eating facilities:* lounge bar open weekdays and weekends, light snacks and full catering available. *Visitors:* welcome at all times except during club competitions, visitors must tee off before 4pm Mondays, Tuesdays and Wednesdays. *Society Meetings:* welcome, booking through Clubhouse (01361 882194). Secretary: Alex Preston (01361 883599).

EYEMOUTH. **Eyemouth Golf Club,** Gunsgreenhill, Eyemouth TD14 5SF (018907 50004). *Location:* eight miles north of Berwick-on-Tweed, one mile off the A1. Superb cliff-top course with spectacular sea views. Play the Par 3 - 6th hole over a vast gully, with crashing waves below. Recently voted "Britain's most extraordinary Golf Hole'. 18 holes, 6520 yards, Par 72. Practice area. *Green Fees:* weekdays £25.00 per round, £35.00 per day; weekends £30.00 per round, £40.00 per day. Winter £15.00 per round or day, 7 days. *Eating facilities:* full catering facilities with the `Bay View' restaurant specializing in local sea food. *Visitors:* very welcome, phone Professional for booking. Games room, changing rooms, showers. *Society Meetings:* golfing groups and society packages very welcome. Professional: Michael Hackett (018907 50004). Secretary: Mrs M. Gibson (018907 50551

GALASHIELS. **Galashiels Golf Club,** Ladhope Recreation Ground, Galashiels TD1 2NJ (01896 753724). *Location:* north end of town, quarter of a mile off A7 on Ladhope Drive. Parkland with hill connecting two halves. 18 holes, 5185 yards. Par 67. Practice area. *Green Fees:* information not available. Package deals available for parties on application to the Visitors Contact. *Eating facilities:* catering midweek by arrangement only. *Visitors:* welcome anytime, booking essential for weekends. Ladies' night Tuesday 5pm to 7.30pm. *Society Meetings:* catered for. Contact: Secretary (01896 753724).*

GALASHIELS. **Torwoodlee Golf Club,** Edinburgh Road, Galashiels TD1 2NE (01896 752260). *Location:* leave Galashiels on A7 for Edinburgh. Entrance to course one mile on left. Parkland with wooded greens alongside river and splendid par 5. Designed by Willie Park/John Garner. 18 holes, 6021 yards. S.S.S. 70. *Green Fees:* weekdays £30.00 per round, £40.00 per day; weekends £35.00 per round, £45.00 per day. Subject to review. *Eating facilities:* bar, dining room. *Visitors:* welcome except 8.30 to 9.30, 12.00 to 13.30 weekdays or 07.30 to 10.15, 12.15 to 15.00 and 16.15 to 17.00 Saturdays. Showers available. *Society Meetings:* bookings required in advance, packages available. Administrator: L. Moffat (01896 752260). e-mail: thesecretary@torwoodleegolfclub.org.uk website: www.torwoodleegolfclub.org.uk

HAWICK. **Hawick Golf Club,** Vertish Hill, Hawick TD9 9JY (01450 372293). *Location:* north along A7 from Carlisle or south on A7 from Edinburgh. Course situated half a mile south-west of town. Hill course with spectacular views. 18 holes, 5929 yards, 5422 metres. S.S.S. 69. Restricted practice area. *Green Fees:* information not provided. *Eating facilities:* full bar and catering daily. *Visitors:* welcome Saturdays and after 10am Sundays. *Society Meetings:* catered for, advisable to book in advance. Secretary: J. Reilly (01450 375594).

HAWICK. **Minto Golf Club,** Denholm, Hawick TD9 8SH (01450 870220). *Location:* five miles north-east of Hawick leaving A698 at Denholm village. Parkland, trees. 18 holes, 5542 yards, 4992 metres. S.S.S. 67. Practice area. *Green Fees:* information not available. *Eating facilities:* full facilities, except Thursday. *Visitors:* welcome, with prior booking. *Society Meetings:* accepted with Handicap Certificate (weekends difficult). Secretary: John Simpson.

INNERLEITHEN. **Innerleithen Golf Club,** Leithen Water, Leithen Road, Innerleithen EH44 6NL (01896 830951). *Location:* 25 miles south of Edinburgh, six miles south of Peebles, off A72 less than one mile from main street. Attractive 9 hole course set in valley with lovely views of surrounding hills, easy walking but challenging. 9 holes, 3033 yards, 2773 metres. S.S.S. 69. Practice ground. *Green Fees:* information not available. *Eating facilities:* by prior arrangement. *Visitors:* welcome without reservation, though parties should book. *Society Meetings:* catered for by arrangement, limit 40. Secretary: Norman Smith (01896 830050).

JEDBURGH. **Jedburgh Golf Club,** Dunion Road, Jedburgh TD8 6TA (01835 863587). *Location:* one mile south of Jedburgh on Dunion Road to Hawick. Undulating course with trees. New 18 hole course. Parkland style with natural areas of gorse and broom. An undulating course with trees and water features. 5819 yards, S.S.S. 69. *Green Fees:* information not available. *Eating facilities:* bar and catering facilities available 11am to 11pm Wednesday to Sunday or by prior arrangement. *Visitors:* welcome. Buggy, trolley hire. *Society Meetings:* group discount on application. All enquiries please telephone 01835 863587.*

KELSO. **Kelso Golf Club,** Golf Course Road, Kelso TD5 7SL (01573 223009). *Location:* one mile north-east of town within Kelso Racecourse. Flat parkland course. 18 holes, 6032 yards. S.S.S. 70. Practice ground. *Green Fees:* information not available. *Eating facilities:* snacks available daily from 11.30am until 2pm. Special packages available to groups of 8 or more. *Visitors:* daily bookings through Starter. *Society Meetings:* bookings through Office Administrator, 9.30am to 12.30pm weekdays.*

KELSO. **The Roxburghe Golf Club,** The Roxburghe Hotel, Heiton, by Kelso TD5 8JZ (01573 450333; Fax: 01573 450611). *Location:* eight miles east of Jedburgh on the A698, three miles south of Kelso. Parkland, woodland course with water set in 200 acres alongside the River Teviot; designed by Dave Thomas to USPGA specifications. The Championship Course is home to the Scottish Seniors Open. 18 holes, 7111 yards. Chipping area, putting green, practice ground. *Green Fees:* £65.00, day ticket £85.00. Subject to review. It is advisable to pre-book tee times. *Eating facilities:* spike bar, fine dining. *Visitors:* welcome at all times, Handicap Certificate required. *Society Meetings:* welcome by prior arrangement. Accommodation available; tuition, clay pigeon shooting. The course is owned by the Duke and Duchess of Roxburghe. Professional: Craig Montgomerie. General Manager: Mr George Mack.
e-mail: hotel@roxburghe.net
website: www.roxburghe.net

LAUDER. **Lauder Golf Club,** Galashiels Road, Lauder TD2 6RS (01578 722240). *Location:* off A68, 28 miles south of Edinburgh. Undulating course, originally designed by W. Park of Musselburgh, on Lauder Hill. 9 holes, 6050 yards. S.S.S. 69. Practice ground. *Green Fees:* £15.00 all day, anyday. *Eating facilities:* none — good Hotels in Lauder. *Visitors:* individuals, groups and parties welcome. Telephone to book your tee time. Secretary: D. Dickson (01578 722526).

MELROSE. **Melrose Golf Club,** Dingleton Road, Melrose (01896 822855). *Location:* 4 miles south of Galashiels, less than one hour from Edinburgh. Tree-lined parkland course situated beneath Eildon Hills. 9 holes, 5562 yards, 5075 metres. S.S.S. 68. *Green Fees:* £25.00 per round/day. Juniors £10.00. *Eating facilities:* bar open at given times, catering on request for larger parties. *Visitors:* welcome anytime when no competitions taking place, Ladies have priority on Tuesdays; Juniors have priority on Wednesday mornings during school holidays. Locker room, shower. *Society Meetings:* welcome by arrangement. Secretary: Les Wallace (01835 823553).

NEWCASTLETON. **Newcastleton Golf Club,** C/o 5 Union Street, Newcastleton TD9 0QS. *Location:* midway between Carlisle 25 miles and Hawick 21 miles; off A7 at Canonbie. Hilly course with picturesque views, first three holes uphill. 9 holes, 5483 yards. S.S.S. 70. *Green Fees:* £12.00; weekly ticket £35.00. *Eating facilities:* can be arranged. *Visitors:* welcome, no restrictions except competition days. *Society Meetings:* welcome. Secretary: G.A. Wilson (013873 75608).

THE APPEARANCE OF AN ASTERISK (*) AT THE END OF A CLUB OR COURSE ENTRY INDICATES THAT UP-TO-DATE INFORMATION HAS NOT BEEN SUPPLIED

PEEBLES. **Macdonald Cardrona Hotel, Golf and Country Club,** Cardrona, Peebles EH45 6LZ (01896 831971; Fax: 01896 831166). *Location:* from Edinburgh take 'Bridges' road to Cameron Toll; turn right at roundabout; heading to Penicuik take A703 to Peebles, turn left to Innerleithen. Club situated 3 miles out of Peebles. Flat parkland/woodland championship standard course. 18 holes, 6856 yards. S.S.S. 72. Putting/practice area. *Green Fees:* information not available. *Eating facilities:* Spikes Bar. *Visitors:* welcome at any time. *Society Meetings:* welcome at any time, special rates on request. 100-bedroom de luxe hotel on site. Director of Golf: Ross Harrower (01896 833701; Fax: 01896 831166).*
e-mail: cardrona@macdonald-hotels.co.uk
website: www.macdonald-hotels.co.uk

PEEBLES. **Peebles Golf Club,** Kirkland Street, Peebles EH45 8EU (01721 720197). *Location:* 51 miles from Glasgow, off A72 at west side of town, 23 miles from Edinburgh. Undulating parkland with panoramic views. 18 holes, 6137 yards. S.S.S. 70. *Green Fees:* weekdays £38.00 per round, £50.00 per day; weekends £44.00 per round, £60.00 per day. Generous discounts for society bookings. *Eating facilities:* full catering daily. *Visitors:* welcome subject to tee availability. Golf buggy hire April to September. *Society Meetings:* catered for subject to prior booking, groups of up to 40 persons catered for. Secretary: Hugh Gilmore.

ST BOSWELLS. **St Boswells Golf Club,** Braeheads, St Boswells, Melrose TD6 0DE (01835 823527). *Location:* quarter of a mile off trunk route A68 at St. Boswells Green. Flat attractive scenery along the banks of the River Tweed. 9 holes, 5250 yards. S.S.S. 66. *Green Fees:* £20.00, £12.00 for 9 holes (subject to review). *Visitors:* no visitors after 4pm on a weekday and when competitions are being held. Secretary: Linda Cessford (01835 823527).

SELKIRK. **Selkirk Golf Club,** The Hill, Selkirk TD7 4NW (01750 20621). *Location:* one mile south of Selkirk on A7 road. Heather covered hill course, superb views of Border valleys. 9 holes, 5620 yards. S.S.S. 68. *Green Fees:* information not available. *Eating facilities:* bar, open evenings. *Visitors:* welcome morning and afternoon weekdays, weekends booking needed. *Society Meetings:* welcome. Secretary: J. M. Hay (01750 20621, 01750 20857 pm).*

WEST LINTON. **Rutherford Castle Golf Club,** West Linton EH46 7AS (Tel & Fax: 01968 661233). *Location:* A702 ten miles south of Edinburgh City Bypass. Undulating parkland course at the foot of the Pentland Hills. 18 holes, 6525 yards, 5872 metres. S.S.S. 71. *Green Fees:* £15.00 weekdays, £25.00 weekends. *Visitors:* no restrictions. Buggy and trolley hire. Contact: (01968 661233).
e-mail: rcgc@BTconnect.com

WEST LINTON. **West Linton Golf Club,** West Linton EH46 7HN (01968 660970). *Location:* A702 road 17 miles south west of Edinburgh. Scenic moorland course. 18 holes, 6161yards, 5633 metres. S.S.S. 70. Two practice areas. *Green Fees:* weekdays £30.00 per round, £40.00 per day; weekends £40.00 per round (group discounts available). Weekly ticket (Mon-Fri) £100.00. Season ticket (10 rounds) £150.00. Fees subject to review. *Eating facilities:* lunches, bar snacks, high teas, morning coffee, bar. *Visitors:* welcome at all times except on Medal days and weekends before 1pm. Buggy and carts for hire. *Society Meetings:* catered for weekdays. Professional: I. Wright (01968 660256). Secretary: John Johnson (01968 660970).

Jedburgh Golf Club

Dumfries & Galloway

ANNAN. **Powfoot Golf Club,** Cummertrees, Annan DG12 5QE (01461 204100; Fax: 01461 204111). *Location*: three miles from Annan on the B724, turnoff in the village of Cummertrees. Semi-links course on Solway shore with outstanding views. 18 holes, 6255 yards (white). S.S.S. 71. Two practice grounds. *Green Fees*: information not available. *Eating facilities*: morning coffee, lunches and teas in clubhouse - ordering in advance essential for large parties. Steward (01461 207521). *Visitors*: welcome weekdays 9am till 11am, 1pm till 3.30pm. Saturday 2.30pm to 3.30pm. Sundays 10.30am to 11.15am, 1pm to 3.30pm. All bookings through the office. *Society Meetings*: as per visitors. Office Manager: Steven Gardner.
e-mail: info@powfootgolfclub.com
par71@powfootgolfclub.fsnet.co.uk
website: www.powfootgolfclub.com

CASTLE DOUGLAS. **Castle Douglas Golf Club,** Abercromby Road, Castle Douglas DG7 1BA (01556 502801). *Location:* half a mile from town centre on A713 Castle Douglas to Ayr Road. Parkland course featuring the region's longest par 5, the 603-yard 6th hole. A challenge for golfers of all standards. 9 holes, 6254 yards. S.S.S. 71. *Green Fees:* £17.00 per day; 9 holes £12.00; Juniors (under 16 years) half price. *Eating facilities:* catering and bar facilities available all day April through September. *Visitors:* welcome without reservation April through September, except Tuesdays or Thursdays after 3pm. *Society Meetings:* welcome by arrangement with the Secretary; special packages for groups of 8 or more. Secretary: James Greenfield (01556 502509).
e-mail: cdgolfclub@aol.com
website: www.cdgolf.co.uk

> **THE APPEARANCE OF AN ASTERISK (*) AT THE END OF A CLUB OR COURSE ENTRY INDICATES THAT UP-TO-DATE INFORMATION HAS NOT BEEN SUPPLIED**

DALBEATTIE. **Colvend Golf Club,** Sandyhills, Colvend, By Dalbeattie DG5 4PY (01556 630398). *Location:* six miles from Dalbeattie on the A710, Solway Coast road, between Dalbeattie and Dumfries. Picturesque course on the Solway Coast with superb views over Galloway Hills and the Solway Firth. 18 holes visitors' tees,5035 yards, 4616 metres. S.S.S. 66; medal tees 5297 yards 4856 metres, S.S.S. 67. *Green Fees:* £25.00. Juniors £10.00. *Eating facilities:* modern clubhouse with full changing, catering and bar facilities. *Visitors:* all welcome. Buggies available. *Society Meetings:* welcome by booking through the club. Secretary: (01556 630398).

DALBEATTIE. **Dalbeattie Golf Club,** c/o The Secretary, 19 Maxwell Park, Dalbeattie DG5 4LR (Tel & Fax: 01556 610666; mobile: 07702 849945). Clubhouse (01556 611421 – not always manned). *Location*: signed off the B794 Haugh of Urr Road on the outskirts of Dalbeattie. Slightly undulating parkland course. 9 holes, 5710 yards (18 holes). S.S.S. 68. *Green Fees*: information not available. *Eating facilities*: bar and food available. *Visitors*: very welcome anytime and should club competitions be in progress, every effort will be made to accommodate them. *Society Meetings*: all welcome. Contact Secretary for further information regarding tee times, accommodation, restaurants, etc. website: www.dalbeattiegc.co.uk

DUMFRIES. **Crichton Golf Club,** Bankend Road, Dumfries DG1 4TH (01387 247894). *Location:* directly opposite Dumfries and Galloway Royal Infirmary, one mile outside Dumfries on Bankend Road. Wooded parkland. 9 holes, 5952 yards. S.S.S. 69. *Green Fees:* information not available. *Visitors:* welcome, restrictions depending on club competitions, Thursdays last tee off time 1pm. *Society Meetings:* on application to the Administrator. Match Secretary: Lee Sterritt.*

DUMFRIES. **Dumfries and County Golf Club,** Nunfield, Edinburgh Road, Dumfries DG1 1JX (01387 253585). *Location:* one mile north-east town centre on A701. 18 holes, 5918 yards. S.S.S. 69. Limited practice facilities. *Green Fees:* (under review for 2008). *Eating facilities:* restaurant and bar snacks. *Visitors:* welcome except on competition days. *Society Meetings:* by arrangement with Club Professional. Professional: S.J. Syme (Tel & Fax: 01387 268918). Secretary: B.R.M. Duguid (Tel & Fax: 01387 253585).
e-mail: dumfriesc@aol.com
website: www.thecounty.org.uk

DUMFRIES. **Dumfries and Galloway Golf Club,** 2 Laurieston Avenue, Dumfries DG2 7NY (01387 253582). *Location:* one mile from Dumfries on Castle Douglas road, A780. Parkland course. 18 holes, 6222 yards. S.S.S. 71. Practice area. Putting green. *Green Fees:* weekdays £30.00 per round, £38.00 per day; weekends £35.00 per round, £45.00 per day (under review.) *Eating facilities:* full catering during bar hours. *Visitors:* welcome, except on competition days. Ladies' Day Tuesday. *Society Meetings:* catered for weekdays, except Tuesdays or Saturdays. Professional: Joe Fergusson (01387 256902; Fax: 01387 276297). Secretary: Alasdair T. Miller (Tel & Fax: 01387 263848).
e-mail: info@dandggolfclub.co.uk
website: www.dandggolfclub.co.uk

DUMFRIES. **The Pines Golf Centre,** Lockerbie Road, Dumfries DG1 3PF (Tel & Fax: 01387 247444). *Location:* beside A75 Dumfries bypass off Lockerbie Road roundabout. Mixed park and heathland with mature trees and water features. 18 holes, 5940 yards. S.S.S.68. 20 bay driving range with video teaching facility. Short game practice area and large undulating putting green. *Green Fees:* adults £22.00, juniors £10.00. *Eating facilities:* bar with meals. *Visitors:* welcome. *Society Meetings:* welcome. Professionals: Stuart Syme, Gareth Dick and Richard Clark.

DUMFRIES. **Southerness Golf Club,** Southerness, Kirkbean, Dumfries DG2 8AZ (01387 880677; Fax: 01387 880644). *Location:* 16 miles south west of Dumfries on A710 (Solway Coast Road). Natural challenging Championship links, designed by MacKenzie Ross, with panoramic views of Solway Firth and Galloway hills. Hosted British Ladies' Amateur 1989 and British Youths' 1990. Scottish Amateur 1995. Scottish Amateur Stroke-play 2002. 18 holes, 6566 yards. S.S.S. 73. Practice ground. *Green Fees:* information not provided. *Eating facilities:* full bar and catering facilities. *Visitors:* welcome every day other than 9 days when there are Open Competitions, other golf club members only with Handicap Certificates. Trolley hire. *Society Meetings:* welcome by prior arrangement. Secretary: I.A. Robin.

PORTPATRICK. **Portpatrick Golf Club,** Clubhouse, Golf Course Road, Portpatrick DG9 8TB (01776 810273; Fax: 01776 810811). *Location:* A77 to Stranraer, follow signs to Portpatrick; A75 fork left one and a half miles after Glenluce bypass, follow signs to Portpatrick. Enter village, fork right at war memorial, then 300 yards on right. Cliff top links-type course. "Dunskey" 18 holes, 5913 yards. S.S.S. 69; "Dinvin" 9 holes, 1346 yards. S.S.S. 27. Practice ground. *Green Fees:* weekdays £32.00 per round, £42.50 per day; weekends £37.50 per round, £48.00 per day. Winter rates apply November to mid-March. *Eating facilities:* bar and catering available all year round. *Visitors:* advisable to book in advance (members times). Handicap Certificate required for Dunskey Course. *Society Meetings:* catered for by prior arrangement. Secretary: J. McPhail (01776 810273; Fax: 01776 810811).
e-mail: enquiries@portpatrickgolfclub.com
website: www.portpatrickgolfclub.com

PORT WILLIAM. **St Medan Golf Club,** Monreith, Port William, Newton Stewart DG8 8NJ (01988 700358). *Location:* on A747, three miles south of Port William. Seaside links course with panoramic views of Mull of Galloway and Isle of Man - Scotland's most southerly course. 9 holes, 18 tees 4520 yards. S.S.S. 63. Practice driving net and green. *Green Fees:* 9 holes £12.00, 18 holes £18.00, day £25.00; weekly £60.00. *Eating facilities:* available (also bar), summer only. *Visitors:* welcome without reservation. Telephone clubhouse for further information.

SANQUHAR. **Sanquhar Golf Club,** Euchan Course, Barr Road, Sanquhar DG4 6JZ (01659 50577). *Location:* situated quarter-of-a-mile from A76 Dumfries-Kilmarnock trunk road. Undulating parkland with views across the town. Practice areas/net. 9 holes, 5144 metres. S.S.S. 68. *Green Fees:* weekdays £10.00 per day; weekends £12.00 per day. Subject to review. *Eating facilities:* bar available if requested in advance. *Visitors:* welcome without reservation. Licensed clubhouse with full-size snooker table. *Society Meetings:* Golf package including catering for parties of 12 and over £25.00 per person.

SOUTHERNESS. **Solway Links Golf Club,** Southerness, Kirkbean, Dumfries DG2 8BE (01387 880323; Fax: 01387 880555). *Location:* 12 miles south-west of Dumfries on A710 (500 yards from Southerness Golf Course). Built on an ancient raised beach, in a stunning location overlooking the Solway Firth and Lake District hills. The fairways have received lots of praise for their spongy grass and generous width. 18 holes, 5037 yards. Par 67. 9-hole option and 9 holes of GolfCross Game (1st in UK). *Green Fees:* information not available. *Visitors:* welcome. Buggy and club hire available.*
e-mail: info@solwaylinks.co.uk
website: www.solwaylinks.co.uk

www.uk-golfguide.com

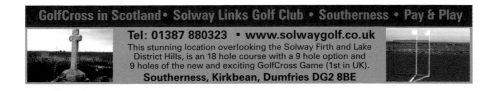

STRANRAER. **Stranraer Golf Club,** Creachmore, Leswalt, Stranraer DG9 0LF (01776 870245; Fax: 01776 870445). *Location:* three miles from Stranraer on the Kirkcolm Road (A718). Parkland, seaside – the last course James Braid designed. 18 holes, 6308 yards. S.S.S. 72. Practice area and putting green. *Green Fees:* weekdays £30.00 per round, £40.00 per day; weekends £35.00 per round, £45.00 per day. 27 holes: weekdays £31.00; weekends £36.00. Fees subject to review. *Eating facilities:* full catering all day, lounge bar overlooks course. *Visitors:* weekdays 9.15am to 12.30pm then 1.30 to 5pm; weekends 9.30am to 11.45am then 1.45pm to 5pm. Pull trolleys and golf carts available for hire. *Society Meetings:* all welcome with prior arrangement. Secretary: Bryce C. Kelly (01776 870245; Fax: 01776 870445).
e-mail: stranraergolf@btclick.com
website: www.stranraergolfclub.net

THORNHILL. **Thornhill Golf Club,** Blacknest, Thornhill DG3 5DW (01848 330546) *Location:* 14 miles north of Dumfries on A76, 1 mile east of village. Parkland/open moorland. 18 holes, 6085 yards. S.S.S. 70. Practice ground (two areas). *Green Fees:* information not available. *Eating facilities:* catering available, bar facility. *Visitors:* welcome without reservation, but please contact the club steward to ensure tee times are available. Buggies. *Society Meetings:* welcome, contact Alex Hillier (01848 331779).
e-mail: info@thornhillgolfclub.co.uk
website: www.thornhillgolfclub.co.uk

WIGTOWN. **Wigtown and Bladnoch Golf Club,** Lightlands Terrace, Wigtown, Newton Stewart DG8 9DY (01988 403354). *Location:* 200 yards from square in Wigtown. Parkland course. 9 holes, 5400 yards. S.S.S. 67. Practice bays. *Green Fees:* £20.00 for 18 holes, £12.00 for 9 holes; Senior Citizens £15.00 (9 or 18 holes), £25.00 per day; Juniors £10.00 (9 or 18 holes). Five day ticket £52.00. *Visitors:* welcome most days, tee reserved for open competitions occasional weekends. No prior booking necessary. *Society Meetings:* welcome by arrangement.

Dunbartonshire

ALEXANDRIA. **Vale of Leven Golf Club,** Northfield Road, Bonhill, Alexandria G83 9ET (01389 752351). *Location:* A82 to Dumbarton, follow signs at roundabout at Dumbarton for Bonhill then club signs. Parkland with splendid views of Loch Lomond. 18 holes, 5277 yards. S.S.S. 67. *Green Fees:* weekdays £20.00 per round, £30.00 per day; weekends £25.00 per round, £37.50 per day. Weekly ticket (Monday to Friday) £70.00. *Eating facilities:* catering and bar available. *Visitors:* welcome all year round. Full changing and locker facilities. Shop: Barry Campbell. *Society Meetings:* on application. Club Administrator: Richard Barclay (01389 752351).
e-mail: rbarclay@volgc.org
website: www.volgc.org

CARDROSS. **Cardross Golf Club,** Main Road, Cardross G82 5LB (01389 841213). *Location:* on A814 west of Dumbarton. Championship parkland course. 18 holes, 6469 yards. S.S.S. 72. Practice ground. *Green Fees:* weekdays £35.00 per round, £50.00 day ticket. *Eating facilities:* lunches/bar snacks available. *Visitors:* weekdays only (by phoning Professional to book time). *Society Meetings:* catered for weekdays by arrangement. Professional: Robert Farrell (01389 841350). Secretary: Iain T. Waugh (01389 841754; Fax: 01389 842162).
e-mail: golf@cardross.com
website: www.cardross.com

CLYDEBANK. **Clydebank and District Golf Club,** Glasgow Road, Hardgate, Clydebank G81 5QY (01389 383831). *Location:* Hardgate village. Off A82 10 miles west of Glasgow (off Great Western Road). 18 holes, 5832 yards, 5325 metres. S.S.S. 69. *Green Fees:* £20.00. *Eating facilities:* catering as required. *Visitors:* welcome weekdays only. Professional: Alan Waugh (01389 383835). Secretary: Mrs K. Stoddart (01389 383831; Fax: 01389 383831 by request).

CLYDEBANK. **Clydebank Municipal Golf Course,** Overtoun Road, Clydebank G81 3RE (0141-952 6372). *Location:* one mile west of Clydebank centre off Duntocher Road. Parkland course - one of the best Par 3s in Scotland. 18 holes, 5349 yards. S.S.S. 66. *Green Fees:* information not available. *Eating facilities:* tearoom. *Visitors:* municipal course, tee closed Saturdays 7.30am till 10.00am and 11.00am to 3.00pm. *Society Meetings:* contact District Council. Secretary: District Council (01389 738762).*

DUMBARTON. **Dumbarton Golf Club,** Broadmeadow, Dumbarton G82 2BQ (01389 765995). *Location:* off A82, one mile from town centre. Flat parkland. 18 holes, 6017 yards. S.S.S. 69. Practice area. *Green Fees:* weekdays £22.00 per round, £32.00 per day. *Eating facilities:* catering and bar available. *Visitors:* welcome weekdays not Saturday, Sunday or Bank Holidays. No jeans or shellsuits on course or in clubhouse. *Society Meetings:* all welcome with prior bookings through Secretary. Secretary: W. McMonagle.

HELENSBURGH. **Helensburgh Golf Club,** 25 East Abercromby Street, Helensburgh G84 9HZ (01436 674173; Fax: 01436 671170). *Location:* A82 from Dumbarton. Moorland course with panoramic views across Loch Lomond and The Clyde Estuary. 18 holes, 5942 yards. S.S.S. 69 Practice area and putting green. *Green Fees:* £30.00 per round, £40.00 per day weekdays. Winter conditions £15.00 per day. *Eating facilities:* full catering and bar. *Visitors:* welcome weekdays only, dress in recognised golfing attire, no denims or trainers. Clubs for hire. *Society Meetings:* welcome by arrangement. Professional: Fraser Hall (Tel & Fax: 01436 675505). Secretary: David Deas (01436 674173; Fax: 01436 671170).

KIRKINTILLOCH. **Kirkintilloch Golf Club,** Todhill, Campsie Road, Kirkintilloch G66 1RN (0141-776 1256). *Location:* from Glasgow to Bishopbriggs, then straight on to Kirkintilloch. Undulating, parkland course. 18 holes, 5860 yards. S.S.S. 69. Par 70. Putting green and practice areas. *Green Fees:* on application. *Eating facilities:* dining room and bar. *Visitors:* phone Secretary for tee times. *Society Meetings:* catered for Monday to Friday, information from Secretary including catering. Secretary: T. Cummins (0141-775 2387).

LENZIE. **Lenzie Golf Club,** 19 Crosshill Road, Lenzie, Glasgow G66 5DA (0141-776 1535; Fax: 0141-777 7748). *Location:* two miles from M80/A80 Junction to Kirkintilloch. Parkland. 18 holes, 5982 yards. S.S.S. 69. Practice ground. *Green Fees:* information not available. *Eating facilities:* bar and catering facilities available. *Visitors:* welcome any day except weekends. Carts for hire. Private room available for meetings or dinners. *Society Meetings:* welcome. Professional: James McCallum (Tel & Fax: 0141-777 7748). Secretary: Scott M. Davidson (0787 296 1305). website: www.lenziegolfclub.co.uk

Edinburgh & Lothians

East Lothian

EAT DRINK SLEEP GOLF

A golfers' paradise of 21 courses, including the world famous links at Muirfield, Gullane and North Berwick.

There's always a warm welcome waiting with friendly clubhouses, affordable green fees, a great variety of accommodation and outstanding restaurants.

For further information visit:
www.golfeastlothian.com

ABERLADY. **Craigielaw Golf Club,** Aberlady EH32 0PY (01875 870800; Fax: 01875 870620). *Location:* half mile west of Aberlady on A198. Links course. 18 holes, 6601 yards, S.S.S. 71, Par 71. Golf Academy and short course. *Green Fees:* information not available. *Eating facilities:* full catering all day; restaurant open to public. *Visitors:* welcome anytime except competition days; advisable to book in advance. Club and buggy hire. *Society Meetings:* society and group bookings welcome.* website: www.craigielawgolfclub.com

ABERLADY. **Kilspindie Golf Club,** The Clubhouse, Aberlady, East Lothian EH32 0QD (01875 870358). *Location:* A198 North Berwick Road (off A1 East of Edinburgh). Club's access road sign posted at east end of Aberlady, overlooking nature reserve and Aberlady Bay. Traditional Scottish links course. 18 holes, 5502 yards, S.S.S. 66, Par 69. *Green Fees:* weekdays £34.00 per round, £52.50 per day; Saturdays and Sundays £43.00 per round, £62.50 per day. *Eating facilities:* dining room with full catering and licensed bar. *Visitors:* welcome booking advisable. *Society Meetings:* welcome, prior booking essential (01875 870358 or e-mail). Professional: Graham Sked (Tel & Fax: 01875 870695). General Manager: P.B. Casely (01875 870358). e-mail: kilspindie@btconnect.com website: www.golfeastlothian.com

ABERLADY. **Luffness New Golf Club,** Aberlady EH32 0QA (01620 843336; Fax: 01620 842933). *Location:* A198 - 17 miles east of Edinburgh. One mile from Gullane. Links course, 18 holes, 6328 yards. S.S.S. 71. *Green Fees:* £70.00 per round, £95.00 per day. *Eating facilities:* dining room except Mondays. *Visitors:* weekdays only (require introduction). *Society Meetings:* by prior arrangement. Secretary: Group Captain A.G. Yeates (01620 843336; Fax: 01620 842933). e-mail: secretary@luffnessnew.com website: www.luffnessgolf.com

BATHGATE. **Bathgate Golf Club,** Edinburgh Road, Bathgate EH48 1BA (01506 652232; Fax: 01506 636775). *Location:* three miles from M8, 400 yards east of George Square, the town centre and railway station. Flat course. 18 holes, 6328 yards. S.S.S. 71. Practice area. *Green Fees:* weekdays £20.00 per round, £25.00 per day; weekends £25.00 per round, £35.00 per day. *Eating facilities:* dining room facilities open all week. *Visitors:* welcome without reservation except on Competition days at weekends. Handicap Certificates preferred. Electric buggies available. *Society Meetings:* welcome, numbers limited at weekends. Professional: Stuart Callan (01506 630553). Secretary: W. Allan Osborne (01506 630505; Fax: 01506 636775).

BO'NESS. **West Lothian Golf Club,** Airngath Hill, Bo'ness EH49 7RH (01506 825060; Fax: 01506 826462). *Location:* situated midway between Linlithgow and Bo'ness. Undulating parkland course with panoramic views over River Forth beyond Stirling to below the Bridges. 18 holes, 6249 yards. S.S.S. 70. Practice ground. *Green Fees:* weekdays £25.00 per round, £33.00 per day; weekends £36.00 per round. *Eating facilities:* bar and catering service. *Visitors:* welcome, advisable to phone weekends. Trolleys and buggies. *Society Meetings:* welcome by arrangement. Professional: Alan Reid (01506 825060). Secretary: Ian Osborough.

BONNYRIGG. **Broomieknowe Golf Club Ltd,** 36 Golf Course Road, Bonnyrigg EH19 2HZ (0131-663 9317; Fax: 0131-663 2152). *Location:* south of Edinburgh, A6094 from Dalkeith. Flat parkland course. 18 holes, 6150 yards. S.S.S. 70. Practice ground. *Green Fees:* weekdays £28.00 per round, £42.00 per day; £32.00 per round at weekends. *Eating facilities:* meals and snacks. *Visitors:* welcome Monday to Friday 9.30am to 4pm, weekends by prior arrangement. *Society Meetings:* welcome weekdays by arrangement. Professional: Mark Patchett (0131-663 9317). Secretary: John D. Fisher (0131-663 9317; Fax: 0131-663 2152). e-mail: administrator@broomieknowe.com website: www.broomieknowe.com

DALKEITH. **Newbattle Golf Club Ltd,** Abbey Road, Dalkeith EH22 3AD (0131-663 2123). *Location:* approximately seven miles south-east of Edinburgh A7 to Eskbank Toll (Newbattle exit). Parkland, wooded course. 18 holes, 6012 yards, 5498 metres. S.S.S. 69. Small practice area. *Green Fees:* £25.00 per round, £35.00 per day. Package deals available. *Eating facilities:* full catering available on request. *Visitors:* weekdays 9.30am to 4.00pm. Limited numbers Sunday afternoons. No jeans/trainers on course or in clubhouse. *Society Meetings:* welcome. Professional: S. McDonald (0131-660 1631). Secretary: H.G. Stanners (0131-663 1819).

DUNBAR. **Dunbar Golf Club,** East Links, Dunbar EH42 1LL (01368 862317; Fax: 01368 865202). *Location:* on coast half a mile east of Dunbar. Seaside links, used for final qualifying 1992 and 2002 Open Championship. 18 holes, 6404 yards, 5855 metres. S.S.S. 71. *Green Fees:* weekdays £50.00 per round, £65.00 per day; weekends £60.00 per round, £85.00 per day. Twilight golf (after 3pm) weekdays £30.00, weekends £40.00. Fees subject to review for 2008. *Eating facilities:* full catering facilities. *Visitors:* no visitors on Thursdays or before 9.30am and between 12.30pm and 2pm weekdays; or before 10am and between 12 noon and 2pm weekends. *Society Meetings:* welcome. Professional: Jacky Montgomery (01368 862086). Manager: Kevin Johnston (01368 862317; Fax: 01368 865202). e-mail: secretary@dunbargolfclub.sol.co.uk website: www.dunbar-golfclub.co.uk

DUNBAR. **Winterfield Golf Club,** St. Margarets, North Road, Dunbar EH42 1AU (01368 862280). Seaside course. 18 holes, 4686 metres. S.S.S. 65. *Green Fees:* information not available. *Eating facilities:* Full catering and bar facilities. *Visitors:* welcome without reservation or restriction. Secure changing facilities. *Society Meetings:* welcome without reservation. Pro Shop: (01368 863562). Professional: Kevin Phillips (01368 863562) Vice Captain: E. Coulter; Captain: W. G. Kerr (01368 862280).*

EDINBURGH. **Baberton Golf Club,** 50 Baberton Avenue, Juniper Green, Edinburgh EH14 5DU (0131-453 4911). *Location:* five miles west of Edinburgh on the A70. 18 holes, 6123 yards. S.S.S. 70. *Green Fees:* weekdays £27.00 per round, £37.00 per day; weekends £30.00 per day. *Eating facilities:* by arrangement (phone Andrew Grieve (0131-453 4911). *Visitors:* welcome by arrangement with Secretary. *Society Meetings:* catered for. Professional: K. Kelly (Tel & Fax: 0131-453 3555). Club Manager: B.M. Flockhart (0131-453 4911; Fax: 0131-453 4678). e-mail: manager@baberton.co.uk website: www.baberton.co.uk

EDINBURGH. **Braid Hills Golf Course,** Braid Hills Approach, Morningside, Edinburgh EH10 6JY *Location:* Braid Hills on south side of Edinburgh. 18 holes, 5865 yards. S.S.S. 68. *Green Fees:* information not available. *Visitors:* welcome. Public courses, clubs on hire. Braids United Golf Club, Edinburgh Thistle Golf Club, Edinburgh Western Golf Club and Harrison Golf Club all have clubhouses at Braid Hills and welcome visitors. Catering available on request. Managed by Edinburgh Leisure.*

EDINBURGH. **Bruntsfield Links Golfing Society Ltd,** The Clubhouse, 32 Barnton Avenue, Edinburgh EH4 6JH (0131-336 2006). *Location:* off A90 at Davidson's Mains. Mature parkland course with magnificent views to north over Firth of Forth and to the west. 18 holes, 6428 yards. S.S.S. 71. Excellent practice facilities. *Green Fees:* weekdays £55.00 per round, £80.00 per day; weekends £65.00 per round, £85.00 per day. *Eating facilities:* morning coffee, lunches, dinner by arrangement. *Visitors:* welcome - telephone Professional to arrange times. *Society Meetings:* catered for by arrangement. Professional: Brian MacKenzie (0131-336 4050). Secretary: Cdr D.M. Sandford (0131-336 1479; Fax: 0131-336 5538). e-mail: secretary@bruntsfield.sol.co.uk

EDINBURGH. **Carrick Knowe Golf Course.** *Location:* situated on the west side of the city on Glendevon Park. Undulating parkland course which has recently undergone a major remodelling. 18 holes, 6150 yards. S.S.S. 69. *Green Fees:* information not available. *Visitors:* welcome. Managed by Edinburgh Leisure.*

EDINBURGH. **City of Edinburgh Golf Club,** Craigentinny Golf Course, Fillyside Road, Edinburgh EH7 6RG. *Location:* Club plays over the following pay and play courses - Carrick Knowe: 18 holes, 6150 yards. S.S.S. 69; Braid Hills: 18 holes, 5692 yards. S.S.S. 67; Silverknowes: 18 holes, 6198 yards. S.S.S. 69; Craigentinny: 18 holes, 5413 yards. S.S.S. 66; Portobello: 9 holes, 4816 yards. S.S.S. 64; Princes: 9 holes, 3800 yards. Par 60. *Green Fees:* from £13.50 weekdays, £16.00 weekends. *Visitors:* welcome all year round. Secretary: Peter Long (0131-554 7501) website: www.edinburghleisure.co.uk

EDINBURGH. **Craigentinny Golf Course.** *Location:* Situated on the east side of the city on Fillyside Road. Undulating parkland course. 18 holes, 5413 yards. S.S.S. 66. *Green Fees:* information not available. *Visitors:* welcome. Managed by Edinburgh Leisure.*

EDINBURGH. **Craigmillar Park Golf Club,** 1 Observatory Road, Edinburgh EH9 3HG (0131-667 2837). *Location:* A702 from City Centre on Mayfield Road, right at King's Buildings. Parkland. 18 holes, 5825 yards, 5350 metres. S.S.S. 68. *Green Fees:* information not available. *Eating facilities:* lunches, snacks, high teas and dinners. *Visitors:* welcome weekdays only before 4pm and on Sunday after 2.30pm. *Society Meetings:* catered for by previous arrangement. Professional: S. Gourlay (0131-667 2850). Secretary: A.Crabbe (0131-667 0047).

EDINBURGH. **Duddingston Golf Club Ltd,** Duddingston Road West, Edinburgh EH15 3QD (0131-661 1005). *Location:* adjacent to A1 Willowbrae Road, turn right at Duddingston crossroads then one mile on Duddingston Road West. Undulating parkland with stream. 18 holes, 6487 yards. S.S.S. 72. *Green Fees:* weekdays only £38.00 per round, £48.00 per day. *Eating facilities:* full catering and bar facilities. *Visitors:* welcome weekdays only. *Society Meetings:* by arrangement (rates on request). Professional: Alistair McLean (0131-661 4301). General Manager:Terry Christie (0131-661 7688).
e-mail: admin@duddingstongolf.co.uk

EDINBURGH. **Kingsknowe Golf Club,** 326 Lanark Road, Edinburgh EH14 2JD (0131 4411144). *Location:* on the western boundary of Edinburgh with easy access from the City Bypass (Calder Junction). The Clubhouse is located on the A70 Lanark Road. Designed by 1902 Open Champion Alec Herd, Kingsknowe offers a picturesque challenge for all players. The clubhouse offers excellent facilities, including a warm welcome upon completion of your round. Parkland course. 18 holes, 5981 yards. Par 69. Practice area. *Green Fees:* weekdays £25.00 per round, £32.00 per day; weekends £35.00 per round (after 3pm). *Eating facilities:* full catering and bar services available. *Visitors:* welcome Monday to Friday, also weekends subject to availability. *Society Meetings:* prices available on request. Professional: Chris Morris (0131-441 4030). Secretary/Manager: L.I. Fairlie (0131-441 1145).

EDINBURGH. **Liberton Golf Club,** 297 Gilmerton Road, Edinburgh EH16 5UJ (0131-664 3009; Fax: 0131-666 0853). *Location:* Corporation transport to Lodge Gate, buses 3 and 8 from Edinburgh. By car on A7 (Visitors' car park). Parkland, rolling. 18 holes, 5344 yards, 4888 metres. S.S.S. 66. *Green Fees:* information not provided. *Eating facilities:* full catering and bar service. *Visitors:* phone professional. *Society Meetings:* catered for by arrangememt except weekends. Professional: I. Seath (0131-664 1056). Secretary: Duncan Ireland (0131-664 3009).
e-mail: info@libertongc.co.uk
website: www.libertongc.co.uk

EDINBURGH. **Lothianburn Golf Club,** 106a Biggar Road, Edinburgh EH10 7DU (0131 445 2206). *Location*: south on the A702 approximately four miles from city centre or easily reached from Edinburgh bypass road coming off at Lothianburn junction. Hill course close to Pentland Hills. 18 holes, 5662 yards. S.S.S. 69. Practice ground. *Green Fees:* £20.00 per round weekdays; £26.00 weekends. *Eating facilities:* normal bar hours, no hot food on Wednesdays. *Visitors*: welcome mid-week, weekends restricted. *Society Meetings*: catered for by prior arrangement with the Secretary. Professional: Kurt Mungall (0131-445 2288). Secretary: D.P. Maclaren (0131-445 5067).
website: www.lothianburngc.co.uk

EDINBURGH. **Melville Golf Centre, Golf Course, Range and Shop,** Lasswade, Near Edinburgh EH18 1AN (0131-663 8038; Fax: 0131-654 0814). *Location:* three minutes from Edinburgh City Bypass (signposted), on A7. Short but challenging parkland course with large tees and greens, lying in the Esk Valley with panoramic views. 9 holes, 2265 yards, 2070 metres. Par 66. S.S.S. 62. Built to USPGA standard. Floodlit range, 9-hole pay and play course, 4-hole practice/short game area, bunker and putting green. *Green Fees:* weekdays 9 holes £11.00, 18 holes £19.00; weekends 9 holes £13.00, 18 holes £23.00. *Eating facilities:* vended hot and cold drinks and confectionery. *Visitors:* welcome at all times. 24 hour bookings available, full club equipment and shoe hire, PGA tuition. Golf shop; fully stocked ladies, gents, and juniors. Tuition available. A Junior Golf Foundation Starter Centre. *Society Meetings:* welcome, advance bookings arranged. Professional: Gary Carter. Contact Mr & Mrs MacFarlane (0131-663 8038 course; Fax: 0131-654 0814).
e-mail: golf@melvillegolf.co.uk
website: www.melvillegolf.co.uk

EDINBURGH. **Merchants Of Edinburgh Golf Club,** 10 Craighill Gardens, Edinburgh EH10 5PY (0131-447 1219; Fax: 0131-446 9833). *Location:* car park Glenlockhart Road, Edinburgh EH10. Hilly, parkland. 18 holes, 4889 yards. S.S.S. 64. *Green Fees:* information not available. *Eating facilities:* full catering available daily. *Visitors:* welcome weekdays, weekends by arrangement. *Society Meetings:* catered for except weekends. Professional: N.E.M. Colquhoun (0131 447 8709). Administrator: John Leslie (0131 447 1219).
e-mail: admin@merchantsgolf.com
website: www.merchantsgolf.com

www.uk-golfguide.com

EDINBURGH. **Mortonhall Golf Club,** 231 Braid Road, Edinburgh EH10 6PB. *Location:* take A702 south from City to Morningside traffic lights, up Braid Road one mile, course on left. Moorland course with scenic views. 18 holes, 6523 yards. S.S.S. 72. *Green Fees: weekdays* £40.00 per round, £60.00 per day; weekends £45.00 per round. *Eating facilities:* lunch and bar snacks available. *Visitors:* welcome. *Society Meetings:* catered for (not at weekends). Professional: Malcolm Leighton. Club Manager: Bernadette M. Giefer (0131-447 6974).
e-mail: clubhouse@mortonhallgc.co.uk
website: www.mortonhallgc.co.uk

EDINBURGH. **Murrayfield Golf Club Ltd,** 43 Murrayfield Road, Edinburgh EH12 6EU (0131-337 3478; Fax: 0131-313 0721). *Location:* Corstorphine Road, two miles west of city centre. Parkland on east side of Corstorphine Hill. 18 holes, 5799 yards. S.S.S. 69. Practice area, net and putting green. *Green Fees:* weekdays £35.00 per round, £45.00 per day. *Eating facilities:* lunch each day, snacks in casual bar, also full bar facilities. *Visitors:* welcome playing with member or by prior arrangement only. No visitors weekends. *Society Meetings:* catered for by prior arrangement. Professional: K. Stevenson (Tel & Fax: 0131-337 3479). Club Manager: Mrs M.K. Thomson (0131-337 3478; Fax: 0131-313 0721).
e-mail: info@murrayfieldgolfclub.co.uk

EDINBURGH. **Portobello Golf Course,** Stanley Street, Portobello, Edinburgh EH15 1JJ (0131-669 4361). *Location:* on A1 at Milton Road East. Parkland course. 9 holes, 2400 yards, 2167 metres. S.S.S. 32. *Green Fees:* £5.50 per round (9 holes) weekdays; £6.50 per round (9 holes) weekends. Reductions for Juniors and Senior Citizens. *Visitors:* welcome. *Society Meetings:* not catered for. Managed by Edinburgh Leisure.

EDINBURGH. **Prestonfield Golf Club,** 6 Priestfield Road North, Edinburgh EH16 5HS (0131-667 9665; Fax: 0131-777 2727). *Location:* off Dalkeith Road, near Royal Commonwealth Pool on A7. Parkland. 18 holes, 6207 yards. S.S.S. 70, Par 70. *Green Fees:* information not available. *Eating facilities:* full catering. *Visitors:* welcome all day weekdays; weekends only after 3pm. Petrol buggies available. *Society Meetings:* welcome all day weekdays; weekends only after 3pm. Professional: Gavin Cook (0131-667 8597). General Manager: John I. Archibald.*
e-mail: generalmanager@prestonfieldgolf.com
website: www.prestonfieldgolf.com

EDINBURGH. **Princes Golf Course,** Braid Hills Road, Edinburgh EH16 6NS (0131-447 3568). *Location:* Braid Hills on south side of Edinburgh. 9-hole course, ideal for beginners, children and families. Managed by Edinburgh Leisure. *Green Fees:* information not available.*

Mortonhall Golf Club

Founded in 1892, this is the oldest course on which golf is still played in the city of Edinburgh. It is one of outstanding scenic beauty, emerging from a narrow valley to an open area bounded by a wood on the south and the Braid Hills in the north. At 6523 yards, it is the longest course in the city, and at 600ft above sea level, the wind can make it a formidable challenge.

The well appointed clubhouse contains many interesting photographs and golfing memorabilia. *Bar and catering facilities available.*

Vistors are welcome to play this picturesque and challenging course.

231 Braid Road, Edinburgh EH10 6PB
Tel: 0131 447 6974 •• Fax: 0131 447 8712
www.mortonhallgc.co.uk •• clubhouse@mortonhallgc.co.uk

Prestonfield Golf Club

6 Priestfield Road North, Edinburgh EH15 5HS

A testing par 70 course of 6207 yards, set in beautiful parkland within the heart of Edinburgh, beneath Arthur's Seat, next to Holyrood Park and Duddingston Loch. This easy to walk golf course, created by James Braid, is playable all year round. Visitors, Societies and Corporate Parties always welcome. Catered packages available, contact General Manager for details.

Tel: 0131 667 9665 • Fax: 0131 777 2727 • e-mail: generalmanager@prestonfieldgolf.com
www.prestonfieldgolf.com

EDINBURGH. **Ratho Park Golf Club Ltd,** Ratho, Edinburgh EH28 8NX (0131-335 0069). *Location:* west side of Edinburgh near Airport, access from A71 or A8. Flat parkland course of outstanding natural beauty. 18 holes, 5960 yards. S.S.S. 68. *Green Fees:* weekdays £32.00 per round, £45.00 per day; weekends £45.00 per round. *Eating facilities:* full catering available. *Visitors:* very welcome, please telephone Professional in advance. *Society Meetings:* welcome Monday-Friday, up to 40, subject to availability. Professional: Alan Pate (0131-333 1406). Secretary/Manager: Craig R Innes (0131-335 0068). e-mail: secretary@rathoparkgolfclub.co.uk website: www.rathoparkgolfclub.co.uk

EDINBURGH. **Ravelston Golf Club Ltd,** 24 Ravelston Dykes Road, Blackhall, Edinburgh EH4 3NZ (Tel & Fax: 0131-315 2486). *Location:* A90 Queensferry Road (leading to Forth Road Bridge). Left at traffic lights by Blackhall junction to Strachan Road, cross Craigcrook Road, clubhouse on right. Parkland course. 9 holes, 2585 yards. S.S.S. 66. *Green Fees:* £25.00 weekdays. Subject to review. Eating facilities; tea, coffee, soft drinks and light snacks. *Visitors:* welcome during quiet periods weekdays only. *Society Meetings:* permitted by special application only. Secretary: Jim Lowrie.

EDINBURGH. **Royal Burgess Golfing Society of Edinburgh,** 181 Whitehouse Road, Barnton, Edinburgh EH4 6BU. *Location:* A90 to Forth Road Bridge, behind Barnton Hotel. Parkland. 18 holes, 6494 yards. S.S.S. 71. *Green Fees:* weekdays £55.00 per day/round, weekends £75.00 per day/round. *Eating facilities:* snacks and lunches available. *Visitors:* welcome all week; Saturdays after 2.30pm, Sundays after 12 noon. *Society Meetings:* catered for Tuesdays, Thursdays and Fridays. Professional: Steven Brian (0131-339 6474). Secretary: Graeme Seeley (0131-339 2075; Fax: 0131-339 3712). e-mail: secretary@royalburgess.co.uk website: www.royalburgess.co.uk

EDINBURGH: **Silverknowes Golf Course,** Silverknowes, Parkway, Edinburgh EH4 5ET (0131-336 5359). *Location:* nearest main road Queensferry Road; signs Davidson Mains, Silverknowes. Parkland, flat. 18 holes, 6216 yards. S.S.S. 71. *Green Fees:* information not available. *Eating facilities:* catering available on request. Managed by Edinburgh Leisure.*

EDINBURGH. **Swanston Golf Course,** 111 Swanston Road, Edinburgh EH10 7DS (0131-445 2239). *Location:* five miles from centre of Edinburgh, west of Biggar Road (A702) on the lower slopes of the Pentland Hills. Parkland course. 18 holes, 5024 yards. S.S.S. 66. *Green Fees:* weekdays £15.00 per round, £20.00 day ticket; weekends £20.00 per round, £30.00 day ticket. *Eating facilities:* full catering facilities. *Visitors:* welcome without reservation weekdays, weekends restricted. *Society Meetings:* catered for. Golf carts available. website: www.swanstongolf.co.uk

EDINBURGH. **Torphin Hill Golf Club,** Torphin Road, Edinburgh EH13 0PG (0131-441 4061). *Location:* south west of Colinton Village at terminus of No. 10 bus. Holes 5 to 15 on plateau with outstanding views of Edinburgh. 18 holes, 5285 yards. Par 68. Practice area. *Green Fees:* weekdays £15.00 per round; weekends £20.00 per round (subject to review.) *Eating facilities:* dining room and bar snacks. *Visitors:* welcome without reservation except on Competition Days. *Society Meetings:* catered for except Tuesday. Reduced rates for parties over 20. Professional: Jamie Browne (0131-441 4061). Secretary: Willie McCathie (0131-441 1100; Fax: 0131 441 7166). e-mail: torphinhillgc@btconnect.com website: www.torphinhillgolfclub.co.uk

EDINBURGH. **Turnhouse Golf Club,** Lennie Park, 154 Turnhouse Road, Edinburgh EH12 0AD (0131-339 1014). *Location:* towards RAF Turnhouse on west side. James Braid designed course. 18 holes, 6153 yards. S.S.S. 70. Par 69. *Green Fees:* information not available. *Eating facilities:* full service. *Visitors:* welcome, contact Professional. *Society Meetings:* welcome by prior arrangement with Secretary. Professional: John Murray (0131-339 7701). Secretary: David Cullum (07792 399069).* e-mail: secretary@turnhousegc.com website: www.turnhousegc.com

EDINBURGH (SOUTH). **Whitehill House Golf Club,** Rosewell, Midlothian EH24 9EG (0131 440 0594; Fax: 0131 440 1736). *Location:* twenty minutes south of central Edinburgh; may be reached by a short trip through Lasswade from A720 bypass to Rosewell. Parkland course in mature woodland setting. Located in the grounds of Whitehill House, one of Scotland's most historic houses. 18 holes, 6324 yards. Par 70. Practice holes and driving area, tuition available from resident professional. *Green Fees:* weekdays 9 holes £13.00, 18 holes £18.00; weekends 9 holes £14.00, 18 holes £20.00. Annual memberships, no waiting lists. Concessions available. *Eating facilities:* hot and cold drinks. *Visitors:* welcome at all times, no restrictions. Club and trolley hire. Lockers and Pro Shop. *Society Meetings:* by prior arrangement, catering for groups provided by nearby Melville Castle Hotel. e-mail: info@whitehillhousegolf.com website: www.whitehillhousegolf.com

FAULDHOUSE. **Greenburn Golf Club,** 6 Greenburn Road, Fauldhouse EH47 9HJ (01501 770292). *Location:* four miles south of Junctions 4 and 5 of M8 motorway. Undulating course, a mixture of moorland and parkland settings. 18 holes, 6055 yards. S.S.S. 70. Practice area. *Green Fees:* weekdays £22.00 per round, £29.00 per day. Weekends £28.00 per round, £35.00 per day; prices include £0.50 liability insurance. *Eating facilities:* catering available all week. *Visitors:* welcome. *Society Meetings:* welcome by arrangement with Administrator. Professional: Scott Catlin (01501 771187). Club Administrator: Adrian McGowan.

GULLANE. **Gullane Golf Club,** West Links Road, Gullane EH31 2BB (01620 842255; Fax: 01620 842327). *Location:* 18 miles east of Edinburgh on A198 Edinburgh to North Berwick Road. Links. Three 18 hole courses. No. 1 - (Medal) 6466 yards, 5913 metres. S.S.S. 72; (FWD) 6077 yards, 5557 metres. S.S.S 70. No. 2 - 6244 yards, 5710 metres. S.S.S. 71. No. 3 - 5252 yards, 4775 metres. S.S.S. 66. Practice, driving range. *Green Fees:* weekdays: No. 1 course £85.00 per round, £120.00 per day; No. 2 course £40.00 per round, £50.00 per day; No. 3 course £24.00 per round, £30.00 per day; weekends No. 1 £100.00 per round, No. 2 £45.00 per round, £65.00 per day, No. 3 £30.00 per round, £40.00 per day (prices increase on 1st March 2007). Weekly and combination rates available. *Visitors:* welcome. Call Office for bookings. *Society Meetings:* catered for. Professional: Alasdair Good (01620 843111; Fax: 01620 843090). Office: (01620 842255; Fax: 01620 842327).
e-mail: bookings@gullanegolfclub.com
website: www.gullanegolfclub.com

GULLANE. **The Honourable Company Of Edinburgh Golfers,** Muirfield, Gullane EH31 2EG (01620 842123; Fax: 01620 842977). *Location:* 20 miles from Edinburgh along the coast road to North Berwick. Championship links course. 18 holes, 6601 yards. S.S.S. 73. *Green Fees:* (2008) £160.00 18 holes, £200.00 36 holes. *Eating facilities:* morning coffee, lunches and afternoon teas if ordered in advance. *Visitors:* welcome Tuesdays and Thursdays, maximum Handicap 18 for men, 20 for ladies. Secretary: A.N.G. Brown.
e-mail: hceg@muirfield.org.uk

HADDINGTON. **Castle Park Golf Club,** Gifford EH41 4PL (01620 810733; Fax: 01620 810691). *Location:* B6369 from Haddington to Gifford, Castle Park is 2 miles south of Gifford, well signposted. Originally 9 holes, now extended to 18 (opened in 2002) combines a unique test of golf with stunning views. 6443 yards (blue), 6202 yards (white), 5851 yards (yellow), S.S.S. 71. 7 bay driving range, 6 hole putting green and practice bunker. *Green Fees:* from £20.00. *Eating facilities:* bar with full catering available. *Visitors:* welcome. Buggies available for hire. *Society Meetings:* welcome. Professional: Derek Small (01368 862872; mobile: 07968 209167). Secretary: Jim Wilson.
e-mail: castleparkgolf@hotmail.com
website: www.castleparkgolfclub.co.uk

HADDINGTON. **Haddington Golf Club,** Amisfield Park, Haddington EH41 4PT (01620 822727). *Location:* three-quarters of a mile from A1, 17 miles east of Edinburgh. Wooded parkland, slightly undulating. 18 holes, 6335 yards. S.S.S. 71, Par 71. Practice area. *Green Fees:* midweek £25.00 per round, £40.00 per day; weekends £35.00 per round, £50.00 per day. *Eating facilities:* two bars and dining room. *Visitors:* welcome, midweek no restrictions, weekends permitted 10am-12 noon, 2-4pm. *Society Meetings:* packages available on request. Professional: J. Sandilands (01620 822727). Club Manager: K. Nicholson (01620 823627; Fax: 01620 826580).
e-mail: info@haddingtongolfclub.co.uk
website: www.haddingtongolf.co.uk

HADDINGTON near. **Gifford Golf Club,** Edinburgh Road, Gifford, Near Haddington EH41 4JE (0162-810 591). *Location:* quarter of a mile west of village. Undulating parkland with burn crossing the course. 9 holes, 6050 yards. S.S.S. 69. *Green Fees:* £20.00 18 holes, £14.00 9 holes; day ticket £30.00; Juniors (under 18s) £5.00. *Visitors:* closed all day first Sunday in the month. Secretary: R. Stewart (01620 810267). Starter (01620 810 591).

KIRKNEWTON. **Marriott Dalmahoy Hotel and Country Club,** Kirknewton, Midlothian EH27 8EB (Hotel 0131-333 1845; Fax: 0131-333 1433). *Location:* seven miles west of Edinburgh on A71. Parkland courses. East Course: (Championship) host to many major tournaments, 18 holes, 7044 yards. S.S.S. 72. West Course: with a finish around the Gogar Burn that will test your nerve. 18 holes, 5185 yards. S.S.S. 66. Driving range, extensive practice area. *Green Fees:* from £30.00 per person. *Eating facilities:* The Long Weekend Restaurant and Club Bar in Country Club, restaurant and bars in Hotel also. *Visitors:* welcome 7 days. Hotel accommodation. Golf buggies, trolleys and clubs for hire. Country Club facilities include swimming pool, two outdoor tennis courts, sauna, steam room, spa, gymnasium, fitness and aerobics studio. *Society Meetings:* welcome weekdays only. Director of Golf: Neal Graham (0131-335 8010). Secretary: Gordon Watt (0131-335 8010).

www.uk-golfguide.com

LASSWADE. **Kings Acre Golf Course and Academy,** Lasswade, EH18 1AU (0131 663 3456; Fax: 0131 663 7076). *Location*: A720 Edinburgh City Bypass. Lasswade is two minutes from City Bypass. Parkland course with matured woodland and large contoured greens, set in picturesque countryside close to Edinburgh City Bypass.18 holes (pay and play), 6031 yards. S.S.S. 69. State of the art practice facility. *Green Fees*: weekdays £25.00 per round, £35.00 per day; weekends £34.00 per round, £48.00 per day (2007 rates). *Eating facilities*: spike bar, fully licensed restaurant. *Visitors*: all visitors welcome all year (no restrictions), accommodation available on site. PGA tuition, buggy and club hire. *Society Meetings:* all welcome. Director of Golf: Alan Murdoch. Secretary: Alan Murdoch.
e-mail: info@kings-acregolf.com
website: www.kings-acregolf.com

LINLITHGOW. **Bridgend & District Golf Club,** Willowdean, Bridgend, Linlithgow EH49 6NW (01506 834140; Fax: 01506 834706). *Location*: between Winchburgh and Linlithgow, signposted on main road. 9 holes, 5451 yards, S.S.S. 66. *Green Fees*: information not available. *Eating facilities*: no catering on Tuesdays, bar facilities all week. *Visitors*: welcome any time. Buggies for hire. Secretary: George Green.*

LINLITHGOW. **Linlithgow Golf Club,** Braehead, Linlithgow EH49 6QF (01506 844356; Fax: 01506 842764). *Location:* M8, M9, 20 miles west of Edinburgh, west end of Linlithgow - fork left. Parkland and wooded course with panoramic views. 18 holes, 5729 yards, 5239 metres. S.S.S. 68. Practice area. *Green Fees:* information not available. *Eating facilities:* full catering available, bar open every day. *Visitors:* welcome except Saturdays. *Society Meetings:* welcome by arrangement with Secretary. Professional: Steven Rosie (01506 844356). Secretary: T.I. Adams (01506 842585).*

LIVINGSTON. **Deer Park Golf & Country Club,** Golf Course Road, Carmondeans, Livingston EH54 8AB (01506 446699; Fax: 01506 435608). *Location:* off M8 Junction 3 onto Deer Park roundabout. Parkland course, first 9 holes flat, back 9 holes hilly. 18 holes, 6688 yards. S.S.S. 72. *Green Fees:* information not available. *Eating facilities:* four bars, catering seven days. *Visitors:* welcome. Snooker, ten pin bowling. *Society Meetings:* catered for. Professional: Brian Dunbar.*

LIVINGSTON. **Pumpherston Golf Club,** Drumshoreland Road, Pumpherston, Livingston EH53 0LQ (01506 432869). *Location:* one mile east of Livingston, one and a half miles south of M8. Challenging parkland course, recently redeveloped. 18 holes, 6006 yards, 5492 metres. Par 70, S.S.S. 69. Practice area with pitching and bunker facilities, putting green, designed particularly for juniors. *Green Fees:* on application. *Eating facilities:* new clubhouse with bar, dining room and entertainment facilities; junior lounge. *Visitors:* welcome. *Society Meetings:* Mondays to Thursdays, maximum number 30. Professional: R. Fyvie (01506 433337). Secretary: G. C. Walker (01506 882904).
website: www.pumpherstongolfclub.co.uk

LONGNIDDRY. **Longniddry Golf Club Ltd,** Links Road, Longniddry EH32 0NL (01875 852141; Fax: 01875 853371). *Location:* at the foot of Links Road in Longniddry village. Unique combination of woodland and links. Superb views over the Firth to Edinburgh and Fife. 18 holes, 6260 yards, 5690 metres. S.S.S. 70. Practice area, putting green, nets. *Green Fees:* weekdays £42.00 per round, £65.00 per day; weekends £60.00 per round. Subject to review. *Eating facilities:* catering available seven days, two bars and dining room. *Visitors:* welcome daily, though limited availability at weekends; advance booking recommended. *Society Meetings:* welcome Monday to Friday with Handicap Certificates. Professional: John Gray (01875 852228). Secretary: Bob Gunning (01875 852141)   .
e-mail: secretary@longniddrygolfclub.co.uk
website: www.longniddrygolfclub.co.uk

MUSSELBURGH. **Musselburgh Golf Club,** Monktonhall, Musselburgh EH21 6SA (0131-665 2005). *Location:* from the A1 end of the Edinburgh City bypass, on B6415 to Musselburgh. Wooded parkland, rivers. 18 holes, 6725 yards. S.S.S. 72. *Green Fees:* on application. *Eating facilities:* catering available. *Visitors:* welcome with reservation. *Society Meetings:* catered for. Professional: F. Mann (0131-665 7055).
e-mail: secretary@themusselburghgolfclub.com

MUSSELBURGH. **Musselburgh Old Course Golf Club,** 10 Balcarres Road, Musselburgh EH21 7SD (0131-665 6981). *Location*: A199 road at Musselburgh racecourse one-and-a-half miles east of town centre. Seaside links course. 9 holes, 2887 yards. S.S.S. 69. Large practice area. *Green Fees*: information not available. *Eating facilities*: available. *Visitors*: welcome. Starter (0131-665 5438). Secretary: R. McGregor (0131 665 6981).*
e-mail: mocgc@breathemail.net
website: www.musselburgholdlinks.co.uk

NORTH BERWICK. **Glen Golf Club,** East Links, Tantallon Terrace, North Berwick EH39 4LE (01620 892726; Fax: 01620 895447). *Location:* one mile east of town centre, off A198. Seaside links with magnificent panoramic views. 18 holes, 6243 yards. S.S.S. 70. Practice ground, putting green. *Green Fees:* midweek £37.00, weekends £49.00. *Eating facilities:* full facilities available. *Visitors:* welcome anytime, no restrictions. Pro Shop. Trolleys and caddies available. *Society Meetings:* welcome, advance booking required. Secretary: Kevin Fish (01620 892726; Fax: 01620 895447). Starter: (01620 892726).
website: www.glengolfclub.co.uk

> THE APPEARANCE OF AN ASTERISK (*) AT
> THE END OF A CLUB OR COURSE ENTRY
> INDICATES THAT UP-TO-DATE
> INFORMATION HAS NOT BEEN SUPPLIED

NORTH BERWICK. **The North Berwick Golf Club,** New Clubhouse, Beach Road, North Berwick EH39 4BB (01620 895040; Fax: 01620 890312). *Location*: 24 miles east of Edinburgh via Meadowmill roundabout then A198 to North Berwick. Seaside links. 18 holes, 6420 yards. S.S.S. 72. Practice ground. *Green Fees:* weekdays £65.00 per round, £95.00 per day; weekends £85.00 per round. *Eating facilities:* diningroom and bar. *Visitors:* welcome from 10am, advance bookings (01620 892135) Saturdays – restricted when there are club fixtures. Lounge and changing rooms available. *Society Meetings:* catered for by arrangement. Professional: D. Huish (01620 893233). Secretary: C. J. Spencer (01620 895040). Advance Bookings: (01620 892135). e-mail: secretary@northberwickgolfclub.com
website: www.northberwickgolfclub.com

PENICUIK. **Glencorse Golf Club,** Milton Bridge, Penicuik EH26 0RD (01968 677177). *Location:* A701 nine miles south of Edinburgh on Peebles Road. Voted one of Scotland's hidden gems by U.S. Sports Illustrated magazine. Parkland course with stream affecting 10 holes. 18 holes, 5217 yards. S.S.S. 66. *Green Fees:* weekdays £25.00 per round, £32.00 per day; weekends £32.00 per round. Package deals available. *Eating facilities:* all day catering and bar. *Visitors:* welcome at all times subject to Club Competitions. *Society Meetings:* catered for Mondays to Fridays and Sunday afternoons. Professional: Cliffe Jones (01968 676481). Secretary: Bill Oliver (01968 677189; Fax: 01968 674399).

FHG Guides

publish a large range of well-known accommodation guides.
We will be happy to send you details or you can use
the order form at the back of this book.

PRESTONPANS. **Royal Musselburgh Golf Club,** Prestongrange House, Prestonpans EH32 9RP (Tel & Fax: 01875 810276). *Location*: B1361 North Berwick Road, Prestonpans. Fairly flat parkland, wooded course. 18 holes, 6254 yards. S.S.S. 70. *Green Fees:* information not available. *Visitors:* welcome. *Society Meetings:* welcome by arrangement with the Management Secretary. Professional: John Henderson (Tel & Fax: 01875 810139). Management Secretary: Thos. H. Hardie (Tel & Fax: 01875 810276). Competition Secretary: J. Hanratty (01875 819000). e-mail: enquiries@royalmusselburgh.co.uk website: www.royalmusselburgh.co.uk

SOUTH QUEENSFERRY. **Dundas Parks Golf Club,** Dundas Estate, South Queensferry, West Lothian EH30 9SS. *Location:* five miles west of Edinburgh, on South Queensferry to Kirkliston road on right of A8000. Parkland course in open countryside. 9 holes (x 2), 6024 yards, 5510 metres. S.S.S. 70. Small practice area. *Eating facilities:* no bar or food facilities. *Visitors:* welcome with member, or by prior arrangement with Club Administrator. *Society Meetings:* by prior arrangement with Club Administrator. Club Administrator: Christine Wood (0131-319 1347).

UPHALL. **Uphall Golf Club,** Uphall, West Lothian EH52 6JT (01506 856404; Fax: 01506 855358). *Location:* eight miles west of Edinburgh Airport on the A89 Edinburgh to Glasgow road. Established parkland course. 18 holes, S.S.S. 67. *Green Fees:* information not available. *Eating facilities:* hot and cold snacks, lunches, high teas and bars, à la carte available Saturday evenings. *Visitors:* welcome weekdays without reservation. A booking through the Professional is required at weekends. *Society Meetings:* catered for. Professional: Gordon Law (01506 855553). Club Administrator: Mima O'Connor: (01506 856404; Fax: 01506 855358). e-mail: uphallgolfclub@btconnect.com

WEST CALDER. **Harburn Golf Club,** Harburn, West Calder EH55 8RS (01506 871256). *Location:* two miles south of West Calder on B7008. Parkland course. 18 holes, 6125 yards. S.S.S. 70. Practice ground. *Green Fees:* Monday to Thursday £25.00 per round, £30.00 per day; Friday £30.00 per round, £35.00 per day; weekends £35.00 per round, £40.00 per day. *Eating facilities:* full catering and bar service

available. *Visitors:* welcome any time, no restrictions. *Society Meetings:* special terms on request. Professional: S.J. Mills (01506 871582). Secretary: Mr Stuart More (01506 871131; Fax: 01506 870286). e-mail: info@harburngolfclub.co.uk website: www.harburngolfclub.co.uk

WHITBURN. **Polkemmet Golf Course,** Polkemmet Country Park, Whitburn, West Lothian (01501 743905). *Location:* off B7066, one mile west of Whitburn. Inland course set within old private estate, mature varied woodland with belts of rhododendrons. 9 holes, 2946 metres. Par 37. 15 bay floodlit driving range. *Green Fees:* weekdays (summer) £5.60 per round, concessions £4.20; weekends and Public Holidays (summer) £6.70 per round, concessions £5.00. *Eating facilities:* not functioning at present. *Visitors:* welcome. Public course. Facilities include bowling green, picnic areas, etc. Caddy cart hire £1.25. Secretary: West Lothian Council, Countryside Section, Property Services, Development and Environmental Services, Lammermuir House, Livingston.

WHITEKIRK. **Whitekirk Golf & Country Club,** Whitekirk, Near North Berwick EH39 5PR (01620 870300; Fax: 01620 870330). *Location*: East of North Berwick, off the main A1 Edinburgh - Berwick upon Tweed road, on the A198. Heathland, wooded, lakes, commanding views over East Lothian. 18 holes, 6526 yards. S.S.S. 72. *Green Fees*: information not provided. *Eating facilities*: lunches, dinners, bar snacks. *Visitors*: welcome, no restrictions. Golf academy; buggies and carts available. *Society Meetings*: welcome seven days, special rates available. Professional: Paul Wardell (01620 870300; Fax: 01620 870330) Secretary: David Brodie (01620 870300; Fax: 01620 870330). e-mail: countryclub@whitekirk.com website: www.whitekirk.com

WINCHBURGH. **Niddry Castle Golf Club,** Castle Road, Winchburgh, Broxton EH52 6RQ (01506 891097). *Location:* 10 miles west of Edinburgh on B9080 between Kirkliston and Linlithgow. Wooded, natural parkland. 18 holes, 5914 yards. S.S.S. 69. Practice net. *Green Fees:* information not provided. *Eating facilities:* full catering; bar. *Visitors:* welcome weekdays before 4.30pm, weekends on competition days after 2.30pm. *Society Meetings:* by arrangement. Secretary: Tom. S. MccCabe.

Fife

ABERDOUR. **Aberdour Golf Club,** Seaside Place, Aberdour KY3 0TX (01383 860080; Fax:01383 860050 *Location:* take Shore Road from centre of village. Parkland course situated along the shoreline of the River Forth. 18 holes, 5460 yards. S.S.S. 67. *Green Fees:* information not available. *Eating facilities:* full catering. *Visitors:* welcome. *Society Meetings:* catered for on weekdays and Sundays. On Sundays, maximum size of group 24. Professional: David Gemmell (01383 860256). Manager. (01383 860080; Fax: 01383 860050).
e-mail: info@aberdourgolfclub.co.uk
website: www.aberdourgolfclub.co.uk

ANSTRUTHER. **Anstruther Golf Club,** Marsfield, Shore Road, Anstruther KY10 3DZ (01333 310956). *Location:* nine miles south of St Andrews, west side of Anstruther. Seaside links course. 9 holes, 4532 yards. S.S.S. 63. *Green Fees:* 9 holes £14.00. 18 holes £20.00. *Eating facilities:* lounge bar and dining room. *Visitors:* welcome except during club competitions. *Society Meetings:* welcome except Saturdays and competition days. Secretary: S. Gardner (01333 310956).

BURNTISLAND. **Burntisland Golf House Club,** Dodhead, Burntisland KY3 9LQ (01592 874093). *Location*: Rossend Castle, near Kirkcaldy. Parkland with some hills. 18 holes, 5965 yards. S.S.S. 70. Practice ground and net. *Green Fees:* information not available. *Eating facilities:* all day bar and catering. *Visitors*: all parties catered for. Changing room. *Society Meetings*: welcome with advance bookings. Professional: P. Wytrazek (01592 872116).

CARDENDEN. **Auchterderran Golf Club,** Woodend Road, Cardenden KY5 0NH (01592 721579). *Location:* six miles north of Kirkcaldy. Flat course. 9 holes, 5252 yards. S.S.S. 66. *Green Fees:* weekdays £8.00 per round, weekends £10.00 per round. Concessionary ticket available. *Eating facilities:* clubhouse bar facilities, meals available on request, snacks available most times. *Visitors*: all welcome, Saturdays and some Sundays members' competitions held from 7am to 11am and 1pm to 3pm. *Society Meetings:* welcome. Secretary: Charles Taylor (01592 720080).

COLINSBURGH. **Charleton Golf Club,** Colinsburgh Golf Ltd, Charleton, Colinsburgh KY9 1HG (01333 340505; Fax: 01333 340583). *Location:* B942, Colinsburgh (near Elie). Parkland course. 18 holes, 6216 yards, 5684 metres. S.S.S. 72. Driving range, bunker practice area, putting green. *Green Fees:* information not provided. *Eating facilities:* fully licensed clubhouse with restaurant. *Visitors:* all welcome, pay as you play, no restrictions, please book. Carts, buggies. *Society Meetings:* all welcome. Professional: George Finlayson. Secretary: James Bruce.

COWDENBEATH. **Cowdenbeath Golf Club,** Seco Place, Cowdenbeath KY4 8PD (01383 511918). *Location:* just off the A92 after Dunfermline. Parkland course. 18 holes, 6212 yards. S.S.S. 71. Practice ground and putting green. *Green Fees:* weekdays £19.00, weekends £24.00. *Eating facilities:* catering available weekends, midweek by arrangement only. *Visitors:* welcome at any time. *Society Meetings:* booking available by telephone (01383 513079/01383 511918). Secretary: Mr L. Connelly.

COWDENBEATH. **Dora Golf Course,** Cowdenbeath KY4 8PD (01383 513079). Parkland course, 18 holes. Par 71. *Green Fees: weekdays £19.00, between 2pm - 4pm £13.00; weekends £24.00* . *Eating facilities:* bar available, catering by arrangement.

CRAIL. **Crail Golfing Society,** Balcomie Clubhouse, Fifeness, Crail KY10 3XN (01333 450686; Fax: 01333 450416). Instituted 1786. *Location:* eleven miles south-east of St Andrews on A917. Traditional links courses. Balcomie Links: 18 holes, 5922 yards. S.S.S. 70. Par 69. Craighead Links: 18 holes, 6728 yards. S.S.S. 74. Par 72. Practice ground. *Green Fees:* weekdays £45.00 per round, £60.00 per day; weekends and Public Holidays £55.00 per round, £70.00 per day. *Eating facilities:* quality catering and bar. *Visitors:* welcome. *Society Meetings:* advance booking available for parties. Professional: Graeme Lennie (01333 450960). Secretary: (01333 450686; Fax: 01333 450416). e-mail: info@crailgolfingsociety.co.uk website: www.crailgolfingsociety.co.uk

CUPAR. **Cupar Golf Club,** Hilltarvit, Cupar KY15 5JT (01334 653549). *Location:* near cemetery on Ceres Road. Hillside/parkland course. 9 holes, 5153 yards. S.S.S. 66. Practice putting green. *Green Fees:* £20.00; weekly £50.00. Family per day £30.00. *Eating facilities:* full catering/bar. *Visitors:* welcome, except Saturdays. *Society Meetings:* by arrangement with Secretary. Secretary: Paul. P. Harryman. (01334 653549). e-mail: cupargc@fsmail.net website: www.cupargolfclub.co.uk

CUPAR. **Elmwood,** Stratheden, Near Cupar KY15 5RS (01334 658780; Fax: 01334 658781). *Location:* signposted from both A91 and A914, one mile west of Cupar, nine miles from St Andrews. Gently undulating parkland. 18 holes, 5951 yards. S.S.S 68. *Green Fees:* weekdays £22.00 per round, £32.00 per day; weekends: £25.00 per round, £35.00 per day (until 31st March 2008). Rates for concessions and Juniors. *Eating facilities:* full catering and bar. New lounge. *Visitors:* welcome anytime. Trolleys and buggies available. New indoor Golf Swing Analysis Studio. *Society Meetings:* welcome, advance bookings and special rates. Golf Administrator: Sharif Sulaiman.
e-mail: clubhouse@elmwood.ac.uk
website: www.elmwoodgc.co.uk

DUNFERMLINE. **Canmore Golf Club,** Venture Fair, Dunfermline (01383 724969). *Location:* one mile north of town centre on A823. Parkland, undulating. 18 holes, 5347 yards. S.S.S. 66. *Green Fees:* weekdays £22 per round, Sundays £27.00. Subject ro review. *Eating facilities:* full catering and bar. *Visitors:* welcome weekdays, limited Sundays. *Society Meetings:* we welcome visiting societies with prior reservation (not on Saturdays). Professional: David Gemmell (01383 728416). Secretary: Andrew Watson (01383 724969).

DUNFERMLINE. **Dunfermline Golf Club,** Pitfirrane, Crossford, By Dunfermline KY12 8QW (01383 723534). *Location:* two miles west of Dunfermline on A994 to Kincardine Bridge. Undulating parkland. 18 holes, 6121 yards, 5597 metres. S.S.S. 70. Practice area. *Green Fees:* £28.00 per round, £40.00 per day weekdays; £35.00 per round Sundays. *Eating facilities:* full catering, bar snacks available. *Visitors:* welcome 9.30am to 4pm weekdays and Sunday. Must have official Club Handicap. *Society Meetings:* accepted weekdays and Sunday by prior arrangement. Professional: Chris Nugent (01383 729061). Secretary: Robert De Rose (01383 723534).

DUNFERMLINE. **Forrester Park Resort,** Pitdinnie, Cairneyhill KY12 8RF (01383 880505; Fax: 01383 882505). Parkland course with gentle undulations and lots of water features. 300m driving range, practice bunkers. *Green Fees:* information not available. *Eating facilities:* Acanthus 5 star à la carte restaurant and bar/bistro. New members area, sports bar, X Golf. *Visitors:* welcome, no restrictions. *Society Meetings:* always welcome. Tuition, golfshop, showers available. Professional: Paul Edgecombe. Secretary: Robert Forrester.
e-mail: forresterpark@aol.com
website: www.forresterparkresort.com

DUNFERMLINE. **Pitreavie (Dunfermline) Golf Club,** Queensferry Road, Dunfermline KY11 8PR (Tel & Fax: 01383 722591). *Location:* M90 Edinburgh/Perth, leave at Junction 2 for Dunfermline. Undulating parkland with views across Firth of Forth. 18 holes, 6008 yards. S.S.S. 69. Practice ground. *Green Fees:* weekday £25.00 per round, £35.00 per day; weekend £30.00 per round, £40.00 per day. *Eating facilities:* full catering and bar facilities. *Visitors:* welcome. Please

phone the Professional in advance, must have recognised Golf Union Handicap. Trolleys and carts available. *Society Meetings:* catered for, must be booked through Secretary. Professional: Paul Brookes (01383 723151). Secretary: Eddie Comerford (01383 722591).

DUNFERMLINE. **Saline Golf Club,** Kinneddar Hill, Saline KY12 9LT (01383 852591). *Location:* turn off M90 at Junction 4, 7 miles along B914 to Dollar. Hillside parkland course. 9 holes, 5302 yards. S.S.S. 66. Practice net, putting green. *Green Fees:* adults £7.50 per 9 holes weekdays and Sundays; day ticket £11.50 weekdays, £14.00 Sundays. Juniors and Senior Citizens £5.50 weekdays and Sundays. Members' guests £5.50. *Eating facilities:* bar snacks; meals by prior arrangement. *Visitors:* welcome, restricted Saturdays and Thursdays. *Society Meetings:* catered for midweek or Sundays; maximum 24. Secretary: Mrs. Adrienne Lyon.

ELIE. **Earlsferry Thistle Golf Club,** Melon Park, Elie (01333 330301). *Location:* A917 golf course signs in Elie. Seaside links. 18 holes, 6250 yards. S.S.S. 70. *Green Fees:* information not available. *Visitors:* welcome weekdays. The course belongs to Elie Golf House Club, also played by Earlsferry Thistle.

ELIE. **Golf House Club,** Elie KY9 1AS (01333 330301; Fax: 01333 330895). *Location:* 10 miles south of St Andrews on A917. Links course. 18 holes, 6273 yards. S.S.S. 70. *Green Fees:* (2007) weekdays £60.00 per round, £80.00 per day; weekends £70.00 per round, £90.00 per day. Subject to review. *Eating facilities:* lunches, teas, etc. *Visitors:* welcome with reservation. Elie Sports Centre nearby with leisure facilities and cafeteria. *Society Meetings:* catered for except at weekends. Professional: Ian Muir (01333 330955). Secretary: Graham Scott (01333 330301; Fax: 01333 330895).
website: www.golfhouseclub.org

FALKLAND. **Falkland Golf Club,** The Myre, Falkland KY15 7AA (01337 857404). *Location:* entrance on A912, 12 miles from Kirkcaldy – approximately 20 minutes from St. Andrews. Lies at the foot of East Lomond Hills. Flat meadowland, beautiful views. 9 holes, 4988 yards, 4560 metres. S.S.S. 65 for 18 holes. *Green Fees:* contact clubhouse. *Eating facilities:* by arrangement. *Visitors:* welcome.

GLENROTHES. **Glenrothes Golf Club,** Golf Course Road, Glenrothes KY6 2LA (01592 758686). *Location:* at the western end of town, near airfield. Parkland, wide fairways, with burn crossing four fairways on back nine holes. 18 holes, 6444 yards, 5984 metres. S.S.S. 71. *Green Fees:* information not available. *Eating facilities:* full catering service and bar. Temporary day membership of club available to visitors. *Visitors:* welcome, some restrictions weekends. *Society Meetings:* welcome, advance booking, numbers 12-40. Hon. Secretary: Claire Dawson (01592 754561).*
website: www.glenrothesgolf.org.uk

KINCARDINE. **Tulliallan Golf Club,** Alloa Road, Kincardine on Forth, by Alloa FK10 4BB (01259 730396). *Location:* on A908 five miles east of Alloa, one mile north of Kincardine Bridge. Parkland, slightly wooded, burn winds through the course. 18 holes, 6000 yards. S.S.S. 69. Practice ground. *Green Fees:* £22.00 per round, £36.00 per day; Sunday £26.00 per round, £43.00 per day, with catering £45.00. *Eating facilities:* dining room, bar 11am to 11pm. *Society Meetings:* catered for by phoning Pro shop. Professional: Steve Kelly (Tel & Fax: 01259 730798). Secretary: Amanda Aitken (01259 730396).

KINGHORN. **Kinghorn Municipal Golf Club,** MacDuff Crescent, Kinghorn KY3 9RE (01592 890345). *Location:* bus stop at course, railway station three minutes away. Semi links course with hills. 18 holes, 5166 yards, S.S.S. 66. *Green Fees:* weekdays £19.00 per round, £30.00 per day; weekends £24.00 per round, £42.00 per day. *Eating facilities:* meals at clubhouse on request, local hotels. *Visitors:* welcome at any time; no large parties on Saturdays. *Society Meetings:* catered for by arrangement. Secretary: Gordon Tulloch (01592 891008). Starter: (01592 890978).

KINGSBARNS. **Kingsbarns Golf Links,** Kingsbarns, St Andrews KY16 8QD (01334 460860; Fax: 01334 460877). *Location:* on the coast near the village of Kingsbarns, 10 miles south-east of St Andrews. 18 holes, 6174 yards, Par 72. Driving range. *Green Fees:* information not available. *Eating facilities:* bar; light meals available. *Visitors:* welcome. Maximum handicap 28 (Men), 36 (Ladies). Fully stocked Pro Shop; locker lounges with showers and changing facilities.* website: www.kingsbarns.com

KIRKCALDY. **Dunnikier Park Golf Club,** Dunnikier Way, Kirkcaldy KY1 3LP (01592 261599 (Clubhouse). *Location:* one mile off A92 on the B981 north side of Kirkcaldy. Municipal parkland course, not hilly. 18 holes, 6601 yards, 6036 metres. S.S.S. 72. Practice ground. *Green Fees:* weekdays £16.00 per round, £26.00 per day; weekends £21.00 per round, £37.00 per day. Large concessions for over 60s and visiting parties over 8. *Eating facilities:* full bar and catering facilities. *Visitors:* welcome, no restrictions. *Society Meetings:* welcome by arrangement with Secretary (min. 12, max. 30). Professional: Gregor Whyte (01592 642121). Secretary: Raymond Johnston (01592 261599).
e-mail: dunnikierparkgolfclub@btinternet.com
website: www.dunnikierparkgolfclub.com

KIRKCALDY. **Kirkcaldy Golf Club,** Balwearie Road, Kirkcaldy KY2 5LT (01592 205240). *Location:* west end of town adjacent to Beveridge Park. Challenging parkland layout in rural setting with views across Firth of Forth. 18 holes, 6004 yards. S.S.S. 69 – Par 71. Practice ground. *Green Fees:* information not available. *Eating facilities:* bar and full catering facilities. Magnificent clubhouse. *Visitors:* welcome except Saturdays, restricted Tuesdays. Professional's shop. Trolleys for hire. *Society Meetings:* welcome but please phone or write in advance. Professional: Anthony Caira (01592 203258). Secretary: Andrew Wood (01592 205240).*

LADYBANK. **Ladybank Golf Club,** Annsmuir, Ladybank KY15 7RA (01337 830814). *Location:* on A92 off A91, 15 miles St. Andrews. Wooded heathland. 18 holes, 6641 yards. S.S.S. 72. Practice ground. *Green Fees:* weekdays £49.00 per round, £70.00 per day; weekends £60.00 very limited. *Eating facilities:* full catering facilities and bar. *Visitors:* welcome without reservation. Party bookings by arrangement with Secretary. *Society Meetings:* by arrangement. Professional: Sandy Smith (Tel & Fax: 01337 830725). Secretary: Fraser McCluskey (01337 830814; Fax: 01337 831505).

LESLIE. **Leslie Golf Club,** Balsillie Laws, Leslie, Glenrothes KY6 3EZ (01592 620040). Parkland with small stream running through some fairways. 9 holes, 4940 yards. S.S.S. 65. *Green Fees:* information not available. *Eating facilities:* bar open all day. *Visitors:* always welcome, some restrictions on competition days.*

LEUCHARS. **St Michaels Golf Club,** Gallowhill, Leuchars KY16 0DX (01334 839365; Fax: 01334 838789). *Location:* quarter of a mile outside Leuchars on A919 towards Dundee. Undulating parkland course surrounded by plantations. 18 holes, 5802 yards. S.S.S. 68. *Green Fees:* information not available. *Eating facilities:* bar and catering available. *Visitors:* welcome anytime but not before 12 noon Sundays. Changing rooms and showers. Trolley hire and electric carts. *Society Meetings:* by prior arrangement. A booking fee is payable before confirmation of reservation. Secretary: Mr G. Dignan (01334 838666; Fax: 01334 838789).

LEVEN. **Leven Golfing Society,** PO Box 14609, Links Road, Leven KY8 4HS (01333 426096; Fax: 01333 424229). *Location:* 14 miles south west of St Andrews. Championship Links course used for national and international events, including open qualifying. 18 holes, 6506 yards. S.S.S. 72. *Green Fees:* weekdays £45.00 per round, £60.00 per day; weekends £55.00 per round, £70.00 per day. *Eating facilities:* full catering available. *Visitors:* welcome except Saturdays. *Society Meetings:* by arrangement, please contact the Secretary, Links Joint Committee, Promenade, Leven KY8 4HS (01333 428859). Secretary: Verne Greger (Tel & Fax: 01333 424229).

LEVEN. **Leven Thistle Golf Club,** Balfour Street, Leven KY8 4JF (01333 426333; Fax: 01333 439910). *Location:* 10 miles south west of St. Andrews. Top championship links used for national and international events including Open qualifying. 18 holes, 6506 yards. S.S.S. 72. *Green Fees:* weekdays £40.00 per round, £55.00 per day; weekends £50.00 per round, £65.00 per day. *Eating facilities:* full catering available, two bars, function hall. *Visitors:* welcome without reservation, except Saturdays. *Society Meetings:* for group bookings contact Leven Links Joint Committee, Promenade, Leven, Fife KY8 4HS (01333 428859). Secretary: J. Scott. Links Secretary: Mr R. Bissett.

LEVEN. **Scoonie Golf Club,** North Links, Leven KY8 4SP (01333 307007). *Location:* nearest town Leven on coastal road to St Andrews. Flat, typical seaside bunkers. 18 holes, 4979 metres. S.S.S. 65. *Green Fees:* information not available. *Eating facilities:* full catering available, bar open normal hours. *Visitors:* welcome anytime. *Society Meetings:* welcome by bookings except Saturdays. Secretary: S. Kuczerepa (01333 307007; Fax: 01333 307008).

LOCHGELLY. **Lochgelly Golf Club,** Cartmore Road, Lochgelly (01592 780174). *Location:* take M90 to Junction 4 Halbeath Interchange, follow signs. Parkland. 18 holes, 5491 yards, 5063 metres. S.S.S. 67. *Green Fees:* information not available. *Eating facilities:* catering available. *Visitors:* welcome, no restrictions weekdays, weekends parties limited to 24. Professional: Martin Goldie (01592 782589). Secretary: G. Haldane (01383 512238).

LUNDIN LINKS. **Lundin Ladies Golf Club,** Woodielea Road, Lundin Links KY8 6AR. *Location:* at Lundin Links on A915, turn into road opposite Royal Bank of Scotland. Excellent parkland course, with famous standing stones. 9 holes, 2365 yards. S.S.S. 68. *Green Fees:* weekdays £8.00 9 holes, £15.00 18 holes; weekends £9.00 9 holes, £17.00 18 holes. Member's guest £6.00; reductions for Juniors; weekly tickets available. *Eating facilities:* none available, but local hotels within walking distance. *Visitors:* welcome, restricted tee times on Wednesdays during season. Starter (01333 320022). Clubhouse: (01333 320832).

Leven Links

The Promenade, Leven, Fife KY8 4HS

Leven Links, in part one of the oldest pieces of golfing ground in the world, is a true seaside links course. It has hosted many national and international events and is used as a final qualifying course for the Open Championship when it is held at St Andrews. The strength of Leven Links lies in its fine variety of links-type holes combined with large greens; turning into the prevailing west wind at the 13th leaves the golfer with a lot of work to do before reaching one of the finest finishing holes in golf.

Tel/Fax: 01333 428859 • www.leven-links.com
e-mail: secretary@leven-links.com

LUNDIN LINKS. **Lundin Golf Club,** Golf Road, Lundin Links KY8 6BA (01333 320202). *Location:* three miles east of Leven, 12 miles SW of St Andrews. Seaside links. 18 holes, 6371 yards. S.S.S. 71. Practice ground. *Green Fees:* £47.00 per round, £65.00 per day weekdays; Saturdays and Sundays after 2.30pm £50.00 per round (subject to review for 2008). *Eating facilities:* bar and dining room. *Visitors:* welcome Monday/ Thursday 9am to 3.30pm; Friday 9am to 3pm; Saturdays no visitors before 2.30pm; limited Sunday golf available. Professional: David K. Webster (01333 320051). Secretary: A.J. McDonald (01333 320202).
e-mail: secretary@lundingolfclub.co.uk
website: www.lundingolfclub.co.uk

MARKINCH. **Balbirnie Park Golf Club,** The Clubhouse, Balbirnie Park, Markinch, Glenrothes KY7 6NR (01592 612095; Fax: 01592 612383). *Location:* outside Markinch near the A92. Wooded parkland course. 18 holes, 6334 yards. S.S.S. 71. *Green Fees:* information not provided. *Eating facilities:* snacks, lunch, high tea and full meals available during clubhouse hours. *Visitors:* no restrictions at present other than maximum number of 24 at weekends and no visitors before 10am weekends. *Society Meetings:* welcome. Professional: Craig Donnelly (Tel & Fax: 01592 752006). Club Administrator: Steve Oliver (01592 612095; Fax: 01592 612383). Starter: (01592 752006).
e-mail: craigfdonnelly@aol.com
website: www.balbirniegolf.com

ST ANDREWS. **Old Course,** St Andrews KY16 9SF (01334 466666; Fax: 01334 466664). *Location:* go into St Andrews on the A91, follow signs to West Sands. Approximately 50 miles from Edinburgh. Public links. 18 holes, 6721 yards. S.S.S. 73. 60 bay driving range, practice facilities. *Green Fees:* information not avilable. *Eating facilities:* Links Clubhouse with full facilities; there is a buggy shuttle run from the clubhouse to the Old Course. *Visitors:* Handicap Certificate required. Handicap limit 24 or less (Men), 36 or less (Ladies). Trolleys allowed after 12 noon from May to September.*

ST ANDREWS. **Balgove Course,** St Andrews Links Trust, St Andrews KY16 9SF (01334 466666; Fax: 01334 466664). *Location:* A91 to St Andrews, turning is on the left just before the town. Public 9 hole beginners' course, 1520 yards. S.S.S. 60 (18 holes). *Green Fees:* information not available. *Eating facilities:* adjacent Eden Clubhouse with full facilities. Children's room. *Visitors:* welcome with or without reservation. Trolleys £3.00 per round. *Society Meetings:* welcome.*

ST ANDREWS. **The Castle Course,** St Andrews Links Trust, Pilmour House, St Andrews KY16 9SF (01334 466666; Fax: 01334 466664). Open April to October. *Location:* from St Andrews take the A917, the course is on the left. Public clifftop course. 18 holes, 5600-7200 yards. Par 71. *Green Fees:* £120.00. *Eating facilities:* The Castle Clubhouse with full facilities. *Visitors:* welcome. Trolleys £3.00 per round. *Society Meetings:* welcome.

ST ANDREWS. **Drumoig Hotel and Golf Resort,** Drumoig, Leuchars, St Andrews KY16 0BE (Tel & Fax: 01382 541898). *Location:* on A92 (St Andrews to Dundee), four miles south of Dundee. Natural free draining, rolling countryside over sandy based ground featuring spectacular water holes. Unusual quarry greens and views of St Andrews Bay and Carnoustie. 18 holes, 6835 yards. S.S.S 72. Driving Range. *Green Fees:* information not available. *Eating facilities:* bar and restaurants. *Visitors:* welcome. 29 bedroom hotel, all en suite (5 executive suites). *Society Meetings:* welcome.*

ST ANDREWS. **The Duke's,** Craigtoun, St Andrews KY16 8NS (01334 470214; Fax: 01334 479456). *Location:* 2½ miles from town centre, signposted on A91. Heathland championship tree-lined course with undulating fairways, spectacular bunkers and stunning views over 'The Auld Grey Toon'. Multiple tees to suit all golfers. 18 holes, 7500+ yards. Par 71. Grassed practice range and short game area. *Green Fees:* information not available. *Eating facilities:* restaurant and bar; private dining/meeting facilities. *Visitors:* all welcome, no restrictions. Trolley, club, shoe and cart hire available from the comprehensively stocked Pro Shop. *Society Meetings:* please call for details of packages. Professional: Ron Walker. Events and Membership Co-ordinator: Alan McColm.*
e-mail: reservations@oldcoursehotel.co.uk
website: www.oldcoursehotel.co.uk

www.uk-golfguide.com

ST ANDREWS. **Eden Course,** St Andrews Links Trust, Pilmour House, St Andrews KY16 9SF (01334 466666; Fax: 01334 466664). *Location:* A91 main road into St Andrews, turning is left just before the town; approximately 50 miles from Edinburgh. Public links. 18 holes, 6195 yards. S.S.S. 70. 60 bay driving range. Practice facilities. *Green Fees:* information not available. *Eating facilities:* Eden Clubhouse, lounge bar, dining room children's room. *Visitors:* welcome with or without reservation. Trolleys £3.00 per round. *Society Meetings:* always welcome.*

ST ANDREWS. **Jubilee Course,** St Andrews Links Trust, Pilmour House, St Andrews KY16 9SF (01334 466666; Fax: 01334 466664). *Location:* go into St Andrews on the A91, follow signs to West Sands; approximately 50 miles from Edinburgh. Public links. 18 holes, 6742 yards. S.S.S. 73. 60 bay driving range, practice facilities available. *Green Fees:* information not available. *Eating facilities:* Links Clubhouse, dining room. *Visitors:* always welcome. Trolleys £3.00 per round. *Society Meetings:* welcome.*

ST ANDREWS. **New Course,** St Andrews Links Trust, Pilmour House, St Andrews KY16 9SF (01334 466666; Fax: 01334 466664). *Location:* go into St Andrews on the A91, follow signs to West Sands; approximately 50 miles from Edinburgh. Public links course. 18 holes, 6625 yards. S.S.S. 72. 60 bay driving range, practice ground. *Green Fees:* information not available. *Eating facilities:* Links Clubhouse, dining room. *Visitors:* welcome. Buggies may be hired, trolleys are £3.00 per round. *Society Meetings:* welcome.*

www.uk-golfguide.com

ST ANDREWS. **Strathtyrum Course,** St Andrews Links Trust, Pilmour House, St Andrews KY16 9SF (01334 466666; Fax: 01334 466664). *Location:* A91 main road into St Andrews, turning is on the left just before the town. Approximately 50 miles from Edinburgh. Public links course, 18 holes, 5620 yards. S.S.S. 65. 60 bay driving range, practice ground. *Green Fees:* information not available. *Eating facilities:* Eden Clubhouse with full facilities. Children's room. *Visitors:* welcome. Buggies may be hired, trolleys are £3.00 per round. *Society Meetings:* welcome.*

TAYPORT. **Scotscraig Golf Club,** Golf Road, Tayport DD6 9DZ (01382 552515; Fax: 01382 553130). *Location:* ten miles north of St Andrews. Links/parkland. 18 holes, 6550 yards. S.S.S. 72. *Green Fees:* information not available. *Eating facilities:* lunches and high teas. *Visitors:* welcome on weekdays or weekends by prior arrangement. *Society Meetings:* catered for subject to approval. Company Days available. Professional: Craig Mackie (01382 552855). Secretary: B.D. Liddle (01382 552515). e-mail: scotscraig@scotscraiggolfclub.com website: www.scotscraiggolfclub.com

THORNTON. **Thornton Golf Club,** Station Road, Thornton KY1 4DW (01592 771111 office, 771173 starter). *Location:* southeast Fife located off A92, midway between Glenrothes and Kirkcaldy. Easily walked parkland course bounded by River Ore. Renowned for condition of greens. 18 holes, 6219 yards. S.S.S. 69. Practice area, chipping and putting areas. *Green Fees:* Monday to Friday (am) £25.00 per round, £35.00 per day; Friday (pm) to Sunday £35.00 per round, £50.00 per day. Parties of 18 or more get one free place. *Eating facilities:* full catering service and bar. *Visitors:* very welcome, restricted weekends before 10am and between 12 noon and 2.30pm. Recently built clubhouse; buggies for hire. *Society Meetings:* catered for. Secretary: W.D. Rae.

Glasgow & District

BISHOPBRIGGS. **The Bishopbriggs Golf Club,** Brackenbrae Road, Bishopbriggs G64 2DX (0141-772 1810). *Location:* quarter mile from Bishopbriggs Cross off Glasgow-Kirkintilloch road. Fairly flat parkland course. 18 holes, 6414 yards. S.S.S. 71. *Green Fees:* information not available. *Eating facilities:* full service always available. *Visitors:* weekends/Public Holidays with member only, other times apply to Secretary. *Society Meetings:* catered for Monday to Friday, application to committee at least one month in advance. Secretary: Andrew Smith (0141-772 8938).*

CUMBERNAULD. **Palacerigg Golf Club,** Palacerigg Country Park, Cumbernauld, Near Glasgow G67 3HU (01236 734969). *Location:* Cumbernauld off A80 between Glasgow and Stirling, Palacerigg Road, three miles south of Cumbernauld. Wooded parkland with good views to Campsie Hills, designed by Henry Cotton. 18 holes, 6444 yards, 5894 metres. S.S.S. 72. Practice area. *Green Fees:* weekdays £8.00; weekends £10.00. Full membership available contact Secretary. *Eating facilities:* full catering facilities. *Visitors:* welcome, advance booking recommended for individual rounds. *Society Meetings:* welcome weekdays, full days golf and catering £28.00. Other packages available contact Secretary or club steward. Starter: John Murphy (Tel & Fax: 01236 721461). Secretary: David S.A. Cooper (01236 734969; Fax: 01236 721461).
e-mail: palacerigg-golfclub@lineone.net
website: www.palacerigggolfclub.co.uk

CUMBERNAULD. **The Westerwood Hotel, Golf and Country Club,** Westerwood, Cumbernauld G68 0EW (01236 457171; Fax: 01236 738478). *Location:* between Glasgow and Stirling, off A80 towards Dullatur. Parkland, rolling American style; designed by Seve Ballesteros and Dave Thomas. 18 holes, 6616 yards. S.S.S. 72. *Green Fees:* weekdays £35.00, weekends £40.00. *Eating facilities:* full catering facilities. *Visitors:* welcome at all times, no restrictions. Advance booking of tee times recommended. 150 bedroom Hotel, full leisure facilities and indoor pool. *Society Meetings:* welcome by arrangement, packages available, including corporate membership. Golf Events Manager: Sam Cairns (01236 457171; Fax: 01236 738478).
e-mail: wesgolf@qhotels.co.uk
website: www.qhotels.co.uk

GLASGOW. **Alexandra Golf Club,** Alexandra Park, Alexandra Parade, Glasgow G31 8SE (0141-556 1294). *Location:* M8 off ramp to Alexandra Parade. Wooded Parkland, very hilly. 9 holes, 1965 yards, S.S.S. 35. Practice area. *Green Fees:* available on request. *Visitors:* welcome at all times. Blind Club and Unemployed Club use this course. Room available for functions, to book phone 0141-770 0519 (24 hours notice is required). Bowling greens available from Easter to September. Professional: Paul West (0141-556 1294). Secretary: G. Campbell (0141-556 1294).

GLASGOW. **Balmore Golf Club,** Balmore, Torrance G64 4AW (01360 620240; Fax: 01360 622742). *Location:* A803 then A807 from Glasgow. Parkland. 18 holes, 5530 yards. S.S.S. 67. Practice area. *Green Fees:* weekdays £30.00 per round, £40.00 day ticket. *Eating facilities:* catering and bar facilities. *Visitors:* welcome. *Society Meetings:* welcome Monday to Friday only. Professional: Paul Morrison (01360 620123). Secretary: C. Campbell (01360 620284).
e-mail: balmoregolf@btconnect.com
website: www.balmoregolfclub.co.uk

GLASGOW. **Bearsden Golf Club,** Thorn Road, Bearsden G61 4BP. *Location:* seven miles north-west of Glasgow. Parkland. 9 holes, 6014 yards. S.S.S. 69. *Green Fees:* information not available. *Visitors:* welcome, but must be accompanied by member. Secretary: Alan Harris (0141 586 5300).

GLASGOW. **Blairbeth Golf Club,** Fernbrae Avenue, Rutherglen, Glasgow G73 4SF (0141-634 3355). *Location:* two miles south of Rutherglen off Burnside Road. Parkland. 18 holes, 5518 yards. S.S.S. 68. *Green Fees:* on application. *Eating Facilities:* available. *Visitors:* welcome weekdays only. *Society Meetings:* on application. Hon. Secretary/Treasurer: John Bell (0141-634 3325).
e-mail: bgc1910@yahoo.co.uk
website: www.blairbeth.com

GLASGOW. **Bonnyton Golf Club,** Eaglesham, Glasgow G76 0QA (01355 302645; Fax: 01355 303151). *Location:* B764. Moorland course. 18 holes, 6252 yards. S.S.S. 71. *Green Fees:* £40.00 per day. *Eating facilities:* full diningroom and snack facilities. *Visitors:* welcome except weekends. Professional: Kendal McWade (01355 302256). Secretary: A. Hughes (01355 302781).

GLASGOW. **Bothwell Castle Golf Club,** Uddingston Road, Bothwell G71 8TD (Tel & Fax: 01698 801971). *Location:* adjacent to M74, three miles north of Hamilton. Flat parkland course. 18 holes, 6230 yards. S.S.S. 70. Golf clubs and caddy cars for hire. Practice ground. *Green Fees:* £28.00 per round, £38.00 per day. (Playing times must be booked with Professional). *Eating facilities:* full catering and bar. *Visitors:* welcome Fridays only between 10am and 12 noon. *Society Meetings:* catered for, courtesy granted by application. Professional: A. McCloskey (01698 801969). Secretary: David McNaught (Tel & Fax: 01698 801971).

> **THE APPEARANCE OF AN ASTERISK (*) AT THE END OF A CLUB OR COURSE ENTRY INDICATES THAT UP-TO-DATE INFORMATION HAS NOT BEEN SUPPLIED**

GLASGOW. **Buchanan Castle Golf Club,** Buchanan Estate, Drymen, Glasgow G63 0HY (01360 660307). *Location:* A811, one mile beyond Croftamie village. Flat parkland course. 18 holes, 6052 yards. S.S.S. 69. 9 hole putting area. *Green Fees:* weekdays £35.00 per round, £50.00 per day; weekends £35.00 per round. *Eating facilities:* full catering and bar available. *Visitors:* welcome except Tuesday and Saturday mornings. *Society Meetings:* welcome Thursdays and Fridays only. Professional: Keith Baxter (01360 660330). Secretary: Janet Dawson (01360 660307; Fax: 01360 870382).
e-mail: buchanancastle@sol.co.uk
website: www.buchanancastlegolfclub.com

GLASGOW. **Cambuslang Golf Club,** 30 Westburn Drive, Cambuslang (0141-641 3130). *Location:* half a mile north of Cambuslang main street. Parkland. 9 holes, 6146 yards. S.S.S. 69. *Green Fees:* information not available. *Eating facilities:* bar snacks, lunches, evening meals. *Visitors:* welcome if introduced by a member. *Society Meetings:* by arrangement. Secretary: R.M. Dunlop.*

GLASGOW. **Cathcart Castle Golf Club,** Mearns Road, Clarkston, Glasgow G76 7YL (0141-638 9449). *Location:* one and a half miles from Clarkston Toll. Undulating parkland course. 18 holes, 5832 yards. S.S.S. 69. *Green Fees:* £30.00 weekdays. *Eating facilities:* full catering available, lounge bar. *Visitors:* welcome weekdays by prior arrangement. *Society Meetings:* weekdays by application. Professional: Stephen Duncan (0141-638 3436). Secretary: I.G. Sutherland (0141-638 9449).

GLASGOW. **Cathkin Braes Golf Club,** Cathkin Road, Rutherglen, Glasgow G73 4SE (0141-634 6605). Moorland course. 18 holes, 6208 yards. S.S.S. 71. Practice ground. *Green Fees:* £35.00 per round. *Eating facilities:* available. *Visitors:* welcome Monday to Friday by prior arrangement. *Society Meetings:* catered for. Professional: Stephen Bree (0141-634 0650). Secretary/Treasurer: David Moir.
e-mail: secretary@cathkinbraesgolfclub.co.uk
website: www.cathkinbraesgolfclub.co.uk

GLASGOW. **Cawder Golf Club,** Cadder Road, Bishopbriggs, Glasgow G64 3QD (0141-761 1280; Fax: 0141-761 1285). *Location:* A803 north of city. Parkland. Cawder: 18 holes, 6279 yards, 5741 metres. S.S.S. 70. Keir: 18 holes, 5878 yards, 5374 metres. S.S.S. 68. Practice area. *Green Fees:* information not provided. *Eating facilities:* lunches, high teas, dinners available. *Visitors:* welcome when playing with member. *Society Meetings:* catered for mid-week. Professional: Gordon Stewart (0141-772 7102). Secretary: Lesley M. Giblin (0141-761 1283).
e-mail: lesley.giblin@cawder.co.uk
website: www.cawdergolfclub.co.uk

GLASGOW. **Clober Golf Club,** Craigton Road, Milngavie G62 7HP (0141-956 1685). *Location:* five minutes from Milngavie centre, seven miles from Glasgow city centre. Parkland course. 18 holes, 4963 yards. S.S.S. 65. *Green Fees:* weekdays £22.00 per round. *Eating facilities:* morning coffee, lunches, high teas. *Visitors:* welcome Monday to Thursday before 4pm, some Fridays also before 4pm; not at weekends unless introduced by a member. *Society Meetings:* catered for. Professional: Gary McFarlane. (0141-956 6963). Secretary: Brian Davidson (0141-956 1685).
e-mail: clobergolfclub@btopenworld.com
website: www.clober.co.uk

GLASGOW. **Cowglen Golf Club,** 301 Barrhead Road, Glasgow G43 1AU (0141-632 0556). *Location:* south-west Glasgow, follow M77 from Glasgow taking Pollok turnoff, turn left at traffic lights. Course half mile on right. Undulating parkland course. 18 holes, 6079 yards, 5559 metres. S.S.S. 69. Extensive practice facilities available. *Green Fees:* £35.00 per round, £45.00 per day. *Eating facilities:* full catering facilities available. *Visitors:* welcome if arranged beforehand with Secretary. Lockers and showers available. *Society Meetings:* restricted numbers, apply to Secretary. Professional: Simon Payne (0141-649 9401). Secretary: Ronald J.G. Jamieson C.A. (Tel & Fax: 01505 503000).
e-mail: r.jamieson-accountants@fsmail.net

GLASGOW. **Crow Wood Golf Club,** Garnkirk House, Cumbernauld Road, Muirhead G69 9JF (0141-779 2011). *Location:* on A80 on Stirling Road, 6 miles north east of Glasgow. Wooded parkland. 18 holes, 6160 yards. S.S.S. 70. Practice area. *Green Fees:* weekdays £30.00 per round, £40.00 per day (incl. third-party insurance). *Eating facilities:* fully licensed, snacks or full meals served all day. *Visitors:* welcome Monday to Friday except Bank Holidays and only by arrangement with Secretary. *Society Meetings:* catered for as visitors. Professional: Brian Moffat (0141-779 1943). Secretary: G. Blyth (0141-779 4954).

GLASGOW. **Douglas Park Golf Club,** Hillfoot, Bearsden, Glasgow G61 2TJ (0141-942 2220). *Location:* adjacent to railway station, Hillfoot, Bearsden, off Milngavie Road. Undulating parkland course. 18 holes, 5962 yards. S.S.S. 69. *Green Fees:* £25.00 per round, £35.00 per day. *Eating facilities:* full service available, usual licensing hours. *Visitors:* must be introduced and play with member. *Society Meetings:* midweek only on application to Secretary. Professional: David B. Scott (0141-942 1482). Secretary: J.G. Fergusson (Tel & Fax: 0141-942 0985).

GLASGOW. **Dullatur Golf Club,** 1A Glen Douglas Drive, Cumbernauld G68 0DW (01236 723230; Fax: 01236 727271). *Location:* 12 miles east of Glasgow - leave A80 for Dullatur then off third roundabout (Craigmarloch). Moorland, rolling courses. Two courses Antonine, 5205 yards and Carrickstone, 5673 yards. 36 holes, S.S.S. 70. *Green Fees:* information not provided. *Eating facilities:* full catering facilities. *Visitors:* welcome. Smart casual dress required in clubhouse. Full leisure centre. *Society Meetings:* welcome, book through Secretary. Professional: Duncan Sinclair (01236 723230; Fax: 01236 727271). Secretary: William Crombie.

GLASGOW. **East Kilbride Golf Club,** Chapelside Road, Nerston, East Kilbride G74 4PH (013552 20913). *Location:* Glasgow Road exit from East Kilbride. Parkland course with variable topography. 18 holes, 6419 yards. S.S.S. 71. *Green Fees:* weekdays £25.00 per round, £35.00 per day. *Eating facilities:* full bar and catering facilities seven days per week. *Visitors:* welcome weekdays only. *Society Meetings:* catered for weekdays only. Professional: Paul McKay (01355 222192). Secretary: W.G. Gray (01355 247728).

GLASGOW. **The East Renfrewshire Golf Club,** Pilmuir, Newton Mearns, Glasgow G77 6RT (01355 500256). *Location:* off M77, on A77, one and a half miles south of Newton Mearns. Moorland course with plantations of evergreen trees. 18 holes, 6107 yards, 5584 metres. S.S.S. 70. Practice ground. *Green Fees:* weekdays £40.00 per round, £50.00 per day. *Eating facilities:* by prior arrangement with club caterer. *Visitors:* welcome except Saturdays but always by prior arrangement with Professional. *Society Meetings:* welcomed weekdays on prior application. Professional: Stewart Russell (01355 500206). Secretary: Graham Tennant (01355 500256; Fax: 01355 500323).
e-mail: secretary@eastrengolfclub.co.uk
website: www.eastrengolfclub.co.uk

GLASGOW. **Eastwood Golf Club,** Muirshield, Loganswell, Newton Mearns, Glasgow G77 6RX (01355 500261). *Location:* on A77 road to Kilmarnock two miles south of Newton Mearns. Moorland course. 18 holes, 6071 yards. S.S.S. 70. Par 70. Practice area. *Green Fees:* weekdays £30.00 per round, £40.00 per day. *Eating facilities:* snacks or full meals available. *Visitors:* welcome weekdays on application to Secretary. *Visiting parties:* welcomed on prior application. Professional: I.J. Darroch (01355 500285). Secretary: I.M. Brown (01355 500280).

GLASGOW. **Esporta (Dougalston Golf Club),** Strathblane Road, Milngavie, Glasgow G62 8HA (0141-955 2404; Fax: 0141-955 2406). *Location:* A81 half a mile from Milngavie. Parkland course set in woodland estate. 18 holes, 6040 yards. S.S.S. 70, par 71. Practice ground, putting green, practice nets. *Green Fees:* weekdays £25.00, weekends £28.00. Subject to review for 2007. *Eating facilities:* restaurant, sports bar and leisure facilities. *Visitors:* welcome weekdays 8am to 4.30pm. Buggies available. *Society Meetings:* welcome weekdays. Weekends subject to availability. Other facilities include 25 metre swimming pool, along with a health suite, aerobic studios, air-conditioning fitness area, gymnasium, indoor - outdoor tennis, Sports Bar and banqueting facilities. Professional: Craig Everett (0141-955 2404; Fax: 0141-955 2406). Secretary: Hilda Everett (0141-955 2404; Fax: 0141-955 2406).

GLASGOW. **Glasgow Golf Club,** Killermont, Bearsden, Glasgow G61 2TW (0141-942 1713). *Location:* taking Maryhill Road out of Glasgow turn right at Killermont Avenue, half a mile before Canniesburn Toll and then turn immediately right again. Tree-lined parkland. 18 holes, 5977 yards. S.S.S. 69, Par 70. *Green Fees:* on application. *Eating facilities:* bar and dining room. *Visitors:* only if introduced by member; no visitors at weekends. *Society Meetings:* by application to Managing Secretary. Professional: Jack Steven (0141-942 8507). Secretary: D.W. Deas (0141-942 2011; Fax: 0141-942 0770).
e-mail: secretary@glasgow-golf.com

GLASGOW: **Haggs Castle Golf Club,** Dumbreck Road, Dumbreck, Glasgow G41 4SN (0141-427 0480). *Location:* off Junction 1 of M77 from Glasgow. Flat, tree-lined course. 18 holes, 6426 yards. S.S.S. 71. Practice area and putting green. *Green Fees:* weekdays £40.00 per round, £50.00 per day. Weekends, members only. *Eating facilities:* full catering available. *Visitors:* welcome except weekends; must book through Professional. Handicap Certificate required. Golf shoes must be worn. *Society Meetings:* by arrangement through Secretary. Professional: C. Elliott (0141-427 3355). Secretary/Manager: Alan Williams (Tel & Fax: 0141-427 1157).

GLASGOW. **Hayston Golf Club,** Campsie Road, Kirkintilloch, Glasgow G66 1RN (0141-776 1244). *Location:* 10 miles north-east of Glasgow and one mile north of Kirkintilloch. Parkland course with tree-lined fairways. 18 holes, 6042 yards. S.S.S. 70. Practice area. *Green Fees:* information not provided.*Eating facilities:* lunches, dinners, bar snacks. *Society Meetings:* Tuesdays, Wednesdays and Thursdays on application to Secretary, max 24. Professional: Steve Barnett (0141-775 0882). Secretary: R. Bryan (0141-775 0723; Fax: 0141-776 9030).
e-mail: secretary@haystongolf.com
website: www.haystongolf.com

GLASGOW. **Hilton Park Golf Club,** Stockiemuir Road, Milngavie, Glasgow G62 7HB (0141-956 4657). *Location:* on A809. Moorland courses. Allander course: 18 holes, 5487 yards. S.S.S. 67. Hilton course: 18 holes, 6054 yards. S.S.S. 70. Practice area. *Green Fees:* information not available. *Eating facilities:* full catering and bar. *Visitors:* on application to the Secretary (not at weekends). *Society Meetings:* as visitors. Professional: W. McCondichie (0141-956 5125). Secretary: Mrs J.A. Dawson (0141-956 4657/5124).*

GLASGOW. **Kirkhill Golf Club,** Greenlees Road, Cambuslang, Glasgow G72 8YN (0141-641 3083). *Location:* between Rutherglen and East Kilbride adjacent to A749, three miles from East Kilbride. Slightly hilly parkland course. 18 holes, 6030 yards. S.S.S. 70. Practice area. *Green Fees:* information not provided. *Eating facilities:* dining room and bar. *Visitors:* welcome weekdays only. *Society Meetings:* welcome weekdays only. Professional: D. Williamson (0141-641 7972). Hon. Secretary: Carol Downes (Tel & Fax: 0141-641 8499).
e-mail: secretary@kirkhillgolfclub.org.uk
website: www.kirkhillgolfclub.org.uk

GLASGOW. **Knightswood Golf Club,** Lincoln Avenue, Glasgow G13 3DN (0141-959 6358). *Location:* west along Great Western Road, turn left into Lincoln Avenue. Flat parkland course. 9 holes, 2792 yards. S.S.S. 67. *Green Fees:* information not available. *Visitors:* tee reserved for Club Wednesdays and Fridays 8am to 9am and 10am to 11am, otherwise no restrictions. 24 hours' notice required. Ladies' and gents' changing areas. *Society Meetings:* welcome, as for visitors. Secretary: James Lavery (0141-954 8614).*

GLASGOW. **Lethamhill Golf Course,** 1240 Cumbernauld Road, Glasgow G33 1AH (0141-770 6220; Fax: 0141-770 0520). *Location:* 100 yards off M8 Junction 12. Parkland, many holes with views of Hogganfield Loch. 18 holes, 5836 yards. S.S.S. 68. 18 holes pitch and putt course. *Green Fees:* information not available. *Visitors:* welcome at all times - this is a public course, 24 hour in advance booking system. Ladies and gents changing. *Society Meetings:* contact Golf Professional G. Taggart (0141-770 7135).*

GLASGOW. **Linn Park Golf Club,** Simshill Road, Glasgow G44 5EP (0141-633 0377). *Location:* five miles south of city centre near Carmunnock Road, near Croftfoot roundabout. Parkland. 18 holes, 5005 yards. S.S.S. 66. *Green Fees:* information not available. *Visitors:* welcome, 24 hours notice required. *Society Meetings:* all welcome. Secretary: T. Dunn (0141-633 0377).*

GLASGOW. **Littlehill Golf Club,** Auchinairn Road, Bishopbriggs, Glasgow G64 1UT. *Location:* from Glasgow on A803, turn off for Stobhill Hospital. Flat, parkland. 18 holes, 6364 yards. S.S.S. 70. Small practice area. *Green Fees:* information not available. *Eating facilities:* canteen open five days weekly in season, three outwith. *Visitors:* welcome without reservation - pay and play. *Society Meetings:* no restrictions. Professional: Kevin Hughes (0141-762 3998). Secretary: W. Burke.

GLASGOW. **Milngavie Golf Club,** Laighpark, Milngavie, Glasgow G62 8EP (0141-956 1619; Fax: 0141-956 4252). *Location:* situated off Glasgow to Drymen road approximately one mile past Stockiemuir Service Station, turn right at signpost. Moorland course. 18 holes, 5818 yards. S.S.S. 68. *Green Fees:* information not available. *Eating facilities:* catering available. *Visitors:* welcome when introduced by member or by prior arrangement with the Secretary. *Society Meetings:* catered for. Secretary: S. Woods.

GLASGOW. **Pollok Golf Club,** 90 Barrhead Road, Glasgow G43 1BG (0141-632 1080; Fax: 0141-649 1398). *Location:* Junction 2 M77. Wooded parkland. 18 holes, 6358 yards. S.S.S. 70. *Green Fees:* £50.00 per round. *Eating facilities:* dining room and bar. *Visitors:* welcome with reservation by letter or telephone to Secretary. No visitors Saturday or Sunday. *Society Meetings:* catered for by letter. Secretary: David Morgan (0141-632 4351; Fax: 0141-649 1398).

GLASGOW. **Rouken Glen Golf Centre,** Stewarton Road, Thornliebank, Glasgow G46 7UZ (0141-638 7044 or 0141-620 0826). *Location:* on Stewarton Road at Rouken Glen Park, only 250 yards from the A726. Parkland with wooded features, designed by James Braid. 18 holes, 4800 yards. S.S.S. 63 (Par 64). 15-bay floodlit driving range. *Green Fees:* information not available. *Eating facilities:* catering and bar facilities available. *Visitors:* welcome all week. Shop, club hire, etc. *Society Meetings:* bookings taken. Professional: (0141-638 7044). Secretary: Christine Cosh (0141-632 6816).*

GLASGOW. **Sandyhills Golf Club,** 223 Sandyhills Road, Glasgow G32 9NA (0141-778 1179). *Location:* three miles east from centre of Glasgow. Parkland. 18 holes, 6253 yards. S.S.S. 71. *Green Fees:* information not provided. *Eating facilities:* full catering facilities available. *Visitors:* welcome when introduced by a member. *Society Meetings:* welcome by prior arrangement. Secretary: C.J. Wilson C.A. (01698 282062; Fax: 01698 425840).

GLASGOW. **Whitecraigs Golf Club,** 72 Ayr Road, Giffnock, Glasgow G46 6SW (0141-639 4530; Fax: 0141-616 3648). *Location:* on A77 south of city, two miles from Eastwoodmains roundabout. Parkland course. 18 holes, 6013 yards. S.S.S. 70. *Green Fees:* £40.00 per round, £50.00 per day. *Eating facilities:* restaurant and lounge bar. *Visitors:* welcome midweek, letter of introduction required. *Society Meetings:* catered for Wednesday only. Professional: Alastair Forrow (0141-639 2140). Secretary: Alan Keith (0141-639 4530).

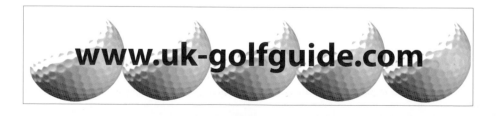

GLASGOW. **Williamwood Golf Club,** Clarkston Road, Glasgow G44 3YR (0141-637 1783; Fax: 0141-571 0166). *Location:* behind service station on Clarkston Road. Attractive parkland course designed by James Braid. 18 holes, 5878 yards. S.S.S. 69. Practice area and putting. *Green Fees:* £30.00 per round, £40.00 per day. *Eating facilities:* meals must be ordered. *Visitors:* welcome by arrangement with Secretary or Professional. *Society Meetings:* weekdays only by arrangement. Professional: Stewart G. Marshall (0141-637 2715; Fax: 0141-637 2600). Managing Secretary: L. W. Conn (0141-637 1783; Fax: 0141-571 0166).

GLASGOW. **Windyhill Golf Club,** Baljaffray Road, Bearsden, Glasgow G61 4QQ (0141-942 2349; Fax: 0141-942 5874). *Location:* one mile north from Bearsden Cross. Undulating parkland course. 18 holes, 6254 yards. S.S.S. 70. Practice area. *Green Fees:* £35.00; weekends £6.00 with member only. *Eating facilities:* full catering and bar. *Visitors:* welcome weekdays only. *Society Meetings:* welcome weekdays by arrangement. Professional: Christopher Duffy (0141-942 7157; Fax: 0141-942 5874). Secretary: James M. Young (0141-942 2349; Fax: 0141-942 5874).

KILSYTH. **Kilsyth Lennox Golf Club,** Tak-Ma-Doon Road, Kilsyth, Glasgow G65 0RS (01236 824115). *Location:* 12 miles from Glasgow on A80. Parkland/moorland, undulating ground with superb views across central Scotland. 18 holes, 6225 yards. S.S.S. 71. *Green Fees:* weekdays £23.00 per round, £33.00 per day; weekends £28.00 per round, £38.00 per day. *Eating facilities:* new clubhouse. *Visitors:* welcome weekdays up to 5.00pm, Saturdays after 3.00pm and Sundays. *Society Meetings:* welcome, details on application. Secretary: Helen Ann Barrie.
e-mail: mail@klgc.co.uk
website: www.kilsythlennox.com

Highlands (North)

The Royal Dornoch Golf Club
Golf Road, Dornoch IV25 3LW
Tel Reservations: 01862 810219 Ext185
Fax: 01862 810792
e-mail: bookings@royaldornoch.com
www.royaldornoch.com

At Royal Dornoch, golfers are challenged on both the Championship Course – rated 3rd in the World outside the USA – and on the Struie Course to create shots.

BONAR BRIDGE. Bonar Bridge-Ardgay Golf Club, Market Stance, Migdale Road, Bonar Bridge IV24 3EJ (01863 766199). *Location:* off the A9, driving north cross Bonar Bridge, straight up hill for half a mile. Wooded heathland. 9 holes, 5284 yards. S.S.S. 65. *Green Fees:* £15.00 per day (2006). Subject to review. *Eating facilities:* limited catering available May to September. *Visitors:* always welcome. *Society Meetings:* limited to weekdays. Joint Secretary: Bert Thomson (01862 892443).
e-mail: bonar-ardgay-golf@tiscali.co.uk

BRORA. Brora Golf Club, 43 Golf Road, Brora KW9 6QS (+44 (0)1408 621417; Fax: +44 (0)1408 622157). *Location:* 52 miles north of Inverness on A9 trunk road. Traditional links course designed by James Braid. 18 holes, 6110 yards. S.S.S. 70. Practice ground available. *Green Fees:* (2007) weekdays £35.00 per round, £45.00 per day; weekends £40.00 per round, £50.00 per day. *Eating facilities:* full catering, bar facilities April to October. *Visitors:* welcome anytime except on tournament days, advisable to book tee times in season. Welcome to participate in open events (Certificate of Handicap required). Carts, caddies, etc available. *Society Meetings:* by arrangement with Secretary. Secretary: Tony Gill (01408 621417; Fax: 01408 622157).
e-mail: secretary@broragolf.co.uk
website: www.broragolf.co.uk

DORNOCH. **Royal Dornoch Golf Club,** Golf Road, Dornoch IV25 3LW (01862 810219; Fax: 01862 810792). *Location:* one mile from A9 between Tain and Golspie. Seaside links. Championship Course and Struie Course. Championship: 18 holes, 6514 yards, 5958 metres. S.S.S. 73; Struie: 18 holes, 6276 yards, 5793 metres. S.S.S. 70. Practice area. *Green Fees:* Championship Course: weekdays £78.00 per round, weekends £88.00 per round. Struie Course: £35.00 per round, £45.00 day ticket. Combination Day Ticket (one round each course) £93.00 weekdays, £103.00 weekends. All green fees discounted £10.00 in April and October and are subject to alteration. *Eating facilities:* available. *Visitors:* welcome, no major restrictions other than competitions – bookings can be heavy. Saturdays members only until late afternoon. Handicap requirement – Men 24, Ladies 35. *Society Meetings:* must be arranged through the Secretary. J.S. Duncan (01862 810219; Fax: 01862 810792). Professional: A. Skinner (01862 810902; Fax; 01862 811095).
e-mail: bookings@royaldornoch.com
website: www.royaldornoch.com

DORNOCH. **The Carnegie Golf Club at Skibo Castle,** Skibo Castle, Dornoch (01862 894600; Fax: 01862 894601). *Location*: off A9 between Tain and Dornoch. Links course, built on peninsula, naturally contoured; Donald Steel designed. 18 holes, 6671 yards. S.S.S. 72. Practice facilities. *Green Fees*: information not available. *Eating facilities*: bar, luncheon table. *Visitors*: by prior arrangement, write or telephone only. Private members club, daily golf membership available, must be booked in advance. *Society Meetings*: welcome. Accommodation available, charges on request. Golf Secretary: Sharon Stewart. Professional: David Thomson (01862 881260).*
e-mail: sharon.stewart@carnegieclubs.com

DURNESS. **Durness Golf Club,** Balnakiel, Durness. *Location:* 57 miles northwest of Lairg on A838. Links course with final hole played over deep gully. 9 greens, 18 tees, 5555 yards. S.S.S 69. *Green Fees:* £15.00 per day. Weekly ticket £50.00. *Eating facilities:* snacks available 12-5pm June to September. *Visitors:* welcome without reservation, only restriction on Sunday mornings. *Society Meetings:* by arrangement. Secretary: Lucy MacKay (01971 511364).

GOLSPIE. **Golspie Golf Club,** Ferry Road, Golspie KW10 6ST (01408 633266; Fax: 01408 633393). Location: 53 miles on A9 north of Inverness. Fairly flat course, seaside links and wooded. 18 holes, 5990 yards. S.S.S. 68. Practice area available. Green Fees: £30.00 per round, £40.00 per day (7 days). Eating facilities: bar and catering service, available during season. Visitors: welcome, no restrictions except on competition days. Carts, caddies must be booked in advance. Self-catering holiday apartment adjacent to clubhouse, sleeps four, free golf-package available. Society Meetings: welcome by prior arrangement, packages available. Golf Shop.
e-mail: info@golspie-golf-club.co.uk
　　　　miller12@icscotland.net (accommodation)
website: www.golspie-golf-club.co.uk

GRANTOWN-ON-SPEY. **Grantown-on-Spey Golf Club,** The Clubhouse, Golf Course Road, Grantown-on-Spey PH26 3HY (01479 872079; Fax: 01479 873725). Location: turn off main road opposite police station. Parkland and woodland. 18 holes, 5710 yards, S.S.S. 68, Par 70. Practice ground and putting green. Green Fees: information not available. Eating facilities: full bar and catering facilities. Visitors: welcome, members have priority before 10am weekends. Shop. Society Meetings: welcome except before 10am weekends. Secretary: Paul Mackay (01479 872079/ 873154; Fax: 01479 873725).*
e-mail: secretary@grantownonspeygolfclub.co.uk
website: www.grantownonspeygolfclub.co.uk

HELMSDALE. **Helmsdale Golf Club,** Golf Road, Helmsdale KW8 6JA. Location: on A9, 28 miles north of Dornoch, follow signs for Melvich. undulating parkland/moorland course. 9 holes, 3720 yards. S.S.S. 61 (2 x 9 holes). Green Fees: information not available. Life membership now available, contact Secretary. Visitors: welcome at all times. Society Meetings: welcome by appointment. Secretary: Ronald Sutherland (01431 821063).*

THE APPEARANCE OF AN ASTERISK (*) AT THE END OF A CLUB OR COURSE ENTRY INDICATES THAT UP-TO-DATE INFORMATION HAS NOT BEEN SUPPLIED

LYBSTER. **Lybster Golf Club,** Main Street, Lybster. Location: 14 miles south from Wick on A9, half-way down village street. One of smallest courses in Scotland, heathland/parkland. 9 holes, 1929 yards. S.S.S. 61. Green Fees: £10.00 per round/day (adults); £5.00 per round/day (juniors). Eating facilities: at nearby hotels in village. Visitors: welcome anytime. Society Meetings: welcome anytime. Full membership available. Secretary: Alex Calder.
website: www.lybstergolfclub.co.uk

REAY. **Reay Golf Club,** Clubhouse, Reay, By Thurso KW14 7RE (01847 811288). Location: 12 miles west of nearest main town of Thurso. Most northerly 18 hole seaside links. 18 holes, 5831 yards. S.S.S. 69. Green Fees: £25.00 per round, £35.00 per day, £90.00 per week – information from Secretary. Eating facilities: restricted: bar open 12-3pm, 8-11pm daily July/August. Visitors: welcome anytime, restricted during competitions. Society Meetings: welcome, advance bookings via Secretary. Captain: Ian Ross. Secretary: Bill McIntosh (01847 811288).
e-mail: info@reaygolfclub.co.uk
website: www.reaygolfclub.co.uk
　　　　www.caithnessgolfweek.co.uk
　　　　www.scottishopengolf.co.uk

THURSO. **Thurso Golf Club,** Newlands of Geise, By Thurso, KW14 7XF (01847 893807). Location: two miles from Railway Station, on road to Reay via Westfield. Flat parkland with newly planted trees. 18 holes, 5828 yards, 5290 metres. S.S.S. 69. Green Fees: information not available. Eating facilities: snacks available in the bar during the day June to August. Visitors: welcome, no restrictions. Society Meetings: welcome, notice required. Secretary: R.M. Black (01847 892575).*

WICK. **Wick Golf Club,** Reiss, By Wick KW1 4RW (01955 602726). Location: three miles north of Wick on A9. Seaside links course. 18 holes, 6123 yards. S.S.S. 71. Practice area. Green Fees: information not available. Eating facilities: licensed; snacks available. Visitors: welcome. Society Meetings: catered for. Secretary: I. Miller (01955 605680).*

Highlands (Mid)

ALNESS. Alness Golf Club, Ardross Road, Alness IV17 0QA (01349 883877). *Location:* 20 miles from Inverness; turn into Alness from A9 (north). Beautiful surroundings with views over Cromarty Firth and Alness River. 18 holes, 4886 yards. S.S.S. 64. Practice green available. *Green Fees:* (2007) weekdays £23.00 per round, £28.00 per day; weekend £25.00 per round, £30.00 per day. *Eating facilities:* licensed bar. *Visitors:* welcome all week. Changing rooms, hot showers; clubs and trolleys for hire. PGA Pro Shop, lessons available. *Society Meetings:* welcome with advance notice. Secretary: Dawn Fraser. website: www.alness-golfclub.co.uk

FORTROSE. Fortrose and Rosemarkie Golf Club, Ness Road East, Fortrose IV10 8SE (Office: 01381 620529, Shop: 01381 620733; Fax: 01381 621328). *Location:* on the Black Isle. A9 north from Inverness, across Kessock Bridge, through Munlochy, follow signs to Fortrose. James Braid designed links course, sea both sides, founded 1888. 18 holes, 5890 yards. Par 71, S.S.S. 69. Practice area available Summer. *Green Fees:* weekdays £32.00, weekends £38.00; day tickets £45.00. *Eating facilities:* catering available. *Visitors:* welcome without reservation. *Society Meetings:* catered for. e-mail: secretary@fortrosegolfclub.co.uk website: www.fortrosegolfclub.co.uk

GAIRLOCH. Gairloch Golf Club, Gairloch IV21 2BE (01445 712 407). *Location:* 75 miles west of Inverness on the A832. Seaside links with superb views. 9 holes, 4108 yards. S.S.S. 62 over 18 holes. Practice net. *Green Fees:* £16.00 per round, £20.00 per day, £60.00 per week. Juniors £10.00 per day, £35.00 per week. Subject to review. *Eating facilities:* licensed bar and light refreshments available. *Visitors:* welcome anytime but must be regular golfers. Tee times must be booked during the summer season – call clubhouse for details. *Society Meetings:* welcome, no restrictions. Secretary: B. Jeffrey (01445 731 680). e-mail: gairlochgolfclub@hotmail.co.uk website: www.gairlochgolfclub.com

INVERGORDON. Invergordon Golf Club, King George Street, Invergordon IV18 0BD (01349 852715). *Location:* A9 (B817), two miles, west side of town. Relatively flat, parkland. 18 holes, over 6020 yards. S.S.S. 69. Practice area. *Green Fees:* £25.00 per round, £30.00 per day ticket. *Eating facilities:* bar, bar snacks - normal licensing hours. *Visitors:* welcome without restrictions other than club competition times. Locker rooms. Club/caddy carts for hire. *Society Meetings:* welcome by prior arrangement. Clubhouse Manager: J. Ross (01349 852715). e-mail: invergordongolf@tiscali.co.uk

LOCHCARRON. Lochcarron Golf Club, Lochcarron, Ross-shire IV54 8YS. *Location:* one mile east of Lochcarron village by A896. Seaside course, combined parkland and shore. Interesting opening hole. A short course but great accuracy required. 9 holes with some alternative tees for second nine. 3575 yards (18 holes). S.S.S. 60. *Green Fees:* £14.00 per day; £55.00 per week. Juniors (under 16 years old) half price. Fees subject to review for 2008. *Eating facilities:* snacks and refreshments available in clubhouse. *Visitors:* welcome anytime except Saturdays between 2pm and 5pm. Bookings not required. Clubs for hire. *Society Meetings:* welcome. Secretary: Gerald Arscott (01599 577219).

MUIR OF ORD. **The Muir of Ord Golf Club,** Great North Road, Muir of Ord IV6 7SX (01463 870825; Fax: 01463 871867). *Location:* 15 miles north of Inverness beside A862, 12 miles north of Inverness on A832. Heathland, moorland course, excellent greens. 18 holes, 5559 yards. S.S.S. 68. Practice area. *Green Fees:* weekdays £20.00 per round, £25.00 per day; weekends £30.00 per round, £40.00 per day. Subject to review. Discounts of £1.00 per player if more than 14 players in party; weekends by appointment. *Eating facilities:* lounge bar (snacks all day), meals weekends or by appointment. *Visitors:* welcome weekdays outwith competition times, weekends by appointment. Trolleys available; buggy hire. *Society Meetings:* welcome. Shop (01463 871311). Secretary/Administrator: Mrs J. Gibson (01463 870825).
e-mail: muirgolf@supanet.com
website: www.muir-of-ordgolfclub.co.uk

PORTMAHOMACK. **Tarbat Golf Club,** Tarbatness Road, Portmahomack, Tain IV20 1YB. *Location:* 10 miles east of Tain. B9165 off A9. Seaside links course with scenic views. 9 holes, 5082 yards. S.S.S. 65. Practice area. *Green Fees:* £18 per day. *Eating facilities:* catering April-October, light snacks; local hotels. *Visitors:* welcome, some restrictions Saturdays. *Society Meetings:* welcome, please telephone Secretary. Secretary: John Mackay (01862 871325).

STRATHPEFFER. **Strathpeffer Spa Golf Club,** Golf Course Road, Strathpeffer IV14 9AS (01997 421219 or 01997 421011). *Location:* 20 minutes north of Inverness by A9, 5 miles west of Dingwall, quarter of a mile north of Strathpeffer Square (signposted). Upland course, panoramic views of moorland and mountain; water hazards at 3rd, 10th and 11th. 18 holes, 4956 yards. S.S.S. 66. Small practice area and putting green. *Green Fees:* weekdays £20.00 per round, £30.00 per day; weekends £25.00 per round, £35.00 per day. Discounts for groups of over 12. *Eating facilities:* bar and catering available seven days a week. *Visitors:* welcome without reservation, but check weekends and competition days. Club, buggy and trolley hire. *Society Meetings:* catered for by arrangement. Clubhouse (Bookings): 01997 421219.
e-mail: mail@strathpeffergolf.co.uk
website: www.strathpeffergolf.co.uk

TAIN. **Tain Golf Club,** Chapel Road, Tain IV19 1JE (01862 892314; Fax: 01862 892099). *Location:* off A9, 34 miles north of Inverness. Travelling north, turn right in middle of High Street - Golf Club one mile. Traditional links course designed by Old Tom Morris. 18 holes, 6404 yards. S.S.S. 71. All practice facilities available. *Green Fees:* weekdays £40.00 per round, £55.00 per day; weekends £45.00 per round, £60.00 per day. Discounts for parties of 12 or more. All green fees are subject to alteration. *Eating facilities:* full catering, licensed. *Visitors:* welcome anytime except when competitions are being held. Electric buggy, trolley, club hire and shop. *Society Meetings:* catered for. Secretary: Mrs Joanna Bell.
e-mail: info@tain-golfclub.co.uk
website: www.tain-golfclub.co.uk

ULLAPOOL. **Ullapool Golf Club,** North Road, Ullapool IV26 2TH (01854 613323; Fax: 01854 613133). *Location:* situated at the northern outskirts of the village. Parkland seaside course. 18 tees, 9 holes, 5338 yards, S.S.S. 67. 3 hole practice course, bunker. *Green Fees:* £18.00 per day adults, £9.00 per day juniors. *Eating facilities:* catering/bar only available at open competitions and club events. *Visitors:* welcome except during competitions. *Society Meetings:* welcome, group rates by negotiation. Secretary: A. Paterson.
e-mail: info@ullapool-golf.co.uk
website: www.ullapool-golf.co.uk

Highlands (South)

ARISAIG. **Traigh Golf Course,** Traigh, Arisaig PH39 4NT (01687 450 337). *Location:* on A830 Fort William to Mallaig Road, 3 miles north of Arisaig. Seaside links, close to sandy beaches on the beautiful Morar coast. 9 holes, 2456 yards. S.S.S 65. Practice green. *Green Fees:* £16.00 per day. *Eating facilities:* unlicensed, soft drinks and confectionery only. *Visitors:* welcome at all times. Clubs may be hired. *Society Meetings:* by arrangement. Manager: Bill Henderson (01687 450337/450645).
website: www.traighgolf.co.uk

BEAULY. **Aigas Golf Course,** By Beauly IV4 7AD (01463 782942 or 782423). *Location:* A831, five miles from Beauly village. Aigas nestles spectacularly between the River Beauly and Aigas Foret in beautiful Strathglass. Challenging parkland course.9 holes, 2439 yards, S.S.S. 63 (2 x 9 holes). Practice area. *Green Fees:* Monday to Friday 9 holes £11.00, 18 holes £16.00, day ticket £20.00; weekends 9 holes £13.00, 18 holes £18.00, day ticket £22.00. Subject to review. *Eating facilities:* coffee shop for light refreshments. *Visitors:* welcome almost anytime, booking at weekends advisable. Club and trolley hire.
e-mail: info@aigas-holidays.co.uk
website: www.aigas-holidays.co.uk

BOAT OF GARTEN. **Boat of Garten Golf and Tennis Club,** Boat of Garten PH24 3BQ (01479 831282; Fax: 01479 831523). *Location:* A9 six miles from Aviemore. Highly rated, beautiful, challenging course, designed by James Braid, cut through moorland and birch forest and set amid stunning scenery of Cairngorms National Park. 18 holes, 5876 yards, 5373 metres. S.S.S. 69. Practice net. *Green Fees:* weekdays £32.00 per round, £37.00 per day; weekends £42.00 per round, £47.00 per day. *Eating facilities:* catering facilities open 9.00am to 8.00pm, bar open from 11am daily. *Visitors:* welcome 9.30am to 5.30pm. Two tennis courts. *Society Meetings:* catered for. Professional: Ross Harrower (01479 831282; Fax: 01479 831523). Secretary: (01479 831282; Fax: 01479 831523).
e-mail: office@boatgolf.com
website: www.boatgolf.com

CARRBRIDGE. **Carrbridge Golf Club,** Inverness Road, Carrbridge PH23 3AU (08444 141415). *Location:* off A9, 27 miles south of Inverness. Moorland/parkland. 9 holes, 5402 yards. S.S.S. 68, Par 71. *Green Fees:* April-September £20.00 weekdays; £22.00 weekends. 9-hole tickets and reduced rates for Juniors. *Eating facilities:* breakfast, morning coffee, lunch, afternoon tea and dinner by arrangement. Clubhouse open April to October only. *Visitors:* always welcome. Tee booking system in operation, call first to avoid delay. *Society Meetings:* group bookings very welcome. Secretary: Mrs Katie Fenton. e-mail: katie@carrbridgegolf.co.uk
website: www.carrbridgegolf.com

CAWDOR CASTLE. **Cawdor Castle Golf Course,** Cawdor Castle, Nairn IV12 5RD (01667 404401; Fax: 01667 404674). *Location:* situated between Inverness and Nairn on the B9090 off A96. Parkland. 9 holes, 1303 yards. S.S.S. 32. *Green Fees:* £10.00 (2007). Subject to review. *Eating facilities:* licensed Courtyard Restaurant in Castle, snack bar in grounds. *Visitors:* welcome every day from 1st May to second Sunday in October, 10am to 5pm. e-mail: info@cawdorcastle.com
website: www.cawdorcastle.com

FORT AUGUSTUS. **Fort Augustus Golf Club,** Markethill, Fort Augustus PH32 4DS (01320 366660). *Location:* half-a-mile south of village on A82. Moorland course, tree lined to north, heather covered hills to the south. 9 holes (18 tees), 5379 yards. S.S.S. 67. *Green Fees:* £15.00 per round, £20.00 per day. *Eating facilities:* hot and cold snacks, lounge bar. *Visitors:* welcome anytime except Saturday afternoons from 12 noon to 4.30pm. Clubs and caddy cars for hire. *Society Meetings:* welcome, please book in advance. Secretary: Kevin Cheeseman (01320 366771) e-mail: fortaugustusgc@aol.com.

FORT WILLIAM. **Fort William Golf Club,** Torlundy, Fort William PH33 6SN (01397 704464). *Location:* north from Fort William, approx. 3 miles through town. Parkland course. 18 holes, 6217 yards, S.S.S 71. Practice area. *Green Fees:* £20.00 per round, £25.00 per day. *Eating facilities:* snacks available from the bar. *Visitors:* welcome all week except Saturday and Sunday between 8am and 11am. *Society Meetings:* welcome, discount available for parties of more than 15. Secretary: Miss Rosemary MacIntyre.

INVERNESS. **Inverness Golf Club,** The Clubhouse, Culcabock Road, Inverness IV2 3XQ (01463 239882). *Location:* one mile south of town centre. Parkland course. 18 holes, 6256 yards. S.S.S. 70. Two practice grounds. *Green Fees:* £35.00 per round, £48.00 per day. Weekly, fortnightly and monthly tickets by arrangement. Subject to review. *Eating facilities:* sandwiches, lunches, high teas and dinners served at club. *Visitors:* welcome. Pre-booking advised. Caterer: (01463 233259). Professional:(01463 231989). Club Secretary/Manager:(01463 239882; Fax: 01463 240616). e-mail: igc@freeuk.com
website: www.invernessgolfclub.co.uk

Nairn Dunbar Golf Club, Nairn

INVERNESS. **Loch Ness Golf Course,** Fairways, Castle Heather, Inverness IV2 6AA (01463 713335; Fax: 01463 712695). *Location:* on the outskirts of Inverness, heading west along new Ring Road. Parkland course with panoramic views over Inverness and Moray Firth. 27 holes. Old Course 6493 yards (yellow), 6797 yards (white); New Course 5624 yards (yellow), 5907 yards (white); 9-hole family course 1442 yards. *Green Fees:* Old and New Courses - weekdays £25.00 per round; weekends £30.00 per round. 9-hole course £10.00 per round at all times. *Eating facilities:* lounge bar, sports bar, full catering facilities. *Visitors:* welcome. Buggies and carts available. *Society Meetings:* most welcome by prior arrangement. Professional: Martin Piggot (01463 713334). Secretary: Neil D. Hampton (01463 713335; Fax: 01463 712695).
e-mail: info@golflochness.com
website: www.golflochness.com

THE APPEARANCE OF AN ASTERISK (*) AT THE END OF A CLUB OR COURSE ENTRY INDICATES THAT UP-TO-DATE INFORMATION HAS NOT BEEN SUPPLIED

INVERNESS. **Torvean Golf Club,** Glenurquhart Road, Inverness IV3 8JN (Starter: 01463 711434). *Location:* A82 towards Fort William, approximately one mile from town centre. Parkland course. 18 holes, 5799 yards, S.S.S. 69. *Green Fees:* weekdays £24.00 (Adults), weekends £28.50 (Adults). *Eating facilities:* all day catering provided year round. *Visitors:* booking preferred, especially at weekends (01463 711434; Fax 01463 711417 – Starters Office). Clubs and trolleys for hire. *Society Meetings:* discounts for parties over 10. Club Manager: Susan Menzies.
e-mail: info@torveangolfclub.com

KINGUSSIE. **Kingussie Golf Club,** Gynack Road, Kingussie PH21 1LR (01540 661600). *Location:* half a mile from Kingussie High Street, turning at Duke of Gordon. 18 holes, 5643 yards. S.S.S. 68. *Green Fees:* weekdays £26.00 per round, £34.00 per day; weekends £30.00 per round, £36.00 per day. Juniors £12.00. Weekly (seven days) £80.00. Subject to review. *Eating facilities:* bar and excellent catering. *Visitors:* welcome. *Society Meetings:* welcome at all times, book in advance. Secretary: Ian Chadburn (01540 661600).
e-mail: sec@kingussie-golf.co.uk
website: www.kingussie-golf.co.uk

NAIRN. **Nairn Dunbar Golf Club,** Lochloy Road, Nairn IV12 5AE (01667 452741; Fax: 01667 456897). *Location:* off A96, at east end of town. Championship links. 18 holes, 6765 yards. S.S.S. 74. *Green Fees:* information not available. *Eating facilities:* new spacious clubhouse with full catering and visitors facilities. *Visitors:* welcome, also groups. Secretary: Mr Scott Falconer (01667 452741; Fax: 01667 456897). Professional: David Torrance. (01667 453964).*
e-mail: secretary@nairndunbar.com
website: www.nairndunbar.com

NETHY BRIDGE. **Abernethy Golf Club,** Nethy Bridge PH25 3EB (01479 821305). *Location:* 10 miles from Aviemore lying on the B970 between Boat of Garten and Grantown-on-Spey. Delightful nine hole course close to pine woods and with commanding view of the valley of the River Spey. 9 holes, 5068 yards. S.S.S. 66. *Green Fees:* weekdays £17.00, weekend £19.00. Late weekdays £10.00, late weekend £12.00. Juniors half price. *Eating facilities:* clubhouse is unlicensed but there are full catering facilities available. *Visitors:* welcome subject to short restrictions when club competitions being held. Secretary: Mrs Janette McCool.
e-mail: info@abernethygolfclub.com
website: www.abernethygolfclub.com

NEWTONMORE. **Newtonmore Golf Club,** Golf Course Road, Newtonmore PH20 1AT (Tel & Fax: 01540 673878). *Location:* turn off A9 at Newtonmore, course in centre of village, 45 miles south of Inverness. Mainly flat course set by River Spey amidst beautiful scenery. 18 holes, 6029 yards. S.S.S. 69. Practice green. *Green Fees:* weekdays £27.00 per round, £32.00 per day; weekends £29.00 per round, £37.00 per day. Subject to review. Special midweek breaks available, apply Secretary. *Eating facilities:* full catering (except Tuesdays) and bar facilities. Locker and shower facilities. *Visitors:* welcome. *Society Meetings:* all welcome. Professional: Robert Henderson (01540 673611). Secretary: Charles Bisset (Tel & Fax: 01540 673878).

SPEAN BRIDGE. **Spean Bridge Golf Club,** Station Road, Spean Bridge PH34 4EU. *Location:* on main A82, eight miles north of Fort William. Wooded course set on the hillside, full view of Nevis Range ski slopes and Ben Nevis. 9 holes, 2271 yards. S.S.S. 63. *Green Fees:* £15.00 day ticket. *Eating facilities:* Hotel nearby. *Visitors:* welcome, tees reserved Sundays 12 noon to 4pm. *Society Meetings:* all welcome. Secretary: K. Dalziel (07710 105478).

Lanarkshire

AIRDRIE. **Airdrie Golf Club,** Glenmavis Road, Airdrie ML6 0PQ (01236 762195). *Location:* one mile north of Airdrie Cross. 18 holes, 5772 yards. S.S.S. 68. *Green Fees:* information not available. *Eating facilities:* available. *Visitors:* welcome only on application to the Secretary. Professional: S. McLean (01236 754360). Secretary: W. Campbell.

AIRDRIE. **Easter Moffat Golf Club,** Plains, Airdrie ML6 8NP (01236 842878; Fax: 01236 842904). *Location:* three miles east of Airdrie on old Edinburgh Road. 18 holes, 6221 yards. S.S.S. 70. Practice ground. *Green Fees:* £23.00 per round, £35.00 per day. *Eating facilities:* bar and dining room. *Visitors:* welcome except weekends. *Society Meetings:* welcome. Professional: Graham King (01236 843015). Secretary: Gordon Miller (01236 620972).

BELLSHILL. **Bellshill Golf Club,** Community Road, Orbiston, Bellshill ML4 2RZ (01698 745124). *Location:* Bellshill to Motherwell road, turn right. Parkland course. 18 holes, 5852 yards. S.S.S. 69. *Green Fees:* May to October, midweek £20.00 per round, £25.00 per day, juniors (accompanied by adult) £5.00 per round; weekends and Public Holidays £30.00 per round, £35.00 per day, juniors (with adult) £10.00. November to March £12.00 per round. Half price rates for students. Midweek packages for visiting parties of 8 or more: two rounds of golf plus coffee, soup and rolls, and high tea £35.00; one round of golf plus coffee and a meal £25.00. All prices subject to review. *Eating facilities:* by prior arrangement with Clubmaster. *Visitors:* welcome, Sundays by prior arrangement, parties by prior application (not competition days). *Society Meetings:* by prior arrangement with Administrator (A. Coghlan) or Secretary. Secretary: Tom McLaughlin.

BIGGAR. **Biggar Golf Club,** Broughton Road, Biggar ML12 6HA (01899 220618 (Clubhouse)). *Location:* from Edinburgh A702, from Glasgow A74 or M8, turn off at Newhouse. Flat, scenic parkland course. 18 holes, 5416 yards. S.S.S. 66. *Green Fees:* information not available. *Eating facilities:* all day licence, full catering, snacks only on Tuesdays. *Visitors:* unrestricted, casual dress – no jeans. All weather tennis courts and caravan park. Buggies and carts available. *Society Meetings:* welcome, early reservation essential. Secretary: Tom Rodger. Tee Reservations: (01899 220319). *

CARLUKE. **Carluke Golf Club,** Maudslie Road, Hallcraig, Carluke ML8 5HG (01555 771070). *Location:* Carluke Cross, go west along Clyde Street for two miles. Parkland course. 18 holes, 5800 yards. S.S.S. 68. Practice area. *Green Fees:* information not available. *Eating facilities:* available. *Visitors:* till 4pm weekdays, no visitors weekends. Tuition. *Society Meetings:* by written application to the Secretary, restriction on numbers. Professional: Craig Ronald (01555 751053). Administration: Tom Fraser (01555 770574). website: www.carlukegolfclub.com

CARNWATH. **Carnwath Golf Club,** 1 Main Street, Carnwath ML11 8JX (01555 840251; Fax: 01555 841070). *Location:* on main Ayr/Edinburgh Road. Fairly hilly inland course. 18 holes, 5963 yards. S.S.S. 69. *Green Fees:* weekdays £20.00 per round, £30.00 per two rounds; Sundays £26.00 per round, £36.00 per two rounds. Subject to review. *Eating facilities:* lounge bar and dining room daily. *Visitors:* welcome. Not Saturdays or after 4pm weekdays. Sunday with prior booking. *Society Meetings:* catered for by prior arrangement. Secretary: Mrs L. McPate (01555 840251). e-mail: carnwathgc@hotmail.co.uk

COATBRIDGE. **Drumpellier Golf Club,** Drumpellier Avenue, Coatbridge ML5 1RX (01236 424139). *Location:* one mile from town centre. Parkland, wooded. 18 holes, 6227 yards. S.S.S. 70. Practice area. *Green Fees:* £35.00 per round, £50.00 per day weekdays. *Eating facilities:* available seven days. *Visitors:* welcome daily except weekends. *Society Meetings:* catered for by arrangement. Professional: I. Taylor. Secretary: J.M. Craig (01236 424139; Fax: 01236 428723). e-mail: administrator@drumpelliergc freeserve.co.uk

DOUGLAS WATER. **Douglas Water Golf Club,** Ayr Road, Rigside, Lanark (01555 880361). *Location:* five miles south of Lanark on A70, Junction 11 from M74. Hilly course, small greens, undulating fairways. 9 holes, 2947 yards, 2694 metres. S.S.S. 69. *Green Fees:* information not provided. *Visitors:* welcome any time, except Saturdays because of competitions. *Society Meetings:* contact Secretary. Secretary: D. Hogg (01698 882432).

EAST KILBRIDE. **Torrance House Golf Club,** Calderglen Country Park, Strathaven Road, East Kilbride G75 0QZ (013552 49720). *Location:* East Kilbride boundary on main Strathaven road. Parkland. 18 holes, 6423 yards. S.S.S. 71. Practice area. *Green Fees:* information not available. *Eating facilities:* private clubhouse. *Visitors:* welcome midweek only. *Society Meetings:* details on request. Secretary: M.D. McKerlie (013552 49720). Booking Office: (01355 248638).*

GARTCOSH. **Mount Ellen Golf Club,** Johnstone Road, Gartcosh, Glasgow G69 8EY (01236 872277; Fax: 01236 872249). *Location:* approximately six miles north-east of Glasgow, near old Gartcosh steelworks. Parkland. 18 holes, 5525 yards. S.S.S. 66. *Green Fees:* information not available. *Eating facilities:* bar and full catering service. *Visitors:* welcome weekdays from 9am to 4pm, no weekend visitors. Carts available for hire. *Society Meetings:* weekdays by arrangement with Secretary. Professional: I. Bilsborough (01236 872632). Secretary: Archie Wylie (01236 434310).

HAMILTON. **Hamilton Golf Club,** Carlisle Road, Ferniegair, Hamilton ML3 7UE (01698 282872). *Location:* off M74 Hamilton turn-off, one and a half miles up Larkhall road. Parkland course. 18 holes, 6500 yards. S.S.S. 71. *Green Fees:* £35.00 per round, day ticket £45.00. *Eating facilities:* meals must be ordered. *Visitors:* by arrangement, please contact Secretary. *Society Meetings:* visitors by arrangement, contact Secretary. Professional: Derek Wright (01698 282872). Secretary: Graham Chapman (01698 282872; Fax: 01698 204650).

HAMILTON. **Strathclyde Park Golf Club,** Motehill, Hamilton ML3 6BY (01698 429350). *Location:* Hamilton/Motherwell exit off M74 to roundabout second exit East Kilbride, to new roundabout second exit, to third roundabout third exit straight ahead, to golf course passing ice rink on left hand side. Wooded parkland course surrounded by race course on one side and nature reserve on other. 9 holes, 3128 yards. S.S.S. 70. Large practice area, putting green and driving range (24 bays). *Green Fees:* weekdays £4.00, Juniors/Senior Citizens £2.00; weekends & public holidays £4.60, Juniors/Senior Citizens £2.30. (Subject to review). *Eating facilities:* bar within complex. *Visitors:* welcome, same day booking system in operation. Course opens 7am Summer, 8am Winter. *Society Meetings:* welcome by arrangement through management (01698 429350). Professional: W. Walker. Secretary: K. Will (01698 429350).

LANARK. **Kames Golf Club,** Eastend, Cleghorn ML11 8NR (01555 870015; Fax: 01555 870022). *Location:* situated on the A721 between Carluke and Carnwath. Home of the championship Mouse Valley Golf Course, 18 holes, 6300 yards. S.S.S. 72, and the delightful Kames Course, 9-holes, 2500 yards par 33 (extending to 18 holes summer 2006.) *Green Fees:* information not available. *Eating facilities:* full bar and catering. *Visitors:* welcome. *Society Meetings:* all welcome, weekend bookings taken.*
e-mail: info@kames-golf-club.com
website: www.kames-golf-club.com

LANARK **Lanark Golf Club,** The Moor, Whitelees Road, Lanark ML11 7RX (01555 663219). *Location:* off A73. Tough moorland course. 18 holes, 6306 yards. S.S.S. 71. Also 9-hole course. Two practice grounds. *Green Fees:* weekdays £40.00 per round, £50.00 per day. 2007 prices, subject to review. *Eating facilities:* full catering and bar. *Visitors:* welcome daily until 4pm, no visitors weekends. *Society Meetings:* groups of 8/40 and over catered for Monday to Friday. Professional: Alan White (01555 661456). Secretary: G.H. Cuthill.

LANARK. **Mouse Valley Golf Course,** East End, Cleghorn, Lanark ML11 (01555 870015; Fax: 01555 870022). *Location:* 5 miles from Carluke on A721 Peebles Road. Pay as you play. Links style course, inland undulating terrain. Mouse Water (river) runs through the course. Two courses - Mouse Valley 18 holes, 6376 yards, Par 70 and Kames course - 9 holes, 2538 yards, Par 33 Practice ground. *Green Fees:* information not available. *Eating facilities:* full bar and catering. *Visitors:* welcome, no restrictions. *Society Meetings:* welcome at all times. Company days. Contact: (01555 870015).*

LARKHALL. **Larkhall Golf Club,** Burnhead Road, Larkhall ML9 2AA (01698 889597). *Location:* on A74, close to M74. Parkland. 9 holes, 6432 yards. S.S.S. 70. *Green Fees:* information not provided. *Eating facilities:* bar, lunch only on Saturdays. *Visitors:* welcome, but check beforehand; not Saturdays. Secretary: Malcolm Mallinson; Booking Office (01698 881113).

LEADHILLS. **Leadhills Golf Club,** The Lowthers, Horners Place, Leadhills, Biggar ML12 6AR (01659 74456). *Location:* seven miles south of Abington on B797. This short but testing course is the highest in Scotland. 9 holes, 4404 yards. S.S.S. 64. *Green Fees:* per round/day – adults £10.00, Juniors £7.00. *Eating facilities:* hotel nearby. *Visitors:* welcome any time. *Society Meetings:* welcome. Secretary: Harry Shaw (01659 74456).
e-mail: harry@glenfranka.fsnet.co.uk

LESMAHAGOW. **Hollandbush Golf Club,** Acretophead, Lesmahagow ML11 0JS (01555 893484). *Location:* off M74 (Junction 9). Golf course is between Lesmahagow and Coalburn. 18 holes, 6246 yards. S.S.S. 70. Practice area. *Green Fees:* information not available. *Eating facilities:* meals at club. *Visitors:* welcome without restriction. *Society Meetings:* catered for. Starter's Office (01555 893646). Secretary: Robert Lynch (01555 893484). *

MOTHERWELL. **Colville Park Golf Club,** Jerviston Estate, Merry Street, Motherwell ML1 4UG (01698 263017; Fax: 01698 230418). *Location:* one mile from town centre and train station (Merry Street, Motherwell). Parkland, wooded first six holes. 18 holes, 6301 yards. S.S.S. 71. *Green Fees:* information not available. *Eating facilities:* full facilities. *Visitors:* welcome between 11am and 3pm Mondays to Thursdays only. Advance booking not required. *Society Meetings:* by prior written arrangement, weekdays only. £27.00 day ticket. Professional Shop: (01698 265779). Secretary: Leslie Innes (01698 262808).*

MOTHERWELL. **Dalziel Park Golf & Country Club,** 100 Hagen Drive, Motherwell ML1 5RZ (01698 862862; Fax: 01698 862863). *Location:* four miles from Motherwell with good access to M74 and M8 at Junction 6. Midway between Glasgow and Edinburgh. Wooded Parkland. 18 holes, 6300 yards, S.S.S. 70. 15 bay floodlit driving range and extensive dry and outdoor sports facilities. *Green Fees:* information not provided. *Eating facilities:* Italian and Scottish restaurants, bars and lounges. 10 bedrooms, conference facilities and all functions catered for in Country Club. *Visitors:* all welcome, only restricted on Saturday morning (during Men's medal day). *Society Meetings:* welcome at all times. Secretary: Russell Weir (01698 862862: Fax: 01698 862863).

THE APPEARANCE OF AN ASTERISK (*) AT THE END OF A CLUB OR COURSE ENTRY INDICATES THAT UP-TO-DATE INFORMATION HAS NOT BEEN SUPPLIED

SHOTTS. **Shotts Golf Club,** Blairhead, Benhar Road, Shotts ML7 5BJ (01501 822658). *Location:* off M8 at Junction 5, one and a half miles south. Semi-flat moorland/wooded course. 18 holes, 6204 yards. S.S.S. 70. Practice area, professional tuition. *Green Fees:* £20.00 per round, £28.00 per day. *Eating facilities:* full catering and bar service. *Visitors:* welcome anytime except Saturdays, Sundays (prior booking needed) or Public Holidays. *Society Meetings:* weekdays only (not Public Holidays) by arrangement. Professional: John Strachan (01501 822658). Secretary: George Stoddart (01501 825868). e-mail: info@shottsgolfclub.co.uk website: www.shottsgolfclub.co.uk

STRATHAVEN. **Strathaven Golf Club,** Overton Avenue, Glasgow Road, Strathaven ML10 6NL. *Location:* on A726 on outskirts of town. 18 holes, 6250 yards. S.S.S. 71. *Green Fees:* please contact Secretary for information. *Eating facilities:* full catering and bar. *Visitors:* welcome weekdays, casual visitors before 4pm; party bookings Tuesdays only by prior arrangement. Professional: Stuart Kerr (01357 521812). General Manager: I.F. Neil (01357 520421).

UDDINGSTON. **Calderbraes Golf Club,** 57 Roundknowe Road, Uddingston G71 7TS (01698 813425). *Location:* at end of M74, overlooking Calderpark Zoo. 9 holes, 3425 yards. S.S.S. 67. *Green Fees:* day ticket £13.00. *Eating facilities:* catering available at all times. *Visitors:* welcome weekdays only; must be off course by 5pm. *Society Meetings:* welcome, contact Secretary. Secretary: S. McGuigan,

WISHAW. **Wishaw Golf Club,** 55 Cleland Road, Wishaw ML2 7PH (01698 372869). *Location:* 400 yards from Wishaw Main Street at West Cross. Tree-lined parkland course. 18 holes, 5999 yards. S.S.S. 69. Practice area. *Green Fees:* weekdays £25.00 per round, £35.00 per day; Sundays £29.00 per round; £39.00 per day. *Eating facilities:* full catering, two bars, and dining room. *Visitors:* welcome before 4pm weekdays, after 10.30am Sundays, no visitors Saturdays. *Society Meetings:* by application. Professional: Stuart Adair (01698 358247). General Manager: James W. Douglas (01698 357480). e-mail: jwdouglas@btconnect.com

Perth & Kinross

ALYTH. **Glenisla Golf Centre,** Pitcrocknie, Alyth PH11 8JJ (01828 632445; Fax: 01828 633749). *Location:* five miles east of Blairgowrie on the B954. Parkland, with undulating, rolling fairways, and featuring over 40 bunkers and 5 water hazards. 'One of Scotland's favourite courses' (Insider Business Magazine Top 500 Survey, March 2001). 18 holes, 6402 yards. S.S.S. 71. *Green Fees:* information not available. *Eating facilities:* superbly appointed, fully licensed clubhouse with panoramic bar and restaurant overlooking the course. *Visitors:* always welcome. Conference and Function facilities and on site B&B and self-catering cottages available. *Society Meetings:* always welcome. Golf Administrator: Ewan Wilson.
e-mail: info@golf-glenisla.co.uk
website: www.golf-glenisla.co.uk

AUCHTERARDER. **Gleneagles Hotel Golf Courses,** Auchterarder PH3 1NF (Golf Office: 01764 694469; Fax: 01764 694383). *Location:* 20 miles south of Perth, 20 miles north of Stirling. Gleneagles offers two moorland 18 hole courses and a third parkland/moorland course. King's Course: 6125 yards par 68; Queen's Course: 5660 yards par 68; PGA Centenary Course: 18 holes, 6141 yards S.S.S. 72 and a 9 hole course, The Wee Course: 1481 yards par 27. *Green Fees:* information not available. *Eating facilities:* at The Dormy Clubhouse (Bar & Restaurant) and The Gleneagles Hotel. *Visitors:* welcome. Professional: Russell Smith. Hotel General Manager: Patrick Elsmie (01764 662231). Golf Contact: (01764 694469; Fax: 01764 662134).*

ABERFELDY. **Aberfeldy Golf Club,** Taybridge Road, Aberfeldy PH15 2BH (01887 820535). *Location:* A9 from Ballinluig. Scenic riverside course. 18 holes, 5283 yards. S.S.S. 66, Par 68. *Green Fees:* information not provided. *Eating facilities:* high teas, lunches, etc. *Visitors:* welcome anytime. Buggy and trolley hire. *Society Meetings:* catered for. Secretary: (01887 820535).

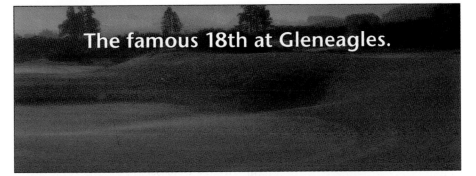

The famous 18th at Gleneagles.

And the other one.

And the other one.

There is only one place in Scotland that can boast three championship golf courses. It's a place where you don't even have to stay to play; a place where there's a spa, riding, fishing, shooting and off-road driving all available amongst some of Scotland's most stunning scenery. Not to mention a choice of four restaurants including the Michelin starred 'Andrew Fairlie at Gleneagles'. That place is Gleneagles. (There is no other like it.) Book online or call us free on 0800 328 4010 for more information.

THE GLENEAGLES HOTEL

Auchterarder, Perthshire, Scotland PH3 1NF. Just 1 hour from Edinburgh / Glasgow.

Telephone + 44 (0) 1764 662231 Fax + 44 (0) 1764 662134   www.gleneagles.com

The GLENEAGLES word and EAGLE Device are trade marks.   A member of *The Leading Hotels of the World*   Ref: GOLF GUIDE

AUCHTERARDER. **Auchterarder Golf Club,** Orchil Road, Auchterarder PH3 1LS (Tel & Fax: 01764 662804). *Location:* off A9 to southwest of town, next to Gleneagles. Flat parkland, part wooded. 18 holes, 5778 yards. S.S.S. 68. Small practice area. *Green Fees:* weekdays £27.50 per round, £39.00 per day; weekends £33.00 per round, £50.00 per day; weekdays weekly ticket (one round per day) £85.00. *Eating facilities:* lounge, dining room, bar. *Visitors:* welcome without reservation except major competition days. *Society Meetings:* welcome, must book 3 months in advance. Professional: Gavin Baxter (01764 663711). Secretary: W.M. Campbell (01764 662804; Fax: 01764 664423).
e-mail: secretary@auchterardergolf.co.uk
website: www.auchterardergolf.co.uk

BLAIR ATHOLL. **Blair Atholl Golf Club,** Blair Atholl, Pitlochry PH18 5TG (01796 481407; Fax: 01796 481751). *Location:* off A9 Perth/Inverness Road, down Invertilt Road. Flat parkland. 9 holes, 5816 yards, 5322 metres. S.S.S. 68. *Green Fees:* weekdays £21.00 per day, weekends £23.00 per day, weekly ticket £133.50. All rates include insurance. *Eating facilities:* meals/bar. *Visitors:* welcome at all times. Carts and clubs available. *Society Meetings:* by arrangement with Secretary. Secretary: D.A. Boon.

BLAIRGOWRIE. **The Alyth Golf Club,** Pitcrocknie, Alyth, Blairgowrie PH11 8HF (01828 632268; Fax: 01828 633491). *Location:* five miles from Blairgowrie on B954. Parkland/heathland course with interesting dog leg Par 4 5th played to a plateau green with out-of-bounds on right. 18 holes, 6205 yards, 5676 metres. S.S.S. 71. Large practice area. *Green Fees:*

information not available. *Eating facilities:* all day catering and bar. *Visitors:* welcome, phone 01828 632411 six days ahead. *Society Meetings:* welcome, prior booking essential. Professional: Tom Melville (01828 632411). Secretary: Jim Docherty (01828 632268; Fax: 01828 633491).*
e-mail: enquiries@alythgolf.co.uk
website: www.alythgolfclub.co.uk

BLAIRGOWRIE. **Blairgowrie Golf Club,** Golf Course Road, Rosemount, Blairgowrie PH10 6LG (01250 872622; Fax: 01250 875451). Location: take A923 out of Perth, turn right at "Rosemount" sign. Gently undulating heathland. Rosemount Course: 18 holes, 6590 yards. S.S.S. 72. Lansdowne Course: 18 holes, 6834 yards. S.S.S. 74. Wee Course: 9 holes, 4704 yards. S.S.S. 63. Two practice grounds. Green Fees: on application. Eating facilities: full catering available. Visitors: welcome by appointment. Handicap Certificate required. Society Meetings: catered for by application to Office. Professional: Charles Dernie (01250 873116). Secretary/Manager: David Swarbrick (01250 872622).
e-mail: office@theblairgowriegolfclub.co.uk
website: www.theblairgowriegolfclub.co.uk

BLAIRGOWRIE. **Dalmunzie Golf Course,** Spittal O' Glenshee, Blairgowrie PH10 7QE (01250 885226). *Location:* A93 Blairgowrie to Braemar road, left at Spittal O' Glenshee. A small well-kept hill course amid glorious scenery. 9 holes, 2099 yards. *Green Fees:* £14.00 per day. Under 8 free, 8–16 half price (we like young golfers). *Eating facilities:* restaurant facilities at Dalmunzie Hotel. Bar. *Visitors:* welcome without reservation. Self-catering cottages available. *Society Meetings:* catered for. Secretary: Simon Winton

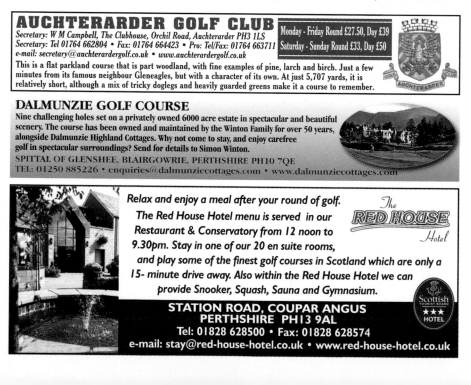

The Blairgowrie
GOLF CLUB

1889

The Blairgowrie Golf Club was founded as a private members' club in 1889 and is situated in the heart of the magnificent Perthshire countryside. The Club features the renowned Rosemount and Lansdowne championship courses plus a very attractive 9-hole course set in heather-lined avenues of pine and silver birch.

The magnificent clubhouse is synonymous with Blairgowrie Golf Club and is rightly acclaimed in all four corners of the golfing world. It offers visitors a warm welcome at the bar and good food in fitting surroundings. A mouth-watering selection of appetizing dishes is available, with special menus for visiting parties available on request. Our club steward and his staff are on hand to dispense drinks from our well stocked gantry.

The courses of The Blairgowrie Golf Club are virtually unique and have that wonderful charm found at very few courses, where each hole is unaffected and untouched by another. The combination of heathland and woodland provides each hole with a peace and tranquillity completely unspoilt by preceding or following games.

The Rosemount Course, described by Tom Morris as, "The most beautiful inland green I have ever seen", certainly lives up to its reputation. Rosemount has played host to a number of prestigious professional and amateur tournaments. Rosemount was voted 11th best course to play in Scotland by the readers of Scotland's premier golf magazine.

The Lansdowne Course is more modern than the Rosemount course in layout, and offers a more challenging test. It was designed by the respected partnership of Peter Allis and Dave Thomas and officially opened in 1979. The course provides a challenging but pleasurable test for all levels of golfer.

The Wee Course formed part of the original layout designed by Dr Alistair McKenzie of Augusta National and Cypress Point fame. The nine-hole layout is heathland in character, comprising 4 par 3s and 5 par 4s, and provides a delightful and charming contrast to Rosemount and Lansdowne.

The Blairgowrie Golf Club
**Golf Course Road, Rosemount,
Blairgowrie, Perthshire PH10 6LG
Tel: 01250 872622 • Fax: 01250 875451
e-mail: office@theblairgowriegolfclub.co.uk • www.theblairgowriegolfclub.co.uk**

BLAIRGOWRIE. **Strathmore Golf Centre,** Leroch, Alyth, Blairgowrie (01828 633322; Fax: 01828 633533). *Location:* one mile south of Alyth off A926 Blairgowrie to Kirriemuir road. Rolling parkland course with magnificent views over the valley of Strathmore. Two courses - Rannaleroch Course: 18 holes, 6454 yards, 5901 metres. Par 72. S.S.S. 72; Leitfie Links Course: 9 holes, 1719 yards, 1572 metres. Par 29. S.S.S. 29. Driving range adjacent. *Green Fees:* information not provided. *Eating facilities:* friendly clubhouse with bar and restaurant. *Visitors:* always welcome. *Society Meetings:* always welcome.
e-mail: enquiries@strathmoregolf.com
website: www.strathmoregolf.com

CALLANDER. **Callander Golf Club,** Aveland Road, Callander FK17 8EN (01877 330090; Fax: 01877 330062). *Location:* M9 Stirling, Junction 10 Crianlarich exit to A84 to Callander. Parkland, partly wooded, with panoramic views. 18 holes, 5185 yards. S.S.S. 65. Small practice ground and putting green. *Green Fees:* from £22.00. P.O.A. *Eating facilities:* bar snacks, lunches, high teas, dinners by arrangement. *Visitors:* welcome, no restrictions. Handicap Certificate required Sundays. *Society Meetings:* welcome, book in advance. Professional: A. Martin (01877 330975). Secretary: Miss E. MacDonald (01877 330090; Fax: 01877 330062).
e-mail: callandergolf@btconnect.com
website: www.callandergolfclub.co.uk

CRIEFF. **Comrie Golf Club,** Laggan Braes, Comrie PH6 2LR (01764 670055). *Location:* six miles west of Crieff on A85 at east end of village. Parkland, wooded course with two long and tricky Par 3 holes (3rd and 5th) and well guarded Par 5 (6th). 9 holes, 6040 yards.

S.S.S. 70. *Green Fees:* information not available. *Eating facilities:* light refreshments and meals during summer months. *Visitors:* welcome at all times. Club Medals - Monday 1pm and 4.30pm, Ladies Tuesdays 1pm. *Society Meetings:* always welcome. Secretary: Spike Gaden (01764 670055).*
e-mail: enquiries@comriegolf.co.uk

CRIEFF. **Crieff Golf Club,** Ferntower, Perth Road, Crieff PH7 3LR (01764 652397; Fax: 01764 655096). *Location:* A85 north-east outskirts of Crieff. Ferntower Course - 18 holes, 6402 yards. S.S.S. 72. Dornock Course - 9 holes, 2386 yards. S.S.S. 63. Two practice areas. *Green Fees:* information not provided. *Eating facilities:* full restaurant facilities by arrangement (phone 01764 652397) and bar snacks. *Visitors:* welcome with reservation, prior arrangement advisable by phone. *Society Meetings:* book by phone (01764 652909) and confirm in writing. Professional: David Murchie (01764 652909; Fax: 01764 655096). Managing/Secretary: J.S. Miller
website: www.crieffgolf.co.uk

CRIEFF. **Culcrieff Golf Club,** Ferntower Road, Crieff PH7 3LQ (01764 651615; Fax: 01764 653087). *Location:* set high in the Strathearn Valley. A85 from Perth, A822 from Stirling. Parkland course. 18 holes, 4876 yards, S.S.S. 64, Par 66. 8-bay driving range, practice green, 6-hole pitch and putt course. *Green Fees:* information not available. *Eating facilities:* licensed clubhouse with restaurant. *Visitors:* welcome. *Society Meetings:* welcome with advance reservation. Contact Andrew Devine for details.*
e-mail: enquiries@crieffhydro.com
website: www.crieffhydro.com.

CRIEFF. **Foulford Inn Golf Course,** Foulford Inn, Sma' Glen, Crieff PH7 3LN (Tel & Fax: 01764 652407). *Location*: 5 miles north of Crieff on the A822 in the direction of Dunkeld. Upland course with water hazards. 9 holes, 916 yards, S.S.S. 27. *Green Fees*: £5.00 per round, £8.00 per day. (under review). *Eating facilities*: bar/restaurant. *Visitors*: welcome anytime, accommodation available in Inn. Course free to residents. *Society Meetings*: welcome, on application. Secretary: B.A. Beaumont.
e-mail: foulford@btconnect.com
website: www.foulfordinn.co.uk

CRIEFF. **Muthill Golf Club,** Peat Road, Muthill, Crieff PH5 2DA (01764 681523; Fax: 01764 681557). *Location:* two miles from Crieff at entrance to Muthill. Parkland course with magnificent views. 9 holes, 4700 yards. S.S.S. 63. *Green Fees:* information not available. *Eating facilities:* full meals service available. *Visitors:* no restrictions except after 5pm Wednesday and Thursdays (club competitions). Trolleys available. *Society Meetings:* welcome. Secretary: Jacq Scott (01764 681523; Fax: 01764 681557).*
e-mail: muthillgolfclub@lineone.net

DUNBLANE. **Dunblane New Golf Club,** Perth Road, Dunblane FK15 0LJ (01786 821521; Fax: 01786 821522). *Location:* two miles off main road M9 at Fourways Roundabout. Parkland/undulating. 18 holes, 5936 yards. S.S.S. 69. *Green Fees:* £30.00 per round, £40.00 per day. *Eating facilities:* available seven days a week. *Visitors:* welcome, 9.30am-12 noon, 2.30pm-4pm. *Society Meetings:* catered for weekdays only except Tuesdays. Professional: R.M. Jamieson (01786 821521; Fax: 01786 821522). Secretary: Roddy Morrison (01786 821527; Fax: 01786 825066).

DUNKELD. **Dunkeld and Birnam Golf Club,** Fungarth, Dunkeld PH8 0ES (01350 727524; Fax: 01350 728660). *Location:* one mile north of Dunkeld on the A923. Heathland course with panoramic views. 18 holes, 5508 yards. S.S.S. 67. Practice area. *Green Fees:* on application. *Eating facilities:* bar and full catering facilities. *Visitors:* welcome; buggies available. *Society Meetings:* catered for. Secretary: (01350 727524: Fax: 01350 728660).
e-mail: secretary-dunkeld@tiscali.co.uk

DUNNING. **Dunning Golf Club,** Rollo Park, Station Road, Dunning PH2 0QX (01764 684747). *Location:* 10 miles south-west of Perth, two miles from A9. Parkland, gently undulating. 9 holes, 4885 yards. S.S.S. 63. Small practice area. *Green Fees:* £18.00 per round. *Eating facilities:* tea/ coffee, soft drinks, snacks. Meals can be arranged with the Dunning Hotel at a 10% discount on production of a visitor's ticket. *Visitors:* welcome, no restrictions apart from club competitions. *Society Meetings:* welcome weekdays and most Sundays. Secretary: A. D. Cantlay (01738 812844).

DUNNING. **Whitemoss Golf Club,** Whitemoss Road, Dunning PH2 0GX (01738 730300; Fax: 01738 730490). *Location:* 10 miles south-west of Perth, two miles from A9. Parkland course. 18 holes, 5968 yards, S.S.S. 69. Practice range, chipping bunkers, practice net and putting green. *Green Fees:* Information not available. *Eating facilities*: New clubhouse with restaurant and bar. *Visitors:* welcome all the time, on medal days after 10am. *Society Meetings:* Welcome, after 10am on medal days. Tuition on request. Shower facilities. Secretary: Victor Westwood (01738 730300).*

KENMORE. **Taymouth Castle Golf Course,** Kenmore, by Aberfeldy PH15 2NT (01887 830228). *Location:* six miles west of Aberfeldy. Parkland set in scenic mountain terrain. 18 holes, 6066 yards. S.S.S. 69. Practice area. *Green Fees:* £25.00 per round, £40.00 per day weekdays; £30.00 per round, £50.00 per day weekends. *Eating facilities:* restaurant and bar. *Visitors:* welcome, tee reservations necessary (phone or letter). Tuition available, motorised buggies. *Society Meetings:* parties welcome; catered for by previous arrangement only. PGA Professional: Gavin Dott (01887 830228).
e-mail: taymouthcastlegolf@hotmail.com

THE APPEARANCE OF AN ASTERISK (*) AT THE END OF A CLUB OR COURSE ENTRY INDICATES THAT UP-TO-DATE INFORMATION HAS NOT BEEN SUPPLIED

KENMORE. **Kenmore Golf Course,** Mains of Taymouth, Kenmore, Aberfeldy PH15 2HN (01887 830226; Fax: 01887 830775). *Location:* west off A9 at Ballinluig on A827, six and a half miles west of Aberfeldy through village of Kenmore on RHS. Testing well kept course on natural undulating terrain, lovely scenery and first class facilities. 9 holes, 6052 yards, 5600 metres. S.S.S. 70. Practice facilities, putting green. *Green Fees:* weekdays 9 holes £15.00, 18 holes £20.00; weekends 9 holes £17.00, 18 holes £25.00. Weekly Ticket £75.00. *Eating facilities:* full bar and restaurant facilities in pleasant surroundings. *Visitors:* welcome anytime. Cottages to let (self-catering included). Pro shop; club and trolley hire; changing and shower facilities. *Society Meetings:* all welcome, please book. Secretary: Robin Menzies.
e-mail: info@taymouth.co.uk
website: www.taymouth.co.uk

KILLIN. **Killin Golf Club,** Killin FK21 8TX (01567 820312). *Location:* west end of Loch Tay. Hilly parkland amongst beautiful scenery. 9 holes, 2510 yards. S.S.S. 65. Small practice area includes bunker and net. *Green Fees:* £18.00 per round (under review). *Eating facilities:* available all day. *Visitors:* welcome. *Society Meetings:* catered for by arrangement. Secretary: Steve Edwards (07703 069084).
e-mail: bookings@killingolfclub.co.uk
website: www.killingolfclub.co.uk

KINNESSWOOD. **Bishopshire Golf Club,** Kinnesswood, By Kinross KY13 9HX. *Location:* take road to Glenrothes from M90, three miles. Course has panoramic views overlooking Loch Leven. 10 holes, 4830 yards, 2268 metres. S.S.S. 63. *Green Fees:* information not provided. *Eating facilities:* by arrangement or available at the hotel 400 yards away. *Visitors:* welcome, no restrictions. *Society Meetings:* by arrangement. Secretary: Ian Davidson (01592 773224).

KINROSS. **Kinross Golf Courses,** owned and operated in conjunction with The Green Hotel and The Windlestrae, The Muirs, Kinross KY13 8AS (01577 863407). *Location:* turn left in Kinross off M90 Junction 6, courses 500 yards on right. Set in beautiful unspoilt parkland bordering Loch Leven. Two courses: Montgomery 18 holes, 6452 yards, 5900 metres. S.S.S. 72; Bruce 18 holes, 6231 yards, 5698 metres. S.S.S. 71. Practice ground. *Green Fees:* weekdays £27.00-£32.00 per round, £38.00-£48.00 per day; weekends £37.00-£42.00 per round, £48.00-£58.00 per day. 50% discount to all hotel residents. *Eating facilities:* in clubhouse, Green Hotel or The Windlestrae. *Visitors:* welcome any time. Accommodation and leisure facilities available. *Society Meetings:* welcome by prior arrangement. Professional: Greg Sporran (01577 865125). Secretary: Eileen Gray (01577 863407; Fax: 01577 863180).
e-mail: bookings@golfkinross.com
website: www.golfkinross.com

MILNATHORT. **Milnathort Golf Club Ltd,** South Street, Milnathort KY13 9XA (01577 864069). *Location:* one mile north of Kinross, M90 Junction 6 (north) or Junction 7 (south). Undulating inland course with lush fairways and excellent greens, with the addition of extra trees around the margins along with current plantations. Strategically placed copses of trees require acurate tee shots. The course is being made more interesting by the addition of extra tees/greens for some holes. 9 holes, 5973 yards. S.S.S. 69. Practice ground/green. *Green Fees:* weekdays £15.00 per round, £22.00 per day; weekends £17.00 per round, £25.00 per day. 9 hole sundowner ticket £8.00 weekends, £7.00 weekdays (subject to review). *Eating facilities:* full bar available, catering by arrangement. *Visitors:* welcome but suggest you phone. Dress code. *Society Meetings:* must be booked in advance. Secretary: via Club House.

PLEASE MENTION **THE GOLF GUIDE** WHEN YOU WRITE
OR PHONE TO ENQUIRE ABOUT CLUBS OR ACCOMMODATION

PERTH. **Craigie Hill Golf Club (1982) Ltd,** Cherrybank, Perth PH2 0NE (01738 624377). *Location:* at west end of town, easy access from M90 and A9. Parkland course with stunning view of Perth and surrounding hills. 18 holes, 5386 yards. S.S.S. 67. Practice ground and putting green. *Green Fees:* information not available. *Eating facilities:* dining room, full catering facilities and lounge bar. *Visitors:* welcome Mondays to Fridays; Sundays by arrangement. *Society Meetings:* catered for by written application in first instance. Car park. Professional: Kris Esson (01738 622644). Administration: (01738 620829).*
e-mail: admin@craigiehill.co.uk

PERTH. **King James VI Golf Club,** Moncreiffe Island, Perth PH2 8NR (01738 625170). *Location:* situated on Island in River Tay, access by Footbridge alongside railway from Tay Street, Perth. Flat parkland course, surrounded by River Tay. 18 holes, 6038 yards. S.S.S. 69. Practice nets. *Green Fees:* weekdays £24.00 per round, £32.00 per day; weekends £26.00 per round, £34.00 per day. April/July/October £15.00 per round, £20.00 per day. *Eating facilities:* full catering. *Visitors:* welcome, phone for reservation, no visitors on Saturday mornings. Carts available. *Society Meetings:* catered for by prior booking. Fully stocked golf shop. Professional: Andrew Crerar (01738 632460). Secretary: (Tel & Fax: 01738 445132).
e-mail: mansec@kingjamesvi.com
website: www.kingjamesvi.com

PERTH. **North Inch Golf Course.** Hay Street, Perth. *Location:* on the historic North Inch, beside the River Tay. A9 entering Perth, follow signs for Bell's Sports Centre, Hay Street. Parkland course with tight greens guarded by well placed bunkers. Truly lovely setting offering a subtle and mature challenge, starting close to city centre. 18 holes, 5500 yards. S.S.S. 66. *Green Fees:* information available by calling Starter (01738 636481). *Eating facilities:* Sport Active Restaurant, Bell's Sports Centre.

PITLOCHRY. **Pitlochry Golf Course,** Pitlochry PH16 5QY (01796 472792). *Location:* half mile from centre of Pitlochry on A9. 18 holes, 5670 yards, S.S.S. 69. *Green Fees:* low season - weekdays £35.00 per day, £25.00 per round; weekends £43.00 per day. £33.00 per round. High season - weekdays £37 per day, £27.00 per round; weekends £45.00 per day, £35.00 per dound. Subject to review. Restricted course (1st November to 31st March). *Eating facilities:* licensed clubhouse. *Visitors:* welcome. Caddy cars available for hire, fully refurbished clubhouse facilities. *Society Meetings:* catered for. Phone Professional for all bookings. Professional: Mark Pirie (01796 472792). Golf Club Secretary: T.C. Leadbetter (01796 472314; Fax: 01796 473947).

www.uk-golfguide.com

ST FILLANS. **St Fillans Golf Club,** South Loch Earn Road, St Fillans, Loch Earn PH6 2NJ (01764 685312). *Location:* 13 miles west of Crieff on A85; turn off at east end of village, club 300 yards on left. A testing parkland course nestling between magnificent Perthshire mountains with one elevated tee and green. 9 holes length (18 holes), 6054 yards. S.S.S. 69. Practice facilities and putting green. *Green Fees:* (2007) Monday to Friday £16.00, weekend £20.00. *Eating facilities:* full meals and snacks available throughout the day; licensed restaurant. Golf trolleys, powered trolleys, buggies and clubs for hire. *Visitors:* welcome at all times except when matches on. *Society Meetings:* welcome with advance booking. Managing Secretary: Gordon Hibbert.

SCONE. **Murrayshall Golf Course,** Murrayshall, Scone, By Perth PH2 7PH (01738 551171). *Location:* three miles north of Perth on A94 Coupar Angus Road. Undulating wooded parkland. 18 holes, 6043 yards. S.S.S. 72. Covered golf driving range, a second 18 hole course has been available since July 2000. *Green Fees:* information not available. *Eating facilities:* clubhouse open all day. *Visitors:* welcome, no restrictions - advance booking essential. *Society Meetings:* welcome - must pre-book. Professional: Alan Reid (01738 552784).*
website: www.murrayshall.com

STRATHTAY. **Strathtay Golf Club,** c/o Secretary, Upper Derculich, Strathtay, Pitlochry PH9 0LR. *Location:* on the right, three-quarters of a mile westwards on the minor road to Weem off the A827 Ballinluig to Grandtully. Wooded, mainly hilly course with beautiful panoramic views. 9 holes, 1887 yards. S.S.S. 61. *Green Fees:* £12.00 per day, £15.00 weekends and public holidays. *Visitors:* welcome at any time without restrictions. Changing room, toilets. *Society Meetings:* must be arranged in advance. Secretary: Alistair Robinson. (01887 840373).

Renfrewshire

BARRHEAD. **Fereneze Golf Club,** Fereneze Avenue, Barrhead, Glasgow G78 1HJ (0141-881 1519). *Location:* nine miles south west of Glasgow. Hilly moorland. 18 holes, 5962 yards. S.S.S. 70 *Green Fees:* weekdays £30.00 per round, £35.00 per day. *Eating facilities:* full catering/lounges *Visitors:* welcome by arrangement. *Society Meetings:* welcome, bookings arranged in advance. Professional: James Smallwood (0141-880 7058). Secretary: Graham McCreadie (Tel & Fax: 0141-881 7149).

BISHOPTON. **Erskine Golf Club,** Bishopton PA7 5PH (01505 862302). *Location:* club situated on south bank of the River Clyde. Leave M8 at Junction 30 onto M898 then left onto B815 (before bridge toll barriers), follow sign for Bishopton, Club approximately one mile on right. Parkland course, with breathtaking views over the river to the hills beyond. 18 holes, 6371 yards. S.S.S. 71. Putting green and practice area. *Green Fees:* £31.00 per round, £42.00 per day ticket (2006). *Eating facilities:* restaurant and bar, lunches, teas and dinners served at club. *Visitors:* welcome Monday to Friday by prior arrangement. Professional: Peter Thomson. Secretary: Donald F. McKellar.

BRIDGE OF WEIR. **Old Course Ranfurly Golf Club Ltd,** Ranfurly Place, Bridge of Weir PA11 3DE (01505 613612). *Location:* five miles west of Glasgow Airport. Moorland course. 18 holes, 6089 yards. S.S.S. 70. *Green Fees:* information not available; weekends only if introduced by and playing with a member. *Eating facilities:* dining room, lounge. *Visitors:* welcome weekdays, should contact club beforehand. Must be members of recognised golf clubs with Handicap Certificates. *Society Meetings:* on written application only. Secretary: J. W. Campbell (Tel & Fax: 01505 613214).
e-mail: secretary@oldranfurly.com
website: www.oldranfurly.com

BRIDGE OF WEIR. **Ranfurly Castle Golf Club Ltd,** Golf Road, Bridge of Weir PA11 3HN (01505 612609). *Location:* M8 from Glasgow exit Junction 29, A240 and A761 to Bridge of Weir. Moorland. 18 holes, 6284 yards. S.S.S. 71. Practice ground. *Green Fees:* weekdays £30.00 per round, £40.00 day ticket. *Eating facilities:* bar snacks all day; lunches, high teas, etc by arrangement. *Visitors:* welcome weekdays, at weekends only if accompanied by member. *Society Meetings:* catered for weekdays only. Professional: Tom Eckford (01505 614795; Fax: 01505 612609). Secretary: J. King (01505 612609).
e-mail: secretary@ranfurlycastlegolfclub.co.uk
website: www.ranfurlycastlegolfclub.co.uk

ELDERSLIE. **Elderslie Golf Club,** 63 Main Road, Elderslie PA5 9AZ (01505 322835). *Location:* off M8 at Linwood turn-off, continue to roundabout, follow Elderslie signs A737. Club on main road. Parkland course. 18 holes, 6175 yards. S.S.S. 70. Practice area. Green Fees: information not available. Eating facilities: full meals and bar meals. Visitors: welcome weekdays, no visitors weekends. Caddy hire. Society Meetings: welcome weekdays, book through Secretary. Professional: R. Bowman (01505 320032). Secretary: Mrs A. Anderson (01505 323956; Fax: 01505 340346).*
e-mail: eldersliegolfclub@btconnect.com
website: www.eldersliegolfclub.net

GOUROCK. **Gourock Golf Club,** Cowal View, Gourock PA19 1HD (01475 631001; Fax: 01475 631001). *Location:* two miles west of Gourock Station above Yacht Club. Heathland/parkland with spectacular views. 18 holes, 6408 yards. S.S.S. 72. *Green Fees:* information not available. *Eating facilities:* restaurant, full meals also bar snacks. *Visitors:* welcome; Saturdays not before 4 pm. *Society Meetings:* catered for on application. Professional: Derek Watters (01475 636834). Secretary: Alan D. Taylor (01475 631001).

GREENOCK. **Greenock Golf Club,** Forsyth Street, Greenock PA16 8RE (01475 720793). *Location:* one mile from town centre. Moorland course. 18 holes, 5835 yards. S.S.S. 68. *Green Fees:* information not available. *Eating facilities:* available. *Visitors:* welcome weekdays, not Saturdays. *Society Meetings:* advance booking required. Starter: Jim Duncan (01475 787236). Secretary: Eric J. Black (01475 720793).

GREENOCK. **Greenock Whinhill Golf Club,** Beith Road, Greenock PA16 9LN (01475 724694). *Location:* off Old Largs Road from Drumfrochar Road, Upper Greenock. Municipal course. Situated in hills high above Greenock, panoramic views of River Clyde and the surrounding area. 18 holes, 5504 yards. S.S.S. 67. *Green Fees:* information not available. *Visitors:* welcome except Saturdays. Secretary: Joe Blyth.*

JOHNSTONE. **Cochrane Castle Golf Club,** Scott Avenue, Craigston, Johnstone PA5 0HF (01505 320146; Fax: 01505 325338). *Location:* turn left off Beith Road at Rannoch Road, second on right to end of Scott Avenue. Parkland course, fairly hilly wth excellent views to north. 18 holes, 6194 yards. S.S.S. 71. Practice area and green. *Green Fees:* weekdays £22.00 per round, £30.00 per day; weekends by introduction only. *Eating facilities:* full catering and bar. *Visitors:* welcome Monday to Friday, limited to 24. Arrangement by letter to Secretary. Trolleys. *Society Meetings:* catered for by arrangement, weekdays only. Professional: Alan J. Logan (01505 328465). Secretary: Mrs P. I. J. Quin (01505 320146)

www.uk-golfguide.com

KILMACOLM. **Kilmacolm Golf Club,** Porterfield Road, Kilmacolm PA13 4PD (01505 872139). *Location:* A761. Moorland course. 18 holes, 5964 yards. S.S.S. 69. Practice area. *Green Fees:* information not available. *Eating facilities:* diningroom and bar. *Visitors:* welcome on weekdays. *Society Meetings:* catered for. Professional: Iain Nicholson (01505 872695). Secretary: D.W. Tinton.*

LANGBANK. **Gleddoch Golf Club,** Langbank PA14 6YE (01475 540304; Fax: 01475 540201). *Location:* M8 west to Greenock/Langbank, exit B789 signposted Langbank/Houston. Parkland/moorland. 18 holes, 6357 yards. S.S.S. 71. Practice area, putting green. *Green Fees:* information not available. *Eating facilities:* bar, lounge and restaurant open all day. *Visitors:* welcome weekdays, restrictions only when competitions. Gleddoch House Hotel, 39 bedrooms plus self catering lodges. *Society Meetings:* welcome weekdays only excluding Bank Holidays. Professional: Keith Campbell (01475 540704; Fax: 01475 540201). Secretary: D.W. Tierney (01475 540304; Fax: 01475 540201). *

LOCHWINNOCH. **Lochwinnoch Golf Club,** Burnfoot Road, Lochwinnoch PA12 4AN (01505 842153; Fax: 01505 843668). *Location:* between Johnstone and Beith, off A737 on Largs road A760. Parkland, extremely scenic, set in quiet country village. 18 holes, 6243 yards. S.S.S. 71. Practice area. *Green Fees:* £25.00 per round, £35.00 per day. *Eating facilities:* licensed bar and catering every day. *Visitors:* welcome weekdays, weekends restricted. *Society Meetings;* welcome weekdays. Professional: Gerry Reilly (01505 843029). Administrator: R.J.G. Jamieson. e-mail: enquiries@lochwinnochgolf.co.uk website: www.lochwinnochgolf.co.uk

PAISLEY. **Barshaw Golf Club,** Barshaw Park, Glasgow Road, Paisley (0141-889 2908). *Location:* one mile from Paisley Cross travelling east towards Glasgow (Glasgow Road). Parkland course, flat/hilly. 18 holes, 5703 yards. S.S.S. 67. Putting green. *Green Fees:* information not available. *Eating facilities:* mobile van rear of clubhouse. *Visitors:* welcome anytime, must have a bag of clubs. *Society Meetings:* apply to Mr Bernard J. Forteath, Director of Environmental Services, Paisley. Secretary: W. Collins (0141-884 2533).*

PAISLEY. **Paisley Golf Club,** Braehead Road, Paisley PA2 8TZ (0141-884 3903). *Location:* up Causeyside Street, Neilston Road, turn right into Glenburn, left at roundabout. Moorland course. 18 holes, 6466 yards. S.S.S. 72. Practice area. *Green Fees:* weekdays £30.00 per round, £40.00 per day. Full day golf package available. *Eating facilities:* bar snacks and full meals. *Visitors:* welcome by prior arrangement with Handicap Certificate, midweek not after 4pm and not at weekends or Public Holidays. *Society Meetings:* by arrangement with Secretary. Professional: David Gordon (0141-884 4114). Club Manager: John Hillis (0141-884 3903).

PAISLEY. **Ralston Golf Club,** Strathmore Avenue, Ralston, Paisley PA1 3DT (0141-882 1349; Fax: 0141 883 9837). *Location:* Glasgow Road, two miles east of Paisley Cross. Parkland course. 18 holes, 6091 yards. S.S.S. 69. *Green Fees:* information not provided. *Eating facilities:* dining room, bar. *Visitors:* welcome subject to course availability. *Society Meetings:* catered for on application subject to course availability. Professional: Colin Munro (0141-810 4925). Secretary: J. Pearson (0141-882 1349; Fax: 0141-883 9837). e-mail: thesecretary@ralstongolf.co.uk

PORT GLASGOW. **Port Glasgow Golf Club,** Devol Road, Port Glasgow PA14 5XE (01475 704181). *Location:* M8 to Newark Castle to roundabout, follow signs for Industrial Estate. Heathland with panoramic views of the Clyde and Argyll Hills. 18 holes, 5712 yards, 5224 metres. S.S.S. 68. *Green Fees:* weekdays £22.00 a round, £30.00 per day; weekends £25.00 a round, £35 per day. Buggies will be available for 2008 season. *Eating facilities:* full catering service. *Visitors:* welcome, only by prior arrangement. *Society Meetings:* welcome by prior arrangement with Hon. Secretary (36 maximum), full catering available. Hon. Secretary: Tommy Rodger (01475 704181).

RENFREW. **Renfrew Golf Club,** Blythswood Estate, Inchinnan Road, Renfrew PA4 9EG (0141-886 6692). *Location:* A8 Renfrew, turn in at Normandy Hotel. Flat parkland, wooded. 18 holes, 6818 yards, 6231 metres. S.S.S. 72. *Green Fees:* £35.00 per round, £45.00 per day. *Eating facilities:* daily restaurant facilities and bar. *Visitors:* welcome on introduction by members. Visiting parties by arrangement. *Society Meetings:* catered for on Mondays, Tuesdays and Thursdays only by written application to Secretary. Professional: David Grant (0141-885 1754). Managing Secretary: David Cameron (0141-886 6692; Fax: 0141-886 1808).

UPLAWMOOR. **Caldwell Golf Club Ltd,** Uplawmoor, Glasgow G78 4AU (01505 850329; Fax: 01505 850604). *Location:* five miles south of Barrhead, Glasgow on A736 Irvine Road. Parkland bounded by mature trees and a natural water hazard. 18 holes, 6335 yards, 5793 metres. S.S.S. 71. Practice area. *Green Fees:* information not available. *Eating facilities:* every day bar menu - filled rolls on Thursdays. *Visitors:* welcome weekdays only before 4.30pm, not weekends and Public Holidays (local and national). *Society Meetings:* weekdays only by prior arrangement. Professional: Stephen Forbes (Tel & Fax: 01505 850616). Secretary: K. Morrison (01505 850366; Fax: 01505 850604).* e-mail: CaldwellGolfClub@aol.com website: www.caldwellgolfclub.i8.com

THE APPEARANCE OF AN ASTERISK (*) AT THE END OF A CLUB OR COURSE ENTRY INDICATES THAT UP-TO-DATE INFORMATION HAS NOT BEEN SUPPLIED

Stirling & The Trossachs

ABERFOYLE. **Aberfoyle Golf Club,** Braeval, Aberfoyle, By Stirling FK8 3UY (01877 382493). *Location:* A81 Glasgow–Stirling. Parkland. 18 holes, 5204 yards. S.S.S. 66. *Green Fees:* available on request. *Eating facilities:* bar and catering available all day April to October; restricted service October to March. *Visitors:* welcome anytime but restrictions at weekends. Club Steward: Duncan Brown.

ALLOA. **Alloa Golf Club,** Schawpark Golf Course, Sauchie, Alloa FK10 3AX (01259 722745 Fax: 01259 218796). *Location:* on A908 between Alloa and Tillicoultry. Parkland, tree lined fairways with spectacular views of Ochil Hills and beyond. 18 holes, 6229 yards, 5695 metres. S.S.S. 70. *Green Fees:* weekdays £28.00 per round, £38.00 per day; weekends £34.00 per round, £44.00 per day. *Eating facilities:* restaurant and lounge bar. *Visitors:* welcome. Phone to confirm booking. Guaranteed tee times can be booked. Ladies and gents changing rooms. *Society Meetings:* welcome weekdays only. Package: morning coffee, lunch, high tea, and two rounds of golf £44.00. Professional/Bookings: David Herd (Tel & Fax: 01259 724476). Secretary: T. White (01259 722745; Fax: 01259 218796).

ALLOA. **Braehead Golf Club,** Cambus, By Alloa FK10 2NT (01259 725766). *Location:* one mile west of Alloa on A907. Gently undulating parkland course with scenic views and a variety of challenging holes. 18 holes, 6053 yards. S.S.S. 69. Practice area. *Green Fees:* weekdays £24.00 per round, £32.00 per day; weekends £32.00 per round, £40.00 per day. *Eating facilities:* bar/full catering available all day during Summer months; slightly restricted during Autumn/ Spring. *Visitors:* no restrictions but advisable to telephone in advance. Buggy and cart hire. *Society Meetings:* catered for with prior booking. Professional: Jamie Stevenson. Starter's Shop (01259 722078). Secretary: Ron Murray.

ALVA. **Alva Golf Club,** Beauclerc Street, Alva FK12 5LH (01259 760431). *Location:* seven miles from Stirling on A91 Stirling to St Andrews Road - course lies at foot of Ochil Hills. Inland wooded hillside course with fast greens. 9 holes, 2423 yards, 2213 metres. S.S.S. 64. *Green Fees:* information not available. *Eating facilities:* snacks during bar hours. *Visitors:* welcome at all times. Secretary: A. Walker.*

BALFRON. **Balfron Golf Society,** Kepculloch Road, Balfron, By Glasgow G63 0PZ. *Location:* situated at the north end of the village on the A875, 18 miles from Glasgow and 18 miles from Stirling. Interesting, undulating upland course with splendid views. 18 holes, 5903 yards, S.S.S. 68. *Green Fees:* information not available. *Visitors:* welcome weekdays until 4pm, and at weekends, restrictions during competition days. *Society Meetings:* welcome subject to prior booking. Secretary: Brian Davidson (01360 550613).* website: www.balfrongolfsociety.org.uk

DOLLAR. **Dollar Golf Club,** Brewlands House, 2 Back Road, Dollar FK14 7EA (01259 742400). *Location:* off A91 in Dollar, signposted. Hillside course without bunkers as designed by Ben Sayers in 1908. 18 holes, 5242 yards, 4796 metres. S.S.S. 66. *Green Fees:* information not provided. *Eating facilities:* full catering (except Tuesdays) and bar. *Visitors:* welcome, booking in advance advisable weekends. Snooker table available. *Society Meetings:* welcome (maximum 30). Secretary: W.S. Morrison.

DRYMEN. **Strathendrick Golf Club,** Glasgow Road, Drymen, Glasgow G63 0AA (01360 660695). *Location:* one mile south of Drymen on A811. Undulating course, designed by Willie Fernie in 1901. 9 holes, 5116 yards. S.S.S. 64. *Green Fees:* weekdays £15.00 per 18 holes, £16.00 per day (under review). *Visitors:* welcome 8.30am to 3.30pm weekdays only May to September. *Society Meetings:* by arrangement with Secretary. Visitors' Convener: John Greig (01389 830622).

FALKIRK. **Bonnybridge Golf Club,** Larbert Road, Bonnybridge FK4 1NY (01324 812822). *Location*: five miles west of Falkirk. Parkland. 9 holes, 6132 yards. S.S.S. 70 Par 72. Practice area. *Green Fees:* information not available. *Eating facilities:* bar open lunchtimes and evenings; all day Saturday and Sunday. *Visitors:* welcome with prior permission, or accompanied by a member. *Society Meetings*: by arrangement with Hon. Secretary. Secretary: J. Mullen (01324 812323).*

FALKIRK. **Falkirk Golf Club,** Carmuirs, 136 Stirling Road, Camelon, Falkirk FK2 7YP (01324 611061; Fax: 01324 639573). *Location:* one and a half miles west of town centre on A9. Parkland with streams. 18 holes, 6282 yards. S.S.S. 70. *Green Fees:* weekdays £25.00 per round, £35.00 per day; Sundays £30.00 per round, £40.00 per day. Special rates for societies. *Eating facilities:* full catering and bar facilities. *Visitors:* welcome Monday to Friday up to 4.00pm unaccompanied, with member only at weekends. *Society Meetings:* weekdays except Saturdays. Make arrangements with Starter (01324 612219). Professional: Stewart Craig. Secretary: John Elliott (01324 634118). e-mail: falkirkgolfclub@btconnect.com

FALKIRK. **Polmont Golf Club,** Manuelrigg, Maddiston, Falkirk FK2 0LS (01324 711277; Fax: 01324 712504). *Location:* first turn to the right past Fire Brigade HQ in Maddiston. Undulating course. 9 holes, 6603 yards. S.S.S. 70. *Green Fees:* weekdays £10.00, Saturdays after 4.30pm and Sundays £15.00. *Eating facilities:* lunches and high teas. *Visitors:* welcome without reservation, no visitors after 5pm weekdays or all day Saturday. *Society Meetings:* catered for. Secretary: John Ingram (01324 711277).

LARBERT. **Falkirk Tryst Golf Club,** 86 Burnhead Road, Stenhousemuir, Larbert FK5 4BD (01324 562415). *Location:* three miles from Falkirk (A9/A88), one mile from Larbert Station. Flat/seaside links style surface. 18 holes, 6053 yards, 5533 metres. S.S.S. 69. Practice area. *Green Fees:* information not available. *Eating facilities:* full catering - lunches, high teas, bar service. *Visitors:* welcome weekdays only except Bank and local Holidays. *Society Meetings:* catered for weekdays only except Bank and local Holidays. Professional: Mr Steven Dunsmore (01324 562091). Secretary: Mr R.C. Chalmers (01324 562054).*

LARBERT. **Glenbervie Golf Club Ltd,** Stirling Road, Larbert FK5 4SJ (01324 562725). *Location:* one mile north of Larbert on A9 Falkirk to Stirling road. Parkland course. 18 holes, 6438 yards. S.S.S. 71. Two practice areas. *Green Fees:* £35.00 per round, £50.00 per day. *Eating facilities:* lunches and high teas, bar snacks. *Visitors:* welcome weekdays until 4pm. Weekends as members' guests only. *Society Meetings:* up to 50 competitors catered for, Tuesdays and Thursdays only. Professional: David Ross (01324 562725). Secretary: Ian R. Webster CA (01324 562605; Fax: 01324 551054). e-mail: secretary@glenberviegolfclub.com

LENNOXTOWN. **Campsie Golf Club,** Crow Road, Lennoxtown, Glasgow G66 7HX (01360 310244). *Location:* on B822 Lennoxtown to Fintry. Hillside course with panoramic views. 18 holes, 5509 yards. S.S.S. 68. Practice fairway, bunker and putting green. *Green Fees:* £15.00 weekdays, £20.00 weekends. *Eating facilities:* full catering available. *Visitors:* welcome, weekdays unrestricted, weekends by prior arrangement. *Society Meetings:* catered for by arrangement. Professional: Mark Brennan (01360 310920). Club Manager: H.B. Weston.

MUCKHART. **Muckhart Golf Club,** Muckhart, By Dollar FK14 7JH (01259 781423; Fax: 01259 781544). *Location:* off A91 east from Stirling, three miles north of Dollar. Undulating heathland. 27 holes played as 3 x 18 holes in rotation. 6069 yards, 6086 yards and 6485 yards – the other 9 hole course is always available. Practice ground. *Green Fees:* 18 holes weekday £25.00, day ticket £35.00, 18 holes weekend £30.00, day ticket £40.00. *Eating facilities:* 11am until 8.45pm (except Monday), bar available. *Visitors:* Welcome. Trolley hire. *Society Meetings:* catered for. Professional: Keith Salmoni (Tel & Fax: 01259 781493). Club Secretary: Alison Houston. e-mail: enquiries@muckhartgolf.com website: www.muckhartgolf.com

POLMONT. **Grangemouth Golf Club,** Polmonthill, Polmont, Falkirk FK2 0YA (01324 711500). *Location:* quarter of a mile north of Junction 4 M9 motorway. Parkland course. 18 holes, 6314 yards. S.S.S. 70. Practice area. *Green Fees:* information not provided. *Eating facilities:* catering and bar facilities available, open all day during season. *Visitors:* welcome, no restrictions. *Society Meetings:* welcome any day except Saturday. Professional: Greg McFarlane (01324 503840). Secretary: Jim McNairney (01324 713612) e-mail: jim.mcnairney@btinternet.com

STIRLING. **Bridge Of Allan Golf Club,** Sunnylaw, Bridge of Allan FK9 4LY (Tel & Fax: 01786 832332). *Location:* from Stirling, three miles, turn right at Bridge, keep taking the high road. Hilly course, spectacular views. 9 holes, 4932 yards, 4508 metres. S.S.S. 66. *Green Fees:* weekdays £15.00, weekends £20.00. *Eating facilities:* catering available during season or by arrangement outwith season. Licensed bar. *Visitors:* welcome without reservation, Saturdays after 4pm. *Society Meetings:* catered for by arrangement, phone in advance.
e-mail: secretary@bofagc.com
website: www.bofagc.com

STIRLING. **Brucefields Family Golf Centre,** Pirnhall Road, Bannockburn, Stirling FK9 4PU (01786 818184; Fax: 01786 817770). *Location:* half-a-mile from M9 and M80 interchange on A91. Parkland. 9 holes, 5025 yards. S.S.S. 66, Par 68; 9 hole par 3 course; driving range; putting green. *Green Fees:* weekdays; 9 holes £11.00, 18 holes £18.00, weekends, 9 holes £12.00, 18 holes £20.00. *Eating facilities:* Clive Ramsay Cafe Bar. *Visitors:* welcome. *Society Meetings:* welcome. Corporate Membership and packages available. Managing Director: Kirsty Stewart. Secretary: Christine Frost.

STIRLING. **Stirling Golf Club,** Queen's Road, Stirling FK8 3AA (01786 464098; Fax: 01786 460090). *Location:* one mile from town centre, rail and bus stations; two miles from Junction 10 M9. Rolling parkland course. 18 holes, 6400 yards. S.S.S. 71. Practice area. *Green Fees:* £30.00 per round; £45.00 per day. *Eating facilities:* full bar and catering. *Visitors:* visiting parties welcome midweek. Casual visitors may reserve tee times only at weekends. *Society Meetings:* welcome. Professional: Ian Collins (01786 471490). Secretary: Alan Rankin (01786 464098; Fax: 01786 460090).
e-mail: enquiries@stirlinggolfclub.tv

STIRLING. **Tillicoultry Golf Club,** Alva Road, Tillicoultry FK12 6BL (01259 750124). *Location:* on A91, nine miles east of Stirling. Parkland at foot of Ochil Hills. 9 holes, 5358 yards, 4904 metres. S.S.S. 67. *Green Fees:* weekdays £12.00 per round, £13.00 after 4pm; weekends £17.00 per round. *Eating facilities:* clubhouse bar, bar lunches. *Visitors:* welcome at all times outwith competitions. No children under 15 weekends until 4pm. *Society Meetings:* welcome by booking through Club Manager. Club Manager: (01259 750124).

Scottish Islands

COLONSAY

ISLE OF COLONSAY. **Colonsay Golf Club,** Machrins, Isle of Colonsay PA61 7YP. *Location:* two miles from ferry terminal. Traditional links course, reputedly 200 years old, natural, challenging and fun course. The 10th green has one of the best views in golf. 18 holes, 4775 yards. S.S.S. 72. *Green Fees:* information not available. *Eating facilities:* none on course, bar/ cafe/shop two miles away. *Visitors:* always welcome. *Society Meetings:* always welcome. Secretary: Donald MacAllister (01951 200307; Fax: 01951 200232).*
e-mail: donald@macallister4666.fslife.co.uk

CUMBRAE

MILLPORT. **Millport Golf Club,** Golf Road, Millport KA28 0HB (Tel & Fax: 01475 530306). *Location:* Caledonian McBrayne car ferry Largs slip to Cumbrae slip (seven minutes). Millport town four miles. On hill overlooking Firth of Clyde over Bute and Arran to Mull of Kintyre. Heathland with panoramic views. 18 holes, 5828 yards. S.S.S. 69. Large practice area. *Green Fees:* weekdays from £22.00 ; weekends and Bank Holidays from £28.00. *Eating facilities:* full à la carte and bar menu. *Visitors:* welcome without reservation. Tee reservations available for parties. Well stocked Professional's shop. Starter's telephone (01475 530305). *Society Meetings:* catered for. Special open amateur competition, Cumbrae Cup. Professional: (01475 530305). Secretary: William Reid (Tel & Fax: 01475 530306).
e-mail: secretary@millportgolfclub.co.uk
website: www.millportgolfclub.co.uk

GIGHA

.ISLE OF GIGHA. **Isle of Gigha Golf Club,** The Croft, Isle of Gigha PA41 7AA (01583 505287). *Location:* by ferry from Tayinloan to Gigha, course half a mile north from Post Office. Seaside course with scenic views looking over the Sound of Gigha and the Kintyre coast. 9 holes, 5042 yards (18 holes). S.S.S. 65. *Green Fees:* £12.50 per round. Phone for special rates. *Eating facilities:* available at Gigha Hotel. *Visitors:* always welcome. *Society Meetings:* welcome. Secretary: John Bannatyne (01583 505242).

HARRIS

SCARISTA. **Harris Golf Club,** Scarista, Isle of Harris. *Location:* 10 miles south of Tarbert, 50 miles south of Stornoway. Seaside links course on machair land, in an Area of Outstanding Natural Beauty. 9 holes, 2432 yards. S.S.S. 64 (18 holes). *Green Fees:* day ticket £12.00. *Visitors:* welcome, no restrictions. Secretary: John MacLean (01859 550226).

ISLAY

PORT ELLEN. **Islay Golf Club,** 25 Charlotte Street, Port Ellen PA42 7DQ (01496 300094; Fax: 01496 302117). *Location:* five miles north of Port Ellen. Championship course. 18 holes, 6235 yards, 5695 metres. S.S.S. 70. Practice area. *Green Fees:* information not available. *Eating facilities:* full range at adjoining Machrie Hotel. *Visitors:* welcome anytime. Trolleys, caddies by arrangement. *Society Meetings:* all welcome.*

PORT ELLEN. **Machrie Golf Links,** The Machrie Hotel and Golf Links, Port Ellen PA42 7AN (01496 302310; Fax: 01496 302404). *Location:* adjacent Airport. Classic links. 18 holes, 6324 yards. S.S.S. 71. *Green Fees:* £49.00. *Eating facilities:* full service in hotel. *Visitors:* welcome any day without reservation. *Society Meetings:* any number catered for. Golf packages available. Manager: Ian Brown. e-mail: machrie@machrie.com website: www.machrie.com

LEWIS

STORNOWAY. **Stornoway Golf Club,** Lady Lever Park, Stornoway, Isle of Lewis HS2 0XP (01851 70 2240). *Location:* close proximity to town of Stornoway, in grounds of Lews Castle. Hilly parkland course with good views. 18 holes, 5252 yards. S.S.S. 67. *Green Fees:* £20.00 day ticket. Weekly tickets available - no Sunday golf. *Eating facilities:* light bar snacks available. *Visitors:* welcome. Car ferry daily (except Sunday) from Ullapool. Air services daily from Glasgow, Inverness, Aberdeen and Edinburgh. *Society Meetings:* welcome, book through Secretary. Secretary: K.W. Galloway (01851 702240). e-mail: admin@stornowaygolfclub.co.uk website: www.stornowaygolfclub.co.uk

MULL

CRAIGNURE. **Craignure Golf Club,** Scallastle, Craignure PA65 6AY (01680 300402). *Location:* one mile from Oban/Mull main ferry terminal. Links course - first layout 1895, superb natural setting. 9 holes, 18 tees, 5351 yards. S.S.S. 66. Small practice area. *Green Fees:* information not available. *Eating facilities:* three-quarters-of-a-mile from MacGregor's Road House and Craignure Inn. *Visitors:* always welcome, except for Club inter-match days - please phone for details. Clubs, trolleys for hire, balls for sale. *Society Meetings:* welcome, discounts available. Secretary: Michael Timms (mobile: 07710 767895).*

TOBERMORY. **Tobermory Golf Club,** Erray Road, Tobermory PA75 6PG. *Location:* situated on the cliffs above the town to the north west. Panoramic views of Sound of Mull; beautifully maintained and challenging course. 9 holes, 4921 yards, 4362 metres. S.S.S. 64. Practice ground. *Green Fees:* £18.00 per day, Juniors (under 18) £9.00 per day. *Eating facilities:* Club licence. Catering April–Oct. Green Fee ticket includes temporary membership. *Visitors:* unrestricted except for some competition days. Membership available, contact Secretary. Club and trolley hire available. *Society Meetings:* welcome. Secretary: Mr Mike Campbellr (01688 302743; Fax: 0870 0523091). e-mail: secretary@tobermorygolfclub.com website: www.tobermorygolfclub.com

ORKNEY

KIRKWALL. **Orkney Golf Club,** Grainbank, Kirkwall KW15 1RD (01856 872457). *Location:* half-a-mile west of Kirkwall. Parkland with good views over Kirkwall Bay and North Isles. 18 holes, 5411 yards, 4964 metres. S.S.S. 67. Practice area. *Green Fees:* information not available. *Eating facilities:* bar lunches during summer months. *Visitors:* welcome at all times, restrictions only during competitions. *Society Meetings:* welcome, booking advised. Secretary: Andrew Bonner (01856 741317).*
website: www.orkneygolfclub.co.uk

STROMNESS. **Stromness Golf Club Ltd,** Ness, Stromness KW16 3DU (01856 850772). Location: situated at south end of town. Seaside course bordering Hoy Sound. 18 holes, 4762 yards. S.S.S 63. Green Fees: £20.00 per day. Eating facilities: clubhouse with full facilities. Visitors: welcome, no restrictions. Bowling and tennis. Society Meetings: welcome by arrangement through Secretary. Secretary: G.A. Bevan (01856 850885). website: www.stromnessgc.co.uk

WESTRAY. **Westray Golf Club,** Westray, Orkney Islands KW17 2DH (01857 677373). *Location:* half a mile from Pierowall Village. Seaside links course. 9 holes, 2316 yards, 2084 metres. S.S.S. 33. *Green Fees:* information not available. *Visitors:* welcome anytime. Secretary: Mr John Cable (01857 677287).*

SHETLAND

Shetland Golf Club, Dale, Gott, Shetland ZE2 9SB (01595 840369). *Location:* four miles north of Lerwick on the A970. Parkland. 18 holes, 5562 yards. Par 68. S.S.S 68. Practice nets, chipping green and putting green. Driving range three miles away. *Green Fees:* £20.00 a day. *Eating facilities:* bar with sandwiches and snacks at lunchtimes, evenings and weekends. *Visitors:* welcome, no restrictions except on club competition days. Club and trolley hire available. Changing rooms, showers. *Society Meetings:* in writing by letter or e-mail. Secretary: Mrs J. Wishart. e-mail: info@shetlandgolfclub.co.uk website: www.shetlandgolfclub.co.uk

WHALSAY. **Whalsay Golf Club,** Skaw Taing, Whalsay ZE2 9AL (01806 566259). *Location:* five miles from Symbister ferry terminal - ferries run from Laxo to Symbister. Seaside course with wonderful scenery and birdlife in abundance - Britain's most northerly 18 holes. 18 holes, 6140 yards. S.S.S. 69. Changing rooms. *Green Fees:* £20.00 per round; weekly ticket £50.00 (subject to review). *Eating facilities:* lunch/ dinner available by arrangement. *Visitors:* welcome. Trolleys for hire £2.00. Saturday/Sunday competitions, check before travelling. Secretary: Charles Hutchison (01806 566450) and Harry Sandison (01806 566481)

SKYE

SCONSER. **Isle of Skye Golf Club,** Sconser IV48 8TD (01478 650414). *Location:* on A87 halfway between Broadford and Portree, 20 miles from Skye Bridge. Seaside course with spectacular views to Isle of Raasay and North Skye. 9 holes (with different tee settings on back 9), 4677 yards, 4277 metres. S.S.S. 64. *Green Fees:* 9 holes £14.00, 18 holes £21.00. Subject to review for 2008. *Eating facilities*: tearoom serving light snacks. *Visitors:* welcome at all times. Changing and toilet facilities, trolleys and clubs for hire, small shop. *Society Meetings:* welcome. Secretary: B. Sandy (01478 650414).
e-mail: info@isleofskyegolfclub.co.uk
website: www.isleofskyegolfclub.co.uk

SKEABOST BRIDGE. **Skeabost Golf Club,** Skeabost House Hotel, Skeabost Bridge IV51 9NP (01470 532202; Fax: 01470 532454). *Location:* A850 Portree to Dunvegan Road. Woodland course. 9 holes, 3114 yards. S.S.S. 59 (for 18 holes). *Green Fees:* information not available. *Eating facilities:* lunch, evening meals in hotel; bar food in public bar. *Visitors:* welcome, under 13s must be accompanied by an adult. *Society Meetings:* accepted. Club Captain: D. Sutherland. Secretary: D.J. Matheson.*
e-mail: reception@skeabostcountryhouse.com

SOUTH UIST

LOCHBOISDALE. **Askernish Golf Club,** Askernish, Lochboisdale. *Location:* off South Uist main road B888. Seaside, undulating, designed by Tom Morris Senior 1891. 9 holes, 18 tees, 5042 yards. S.S.S. 68. *Green Fees:* information not available. *Visitors:* welcome. Secretary: Neil Elliot (01878 700298).*
e-mail: askernish.golf.club@cwcom.net

TIREE

SCARINISH. **Vaul Golf Club,** Scarinish, Isle of Tiree PA77 6XH. *Location:* two miles from Scarinish and half a mile from Lodge Hotel, ferry from Oban four hours and plane from Glasgow 45 minutes. Links course with crystal white beaches to north and south with beautiful views on all sides. 9 holes, 5674 yards (18 holes). S.S.S. 68 (18 holes). *Green Fees:* information not available. *Visitors:* welcome, no restrictions. Enquiries and fees to R. Omand, Royal Bank of Scotland, Scarinish. Secretary: Mrs S. Sweeney (01879 220729).*

Golf in Wales

Chris Smart

Anglesey & Gwynedd • North Wales
Carmarthenshire • Ceredigion • Pembrokeshire
Powys • South Wales

'**WINNING THE BID** to host the 2010 Ryder Cup has given Wales the opportunity to tell the world what it has to offer.' The words of Wales' most famous golfing son, Ian Woosnam.

The Principality has a golfing tradition that scholars of the game will be well aware of, but now, as Woosie points out, the whole world is starting to sit up and take notice of this green and pleasant land.

How could anyone fail to take notice of the centrepiece of the Wales 2010 campaign, the Celtic Manor Resort? Drive across the iconic Severn Bridge into Wales and you will soon be greeted by another structure that has become

Cottrell Park Golf Club, Cardiff, Mackintosh Course, 9th hole

a modern-day landmark. The imposing sight of Sir Terry Matthews' five-star resort hotel has fast become a sporting mecca, with golf at its beating heart. The seemingly endless stream of additions and improvements to the Celtic Manor have made it a benchmark for the game, not just in Wales, but worldwide. Golfers can sample the newly redesigned Ryder Cup layout, spawned from the existing Wentwood Hills course, the Roman Road, which hosted the Celtic Manor Wales Open from 2005-2007, and the Montgomerie course, a reworking of the Coldra Woods layout by European great, Colin Montgomerie. The luxurious hotel, spa and conference facilities mean that there is, quite literally, something for everyone.

Celtic Manor quite rightly demands its fair share of attention, but, within a Tiger Woods' drive of the resort, Gwent has plenty more for the golfer to appreciate. The Monmouthshire Club at Abergavenny, the spectacular Rolls of Monmouth, the ever-challenging Newport course at Rogerstone, and St Pierre, Wales'

first flagship resort and venue for a string of major championships, are all worth a visit.

Just along the M4, west from the Celtic Manor, is Wales' vibrant capital city, Cardiff. Accommodation with most of the major hotel chains can be found in and around the city, and golf courses are dotted to the north, south, east and west of the central zone. Cardiff, Radyr, Glamorganshire, Llanishen and Whitchurch are among the area's long-established clubs.

Just eight miles west of Cardiff lies the picturesque Vale of Glamorgan, one of Wales' most affluent areas, and home to the Vale Hotel resort. Just as Sir Terry Matthews has striven to bring excellence to all things at the Celtic Manor, Gerald Leeke has done likewise at the Vale. Two championship courses, the Lakes and the Wales National, have hosted European Challenge Tour and Seniors' Tour events, and the resort is the home of both the Welsh national rugby and soccer teams.

Heading west again brings you to what is arguably Wales' best-known and best-loved

16th green at Ashburnham Golf Club, Carmarthenshire, with the Gower Peninsula beyond

golfing stretch. The traditional seaside town of Porthcawl is home to Royal Porthcawl, the most majestic of links, with its unique sea view from every hole. The Royal has always been, and will no doubt continue to be, a fitting venue for major championships – the 2007 Glenmuir Club Professionals' finals the most recent - and its close neighbours, Pyle and Kenfig and Southerndown, complete the region's 'holy trinity'.

Further west, and the Machynys Peninsula resort near Llanelli, home to one of the flagship events of the Ladies' European Tour, is another lavish complex that shows Wales is now hitting with the big guns. Machynys has also hosted the Welsh Open Stroke-play Championship and the Boys' home internationals. Machynys boasts Wales' first Jack Nicklaus-designed course and has won a string of plaudits in its fledgling years. More traditional links, such as those at Pennard and Langland Bay on the Gower coast, and

Ashburnam and Tenby further west, continue to draw the travelling golfer.

Mid-Wales has its own gems, such as Cradoc, Brecon, Builth Wells, Borth and Ynyslas, and Llandrindod Wells.

That brings us to the north of the Principality, where there are plenty more ingredients to add to the mix. Royal St David's at Harlech – the Porthcawl of the north in its stature and tradition – is an awe-inspiring links, with Harlech Castle as its permanent watchtower. Aberdovey, a course much written about by famous journalist Bernard Darwin, is another superb links layout, while Nefyn, which has come into the spotlight as a host on the European Challenge Tour, and Conwy, head the impressive supporting cast. Finally there are the two Llandudno courses – North Wales and Maesdu – and on Anglesey gems such as Trearddur Bay and Bull Bay.

The dragon is awake and breathing fire!

Anglesey & Gwynedd

ABERDOVEY. **Aberdovey Golf Club,** Aberdovey LL35 0RT (01654 767493; Fax: 01654 767027). *Location*: west end of Aberdovey on A493, adjacent to railway station. Seaside links, easy walking. 18 holes, 6445 yards, 5893 metres. S.S.S. 71. Practice ground, limited. *Green Fees*: information not available. *Eating facilities*: restaurant, bar and lounge. *Visitors*: welcome on production of Handicap Certificate, restrictions some weekends. *Society Meetings*: catered for by prior arrangement (not August or Bank Holidays). Professional: John Davies (01654 767602). Secretary: J.M. Griffiths (01654 767493; Fax: 01654 767027).*
website: www.aberdoveygolf.co.uk

ABERSOCH. **Clwb Golff Abersoch,** Golf Road, Abersoch LL53 7EY (01758 712622; Fax: 01758 712777). *Location:* A55 to Bangor, coast road to Abersoch. Parkland and seaside links course. 18 holes, 5671 yards. S.S.S. 68, Par 69. Practice area, putting green. *Green Fees:* information not provided. *Eating facilities:* full catering and bar service. *Visitors:* welcome, Ladies' day Thursdays, Gents' competition day Sundays. Handicap Certificate required. Shop. Buggies, carts. *Society Meetings:* welcome by prior arrangement. Professional/Manager: Alan Drosinos Jones (01758 712622; Fax: 01758 712777).
e-mail: pro@abersochgolf.co.uk
website: www.abersochgolf.co.uk

ANGLESEY. **Baron Hill Golf Club Ltd,** Beaumaris, Anglesey LL58 8YW (01248 810231). *Location:* turn left on approach to Beaumaris from Menai Bridge on A545. Moorland course with panoramic view of Snowdonia and Menai Straits. 9 holes, 5570 metres. S.S.S. 69. *Green Fees:* £16.00, £10.00 with a member. *Eating facilities:* comprehensive menu (closed Mondays). *Visitors:* welcome, competitions most Sundays, Ladies' Day on Tuesday mornings. *Society Meetings:* welcome by prior arrangement - special rates and packages available. Secretary: Alwyn Pleming.

ANGLESEY. **Bull Bay Golf Club Ltd,** Bull Bay, Amlwch, Isle of Anglesey LL68 9RY (01407 830213). *Location:* one mile west of Amlwch on A5025 coastal road towards Cemaes Bay and Holyhead. Coastal heathland championship course; Wales' northernmost golf course. 18 holes, 6217 yards. S.S.S. 70. Practice ground and putting green. *Green Fees:* (2007) £27.00 per round, £30.00 per day weekdays; £33.00 per round, £36.00 per day weekends and Bank Holidays (subject to review for 2008). *Eating facilities:* bar snacks, dining room; limited facilities on Mondays. *Visitors:* welcome, competitions permitting; advance bookings advised. Snooker and pool. *Society Meetings:* welcome, booking essential. Professional: John Burns (01407 831188). Secretary/Manager: (01407 830960; Fax: 01407 832612).

ANGLESEY. **Penrhyn Golf Complex,** Llanddaniel - Fâb LL60 6NN (01248 421150). *Location:* A5 turn off at Star Crossroads taking Llanddaniel road. Follow Brown Tourism signs from the village. Parkland with some small hills. 9 holes, Par 3. 14 bay covered and floodlit driving range and putting area. *Green Fees:* £4.00 9 holes, £6.00 18 holes (as from January 2006). Pay-as-you-play course. Special rates weekdays 10am-5pm for 18 holes. *Visitors:* no restrictions. Professional: Paul Lovell (Visiting). Owner: W.R. Carter.

BALA. **Bala Golf Club,** Penlan, Bala LL23 7YD (01678 520359; Fax: 01678 521361). *Location:* turn right before coming to Bala Lake on the main Bala-Dolgellau road. Upland course with superb views in the Snowdonia National Park. 10 holes, 4970 yards, 4512 metres. S.S.S. 64. *Green Fees:* £20.00 weekdays £30.00 weekends. *Eating facilities:* bar with snacks available. *Visitors:* welcome all year, some restrictions Bank Holidays and weekends. Snooker table and small golf shop. *Society Meetings:* very welcome by prior arrangement. Professional: Tony Davies (visiting). Secretary: G. Rhys Jones.
e-mail: balagolfclub@onetel.com
website: www.golffbala.co.uk

BANGOR. **St Deiniol Golf Club,** Penybryn, Bangor LL57 1PX (01248 353098; Fax: 01248 370792). *Location:* at A5/A55 Junction 11 intersection, follow A5122 for one mile to eastern outskirts of Bangor. Parkland course with magnificent views. 18 holes, 5654 yards, 5068 metres. S.S.S. 67. *Green Fees:* weekdays £20.00, weekends and Bank Holidays £25.00. *Eating facilities:* two bars; full catering Mondays excepted. *Visitors:* welcome without reservation, restrictions at weekends. Golf buggies available for hire. *Society Meetings:* welcome by prior arrangement. Secretary: Bob Thomas M.B.E.
e-mail: secretary@st-deiniol.co.uk
website: www.st-deiniol.co.uk

BEAUMARIS. **Henllys Golf Course,** Henllys Hall, Beaumaris, Anglesey LL58 8HU (01248 811717; Fax: 01248 811511). *Location:* quarter of a mile through Beaumaris town centre. Parkland course. 18 holes, 6062 yards, S.S.S. 70. Practice ground. *Green Fees:* weekdays £24.00, weekends and Bank Holidays £30.00. *Visitors:* welcome, please telephone before. Tuition from PGA Professionals available. Professionals: Peter Maton/ David Gadsby (01248 811717; Fax: 01248 811511). Director of Golf: Peter Maton.
e-mail: HG@HPB.co.uk

BRYNTEG. **Storws Wen Golf Club,** Brynteg LL78 8JY (01248 852673). *Location:* one-and-three-quarter miles along the B5108 from Benllech to Brynteg. Parkland course with a stream, three lakes and spectacular views. 9 holes, 5002 yards. S.S.S. 64. *Green Fees:* call for details. *Eating facilities:* clubhouse with full facilities. *Visitors:* always welcome. *Society Meetings:* welcome, terms on request. General Manager: Enyr Rowlands.

CAERNARFON. **Royal Town of Caernarfon Golf Club,** Aberforeshore, Llanfaglan, Caernarfon LL54 5RP (Tel & Fax: 01286 673783). *Location:* less than a mile from the historic Royal town of Caernarfon. Parkland course in superb sea and mountain setting. 18 holes, 5941 yards. S.S.S. 68. *Green Fees:* Monday £20.00 per round, Tuesday to Friday £25.00 per round (April-May), £30.00 per round (June-Sept), Saturday £30.00 per round (April-May), £35.00 per round (June-Sept), Sunday £27.00. *Eating facilities:* excellent catering and bar facilities, except Mondays. *Visitors:* welcome with no restrictions except Saturdays, please contact Professional to reserve tee time. Tuition, shop. *Society Meetings:* welcome, subject to pre-arranged bookings. Professional: Aled Owen (01286 673783). Secretary/Manager: E.G. Angel

CRICCIETH. **Criccieth Golf Club,** Ednyfed Hill, Criccieth LL52 0PH (01766 522154). *Location:* in High Street (A497) turn right past Memorial Hall, keep going up lane to Club. 18 holes, 5755 yards. S.S.S. 68. *Green Fees:* from £20.00. *Eating facilities:* light meals available. *Visitors:* welcome without reservation. *Society Meetings:* catered for with prior reservation. Secretary: G.I. Owen.
e-mail:criccieth golfclub.co.uk

www.uk-golfguide.com

DOLGELLAU. **Dolgellau Golf Club,** Pencefn Road, Dolgellau LL40 2ES (01341 422603). *Location:* half-a-mile from town centre. Parkland with panoramic views. 9 holes and alternate tees, 4671 yards. S.S.S. 63. Practice facility. *Green Fees:* weekdays £18.00, weekends and Bank Holidays £22.50. *Eating facilities:* catering facilities available. *Visitors:* welcome without reservation. *Society Meetings:* catered for. Special packages available. Secretary: Richard Stockdale (01341 422603).
website: www.dolgellaugolfclub.com

FFESTINIOG. **Clwb Golff Ffestiniog,** Y Cefn, Ffestiniog LL41 4PS (01766 762637). *Location:* located on B4391, one mile from Ffestiniog village. Upland course. 9 holes, 4570 yards. S.S.S. 66. *Green Fees:* weekdays £10.00, weekends £10.00. *Visitors:* welcome at any time, some restrictions mainly at weekends during club competitions. *Society Meetings:* by prior arrangement. Secretary: Andrew Roberts.
e-mail: info@ffestinioggolf.org

HARLECH. **Royal St David's Golf Club,** Harlech LL46 2UB (01766 780203). *Location:* A496 lower Harlech road. Championship links course. 18 holes, 6601 yards. S.S.S. 73. Large practice ground. *Green Fees:* weekdays £47.00 per round; weekends £57.00 per round; reduced rates in winter months. *Eating facilities:* full catering and bar facilities available. *Visitors:* must be members of bona fide golf clubs with Handicap - booking essential. *Society Meetings:* catered for by prior arrangement. Professional: John Barnett (01766 780857). Secretary: D.L. Morkill (01766 780361; Fax: 01766 781110).
e-mail: secretary@royalstdavids.co.uk
website: www.royalstdavids.co.uk

LLANGEFNI. **Llangefni Public Golf Course,** Clai Road (B5111), Llangefni, Isle of Anglesey LL77 8YQ. Parkland course, eight Par 3s, one Par 4. 9 holes, 1467 yards, 1342 metres. Practice net. *Green Fees:* information not available. *Eating facilities:* light refreshments only. *Visitors:* welcome at all times, no restrictions. Fully stocked Discount Golf Shop. Professional: Paul Lovell (01248 722193).

MORFA BYCHAN. **Porthmadog Golf Club,** Morfa Bychan, Porthmadog LL49 9UU (Tel & Fax: 01766 514124). *Location:* turn in Porthmadog High Street at Woolworths towards Black Rock Sands, club on left hand side of road one mile west. Part parkland, part seaside links. 18 holes, 6322 yards. S.S.S. 71. Two practice grounds. *Green Fees:* per round £30.00 weekdays, £35.00 weekends and Bank Holidays; £37.00 and £42.00 for day tickets. Discounts available for larger parties (2008 fees under review). *Eating facilities:* lounge bar, golfers' bar and large restaurant. *Visitors:* welcome, no restrictions except for competition days. Snooker room. *Society Meetings:* catered for by prior arrangement. Bookings via Office Manager: Åse Richardson (01766 514124). Professional: Peter L. Bright (01766 513828). Club Manager: Gwilym Jones.
e-mail: secretary@porthmadog-golf-club.co.uk
website: www.porthmadog-golf-club.oo.uk

NEFYN. **Nefyn and District Golf Club,** Golf Road, Morfa Nefyn, Pwllheli LL53 6DA (Fax: 01758 720476). *Location:* north coast of Lleyn Peninsula, two miles west of Nefyn. Seaside course. 27 holes. Main Course - 18 holes, 6548 yards. S.S.S. 71. Practice area. *Green Fees:* (2007) Weekday (Monday to Thursday) £35.00 per round, £46.00 per day; Weekend (including Friday and Bank Holidays) £42.00 per round, £55.00 per day. 10% discount for parties of 12 or more players. *Eating facilities:* full restaurant facilities and two bars. *Visitors:* welcome without reservation, except club competition days. Snooker. *Society Meetings:* catered for by arrangement with Secretary. Professional: John Froom (01758 720102). Secretary: S. Dennis (01758 720966).

PENMAENMAWR. **Penmaenmawr Golf Club,** Conwy Old Road, Penmaenmawr LL34 6RD (01492 623330). *Location:* A55 expressway three miles west of Conwy. Parkland with panoramic views. 9 holes (18 tees), 5306 yards. S.S.S. 67. Two practice areas. *Green Fees:* £15.00 weekdays, £20.00 weekends. *Eating facilities:* bar and bar snacks, meals available daily except Tuesdays. *Visitors:* welcome anytime except Saturdays. *Society Meetings:* welcome by arrangement (not Saturdays). Secretary: A. Greenwood (01492 623330).

Pwllheli Golf Club

Golf Road, Pwllheli
Gwynedd LL53 5PS
Office: 01758 701644
Professional: 01758 701644

Excellent 18-hole course combining both parkland and links, with superb views of the Snowdonia and Cambrian mountain ranges, and across Cardigan Bay.

Green Fees: on request

Societies welcome and special rates are available for parties of 10 or more players.

admin@pwllheligolfclub.co.uk
www.pwllheligolfclub.co.uk

PWLLHELI. **LLyn Golf,** Pen-y-Berth, Penrhos, Pwllheli LL53 7HG (01758 701200). *Location*: off A499 between Pwllheli and Abersoch. New 9-hole pay and play course. 1782 yards, Par 3 and 4. 14-bay driving range, bunker practice area. *Green Fees:* information not available. *Eating facilities:* refreshments available. *Visitors:* welcome. Open daily. Clubs for hire. *Society Meetings:* welcome. website: www.pen-y-berth.co.uk

PWLLHELI. **Pwllheli Golf Club,** Golf Road, Pwllheli LL53 5PS (01758 701644). *Location:* A499 from Caernarvon (20 miles). Parkland/seaside links. 18 holes, 6108 yards. S.S.S. 70. Two practice areas and putting green. *Green Fees:* weekday £34.00, weekend £39.00; twilight after 4pm £25.00. *Eating facilities:* two large lounge bars and diningroom. Steward: (01758

701633). *Visitors:* welcome without reservation. Pro shop. *Society Meetings:* welcome. Professional: S. Pilkington (01758 701644). General Manager: Mr Dennis Moore (01758 701644).
e-mail: admin@pwllheligolfclub.co.uk
website: www.pwllheligolfclub.co.uk

RHOSNEIGR. **The Anglesey Golf Club Ltd,** Station Road, Rhosneigr, Anglesey LL64 5QX (Tel & Fax: 01407 811202; Club House 01407 810219). *Location*: turn south off A55 Junction 5 signposted Rhosneigr, Aberffraw. In about three miles turn right at Llanfaelog church about one mile from course. Flat links course with sand dunes and heathland. 18 holes, 6300 yards. S.S.S. 71. *Green Fees*: please phone for current prices. *Eating facilities*: catering facilities available all day. *Visitors*: welcome, advanced booking advisable. Dress smart casual. *Society Meetings*: club societies welcome. Professional tuition. Contact Matthew Parry for further details (01407 811202).
e-mail: info@theangleseygolfclub.com
website: www.angleseygolfclub.co.uk

TENBY. **Trefloyne Golf Club,** Trefloyne Park, Penally, Tenby SA70 7RG (01834 842165). *Location:* on edge of village of Penally, just off A4139 Tenby/Pembroke road, about one mile from Tenby. Men's course - 18 holes, 6635 yards, 6068 metres, S.S.S. yellow tees 72, white 73, Par 71. Ladies' course - 18 holes, 5764 yards, 5271 metres, S.S.S. 73, Par 73. Practice ground. *Green Fees:* information not available. *Eating facilities:* full restaurant and bar service, with breakfast and snack menu. *Visitors:* always welcome. Full equipment hire, clubs, trolleys and motorised buggies. Club Professional: Christine Burton PGA, Pro Shop: (01834 845639). Course Manager: Sarah Beynon.*
website: www.trefloyne.com

TREARDDUR BAY. **Holyhead Golf Club,** Trearddur Bay, Anglesey LL62 2YL (Tel & Fax: 01407 763279). *Location:* A55 to Holyhead, turn left at roundabout on B4545 for 1 mile, left for Trearddur Bay. Heathland, heavy gorse cover, superb sea views. Course designed by James Braid. 18 holes, 6058 yards. S.S.S. 70. *Green Fees:* information not provided. *Eating facilities:* restaurant/bar. *Visitors:* welcome. *Society Meetings:* catered for weekdays. Dormy House accommodation available for up to 14. Professional: Steve Elliot (01407 762022). Managing Secretary: Richard D. Barrance.
website: www.holyheadgolfclub.co.uk

North Wales

ABERGELE. **Abergele Golf Club,** Tan-y-Gopa Road, Abergele, Conwy LL22 8DS (01745 824034; Fax: 01745 824772). *Location:* A55 from Chester. Below Gwrych Castle, Abergele. Parkland in scenic setting. 18 holes, 6256 yards. S.S.S. 70. USGA greens. Practice ground and indoor practice nets. *Green Fees:* information not provided. *Eating facilities:* restaurant and bar. *Visitors:* welcome, avoid Tuesdays (Ladies' Day) and Saturdays difficult due to club competitions. Buggy hire available, trolleys. *Society Meetings:* visiting party packages available. Professional: Iain R. Runcie (Tel & Fax: 01745 823813). Secretary: Chris Langdon (01745 824034; Fax: 01745 824772).
website: www.abergelegolfclub.co.uk

BETWS-Y-COED. **Betws-y-Coed Golf Club,** The Clubhouse, Betws-y-Coed LL24 0AL (01690 710556). *Location:* take Railway Museum Road in centre of the village. Parkland, flat scenic course on valley floor of River Conwy. 9 holes, 18 tees, 4998 yards. S.S.S. 63. *Green Fees:* information not available. *Eating facilities:* bar open from 12 noon onwards. *Visitors:* no restrictions provided there are no club competitions. *Society Meetings:* welcome. Secretary: Dafydd Hughes.
e-mail: info@golf-betws-y-coed.co.uk
website: www.golf-betws-y-coed.co.uk

BODELWYDDAN. **Kinmel Park Golf Complex,** Abergele Road, Bodelwyddan LL18 5SR (01745 833548). *Location:* Junction 25 off A55 Expressway at the famous White Marble church. Flat parkland course. 9 holes, 1550 yards. S.S.S. 58. 25 bay undercover and floodlit driving range. Practice chipping and putting green. *Green Fees:* Pay and Play course £5.00 weekdays, £6.00 weekends. Subject to review. *Visitors:* welcome. Golf lessons available. *Society Meetings:* Welcome, special rates. Professional: Rhodri Lloyd Jones. Director: Mrs Fetherstonhaugh.
website: www.kinmelgolf.co.uk

CHESTER near. **Northop Country Park Golf Club,** Northop, Near Chester CH7 6WA (01352 840440; Fax: 01352 840445). *Location:* travel west on M56, follow signs for North Wales. A494/A55 for Northop. Parkland course set amongst 300 year old oak trees, designed by John Jacobs. 18 holes, 6735 yards, 6128 metres. S.S.S. 74. Practice range and academy. *Green Fees:* information not available. *Eating facilities:* clubroom for snacks, club restaurant for full meals. *Visitors:* welcome. St David's Park Hotel only five minutes away for accommodation. *Society Meetings:* welcome depending on availability. Professional: Matthew Pritchard. Director of Golf: Neil Sweeney.*

CHIRK. **Chirk Golf Club,** Chirk, Near Wrexham LL14 5AD (01691 774407; Fax: 01691 773878). *Location:* just off A5 towards Llangollen. Generally flat course. 18 holes, 6541 yards. S.S.S. 72. 9 hole Par 3 course, 15 bay driving range. *Green Fees:* information not available. *Eating facilities:* bar and restaurant. *Visitors:* welcome seven days a week. *Society Meetings:* all welcome. Professional: M. Maddison (01691 774407).*

COLWYN. **Old Colwyn Golf Club,** The Clubhouse, Woodland Avenue, Old Colwyn LL29 9NL (01492 515581). *Location:* signposted at main Abergele road, Old Colwyn. Parkland. 9 holes (x 2), 5263 yards. S.S.S. 68. *Green Fees:* information not available. *Eating facilities:* bar and meals by arrangement. *Visitors:* welcome except Saturday afternoons or Wednesday evenings. *Society Meetings:* welcome by arrangement with Secretary. Secretary: D.A. Jones. *

THE APPEARANCE OF AN ASTERISK (*) AT THE END OF A CLUB OR COURSE ENTRY INDICATES THAT UP-TO-DATE INFORMATION HAS NOT BEEN SUPPLIED

CONWY. **Conwy (Caernarvonshire) Golf Club,** Morfa, Conwy LL32 8ER (01492 592423). *Location:* follow signs for Conwy Marina off A55 Junction 17. Seaside links. 18 holes, 6647 yards. S.S.S. 72. Practice facilities. *Green Fees:* Winter package (coffee on arrival, 18 holes plus meal) - please contact Secretary; Summer (April to October) - £45.00 per round, £50.00 per day all week. *Eating facilities:* available daily April to October. *Visitors:* welcome with reservation, restrictions at weekends. *Society Meetings:* catered for on application to Secretary. Professional: Peter Lees (Tel & Fax: 01492 593225). Secretary: D.L. Brown (01492 592423; Fax: 01492 593363).
e-mail: secretary@conwygolfclub.co.uk
website: www.conwygolfclub.co.uk

DENBIGH. **Denbigh Golf Club,** Henllan Road, Denbigh LL16 5AA (01745 816669. Fax: 01745 814888). *Location:* one mile from Denbigh town centre on the B5382 road. Parkland with excellent views. 18 holes, 5746 yards. S.S.S. 68. *Green Fees:* weekdays from £24.00, weekends from £30.00. Subject to review. *Eating facilities:* catering daily, bar. *Visitors:* welcome. *Society Meetings:* by arrangement. Professional: M.D. Jones (01745 814159). Manager: John Williams.
e-mail: denbighgolfclub@aol.com
website: www.denbighgolfclub.co.uk

DENBIGH near. **Bryn Morfydd Hotel Golf Club,** Llanrhaeadr, Near Denbigh LL16 4NP (01745 589090; Fax: 01745 589093). *Location:* off A525 between Denbigh and Ruthin. Mature parkland course overlooking Vale of Clwyd. The Duchess Course: 9 holes, 1146 yards. Par 27. The Duke's Course: 18 holes, 5685 yards. S.S.S. 67, Par 70. Practice area. *Green Fees:* information not provided. *Eating facilities:* courses attached to three star Hotel, two restaurants, two bars, clubhouse. *Visitors:* welcome by arrangement. Hotel with 25 rooms en suite. *Society Meetings:* welcome by arrangement all year. Secretary/ Director of Golf: C. Henderson. Proprietors: D. & S. Frith.

FLINT. **Flint Golf Club,** Cornist Park, Flint CH6 5HJ (01352 732327). *Location:* A548 coast road, one mile from town centre. Hilly parkland. 9 holes, 5927 yards. S.S.S. 69. Practice area. *Green Fees:* information not available. *Eating facilities:* full bar and catering 11am to 11pm. *Visitors:* welcome except Sundays. *Society Meetings:* welcome by arrangement. Secretary: Mr Geoff Hughes (01352 735245).*

HAWARDEN. **Hawarden Golf Club,** Groomsdale Lane, Hawarden CH5 3EH (01244 531447. Fax: 01244 536901). *Location:* A55, left at Ewloe interchange, follow Hawarden signs. Undulating parkland. 18

Conwy (Caernarvonshire) Golf Club

Morfa, Conwy LL32 8ER
Tel: (Secretary): 01492 592423 • Fax: 01492 593363
e-mail: secretary@conwygolfclub.co.uk
www.conwygolfclub.co.uk

A truly magnificent and spectacular setting for golf, in the shadow of Conwy Mountain overlooking the estuary towards Llandudno.
A flat, links layout, the first Welsh course to be a final qualifying course for the Open Championship.
"tough but very fair"

Modern Clubhouse with bars, lounge, snooker room and excellent dining facilities.

Visitors and Societies welcome.
For reservations contact the Secretary

18-hole parkland course offering a challenging round of golf, combined with superb panoramic views along the Vale of Clwyd to the coast.

Visitors and Societies welcome
Packages start from £24.00

Denbigh Golf Club
Henllan Road, Denbigh,
North Wales LL16 5AA
Secretary: 01745 816669
denbighgolfclub@aol.com
www.denbighgolfclub.co.uk

holes, 5842 yards, 5340 metres. S.S.S. 69, Par 69. *Green Fees:* information not available. *Eating facilities:* full bar and catering. *Visitors:* welcome by arrangement. Some restrictions Wednesday (Ladies' Day). *Society Meetings:* catered for by prior arrangement. Summer and Winter packages available. Professional: Alex Rowlands (01244 520809). Secretary: Malcolm Coppack.*

HOLYWELL. **Holywell Golf Club,** Brynford, Near Holywell CH8 8LQ (01352 713937). *Location:* turn off A55 at Junction 32 onto A5026, turn left at traffic lights, signed for Brynford, up hill for one and a half miles, turn right at crossroads. Flat natural terrain, links type course, a good test of golf. 18 holes, 6100 yards. S.S.S. 70. *Green Fees:* weekdays £20.00, weekends and Bank Holidays £25.00. Special rates between November and March. *Eating facilities:* full bar facilities and catering. *Visitors:* welcome weekdays without reservation; Bank Holidays and weekends by prior arrangement with Secretary. Snooker table. *Society Meetings:* by prior arrangement with Secretary. Professional: Matthew Parsley (01352 710040). Hon Secretary: Bob Fiddaman (Tel & Fax: 01352 713937).
e-mail: holywell_golf_club@lineone.net

HOLYWELL **Kinsale Golf Course,** Llanerchymor, Holywell CH8 9DX (01745 561080; Fax: 01745 561079). *Location:* A55 expressway, Holywell to A548; opposite White Shlp Abakham Textiles. Magnificent view over Dee Estuary towards the Wirral. 9 holes, 5944 yards. S.S.S. 69. Driving range. *Green Fees:* 9 holes £8.00, 18 holes £12.00. *Eating facilities:* snacks in clubhouse. *Visitors:* always welcome; pay as you play course.

LLANDUDNO. **Llandudno Golf Club (Maesdu) Ltd,** Hospital Road, Llandudno LL30 1HU (Tel & Fax: 01492 876450). *Location:* Llandudno General Hospital. A55 and then A470. Parkland. 18 holes, 6545 yards. S.S.S. 72. Practice ground. *Green Fees:* weekdays £25.00 per round, £35.00 per day; weekends and Bank Holidays £30.00 per round, £40.00 per day. *Eating facilities:* full catering, bar (large) available. *Visitors:* welcome, must book. Buggies, electric trolleys for hire. *Society Meetings:* must be booked. Professional: S. Boulden (01492 875195). Secretary: George Dean (01492 876450)
e-mail: secretary@maesdugolfclub.co.uk
website: www.maesdugolfclub.co.uk

The Imperial Hotel

Conferences • Seminars • Luncheons • Dinner Dances • Golf Breaks

Christmas Functions • Weddings • Civil Weddings • Social Weekends

MINT *Condition*

Health and Fitness Centre:
45' Heated Pool - Sauna - Steam Room - 2 Gyms

The Promenade, Llandudno LL30 1AP Tel: 01492 877466 Fax: 01492 870552
sales@theimperial.co.uk www.theimperial.co.uk

LLANDUDNO. **North Wales Golf Club Ltd,** 72 Brynlau Road, West Shore, Llandudno LL30 2DZ. *Location:* two miles off the A55 expressway on the A470 Junction. Seaside links with wonderful views of Conwy estuary and mountains. 18 holes, 6287 yards, S.S.S. 71. Practice ground. *Green Fees:* information not available. *Eating facilities:* full bar and catering facilities. *Visitors:* welcome after 9.30am weekdays, 10.30am weekends. Buggies, carts and clubs for hire. *Society Meetings:* catered for by arrangement. Professional: R.A. Bradbury (01492 876878; Fax: 01492 872420). General Manager: Gren Jones (01492 875325; Fax: 01492 873355).*
e-mail: golf@nwgc.freeserve.co.uk
website: www.northwalesgolfclub.co.uk

LLANDUDNO. **Rhos-on-Sea Residential Golf Club**, Penrhyn Bay, Llandudno LL30 3PU (01492 549641; Fax: 01492 549100). *Location:* A55 to Colwyn Bay follow signs to Rhos-on-Sea, one mile past Rhos-on-Sea on coast road in Penrhyn Bay. Flat seaside parkland course. 18 holes, 6064 yards. S.S.S. 69. *Green Fees:* information not available. *Eating facilities:* full catering available 8.30am tp 9pm, 7 days a week. Licensed bar with new licensing hours available. *Visitors:* welcome 7 days a week, prior booking required. Dormy house hotel with 12 bedrooms, sleeping up to 24 all ensuite with televisions. Licensed for weddings. Snooker tables, TV lounge. Trolley and buggy hire available. *Society Meetings:* all welcome. Professional: Jonathan Kelly (01492 548115). Secretary: Gordon Downs.*

LLANFAIRFECHAN. **Llanfairfechan Golf Club**, Llannerch Road, Llanfairfechan LL33 0EB (01248 680144 evenings and after 11am at weekends, 07737385070 anytime). *Location:* signposted off old A55, 300 yards west of traffic lights. Hillside parkland. 9 holes (14 tees & 12 greens), 3103 yards. Par 54, S.S.S. 57. *Green Fees:*information not available. *Eating facilities:* no eating facilities at club without prior arrangement, (available in village); bar opens weekday evenings (afternoons June - August) and from 11am weekends. *Visitors:* welcome anytime except Sundays and most Saturdays from June - September. *Society Meetings:* by arrangement, weekdays only in Summer. Secretary: R .C . Ingham.*
e-mail: hon.sec.llgc@btconnect.com

LLANGOLLEN. **Vale of Llangollen Golf Club Ltd.**, The Clubhouse, Llangollen LL20 7PR (01978 860906; Fax: 01987 869165). *Location:* one and a half miles east of town on the A5. Course is set on the valley floor bordered by the River Dee. 18 holes, 6656 yards, 6086 metres. S.S.S. 73. Practice ground. *Green Fees:* weekdays £35.00 per round, £40.00 per day, weekends £40.00 per round, £45.00 per day. Subject to review. *Eating facilities:* full catering service. *Visitors:* welcome any day subject to availability, Handicap Certificate essential. *Society Meetings:* welcome. Professional: David Vaughan (01978 860906). Secretary: Bob Hardy (01978 860906; Fax: 01987 869165).
e-mail: info@vlgc.co.uk

MOLD. **Mold Golf Club**, Cilcain Road, Pantymwyn, Mold CH7 5EH (01352 741513; Fax: 01352 741517). *Location:* 14 miles west of Chester. Take A55 from Chester for Mold. Follow Pantymwyn signs from Mold. Uplands course offering extensive views of Cheshire, Liverpool, Peak District. 18 holes, 5628 yards. S.S.S. 67. Practice ground and practice green. *Green Fees:* information not provided. *Eating facilities:* extensive restaurant and bar facilities.

Visitors: welcome by prior arrangement. Tee bookings advised at weekends. Trolley hire. *Society Meetings:* welcome, subject to tee availability. Professional: Mark Jordan (01352 740318) (Lessons by appointment). Secretary: C. Mills (01352 741513; Fax: 01352 741517).
e-mail: info@moldgolfclub.co.uk

MOLD. **Padeswood and Buckley Golf Club,** The Caia, Station Lane, Padeswood, Near Mold CH7 4JD (01244 550537). *Location*: A5118 Chester - Mold, one mile west of Castle Cement Works, half a mile off main road. Flat parkland; river, lakes. 18 holes, 6042 yards. S.S.S. 69. Practice ground. *Green Fees:* £25.00 weekdays. *Eating facilities:* bar all day every day, catering daily. *Visitors*: welcome except on Sundays. Buggies, carts for hire; two snooker tables. *Society Meetings:* welcome, enquiries through Secretary; packages available. Professional: David Ashton (01244 543636). Secretary: Mrs S.A. Davies (01244 550537).

PADESWOOD. **Old Padeswood Golf Club Ltd,** Station Road, Padeswood, Near Mold CH7 4JD (01244 547701). *Location:* off A5118 Chester to Mold road, eight miles from Chester and three miles from Mold. Situated in the beautiful Alyn Valley - nine holes flat parkland, nine holes slightly undulating. 18 holes, 6668 yards, 6079 metres. S.S.S. 72/Ladies 73. Practice ground. *Green Fees:* weekdays £25.00, with member £13.00; weekends £30.00, with member £15.00. *Eating facilities:* diningroom, bar meals - two bars. *Visitors:* welcome anytime subject to tee availability. *Society Meetings:* welcome, written applications or telephone Steve Shaw on (01244 547701). Professional: Tony Davies (01244 547401). Co-Secretary: Mrs B. Jones (01244 550414; Fax: 01244 545082). Hon. Secretary: Mr B. Slater (01244 816573; Fax: 01244 545082).
e-mail: oldpad@par72.fsbusiness.co.uk
website: www.oldpadeswoodgolfclub.co.uk

PRESTATYN. **Prestatyn Golf Club,** Marine Road East, Prestatyn LL19 7HS (01745 854320). Location: A548, on approaching Prestatyn from Chester direction turn right at sign for Pontins Holiday Village and follow club sign. Seaside links Championship course. 18 holes, 6564 yards, 5959 metres. S.S.S. 72. Practice areas. Green Fees: information not available. Eating facilities: full catering available, bar. Visitors: welcome. Society Meetings: special "all-in" arrangement for 27 holes. Professional: D. Ames (01745 854320). Manager: S.L. Owen (Tel & Fax: 01745 854320).*
e-mail: prestatyngcmanager@freenet.co.uk
website: www.prestatyngolfclub.co.uk
          www.ukgolfer.org

PRESTATYN. **St Melyd Golf Club,** The Paddock, Meliden Road, Prestatyn LL19 8NB (01745 854405; Fax: 01745 856908). *Location:* on main Prestatyn to Rhuddlan road, just outside Meliden. Parkland course with tight fairways and varied greens, set twixt the hills and the sea. 9 holes, 5811 yards. S.S.S. 68. *Green Fees:* information not provided. *Eating facilities:* full range of catering facilities except Tuesdays which is by arrangement. *Visitors:* welcome without reservation but advise phone call first in summer season. Restriction Saturdays Competition Day; Thursdays Ladies' Day. Snooker room. *Society Meetings:* catered for by arrangement with Secretary (various golf packages). Golf coaching available from PGA Professional: Carl Edwards. Administrator: Jean McCormick.
e-mail: info@stmelydgolf.co.uk
website: www.stmelydgolf.co.uk

RHUDDLAN. **Rhuddlan Golf Club,** Meliden Road, Rhuddlan LL22 9DP (01745 590217). *Location:* leave A55 at St Asaph for Rhuddlan, clubhouse 100m from roundabout at Prestatyn end of Rhuddlan. Gently undulating, parkland course with natural hazards; set amid splendid scenery with fine views of the Clwydian Hills. 18 holes, White 6473 yards. S.S.S. 71; Yellow 6291 yards, S.S.S. 70; Ladies 5768 yards, Par 70. Extensive practice ground. *Green Fees:* £30.00 to £35.00. *Eating facilities:* full restaurant facilities daily. *Visitors:* welcome at all times when course demand permits. Sundays with member only. No denim. Snooker table. *Society Meetings:* weekdays only, maximum 50. Professional: A.Carr (01745 590898). Secretary: Jill Roberts (01745 590217; Fax: 01745 590472).
e-mail: secretary@rhuddlangolfclub.co.uk
website: www.rhuddlangolfclub.co.uk

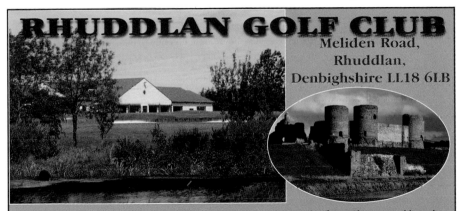
For full details of clubs and courses, plus convenient accommodation
www.uk-golfguide.com

RHYL. **Rhyl Golf Club,** Coast Road, Rhyl LL18 3RE (01745 353171; Fax: 01745 360007). *Location:* situated alongside A548, the Rhyl/ Prestatyn coast road. Flat links. 9 or 18 holes, 6220 yards. S.S.S. 71. Practice ground. *Green Fees:* information not available. *Eating facilities:* dining room, catering and bar snacks available. *Visitors:* always welcome; some restrictions when club competitions in play. Trolleys for hire. *Society Meetings:* society specials available, maximum 60; discounts for 10 or more. Professional: John Stubbs Secretary: Mrs Gill Davies (01745 353171).
e-mail: rhylgolfclub@i12.com
website: www.rhylgolfclub.com

RUTHIN. **Ruthin Pwllglas Golf Club,** Pwllglas, Near Ruthin LL15 2PE (01824 702296). *Location:* Corwen Road (A494), two miles south of Ruthin. Parkland. 10 holes, 5418 yards. S.S.S. 66. Practice area. *Green Fees:* weekdays £16.00, weekends and Bank Holidays £22.00. *Eating facilities:* Bar. Secretary can arrange catering for visiting parties. *Visitors:* welcome without reservation, phone call advisable in high season and at weekends. *Society Meetings:* catered for. Hon. Secretary: Eric Owen (01824 702383).

WREXHAM. **Moss Valley Golf Club,** Moss Road, Wrexham LL11 6HA (Tel & Fax: 01978 720518). Private members' club. *Location:* off A541 from Wrexham roundabout. Parkland course meandering through wooded valley. 9/18 holes (twin tees on every hole), 2531 yards. S.S.S. 67. *Green Fees:* information not available. *Visitors:* welcome, booking required at weekend. *Society Meetings:* contact in advance. Manager/Secretary: John Parry.*
e-mail: info@mossvalleygolf.com
website: www.mossvalleygolf.com

WREXHAM. **Plassey Golf Course,** Eyton, Wrexham LL13 0SP (01978 780020; Fax: 01978 781397). *Location:* 4 miles south-east of Wrexham. Take B5426 and follow brown "Tourist Attraction" signs to "Plassey" from A483 Wrexham by-pass. Undulating parkland course. 9 holes, 4961 yards, Par 66. Practice area, driving net, pitch and putt. *Green Fees:* information not available. *Visitors:* most welcome. Please book start times at weekends. Full bar and catering facilities. Golf course is part of Plassey Leisure Park which includes shops, boutiques, craft centre, brewery, garden centre, blacksmith and award-winning Caravan & Campsite. *Society Meetings:* most welcome (please book start times at weekends). Proprietor/Professional: Simon Ward (PGA Qualified).*
website: www.plasseygolf.co.uk

WREXHAM. **Wrexham Golf Club,** Holt Road, Wrexham LL13 9SB (01978 351476; Fax: 01978 362168). *Location:* A543 north east of Wrexham. 18 holes, 6263 yards. S.S.S. 70. Practice facilities. *Green Fees:* information not available. *Eating facilities:* daily. *Visitors:* welcome, subject to competitions and Society bookings. *Society Meetings:* catered for Monday, Wednesday, Thursday and Fridays only. Professional: P. Williams (01978 351476). Secretary: Jim Johnson (01978 364268).

> THE APPEARANCE OF AN ASTERISK (*) AT THE END OF A CLUB OR COURSE ENTRY INDICATES THAT UP-TO-DATE INFORMATION HAS NOT BEEN SUPPLIED

Rhuddlan Golf Club, Rhuddlan

Carmarthenshire

AMMANFORD. **Glynhir Golf Club,** Glynhir Road, Llandybie, Ammanford SA18 2TF (Tel & Fax: 01269 851365). *Location:* seven miles from end of M4, between Ammanford and Llandybie on the A483. Turn right up Glynhir Road and proceed for about two miles. Undulating wooded parkland course. 18 holes, 6010 yards. S.S.S. 70. *Green Fees:* information not available. *Eating facilities:* full catering available. *Visitors:* welcome. *Society Meetings:* welcome anytime by prior arrangement with the Secretaries (special rates available). Professional: Richard Herbert (01269 851010). Joint Secretaries: C. Edwards, B. Thorpe (01269 851365).*
e-mail: glynhir.golfclub@virgin.net
website: www.glynhirgolf.co.uk

CARMARTHEN. **Carmarthen Golf Club,** Blaenycoed Road, Carmarthen SA33 6EH (01267 281588). *Location:* four miles north-west of town. Undulating heathland - a good test of golf. 18 holes, 6210 yards. S.S.S. 71. Large practice ground. *Green Fees:* weekdays £25.00, weekends £30.00. *Eating facilities:* catering every day. *Visitors:* welcome, telephone call advisable at weekends. *Society Meetings:* by arrangement. Professional: Jon Hartley (01267 281493). Secretary: Peter Ward (01267 281588).
e-mail: info@carmarthengolfclub.co.uk
website: www.carmarthengolfclub.co.uk

CARMARTHEN. **Derllys Court Golf Club,** Llysonnen Road, Bancyfelin, Carmarthen SA33 5DT (Tel. & Fax: 01267 211575). *Location:* three miles west of Carmarthen on A40, signposted. Gently undulating parkland. 18 holes, 5650 yards. Practice area. *Green Fees:* information not provided. *Eating facilities:* bar/lounge and restaurant. *Visitors:* welcome at all times. *Society Meetings:* welcome by prior arrangement. Secretary: Rhian Walters.
e-mail: derllys@hotmail.com
website: www.derllyscourtgolfclub.com

KIDWELLY/LLANELLI. **Glyn Abbey Golf Club,** Trimsaren, Kidwelly SA17 4LB (01554 810278; Fax: 01554 810889). *Location:* five miles north west of Llanelli on the B4317 between Trimsaran and Carway. Parkland course with spectacular views, Hawtree design, mature woodland. 18 holes, 6173 yards, Par 70. S.S.S. 70. *Green Fees:* £18.00 midweek, £25.00 weekends. *Eating facilities:* fully licensed clubhouse and restaurant. *Visitors:* welcome at all times with no restrictions. Advisable to phone ahead and book. *Society Meetings:* always very welcome by prior arrangement. Professional: Darren Griffiths. Managing Director: Martin Lane
e-mail: course-enquiries@glynabbey.co.uk
website: www.glynabbey.co.uk

LLANDYSUL. **Saron Golf Course,** Penwern, Saron, Llandysul SA44 5EL (01559 370705). *Location:* midway between Carmarthen and Newcastle Emlyn on the A484. Parkland course in the Teifi Valley set in 50 acres. 9 holes 18 tees. 9 holes 2091 yards, 18 holes 4412 yards. *Green Fees:* 9 holes £9.00, under 15s £5.00, 18 holes £12.00, under 15s £6.00. *Visitors:* welcome at all times. Three cottages on course, sleeping six/ four/two. *Society Meetings:* welcome. Secretary: Mr C. Searle (01559 370705).
e-mail: c9mbl@sarongolf.freeserve.co.uk
website: www.saron-golf.com

LLANELLI. **Ashburnham Golf Club,** Cliffe Terrace, Burry Port SA16 0HN (01554 833846). *Location:* south side of A484, four miles west of Llanelli. Seaside links with Championship status. 18 holes. S.S.S. 73. Practice area. *Green Fees:* Monday to Friday £50.00, Saturday and Sunday after 3pm only, £39.00. *Eating facilities:* catering except Mondays, two bars. *Visitors:* welcome, up to seven days in advance; starting times available from the Pro Shop. Handicap Certificates required. Carts available. *Society Meetings:* by arrangement with Secretary. Professional: Martin Stimson (01554 833846). Secretary: Ian K. Church (01554 832269).
e-mail: golf@ashburnhamgolfclub.co.uk
website: www.ashburnhamgolfclub.co.uk

Carmarthen Golf Club

Ceredigion

ABERYSTWYTH. **Aberystwyth Golf Club,** Brynymor Road, Aberystwyth SY23 2HY (01970 615104; Fax: 01970 626622). *Location:* north end of Promenade, access near to cliff railway. Undulating meadowland designed by Harry Vardon. 18 holes, white - 6119 yards. S.S.S. 71. Practice ground. *Green Fees:* information not available. *Eating facilities:* restaurant and bar. *Visitors:* welcome at all times, pre-booking helpful. *Society Meetings:* welcome, Special Deals available. Professional: (01970 625301). Secretary: (01970 615104).t

BORTH. **Borth and Ynyslas Golf Club Ltd,** Borth, Ceredigion SY24 5JS (Tel & Fax: 01970 871202). *Location:* A487 Machynlleth to Aberystwyth, turn off to Borth. Gently undulating links. 18 holes, 6116 yards. S.S.S. 70 men, 72 ladies. Practice ground. *Green Fees:* information not available. *Eating facilities:* clubhouse with full catering and bar. *Visitors:* welcome at all times. *Society Meetings:* by prior arrangement with the Secretary, special rates available. Professional: J.G. Lewis (01970 871557). Secretary: G.J. Pritchard (01970 871202).*
e-mail: secretary@borthgolf.co.uk

CARDIGAN. **Cardigan Golf Club,** Gwbert-on-Sea, Cardigan SA43 1PR (01239 612035). Location: three miles from Cardigan. Seaside links course. 18 holes, 6687 yards. S.S.S. 73. Green Fees: weekdays £27.50, weekends and Bank Holidays £35.00. Eating facilities: catering and bar facilities available. Visitors: welcome. Tee reserved for members 1pm–2pm. Society Meetings: very welcome. Reductions on application. Professional: S. Parsons (01239 615359). Secretary: Mr J. Jones (Tel & Fax: 01239 621775).*
e-mail: golf@cardigan.fsnet.co.uk
website: www.cardigangolf.co.uk

LAMPETER. **Cilgwyn Golf Club,** Llangybi, Lampeter SA48 8NN (01570 493286). *Location:* five miles north-east of Lampeter, off A485 Tregaron Road at Llangybi. Flat parkland course with natural hazards. 9 holes, 5309 yards, S.S.S. 66. Large practice ground and putting green. *Green Fees:* weekdays £12.00, weekends £17.00. *Eating facilities:* full bar and snacks. *Visitors:* welcome without restrictions – please telephone at weekends April to September. Trolley hire, pool table, TV. Caravan parking and golf for Caravan Club members. *Society Meetings:* welcome Wednesdays and Fridays by prior arrangement. Package deals for parties of six or more. Secretary: J.D. Morgan (01570 423226).

LLANDYSUL. **Cwmrhydneuadd Golf Club,** Pentregat, Plwmp, Llandysul SA44 6HD (01239 654933). *Location:* follow the Aberystwyth to Cardigan A487 trunk road to the village of Pentregat, then follow signs to golf club. Parkland course set in picturesque, secluded valley, surrounded by wooded hills. Includes three small lakes. 9 holes, 4061 yards. S.S.S. 62. *Green Fees:* information not provided. *Eating facilities:* club house; home-made snacks, meals. *Visitors:* welcome, no restrictions. *Society Meetings:* welcome. Secretary: J. Curry (01559 362253).

LLANRHYSTYD. **Penrhos Golf and Country Club,** Llanrhystyd SY23 5AY (01974 202999; Fax: 01974 202100). *Location:* nine miles south of Aberystwyth on A487. Parkland and meadowland with lakes and panoramic views of the Welsh countryside and Cardiagan Bay. 18 holes, 6641 yards. S.S.S. 73. Floodlit driving range, practice ground, 9 holes Par 3, Par 4. *Green Fees:* from £15.00. *Eating facilities:* bar meals and table d'hôte restaurant. *Visitors:* welcome at all times. Accommodation in en suite hotel on site with full leisure facilities. *Society Meetings:* welcome all week by appointment. Professional: Paul Diamond. Secretary: R. Rees-Evans. e-mail: info@penrhosgolf.co.uk website: www.penrhosgolf.co.uk

THE APPEARANCE OF AN ASTERISK (*) AT THE END OF A CLUB OR COURSE ENTRY INDICATES THAT UP-TO-DATE INFORMATION HAS NOT BEEN SUPPLIED

Pembrokeshire

FISHGUARD/HAVERFORDWEST. **Priskilly Forest Golf Club,** Castlemorris, Haverfordwest SA62 5EH (Tel & Fax: 01348 840276). *Location*: A40 Haverfordwest to Fishguard road, left turn at Letterston B4331 towards Mathry. Picturesque undulating parkland surrounded by rhododendrons, etc – a challenging course. 9 holes, 5874 yards. S.S.S. 69. Practice net and ground, trolleys and buggy for hire. *Green Fees:* £14.00 for 9 holes, £20.00 for 18 holes, £24.00 per day. Special winter rates/packages available. *Eating facilities:* licensed bar, light refreshments. *Visitors:* a warm welcome is assured. Accommodation with golf inclusive packages on site in 4-Star country house. Buggies for hire £18.00 for 18 holes. *Society Meetings:* welcome. Secretary: P. Evans. e-mail: jevans@priskilly-forest.co.uk website: www.priskilly-golfclub.co.uk

HAVERFORDWEST. **Haverfordwest Golf Club,** Arnolds Down, Haverfordwest SA61 2XQ (01437 763565). *Location:* one mile east of town on A40 trunk road. A parkland course set in Pembrokeshire National Park – challenging but easy walking. 18 holes, 5986 yards. S.S.S. 69. Practice area and putting green. *Green Fees:* contact for current rate. *Eating facilities:* dining room, bar snacks 11am to 9pm. *Visitors:* welcome. *Society Meetings:* welcome by arrangement. Professional: Alex Pile (01437 768409). Secretary: Mike Foley (01437 764523; Fax: 01437 764143). Full details on our website. e-mail: haverfordwestgc@btconnect.com website: www.haverfordwestgolfclub.co.uk

MILFORD HAVEN. **Dawn till Dusk Golf Club**, Furze Hill Farm, Rosemarket, Milford Haven SA73 1JY (01437 890281). *Location*: from Haverfordwest Bypass take A4076 as far as Johnston, turn left, signposted Rosemarket, one and a quarter miles to crossroads, turn right, one mile on left side of road. Flat parkland course. 9 holes (18 tees), 6373 yards, S.S.S. 71. Putting green, bunkers. *Green Fees*: information not available. *Visitors*: welcome at all times. *Society Meetings*: welcome, rates negotiable for larger groups. Grass airstrip available, by prior arrangement.* website: www.dawntilldusk.co.uk

MILFORD HAVEN. **Milford Haven Golf Club Ltd,** Woodbine House, Clay Lane, Hubberston, Milford Haven SA72 3RX (01646 697762). *Location:* one mile west of Milford Haven on Dale Road. Parkland overlooking magnificent harbour. 18 holes, 6035 yards. S.S.S. 70. Practice area. *Green Fees:* information not available. *Eating facilities:* bar and restaurant facilities. *Visitors:* welcome at all times, please ring Pro shop to check availability. *Society Meetings:* welcome, special rates available. Professional: Martin Stimson (01646 697762). Secretary/Administrator: Mr C. Pugh (01646 697822; Fax: 01646 697870).* e-mail: cerithmhgc@aol.com website: www.mhgc.co.uk

Haverfordwest Golf Club

Arnolds Down, Haverfordwest, Pembrokeshire SA61 2XQ

Set near the Pembrokeshire National Park and boasting magnificent views of the Preseli Hills, Haverfordwest Golf Club offers a real challenge to golfers of all abilities. Easily reachable on the A40 one mile east of Haverfordwest, this course is located in majestic parkland, and despite being an easy walk, there are a few holes that test the golfer's skill. The clubhouse, built in 1994, has excellent facilities including pro shop, locker rooms, lounge, bars and full catering facilities. **Full details on our website: www.haverfordwestgolfclub.co.uk**

• Club founded 1904 • 18 holes • Parkland • 5986 yards • Par 70
• Societies welcome by arrangement • Green Fee Visitors Welcome • Special Winter Rate Packages
Contact: Alex Pile or Mike Foley on 01437 768409 or 01437 764523 • Fax: 01437 764143

NEWPORT. **Newport Links Golf Club Ltd,** The Golf Club, Golf Course Road, Newport SA42 ONR (01239 820244; Fax: 01239 820085). *Location:* two miles off A487 Cardigan-Fishguard at Newport, Pembrokeshire. Flat seaside links course with breathtaking views over the mountains and bay. 9 holes, 6003 yards. S.S.S. 69. Driving range. *Green Fees:* information not available. *Eating facilities:* full catering and bar facilities available. *Visitors:* welcome, tee times must be booked and Handicap Certificate may be required; Pro shop and buggy hire. Self-catering accommodation available in adjoining clubhouse. *Society Meetings:* welcome by arrangement, please phone Amanda Payne (01239 820244). Professional: Julian Noott PGA (01239 820244). Operations Manager: Amanda Payne (01239 820244). Fax: 01239 820085).
e-mail: newportgc@lineone.net

PEMBROKE DOCK. **South Pembrokeshire Golf Club,** Military Road, Pennar, Pembroke Dock SA72 6SE (01646 621453). *Location*: on headland overlooking Pembroke Dock and The Haven. 18 holes, 6100 yards. S.S.S. 69. Practice facilities. *Green Fees:* weekdays and weekends £20.00. *Eating facilities*: bar, please book for food. *Visitors:* welcome except during club competitions, please telephone. *Society Meetings*: welcome by arrangement.
e-mail: spgc06@tiscali.co.uk
website: www.southpembsgolf.co.uk

ST DAVIDS. **St Davids City Golf Club,** Whitesands Bay, St Davids SA62 6PT (01437 721751). *Location:* follow signs to Whitesands Bay, on Fishguard Road out of St Davids, for two miles. Car park is situated on crossroads with club sign at entrance. If you reach the beach you've gone too far! Seaside links course with spectacular panoramic views over Whitesands Bay and St David's Head. 9 holes, 6117 yards. S.S.S.

70. *Green Fees:* weekdays £18.00 for 18 holes. *Visitors:* welcome at all times but please check at weekends and Bank Holidays; Ladies' Day Friday afternoons, Seniors' Day Thursday afternoon. *Society Meetings:* welcome, book with Secretary. Secretary: James Wilcox (01437 721751).

TENBY. **Tenby Golf Club,** The Burrows, Tenby SA70 7NP *Location:* on A478, near Tenby Railway Station. Seaside links, Championship course, oldest affiliated club in Wales. 18 holes, 6224 yards. S.S.S. 71. Practice ground. *Green Fees:* midweek £20.00-£36.00, weekends £26.00-£45.00. *Eating facilities:* complete dining facilities; licensed bar. *Visitors:* always welcome, subject to club competitions. Handicap Certificate required. Billiards rooms. *Society Meetings:* catered for by advance booking. Professional: Mark Hawkey PGA (01834 844447). Secretary: D. Hancock (Tel & Fax: 01834 842978).
e-mail: tenbygolfclub@uku.co.uk
website: www.tenbygolf.co.uk

TENBY. **Trefloyne Golf Club,** Trefloyne Park, Penally, Tenby SA70 7RG (01834 842165). *Location:* on edge of village of Penally, just off A4139 Tenby/Pembroke road, about one mile from Tenby. Men's course - 18 holes, 6635 yards, 6068 metres, S.S.S. yellow tees 72, white 73, Par 71. Ladies' course - 18 holes, 5764 yards, 5271 metres, S.S.S. 73, Par 73. Practice ground. *Green Fees:* information not available. *Eating facilities:* full restaurant and bar service, with breakfast and snack menu. *Visitors:* always welcome. Full equipment hire, clubs, trolleys and motorised buggies. Club Professional: Christine Burton PGA, Pro Shop: (01834 845639). Course Manager: Sarah Beynon. Club Secretary: Tony Hopkins.*
website: www.trefloyne.com

Newport Links Golf Club

Golf Course Road, Newport, Pembrokeshire SA42 0NR

Newport Links is situated in Pembrokeshire's Coastal National Park. Sitting proudly on the coast, we are a two minute drive from the town of Newport, nestled under Carningli (mountain of the Angels) on the Nevern estuary.

Newport attracts all kinds of people, from walkers and bird watchers to golfers and fishermen. With its well publicised arts and crafts shops and extremely friendly Welsh pubs, we believe Newport has everything you want from your holiday.

To stay with us does not mean you have to play golf. We pride ourselves on our friendly staff who will endeavour to help arrange the perfect break for you.

Whether you want to play on our outstanding 80 year-old links golf course, to salmon fish on the best river in Wales or simply walk the best coastline in Britain, our location makes this all so easy to get to.

Having recently undergone a £1.5 million development, the club offers accommodation of 12 fabulous twin bedrooms and three luxury suites.

With the club moving to 18 holes in 2008 we have decided upon heavily discounted packages for this coming year. The new development enhances the quality of the environment and in no way spoils the unique ambience we have created.

Try Newport Links for yourself and you will see what we mean.

Visitors and societies always receive a warm welcome.

Tel: 01239 820244 • Fax: 01239 820085
newportgc@lineone.net • www.newportlinks.co.uk

Powys

BRECON. **Brecon Golf Club,** Newton Park, Brecon LD3 8PA (01874 622004). *Location:* A40 west of town, half a mile from town centre. Flat parkland course. 9 holes, 5476 yards. S.S.S. 70, Par 70. *Green Fees:* weekdays £15.00, weekends and Bank Holidays £18.00. *Eating facilities:* bars and catering available. *Visitors:* welcome, some restriction Sundays when prior arrangement advisable. *Society Meetings:* by arrangement. Secretary: T. J. Richards. (01874 622004). website: www.brecongolfclub.co.uk

BUILTH WELLS. **Builth Wells Golf Club,** Golf Club Road, Builth Wells LD2 3NF (01982 553296). *Location*: off A483, on outskirts of town on Llandovery Road. Parkland, easy walking. 18 holes. S.S.S. 66. Practice area. Host to the 2005 PGA Welsh Young Professionals Championship. *Green Fees*: £22.00 per round, £30.00 per day weekdays; £25.00 per round, £32.00 per day weekends and Bank Holidays. Three-day ticket £55.00, Five-day ticket £95.00, – prices subject to change. *Eating facilities*: catering all day, two bars. *Visitors*: welcome. *Society Meetings*: welcome, Handicap Certificate required. Professional/Secretary: Simon Edwards (01982 553296; Fax: 01982 551064). e-mail: info@builthwellsgolf.co.uk website: www.builthwellsgolf.co.uk

CRADOC. **Cradoc Golf Club,** Penoyre Park, Cradoc, Brecon LD3 9LP (01874 623658; Fax: 01874 611711). *Location:* about two miles north of the market town of Brecon, off B4520 Upper Chapel Road (signposted) past Brecon Cathedral. Attractive parkland course adjoining the Brecon Beacons National Park, scenic views. 18 holes, 6188 yards. S.S.S. 71. (off back tees) 10-bay floodlit driving range. Welsh Golf Club of the Year 2005. Home of the Coors Champion of Champions Tournament. *Green Fees:* weekdays £26.00 per day, weekends and Bank Holidays £32.00 per day. *Eating facilities:* full catering facilities daily. *Visitors:* welcome daily but restricted on Sundays. Electric trolley/buggy hire. *Society Meetings:* welcome any day; prior arrangement advised especially for Sundays. Special packages available. Professional: R.W. Davies (01874 625524). Club Manager: Bob Barnes (01874 623658). e-mail: secretary@cradoc.co.uk website: www.cradoc.co.uk

CRICKHOWELL. **Old Rectory Hotel and Golf Club,** Llangattock, Crickhowell NP8 1PH (01873 810373). *Location:* A40 to Crickhowell. Course is on a hill with spectacular views. 9 holes, 2878 yards. S.S.S. 54. *Green Fees:* information not available. *Eating facilities:* restaurant, bar meals, two bars. *Visitors:* welcome at all times, no restrictions. Accommodation available in 20 en suite bedrooms. *Society Meetings:* welcome. Secretary: G. Crawford.*

KNIGHTON. **Knighton Golf Club,** The Ffrydd, Knighton LD7 1DL (01547 528646). *Location:* on the A488 to Llandrindod Wells, signposted. Undulating wooded hill course with spectacular views. 9 holes, 5362 yards. S.S.S. 66. *Green Fees:* weekdays £10.00; weekends £15.00, discounts of £5.00 off day rate if playing with a member. *Eating facilities:* bar, meals available; contact Steward (01547 528646). *Visitors:* welcome, no visitors before 4.30pm on Sundays. *Society Meetings:* catered for by prior arrangement. Secretary: Mr D. B. Williams (01547 528046).

LLANDRINDOD WELLS. **Llandrindod Wells Golf Club,** The Clubhouse, Llandrindod Wells LD1 5NY (01597 823873). *Location:* signposted off A483 at south east of town. An 'Inland Links' course set in the rolling hills of mid Wales and patrolled by Red Kites and Buzzards. 18 holes, Men 5759 yards white, 5543 yards yellow, Par 69. Ladies 5143 yards, Par 72. Floodlit driving range. *Green Fees:* weekdays £24.00 per round, £32.00 per day; weekends and Bank Holidays £30.00 per round, £36.00 per day. Five day ticket £100.00; seven day ticket £130.00. Subject to review. Winter packages 1st November to 31st March. *Eating facilities:* full catering daily except Tuesdays when bar snacks only available, two bars. *Visitors:* welcome at all times, no restrictions. Buggy, trolley hire. *Society Meetings:* welcome any day, booking essential. Golf Shop: (01597 822247). Secretary: (Tel & Fax: 01597 823873). e-mail: secretary@lwgc.co.uk website: www.lwgc.co.uk

LLANIDLOES. **St Idloes Golf Club,** Penrallt, Llanidloes SY18 6LG (01686 412559). *Location:* signposted from the town. Take road to Trefeglwys from Llanidloes for one mile, turn left at sharp bend before house. Heathland and elevated course. 9 holes, 5510 yards. S.S.S. 66. Practice putting area. *Green Fees:* £10.00 per 9 holes, £15.00 per 18 holes, £20 per day. *Eating facilities:* Bar snacks available during opening hours, full meals by arrangement for large group, please phone first. *Visitors:* welcome anytime except Sunday mornings or special competitions. *Society Meetings:* welcome, packages available. Please ring the clubhouse.

MACHYNLLETH. **Machynlleth Golf Club,** Felingerrig, Machynlleth SY20 8UH (01654 702000). *Location*: A489 from Newtown, left hand turn before the speed restriction sign on entering Machynlleth. Undulating moorland course. 9 holes, 5726 yards, 5285 metres. S.S.S. 68. Small practice area. *Green Fees*: £18.00 per day. *Eating facilities*: bar. *Visitors*: welcome except during competition days. *Society Meetings*: welcome.

NEWTOWN. **St Giles Golf Club,** Pool Road, Newtown SY16 3AJ (01686 625844). *Location:* convenient to town centre, quarter-of-a-mile north east on A483 from Newtown. Challenging riverside course. 9 holes, 6012 yards. S.S.S. 70. *Green Fees:* information not included. *Visitors:* welcome, with reservation Saturday afternoons and Sunday mornings. 2-Fore-1 welcome. *Society Meetings:* catered for.*

RHOSGOCH. **Rhosgoch Golf Club,** Rhosgoch, Near Hay-on-Wye, Builth Wells LD2 3JY (01497 851251). *Location:* 6 miles north west of Hay-on-Wye, half-a-mile south east of the B4594. Parkland course in beautiful picturesque valley. 9 holes, 4955 yards, Par 68. S.S.S. 66. *Green Fees:* £10.00 weekdays; £12.00 weekends. Membership £170.00. *Eating facilities:* bar/restaurant meals. *Visitors:* welcome anytime. *Society Meetings:* welcome weekdays and Saturdays. Club Steward: Andrew Davies. Secretary: Chris Dance.

WELSHPOOL. **Welsh Border Golf Club,** Bulthy Farm, Middletown, Welshpool SY21 8ER (01743 884247). *Location:* situated off the A458. Parkland course. 9 holes, 6114 yards. S.S.S. 69. Driving range. *Green Fees:* information not available. *Eating facilities:* lunchtime only unless otherwise arranged. *Visitors:* welcome, but tee times must be booked. *Society Meetings:* welcome by prior arrangement. Secretary: Keith Farr (0796 663 0042).

WELSHPOOL. **Welshpool Golf Club,** Y Golfa, Golfa Hill, Welshpool SY21 9AQ (01938 850249). *Location:* A458 out of Welshpool, approximately three and a half to four miles on right. Rather hilly but spectacular views. 18 holes, 5708 yards. S.S.S. 69. *Green Fees:* weekdays £15.50 all year; weekends and Bank Holidays £15.50 1st November to 31st March, £25.50 1st April to 31st October. *Eating facilities:* open most of the day for food and drink. *Visitors:* welcome, some weekend restrictions. Buggies now available. *Society Meetings:* welcome by arrangement, contact Don Lewis. Professional: Bob Barlow. Secretary: Don Lewis.

Builth Wells Golf Club

South Wales

ABERDARE. **Aberdare Golf Club,** Abernant, Aberdare CF44 0RY (01685 871188; Fax: 01685 872797). *Location:* half a mile from town centre. Mountain course with parkland features and view of whole Cynon Valley. 18 holes, 5875 yards. S.S.S. 69. *Green Fees:* weekdays £17.00, (with member £10.00); weekends and Bank Holidays £21.00, (with member £12.00). *Eating facilities:* bar, lounge and dining room. *Visitors:* welcome without reservation weekdays (see Professional). Saturdays and Sundays by prior arrangement with Secretary. Handicap Certificates required. Snooker room, and changing room. *Society Meetings:* catered for by prior arrangement with Secretary. Professional: A. Palmer (01685 878735). Secretary: Tony Mears (01685 872797).

ABERGAVENNY. **Monmouthshire Golf Club, Llanfoist, Abergavenny NP7 9HE. *Location:* two miles from A465 on Llanfoist – Llanellen Road (B4269).** Parkland with scenic mountain views. **18 holes, 5776 yards. S.S.S. 70. Practice ground. *Green Fees:* Monday to Friday £35.00, weekends and Bank Holidays £40.00. *Eating facilities:* bar snacks available, evening meals by arrangement. *Visitors:* welcome. *Society Meetings:* catered for by arrangement. Professional: Brian Edwards (Tel & Fax: 01873 852532). Secretary: R.F. Bradley (01873 852606; Fax: 01873 850470).**
website: www.themonmouthshiregolfclub.com

ABERGAVENNY. **Wernddu Golf Club,** Old Ross Road, Abergavenny NP7 8NG (01873 856223; Fax: 01873 852177). *Location:* one and a half miles east of Abergavenny on B4521 (off A465). Sloping, well drained site with pond hazards on four holes and magnificent views. 18 holes, 5413 yards. S.S.S. 68. 24-bay covered floodlit driving range, 9 hole pitch and putt, practice putting and bunker area. *Green Fees:* £18.00 per 18 holes. *Eating facilities:* lounge bar, light snacks. *Visitors:* welcome. *Society Meetings:* welcome. Professional: Tina Tetley (Ladies European Tour) (01873 856223; Fax: 01873 852177). Secretary: Lyn Turvey (01495 308161).
e-mail: info@wernddu-golf-club.co.uk
website: www.wernddu-golf-club.co.uk

BARGOED. **Bargoed Golf Club,** Heolddu, Bargoed CF81 9GF (01443 830143). *Location:* A469 to Bargoed town centre - Moorland Road. Flat mountain top course. 18 holes, 6210 yards. S.S.S. 70. Practice area, nets, etc. *Green Fees:* information not available. *Eating facilities:* full catering and bar. *Visitors:* welcome, only with member at weekends, no other restrictions. *Society Meetings:* catered for weekdays only by prior arrangement. Professional: C Easton (01443 836179).*

BARRY. **Brynhill (Barry) Golf Club,** Port Road East, Colcot, Barry CF62 8PN (01446 720277). *Location:* leave M4 at Junction 33 (A4232), follow signs for Barry and Cardiff (Wales) Airport onto the A4050. Club on right of road, just before a roundabout. Challenging, undulating meadowland course. 18 holes, 6352 yards. S.S.S. 71. Par 72. *Green Fees:* Mondays to Fridays £30.00, Saturdays £35.00, with member £15.00. *Eating facilities:* Steve, our caterer, extends a warm welcome, and will provide lunches between 12 noon and 2pm, and dinner from 5pm. Your order prior to playing is requested. *Visitors:* welcome, except Sundays; must produce membership card and Handicap Certificate. *Society Meetings:* by arrangement with Secretary – no Sundays, must be members of a golf club. Competitive rates available. Professional: Duncan Prior (01446 720277). Secretary: Rita Cook (01446 720277; Fax: 01446 740422).
e-mail: postbox@brynhillgolfclub.co.uk
website: www.brynhillgolfclub.co.uk

BARRY. **RAF St Athan Golf Club,** Clive Road, St Athan CF62 4JD (01446 751043). *Location:* eight miles from Barry, turn right through St. Athan Village. Parkland. 9 holes, 6452 yards. S.S.S. 72. Practice area and nets. *Green Fees:* information not provided. *Eating facilities:* available. *Visitors:* welcome except Sundays, telephone for information. *Society Meetings:* apply through the Secretary. Secretary: P.F. Woodhouse (01446 751043; Fax: 01446 751862).

www.uk-golfguide.com

BARRY. **St Andrews Major Golf Club,** Coldbrook Road East, Near Cadoxton, Barry CF63 1BL (01446 722227; Fax: 01446 748953). *Location:* off Barry Docks Link Road, Junction 33 M4. Flat parkland course with excellent greens, full 18 holes, 5500 yards, Par 69. 12-bay floodlit driving range open 7.30am to 9.30am. *Green Fees:* £18.00 weekdays, £20.00 weekends. Full membership packages available to cater for all needs. *Eating facilities:* restaurant and snacks; full bar facilities, specialise in large functions up to 150 people, weddings, birthdays etc. *Visitors:* welcome anytime, but advisable to ring for bookings (especially at weekends). *Society Meetings:* we specialise in society meetings, special packages available on request. Contact Andrew Edmunds.
e-mail: enquiries@standrewsmajorgolfclub.com
website: www.standrewsmajorgolfclub.com

BLACKWOOD. **Blackwood Golf Club,** Cwmgelli, Blackwood NP12 1EL (01495 222121/223152). *Location:* quarter of a mile north of Blackwood on A4048. 9 holes, 5350 yards. S.S.S. 67. *Green Fees:* information not available. *Visitors:* welcome weekdays only. *Society Meetings:* by arrangement. Secretary: Mr G.A. Batty (01495 222121 or 223152).*

BRIDGEND. **Coed-y-Mwstwr Golf Club,** The Clubhouse, Coychurch, Bridgend CF31 6AF (01656 862121; Fax: 01656 864934). *Location:* Junction 35 M4, A473 towards Bridgend. Turn right into Coychurch. Parkland, south facing. 18 holes, 5703 yards. Par 69. Practice nets, putting green and chipping area. *Green Fees:* information not available. *Eating facilities:* bar meals and snacks. *Visitors:* members' guests only on Saturdays. *Society Meetings:* by prior arrangement. Secretary: (Tel & Fax: 01656 864934).*
website: www.coed-y-mwstwr.co.uk

CAERLEON. **Caerleon Public Golf Course,** The Broadway, Caerleon, Newport NP18 1AY (01633 420342). *Location:* three miles off M4 at turnoff for Caerleon. Flat parkland. 9 holes, 3000 yards. S.S.S. 34 yellow, 35 white. Driving range, putting green. *Green Fees:* information not available. *Eating facilities:* bar, light meals (kitchen facilities) available all day. *Visitors:* welcome. *Society Meetings:* welcome. PGA Teaching Professional: Joe Pritchard. Secretary: R. Jones (01633 420342).

CAERPHILLY. **Caerphilly Golf Club,** Pencapel, Mountain Road, Caerphilly CF83 1HJ (029 2088 3481). *Location:* seven miles north of Cardiff on A469, 250 yards south of both railway and bus stations. Situated opposite Magistrates' Court. Mountainside course with undulating features and wooded areas. 18 holes, 5728 yards (white tees). S.S.S. 69. Limited practice facilities. *Green Fees:* information not available. *Eating facilities:* member' and guests' bar, ladies' lounge, mixed lounge and dining room. *Visitors:* welcome weekdays (not Bank Holidays); weekends with member only. *Society Meetings:* most welcome; society packages on request. Professional: James Lee (029 2086 9104). Secretary: Roger Chaffey (029 2086 3441).*
e-mail: secretary@caerphillygolfclub.com
website: www.caerphillygolfclub.com

CAERPHILLY. **Castell Heights Golf Club,** Blaengwynlais, Caerphilly CF83 1NG (029 2088 6686). *Location:* 5 minutes from Junction 32 on M4. Flat parkland, many trees. 9 holes, 2688 yards. *Green Fees:* information not available. *Eating facilities:* snacks, lunches and afternoon tea available. *Visitors:* welcome anytime, only members can book times. Secretary: Gareth Richards (029 2086 1128; Fax: 029 2086 9030).*

CAERPHILLY. **Mountain Lakes Golf Club,** Blaengwynlais, Caerphilly CF83 1NG (029 2086 1128). *Location:* take exit 32, M4. Last exit of roundabout "Tongwynlais", right at Lewis Arms, past Castell Coch, three miles up road on left. Part parkland, part wooded, undulating. 20 water hazards, large penncross greens. 18 holes, 6500 yards. S.S.S. 73. *Green Fees:* information not available. *Visitors:* welcome at all times but must have registered Handicap. *Society Meetings:* welcome at all times but must book. Professional: Sion Bebb (029 2088 6666). Director of Golf: P. Page (029 2086 1128; Fax 029 2086 9030).*

CAERPHILLY. **Ridgeway Golf Club,** Thornhill, Caerphilly CF83 1LY (029 2088 2255). *Location:* driving out of Cardiff towards Caerphilly over Caerphilly mountains, take first left after Traveller's Pub. Mountain course but not too steep. 9 holes, 2314 yards. S.S.S. 65. Driving range. *Green Fees:* £10.00 for 9 holes. *Eating facilities:* bar with snacks available. *Visitors:* welcome. *Society Meetings:* weekdays only by arrangement. Professionals: P. Johnson/R. Johnson. Secretary: Tim James.
e-mail: petethepro@tiscali.co.uk.

CAERPHILLY. **Virginia Park Golf Club,** Virginia Park, Caerphilly CF83 3SW (029 2086 3919). *Location:* off Pontygwindy Road, near Caerphilly recreation centre. Flat parkland, Easy walking but challenging. 9 holes, 4661 yards, S.S.S. 63. 20 bay covered, floodlit, driving range. Practice putting green. *Green Fees:* information not available. *Eating facilities:* catering available every day. *Visitors:* welcome but must observe dress code. Function room. *Society Meetings:* Telephone bookings. Professional: Katherine Price. Members' Secretary: Graham Taylor (02920 863919).

CARDIFF. **Cardiff Golf Club,** Sherborne Avenue, Cyncoed, Cardiff CF23 6SJ (029 2075 3320). *Location:* two miles north of city centre or M4, A48 or A48M from east to Pentwyn exit on Eastern Avenue, and take Pentwyn Industrial Road to top of hill at Cyncoed Village, turn left at Spar shop into Sherborne Avenue. Undulating parkland, all greens bunkered. 18 holes. S.S.S. 70. *Green Fees:* £50.00. *Eating facilities:* catering and bars available from 11am every day. *Visitors:* welcome; Saturdays must play with a member. Snooker. *Society Meetings:* by arrangement - dining facility for up to 130 people. Professional: Terry Hanson (029 2075 4772). Secretary: Kenvyn Newling (029 2075 3320; Fax: 029 2068 0011).

CARDIFF. **Cottrell Park Golf Club,** St Nicholas, Cardiff CF5 6SJ (01446 781781; Fax: 01446 781187). *Location:* four miles west of Cardiff on A48 main road. Two parkland courses. Driving range (20 bays) - clubhouse. Two courses: Mackintosh - 18 holes, 6313 yards off white tees. S.S.S. 72; Button - 18 holes, 6156 yards off white tees. S.S.S. 70. *Green Fees:* on application. *Eating facilities:* all day. *Visitors:* welcome anytime. Professional: Steve Birch.
e-mail: sales@golfwithus.com
website: www.golfwithus.com

CARDIFF. **Creigiau Golf Club,** Llantwit Road, Creigiau, Cardiff CF15 9NN (029 2089 0263). *Location:* seven miles north-west of Cardiff, two miles off A4199, M4 Junction 34 two miles. 18 holes, 6063 yards. S.S.S. 70 (Par 71). Limited practice facilities. *Green Fees:* £35.00 per day. *Eating facilities:* bars and full catering available. *Visitors:* welcome weekdays except Tuesdays, prior phone call requested; weekends with members only. Must hold Handicap Certificate. *Society Meetings:* catered for by prior arrangement (maximum 40). Professional: Ian Luntz (029 2089 0263). Secretary: (029 2089 0263; Fax: 029 2089 0706). Caterer: (029 2089 0263).
e-mail: manager@creigiaugolf.co.uk
website: www.creigiaugolf.co.uk

CARDIFF. **Llanishen Golf Club,** Heol Hir, Cardiff CF14 9UD (029 2075 5078; Fax: 029 2076 5253). *Location:* five miles north of Cardiff city centre, one mile north of Llanishen village. Wooded undulating course with spectacular views. 18 holes, 5338 yards, 4881 metres. S.S.S. 67, Par 68. *Green Fees:* information not available. *Eating facilities:* full bar and catering, except Mondays. *Visitors:* welcome weekdays; weekends only with member. Handicap Certificate required. *Society Meetings:* catered for Thursday and Friday, on written application. *Visitors* must be bona fide members of a golf club. Professional: Adrian Jones (029 2075 5076). Manager: Colin Duffield
e-mail: secretary.llanishengc@virgin.net
website: llanishengc.co.uk

CARDIFF. **Peterstone Lakes Golf Club & Hotel,** Peterstone, Wentloog, Cardiff CF3 2TN (01633 680009; Fax: 01633 680563). *Location:* in between Newport and Cardiff off the A48 at Castleton. Parkland/links course bordering the Bristol Channel. 18 holes, 6555 yards. S.S.S. 72. Indoor teaching academy. *Green Fees:* information not available. *Eating facilities:* lounge bar, Cinnamon Tree Restaurant, Crystal Suite. *Visitors:* welcome, strongly recommend telephone enquiry for a tee time. *Society Meetings:* welcome. Professional: Paul Glynn (01633 680075; Fax: 01633 680563). Manager: Peter Millar.*

CARDIFF. **Radyr Golf Club,** Drysgol Road, Radyr, Cardiff CF15 8BS (029 2084 2408). *Location:* Junction 32 M4, A470 to Merthyr Tydfil, first exit. Parkland course. 18 holes, 6015 yards. S.S.S. 70. *Green Fees:* £40.50. Special rates for societies, please enquire. *Eating facilities:* snacks, lunches and evening meals. *Visitors:* welcome. *Society Meetings:* catered for Mondays, Wednesdays and Thursdays only. Professional: Simon Swales (029 2084 2476; Fax: 029 2084 3914). Club Manager: Sarah Rodgers (029 2084 2408; Fax: 029 2084 3914).
e-mail: manager@radyrgolf.co.uk

CARDIFF. **St Mellons Golf Club,** St Mellons, Cardiff CF3 2XS (01633 680408; Fax: 01633 681219). *Location:* Junctions 28 and 30 of M4 to A48 between Cardiff and Newport. 70 year old parkland course. 18 holes, 6225 yards. S.S.S. 70. *Green Fees:* telephone for special rates. *Visitors:* welcome by arrangement. *Society Meetings:* catered for on written or telephone application. Professional: Barry Thomas (01633 680101). Secretary: R.H. Boyce (01633 680408; Fax: 01633 681219).

CARDIFF. **Wenvoe Castle Golf Club,** Wenvoe, Near Cardiff CF5 6BE (029 2059 1094; Fax: 029 2059 4371). *Location:* exit Junction 33 M4, follow signs for Cardiff Airport. Parkland course founded in 1936, fairly open layout with hilly front 9, hosted first PGA Welsh Classic. 18 holes, 6544 yards. S.S.S. 72. Practice areas. *Green Fees:* information not provided. *Eating facilities:* bar snacks and restaurant meals. *Visitors:* welcome weekdays and weekends. *Society Meetings:* catered for weekdays only, parties of 16 or more. Professional: Jason D. Harris (029 2059 3649). Secretary: Nicola Sims (Tel & Fax: 029 2059 4371).
e-mail: enquiries@wenvoecastlegolfclub.com
website: www.wenvoecastlegolfclub.com

CARDIFF. **Whitchurch (Cardiff) Golf Club,** Pantmawr Road, Whitchurch, Cardiff CF14 7TD (029 2062 0985). *Location:* three miles north west of Cardiff on A470, 600 metres Junction 32 M4. Parkland, undulating and easy walking with panoramic views of Cardiff. A championship course with Ian Woosnam holding course record of 62. 18 holes - white tees 6278 yards. S.S.S. 71. Practice facilities. *Green Fees:* £40.00 per day weekdays; £45.00 per day weekends and Bank Holidays. *Eating facilities:* restaurant and bars. *Visitors:* welcome please phone first. Trolleys for hire. *Society Meetings:* catered for by arrangement with Club Manager. Professional: Rhys Davies (029 2061 4660). Club Manager: Graham Perrott (029 2062 0985; Fax: 029 2052 9860).
e-mail: secretary@whitchurchcardiffgolfclub.com

CHEPSTOW. **Dewstow Golf Club,** Caerwent, Monmouthshire NP26 5AH (01291 430444; Fax: 01291 425816). *Location*: off A48 at Caerwent, between Chepstow and Newport, five miles from the Old Severn Bridge. Two 18-hole parkland courses, special features include Totem pole, Ekki bridge, 26- bay golf range. The Valley Course–Par 72, 6100 yards, The Park Course–6200 yards. *Green Fees*: information not available. *Eating facilities*: restaurant, function rooms and bar snacks available all day. *Visitors*: welcome at all times. Trolley and buggy hire in season. *Society Meetings*: Society and corporate days are our speciality (from £27.00pp). Bookings and information: Emma Corner (01291 430444). Professional: Steve Truman. Golf Secretary: Dave Bradbury.*
e-mail: info@dewstow.com
website: www.dewstow.com

CHEPSTOW. **Marriott St Pierre Hotel and Country Club,** St Pierre Park, Chepstow, Monmouthshire NP16 6YA (01291 635205; Fax: 01291 629975). *Location*: Junction 2 of M48, A466 Chepstow, A48 Caerwent. 400 acres of beautiful parkland, some of the rarest and oldest trees in Britain. Old Course: 18 holes, 6818 yards. S.S.S. 73 off white, 71 off yellow, 75 Ladies. Mathern Course: 18 holes, 5762 yards, S.S.S. 68. 13-bay driving range with computerised tuition facilities. *Green Fees:* information not available. *Eating facilities:* Trophy Bar serves light bites during day, Long Weekend Cafe Bar, private suites for groups. *Visitors*: welcome, book 10 days in advance for weekdays and 48 hours in advance for weekends. *Society Meetings:* weekdays only except when resident in hotel which has 148 bedrooms all en suite, conference rooms and extensive leisure facilities. Director of Golf: Ben Laing.

CWMBRAN. **Greenmeadow Golf and Country Club,** Treherbert Road, Croesyceiliog, Cwmbran NP44 2BZ (01633 869321; Fax: 01633 868430). *Location:* M4 Junction 26 north on A4042, turn right at brown tourist sign for Golf Course and Driving Range. Next to Gwent Crematorium. Parkland course with undulating fairways, mature woodlands, strategically positioned lakes and bunkers. 18 holes, 6200 yards. S.S.S. 71. 26 bay floodlit driving range (8am to 10pm), putting green, six all-weather tennis courts. *Green Fees:* information not available. *Eating facilities:* lounge bar, patio coffee lounge and restaurant. Private function room available if required. *Visitors:* welcome, telephone golf shop for tee time. *Society Meetings:* always welcome, bookings via our golf shop. Package deals with meals available. Professional: Dave Woodman (01633 862626). Secretary: P.J. Richardson (Fax: 01633 868430).*

CWMBRAN. **Llanyrafon Golf Course,** Llanfrechfa Way, Cwmbran NP44 8HT (01633 874636). *Location*: M4 Junction 26, A4042 to Cwmbran. Flat, parkland, wooded, river enclosed course. 9 holes, 1283 yards. Practice nets, putting green. *Green Fees*: information not available. *Visitors*: always welcome. Tuition available. Professional Golf Shop. Professional: David Woodman (01633 874636).

DINAS POWIS. **Dinas Powis Golf Club,** Golf House, Highwalls Road, Dinas Powis CF64 4AJ *Location*: M4 Cardiff, Junction Cardiff West, thereafter signposted Dinas Powis, Penarth and Barry. Mostly parkland, a challenging course. 18 holes, 5532 yards. S.S.S. 67. *Green Fees:* Monday to Friday £25.00, Saturday and Sunday £30.00 (discounts playing with member). *Eating facilities:* dining room/bar snacks. *Visitors:* welcome weekdays, weekends by arrangement. Separate function room with bar available for hire. *Society Meetings:* call for details. Professional: G. Bennett (029 2051 3682). Secretary: C. Miller (Tel & Fax: 029 2051 2727); Club (029 2051 2157).

GLYNNEATH. **Glynneath Golf Club,** 'Penygraig', Pontneathvaughan, Near Glynneath SA11 5UH (01639 720452). *Location*: A465 trunk road to Glynneath onto B4242 to Pontneathvaughan, one and a half miles. Picturesque course overlooking Vale of Neath, in Brecon Beacons National Park, reasonably flat, half woodland, half parkland. 18 holes - white tees 6122 yards. S.S.S. 71. *Green Fees*: Monday £10.00, Tuesday to Friday £18.00; Saturday, Sunday £23.00. (2007 fees, subject to revision.) *Visitors*: welcome, trolleys and buggies available; catering; snooker. *Society Meetings*: welcome weekdays and weekends, only by arrangement. Professional: Shane McMenamin (01639 720452). Secretary: T.A. Roberts (01639 720452).
website: www.newportgolfclub.org.uk

HENGOED. **Bryn Meadows Golf Club,** Maesycwmmer, Near Hengoed CF82 7SN (01495 225590; Fax: 01495 228272). *Location:* just off A472 near Blackwood, 15 minutes to M4 Junction 28. Parkland course, spectacular views, new challenge from every tee. 18 holes, 6100 yards. Par 72. *Green Fees:* information not available. *Eating facilities:* à la carte restaurant, bar snacks, etc. *Visitors:* welcome weekdays, weekends by prior arrangement only. Award-winning hotel and leisure club. Buggy hire. *Society Meetings:* welcome weekdays, weekends by prior arrangement. For all golf enquiries please contact: Bruce Hunter (01495 221905/225590).*
website: www.brynmeadows.com

HENSOL. **The Vale Hotel, Golf and Spa Resort,** Hensol Park, Hensol, Near Cardiff CF72 8JY (01443 667800). *Location*: set in over 650 acres of beautiful countryside yet only three minutes from Junction 34 of M4, 15 minutes from Cardiff city centre and International airport. Home to the Welsh PGA. 2 Championship standard courses - Lake Course, 6436 yards, and Wales National Course, 7433 yards, Par 72, water features, greens to USGA standard. 16 bay driving range, short play area. *Green Fees:* information not provided. *Eating facilities*: superb eating facilities in the clubhouse and AA Rosette Mediterranean restaurant. *Visitors:* welcome – Handicap Certificate required. Coaching available using latest video technology; Pro shop. spike and lounge bar. Buggy and trolley hire. *Society Meetings:* welcome, corporate days with full management service. Accommodation available in four-star hotel. website: www.vale-hotel.com

LLANWERN. **Llanwern Golf Club (Est 1929),** Llanwern Village, Newport NP18 2DY (Tel & Fax: 01633 412 029). *Location:* four miles east of Newport city centre, one mile from M4 Junction 24. Mature parkland course in a picturesque village setting, established in 1928. 18 holes, 6177 yards, S.S.S. 70 Men; 5214 yards, S.S.S. 71 Ladies. Extensive practice facilities. *Green Fees:* on application; various summer and winter packages. *Eating facilities:* full catering and bar. *Visitors:* welcome Monday to Friday and by arrangement on Saturday (no Sundays). Bookings: (01633 412029). Professional: (01633 413233). e-mail: llanwerngolfclub@btconnect.com website: www.llanwerngolfclub.co.uk

MAESTEG. **Maesteg Golf Club,** Mount Pleasant, Neath Road, Maesteg CF34 9PR (01656 732037). *Location:* half a mile out of Maesteg town centre on the Port Talbot road (B4282). Reasonably flat hilltop course with scenic views over wooded hills and valleys down to Swansea Bay. 18 holes, 5929 yards. S.S.S. 69. Practice area and putting green. *Green Fees:* information on request. *Eating facilities:* meals available in restaurant overlooking the course, bar meals and snacks throughout the day. *Visitors:* welcome without reservation, groups of more than 12 by arrangement. *Society Meetings:* catered for weekdays only by arrangement. Secretary: (01656 734106).

MERTHYR TYDFIL. **Merthyr Tydfil Golf Club,** Cloth Hall Lane, Cefn Coed, Merthyr Tydfil CF48 2NU (01685 723308). *Location:* off A470 Merthyr Tydfil to Brecon Road. Mountain top course in Brecon Beacons National Park area with outstanding views. 18 holes, 5625 yards. S.S.S. 68. *Green Fees:* £10.00 weekdays; £15.00 weekends. *Eating facilities:* available by prior arrangement. *Visitors:* welcome anytime except competition days (usually Sundays). *Society Meetings:* catered for by prior arrangement. Secretary: Vivian Price.

MERTHYR TYDFIL. **Morlais Castle Golf Club,** Pant, Dowlais, Merthyr Tydfil CF48 2UY (01685 722822). *Location:* near "Heads of Valley Road", Dowlais roundabout, follow signs for Brecon Mountain Railway. Very pleasant moorland course with excellent views. 18 holes, 6320 yards, 5744 metres. S.S.S. 71. Practice area. *Green Fees:* weekdays £18.00 per day, £12.00 with member; weekends £22.00, £16.00 with a member. *Eating facilities:* clubhouse offers excellent eating facilities; lounge, bars and restaurant. *Visitors:* welcome, weekends by prior arrangement with/or by application to the Secretary. *Society Meetings:* please contact Secretary. Professional: H. Jarrett (01685 388700). Secretary: Steven Jones. website: www.morlaiscastlegolf.co.uk

MONMOUTH. **Monmouth Golf Club,** Leasbrook Lane, Monmouth NP25 3SN (01600 712212). *Location:* outskirts of town on Monmouth - Ross-on-Wye dual carriageway, left turn 100 yards from roundabout; signposted. Undulating parkland, very scenic. 18 holes, 5700 yards. S.S.S. 69. Practice area, putting green. *Green Fees:* weekdays £20.00 per round, £28.00 per day; £10.00 with member; weekends and Bank Holidays £24.00 per round. £30.00 per day, £14.00 with member; Juniors £10.00 at all times. *Eating facilities:* bar snacks, dining room facilities daily. *Visitors:* welcome at all times. Trolley and buggy hire. *Society Meetings:* contact the Secretary in advance. Secretary: Peter Tully (01600 712212; Fax: 01600 772399).
e-mail:sec.mongc@barbox.net
website: www.monmouthgolfclub.co.uk

MONMOUTH. **The Rolls of Monmouth Golf Club,** The Hendre, Monmouth NP25 5HG (01600 715353; Fax: 01600 713115). *Location:* B4233 old Monmouth/ Abergavenny road. Arboretum wooded, hilly parkland course on private estate. 18 holes, 6283 yards. S.S.S. 71. Practice area, putting green. *Green Fees:* weekdays £40.00; weekends £44.00. Monday Special £38.00. Subject to review. *Eating facilities:* bar and catering facilities seven days a week. *Visitors:* welcome any day. Buggies and trolleys for hire. *Society Meetings:* welcome on any day including weekends. Secretary: Mrs Sandra Orton. e-mail: sandra@therollsgolfclub.co.uk

MOUNTAIN ASH. **Mountain Ash Golf Club,** Cefn Pennar, Mountain Ash CF45 4DT (01443 479459). *Location:* A470 Pontypridd to Aberdare road, approximately 10 miles from Pontypridd, four miles north of Abercynon. Picturesque heathland course. 18 holes, 5553 yards. S.S.S. 67. *Green Fees:* please ring for details. *Eating facilities:* catering at club. *Visitors:* welcome anytime without reservation. *Society Meetings:* catered for, special rates by arrangement. Secretary: Sharon Rees (01443 479459).

> **THE APPEARANCE OF AN ASTERISK (*) AT THE END OF A CLUB OR COURSE ENTRY INDICATES THAT UP-TO-DATE INFORMATION HAS NOT BEEN SUPPLIED**

NANTYGLO. **West Monmouthshire Golf Club,** Pond Road, Nantyglo, Brynmawr NP23 4QT (01495 310233). *Location:* Heads of the Valleys Road to Brynmawr, roundabout to Nantyglo, signposted. Mountain and heathland course. Now recognised as the highest golf course in Great Britain. 18 holes, 6118 yards. S.S.S. 69. *Green Fees:* information not available. *Eating facilities:* 24 hours notice required. *Visitors:* welcome. *Society Meetings:* welcome. Special package for parties – details on request. Secretary: S.E. Williams (01495 310233).*

NEATH. **Earlswood Golf Club,** Jersey Marine, Neath SA10 6JP (01792 321578). *Location:* half a mile southeast of Jersey Marine village, take B4290 turning off A483 then first right. Scenic, gently undulating course. 18 holes, 5174 yards. S.S.S. 68. *Green Fees:* £10.00. *Visitors:* pay as you play course, all visitors welcome. *Society Meetings:* by arrangement.

NEATH. **Neath Golf Club,** Cadoxton, Neath SA10 8AH (01639 643615). *Location:* two miles from Neath town centre. James Braid designed (1934) mountain/ heathland course – gentle slopes, magnificent views of Brecon Beacons and Bristol Channel. 18 holes, 6490 yards. S.S.S. 72, Par 72. *Green Fees:* information not available. *Eating facilities:* full catering facilities Tuesday to Sunday. *Visitors:* welcome at any time; phone Secretary in advance. Buggy (£15.00) and trolley hire available. *Society Meetings:* welcome at any time by prior arrangement with Secretary. Professional: R.M. Bennett (01639 633693). Secretary: D.R. Thomas (01639 632759).*
e-mail: neathgolf@btconnect.com
website: www.neathgolfclub.com

NEATH. **Swansea Bay Golf Club,** Jersey Marine, Neath SA10 6JP (01792 812198). *Location:* exit 42 off M4. At 1st roundabout, take B4290 turning off A483 then first right. Seaside links. 18 holes, 6605 yards. S.S.S. 72. *Green Fees:* weekdays £18.00; weekends and Bank Holidays £25.00. *Eating facilities:* bar/catering available every day from 11.00am; dinners by arrangement. *Visitors:* welcome without reservation. *Society Meetings:* by arrangement. Professional: M. Day (01792 816159). Secretary: Mrs D. Goatcher (01792 814153).

Monmouth Golf Club
Leasbrook Lane, Monmouth NP25 3SN
Tel: 01600 712212 • Fax: 01600 772399
sec.mongc@barbox.net
www.monmouthgolfclub.co.uk

Monmouth Golf Club is situated on the A40, half a mile north of the town. It was extended to an 18-hole course in 1992, when a new clubhouse was opened, offering a most comfortable location for a drink or a meal, with magnificent views of the course and the surrounding countryside. Monmouth certainly has every justification for its claim to be one of the prettiest courses in Wales, and is renowned for the warm welcome offered to its guests.

Standing on high ground above the town, the undulating parkland course plays 5698 yards off white tees, 5507 off yellow, and 5118 off red (ladies). Each aptly named hole offers a different challenge. The 8th (Cresta Run) was recently included in "Britain's 100 most extraordinary golf holes" which also nominated Monmouth as having the best value green fees in the country.

As you leave the clubhouse you become aware of the tranquillity of the verdant surroundings, mature trees, wild flowers and an abundance of wildlife.

Visit the Monmouth Golf Club- you will not be disappointed.

CELTIC MANOR
R E S O R T

Host venue for The Ryder Cup in 2010, The Celtic Manor Resort's 1400 acres of parkland offers the ultimate golfing experience, with the choice of three championship golf courses, two large and luxurious clubhouses, and a state-of-the-art Golf Academy.

With 400 bedrooms in two hotels, two exceptional spas, two state-of-the-art health clubs, tennis courts, shooting, fishing, mountain biking, walking trails, a kids' club and crèche, and four outstanding restaurants, The Celtic Manor Resort is the ideal place to unwind off the golf course as well as on it.

The new Twenty Ten Course, built for hosting The Ryder Cup, opened for play in July 2007. With water hazards on half of its holes, the course presents many memorable risk-and-reward dilemmas and is destined to become one of the world's must-play layouts.

The Montgomerie, designed by the Ryder Cup legend, also opened in 2007 and features some spectacular tee shots over ravines and dramatic descents to greens. The Resort's original Roman Road course, designed by Robert Trent Jones Sr, has hosted The Celtic Manor Wales Open for the last three years as well as The All★Star Cup.

The Celtic Manor Resort
Coldra Woods, The Usk Valley
Newport, South Wales NP18 1HQ

Tel: 01633 413 000 Fax: 01633 412 910
E-mail: bookings@celtic-manor.com • www.celtic-manor.com

NELSON. **Whitehall Golf Club,** The Pavilion, Nelson, Treharris CF46 6ST (01443 740245). *Location:* 15 miles north of Cardiff, take A4054 off A470. Hillside course with pleasant views. 9 holes (x2), 5666 yards. S.S.S. 68. *Green Fees:* Monday to Friday £10.00, with or without a member. Saturdays £12.00 with or without a member, but Captain's permission must be requested. Sundays/Bank Holidays by arrangement with Hon Secretary. *Eating facilities:* available, contact Stewardess for cooked meals. *Visitors:* welcome weekdays, weekends with members. *Society Meetings:* by prior arrangement with Secretary. Secretary: P.M. Wilde. (01443 451357).

NEWPORT. **The Celtic Manor Resort,** Coldra Woods, The Usk Valley, South Wales NP18 1HQ (Resort Enquiries 01633 413000; Fax: 01633 410269). *Location:* 90 minutes from London, off Junction 24 of the M4 motorway, five minutes from new Severn Bridge. The Resort is the home of The Celtic Manor Wales Open and the venue for the 2010 Ryder Cup. It features three very different and challenging championship courses. The new Ryder Cup course is the world's first-ever course designed specifically for golf's most prestigious tournament. Roman Road has played host to The Celtic Manor Wales Open and the celebrity All*Star Cup. The newly designed Montgomerie Course is the latest addition to the Resort's world class golf facilities. The Golf Academy offers comprehensive practice and coaching facilities, a two-tier floodlit driving range, 3 coaching bays with A-star video graphics, practice range, Pro Shop and short play areas. *Green Fees:* information not available. *Eating facilities:* superb dining facilities at The Lodge and hotels. *Visitors:* welcome. Meeting and banqueting rooms available. *Society Meetings:* welcome. Full event management service for Corporate Golf Days. Accommodation available at 330 room Resort Hotel or 70 room Manor House. Director of Golf Courses and Estates: Jim McKenzie. For tee times, call reservations (01633 410262).*

NEWPORT. **Newport Golf Club,** Great Oak, Rogerstone, Newport NP10 9FX (01633 892643; Fax: 01633 896676). *Location:* M4 Junction 27, take B4591 to RISCA, one and a half miles on right. Rolling parkland. 18 holes, white tees 6500 yards, S.S.S. 72 yellow tees 6273 yards. S.S.S. 71. Two practice areas. *Green Fees:* information not available. *Eating facilities:* full dining facilities at club. *Visitors:* welcome Saturdays with members only, welcome other days; advisable to ring in advance. *Society Meetings:* welcome Thursday or Friday mornings, book through Secretary. Professional: Paul Mayo (01633 893271). Secretary: Russell Thomas (01633 892643; Fax: 01633 896676). website: www.newportgolfclub.org.uk

NEWPORT. **Parc Golf Club.** Church Lane, Coedkernew, Newport NP10 8TU (01633 680933; Fax: 01633 681011). *Location:* Junction 28 M4, then A48 three miles from Newport. Flat parkland course. 18 holes, 5619 yards, S.S.S. 68. Golf range 38 bays, 9 hole short course, practice putting greens (grass and astro turf). *Green Fees:* £18.00 mid-week, £23.00 weekends. *Eating facilities:* bar, conservatory, function room (can cater for 120 plus). *Visitors:*

always welcome, must pre-book. Golf days arranged, weddings, conference facilities, exhibitions etc. *Society Meetings:* minimum 10 persons. Professionals: Richard Dinsdale & John Wills. Secretary: M.V. Cleary. Manager: Carl Hicks. e-mail: enquiries@parcgolfclub.co.uk website: www.parcgolf.co.uk

NEWPORT. **Tredegar Park Golf Club Ltd,** Parc-Y-Bryn, Rogerstone, Newport NP10 9TG (01633 894433). *Location:* north of M4 between Junctions 26 and 27. Parkland course. 18 holes, 6400 yards, 5850 metres. S.S.S. 72. Practice area. *Green Fees:* midweek £26.00, weekends £31.00. *Eating facilities:* restaurant and bar. *Visitors:* welcome, must be member of affiliated club. *Society Meetings:* groups of 16 and over catered for. Professional: Mark Phillips General Manager: Stuart Salway (01633 894433; Fax: 01633 897152).

OAKDALE. **Oakdale Golf Course,** Llwynon Lane, Oakdale NP12 0NF (01495 220044). Parkland course, 9 holes. Pay & Play course. 18 bay floodlit driving range. *Green Fees:* Adult £6.50, junior £5.50, friendly welcome always. *Eating facilities:* licensed bar, snacks. Full-sized snooker tables. *Visitors:* welcome. *Society Meetings:* welcome.

PENARTH. **Glamorganshire Golf Club,** Lavernock Road, Penarth CF64 5UP (Tel & Fax: 029 2070 1185). *Location:* five miles west Cardiff, one mile west Penarth Centre. Parkland course overlooking Bristol Channel. 18 holes, 6150 yards. S.S.S. 70. Practice area. *Green Fees:* information not available. *Eating facilities:* full restaurant and bar snacks, Men's bar and mixed lounge bar. *Visitors:* welcome providing no competitions in progress and/or Societies on course. Telephone call recommended. All visitors must possess current Handicap Certificate. *Society Meetings:* applications to Secretary/Manager. Reductions for parties exceeding 20. Professional: Mr A.K. Smith (029 2070 7401). Secretary/Manager: B.M. Williams (029 2070 1185).*

PENCOED. **St Mary's Golf Club,** St Mary's Hill, Pencoed CF35 5EA (01656 861100; Fax: 01656 863400). *Location:* Junction 35 of M4 and take third exit at roundabout, follow A473, take road signposted Felindre for about 300 yards, we are on left. Parkland course. 18 holes, 5291 yards. S.S.S. 66. Kingfisher 12 hole Public Course, practice area, driving range. *Green Fees:* information not available. *Eating facilities:* restaurant, three bars. *Visitors:* welcome weekdays 9am to 4pm; weekends 1pm to 4pm. 24 bedroom hotel. *Society Meetings:* welcome weekdays, restricted times at weekends. Society Secretary: Leighton Janes (01656 860280).*

PONTYPOOL. **Pontypool Golf Club,** Lasgarn Lane, Trevethin, Pontypool NP4 8TR (01495 763655). *Location:* Pontypool A4042 to St. Cadoc's Church, Trevethin. Undulating hillside course, with mountain turf and fine views. 18 holes, yellow tees 5838 yards. S.S.S. 69. Practice area, Indoor teaching academy. *Green Fees:* information not available. *Eating facilities:* diningroom and bar snacks. *Visitors:* welcome, must have Handicap Certificates. *Society*

Meetings: special packages available. Professional: Neil Matthews (01495 755544). Secretary: Les Dodd (01495 763655).*

e-mail: pontypoolgolf@btconnect.com
website: www.pontypoolgolf.co.uk

PONTYPOOL. **Woodlake Park Golf and Country Club,** Glascoed, Pontypool NP4 0TE (01291 673933; Fax: 01291 673811). *Location:* three miles from Usk overlooking Llandegfedd Reservoir. Undulating parkland with superb greens built to USGA specification. 18 holes, 6400 yards. S.S.S. 72. *Green Fees:* weekdays £22.50; weekends £30.00 (summer); weekdays £15.00, weekends £18.00 (winter). *Eating facilities:* spikes bar, lounge bar. *Visitors:* welcome, no restrictions. Function room for 130, private diningroom for up to 36 adjacent to Spikes Bar. *Society Meetings:* welcome, must pre-book, can cater for up to 100. Professional: Leon Lancey. Secretary: M.J. Wood BSc.

PONTYPRIDD. **Pontypridd Golf Club,** Ty Gwyn Road, Pontypridd CF37 4DJ (01443 402359). *Location:* east side of town, off A470, 12 miles from Cardiff. Wooded mountain course. 18 holes, 5881 yards, 5378 metres. S.S.S. 68. *Green Fees:* information not provided. *Eating facilities;* bar, restaurant (restaurant closed Thursdays, snacks available). *Visitors:* welcome weekdays, Ladies' Day Tuesdays; weekends with member only. Must be member of recognised golf club in possession of Handicap Certificate. *Society Meetings:* catered for

weekdays with prior reservation. Professional: Wade Walters (01443 491210). Secretary: Vikki Hooley (01443 409904; Fax: 01443 491622).

PORTHCAWL **Grove Golf Club Ltd.,** South Cornelly, Porthcawl, Mid Glamorgan CF33 4RP (01656 788771; Fax: 01656 788414). *Location:* near the Glamorgan Heritage Coast at Porthcawl on A4229 two minutes from Junction 37 off M4. Parkland course with spectacular views. 18 holes, 6128 yards, S.S.S. 69. *Green Fees:* information not provided. *Eating facilities:* Full restaurant and bar snacks from 8am daily. *Visitors:* welcome every day, bookings advisable. *Society Meetings:* welcome by arrangement. A variety of packages available. Secretary: Mike Thomas (01656 788771).

e-mail: enquiries@grovegolf.com
website: www.grovegolf.com

PORTHCAWL. **Pyle and Kenfig Golf Club,** Waun-y-Mer, Kenfig, Bridgend CF33 4PU (01656 783093; Fax: 01656 772822). *Location:* one mile off M4 at Junction 37, follow Porthcawl signs. Undulating dune and downland course. 18 holes, 6588 yards (white tees). S.S.S. 73. Five practice holes, practice range. *Green Fees:* £50.00, £70.00 Sundays. *Eating facilities:* full catering facilities. *Visitors:* welcome weekdays and Sundays. *Society Meetings:* welcome by arrangement. Professional: Robert Evans (Tel & Fax: 01656 772446). Secretary: David Fellowes (01656 783093; Fax: 01656 772822).

e-mail: secretary@pandkgolfclub.co.uk
website: www.pandkgolfclub.co.uk

PORTHCAWL. **Royal Porthcawl Golf Club,** Rest Bay, Porthcawl CF36 3UW (01656 782251; Fax: 01656 771687). *Location:* Junction 37 M4, head towards Porthcawl (three miles), club located at Rest Bay. Links course. 18 holes, 6829 yards. S.S.S. 74. 27-acre practice area. *Green Fees:* weekdays £80.00 per round, £120.00 per day; weekends £100.00 per round, Sunday pm only unless residents. *Eating facilities:* full catering and bars. *Visitors:* accepted Monday afternoons, Tuesdays, Thursdays and Fridays; limited weekend availability. Dormy House – six single rooms (£45.00 B&B), three twin rooms (£80.00 B&B). *Society Meetings:* welcome. Professional: Peter Evans (01656 773702). Secretary: Mr Martin Bond.

PORT TALBOT. **Corus (Port Talbot),** Groes Fields, Margam, Port Talbot SA13 2NF (01639 871111 Ext. 3368). *Location*: Margam Park exit from M4. Flat course. 12 holes, 5020 yards. S.S.S. 64. *Green Fees*: information not available. *Eating facilities*: bar meals available if ordered in advance. *Visitors:* welcome midweek, weekends by arrangement with Secretary. Secretary: David Wilkinson (01639 793194).*

PORT TALBOT. **Lakeside Golf Club,** Water Street, Margam, Port Talbot SA13 2PA (01639 899959). *Location:* Junction 38 of M4 Port Talbot, Margam Country Park. Flat parkland course. 18 holes, 4390 yards, S.S.S. 63. 20 bay driving range. *Green Fees:* information not available. *Eating facilities:* bar meals, restaurant. *Visitors:* welcome. *Society Meetings:* welcome. Professional: Matthew Wootton (07940 167202). Secretary: Brian Channell.*

RAGLAN. **Raglan Parc Golf Club,** Parc Lodge, Raglan NP15 2ER (01291 690077; Fax: 01291 690075). *Location:* near junction A40 and A449. 18 holes, 6604 yards, Par 73. *Green Fees:* information not available. *Visitors:* welcome. *Society Meetings:* welcome; packages available. Professional: Chris Murphy.* e-mail: golf@raglanparc.freeserve.co.uk website: www.raglanparc.co.uk

RHONDDA. **Rhondda Golf Club,** Golf House, Penrhys, Ferndale, Rhondda CF43 3PW (01443 441384). *Location:* on the Penrhys road joining Rhondda Fach and Rhondda Fawr. Mountain course. 18 holes, 6206 yards. S.S.S. 70. *Green Fees:* details on request. *Eating facilities:* all facilities daily except Mondays during winter months. *Visitors:* welcome. please telephone regarding availablilty. Handicap Certificate required. *Society Meetings:* welcome, please telephone for availability. Handicap Certificate required. Golf Shop: (01443 441384). Secretary: Mr Ian Ellis (01443 441384). e-mail: rhonddagolf@aol.com website: www.rhonddagolf.co.uk

RHYMNEY. **Tredegar and Rhymney Golf Club,** Cwmtysswg, Rhymney NP2 3BQ (01685 840743). *Location:* A4048 Rhymney, Heads of the Valley road. Very scenic mountain course, lots of hazards. 18 holes, 6120 yards. S.S.S. 67. *Green Fees:* information not provided. *Eating facilities:* bar snacks, meals by prior arrangement. *Visitors:* welcome at all times except Sunday mornings. *Society Meetings:* welcome at all times except Sunday mornings. Special rates. Secretary: Will Price (07761 005184). e-mail: tandrgc@googlemail.com

SOUTHERNDOWN. **Southerndown Golf Club,** Ogmore by Sea, Bridgend CF32 0QP (01656 880476; Fax: 01656 880317). *Location:* three miles from Bridgend on the Ogmore Road. Downland links overlooking Bristol Channel. 18 holes, 6449 yards. S.S.S. 72. Practice area. *Green Fees:* £50.00 weekdays; £70.00 weekends. *Eating facilities:* full dining room and bar facilities. *Visitors:* welcome any time except competition days (check with Secretary). Handicap Certificate required. *Society Meetings:* catered for by arrangement with Secretary. Special rates dependent on number. Professional: D. McMonagle (01656 881112). Secretary: (01656 881111). e-mail: southerndowngolf@btconnect.com

SWANSEA. **Allt-y-Graban Golf Club,** Allt-y-Graban Road, Pontlliw, Swansea SA4 1DT (01792 885757). *Location:* two miles from Junction 47 M4 turn left off A48 towards Pontarddulais, half mile past Glamorgan Arms. Parkland course. 9 holes, 4486 yards. S.S.S. 63. *Green Fees:* information not available. *Eating facilities:* full club house facilities including licensed bar and meals. *Visitors:* welcome. Secretary: S. Holston.*

SWANSEA. **Clyne Golf Club,** 120 Owls Lodge Lane, The Mayals, Swansea SA3 5DP (01792 401989; Fax: 01792 401078). *Location:* west of Swansea, right off Mumbles Road, signposted. Moorland course with extensive sea views. 18 holes, 6334 yards. S.S.S. 72. Large practice area, indoor and outdoor driving nets and chipping and putting green. *Green Fees:* weekdays £35.00; weekends £40.00. Winter offer - £20.00 including two course meal. *Eating facilities:* full catering facilities, fully licensed. *Visitors:* welcome except during competition days - check with Secretary. *Society Meetings:* welcome by application, reduction in fees for societies of 20 or more. Professional: Jonathan Clewett (01792 402094). Manager: Dave Thomas.
e-mail: clynegolfclub@supanet.com
website: www.clynegolfclub.com

SWANSEA. **Fairwood Park Golf Club Ltd,** Blackhills Lane, Upper Killay, Swansea SA2 7JN (01792 297849). *Location:* A4118 road - follow signs to "Sketty" and "Killay"; road to club opposite Swansea Airport. Parkland Championship course twice hosted the Welsh PGA. 18 holes, 6650 yards. S.S.S. 73. Practice facilities available. *Green Fees:* £22.00 weekdays; £27.00 Fridays and weekends. *Eating facilities:* every day all day full range, from bar snacks to three-course meals in restaurant, two licensed bars. *Visitors:* always welcome. *Society*

Meetings: always welcome. Professional: Gary Hughes (Tel & Fax: 01792 299194). Secretary: Mrs C.J. Beer (01792 297849).
e-mail: info@fairwoodpark.com
website: www.fairwoodpark.com

SWANSEA. **Gower Golf Club,** Cefn Goleu, Three Crosses, Swansea (01792 872480). *Location:* Junction 47 follow signs to Gowerton. Signposted in Gowerton and Three Crosses. Rolling parkland course. 18 holes, 6441 yards. S.S.S. 72. Practice facilities. *Green Fees:* information not available. *Eating facilities:* licensed bar, full catering facilities. *Visitors:* welcome, members start times 10am to 11am. 4 star Wales Tourist Board accommodation available for visitors. Bookings via Pro Shop (01792 879905). Tuition area. *Society Meetings:* welcome, packages arranged. Professional: Alan Williamson.

SWANSEA. **Gowerton Golf Centre,** Victoria Road, Gowerton, Swansea SA4 3AB (01792 875188; Fax: 01792 874288). Flat wooded course with rivers and bunkers. 9 holes, 1000 yards, S.S.S. 27. *Green Fees:* information not provided. *Eating facilities:* Diner, hot and cold meals provided. *Visitors:* open to the public. Lessons available. *Society Meetings:* welcome, group discounts. Professional: Mike Hobbs.
e-mail: waynebattye@yahoo.com
website: www.gowertongolf-range.com

SWANSEA. **Inco Golf Club,** Clydach, Swansea SA6 5QR (01792 841257. *Location:* easily accessible from M4. Two minutes from Junction 45 on A4067 towards Pontardawe. A flat easy-walking parkland course bordered by the meandering River Tawe. 18 holes, 6064 yards. S.S.S 69. *Green Fees:* weekdays £18.00, weekends £23.00. *Eating facilities:* full catering facilities. *Visitors:* welcome at all times. *Society Meetings:* welcome, group discounts. Secretary: D.E. Jones (01792 842929).

SWANSEA. **Langland Bay Golf Club,** Langland Bay Road, Langland, Swansea SA3 4QR (01792 361721). *Location:* M4 Junction 42, A483 Swansea, A4067 to Mumbles, followed by Langland Bay. Parkland/seaside course. 18 holes, 5857 yards. S.S.S. 70. *Green Fees:* information not provided. *Eating facilities:* full catering and refreshment service provided; limited on Mondays (01792 366023). *Visitors:* welcome best to check for availability. *Society Meetings:* parties over 12 are required to book in advance. Professional: Mark Evans (01792 366186). Secretary: Mrs Lynne Coleman (01792 361721; Fax: 01792 361082).
e-mail: info@langlandbaygolfclub.com
website: www.langlandbaygolfclub.com

SWANSEA. **Morriston Golf Club,** 160 Clasemont Road, Morriston, Swansea SA6 6AJ (01792 771079). *Location:* off Junction 46 M4, turn first left and follow road for one mile, clubhouse on left hand side of road. Parkland course, rather difficult. 18 holes, 5708 yards. S.S.S. 68. Practice area. *Green Fees:* see website for information. *Eating facilities:* restaurant and three bars. *Visitors:* welcome most days on application. Trolleys and buggies for hire. *Society Meetings:* welcome. Professional: M. Govier (01792 772335). Secretary: David Fellowes (Tel & Fax: 01792 796528). e-mail: morristongolf@btconnect.com
website: www.morristongolfclub.co.uk

SWANSEA. **Palleg Golf Club,** Palleg Road, Lower Cwmtwrch, Swansea SA9 2QQ (01639 842193). *Location:* off A4067 (A4068) north of Swansea 14 miles, 25 miles Brecon. Parkland course, open to the public 7 days a week. 18 holes, 5902 yards. S.S.S. 70. *Green Fees:* £15.00. *Eating facilities:* to be arranged with Steward. *Visitors:* welcome through week, check Pro Shop for weekends. *Society Meetings:* welcome if arranged. Club Professional: Baden Jones. Professional/Director: Graham Coombe.

SWANSEA. **Pennard Golf Club,** 2 Southgate Road, Southgate, Swansea SA3 2BT (01792 233131; Fax: 01792 234797). *Location:* eight miles west of Swansea A4067, B4436. Seaside links. 18 holes, 6267 yards. S.S.S. 72, Par 71. Practice areas. *Green Fees:* weekdays £40.00, weekends and Bank Holidays £50.00. *Eating facilities:* dining room and two bars. *Visitors:* welcome at any time. Snooker room. *Society Meetings:* by arrangement. Professional: M.V. Bennett (01792 233451). Secretary: E.M. Howell (01792 233131).
e-mail: sec@pennardgolfclub.com
website: www.pennardgolfclub.com

Monmouth Golf Club

SWANSEA. **Pontardawe Golf Club,** Cefn Llan, Pontardawe, Swansea SA8 4SH (01792 863118). *Location:* four miles north of M4 Junction 45 on A4067 Swansea-Brecon road. Wooded course. 18 holes, 6038 yards. S.S.S. 70. *Green Fees:* £20.00. *Eating facilities:* restaurant open daily except Mondays. *Visitors:* welcome, weekends by prior arrangement only. Handicap Certificate required. *Society Meetings:* catered for by application/ appointment, parties of 20 or more - £18.00 per person for 18 holes. Professional: G. Hopkins (Tel & Fax: 01792 830977). Secretary: Nigel Bowden. Administrator: Mrs M. Griffiths (01792 863118; Fax: 01792 830041).

TALBOT GREEN. **Llantrisant and Pontyclun Golf Club,** Talbot Green, Pontyclun CF72 8AL (01443 222148). *Location:* 10 miles north of Cardiff, two miles north of Junction 34 M4. Parkland. 18 holes, 5418 yards. S.S.S. 66. *Green Fees:* information not available. *Eating facilities:* available. *Visitors:* welcome weekdays. *Society Meetings:* catered for by arrangement. Professional: Andrew Bowen (01443 228169). Ofiice: Theresa Morgan (01443 224601).*
e-mail: golf@lpgc.wanadoo.co.uk

USK. **Alice Springs Golf Club,** Kemeys Commander, Usk NP15 1PP (Fax: 01873 881381). *Location:* three miles north of Usk on B4598. Undulating parkland course with beautiful views across the Usk Valley. Usk Course: 18 holes, 6185 yards. S.S.S. 72. Monnow Course: 18 holes, 6041 yards. S.S.S. 69. Driving range. *Green Fees:* £17.00 to £25.00. Buggies (40) available, all with G.P.S., from £12.00 per buggy. *Eating facilities:* restaurant facilities all day; function room. *Visitors:* welcome at all times; telephone for tee time. *Society Meetings:* catered for, special packages available. Professional: (01873 880914). Managing Director: David Rowlands (01873 880708; Fax: 01873 881381). e-mail: alice_springs@btconnect.com
website: www.alicespringsgolfclub.co.uk

> THE APPEARANCE OF AN ASTERISK (*) AT THE END OF A CLUB OR COURSE ENTRY INDICATES THAT UP-TO-DATE INFORMATION HAS NOT BEEN SUPPLIED

Looking for Holiday Accommodation?

for details of hundreds of properties throughout the UK, visit our website

www.holidayguides.com

The K Club, Co Kildare

Irish Golf

Philip Reid • for Fáilte Ireland

WHO KNOWS what thoughts swirled around Leonardo Da Vinci's mind after he painted the *Mona Lisa*; or James Joyce's head after he finished *Ulysses*? When you produce a masterpiece, what comes next? Likewise, the hugely successful staging of the 2006 Ryder Cup at The K Club on the banks of the River Liffey in Co Kildare left an exhilarating afterglow in Irish golf – but also, something of a void. What could fill it?

To be sure, in a golfing context, Ireland is spoilt. Sure, didn't Mother Nature provide Ireland with natural terrain that sees no fewer than one-third of all the links courses on the planet in this one country? And these magnificent seaside courses have been augmented with world class parkland creations that various golf course designers – both Irish and international – have created in recent decades.

It is at one of these parkland creations, Killeen Castle in Dunsany in Co Meath, a course designed by the legendary golfer Jack Nicklaus, that the 2011 Solheim Cup will be staged, as Ireland maintains its position as the foremost golfing destination not only for

golf tourism but also for big-time tournaments.

Securing the Solheim Cup, the women's equivalent of the Ryder Cup for professional golfers, is the final piece in one jigsaw that will see Ireland play host to all of golf's major team competitions, having also successfully staged the Canada Cup, now known as the World Cup (in 1960); the Walker Cup (in 1991), the Curtis Cup (in 1996), and, of course, the Ryder Cup in 2006.

While the 2007 Walker Cup takes place in September over the famed dunes and sand hills of Royal County Down, with the imposing presence of Slieve Donard overlooking the links, Irish golf fans – and visitors – can also watch the world's great players in action in the Irish Open at Adare Manor resort in May, the Smurfit Kappa European Open over the Smurfit Course at The K Club in July, and the Challenge of Ireland at Glasson in August. And a number of the winning Europe Ryder Cup team will be back again in September for the Seve Trophy when it is played at The Heritage at Killenard in Co Laois.

This diet of tournament golf in Ireland, over

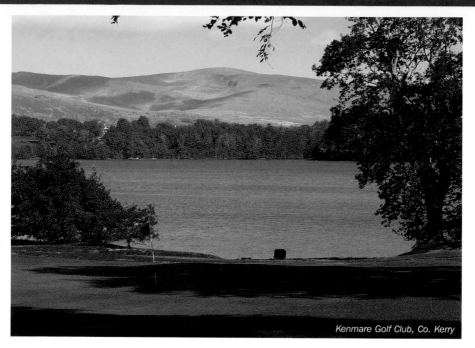

Kenmare Golf Club, Co. Kerry

THERE ARE FEW, if any, countries in the world that can offer the same golf facilities as Ireland. From the top-of-the-range courses like Mount Juliet, Doonbeg, Old Head, Carton House, etc. to the humbler nine-holers that are dotted around, there are over 500 courses in the Emerald Isle.

Ireland has the greatest number of links courses of any country in the world, with an almost perfect mixture of links and parkland, but there is a growing feeling among the Irish that possibly the development of new venues will have to be called to a halt. It is felt in some quarters that saturation point is fast approaching - there are too many courses in Ireland some will argue.

That, of course, is good news for the visitor, who can pick the type of course he or she wishes to play. It also means that, unlike some places abroad, courses are not crowded and visitors can have a leisurely stroll around 18 holes.

Knightsbrook and Killeen Castle in Co Meath, Moyvalley in Westmeath, Blarney Golf Resort in Cork and Castle Dargan, designed by Darren Clarke, in Co Sligo are some of the newer ones that have come on stream recently.

The East Coast in particular, from Greenore in Co Louth to Tramore in Co Waterford, has a long line of courses that will often challenge but always delight the players. Most of these are friendly to the player on holiday – friendly in the sense that they don't make play so difficult that it is not enjoyable. Indeed, all four provinces have a wide selection to choose from.

Up north, the high-profile Nick Faldo-designed Lough Erne Course will be opened in 2008. The triple British Open champion and three times winner of the US Masters has left his indelible mark on the new course, a big brother to the Castle Hume Club, outside Enniskillen in Co Fermanagh. This jewel in the north will be one of the most scenic and interesting clubs in the British Isles, and even further afield. Weaving around the shores of Lough Erne, the scenery is breath-taking. Fourteen holes are built around the lough, with the elevated 16th green having a fantastic view across the lake and some of its 365 islands. The course has been mainly hewed out of the hills and woodland of Ely Lodge Estate, a noted British Air Force base during World War II.

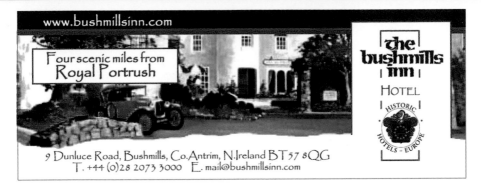

www.bushmillsinn.com

Four scenic miles from
Royal Portrush

the
bushmills
inn
HOTEL

HISTORIC

HOTELS - EUROPE

9 Dunluce Road, Bushmills, Co.Antrim, N.Ireland BT57 8QG
T. +44 (0)28 2073 3000 E. mail@bushmillsinn.com

"This is real tranquillity," enthused Faldo, "and this will be one of the greatest courses in these islands. It's the Loch Lomond of Ireland."

A 75-room, five-star hotel adjacent to the course opened in 2007, and there are 25 lodges and 60 chalets nestling among the trees that divide the Castle Hume and Lough Erne Clubs. There is an International Membership, confined to 100, at a cool £25,000 plus an annual fee of £1,000. That's not for everyone, nor is the Lough Erne course, as it will be a real challenge to the lowest of handicappers.

This is just another addition to the many super courses and golf facilities that are available to the holidaymaker as state-of-the-art courses are completed all over the island. Upgraded Doonbeg in Co Clare and Hangman's Point in Co Kerry are other plush centres. Making his Irish designing debut was Ernie Els, who gave his signature to the 200 million development at Kenmare. The name of the club, at this historic spot in the Kingdom, conjures up thoughts of stagecoach robbers...

In Co Cork is Old Head, a very exclusive club poised on a cliff edge, but not really for the casual visitor or anyone afraid of heights. It still could be worth a look if you have money to spend.

There is no shortage of this type of club around the island, with Adare Manor in Co Clare, scene of Padráig Harrington's great win in the 2007 Irish Open Championship, Mount Juliet in Kilkenny, the Seve Ballesteros-designed Heritage in Co Laois, Druid's Glen and Druid's Heath, Carton House and the nearby K Club where Europe retained the Ryder Cup, and others of worldwide reputation.

Incidentally, Adare Manor is situated at the edge of Adare village, arguably the loveliest village in Ireland with its thatched houses and shops along the main street, just outside the gates of the golf club and the Manor House, built in the 1720s.

Those courses are usually visited by extremely low handicap players, especially Americans, who make a practice of adding the big names

Bushmills Inn

Set between The Giant's Causeway and Royal Portrush Golf Club, in the village that is home to the world's oldest distillery, Bushmills Inn provides a relaxing environment for couples, small groups of friends or golfing parties. The area is a golfers' paradise, with eight courses within easy driving distance. The spectacular coastline of Giant's Causeway is home to a wealth of wildlife, and sandy beaches, grassy dunes and fishing harbours abound. There are 10 bedrooms in the inn itself, and 22 cottage-style rooms, each with private sitting area, in the adjoining Mill House. The award-winning restaurant serves a unique blend of classical and new Irish cuisine, and visitors are welcome all day for a wide selection of meals or snacks prepared from the best Co. Antrim produce.

to their conquests. A better alternative for the ordinary golfer is to visit the more handicap-friendly tracks, and there are plenty of those to choose from.

One club that falls somewhere between the two types is The European Club at Brittas Bay, a famed holiday resort in Co Wicklow. This Pat Ruddy-designed jumbo has to be visited and you will get a very warm welcome from Pat and his entire family, who run the business as a really friendly, family affair.

The Irish Amateur Close Championship, won for the second year in a row by Holywood teenager Rory McIlroy, was played at The European Club in 2005, and the PGA Irish Championship was hosted in July 2007. A massive 7,355 yards off the Blue tees with some card-wrecking holes included, the course is still an enjoyable trip for the average golfer. Better to play matchplay on this superb, scenic track, and you will certainly enjoy the experience of the idyllic seaside journey.

In 2000, it was named 24th in the World's 100 Greatest Golf Courses of the 20th century, while holes seven, 13 and 14 appeared in the World's Top 100 Best Golf Holes. "It is the first links I have played with 10 par fives (there are only two)!" joked 1976 British Open winner Johnny Miller. "I would love to see the British Open played at The European Club."

An added bonus to playing golf in Ireland is the vast improvement in roads, mostly uncluttered outside the cities and large towns. A new motorway now runs from Dublin to between Dundalk and Newry – a little over an hour's drive – and this carriageway is being extended towards Newry. There are other motorways or dual carriageways heading south towards Limerick and Cork and west to Galway. Up north the roads are excellent, too, with motorways included.

Nowadays, one can drive from Belfast to Limerick or Cork in between five and six hours, either via Dublin or through the centre of Ireland, where the scenery is more pleasing. From Dublin to Galway is also a fast drive.

There is always a welcome on the mat and the traditional nightlife that can be experienced throughout Ireland is second to none. Irish music and dancing is widespread, especially in the west of the country with sessiuns – music, song, dance and craic - organised in most tourist areas. Also many golf clubs are adjacent to historical sights and ancient ruins.

17th at Moyola Park Golf Club, Magherafelt, Northern Ireland

Wicklow Golf Club, Co. Wicklow

Of special interest to Scottish people is surely the Roe Park Resort at Limavady in Co Londonderry. There is much history there, too. One spot on the course is unique - that's the mound, Mullagh Hill, where St Columba addressed the High Kings of Ireland at the Convention of Drumceatt in 575AD. He arrived from Scotland to sort out a tax argument between the Irish and Scots and a special room in the adjoining Radisson Roe Hotel is named after him.

Roe Park Resort has a lot to offer to the touring golfer. It's parkland with links views and for years Norman Wisdom stayed at the hotel and enjoyed his round of golf. Just over an hour from Belfast and less from Derry City, Roe Park is the tail of the North Coast chain with neighbours Castlerock, Portstewart, Royal Portrush and Ballycastle all along the line. Bushfoot, where Darren Clarke's mother Heidi was Lady Captain, is nestled in there, too, and also Brown Trout, a few miles from Coleraine.

This web of courses, allied to the large range of accommodation, from the likes of the Radisson Roe Hotel with its leisure centre, beauty salon, restaurants and golf academy, to the popular B&Bs (bed and breakfast – not bread and butter!) guest houses, offers the holidaymaker a wide selection of activities. Economically priced B&Bs are dotted throughout Ireland.

Up to three of the north coast courses can be played in one day, if energy allows, but pre-booking is advisable at the likes of Royal Portrush, which is one of the most famous clubs in the world. The British Open Championship was played there in 1951 when Max Faulkner was the winner. Ironically, Max's son-in-law Brian Barnes won the British Seniors, also on the jumbo Dunluce links that features the famous Calamity Corner – the short 14th hole.

With the north coast reasonably close to Belfast International and George Best Belfast City Airports, and Belfast Docks, it is obvious

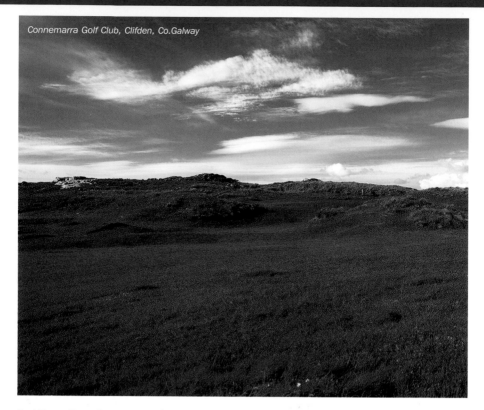
Connemarra Golf Club, Clifden, Co.Galway

that these famed courses are busy during the height of the tourist season, but on the way north there are many more pleasant courses to visit.

The Hilton Golf Club and Hotel at Templepatrick is quite a tough track where the Northern Ireland Ladies' Professional Open Tournament was played in June 2007.

Belfast has 14 clubs, with Shandon Park, Malone and Belvoir Park among the most famous. But don't forget suburban Dunmurry that won the AIB Club of the Year in 2003.

Trees play a big part on the Malone and Shandon Park courses and also at Belvoir Park from where there is a superb view over the city to the Black Mountain from the elevated clubhouse.

Royal County Down, with its magnificent backdrop of the majestic Mourne Mountains, hosted the 2007 Walker Cup but it would not be the choice of the high handicap golfer. There are many tough holes here, with the deep gorse

and heather gobbling up balls constantly. However, the par four ninth hole must be one of the most spectacular of any in the land. Here the drive disappears over a hill and drops into an angled valley about 80 feet below.

Deeper into the province one finds the likes of up-market Slieve Russell at Ballyconnell in Co Cavan. The Sean Quinn Complex – a non-golfer himself, Sean now owns The Belfry! – was created out of the Breffni Drumlin country. The plush hotel is attached to an excellent course where PGA events are staged annually. Liam McCool wears two hats as he is head golf pro and Golf Director. His sister, Lynn, is the teaching pro at The K Club, a rare brother-sister act.

Further west, Donegal has 17 clubs, from Ireland's most northerly course at Ballyliffin to Bundoran at the bottom end of the county.

Co Sligo, at Rosses Point, hosts the West of Ireland Championship every Easter. Set among sand dunes on cliffs overlooking three beaches, the wind factor plays a big part on Rosses Point, while a burn meanders through the course and comes into play at a number of holes. The famous Benbulben, close to the grave of William B Yeats at Drumcliffe, towers in the distance to the north, with the Ox Mountains to the west giving a panoramic view to relax golfers who may be having a bad day.

Westport Town and the local golf club are among the busiest and friendliest in the country. This is a tourists' paradise where sport and entertainment mingle daily. Traditional music pumps out from Matt Molloy's pub on the main street and if you don't know who Matt Molloy is I'll tell you. He's the celebrated flute player with the Chieftains.

The Westport course commands a superb view of Clew Bay and is overshadowed by famous Croagh Patrick, the holy mountain to which visitors flocks in their thousands throughout the year. The 15th hole, a jumbo par five of 580 yards, is played over an inlet of Clew Bay.

Christy O'Connor Jnr was the architect of the Galway Bay course on the Renville Peninsula, where one needs to ignore the beautiful scenery if a good score is to be carded. When visiting this rugged area of Ireland, no self-respecting tourist could miss out on playing Connemara, a remote course on the western seaboard, nine miles from Clifden, famous for its Pony Show, and past the old Marconi Wireless Station where Alcock

and Brown landed after their trans-Atlantic flight in 1919. Big hitters will enjoy the Connemara Course.

The south-west corner of the country is littered with up-market clubs and courses but one that most visitors like to play is Lahinch. Nestling on the Co Clare coast beside the Shannon, as with many clubs there are two courses to choose from. Sand dunes are the norm and one superb hole on the Old Course is 'The Dell', a great par three with the hidden hole in a basin well below the tee. 'The Klondyke' is another aptly named hole.

Fota Island, adjacent to the Wild Life Park on the outskirts of Cork City and nearby Little Island – alias Cork Golf Club – should be visited.

In the Kingdom of Kerry are the famed Killarney, Ballybunion and Waterville courses, backed up by many lesser lights such as Tralee and Killorglin, while inland at Dundrum House is Co Tipperary Golf Club where Willie Crowe will make you especially welcome. Tramore and Faithlegg in Waterford are also courses suited to the traveller.

In the south-east corner of Ireland there is a wide selection of courses for visitors to play. Mount Juliet in Co Kilkenny and sister clubs Druid's Glen and Druid's Heath up the coast in Co Wicklow, are, of course, the doyens, but maybe not for the high handicapper.

Easier tracks like Courtown and St Helen's Bay to name just two that attract much

18th fairway, Seapoint Golf Club, Drogheda, Co. Louth

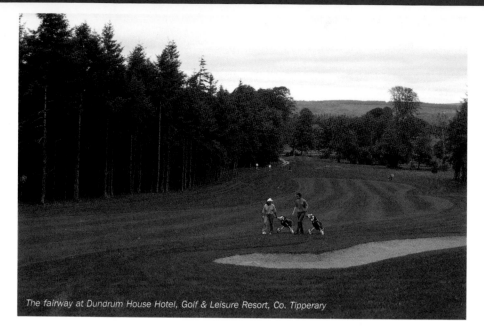

The fairway at Dundrum House Hotel, Golf & Leisure Resort, Co. Tipperary

attention are more for the holidaymaker. Further in-country in Leinster there is a big selection like Glasson, Headfort and Mullingar.

Apart from the likes of Hermitage in south city and Portmarnock in north city Dublin, there are over 20 other courses to choose from in the Irish capital.

One of the most popular courses on the east coast is the Par 73 Co Louth, the scene of many big tournaments. The East of Ireland Championship is played there annually and the Irish Open was held there in 2004. This is Des Smyth country and just 'over the hedge' from Co Louth is the equally attractive Seapoint.

This is only a thumbnail glimpse of what Ireland has to offer the holiday golfer. It would take more than the thickness of this Golf Guide to give anything like a comprehensive view of the playing facilities that are on offer.

By the way, what should interest many people is that the holidaymaker can travel by water from Lough Erne in Co Fermanagh to the mouth of the Shannon River in Co Clare. Cruises are for hire, and along the route there are plenty of stopping off places where the traveller can have a game of golf and also enjoy a night's craic.

NORTHERN IRELAND

Antrim

ANTRIM. **Massereene Golf Club,** 51 Lough Road, Antrim BT41 4DQ (028 9442 9293). *Location:* one mile S.W. of town, 3 miles from Aldergrove Airport, situated alongside the shores of Lough Neagh. 18 holes, 6602 yards. S.S.S. 72. *Green Fees:* weekdays £22.00, weekends £30.00. *Eating facilities:* full catering facilities 12 noon till 9pm. *Visitors:* welcome. Buggies for hire, *Society Meetings:* catered for. Professional: Jim Smyth (028 9446 4074). Secretary/Manager: Mr Gary Henry (028 9442 8096).

BALLYCASTLE. **Ballycastle Golf Club,** Cushendall Road, Ballycastle BT64 6QP (028 2076 2536). *Location:* approximately 40 miles along the coast road west of Larne Harbour. Seaside links/undulating. 18 holes, 5744 yards, 5228 metres. S.S.S. 69. *Green Fees:* weekdays £25.00 (with member £10.00); weekends and Public Holidays £35.00 (with member £15.00). Subject to review. *Eating facilities:* catering available (028 2076 2536). *Visitors:* welcome weekdays and afternoons at weekends. *Society Meetings:* by arrangement. Professional: I. McLaughlin (028 2076 2506). Hon. Secretary: B.J. Dillon (028 2076 2536; Fax: 028 2076 9909).
e-mail: info@ballycastlegolfclub.com
website: www.ballycastlegolfclub.com

BALLYCLARE. **Ballyclare Golf Club,** 25 Springvale Road, Ballyclare BT39 9JW (028 9332 2696/9334 2352). *Location:* one and a half miles north of Ballyclare. Parkland, lakes and river, 18 holes, 6339 yards. S.S.S. 71. Practice ground. *Green Fees:* weekdays £22.00, with member £14.00; weekends £28.00, with member £18.00. *Eating facilities:* catering available. *Visitors:* welcome weekdays except Thursday. *Society Meetings:* catered for. Special rates for 15 plus. Professional: Colin Lyttle (028 9332 4541). Secretary Manager: Michael Stone (028 9332 2696)

BALLYCLARE. **Greenacres Golf Club,** 153 Ballyrobert Road, Ballyclare BT39 9RT (028 9335 4111; Fax: 028 9335 4166). *Location:* three miles from Corrs Corner on B56. Parkland course, 18 holes. Par 71. S.S.S. 68. Floodlit driving range. *Green Fees:* information not available. *Eating facilities:* bar and catering available.*

BALLYMENA. **Ballymena Golf Club,** 128 Raceview Road, Ballymena BT42 4HY (028 2586 1207). *Location:* two miles north east of town on A42. Flat/parkland/heathland. 18 holes, 5299 metres. S.S.S. 67. *Green Fees:* information not available. *Eating facilities:* restaurant and bar snacks. *Visitors:* welcome at all times, except Tuesdays and Saturdays. *Society Meetings:* catered for Tuesdays and Saturdays.. Professional: Ken Revie (028 2586 1652). Secretary: George Small (Tel & Fax: 028 2586 1487).*

BALLYMENA. **Galgorm Castle Golf Club,** Galgorm Castle, Ballymena BT42 1HL (028 2564 6161; Fax: 028 2565 1151). *Location:* one mile south of Ballymena on A42 to Galgorm village. Mature parkland course in the grounds of one of Ireland's most historic castles. 18 holes, 6736 yards, S.S.S. 72. Driving range, practice area. *Green Fees:* Golf only, Monday-Thursday £33.00, Friday £35.00, Saturday-Sunday £45.00, group rates available. *Eating facilities:* full restaurant and bar. *Visitors:* welcome. Accommodation and tuition available. Fully equipped golf shop, hire facilities including buggies with GPS satellite navigation. *Society Meetings:* welcome, special rates available. Professional: Phil Collins (028 2564 6161; Fax: 028 2565 1151). Secretary: Barbara McGeown (028 2565 0210).
e-mail: golf@galgormcastle.com
website: www.galgormcastle.com

BALLYMONEY. **Gracehill Golf Club,** 141 Ballinlea Road, Stranocum, Ballymoney BT53 8PX (028 2075 1209; Fax: 028 2075 1074). *Location:* Ballymoney; International Airport (40 minutes). Parkland. Opened May 1995 with American-style water hazards. 18 holes, 6525 yards. S.S.S. 73. Practice area. Driving range adjacent to course. *Green Fees:* Monday to Friday £25.00, Saturday/Sunday £30.00. *Eating facilities:* restaurant/bar. *Visitors:* telephone for tee time. *Society Meetings:* all welcome. Secretary/ Manager: M. McClure.
website: www.gracehillgolfclub.co.uk

BELFAST. **Castlereagh Hills Golf Club,** Upper Braniel Road, Castlereagh, Belfast BT5 7TX (028 9044 8477). *Location:* two miles from city centre, east Belfast. Parkland. 18 holes. 5398 metres. S.S.S. 67. Practice area and putting green. *Green Fees:* information not available. *Eating facilities:* every day. *Visitors:* welcome, no restrictions. Club hire *Society Meetings:* all welcome. Professional: K. Gray (028 9044 8477). Secretary: A. Carson (028 9065 9653).

BELFAST. **Cliftonville Golf Club,** 44 Westland Road, Belfast BT14 6NH (028 9074 4158). Parkland with rivers bisecting three fairways. 9 holes, 6210 yards, 5672 metres. S.S.S. 70. Practice fairway and nets. *Green Fees:* information not available. *Eating facilities:* bars, catering on request. *Visitors:* no visitors after 5pm weekdays, until 6pm on Saturdays, and until 1.30 pm Sundays. *Society Meetings:* very welcome, especially by arrangement. Professional: Peter Hannah. Hon. Secretary: E. Lusty O.B.E (028 9074 6595).*

THE APPEARANCE OF AN ASTERISK (*) AT THE END OF A CLUB OR COURSE ENTRY INDICATES THAT UP-TO-DATE INFORMATION HAS NOT BEEN SUPPLIED

BELFAST. **Dunmurry Golf Club,** 91 Dunmurry Lane, Dunmurry, Belfast BT17 9JS (028 9061 0834; Fax: 028 9060 2540). *Location:* off M1 at Dunmurry, to village, turn left past Tesco, one and a half miles to right. Parkland, partially wooded. 18 holes, 6080 yards. S.S.S. 69. Practice area. *Green Fees:* Monday-Friday £27.00, Sundays and Bank Holidays £37.00. *Eating facilities:* restaurant (not Mondays) and bar. *Visitors:* welcome by arrangement; not Fridays (Ladies' Day) and not Saturdays. Trolleys available. *Society Meetings:* welcome by written application; 20 or more £23.00. Professional: John Dolan (028 9062 1314; Fax: 028 9060 2540). Golf Manager: Tony Cassidy (028 9061 0834; Fax: 028 9060 2540).

BELFAST. **Fortwilliam Golf Club,** Downview Avenue, Belfast BT15 4EZ (028 9077 6798). *Location:* one mile Fortwilliam Junction M2. Parkland. 18 holes, 6030 yards. S.S.S. 69. *Green Fees:* weekdays £22.00; weekends £29.00. *Eating facilities:* excellent catering and bar. *Visitors:* welcome every day except Saturdays. *Society Meetings:* catered for Tuesdays and Thursdays, special rates available. Golf cart available, £20.00 per round. Professional: Peter Hanna (Tel & Fax: 028 9077 0980). Secretary: M. Purdy (028 9037 0770; Fax: 028 9078 1891).

BELFAST. **Malone Golf Club,** 240 Upper Malone Road, Dunmurry, Belfast BT17 9LB (028 9061 2758; Fax: 028 9043 1394). *Location:* five miles south of Belfast city centre, opposite Lady Dixon Park. Parkland, wooded course with large lake. 18 holes, 6706 yards. S.S.S. 72. 9 holes, 6320 yards. S.S.S. 70 (9 holes x 2). Practice ground, putting green. *Green Fees:* Weekdays £65.00 per day, weekends £75.00 per day. *Eating facilities:* bar, bar snacks and restaurant. *Visitors:* welcome weekdays except Tuesdays (Ladies' Day); time sheet on weekends. Dress code observed on course and in clubhouse. Golf carts for hire. *Society Meetings:* welcome by arrangement Mondays and Thursdays. Professional: Michael McGee (Tel & Fax: 028 9061 4917). Manager: J.N.S. Agate (028 9061 2758; Fax: 028 9043 1394). website: www.malonegolfclub.co.uk

CARRICKFERGUS. **Carrickfergus Golf Club,** 35 North Road, Carrickfergus BT38 8LP (028 9336 3713; Fax: 028 9336 3023). *Location:* North Road, one mile from main shore road. Fairly flat parkland course, partially wooded. 18 holes, 5768 yards. S.S.S. 68. *Green Fees:* weekdays £19.00, weekends and Bank Holidays £25.00. *Eating facilities:* full catering and bar facilities. *Visitors:* welcome except on Saturdays. *Society Meetings:* catered for. PGA Professional: G. Mercer PGA (028 9336 3713; Fax: 028 9336 3023). Secretary: I. McLean (028 9336 3713; Fax: 028 9336 3023).

CARRICKFERGUS. **Greenisland Golf Club,** 156 Upper Road, Greenisland, Carrickfergus BT38 8RW (028 9086 2236). *Location:* situated at the foot of Knockagh Hill and on the edge of Carrickfergus town, one of the best features is the scenic view over Belfast Lough. Parkland course. 9 holes, 5624 metres. S.S.S. 69. *Green Fees:* information not available. *Eating facilities:* lunch and evening meals available, bar snacks. *Visitors:* welcome; Saturdays not before 5.30pm. *Society Meetings:* welcome by prior arrangement. Hon. Secretary: W.J. McLaughlin.

CARRICKFERGUS. **Whitehead Golf Club,** McCrea's Brae, Whitehead, Carrickfergus BT38 9NZ (028 9337 0822). *Location:* Whitehead, 15 miles from Belfast, 10 miles from Larne. 18 holes, 6050 yards. S.S.S. 69, par 70. *Green Fees:* information not available. *Eating facilities:* by arrangement with Caterer. *Visitors:* welcome Monday to Friday, weekends with a member only. *Society Meetings:* by prior arrangement. Professional: C. Farr (028 9337 0821. Secretary/Manager: (028 9337 0820 9am-5pm; Fax: 028 9337 0825). Caterer (028 9337 0823).*

CUSHENDALL. **Cushendall Golf Club,** 21 Shore Road, Cushendall BT44 0NG (028 2177 1318). *Location:* 25 miles north on Antrim coast road from Larne Harbour. Seaside wooded course; river comes into play in seven out of nine holes. 9 holes, 4384 metres. S.S.S. 63. *Green Fees:* weekdays £13.00 per day, weekends and Bank Holidays £18.00; £5.00 concession if playing with member. *Eating facilities:* normal bar hours, bar snacks, full catering by arrangement. *Visitors:* welcome without reservation, avoid Wednesday afternoons, Thursday Ladies' Day, time sheet in operation at weekends. *Society Meetings:* welcome. Hon. Secretary: Shaun McLaughlin (028 2175 8366).

LARNE. **Cairndhu Golf Club Ltd,** 192 Coast Road, Ballygally, Larne BT40 2QG (028 2858 3954; Fax: 028 2858 3324). *Location:* three miles north of Larne on the famous Antrim Coast road leading to the Glens of Antrim. Parkland course with stunning views. 18 holes, 5611 metres. S.S.S. 69. Practice area, driving range. *Green Fees:* weekdays £20.00, weekends £25.00. *Eating facilities:* restaurant and bar. *Visitors:* welcome except Saturdays. *Society Meetings:* welcome. Professional: Stephen Hood (Tel & Fax: 028 2858 3954). Office Manager: Mrs Kerry Craig.

LARNE. **Larne Golf Club,** 54 Ferris Bay Road, Islandmagee, Larne BT40 3RT (028 9338 2228; Fax: 028 9338 2088). *Location:* six miles north of Whitehead on Browns Bay Road. Part links, part parkland. 9 holes, 18 tee boxes, 6288 yards. S.S.S. 70. Practice ground. *Green Fees:* information not available. *Eating facilities:* bar, restaurant. *Visitors:* welcome Mondays to Thursdays, and Sundays. Snooker table. *Society Meetings:* welcome on application (not Friday or Saturday). 10% reduction for societies of 20 or more. Hon. Secretary: K.J. Hedley. Club Manager: L.I. Oldfield.

LISBURN. **Lisburn Golf Club,** Blaris Lodge, 68 Eglantine Road, Lisburn BT27 5RQ (028 9267 7216; Fax: 028 9260 3608). *Location:* three miles south of Lisburn on A1. Parkland. 18 holes, 6647 yards. S.S.S. 72. Practice area. *Green Fees:* information not available. *Eating facilities:* bar and restaurant. *Visitors:* welcome weekdays, Tuesdays Ladies have preference. Saturday after 5.30pm only, Sundays with member only. Snooker room. *Society Meetings:* Mondays and Thursdays only. Professional: S. Hamill (028 9267 7217). Manager: G.E. McVeigh (028 9267 7216).* e-mail: lisburngolfclub@aol.com

MAZE. **Down Royal Park Golf Course,** 6 Dunygarton Road, Maze BT27 5RT (Tel & Fax: 028 9262 1339). *Location:* Belfast–Hillsborough road. Lisburn–Moira road. Heathland. 27 holes, 6824 metres. S.S.S. 72. *Green Fees:* weekdays £15.00, weekends and Bank Holidays £20.00. *Eating facilities:* available. *Visitors:* G.U.I. dress code applies. Budget accommodation available. *Society Meetings:* all welcome.

NEWTOWNABBEY. **Ballyearl Golf and Leisure Centre,** 585 Doagh Road, Newtownabbey BT36 8RZ (028 9084 8287; Fax: 028 9084 4896). *Location:* eight miles north of Belfast, 15 miles south of Larne. From Belfast follow signs to Larne via M2 (A8), turn right to Mossley approximately one miles from Corrs Corner Pub. Ballyearl is one mile on left. Parkland. 9 holes, 2402 yards, 2196 metres. Par 3. 27 bay covered floodlit driving range, outdoor grass teeing area. *Green Fees:* information not available. *Eating facilities:* snacks available in Squash Club bar. *Visitors:* no restrictions – pay and play. Squash courts, hi-tech fitness suite and arts theatre. Golf lessons available by appointment, golf equipment tailored to individual requirements and can be tested on driving range. Professional: Richard Johnston (028 9084 0899).*

PORTBALLINTRAE. **Bushfoot Golf Club,** 50 Bushfoot Road, Portballintrae BT57 8RR (028 2073 1317; Fax: 028 2073 1862). *Location:* off Ballaghmore Road, Portballintrae. Seaside links course. 9 holes, 6075 yards. S.S.S 67. *Green Fees:* weekdays £16.00; weekends £20.00. *Eating facilities:* full dining room, bars. *Visitors:* welcome, restrictions weekends July to September. *Society Meetings:* all welcome weekdays. Secretary/ Manager: J. Knox Thompson.

PORTRUSH. **Rathmore Golf Club,** Bushmills Road, Portrush BT56 8JG (028 7082 2285). *Location:* north east coast - six miles from Coleraine, beside roundabout on road to Bushmills. Royal Portrush Golf Club (valley links). Flat seaside links. 18 holes, 6304 yards. S.S.S. 70. *Green Fees:* Information not available. *Eating facilities:* bar but no eating facilities. *Visitors:* Saturday and Sunday 1.30 to 2.30pm, Monday to Friday no restrictions except Tuesday after 11am September to March and Thursday from 4-6pm May to August. *Society Meetings:* must register at Royal Portrush Golf Club and pay green fees before commencement of play. Professional: Gary McNeill (R.P.G.C.) (028 7082 2311). Club Administrator: Willie McIntyre (Tel & Fax: 028 7082 2996).

PORTRUSH. **Royal Portrush Golf Club,** Dunluce Road, Portrush BT56 8JQ (028 7082 2311). *Location:* one mile from Portrush on the main Portrush/ Bushmills Road. Dunluce Course-natural seaside links. 18 holes, 6845 yards. S.S.S. 73. Valley Course - flat seaside links. 18 holes, 6304 yards. S.S.S 71. Two practice grounds. *Green Fees:* Dunluce £110.00 weekdays, £125.00 weekends; Valley £35.00 weekdays, £40.00 weekends. *Eating facilities:* three bars, restaurant with snacks and à la carte. *Visitors:* Dunluce Course: must contact Secretary prior to visit. Restrictions Monday, Wednesday and Friday afternoons and Saturday and Sunday mornings. Valley Course: welcome weekdays, plus limited tee times at weekends. *Society Meetings:* accepted with prior bookings. Professional: Gary McNeill (028 7082 3335). Secretary: Miss W. Erskine (028 7082 2311; Fax: 028 7082 3139). e-mail: info@royalportrushgolfclub.com8 4482 8428).

TEMPLEPATRICK. **Hilton Templepatrick Golf Club,** Paradise Walk, Castle Upton Estate, Templepatrick BT39 0DD (02894 435542; Fax: 02894 435511). *Location:* 5 miles from Belfast International Airport, 15 miles from Belfast city centre. Parkland course - USGA greens. 18 holes, 7010 yards. S.S.S. 71. Driving range and putting green. *Green Fees:* Information not available. *Eating facilities:* à la carte Restaurant and Bar Brasserie in 4 star hotel. *Visitors:* welcome. 129 bedroomed hotel, Livingwell Health Club, Tuition package. *Society Meetings:* welcome, no restrictions. Professionals: Eamonn Logue/Lynn McCool (02894 435542; Fax: 02894 435511). Director of Golf: Lynn McCool (02894 435510).* e-mail: lynn.mccool@hilton.com

FHG Guides

publish a large range of well-known accommodation guides. We will be happy to send you details or you can use the order form at the back of this book.

Armagh

ARMAGH. **County Armagh Golf Club,** 7 Newry Road, Armagh BT60 1EN (028 3752 2501). *Location:* Armagh/Newry road. Parkland course. 18 holes, 6212 yards. S.S.S. 69. Practice area available. *Green Fees:* £17.00 weekdays, £22.00 weekends. November to February (incl.) reduction of £1.00. *Eating facilities:* diningroom/bar meals Tuesdays to Sundays, bar facilities daily. *Visitors:* welcome by arrangement. Not Saturdays or Thursdays. Carts and buggies. *Society Meetings:* welcome by arrangement except Saturdays or Thursdays. Professional: Alan Rankin (Tel & Fax: 028 3752 5864). Secretary: Lynne Fleming (Tel & Fax: 028 3752 5861).

CRAIGAVON. **Craigavon Golf and Ski Club,** Turmoyra Lane, Lurgan, Craigavon (028 3832 6606; Fax: 028 3834 7272). *Location:* half a mile from motorway, one mile from town centre, adjacent to ski slope. Parkland/wooded. 18 holes, 5901 meters. S.S.S. 72. 9 hole Par 3. 12 hole pitch and putt. Driving range. *Green Fees:* information not available. *Eating facilities:* full restaurant facilities. *Visitors:* always welcome. Modern clubhouse, showers and lockers. *Society Meetings:* welcome - book beforehand. Professional: S.Dickson.*

CRAIGAVON. **Edenmore Golf and Country Club,** Edenmore House, 70 Drumnabreeze Road, Magheralin, Craigavon BT67 0RH (028 9261 9241; Fax: 028 9261 3310). *Location*: take main road for Lurgan, coming off M1 at Moira Exit. Signposted from village of Magheralin on main Moira – Lurgan Road. Undulating, parkland course with panoramic views. Well drained. 18 holes, 6244 yards. S.S.S. 70. Practice facilities, putting green. *Green Fees*: weekdays £18.00, weekends and Bank Holidays £24.00. Subject to review. *Eating facilities:* Bailies restaurant. *Visitors*: Edenmore is a friendly, welcoming club. Visitors at all times except Saturdays before 3pm. Well stocked Pro Shop, lessons available. *Society Meetings:* welcome. Ring to book. PGA Professional: Andrew Manson. Secretary: Kenneth Logan (028 9261 1310; Fax: 028 9261 3310).
e-mail: info@edenmore.com
website: www.edenmore.com

CULLYHANNA. **Ashfield Golf Club,** Freeduff Road, Cullyhanna, Newry BT35 0JJ (028 3086 8180; Fax: 028 3086 8611). *Location:* A29 road, from Newry to Crossmaglen, 15 miles distance. Parkland course, lake, water hazard, bunkers. 18 holes, 5616 yards. S.S.S. 67. Par 69. Driving range. *Green Fees:* £15.00 weekdays, £20.00 weekends. Discounts for students, Seniors and juveniles. *Eating facilities:* licensed restaurant. *Visitors:* welcome at all times except before 11am on Sundays. *Society Meetings:* welcome, special rates available. Secretary: Seamus McNulty.

LURGAN. **Lurgan Golf Club,** The Demesne, Lurgan, Craigavon BT67 9BN (028 3832 2087; Fax: 028 3831 6166). *Location:* one mile from motorway, half a mile from town centre. Parkland. 18 holes, 5895 metres. S.S.S. 69. Small practice area, putting green. *Green Fees:* weekdays £17.00; weekends £22.00. Reductions if playing with a member. Students £14.00, under 18s £6.00. *Eating facilities:* restaurant and lounge bar. Caterer: (028 3832 2087). *Visitors:* welcome Monday to Friday, and Sundays after 3pm. *Society Meetings:* welcome as per visitors. Professional: Des Paul (028 3832 1068). Secretary: Muriel Sharpe (028 3832 2087; Fax: 028 3831 6166).

PORTADOWN. **Portadown Golf Club,** 192 Gilford Road, Portadown BT63 5LF (028 3835 5356). *Location:* on main Gilford Road out of Portadown. Parkland. 18 holes, 5649 metres. S.S.S. 69 off white tees; 68 off green tees, 72 off red tees. *Green Fees:* information not available. *Eating facilities:* Contact caterer on 028 3835 2214. *Visitors:* welcome at all times except Tuesdays and Saturdays. Squash, indoor bowling and snooker. *Society Meetings:* catered for by booking. Professional: Paul Stevenson (028 3833 4655). Secretary: Mrs Lily Holloway (028 3835 5356).*

TANDRAGEE. **Tandragee Golf Club,** Markethill Road, Tandragee, Craigavon BT62 2ER (028 3884 1272; Fax: 028 3884 0664). *Location*: approximately five miles from Portadown on road to Newry and Dublin. Hilly parkland and wooded. 18 holes, 5754 metres. S.S.S. 70, Par 71. Practice ground and net. *Green Fees*: information not available. *Eating facilities*: full catering except Mondays; two lounges. *Visitors*: welcome all days except Thursdays (Ladies' Day) and Saturdays (competition day). Carts and buggies available. *Society Meetings*: welcome by arrangement. Professional: D. Keenan (028 3884 1761). Administrative Assistant: Mrs Ashley Stewart.
e-mail: office@tandragee.co.uk
website: www.tandragee.co.uk

Co. Down

ARDGLASS. Ardglass Golf Club, 4 Castle Place, Ardglass BT30 7TP (028 4484 1219; Fax: 028 4484 1841). *Location:* nearest town – Downpatrick. Situated on the coast 30 miles due south of Belfast. Seaside links. 18 holes, White markers - 6231 yards. S.S.S. 70, Par 70. *Green Fees:* information not available. *Eating facilities:* bar and dining room. *Visitors:* welcome all week. *Society Meetings:* welcome except Saturdays, advance booking necessary. Professional: Philip Farrell (028 4484 1022). Club Manager: Miss Deborah Polly (028 4484 1219; Fax: 028 4484 1841).*
e-mail: info@ardglassgolfclub.com
website: www.ardglassgolfclub.com

BALLYNAHINCH. Spa Golf Club, 20 Grove Road, Ballynahinch BT24 8PN (028 9756 2365; Fax: 028 9756 4158). *Location:* Ballynahinch half mile, 11 miles south of Belfast. Parkland, wooded course with panoramic views. 18 holes, 6469 yards. S.S.S. 72. Practice area. *Green Fees:* weekdays £20.00; weekends £25.00. *Eating facilities:* bar snacks/restaurant service. *Visitors:* welcome except Saturdays. *Society Meetings:* welcome, discount for large parties. Secretary: T.G. Magee (028 9756 2365).

BANBRIDGE. Banbridge Golf Club, Huntly Road, Banbridge BT32 3UR. *Location:* half-a-mile from town centre on the Huntly Road. Parkland. 18 holes, 5590 yards. S.S.S. 67. Practice ground. *Green Fees:* information not available. *Eating facilities:* full catering and bar facilities. *Visitors:* welcome, restrictions on Ladies' Day (Tuesdays) and men's competition day (Saturdays). *Society Meetings:* catered for; arrange with Secretary/Manager: Mr J. McKeown (028 4066 2211).
e-mail: banbridgegolf@btconnect.com

BANGOR. Bangor Golf Club, Broadway, Bangor BT20 4RH (028 9127 0922; Fax: 028 9145 3394). *Location:* one mile from town centre off Donaghadee Road. Parkland. 18 holes, 6424 yards. S.S.S. 71. Practice facilities. *Green Fees:* information not available. *Eating facilities:* lunches and evening meals. *Visitors:* welcome except Saturdays; Tuesday is Ladies' Day. Trolleys and buggies available. *Society Meetings:* advance booking necessary. Professional: Michael Bannon (028 9146 2164).*
e-mail: bangorgolfclubni@btconnect.com
website: www.bangorgolfclubni.co.uk

BANGOR. Blackwood Golf Centre, 150 Crawfordsburn Road, Bangor BT19 1GB (028 9185 2706). *Location:* west of Bangor. Two 18-hole courses. Driving range. *Green Fees:* weekdays £20.00, weekends £25.00. *Visitors:* welcome.

BANGOR. Carnalea Golf Club, Station Road, Bangor BT19 1EZ (028 9146 5004). *Location:* one minute walk from Carnalea Railway Station. Seaside parkland. 18 holes, 5574 yards. S.S.S. 67. *Green*

Fees: information not available. *Eating facilities:* full restaurant and two bars. *Visitors:* welcome without reservation. *Society Meetings:* catered for. Golf Shop (028 9127 0122). Professional: Tom Loughran (028 9127 0122). Secretary: G. Steele (028 9127 0368; Fax: 028 9127 3989).*

BANGOR. Helen's Bay Golf Club, Golf Road, Helen's Bay, Bangor BT19 1TL (028 9185 2815). *Location:* A2 from Belfast - 9 miles. Parkland. 9 holes, 5643 yards. S.S.S. 67. *Green Fees:* information not available. *Eating facilities:* available - full restaurant, bar and lounge bar (028 9185 2816). *Visitors:* welcome Sunday, Monday, Wednesday and Friday; Tuesday is Ladies' Day. *Society Meetings:* catered for by prior booking confirmed by the Secretary Manager (maximum 40). Secretary Manager: (Tel: 028 9185 2815; Fax: 028 9185 2660).*

BELFAST. Balmoral Golf Club Ltd, 518 Lisburn Road, Belfast BT9 6GX (028 9038 1514). *Location:* M1 from Belfast exit Balmoral, turn right at lights Lisburn Road, quarter mile on left beside Kings Hall or two/three miles south of Belfast on main Lisburn Road next to Kings Hall. A flat undulating course with 44 plus bunkers and a stream to contend with. Excellent greens, approached by tree-lined fairways. 18 holes, 6034 metres. S.S.S. 70 Medal, 69 regular. Practice ground and nets. *Green Fees:* (2007) Visitor midweek £27.00, weekend £40.00; Society midweek £22.00, weekend £27.00. *Eating facilities:* restaurant, lunch, dinner, snacks à la carte, two bars. *Visitors:* welcome except Saturdays; restricted on Sundays. *Society Meetings:* Mondays, Thursdays and Sunday afternoons. Professional: Geoff Bleakley (028 9066 7747). Chief Executive: Terry Graham (028 9038 1514; Fax: 028 9066 6759).
website: www.balmoralgolf.com

BELFAST. Belvoir Park Golf Club, 73/75 Church Road, Newtownbreda, Belfast BT8 7AN (028 9049 1693; Fax: 028 9064 6113). *Location:* two miles from city centre, Saintfield Road. Parkland, well wooded. 18 holes, 6597 yards. S.S.S. 71. Practice area. *Green Fees:* information not available. *Eating facilities:* full catering and bar. *Visitors:* welcome except Saturday. *Society Meetings:* by prior booking only. Professional: Michael McGivern (028 9064 6714). Secretary: Ann Vaughan (028 9049 1693).*

BELFAST. Knock Golf Club, Summerfield, Dundonald, Belfast BT16 2QX (028 9048 2249; Fax: 028 9048 7277). *Location:* Upper Newtownards Road in east of the city of Belfast. Parkland with huge trees, large bunkers and a stream running through the course. 18 holes, 6435 yards. S.S.S. 71. Practice ground. *Green Fees:* information not available. *Eating facilities:* full catering and bar facilities available. *Visitors:* welcome except Saturday but it is advisable to ring Professional first. Trolleys available. *Society Meetings:* catered for Mondays and Thursdays. Advance booking required. Professional: G. Fairweather (028 9048 3825). Secretary/Manager: Mrs A. Armstrong (028 9048 3251).*

BELFAST. **Ormeau Golf Club,** 50 Park Road, Belfast BT7 2FX (028 9064 0700; Fax: 028 9064 6250). *Location:* Belfast south/east; Ravenhill Road. Flat, parkland wooded course. 9 holes, 2783 yards, 2542 metres. S.S.S. 67. *Green Fees:* information not available. *Eating facilities:* bars and restaurant. *Visitors:* welcome, restrictions on Tuesdays and Saturdays. Snooker. *Society Meetings:* welcome most days. Shop Manager: S. Rourke (028 90 640999). Manager: W. Lynn (028 9064 0700). Caterer: (028 9064 1999).

BELFAST. **Shandon Park Golf Club,** 73 Shandon Park, Belfast BT5 6NY (028 9080 5030). Parkland. 18 holes, 6460 metres. S.S.S. 70. *Green Fees:* information not available. *Eating facilities:* restaurant facilities, bar snacks. *Visitors:* welcome except Saturdays subject to advance clearance by Professional. *Society Meetings:* Mondays, Thursdays, Fridays and Sundays. Professional: Barry Wilson (028 9080 5031). Secretary/Manager: Greg Bailie (028 9080 5030; Fax: 028 9080 5999).

DONAGHADEE. **Donaghadee Golf Club,** 84 Warren Road, Donaghadee BT21 0PQ (028 9188 8697). *Location:* five miles south of Bangor on main coast road. Part links and inland park with scenic views over Copeland Islands and Scottish coast. 18 holes, 6000 yards, 5561 metres. Par 71, S.S.S. 69. Practice ground and putting green. *Green Fees:* information not available. *Eating facilities:* full catering available, seven days in summer, Tuesday to Sunday in winter. *Visitors:* welcome on any weekday and Sundays; Members only on Saturdays. Ladies welcome on Tuesdays. Juveniles must be accompanied by an adult. Pro shop. Club and trolley hire. Lessons available by prior arrangement. *Society Meetings:* welcome any day except Saturday. Special rates available. Professional: Gordon Drew (028 9188 2392). General Manager: (028 9188 3624; Fax: 028 9188 8891) e-mail: deegolf@freenet.co.uk.

> **THE APPEARANCE OF AN ASTERISK (*) AT THE END OF A CLUB OR COURSE ENTRY INDICATES THAT UP-TO-DATE INFORMATION HAS NOT BEEN SUPPLIED**

DOWNPATRICK. **Bright Castle Golf Club,** 14 Coniamstown Road, Bright, Downpatrick BT30 8LU (028 4484 1319). *Location:* turn right off the main B176, signposted to Bright/Minerstown. Bright Castle is an 18 hole mature woodland course featuring 4 formidable par 5s - your driving accuracy will be tested to the limit on the sloping, densely tree-lined fairways. 6645 yards. SSS 73. *Green Fees:* information not available. *Eating facilities:* Restaurant and bar available. *Visitors:* Welcome. *Society Meetings:* Welcome, must book in advance. Secretary: Thomas Johnston (028 4482 8428).* e-mail: bright.castle@virgin.net

DOWNPATRICK. **Downpatrick Golf Club,** 43 Saul Road, Downpatrick BT30 6PA (028 4461 5947; Fax: 028 4461 7502). *Location:* one and a half miles from town centre, south-east direction. Parkland, challenging upland course. 18 holes, 6120 yards. S.S.S. 69. Practice area and putting area. *Green Fees:* information not available. *Eating facilities:* two lounges and diningroom. Catering: (028 4461 5244). *Visitors:* welcome, but advisable to make arrangements in advance for weekends. Snooker room. *Society Meetings:* welcome by prior arrangement. Professional: Robert Hutton (028 4461 5167). Office Manager: Elaine Carson.

HOLYWOOD. **Holywood Golf Club,** Nuns Walk, Demesne Road, Holywood BT18 9LE (028 9042 3135/2138; Fax: 028 9042 5040). Parkland. 18 holes, 5430 yards. S.S.S. 68. *Green Fees:* information not available. *Eating facilities:* bars and restaurant. *Visitors:* welcome, Thursday is Ladies' Day. *Society Meetings:* welcome Mondays, Tuesdays, Wednesdays and Fridays and between 8am and 9am Sundays. Professional: Paul Gray (028 9042 5503; Fax: 028 9042 5040). Secretary: (028 9042 3135; Fax: 028 9042 5040).*

HOLYWOOD. **The Royal Belfast Golf Club,** Station Road, Craigavad BT18 0BP (028 9042 8165; Fax: 028 9042 1404). *Location:* two miles past Holywood, off main Belfast to Bangor Road. Mainly parkland, bordering shores of Belfast Lough. 18 holes, 5961 yards. S.S.S. 69. Practice ground. *Green Fees:* £60.00 weekdays, £70.00 weekends. *Eating facilities:* full catering and bar facilities. *Visitors:* with letter of introduction and by arrangement only. *Society Meetings:* by arrangement. Professional: A. Ferguson (028 9042 8586). Secretary/Manager: Mrs S.H. Morrison (028 9042 8165).

KILKEEL. **Kilkeel Golf Club,** Mourne Park, Kilkeel BT34 4LB (028 4176 5095; Fax: 028 4176 5579). *Location:* Kilkeel to Newry road approximately three miles from Kilkeel. Parkland situated at the foot of Mourne Mountains. 18 holes, 6615 metres. S.S.S. 72. Practice area available. *Green Fees:* weekdays £23.00, weekends £28.00. *Eating facilities:* restaurant and bar. *Visitors:* welcome, club competitions on Tuesday, Thursday and Saturday. Booking for Saturday late afternoons and Sundays. *Society Meetings:* catered for by prior arrangement.

KILLYLEAGH. **Ringdufferin Golf Course,** 36 Ringdufferin Road, Toye, Killyleagh BT30 9PH (Tel: 028 4482 8812; Fax: 028 4482 8972). *Location*: 2 miles north of Killyleagh on Comber Road. Drumlin course. 18 holes, 5113 yards, 4641 metres. S.S.S. 66. Practice facilities. *Green Fees:* £16.00. *Eating facilities*: licensed restaurant. *Visitors*: welcome, except Saturdays between 7am - 12.30pm. *Society Meetings*: welcome. Secretary: Willis Marshall (Tel : 028 4482 8812; Fax: 028 4482 8972).

KNOCKBRACKEN. **Mount Ober Golf and Country Club,** 24 Ballymaconaghy Road, Knockbracken, Belfast BT8 6SB (028 9079 5666; Fax: 028 9070 5862). *Location:* 15 minutes from centre of Belfast; Saintfield Road, Cairnshill Road, Four Winds Roundabout. Parkland on undulating ground. 18 holes, 5022 yards, S.S.S. 66. Golf academy, floodlit driving range. *Green Fees:* Monday to Friday £17.00, Sunday and Bank Holidays £19.00. *Eating facilities:* full catering and bar service at all times; excellent restaurant. *Visitors:* welcome anytime, except Saturdays before 3pm. *Society Meetings:* welcome except Saturdays before 3pm. Professional: Wesley Ramsay (028 9070 1648; Fax: 028 9070 5862). Secretary: Ena Williams (028 9040 1811; Fax: 028 9070 5862).
e-mail: mt.ober@ukonline.co.uk

NEWCASTLE. **Royal County Down Golf Club,** Newcastle BT33 0AN. *Location:* adjacent to north side of Newcastle, approach from town centre. Championship Course: 18 holes, 7181 yards, S.S.S. 74. Annesley Links Course: 18 holes, 4681 yards. S.S.S. 66. *Green Fees:* information not available. *Eating facilities:* light lunches and bar, weekdays only. *Visitors:* welcome with prior reservation. *Society Meetings:* catered for. Professional: Kevan J. Whitson (028 4372 2419). Secretary: J.H. Laidler (028 4372 3314; Fax: 028 4372 6281).
website: www.royalcountydown.org

NEWTOWNARDS. **Clandeboye Golf Club,** Tower Road, Conlig, Newtownards BT23 3PN (028 9127 1767). *Location:* Conlig village off A21 between Bangor and Newtownards. Wooded, undulating parkland/heathland. Two courses: Dufferin – 18 holes, 6559 yards, S.S.S. 71; blue tees - 6742 yards, S.S.S. 72. Ava – 18 holes, 5755 yards, S.S.S. 68. Practice ground. Host to the Irish Seniors 2001; N.I. Masters, won by Darren Clarke. *Green Fees:* information not available. *Eating facilities:* full catering and bar. *Visitors:* welcome weekdays; no play before 3pm Saturdays, before 10.30am Sundays. Visitors changing facility. *Society*

Meetings: welcome weekdays except Thursdays. Professional: Peter Gregory (028 9127 1750). General Manager: J. W. Thomson (028 9127 1767; Fax: 028 9147 3711).*

NEWTOWNARDS. **Kirkistown Castle Golf Club,** 142 Main Road, Cloughey, Newtownards BT22 1JA (028 4277 1233). *Location:* approximately 45 minutes from Belfast, 16 miles from Newtownards on the A2. 18 holes, Par 69, S.S.S. 70. *Green Fees:* £25.00 weekdays; £30.00 weekends and Public Holidays. Tourists 10% discount in approved accommodation. *Eating facilities:* full catering and snacks. *Visitors:* welcome. *Society Meetings:* outings welcome by arrangement. Secretary/Manager: Rosemary Coulter (028 4277 1233). Professional: Andrew Ferguson (028 9177 1004). Caterer: Marion Smyth (028 4277 2395; Fax: 028 4277 1699).
e-mail: kirkistown@supanet.com
website: www.linksgolfkirkistown.com

NEWTOWNARDS. **Mahee Island Golf Club,** Mahee Island, Comber, Newtownards BT23 6EP (028 9754 1234). *Location:* Comber/Killyleagh Road. After half a mile turn left signposted Ardmillan/Mahee Island. Keep left for six miles to course. Parkland course set on an island with magnificent views over Strangford Lough. 9 holes, 5822 yards, 5108 metres. S.S.S. 70. Par 71 over 18 holes. Putting green and pitching area. *Green Fees:* weekdays £13.00; weekends £18.00. *Eating facilities:* Sunday, Monday, Wednesday and Saturday, other times by arrangement with caterer (07968 449932). *Visitors:* welcome, restricted Saturdays until 5pm. *Society Meetings:* welcome, by prior arrangement. Professional: (Shop) Colin Macaw (028 9754 1234). Secretary: Mervyn Marshall (028 9145 7385).

NEWTOWNARDS. **Scrabo Golf Club,** 233 Scrabo Road, Newtownards BT23 4SL (028 9181 2355). *Location:* approximately 10 miles from Belfast off main Belfast to Newtownards dual carriageway, follow signs to Scrabo Country Park. Upland course. 18 holes, 5699 metres. S.S.S. 71. Practice area. *Green Fees:* call for details. *Eating facilities:* full catering (closed Mondays). *Visitors:* welcome except Saturdays and avoid Wednesdays 4.30pm to 6.30pm. *Society Meetings:* over 12 players, welcome. General Manager: Bill Brown (028 9181 2355; Fax: 028 9182 2919).

WARRENPOINT. **Warrenpoint Golf Club,** Lower Dromore Road, Warrenpoint BT34 3LN (028 4175 3695; Fax: 028 4175 2918). *Location:* five miles south of Newry on coast road. Parkland. 18 holes, 5700 metres. S.S.S. 70. Practice ground. *Green Fees:* information not available. *Eating facilities:* full catering and bar facilities. *Visitors:* welcome Sunday, Monday, Thursday, Friday. Snooker facilities available. *Society Meetings:* catered for by prior arrangement. Professional: Nigel Shaw (Tel & Fax: 028 4175 2371). Secretary: Marian Trainor. *
e-mail: office@warrenpointgolf.com

www.uk-golfguide.com

Fermanagh

ENNISKILLEN. **Castle Hume Golf Club,** Belleek Road, Enniskillen BT93 7ED (028 6632 7077; Fax: 028 6632 7076). *Location:* on A46 Belleek/Donegal Road, just a few minutes' drive from Enniskillen. Fast emerging as one of the best golfing facilities the North has to offer, this Championship Course provides golfers of all skill levels with a very enjoyable yet testing challenge. Hosted the Ulster PGA Championship 1996-1998 and 2003-2006. 18 holes, 5932 metres. Floodlit driving range. *Green Fees:* information not available. *Eating facilities:* excellent hospitality in the bar and restaurant. *Visitors:* welcome. Fully stocked Pro Shop. *Society Meetings:* welcome. Resident PGA Professional: Shaun Donnelly. Visit our website for Open Days and Open Week.*
website: www.castlehumegolf.com
          www.lougherneegolfresort.com

ENNISKILLEN. **Enniskillen Golf Club,** Castlecoole, Enniskillen BT74 6HZ (028 6632 5250). *Location:* off Enniskillen to Tempo Road on outskirts of town. Scenic parkland course with views of market town of Enniskillen on front nine, many mature trees on back nine. 18 holes, 6189 yards. S.S.S. 69. *Green Fees:* information not available. Reduction if playing with member. *Eating facilities:* catering by arrangement. *Visitors:* welcome at all times; some restriction on Tuesdays (Ladies' Day) and weekends. *Society Meetings:* welcome at all times, special rates available. Hon. Secretary: David McKechnie. Club Steward Daryll Robinson (028 6632 5250).

Londonderry

CASTLEROCK. **Castlerock Golf Club,** 65 Circular Road, Castlerock, Coleraine BT51 4TJ (028 7084 8314). *Location:* A2, six miles west of Coleraine. Seaside links, stream in play at four holes. 18 holes, 6687 yards, S.S.S. 72. 9 holes, 2457 metres. S.S.S. 67. Practice area. *Green Fees:* weekdays £60.00 per round, weekends and Bank Holidays £75.00. Subject to review. *Eating facilities:* full restaurant facilities, two bars. *Visitors:* welcome weekdays Monday to Friday and weekends by arrangement. *Society Meetings:* welcome Monday to Friday. Professional: Ian Blair (028 7084 9424). Secretary: Mark Steen (028 7084 8314; Fax: 028 7084 9440).

COLERAINE. **Brown Trout Golf and Country Club,** 209 Agivey Road, Aghadowey, Near Coleraine BT51 4AD (028 7086 8209; Fax: 028 7086 8878). *Location:* on A54 between Kilrea and Coleraine. Parkland course, heavily wooded, crossing water seven times in nine holes. 9 holes, 2755 metres. S.S.S. 68. *Green Fees:* information not available. *Eating facilities:* à la carte restaurant, bar snacks, barbecues. *Visitors:* always welcome. 15 new luxurious en suite bedrooms and four new five-star cottages available. *Society Meetings:* welcome. Professional: Ken Revie. Secretary/ Manager: Bill O'Hara.
e-mail: bill@browntroutinn.com
website: www.browntroutinn.com

LIMAVADY. **Benone Golf Course,** 53 Benone Avenue, Benone, Limavady BT49 0LQ (028 7775 0555). *Location:* situated on the A2 coast road, 12 miles from Limavady. Parkland course. 9 holes, 1458 yards, 1334 metres. S.S.S. 27. Practice range, putting green. *Green Fees:* information not available. *Eating facilities:* coffee shop open July/ August, restaurant and bars within one mile. *Visitors:* welcome. Club hire available. *Society Meetings:* welcome. Secretary: M. Clark (028 7775 0555; Fax: 028 7775 0919).

LIMAVADY. **Roe Park Golf Club,** Radisson SAS Roe Park Resort, Roe Park, Limavady BT49 9LB (028 7772 2222; Fax: 028 7772 2313). *Location:* on main A2 Londonderry-Limavady road, 16 miles from Londonderry and one mile from Limavady. (028 777 60105). Parkland. 18 holes, 6318 yards. S.S.S. 69. Floodlit driving range; putting green; equipment hire. *Green Fees:* information not available. *Eating facilities:* Coach House Brasserie. *Visitors:* welcome with some restrictions at weekend. *Society Meetings:* welcome; society packages available. Accommodation on site. Professional: Shaun Devenney. Golf Manager: Jim Cullen.

LONDONDERRY. **Foyle International Golf Centre,** 12 Alder Road, Londonderry BT48 8DB (028 7135 2222; Fax: 028 7135 3967). *Location:* one-and-a-half miles from Foyle Bridge heading towards Moville, Co Donegal. Parkland Championship standard Par 71, notable holes with water coming into play are third Par 3, 10th and 11th. 18 holes, 6678 yard, 6164 metres. S.S.S. 71, Par 71. 9 hole course, Par 3. Indoor floodlit driving range, putting greens. *Green Fees:* weekdays £16.00; weekends £19.00. 10% discount for groups over 12. *Eating facilities:* Pitchers Wine Bar and Restaurant within club house. *Visitors:* welcome anyday, anytime. Carts, caddies available. Golf academy with video analysis teaching system. *Society Meetings:* welcome. Professionals: Derek Morrison and Sean Young. Secretary: Margaret Lapsley.
e-mail: mail@foylegolf.club24.co.uk
website: www.foylegolfcentre.co.uk

MAGHERAFELT. **Moyola Park Golf Club,** 15 Curran Road, Castledawson, Magherafelt BT45 8DG (028 7946 8468; Fax: 028 7946 8626). *Location:* 35 miles north of Belfast on M2; off middle of Main Street, Castledawson. Attractive, spacious mature parkland. 18 holes, 6519 yards. S.S.S. 71. Practice ground, putting green. *Green Fees:* Mondays to Thursdays £24.00, Fridays £30.00, weekends and Bank Holidays £30.00. Eating facilities: bars and restaurant. *Visitors:* welcome with prior notice. *Society Meetings:* welcome with prior notice. Professional: Bob Cockcroft (028 7946 8830). Secretary/Manager:Michael Gribbin.

PORTSTEWART. **Portstewart Golf Club,** Strand Road, Portstewart, BT55 7PG (028 7083 2015; Fax: 028 7083 4097). *Location:* north from Coleraine. Coastal links. No 1 Strand - 18 holes, 6784 yards, S.S.S. 73. No 2 Riverside - 9 holes, 2622 yards. No 3 Old - 18 holes, 4733 yards, S.S.S. 64. Practice area. *Green Fees:* information not available. *Eating facilities:* meals available - advance orders; no catering on Mondays. *Visitors:* welcome Mondays to Fridays; limited Wednesdays. Prior booking essential on Strand. Enquire about special rates for parties. *Society Meetings:* catered for by arrangement. Professional: Alan Hunter (Tel & Fax: 028 7083 2601). Secretary: Michael Moss (028 7083 2015; Fax: 028 7083 4097).*
e-mail: michael@portstewartgc.co.uk.*

PREHEN. **City of Derry Golf Club,** 49 Victoria Road, Prehen BT47 2PU (028 7134 6369). *Location:* three miles from city centre on the road to Strabane - follow the River Foyle. Parkland, wooded. 18 holes, 5877 metres. S.S.S. 71, Par 71. Also 9 hole (Dunhugh) course, 4305 metres. Par 66. Practice area. *Green Fees:* information not available. *Eating facilities:* catering and bar facilities available. *Visitors:* welcome on weekdays up to 4.30pm, weekends please contact Professional. Convenient for hotels and guest houses. *Society Meetings:* welcome, please contact Manager's Office. Professional: Mr Michael Doherty (028 7131 1496). Hon. Secretary: Mr G. Mills (028 7134 6369). Secretary: Noreen Allen (028 7134 6369).*

Tyrone

COOKSTOWN. **Killymoon Golf Club,** 200 Killymoon Road, Cookstown BT80 8TW (Tel & Fax: 028 8676 3762). *Location:* private road off A29. Signposted at Dungannon end of town opposite Drum Road. Mainly flat parkland. 18 holes, 6202 yards. S.S.S. 70. Practice ground. *Green Fees:* Mondays £16.00 (excluding Bank Holidays); Tuesdays to Fridays £22.00; weekends and Bank Holidays £28.00. *Eating facilities:* full catering at club (large groups please book). *Visitors:* welcome, after 4pm Saturdays, Thursday is Ladies' Day. *Society Meetings:* welcome. Booking essential. Professional: Gary Chambers (Tel & Fax: 028 8676 3460); Secretary: Brian Rouse (Tel & Fax: 028 8676 3762). General Manager: Norman Weir (028 8676 3762).

DUNGANNON. **Dungannon Golf Club,** 34 Springfield Lane, Dungannon BT70 1QX (028 8772 2098; Fax: 028 8772 7338). *Location:* a short distance from Dungannon along Donaghmore Road. Flat first 9, hilly second 9. Parkland course with some water hazards newly positioned. 18 holes, 6155 yards (white markers.) S.S.S. 69. *Green Fees:* weekdays £20.00; weekends and Bank Holidays £25.00. As a guest of a member £14.00 weekdays, £16.00 weekends and Bank Holidays. *Eating facilities:* bar snacks and licensed restaurant. *Visitors:* always welcome but please telephone first; precluded by timesheets at weekends, Ladies' Day Tuesdays. *Society Meetings:* welcome by prior arrangement; apply in writing. Professional: Vivian Teague. Secretary: S.T. Hughes.

FINTONA. **Fintona Golf Club,** 1 Kiln Street, Ecclesville Demesne, Fintona BT78 2BJ (Tel & Fax: 028 8284 1480). *Location:* eight miles south of Omagh, county town of Tyrone. An attractive parkland course, its main features being a trout stream; rated one of the top nine hole courses in the Province. 9 holes, 5765 metres. S.S.S. 70. Putting green. *Green Fees:* £15.00. Weekends by arrangement. *Eating facilities:* bar snacks, meals on request. *Visitors:* welcome weekdays, weekends by arrangement. *Society Meetings:* welcome weekdays, book in advance.

NEWTOWNSTEWART. **Newtownstewart Golf Club,** 38 Golf Course Road, Newtownstewart, Omagh BT78 4HU (028 8166 1466; Fax: 028 8166 2506). *Location:* signposted from Strabane Road (A57) at Newtownstewart, two miles west of Newtownstewart on B84. Parkland and wooded course. 18 holes, 5320 metres. S.S.S. 69. Practice ground. *Green Fees:* weekdays £17.00; weekends and Bank Holidays £25.00. *Eating facilities:* available. *Visitors:* welcome at all times. Accommodation available in chalets beside clubhouse. Buggies available. *Society Meetings:* all welcome. Special packages available. Golf Shop: (028 8166 2242; Fax: 028 8166 2506). Club Administrator/Secretary: Mrs Lorraine Donnell (028 8166 1466; Fax: 028 8166 2506). e-mail: newtown.stewart@lineone.net
website: www.globalgolf.com/newtownstewart

OMAGH. **Omagh Golf Club,** 83a Dublin Road, Omagh BT78 1HQ (Tel & Fax: 028 8224 3160). *Location:* one mile from Omagh town centre on Belfast/Dublin Road. Parkland. 18 holes, 5638 metres. S.S.S. 70. *Green Fees:* information not available. *Eating facilities:* snacks and bar facilities. *Visitors:* welcome any day except Tuesday and Saturday. *Society Meetings:* welcome. Hon. Secretary: Joseph A. McElholm. Secretary: Florence E.A. Caldwell (Tel & Fax: 028 8224 3160).*

STRABANE. **Strabane Golf Club,** 33 Ballycolman Road, Strabane BT82 9PH (028 7138 2271/2007; Fax: 028 7188 6471). *Location:* A5 half mile from Strabane towards Omagh. Parkland. 18 holes, 5610 metres. S.S.S. 69. *Green Fees:* information not available. *Eating facilities:* two bars, catering by arrangement. *Visitors:* welcome, except Saturdays. Practice putting green and chipping area. *Society Meetings:* by arrangement. Secretary: Gerry Glover (028 7138 2007).*

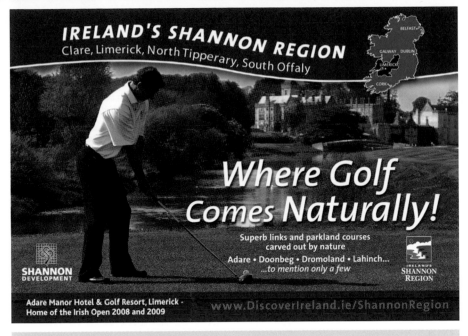

Ireland's Shannon Region

Ireland's Shannon Region – Counties of Clare, Limerick, North Tipperary and South Offaly - has been carved by nature itself, and its dramatic Atlantic coastline and unspoiled greenery is the perfect setting for superb golf courses. Golfers can test their skills on the windswept dunes of a championship links, challenge the water-traps and other hazards of courses created by some of the world's most famous designers, or just play a relaxing eighteen holes on a parkland course of tree-lined fairways.

There are twenty-five courses to choose from in the Shannon Region. Established in 1892, the Lahinch links course in Co. Clare is often referred to as 'the St Andrews of Ireland' with its famous holes such as 'The Dell'. A little further south along the Clare coast is another links gem, Doonbeg, with its massive dunes, designed by Australian legend, Greg Norman. When you travel inland, the choices are equally impressive. There are superb courses on the estates of the luxurious hotels, Dromoland Castle, Co. Clare and Adare Manor, Co. Limerick. Other options include Birr, Co. Offaly, with magnificent views of the Slieve Bloom Mountains, Nenagh, North Tipperary with some fine panoramic views, and East Clare, Co. Clare. You have four excellent choices close to Limerick City, including Limerick County Golf & Country Club with its own indoor teaching facility.

Another great reason to visit the Shannon Region – Adare Manor Hotel and Golf Resort will host the Irish Open from the 15th to 18th May 2008.

Fly from the UK to Shannon Airport in less than 60 minutes, with a choice of direct flights from Birmingham, Bristol, East Midlands, Edinburgh, Glasgow (Prestwick), Leeds-Bradford, Liverpool; and from London Gatwick, Luton and Stanstead; and Manchester.

For further information visit: www.DiscoverIreland.ie/ShannonRegion or request a brochure from Tourism Marketing, Shannon Development, Shannon, Co. Clare, Ireland

Tel: +353 61 317522, Fax: +353 61 363180

REPUBLIC OF IRELAND

Co. Carlow

BORRIS. **Borris Golf Club,** Deer Park, Carlow (059 9773310; Fax: 059 9773750). Scenic parkland course with tree lined fairways and modern sandbased greens. 10 holes, 5680 yards, S.S.S. 69. Practice area and putting green. *Green Fees*: information not available. *Eating facilities*: bar meals available. *Visitors*: welcome weekdays by prior arrangement, restrictions Thursdays and weekends. *Society Meetings*: welcome by prior arrangement. Secretary: Nollaig Lucas (059 9773310; Fax: 059 9773750).*

CARLOW. **Carlow Golf Club**, Deer Park, Carlow (0503 31695; Fax: 0503 40065). *Location*: N9 2.5 miles north of Carlow town. Parkland, undulating, sandy sub-soil. 18 holes, 5974 metres. S.S.S. 71. Practice ground. New 9 hole golf course. *Green Fees*: information not available. *Eating facilities*: bar and restaurant. *Visitors*: always welcome, weekends difficult, pre-booking advisable. Carts, caddies and club hire. *Society Meetings*: must be pre-booked with Secretary. Professional: Andrew Gilbert (059 9141745; Fax: 059 9140065). General Manager: Donard MacSweeney (059 9131695; Fax: 059 9140065).*
e-mail: carlowgolfclub@eircom.net
website: www.carlowgolfclub.com

Co. Cavan

BALLYCONNELL. **Slieve Russell Hotel & Golf Club,** Ballyconnel (049 952 5090; Fax: 049 952 6640). Mature parkland European tour Championship course on 350 acres. 18 holes, 7053 yards, 6412 metres. Driving range and practice ground. *Green Fees*: information not available. *Eating facilities*: Summit Bar and restaurant. *Visitors*: welcome everyday, pre-booking essential. Limited availablity on Saturdays. 4 Star Hotel on site. *Society Meetings*: welcome, please contact for details. Professional: Liam McCool. Golf Director: Ivan Hewson (049 952 6458; Fax: 049 952 6640).*
e-mail: slieve-golf-club@quinn-hotels.com
e-mail: hewsoni@quinn-hotels.com

BELTURBET. **Belturbet Golf Club,** Erne Hill, Belturbet (00 353 49 9522287). *Location*: quarter-of-a-mile from Belturbet town centre on main N3 Cavan-Dublin road. Parkland with elevated greens. 9 holes, 5204 yards. S.S.S. 65. Practice area and putting green. *Green Fees*: information not available. *Eating facilities*: clubhouse and bar; catering available. *Visitors*: welcome at all times. *Society Meetings*: welcome at all times. Club/trolley hire. Various classes of Membership available, including distance/overseas. All enquiries to 00 353 49 9522287.*

BLACKLION. **Blacklion Golf Club,** Toam, Blacklion, via Sligo (071 985 3024). *Location*: Blacklion/Belcoo on Enniskillen to Sligo Road. Flat parkland, wooded copses, lake partially in play, scenic. 9 holes, 6175 yards, 5614 metres. S.S.S. 69. *Green Fees*: information not available. *Eating facilities*: full catering available. *Visitors*: welcome. Course surrounded on four holes by Loch McNean. Safe swimming in lake. Scenic hill walks. *Society Meetings*: by arrangement. Hon. Secretary: Pat Gallery.*

CAVAN. **County Cavan Golf Club,** Arnmore House, Drumelis, Cavan (049 4331541). *Location*: on Killeshandra road from Cavan. Parkland course. 18 holes, 5634 metres. S.S.S 69. Practice area, driving range. *Green Fees*: (2007) Monday to Thursday €30, Friday to Sunday €35; open day every Thursday. *Eating facilities*: full catering facilities including bar snacks. *Visitors*: welcome; limited availablility on Wednesdays and weekends. *Society Meetings*: on application to Professional. Professional: Bill Nobel (049 4331388). Club Secretary: Seamus McConnon (Tel & Fax: 049 4331541).
e-mail: cavangc@iol.ie
website: www.cavangolf.ie

THE APPEARANCE OF AN ASTERISK (*) AT THE END OF A CLUB OR COURSE ENTRY INDICATES THAT UP-TO-DATE INFORMATION HAS NOT BEEN SUPPLIED

Co. Clare

CLONLARA. **Clonlara Golf and Leisure,** Clonlara (061 354141; Fax: 061 354143). *Location:* 7 miles from Limerick on Corbally to Killaloe road. Parkland. 12 holes. S.S.S.67. *Green Fees:* information not available. *Eating facilities:* fully licensed bar with bar food. *Visitors:* welcome. *Society Meetings:* welcome. No walkers, caddies, or children under 14 allowed on the course. Tennis courts, sauna, children's play area, crazy golf. Self-catering apartments available. Secretary: Ms A. O'Grady (061 354141; Fax: 061 354143).*
e-mail: tmcmahon@circom.net

DOONBEG. **Doonbeg Golf Club,** Doonbeg (353 65 9055246; Fax: 353 65 9055247). *Location:* The highly acclaimed Doonbeg Golf Club is situated between two of Ireland's greatest Links courses - Ballybunion and Lahinch. Designed by Greg Norman and host of the 2002 Palmer Cup matches, it is set along 1.5 miles of crescent-shaped beach encircling Doughmore Bay, providing magnificent views. Links course. 18 holes, 6885 yards, par 72. Practice green, putting green. *Green Fees:* information not available. *Eating facilities:* restaurant. *Visitors:* welcome. On site accommodation expected 2006.*
e-mail: links@doonbeggolfclub.com

ENNIS. **Ennis Golf Club,** Drumbiggle, Ennis (065 6824074; Fax: 065 6841848). *Location:* half a mile from Ennis town centre. Parkland course set in rolling hills with five challenging Par 3s. 18 holes, 6240 yards, 5706 metres. Par 70. *Green Fees:* €40. Groups rates on request. *Eating facilities:* full catering facilities and bar. *Visitors:* Monday, Thursday, Saturday with some restrictions Tuesday and Wednesday. New Club House. Carts, clubs and caddies available. *Society Meetings:* welcome; 30 euros. Club Manager: Pat McCarthy (065 6824074; Fax: 065 6841848).
e-mail: info@ennisgolfclub.com
website: www.ennisgolfclub.com

ENNIS. **Woodstock Golf and Country Club,** Shanaway Road, Ennis (00353 656 829463; Fax: 00353 656 820304). *Location:* from Ennis town take Lahinch Road, 18 miles Shannon Airport. Parkland course. 18 holes, 5879 metres. S.S.S. 71. *Green Fees:* information not available. *Eating facilities:* bar food served daily, The Tenth Tee Bar, G/B's Restaurant (065 44430). *Visitors:* welcome at all times, telephone in advance advisable at weekends. Hotel on site. *Society Meetings:* all welcome, special rates available. Contact: Anne Marie Russell (+ 353 65 682 9463; Fax: + 353 65 682 0804).
e-mail: proshopwoodstock@eircom.net
website: www.woodstockgolfclub.com

Doonbeg Golf Club, Doonbeg

KILKEE. **Kilkee Golf Club,** East End, Kilkee (065 9056048; Fax: 065 9056977). *Location:* right on seafront at end of promenade. Seaside course with many cliff top tees and greens. 18 holes, 5960 metres. S.S.S. 71. *Green Fees:* €30. *Eating facilities:* fully licensed restaurant and bar. *Visitors:* very welcome every day. Golf shop. *Society Meetings:* Society outings welcome, special reduced rates. Secretary/ Manager: Michael Culligan (065 9056048; Fax: 065 9056977).
e-mail: kilkeegolfclub@eircom.net
website: www.kilkeegolfclub.ie

KILRUSH. **Kilrush Golf Club,** Kilrush (065 905 1138; Fax: 065 905 2633). *Location:* On main Ennis/Kilrush Road - 1km from Kilrush. Parkland course. 18 holes, 5960 yards. S.S.S. 70. *Green Fees:* from €20. *Eating facilities:* full bar and catering facilities. *Visitors:* always welcome - please book in advance. *Society Meetings:* welcome. Secretary/Manager: Denis F. Nagle (087 623 7557).
website: www.kilrushgolfclub.com

LAHINCH. **Lahinch Golf Club,** Lahinch (065 7081003). *Location:* 32 miles north west of Shannon Airport, 200 yards from Lahinch Village on Lisconner Road. Links course. Old Course - 18 holes, 6950 yards. S.S.S. 74; Castle Course - 18 holes, 5594 yards. S.S.S. 67. *Green Fees:* information not available. *Eating facilities:* bar and restaurant. *Visitors:* welcome. *Society Meetings:* catered for by arrangement. Professional: Robert McCavery (065 7081003). Secretary: Alan Reardon (065 7081003; Fax: 065 7081592). *
e-mail: info@lahinchgolf.com

MILTOWN MALBAY. **Spanish Point Golf Club,** Spanish Point, Miltown Malbay (065-708 4198). *Location:* two miles south of Miltown Malbay at Spanish Point Beach. Links course. 9 holes, 2312 metres, S.S.S. 63. Practice facilities. *Green Fees:* information not available. *Eating facilities:* bar snacks. *Visitors:* welcome at all times, not before noon on Sundays. *Society Meetings:* welcome weekdays excluding July and August. Secretary: David Fitzgerald (086-812 5742).*
e-mail: david@spanish-point.com
e-mail: dkfitzgerald@tinet.ie
website: www.spanishpointgolf.com

NEWMARKET-ON-FERGUS. **Dromoland Castle Golf & Country Club,** Newmarket-on-Fergus (061 368444; Fax: 061 368498). *Location:* part of the Dromoland Castle Estate, 10 minutes' drive from Shannon Airport. 400 acres of wooded parkland, with the River Rine flowing through. Course designed by Ron Kirby and Joe Carr. 18 holes, 6824 yards. *Green Fees:* from €60 - €110. *Eating facilities:* available. *Visitors:* welcome. *Society Meetings:* welcome.
e-mail: golf@dromoland.ie
website: www.dromoland.ie

SHANNON. **Shannon Golf Club,** Shannon (061 471849; Fax: 061 471507). *Location:* from Limerick take Airport road, course is 200 yards past Airport. Parkland. 18 holes, 6271 yards. S.S.S. 72. Practice area, club hire, buggy hire. *Green Fees:* information not available. *Eating facilities:* full bar and catering services. *Visitors:* welcome with prior booking. *Society Meetings:* welcome. Professional: Artie Pyke (061 471551). General Manager: Michael Corry.*

Co. Cork

BANDON. **Bandon Golf Club,** Castlebernard, Bandon (023 41111; Fax: 023 44690). *Location:* one mile west of Bandon town centre. Undulating parkland course with scenic views of West Cork. 18 holes, 6421 yards, 5780 metres. S.S.S. 70. Practice ground. *Green Fees:* information not available. *Eating facilities:* available, menu at bar. *Visitors:* welcome, restriction at weekends. Clubs, buggies and carts for hire. *Society Meetings:* welcome except Wednesdays and Sundays. Professional: Paddy O'Boyle (023 42224; Fax: 023 44690).
e-mail: enquiries@bandongolfclub.com

BANTRY. **Bantry Bay Golf Club,** Bantry, West Cork (353 (0) 27 50579/53773/53790; Fax: 353 (0) 27 53790). *Location:* approximately 1 mile from Bantry on N71 Killarney road. Clifftop parkland championship course to USGA standards. 18 holes, 6700 yards, 6100 metres. S.S.S. 72. *Green Fees:* €35 to €50. *Eating facilities:* full bar and restaurant open all year. *Visitors:* welcome, with restrictions at weekend. Trolley, buggy and club hire. *Society Meetings:* rates on request. Secretary: John O'Sullivan.
e-mail: info@bantrygolf.com
website: www.bantrygolf.com

BLARNEY. **Blarney Golf Resort,** Tower, Blarney (00353 21 438 4477; Fax: 00353 21 451 6453). *Location:* close to the town of Blarney, and only 8 miles from Cork. A challenging course with some of the best greens in Ireland. 18 holes, 6712 yards. Par 71. Fully equipped clubhouse. Accommodation in 56 two-bedroom Club Lodges or 62-bedroom hotel.
e-mail: reservations@blarneygolfresort.com
website: www.blarneygolfresort.com

CARRIGALINE. **Fernhill Golf & Country Club,** Carrigaline (00 353 (0)21 4372226; Fax: 00 353 (0)21 437 1011). *Location:* 20 minutes from Cork city and Airport, 10 minutes from Ringaskiddy Ferry Port. From city/airport follow sign to Ringaskiddy Ferry Port until roundabout with sign for Carrigaline - take Ringaskiddy exit, 2nd right, club is on left on this road. Parkland course. 18 holes, 6340 yards, S.S.S. 67. *Green Fees:* Monday - Thursday €20, Friday - Sunday €30. *Eating facilities:* fully licensed clubhouse, bar and restaurant, barbecue area. *Visitors:* always welcome. Booking advised at weekends. 40 bedroom hotel on site, plus 10 holiday homes, tennis court, indoor pool and sauna. Pro shop. Golf packages available. *Society Meetings:* always welcome. Booking advised at weekends. General Manager: Mr Alan Bowes.
e-mail: info@fernhillgolfhotel.com
website: www.fernhillcountryclub.com

CASTLETOWNBERE. **Berehaven Golf Club and Amenity Park,** Filane, Castletownbere, Beara (027 70700). *Location:* on main Castletownbere - Glengarriff Road, three miles from Castletownbere. Scenic course overlooking Bantry Bay. 9 holes, 2598 metres, S.S.S. 65. *Green Fees:* information available. *Eating facilities:* bar and restaurant. *Visitors:* welcome at all times. Tennis, crazy golf, sauna, caravan park. Club hire available. *Society Meetings:* welcome by appointment, special rates. Hon. Secretary: J. J. McLaughlin (027 70700).*

CHARLEVILLE. **Charleville Golf Club,** Charleville (063 81257; Fax: 063 81274). *Location:* Two kilometres west of Charleville town which is on main Cork/Limerick road. Parkland, heavily wooded. 27 holes. 18 holes 6430 yards. S.S.S. 70. 9 holes 3451 yards. Driving range. *Green Fees:* information not available. *Eating facilities:* full bar and restaurant facilities. *Visitors:* welcome, weekends by appointment. *Society Meetings:* welcome. Special rates apply. Professional: David Keating (063 81257). Secretary/Manager: Patrick Nagle. *
e-mail: charlevillegolf@eircom.net
website: www.charlevillegolf.com

COBH. **Cobh Golf Club,** Ballywilliam, Cobh (021-481 2399; Fax: 021-481 2615). Parkland course. 9 holes, 5006 yards, 4576 metres, S.S.S. 64. *Green Fees:* information not available. *Eating facilities:* available. *Visitors:* welcome mid week, restricted weekends and Tuesdays (Ladies' Day).*

DONERAILE. **Doneraile Golf Club,** Doneraile (022 24137). *Location:* three-and-a-half miles off main Cork/Limerick Road. Parkland, mature trees. 9 holes, 5768 yards. S.S.S.67. *Green Fees:* information not available. *Eating facilities:* by request. *Visitors:* welcome weekdays. *Society Meetings:* welcome Saturdays and weekdays. Secretary: Jimmy O'Leary (022 24379).*

DOUGLAS. **Douglas Golf Club,** Douglas (021 4891086; Fax: 021 4367200). *Location:* Douglas is on the main road from Cork to ferry port at Ringaskiddy, three miles south of Cork City. Beautifully maintained flat parkland course, greens and tees to full USGA spec – the views from the Clubhouse are some of the most panoramic in the country. 18 holes, 6669 yards, 5972 metres. S.S.S. 71. Practice ground. *Green Fees:* €50 all week. Groups of 20 or more €45. Subject to review. *Eating facilities:* full restaurant and bar available from 11am. *Visitors:* Monday, Wednesday, Thursday, Friday (mornings preferably); Saturday and Sunday after 2pm. Advisable to check in advance. *Society Meetings:* welcome but bookings should be made by end of April each year. Professional: Gary Nicholson (021 4362055). Secretary/Manager: Ronan Burke (021 4895297; Fax:021 4367200).

The Blarney Golf Resort.

The Blarney Golf Resort's impressive signature championship golf course was co-designed by two-times Major winner, John Daly. Enjoy some of the best greens in Ireland as you wind your way along this 6,712 yard, par 71 course. Its location nestled in the stunning Shournagh Valley creates the most wonderful atmosphere and breathtaking views where you can't help but feel at one with your natural surroundings. With saunas located in both the ladies and gents locker rooms, the Lions Den Bar, a full service clubhouse, a fully equipped professional shop, restaurant and private function rooms, we're certain your every request can be catered for by our Professional Golf Team. Finally, with 56 beautifully constructed self-contained Golf Lodges at the Blarney Golf Resort, you'll never be far from home.

John Daly

BLARNEY
GOLF RESORT

Blarney Golf Resort
Tower, Blarney, Co. Cork, Ireland
Tel: +353 21 438 4477
Fax: +353 21 451 6453
Email: reservations@blarneygolfresort.com
www.blarneygolfresort.com

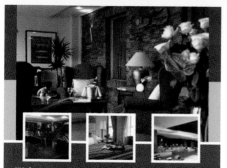

GLENGARRIFF. Glengarriff Golf Club, Glengarriff (027 63150). Parkland course. 9 holes, Par 33. *Green Fees*: information not available. *Eating facilities*: light snacks available in the clubhouse. *Visitors*: welcome at all times. *Society Meetings*: welcome. Secretary: Noreen Deasy (027 50315). *

KINSALE. Kinsale Golf Club, Farrangalway, Kinsale (021 4774722; Fax: 021 4773114). *Location*: beautifully situated in meadowland and parkland. Two courses. 18 holes and 9 holes. *Green Fees*: Monday to Friday (1pm) €35.00; Friday (after 1pm) to Sunday, and Bank Holidays €40.00; Early Bird (Monday-Friday before 10 am) €25.00. *Eating facilities*: full bar and catering. *Visitors*: welcome. e-mail: office@kinsalegolf.com website: www.kinsalegolf.com

KINSALE. Old Head Golf Links, Kinsale (+353 (0) 21 4778444; Fax: +353 (0) 214778022). *Location*: from Cork Airport follow R600 from Cork to Kinsale on to Old Head. 15 minutes south, signposted. Spectacular links course at an elevation of 200-300 ft. Practice ground, putting green, chipping green. 18 holes, 7200 yards. S.S.S. 72. *Green Fees*: 18 holes €295 (2007). *Eating facilities*: full bar and restaurant facilities. *Visitors*: no restrictions. Buggy hire and Caddies available.Pro shop, shower and changing facilities *Society Meetings*: welcome subject to availability, Special rates available for groups over 24. Course closed November to April. Golf Operations: Danny Brassil. General Manager: John Dwyer. e-mail: info@oldhead.com website: www.oldhead.com

FERMOY. Fermoy Golf Club, Corrin, Fermoy (025 32694; Fax: 025 33072). *Location*: 2km from Dublin to Cork main route. Parkland, wooded course. 18 holes, 5847 metres. S.S.S. 68. Practice ground. *Green Fees*: information not available. *Eating facilities*: full bar and restaurant. *Visitors*: welcome, Mondays very limited, weekends by reservation. Caddies. *Society Meetings*: welcome, booking essential. Professional: Brian Moriarty (025 31472; Fax: 025 33072). Secretary: Kathleen Murphy.* e-mail: fermoygolfclub@eircom.net

FOTA ISLAND. Fota Island Resort, Cork (021 4883700; Fax: 021 4883713). *Location*: take N25 east from Cork City (9 miles), turn off for Fota and Cobh. Gently undulating parkland bordered by mature woodland, very traditional in design. Championship courses, venue for the 2001 and 2002 Murphy's Irish Open. Voted 'Golf Course of the Year' 2002 by the Irish Golf Tour Operators. 27 holes, Deerpark course, 6927 yards, Par 72; Barryscourt course, 7362 yards, Par 74; Belvelly course, 7121 yards, Par 72. Practice range and putting green. *Green Fees*: Low season €75 - €95, High season €90 - €120. *Eating facilities*: restaurant and bar. *Visitors*: welcome everyday, telephone or e-mail for tee times. Metal spikes not allowed. Buggies, carts and caddies available. *Society Meetings*: welcome everyday, but limited availability on weekends. Professional: Kevin Morris (021 4883700; Fax: 021 4883713). e-mail: reservations@fotaisland.ie website: www.fotaisland.ie

LITTLE ISLAND. Cork Golf Club, Little Island (021 4353451; Fax: 021 4353410). *Location*: five miles east of Cork City N25, signposted. Parkland, very scenic championship course. 18 holes, 6065 metres. S.S.S. 72, 70. Practice ground. *Green Fees*: information not available. *Eating facilities*: full catering facilities, bar. *Visitors*: welcome Mondays, Tuesdays, Wednesdays and Fridays except 12.30 to 2pm; Thursdays, weekends ring in advance. *Society Meetings*: catered for, arrange with General Manager. Professional: Peter Hickey (021 4353421). General Manager: Matt Sands (021 4353451; Fax: 021 4353410).* e-mail: corkgolfclub@eircom.net website: www.corkgolfclub.ie

LITTLE ISLAND. Harbour Point Golf Club, Clash Road, Little Island (021 4353094; Fax: 021 4354408). *Location*: follow signs for Rosslare from Cork City and then take exit for Little Island (approx 6 miles from city). Parkland course by banks of River Lee. 18 holes, 6163 metres. S.S.S. 72. 21 bay floodlit driving range. *Green Fees*: information not available. *Eating facilities*: full bar and catering facilities. *Visitors*: welcome anytime, please book tee times. Carts, buggies and caddies for hire. Fully stocked golf store. *Society Meetings*: very welcome, special rates available. Professional: Morgan O'Donovan. General Manager: Aylmer Barrett (021 4353094; Fax: 021 4354408). e-mail: info@harbourpointgolfclub.com website: www.harbourpointgolfclub.com

MACROOM. **Macroom Golf Club,** Lackaduve, Macroom (026 41072; Fax: 026 41391). *Location:* through castle gates at town centre. Parkland. 18 holes, 5574 metres. S.S.S. 69. *Green Fees:* weekdays €35, weekends €40; early bird €20, Juniors €15. *Eating facilities:* full catering with restaurant and bar. *Visitors:* welcome, booking essential. *Society Meetings:* welcome March to October, booking essential. Manager: Cathal O'Sullivan.
e-mail: macroomgc@iol.ie
website: www.macroomgolfclub.com

MALLOW. **Mallow Golf Club,** Ballyellis, Mallow (022 21145; Fax: 022 42501). *Location:* one mile from town, east, on the Killavullen road. Parkland course. 18 holes, 5960 metres, S.S.S.72. *Green Fees:* weekdays €45, weekends and Public Holidays €50. *Eating facilities:* available. *Visitors:* welcome Monday to Friday, restrictions on weekends and Public Holidays, please check for details. *Society Meetings:* welcome, please telephone for details. Professional: Sean Conway (022 43424). Secretary/Manager: David Curtin (022 21145; Fax: 022 42501).
e-mail: mallowgolfclubmanager@eircom.net
website: www.mallowgolfclub.net

MIDLETON. **East Cork Golf Club,** Gortacrue, Midleton (021 463 1687; Fax: 021 461 3695). *Location:* two miles off main Waterford to Cork road. Exit at Midleton 13 miles east of Cork city. Parkland course. 18 hole, 5491 yards. S.S.S. 67. Driving range. *Green Fees:* weekdays €30, weekends €35. *Visitors:* welcome all year round. *Society Meetings:* special rates available. Professional: Don MacFarlane (021 463 3667). Secretary: Maurice Maloney.

MITCHELSTOWN. **Mitchelstown Golf Club,** Limerick Road, Gurrane, Mitchelstown (025 24072). *Location:* one kilometre from Mitchelstown (main Dublin/Cork route). Flat parkland. 18 holes, 6008 metres. S.S.S. 70. Practice area. *Green Fees:* information not available. *Eating facilities:* bar food evenings/weekends. *Visitors:* welcome. Caddie car hire. *Society Meetings:* welcome. Secretary: D. Stapleton. (025 24072).*

MONKSTOWN. **Monkstown Golf Club,** Parkgarriff, Monkstown (021 4841376; Fax: 021 4841722). *Location:* 7 miles from Cork city, just 10 minutes' drive from the Cork/Swansea Ferry. Demanding parkland course for golfers of all levels and the greens have been noted for being amongst the best in the country. 18 holes, 5640 metres. S.S.S. 69. Practice ground. *Green Fees:* Monday to Thursday: €43 (day), Friday to Sunday €50 (day). *Eating facilities:* full bar and restaurant available. *Visitors:* welcome, avoid Tuesday (Ladies' Day) and Bank Holiday Mondays. Phone at weekends. *Society Meetings:* welcome with restrictions. General Manager/Secretary: Hilary Madden.
e-mail: office@monkstowngolfclub.com
website: www.monkstowngolfclub.com

MUSKERRY. **Muskerry Golf Club,** Carrigrohane (021 4385297; Fax: 021 4516860). *Location:* seven and a half miles north west of Cork City, two and a half miles from Blarney. Parkland/wooded, two rivers. 18 holes, 5785 metres. S.S.S. 71. *Green Fees:* information not available. *Eating facilities:* available. *Visitors:* welcome; Monday and Tuesday all day, Wednesday up to 10.30am, Thursday after 1.30pm and Friday up to 3.30pm; weekends as available. Members' hour weekdays 12.30pm to 1.30pm. *Society Meetings:* welcome; 32 euros weekdays, 37 euros weekends. Professional: W.M. Lehane (021 4381445). Manager: Hugo Gallagher (021 4385297; Fax: 021 4516860).

OVENS. **Lee Valley Golf & Country Club,** Clashanure, Ovens (Tel & Fax: 00 353 (0)21 7331721). *Location:* eight miles from Cork on N22, turn right at Dan Sheehans. Parkland. 18 hole championship golf course designed by Ryder Cup star Christy O'Connor Jnr. 6725 yards. Par 72. *Green Fees:* from €30 - €65. *Eating facilities:* bar and full restaurant. *Visitors:* welcome. Club shop; club hire, caddy car hire and caddies and buggies available. *Society Meetings:* welcome. Corporate days. Lee Valley Bus available to cater for all your transport needs. 20 x 4 Star Self catering cottages on site overlooking the golf course, available for long and short breaks. Proprietor: Jerry Keohane.
e-mail: reservations@leevalleygcc.ie
website: www.leevalleygcc.ie

SCHULL. **Coosheen Golf Club,** Coosheen, Schull (028 28182). *Location:* one mile from Schull. Seaside parkland. 9 holes, 2023 metres. S.S.S. 58. Club hire, trolley hire. *Green Fees:* information not available. *Eating facilities:* seasonal bar and daily lunches. *Visitors:* welcome. *Society Meetings:* welcome. Secretary: A. Good or Donal Morgan. *

YOUGHAL. **Youghal Golf Club,** Knockaverry, Youghal (024 92787; Fax: 024 92641). *Location:* N25 main road from Rosslare to Cork. Seaside course with panoramic views of Youghal Bay/Blackwater Estuary. 18 holes, 6102 metres. S.S.S. 70. *Green Fees:* information not available. *Eating facilities:* full bar and restaurant facilities. *Visitors:* welcome mid-week, phone re weekends and Wednesdays (Ladies' Day). *Society Meetings:* welcome, please phone. Special rates available. Professional: Liam Burns (024 92590). Secretary: Margaret O'Sullivan.*

THE APPEARANCE OF AN ASTERISK (*) AT THE END OF A CLUB OR COURSE ENTRY INDICATES THAT UP-TO-DATE INFORMATION HAS NOT BEEN SUPPLIED

Co. Donegal

BALLYLIFFIN. **Ballyliffin Golf Club,** Ballyliffin, Inishowen. (00 353 74 93 76119; Fax: 00 353 74 93 76672). *Location:* Carndonagh from Derry, Buncrana from Letterkenny. 2 Championship Links. Glashedy; 18 holes, 7250 yards. S.S.S. 72. Old Links; 18 holes, 6612 yards. S.S.S. 71. Practice ground and three practice holes. *Green Fees:* €65-€85, or check website. *Eating facilities:* bar and restaurant. *Visitors:* welcome, booking advisable. *Society Meetings:* concessions for groups of 16 and over. Manager: John Farren (00 353 74 93 76119; Fax: 00 353 74 93 76672). Professional: John Dolan.
e-mail: info@ballyliffingolfclub.com
website: www.ballyliffingolfclub.com

BUNCRANA. **Buncrana Golf Club,** Ballymacarry, Buncrana (07493 20749). *Location:* on entry to Buncrana town take first left after Inishowen Gateway Hotel. Links course. 9 holes, 4310 yards, S.S.S. 62. *Green Fees:* Adults: gentlemen €13.00, ladies €8.00, juveniles €5.00. *Visitors:* welcome Monday to Friday, weekends by prior arrangement. *Society Meetings:* welcome. Professional: J. Doherty (07493 62279). Secretary: Francis McGrory (07493 20749).

BUNCRANA. **North West Golf Club,** Lisfannon, Buncrana (07493 61027; Fax: 07493 63284). *Location:* eight miles north west of Derry, one mile Buncrana - main Derry/Buncrana Road. Traditional links course, established 1891 founder member of G.U.I. **18 holes, 5968 yards. S.S.S. 70.** Putting green. *Green Fees:* information not available. *Eating facilities:* full bar and restaurant; bar snacks. *Visitors:* welcome anytime, phone in advance for weekends and Wednesdays. Caddies, carts available. *Society Meetings:* all welcome, booking essential. Professional: Seamus McBriarty (07493 61715). Hon. Secretary: Dudley Coyle.*

www.uk-golfguide.com

BUNDORAN. **Bundoran Golf Club,** Bundoran (071 9841302; Fax: 071 9842014). *Location:* 22 miles north of Sligo on edge of Bundoran Town. Parkland, seaside; not wooded. 18 holes, 5688 metres. S.S.S. 70. Practice ground. *Green Fees:* information not available. *Eating facilities:* tea, coffee and sandwiches in bar. *Visitors:* anytime with due notice but preferably Monday to Thursday. Buggies and carts. *Society Meetings:* very welcome with due notice. Professional: David T. Robinson (071 9841302). Secretary: John McGagh.*

DONEGAL. **Donegal Golf Club,** Murvagh, Laghey (074 9734054; Fax: 074 9734377). *Location:* N15 off main Donegal/Ballyshannon Road. Seaside links course, Murvagh Peninsula. 18 holes, 6874 yards, 6249 metres. S.S.S. 73. Practice area. *Green Fees:* Monday to Friday €55, Saturday and Sunday €70. *Eating facilities:* restaurant and bar. *Visitors:* welcome, restrictions weekends and Mondays. Buggies, carts available, caddies on request. Administrator: (074 9734054; Fax: 074 9734377).
e-mail: info@donegal-golfclub.ie

DOWNINGS **Rosapenna Hotel & Golf Links,** Rosapenna, Downings (074 915 5301; Fax: 074 915 5128). *Location:* 25 miles from Letterkenny. Links course, designed by Old Tom Morris. 18 holes, 6271 yards, 5735 metres. S.S.S. 71. New 18 holes opened June 2003. *Green Fees:* information not available. *Eating facilities:* available at hotel. *Visitors:* welcome all times. Four star Hotel on course. *Society Meetings:* welcome, must have Club Handicap. Secretary: Michael Bonner. Hotel and Course Manager: Frank T. Casey.

DUNFANAGHY. **Dunfanaghy Golf Club,** Kill, Dunfanaghy, Letterkenny (074 9136335; Fax: 074 9136684). *Location:* on main Letterkenny-Dunfanaghy Road N56. Seaside links course overlooking Sheephaven Bay and overshadowed by Horn Head. 18 holes, 5000 metres. S.S.S. 66. *Green Fees:* weekdays €30, weekends €40. Subject to review. *Eating facilities:* bar snacks - soup, tea and sandwiches. *Visitors:* welcome most days. Time sheet in operation at weekends, Bank Holidays (North & South) and Summer months. Buggies, carts and caddies by request. *Society Meetings:* all welcome. Club Secretary: Sandra McGinley (074 9136335). Hon. Secretary: Cairns Witherow.
e-mail: dunfanaghygolf@eircom.net

KINCASSLAGH. **Cruit Island Golf Club,** Cruit Island, Kincasslagh (074 9543296). *Location:* five miles north of Dunglue, turn off opposite Daniel O'Donnell's Viking House Hotel, three miles to the clubhouse. Seaside links with 9 holes, spectacular views hugging ragged coastline. 9 holes, 4860 metres. S.S.S. 66. Practice green. *Green Fees:* information not available. *Eating facilities:* full menu available if pre-booked. *Visitors:* welcome all year. Secretary: Dermot Devenney (074 9548872).*

LETTERKENNY. **Letterkenny Golf Club,** Barnhill, Letterkenny (074 21150). *Location:* Off Ramelton Road out of Letterkenny. Parkland/wooded course by the river. Practice area, putting green. 18 holes, 6239 yards. S.S.S. 71. *Green Fees:* Monday to Friday €25, weekends €30, *Eating facilities:* bar snacks; full à la carte menu available. *Visitors:* always welcome. *Society Meetings:* special reduced rates available, phone for details. Secretary: Brian O'Donnell (074 9121150).

NARIN/PORTNOO. **Narin and Portnoo Golf Club,** Narin, Portnoo (074 9545107; Fax: 074 9545994). *Location:* 6 miles north of Ardara adjacent to Blue Flag beach. Links course. 18 holes, 6269 metres. *Green Fees:* weekdays €40, weekends €45 (subject to review for 2008). *Eating facilities:* full catering. *Visitors:* welcome seven days a week, please ring or e-mail for a tee time. *Society Meetings:* very welcome with special rates. Secretary: Willie Quinn. e-mail: narinportnoo@eircom.net website: www.narinportnoogolfclub.ie

PORTSALON. **Portsalon Golf Club,** Portsalon, Fanad (074 9159459; Fax: 074 9159919). *Location:* 22 miles north of Letterkenny via Ramelton. Milford, Kerrykeel to Portsalon. Seaside links. 18 holes, white markers 6185 metres. S.S.S. 72, par 72. *Green Fees:* weekdays €40; weekends and Bank Holidays €50. Subject to review. Phone for special rates. *Eating facilities:* diningroom and bar in clubhouse. *Visitors:* phone in advance. *Society Meetings:* welcome weekdays and some weekends, must book in advance - contact Cathal. Secretary: Peter Doherty (074 9159459; Fax: 074 9159919).

RATHMULLAN. **Otway Golf Club,** Saltpans, Rathmullan (074 9158319). *Location:* from Rathmullan take road to Portsalon, course is two miles out on right. Seaside links course. 9 holes, 4234 yards. S.S.S. 64. *Green Fees:* €15. *Eating facilities:* bar. *Visitors:* always welcome. *Society Meetings:* by arrangement. Secretary: Kevin Toland (074 9151665). e-mail: tolandkevin@eircom.net.

REDCASTLE. **Redcastle Golf Club,** Redcastle (074 9382073; Fax: 074 9382214). *Location:* 4 miles from Moville on Londonderry Road. Parkland. 9 holes, 6152 yards, 5700 metres. S.S.S. 69. *Green Fees:* information not available. *Eating facilities:* Redcastle Hotel. *Visitors:* Always welcome. *Society Meetings:* special group rates if pre-booked. 35 bedroom 3 star hotel. Secretary: Mark Wilson.*

www.uk-golfguide.com

Co. Dublin

BALBRIGGAN. **Balbriggan Golf Club,** Blackhall, Balbriggan (8412173; Fax: 8413927). *Location:* quarter of a mile south of Balbriggan on main Belfast/Dublin Road. Parkland course with fine views of Cooley Peninsula and Mourne Mountains. 18 holes, 5922 metres. S.S.S. 71. *Green Fees:* information not available. *Eating facilities:* full restaurant facilities and bar. *Visitors:* welcome, Tuesday Ladies' Day, Saturdays and Sundays not good as club competitions take place. *Society Meetings:* catered for Mondays, Wednesdays, Thursdays and Fridays. Secretary: Michael O'Halloran (8412229).*

BALCARRICK. **Donabate Golf Club,** Balcarrick, Dublin (8434346; Fax: 8434488). *Location:* 5 miles north of Dublin Airport. Tree-lined parkland course, water in 9 holes. All sand based greens. 27 holes, 6085 metres. S.S.S. 73. Practice area including pitching and putting green. *Green Fees:* information not available. *Eating facilities:* full catering and bar facilities. *Visitors:* welcome every day. Must book in advance. Tuition available. Buggy hire. New ultra-modern clubhouse opened in 2003, with panoramic views of the course. *Society Meetings:* welcome every day, some restrictions at weekends. Professional: Hugh Jackson (8436346; Fax: 8434488).
e-mail: info@donabategolfclub.com
website: www.donabategolfclub.com

BALLYBOUGHAL. **Hollywood Lakes Golf Club,** Ballyboughal (8433407; Fax: 8433002). *Location:* 15 minutes north of Dublin Airport via N1 and the R129 to Ballyboughal, right at 'T' junction then two miles on right. Parkland course with water features on 11 holes. 18 holes, 5763 metres. S.S.S. 71. Practice ground, putting greens. *Green Fees:* information not available. *Eating facilities:* bar and restaurant. *Visitors:* welcome, not before 1pm at weekends, not after 4pm Wednesdays. *Society Meetings:* welcome, rates negotiable. Secretary: Sid Baldwin PGA (8433407; Fax: 8433002).*

BRITTAS. **Slade Valley Golf Club,** Lynch Park, Brittas (01-458 2183; Fax: 01-458 2784). *Location:* signposted from Saggart Village (approx. 4 miles). Parkland course with spectacular views over Dublin City. 18 holes, 5960 yards, 5457 metres, Par 69, S.S.S. 68. Putting green, driving net. *Green Fees:* information not available. *Eating facilities:* bar/restaurant. *Visitors:* welcome weekdays. Professional available for lessons. *Society Meetings:* welcome weekdays - rates negotiable. Professional: John Dignam. Secretary: Dermot Clancy.*

BRITTAS. **South County Golf Club,** Lisheen Road, Brittas (01 458 2965; Fax: 01 458 2842). *Location:* on the Blessington road - N81, 7 miles from the M50 and 30 minutes from Dublin city centre. Parkland course. 18 holes, 7007 yards. S.S.S. 72. *Green Fees:* weekday 50, weekend 60. *Eating facilities:* clubhouse with catering. *Visitors:* welcome. Fully stocked Pro shop. *Society Meetings:* welcome.
e-mail: info@southcountygolf.ie
website: www.southcountygolf.com

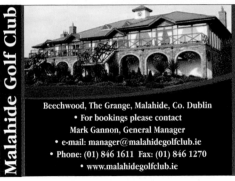

CASTLEKNOCK. **Luttrellstown Castle Golf and Country Club,** Castleknock, Dublin 15 (353 1 8089988; Fax: 353 1 8089989). *Location:* six miles from Dublin City. 18 holes Championship parkland course with magnificent lakes and well manicured greens. 18 holes, 7091 yards, 6384 metres. S.S.S. 72. Practice ground. *Green Fees:* information not available. *Eating facilities:* restaurant and bar. *Visitors:* some tee times reserved for members, please phone in advance. Accommodation available at Luttrellston Castle and in stable yard apartments. *Society Meetings:* welcome subject to availability. Professional: Edward Doyle.*

DONABATE. **Balcarrick Golf Club,** Corballis, Donabate (8436957; Fax: 8436228). *Location:* from Dublin take the M1 motorway north past Dublin Airport and Swords and take the first exit signposted Donabate/Skerries/Lusk; turn right in the village of Donabate, travel 1.5km and turn right again, Balcarrick is 1km on the right hand side. Parkland course. 18 holes, 6191 metres. Par 72. *Green Fees:* information not available. *Eating facilities:* full catering and bar facilities available. *Visitors:* welcome, please telephone Professional for time sheet details. *Society Meetings:* welcome. Professional: Stephen Rayfus (8434034).*

DONABATE. **Beaverstown Golf Club,** Beaverstown Road, Donabate (00 353 1 843 6439/843 6721; Fax: 00 353 1 843 5059). *Location:* on the shores of Rogerstown Estuary in North Dublin, 6km north of Dublin Airport. Attractive course set in 140 acres of lush parkland, with orchards bordering the tees and fairways. Water comes into play on 12 holes. 18 holes, 5972 metres. S.S.S. 72, Par 72. Practice facilities. *Green Fees:* Monday to Friday €50, Saturdays and Sundays €60, weekdays early bird €27. *Eating facilities:* bar, catering. *Visitors:* welcome. Please contact Club Manager in advance. Ladies' Day Tuesday. *Society Meetings:* welcome most Saturdays. e-mail: manager@beaverstown.com website: www.beaverstown.com

DONABATE. **Corballis Golf Links,** Donabate (8436583). *Location:* main Dublin to Belfast Road. Links course. 18 holes, 4971 yards. S.S.S. 64. Putting green. *Green Fees:* information not available. *Eating facilities:* snack food. *Visitors:* welcome anytime. Carts available. *Society Meetings:* welcome. Manager: Austin Levins.*

DONABATE. **The Island Golf Club,** Corballis, Donabate (00 353 (01)1 8436205; Fax: 00 353 (01)1 8436860). *Location:* 15 minute drive from Dublin Airport, across the estuary from the village of Malahide. Links course with challenging greens. Ranked 26th in World by *Golf Weekly* (Nov. 05 issue). 18 holes, 6236 metres, S.S.S. 73, Par 71. *Green Fees:* €125 per round; early bird rate 8.30-9.30am €95. *Visitors:* warmly welcomed. e-mail: info@theislandgolfclub.com website: www.theislandgolfclub.com

KILLINEY. **Killiney Golf Club,** Ballinclea Road, Killiney (Tel. & Fax: 01 2852823). *Location:* south Dunlaoghaire. Parkland. 9 holes, 5655 metres. S.S.S. 70. *Green Fees:* information not available. *Eating facilities:* snacks available. *Visitors:* welcome with restrictions. Professional: P. O'Boyle. Secretary: M.F. Walsh.*

KILSALLAGHAN. **Corrstown Golf Club,** Corrstown, Kilsallaghan (01 864 0533/4; Fax: 01 864 0534). *Location*: 10 minutes north of Dublin Airport. Parkland course. 27 holes. Practice green and nets. *Green Fees*: weekdays €50, weekends €60. *Eating facilities*: full bar and restaurant. *Visitors*: welcome Monday to Friday; Saturday and Sunday when available. *Society Meetings*: outings welcome. Professional: Pat Gittens (01 864 3322; Fax: 01 864 0537). Office: (01 864 0533; Fax: 01 864 0537). e-mail: info@corrstowngolfclub.com website: www.corrstowngolfclub.com

MALAHIDE. **Malahide Golf Club,** Beechwood, The Grange, Malahide (8461611; Fax: 8461270) *Location:* 15 minutes from Dublin city, 7 miles from Dublin Airport. Parkland. 27 holes, 6066 metres. S.S.S. 71. Practice area, Proshop. *Green Fees:* weekdays €60, group rates available. *Eating facilities:* full bar and restaurant available. *Visitors:* welcome, must book in advance. *Society Meetings*: society outings welcome. Professional: John Murray (8460002; Fax: 8461270). General Manager: Mark Gannon. e-mail: manager@malahidegolfclub.ie website: www.malahidegolfclub.ie

PORTMARNOCK. **Portmarnock Hotel & Golf Links,** Strand Road, Portmarnock (8461800; Fax: 8461077). *Location:* 8 miles north east of Dublin, 15 minutes from Dublin Airport. Seaside links designed by Bernhard Langer. 18 holes, 6350 metres. S.S.S. 73. Pitching area with bunker and putting green. *Green Fees:* information not available. *Eating facilities:* two restaurants and three bars. *Visitors:* no restrictions. Four star de luxe hotel, 138 bedrooms and conference facilities. *Society Meetings:* group rates and corporate packages available on request. Golf Director: Moira Cassidy. e-mail: golfres@portmarnock.com website: www.portmarnock.com

RATHCOOLE. **Beech Park Golf Club,** Johnstown, Rathcoole (4580522; Fax: 4588365). Gently undulating parkland course. 18 holes, 5762 metres. S.S.S. 70. *Green Fees:* €42 per round. *Eating facilities:* bar and restaurant. *Visitors:* welcome Monday-Friday. *Society Meetings:* welcome Monday, Thursday, Friday. General Manager: Gay Nolan. e-mail: info@beechpark.ie website: www.beechpark.ie

RATHFARNHAM. **Stackstown Golf Club,** Kellystown Road, Rathfarnham, Dublin 16 (01-494 1993; Fax: 01-493 3934). *Location:* one mile from Exit 13 on M50 towards Rathfarnham. Parkland course situated on slopes of Dublin mountains. Home club of Padraig Harrington. 18 holes, 6152 yards, S.S.S. 70. Practice fairway, putting green, driving nets. *Green Fees:* weekdays €30, weekends €40. *Eating facilities*: full catering and bar facilities. *Visitors*: welcome everyday except Tuesday (Ladies' Day), Wednesday afternoons, Saturday, Sunday subject to availability. Professional tuition available. Fully stocked shop, buggies, clubs, trolley for hire. *Society Meetings*: welcome Monday, Thursday, Friday and Sunday, special rates available. Professional: Michael Kavanagh (01-494 4561; Fax: 01-493 3934). General Manager: Larry Clarke (01 494 1993; Fax: 01-493 3934). e-mail: stackstowngc@eircom.net website: www.stackstowngolfclub.com

ST MARGARET'S. **St Margaret's Golf and Country Club,** St Margaret's, Dublin (8640400; Fax: 8640289). *Location:* 10 minutes from Dublin Airport and 25 minutes from Dublin city centre. Parkland, championship course, ultra-modern design by Craddock and Ruddy. 18 holes, 6629 yards. S.S.S. 73. Putting and practice areas. *Green Fees:* information not available. *Eating facilities:* full bar and restaurant facilities. *Visitors:* welcome at all times. Cobra Golf Academy. *Society Meetings:* welcome. Professional: David O'Sullivan.* e-mail: reservations@stmargaretsgolf.com website: www.stmargaretsgolf.com

ST MARGARET'S. **The Open Golf Centre,** Newtown House, St Margarets (8640324; Fax: 8341400). *Location:* 2km from Dublin Airport, adjacent to N2 (Derry road). Inviting parkland course, three lakes feature prominently. 27 holes, 9500 yards. S.S.S. 69/31. 20 bay driving range. *Green Fees:* information not available. *Eating facilities*: coffee shop. *Visitors*: welcome everyday. Teaching auditorium. *Society Meetings*: welcome. Professional: R. Machin (8640324; Fax: 8341400). Secretary: R. Yates (8640324 Fax: 8341400).*

SKERRIES. **Skerries Golf Club,** Hacketstown, Skerries (01 8491567: Fax: 01 8491591). *Location:* east of Dublin/Belfast road, approximately six miles. Parkland course close to sea with undulating fairways. 18 holes, 6081 metres. Par 73. Practice ground. *Green Fees:* information not available. *Eating facilities:* restaurant, snack bar, bar, lounge. *Visitors:* welcome Mondays, Thursdays, Fridays; weekends by arrangement. *Society Meetings:* welcome. Professional: Jimmy Kinsella (01 8490925). General Manager: Billy Meehan (01 8491567; Fax: 01 8491591).*

SUTTON. **Howth Golf Club,** St. Fintan's, Carrickbrack Road, Sutton, Dublin 13 (8323055; Fax: 8321793). *Location:* one and a half miles from Sutton Cross on city side of Hill of Howth. Moorland course with scenic views of Dublin Bay. 18 holes, 5672 metres. S.S.S. 69. Practice ground. *Green Fees:* information not available. *Eating facilities:* restaurant facilities every day from midday. *Visitors:* welcome weekdays except Wednesdays and Thursdays. Carts. *Society Meetings:* bookings accepted by arrangement with Club Manager. Reduced rates for large groups. Professional: John McGuirk (8392617). Club Manager: Paul Kennedy.*
e-mail: secretary@howthgolfclub.ie
website: www.howthgolfclub.ie

SWORDS. **Swords Open Golf Course,** Balheary Avenue, Swords (Tel & Fax: 01 8409819). *Location:* three miles west of Swords. Parkland. Broadmeadow river divides course. No climbing, flat course. 18 holes, 5631 metres. S.S.S. 69. Putting green. *Green Fees*: weekdays €20, weekends €25. *Eating facilities*: coffee shop. *Visitors:* any time, very welcome. *Society Meetings:* very welcome. Secretary: Orla McGuinness.
e-mail: info@swordsopengolfcourse.com
website: www.swordsopengolfcourse.com

Co. Galway

ANNAGHVANE. **Connemara Isles Golf Club,** Annaghvane, Lettermore (091 572498). *Location:* Take the coast road from Galway City, at Casla (Costello) take the first right after the Texaco Station. Continue on that road for four and a half miles until you pass "An Hooker Bar" (on a bend). The golf course is 500 metres ahead. Seaside links Championship course. *Green Fees:* information not available. *Visitors:* always welcome. *Society Meetings:* welcome. Manager Anthony Lynch.*

ATHENRY. **Athenry Golf Club,** Palmerstown, Oran More (091 794466; Fax: 091 794971). *Location:* 8 miles from Galway city. Parkland. 18 holes, 5687 metres. Par 70, S.S.S. 70. Practice ground. *Green Fees:* information not available. *Eating facilities:* full bar and catering. *Visitors:* welcome except Sunday. Deals available with local hotels. Club hire and tuition. *Society Meetings:* welcome. Pro shop (091 790599). Professional: R. Ryan. Secretary/Manager: Padraig Flattery.*
e-mail: athenrygc@eircom.net
website: www.athenrygolfclub.net

BALLINASLOE. **Ballinasloe Golf Club,** Rossgloss, Ballinasloe (0905 42126; Fax: 0905 42538). *Location:* 2 miles from Ballinasloe town on Portumna side. Ballinasloe on main Dublin-Galway Road, two hours from Dublin. Mature parkland course, 18 holes, 5865 metres, Par 72. Practice area, putting green. *Green Fees:* information not available. *Eating facilities:* full bar and catering facilities. Buggy and cart hire. *Society Meetings*: welcome Monday-Saturday. Secretary: Dr Conor Corr (0905 42126).*
e-mail: ballinasloegolfclub@eircom.net
website: www.ballinasloegolfclub.com

THE APPEARANCE OF AN ASTERISK (*) AT THE END OF A CLUB OR COURSE ENTRY INDICATES THAT UP-TO-DATE INFORMATION HAS NOT BEEN SUPPLIED

FHG Guides
publish a large range of well-known accommodation guides. We will be happy to send you details or you can use the order form at the back of this book.

CLIFDEN. **Connemara Golf Club,** Ballyconneely, Near Clifden (095 23502/23602; Fax: 095 23662). *Location:* from Clifden to Ballyconneely, 4 miles on the right. Seaside links Championship course. 27 holes, 6611 metres. S.S.S. 73. 220 yard Par 3 13th is feature hole. Practice fairway, putting green and driving net. *Green Fees:* April €45, May €50, June/July/August €60, September €60, October €45. November-March €35. *Eating facilities:* full restaurant and bar facilities. *Visitors:* always welcome. Fully equipped Pro Shop. *Society Meetings:* groups of 20 or more welcome. Professional: Hugh O'Neill. Secretary: Richard Flaherty.
e-mail: info@connemaragolflinks.net
website: www.connemaragolflinks.com

GORT. **Gort Golf Club,** Castlequarter (091 632244; Fax: 091 632387). Location: 20 minutes Galway Airport, 40 minutes Shannon Airport, 60 minutes Knock Airport, on edge of world-famous Burren, overlooking Coole Lake. Undulating parkland. 18 holes, 5974 metres. S.S.S.71. Green Fees:information not available. Eating facilities: full bar and restaurant. Visitors: welcome all year, restrictions on Sundays. Society Meetings: welcome with prior booking. Time Sheet in operation every day. Administrator: Pauline Faithfull (091 632244). Designer: Christy O'Connor Jnr.*
e-mail: info@gortgolf.com
website: www.gortgolf.com

LOUGHREA. **Loughrea Golf Club,** Craigue, Loughrea (091 841049). *Location:* one and a half miles north east of town, on New Inn Road. Parkland, undulating, with beautiful views of town and Slieve Aughty Mountains in background. 18 holes, 5261 yards. Par 67. Practice area. *Green Fees:* information not available. *Eating facilities:* tea, coffee, sandwiches at bar. New clubhouse with full catering under construction. *Visitors:* welcome weekdays and weekends with advance booking. *Society Meetings:* welcome, please telephone. Secretary: Vinny Ryan.*

ORANMORE **Galway Bay Golf and Country Club Hotel,** Renville, Oranmore (091 790500; Fax: 091 790510). *Location:* seven miles from Galway City, through Oranmore Village. Parkland by the sea, many water hazards with the Atlantic Ocean surrounding on three sides. 18 holes, 7144 yards, 6533 metres. S.S.S. 73. Putting green, chipping green, practice area, indoor practice bays academy. *Green Fees:* information not available. *Eating facilities:* restaurant, spike bar, cocktail bar. *Visitors:* welcome daily. *Society Meetings:* welcome daily, reduced rates for groups. Professional: Eugene O'Connor (091 790503). Director of Golf: Anne Hanley (091 790503).*
e-mail: maryhawkins@galwaybaygolfresort.com
website: www.gbay-golf.com

OUGHTERARD. **Oughterard Golf Club,** Gortreevagh, Oughterard (091 552131; Fax: 091 552733). *Location:* 15 miles west of Galway City on N59 to Connemara. Parkland, newly re-modelled with Greens to USPGA Standards. 18 holes, 5876 metres. S.S.S. 70. Practice area and putting green. *Green Fees:* information not available. *Eating facilities:* full dining facilities during daylight hours. *Visitors:* welcome. *Society Meetings:* welcome, for further information contact Pro Shop. (091 557352). Administration Office (091 557354).*
e-mail: oughterardgc@eircom.net
website: www.oughterardgolf.com

SALTHILL. **Galway Golf Club,** Blackrock, Salthill (091 522033; Fax: 091 529783) *Location*: three miles west of Galway city. Parkland. 18 holes, 5832 metres. S.S.S. 71. *Green Fees:* information not available. *Eating facilities:* full bar and catering facilities. *Visitors*: welcome, avoid Tuesdays and weekends. *Society Meetings:* all welcome. Professional: Don Wallace (091 523038) Secretary: Padraic Fahy (091 522033; Fax: 091 529783).

Co. Kerry

BALLYBUNION. **Ballybunion Golf Club,** Sandhill Road, Ballybunion (068 27146; Fax: 068 27387). *Location:* 20 miles from Tralee, 10 miles from Listowel. Links course established 1893, ranked in top ten in world. Two courses - Old and Cashen. 36 holes, 6800 yards. S.S.S. 71. *Green Fees:* 2007 - Old Course €165 per round, Cashen Course €110 per round, both courses same day €240. Subject to review. *Eating facilities:* full bar and catering facilities. *Visitors:* welcome weekdays, some weekends; telephone bookings in advance. Carts and caddies for hire. *Society Meetings:* catered for. Professional: Brian O'Callaghan. Secretary: Jim McKenna.

BALLYFERRITER. **Dingle Golf Links/Ceann Sibeal,** Ballyferriter (066 915 6255; Fax: 066 915 6409). *Location:* turn right quarter of a mile after Ballyferriter, 40 miles Tralee, 10 miles Dingle. Traditional links, most westerly golf course in Europe. 18 holes, 6696 yards. S.S.S. 71. Practice ground. *Green Fees:* information not available. *Eating facilities:* full bar and dining room. *Visitors:* welcome at all times, book in advance. *Society Meetings:* all welcome. Secretary: Steve Fahy (066 9156255; Fax: 066 9156409).*
e-mail: dinglegc@iol.ie
website: www.dinglelinks.com

CASTLEGREGORY. **Castlegregory Golf Club,** Stradbally, Castlegregory (066 7139444). *Location:* main Tralee Conor pass Dingle Road. Scenic links course with water features. 9 holes, 5264 metres, S.S.S. 67. Putting green. *Green Fees:* information not available. *Eating facilities:* tea and snacks available. *Visitors:* welcome at all times. *Society Meetings:* welcome.

THE APPEARANCE OF AN ASTERISK (*) AT THE END OF A CLUB OR COURSE ENTRY INDICATES THAT UP-TO-DATE INFORMATION HAS NOT BEEN SUPPLIED

GLENBEIGH. **Dooks Golf Links,** Glenbeigh (066 9768205; Fax: 066 9768476). *Location:* on the N70 between Killorglin and Glenbeigh. Links course. 18 holes, 6586 yards. Par 71, S.S.S. 70. Putting green. *Green Fees:* €80. Subject to review. *Eating facilities:* bar and restaurant. *Visitors:* welcome Monday to Saturday. *Society Meetings:* welcome with advance booking. Secretary/Manager: Declan Mangan.
e-mail: office@dooks.com
website: www.dooks.com

KENMARE. **Ring of Kerry Golf and Country Club,** Templenoe, Kenmare (00 353 6442000; Fax: 00 353 6442533). *Location:* take the N70 Ring of Kerry road from Kenmare. Club is three miles on right. Parkland/ links course. 18 holes, 6869 yards. S.S.S. 73. Driving range, putting green. *Green Fees:* under review. Special group, society and ad hoc rates on application. *Eating facilities:* full bar and à la carte restaurant with terrace overlooking 17th/18th holes and bay. *Visitors:* welcome anytime. Pre-booking at weekends advisable. Some restrictions throughout the year. Tuition available. Clubhouse can be hired for private and corporate functions. On-course holiday homes. *Society Meetings:* welcome anytime with advance notice, contact club for details. Professional Adrian Whitehead. Manager: James Mitchell.
e-mail: reservations@ringofkerrygolf.com
marketing@ringofkerrygolf.com
website: www.ringofkerrygolf.com

KENMARE. **Kenmare Golf Club,** Kenmare (064 41291; Fax: 064 42061). *Location:* turn left at top of Main Street in town, on main Cork/Kilgarvan Road. Partly links, partly parkland surrounded by some breathtaking views. 18 holes, 6083 yards, S.S.S. 69. Putting green, driving net. *Green Fees:* information not available. *Eating facilities:* snacks in bar only. *Visitors:* welcome at all times, enquire for weekends. Booking in advance is advisable. Club hire, pull-cart hire. *Society Meetings:* welcome, booking in advance is advisable. Manager: Joy Clifford.*
e-mail: info@kenmaregolfclub.com
website: www.kenmaregolfclub.com

PLEASE MENTION THE GOLF GUIDE WHEN YOU WRITE OR PHONE TO ENQUIRE ABOUT CLUBS OR ACCOMMODATION

KILLARNEY. **Beaufort Golf Club,** Churchtown, Beaufort, Killarney (064 44440; Fax: 064 44752). *Location:* seven miles west of Killarney town, just off the N72. Parkland course in unique setting surrounded by the Kerry Mountains. 18 holes, 6587 yards, 6023 metres. S.S.S. 72. Practice facilities. *Green Fees:* information not available. *Eating facilities:* large bar and full food menu. *Visitors:* welcome seven days, but please pre-book. Electric buggies and carts. *Society Meetings:* welcome. Special rates available on request. Secretary: Colm Kelly (064 44404).
e-mail: beaufortgc@eircom.net
website: www.beaufortgolfclub.com

KILLARNEY. **Dunloe Golf Club,** Gap of Dunloe, Kilarney (00353 64 44578). *Location:* 10 minutes from Killarney town. Take N72 (main Killarney/ Killorglin Road); first left after passing Hotel Europe. Outstanding parkland layout with spectacular views of Killarney's lakes and mountains. 9 holes. Par 34. *Green Fees:* information not available. *Eating facilities:* snack bar from 8am to 9pm (from 10am in winter). Professional: Kieran P. Crehan.*
e-mail: enquiries@dunloegc.com

KILLARNEY. **Killarney Golf and Fishing Club,** Mahony's Point, Killarney (64 31034; Fax: 64 33065). *Location:* Killarney town, two miles west on Ring of Kerry road. Undulating parkland courses - lakeside. Mahony's Point: 18 holes, 6152 metres. S.S.S. 72. Killeen: 18 holes, 6474 metres. S.S.S. 73. Lackabane Course, 18 holes, 6410 metres. Practice area. *Green Fees:* information not available. *Eating facilities:* available all day. *Visitors:* welcome at all times, reservations in advance, Handicap Certificate required. *Society Meetings:* welcome. Professional: T. Coveney (64 31615). Secretary: T. Prendergast.*
e-mail: reservations@killarney-golf.com
website: www.killarney-golf.com

KILLARNEY. **Ross Golf Club,** Ross Road, Killarney (064-31125; Fax: 064-31860). *Location:* from town centre follow signs to Muckross House, take first right on Muckross Road to Ross Castle and Ross Golf Club. Parkland, wooded course. 9 holes, 6450 yards, S.S.S. 73. Practice area and putting green. *Green Fees:* information not available. *Eating facilities:* full bar and snack bar serving soup and sandwiches. *Vistors:* welcome. PGA tuition and accommodation can be arranged. *Society Meetings:* welcome, special rates available. Professional & Secretary: Alan O'Meara (064 31125; Fax: 064 31860).*
e-mail: info@rossgolfclub.com
website: www.rossgolfclub.com

KILLORGLIN. **Killorglin Golf Club,** Stealroe, Killorglin (066 9761979; Fax: 066 9761437). *Location:* just 20 minutes from Killarney and from Kerry Airport, three kilometres from the bridge at Killorglin on N70 road to the county town of Tralee. Parkland course overlooking Dingle Bay. 18 holes, 6464 yards. S.S.S. 71. *Green Fees:* weekdays €35; weekends €35, 9 holes €25. Group rates available on request. *Eating facilities:* bar and restaurant facilities all day. *Visitors:* always welcome, booking necessary at weekends. Accommodation can be arranged; all major credit cards accepted. *Society Meetings:* all welcome, rates on request. Manager: Billy Dodd.
e-mail: kilgolf@iol.ie
website: www.killorglingolf.ie

> THE APPEARANCE OF AN ASTERISK (*) AT THE END OF A CLUB OR COURSE ENTRY INDICATES THAT UP-TO-DATE INFORMATION HAS NOT BEEN SUPPLIED

SNEEM. **Parknasilla Golf Club,** Parknasilla, Sneem (064 45195; Fax: 064 45323). *Location:* on the Ring of Kerry route, two miles east of Sneem Village. Hilly seaside course, wooded. 12 holes, 5284 metres. S.S.S. 67. Practice ground. *Green Fees:* information not available. *Eating facilities:* available at Great Southern Hotel, 10 minutes' walk. *Visitors:* welcome, no restrictions. Caddy cars available. *Society Meetings:* contact 064 45195. Secretary/Manager: Maurice Walsh (064 45233).*

TRALEE. **The Kerries Golf Club,** Kerries East, Tralee (667 122112; Fax: 667 120085). *Location:* one mile from Tralee town. Parkland, overlooking Tralee Bay. 9 holes. S.S.S. 68. *Green Fees:* information not available. *Eating facilities:* snacks and wine bar. *Visitors:* welcome daily except Sundays 8am-12.30 pm. *Society Meetings:* welcome. Secretary: Helen Barrett.*

TRALEE. **Tralee Golf Club,** West Barrow, Ardfert, Tralee (066 7136379; Fax: 066 7136008). *Location:* Tralee to Barrow via the Spa and Churchill. Seaside links. 18 holes, 6975 yards, S.S.S. 73. *Green Fees:* €170. Subject to review. *Eating facilities:* bar and restaurant. *Visitors:* welcome except Wednesdays of June, July and August. Other months Wednesdays 7.30-10.30pm, Saturdays 10.00am-1.30pm, no visitors on Sundays or Bank Holidays. General Manager: Anthony Byrne.
e-mail: info@traleegolfclub.com
          reservations@traleegolfclub.com
website: www.traleegolfclub.com

WATERVILLE. **Waterville House and Golf Links,** Waterville (066 947 4102; Fax: 066 947 4482). *Location:* 55 miles from Killarney and Tralee, halfway round the Ring of Kerry. Links course, established in 1889 - Awards: Golf Monthly Top 5 British Isles, Golf Digest Top 100 World, Golf Digest No.1 Ireland, Golf Magazine - Best International Resorts. 7325 yards. S.S.S. 74. *Green Fees:* (2007) €165 pp; early/late €115 pp. (2008 under review). *Eating facilities:* bar and restaurant facilities available. *Visitors:* welcome every day. *Society Meetings:* welcome every day. Carts and caddies available on request. Secretary/ Manager: Noel Cronin (066 947 4102; Fax: 066 947 4482.
e-mail: wvgolf@iol.ie
website: www.watervillegolflinks.ie

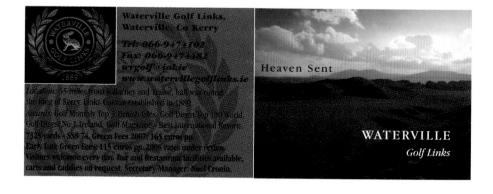

PLEASE NOTE

All the information regarding Golf Clubs in this guide is given in good faith in the belief that it is correct. However, the publishers cannot guarantee the facts given in these pages, neither are they responsible for changes in ownership or facilities, such as green fees, that may take place after the date of going to press. Readers should always satisfy themselves that the facilities they require are available and that the terms, if quoted, still apply.

Co. Kildare

CARBURY. **Highfield Golf Course,** Carbury (Tel & Fax: 046 9731021). *Location*: 10km from N4, nearest major town is Edenderry. Parkland course set in quiet countryside. 18 holes, 6292 yards, 5720 metres, S.S.S. 70. Open-air driving range. *Green Fees*: information not available. *Eating facilities*: full bar and restaurant. *Visitors*: welcome. Tuition available. *Society Meetings*: welcome.*
e-mail: highfieldgolf@eircom.ie
website: www.highfield-golf.ie

CLANE. **Millicent Golf & Country Club,** Millicent Road, Clane (045 893279; Fax: 045 868369). *Location*: drive through Clane, take right after Corner House pub. Golf course on left after one mile. Parkland course, playable all year round. 18 holes, 7063 metres, S.S.S. 73. Driving range, chipping and putting greens. *Green Fees*: information not available. *Eating facilities*: bar and restaurant. *Visitors*: welcome every day, except Saturday between 8-9am and Sundays between 8-10am. *Society Meetings*: welcome every day,rates depending on numbers. Secretary: Niamh Killian.*
e-mail: info@millicentgolfclub.com
website: www.millicentgolfclub.com

CURRAGH. **The Curragh Golf Club,** Curragh, Newbridge (045 441238; Fax: 045 442476). *Location*: three miles south of Newbridge. Hilly parkland course. 18 holes, 6586 yards. S.S.S. 72. Practice ground. *Green Fees*: €35 per person weekdays. *Eating facilities*: bar and restaurant. *Visitors*: restricted, please check in advance for course availability. *Society Meetings*: by appointment. Society package €60 including meal, minimum 25 players (weekends only). Society weekday green fee only €35. Professional: Gerry Burke (045 441896). Secretary: Ann Culleton (045 441714; Fax: 045 442476).
e-mail: curraghgolf@eircom.net

DONADEA. **Knockanally Golf and Country Club,** Donadea, North Kildare (Tel & Fax: 045 869322). *Location*: three miles off N4 between Enfield and Kilcock. Parkland, home of the Irish International Professional Championship. 18 holes, 6495 yards. S.S.S. 72. *Green Fees*: weekdays €35, weekends €45. *Eating facilities*: bar and restaurant. *Visitors*: welcome, no restrictions. *Society Meetings*: by arrangement. Professional: Martin Darcy (045 869322). Secretary: Declan M. Monaghan (045 869322).
e-mail: golf@knockanally.com
website: www.knockanally.com

KILKEA. **Kilkea Castle Hotel & Golf Club,** Kilkea, Castledermot (00353 503 45555). *Location*: southbound on N7, onto M9, then N78 to Athy. Before entering Athy look for Ford garage on right. Kilkea is signposted on the left. 18 holes. Par 70. *Green Fees*: information not available. *Eating facilities*: available all day. Award-winning restaurant.*
e-mail: kilkeagolf@eircom.net

KILL. **Killeen Golf Club,** Kill (045 86603; Fax: 045 875881). *Location*: South from Dublin on N7, turn right at Kill village. Parkland course with abundant wildlife. 18 holes, 6732 yards. S.S.S. 72. *Green Fees*: information not available. *Eating facilities*: restaurant and bar. *Visitors*: welcome. *Society Meetings*: welcome. For bookings contact Manager: Maurice Kelly.*
e-mail: admin@killeengc.ie
website: www.killeengolf.com

MAYNOOTH. **Carton House,** Maynooth, Co. Kildare (00353 1 5052000; Fax: 00353 1 6286555). *Location*: from Dublin take the N4. The Lexlip West exit from the N4 and follow signs to Carton House. O'Meara, Parkland course; The Montgomerie, inland links course. The Montgomerie course home to the 2005 & 2006 Nissan Irish Open. O'Meara 18 holes, 6400 metres, S.S.S. 74; Montgomerie 18 holes, 6700 metres, S.S.S. 74. Practice range and putting green. Golfing Union of Ireland Academy. *Green Fees*: Summer 135 per person, Winter 75 per person. *Eating facilities*: clubhouse restaurant. *Visitors*: always welcome, 165 bedroom hotel with conference and spa facility. *Society Meetings*: always welcome, rates from €95. Professional: Francis Howley. Secretary: John Lawler (00353 1 5052000; Fax: 00353 1 6286555).
e-mail: golfreservations@cartonhouse.com
website: www.cartonhouse.com

NAAS. **Craddockstown Golf Club,** Blessington Road, Naas (045 897610; Fax: 045 896968). *Location*: off the southbound N7 turn left before Naas and take Blessington road, club one mile on right. Parkland course with meandering fairways, bunkers and many water features. Newly redeveloped golf course opened in May 2004. 18 holes, Par 71. Practice area. *Green Fees*: weekdays €43, weekends and Public Holidays €48. *Eating facilities*: Bar/snacks; lunch, dinner. *Visitors*: welcome Mondays, Thursdays and Fridays. Trolley and buggy hire. *Society Meetings*: welcome. Special group rates on request. Trolley and buggy hire. Contact club office (00353 45897610)
e-mail: enquiries@craddockstown.com

NAAS. **Naas Golf Club,** Kerdiffstown, Naas (045 897509; Fax: 045 896109). *Location*: take Sallins turn off, the N7 from Dublin. Approx. one and a half kilometres on right hand side. Parkland. 18 holes,6232 yards. S.S.S. 71. Practice ground. Public driving range within 200 metres. *Green Fees*: (2007) midweek €40, weekends and Bank Holidays €45. (subject to review). *Eating facilities*: 10.30am-11.00pm. *Visitors*: welcome. Contact club in advance. Dress code applies. *Society Meetings*: welcome. Manager: Denis Mahon (045 874644).

NAAS. **Woodlands Golf Club,** Coill Dubh, Cooleragh (045 860777; Fax: 045 860988). *Location:* From Naas, main Road to Sallins on to Clane village, left onto prosperous village, on to public house (Dagwelds) then turn right one mile ahead. Parkland, wooded with seven lakes. 18 holes. Putting green plus 9 hole pitch & putt course. *Green Fees:* Monday to Wednesday €25, Thursday and Friday €30; Saturday, Sunday and Bank Holidays €35 (to be reviewed). *Visitors:* welcome except Saturday pm and Sunday am. Always phone in advance. *Society Meetings:* always welcome, rates depend on number playing. Secretary: Pat O'Rourke.
e-mail: woodlandsgolf@eircom.net

SALLINS. **Bodenstown Golf Club,** Sallins (045 897096). *Location:* Naas dual carriageway, turn left at No.7 exit. 36 holes. **S.S.S. 72.** Practice green. *Green Fees:* €25. *Eating facilities:* full catering and bar. *Visitors:* welcome, no restrictions. *Society Meetings:* please telephone. Secretary: Bernadette Curtin (045 897096).

STRAFFAN. **Castlewarden Golf and Country Club,** Castlewarden, Straffan (3531 4589254; Fax: 3531 4588972). *Location:* on the N7 Dublin to Naas road, take the second right after Blackchurch Inn. Parkland. 18 holes, 6690 yards. S.S.S. 71. Practice area and putting green. *Green Fees:* information not available. *Eating facilities:* full catering and bar. *Visitors:* welcome, booking advisable. *Society Meetings:* welcome. Professional: Brian O'Brien (3531 4588219). Secretary: Fiona Kane (3531 4589838).*
e-mail: castlewarden@clubi.ie
website: www.castlewardengolfclub.com

STRAFFAN. **The K Club,** Straffan, Co. Kildare (6017300; Fax: 6017399). *Location:* N7 south of Dublin to Kill, turn right, five miles from Junction. Signposted. Parkland course with trees, lakes, River Liffey – absolute Championship course. 18 holes, 7178 yards. S.S.S.76. Driving range. *Green Fees:* information not available. *Eating facilities:* Legends Restaurant and Bar, The Arnold Palmer Room, Snack Bar and Members' Restaurant. *Visitors:* members' hours Winter 11am to 1pm; Summer 1.30pm to 3.30pm weekdays. Golf shop, trolleys, clubs and shoe hire. The Kildare Hotel (within complex) AA 5 Red Star; 69 bedrooms. Professional: John McHenry (6017321; Fax: 6017399). Director of Golf: Paul Crowe.*
e-mail: golf@kclub.ie
website: www.kclub.ie

Co. Kilkenny

CALLAN. **Callan Golf Club,** Geraldine, Callan (056 25136/25949; Fax: 056 55155). *Location*: One mile from Callan on the Knocktopher Road. Parkland course with many water features. 18 holes, 6400 yards. S.S.S. 70. Practice area. *Green Fees*: information not available. *Eating facilities*: food available all day, bar. *Visitors*: welcome – best to check with Golf Shop in advance. *Society Meetings*: all welcome. Secretary/Manager: Liam Duggan (056 25136)*
e-mail: info@callangolfclub.com
website: www.callangolfclub.com

CASTLECOMER. **Castlecomer Golf Club,** Drumgoole, Castlecomer (00 353 564441575; Fax: 00 353 564441139). *Location*: Main Castlecomer to Kilkenny Road. Parkland course beside the River Deen. 18 holes, 6175 metres. S.S.S. 72. Par 72. Practice ground. *Green Fees*: weekdays €35, weekends €40. *Eating facilities*: catering available. *Visitors:* always welcome. *Society Meetings*: welcome, society and group rates available. Secretary: Matt Dooley (00 353 567 727480).
e-mail: castlecomergolf@eircom.net
website: www.castlecomergolf.com

GOWRAN. **Gowran Park,** Gowran (056 7726699; Fax: 056 7726173). *Location:* on main Waterford–Dublin road (N9), half a mile on the Waterford side of Gowran. Parkland, part of old Annally Estate, with woodland and lakes. 18 holes, 6100 metres. S.S.S. 72 (Blue), 70 (White), 68 (Green). Putting green, practice range. *Green Fees:* €40 weekdays, €50 weekends. *Eating facilities:* full catering available. *Visitors:* welcome daily (some restrictions at weekends). *Society Meetings:* welcome daily. Rates €35-€45 for groups of 20+. Secretary: Michael O'Sullivan.
e-mail: gowranparkltd@eircom.net
website: www.gowranpark.ie

KILKENNY. **Kilkenny Golf Club,** Glendine, Kilkenny (056 7765400; Fax: 056 7723593). *Location:* off Castlecomer Road two kilometres from centre of city. Parkland. 18 holes, 5133 metres. S.S.S. 71. Practice area. *Green Fees:* €35-€45. *Eating facilities:* available. *Visitors:* welcome, weekends by arrangement. *Society Meetings:* welcome, by arrangement. Professional: Jimmy Bolger (056 7761730). Manager: Sean Boland (056 7765400).
e-mail: enquiries@kilkennygolfclub.com

THOMASTOWN. **Mount Juliet Golf Club,** Thomastown (056 7773064; Fax: 056 7773078). *Location:* Thomastown - on main Dublin to Waterford Road. Parkland, designed by Jack Nicklaus, home of the 1993-95 Irish Open. Home of the American Express World Golf Championship 2002 won by Tiger Woods and in 2004 won by Ernie Els. Voted Golf Course of the Year 2003. 18 holes, 7260 yards. S.S.S. 75, 73, 72. Golf academy and driving range, also Europe's first 18 hole putting course with a par of 53. *Green Fees:* €75 - €160. *Eating facilities:* hotel, Spike bar, President's bar, two restaurants. *Visitors:* welcome, no restrictions but please book in advance. Handicap Cards preferred. 59 bedroom de luxe Hotel. *Society Meetings:* please book in advance. Professional: Sean Cotter.

Co. Laois

The Heritage, a par 72 championship golf course, designed by Seve Ballasteros and Jeff Howes, is set in beautiful rolling countryside, just one hour from Dublin. Five lakes and a stream meander through the course, and 98 bunkers and 7,000 trees adorn the landscape.

- Seve Ballasteros 'Natural' Golf School
- Hotel with superbly appointed rooms and suites.
- Resort Spa with over 70 treatments to choose from
- Health Club • Heritage Spa Experience
- Variety of restaurants and bars
- Tennis • International indoor and outdoor bowls
- On-course 2 bedroom luxury penthouse apartments.

Host Venue for the Seve Trophy 2007 & 2009.

The Heritage Golf & Spa Resort, Killenard, Co Laois • Tel: 057 864 5500
e-mail: info@theheritage.com
www.theheritage.com

THE HERITAGE
GOLF & SPA RESORT
★ ★ ★ ★ ★

Continental Europe & Great Britain & Ireland
SEVE TROPHY 2007
THE HERITAGE
GOLF & SPA RESORT

ABBEYLEIX. **Abbeyleix Golf Club,** Rathmoyle, Abbeyleix (0502 31450; Fax: 0502 30108). *Location*: quarter mile outside town of Abbeyleix on Ballyroan Road. Parkland course with many water features. Practice chipping and putting green. 18 holes, 6020 yards. S.S.S. 70. *Green Fees*: Monday-Friday €25, weekends €30 (under review). *Eating facilities*: bar/restaurant (by arrangement). *Visitors*: welcome weekdays, weekends after 5pm. Secretary: Malady Fogarty (0502 31546).
website: www.abbeyleixgolfclub.com

MOUNTRATH. **Mountrath Golf Club,** Knockanina, Mountrath (0502 32558 (Public) or 0502 32643 (Office) or Fax: 0502 56735). *Location:* one kilometre off Dublin/Limerick Road, turn left outside Mountrath, signposted. Undulating parkland course with river flowing through it. 18 holes, 5643 metres. S.S.S. 69. Putting green, chipping green and practice area. *Green Fees:* information not available. *Eating facilities:* available everyday and by arrangement. Bar everyday. *Visitors:* welcome weekdays, and weekends after 4pm, phone beforehand. *Society Meetings:* welcome, contact office. Secretary: Lar Scully.*

PORTARLINGTON. **Portarlington Golf Club,** Garry Hinch, Portarlington (057 8623115; Fax: 057 8623044). *Location*: two and a half miles from Portarlington on the Mount Mellick Road. Parkland course with tree lines fairways. Practice ground. 18 holes, 5906 metres. S.S.S. 71. *Green Fees*: information not available. *Eating facilities*: bar and catering facilities available throughout the day. *Visitors:* welcome restricted at weekends. *Society Meetings:* welcome, rates available.*
e-mail: portarlingtongc@eircom.net
website: www.portarlingtongolf.com

PORTLAOISE. **The Heath Golf Club,** The Heath, Portlaoise (057 86 46533; Fax: 057 86 46735). *Location:* three-and-a-half miles northeast of Portlaoise, off main Dublin road. Relatively flat with furze, gorse and three lakes. 18 holes, 5736 metres. S.S.S. 71. 10 bay all-weather floodlit driving range and practice area. *Green Fees:* weekdays €20, weekends €30. *Eating facilities:* full bar and catering facilities available. *Visitors:* welcome at all times but advance booking required for weekends and Public Holidays. *Society Meetings:* welcome by prior arrangement. Professional: Mark O'Boyle.

PORTLAOISE. **Rathdowney Golf Club,** Rathdowney, Portlaoise (0505 46170 or Tel & Fax: 0505 46065 office). *Location*: half a mile from Rathdowney, signposted from the square. Parkland course with gentle sloping hills; good test for most golfers (second 9 holes opened June 1997). 18 holes, 5894 metres, S.S.S. 70, Par 71. *Green Fees*: €30. *Eating facilities:* bar open daily (afternoon), catering by prior arrangement. *Visitors:* welcome any time during the week, Sundays after 4.30pm, Saturday mornings reserved for societies. *Society Meetings:* welcome by appointment through Hon. Secretary. Hon. Secretary: Sean Bolger.
website: www.rathdowneygolf.com

Co. Leitrim

BALLINAMORE. **Ballinamore Golf Club,** Ballinamore (00353 7 196 44346). *Location:* one-and-a-half miles north-west of town alongside Shannon/Erne waterway. Parkland. 9 holes, 6142 yards, 5514 metres. S.S.S.68. *Green Fees:* information not available *Eating facilities:* bar with snacks. *Visitors:* welcome with some restrictions on certain weekends. *Society Meetings:* welcome with restrictions on certain weekends. Captain: Aiden Wynne (087 2324196). Secretary: Gerry Mahon (071 9644031 or 087 7678392).

Co. Limerick

ABBEYFEALE. **Abbeyfeale Golf Club,** Dromtrasna Collins, Abbeyfeale (068 32033). *Location*: two miles from Abbeyfeale. Parkland. 9 holes, 4072 yards. S.S.S. 64. 20 bay indoor driving range, practice putting green. *Green Fees*: information not available. *Eating facilities*: by appointment. *Visitors*: welcome everyday. *Society Meetings*: societies/companies/ groups always welcome. Professional: (068 32033). Hon. Secretary: Conleth Dillon (068 31454).*
e-mail: abbeyfealegolf@eircom.net

ADARE. **Adare Golf Club,** Adare Manor Hotel & Golf Resort, Adare (061 605274; Fax: 061 605271). *Location:* from Limerick take the N21.Parkland. Robert Trent Jones designed Championship course, home to the Irish Open 2007 - 2009. 18 holes, 7453 yards. S.S.S. 69. *Green Fees:* weekdays €150, sunsetter rate €85 (after 4pm). *Eating facilities:* clubhouse bar and restaurant. *Visitors:* always welcome. Putting green, short game practice area and driving range. *Society Meetings:* welcome. Professional: John Coyle
e-mail: golf@adaremanor.com
website: www.adaregolfclub.com

ADARE. **Adare Manor Golf Club,** Adare (353 61 396204; Fax: 353 61 396800). *Location*: main Limerick to Killarney road, 10 miles from Limerick. Parkland course. 18 holes, 5764 yards. S.S.S. 69. Putting green, chipping area. *Green Fees*: €37. *Eating facilities*: full bar and restaurant. *Visitors*: welcome all year round. Check with club for times at weekends. *Society Meetings*: societies welcome all year round. €26.50 per visitor, €16 per member in society. Hon. Secretary: T.P. Healy (353 61 396204; Fax: 353 61 396800).
e-mail: info@adaremanorgolfclub.com
website: www.adaremanorgolfclub.com

ARDAGH. **Newcastle West Golf Club,** Ardagh (00-353-6976500; Fax: 00-353-6976511). *Location:* Off N21 roadway linking Shannon, Limerick and Killarney beyond Rathkeale. Parkland course. 18 holes, 6400 yards. S.S.S. 72. Flood-lit driving bays, practice green and bunker. *Green Fees:* €35 weekdays, €45 weekends and Bank Holidays. *Eating facilities:* Bar and restaurant. *Visitors:* welcome. *Society Meetings:* welcome - green fee reductions. Professional: Conor McCormick (Tel & Fax: 00-353-6976500) Secretary/Manager: William Hickey (Tel & Fax: 00-353-6976500).
website: www.newcastlewestgolf.com

BALLYNEETY. **Limerick County Golf and Country Club,** Ballyneety (061 351881; Fax: 061 351384). *Location:* five miles from Limerick City, R512 direction of Lough Gur/Kilmallock. Championship standard, parkland course with water hazards bordering 8 holes. 18 holes, 5876 metres. S.S.S. 71. Driving range, putting greens, 3 hole short game area, golf school with professional tuition. *Green Fees:* midweek €40, weekend €50. *Eating facilities:* excellent restaurant serving international cuisine, light snacks, lunch and dinner menus, full bar service. *Visitors:* always welcome, telephone in advance to assure tee space. Play and Stay packages available. *Society Meetings:* welcome. Professional: Donal McSweeney (061 351881). Manager: Gerry McKeon (061 351881; Fax: 061 351384).
e-mail: teetimes@limerickcounty.com
website: www.limerickcounty.com

CASTLETROY. **Castletroy Golf Club,** Golf Links Road, Castletroy, Limerick City (061 335261; Fax: 061 335753; Fax: 061 335373). *Location:* three miles from Limerick City on N7 (Dublin Road). Popular parkland course redeveloped to USGA specification in 2005. 18 holes, 6274 metres. *Green Fees:* information not available. *Eating facilities:* full catering and bar service. *Visitors:* welcome all week except Tuesday and Thursday - advisable to phone Golf Shop (061 330450). *Society Meetings:* welcome Monday, Wednesday, Friday and Saturday; group rates available. Golf Shop: (061 330450). General Manager: Patrick Keane.*
e-mail: cgc@iol.ie

LIMERICK. **Limerick Golf Club,** Ballyclough, Limerick (061 414083; Fax: 061 319219). *Location*: five km from Limerick city on Fedamore Road. Parkland. 18 holes, 5932 metres. S.S.S. 71. *Green Fees:* €50 Monday to Thursday, €70 Friday to Sunday and Bank Holidays. *Eating facilities*: full bar and dining facilities. *Visitors*: welcome Mondays, Wednesdays, Thursdays, Fridays up to 4pm. *Society Meetings:* advance booking required. Professional: Lee Harrington (061 412492). General Manager: Pat Murray (061 415146).
e-mail: lgc@eircom.net
website: www.limerickgc.com

NEWCASTLE WEST. **Killeline Golf Club,** Newcastle West (069 61600; Fax: 069 77428). *Location:* quarter-of-a-mile off the main Limerick to Kerry road on Drumcollier road. Flat parkland. 18 holes, 7000 metres. S.S.S. 72. *Green Fees:* information not available. *Eating facilities:* two bars and restaurant. *Visitors:* welcome. *Society Meetings:* welcome. Leisure facilities include swimming pool, sauna, gymnasium. 32 bedroom lodge. Secretary: Paul O'Toole. Director of Golf: Kevin Dorrian.*

PLEASE MENTION **THE GOLF GUIDE** WHEN YOU WRITE OR PHONE TO ENQUIRE ABOUT CLUBS OR ACCOMMODATION

Co. Longford

LONGFORD. **County Longford Golf Club,** Glack, Dublin Road, Longford (043 46310); Fax: 043 47082). *Location:* one mile from centre of town on Dublin road. 18 holes, 5981 metres. S.S.S. 73. *Green Fees:* weekdays €25.00, weekends and Bank Holidays €30.00. *Eating facilities:* full catering and bar. *Visitors:* welcome at all times subject to availability. Buggies and carts available. *Society Meetings:* all welcome. Secretary: Mark Glancy.
e-mail: colonggolf@eircom.net

Co. Louth

ARDEE. **Ardee Golf Club,** Townparks, Ardee (041 6853227; Fax: 041 6856137). Parkland, wooded course with beautiful mature trees and exquisite greens. 18 holes, 6348 yards, S.S.S. 71. Large practice area. *Green Fees:* information not available. *Eating facilities:* restaurant and bar. *Visitors:* welcome. Carts for hire, caddies by arrangement. *Society Meetings:* welcome Mondays to Saturdays. Professional: Scott Kirkpatrick (041 6857472). Hon Secretary: E. Roe. Secretary/Manager: Seamus Rooney (041 6853227; Fax: 041 6856137).*

DROGHEDA. **Seapoint Golf Club,** Termonfeckin, Drogheda (041 982333; Fax: 041 982331). *Location:* Dublin–Belfast–Drogheda to Termonfeckin Road. Links course. 18 holes, 6339 metres. S.S.S. 74. Practice range and putting green. *Green Fees:* information not available. *Eating facilities:* restaurant and bar. *Visitors:* welcome at all times; members' tee times 1-2pm daily and up to 10.30am weekends. *Society Meetings:* welcome, discounts available. Trolleys and caddies available. Professional: David Carroll. Secretary: Kevin Carrie.*
e-mail: info@seapointgolfclub.com
website: www.seapointgolfclub.com

DROGHEDA. **County Louth Golf Club,** Baltray, Drogheda (041 9881530; Fax: 041 9881531). *Location:* Drogheda, five miles north east. Championship links course. 18 holes, 7035 yards. S.S.S. 74. *Green Fees:* weekdays €120; weekends €140. *Eating facilities:* restaurant, coffee shop and bar. *Visitors:* welcome weekdays except Tuesdays on application, weekends restricted. Residential accommodation available for 20 persons. *Society Meetings:* on application. Professional: Paddy McGuirk (041 9881536). Secretary: Michael Delany (041 9881530; Fax: 041 9881531).

DUNDALK. **Dundalk Golf Club,** Blackrock, Dundalk (042 9321731; Fax: 042 9322022). *Location:* Dundalk coast road to Blackrock, two miles. Championship parkland course with tree-lined fairways. Hosted All Ireland Finals in 1997 and 2000. Attracts country's top players to Senior Scratch Cup. Hosts major PGA Pro-Am and Ladies' Home Internationals. Celebrated Centenary in 2005. 18 holes, 6776 yards, 6160 metres. S.S.S. 72 (Par 72). Six acre field practice ground. *Green Fees:* €60. *Eating facilities:* full restaurant and bar. *Visitors:* welcome Mondays, Wednesdays, Thursdays and Fridays, restrictions weekends and Tuesday Ladies' Day. *Society Meetings:* welcome by appointment. Professional: Leslie Walker (042 9322102). Secretary/Manager: Terry Sloane (042 9321731; Fax: 042 9322022).
e-mail: manager@dundalkgolfclub.ie
website: www.dundalkgolfclub.ie

GREENORE. **Greenore Golf Club,** Greenore (042 93 73212/73678; Fax: 042 9383898). *Location:* Dundalk/ Newry, Dundalk 15 miles, Newry 12 miles. Flat semi-links course with heathland features, pine trees, rivers, ponds – very scenic, Carlingford Mountains and Mountains of Mourne. 18 holes, 6647 yards. S.S.S. 73. *Green Fees:* weekdays €40.00; weekends and Bank Holidays 50 euros; subject to review. *Eating facilities:* full catering and bar facilities (daylight hours). *Visitors:* always welcome, prior booking advisable. Caddies on request, trolley and golf buggy available for hire. *Society Meetings:* very welcome by prior arrangement. Professional: Robert Giles. Secretary: Linda Clarke (042 9373678).
e-mail: greenoregolfclub@eircom.net
website: www.greenoregolfclub.com

KILLIN. **Killin Park Golf & Country Club,** Killin, Dundalk (00353 42 9339303). *Location:* two miles west of Dundalk. Undulating parkland with mature trees. The 4th and 6th holes are surrounded by the Castletown River. 18 holes. Par 69. *Green Fees:* information not available. *Eating facilities:* available from dawn till dusk.*

Co. Mayo

ACHILL. Achill Golf Club, Keel, Achill Island (098 43456). *Location:* N59 from Westport and R319 from Mulranny to Achill. Flat seaside links in scenic setting. 9 holes, 2947 yards, 2689 metres. S.S.S. 67. *Green Fees:* €15. *Visitors:* welcome at all times, no restrictions. *Society Meetings:* by prior arrangement. Secretary: Michael McGinty (085 1743571.

BALLINA. Ballina Golf Club, Mossgrove, Shanaghy, Ballina (Tel & Fax: 096 21050). *Location:* on Bonniconlon Road. Parkland course. 18 holes, 6103 yards. S.S.S. 69. *Green Fees:* information not available. *Eating facilities:* bar, snacks. *Visitors:* welcome every day, Sundays 11am to 1.30pm. *Society Meetings:* weekdays to 4pm, Saturdays 10am to 12 noon, Sundays 11am to 1.30pm. Secretary: Padhraig Connolly (096 21050; Fax: 096 2178).*
e-mail: ballinagc@eircom.net
website: www.ballinagolfclub.com

BALLINROBE. Ballinrobe Golf Club, Cloonacastle, Ballinrobe (09495 41118; Fax: 09495 41889). *Location:* off N84 at Ballinrobe onto the R331 to Claremorris. Parkland course with trees and man-made lakes. 18 holes, 6354 metres. S.S.S. 73. Practice ground, driving range. *Green Fees:* information not available. *Eating facilities:* catering and bar facilities. *Visitors:* welcome at all times but is advisable to book tee times in advance. Buggies and carts available. Excellent fishing. *Society Meetings:* welcome by arrangement. Secretary/Manager: John McMahon.*
website: www.ballinrobegolfclub.com
http:// www.iol.ie

BELMULLET. Carne Golf Links, Belmullet (097 82292; Fax: 097 81477) *Location:* on N59 three km from centre of Belmullet town. Pure links course - feature holes 9th, 14th and 18th. 18 holes, 6119 metres. Medal S.S.S 72; Championship. S.S.S 72, Par 72. Practice ground and putting green. *Green Fees:* information not available. *Eating facilities:* full restaurant and bar facilities. *Visitors:* very welcome at all times. Buggies and caddies available. *Society Meetings:* by arrangement. Secretary/Manager: James O'Hara (097 82292; Fax: 097 81477).*
e-mail: carngolf@iol.ie
website: www.carnegolflinks.com

CASTLEBAR. Castlebar Golf Club, Rocklands, Castlebar (353 94 9021649; Fax: 353 94 9026088). *Location:* situated on the Galway road out of town. Championship, parkland course with abundance of water and trees. 18 holes, 6500 yards, S.S.S. 70. *Green Fees:* Monday to Thursday €25, Friday/ Saturday/Sunday €35. *Eating facilities:* full catering facilities. *Visitors:* welcome every day, except Sunday before 1.30pm. *Society Meetings:* welcome every day except Sunday. Honorary Secretary: Paul Kilcourse (353 87 8109535).

CLAREMORRIS. Claremorris Golf Club, Castlemacgarrett, Claremorris (094 9371527). *Location:* on N17, Galway 35 miles, Claremorris two miles, Knock airport 20 miles. Parkland/wooded course designed by Tom Craddock; numerous water hazards and excellent sand-based greens. 18 holes, 7000 yards. S.S.S. 72. Practice ground. *Green Fees:* weekdays €32, weekends €40. *Visitors:* welcome weekdays, weekends on request. *Society Meetings:* welcome, booking required. Admin Manager: Christina Rush (094 9371527)
e-mail: info@claremorrisgolfclub.com
website: www.claremorrisgolfclub.com

SWINFORD. Swinford Golf Club, Brabazon Park, Swinford (094 92 51378). *Location:* on Kiltimagh Road beside Swinford town. Parkland. 9 holes, S.S.S. 68. Practice green and pitching area. *Green Fees:* information not available. *Eating facilities:* bar with catering by arrangement. *Visitors:* welcome with some restrictions. *Society Meetings:* Golf societies welcome, prices on application. Secretary: John Sheahan (087 9100 572).*
e-mail: sheetsjj@eircom.net

WESTPORT. Westport Golf Club, Carrowholly, Westport (098 28262/27070; Fax: 098 27217). Parkland championship course. 18 holes. Practice area, 9 bay floodlit driving range. *Green Fees:* information not available. *Eating facilities:* bar and restaurant. *Visitors:* welcome with restrictions. *Society Meetings:* welcome. Professional: Alex Mealia. Club Administrator: Margaret Walsh. Secretary: Karen Walsh. Manager: Paul O'Neil.
e-mail: info@westportgolfclub.com

www.uk-golfguide.com

FHG Guides
publish a large range of well-known accommodation guides.
We will be happy to send you details or you can use
the order form at the back of this book.

Co. Sligo

BALLYMOTE. **Ballymote Golf Club**, Ballinascarrow, Ballymote (071 9183504/9183089). *Location:* 15 miles south of Sligo town, 12 miles west of Boyle. Undulating parkland with pleasant views. 9 holes, 2651 metres. S.S.S. 67 (for 18 holes). *Green Fees:* information not available. Trolleys available for hire 2 euros, buggies 3 euros. *Society Meetings:* please telephone John O'Connor (087 2187054).*

ENNISCRONE. **Enniscrone Golf Club,** Enniscrone (096 36297 three lines; Fax: 096 36657). *Location:* on coast road from Sligo to Ballina, about 13 km from Ballina. Championship links course - host to the Irish Close Championship 1993 - host to West of Ireland Championship 1997-1999 - host to Senior Inter Provincials 1999. 18 holes, 6857 yards. Par 73. Practice area and putting green. *Green Fees:* information not available. *Eating facilities:* bar and full catering facilities. *Visitors:* welcome, please phone beforehand. Professional: Charlie McGoldrick (096 36666). Hon. Secretary: Brian Casey (096 36414). Administrator: Anne Freeman. Secretary/ Manager: Mick Staunton. Rated number 66 in Top 100 Courses in Great Britain and Ireland - Golf World.*
e-mail: enniscronegolf@eircom.net
website: www.enniscronegolf.com

ROSSES POINT. **County Sligo Golf Club,** Rosses Point (+353 (0)71 9177134; Fax: +353 (0)71 9177460). *Location:* 8km west of Sligo city at Rosses Point village. Championship links course which has hosted all of Ireland's major championships - rates No 58 in Golf World's 100 Best Courses (2006). 18 holes, 6136 metres. S.S.S. 72. Large practice area. *Green Fees:* information not available. *Eating facilities:* full 80 seat restaurant, spacious lounge bar. *Visitors:* welcome seven days, Tuesdays Ladies' Day. Additional 9 holes Par 35. Ten electric buggies available at €40 per round. *Society Meetings:* welcome. Professional: Jim Robinson (+353 (0)71 9177171). Manager: Hugh O'Neill. Reservations: Teresa Banks (+353 (0)71 9177134; Fax: +353 (0)71 9177460).*
e-mail: teresa@countysligogolfclub.ie
website: www.countysligogolfclub.ie

SLIGO. **Castle Dargan Estate,** Ballygawley (00353 71 9118080; Fax: 00353 71 9118090). *Location:* ten minutes south of Sligo town. Darren Clarke designed parkland championship course. 18 holes, 7000 metres, S.S.S. 71. Practice academy, driving bays, chipping green and putting green. *Green Fees:* information not available. *Eating facilities:* club bar, restaurant and conference facility. *Visitors:* always welcome. 22-bedroom 4-star hotel and self-catering apartments. *Society Meetings:* welcome all year round, rates from €45 - €60. Secretary: David O'Donovan.*
e-mail: golf@castledargan.com
website: www.castledargan.com

Co. Tipperary

CAHIR. **Cahir Park Golf Club,** Kilcommon, Cahir (052 41474; Fax: 052 42717). *Location:* half-a-mile from Cahir town on Clogheen road. Parkland. 18 holes, 5740 metres. S.S.S. 71. *Green Fees:* weekdays €30, weekends €35. Open Singles for men from March 17th to October. *Eating facilities:* meals available, bar, dining room in new clubhouse. *Visitors:* welcome. Practice area. Locker rooms. Buggy available for hire. *Society Meetings:* welcome. PGA Professional: David Ryan

CARRICK-ON-SUIR. **Carrick-on-Suir Golf Club,** Garravoone, Carrick-on-Suir (051 640047; Fax: 051 640558). *Location:* one mile from Carrick-on-Suir on Dungarvan Road. Parkland course set against the backdrop of the Comeragh Mountains on one side and the Suir Valley on the other. 18 holes, 6061 yards. S.S.S. 70, Par 72. *Green Fees:* information not available. *Eating facilities:* full facilities, bar open 9am to 11.30pm. *Visitors:* welcome thoughout the week except during competition times on Wednesday, Tuesday and Sunday. Sean Kelly's (cyclist) home club. One buggy for hire and carts. *Society Meetings:* all welcome by prior arrangement. Secretary/Manager: Aidan Murphy (051 640047).*

CLONMEL. **Clonmel Golf Club,** Lyreanearla, Mountain Road, Clonmel (052 24050; Fax: 052 83349). *Location:* three miles up the mountain road from Clonmel town. Parkland set on the scenic slopes of the Comeragh Mountains. 18 holes, 6347 (white), 6068 (green) yards. S.S.S. 71 white, 70 green. Practice area. *Green Fees:* Monday - Friday €30pp, Sat/Sun and Bank Holidays €35pp. *Eating facilities:* bar food, sit-down meals available on request. *Visitors:* always welcome but contact Secretary/ Manager re weekends. Ladies' Day Wednesdays. Golf Buggy available for hire, contact professional. *Society Meetings:* welcome, contact Secretary/ Manager for weekends. Course information (052 83344). Professional: Robert Hayes (052 24050). Secretary/ Manager: Ms Aine Myles Keating (052 24050; Fax: 052 83349).
e-mail: cgc@indigo.ie
website: www.clonmelgolfclub.com

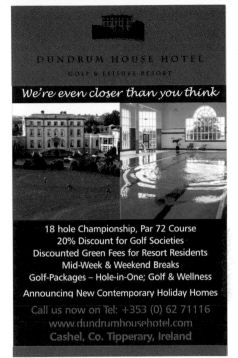

DUNDRUM. **Co. Tipperary Golf & Country Club,** Dundrum House Hotel, Golf & Leisure Resort, Dundrum (00 353 (0)62 71717; Fax: 00 353 (0)62 71718). *Location:* 7 miles west of Cashel Town. Parkland course, 18 holes, 6800 yards (Championship course). *Green Fees:* €50pp weekdays, €60pp weekends; €40 midweek (groups over 20), €50 weekend. *Eating facilities:* full bar and food facilities available. *Visitors:* welcome anytime. Club house with changing facilities. Putting Green and chipping area. *Society Meetings:* welcome.
website: www.dundrumhousehotel.com

MONARD. **Ballykisteen Golf and Country Club,** Monard, Tipperary (052 33333; Fax: 062 82587). *Location:* on the N24 20 minutes' drive from Limerick City, two miles from Tipperary town and 500 metres from Limerick Junction railway station. 4 Star rated Ramada Hotel and Suites with Leisure Centre and 18 hole Championship golf course. 6765 yards, Par 73. Driving range and practice green. *Green Fees:* information not available. *Eating facilities:* full restaurant and bar facilities. *Visitors:* welcome at all times. *Society Meetings:* all welcome. Bookings to John O'Dwyer (062 33333).*
website: www.ballykisteenramada.com

TEMPLEMORE. **Templemore Golf Club,** Manna South, Templemore (0504 31400; Fax: 0504 31913). *Location:* beside N62 (South) half-a-mile from town centre. Flat parkland course, short distance between greens and tees, easy to walk. 9 holes, 5443 metres. S.S.S. 68. *Green Fees:* information not available. *Visitors:* welcome at all times, some restrictions Sundays. *Society Meetings:* welcome. Secretary: Jim Tobin (087 6882618).*

THURLES. **Thurles Golf Club,** Turtulla, Thurles (0504 21983; Fax: 0504 24647). *Location:* one mile from town centre on Cork Road. Sloping parkland course. 18 holes, 6465 yards. S.S.S.71. *Green Fees:* information not available. *Eating facilities:* restaurant and bar. *Visitors:* welcome except Tuesday and Sunday. *Society Meetings:* welcome, special rates available. Professional: Sean Hunt. Hon. Secretary: Michael O'Sullivan (0504 21983; Fax: 0504 90806).*

Co. Waterford

DUNGARVAN. **Dungarvan Golf Club,** Knocknagranagh, Dungarvan (00 353 5843310 /5841605; Fax: 00 353 5844113). *Location:* four kilometres east of Dungarvan on N25 to Waterford. Parkland course adjacent to Dungarvan Bay. 18 holes, 6785 yards, 6204 metres. S.S.S. 73. Practice ground. *Green Fees:* information not provided. *Eating facilities:* Full bar and catering services by prior arrangement. *Visitors:* welcome but booking advisable. *Society Meetings:* welcome, special rates. Professional: David Hayes (00 353 5844707). Manager: Irene Howell (00 353 5843310).
e-mail: dungarvangc@eircom.net
website: www.dungarvangolfclub.com

DUNGARVAN. **Gold Coast Golf Club,** Ballinacourty, Dungarvan (Tel & Fax: 00 353 58 44055). *Location:* 45 miles east of Cork city, 30 miles south of Waterford city, on N25, 2 miles from Dungarvan town, on the coast. Scenic and challenging course bordering the Atlantic Ocean with unrivalled panoramic views of Dungarven Bay and Comeragh Mountains. 18 holes,

6788 yards, 6171 metres. S.S.S. 72. *Green Fees:* weekdays from €35, weekends from €45. *Eating facilities:* full hotel and leisure facilities. *Visitors:* welcome anytime. *Society Meetings:* welcome, special rates available. Secretary: Tom Considine (Tel & Fax: 00 353 58 44055).
e-mail: info@goldcoastgolfclub.com
website: www.goldcoastgolfclub.com

DUNGARVAN. **West Waterford Golf & Country Club,** Dungarvan (058 43216/41475; Fax: 058 44343). *Location:* 4km west of Dungarvan, off N25 bypass on Aglish Road. Challenging parkland course with natural water hazards, mature trees, abundant wildlife. 18 holes, 6712 yards. S.S.S. 72 blue. Large practice area and putting green. *Green Fees:* weekdays €35; weekends and Bank Holidays €45. Discounts for groups and societies. *Eating facilities:* full restaurant and catering facilities. *Visitors:* always welcome, but reservations are necessary. *Society Meetings:* always welcome, pre-booking essential. Secretary: Tom Whelan (00353 58 43216/41475; Fax: 00353 58 44343).
e-mail: info@westwaterfordgolf.com
website: www.westwaterfordgolf.com

DUNMORE EAST. **Dunmore East Golf Club,** Dunmore East (Tel. & Fax: 00 353 51 383151). *Location:* at the entrance to Dunmore village take first left to Strand and follow signpost to Club. Seaside parkland. 18 holes, 6070 metres. S.S.S. 70. *Green Fees:* from €25. *Eating facilities:* full bar and catering facilities. *Visitors:* always welcome. Self-catering accommodation on-site. *Society Meetings:* welcome, prices on request. Distance membership available. Club Professional: Derry Kiely. Secretary: Sadie Whittle (Tel & Fax: 00 353 51 383151).
e-mail: info@dunmoreeastgolfclub.ie
website: www.dunmoreeastgolfclub.ie

LISMORE. **Lismore Golf Club,** Ballyin, Lismore (058 54026; Fax: 058 53338). *Location:* one kilometre north of Lismore Heritage Town, just off the N72. Undulating parkland with mature trees, course surrounded by woodlands. 9 holes, 5871 metres. S.S.S. 68. *Green Fees:* €20. *Eating facilities:* tea, coffee, snacks. *Visitors:* welcome weekdays, restriction may apply on Wednesday (Ladies' Day) and weekends. *Society Meetings:* welcome. Secretary: Katherine Moynihan.

TRAMORE. **Tramore Golf Club,** Newtown Hill, Tramore (051 386170; Fax: 051 390961). *Location:* seven miles from Waterford city. Parkland. 18 holes, 5918 metres. S.S.S. 72. *Green Fees:* information not available. *Eating facilities:* full catering and bar. *Visitors:* welcome Monday to Saturday. No visitors on Sundays. *Society Meetings:* welcome on application. Professional: Deirdre Brennan. Club Manager: David Murray.
website: www.tramoregolfclub.com

THE APPEARANCE OF AN ASTERISK (*) AT THE END OF A CLUB OR COURSE ENTRY INDICATES THAT UP-TO-DATE INFORMATION HAS NOT BEEN SUPPLIED

Ballykisteen Hotel & Golf Resort
BALLYKISTEEN, LIMERICK JUNCTION, CO. TIPPERARY

Set in the Shadow of the Galtee Mountains this stunning 4 star Hotel is the ideal venue for a leisurely break. Boasting a charming mix of course side lodges and well appointed guest rooms, most of which overlook our 18 Hole Championship Golf Course.

The Course was designed by Ex European Tour and Ryder Cup star Des Smyth, it is a visually appealing course with an abundance of water hazards and bunkers. Ballykisteen is a memorable course which is friendly to all grades of golfers. Golf societies are welcome all year round. Academy Style lessons are available on site from our Golf Pro.

For more information please contact:

Tel: 353 (0) 62 33333 / 32117

Fax: 353 (0) 62 31555

e-mail: Info@ballykisteenhotel.com

www.ballykisteenhotel.com

WATERFORD. **Faithlegg Golf Club,** Faithlegg House, Waterford (051 380587; Fax: 051 382010). *Location:* 6 miles from Waterford city centre on Dunmore road; head for Cheek Point. Premier course in the south-east, a challenge to all levels of golfer, with superb views. Ranked in the top ten best new courses in Britain and Ireland by Golf World Magazine in 1993. Hosted Ladies Irish Open in 1999 and 2000,Europro event 2007. 18 holes, 6649 yards. S.S.S. 72. Practice ground and putting green. *Green Fees:* information not available. *Eating facilities:* full bar and restaurant facilities available every day. *Visitors:* always welcome. Hotel on site. *Society Meetings:* always welcome, booking advisable. Professional: Derry Kiely (051 380587; Fax: 051 382010). Corporate and Events Manager: Tracy McDaid (051 380581). General Manager: Ryan Hunt (051 380588).
e-mail: golf@faithlegg.com
website: www.faithlegg.com

WATERFORD. **Waterford Castle Golf Club,** The Island, Ballinakill, Waterford City (00 353 51 871633; Fax: 00 353 51 871634). *Location:* one mile east of Waterford City on the R683. A unique island course surrounded by River Suir and accessed by private ferry. Parkland course, internal water features, mature woodlands and a Swilken Bridge. 18 holes, 6814 yards, 6231 metres. S.S.S. 73. Driving range, practice ground, chipping area. *Green Fees:* information not provided. *Eating facilities:* full bar and bar food. *Visitors:* welcome, no restrictions subject to availability. Accommodation available at five star Waterford Castle Hotel with all its facilities including all-weather tennis courts. Golf buggies, trolleys available. *Society Meetings:* welcome, special rates available. Director of Golf: Michael Garland (051 871633).
e-mail: directorofgolf@waterfordcastle.com
e-mail: golf@waterfordcastle.com
website: www.waterfordcastle.com

Co. Westmeath

ATHLONE. **Glasson Golf and Country Club,** Glasson, Athlone (090 6485120; Fax: 090 6485444). *Location*: take the N55 from Athlone to Glasson village and turn left. Parkland course bordering Lough Ree and the Shannon – spectacular scenery and 555 yard 14th hole. 18 holes, 6836 yards. S.S.S. 74. 3 hole golf academy. *Green Fees*: Monday to Thursday €60, Friday and Sunday €65, Saturday €75. *Eating facilities*: restaurant, spike bar, snack bar and private rooms available. *Visitors*: welcome every day. *Society Meetings:* welcome, no restrictions, all facilities available. Office: Fidelma Reid (090 6485120; Fax: 090 6485444).
e-mail: info@glassongolf.ie
website: www.glassongolf.ie

MOATE. **Mount Temple Golf Club,** Mount Temple Village, Moate (09064 81841/81545). *Location:* four miles off N6 Dublin/Galway road signposted to Mount Temple village. Parkland. 18 holes, 5927 metres. S.S.S. 72. Three hole practice area. New Golf Academy/golf range *Green Fees:* information not available. *Eating facilities:* snacks and farmhouse cuisine, dinner by arrangement, wine licence, pub 100 yards. *Visitors:* welcome but possible restrictions at weekends. *Society Meetings:* welcome. Professional: David Keenan (044 44728). Secretary: Michelle Allen (090 648 1841).*
e-mail: mttemple@iol.ie
website: www.mounttemplegolfclub.com

Co. Wexford

ENNISCORTHY. **Enniscorthy Golf Club,** Knockmarshal, Enniscorthy (053 92 33191). *Location:* one mile from Enniscorthy town on New Ross Road. Parkland course, renowned for excellent greens. 18 holes, 6115 metres. S.S.S. 72. Practice ground. *Green Fees:* Monday to Thursday €30, Friday to Sunday/Public Holidays €40. *Eating facilities:* bar and restaurant facilities. *Visitors:* welcome. Please telephone for bookings. Golf buggies available, must be pre-booked. Carts available. *Society Meetings:* welcome, must be pre-booked. Professional: Martin Sludds (053 92 37600). General Manager: A. P. Colley (053 92 33191).
e-mail: info@enniscorthygc.ie
website: www.enniscorthygc.ie

GOREY. **Seafield Golf and Country Club,** Ballymoney, Gorey (053 9424777; Fax: 053 9424837). *Location:* in the north Wexford coastal village of Ballymoney. Challenging parkland course with mature woodland and water features and beautiful cliff top holes. 18 holes, 6814 yards, Par 71. *Green Fees:* on application: *Visitors:* welcome.
e-mail: info@seafieldgolf.com
website: www.seafieldgolf.com

ROSSLARE. **Rosslare Golf Club,** Rosslare Strand, Wexford (053 32203; Fax: 053 32263). *Location:* 6 miles from ferry terminal at Rosslare Harbour. 10 miles south of Wexford. Seaside links course, beside Irish Sea. Old Course – 18 holes, 6608 yards. S.S.S. 72. New Course – 12 holes, 3983 yards. S.S.S. 70. Practice ground. *Green Fees:* Old Course: €50 and €70, New Barrow Course €20 and €25. *Eating facilities:* available all day. *Visitors:* welcome, telephone for booking. *Society Meetings:* welcome, telephone for booking. General Manager: J.P. Hanrick (053 32203).
e-mail: office@rosslaregolf.com

ROSSLARE HARBOUR. **St Helen's Bay Golf Resort,** St Helens Bay, Kilrane, Rosslare Harbour ((053) 9133234; Fax: (053) 9133803). *Location:* six miles from ferry terminal at Rosslare Harbour, 10 miles south of Wexford. Championship seaside parkland and links course with several water features. Additional 9 hole pay 'n' play course and driving range. 18 holes, 6608 yards, S.S.S. 72. *Green Fees:* information not available. *Eating facilities:* newly refurbished fully licensed bar and restaurant. *Visitors:* always welcome with no restrictions. Advisable to book in advance, especially in high season. Self-catering cottage and B&B accommodation on site. *Society Meetings:* play and stay specialists. Meetings/ conferences welcome. Secretary: Kevin Doherty.*
e-mail: info@sthelensbay.com
website: www.sthelensbay.com

Co. Wicklow

ARKLOW. **Coollattin Golf Club**, Shillelagh, Arklow (053 94 29125; Fax: 053 94 29930) *Location*: take N11 from Dublin to Rathnew, then travel to Rathdrum, Aughrim, Tinahely and Coollattin. Parkland with large oak trees being a special feature of the course. 18 holes, 5831 yards, par 70. S.S.S. 68. *Green Fees*: information not available. *Eating facilities*: full bar and catering facilities. *Visitors*: by arrangement with Professional. *Society Meetings*: by arrangement with Dave Masterson. Professional: Peter Jones. Secretary: Billy Stamp (053 94 29938).*
e-mail: coollattingolfclub@eircom.net
website: www.coollattingolfclub.com

BALTINGLASS. **Baltinglass Golf Club**, Stratford Lodge, Baltinglass (059 6481350; Fax: 059 6482842). *Location:* just outside Baltinglass on main Dublin road (N81). Picturesque course with mature trees and breathtaking views. 18 holes, 5912 yards. Par 71. *Green Fees:* information not available. *Eating facilities:* bar and catering facilities available. *Visitors:* welcome. *Society Meetings:* booking now for 2006. Contact Hon. Secretary, Genevieve or Patricia at Club Office.*
e-mail: baltinglassgc@eircom.net
website: www.baltinglass.com

BLAINROE. **Blainroe Golf Club**, Blainroe (0404 68168; Fax: 0404 69369). *Location:* three miles south of Wicklow town on coast road. Parkland terrain with extensive views of the sea. 18 holes, 6175 metres, S.S.S. 72. Practice area, putting green. *Green Fees:* information not available. *Eating facilities:* full bar and restaurant facilities. *Visitors:* welcome with previous booking. Buggies, carts and caddies available. *Society Meetings:* welcome. Professional: John McDonald (0404 66470). General Manager: Patrick Bradshaw.*

BLESSINGTON. **Tulfarris Golf Club**, Blessington Lakes, Blessington (045 867600; Fax: 045 867565). *Location*: through Blessington village take N81, 4 miles outside town, turn left after Poulaphuca House. Parkland course built on 3 peninsulas, surrounded by Poulaphuca Lake. 18 holes, 7116 yards, S.S.S. 72. Practice range, chipping area, putting green. *Green Fees*: information not available. *Society Meetings*: welcome, rates available on request. Director of Golf: David Murray (045 867654).*
e-mail: golf@tulfarris.com
website: www.tulfarris.com

BRAY. **Bray Golf Club**, Greystones Road, Bray (00 353 1 276 3200; Fax: 00 353 1 276 3262). *Location*: from N11 take turnoff for Bray & Greystones. Turn right at roundabout, continue on to Ramada Hotel, turn right at roundabout. Golf club is 700 yards up on the left. Partly wooded, parkland course. 18 holes, 6750 yards, 5645 metres. S.S.S 71. Putting green, chipping green and practice range. *Green Fees:* weekdays €25 to €50, weekends €70. Limited on Saturdays. *Eating facilities:* full bar and restaurant. *Visitors:* welcome Mondays, Thursdays and Fridays. No green fees after 4.30pm. Limited on Saturdays. Lessons available. Meeting rooms for hire. *Society Meetings:* welcome Mondays, Thursdays and Fridays; limited on Saturdays. Rates vary according to numbers - telephone office for details. Professional: Ciaran Carroll (00 353 1 276 3200) Secretary: Alan Threadgold (00 353 1 276 3200; Fax 00 353 1 276 3262).
e-mail: info@braygolfclub.com
          alan.threadgold@braygolfclub.com
website: www.braygolfclub.com

BRAY. **Woodbrook Golf Club**, Dublin Road, Bray (003531 2824799; Fax: 003531 2821950). *Location:* Bray, Co Wicklow. Flat parkland course on the cliff above Bray harbour. 18 holes, 6800 yards, S.S.S. 72.

Green Fees: information not available. *Eating facilities:* bar/restaurant. *Visitors:* welcome Monday, Tuesday and Friday. *Society Meetings:* welcome Monday, Tuesday and Friday. Professional: Billy Kinsella (0035312 820205). Secretary: Jim Melody. * e-mail: woodbrook@internet-ireland.ie website: www.woodbrook.ie

BRAY. **Old Conna Golf Club**, Ferndale Road, Bray (01282 6055; Fax: 01282 5611). *Location:* two miles from Bray town, 12 miles south of Dublin route N11. Parkland course set in wooded hillside terrain with panoramic views of Irish Sea and Wicklow. 18 holes, 6650 yards. S.S.S 72. *Green Fees:* on application. *Eating facilities:* full catering facilities. *Visitors:* welcome, Tuesdays Ladies' Day, semi open Wednesdays. Hire of clubs/caddy car. *Society Meetings:* society outings welcome Mondays, Thursdays and Fridays. Professional: Michael Langford (01272 0022; Fax: 01282 5611). General Manager: Tom Sheridan.

BRITTAS BAY. **The European Club**, Brittas Bay, Wicklow (0404 47415). *Location:* one mile south of main Brittas Bay beach on coast road, 40 miles south of Dublin City Centre. Rolling linksland overlooking Arklow Bay, designed and owned by Pat Ruddy. Ranked No. 2 among Ireland's 100 greatest golf courses by Golf Digest (2006); 24th Greatest Golf Course of the 20th Century (Golfer's Companion Jan. 2000). 18 holes, 7323 yards. S.S.S. 73. Extensive practice areas. *Green Fees:* information not available. *Eating facilities:* full services. *Visitors:* welcome to all golfers, advisable to book. *Society Meetings:* welcome. Secretary: Sidon Ruddy (0404 47415; Fax: 0404 47449).* e-mail: info@theeuropeanclub.com

DELGANY. **Delgany Golf Club**, Delgany (01287 4536; Fax: 01287 3977). *Location:* half an hour from Dublin city centre just off the N11 to Wexford in Delgany village. Wooded parkland course with splendid hill and sea views. 18 holes, 5473 metres. S.S.S. 69. *Green Fees:* €45 midweek, €55 weekends. Subject to review. *Eating facilities:* restaurant and bar food. Mondays bar snacks only. *Visitors:* particularly welcome Mondays, Wednesdays, Thursdays and Fridays. Carts for hire, three motor buggies. Special packages with local hotels see website. *Society Meetings:* welcome. Professional: Gavin Kavanagh (01287 4697; Fax: 01287 3977). General Manager: Peter Ribeiro. e-mail: delganygolf@eircom.net website: www.delganygolfclub.com

DELGANY. **Glen of the Downs Golf Club**, Coolnaskeagh, Delgany (01287 6240; Fax: 01287 0063). *Location:* off the N11, 35 minutes from Dublin. Parkland course. 18 holes, 6443 yards. Practice area. *Green Fees:* information not available. *Eating facilities:* Pavilion with restaurant and bar. *Visitors:* welcome. Golf shop, locker rooms; clubs, buggies and caddy cars for hire. *Society Meetings:* welcome. e-mail:info@glenofthedowns.com website: www.glenofthedowns.com

DUNLAVIN. **Rathsallagh Golf Club**, Dunlavin (045 403316; Fax: 045 403295). *Location:* take M7 south from Naas, exit onto M9 southbound, turn left eight miles south of Kilcullen. Set on 270 acres of mature rolling parkland of which the golf course takes up 252 acres, surrounded by thousands of trees, water on five holes. 18 holes, 6920 yards. S.S.S. 72. Practice tees, putting green, driving range. *Green Fees:* midweek: €65, weekends €80. *Eating facilities:* full bar and restaurant. *Visitors:* welcome all week. Reservation essential, no handicap required. 29 bedrooms. Golf Academy. *Society Meetings:* welcome all week. Club Professional: Brendan McDaid (045 403316; Fax: 045 403295). Secretary: Joe O'Flynn (045 403316; Fax: 045 403295). e-mail: info@rathsallagh.com website: www.rathsallagh.com

ENNISKERRY. **Powerscourt Golf Club**, Powerscourt Estate, Enniskerry (2046033; Fax: 2761303). *Location:* 12 miles south of Dublin city centre just off N11, south of Bray adjacent to Enniskerry village. Two parkland courses (East designed by Peter McEvoy, West by David McLay Kidd) located in Powerscourt Estate with links characteristics, exceptional tiered greens, selection of 5 tee boxes on each course. Practice range,short game practice area. *Green Fees:* information not available. *Eating facilities:* restaurant and bar food available, full bar facilities. *Visitors:* welcome daily. Five studio apartments (sleeping two/three per apartment) available. Buggies, carts and caddies available. Conference facilities available. Professional: Paul Thompson. Manager: Bernard Gibbons.* website: www.powerscourt.ie

GREYSTONES. **Charlesland Golf Club,** Greystones. *Location*: 45 minutes south of Dublin just off the M50/N11. Charlesland boasts a magnificent location beside the sea, in the shadow of the Wicklow mountains. 18 hole parkland Championship Course 6169 metres. S.S.S. 72. Large practice area, putting green, public driving range available within 500 metres. *Green Fees*: April to October – weekdays €50, weekends €60. 2007 rates, subject to review. *Eating facilities*: restaurant and bar food available. Full bar facilities. *Visitors*: welcome daily. Please make prior booking. Neat dress essential. Buggies and handcarts for hire from our well-stocked Golf Shop. 12 en suite bedrooms; boardroom and conference facilities. For reservations phone 01-2878200; Fax: 01-2870078. *Society Meetings*: corporate, society and group rates available on request. For golf bookings phone (01-2874350; 01-2874360). Club Administrator: Rosaleen Horan.
e-mail: teetimes@charlesland.com
website: www.charlesland.com

GREYSTONES. **Greystones Golf Club,** Whitshed Road, Greystones (01-287 4136; Fax: 01-287 3749). Parkland course. 18 holes, 5322 metres, S.S.S. 69. Practice facilities. *Green Fees*: information not available. *Eating facilities*: full catering available. *Visitors*: welcome Monday, Tuesday, Friday and Sunday. *Society Meetings*: especially welcome, please contact the Secretary for details. Professional: Karl Holmes (01-287 5308). Secretary: Jim Melody (01-287 4136).*
e-mail: secretary@greystonesgc.com
website: www.greystonesgc.com

KILCOOLE. **Kilcoole Golf Club,** Kilcoole (01 2872066; Fax: 01 2010497). *Location:* two miles from Greystones off N11. Flat course one mile from sea. 9 holes, 5506 metres. S.S.S. 69. Practice area. *Green Fees:* information not available. *Eating facilities:* bar with meals available. *Visitors:* welcome, booking advisable. *Society Meetings:* welcome, special rate available. Secretary/Manager: Eddie Lonergan.*

NEWTOWNMOUNTKENNEDY. **Druids Glen Golf Club,** Newtownmountkennedy (00 353 1 287 3600; Fax: 00 353 1 287 3699). *Location:* 20 miles south of Dublin. Two great championship courses: Druids Glen and Druids Heath. 18 holes, par 71. New golf academy. *Green Fees*: information not available. *Eating facilities*: available. *Visitors:* welcome. Five-star Marriott hotel on site. Professional: George Henry. General Manager: Donal Flinn. Golf Director: John Kinsella.

NEWTOWNMOUNTKENNEDY. **Druids Heath Golf Club,** Newtownmountkennedy (00 353 1 281 2278; Fax: 00 353 1 281 2279). *Location:* 20 miles south of Dublin. Two great championship courses: Druids Glen and Druids Heath. 18 holes, par 71. New golf academy. *Green Fees*: information not available. *Eating facilities*: available. *Visitors:* welcome. Five-star Marriott hotel on site. Professional: George Henry. General Manager: Donal Flinn. Golf Director: Barry Dowling.*

NEWTOWNMOUNTKENNEDY. **Roundwood Golf Club,** Newtownmountkennedy (01 281 8488; Fax: 01 284 3642). Location: on the Glendalough/Roundwood road, in the heart of County Wicklow, just 35 minutes' drive from the ferry port at Dun Laoghaire. Parkland/heathland course with all-weather greens built to USGA standards. 18 holes, 6685 yards, Par 72. *Green Fees:* available on request. *Eating facilities:* five-star clubhouse catering for all requirements. *Visitors:* welcome. *Society Meetings:* welcome.
e-mail: rwood@indigo.ie
website: www.roundwoodgolf.com

Roundwood Golf Club

This links-like parkland course, built to the highest standards with sand-based USGA greens, has water and forestry coming into play on many holes. The 502 yards, Par five 15th is the feature hole and the lake-fronted green on the second hole would prove a challenge for any golfer. After the game, golfers can relax in the 5-star clubhouse which is set in beautiful surroundings with panoramic views of the course and the Wicklow Mountains.

DERRYBAWN HOUSE

The moment you set foot in the grounds of Derrybawn House, you know you are about to experience something special. With its long driveway, woodland backdrop and manicured lawns, this 96 acre private hideaway in the Wicklow mountains casts a spell of serene enchantment and soul-soothing tranquillity.

Beautiful, individually designed en suite bedrooms, all non-smoking and each unique in style and character.

Derrybawn offers guests a variety of dining experiences – from a formal dinner in the elegantly classic Dining Room to a simple home-cooked meal enjoyed in the large country kitchen. The beauty of this exclusive-use house is that guests can be left to their own devices, – or waited on hand and foot.

The perfect venue for successful and stimulating business events of all kinds, from conferences to executive weekends, motivation and teambuilding days, adventure and fun.

• Archery • Quad biking
• Fishing • Horse riding • Clay shooting.
• Hill walking and Orienteering.
• Golf clinics on a professionally designed green.
• Midweek golf packages, playing three of Ireland's top courses.
• Reflexology • Aromatherapy • Massage.

Truly individual weddings, created with the knowledge, creative flair and expertise of the staff at Derrybawn.

If you crave nature, harmony and effortless luxury, youl will find it at Derrybawn House.

Derrybawn House, Laragh, Co. Wicklow, Ireland
Tel: 00 353 404 450 73 • Fax: 00 353 404 450 77
e-mail: enquiries@derrybawnhouse.com
www.derrybawnhouse.co.uk

RATHDRUM. **Glenmalure Golf Club,** Greenan, Rathdrum (0404 46679). *Location:* two miles west of Rathdrum - signposted. Parkland, hilly course. 18 holes, 5500 yards. S.S.S. 66. *Green Fees:* information not available. *Eating facilities:* full facilities. *Visitors:* welcome, no restrictions. Self catering Scandinavian Lodges available. Buggies, carts available, caddy on notice. *Society Meetings:* welcome weekdays and Saturdays. Secretary: Kathleen Byrne (0404 46679).*

REDCROSS. **Millbrook Golf Course,** Redcross (0404 41647). *Location:* in Redcross village, two miles off N11, eight miles south of Wicklow town. Parkland, Par 3 course. 18 holes, 2009 yards. S.S.S 55. *Green Fees:* information not available. *Eating facilities:* full bar, restaurant, takeaway and wine bar. Clubs for hire. River Valley Caravan and Camping Park with mobile homes to let; many other facilities also available.*

WICKLOW. **Wicklow Golf Club,** Dunbur Road, Wicklow. *Location:* Wicklow Town, off N11. Parkland course by the seaside. 18 holes, 5695 metres. S.S.S. 70. *Green Fees:* information not available. *Eating facilities:* full facilities available. *Visitors:* welcome; some restrictions Wednesday and Thursday evenings and Sunday. Caddy cars. *Society Meetings:* welcome, prior arrangement with Secretary advisable. Information brochure sent on request. Professional: Darren McLoughlin (00 353 404 66122). Secretary: Joe Kelly (00353 404 67379; Fax: 00353 404 64756).* e-mail: info@wicklowgolfclub.ie website: www. wicklowgolfclub.ie

> **THE APPEARANCE OF AN ASTERISK (*) AT THE END OF A CLUB OR COURSE ENTRY INDICATES THAT UP-TO-DATE INFORMATION HAS NOT BEEN SUPPLIED**

Isle of Man

CASTLETOWN. **Castletown Golf Links,** Derbyhaven, Castletown IM9 1UA (01624 822220). *Location:* five minutes from Ronaldsway Airport and 20 minutes from Douglas. Championship links course voted in the Top 100 in the UK by 'Golf World' magazine. Host to the Duke of York Young Champions Trophy in 2003 and 2005. 18 holes, 6707 yards. S.S.S. 72. *Green Fees:* please refer to website. *Visitors:* most welcome but must be pre-booked. *Society Meetings:* welcome, must be pre-booked. Golf Director: Michael Brooks (01624 822220; Fax: 01624 829661).
website: www.golfiom.com

DOUGLAS. **Douglas Golf Club,** Pulrose Road, Douglas IM2 1AE (01624 675952). *Location:* one mile out of Douglas near Pulrose Power Station. Parkland - 17th hole tee off 200ft above green (214 yards). 18 holes, 5982 yards. S.S.S. 69. *Green Fees:* mid-week £12.50, weekends £15.00 adult, £5.90 junior. *Visitors:* welcome, but not before 10am Sundays. Dress code in bar, no jeans. *Society Meetings:* catered for by arrangement with Pro Shop (01624 661558). Manager/Professional: Mike Vipond. Secretary: Elaine Vincent (Tel & Fax: 01624 616865).

DOUGLAS. **Pulrose Golf Course,** Pulrose Park, Douglas IM2 1AE (01624 675952). *Location:* one mile from town centre. Undulating parkland with memorable 17th hole. 18 holes, 5922 yards. S.S.S. 68. Putting and practice area. *Green Fees:* information not available. *Eating facilities:* bar; snacks available at all times. *Visitors:* welcome, not before 10am on Sundays. Dress code in bar - no jeans. *Society Meetings:* by arrangement with Professional: Mike Vipond (01624 661558).*

ONCHAN. **King Edward Bay Golf Club,** Groudle Road, Howstrake, Onchan (01624 672709). *Location:* north headland of Douglas Bay. Stunning views from Headland links course. Watered greens, excellent fairways. 18 holes, 5450 yards. S.S.S. 67. Practice area. *Green Fees:* information not available. *Eating facilities:* full catering available (except Mondays), three bars. *Visitors:* welcome without reservation but not before 9.30am Sundays. *Society Meetings:* most welcome by arrangement. Special rates. Professional: Donald

Jones (01624 672709). Secretary: Cyril Kelly (01624 827726; Fax: 01624 827724).*

PEEL. **Peel Golf Club,** Rheast Lane, Peel IM5 1BG (01624 842227). *Location:* outskirts of Peel on main Douglas Road. Combination of links and heathland. 18 holes, 5850 yards. S.S.S. 69. Practice ground. *Green Fees:* weekdays £22.00, weekends £30.00. *Eating facilities:* full bar service and meals. *Visitors:* welcome, but check in advance for weekend availability. *Society Meetings:* catered for, check in advance. Pro Shop. Professional: Paul O'Reilly (01624 844232). Secretary/Manager: Neil Richmond (01624 843456).

PORT ERIN. **Rowany Golf Club,** Rowany Drive, Port Erin IM9 6LN (Tel & Fax: 01624 834072). *Location:* off the Promenade, five minutes from Port Erin. Hilly setting and meadowland. 18 holes, 5774 yards. S.S.S. 69. Practice ground. *Green Fees:* weekdays £22.00 per round, weekends £28.00 per round (under review). *Eating facilities:* restaurant and bar meals. *Visitors:* welcome by arrangement, few restrictions. Accommodation can be arranged. *Society Meetings:* welcome. Secretary: K. O'Loughlin. General Manager: C.A. Corrin (Tel & Fax: 01624 834072).

PORT ST MARY. **Port St Mary Golf Club,** Kallow Point Road, Port St Mary (01624 834932). *Location:* clearly signposted after entering Port St Mary. Seaside links with beautiful panoramic views. 9 holes, 2885 yards. S.S.S. 68. *Green Fees:* weekdays £15.00; weekends £17.00. Twilight or with member £9.00. 10% discount for Societies. *Eating facilities:* restaurant and bar open all day. *Visitors:* welcome at all times, only restrictions weekends between 8am to 10.30am. Handicap Certificate required. Secretary: T. M. Boyle (01624 837231; 07624 497387).

RAMSEY. **Ramsey Golf Club,** Brookfield, Ramsey (01624 812244; Fax: 01624 815833). *Location:* west boundary of Ramsey. Parkland. 18 holes, 5982 yards. S.S.S. 69. Practice area. *Green Fees:* information not available. *Eating facilities:* bar and restaurant. *Visitors:* welcome. *Society Meetings:* welcome weekdays only. Professional: Andrew Dyson (01624 814736).

SANTON. **Mount Murray Golf Club,** Mount Murray, Santon (01624 661111; Fax: 01624 661116). *Location:* three miles from Douglas on the Castletown road. Wooded parkland set on hills with panoramic views. 18 holes, 6361 yards. S.S.S. 71. 24-bay driving range, two-tier putting green. *Green*

Fees: information not available. *Eating facilities:* full hotel catering, bistro, dining room, two bars. *Visitors:* welcome at any time by arrangement with the Professional. 90 bedroomed four star hotel. *Society Meetings:* welcome at any time by arrangement with the Secretary. Professional: Andrew Dyson.*

Channel Islands

ALDERNEY. **Alderney Golf Club,** Route des Carrieres, Alderney (01481 822835; Fax: 01481 823609). *Location:* one mile east of St Annes. Seaside links with sea views from every hole. 9 holes, 2528 yards. S.S.S. 65. Putting green and practice range, *Green Fees:* available on request. *Eating facilities:* friendly lounge bar with bar meals all day. *Visitors:* welcome all year, tees reserved for competitions only. *Society Meetings:* welcome by arrangement. Hon. Secretary: L.N. Stewart.

GUERNSEY. **La Grande Mare Golf Club,** Vazon Bay, Castel, Guernsey GY5 7LL (01481 253544; Fax: 01481 255194). *Location:* on west coast main road. Parkland course. 18 holes, 5112 yards. S.S.S. 67. *Green Fees:* information not available. *Eating facilities:* full hotel facilities, restaurant, bar, leisure club. *Visitors:* welcome at most times by prior booking. La Grande Mare Hotel. Changing facilities and Pro Shop. Trolleys, clubs for hire. *Society Meetings:* welcome. Professional: Matt Groves (01481 253432; Fax: 01481 255194). Secretary: Mr Nick Graham (01481 253544; Fax: 01481 255194).*

GUERNSEY. **Royal Guernsey Golf Club,** L'Ancresse, Vale, Guernsey GY3 5BY (01481 247022). *Location:* three miles north of St Peter Port. Seaside links. 18 holes, 6215 yards. S.S.S. 70. Driving range. *Green Fees:* £45.00 per round or day, £30.00 with member. *Eating facilities:* restaurant and bar. *Visitors:* welcome except Thursday and Saturday afternoons and Sundays unless playing with a member. Must have Handicap Certificate. Professional: Chris Douglas (01481 245070). Secretary: Roy Bushby (01481 246523; Fax: 01481 243960).

GUERNSEY. **St Pierre Park Golf Club,** Rohais, St. Peter Port, Guernsey (01481 727039; Fax: 01481 712041). *Location:* 10 minutes' drive from town

centre. Wooded parkland with numerous lakes. 9 holes, 1323 yards, 1210 metres. S.S.S. 50. Driving range, putting green. *Green Fees:* information not available. *Eating facilities:* two restaurants and two bars. *Visitors:* welcome, all times bookable. Subject to rules and regulations on display. Hotel accommodation in 135 luxurious rooms and suites. Tennis. Pro Shop/ Club Manager: G. Roberts.

JERSEY. **Jersey Recreation Grounds,** Plat Douet Road, St Clement, Jersey (01534 721938). *Location:* inner coast road near St Helier. Flat course with some water hazards. 9 holes, 2149 yards. S.S.S. 30. Practice green and putting green. *Green Fees:* information not provided. Clubs available to hire. *Eating facilities:* licensed buffet. *Visitors:* welcome at all times. *Society Meetings:* welcome. Manager: H. Cooper.

JERSEY. **Les Mielles Golf and Country Club,** St Ouen's Bay, Jersey JE3 7FQ (01534 482787; Fax: 01534 485414). *Location:* centre of St Ouen's Bay. Set in an American styled seaside parkland course with "bent grass" greens and fairways of "dwarf rye". The 18 hole course plays 5758 yards, Par 70 gents, 5253 yards, Par 71 ladies. Other facilities include: 25 bay covered driving range, practice putting green, 75 yard short hole practice hole. *Green Fees:* information not available. *Eating facilities:* Rocco's on site 120- seater restaurant, Rocco's bar, BBQ and seasonal patio area. *Visitors:* always welcome, pre-booking necessary. Smart golfing attire required; no jeans. VAT Free Pro Shop, miniature golf, laser clay pigeon shooting, Segway Rally, hire equipment available - carts, buggies, clubs. *Society Meetings:* welcome, packages available. Professionals: Wayne Osmand, Lynne Cummins and Adam Jones (ATZ) (01534 483252). Administration, Enquiries & Corporate Bookings: please call (01534 485984).* e-mail: enquire@lesmielles.co.je website & online booking: www.lesmielles.com

JERSEY. **Les Ormes Golf & Leisure Club,** Mont à la Brune, St. Brelade JE3 8FL (01534 497000; Fax: 01534 499122). *Location:* on top of Mont à la Brune, adjacent to the airport. Attractive elevated course with beautiful coastal views. 9 hole course, 2509 yards, S.S.S. 65 white, 63 yellow. 17 bay covered driving range, practice bunkers and putting green. *Green Fees:* information not available. *Eating facilities;* restaurant and bar with terrace. *Visitors:* welcome, pre-booking advisable. Health and fitness complex, eight indoor tennis courts and LTA qualified coaches. Hair and Beauty salon on site. *Society Meetings:* welcome by arrangement. Professional: Andrew Chamberlain (01534 744464). General Manager: Mike Graham (01534 497002). Secretary: Frank Le Quesne (01534 853809).*

JERSEY. **La Moye Golf Club,** St Brelade, Jersey JE3 8GQ (01534 743401; Fax: 01534 747289). *Location*: on road to Corbiere Lighthouse at La Moye, St Brelade. Turn right at airport crossroads, right again at crossroads traffic lights. Seaside links championship course. 18 holes, 6664 yards. S.S.S. 72. Practice ground. *Green Fees*: weekdays £60.00; weekends £65.00. *Eating facilities*: full restaurant/ snack facilities, three bars. *Visitors*: weekdays 9.30 to 11am and 2 to 3.30pm, weekends 2.30pm onwards. Must have Handicap Certificate. *Society Meetings*: by prior appointment only. Professional: Mike Deeley (01534 743130; Fax: 01534 7499565). Secretary/Manager: Ian Prentice (01534 743401). Course Ranger's Office: (01534 747166).
e-mail: secretary@lamoyegolfclub.co.uk
website: www.lamoyegolfclub.co.uk

JERSEY. **Royal Jersey Golf Club,** Grouville, Jersey JE3 9BD (01534 854416; Fax: 01534 854684). *Location:* take coast road from St Helier, head towards Gorey. Seaside links course. 18 holes, 6100 yards. S.S.S. 70. *Green Fees:* information not available. *Eating facilities:* restaurant and bar. *Visitors:* welcome weekdays between 10am and 12 noon or 2pm to 4pm; weekends after 2.30pm. Handicap Certificate required. *Society Meetings:* welcome by prior arrangement. Professional: D Morgan (01534 852234; Fax: 01534 854684). Secretary: D.J. Attwood.

JERSEY. **Wheatlands Golf Course and Country Hotel,** Off Old Beaumont Hill, St Peter, Jersey JE3 7ED (01534 888844; Fax: 01534 69880). *Location:* Le Vieux Beaumont, which is road forking off to right by Cannon, and then first right at top of hill. Officially opened by Ryder Cup Captain Ian Woosnam in 1994, Jersey's only inland/parkland course; undulating setting with pond features and extensive countryside views. 9 holes (18 tees), 2767 yards, S.S.S. 54. Practice nets. *Green Fees:* information not available. *Eating facilities:* "Tenth Hole Bar", "Garden Terrace" - snacks and meals. *Visitors:* always welcome. Accommodation available in 20 en suite rooms. Hire equipment available - clubs, shoes, carts; VAT free shop. Professional tuition. *Society Meetings:* welcome. Professional: Terry Le Brocq.*
e-mail: info@wheatlandsjersey.com
website: www.wheatlandsjersey.com

Holiday Golf in France

Michael Gedye

PACKING YOUR GOLF CLUBS in the car for a short or extended break across the Channel is only continuing something that had its origins more than a century ago. Long before car ownership became the norm, the elite of European society used to patronise the northern French coast in the summer months, for the casinos, horse racing, luxury hotels and golf. They came by boat and train, gravitating to the milder south-west and Côte d'Azur in the Mediterranean south in the winter.

Although the sport (and the choice of places to play) has changed dramatically in recent decades, one of the charms of golfing in France is the fact that many of the early courses have stood the test of time and offer their subtle, historic charms alongside the wealth of new arrivals. More than any other country in the world outside of the British Isles, France can present a broad selection, from ancient seaside links to château-dominated parkland; from fairways amid snow-capped mountain splendour to modern, dramatically-designed challenges built with the very latest technology. More than 500 courses, spread fairly evenly throughout this large and varied landscape, offer a warm welcome to visitors, with moderate charges and inevitable Gallic flair.

Although the sport has started to make inroads as a domestic activity, most golf

Sweeping Fairway at Golf de Royan, Saint Palais-Sur-Mer

Mont Blanc towers over Golf de Chamonix, Rhone Alps

courses were built with the visitor (rather than club member) in mind. A good number lie near seaside resorts and providing you avoid the traditional French holiday month of August, provide uncluttered fairways, relaxed starting times and clubhouses that are often temples of gastronomy. The British may head for the bar; in France, serious consideration of the restaurant menu and extensive wine list may well take priority over one's scorecard. For example, at Golf du Médoc, in the middle of the Bordeaux vineyards, the yardage markers are outsize wine bottles, the club logo depicts golf balls clustered as a bunch of grapes and the thirty-six holes are sponsored by world-famous châteaux, all of which appear on the clubhouse wine list. At another club, with some holes alongside the sea, an annual event has eighteen local chefs preparing their specialities behind each green as an integral part of the competition. At yet another, a club stableford is immediately followed by a cooking competition between the same competitors, worth half the final result.

The French Golf Federation, in conjunction with the Tourist Board, promotes those tourist-friendly clubs which have good facilities and are multi-lingual. It is quite normal for many clubs to have regular competitions open to all holiday visitors, including locally-sponsored prizes and a lavish buffet, which may well include oysters, pâté and champagne. Playing the game the French way provides many refreshing surprises and a new perspective on the social as well as competitive aspects.

In recent years, holiday golf has become synonymous with a winter-season escape by plane to warmer climes much further south. A big advantage of playing in France is that the game can be enjoyed all year round and access can be in your own car, either by ferry or the Channel tunnel. Golfers can take a weekend break or follow an extended tour, not only of scenic courses but also of ancient châteaux, historic museums and art galleries, do a bit of wine tasting or search out tasty produce in local markets to bring back home.

There are more golf courses available to the holiday visitor in France, especially along or near the coast, than all the resort golf on offer throughout the rest of Europe combined. Whether you choose the convenient charms of the northern coast and familiar Brittany; swing beneath spectacular alpine vistas or through rural woodland; search out the treasure trove of golf laid out in south-western Aquitaine or

Historic setting at Golf du Château des Sept Tours

play beside fabled Mediterranean film locations – there is golf to suit all tastes and handicaps. Courses with a unique blend of old and new, historic and modern, demanding and relaxed – and all overlaid with quintessentially French charm.

We have divided France into seven regions. The **NORTH**, which covers the Channel coast, is steeped in history and memories of historic conflicts. The areas of Pas-de-Calais, Picardy and Normandy can boast the traditional delights of Le Touquet, Hardelot, Wimereux or Deauville alongside the modern examinations of Belle Dune and Champ de Bataille.

Historically linked with the West Country of England, are the regions of the **NORTH-WEST.**

Spectacular but demanding golf at Seignosse, Aquitaine

Four Seasons Resort, Provence, 11th hole, Le Château course

Traditionalists will enjoy the coastal golf of Brest Iroise and St Jean de Monts or, by contrast, inland you can discover wooded charm and parkland with aged châteaux at La Freslonièrre, Golf de la Bretesche and Golf International Barrière La Baule. Visiting Paris, the bright lights and shopping opportunities need not exclude golf. You can sample the gentle parkland of Golf des Yvelines or tackle the links-style challenge of Golf National, regular venue of the French Open.

The region of **WEST & CENTRE** follows the historic course of the River Loire. This is châteaux country, with golf on offer in Poitou Charentes, Limousin and Auvergne. For something special, test your game over Les Bordes, Château des Sept Tours and the plunging fairways of Royan near the sea. Further inland is the **EAST,** the large area comprising Champagne-Ardennes, Lorraine, Alsace, Burgundy, Franche Compte, French Alps and the Rhone Valley. Here you can discover courses in highly photogenic settings but also superb cuisine and wines to enjoy against a backdrop of crystal lakes and snow-capped peaks.

The best concentration of resort golf lies along the pinewoods of the **SOUTH-WEST.** Aquitaine, firmly fixed in British history, also boasts truffles, foie gras and arguably the finest red wines in the world around Bordeaux. Golfing tradition is well-represented in the famous fairways of Pau (celebrating 150 years in 2006), Biarritz, Chiberta, Chantaco, Hossegor and La Nivelle. In contrast, sample more modern layouts at the 36-holes of Golf du Médoc, Château des Vigiers, Pessac, Gujan Mestras and Moliets or, a little further south, the demanding challenges of Seignosse and Arcangues.

Upmarket glamour has been a byword for the Mediterranean holiday coastline of the **SOUTH.** It also offers an excellent selection of golf, both old and new. Discover Cap d'Agde, La Grande-Motte, Massane, Nîmes, Riviera, the craggy slopes of Fregate or the gentler parkland of Royal Mougins. Offshore, the clifftop layout by Robert Trent Jones, at Sperone in Corsica, is truly spectacular.

NORTH

BOULOGNE. **Golf de Wimereux,** Route d'Ambleteuse, 62930 Wimereux (03 21.32.43.20). *Location:* just off motorway A16 between Calais and Boulogne, North of Wimereux on the D940, seven km north of Boulogne. Venerable Scottish-style links course with broad fairways between sea and dunes. 18 holes, 6150 metres, Par 72. Two practice grounds, putting green, training bunker. *Green Fees:* information not available. *Eating facilities:* bar and restaurant (closed Mondays in low season). *Visitors:* welcome. Trolley and buggy hire. *Society Meetings:* welcome weekdays, special rates. Professional: Alexandre Devaux. Office: Nicolas Bouzin (03 21.32.43.20; Fax: 03 21.33.62.21).*
e-mail: golf.wimereux@wanadoo.fr

CAEN. **Golf de Caen,** Le Vallon, 14112 Bieville Beuville (02 31.94.72.09; Fax: 02 31.47.45.30). *Location:* follow road to Guistreham car ferries, first on your right to Château de Beauregard. A hilly course, wooded. 18 holes, 6155 metres, Par 72; 9 holes, 2950 metres, Par 36. Practice area, putting green. *Green Fees:* information not available. *Eating facilities:* available except Tuesdays. Pro shop. Professional: Christian Carle (02 31.95.17.70). Secretaries: Corinne/Elizabeth (02 31.94.72.09).*

DEAUVILLE. **Golf de Deauville,** Le Mont Saint-Jean, 14130 St Gatien (02 31.65.19.99; Fax: 02 31.65.11.24). 18 holes, 6171 metres, Par 72. 9 holes, 2969 metres, Par 36. Practice ground(60 places), putting and chipping green. *Green Fees:* from 31 to 58. *Eating facilities:* bar and restaurant in clubhouse; all facilities at the adjoining Golf Hotel. *Visitors:* welcome, Handicap Certificates required. Reservations 24 hours in advance. Pro shop; cart and trolley hire. Secretary: Pierre Peltier.
website: www.golfdeauville.com

GRANVILLE. **Golf de Granville - Baie du Mont Saint Michel,** Route de la Plage, 50290 Breville-sur-Mer (02 33.50.23.06; Fax: 02 33.61.91.87). *Location:* near Granville, towards Coutances and Cherbourg. Seaside links. 18 holes, 5834 metres, Par 71. 9 holes, 2186 metres, Par 33. Driving range, putting green. *Green Fees:* information not available. *Eating facilities:* bar and restaurant in clubhouse. Pro shop; trolley and club hire. *Visitors:* welcome, no restrictions. Special rates for groups over 10.*
e-mail: granville@best-channel-golfs.com
www.best-channel-golfs.com/granville/acces.htm

HARDELOT. **Golf d'Hardelot "Les Dunes",** 3 Avenue du Golf, 62152 Hardelot (03 21.91.90.90; Fax: 03 21.83.24.33). *Location:* at Hardelot Plage, 15km south of Boulogne. Gently sloping dunes with attractive pine trees. 18 holes, 6031 metres, Par 73. Golf academy, practice facilities. *Green Fees:* information not available. *Eating facilities:* available. *Visitors:* welcome. Handicap Certificate required. *Society Meetings:* welcome. Professionals: Louis Maisonnave/ David Amat (06.83.34.70.62/ 06.87.45.72.27). Secretary: B. Blempain (03 21.83.73.10; Fax: 03 21.83.24.33). Director of Golf: Ken Strachan.*
e-mail: hardelot@opengolfclub.com
website: www.opengolfclub.com

HARDELOT. **Golf d'Hardelot "Les Pins",** 3 Avenue du Golf, 62152 Hardelot (02 21.83.73.10; Fax: 03.21.83.24.33). *Location:* the beach-resort of Hardelot Plage is 15 km south of Boulogne. Attractive course carved through a pine forest. 18 holes, 5926 metres, Par 73. Practice ground, putting green. *Green Fees:* information not available. *Eating facilities:* clubhouse with bar and fine restaurant. Handicap Certificate required. Pro shop; club and trolley hire. Professionals: Louis Maisonnave/David Amat (03 21.91.89.80/ 06.87.45.72.27). Secretary: B. Blempain (03 21.83.73.10; Fax: 03 21.83.24.33). Director of Golf: Ken Strachan.*
e-mail: hardelot@opengolfclub.com
website: www.opengolfclub.com

LAON. **Golf de l'Ailette,** 02860 Cerny-en-Laonnois (03.23.24.83.99). *Location:* about 12km south of Laon, autoroute A26 exit Laon. An interesting course laid out on the edge of a forest flanked by large areas of water. 18 holes, 6127 metres, Par 72. 9 holes, 1753 metres, Par 32. Practice ground, pitch and putt, putting green. *Green Fees:* information not provided. *Eating facilities:* bar and restaurant. *Visitors:* welcome. Handicap required (maximum 35). *Society Meetings:* welcome, 20% to 30% discount for groups. Professional: Eric Censier. Secretaries: Miss Sylvie Dolat and Mrs Marie Christine Harant (03.23.24.83.99; Fax: 03.23.24.84.66).

LE TOUQUET. **Golf du Touquet,** Avenue du Golf - BP41, 62520 Le Touquet (03 21.06.28.00; Fax: 03 21.06.28.01). *Location:* 20km from Boulogne, on the coast, 3km from Le Touquet centre. La Forêt Course created in 1904 set in the heart of an old pine forest - 18 holes, 5827 metres, S.S.S. 71.0, Par 71. La Mer Course, designed by Harry S. Colt (1931), is a championship links course laid out amongst wild sand dunes - 18 holes, 6275 metres. S.S.S 74.9, Par 72. Le Manoir Course is perfect for beginners - 9 holes, 2817 metres, S.S.S. 35, Par 35. Practice range and putting green. *Green Fees:* midweek from €47 to €90, weekends from €59 to €115. *Eating facilities:* bar and restaurant in clubhouse. *Visitors:* welcome. Maximum Handicaps: La Forêt Course 35, La Mer Course 24 Gentlemen, 28 Ladies; no Handicap required for Le Manoir Course. *Society Meetings:* welcome. Pro Shop; carts, caddies. Accommodation available in Le Manoir Hotel (3 Star) facing La Forêt course. Professionals: Didier Behin, Daphné Lesur. Manager: Gilles Grattepanche.

LILLE. **Golf de Bondues,** Château de la Vigne, 59910 Bondues (03 20.23.20.62). *Location:* about 10km north of Lille, west of the N17. In the grounds of an 18th century chateau, the courses have well protected greens with deep bunkers and several water hazards. 18 holes, 6163 metres, Par 73. 18 holes, 6009 metres, Par 72. Driving range, putting green. *Green Fees:* €60 weekdays, €85 weekends . *Eating facilities:* bar and restaurant in clubhouse. *Visitors:* welcome. Closed Tuesdays. Trolley hire. Lessons available. Professional: (03 20.23.13.87). Secretary: (03 20.23.20.62; Fax: 03 20.23.24.11).
e-mail: contact@golfdebondues.com
website: www.golfdebondues.com

NEUBOURG. **Golf Club du Champ de Bataille,** 27110 Le Neubourg (02 32.35.03.72; Fax: 02 32.35.83.10). *Location:* south west of Rouen, about 28km north west of Evreux. A fine test of golf attractively laid out through the wooded estate of the elegant château. Par 3 holes. 18 holes, 6575 yards, 5983 metres, Par 72. Driving range, putting green. *Green Fees:* information not available. *Eating facilities:* bar and restaurant. *Visitors:* welcome, no restrictions. Pro shop; cart, trolley and club hire. Guest house, 800 metres. New clubhouse built on the edge of the wood, independent of the Château, offering a wide range of services. *Society Meetings:* welcome. Secretary: Sophie Prieux.
e-mail: info@champdebataille.com

NORMANDIE. **Golf d'Omaha Beach,** Ferme St. Sauveur, 14520 Port-en-Bessin (02 31.22.12.12; Fax: 02 31.22.12.13). *Location:* from Paris, A13 towards Caen. Don't go into the city, take the ring road towards Bayeux, follow signs to Port-en-Bessin. Hilly course; 9 holes on the sea, above the cliffs and beaches that witnessed the landing of the allied forces in June 1944. 18 holes, 6216 metres. S.S.S. 70; 9 holes, 2693 metres. S.S.S. 36. Driving range, practice area, pitch and putt course. *Green Fees:* information not available. *Eating facilities:* available at the clubhouse. *Visitors:* welcome. Professional: Julien Thomas. Manager: Nicolas Poillot. Secretary: Laure Tancoigne, Severine Aumont (02 31.22.12.12; Fax: 02 31.22.12.13).*

ROUEN. **Golf du Vaudreuil,** 27100 le Vaudreuil (02 32.59.02.60; Fax: 02.32.59.43.88). *Location:* 30km south-east of Rouen, east of the RN15 and the A13, 5 km from Louviers. A flat course, designed by Hawtree in 1961 in wooded parkland. 18 holes, Par 73. Driving range, buggies, trolleys, clubs. *Green Fees:* information not available. *Eating facilities:* beautiful clubhouse with bar and restaurant. On course Hotel du Golf (Two star) offers special Hotel and Golf packages (02.32.59.02.94; Fax: 02 32.59.67.39).*

SAINT-JULIEN-SUR-CALONNE. **Golf & Country Club de Saint-Julien,** B.P. 76, 14130 Pont l'Eveque, Saint-Julien-sur-Calonne (02.31.64.30.30; Fax: 02.31.64.12.43). *Location:* A13 leaving Pont l'Eveque, near Deauville (Normandy). Hilly 18 and 9 hole courses in the heart of the Pays d'Auge in Normandy. 18 hole course 6670 yards, 6065 metres, S.S.S. 72; 9 hole course 2500 yards, 2275 metres, S.S.S. 33. Driving range, putting green, bunker and approach green. *Green Fees:* information not provided. *Eating facilities:* Restaurant open from 12 noon to 4pm from April to September. Bar facilities available. *Visitors:* welcome every day. *Societies:* welcome every day, special rates for groups of more than ten. Driving range, buggies, carts, caddies, trolleys available. Professional: Alain Quibeuf (02.31.64.99.58; mobile: 06.07.01.64.27). Manager: J. M. Bonnet.

ST OMER. **Aa Saint-Omer Golf Club,** Chemin des Bois, Acquin-Westbécourt 62380 Lumbres (03.21.38.59.90; Fax: 03.21.93.02.47). *Location:* from Calais take A26 Autoroute, Junction 3 St Omer, right onto RN42 Expressway, first exit Acquin/Lumbres (30 minutes from Calais). Undulating parkland and mature trees overlooking the valley of the River Aa. La Haute Drève: 9 holes 2015 metres, Par 31; Le Val 18 holes 5979 metres, Par 73. Practice ground and putting green. *Green Fees:* information not available. *Eating facilities:* clubhouse bar and restaurant. *Visitors:* welcome all year, no restrictions. Golf and accommodation packages on request. Pro shop; trolley, buggy and club hire. Course selected by the European Tour. *Society Meetings:* welcome, special packages available. Professional: Sylvain Raout. Manager: Sandrine Grevet.*
e-mail: aa-st-omer.golf@najeti.com
website: www.aa-st-omer-golfclub.com

NORTH WEST

ANGERS. **Anjou Golf and Country Club,** Route de Cheffes, 49330 Champigne (02 41.42.01.01; Fax: 02 41.42.04.37). *Location:* about 20km north of Angers, from Paris A11, exit Durtal. Flat course with a few lakes and trees. 18 holes, 6227 metres, Par 72. Short 6 hole course, 750 metres, Par 19. Practice facilities. *Green Fees:* information not available. *Eating facilities:* "Le Prince Noir" traditional catering; "L'Auberge de Mozé" gastronomic catering. *Visitors:* welcome. Starting times must be booked in advance. Pro shop; cart, trolley and club hire; flats to rent at golf course. Professional/Director: Stephane Guguen. Secretaries: Christelle, Gaëlle, Valérie.*
e-mail: info@anjougolf.com

ANGERS. **Golf de Sablé-Solesmes,** Domaine de l'Outinière, Route de Pincé, 72300 Sablé-sur-Sarthe (02 43.95.28.78; Fax: 02 43.92.39.05). *Location:* east of the A11, exit 10 (Sablé La Flèche), about 40km north of Angers, south-east of Le Mans. Three totally different 9s - Forest and River: 18 holes, 6189 metres, Par 72; Waterfall: 9 holes, 3069 metres, Par 36, radiate from the large clubhouse. Testing and spectacular with park, woodland and lakeside holes. Driving range, putting green. *Green Fees:* information not available. *Eating facilities:* bar and restaurant in clubhouse. Pro shop; cart, trolley and club hire. Professional: Julien Desouches. Director: Yves Pironneau.

AURAY. **Golf de Baden,** Kernic, 56870 Baden (02 97.57.18.96; Fax: 02 97.57.22.05). *Location:* between the village of Baden and the sea, south of the RN 165 at Auray exit. Undulating course partly through pine woods and around lakes. 18 holes, 6112 metres, Par 72. 3 hole, 535 metres pitch and putt course. Practice area, putting green, approach green. *Green Fees:* information not available. *Eating facilities:* bar and restaurant. Pro shop; trolley and club hire; club repair. Neighbouring hotels "Le Gavrinis" and "du Loch" offer year-round golfing breaks. *Society Meetings:* welcome, special rates. Professional: J. F. Le Gall. Secretaries: Mme. Le Quilliec, Mme. Burguin. Director: Mr O. Charmont.*

AURAY. Golf de Saint Laurent, 56400 Ploemel, Auray (02 97.56.85.18; Fax: 02 97.56.89.99). *Location:* about 10 km west of Auray and not far from Carnac with its ancient standing stones. High quality championship course, undulating through mature trees. 18 holes, 6112 metres, Par 72. 9 hole course, 2705 metres, Par 35. Driving range. *Green Fees:* information not available. *Eating facilities:* bar and restaurant in on-course Fairway Hotel St Laurent; also on-course "Maeva" self-catering cottages available. *Visitors:* welcome. Pro shop; cart, trolley and club hire. Professionals: Mr D. Jouan and Mr A. Brien.*

BENODET. Golf de l'Odet,Benodet Menez Groas, Clohars-Fouesnant, 29950 Benodet (02.98.54.87.88; Fax: 02.98.54.61.40). *Location:* 12km south of Quimper, towards the sea at Benodet. An undulating partly wooded course. 18 holes, 6235 metres, Par 72. 9 holes, 1100 metres, Par 27. Driving range, putting green, pitching green, short game area. *Green Fees:* information not available. *Eating facilities:* bar, restaurant and on-site Hotel Eurogreen, whose residents have reduced green fees. *Visitors:* welcome, no restrictions but advisable to book tee times. Other accommodation nearby. Pro shop; cart, trolley and club hire. Professional: C. Olivard. Secretary: Christophe Bodere (02.98.54.87.88; Fax: 02.98.52.61.40).*

BREST. Golf de Brest Iroise, Parc de Loisirs de Lann Rohou, 29800 Landerneau (02 98.85.16.17; Fax: 02 98.85.19.39). *Location:* 10 miles east of Brest, three miles south of Landerneau. A tough course, open to the breeze in a beautiful natural setting. 18 holes, 5672 metres, Par 71. 9 holes, 3329 metres, Par 37. 22 bay driving range, 2 putting greens. *Green Fees:* information not available. *Eating facilities:* bar and restaurant and all facilities at the Golf Hotel d'Iroise. *Visitors:* welcome. Pro shop; cart, trolley and club hire. Golf/Hotel packages. *Society Meetings:* welcome. Professional: Philippe Le Verche. Secretary: Guylene (02 98 85 16 17).*

LA BAULE. Golf de la Bretesche, 44780 Missillac (02 51.76.86.86; Fax: 02 40.88.36.28). *Location:* 20km north-east of La Baule; 50km north of Nantes on the N167. In a wooded and magnificent forest (2600 acres), large fairways and superb greens cover an area of 480 acres and borders the picturesque Chateau de la Bretesche surrounded by a vast lake. 18 holes, 6700 yards, S.S.S. 72. Practice ground, putting green, training bunker. *Green Fees:* information not available. *Eating facilities:* two bars and two restaurants. *Visitors:* welcome. Pro shop, cart, club and trolley hire. *Society Meetings:* welcome. Professional: Thierry Mathon. Manager: Fabrice Gicquiand. Secretary: Stephane Harouard/Francoise Desmarches (02 51.76.86.86; Fax: 02 40.88.36.28).*

LA BAULE. Golf International Barrière La Baule, 44117 St-André-des-Eaux (02.40.60.46.18; Fax: 02.40.60.41.41). *Location:* to the east of La Baule, 3 km from St André des Eaux. Three parkland courses with interesting water features. Red Course: 18 holes, 6055 metres, Par 72. Green Course: 9 hole course, 2961 metres, Par 36. Blue Course 18 hole, 6301 metres, Par 72. Golf Academy: designed by Jack Nicklaus Company. *Green Fees:* information not available. *Eating Facilities:* bar and restaurant. *Visitors:* welcome by reservation booked the day before. Pro shop; cart (GPS), club and trolley hire; target and putting green, approach zone, training bunker and coaching studio. *Society Meetings:* welcome by arrangement.
e-mail:golfinterlabaule@lucienbarriere.com
website: www.lucienbarriere.com

LA ROCHE-SUR-YON. Golf Club de la Domangère, Route de la Rochelle, 85310 Nesmy (02 51.07.65.90; Fax: 02 51.07.65.95). *Location:* approximately 10km south of La Roche-sur-Yon west of the D747. A long and majestic course with plenty of strategic water, mature trees and bordered by the River Yon. 18 holes, 6480 metres, Par 72. 4 hole practice course, driving range, putting green. *Green Fees:* information not available. *Eating facilities:* bar, grill-room. *Visitors:* welcome. Club, cart and trolley hire. Hotel apartments. *Society Meetings:* welcome, booking required. Professional: Mr A. Stephane.*

LORIENT. Golf du Val Quéven, Kerrousseau RD 6, 56530 Quéven (02 97.05.17.96; Fax: 02 97.05.19.18). *Location:* nearest main road RN165, Quéven situated between Lorient and Pont Scorff. Offering an impressive and diversified landscape built around 100 year old trees, the course is very challenging and is one of the best in western France. 18 holes, 6140 metres, Par 72. Driving range, putting green. *Green Fees:* information not available. *Eating facilities:* bar and restaurant. Visitors: welcome. Pro shop; club and trolley hire. *Society Meetings:* welcome. Professional: Mario Zimmermann (02 97.05.17.96; Fax: 02 97.05.19.18). Secretaries: Anita Le Bousseau and M. Frédéric Dellsperger (02 97.05.17.96; Fax: 02 97.05.19.18). Director: Jean Luc Leroux.*

LORIENT. Parcours Formule Golf Ploemeur Ocean, Saint Jude-Kerham, 56270 Ploemeur (02 97.32.81.82; Fax: 02 97.32.80.90). *Location:* RN165 exit Ploemeur, towards Fort Bloque. Seaside links course, huge American style greens, water hazards. 18 holes, 6517 yards, 5957 metres, S.S.S. 72. Covered driving range. *Green Fees:* information not available. *Eating facilities:* bar and restaurant. *Visitors:* welcome. Hotels in immediate surroundings. *Society Meetings:* managed by the Parcours Formule Golf. Professional: Laurent Queffelec. Manager: Jeau Luc Leroux.*

RENNES. Golf de la Freslonnière, 35650 Le Rheu (02 99.14.84.09; Fax: 02 99.14.94.98). *Location:* three km from Rennes towards Lorient. Woodland course with water features and banks of rhododendrons. 18 holes, 5756 metres, Par 72. Practice ground and putting green. *Green Fees:* €39/€52. *Eating facilities:* clubhouse, restaurant and bar (closed Mondays). *Visitors:* welcome, no restrictions. Pro shop; club, cart and trolley hire. Professional: Richard Triaire, Jean-Marie Carret. Director: Romain Hullard.
e-mail: lafreslo@wanadoo.fr
website: www.golfdelafreslonniere.com

RENNES. **Golf de Rennes**, St. Jacques de la Lande, 35136 Rennes (02 99.30.18.18. Fax: 02 99.30.10.25). *Location:* eight km south of Rennes, off the D177 to Redon. Brittany's largest golf course is a championship course, with fast, high quality greens. The narrow fairways have players of all levels thinking carefully about their tactics. This complex has something for everyone. 18 holes, 6713 yards, Par 72. 9 holes, 2262 yards, Par 32. 9 hole pitch and putt course. *Green Fees:* information not available. *Eating facilities:* bar and restaurant in clubhouse. *Visitors:* welcome, no restrictions. Pro shop; buggies; trolley and club hire. Director: Gregory Dudouit.*
e-mail: golf.rennes@formule-golf.com
website: www.formule-golf.com

ST MALO. **Saint Malo Golf Club**, Le Tronchet, 35540 Miniac Morvan (02 99.58.96.69). *Location:* 23km south of St Malo, 12km east of Dinan, south of the N176. The 27 hole golf course is set alongside the lake of Mirloup and the forest of Mesnil and harks back to the days of Robert Surcouf's hunting lands. With a slope of 133, the strategic use of water will really test the good golfers but the rough is cut short to promote faster play and accessibility to all players. 18 holes, 5936 metres, Par 72. 9 holes, 2684 metres, Par 35. Driving range and practice facilities. *Green Fees:* approx between €35 to €55. *Eating facilities:* bar and restaurant on site. *Visitors:* welcome. Charming 3 star hotel on site with 29 spacious air conditioned rooms (approx 30m²) and L'Etang restaurant for evening meal. Ask for packages. Pro shop; trolley, club car and club hire. *Society Meetings:* welcome, bookings required. Professional: Eric Chaperon. General Manager: Philip Petersson.
website: www.saintmalogolf.com

ST JEAN-DE-MONTS. **Golf Club de St Jean-de-Monts**, Avenue des Pays de la Loire, 85160 St. Jean-de-Monts (02 51.58.82.73; Fax: 02 51.59.18.32). *Location:* a partly links-style course along the seaside with pine trees and dunes. On the Atlantic coast some 60/70km south-west of Nantes. 18 holes, 5962 metres, Par 72. Short 5 hole course. Practice ground and putting greens. *Green Fees:* information not available. *Eating facilities:* clubhouse with bar and restaurant. The Hotel de la Plage in nearby Notre Dame de Monts offers golfing breaks. Pro shop; cart, club and trolley hire.*

PARIS

PARIS. **Golf de Forges-les-Bains,** Rue de General Leclerc, 91470 Forges-les-Bains (01 64.91.48.18; Fax: 01 64.91.40.52). *Location:* A10 Orleans, exit Les Ulis then towards Limours and Forges-les-Bains; 35 minutes from Paris. Parkland course with a lot of variety and suitable for all levels of golfers. 18 holes, 6207 metres, Par 72. Driving range, three holes training course. *Green Fees:* weekdays €35, weekends €52 (2007 prices). *Eating facilities:* bar and restaurant in clubhouse. *Visitors:* welcome, no restrictions but reservations preferred. Special rates for groups and societies. David Leadbetter Golf Academy on site. Pro shop; trolley and club hire. Professionals: Yan Massonat, Pedro Chaparreiro. Secretary: Philippe Wibaux.
website: www.golf-forgeslesbains.com

PARIS. **Golf de la Vaucouleurs,** 78910 Civry-la-Forêt (01.34.87.16.04). *Location:* off the A13 at the Mantes interchange, south off the road to Houdan. Two 18 hole courses. "The River" - very varied with trees, water and hills, 6138 metres, Par 73; "The Little Valley" - a links-type course, 5553 metres, Par 70. Practice ground, putting green. *Green Fees:* information not available. *Eating facilities:* bar and restaurant in clubhouse; also at nearby Hotel la Dousseine at Anet. Pro shop; club and trolley hire, buggy available. Professional: Pierre Girard. Secretary: (01.34.87.62.29; Fax: 01 34.87.70.09).*

PARIS. **Golf de St Quentin-en-Yvelines,** RD 912, 78197 Trappes (01.30.50.86.40; Fax: 01.34.82.88.82). *Location:* about 20km west of Paris off the D912. A very popular public facility of 36 holes. White Course - 18 holes, 6100 metres, S.S.S. 72; Red Course - 18 holes, 5700 metres, S.S.S. 69. Also 9 hole compact course, driving range, putting green. *Green Fees:* information not available. *Eating facilities:* bar and restaurant in clubhouse. Pro shop; trolley and club hire. Professional: Jean Marc Lecuona. Secretary: Jerome Lauredi.*

PARIS. **Golf des Yvelines,** Château de la Couharde, 78940 La Queue-les-Yvelines (01 34.86.48.89; Fax: 01 34.86.50.31). *Location:* about 45km west of Paris by N12, near Montfort-l'Amaury. Built around the elegant château, with fairways cut through thick woods. 18 holes, 6344 metres, S.S.S. 72. 9 holes, 2065 metres, S.S.S. 31. Practice ground, putting green. *Green Fees:* information not available. *Eating facilities:* bar and restaurant. *Visitors:* all visitors welcome. Club and trolley hire. Professional: Jean Paul Chardonnet. Secretary: Stephane Bessette.*

PARIS. **Golf National,** 2 Avenue du Golf, 78280 Guyancourt (01 30.43.36.00; Fax: 01 30.43.85.58). *Location:* about 25km south-west of Paris off the A13/A12, six miles from Versailles. A public facility of 45 holes laid out in three courses. "The Albatross" (now the venue for the French Open) - 18 holes, 6500 metres championship course with severe water hazards and winding fairways, Par 72; "The Eagle" - 18 holes, 6000 metres, Par 72 for experienced players; "The Birdie" - 9 holes, 2100 metres beginners' course, Par 32 and driving range; "The Par" - a warm-up, practice course. Putting greens. *Green Fees:* information not available. *Eating facilities:* on-site Hotel Novotel. Two restaurants. *Visitors:* all welcome, public course. Club and trolley hire.*

THE APPEARANCE OF AN ASTERISK (*) AT THE END OF A CLUB OR COURSE ENTRY INDICATES THAT UP-TO-DATE INFORMATION HAS NOT BEEN SUPPLIED

WEST & CENTRE

CHEVERNY. **Golf du Château de Cheverny,** La Roussellère, 41700 Cheverny (33 (0) 2.54.79.24.70; Fax: 33 (0) 2.54.79.25.52). *Location:* to the south of Cheverny 15km south of Blois. Built over the former hunting grounds of the Château with large well-kept greens. 18 holes, 6272 metres, Par 71. 3 hole practice course, driving range, putting green. *Green Fees:* information not available. *Eating facilities:* bar and restaurant in clubhouse. *Visitors:* welcome. Pro shop; club and trolley hire, electric carts. Swimming pool by the bar. *Society Meetings:* 20% reduction on fees. Sister Club: Rolls Of Monmouth (Wales). Professional: Pierre Raguet.*
e-mail: contact@golf-cheverny.com
website: www.golf-cheverny.oom

COGNAC. **Golf du Cognac,** Saint-Brice, 16100 Cognac (05 45.32.18.17; Fax: 05 45.35.10.76). *Location:* five km east of Cognac, north of the N141 across the River Charente. Undulating fairways with views of vineyards and the river; some water hazards. 18 holes, 6142 metres, Par 72. 4 hole practice course, putting green and driving range. *Green Fees:* information not available. *Eating facilities:* clubhouse with restaurant and bar. Pro shop; cart, club and trolley hire. Professional: (05 45.32.37.60). Secretary: (05 45.32.18.17).*

LOUDUN. **Golf de Loudun-Roiffe,** Domaine St Hllaire, 86120 Roiffe (05 49.98.78.06; Fax: 05 49.98.72.57). *Location*: 15km north of Loudun towards Saumur on the D147. An attractive woodland course with a few water hazards and well guarded greens. 18 holes, 6343 metres, S.S.S. 73, Par 72. 6 hole pitch and putt course, driving range, practice green and putting green. *Green Fees*: information not available. *Eating facilities*: restaurant; bar in clubhouse. *Visitors*: welcome, no restrictions. Two-star hotel wlth 64 rooms and 13 self-catering apartments, seminar rooms, entertainment room. Tennis, bicycles for hire, crazy-golf, swimming pool, playground for children, marked trails. Pro shop, trolley and club hire. *Society Meetings*: welcome. Professional: Jean-Marc Warot.*
e-mail: golf-france@interpc.fr
website: www.france-in.com

ORLEANS. **"Les Bordes" Golf International,** 41220 St-Laurent des Eaux (02 54.87.72.13; Fax: 02 54.87.78.61). *Location:* from Paris motorway A10 exit Meung sur Loire. Laid out on a former hunting park. 18 holes, 7041 yards, 6412 metres, Par 72. Driving range, putting green. *Green Fees:* from €50 to €150, special rates for hotel residents . *Eating facilities:* bar and restaurant in clubhouse. *Visitors:* welcome every day. Pro shop; carts, trolleys and clubs for hire. Accommodation on site.

POITIERS. **Golf du Haut-Poitou,** Parc de Loisirs de St Cyr, 86130 Saint Cyr (05 49.62.53.62; Fax: 05 49.88.77.14). *Location:* 20km north of Poitiers and 15km south of Chatellerault. Undulating course with wooded hills, a lake and water hazards. Host of a Professional International Open at the end of October in 2005. 18 holes, 6590 metres, S.S.S. 75. 9 holes, 1800 metres, Par 31. Practice ground, driving range, putting and pitching greens. *Green Fees:* information not available. *Eating facilities:* clubhouse with brasserie and bar; Restaurant (05 49.61.53.56) *Visitors:* welcome without restriction. Pro shop and equipment hire. *Society Meetings:* welcome. Professionals: Martin Guilbaud and David Maxwell. Secretaries: Catherine Marchais and Jessica Guillon (05 49.62.53.62; Fax: 05 49.88.77.14).*
e-mail: contact@golfduhautpoitou.com

ROYAN. **Golf de Royan,** Maine-Gaudin, 17420 St-Palais-sur-Mer (05 46.23.16.24; Fax: 05 46.23.23.38). *Location:* on the D25 coast road, nine km north-west of Royan. An exciting course with narrow fairways undulating through tall pines. Two courses. 18 holes, 5924 metres, S.S.S. 71; 6 hole, 920 metres, S.S.S. 20. Practice ground with driving range, putting green. *Green Fees:* information not available. *Eating facilities:* restaurant and bar in clubhouse. *Visitors:* welcome. Pro shop with equipment hire. *Society Meetings:* welcome by arrangement with the Secretary. Professionals: Gilles Delavallade and Christine Wenandy. Secretaries: Nathalie, Christelle and Valérie (05 46.23.16.24; Fax: 05 46.23.23.38).*
e-mail: golfderoyan@wanadoo.fr
website: www.golfderoyan.com

TOURS. **Blue Green Golf d'Ardrée,** Golf d'Ardrée Tours, 37360 Saint Antoine du Rocher (02 47.56.77.38; Fax: 02 47.56.79.96). *Location:* near Tours north, direction of Le Mans, nearest town St Antoine Du Rocher. Parkland course, wooded with water and bunkers. 18 holes, 5758 metres, Par 70. Practice ground and putting green. *Green Fees:* information not available. *Eating facilities:* restaurant and bar in clubhouse. *Visitors:* welcome but it would be better to reserve the tee two or three days in advance for weekdays, and five days in advance for weekends. *Society Meetings:* welcome but reservatlon a month ln advance please. Professional: Karl Cotteray. Secretaries: Virginie and Corinne.*

TOURS. **Golf du Château des Sept Tours,** 37330 Courcelles de Touraine (02.47.24.69.75; Fax: 02.47.24.23.74). *Location:* 30kms from Tours on the D34 between Château la Vallière and Langeais. A fairly long course but relatively flat with attractive trees and water, excellent greens. 18 holes, 6194 metres, Par 72. Practice ground and putting green. *Green Fees:* information not available. *Eating facilities:* restaurant and bistro in clubhouse. *Visitors:* 4 star Hotel, restaurant and golf club open all year. Pro shop; club and trolley hire. Professional: Pascal Petit.*

EAST

AIX-LES-BAINS. **Golf d'Aix-les-Bains,** Avenue du Golf, 73100 Aix-les-Bains (04 79.61.23.35). *Location:* three km south of Aix by the Lac du Bourget. An attractive parkland course on sloping land surrounded by wooded hills. 18 holes, 5519 metres. S.S.S. 70. Practice, putting green. *Green Fees:* from   45- 62. *Eating facilities:* restaurant (04.79.61.47.20). *Visitors:* welcome. Pro shop; trolley and club hire (04.79.61.31.56). *Professional:* (04 79.35.39.41). Secretary: (Fax: 04 79.34.06.01). e-mail: info@golf-aixlesbains.com
website: www.golf-aixlesbains.com

CHAMONIX. **Golf de Chamonix,** 35 route du Golf, Les Praz, 74400 Chamonix (04 50.53.06.28; Fax: 04 50.53.38.69). *Location:* on the N506 three km north of Chamonix. A subtle and technical course, enhanced by water obstacles and numerous bunkers. Spectacular mountain views including Mont Blanc. 18 holes, 6076 metres, S.S.S. 72. Driving range, putting green. *Green Fees:* information not provided. *Eating facilities:* restaurant. *Visitors:* welcome every day with a Handicap Certificate, tee off times must be booked one day in advance. Pro shop; cart, trolley and club hire. Professional: Jean Claude Bonnaz. Director: Christophe de Carné (04 50.53.06.28; Fax: 04 50.53.38.69).

EVIAN. **Evian Masters Golf Club,** South Bank of Lake Geneva, 74500 Evian-les-Bains (33-(0)4.50.26.85.00; Fax: 33-(0)4.50.75.65.54). *Location:* on high ground above Evian. 8kms from Thonon, 45kms west of Geneva. Hilly fairways overlooking Lake Geneva, sloping greens guarded by deep bunkers. Evian Masters course. 18 holes, 6674 yards, 6006 metres, Par 72. Covered and uncovered practice range, two putting greens, chipping green, pitching green, training bunkers, pitch and putt. *Green Fees:* information not available. *Eating facilities:* restaurant and bar: Le Chalet du Golf. *Visitors:* welcome, Handicap 35 or course authorization. Pro shop; clubs, bags and carts. *Society Meetings:* welcome (up to 180 people). Professional: Christophe Martigniere (courses). Co-Director: Margo Perrolaz. Director: Yannic Le Hec.*

GRENOBLE. **Golf International de Grenoble,** Route de Montavie, Bresson, 38320 Eybens (04 76.73.65.00; Fax: 04 76.73.65.51). *Location:* five km south of Grenoble. A long course with winding fairways, small lakes, trees - architect Robert Trent Jones Jnr. Bresson Course 18 holes, 6343 metres, Par 73; Uriage Course 9 holes, 2005 metres. Practice ground and putting green; driving range. *Green Fees:* information not available. *Eating facilities:* clubhouse and nearby hotel. *Visitors:* welcome at all times. Professional: Loic Landoas. Manager: Herve Segrais.*

LYON. **Golf Club de Lyon,** 38280 Villette d'Anthon (04 78.31.11.33; Fax: 04 72.02.48.27). *Location:* Lyon, Rocade Est exit Meyzieu Grand Large. Brocards - flat, wooded, various sandtraps. Hawtree design(1964), parkland course; Sangliers - typical target golf, various water hazards. Hosted the French Open in 2001. Brocards 18 holes, 6229 metres. Par 72; Sangliers 18 holes, 6727 metres. Par 72. Practice ground, putting green, training centre. *Green Fees:* €45 to €70. *Eating facilities:* bar and restaurant in clubhouse. *Visitors:* welcome anytime. No jeans, no powered trolleys. *Society Meetings:* welcome. Pro shop; equipment hire. Professionals: Raphael Reynaud and Hubert Sauzet (04.78.31.11.33; Fax: 04.72.02.48.27). Secretary: (04.78.31.11.33; Fax: 04 72.02.48.27).
e-mail: gcl2@wanadoo.fr
website: www.golfclubdelyon.com

ST JULIEN (Geneva). **Golf and Country Club de Bossey,** Chateau de Crevin, Bossey, 74160 St-Julien-en-Genevois. *Location:* just near the main road between St. Julien en Genevois and Annemasse about five miles from each of these towns. Just in France on the southern outskirts of Geneva. Challenging mountain golf with fine views. Well wooded with water hazards. 18 holes, 5952 metres, Par 71. Driving range, putting green. *Green Fees:* information not available. *Eating facilities:* bar and restaurant in chateau clubhouse. *Visitors:* welcome weekdays only, maximum of three times a year. Maximum handicap 35. No jeans allowed on course. Contact General Manager for details. Pro shop; cart, trolley and club hire. *Society Meetings:* catered for, contact General Manager. Professional: Mark Cobley (04.50.43.65.66). Secretary: (04.50.43.95.50; Fax: 04.50.95.32.57).*

SOUTH WEST

ALBI. **Golf d'Albi Lasbordes,** Chateau de Las Bordes, 81000 Albi (05.63.54.98.07; Fax: 05.63.47.21.55). *Location:* three minutes from town centre, overlooking the River Tarn and offering beautiful views towards the cathedral. A championship course with trees. 18 holes, 6155 metres, Par 72. *Green Fees:* information not available. *Eating facilities:* bar and restaurant in clubhouse. *Visitors:* welcome all year. Club and trolley hire. Professional: Olivier Doan.*

ANGLET. **Golf de Chiberta,** 104 Boulevard des Plages, 64600 Anglet (05 59.52.51.10; Fax: 05 59.63.30.56). *Location:* three km from Biarritz and from Bayonne. A well-established combination of seashore and wooded parkland. 18 holes, 5650 metres, Par 71. Driving range, putting green. *Green Fees:* information not available. *Eating facilities:* bar and restaurant in clubhouse. *Visitors:* welcome, Handicap Certificate required. Pro shop; trolley and club hire. Professional: H. Brouson, P Dufourg, C. Lecuona. Secretary: (05 59.52.51.10; Fax: 05 59.63.30.56).*

ARCACHON. **Golf de Gujan Mestras,** BP 74, Route de Sanguinet, 33470 Gujan Mestras (05 57.52.73.73; Fax: 05 56.66.10.93). *Location:* autoroute Bordeaux/Bayonne, A66 in the direction of Arcachon. A spectacular course with well located water obstacles. 18 holes, 6225 metres, Par 72. 9 holes, 2630 metres, Par 35. Practice facilities and putting green. *Green Fees:* information not available. *Eating facilities:* restaurant, clubhouse and at nearby hotel. Pro shop; equipment and trolley hire.*

BAYONNE. **Golf de Moliets,** Rue Mathieu Desbieys, 40660 Moliets (05 58.48.54.65; Fax: 05 58.48.54.88). *Location:* about 30km north of Bayonne on the Atlantic coast at Moliets. Part of a leisure seaside complex with links and wooded inland holes. 18 holes, 6164 metres, Par 72. 9 holes, 1905 metres, Par 31. Practice ground, putting green. *Green Fees:* €50 low season, €63 high season. *Eating facilities:* bar and restaurant in clubhouse and in on-site hotels. *Visitors:* welcome. Pro shop; cart, club and trolley hire; tennis. *Society Meetings:* welcome. Professionals: Franck Ducousso, Christophe Berthet. website: www.golfmoliets.com

BAYONNE. **Seignosse Golf Hotel,** Avenue du Belvedere, 40510 Seignosse (05 58.41.68.30; Fax: 05 58.41.68.31). *Location:* about 25km north of Bayonne on the D79 north of Hossegor. Very hilly, exciting and undulating course, a pleasure to look at as well as play. Ranked 21st in the top 100 European courses by 'Golf World International'. 18 holes, 6124 metres, Par 72. Practice ground. *Green Fees:* information not available. *Eating facilities:* two bars and two restaurants. *Visitors:* welcome. 3 Star Hotel. Pro shop; cart, club and trolley hire; swimming pool. *Society Meetings:* welcome. Special golf/hotel packages available 'Golf Pass Biarritz' member. Professional: F. Martin. Director: Armand Gadea. Sales Manager: Sidonie Blanc (05 58.41.68.30).* e-mail: golfseignosse@wanadoo.fr website: www.golfseignosse.com

BIARRITZ. **Golf d'Arcangues,** 64200 Arcangues (05 59.43.10.56; Fax: 05 59.43.12.60). *Location:* three km south-east of Biarritz. A fine rolling test in modern and natural style. Mounded bunkers and strategic water. 18 holes, 6142 metres, Par 72. *Green Fees:* information not available. *Eating facilities:* bar and restaurant in clubhouse. *Visitors:* welcome, no restrictions. Pro shop and equipment hire. Professional: O. Leglise. Secretary: English/French Mme Sylvie Cormier; French Mme Marie-José Dabbadie.* e-mail: golf.arcangues@wanadoo.fr

BIARRITZ. **Golf de Biarritz Le Phare,** 2 Avenue Edith Cavell, 64200 Biarritz (05 59.03.71.80). *Location:* in Biarritz, facing the ocean with cooling breezes. A historic course (1888) with fast greens, level, many bunkers. 18 holes, 5379 metres, S.S.S. 69. Practice ground, putting green. *Green Fees:* information not available. *Eating facilities:* bar and restaurant in clubhouse, the nearby Hôtel du Palais and other hotels. Pro shop; club and trolley hire. Secretary: (05 59.03.71.80; Fax: 05 59.03.26.74).* e-mail: info@golfbiarritz.com

BORDEAUX. **Golf de Bordeaux Cameyrac,** R.N. 89 Bordeaux Libourne No. 5, 33450 Cameyrac (05 56.72.96.79; Fax: 05 56.72.86.56). *Location:* 15km from Bordeaux close to the famous vineyards of St Emilion and Pomerol. Fairways run through forest, alongside ponds and vineyards. 18 holes, 5972 metres, Par 72. 9 holes, 1188 metres, Par 28. Practice ground, putting green. *Green Fees:* under review for 2008. Special fees for couples and students, Green fee packages on demand. *Eating facilities:* bar and restaurant. *Visitors:* welcome every day. Pro shop; equipment hire. *Society Meetings:* welcome. Professionals: Yan Rico. e-mail: contact@golf-bordeaux-cameyrac.com website: www.golf-bordeaux-cameyrac.com

BORDEAUX. **Golf du Médoc,** Chemin de Courmateau, 33290 Le Pian Médoc (05 56 70 11 90; Fax: 05 56 70 11 99). *Location:* 20 minutes by car from Bordeaux International Airport. Vintage golf in Bordeaux Country, 36 holes named after Medoc Wine Chateaux. The "Chateaux Course" 6316 par 71, traditional links course, host of the French Open in 1999 (PGA European Tour), host of the European Amateur Championship in 1998. The "Vignes Course" 6220m par 71 set in a typically regional landscape winding through lakes and pine trees. Practice ground, pitching and putting greens. *Green Fees:* information not available. *Eating facilities:* clubhouse with bar and quality restaurant. *Visitors:* welcome. *Society Meetings:* please contact Secretary. Professionals: Gilles Arnaud and Nicolas Besançon. General Manager; Vincent Paris.* e-mail: info@golf-du-medoc.com

BORDEAUX. **Golf de Pessac,** Rue de la Princesse, 33690 Pessac (05 57.26.03.33; Fax: 05 56.36.52.89). *Location:* on the western outskirts of Bordeaux, four km from the city and close to the airport, St Jean d'Illiac road. A level course with large bunkers and some water. 27 holes providing alternative 9 hole layouts plus 9 hole practice course. 18 holes, 6040 metres. Par 72; 9 holes, 2911 metres. Par 36. Driving range, putting green. *Green Fees:* information not available. *Eating facilities:* restaurant and bar. *Visitors:* welcome at any time. *Society Meetings:* welcome. Pro shop; cart, club and trolley hire. Professionals: Ramuntcho Artola, Nagalie Gaillard. Secretary: Alain Egloff.*

CASTELJALOUX. **Golf de Casteljaloux,** Route de Mont-de-Marsan, 47700 Casteljaloux (05.53.93.51.60; Fax: 05.53.20.90.98). *Location:* situated on the D933 facing Lake Clarens on the road to Mont-de-Marsan, 15km from the exit of the motorway, 90km from Bordeaux, 170km from Toulouse. Flat and wooded on six holes, 12 holes undulating. 18 holes, 6500 yards, 5916 metres, Par 72, S.S.S. 71. Practice holes, bunkers and tees, driving range and putting green. *Green Fees:* information not available. *Eating facilities:* bar and restaurant in clubhouse with fine views. *Visitors:* welcome. Pro shop; club and trolley hire; 3 buggies. 15 bungalows for rent (5 doubles and 10 singles). *Society Meetings:* by arrangement. Professional: Citin Krault. Golf Manager: Denis Muller-Feuga.*
e-mail: golfdecasteljaloux@wanadoo.fr
website: www.golf-casteljaloux.com

DORDOGNE. **Château des Vigiers Golf and Country Club,** 24240 Monestier (05 53.61.50.00; Fax: 05 53.61.50.20). *Location:* about an hour's drive east of Bordeaux on D936, bearing right on D18 at Ste-Foy-la-Grande. Rolling past orchards, vineyards, woods, lakes surrounding a16th century château. 18 holes, 6003 metres. Par 72. 6 hole practice course, driving range and putting green. *Green Fees:* information not available. *Eating facilities:* restaurant and bar. Pro shop, club, cart and trolley rental; luxury hotel. Professional: Vincent Trojani.*
e-mail: reserve@vigiers.com
website: www.vigiers.com

HOSSEGOR. **Golf d'Hossegor,** Avenue du Golf, 40150 Hossegor (05 58.43.56.99; Fax: 05 58.43.98.52). *Location:* about 15km north of Bayonne just west of the A63. Fine classic test of golf over gently undulating, heavily wooded land. 18 holes, 5920 metres, Par 71. Driving range, putting green. *Green Fees:* information not available. *Eating facilities:* bar and restaurant in clubhouse. Pro shop; trolley hire.*

LACANAU-OCEAN. **Golf Hotel ★★★ 3 de Lacanau Ocean,** 33680 Lacanau Océan (05 56.03.92.98; Fax: 05 56.26.30.57). *Location:* between Lac de Lacanau and the sea, 60km west of Bordeaux. Level, within a pine and oak forest, some water hazards. 18 holes, 5900 metres, Par 72. Covered and open practice ground, putting green. *Green Fees:* information not available. *Eating facilities:* regional restaurant, snacks at clubhouse; bar. *Visitors:* welcome all year round. *Society Meetings:* welcome. Pro shop; equipment, trolley, buggy hire. Special packages with Golf–Hotel

and Restaurant. Three Star Hotel, 50 rooms direct onto the course; swimming pool; cottages. (05 56.03.92.92; Fax: 05 56.26.30.57).*

LAVAUR. **Golf des Etangs de Fiac,** Brazis, 81500 Fiac (05.63.70.64.70; Fax: 05.63.75.32.91). *Location:* Toulouse to Lavaur, course is 10km after Lavaur in the direction of Castres. A technically interesting course, very green, with water hazards across natural ponds. 18 holes, 5800 metres. S.S.S. 71. *Green Fees:* information not available. *Eating facilities:* bar and restaurant open all year. *Visitors:* welcome all year. Pro shop, equipment hire. Swimming pool in season (golfers only) Lessons available. Professional: Pierre Crouzet. Secretaries: J. Phillippe and Sandie. Owner: Hilda Stevens.*

MAZAMET. **Golf de Mazamet la Barouge,** 81660 Pont de l'Arn, Mazamet (05.63.61.06.72). *Location:* three km north of Mazamet. A standard course with small wooded areas, set in magnificent surroundings. Notable for tricky and long Par 3s. 18 holes, 5953 metres. Par 70. *Green Fees:* information not available. *Eating facilities:* bar and restaurant in clubhouse. *Visitors:* welcome all year. Buggy hire. Professional: Bruno Michel.*
e-mail: golflabarouge@wanadoo.fr
website: www.golf-mazamet.net

PAU. **Pau Golf Club 1856,** Rue du Golf, 64140 Billere (05 59.13.18.56; Fax: 05 59.13.18.57). *Location:* RN 117 Commune de Billere 5km from Pau towards Bayonne-Biarritz. Founded 150 years ago, the oldest course in continental Europe (1856). Flat, wooded, alongside the River Gave. 18 holes, 5312 metres, Par 69. Practice facilities including pitch and putt. *Green Fees:* information not available. *Eating facilities:* bar and restaurant in clubhouse. *Visitors:* welcome. *Society Meetings:* by arrangement. Secretary: Nicolas Barraud. President: Jean Pierre Mazin.*
e-mail: president.pgc@wanadoo.fr

SAINT-JEAN-DE-LUZ. **Golf de la Nivelle,** Place William Sharp, 64500 Ciboure (05 59.47.19.72; Fax: 05 59.47.21.16). *Location:* two km south of Saint-Jean de Luz on the banks of the River Nivelle. Classic parkland with mature trees and harbour views. 18 holes, 5513 metres, Par 70. Practice ground, putting green. *Green Fees:* information not available. *Eating facilities:* bar and restaurant in clubhouse. *Visitors:* welcome, maximum Handicap 35. Self catering flats on golf course. Pro shop; equipment hire.*

SOUILLAC. **Souillac Country Club,** Lachapelle-Auzac, 46200 Souillac (0871 780 1444 (UK only); 0033 565 275 600). *Location:* in the heart of South West France, within 1½ hours' drive of Toulouse, Limoges and Bergerac Airports. The course follows the contours of a natural valley and enjoys panoramic views of the Perigord Noir. 10-bay driving range and 18-hole putting green. *Green Fees:* on application. *Eating facilities:* clubhouse with terrace bar and brasserie-style restaurant. *Visitors:* welcome. Golf breaks available.
e-mail: rentals@souillaccountryclub.com
website: www.souillaccountryclub.com

TOULOUSE. **Maeva Latitudes Toulouse Seilh,** Route de Grenade, 31840 Seilh (05 62.13.14.14; Fax: 05 61.42.34.17). *Location:* about 12km north-west of Toulouse near the A62. "Yellow" Course of moderate difficulty, 18 holes, 4202 metres, Par 64; "Red" Course of competition standard, 18 holes, 6200 metres, Par 72. Extensive practice and training facilities. *Eating facilities:* bar and restaurant in clubhouse. Pro shop; club, cart and trolley hire. A new hotel with 175 rooms and apartments is now available on site with tennis and private swimming pool (05.62.13.14.15).*
e-mail: toulouse.golf@maeva.fr
website: www.maeva.latitudes.toulouse.com

VILLENEUVE-SUR-LOT. **Villeneuve sur Lot Golf and Country Club,** 47290 Castelnaud de Gratecambe (05. 53. 01. 60.19; Fax: 05. 53. 01. 78. 99). *Location:* on the N21 10km north of Villeneuve, between the scenic valleys of the Lot and the Dordogne. Inland course with water and many trees. 18 holes, 6322 metres, Par 72. Debutants Ecole de Golf 9 hole course. Practice ground, putting green. *Green Fees:* from €49.50 for 18 holes. *Eating facilities:* clubhouse bar, bistro, terrace brasserie/snack restaurant. Pro shop; equipment hire.
e-mail: info@vslgolf.com
website: www.vslgolf.com

For full details of clubs and courses, plus convenient accommodation
www.uk-golfguide.com

SOUTH

AGDE. **Golf du Cap d'Agde,** 4 Avenue des Alizés, 34300 Cap d'Agde (04 67.26.54.40; Fax: 04 67.26.97.00). *Location:* autoroute A9 exit Agde. Seaside links. 18 holes, 6279 metres. S.S.S. 73. Practice ground; 9 hole pitch and putt, 800 metres, S.S.S. 27. *Green Fees:* information not available. *Eating facilities:* bar and restaurant in clubhouse. *Visitors:* welcome, no restrictions. Club, trolley and cart hire. Spikes on shoes forbidden. *Society Meetings:* welcome by reservation. Professionals: Jean Pierre Prieur, Franck Renard. Secretary: Myriam Delcayre.*

AIX-EN-PROVENCE. **Golf International de Château L'Arc,** Domaine de Château L'Arc, 13710 Fuveau (04 42.53.28.38; Fax: 04 42.29.08.41). *Location:* about 15km south-east of Aix-en-Provence just south of the A8. A challenging course of varying terrain through trees, sloping fairways and water hazards. 18 holes, 6200 metres. S.S.S. 71. Driving range, putting green. *Green Fees:* information not available. *Eating facilities:* bar and restaurant in clubhouse. Pro shop; cart, trolley and club hire. *Visitors:* welcome, no restriction but it is necessary to make a reservation for weekends. Professional: Eric Follet. Secretary: Catherine Peter.*

AVIGNON. **Golf de Servanes,** Domaine de Servanes, 13890 Mouries (04 90.47.59.95; Fax: 04 90.47.52.58). *Location:* leave autoroute at Salon and head for Arles; leave at Avignon and head for St. Remy. Undulating course with serveral water hazards. 18 holes, 6121 metres. S.S.S. 72. Practice facilities. *Green Fees:* €65. *Eating facilities:* available. *Visitors:* welcome, no restrictions. *Society Meetings:* welcome. Professional: Alain Brioland.

BANDOL. **Golf de Fregate,** Route de Bandol, RD 559, 83270 St-Cyr-sur-Mer (04 34.29.38.00; Fax: 04 94.29.96.94). *Location:* about 4km from St-Cyr-sur-Mer on the road to Bandol on the right hand side. A dramatic new course in a vineyard setting overlooking the Mediterranean. 18 holes, 6209 metres. Par 72. Also 9 holes, 1500 metres. Par 29. Practice ground and two putting greens. *Green Fees:* visit website. Special rates for golf and hotel packages all year round. *Eating facilities:* bar and restaurant. Also on-site hotel (four star, 133 rooms) by 18th green. Pro shop, club, cart and trolley hire.
website: www.fregate.dolce.com

CANNES. **Golf Club de Cannes-Mandelieu,** Route du Golf, 06210 Mandelieu-la-Napoule (04 92.97.32.00; Fax: 04 93.49.92.90). *Location:* across the mouth of the small River Siagne, about seven km west of Cannes, south of the A8. A short, level course, third oldest and most popular in France. 18 holes, 5867 metres, Par 71. 9 holes, 2409 metres, Par 33. Practice ground, putting green. *Green Fees:* information not available. *Eating facilities:* bar and restaurant in attractive clubhouse. *Visitors:* welcome. *Society Meetings:* welcome. Director: Jean Stefan Camerini.*

CANNES. **Golf Country Club de Cannes-Mougins,** 175 Avenue du Golf, 06250 Mougins (04 93.75.79.13; Fax: 04 93.75.27.60). *Location:* eight km north of Cannes, near the A8. A high-class private course, undulating through wooded hills. 18 holes, 6849 yards, 6263 metres, S.S.S. 72. Driving range, two putting greens, pitching green. *Green Fees:* information not available. *Eating facilities:* restaurant, bar, snacks. *Visitors:* welcome, no restrictions. Sauna. Magasin du Golf; cart, trolley and club hire. Professionals: Roger Damiano, Patrick Lemaire, Richard Sorrell (04 93.75.53.32). Secretaries: Hugues Danjou, Maryline Eynaud, Claudie Valle and Lydie de Rungs (04 93.75.79.13; Fax: 04 93.75.27.60).*

CANNES. **Riviera Golf Club,** Avenue des Amazones, 06210 Mandelieu (04.92.97.49.49; Fax: 04.92.97.66.57). *Location:* less than five km west of Cannes, just south of the A8, Fréjus direction. A new 18 hole course by American master Robert Trent Jones; mostly level, some hills and lakes. 18 holes, 5736 metres, Par 72. Driving range, putting green. *Green Fees:* information not available. *Eating facilities:* in clubhouse. *Visitors:* welcome, Handicap of 35 and insurance required. Professional/Manager: Y. Lecrubier. President: R.G. Boillat.*

CORSICA. **Golf de Sperone,** Domaine de Sperone, 20169 Bonifacio (04 95.73.17.13: Fax: 04 95.73.17.85). *Location:* near Bonifacio, southern point of Corsica. Another new Trent Jones creation, part on rocky maquis inland, part overlooking the Mediterranean. 18 holes, 6106 metres. S.S.S. 72. Practice facilities. *Green Fees:* information not provided. *Eating facilities:* bar and restaurant with panoramic views. *Visitors:* welcome every day, please make a reservation. The golf course is closed on Thursdays from November to March and on Thursday afternoons from April to October. Pro shop, practice area, putting green, car, club and trolley hire; rented accommodation available at course. *Society Meetings:* welcome except July and August. Chairman: Y. Tozzi. Professional: Marc Malrieu. Secretary: Shirley Bailie, Nafissa Bartoli, Brigitte Liechty. website: www.sperone.com

COTE D'AZUR. **Golf Opio-Valbonne,** Route de Roquefort Les Pins, 06650 Opio ([33] 04 93 12 00 08; Fax: [33] 04 93 12 26 00). *Location:* from Nice, A8 to Aix, out Villeneuve-Loubet, D2085, at Roquefort Les Pins, Valbonne, D204. Situated between Riviera coast and mountains, in a natural park of 530 acres. 18 holes, 5782 metres, S.S.S.73. Practice area, putting green. *Green Fees:* information not available. *Visitors:* welcome. Car, club and trolley hire. Instruction school.*
e-mail: opiovalbonne@opengolfclub.com
website: www.opengolfclub.com

GRASSE. **Golf de la Grande Bastide,** Chemin des Picholines, 06740 Chateauneuf de Grasse (04 93.77.70.08; Fax: 04 93.77.72.36). *Location:* autoroute A8 exit Cannes towards Mougin-Valbonne-Opio. Gently rolling, of equal challenge to all grades of player. 18 holes, 6105 metres, S.S.S. 72. Driving range, putting green. *Green Fees:* information not available. *Eating facilities:* bar and restaurant in clubhouse. *Visitors:* welcome anytime. Trolley and club hire. *Society Meetings:* welcome. Professional: S. Damiano (06.07.56.31.57). Manager: Alain Decovan.*

LES BAUX. **Golf des Baux de Provence,** Domaine de Manville, 13520 Les Baux de Provence (04 90.54.40.20; Fax: 04 90.54.40.93). *Location:* 25km from Avignon, 18km from Arles, 80km from Marseilles (Airport), the course is on the D27 between Les Baux and Maussane-les-Alpilles. Designed by the British architect Martin Hawtree, the course is set between pines, olive trees and scented lavender. 9 holes, 2842 metres. Par 36. Practice, putting green. *Green Fees:* 9 holes €36, 18 holes €53. *Eating facilities:* bar and restaurant in clubhouse. *Visitors:* always welcome. Hire of clubs, trolleys and golf carts. Professional: Joël Laggoune.

MARSEILLES. **Golf d'Aix Marseille,** Domaine de Riquetti, 13290 Les Milles (04 42.24.20.41; Fax: 04 42.39.97.48). *Location:* between Marseilles and Aix-en-Provence, west of the A51. A mature parkland course in a natural setting with a wealth of established trees. 18 holes, 6291 metres, Par 73. Driving range, putting green. *Green Fees:* information not available. *Eating facilities:* bar and restaurant in clubhouse. *Visitors:* welcome, closed Tuesdays. Pro shop; trolley and club hire.*

MARSEILLES. **Golf de Marseille La Salette,** Impasse des Vaudrans, Quartier de la Valentine, 13011 Marseille (04.91.27.12.16; Fax: 04.91.27.21.33). *Location:* Autoroute A50 exit La Valentine, follow the signs for "Valentine" then "Golf de la Salette". Hilly parkland course. 18 holes, 5436 metres. Par 71. *Green Fees:* information not available. *Eating facilities:* restaurant. *Visitors:* welcome. *Society Meetings:* welcome - conference and ballrooms available for seminars. Tennis courts and swimming pool. Golf school and buggy hire available.*

MONTE CARLO. **Monte Carlo Golf Club,** Route du Mont Agel, 06320 La Turbie (04 93.41.09.11/ 04 92 41 50 70: Fax: 04 93.41.09.55). *Location:* from Nice, take autoroute A8 Exit for La Turbie. Signpost at end of town, left turn for Mont Agel. Golf course entrance after 5 kms. Picturesque course with exceptional views of the Mediterranean sea and southern Alps. 18 holes, 5700 metres, Par 71. Driving range, practice, putting green. *Green Fees:* information not available. *Eating facilities:* bar and restaurant. *Visitors:* welcome, Handicap Certificate required. *Society Meetings:* welcome by prior arrangement. Professionals: F. Ruffier-Meray, J.M. Loustalan and Sophie Halsall. Secretary: C. Houtart.*

MONTPELLIER. **Golf de la Grande-Motte,** Club House du Golf, 34280 La Grande-Motte ((33) 04.67.56.05.00; Fax: (33) 04.67.29.18.84). *Location:* on the coast, east of Montpellier. Former marshland, now a 42 hole complex with fast greens, water, trees and bunkers. "The Pink Flamingos" - 18 competition class holes, 6161 metres, Par 72; "The Seagulls" - 3220 metres, Par 58; and 6 hole practice green, 560 metres, Par 19. Practice ground, putting green. *Green Fees:* weekdays €48, weekends €56. *Eating facilities:* bar and restaurant in clubhouse and on-course Golf Hotel. Pro shop; trolley and cart hire. Professionals: V. Etchevers, P.H. Milhau, M. Boudou. Manager: J C. Mathieu.
e-mail: golf@lagrandemotte.fr
website: www.ot-lagrandemotte.fr

MONTPELLIER. **Golf de Massane,** Domaine de Massane, 34670 Baillargues (04.67.87.87.87; Fax: 04.67.87.87.90). *Location:* seven km from airport, 10km from Montpellier and two km from autoroute. Tough championship layout which hosts the annual Volvo Tour qualifying. Elevated greens protected by sand and water. 18 holes, 7037 metres, Par 72. 9 hole compact course. Extensive teaching school with large driving range, pitching and putting greens. *Green Fees:* information not available. *Eating facilities:* bar, snacks and restaurant in clubhouse, hotel on course. Pro shop. Leadbetter Academy. *Visitors:* welcome all year. *Society Meetings:* welcome. Professional: Nicolas Armand (04.67.87.87.91). Secretary: M. Brunet (04.67.87.87.87).*

MONTPELLIER. **Golf Hotel de Fontcaude,** Route de Lodève, Domaine de Fontcaude 34990 Juvignao (04.67. 45.90.10; Fax: 04.67.45.90.20). *Location:* at Juvignac, six km west of Montpellier. Undulating over a rolling, scrub-covered landscape, this course provides a fair and interesting challenge. Two courses: International 18 holes, 6292 metres, Par 72. Executive 9 holes, 1290 metres, Par 29. Driving range, putting green, pitching green. *Green Fees:* information not available. *Eating facilities:* bar and restaurant in clubhouse. *Visitors:* welcome, no restrictions. Pro shop; cart, trolley and club hire. *Society Meetings:* welcome. Professional: Bruno Tancogne. Golf Manager: Antony Bonsergent (04 67.45.90.10).*

NANS LES PINS. **Golf de la Sainte-Baume,** Domaine de Chateauneuf, 83860 Nans-les-Pins. (04.94.78.60.12; Fax; 04.94.78.63.52). *Location:* 40 kms from Marseilles, A8 exit Saint-Maximin. 45 kms from Aix-en-Provence. Wooded, undulating course. 18 holes, 6167 metres, Par 72. *Green Fees:* information not available. *Eating facilities:* restaurant. *Visitors:* welcome. *Society Meetings:* welcome. Golf school and pro shop, buggy hire available. Accommodation available in our 4 star Domaine de Châteauneuf "Relais et Chateaux" located in the centre of the course. Managers: Alain Batteux and Marie-Pierre Puisset.*

NIMES. **Golf de Nîmes-Campagne,** Route de Saint-Gilles, 30900 Nîmes (04.66.70.17.37; Fax: 04.66.70.03.14). *Location:* close to the A54, exit Nîmes Garons (Airport). A classic flat parkland course of championship calibre built around a superb clubhouse. 18 holes, 6135 metres, Par 72. Driving range, practice bunker, putting green. *Green Fees:* information not available. *Eating facilities:* bar and excellent restaurant. *Visitors:* welcome with reservation. Pro Shop; buggies and carts for hire. *Society Meetings:* welcome during weekdays with reservation, maximum 12/15 persons. Professionals: Marc Dolisie and Didier Behin. Secretary: Sandra Dombret.*

NIMES. **Golf de Nîmes Vacquerolles,** 1075 Chemin du Golf, 30900 Nîmes ((33)04.66.23.33.33; Fax: (33) 04.66.23.94.94). *Location:* five minutes from Nîmes, autoroute A9, exit Nîmes Ouest, then Le Vigan. Running up a valley and over steeply wooded hills. 18 holes, 6260 metres, Par 73. Practice area, putting green. *Green Fees:* from €55. *Eating facilities:* bar and restaurant in clubhouse. *Visitors:* welcome. Self-catering apartments on the course. *Society Meetings:* welcome. Open Golf Club. Professionals: Eric Rossary, Emmanuel Thomas and David Gonez.
e-mail: vacquerolles.opengolfclub@wanadoo.fr
website: www.opengolfclub.com

PERPIGNAN. **Golf de Saint Cyprien,** Mas d'Huston, 66750 Saint Cyprien Plage (33 04 68 37 63 63; Fax: 33 04 68 37 64 64). *Location:* just south of Perpignan (15mins) and 30 mins from Spain, a renowned course between sea and lake with the Pyrenees mountains in the background. Challenging championship course with water hazards. Etang-Canigou, 18 holes, 6475 metres, Par 73. La Foret - 9 holes, 2963 metres, Par 35. *Green Fees:* day pass from 50 to 65 (2007). *Eating facilities:* bar at clubhouse. Bars, restaurants and accommodation at Le Mas d'Huston, on-course hotel. Hotel 4 Star with 50 rooms. Open all year. Pro shop, golf clinic. Professional: Marc Malafosse, Philippe Tourtrol, Jean Marc Espelt.
e-mail: contact@golf-saint-cyprien.com
website: www.golf-saint-cyprien.com

ST RAPHAEL. **Golf de l'Estérel Latitudes,** Avenue du Golf, 83700 St Raphaël (04 94.52.68.30; Fax: 04 94.52.68.31). *Location:* inland just a few metres north of St Raphaël, close to Golf de Valescure. Not long but rated difficult; many trees, narrow fairways and water hazards protecting beautiful greens. 18 holes, 5921 metres, Par 71. 9 holes, 1400 metres, Par 29. Driving range, 9 hole school. *Green Fees:* information not available. *Eating facilities:* bar, clubhouse and restaurant. *Visitors:* welcome. On-site Hotel Latitudes-Valescure (discounts for residents). Pro shop; club, cart and trolley hire. *Society Meetings:* welcome, pre-booking with hotel. Professional: Hugues Gioux (04.94.44.64.65).*

ST RAPHAEL. **Golf et Tennis Club de Valescure,** BP451, Route de Golf, 83700 St Raphaël (04 94.82.40.46; Fax: 04 94.82.41.42). *Location:* about five km east of St. Raphaël. An established course (1895), winding attractively through the umbrella pine trees. 18 holes, 5067 metres, Par 68. Driving range, putting green. *Eating facilities:* bar and restaurant in period clubhouse and at golf hotel nearby. Pro shop; trolley and club hire.*

VAR. **Four Seasons Resort at Terre Blanche,** Domaine de Terre Blanche, 83440 Tourettes, Var (04 94 39 90 00; Fax: 04 94 39 90 01). *Location:* about 25 minutes inland of Cannes and St Raphael. Two new courses by Dave Thomas wind through pine and oak-clad hills with sweeping mountain views. Le Chateau 18 holes, 6616 metres, Par 72; Le Riou 18 holes, 6005 metres, Par 72. Driving range, putting green, Pro shop, David Leadbetter golf academy. *Green Fees:* €140. Club, cart and trolley hire. *Eating facilities:* Clubhouse restaurant; also restaurants in adjacent luxury resort spa hotel. *Visitors:* welcome.
e-mail: res.provence@fourseasons.com
website: www.fourseasons.com/provence

Holiday Golf in Portugal

Michael Gedye

Sunset serenity at Penha Longa Hotel & Golf Resort, Estoril

ALTHOUGH PEOPLE with the inclination and the means have been going abroad for holidays (which included golf) for many years, the concept of "holiday golf" with specialised resorts and specific travel packages, is a much more recent phenomenon. The idea of taking a vacation where golf is a primary motivation for travel, usually coupled with a seasonal escape to better weather, has taken root, particularly during the winter or off-season. Portugal has become a focal point of golfing travellers who can enjoy the ever-increasing number of excellent, well-designed modern golf courses built specifically to satisfy this holiday demand. Only a relatively small number of local

Portuguese have taken up golf; the demand comes from overseas and this, in turn, has led to welcoming club facilities, multi-lingual staff, international menus and a very home-from-home atmosphere at the most popular clubs, which tend to follow the coastline of the southerly Algarve and the vacation areas south and west of the central capital, Lisbon.

By far the largest contingent of golfers visiting Portugal, particularly during the winter season, come from Great Britain – and with good reason. Only a short flight south, this warm and welcoming country with a longstanding reputation for courtesy and hospitality is inextricably linked with the British Isles by a

Tough test on a sandbar – Trioa Golf, Setubal

mutual history and a fabled seafaring tradition. The British brought the game to the country more than a century ago as a byproduct of commercial involvement with the export of port wine. The growing demand for 'holiday golf in out-of-season sunshine' saw the British in the forefront of development, construction and management of new resort courses, particularly along the southern Algarve. The heady mixture of warm sunshine, verdant fairways, aromatic umbrella pines, fresh grilled seafood and excellent wines brought the players, who returned annually with their friends. Other golfing countries suffering from winter chills joined in – Sweden, Holland and Germany in the main – and a major winter activity transformed this rural coast, formerly known only for agriculture and fishing, into a thriving magnet for players. A further development has been in the construction and sale of holiday and retirement property linked to golf, creating a sizeable expatriate community.

The demand for golf spread north to the environs of the sophisticated capital, Lisbon, and holiday courses have grown along the sandy Atlantic coasts to the west and south, many of genuine international quality. Modern air travel means it is possible, with the right timetable, to fly out and play sunshine golf on the same day. It is certainly perfectly reasonable to consider a long golfing weekend. The coastal aspect of most of the resort courses in the country ensures not only a plethora of fish and seafood restaurants but also gentle breezes to temper the warm sunshine.

The ALGARVE, sheltered to the north by a range of inland mountains, maintains a mild and attractive climate all year. It boasts a unique local culture, combining the best of Portuguese tradition with colourful concepts and cuisine implanted from northern Africa. There are more than thirty courses in play along this pine-studded coast, with more in the pipeline. Many will already be well-known to travelling golfers – Vilamoura, with five courses including the Victoria, venue for the 2005 World Cup, Penina, Vale do Lobo, Quinta do Lago, San Lorenzo, Vila Sol, Parque da Floresta, Pinta and Pinheiros Altos. New arrivals include Castro Marim, Quinta da Ria, Quinta de Cima and Jack Nicklaus' Monte Rei to the east plus Boavista and Golfe do Morgado to the west.

Created for knowledgeable golfing visitors and designed by experts, the courses of Portugal come highly recommended. From the creations of three-times Open champion Sir Henry Cotton

Seaside duneland at Praia D'el Rey Golf & Country Club

and English international Frank Pennink, the roster includes such global masters as Robert Trent Jones, Arnold Palmer, Jack Nicklaus, Rocky Roquemore, Cabel Robinson, Arthur Hills, Ronald Fream and Donald Steel. From tough tests for champions to charming examinations of strategy – there is something for all to enjoy and much more to discover.

LISBON is the focal point for a second wave of holiday golf, both out to the west along the coast past the seaside spa town of Estoril with its elegant casino and further north to the ancient walled city of Obidos, or south down the sandy, wooded calm of the Costa Azul to the fishing port of Setubal. Around Estoril, you can tackle the ageless strategic charm of the Palacio

Manicured fairways at Quinta da Ria, Cacela

Quinta da Ria

Estoril course or more recent additions at Penha Longa, Belas Clube de Campo and Quinta da Marinha Oitavos. A little further north lie Golden Eagle and the natural dune setting of Praia d'El Rey by the sea. Crossing the Tagus river southwards opens up a wealth of golfing treasure. Aroeira I and II, Quinta do Peru and by ferry to a windswept coastal sandbar, easily the most demanding course in the country – Robert Trent Jones' Troia. Great golf, backed by the fresh grilled harvest of the sea and the range of excellent red wines from the Duoro or nearby Alentejo regions.

Portuguese golf began in the **OPORTO** region to the north, thanks to expatriate wine shippers in Oporto in 1888. In a region of ancient castles, variable weather, a wealth of wine and unique handicrafts, there are now a total of nine courses, the best of which is undoubtedly Ponte de Lima. This course, which winds across and over mountain slopes is highly dramatic with some sensational views.

The sub-tropical island of Madeira has two courses at volcanic altitude, often above the clouds, with amazing changes of elevation. One is now a regular stop on the PGA European Tour. Also, just off-shore, on the island of Porto Santo, a new course by Spanish champion Severiano Ballesteros offers 27 holes at sea level. **The AZORES** islands are a mid-Atlantic alternative, with three very playable courses set amid colourful flora.

Historically, Portugal gained a deserved reputation for global exploration and discovery, which in turn influenced much of European development over the centuries. Now, golfers in search of new horizons are discovering the charms of sunny Portugal, with not only a superb selection of resort golf but also a culture offering a unique blend of architecture, art, music and cuisine distilled from contact with Spain, Africa and the New World.

View across the bay at Golf de Palmares, Lagos

ALGARVE

ALBUFEIRA. **Golf de Salgados,** Apartado 2266, Vale Rebelho, 8200-917 Albufeira (00351 289 583030; Fax: 00351 289 591112). *Location:* from Faro on EN125, turn left for Vale de Parra. Next to a nature reserve. Level course carved from seamarsh with plenty of water hazards. 18 holes, 6080 metres. Par 72. Driving range, putting green. *Green Fees:* information not available. *Eating facilities:* bar and restaurant in clubhouse. *Visitors:* welcome. Pro shop; cart, trolley and club hire. *Society Meetings:* all welcome. Professional: John Wood. Director: Pedro Silvestre.*

ALBUFEIRA. **Sheraton Algarve Pine Cliffs Golf and Country Club,** PO Box 644, Praia da Falesia, 8200-909 Albufeira ((+351) 289 500113; Fax: (+351) 289 500117). *Location:* seven km from Vilamoura, situated outside Olhos d'Agua. Seaside links. 9 holes, 2557 yards, 2324 metres, Par (equivalent) 67. 9 holes Par 3 course. *Green Fees:* information not available. *Eating facilities:* bar and restaurants. *Visitors:* welcome, advance booking required. On-line booking available. Golf academy with 3 golf Pros. *Society Meetings:* all groups welcome. Professional/Golf Director: Manuel Baptista.*
e-mail: golf.algarve@starwoodhotels.com
website: www.sheraton-algarve.com/golf

ALMANCIL. **San Lorenzo Golf Club,** Vale de Lobo, 8135-901 Almancil (00 351 89 396 522; Fax: 00 351 89 396 908). *Location:* 20km from Faro Airport towards west. Parkland with seaside view surrounded by wildlife and umbrella pine trees designed by Joseph Lee. 18 holes, 6238 metres. Par 72. Practice range, putting green and driving range. *Green Fees:* information not available. *Eating facilities:* bar and restaurant. *Visitors:* welcome, please reserve 24 hours in advance before wishing to play, Handicap Certificate required - Men 28, Ladies 36. Caddies and cart rental available. Soft spikes required. Pro shop. *Society Meetings:* welcome if staying in Dona Filipa Hotel. Professional: A. Rodrigues. Course Manager: Antonio Santos (00 351 89 396 534).*
e-mail: san.lorenzo@lemeridien-algarve.com
website: www.lemeridien.com/donafilipa

ALMANCIL. **Sociedade do Golfe da Quinta do Lago,** Quinta do Lago, 8135-024 Almancil (+351 289 390700; Fax: +351 289 394013). *Location:* 15 minutes west of Faro airport, nearest town Almancil. Gently undulating sandy site covered with umbrella pines, wild flowers and lakes. 2 courses: Quinta do Lago South and Quinta do Lago North. Both 18 holes, 7136 and 6738 yards, 6488 and 6126 metres. S.S.S. 72. Driving range. *Green Fees:* information not available. *Eating facilities:* clubhouse bar, restaurants (9 Iron and Casa do Lago), and Buggy Bar. *Visitors:* welcome subject to availability, first starting time around 7.30am. Pro Shop and golf academy;

buggies, trolleys and power caddies. *Society Meetings:* welcome subject to availability. Professional: Domingos Silva, Rogério Valente and Jason Hoyles (+351 289 394368; Fax: +351 289 394013. Golf Director: José Capela. General Manager: João Paulo Sousa.*

ALMANCIL. **Vale do Lobo Golf Club,** Vale do Lobo, 8135-864 Vale do Lobo, Almancil (00 351 289 353464 Fax: 00 351 289 353003). *Location:* on the cliff edge, overlooking the sea, 15 minutes' drive west from Faro. 2 courses. "Ocean Course", 18 holes, 6131 metres. Par 73. "Royal Course", 18 holes, 6059 metres. Par 72. Coastline scenery with fairways lined with pine, eucalyptus and almond trees. *Green Fees:* Ocean Course €150, Royal Course €160. *Eating facilities:* clubhouse with restaurant, bar and cafe. *Visitors:* always welcome. *Society Meetings:* welcome. Teaching Professional: Steve Walker. Tour Professionals: Antonio Sobrinho, Jarmo Sandelin and Brian Davis. Golf Director: Ian Church. Golf Manager: Hernani Estevão.
e-mail: golf@vdl.pt
website: www.valedolobo.com

ALVOR. **Alto Golf & Country Club,** Quinta do Alto do Poco, Apartado 100, 8501 906 Alvor - Portimao (282 460870; Fax: 282 460879). *Location:* in Alvor, overlooking the Atlantic Ocean and the Bay of Lagos. A parkland course designed by Sir Henry Cotton with gently undulating fairways and challenging sloping greens. Stunning views of the Monchique Mountains in the background. 18 holes, 5812 metres, S.S.S. 73. Driving range, putting green. *Green Fees:* special offers available all year round. *Eating facilities:* bar and restaurant in clubhouse. *Visitors:* welcome. *Society Meetings:* groups also welcome, Handicap Certificate required. Pro shop; cart, trolley and club hire. Professional: BGLC - Bennets Golf Learning Centre. 3 Pros with all the latest computer teaching software and Explanar training aid. Director: Richard Marshall.
e-mail: golf@altoclub.com

BUDENS/SALEMA. **Parque da Floresta Golf and Leisure Resort,** Vale do Poco, 8650-060 Budens (+351 282 690054; Fax: +351 282 695157). *Location:* EN125, 16km west of Lagos. Located just past Budens on right. Undulating course with spectacular views; member of the Portuguese Golf Federation. 18 holes, 5670 metres. S.S.S. 72. Short game practice area, driving range, golf academy, three putting greens. *Green Fees:* information not available. *Eating facilities:* clubhouse with restaurant and bar overlooking 18th hole. *Visitors:* very welcome but advisable to book. Enquire about Special Rates. Pro shop; swimming pools, tennis court, health and beauty spa. Self-catering villas and townhouses available. *Society Meetings:* welcome, catered for by arrangement with Golf Director. PGA Professionals: Gary Silcock, Scott Catlin. Golf Director: Billy Sim.*
e-mail: b.sim@vigiasa.com OR golf@vigiasa.com
website: www.vigiasa.com

THE APPEARANCE OF AN ASTERISK (*) AT THE END OF A CLUB OR COURSE ENTRY INDICATES THAT UP-TO-DATE INFORMATION HAS NOT BEEN SUPPLIED

CACELA. **Quinta da Ria**, 8900-057 Vila Nova de Cacela, Algarve (351 281 950 580; Fax: 351 281 950 589). *Location*: take N125 east from Faro; after Tavira turn right at sign for Cacela Vehla and golf. Situated in the Ria Formosa Nature Reserve, a spectacular course by Rocky Roquemore, with superb views over the tidal estuary and the sea. 18 holes, 6,016 metres, Par 72. Driving range, golf academy, putting green. *Green fees:* information not available. *Eating facilities:* clubhouse snack bar. *Visitors:* welcome. Electric carts, pull and electric trolleys, club rental. Golf Director: Antonio Cavaco.*
e-mail: info@quintadaria.com

CACELA. **Quinta de Cima**, 8900-057 Vila Nova de Cacela, Algarve (351 281 950 580; 351 281 950 589). *Location*: take N125 east from Faro; after Tavira turn right at sign for Cacela Velha and golf. Highly-rated new course by Rocky Roquemore winding past ancient olive and carob trees, with sea and mountain views. 18 holes, 6,256 metres, Par 72. Driving range, golf academy, putting green. *Green fees:*information not available. *Eating facilities:* clubhouse snack bar. *Visitors*: welcome. Electric carts, pull and electric trolleys, club rental. Golf Director: Antonio Cavaco.*
e-mail: info@quintadaria.com

LAGOA. **Gramacho Course,** Pestana Golf Resorts Algarve, Carvoeiro, Apartado 1011, 8400-908 Lagoa +351 282 340900; Fax: +351 282 340901). *Location:* 2km south of Lagoa, follow signposting. Superbly designed course undulating through olive groves. 18 holes, 27 greens, 6107 metres. Par 72. Pestana Golf Academy. *Green Fees:* from €62.50 to €92.50, (2007). *Eating facilities:* restaurant, bar plus magnificent terrace. *Visitors:* welcome, open all year round. Luxury villas, townhouses and apartments; accommodation available. Professional: Carlos Ribeiro (282 340440; Fax: 282 3409001). Secretary: Rui Gago. Director of Golf: José Matias. weblste:www.pestanagolf.com

LAGOA. **Vale de Pinta Course,** Pestana Golf Resorts Algarve, Carvoeira, Apartado 1011, 8400-908 Lagoa (+351 282 340900; Fax: +351 282 340901). *Location:* 2km south of Lagoa , follow signposting. Situated in ancient olive groves with trees 700 years old. Championship 18 holes, 6115 metres. Par 71. Pestana Golf Academy. *Green Fees:* from €62.50 to €92.50, (2007). *Eating facilities:* new clubhouse, restaurant, bar plus magnificent terrace. *Visitors:* welcome, open all year round, buggies, trolleys, great practice facilities, luxury villas, townhouses and apartments; accommodation available. Professional: Carlos Ribeiro (282 340440; Fax: 282 3409001). Secretary: Rui Gago. Director of Golf: José Matias. website: www.pastanagolf.com

LAGOS. **Boavista Golf Resort,** Apartado 62, 8601-901 Lagos (00 351 282 000111; Fax: 00 351 282 000150). *Location*: 500m west of 2nd roundabout on the Lagos spur (Junction 1) of the Trans-Algarve Highway (A22). Spectacular clifftop golf with stunning views. 18 holes, 6,053 metres, Par 71. Driving range, short game area, putting greens. *Green fees:* information not available. *Eating facilities:* bar and restaurant. *Visitors*: welcome, normal dress code, soft spikes; Handicap Certificate required – maximum 27 men; 34 ladies; booking essential. Carts, trolleys and clubs for rent. Golf Director: Antonio Castelo.*
e-mail: golf.reception@boavistagolf.com

LAGOS. **Palmares Golf,** Apartado 74, Meia Praia, 860-901 Lagos (282 790500; Fax: 282 790509). *Location*: five km from centre of Lagos on main Meia Praia beach road. Five links type holes - very scenic and serene. Magnificent views over Lagos Bay. 18 holes, 5961 metres. S.S.S. 72, Par 71. Driving range, putting green, pitch and putt area. *Green Fees*: high season €89, low season €59. *Eating facilities*: Palmares Restaurant serving international and Portuguese cuisine with fresh fish. Panoramic bar and veranda with spectacular views over the Bay of Lagos. *Visitors*: open to all players with Handicap Certificate all year round. Golf shops, trolleys, buggies and golf lessons available. *Society Meetings*: always welcome at all times. Professionals: Luis Espadinha and José Dias.
e-mail: golf@palmaresgolf.com
website: www.palmaresgolf.com

www.uk-golfguide.com

The Old Course, Vilamoura

PORTIMAO. **Golfe dos Alamos,** Apartado 293, 8501-912 Portimao (351 282 402 150/1; Fax: 351 282 402 153). *Location:* travelling towards Portimao, take Monchique turning (Exit 5). Continue for 5km, turn left at golf course sign and follow signs to clubhouse. Scenic course with tight, undulating fairways bounded by native trees. 18 holes, 5641 metres. Par 71. Driving range, chipping and putting greens. Green Fees: information not available. Eating facilities: bar and restaurant. Visitors: welcome. Clubs, trolley and buggy hire. Professional: Nelson Cavalheiro. Manager: Jorge Papa.*

PORTIMAO. **Golfe do Morgado,** Apartado 293, 8501-912 Portimao (351 282 402 150/1; Fax: 351 282 402 153). Location: from the A22, direction Portimao, take Exit 5 (Portimao/Monchique) and follow direction Monchique. After one km, turn left at 'Golf' sign. A moderately landscaped course, one of the longest in the region, with large greens, lakes and strategic bunkers. 18 holes, 6,399 metres, Par 73. Second course Golfe dos Alamos, 18 holes, 5641 metres, S.S.S. 71. Driving range, putting and chipping greens with practice bunkers. Green fees: information not available. *Eating facilities:* bar and restaurant. *Visitors:* welcome; maximum handicaps – 28 men; 36 ladies. Electric carts, trolleys, club rental. Professional: Nelson Cavalheiro. Manager: Jorge Papa.*
e-mail: playgolf@golfedomorgado.com

PORTIMAO/PENINA. **Penina Golf Club,** Le Meridien Penina Golf & Resort, PO Box 146, Penina, 8501-952 Portimao (351 282 420 200; Fax: 351 282 420 300). *Location:* five km from Portimao, 12km from Lagos. Long, flat course with lakes, trees and bunkers. 18 holes (plus two 9 hole courses), 6935 yards, 6273 metres. S.S.S. 73. Also Resort Course - 9 holes, 3268 yards, 2987 metres. S.S.S. 35 and Academy Course - 9 holes, 2035 yards, 1851 metres. S.S.S. 30. Golf academy, putting greens. Green Fees: please check with hotel. Eating facilities: clubhouse and Hotel restaurants. Visitors: welcome, Handicap Certificate (28 for men and 36 for ladies) and soft spike shoes required to play all courses. Society Meetings: welcome. Professional: José Lourenco, Robin Liddle and José Marcelino. Course Manager: Leonel Rio.
e-mail: reservations.penina@starwoodhotels.com
golf.penina@starwoodhotels.com
website: www.lemeridien.com/penina

QUINTA DO LAGO. **Pinheiros Altos Golf Club,** Quinta do Lago, 8135 Almancil, Algarve (289 359910; Fax: 289 394392). *Location:* south of Almancil just east of the Quinta do Lago and San Lorenzo courses, bear left on first roundabout at Quinta do Lago. Pine trees and water hazards with fast bent grass greens and the island green 17th hole. 18 holes, 6236 metres. Par 72. Driving range areas, three putting greens, two chipping/ bunker areas. Green Fees: information not available. Eating facilities: restaurant, snack bar; drinks buggy. Visitors: welcome, Handicap Certificate required: Men 28, Ladies 36. Pro shop; club hire. 'A' Star equipped Golf Academy. Society Meetings: on request. Professionals: Ross Sutherland, Kenny Fairbairn, Max Evans. Director of Golf: Brian Evans.*

SILVES. **Silves Golf Course,** Pestana Golf Resorts Algarve, Eurogolfe S.A., Vila Fria, 8300 Silves (+351 282 440130; Fax: +351 282 440131). *Location:* 3km south-east of Silves, follow signposting. A strategic masterpiece, undulating through olive groves. 18 holes, 5615 metres Par 70. Pestana Golf Academy. *Green Fees:* €75.00 (2007). *Eating facilities:* Restaurant, bar plus magnificent terrace. *Visitors:* welcome, open all year round, accommodation available. Professional: Carlos Ribeiro (282 340440; Fax: 282 3409001). Secretary: Rui Gago. Director of Golf: José Matias.
website: www.pastanagolf.com

VILAMOURA. **Laguna Golf Course,** Lusotur Golfes SA, 8125 - 507 Vilamoura, Algarve (00 351 289 310 180; Fax: 00 351 289 310 183). *Location:* 20 kms from Faro Airport, 25 kms from Faro. Relatively flat, open course with challenging placement of bunkers and water hazards, designed by Joseph Lee. 18 holes. 6133 metres. Par 72. Practice facilities, putting green, driving range. *Green Fees:* information not available. *Eating facilities:* restaurant and bar. *Visitors:* open to players with Handicap Certificate (max. Men 28, Ladies 36). *Society Meetings:* welcome at all times. Pro shop, equipment hire. Professionals: Abilio Coelho and Joaquim Catarino (089 380724). Bookings: (00 351 289 310 333; Fax: 00 351 289 310 349). Commercial Manager: Alice Carlota. Golf Manager: Eduardo de Sousa.*
e-mail: reservas_golfe@lusotur.pt
website: www.vilamoura.net

VILAMOURA. **Millennium Golf Course, Clube de Golfe Vilamoura,** Lusotur Golfes SA, 8125 - 507 Vilamoura, Algarve (00 351 289 310 188; Fax: 00 351 289 310 183). *Location:* 20km from Faro Airport, 25km from Faro. Narrow fairways through pine woods and natural countryside. 18 holes, 6143 metres. Par 72. Practice and putting greens, driving range. *Green Fees:* information not available. *Eating facilities:* restaurant and bar. *Visitors:* course open to all players with Handicap Certificate (max. Men 24, Ladies 28). Soft spikes only. Pro shop, hire of trolleys. Professional: Abilio Coelho and Joaquim Catarino Bookings: (00 351 289 310 333; Fax: 00 351 289 310 349). Commercial Manager: Alice Carlota. Golf Manager: Eduardo de Sousa.*
e-mail: reservas_golfe@lusotur.pt
website: www.vilamoura.net

VILAMOURA. **The Old Course, Clube de Golfe Vilamoura,** Lusotur Golfes SA, 8125 - 507 Vilamoura, Algarve (00 351 289 310 341; Fax: 00 351 289 310 321). *Location:* 20km from Faro Airport, 25km from Faro. Narrow fairways through pine woods, sea views. 18 holes, 6254 metres. Par 73. Practice and putting greens; driving range. *Green Fees:* information not available. *Eating facilities:* restaurant and bar. *Visitors:* course open to all players with Handicap Certificate (max. Men 24, Ladies 28). Soft spikes only. Pro shop, equipment hire. Professional: Joaquim Sequeira. Bookings: (00 351 289 310 333; Fax: 00 351 289 310 349). Commercial Manager: Alice Carlota. Golf Manager: Eduardo de Sousa.*
e-mail: reservas_golfe@lusotur.pt
website: www.vilamoura.net

VILAMOURA. **Pinhal Golf Course,** Lusotur Golfes SA, 8125 - 507 Vilamoura, Algarve (00 351 289 310 390; Fax: 00 351 289 310 393). *Location:* 20 kms from Faro Airport. Pine wood setting and magnificent sea views, designed by Frank Pennink and Robert Trent Jones. 18 holes, 6353 metres. Par 72. Driving range and putting green. *Green Fees:* information not available. *Eating facilities:* bar and restaurant. *Visitors:* open to players with Handicap Certificate (max. Men 28, Ladies 36), all year round. *Society Meetings:* welcome at any time. Pro shop, equipment hire. Professionals: Manuel Pardal and Francisco Pontes. Bookings: (00 351 289 310 333; Fax: 00 351 289 310 349). Commercial Manager: Alice Carlota. Golf Manager: Maria de Jesus Beltrão.*
e-mail: reservas_golfe@lusotur.pt
website: www.vilamoura.net

VILAMOURA. **Victoria Clube de Golfe,** Lusotur Golfes S.A., Apartado 970. 8126-912 Vilamoura, Algarve (00 351 289 320 100; Fax: 00 351 289 320 104). *Location*: 20 km west from Faro airport on N125. Follow signs on left for Vilamoura and golf. A new links-style championship course by Arnold Palmer, complementing the four existing courses, with indigenous carob, almond and olive trees, and many large water hazards. An excellent strategic test, with superb clubhouse and practice facilities, venue for the World Cup in November 2005. 18 holes, 6,560 metres, Par 72. Driving range, huge putting green, plus bunker and chipping areas. *Green Fees:* information not provided. *Eating facilities:* restaurant, bar, buggy bar on course. *Visitors:* welcome; maximum handicap – men 24, ladies 28. Soft spikes only. Electric and pull trolleys, club rental. Golf Manager: Maria de Jesus Beltrao.
e-mail: reservasgolfea@vilamouragolf.com
website: www.vilamouragolf.com

VILAMOURA. **Vila Sol Spa & Golf Resort,** Morgadinhos, 8125-307, Vilamoura, Algarve (289 300 505/502; Fax: 289 316499). *Location*: just east of Vilamoura off the road leading down to Quarteira. An excellent natural course undulating through umbrella pines with good water hazards and superb greens. Voted "One of the Top 10 European Golf Resorts" by Golf World 2006. 27 holes, 6320 metres - men 5372 metres, ladies 5372 metres. Par 72, S.S.S 72. Driving range, putting green. *Green Fees*: information not available. *Eating facilities*: bar and restaurant in clubhouse and also L'Olive Gourmet restaurant and Piano Bar La Palmeraie. *Visitors*: welcome. Handicap Certificate required. Soft spikes only. (Men 27, Ladies 35). Pro shop; cart, trolley, buggy and club hire; golf academy. Five star Vila Sol Hotel and apartments, Vila Sol Spa, Vila Sol Beach, several bars and restaurants also available.Professional: Peter Lester. Golf Secretary: Miguel Lourenco.*
e-mail: golfsecretary@vilasol.pt
e-mail: golfreservation@vilasol.pt
website: www.vilasol.pt

LISBON

AROEIRA. **Aroeira Golf,** Herdade da Aroeira, 2820 567 Chameca de Caparica, Aroeira, Costa Lisboa (00351 21 2979110; Fax: 00351 21 2971238). *Location:* south from Lisbon across the bridge, turn right to Costa Caparica and follow signs. This well-established course remains one of Portugal's best kept secrets. Venue of Portugal Open-European Tour 1996, 1997; Portuguese Ladies' Open 2002, 2003 and 2004. A superb test through a floral pine forest by Frank Pennink; one for purists to savour. 18 holes, 6040 metres, Par 72. Practice ground with shelters for bad/ hot weather. Aroeira 2 opened in 2000, designed by Donald Steel. *Green Fees:* information not provided. *Eating facilities:* restaurant, snack bar, oocktail bar and lounge. *Visitors:* welcome, no restrictions; subject only to having a valid Handicap and availability of tees. Private apartments with 1,2 or 3 bedrooms available for rental, all facing the Golf Course. Self catering. New golf school specialising in intensive courses, indoor and outdoor facilities. Driving range. Buggies, electric trolleys and golf bags available for hire. Professional: Joaquim Moura. Operations Director: Carlos Fonseca. Commercial Director: Francisco Pinto Leite. President: Pedro Silveira.
e-mail: golf.reservas@aroeira.com
website: www.aroeira.com

AZEITAO. **Quinta do Peru Golf Course,** Alameda da Serra 2, 2975-666 Quinta do Conde (+351 21 213 43 20; Fax: +351 21 213 43 21). *Location*: Cross the bridge "25 de Abril" and follow A2 motorway to Junction 3 (24km from Lisbon). Exit A2 at Junction 3 – pass through toll (portagem) then immediately exit right up slope, signs to "COINA"– then follow signs to Quinta do Peru – Golf. Fine new, American- shaped course laid out through rolling pine woods with lakes and fine views. 18 holes, 6036 metres. S.S.S. 72. Driving range, two putting greens, chipping and bunker practice area. *Green Fees*: weekends €88, weekdays €58. *Eating facilities*: restaurant and bar in clubhouse. *Visitors*: welcome. Pro shop, carts, trolleys, club hire. Professional: António Dantas. Manager: Pedro de Mello Breyner.
e-mail: play@golfquintadoperu.com
website: www.golfquintadoperu.com

BELAS. **Belas Clube de Campo,** Al. Aqueduto, 2605-193 Belas (21 962 6640; Fax: 21 962 6644). *Location:* make your way to the CREL (A9) from either the A1, A5, A8 or IC19. From the CREL take the exit signposted 'Belas', and after the toll, follow signs to N250. At the N250 T-junction turn right. First left over small bridge and then follow signs to Club. Very new, American-designed course built on a grand scale amongst a dramatic rolling landscape. 18 holes, 6380 metres. S.S.S. 72. Pro shop, driving range, short game area, putting green. *Green Fees*: information not available. *Eating facilities*: restaurant and bar. *Visitors*: welcome. Carts, trolleys, club hire. Professional: Keith Barret. Director: Fernando Nunes Pedro.*
e-mail: golfe@planbelas.pt
website: www.belasgolf.com

ESTORIL. **Academia de Golf Estoril Sol,** Estrada da Lagoa Azue, Quinta do Outeiro, Linho, Sintra 2710-314 (00351-21-924 04 44). *Location:* take the main Cascais-Sintra road and turn left at the village of Linho towards Lagoa Azul. 9 holes (18 tees), 1805 metres. S.S.S. 62. Purpose-built golf academy - practice facility, chipping greens, putting green. *Green Fees:* information not available. *Eating facilities:* restaurant and bar. *Visitors:* no restrictions. *Society Meetings:* welcome. Bennett's Golf Learning Centre. Golf Academy with full services. Three Professionals. Golf Director: Tony Bennett.*
e-mail: scoringzone@hotmail.com

ESTORIL. **Golf Do Estoril,** Avenida Da Republica, 2765-273 Estoril (351 214 680176; Fax: 351 214 682796). *Location:* in Estoril. An undulating links course with views of the Atlantic and Sintra Mountains. 18 holes, 5238 metres. S.S.S. 69. *Green Fees:* information not available. Reductions for Estoril Palacio Hotel guests. Driving range. *Eating facilities*: Clubhouse with bar and restaurant. Professionals: Joaquim Rodrigues, Henrique Pallino, Carlos Aleixo. Director: Francisco Pinherio.*

ESTORIL. **Hotel Quinta da Marinha & Villas Golf Resort,** Quinta da Marinha, Casa 36 - 2750 Cascais (351 1 4860180; Fax: 351 1 4869032). *Location:* 3km from Cascais centre, 25km from Lisbon, near Guincho beach. Championship golf course designed by Robert Trent Jones. Open sandy course with pine trees, lakes and spectacular views over the mountains and ocean. 18 holes, 6684 yards. S.S.S. 71. Driving range, putting greens. *Green Fees:* information not available. *Eating facilities:* bar, restaurant and club house. *Visitors:* welcome. Men's Handicap 28, Ladies' Handicap 36. Club hire, trolley rental; Pro shop. Accommodation available in 42 villas or the new 200-bedroom Hotel Quinta da Marinha facing the course, with conference facilities, swimming pools, tennis courts and health centre. *Society Meetings:* not applicable. Professional: Richard Allen. Golf Director: Maria Padrela.*

ESTORIL. **Penha Longa Hotel & Golf Resort,** Estrada da Lagoa Azul, Linho, 2714-511 Sintra (21.524.9031; Fax: 21.924.9024). *Location:* half an hour west of Lisbon, just north of Estoril on the main road to Sintra. Designed by Robert Trent Jones Jnr, laid out over craggy hills, wooded slopes and valleys surrounding an ancient royal palace; the 18 holes hosted the Portuguese Open in 1994 and again in 1995. 18 holes, 6910 yards, 6290 metres. S.S.S. 73. 9 holes, 2845 yards, 2588metres. S.S.S. 35. Driving range, large putting green, chipping green with two bunkers. *Green Fees:* information not available. *Eating facilities:* three bars and four restaurants. *Visitors:* welcome, Handicap Certificate required. Five star Hotel and Country Club; eight tennis courts, squash and bicycles. Golf Academy, Pro shop, cart, trolley, club and shoe hire. Sauna, jacuzzi. No jeans. Professional: Robert Judd/Antonio Dantas. Director: Andrew Glen.*

ESTORIL. **Quinta da Marinha Oitavos Golfe,** Lote 64, 2750-004 Cascais (351 21 486 0606; Fax: 351 21 486 0609). *Location*: from Cascais, take the seaside coast road direction Sintra-Guincho. Entrance to golf on right

about 3 km. A fine new course by Arthur Hills, set among pine woods and reforested dunes in the Sintra-Cascais Natural Park protected environment. Superb views of sea and mountains. 18 holes, 6,379 metres, Par 71. Driving range, short game practice area, two putting greens, golf lessons. *Green Fees:* information not available. *Eating facilities:* bar and restaurant in modern clubhouse with regional, Italian and international menus. Also seaview deck. *Visitors:* welcome. Maximum handicap: 28 men; 36 ladies. Soft spikes. Restricted times weekends and Bank Holidays. Electric carts, manual and electric trolleys, club rental, pro shop. Professional: Philip A'Court. Golf Director: Nuno Teixeira Bastos.*
e-mail: oitavosgolfe@quinta-da-marinha.pt

LISBON. **Lisbon Sports Club,** Casal da Carregueira, Belas - 2605-213 Belas (214 310 077; Fax: 213 312 482). *Location:* 25 km from Lisbon. Parkland. 18 holes, 5233 metres. Par 69. *Green Fees:* information not available. Putting green, pitch area and practice bunker. *Eating facilities:* clubhouse with restaurant, bar and swimming pool, sauna. *Visitors:* welcome, Handicap Certificate required. Trolley, buggy and club hire available.   Lessons available with Professional. Professional: José Baltazar (00 4321474). President: Joao Salgado (00 432 1474).*
e-mail: geral@lisbonclub.com
website: www.lisbonclub.com

OBIDOS. **Praia D'el Rey Golf and Country Club,** Vale de Janelas, Apartado 2, 2510 Obidos (262 905005; Fax: 262 905009). *Location:* from A8 to Obidos, take turnoff 14 to Peniche and follow EN114, turn right at course sign in Sierra D'el Rey. True links course; one of the best in Europe. 18 holes, 6467 metres. S.S.S. 72. Driving range, pitching and putting greens. *Green Fees:* information not available. *Eating facilities:* snack bar, bar, restaurant. *Visitors:* always welcome. Caddies, trolleys, equipment hire.*
e-mail: golf@praia-del-rey.com

PRAIA DE MIRAMAR. **Clube de Golf de Miramar,** Av. Sacadura Cabral, Miramar, 4405-013 Arcozelo (22 7622067; Fax: 22 7627859). *Location*: approximately 13km south of Oporto by A1, N109 direction Espinho. Flat coastal course amongst dunes alongside the beach. 9 holes, 4884 metres. S.S.S. 67. Driving range. *Green Fees*: information not available. *Eating facilities*: clubhouse with restaurant and bar. *Visitors*: welcome, Handicap Certificate required. Hotels, restaurants and casino nearby. Pro shop. Professional: Sergio Ribeiro, Nelson Ribeiro. Secretary: Paula Sousa.*

RIO MAIOR. **Golden Eagle Golf Club,** Golden Eagle, EN 1, Km 63/64, 2040-481 Rio Maior (+351 243 908 148; Fax: +351 243 908 149). *Location:* A1 from Lisbon to Aveiras exit, follow N366, turn right to IC2, and immediately on left, course on right at 63km. Undulating heathland with strategic sand and water. 18 holes, 6623 metres. S.S.S. 72. Driving range, putting green, clubhouse, pro shop. *Green Fees:* information not available. *Eating facilities:* bar, restaurant. *Visitors:* always welcome. Trolley hire available.*

TORRES VEDRAS. **Campo Real,** Edificio da Administracao, 2565-779 Turcifal (351 261 950 200; Fax: 351 261 950 201). *Location*: 30 minutes' drive north-west of Lisbon. Take A8 motorway to Km. 36, then 2 km to 619-1. A new (2005) course by Donald Steel in a dramatic setting of wooded mountains. Strategic golf in a superb inland location. 18 holes, 6011 metres, Par 72. Large driving range and practice putting green, short game area, academy, Pro shop. *Green Fees:* information not available. Carts, trolleys available. *Eating facilities:* restaurant and bar in clubhouse; snacks on course. *Visitors*: welcome. Soft spikes; dress code. Manager: Michael Stagnetto; Professional: Matthew Tipper.*
e-mail: golfe.reservas@camporeal.pt

TROIA. **Troia Golf Club,** Troia, Carvalhal GDL (265 494112; Fax: 265 494315). *Location:* on the Troia Peninsula, 42 km south of Lisbon. From Lisbon, A2/A12 to Setubal, then follow signs for Troia to the ferry boat; in Troia follow EN243-1 to Comporta; golf course signposted. Spectacular links, 30th on list of Europe's 100 best golf courses and a superb challenge to all golfers. Designed by Robert Trent Jones Snr; host to Portuguese Open-European Tour in 1983. 18 holes, 6320 metres Par 72. Driving range, two putting greens, practice area. *Green Fees:* information not available. *Eating facilities:* clubhouse with bar/restaurant. *Visitors:* welcome, Handicap Certificate (27 men, 35 ladies). Hotel accommodation available (265 499030). Special rates for Troia Hotels guests. Pro shop, trolley and buggy rental. Director of Golf : Henrique de Sousa.*

VIMEIRO. **Vimeiro Golf Club,** Praia de Porto Novo, Termas do Vimeiro, 2660 Torres Vedras (+351 261 980 800). *Location:* situated in a wonderful cliff over the Atlantic coast, next to the beach. A level course divided by a river and sheltered by rocky cliffs. 9 holes with 18 tees, 5228 yards. S.S.S. 67. *Green Fees:* information not available. *Eating facilities:* restaurant In hotel Golf Mar, three bars. Caddies and hand trolleys available.*

www.uk-golfguide.com

MADEIRA

FUNCHAL. **Palheiro Golf Club,** Rua Do Balancal No 29, 9060 - 414 Funchal (00 351 291 790120; Fax: 00 351 291 792456). *Location:* take Camacha turn-off from airport road, straight on under bridge, past car inspection centre (I.P.O.). Follow golf signs. A Cabell Robinson design, built on a hill top overlooking Funchal. Parkland course, amazing views with superb trees and flora. 18 holes, 6086 metres. Par 72. Driving range, putting green. *Green Fees:* €92 from 1st October 2007 - 30th September 2008. *Eating facilities:* bar and restaurant – excellent international cuisine. Pro shop; cart, trolley and club hire. Casa Velha, the five-star hotel, is situated on the course. Professional: Philip Talbot PGA.
website: www.palheiroestate.com

MADEIRA. **Campo de Golfe da Madeira,** Santo Antonio da Serra, 9100 Santa Cruz (291 550100; Fax: 291 550105). *Location:* main highway to Airport (Santa Cruz) Machilo. Wooded, mountainous with view over Atlantic Ocean. 27 holes, 6082 metres. Driving range, putting and chipping green. *Green Fees:* information not available. *Eating facilities:* restaurant, snack bar, lounge bar. *Visitors:* welcome to play in tournaments except PGA Madeira Island Open (January). Pro shop; cart, trolley and club hire. Professional: Joao Sousa. Secretary: Anthony Barton (acting).*

PORTO SANTO. **Porto Santo Golfe,** Sitio das Marinhas, 9400-162 Porto Santo, P.O.Box 174 (351 291 983 777; Fax: 351 291 983 508). *Location:* Porto Santo island – 15 minutes' flight from Madeira and one hour from Lisbon. The course is 10 minutes from Porto Santo airport. Designed by Severiano Ballesteros, the course combines length and strategic water hazards with some links-style cliff top holes overlooking the sea. 18 holes, 6,434 metres, S.S.S.Par 72. Driving range, putting green, chipping green with bunkers. *Green fees:* information not available. *Eating facilities:* two bars and restaurant with panoramic verandah views. Buggy bar. *Visitors:* welcome. Golf carts, electric and pull trolleys, club rental. Professional: Andrew Oliveira. Manager: Mario Silva.*
e-mail: sdps@netmadeira.com

Campo de Golfe da Madeira

OPORTO

AMARANTE. **Amarante Golf Clube, Quinta da Deveza,** Fregim, 4600 - 593 Amarante. (+351 255 44 60 60; Fax: +351 255 44 62 02). *Location*: take A4 from Oporto heading to Vila Real, come off at Amarante Oeste, then follow signs for Fregim, the golf course is signposted from here. A true mountain course with spectacular views over surrounding peaks and valleys. 18 holes, 5035 metres. Par 68. Driving range, putting green, bunker and chipping practice area. *Green Fees*: information not available. *Eating facilities*: restaurant and bar in clubhouse. *Visitors*: welcome. Carts, trolleys, club hire. Pro-shop, swimming pools, tennis courts. Hotels – Casa Da Calçada Relais & Chateaux (+351 255 410830; Fax: +351 255 426670); Hotel Navarras (+351 255 431 036; Fax: +351 255 432 991) Professional: João Silva. Golf Director: Pedro Fonseca.*
e-mail: sgagolfeamarante@oninet.pt
website: www.amarantegolfclube.com

ESPINHO. **Oporto Golf Club,** Paramos, 4500 Espinho (227 342008; Fax: 227 346895). *Location*: 18 miles south of Oporto, one mile south of Espinho. Seaside links, few trees, founded in 1890. 18 holes, 5556 metres. Course rating 70.2; Slope rating 127; Par 71. Practice ground. *Green Fees:* information not available. Half price for guests of Hotels mentioned below. *Eating facilities:* bar with snacks (restaurant - members only). *Visitors:* welcome Tuesdays to Fridays (closed Mondays); weekends and Bank Holidays till 10.30am. Handicap Certificate required. Beach, hotels - Hotel Solverde, Hotel Praia - Golf, casino nearby. Professional: Eduardo Maganinho (02 7313649).*

ESPOSENDE. **Golfe de Quinta da Barca,** Gemezes, Barca do Lago, 4740 476 Esposende (+351 253 966723; Fax: +351 253 969068). *Location*: 50km north of Oporto on JC 1, turn right to Esposende and before Esposende turn to Quinta da Barca. A 9 hole course but very demanding. The river, lakes, bunkers and undulating greens make it a precision test. 9 holes, 1927 metres. C.R. 62,2; S.R. 106. Driving range, putting and chipping greens, apart hotel, marina, tennis. *Green Fees*: information not available. *Eating facilities*: restaurant and bar in clubhouse. *Visitors*: welcome. Pro shop, caddies, cart, trolley, club hire. Professional: Manuel Carneiro. Director: Luis Catarino.*
e-mail: lcatarino@quintabarca.com
website: www.quintabarca.com

ESTELA. **Estela Golf Club,** Rio Alto-Estela, 4490 Povoa de Varzim (52 612700/601567; Fax: 52 612701). *Location:* 30 km north of Oporto, 24 km from the international airport. Seaside links. 18 holes, 6095 metres. S.S.S. 73. *Green Fees:* information not available. *Eating facilities:* full bar and catering facilities. *Visitors:* welcome anytime when no competitions taking place. Sopete Hotel guests entitled to special privileges. *Society Meetings:* by arrangement. Professionals: Carlos Alberto, Carlos Henrique. Secretary/Manager: Salete Correia.*

PONTE DE LIMA. **Golfe de Ponte de Lima,** Quinta de Pias, Fornelos, 4990 Ponte de Lima (258 743414; Fax: 258 743424). *Location*: one kilometre north of Ponte de Lima on EN201. Beautiful and scenic; hilly front nine. 18 holes, 6005 metres. S.S.S. 70. Driving range, Putting green, chipping and bunker practice area. *Green Fees*: information not available. *Eating facilities*: restaurant and bar in clubhouse "Beni-Golf". *Visitors*: welcome. Pro shop, caddies, cart, trolley, club hire. Professionals: Manuel Carneiro, Paulo Teixeira. Director: Manuel Farncisco de Miguel.*

VIDAGO. **Vidago Golf Club,** Vidago 5425 (276 999404; Fax: 276 907359). *Location:* mountain valley course, in spa/resort area well inland, only 25 km from Spanish border. Short 9-hole course, 1000ft high, 2678 yards. S.S.S. 63 (18 holes). *Green Fees:* information not available. *Eating facilities:* Vidago Palace Hotel.*

THE AZORES

SAO MIGUEL. **Batalha Golf Course,** Rua do Bom Jesus, Aflitos, 9545-234 Fenais da Luz, Sao Miguel-Azores (296 498559; Fax: 296 498284). *Location:* go north from Ponta Delgada in direction Faja de Cima, turn right for Aflitos before reaching Fenais da Luz. Championship course with sweeping views over large flowing greens with wide and generous fairways. Beautiful surroundings and fabulous scenery. 18 holes, 6435 metres. S.S.S. 72. Driving range, two large putting greens, chipping area. *Green Fees:* information not provided. *Eating facilities:* modern clubhouse with classic island architecture; bars and restaurant. *Visitors:* welcome. Complete range of support services. Caddies, carts, trolleys, club hire. Professional: Rui Indio. Golf Director: Luis Indio (296 498559).
e-mail: geral@azoresgolfislands.com

SAO MIGUEL. **Furnas Golf Course,** Achada das Furnas, 9675-030 Furnas, Sao Miguel-Azores. (296 584341; Fax: 296 498284). *Location:* 40 minutes from Ponta Delgada. Designed originally by McKenzie Ross and extended by Bob Cameron. Unique style and characteristics, with fairways flanked by trees and fiendishly undulating greens. 18 holes, 6232 metres. Par 72. *Green Fees:* information not available. *Eating facilities:* modern clubhouse; bar, restaurant. *Visitors:* always welcome. Carts, trolleys, club hire. Professional: Rui Indio. Golf Director: Luis Indio (296 584341).*

TERCEIRA. **Terceira Golf Club,** Caixa Postal 15, 9760 Praia da Vitoria, Terceira (00351 295 902444/902299; Fax: 00351 295 902445). *Location:* a few kilometres from Angra do Heroismo and Praia da Vitoria on the island of Terceira in the Azores. Landscaped course through trees and low hills, with small lakes. 18 holes, 6227 metres. S.S.S. 70. Practice facilities. *Green Fees:* (2007) 58. *Eating facilities:* available. *Visitors:* always welcome. Hotel accommodation nearby. *Society Meetings:* always welcome. Professional: Eduardo Correia. General Director: Antonio P. Camara.

A scenic delight – Aloha Golf Club, Marbella

Holiday Golf in Spain

Michael Gedye

DESPITE THE FACT that some of the most successful and colourful performers in the game have been Spanish - Ballesteros, Olazabal and Garcia for example – the nation as a whole has just started to play the game in any depth. But there is a clear distinction between members' clubs, mostly sited near the larger inland cities, and the attractive range of holiday golf courses, built in an ever-expanding chain around the whole of the Mediterranean coastline. For most, Spanish golf remains an elite and expensive pastime, with football and bullfighting still the most popular spectator sports. Although golf has been played here for more than century, only in the last forty years has there been a real

expansion and that has primarily been to accommodate tourists and foreign retirees. No less than 65% of the country's courses are to be found in the five most popular holiday areas – Andalucia, Murcia, Valencia, Catalonia and Majorca.

Since the introduction of cheap charter flights and tour packages nearly fifty years ago, the plethora of highly- developed coastal resorts has grown to meet a steadily rising demand from an eclectic summer holiday market. Such rapid development brought inevitable problems in its wake. How to provide off-season employment for the myriad hotels, restaurants and related staff geared to a seasonal, cosmopolitan business. Golf provided the solution, appealing to a different sector able not only to travel in the off-peak season, but also able to afford to buy second homes or retirement property alongside the sun-drenched, newly-constructed fairways.

Golf courses, the number approaching the 200 mark, sprouted like mushrooms around the prime coastal locations. From an initial foothold in the north-eastern Costa Brava, they crept inevitably down to the southern sunshine coast, the Costa del Sol. In a European mirror-image of the hugely popular coast of Myrtle Beach in the U.S.A., a raft of mainly economy-class hotels fronted an inland wealth of verdant treasure, newly-constructed golf courses, many of genuine quality, designed by some of the best-known names in the business. Visitors can test themselves over layouts designed by international maestros Jack Nicklaus, Robert Trent Jones (both father and son), Cabel Robinson, Gary Player and Perry Dye or the domestic achievements of Severiano Ballesteros, Javier Arana, Jose Maria Olazabal, Pepe Gancedo and Manuel Pinero. Many major tournaments have been played here, including two World Cups (Real Club de Golf Las Brisas), the Ryder Cup (Valderrama), many Spanish Opens and other PGA European Tour events.

Spain is a large, mainly arid country, built on history and steeped in legend. It has proved hugely popular as a tourist venue with northern Europeans, especially the British, Swedish and Germans. Proud, brash and colourful, this land of tapas and tortillas, sangria and sherry can offer golf for all – from difficult tests of genuine championship calibre, through attractive courses where well-watered green ribbons of fairway snake past low hills dotted with cork oak and olive trees to a number of well-equipped teaching academies, even 24-hour floodlit golf for insomniacs! In an attractive Mediterranean climate, Spain offers a convenient escape to off-season sunshine, a vibrant culture and golf to suit players of all levels of ability.

The focal point for most real holiday golfers is **ANDALUCIA** and the ever-expanding Costa del Sol in the south, nicknamed the "Costa del Golf". To the west, in the Costa del Luz, are a number of courses including the Tour Championship venue of Montecastillo, Novo Sancti Petri, classic Sotogrande amid its rolling cork oaks and the Ryder Cup location of Valderrama. More recent arrivals include San Roque and the Sherry Golf club near Jerez. Centrally, enjoy the class of Las Brisas, La

Sea vistas at Alcanada Club de Golf, Majorca

Panoramic view – golf at Pals, Costa Brava

Quinta and Los Arqueros and the dramatic settings of La Cala and Monte Mayor. To the east, the serene seaside pleasures of Anoreta and Golf Almerimar.

Turn north along the coast to **MURCIA** and discover the La Manga resort. Along with a range of other sports facilities, three excellent palm-fringed courses lie beneath a series of low hills. Further on is **VALENCIA,** home of paella and a superb state-owned course and parador hotel, El Saler, designed by Javier Arana. Nearby, you can play attractive Golf Escorpion, Villamartin and demanding El Bosque.

The north-eastern region of Girona and the popular Costa Brava is covered by **CATALONIA.** There are number of very playable courses in the area, with the two at Pals, tucked discreetly amongst rolling pinewoods by the sea, offering a peaceful challenge.

The most frequented island, **MAJORCA,** in the Balearics, also offers the widest selection of resort golf. The latest arrival is Son Muntaner, ranging over the wooded slopes near Son Vida, itself a long-established golfing favourite. Another new location is the Robert Trent Jones Jr-designed layout of Alcanada in the north-west of the island, offering attractive golf sloping gently down to views of distant islands and the Sierra Levante mountains. Other good tests include Santa Ponsa. Poniente and Capdepera. Sun-kissed but tempered by sea breezes, this a good destination for those looking for relaxation and a tan as well as a good score.

ANDALUCIA – CENTRAL

BENAHAVIS. La Quinta Golf and Country Club, Urb La Quinta, s/n 29660 Nueva, Andalucia (Marbella), Malaga (95.276.23.90; Fax: 95.276.23.99). *Location:* on main road to Ronda, 3.5km from N340 coast road. Inland hilly course. 18 holes, 5517 metres, Par 72, S.S.S. 71; also 9 hole course, 2848 metres. Par 36, S.S.S. 71. *Green Fees:* information not available. *Eating facilities:* clubhouse, restaurant. *Visitors:* welcome, please book in advance. Golf Academy, Pro-shop, table tennis, squash, sauna, swimming pool, fitness centre, therapic and static centre. *Society Meetings:* welcome. Professional: Manuel Pinero. Director: D. Marcos Lería Couderc.*

BENAHAVIS. Monte Mayor Golf Club, Apartado 962, 29679 Benahavis (Malaga) (952 937111; Fax: 952 937112. *Location:* in the hills between San Pedro de Alcantara and Estepona; inland from Ctra. N-340, km. 165.6. Possibly the Costa del Sol's most spectacular course, a challenging layout over mountainous terrain for the bold and accurate. 18 holes, 5652 metres, Par 71. *Green Fees:* information not available. *Eating facilities:* bar and restaurant in clubhouse. Pyr Hotel, Puerto Banos - very good package for golfers.*

BENALMADENA. Golf Torrequebrada, Edif Club de Golf, 29630 Benalmadena (95 244 27 42; Fax: 95 256 11 29). *Location:* Exit CN 340 at junction 222. Undulating terrain, lots of vegetation, superb views over Mediterranean Sea. 18 holes, 5852 metres, Par 72. Driving range. *Green Fees:* information not available *Eating facilities:* full bar and restaurant. *Visitors:* welcome at all times. Handicap Certificate required, maximum 27 men, 35 ladies. Pro shop, changing rooms. One of the Costa's favourite golf courses, has hosted two Spanish PGA Championships. Professional: Juan Jimenez. Commercial Director: Eddie MacLean.*

ESTEPONA. Atalaya Golf & Country Club Estepona-Malaga, Ctra de Benahavis, 29688 Estepona, Malaga (95 2882812; Fax: 95 2887897). *Location:* between Marbella and Estepona, off N340 going west, turn inland for Benahavis just past Guadalmina. Two courses Atalaya Old and New. The fairly open parkland holes are lined with eucalyptus and pine. 36 holes, 6142 metres, Par 72. Large practice ground and putting greens. *Green Fees:* information not available. *Eating facilities:* bar and restaurant in clubhouse. Pro shop; club, cart and trolley hire. Professional: (95 2882812; Fax: 95 2887897). Secretary: Maribel Martin (95 2882812/95 2882811; Fax: 95 2887897). Golf Director: Andres Sanchez.*

THE APPEARANCE OF AN ASTERISK (*) AT THE END OF A CLUB OR COURSE ENTRY INDICATES THAT UP-TO-DATE INFORMATION HAS NOT BEEN SUPPLIED

ESTEPONA. El Paraiso Golf Club, Carretera de Cadiz-Malaga 29680 Estepona, Malaga (95.288.38.35; Fax: 95.288.58.27). *Location:* west on N340, turn right at Benavista then inland 3 km. A fine rolling parkland style course opened in 1974. The holes run over and around a hill surmounted by the El Paraiso Hotel. 18 holes, 6116 metres, Par 71. Practice ground and putting green. *Green Fees:* under review contact club for details. *Eating facilities:* bar and restaurant. Pro shop; club, cart and trolley hire. Professional: Daniel Westermark. Golf Director: Colin Christison.
e-mail: info@elparaisogolfclub.com
website: www.elparaisogolfclub.com

MALAGA. Guadalhorce Club de Golf, Ctra de Cartama, Apartado 48, 29590 Campanillas, Malaga (952 179378; Fax: 952 179372). *Location:* east towards Malaga on N340 past airport; turn right at sugar refinery taking underpass towards Bacardi distillery. A combination of classic parkland on level land with sculptured holes with raised greens and strategic water. 18 holes, 6194 metres, Par 72. Practice ground and putting green. Also 9 short holes. *Green Fees:* information not available. *Eating facilities:* bar and restaurant in classical 19th century Andalucian manor house. Pro shop; club, buggies and trolley hire. Professional: S. Bruna. Director of Golf: G Alvarez.*

MARBELLA. Aloha Golf Club, Nueva Andalucia, 29660 Marbella, Malaga (952-90 70 85/86; Fax: 952-81 23 89). *Location:* 3 km inland from Puerto Banus, 8km west of Marbella. Very tight driving course with tree-lined fairways and very strategically placed lakes and streams. 18 holes, 6293 metres, S.S.S. 74 (back tees). Practice area. *Green Fees:* information not available. *Eating facilities:* bar and restaurant (952-61 23 50). *Visitors:* basically a members' club. Pro shop; club, cart and trolley hire. Professional and Sport Director: Jose Luis Mangas (952 81 47 55; Fax: 952 81 23 89).*

MARBELLA. Golf Rio Real, Apartado 82, 29600 Marbella (952-76 57 33; Fax: 952-77 21 40). *Location:* 5km east from Marbella on N340, situated in a very nice valley with sea views and crossed by the Rio Real Creek. A relatively gentle test of golf. Well-cared for and closely linked to the five star Rio Real Golf Hotel. 18 holes, 6166 metres, Par 72. Practice ground and putting green. *Green Fees:* information not available. *Eating facilities:* restaurant and bar.*
e-mail: golf@rioreal.com
website: www.rioreal.com

MARBELLA. Guadalmina Club de Golf, Urb. Guadalmina Alta, 29678 S. Pedro Alcantara, Malaga (952 883375; Fax: 952 883483). *Location:* turn right off N340 approximately 1km west of San Pedro de Alcantara. A development which now boasts 45 holes - the original South course, the North which is more open despite some strategic water, and a short 9 hole layout. North: 18 holes, 5825 metres, Par 71. South: 18 holes, 6021 metres, Par 72. Driving range and putting greens. *Green Fees:* information not available. *Eating facilities:* spike bar and restaurant. *Visitors:* welcome, Handicaps 27 men, 35 ladies. Pro shop; club, cart and trolley hire. Professional: F. Hernandez. Secretary: Alvaro Beamonte (2883455/2883375; Fax: 2883483).*

MARBELLA. **Los Naranjos Golf Club**, Apartado 64, 29660 Nueva Andalucia, Malaga (952-81 24 28; Fax: 952-81 14 28). *Location:* turn right off N340 (going west) at Puerto Banus. Pass bullring and go over hill for 2km. The front nine holes run in a quiet undulating landscape and second nine through an orange grove giving the name to the course. 18 holes, 6038 metres, Par 72. Practice ground and putting green. *Green Fees:* information not available *Eating facilities:* bar and restaurant in new clubhouse. Pro shop, club, cart and trolley hire. *Visitors:* Handicap Certificates required. Manager: Jan Sonneri.*

MARBELLA. **Real Club de Golf Las Brisas**, Apartadode Correos 147, Nueva Andalucia, 29660 Marbella, Malaga (952-81 08 75; Fax: 952-81 55 18). *Location:* turn right off N340 at Puerto Banus. Over hill past bullring, then right and follow signs to Hotel Del Golf. A fine course which has played host to two World Cups and numerous other major Opens. Tough, with plenty of water and fast, sloping greens. 18 holes, 6163 metres, Par 72. Practice ground and putting green. *Green Fees:* information not available. *Eating facilities:* bar and restaurant. Pro shop; club, cart and trolley hire.*

MIJAS. **La Cala Resort**, Apdo de Correos 106, La Cala de Mijas, 29649 Mijas Costa, Malaga (34 952669000; Fax: 34 952669034). *Location:* situated between Fuengirola and Marbella, on N340 highway, turn at La Cala Village, "Cala de Mijas" 6km inland. La Cala offers elevated greens, large bunkers, playable and challenging holes and some magnificent views. 54 holes: Campo America 6187 metres, Par 73; Campo Asia 5966 metres, Par 72. Campo Europa 6014metres; plus top quality 6 hole Par 3 course. David Leadbetter Academy, one driving range, football academy. *Green Fees:* available on request (34 952 669 033; Fax 34 952 669 034). *Eating facilities:* bars and restaurants. *Visitors:* always welcome. Pro shop. Squash and tennis. La Cala Five Star Hotel and Caracala Spa. *Society Meetings:* welcome. Golf Director: Alan Saunders (34 952669036; Fax: 34 952669034).
e-mail: golf@lacala.com
website: www.lacala.com

MIJAS. **Mijas Golf International**, Apartado 145, 29640 Fuengirola, Malaga (0034 52 47 6843; Fax: 0034 52 46 7943). *Location:* from Marbella on N340 take the Fuengirola bypass and turn left at underpass. Then drive for two km before turning right. Two excellent courses: Los Lagos - 18 holes, 6348 metres, Par 71; and Los Olivos - 18 holes, 5896 metres, Par 72. The former course is relatively open although the greens are well protected by sand and water; the latter is narrower with smaller greens, favouring finesse over power. Driving range and putting green. *Green Fees:* information not available. *Eating facilities:* excellent food and bars. *Visitors:* welcome at anytime subject to availability. Pro shop; club, cart and trolley hire. Secretary: Felipe Perez.*
website: www.mijasgolf.org

www.uk-golfguide.com

ANDALUCIA – EAST

ALMERIA. **Golf Almerimar**, Urb Almerimar, 04700 El Ejido, Almeria (950 497454; Fax: 950 497146). *Location:* 7 km from El Ejido, which is some 35 km from Almeria on the main Malaga road. This is a well-established course in a relatively level situation, with a wealth of trees and the chance of a breeze from the sea alongside. 27 holes. Practice ground and putting green. *Green Fees:* information not available. *Eating facilities:* snack bar and restaurant. Pro shop; club, cart and trolley hire. Professional: Juan Parron.*

RINCON DE LA VICTORIA. **Anoreta Golf,** Avda. del Golf, s/n, 29730 Rincon de la Victoria, Malaga (952-40 40 00; Fax: 952-40 40 50). *Location:* 12 km east of Malaga at Rincon de la Victoria, only second course to be built east of Malaga. Seaside/parkland course. 18 holes, 5976 metres, Par 71. Driving range and putting green. *Green Fees:* information not available. *Eating facilities:* bar and restaurant. *Visitors:* welcome, no restrictions. Pro shop; club, cart and trolley hire.*

ANDALUCIA – WEST

CADIZ. **Club de Golf Novo Sancti Petri**, Urb. Novo Sancti Petri, Playa de la Barrosa, 11130 Chiclana de la Frontera, Cadiz (0034 956 49 40 05; Fax: 0034 956 49 43 50). *Location:* end of the La Barrosa road at Chiclana. 36 holes divided into three rounds, Course A, B and C, for all levels. Courses with wonderful views overlooking the Atlantic Ocean or bordered by pine trees and olive trees as well as water hazards. Round C is situated nearby and a free shuttle service is provided. Courses A & B designed by Severiano Ballesteros, Course C designed by Robert Trent Jones. All Par 72. 6000 metres. Putting, chipping and pitching facilities. *Green Fees:* High season €78, Low season €63. *Eating facilities:* club house, bar and café. *Visitors:* welcome, no restrictions. Only soft spikes to be worn. Pro shop; club, cart and trolley hire. Academy with 10 PGA Professionals. Director: Uwe Born.
e-mail: sales@golf-novosancti.es
website: www.golf-novosancti.es

CADIZ. **Montecastillo Hotel & Golf Resort**, Ctra de Arcos, 11406 Jerez de la Frontera, Cadiz ([34] 9-56 15 12 00; Fax: [34] 9-56 15 12 09). *Location:* half a mile main road, four miles Jerez, 46 miles Sevilla. A relatively level but rolling layout with a distinct links flavour. Plenty of mounds and elevated tees, vast bunkers and water. 18 holes, 6424 metres, Par 72. Driving range and putting green. *Green Fees:* information not available. *Eating facilities:* restaurant, two coffee shops. *Visitors:* welcome. Special packages available. Tennis court, football pitches, paddle tennis courts and Montecastillo Spa, including indoor swimming pool, jacuzzi, saunas, massage rooms, gym, cafeteria and solarium. *Society Meetings:* welcome. Secretary: Immaculada Fernandez (956 151213; Fax: 956 151215).*

JEREZ. **Sherry Golf Jerez,** Autovia A-4, Km.642, 11407 Jerez de la Frontera, Cadiz (34 956 088 330; Fax: 34 956 088 331). *Location:* 1.5 km. from Jerez; take motorway Jerez-El Puerto de Santa Maria; access to golf after 5 minutes. An interesting course to play for golfers of all levels, with wide fairways and large greens. Also 9-hole Par 3 course. 18 holes, 6,572 metres, Par 72. Driving range, putting green, golf academy. *Green Fees:* €57 18 holes. *Eating facilities:* bar, snack bar, à la carte restaurant. *Visitors:* welcome, with maximum handicap 36. Golf carts, pull trolley, club rental. Professional: Javier Romero. Manager: Emilio Lustau.
e-mail: info@sherrygolf.com
          comercial@sherrygolf.com (groups)

SAN ROQUE. **Real Club de Golf Sotogrande,** Paseo del Parque s/n, 11310 Sotogrande (956 785014). *Location:* 130km on national road N340, turn 2.5km towards sea. Well established (1964) and a major golfing landmark in Europe. Rolling slopes and strategic water are offset by cork oak, eucalyptus, palm and pine, first golf course in Europe designed by Robert Trent Jones. A demanding golfing feast. 18 holes, 6304 metres, Par 72. Also 9-hole short course. Practice ground and putting green. *Green Fees:* information not available. *Eating facilities:* cafeteria and restaurant. *Visitors:* welcome daily from 11am to 12pm. Pro shop; club, cart and trolley hire; tennis, paddle and swimming pool. Professional: Manuel Ocaña. Secretary: D. Rafael Garcia Buitrago.*

SAN ROQUE. **San Roque Club,** CN 340, KM 126, 11360 San Roque, Cadiz ([34] 9-56 613030/60/90; Fax: 613013). *Location:* 3km from Sotogrande towards San Roque village. Undulating first 9 holes, wooded second 9 holes, water hazards. 18 holes, 6494 metres White markers, 6134 metres Yellow, 5588 metres Blue, 5174 metres Red. S.S.S. 74, Par 72. Two-tiered, covered range (28 bays), two pitching areas, putting greens, three practice bunkers. *Green Fees:* information not available. *Eating facilities:* Snack Bar, "El Bolero" Restaurant, "Tappan Yaki" Japanese Restaurant. *Visitors:* welcome anytime but must pre-book tee times. Pro shop, locker facilities, club rental, buggy, trolley rental, golf lessons available. Golf Director: Ian F. Martin.*

SAN ROQUE. **Club de Golf Valderrama,** Avda Los Cortijos, s/n, 11310 Sotogrande, Cadiz ([34] 9-56 791200; Fax: [34] 9-56 796028). *Location:* access through the main Sotogrande entrance (right of N340 going west); then 2.5 km inland. Cork oaks, rolling hills, view to the sea. Ryder Cup venue 1997 and home of the Volvo Masters. 18 holes, 6356 metres, Par 71. Practice ground and putting green. *Green Fees:* information not available. *Eating facilities:* bar and restaurant open to non members for dinner Tuesdays to Saturdays; buffet on Sundays. *Visitors:* tee off times for visitors 12 noon to 2pm, must book in advance. Handicap maximum 24 men, 32 ladies. Soft spikes on golf shoes compulsory. Pro shop. Valderrama hosted the World Golf Championships and the American Express Championships 1999/2000. *Society Meetings:* welcome by prior arrangement. Professional: Miguel Sedeno. Director General: Derek Brown.*

CATALONIA

GIRONA. **Costa Brava Golf Club,** Urb. Golf Costa Brava, "La Masia", 17246 Sta. Cristina D'Aro, Girona (972 83 70 55; Fax: 83 72 72). *Location:* from A7 highway Exit 9. 30km from Girona, five/six km from the coast. From a hilly, wooded first 9 holes with fine views, the back 9 holes slope down by the river to flatter ground. 18 holes, 5625 metres. S.S.S. 70. Putting greens and practice areas. *Green Fees:* information not available. Special rates for groups. *Eating facilities:* restaurant, bar and snack bar. *Visitors:* welcome anytime, no restrictions. Pro shop, changing rooms. Buggies and caddy carts for hire. *Society Meetings:* welcome, discounts available. Professional: Miguel Gil Garcia (Tel & Fax: 83 50 33). Secretary: Ma. Victoria Figueras Garcia (83 71 50; Fax: 83 72 72).*

Club de Golf Valderrama

GIRONA. **Club de Golf Girona,** Urbanitz. Golf Girona, 17481 Sant Julia Ramis (Girona). (00.34.972.17.16.41;Fax:00.34.972.17.16.82). *Location:* four km north of Girona town centre, near the Girona North Exit (6) of the Girona-La Jonquera Motorway (A7). An undulating course around wooded valleys and hills with three man-made lakes. 18 holes, 6100 metres. S.S.S. 72. Driving range, putting green. *Green Fees:* information not available. *Eating facilities:* bar, restaurant, golfer's menu. *Visitors:* welcome all year by arrangement. Pro shop, caddy carts for hire. *Society Meetings:* welcome by arrangement; 10% reduction. Professionals: Pepe Rowerd and Gerard Solano (972.17.00.11; Fax: 972. 17.16.82).*
e-mail: golfgirona@golfgirona.com

GIRONA. **Club de Golf D'Aro Mas Nou,** 17250 Playa de Aro, Costa Brava (Girona) (972 826900; Fax: 972 826906). *Location:* on the Costa Brava, between Playa de Aro and Santa Cristina, 35 km east of Girona. A scenic course with panoramic views of the Costa Brava from its situation on the Les Gavarres mountains. Trees and lakes add to the course's charm. 18 holes, 6218 metres. S.S.S. 72. 9 hole Par 3 course, practice area. *Green Fees:* information not available. *Eating facilities:* clubhouse with bar, snack bar and restaurant. Caddies. Professionals: Piter Runlus, Pedro Martinez. Secretary: Toni Hidalgo (003 4 972 826900/816727; Fax: 972 826906). Manager: Rudolf Glanzmann (003 4 972 826900).*
e-mail: golfdaromasnou@retemail.es

PALS. **Emporda Golf Club,** Ctra. Palafrugell-Torroella de Montgri, 17257 Gualta (Girona) (972 760450; Fax: 972 757100). *Location:* 40km from Girona almost on the coast, between Pals and Torroella. Combination course with dunes, lakes, wooded, flat course. 27 holes. S.S.S. 71. Large driving range, chipping area. *Green Fees:* information not available. *Eating facilities:* clubhouse, restaurant, snack bar. *Visitors:* welcome anytime, no restrictions. Swimming pool. Professional: Jordi Riera. Manager: Isidre Soria. Commercial Director: Jaume Marin.*

PALS. **Golf Platja de Pals,** Ctra. del Golf, s/n, 17256 Pals, Costa Brava (34 972 667739; Fax: 34 972 636799) *Location:* on the coast at Playa de Pals beach, eight km from Begur and 40 km east of Girona. The oldest course on the Costa Brava, requires advanced golfing skills as its fairways are ringed by 100-year old pine trees. 18 holes, 6222 metres. S.S.S. 72/74. Par 73. Practice course with pitching, chipping and putting green areas. *Green Fees:* €60 - €78, depending on season. *Eating facilities:* snack bar, dining area with spectacular golfing views. Mediterranean style menu. *Visitors:* welcome. Clubs, caddy cars and golf carts can be hired. *Society Meetings:* welcome.
e-mail: comercial@golfplatjadepals.com
website: www.golfplatjadepals.com

PALS. **Golf Serres de Pals,** Pals, Girona 17256 (34+ 972 637375; Fax: 34+ 972 667447). *Location:* motorway to Le Bisbal, 3km from Flaça take the first turn on the left and then follow the signs for Golf Serres de Pals. Three different areas with smooth hill top and pine tree forest, and fairways between lakes.

18 holes, 6882 yards, 6263 metres. S.S.S. 72. Driving range with practice areas and three Par 3 holes. *Green Fees:* 18 holes, adults from €48 to €70, juniors €29 to €42; 9 holes, adults from €35 to €47, juniors from €21 to €28; senior days (Mondays and Wednesdays) €38 to €53; day ticket from €80 to €105. *Eating facilities:* restaurant and bar. *Visitors:* always welcome. Closed Christmas Day. Shop, golf school, changing rooms etc. Hotel accommodation on site. Hire of buggies, clubs, trolleys. *Society Meetings:* always welcome. Tailor-made packages. Sales Manager: Albert Valldeperes.
e-mail: info@golfserresdepals.com
website: www. golfserresdepals.com

MURCIA

MURCIA. **La Manga Club,** Los Belones, Cartagena, 30385 Murcia (968 175000; Fax: 968 175058). *Location:* 330 km from Cartagena, 75 km from Murcia and 100 km from Alicante airport. Access off road to Murcia Airport. A true sporting resort in all aspects, with 54 holes of palm-lined golf backed by low hills as well as tennis, squash, bowls, health club and watersports at the Mar Menor close by. Five star La Manga Club hotel on site. Three courses: North 18 holes, 5780 metres, Par 71; South 18 holes, 6361 metres, Par 72; West 18 holes, 5971 metres, Par 72. Driving range and putting green. *Green Fees:* information not available. *Eating facilities:* bar and restaurant. Pro shop; club, cart and trolley hire.*
e-mail: golf@lamangaclub.es

VALENCIA

BETERA. **Club de Golf Escorpion,** Apartado 1, 46117 Betera, Valencia (96-160 12 11; Fax: 96-169 01 87). *Location:* take the road from Valencia to Liria, turning off at San Antonio de Benageber. Go 4 km to the right in the direction of Betera. A fine private club offering parkland-style golf with a mountain backdrop. Tree-lined and interesting. 18 holes, 6319 metres, Par 72. Driving range and putting green. *Green Fees:* information not available. *Eating facilities:* bar and restaurant. Pro shop; club, cart and trolley hire.*

CHIVA. **Club de Golf El Bosque,** Carretera Godelleta, Urban. El Bosque 46370 Chiva, Valencia (96-180 8000; Fax: 96-180 8001). *Location:* take the Nacional III road (Madrid-Valencia) Exit 337, turn off for Godelleta. Wooded course, designed by Robert Trent Jones Snr. 18 holes, 6276 metres, S.S.S. 72. Driving range and putting green. *Green Fees:* information not available. *Eating facilities:* cafeteria, restaurant. *Visitors:* welcome. One, two and three bedroom flats available. Professionals: Alfonso Pinto, Ignecio Briz.*

ORIHUELA. **Campo de Golf Villamartin,** Crta Alicante Cartagena, 03189 Orihuela, Alicante (96 6765127; Fax: 96 6765170). *Location:* 7 km from Torrevieja, 3 km from the beach and 3km from the main road N332. Two courses laid out on interesting coastal sandy land with some pines. A good test of golf, open to the breeze. 18 holes, 6132 metres, Par 72; 18 holes, 5770 metres, Par 72. Driving range and putting green. *Green Fees:* information not provided. *Eating facilities:* bar, coffee shop and restaurant. *Visitors:* welcome. Pro shop; buggies and carts. *Society Meetings:* welcome, 10% discount. Professional: Emilio Rodriguez (96 6765127; Fax: 96 6765158). Secretary: Juan Miguel Buendia (96 6765051; Fax: 96 6765170).
e-mail: golfvillamartin@grupoquara.com

VALENCIA. **Campo de Golf El Saler,** Parador De Turismo "El Saler", El Saler, Valencia (96 161 0384; Fax: 96 162 7366). *Location:* at 18km on the road from Nazaret to Oliva, right by the sea. One of the great Spanish tests of golf, with open links fairways and tight holes lined with umbrella pine; a public facility offering true seaside conditions. 18 holes, 6042 metres, Par 72. Driving range and putting green. *Green Fees:* information not available. *Eating facilities:* bar, restaurant and coffee shop. *Visitors:* welcome. Pro shop; club, cart and trolley and electric trolley hire.*

MAJORCA

CALA D'OR. **Club Vall D'Or Golf,** Ctra Cala d'Or a Portocolom, 07669 S'Horta (971 837068; Fax: 971 837299). *Location:* approximately 60km east of Palma on the road from Porto Colom to Cala D'Or. Undulating, winding course, with trees. 18 holes, 5824 metres. S.S.S. 71. Driving range, club hire. *Green Fees:* information not available. *Eating facilities:* clubhouse, bar and restaurant. *Visitors:* welcome with Handicap. Nearby hotels include Cala D'Or, Rocador, Rocador Playa. Professional: Antonio Gonzalez. Secretary: Olga Diaz (971 837001).*

MAGALLUF. **Golf de Poniente,** Ctra. Cala Figuera S/N, 07181 Calvia (0034971 130148; Fax: 0034971 130176). *Location:* 18km west of Palma, one km from Magalluf on the Andraitx Road. The course is considered long and difficult, surrounded by trees and water, with large and fast greens. 18 holes, 6430 metres. S.S.S. 72. Driving range, putting green. *Green Fees:* information not provided. *Eating facilities:* clubhouse, restaurant and bar. *Visitors:* welcome. Nearby hotels include Son Caliu, Club Galatzo. Professionals: Paco Ruiz, Brian Salter.
e-mail: golf@ponientegolf.com
website: www.ponientegolf.com

PALMA. **Real Golf de Bendinat,** Campoamor S/N, 07181 Bendinat Calvia (971 405200; Fax: 971 700786). *Location:* five km west from Palma centre on the road between Illetas and Portals Nous. Mixed woodland, good vistas. 18 holes, 5650 metres. S.S.S. 71. Driving range, putting green. *Green Fees:* information not available. *Eating facilities:* excellent restaurant. *Visitors:* welcome, limited numbers. Please reserve tee-off times through our Fax No: (971 700786). *Society Meetings:* welcome. Professional: Ricardo Galiano (971 405450; Fax: 971 700786). Secretary: Alison Bradshaw (971 405200; Fax: 971 700786).

PALMA. **Son Vida Golf,** Urb. Son Vida, 07013 Palma de Mallorca (34/971-79.12.10; Fax: 34/971.79.11.27). *Location:* three km from Palma centre, access via de Sinora Exit Son Rapina. Majorca's first course (1964) winding through trees and estate villas with lakes and gentle slopes. 18 holes, 5740 metres. S.S.S. 71. Driving range, Pro Shops, car, trolley and club rental. *Green Fees:* information not available. *Eating facilities:* snacks and lunches in the comfortable clubhouse, excellent restaurant El Pato (The Duck) overlooking 18th hole. *Visitors:* welcome, Handicap Certificate/Card required. Nearby hotels (discount on green fees) include Arabella Golf Hotel (5 stars), Hotel Son Vida (4 stars) on the course, Victoria Sol (4 stars), Palma, Bonanza Playa Illetas, Son Caliu. *Society Meetings:* welcome. Professionals: R. Maer, S. Ruiz. Secretary: Mrs Layda. Manager: Juan Alvarez.*

POLLENSA. **Golf Pollensa,** Ctra. Palma Pollensa, 07460 Pollensa (0034971 533216; Fax: 0034971 533265). *Location:* in the north of the island, 45 km from Palma Airport and 2 km from Pollensa. On the south side of a hill with smooth and beautiful undulations and sea views. 9 holes: White tees 5304 metres S.S.S. 68; Red tees 5116 metres S.S.S. 70, Par 70. Driving range, putting and pitching green. *Green Fees:* information not provided. *Eating facilities:* snack bar, beautiful restaurant, excellent food, 7 days a week. *Visitors:* welcome, tee reservation recommended. Changing room. Golf lessons, club and electric cart rental. *Society Meetings:* welcome. Professional: Carlos Insua. Director: Jonathan James Walpole. website: www.golfpollensa.com

PUERTO DE ALCUDIA. **Club de Golf Alcanada,** Ctra.del Faro s/n, 07410 Puerto de Alcudia, Mallorca (971 54 95 60; Fax: 971 89 75 78). *Location:* near Puerto de Alcudia. Created by Robert Trent Jones Jr, the course slopes gently down past pine, oak and olive trees with views across the sea to Alcanada island and the distant Sierra Levante mountains. 18 holes, 6,499 metres, Par 72. Driving range, pitching and putting green. *Green Fees:* information not available. *Eating facilities:* clubhouse restaurant with large terrace. *Visitors:* welcome. Electric golf carts, pull trolleys, club rental. Professional: Peter Dost. Director of Golf: Kristoff Both.*
e-mail: info@golf-alcanada.com

THE APPEARANCE OF AN ASTERISK (*) AT THE END OF A CLUB OR COURSE ENTRY INDICATES THAT UP-TO-DATE INFORMATION HAS NOT BEEN SUPPLIED

SANTA PONSA. **Santa Ponsa Golf Club One,** Santa Ponsa, 07184 Calvia (971 690211; Fax: 971 693364). *Location:* 18km on motorway from Palma to Andraitx, turn off roundabout Santa Ponsa. Gently sloping fairways with water hazards. 18 holes, 6543 metres. S.S.S. 72 men, 72 ladies. Practice range, two putting greens. *Green Fees:* €78 18 holes. *Eating facilities:* restaurant and bar in clubhouse, also small bar on golf course. *Visitors:* welcome; maximum Handicaps - 28 men, 36 ladies. Guests at the hotel receive 50% reduction on green fees. Accommodation available, swimming pool, paddling pool, tennis. Hotel Golf Santa Ponsa at the golf course. Five star Hotel Vista Port Adriano near golf course. *Society Meetings:* welcome. Professionals: Diego Lopez/Mark Schmidt. Secretaries: Ana, Oda, Pablo, Yolanta. Director: Jose M. Gomez.

SANTA PONSA. **Santa Ponsa Golf Club Two,** Santa Ponza, Calvia (971 690211; Fax: 971 663364). *Location:* as Santa Ponza One. A very interesting and enjoyable course, it has a mixture of holes, some with very tight fairways and others with many water hazards. Designed by Jose Gancedo. 18 holes, 6053 metres. S.S.S. 73, Par 72. Practice range, putting green. *Green Fees:* information not available. *Eating facilities:* as Santa Ponza One. *Visitors:* at moment only open for shareholders.*

SON SERVERA. **Son Servera Golf Club,** Costa de los Pinos, 07550 Son Servera (71 84.00.96; Fax: 71 84.01.60). *Location:* Palma - Manacor - Sant Lloreng - Son Servera. Fairly flat, narrow, seaside course, set among pine trees. 9 holes, 2978 metres. S.S.S. 72. *Green Fees:* information not available. *Eating facilities:* bar and restaurant. *Visitors:* welcome. Handicap Certificate required. Nearby hotels include Eurotel Golf Punta Roja, Flamenco, Royal Mediterranea, Gran Sol. Professional: Jaime Artiach. Secretary: Jose Colom.*

GOLF IN CYPRUS

GUZELYURT. **CMC Golf Club,** Guzelyurt (+90 392 771 7422). *Location:* situated 30 miles west of Kyrenia and bordering the coast, this is the only golf course in Northern Cyprus. *Visitors:* welcome. Clubs available for hire.*

LIMASSOL. **Vikla Golf & Country Club,** Kellaki, Limassol (+357 99 674218; Fax: +357 25 750789). *Location:* near the village of Vikla, 20 km from Limassol.18 holes, 5250 yards, Par 68. *Visitors:* welcome. Clubs and trolleys for hire. No Handicap Certificate required. Club house with drinks and snacks; swimming pool.
website: www.vikla-golf.com

PAPHOS. **Aphrodite Hills Golf Club,** Kouklia (+357 26 82 8200; Fax: +357 26 82 8201). *Location:* in a stunning location overlooking the Mediterranean, on two plateaux cut by a deep ravine. Site includes a five-star hotel, tennis academy and health spa. 18 holes, 6665 metres, Par 71. 3-hole academy course. Green fees include hire of buggy. *Visitors:* welcome. Clubhouse with bar and restaurant.
website: www.aphroditehills.com

PAPHOS. **Secret Valley Golf Club,** Near 'Petratou Romiou' (+357 26 642774/5; Fax: +357 26 642776). *Location:* 18 km east of Paphos and 49km from Limassol. 18 holes, 6120 metres, Par 72. Golf academy. *Visitors:* welcome. Clubs, carts and trolleys for hire. Bar and restaurant.
website: www.cyprusgolf.com

PAPHOS. **Tsada Golf Club,** Tsada, Near Paphos (+357 26 642774/5; Fax: +357 26 642776). *Location:* 20 minutes from Paphos, in the grounds of a 12th century monastery in the hills around Tsada; signposted from village. 18 holes, 6060 metres, Par 72. Driving range and putting green. *Visitors:* welcome. Clubs, carts and trolleys for hire. Bar and restaurant.
website: www.cyprusgolf.com

Holiday Golf in the USA

Michael Gedye

Mountain backdrop at Indian Wells, Palm Springs

IT IS PERFECTLY POSSIBLE for a travelling golfer, given sufficient wanderlust and dedication, to play the game in 119 separate countries. It would also be a theoretical possibility for the same player to tackle 19,200 courses in one country alone – the United States. Roughly two-thirds of all the world's golf lies here, with a range of scenery, climate, topography and choice that is unique.

Most resort golf courses around the world, designed to attract holiday golfers to an attractive, sun-soaked location with the added bonus of fairway plots and retirement homes, are built with foreign visitors in mind. Not so in the USA. For the domestic holiday market, huge

by any standards, there is such a wide choice that no-one need look overseas. There is mountain golf, desert golf, dramatic seashore golf, even palm-fringed oasis golf - enough for players of all standards and budgets – the majority of whom have neither a handicap nor a passport.

A consequence of this substantial domestic demand is that American holiday golfers know what they like and have the purchasing power to expect the vacation resorts to provide precisely what they want. The result is, in a large number of cases, rather formulaic courses, not too challenging, well-irrigated and manicured to five-star standards, where the

True Blue – part of the rich golfing treasure at Myrtle Beach

facilities and quality of service are impeccable, highly commercial and geared to a mass market.

Each golf resort is in direct competition, not so much with its near neighbours, but more with every other holiday golf location across the country. Courses are often found in spectacular settings, backed by highly photogenic scenery – a purple promise to the market of a well-organised, highly efficient holiday golfing experience, American-style.

For European visitors, it can prove a salutary introduction – something of a culture shock. On arrival at a typical course, you will find yourself treated as an honoured guest. Your clubs will be whisked away, to appear later mounted on your personal golf cart (usually obligatory), complete with specified teetime, courtesy tee pegs, scorecard , pencil - maybe even a bucket of ice cubes, divot seed mixture and a satellite navigation system to calculate your position relative to the pin on each hole. A good number of holiday courses have been designed by leading names in golf architecture, with highly scenic holes, usually with many water features. Remember to take your camera.

Expect a large, superbly appointed pro shop, regular stops around the course for snacks and drinks, even a roving bar wagon. Many American golfers on holiday treat the game as a social experience. A round can be more a party than par, slow by any standards. To set against this, you can play in superb conditions on not overly-testing courses. Adopt the American way, smell the flowers and enjoy the regular snack breaks – your score might even surprise you.

There are many advantages in the hugely competitive nature of resort golf in the USA. Prices are low and the customer (with his holiday dollar) is king. Myrtle Beach, boasting around 110 courses clustered along its coastal strand, is easily the most concentrated golfing area in the world. To facilitate play, all accommodation there is linked in with a computerised golf reservation system. If one course is full when you wish to book, they will quickly find you another. After all, there is plenty of choice!

With the current exchange rate for the dollar, golf in the USA, as well as related equipment and clothing, is available at bargain rates. There is the widest possible choice of locations, backed by the security of knowing that, wherever you go, you will be well looked after at some of the best-kept, most attractive, most efficient golf clubs in the world, where the cuisine and language are not unfamiliar and the game is the same, if possibly played at more social and leisurely pace than you may be used to..

With so many destinations to consider, we are spoilt for choice. We have eventually settled on three – all proven and popular holiday areas with a wealth of interesting golf, some quite testing while others are memorably scenic. On the east coast, the two Carolinas beckon plus the sunshine state of Florida, where more than a thousand courses vie for attention. Further west, in a verdant oasis set in the Californian desert, lies the glittering resort of Palm Springs.

FLORIDA has a long history as a sunshine vacation destination. Originally developed as an ideal winter retreat for snowbound travellers from the north-eastern states, it has grown to form an established retirement location and the home of more holiday golf than any equivalent area in the world. We have chosen central Orlando (home of Disney World), the

elegance of Palm Beach north of Atlantic-bordering Miami and the western coast facing the Gulf of Mexico. There is demanding golf at Innisbrook or PGA National in contrast to the relaxing facilities of Saddlebrook and Naples Beach.

An early example of escapist resort golf, Pinehurst in **NORTH CAROLINA** is part of American golfing history. It offers eight courses of genuine quality radiating out under towering pines from the elegant clubhouse, famous for old-fashioned southern hospitality. Try to find time to visit the PGA Hall of Fame and golf museum nearby.

Just down the road, **SOUTH CAROLINA** offers a broad selection of holiday golf, found in two principal locations. Myrtle Beach has the largest selection of playable golf courses (110) along a single coastal strand of anywhere in the world. Behind a cosmopolitan seaside strip of motels, fast food outlets, vibrant nightlife and bargain shopping (including much golf equipment), the range of golf courses , many of them designed by the world's best architects, offers tests to suit all comers, with a warm and efficient welcome in true southern style. A little further south along

Plenty of strategic water at Grenelefe Golf & Tennis Resort, Orlando

Home hole backed by mountains, Westin Mission Hills, Palm Springs

the coast, Hilton Head Island, in complete contrast, is a peaceful community of holiday and beachfront hotels with excellent golf. The most famous is Harbour Town, home of the USPGA Tour Heritage Classic.

Right across the country in California, **PALM SPRINGS**, just an hour and a half east of Los Angeles, is a verdant oasis in the middle of the Mojave desert. Originally a weekend retreat for movie stars, this unbelievably green 25-mile strip of artificial land is pure Hollywood. In a playground for the super-rich, there are over ninety superb golf courses, their tall palms and lush fairways artificially watered from a limitless underground supply. The statistics here are mind-blowing – 160 hotels, 600 tennis courts and 10,000 swimming pools, all encircled by pastel-shaded mountains, with constant sunshine and virtually no humidity. A somewhat pricey but unique golfing experience.

FLORIDA

AVENTURA. **Turnberry Isle Resort & Club,** 19999 West Country Club Drive, Aventura, FL. 33180 (305) 932 6200; Fax: (305) 933 6922. North Miami Beach. This luxurious private resort and country club is the perfect spot for sports enthusiasts. Two Robert Trent Jones, Sr. championship courses keep resort guests and members in the swing. North 6323 yards, Par 70; South 7003 yards, Par 72. Full facilities.*

BOCA RATON. **Boca Raton Resort & Club,** 501 East Camino Real, Boca Raton, Florida 33431 (561-447 3000; Fax: 561-447 5294). *Location:* 22 miles from Palm Beach. Historic golf resort which combines links with the past and contemporary luxury. 36 holes: Country Club Course 6714 yards Par 72. Resort Course 6253 yards, Par 71. Full facilities. *Eating facilities:* beverage carts, snack bars and restaurants. *Green Fees:* information not available. *Visitors:* closed to public, must be a member, guest of a member or staying at the resort. Director of Golf: Bob Coman.*

BONITA SPRINGS. **Pelican's Nest Golf Club at Pelican Landing,** 4450 Pelican's Nest Drive, Bonita Springs FL (239) (947 2282). *Location:* just inside Pelican Landing, a wonderful complement to local amenities. Two, private member-owned, Tom Fazio designed, courses. Gator: 18 holes, 7066 yards, Par 73, Rating 74.7. slope 137. Hurricane: 18 holes, 6894 yards, Par 72, Rating 74.0, slope 137. Memberships available. *Green Fees:* information not provided. website: www.nestgolf.com

LAKE COUNTY. **Mission Inn Golf and Tennis Resort.** *Location:* on the country side of Orlando, less than one hour from central Florida's famous attractions. Mission Inn boasts 36 holes of championship golf on two renowned courses. El Campeon: 18 holes, 6852 yards. Las Colinas: 18 holes, 6879 yards. *Green Fees:* information not available. *Visitors:* Stay & Play golf packages available inclusive of green fees, accommodation, meals, and for green fees and accommodation only. Many other resort facilities are available for guests travelling with golf enthusiasts - tennis, hydro spa, heated outdoor pool, fitness room, bicycle trails, marina, shopping, etc. Reservations made by calling Destination Golf: 0181-891 5151.*

NAPLES. **Lely Resort,** 8202 Lely Resort Boulevard, Naples, Fl. 34113 (941) 793 2200; Fax: (941) 793 3963. 40 miles from Fort Myers. Great golf in substantial homesite development. Golf design by Jones, Player and Trevino. 54 holes Flamingo Course 7171 yards Par 72. Full facilities.*

NAPLES. **Naples Beach Hotel & Golf Club,** 851 Gulf Shore Boulevard North, Naples, Florida 34102 (239.261.2222; Fax: 239.261.7380). *Location:* 30 miles from S.W. Florida International Airport in Fort Myers.

Beachside hotel and golf resort with much tradition. Very popular with British players. 18 holes 6642 yards Par 72. Full facilities. Golf school, driving range and full service spa. Professional: Larry Gantzer.*

ORLANDO. **Grenelefe Golf & Tennis Resort,** 3200 SR 546, Haines City, Fl. 33844 (941) 422 7511. 25 miles south-west of Disney World. A comprehensive golf and tennis resort in a rolling, wooded setting. Popular also for conventions. 54 holes: East 6802 yards, Par 72; South 6869 yards, Par 71; West 7325 yards, Par 72. Full facilities.*

ORLANDO. **The Villas of Grand Cypress One,** North Jacaranda, Orlando, FL 32836 (800/835 7377; Fax: 407/239 7219). *Location:* take I4 to Exit 68 right to SR 535 North. Superb resort complex. Four Courses: New Course 18 holes, 6773 yards Blue, 6181 yards White; North Course 9 holes, Gold 3521, Blue 3143, White 2912, Par 36; South Course 9 holes, Gold 3472 yards, Blue 3212 yards, White 2911 yards, Par 36; East Course 9 holes, Gold 3434 yards, Blue 3151 yards, White 2878 yards, Par 36. Driving range. *Green Fees:* information not provided. *Eating facilities:* The Club restaurant and Sports Bar, Nine18. Locker room. Academy of Golf, Equestrian Centre and racquet club. Director of Golf: Joe Angelino (407 239 1956; Fax: 407 239 1969). Secretary: Lisa Monohan (407 239 1913; Fax: 407 239 1969).

PALM BEACH. **PGA National Golf Club,** 400 Avenue of the Champions, Palm Beach Gardens Fl 33418 (561 627 1800). 15 miles from West Palm Beach. Golf for all levels, including beginners, at a superb resort which hosted the 1983 Ryder Cup. 90 holes: Champion Course 7022 yards Par 72. Full facilities including teaching academy.*

TAMPA. **Saddlebrook Resort,** 5700 Saddlebrook Way, Wesley Chapel Tampa, Fl. 33543-4499 (813 973 1111; Fax: 813 973 4504). *Location:* 33 miles north of Tampa International Airport, take I-75 to SR54, then east one mile. 480 acres of natural countryside surrounded by tall cypress, pines, palm trees, blue lakes and rolling hills. Two courses (both designed by Arnold Palmer): Saddlebrook Course - 18 holes, 6564 yards. Par 70. Palmer Course - 18 holes, 6469 yards. S.S.S. 71. Practice green, practice range. *Green Fees:* information not available. *Eating facilities:* four restaurants, lounge, pool bar and sports bar. *Visitors:* welcome, open all year. Pro shop; Arnold Palmer Golf Academy; cart and club rental. *Society Meetings:* welcome. Professional: Jerry Couzynse.*

TARPON SPRINGS. **Innisbrook Hilton Resort,** 36750 US 19 N, Palm Harbor, Fl. 34684 (813 942 2000/800 456 2000). *Location:* 20 miles from Tampa International Airport. Florida's finest golf resort. The Copperhead course ranks in Florida's top five. 72 holes: Copperhead 7087 yards Par 71; Island 6999 yards Par 72. Three practice ranges. *Green Fees:* information not available. *Eating facilities:* seven restaurants. *Visitors:* welcome. 13 tennis courts, six pools, golf school, children's programme, fitness centre, airport shuttle.*

NORTH CAROLINA

VILLAGE OF PINEHURST. **Pinehurst Resort & Country Club,** PO Box 4000, Carolina Vista, Village of Pinehurst, North Carolina 28374 (800 487-4653). *Location*: 70 miles from Raleigh. Truly historic with great golf, an old world atmosphere and service to match. 8 courses, 24 tennis courts, croquet lawn, bowls and fitness centre. *Green Fees*: information not available. *Eating facilities*: Carolina Dining Room, Donald Ross Grill, Mulligan's Sports Bar and Grill. *Visitors*: Pinehurst is a stay and play facility. Visitors must be a guest of the resort to play on the courses. Four practice ranges and four clubhouses.*

SOUTH CAROLINA

HILTON HEAD. **Harbour Town Golf Links,** Sea Pines Plantation, Hilton Head Island, South Carolina (803) 842 1892. Home of the Heritage Classic and a true thoroughbred regularly ranked in US top 25. 18 holes 6912 yards Par 71. Full facilities.*

HILTON HEAD. **Port Royal Golf Club,** Hilton Head Island, South Carolina (803 686 8801). Three fine courses winding past magnolia and oak to a hospitable plantation-style clubhouse. 54 holes Robber's Row 6711 yards Par 72; Planter's Row 6520 yards Par 72; Barony 6530 yards Par 72. Full facilities.*

HILTON HEAD. **Shipyard Golf Club,** Hilton Head Island, South Carolina (803 785 2402. Plenty of water hazards on these well-established tree-lined holes near the sea. 27 holes: Galleon 3364 yards; Brigantine 3352 yards; Clipper 3466 yards, all Par 36. Full facilities.*

HILTON HEAD ISLAND. **Palmetto Dunes Resort,** Hilton Head Island, South Carolina (803 785 1161). Rolling dunes and fairways make a contrast at this popular golf and vacation resort. 54 holes: Arthur Hills Course 6651 yards, Par 72; George Fazio Course 6873 yards, Par 70; Robert Trent Jones Course 6710 yards, Par 72. Full facilities.*

MYRTLE BEACH. **Burning Ridge Golf Courses**, Highway 501 W, Conway, West Myrtle Beach, S.C. 29579. (843 347 0538; Fax: 843 347 7054). *Location*: follow Route 501 north toward Conway. The course is on the left side on 501 after Legends. Two fine courses by Gene Hamm, laid out in a heavily wooded location. Voted "Myrtle Beach Golf Course of the Year 2006". The West Course is tight, with water in play on most holes; the East Course is more open with small, well-bunkered greens. West Course 18 holes, 6714 yards, Par 72; East Course 18 holes, 6780 yards, Par 72. Driving range, putting green, pro shop. *Green Fees:* information not available. Club and cart hire. *Eating facilities:* on course snacks and clubhouse restaurant. *Visitors*: welcome all year round.*

MYRTLE BEACH. **Litchfield Country Club**, PO Box 379, Pawleys Island, South Carolina 29585 (843 237 3411). *Location:* 20 miles south of Myrtle Beach. Fine plantation-style golf winding past giant oaks, cypress, marshland and strategic lakes. 18 holes 6752 yards Par 70.6/119. Driving range. *Green Fees:* information not available. *Eating facilities:* full clubhouse with grill and bar. *Visitors:* always welcome. Accommodation available; carts for hire. Professional: Bob Vanderbloemen (843 237 3411).*

MYRTLE BEACH. **Pine Lakes International Country Club,** Woodside Drive, Central Myrtle Beach, South Carolina (803 449 6459). Old fashioned service and style colour every aspect of this mature Scottish-designed golf setting. 18 holes 6709 yards Par 71. Full facilities.*

MYRTLE BEACH. **Tidewater Golf Club,** 901 Little River Neck Road, North Myrtle Beach, South Carolina 29582 (800 446 5363). *Location:* from Highway 17, take Cherry Grove Exit. Stop at end of exit ramp, turn left, turn right on to Little River Neck Road (at Harbour Gate). Two miles to Tidewater. Situated on a seaside peninsula, course designed by Ken Tomlinson. 18 holes, 7150 yards Championship, 6530 yards Blue, 6000 yards Men, 5090 yards Ladies, 4665 yards Juniors. *Green Fees:* information not available. *Eating facilities:* full facilities. *Visitors:* welcome, public course. Professional; Paul Kline.*

MYRTLE BEACH. **Wild Wing Plantation,** PO Box 51090, Myrtle Beach, South Carolina 29579 (800 736 9464; Fax: 843 347 5732). *Location:* on US Highway 501, six miles west of the Intracoastal waterway. Parkland setting. Wood Stork Course - 18 holes, 7044 yards; Hummingbird Course - 18 holes, 6853 yards; Avocet Course - 18 holes, 7127 yards; Falcon Course - 18 holes. Extensive practice facility. *Green Fees:* information not available. *Eating facilities:* Wishbones Restaurant, Players' Pub. *Visitors:* always welcome. Wild Wing School of Golf, Golf Villas/Homes (888 398 9464). Director of Golf: Timothy R Tilma.*

MYRTLE BEACH. **The Witch Golf Club,** Highway 544 between Conway and Myrtle Beach, South Carolina (803 448 1300). 5 miles from Myrtle Beach. A natural spellbinding course winding through dense forest and mangrove swamp. 18 holes 6702 yards Par 71. Full facilities.*

PALM SPRINGS

INDIAN WELLS. **Indian Wells Golf Resort,** 44-500 Indian Wells Lane, Indian Wells (00 1 760 346 4653). 36 holes of rolling holiday golf by Ted Robinson, well-watered, manicured, a handicapper's delight. 36 holes: East 6662 yards, West 6478 yards, both Par 72. Driving range, putting green. *Green Fees:* information not available. *Eating facilities:* bar/snacks in clubhouse. Pro shop; cart and club rental. Head Professional: Joe Williams.*

LA QUINTA. **La Quinta Resort & Club (Dunes),** 50-200 Avenue Vista Bonita, La Quinta, Palm Springs (00 1 619 564 7686). A fine resort course by Pete Dye with plenty of hazards. 18 holes, 6251 yards. Par 72. Driving range, putting green. *Green Fees:* information not available. *Eating facilities:* bar and restaurants in low-rise Spanish-style hotel. Pro shop; cart and club hire. Head Professional: Todd Williams.*

LA QUINTA. **La Quinta Resort & Club (Mountain),** 50-200 Avenida Vista Bonita, La Quinta, CA 92253, Palm Springs (00 1 619 564 7686; Fax: 00 1 760 564 2757). Carved into the base of the Santa Rose hills, these Pete Dye courses have been ranked in USA Top 100. 18 holes, 6303 yards. Par 72. Driving range, putting green. *Green Fees:* information not available. *Eating facilities:* bar and restaurants in low-rise Spanish-style hotel. Pro shop; car and club hire. Professional: Randy J. Duncan.*

LA QUINTA. **PGA West Resort Course (Nicklaus),** 55-900 PGA Boulevard, La Quinta, Palm Springs (00 1 619 564 7170). One of Jack Nicklaus's best with rolling mounds, much sand and water. Accuracy is all. 18 holes, 6671 yards. Par 72. Driving range, putting green. *Green Fees:* information not available. Pro shop; cart and club hire. Head Professional: Billy Neal.*

LA QUINTA. **PGA West Resort Course (TPC Stadium),** 55-900 PGA Boulevard, La Quinta, Palm Springs (00 1 619 564 7170). Highly strategic with vast mounds and steep escarpments; a Pete Dye course almost unplayable by mere mortals. 18 holes, 6836 yards. Par 72. Driving range, putting green. *Green Fees:* information not available. *Eating facilities:* bar and restaurant in clubhouse. Pro shop; cart and club hire. Head Professional: Billy Neal.*

NORTH PALM SPRINGS. **Desert Dunes,** 19-300 Palm Drive, Palm Springs (00 1 619 251 5366). *Location:* north west of downtown, approaching the foothills. A course by Robert Trent Jones Jr. full of natural, savage beauty; a contrast to the norm, home from home for real golfers. 18 holes, 6614 yards. Par 72. Driving range, putting green. *Green Fees:* information not available. *Eating facilities:* bar and restaurant. Pro shop, cart and club hire. Head Professional: Tom Connelly.*

PALM DESERT. **Desert Falls Country Club,** 1111 Desert Falls Parkway, Palm Desert, CA (00 1 760 304 5646) Top ten rated course in greater Palm Springs area. Links style course with rolling terrain accented by palms, water and sand hazards. A Ron Fream designed course with panoramic views of the mountains on every hole. 18 holes, 7005 yards. Par 74, 6529 yards Par 72, 5250 yards (Ladies) Par 72. Large practice facility. *Green Fees:* information not available. *Eating facilities:* Restaurant, snackbar and lounge. Full service. Pro shop, club rental (Titleist) available. Head Professional: Terry Ferraro.*

PALM DESERT. **Marriott's Desert Springs Resort and Spa,** 74855 Country Club Drive, Palm Desert, Palm Springs (760 341 1756; Fax: 760 341 1828). Two excellent resort courses rich in tall palms and strategic yet ornamental water features and falls, with island greens by Ted Robinson, backed by vast 884 room hotel. 36 holes: Palms 6381 yards, Valley 6326 yards, both Par 72. Driving range, 18 hole putting course, John Jacobs teaching. *Green Fees:* information not available. *Eating facilities:* 5 restaurants and many bars. Pro shop; cart and club hire. Head Professional: Tim Skogen (760 341 1757). Assistant: Irma Garcia (760 341 6757). *

RANCHO MIRAGE. **Rancho Las Palmas Country Club,** 42-000 Bob Hope Drive, Rancho Mirage, Palm Springs (00 1 619 862 4551). A 27 hole resort complex with hotel on site. Gently rolling land with many established trees. Short and tight, now 20 years old. West/South Course 18 holes, 6128 yards. Par 70. Driving range, putting green. *Green Fees:* information not available. *Eating facilities:* bar and snacks in golf clubhouse. Hotel close by. Pro shop; cart and club hire, daily golf clinics, extensive instruction programme. Head Professional: Troy Sprister.*

RANCHO MIRAGE. **Westin Mission Hills Resort Golf Club,** 71-501 Dinah Shore Drive, Rancho Mirage, Palm Springs (760 328 3198; Fax: 760 770 4984). *Location:* five miles east of Palm Springs. Pete Dye and Gary Player have built two excellent courses here, undulating past colourful shrubs and water with a mountain backdrop. Pete Dye Resort Course, 18 holes, 6706 yards S.S.S.70. Gary Player Signature Course 18 holes, 7062 yards S.S.S.70. Magnificent 15 acre driving range, putting green. *Green Fees:* information not available. *Eating facilities:* bar and restaurants in palatial Moroccan-style clubhouse. Pro-shop, cart and club hire. Professional: Alan Deck.*

Golf in South Africa
Paul Dimmock

The international golf enthusiast will find South Africa is a unique experience. Nowhere else in the world can offer the discerning and adventurous golfer such an array of challenging golf courses. The courses are surrounded by gloriously stunning panoramas which include the splendour of Table Mountain, sweeping views of the Indian Ocean, the mystique of the African bushveld and areas of beautiful lush tropical vegetation inhabited by an amazing display of wildlife. South Africa is a vibrant and emerging world golf destination, with over 400 courses. Many of the courses are championship standard and on a par with major European and North American courses. To complete the South African experience there is a full range of accommodation from luxurious 5 star hotels offering the best of international comfort and cuisine, to the game park lodge with its cultural delights. Thanks to an advantageous exchange rate the visitor from the UK will find South Africa incredible value for money.

For more information see www.southafrica.info

FISH HOEK. **Clovelly Country Club,** P.O. Box 22119, Fish Hoek 7974 (+27 21 784 2111; Fax: +27 21 782 6853). *Location*: 30 minutes drive south of Cape Town to Clovelly in the Clovelly Valley. Excellent fairways, bent grass greens, some sloping. Offers stern challenges on almost every hole. Surrounded by mountains and sand dunes. 18 holes. Men's - Par 72. 5893 metres. Ladies' - Par 72, 5193 metres. *Green Fees*: information not provided. *Eating facilities*: clubhouse, light snacks, restaurant. *Visitors*: welcome, book in advance (+27 21 784 2100). Handicap not required. Luxury accommodation: Ocean View Estate - contact John or Hazel Goatley (+27 21 789 1053). Pro shop. Club Professional: Dave Odendaal. Club Manager: Jeremy Lindquist.
e-mail: clubhouse@clovelly.co.za
website: www.clovelly.co.za

GEORGE. **Fancourt Golf and Country Club Estate,** P.O. Box 2266, Montagu Street, Blanco, George 6530 (+27 (0) 44 804 0000; Fax: +27 (0) 44 804 0700). *Location*: 440km south east of Cape Town on the N2 Garden Route in Blanco on the western boundary of the pretty village of George. Four 18 hole Gary Player designed championship courses including The Links - Home of the Presidents Cup 2003. Warm up area, putting and chipping green, driving range, 4-hole academy course. Member of "Great Golf Resorts of the World Association" and "Preferred Hotels & Resorts Worldwide". *Green Fees*: information not available. *Eating facilities*: clubhouse, light snacks, dining room and four restaurants. *Visitors:* exclusive private club, visiting players must be Fancourt Hotel Guests, advance booking essential. Tennis, swimming, spa.*
e-mail: golf@fancourt.co.za

MOWBRAY. **Mowbray Golf Club,** Raapenberg Road, Mowbray, P.O. Box 38003, Howard Place 7450 (+27 21 685 3018; Fax: +27 21 686 6008). *Location*: south of Cape Town, approximately 10 km or 10 minutes from airport. Parkland course. No steep hills but plenty of trees, bent grass greens, numerous water hazards. The cross-wind on 14 holes is a real test. Beautiful views of Table Mountain, Devils Peak. Host to South Africa Open on a number of occasions. 18 holes, Par 72. Men's 6054/5760 metres, Ladies' 5049 metres. *Green Fees*: information not available. *Eating facilities*: clubhouse, halfway house, restaurant. *Visitors*: advance booking necessary, maximum Handicap men 24, ladies 30. Pro Shop. Professional: Greg McDonald. Manager: Dave Duncan. Secretary: Mrs Ingrid Tait.*
e-mail: info@mowbraygolfclub.co.za

SOMERSET WEST. **Erinvale Country Estate and Golf Course,** Lourensford Road, Somerset West 7129 (+27 24 847 1144; Fax: +27 24 847 1901). *Location*: 40 minutes due south from central Cape Town in the heart of the winelands. Parkland, wide kikuyu fairways and bent/poa annua greens. Front nine mainly flat with elongated greens protected by water hazards, back nine on rolling high ground with spectacular views of mountains, vineyards and False Bay. Hosted 1996 World Cup of Golf and 2003, 2004 SAA Open (European Tour). Gary Player designed course. 18 holes, Par 72. Mens 5892 metres, ladies 5126 metres. *Green Fees*: information not provided. *Eating facilities*: restaurant, Halfway House. *Visitors*: welcome, booking essential. certain days restricted. Maximum Handicap: men 24, ladies 36, and certificate required. Professional: Johan Piek.
e-mail: pro-shop@erinvale.com

SUN CITY. **Gary Player Country Club,** Sun City, Pilansberg, North Western Province (+27 14 557 1000; Fax: +27 14 657 3426). *Location*: 150km north west of Johannesburg. 18 holes, Par 72, rating 76. 6938 metres. The most demanding course in South Africa. Mainly flat but unique hole designs, water hazards and deceptive greens. Kikuyu fairways and bent grass greens. A variety of tees can shorten the course. Venue for Million Dollar Challenge. *Green Fees*: information not available. *Eating facilities*: clubhouse, light snacks, restaurant. *Visitors*: welcome, book in advance. Part of Sun City complex, bowls and casino.*
website: www.milliondollar.co.za/course.asp

WOODBRIDGE ISLAND. **Milnerton Golf Club,** Bridge Road, Woodbridge Island, Milnerton 7441 (+27 21 552 1047; Fax: +27 21 551 5897). *Location*: ten miles due north (Otto du Plessis Drive) from Cape Town. Only true Links course in Western Cape. Nestled between Atlantic Ocean and a lagoon, spectacular views of Table Mountain. Wind direction plays a major role, first nine downwind, second nine almost directly into the wind. 18 holes, Par 72. Men's 5721 metres, Ladies' 5022 metres. *Green Fees*: information not available. *Visitors*: welcome, book in advance. *Eating facilities*: halfway house, Maestro's Restaurant. Pro Shop. Manager: Roger Wilson.*
e-mail: manager@milgolf.co.za

WYNBERG. **Royal Cape Golf Club,** 174 Ottery Road, Wynberg 7800 (+27 21 761 6551; Fax: +27 21 797 5246). *Location*: southern suburbs of Cape Town. 15 minute drive from city centre and 15 minutes from international airport. Flat parkland course. Narrow tree-lined kikuyu fairways. Dominant Bent greens, water on six holes, 58 bunkers. Wind plays a major part on some holes. Host to the South Africa Open 11 times. The oldest golf club in South Africa. Spectacular views. 18 holes, Par 72. Men's 6121 metres, Ladies' 5288 metres. *Green Fees*: information not provided. *Eating facilities*: clubhouse, light snacks and restaurant. *Visitors*: welcome, advance booking necessary. Pro Shop. General Manager: Barbara Pestana. Professional: Richard Pickering.
e-mail: manager@royalcapegolf.co.za
      bookings@royalcapegolf.co.za
website: www.royalcapegolf.co.za

For full details of clubs and courses, plus convenient accommodation
www.uk-golfguide.com

Golf in Dubai

DUBAI is a thriving commercial centre with magnificent hotel and leisure amenities which now include unique opportunities for serious business and holiday golf. The Emirates Club, The Dubai Golf and Racing Club and the Dubai Creek Golf and Yachting Club all have unrivalled facilities for visiting golf, including the Dubai Golf Pass. Details from The Secretary, PO Box 6302, Dubai, United Arab Emirates.

For information about golf in Dubai see www.golfindubai.org

DUBAI. **Dubai Creek Golf and Yacht Club,** PO Box 6302, Dubai (00971 4 2956000; Fax: 00971 4 2956044). *Location:* beside the Al Garhoud Bridge, close to the city centre and airport. Venue of the Dubai desert classic in 1999 and 2000 and voted into the top 100 "must play" courses by 'Golf World' in 2005. Re-designed in 2004 by European Golf Design in association with Thomas Bjorn. Stunning golf course featuring `Creek-side' holes, man-made lakes and large sandy wastes. 6857 yards, S.S.S 72. Floodlit Par 3 course, golf academy, driving range and practice facilities. *Green Fees:* information not provided. *Eating facilities:* Lakeview, Legends Steakhouse, The Aquarium, QD's, Vinees and the Boardwalk. *Visitors*: welcome. Golf carts (with GPS) compulsory. Park Hyatt Dubai Hotel, Swimming pool, gym, yacht club, pro shops and marina. Director of Golf: Alan MacKenzie. Golf Operations Executive: David Gray. e-mail: dcgyc@dubaigolf.com
website: www.dubaigolf.com

DUBAI. **Emirates Golf Club,** PO Box 24040, Dubai (971-4-3802222; Fax: 971-4-3801555). *Location*: Interchange 5, Sheikh Zayed Road. Two Championship standard 18-hole courses. Majlis Course: 7211 yards with palm-edged fairways, lakes and immaculate greens. Home of the Dubai Desert Classic. Wadi Course: currently under renovation having been re-designed by Nick Faldo. Par 3 course. Two driving ranges (both floodlit), 2 floodlit short-game practice areas. Home to the Peter Cowen Academy. *Green Fees:* information not available. *Eating facilities:* Five-star Le Classique restaurant, Spike Bar, Sports Bar and The Terrace. *Visitors:* welcome. Tennis, squash, swimming and gym available. General Manager: Mohamed Buamaim. Assistant General Manager: Chris Turlik. Director of Golf: Andrew Whitelaw.*
e-mail: egc@dubaigolf.com

DUBAI. **Nad Al Sheba Golf Club,** PO Box 52872, Nad Al Sheba, Dubai (971-4-3363666; Fax: 971-4-3363717). *Location:* Nad Al Sheba Racecourse, a few kilometres from the city centre. A course with undulating fairways, heavily bunkered and water comes into play on 14 holes. 18 holes, 6659 yards S.S.S. 71. Fully floodlit. Golf clinics, floodlit driving range, practice area, chipping and putting. *Green Fees:* on application. *Eating facilities:* well equipped clubhouse with licensed steak house and spike bar. *Visitors:* welcome; overseas pass available, open daily. Lessons available. Golfing attire and Handicap Certificates required. General Manager: St John Kelliher. See website for full details.
website: www.nadalshebaclub.com

Holiday Golf in Thailand

Michael Gedye

MOST GOLFERS have a fair concept of paradise. It is a place where the warm sun shines and shines (with no need for waterproofs). Where the courses are plentiful, uncrowded and of genuine world class. Where the immaculate fairways beckon in rich ribbons of green, the bunkers are well-tended white splashes of sand and azure lakes offer shimmering reflections of colourful local flora. A place no further away than the USA or South Africa for the European traveller, yet a world apart in all respects. Where you can pause for drinks and snacks at small shelters every three holes and take time to smell the flowers. A land where charming young lady caddies will help you get the most from your round – giving accurate yardage and the line on the green, will mark and clean your ball, rake the bunker, hold an umbrella to shield you from the sun (not rain!), clean your clubs, even your shoes – all with a warm, friendly smile. You can expect costs that are amongst the lowest in the world of holiday golf. All set against a background of an ancient, historic land with an exotic, colourful culture, tantalising cuisine and more to see and discover than you will ever have time for. Is such a golfing paradise just a dream? Not at all, it lies waiting to amaze you in the fabled Kingdom of Thailand.

Dramatic sea views from Santiburi Samui Country Club, Koh Samui

Floral splendour at Mountain Shadow Golf Club, Chonburi

This enchanting country has over 200 golf courses (more than the Costa del Sol and Algarve put together), most built in recent years in the most popular holiday areas. You can choose between the beachside resorts of Cha-Am and Hua Hin to the south-west of the capital Bangkok or Pattaya and Rayong across the Gulf of Thailand to the south-east. Further south lie the tropical islands of Phuket and Koh Samui. As an alternative, you can sample golf in Kanchanaburi, near the historic River Kwai, among the forested hills of Khao Yai or near the northern cities of Chiang Mai and Chiang Rai, backed by wooded mountains.

Most golf courses in key resort areas are built to the latest technical specifications, the work of such world-class design names as Jack Nicklaus, Pete Dye, Peter Thomson, Ronald Fream, Gary Player, Nick Faldo and Dennis Griffiths. Kept in superb condition all year round by armies of attentive green staff, the courses offer a fascinating choice of terrain. Some meander past tall stands of palm and crystal lakes, some plunge down mountain slopes or negotiate the rim of ancient tin mines under the observation of a quaint hillside temple, while others are set near a sandy beach, cooled by the ocean breeze. There is always a choice of tees to suit your ability, and the opportunity to rent good quality clubs (even shoes) if you have not brought your own. Wherever you choose to play, the low prices will be a refreshing surprise.

Another interesting aspect of Thai golf is the clubhouses. Often more like palaces, they rise in glass and marbled splendour behind the final green, offering a warm welcome and royal treatment. Expect luxury locker rooms, spas and panoramic restaurants offering a choice of Thai, Japanese, Chinese and international menus. Although golf was first played here in 1898 (inevitably through British influence), it is only in recent years that the game has really taken off, fuelled in part by the success of Tiger Woods, whose mother is Thai. Some 400,000 domestic players have taken up the game, more than those playing in Scotland, Ireland, the Netherlands and Spain, which ensures high levels of service both in the clubhouse and on the course and some national idiosyncrasies, such as the six-ball. For the visitor, however, apart from the Bangkok area at weekends, courses around the Kingdom are relatively underplayed and available. No handicap certificate is normally required.

The attractive choice of golf can be divided into six regions, three within a relatively short driving distance of the central capital, Bangkok, where all international flights arrive. Two more are southern tropical island destinations, Koh Samui in the Gulf of Thailand and Phuket edging the Andaman Sea. Finally there are Chiang Mai and Chiang Rai in the north. All these last four are served by regular short internal flights from the capital.

With a choice of upmarket and more popular holiday locations, the southern island of **PHUKET** has a fine selection of quality golf. Best known internationally is the 36-hole complex of Blue Canyon, but Mission Hills Phuket Golf Resort & Spa, a new 27-hole course designed by Jack Nicklaus, offers testing golf with sea breezes and stunning views. No lasting damage was caused to any of the courses by the 2004 tsunami.

KOH SAMUI is a hugely popular island which can now offer one of the world's most dramatic courses in a spectacular setting. The Santiburi Samui Country Club rises and plunges over the upper slopes of a mountainside encrusted with tall palms, offering fantastic views out over the Gulf of Thailand.

Destinations to the west and the environs of Bangkok are covered by the **CENTRAL** region. Be sure to visit the well-established Rose Garden at Nakorn Pathom, with its riverside hotel, enticing 18 holes and colourful daily cultural show. There are courses further to the north-west, near the infamous bridge over the River Kwai at Kanchanaburi, as well as clustered down the coastal strip of Cha-Am and Hua Hin.

Great golf amongst northern hills – Chiangmai Highlands Golf & Spa Resort

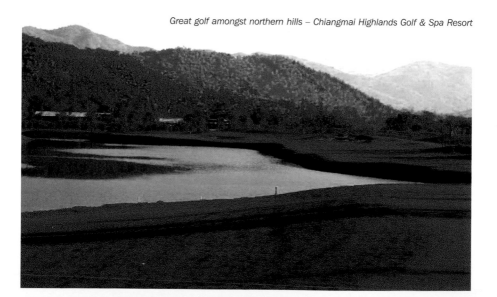

In this peaceful seaside setting, for long the summer retreat of the monarchy, are excellent beachfront hotels, fine sandy beaches, seafood restaurants perched over the water and a good choice of golf.

The **NORTH-EASTERN** region includes the mountainous Khao Yai national park, two hours drive from Bangkok, with its natural wildlife and related golf. Further down the south-eastern coastline of the Gulf of Thailand, the **EASTERN** region offers the largest selection of resort golf and some of the best. Most notable are the 27 holes by Jack Nicklaus at Laem Chabang and Ronald Fream's demanding layout of Mountain Shadow. The nearby resort town of Pattaya offers a wide choice of international dining, hotels and vibrant nightlife.

The mountainous **NORTH**, delightfully cooler during the winter season, cradles the ancient cities of Chiang Mai and Chiang Rai, part of the original Laana kingdom. A number of new courses add to the golfing choice, including the excellent test of Chiangmai Highlands. Arguably the best course in the Kingdom, however, is to be found a short drive to the north-east in Chiang Rai. The Santiburi Country Club, designed by Robert Trent Jones Jr., offers golf of genuine class, immaculately manicured rolling fairways, with superb service on and off the course at very reasonable rates.

Nobody should visit Thailand for golf alone. There is so much more – ancient Bhuddist temples, shimmering Thai silk, graceful classical dancers, tasty complex cuisine and a wealth of history and culture. However, for holiday golf of genuine world class and outstanding value, it truly deserves global recognition.

Pride of the North – immaculate Santiburi Country Club, Chiang Rai

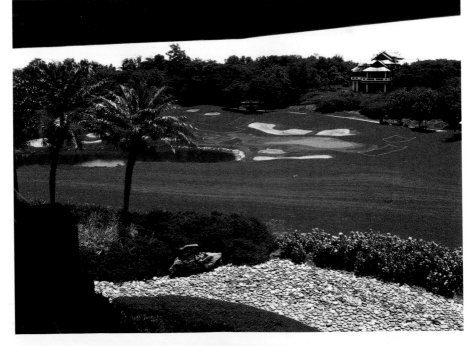

PHUKET

LAGUNA PHUKET. **Laguna Phuket Golf Club,** 34 Moo 4, Tambon Cherngtalay, Amphur Talang, Phuket 83110 (66 76-324 350; Fax: 66 76-324 351). *Location*: part of the Laguna resort complex, 20 minutes south west from Phuket airport. Pleasant, not too demanding modern resort course by Max Wexler and David Abell. Palm trees and water hazards open to the sea breeze. 18 holes, 6768 yards. Par 71. Pro shop, teaching professionals, driving range, chipping areas, putting greens. *Green Fees*: information not available. *Eating facilities*: restaurant and bar in clubhouse. *Visitors*: welcome. Club, shoe, umbrella, chair hire. e-mail: golf-phuket@banyantree.com

PHANG-NGA. **Thai Muang Beach Golf & Marina,** 157/12 Moo 9, Limdul Road, Tambon Thai Muang, Amphur Thai Muang, Phang-Nga 82120 (66 76 571 533/5; Fax: 66 76 571 214). *Location*: off Highway 4, 40 km (30 minutes drive) north of Phuket Airport over road bridge into Phang-Nga. Created by Dye Designs, this is the only true seaside course along the Andaman Sea. Demanding layout in a relaxed, remote setting. 18 holes, 7019 yards. Par 72. Pro shop, driving range, putting green. *Green Fees:* information not available. *Eating facilities:* restaurant and bar in clubhouse. Beach chalet accommodation available. Reservations and Information: (66 76 571 533/4; Fax: 66 76 571 214). Refreshment kiosks on course. *Visitors:* welcome. Carts, club, shoe, umbrella and chair hire.* website: www.thaimuanggolf.com

PHUKET. **Blue Canyon Country Club,** 165 Moo 1, Thepkasattri Road, Maikaw, Thalang, Phuket 83110 (076 327440-7; Fax: 076 327449). *Location:* just 5 minutes drive south of Phuket International Airport. One of the premier golf resorts in Asia. Two dramatic 18-hole courses built around a former tin mine with some spectacular carries and kept in excellent condition. Twice venue of Johnnie Walker Classic. Clubhouse hotel overlooks course from crest of hill. Canyon Course: 18 holes, 7179 yards, Par 72. Lakes Course: 18 holes, 7129 yards, Par 72. Pro shop, Blue Canyon Golf School, driving range, putting greens. *Green Fees:* information not available. Playing rights open only to residents of clubhouse hotel and guests of members. *Eating facilities:* Canyon Restaurant, Golfers' Terrace, Lobby Lounge, Members' Lounge. *Visitors*: only by invitation or as hotel guest. Caddies, club hire.* e-mail: reservation@bluecanyonclub.com website: www.bluecanyonclub.com

PHUKET. **Loch Palm Golf Club Phuket,** 38 Moo 5, Vichitsongkram Road, Kathu District, Phuket 83120 (076 321 930; Fax: 076 321 927/8). *Location:* in Kathu village about 7km from Phuket town and 40 minutes drive from Phuket Airport. Laid out around a large lake on the site of a former tin mine, this is a pleasant course with palm trees and encircled by wooded hills. 18 holes, 6434 yards, Par 72. Pro shop, driving range, chipping and putting green. *Green Fees:* information not available. *Eating facilities:* lakeside restaurant in temporary clubhouse. Four refreshment kiosks on course. *Visitors:* welcome. Cart, club, shoe, umbrella, chair hire.*

PHUKET. **Mission Hills Phuket Golf Resort & Spa,** 195 Moo 4, Pla Khlok, Amphur Talang, Phuket 83110 (76 310 888; Fax: 76 310 899). *Location*: north on highway 402 from Phuket town, turn right at km 25 on route 4027. Course is 4 km on left. Set in the north-east of the island, not far from the airport, this new Jack Nicklaus-designed course boasts two dramatic holes backed by superb ocean views. Plenty of sand and water with night golf available on the 9-hole Bay View course. 18 holes, 6806 yards, Par 72. Also 9-hole course. Driving range, putting green, pro shop. *Green Fees:* information not available. *Eating facilities:* on-course snacks and restaurant in luxury clubhouse hotel. *Visitors:* welcome.* e-mail: info@missionhillssphuket.com website: www.missionhillsphuket.com

PHUKET. **Phuket Country Club,** 80/1 Vichitsongkram Road, Moo7, Katu District, Phuket 83120 (66-76-319200-4; Fax: 66-76-319206). *Location*: 30 minutes from Phuket Airport on main road (4020) to Patong Beach. Two very interesting and well-kept courses. (18 and 9 holes) with plenty of water hazards. Scenic, with mature flowering shrubs and palms in location of former tin mine. Surrounded by wooded hills. Old Course 18 holes, 6483 yards, Par 72. Country Club Course 9 holes, 3575 yards, S.S.S. 37. Pro shop, driving range, putting green. *Green Fees:* 18 holes weekdays and weekends 3,000 Baht per round, 9 holes 1,500 Baht; caddie fee 250 Baht per round. *Eating facilities:* restaurant and bar terrace in clubhouse. Refreshment kiosks on course. *Visitors:* welcome. Club hire. Soft spikes only. General Manager: Mr Keat Lau. e-mail: bookings@phuketcountryclub.com website: www.phuketcountryclub.com

KOH SAMUI

SURATHANI. **Santiburi Samui Country Club**, 12/15 Moo 4, Tambon Maenam, Amphur Koh Samui, Surathani 84330 (66 (0) 7742 1700-8; Fax: 66 (0) 77 421 709). *Location*: on the north coast of the island near Mae Nam, a short drive from the airport. An amazing creation rising to more than 950 feet above spectacular sea views. Embraced by tall coconut palms, this is a world-class course which demands precision, kept in superb condition. 18 holes, 6,881 yards, Par 72. Driving range, golf academy, practice green, pro shop. *Green Fees*: information not available. *Eating facilities*: clubhouse restaurant with panoramic seaview terrace. *Visitors*: welcome. Club rental. Professional: Vuthirut Manee-in. General Manager: Surawut Wannapintu.*
e-mail: proshop@santiburi.com

CENTRAL REGION

AYUTTHAYA. **Bangsai Country Club,** 77/7 Moo 3, Bangplee, Bangsai, Ayutthaya 13190 (035 371 490-7; Fax: 035 371491). *Location*: due north of Bangkok on Route 1 direction Ayutthaya. Near Bangsai follow signs to course. Superbly innovative 18 holes course offering a mixture of parkland and links-style golf in an inland setting. 18 holes, 6923 yards, Par 72. Pro shop, driving range, putting green. *Green Fees*: information not available. *Eating facilities*: clubhouse restaurant, refreshment kiosk on course. *Visitors*: welcome. Cart, club hire.*

BANGKOK. **Muang Ake Golf Club,** 52 Moo 7, Phaholyothin Road, Amphoe Muang, Pathum Thani (02 533 9335; Fax: 02 533 9345). *Location*: take Vibhavadi Rangsit Road north out of the city past Don Muang Airport. Filter left before junction with Phaholyothin road. After 2km turn left at petrol station and then bear right at fork. Pleasant, mature course on fairly compact site with many water hazards. 18 holes, 6398 yards, Par 72. Pro shop, driving range, putting green. *Green Fees*: information not available. *Eating facilities*: restaurant and bar in clubhouse. *Visitors*: welcome. Club, shoe, umbrella hire.*

CHA-AM. **Imperial Lake View Hotel and Golf Club,** 79 Moo 4, Hubkrapong-Praburi, Highway Tambol Samphraya, Cha-Am, Petchburi 76120 (032 456233; Fax: 032 456241). *Location*: 25 minutes north up the coast road from central Hua Hin. Very imaginative and challenging 27 holes of golf by Roger Packard. Rolling mounds, large greens, lakes and palms. 18 holes, 6915 yards. Par 72 plus new 9 holes. Hotel, pro shop, putting green. *Green Fees*: information not available. *Eating facilities*: cafe and restaurant in clubhouse. Refreshment kiosks on course. *Visitors*: welcome. Cart, club, shoe, umbrella hire.*

CHA-AM. **Springfield Village Golf and Spa**, 193 Moo 6 Huay Sai Nua, Cha-am, Petchburi 76120. *Location*: about 110 miles from Bangkok by new highway; 30 minutes north of central Hua Hin and 15 minutes from Springfield Beach resort. This is a golf course of true championship calibre, part of a planned 36 hole layout. This 27 hole facility designed by Jack Nicklaus is a great test for golfers of all skill levels. Opened in 1993. Venue of Thailand Open 2000 and 1995/2000 APGA qualifying schools. 27 stunning holes. Home of Heartland Golf School, lessons and clinics available. Driving range, pitching area, putting greens. *Green Fees*: information not available. *Visitors*: welcome. Soft spikes only. 98 luxurious hotel rooms and full spa available. Director of Golf: Tony Meechai. Head Professional: Michael van Amelsvoort (+66 (0)3270 9259; Fax: +66 (0)32 70 9233).*
e-mail: michael@springfieldresort.com
website: www.springfieldresort.com

HUA-HIN. **Palm Hills Golf Resort and Country Club,** 1444 Petchakasem Highway, Cha-Am District, Petchaburi 76120 Thailand (6632 520801-9; Fax: 6632 520820). *Location*: on Petchakasem highway just 8km before Hua Hin. Links/seaside course. A most pleasant course by Max Waxler with good use of rocks and flowers to decorate holes that mostly follow the natural terrain spilling down from wooded hills behind. 18 holes (Tiff Eagle green), 6373 yards. Par 72. Pro shop, driving range, putting green. *Green Fees*: information not available. *Eating facilities*: international restaurant and executive bar lounges in clubhouse, refreshment kiosks on course. *Visitors*: welcome. Cart, club, shoe, chair hire.*

HUA HIN. **The Majestic Creek Country Club,** Ban Wangkoi, Thumbol Tabtai, Hua Hin District, Prachuap Klirikan (032-520162-6, Fax: 032-520477). *Location*: 25 minutes drive directly inland from Huay Mongkil Road from Hua Hin town, backing up to low hills. Plenty of streams and water hazards on this rolling, challenging but well-maintained course. 18 holes, 6961 yards. Par 72. Pro shop, driving range, putting green. *Green Fees:* information not available. *Eating facilities*: restaurant and bar in clubhouse. Refreshment kiosks on course. *Visitors*: welcome. Cart, club, shoe, umbrella hire. Accommodation is also provided by the Majestic Creek Country Club at the Majestic Beach Resort about 25km from the golf course, by the sea. Transport can be included. (032 520162-6; Fax: 032 520 477).*

HUA HIN. **Royal Hua Hin Golf Course,** Hua Hin District, Prachuapkirikhan 7910 (032 512 475; Fax: 032 513 038). *Location*: in the centre of Hua Hin town right by the railway station. Built in 1922 this is the oldest 'proper' golf course in the Kingdom. Historic, very natural golf running back into wooded hills offering sensational views. 18 holes, 6654 yards. Par 72. Pro shop, driving range, putting green, chipping green. *Green Fees*: 2,000 Baht. *Eating facilities*: restaurant and bar in clubhouse. Refreshment kiosks on course. *Visitors*: welcome. Club, shoe, umbrella hire.

KANCHANABURI. **Mission Hills Golf Club,** 27/7 Moo 7, Tambon Pungtru, Amphur Tha Muang, Kanchanaburi (reservations: 034 644147; Fax: 034 644323). *Location:* about 126 km northwest of Bangkok from Bang Pong, take the left fork and continue 15km towards Tha Maka. At Route 3089 turn left and find course on left. No expense spared on this Jack Nicklaus designed course with waste bunkers, water hazards and mature palms. Course slopes gently away from clubhouse nestling under a wooded hill. 18 holes, 7042 yards. Par 72. Hotel, pro shop, putting green. *Green Fees:* information not available. *Eating facilities:* restaurant and bar in clubhouse. Turf roofed refreshment kiosks on course. *Visitors:* welcome. Club, shoe, umbrella, cart hire.*

KANCHANABURI. **Nichigo Resort & Country Club,** 106 Moo 4, Tambol Wangdong, Ampor Muang, Kanchanaburi 71000 (034 584000; Fax: 034 518518). *Location*: about 25km from Kanchanaburi town (150km north-west of Bangkok) on Ladya-Erawan Falls Road. 27 holes of superb resort golf on land sloping down either side of the Kwai Yai River. Gentle contours, shallow bunkers and few trees offer an attractive round against a backdrop of craggy rock outcrops. Three distinct nines - River, Lake and Mountain courses. Two 18 hole combinations, 7133 and 7260 yards, both Par 72. Hotel, pro shop, driving range, putting green. *Green Fees:* information not available. *Eating facilities:* bar and restaurant in clubhouse; drinks huts on course. *Visitors:* welcome. cart, club hire.*

NAKORN PATHOM. **The Rose Garden Aprime Resort,** Km 32, Pet Kasem Highway, Sampran, Nakorn Pathom 73110 (034 322 588-93; Fax: 034 322 775). *Location:* about one hour north-west of Bangkok on Petchakasem Road Km 32. A unique gem both to visit and to play, where the overall ambience and standards of service only enhance an interesting, mature test of golf over a level site with flowering shrubs, trees and water hazards. A genuine treat – not least from the smiling assistance of over 400 knowledgeable young lady caddies. 18 holes, 7085 yards, Par 72. Riverside hotel, pro shop, driving range, putting green. *Green Fees:* information not available. *Eating facilities:* international restaurant in clubhouse includes sushi bar; refreshment kiosks on course. *Visitors:* welcome. Club, cart, shoe, umbrella hire.*
e-mail: docs@rose-garden.com

NORTH REGION

CHIANGMAI. **Chiangmai-Lamphun Golf Club,** San Kamphaeng-Banthi Road, Chiangmai 50130 (66 (0) 5388 0880-4; Fax: 66 (0) 5388 0888). *Location:* about half-an-hour's drive south-east of Chiangmai. Sheltered in the golden teak valley with delightful trees and many hazards. 18 holes, 6919 yards, Par 72. Golf shop, driving range, putting green. *Green Fees:* information not available. *Eating facilities:* restaurant and bar in clubhouse. *Visitors:* welcome. Cart, club, shoes and umbrella hire.*

CHIANGMAI. **Chiangmai Highlands Golf & Spa Resort,** 167 Moo 2, Tambol On-Nuar, King Amphur Mea-On, Chiangmai 50130 (01 961 0028-9; Fax: 01 951 5233). *Location:* about 30 minutes' drive east of the city. Take the first ring road on Highway 1317 direction Mae-on; the course is on the right after crossing route 1006. A spectacular new course designed by Lee Schmidt in a location surrounded by wooded mountains. Strategic water hazards on the lower holes contrast with dramatic elevation changes on the rolling back nine. 18 holes, 7063 yards, Par 72. Extensive practice area, putting green, pro shop. *Green Fees:* information not available. *Eating facilities:* restaurant in clubhouse. *Visitors:* welcome.*
e-mail: info@chiangmaihighlands.com
website: www.chiangmaihighlands.com

CHIANGMAI. **Royal Chiangmai Golf Resort,** 169 Moo 5, Chiangmai-Phrao Road 26km, Maefak, Sansai, Chiangmai 50290 (053 849301-6; Fax: 053 849310). *Location:* a little north-east of Chiangmai city towards Chiangrai. Attractive course laid out in a valley surrounded by wooded hills. 18 holes, 6969 yards, Par 72. Golf shop, driving range, putting green. *Green Fees:* information not available. *Eating facilities:* restaurant and bar in clubhouse. *Visitors:* welcome. Cart, club hire. Five star 56 room hotel with swimming pool, fitness centre, massage and sauna, snooker, karaoke and function rooms.*
e-mail: rcgc@cm.ksc.co.th
e-mail:golf1@cm.ksc.co.th
website: www.royalchiangmai.co.th

CHIANG RAI. **Santiburi Country Club,** 12 Moo 3, Hoadoi-Sobpao Road, Wiangchai, Chiang Rai 57210 (0-5366 2821-6; Fax: 0-5371 7377). *Location:* take route 1020 south-east from Chiang Rai; turn left route 1152. Follow signs to golf. A magnificent championship layout by Robert Trent Jones Jr, one of the best in the Kingdom, with rolling hills, strategic water and mountain views. Always kept in immaculate condition. 18 holes, 6,982 yards, Par 72. Driving range, putting green, pro shop. *Green Fees:* information not available. *Eating facilities:* clubhouse restaurant with open-air balcony views over the course. Refreshment shelters on course. *Visitors:* welcome. Caddies, electric cart, club and umbrella rental. General Manager: Chotiwut Gajesanandana.*

CHIANG RAI. **Waterford Valley Chiangrai Golf Course & Resort,** 333 Moo 5, Tamboon Pasang, Amphur Wiangchai, Chiangrai 57210 (053 953 440; Fax: 053 953 447). *Location:* about 40 minutes' drive west from Chiang Rai. A well-established course combining holes falling steeply down from the hilltop clubhouse with more level, lake country. 18 holes, 6961 yards, Par 72. Golf shop, driving range, putting green. *Green Fees:* information not available. *Eating facilities:* clubhouse restaurant; refreshment kiosks on course. *Visitors:* welcome. Club, cart hire.*

N. EASTERN REGION

NAKHON RATCHASIMA. **Mission Hills Khao Yai Golf Club,** 151 Moo 5, Tambon Musi, Amphur Pakchong, Nakhon Ratchasima (reservation: 02-226 3390-3; Fax: 02-222 9021). *Location:* up Friendship Highway from Bangkok; turn to Thanaratch (Km 165) then turn right at Km 20 before Khao Yai National Park. Designed by Jack Nicklaus, this gently undulating course, part of a luxurious prestige resort, is protected by dramatic forested crags and hills. Mature trees and some water. 18 holes, 7058 yards, Par 72. Hotel, pro shop, putting green. *Green Fees:* 1,000 Baht per day, weekend 2,000 Baht per day. Cart fee 600 Baht per 18 holes; Caddy fee 200 Baht per 18 holes. *Eating facilities:* coffee shop and restaurant in clubhouse. *Visitors:* welcome as hotel or member's guest. Cart, club hire.

NAKHON RATCHASIMA. **The Country Club Khao Yai,** Km 23 Thanaratch Road, Pakchong District, Nakhon Ratchasima (reservation: 02 255 3979; Fax: 02 255 2168). *Location:* take Friendship Highway from Bangkok; to Pakchong District, turn to Thanaratch Road at Km 165 to Khao Yai National Park. Open nearly five years and designed by Jack Nicklaus, there is plenty of sand and water in this demanding valley course surrounded by wooded mountain environment. 18 holes, 7102 yards, Par 72. Pro shop, putting green. *Green Fees:* information not available. *Eating facilities:* coffee shop and restauraunt in clubhouse. *Visitors:* welcome. Cart, club, shoe hire.*

EASTERN

CHANTABURI. **Soi Dao Highland Golf Club & Resort,** 153/1 Moo 2, Tambon Tabsai, Pong Nam Ron, Chantaburi 22140 (039-320 174-6;Fax: 039-320 177). *Location:* direction Chantabuni on Route 3, turn left to route 317 direction Sao Kaeo. Sign for golf on left at 42 km marker. Gently sloping course surrounded by rain forest below towering Soi Dao mountain. A great design by Dennis Griffiths; well worth the trip. 18 holes, 7,162 yards, Par 72. Driving range, putting green. *Green Fees:* information not available. *Eating facilities:* clubhouse restaurant, snack shelters on course. On-site accommodation. *Visitors:* welcome, advance telephone call suggested. Caddies, cart, club, umbrella and shoe hire.*

CHONBURI. **Laem Chabang International Country Club,** 106/8 Moo 4, Beung, Sriracha, Chonburi 20230 (66 38 372 273; Fax: 66 38 372 275). *Location:* just 120km from Bangkok by the new highway and 30 minutes north of Pattaya. On new Chonburi-Pattaya Road 32km. Three superb nine hole loops by Jack Nicklaus - Lake, Valley and Mountain - of championship quality. Satisfying from the normal tees; tough off the back. Plenty of variety of terrain, plus strategic sand and water. Three x 9 holes, Lake 3472, Valley 3608, Mountain 3486 yards, all Par 36. Golf lodge, pro shop, driving range, putting greens. *Green Fees:* information not available. *Eating facilities:* international restaurant and coffee shop; refreshment kiosks around course. *Visitors:* welcome. Cart, club, shoe, umbrella, chair hire. Swimming pool.*
e-mail: info@laemchabanggolf.com
website: www.laemchabanggolf.com

CHONBURI. **Mountain Shadow Golf Club,** 159/1 Moo 2, Saensuk-Bangpra Road, Ban Muang, Chonburi 20131 (038 393 001/18; Fax: 038 393 019). *Location:* turn left at third exit of Chonburi bypass onto route 36 (keep right onto flyover). At 6km market, turn right and follow road to course. A fine rolling natural design by Ronald Fream, spilling downhill from the clubhouse set against a wooded hill past mature mango trees and palms to several strategic lakes. 18 holes, 6807 yards, Par 72. Pro shop, driving range (irons), putting green. *Green Fees:* information not available. *Eating facilities:* restaurant and bar lounge in clubhouse; refreshment kiosks around course. *Visitors:* welcome. Carts, club, shoe hire.*

CHONBURI. **Crystal Bay Golf Club,** 502 Moo 10, Bangpra, Sriracha, Chonburi 20210 (038 349 370/80; Fax: 038 349 383). *Location:* take routes 34 and 3 from Bangkok through Chonburi (bypass). Course is on left of main road at 109km marker. Well-established 27-hole layout with much use of flowering shrubs, rocks, waterfalls as decoration. Level site with interesting but not overly demanding holes defined by palms and water. 27 holes, A 3526, B 3483, C 3480 yards, all Par 36. Pro shop, driving range, putting green. *Green Fees:* information not available. *Eating facilities:* coffee shop in clubhouse; refreshment kiosks around course. *Visitors:* welcome. Pro-shop, cart, club, shoe, umbrella, chair hire; sports club, fitness centre, Golf Lodge.*

CHONBURI. **Noble Place Golf Resort & Country Club,** 88/8 Moo 6, Tambon Klongkiew Banbung, Chonburi 20220 (038 263458-60; Fax: 01 940 3250). *Location:* leave Bangkok on Bangna-Trad Road, then turn to by-pass 344 and after right on to 331. Club is on left after 5km. Another example of the natural style of Peter Thomson and Michael Wolveridge. Rolling slopes, gentle mounds, pot bunkers and wild grasses create a seaside feel to a palm lined 27 hole course backed by wooded hills. 27 holes - A 3500, B 3500 and C 3565 yards, all Par 72. Pro shop, driving range, putting green, sand bunker practice area. *Green Fees:* information not available. *Eating facilities:* restaurant in clubhouse. *Visitors:* welcome. Cart, club, shoe, umbrella hire. Managing Director: Ekapol Chakshuraksha.*
website: www.babadoogolf.com

CHONBURI. **Plutaluang Navy Golf Course,** Plutaluang, Sattahip, Chonburi (038 701891). *Location*: about 30km south of Pattaya towards Rayong. Take route 331 across 36 and 332, turning right under bridge at 5km, fork left, then right. Established since 1969, the course, 36 holes, is managed by the Royal Thai Navy. Well-established trees and fairly traditional design make for interesting and challenging golf on well-maintained holes in a most attractive setting. 36 holes - South 3274, East 3175, North 3374 and West 3353 yards, all Par 36. Pro shop, putting green. *Green Fees*: information not available. *Eating facilities:* restaurant in clubhouse. *Visitors:* welcome. Cart, club hire.*
e-mail: aree.y@navy.mi
　　　　aree1960@hotmail.com
website: www.geocities.com/plutaluang1969

RAYONG. **Eastern Star Country Club & Resort,** Banchag, Rayong 21130 (038 630 410/7; Fax: 038 630 418). *Location:* take the Bangna-Trad highway towards Rayong and route 3 all the way to 193 km marker, 58 km south of Pattaya and 2 km short of Ban Chang. Enjoyable, gently undulating course by Robert Trent Jones Jr edged with mature palms. Sand is not too penal but some strategic water hazards. 18 holes, 7134 yards, Par 72. Pro shop, driving range, putting green. *Green Fees:* (2008) Weekdays 1,200 Baht, Weekends 1,800 Baht; Cart 600 Baht, Caddy 220 Baht. *Eating facilities:* restaurant and bar in clubhouse, refreshment kiosks on course. *Visitors:* welcome. Cart, club hire.

RAYONG. **Rayong Green Valley Country Club,** 23 Moo 7, Banchang, Rayong 21130 (038 893 838-42, 01 940 8181, 01 940 8228; Fax: 038 893838). *Location:* club is 25 km from North Pattaya. Drive from the end of the Bang Na Expressway to Km15 on highway 36. Wonderfully natural golf created on sloping terrain by Peter Thomson and Michael Wolveridge. Low hills and lush foliage frame the links-style contouring of an interesting layout. 18 holes, Pro 7264 yards Yellow 6856 yards, Am 6835 yards, Ladies 5685 yards. Par 72. Pro shop, driving range, putting green. *Green Fees:* information not available. *Eating facilities:* international menu in clubhouse restaurant. *Visitors:* welcome. Cart, club, shoe, umbrella hire.*

SRIRACHA. **Sriracha Golf Club,** 284-285 Moo 6, Sukhumvit 7, Sriracha, Chonburi 20230 (038 338 375/8; Fax: 038 338 379). *Location:* 40km north-east of Pattaya. From Benga-Trad Highway from Bangkok, turn left onto 3241 at Sriracha, soon after Chonburi. Club on right. Host to the 1996 Thailand Open, this course designed by Gary Player follows relatively level land below the hillside clubhouse. Plenty of mature trees; watch out for the Par 3 3rd hole, 180 yards over a crocodile filled lake! 18 holes, 6227 yards, Par 72. Hotel, pro shop, driving range, putting green. *Green Fees:* information not available. *Eating facilities:* restaurant and lounge in clubhouse. *Visitors:* welcome. Cart, club, shoe hire.*

Mission Hills Golf Club, Kanchanaburi

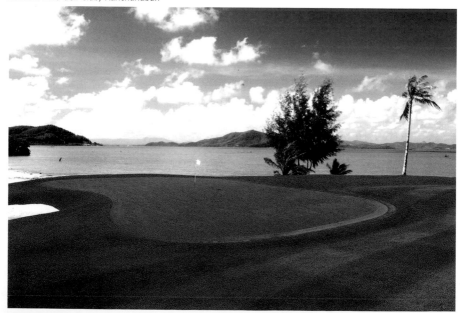

DRIVING RANGES

LONDON

CHINGFORD. **Chingford Golf Range,** Waltham Way, Chingford E4 8AQ (020 8529 2409). *Location:* two miles south of Junction 26 M25. 24 bay floodlit, covered two tier driving range. *Prices:* information not available. *Opening hours:* 8am to 10pm. Practice putting green, practice bunker; indoor academy; video, tuition available at all times. Professional: Gordon Goldie PGA (020 8529 2409).
e-mail: info@chingfordgolfrange.com
website: www.chingfordgolfrange.com

LONDON. **Dukes Meadows Golf Club and Chiswick Bridge Golf Range,** Dukes Meadows, Dan Mason Drive, London W4 2SH (020 8995 0537; Fax: 020 8995 5326). *Location:* Next to Chiswick Bridge on A316, one mile south of the Hogarth Roundabout. Golf Range with 50 covered, floodlit bays and practice bunker. *Prices:* information not available. *Eating facilities:* bar restaurant area. *Opening hours:* weekdays from 9am to 10pm, weekends 8.30am to 10pm. Twelve PGA teaching professionals. Indoor digital tuition studio, individual group and on-course tuition. 9 hole, Par 3 course. Dress code in operation. Practice, putting green. Promenade Suite function room - catering up to 300 people. Professional: Malcolm Henbery (020 8995 0537). General Manager: Scott Margetts (020 8994 3314).

LONDON. **Ealing Golf Range,** Rowdell Road, Northolt, Middlesex UB5 6AG (Tel & Fax: 020 8845 4967). *Location:* A40 Target roundabout, Northolt. Golf range with 35 floodlit, covered bays. Bunker. Artificial putting green. *Prices:* information not available. *Eating facilities:* bar and snack bar. *Opening hours:* 9.30am to 10pm. Five professionals, video tuition, large golf shop, repair shop. Head Professional: Paul O'Brien (Tel & Fax: 020 8845 4967).*
e-mail: pob.golf@cwco.net

NORTHOLT. **Lime Trees Park Golf Club,** Ruislip Road, Northolt UB5 6QZ (020 8845 3180). *Location:* 500 yards south of Polish War Memorial roundabout off A40, two miles inside M25. 20 bay covered, floodlit, grassed driving range. *Prices:* information not available. *Eating facilities:* two bars and bistro (bar open 11am to 11pm). *Opening Hours:* 10am to 10pm. Two PGA Professionals, 'Geoff Buddis' golf superstore, public golf course. Social club with pool and snooker; functions catered for. Professional: Neil MacDonald. Secretary: Adam Phelps (020 8842 0442; Fax: 020 8842 2097).*

NORTHOLT. **London Golf Centre,** Ruislip Road, Northolt UB5 6QZ (020 8845 3180). *Location:* 500 yards south of Polish War Memorial roundabout off A40, two miles inside M25. 20 bay covered, floodlit, grassed driving range. *Prices:* information not available. *Eating facilities:* full bar and catering

facilities (bar open 11am to 11pm). *Opening Hours:* daybreak to sunset. Two PGA Professionals, golf superstore, public golf course. Social club with pool and snooker; functions catered for.*

STANMORE. **Brockley Hill Golf Park,** Brockley Hill, Stanmore HA7 4LR (020 8420 6222; Fax: 020-8420-6333). *Location:* 200 yards down on right hand side from Royal Orthopaedic Hospital, (A5). 38 bay covered floodlit driving range. *Prices:* information not available. *Eating facilities:* sandwiches and soft drinks available. *Opening hours:* Monday to Friday 8am-10pm every day. Group lessons and academy programmes available. Professionals: James Reynolds (Head), Martyn Shoulder and Andrew Stubbs. *

BEDFORDSHIRE

DUNSTABLE. **Tilsworth Golf Centre,** Dunstable Road, Tilsworth, Near Leighton Buzzard LU7 9PU (01525 210721). *Location:* two miles north of Dunstable, off A5 Tilsworth turn. 30 bay covered floodlit range. *Prices:* information not available. *Eating facilities:* restaurant and bar (extensive menu), function suite. *Opening hours:* 10am to 10pm. Large Pro shop, repairs, tuition and group lessons. 18 hole golf course open to public. *Society Meetings:* catered for; prior reservation essential. Professional: Nick Webb (01525 210721; Fax: 01525 210465).

LEIGHTON BUZZARD. **Aylesbury Vale Golf Club,** Stewkley Road, Wing, Leighton Buzzard LU7 0UJ (01525 240196). *Location:* four miles west of Leighton Buzzard between the villages of Wing and Stewkley. 9 bay covered, floodlit range.18 hole golf course, 6612 yards, Par 72. *Prices:* £2.00 per 35 ball bucket. *Eating facilities:* downstairs bar and restaurant, first floor bar and balcony. *Opening hours:* Daylight hours. Please telephone. Group and individual lessons. Professional: Terry Bunyan (07731 966 749). Secretary/ Manager: Chris Wright (01525 240196).

BERKSHIRE

BINFIELD. **Blue Mountain Golf Centre,** Wood Lane, Binfield, Bracknell RG42 4EX (01344 300 200; Fax: 01344 360 960). *Location:* two miles from M4 near Bracknell/Wokingham. 33 bay covered floodlit range. Parkland course with numerous lakes. 18 holes, 6097 yards. S.S.S 70. *Eating facilities:* fully licensed restaurant/bar. New Blues Bar with live jazz and food. *Opening hours:* 7am - 9pm. Manager: Steve Coles (01344 300220).*

MAIDENHEAD. **Bird Hills Golf Centre,** Drift Road, Hawthorn Hill, Near Maidenhead SL6 3ST (01628 771030). *Location:* on A330 Ascot to Maidenhead road. 36 covered, floodlit bays. 18 hole "pay and play"course. Tuition from professional available. *Prices:* information not available. *Opening hours:* 7.30am to 10pm daily. *Eating facilities:* "Elizabethan Restaurant" and Golfers Bar and terrace.*

WARGRAVE. **Hennerton Golf Club,** Crazies Hill Road, Wargrave RG10 8LT (01189 401000; Fax: 01189 401042). *Location:* halfway between Maidenhead and Reading off the A321 to Henley. Scenic course overlooking the Thames valley. 9 holes, 5460 yards. S.S.S. 67. *Visitors:* welcome. Driving range. *Eating facilities:* clubhouse with full facilities. Fully stocked Pro shop. Professional/Manager: William Farrow (01189 404778).

WOKINGHAM. **Downshire Golf Complex,** Easthampstead Park, Wokingham RG40 3DH (01344 302030; Fax: 01344 301020). *Location:* between Bracknell and Wokingham, off the Nine Mile Ride. 30 bay covered floodlit driving range, with PowerTee® installed in 15 bays. *Prices:* 50 balls for £2.95. *Eating facilities:* bar and restaurant, bar snacks available. *Opening hours:* 7.30am to 10pm. 18 hole course, 9 hole pitch and putt; well stocked golf shop, tuition. Societies welcome. Golf Manager: Paul Stanwick. e-mail: downshiregc@bracknell-forest.gov.uk website: www.bracknell-forest.gov.uk/downshiregolf

BUCKINGHAMSHIRE

AYLESBURY. **Aylesbury Golf Centre,** Hulcott Lane, Bierton, Aylesbury HP22 5GA (01296 393644). *Location:* north of Aylesbury on the A418 Leighton Buzzard road. 30 bay covered, floodlit driving range. *Prices:* information not available. *Eating facilities:* bar, bar snacks 11am to 11pm. *Opening hours:* weekdays 8am to 10pm; weekends 7am to 10pm. Professional coaching. 18 hole golf course. General Manager: Kevin Partington. Professional: R. Wooster.

COLNBROOK. **Colnbrook Golf Range,** Galleymead Road, Colnbrook SL3 0EN (01753 682670). *Location:* one mile from Junction 5 M4, one mile Junction 14 M25. 27 bay floodlit, grassed range; 14 covered bays. *Prices:* information not available. *Opening hours:* 9am to 6pm. Professional: Alistair McKay. Full tuition, video assisted lessons given.*

MILTON KEYNES. **Kingfisher Country Club,** Buckingham Road, Deanshanger MK19 6DG (01908 562332; Fax: 01908 260857). *Location:* Between Milton Keynes and Buckingham on A422 opposite Shires Motel. 10 bay covered, grassed driving range. *Prices:* information not available. *Eating facilities:* full clubhouse and lodge facilities. *Opening hours:* 7.30am to 7.30pm Monday to Sunday. Professional tuition by request. Director Golf & Leisure: Major D. M. Barraclough (01908 562332; Fax: 01908 260857).*

MILTON KEYNES. **Windmill Hill Golf Centre,** Tattenhoe Lane, Bletchley, Milton Keynes MK3 7RB (01908 630660; Fax: 01908 630034; Tee reservations: 01908 631113. 7 days in advance). *Location:* M1 South Junction 14/M1 North Junction 13, A421 towards Buckingham. 23 bay covered floodlit driving range, 7 grassed bays. Two putting greens; practice area; two pool tables. *Prices:* information not available. *Eating facilities:* carvery restaurant, cafeteria, two bars, function room. *Opening hours:* 7.30am till dusk. *Society Meetings:* welcome (after 11am weekends and Bank Holidays). Three teaching Professionals, tuition, Pro shop. Professional: Colin Clingan (01908 378623; Fax: 01908 271478). Secretary: Brian Smith (Tel & Fax: 01908 366457).*

STOKE POGES. **The Lanes Golf Course & Driving Range,** Stoke Road, Stoke Poges (01753 554840). *Location:* half-a-mile from Slough Railway Station in direction of Stoke Poges. 18 bay covered, floodlit driving range. Parkland course ideal for the less experienced player. 9 holes. 2074 yds. S.S.S 60 (18 holes). *Eating facilities:* small lounge area with snack facilities. *Opening hours:* contact for details. Clubs for hire. Expert tuition available. A Golf Foundation starter centre. Professional: D. Green (01753 554840).*

STOWE. **Silverstone Golf Club,** Silverstone Road, Stowe MK18 5LH (01280 850005; Fax: 01280 850156). *Location:* A43 Oxford-Northampton opposite Grand Prix Circuit. 11 bay covered range. *Prices:* please telephone for information. *Eating facilities:* Restaurant/bar. *Opening hours:* dawn to dusk. Tuition by teaching professional is available - group or private. Professional: Rodney Holt.

CAMBRIDGESHIRE

CAMBRIDGE. **Cambridge Golf Club,** Station Road, Longstanton, Cambridge CB24 3DS (01954 789388). *Location:* 10 minutes from city, off A14 at Bar Hill, turn right to Longstanton B1050. 12 bay floodlit driving range. Parkland course. 18 holes, 6736 yards, S.S.S. 72. *Prices:* information not available. *Eating facilities:* clubhouse. *Opening hours:* contact for details. Buggies and trolleys for hire. Society meetings catered for. Professional: Geoff Hugget.

HUNTINGDON. **Edrich Driving Range and Old Nene Golf and Country Club,** Muchwood Lane, Bodsey, Ramsey PE26 2XQ (01487 815622). *Location:* halfway between Ramsey and Ramsey Mereside, three quarters of a mile north of Ramsey, half a mile from Rainbow Supercentre. 24 bay driving range, 12 covered, 24 floodlit. *Prices:* information not available. *Eating facilities:* at adjoining club house, open to all. *Opening hours:* summertime, dawn to 9pm, winter to 7pm weekends. Private and group instruction arranged on 9 hole (18 tee) golf course. Coarse fishing on half acre lake and barbecues for summer months arranged. Secretary/Director: M. & G. Stoneman.*

PETERBOROUGH. **Thorney Golf Centre,** English Drove, Thorney, Peterborough PE6 0TJ (01733 270570). *Location*: Heading from Peterborough to Wisbech, left at the middle roundabout off the Thorney bypass and then 1st right. 13 bay covered, floodlit, grassed range. Two 18 hole courses. *Prices*: £2.00 for 50 balls. *Eating facilities*: full bar and restaurant open to public. *Opening hours*: 8am to 9.30pm seven days.

ST NEOTS. **Abbotsley Golf Hotel & Country Club,** Eynesbury, Hardwicke, St Neots PE19 4XN (01480 474000; Fax: 01480 471018). *Location*: A428 St Neots bypass to Abbotsley, south east of St Neots Junction 13 M11. 21 bay floodlit driving range, 300 yard grass driving range. Two 18 hole courses, 9 hole par 3 course. Abbotsley course is regarded by many as one of the finest golf courses in the county and combines the best of both parkland and woodland features. Excellent drainage makes it an ideal venue for all year round corporate and society days. Home of the Denise Hastings School of Golf. *Prices*: information available on request. *Visitors:* welcome. 42 room hotel, gym, squash courts, beauty salon.

CHESHIRE

ADLINGTON. **Adlington Golf Centre,** Sandy Hey Farm, Adlington, Macclesfield SK10 4NG (01625 850660). *Location*: 2 miles south of Poynton off A523. 24 bay covered, floodlit driving range. *Prices*: information not available. *Eating facilities:* tea and coffee available. *Opening hours*: 9am to 10.00pm Monday to Friday, 8.30am to 9.00pm weekends. 9 hole Par 3 course plus 9 hole Academy Course. Reductions for Senior Citizens/Juniors. Tuition available all the time. Professional: John Watson. Proprietor: David Moss (01625 850660).*

CHESTER. **Carden Park Golf Hotel Resort and Spa,** Chester CH3 9DQ (01829 731000; Fax: 01829 731599). *Location*: on A543 east of Wrexham. Golf School. 13 bay covered driving range and short game area. *Eating facilities*: Full Clubhouse facilites and 192 bedroom four star hotel. Nicklaus Course - 7045 yards. Cheshire Course - 6653 yards. Azalea Course 9 hole, Par 3. Professional: Paul Hodgson (01829 731000).*

NORTHWICH. **Hartford Golf Range,** Burrows Hill, Hartford, Northwich CW9 3AP. *Location*: off A556 Northwich, near ICI. 26 bay floodlit driving range, automatic tees. Golf shop. 9 hole pay as you play course now open. Professional: (01606 871162; Fax: 01606 872182).

STOCKPORT. **Cranford Golf Centre,** Harwood Road, Heaton Mersey, Stockport SK4 3AW (0161-432 8242; Fax: 01625 827365). *Location*: five minutes from M60 and M56 motorways. 43 all-weather covered tees, fully floodlit. Two indoor bunkers, 9 hole indoor putting course. *Prices*: £3.80 per bucket (50 balls); £6.50 100 balls. No booking or membership required. School, Junior and group

concessions. *Eating facilities:* drinks and snacks available. *Opening hours:* Monday to Thursday 10am to 10pm, Friday to Sunday 10am to 9.30pm. Hours may vary during Winter months and Bank Holidays. Changing rooms and golf shop. Group facilities and lessons available. Custom club fitting and repair centre now open. Professionals: Tony Murray, Matt Griffin, Granville Ogden and Rob Eastwood. Director: Jeffrey S. Yates.

STYAL. **Styal Golf Driving Range and Par 3 Academy Course,** Home of Cheshire Golf Academy, Styal Golf Club, Station Road, Styal SK9 4JN (Office: 01625 530063; Golf Booking Line: 01625 531359; Pro: 01625 528910). *Location*: five minutes from Manchester Airport. Junction 5 M56, near Wilmslow. 24 bay covered floodlit range plus 12 outdoor bays and practice bunker. 10 bays on the existing range have been fitted with power tee self loading ball dispensers. *Prices*: £4.00 for 50 balls, £6.00 for 100 balls, £15.00 for 300 balls. *Eating facilities:* drinks and snacks available. *Opening hours:* 7.30am to 9.30pm midweek, 7am to 8.30pm weekends. Happy hours are from 10am-12pm and 4pm-6pm Monday to Friday and 5.30pm-7.30pm Saturday and Sunday. Cheshire Golf Academy, tuition available for beginners and established players. Range is fully carpeted with target distances and two-piece premium golf balls. Latest hi-tec teaching and practice facilities. 9 hole deluxe par 3 course, USGA spec greens, 1242 yards, par 27. Professional: Simon Forrest. Secretary: Bill Higham. Golf Director: Glynn Traynor.
e-mail: gtraynor@styalgolf.co.uk
website: www.styalgolf.co.uk

CORNWALL

NEWQUAY. **Merlin Golf Course and Driving Range,** Mawgan Porth, Newquay TR8 4DN (01841 540222). *Location*: on coast road between Newquay and Padstow, after Mawgan Porth take St. Eval Road, golf course and range on right. 6 bay covered, floodlit driving range. *Prices*: information not available. *Eating facilities*: use of the club facilities. *Opening hours*: 8am till dark. Secretary: Richard Burrough.

REDRUTH. **Radnor Golf and Leisure,** Radnor Road, Treleigh, Redruth TR16 5EL (01209 211059). *Location*: two miles north east of Redruth, signposted from A3047 at Treleigh and North Country crossroads. Purpose-built Par 3 - interesting layout. 9 holes, 1312 yards. S.S.S. 52. Covered driving range. *Prices:* information not available. *Eating facilities:* licensed bar, hot and cold food. *Visitors:* welcome. Indoor ski training machine. Small touring site and static caravans. Professional: Scott Richards.*
website: www.radnorgolfandleisure.co.uk

www.uk-golfguide.com

CHATHAM. **Chatham Golf Centre,** Street End Road, Chatham ME5 0BG. *Location*: five minutes' drive from Rochester Airport. Covered, floodlit range, 30 bays. Tuition available. *Prices*: information not available. *Opening hours*: weekdays 10am to 9pm, weekends 9am to 7pm. *Eating facilities:* vending area. Fully stocked Pro Shop. Competitive prices. Pro Shop: (01634 848925).*

CHISLEHURST. **World of Golf,** A20 Sidcup Bypass, Chislehurst BR7 6RP (020 8309 0181). *Location:* six miles from Junction 3 on M25 heading towards London on A20. 54 bay floodlit driving range, Golf School and coaching studio. Par 3 9 hole course, floodlit short game practice area, putting green and bunker, golf shop, club repair service. Adventure putting course, tennis courts, cafe/bar. JJB Sports Golf Store. *Eating facilities:* licensed cafe/bar. *Visitors:* welcome, no restrictions. *Opening hours*: 9am to 10.30pm weekdays; 8am to 10pm weekends. Head Golf Professional: David Young.*
e-mail: sidcup@worldofgolf.biz
website: www.worldofgolf.biz

DARTFORD. **Birchwood Park Golf Centre,** Birchwood Road, Wilmington, Dartford DA2 7HJ (01322 662038; Fax: 01322 667283). *Location:* Take Junction 3 off M25 onto B2173 towards Sidcup, turn right into Birchwood Road at Vauxhall Garage. 41 bay floodlit driving range. *Prices*: information not available. *Eating facilities:* snacks and bar food always available, dining/function room also available. *Visitors:* very welcome. 18 hole course and 9 hole course available teaching professionals and extensive golf shop. Manager: Scott Morley (01322 662038; Fax: 01322 667283).*

GRAVESEND **Gravesend Golf Centre,** Thong Lane, Gravesend DA12 4LG (01474 335002; Fax: 01474 335004). *Location:* only one and a half miles from the A2. 30 bay floodlit, covered driving range with power tees. Teaching Academy, 9 hole Par 3 golf course, mini golf, short game area, golf shop, club repair workshop. *Opening hours:* 9am to 10pm Monday-Friday, 8am-7.30pm Saturday and Sunday. Head Teaching Professional: Stacey Dordoy.

MAIDSTONE. **Maidstone Golf Centre,** Sutton Road, Langley, Maidstone ME17 3NQ (Tel & Fax: 01622 863163). *Location:* south of Maidstone on A274, first turning after Park Wood Industrial Estate. 26 covered, floodlit bays (two heated). *Prices*: information not available. *Opening hours:* 10am to 10pm weekdays, 9.30 am to 7.30 pm weekends. PGA tuition, video coaching, putting green. Fully stocked golf shop. Caravan Club site for tourists. Professional: Cormac McCarthy.

ORPINGTON. **Orpington Golf Centre,** Sandy Lane, St Pauls Cray, Orpington BR5 3HY (01689 871490; Fax: 01689 891428). *Location*: off old A20 at Ruxley Corner. 28 bays, covered, floodlit. *Prices*: information not available. *Opening hours*: 7am to 9pm. *Eating facilities:* breakfast, lunch available, bar open all day. 53 holes, 4 courses.

RAMSGATE. **Manston Golf Centre,** Manston Road, Manston, Ramsgate CT12 5BE (01843 590005). *Location:* quarter of a mile east of Manston village. 20 covered floodlit bays, plus grassed tees and short game area with real greens and bunkers. New 9 hole course open to the public, 4958 yards. Par 66. *Prices:* Midweek 9 holes for £7.50, Weekends 9 holes for £9.50. *Eating facilities:* snacks, coffee, tea, etc. *Opening hours:* 8am till 9.30pm. Specialised teaching unit and short game practice area with real greens and bunkers. Absolute beginners welcome with six PGA qualified "Positive Impact Coaching". Professional /Manager: Philip Sparks.
e-mail: info@manstongolf.co.uk
website: www.manstongolf.co.uk

RAMSGATE near. **Stonelees Golf Centre,** Ebbsfleet Lane, Near Ramsgate CT12 5DJ (01843 823133; Fax: 01843 850569). *Location:* near junction of A256 and B2048. 22 bay covered floodlit/carpeted range. Animated and jackpot range targets. 2 balls free. Practice bunker, putting green and chipping area. *Prices*: £1.30 per 30 balls. *Eating facilities:* licensed bar/restaurant. *Opening hours*: Centre - 8am to 10pm. Range - weekdays 10am to 10pm, weekends 9am to 10pm. Open every day except Christmas Day. PGA Approved teaching centre, golf simulator, three 9 hole courses. Professional: David Bonthron.
e-mail: stonelees@stonelees.com
website: www.stonelees.co.uk.

SITTINGBOURNE. **The Oast Golf Centre Ltd,** Church Road, Tonge, Sittingbourne ME9 9AR (01795 473527). *Location:* one mile north A2 between Faversham and Sittingbourne, take the turning to Tonge at Bapchild. 9-hole Par 3 course; 17 bay covered floodlit driving range. *Prices*: golf 9 holes £5.50, 18 holes £7.50. *Eating facilities:* sandwiches, rolls; licensed bar. *Visitors:* Welcome. Tuition available, golf shop. Two short mat bowls facility.
e-mail: mail@oastgolf.co.uk

SWANLEY. **Olympic Golf Range,** Beechenlea Lane, Swanley BR8 8DR (01322 615126). *Location*: Junction 3 M25, take Swanley exit then first on right. 17 covered, 8 open air bays, all floodlit. Putting green and practice bunker. *Prices*: information not available. *Eating facilities:* bar, restaurant and sun terrace, all open to the public. *Opening hours*: 10am to 10pm. Extensive group tuition by PGA qualified staff. Also snooker centre, bowling green and conference rooms.*

SWANLEY. **Pedham Place Golf Centre,** London Road, Swanley BR8 8PP (01322 867000; Fax: 01322 861646). *Location:* off Junction 3 of M25, A20 towards Brands Hatch. 40-bay floodlit driving range, putting green, practice facilities.18-hole and 9-hole golf courses. *Prices:* information not available. *Eating facilities:* bar; food available daily. *Opening hours:* weekdays and weekends 7am to 10pm.
e-mail: Beverley@ppgc.co.uk
website: www.ppgc.co.uk

TONBRIDGE. **Hilden Golf Centre,** Rings Hill, Hildenborough, Tonbridge TN11 8LX (01732 833607; Fax: 01732 834484). *Location*: take exit off A21 for Tonbridge North/Hildenborough; take second turning right (Watts Cross Road), follow road past station to bottom of the hill, golf centre is on the left. 36 bay covered, floodlit driving range with PowerTee. *Prices:* 20 balls £1.50, 50 balls £3.00, 100 balls £5.00. *Eating facilities:* fully licensed cafe bar open 8am to 10pm. *Visitors:* open to the public all day every day, memberships available. Health and leisure centre, crèche (9.30am to 11.20am weekdays), French boules - Petanque. Teaching academy and large golf discount store stocking all the top brands at discount prices. *Society Meetings:* welcome. Professional: Nicky Way, Nick McNally, Rupert Hunter, Karl Steptoe and Oliver Brown (01732 834404; Fax: 01732 834484). Secretary: Jan Parfett (01732 834404; Fax: 01732 834484).

LANCASHIRE

BLACKBURN. **Blackburn Golf Centre and Driving Range,** Queens Park Playing Fields, Haslingden Road, Blackburn BB2 3HQ. *Location*: east side of Blackburn, one mile from town centre. 27 bay covered, floodlit range. Two bunkers and two greens for outdoor practice. *Prices:* information not available. *Opening hours:* 9am to 9pm weekdays; 9am to 5pm weekends. PGA Professional/Owner Mark M^CEvoy (01254 581996).*

BLACKPOOL. **De Vere Herons' Reach Golf Club,** East Park Drive, Blackpool FY3 8LL (01253 766156; Fax: 01253 798800). Location: leave M55 at Junction 4, follow signs for Stanley Park and Victoria Hospital. Testing championship course with 10 man-made lakes - all year round play course. Herons Reach Course - 18 holes, 6461 yards, S.S.S. 72. 18 bay floodlit driving range, putting and chipping green. *Prices:* information not available. *Eating facilities:* spikes bar serving from 7am to 6pm daily, leisure bar and Cairolis open seven days. *Visitors:* welcome. Handicap Certificate required. 164 bedroomed hotel with extensive conference and banqueting facilities for up to 600 plus leisure complex. *Society Meetings:* welcome. Secretary: Mr P. Heaton.*

LEICESTERSHIRE

BOTCHESTON. **Forest Hill Golf Club,** Markfield Lane, Botcheston LE9 9FJ (01455 824800; Fax: 01455 828522). *Location:* M1 junction 22, take Leicester exit on A50, at first roundabout turn right towards Desford, 3 miles on left. 25 bay floodlit, grassed driving range. 18 hole course. *Prices:* information not available. *Eating facilities:* food available all day. *Society Meetings:* welcome Monday to Thursday. Professional: Glyn Quilter (01455 824800). Secretary: G.D. Hyde (01455 824800; Fax: 01455 828522).*
e-mail: gerry@hyde14.fsnet.co.uk

COALVILLE. **Discovery Golf & Leisure,** Ashby Road, Coalville LE67 3LG (01530 812332). *Location:* Follow the signs to Snibston Discovery Park at Coalville. 18 covered bays with 10 PowerTees, 6 grassed. *Eating facilities:* licensed bar. *Prices:* 50 balls £3.00, 100 balls £5.00. *Opening hours:* Mon to Thurs - 10.30am to 9.00pm, Fri - 10.30am to 7.30pm, Sat/Sun and Bank Holidays - 10.00am to 6pm. Golf shop, tuition, repairs. 9 hole Par 3 golf course. Friendly and pleasant atmosphere.

LEICESTER. **Humberstone Golf Range,** Gipsy Lane, Leicester LE5 (0116 2740033; Fax: 01509 210185). *Location:* Leicester city location, opposite the Hamilton Retail Site, on ring road 5 minutes from A46, A47 and M1 link road. Part of Humberstone Golf Complex. 30 covered, floodlit and heated bays; two grassed. Automatic Power Tees, Video Bays, Multilevel mats. *Prices:* information not available. *Opening hours:* 7am to 9.30pm. *Eating facilities:* bar and restaurant. Tuition by PGA Professionals available.

LINCOLNSHIRE

GRIMSBY. **Great Grimsby Golf Centre (incorporating Willow Park Golf Club),** Cromwell Road, Grimsby DN31 2BH (01472 250555; Fax: 01472 267447). *Location:* two miles from A180 and A46. Four-and-a-half miles from A16. Adjacent to Grimsby Leisure Centre/Auditorium. 27 bay covered, floodlit range. *Prices:* information not available. *Opening Hours:* 9am to 9.30 pm. *Society Meetings:* welcome by prior arrangement. 2500 sq ft golf superstore. All club repairs undertaken. Pay and Play and Membership available for Willow Park Golf Club. Reductions for Juniors and Seniors. European Tour Professional: Stephen Bennett. Secretary: B.J. Hoggett. *

LINCOLN. **Welton Manor Golf Centre,** Hackthorn Road, Welton, Lincoln LN2 3PA (01673 862827). *Location:* six miles north of Lincoln. Off A46 to Welton village, through Welton, turn left at mini roundabout signposted Spridlington, entrance half-a-mile on left. 10-bay floodlit driving range. 18 hole course. *Prices:* £1.50 for 50 balls, £2.50 for 100 balls. *Eating facilities:* licensed bar and restaurant. *Opening hours:* 8am to 9pm. Golf Foundation starter centre. Professional: Gary Leslie.
e-mail: enquiries@weltonmanorgolfcentre.co.uk
website:www.weltonmanorgolfcentre.co.uk

STAMFORD. **Rutland County Golf Club,** Great Casterton, Stamford PE9 4AQ (01780 460330; Fax: 01780 460437). *Location:* on A1 two miles north of Stamford. Part of Rutland County Golf Club. 20 covered, grassed and floodlit bays; bunkers. 9 hole and 18 hole courses, chipping green, putting green. *Prices:* £2.00 per bucket of balls; two buckets for £3.00. *Opening hours:* 8am to 8pm. *Eating facilities:* restaurant and bar. Tuition available. Professional: Ian Melville (01780 460239; Fax: 01780 460437).
e-mail: info@rutlandcountygolf.freeserve.co.uk
website: www.rutlandcountygolf.co.uk

WOODHALL SPA. **National Training Academy,** The Broadway, Woodhall Spa LN10 6PU (01526 351837; Fax: 01526 351817). *Location:* 19 miles South East of Lincoln. Part of Woodhall Spa Golf Club. 20 floodlit bays. *Prices:* £3.00 per basket. *Opening hours:* Monday closed, Summer 8.00am to 7.30pm; 8.30 am to 6.30pm Winter. *Eating facilities:* clubhouse with bar and restaurant. Grass tees and short game academy only available to parties with a PGA professional, must book in advance on (01526 351809). Professional: Andrew Hare, tuition and coaching only (07860 212980).
e-mail: booking@englishgolfunion.org
website: www.woodhallspagolf.com

GREATER MANCHESTER

KEARSLEY. **Kearsley Golf Driving Range,** Moss Lane, Kearsley, Bolton BL4 8SF (01204 575726). *Location:* Two miles north on A666 from Junction 16 on M60. Driving range, 10 covered, 15 grassed tees. Prices: £3.20 for 50 balls. *Opening hours:* weekdays 11am to 9pm; weekends 11am to 4pm. *Visitors:* welcome. Bar. Small 3 hole pitch and putt with practice sand bunker. Open to the public. Professional/Owner: E. Raymond Warburton PGA. 18 hole pay as you play course immediately adjacent.

ROCHDALE. **Castle Hawk Driving Range,** Chadwick Lane, Castleton, Rochdale OL11 3BY (01706 659995). *Location:* five minutes from exit 20 M62. 20 bay covered, floodlit, grassed driving range. 27 hole course. *Prices:* information not available. *Eating facilities:* restaurant available at club. *Opening hours:* 9am to 7.30pm. Professional tuition available. Professionals: Frank Accleton and Craig Bowring.*
e-mail: teeoff@castlehawk.co.uk
website: www.castlehawk.co.uk

MERSEYSIDE

MORETON. **Moreton Hills Golf Centre,** Tarran Way, Moreton, Wirral CH46 4TP (0151-677 6606). *Location:* off Pasture Road, opposite Cadbury's factory. 30 bay covered floodlit driving range. *Prices:* information not available. *Eating facilities:* not available. *Opening hours:* Monday to Thursday 9am to 9pm, Friday to Sunday 9am to 7pm. 6 hole golf course, putting green, practice bunkers, golf shop, PGA Professionals, golf lessons in an undercover academy.
website: www.moretonhills.co.uk

THE APPEARANCE OF AN ASTERISK (*) AT THE END OF A CLUB OR COURSE ENTRY INDICATES THAT UP-TO-DATE INFORMATION HAS NOT BEEN SUPPLIED

NORTHAMPTONSHIRE

CHURCH BRAMPTON. **Brampton Heath Golf Centre,** Sandy Lane, Church Brampton, Northampton NN6 8AX (01604 843939; Fax: 01604 843885). *Location:* 2 miles north east of Kingsthorpe off A5009 (Welford Road). 18 bay covered floodlit driving range. *Prices:* information not available. *Eating facilities:* Spike bar/restaurant. *Opening hours:* Summer: weekdays 8am to 10pm. Weekends 7.30am to 9pm. Winter: 8am to 9pm. Weekends 8am to 8.30pm. Group/individual tuition available. 9 hole Par 3 academy course. Professional: Richard Hudson. Manager: Simon Lawrence (Fax: 01604 843885).*

NORTHAMPTON. **Delapre Golf Centre,** Eagle Drive, Nene Valley Way, Northampton NN4 7DU (01604 764036; Fax: 01604 706378). *Location:* two miles from Junction 15 M1 on A45 towards Wellingborough. 40 bay covered, floodlit range. 18 hole main course Par 70; 9 hole course; two Par 3 courses; pitch and putt course and putting greens. *Prices:* information not available. *Eating facilities:* licensed bar and restaurant, coffee shop. *Opening hours:* 7am to 10.30pm daily. PGA qualified teaching staff available for private or group tuition; golf schools - video, etc. Professional: Greg Iron. Centre Manager: Andrew Coleman 01604 764036.
website: www.jackbarker.com

NOTTINGHAMSHIRE

CALVERTON. **Ramsdale Park Golf Centre,** Oxton Road, Calverton NG14 6NV (01159 655600; Fax: 01159 654105). *Location:* off the A614 from Nottingham to Mansfield. 25 covered, floodlit bays; one bunker. *Prices:* Discount cards available. individual baskets from £1.50. *Opening hours:* 8.30am to 10pm. *Eating facilities:* full bar and catering. Tuition available. Professional: Rob Macey (01159 655600; Fax: 01159 654105).
e-mail: info@ramsdaleparkgc.co.uk
website: www.ramsdaleparkgc.co.uk

LONG EATON. **Trent Lock Golf Centre,** Lock Lane, Sawley, Long Eaton, Nottingham NG10 2FY (0115 946 4398; Fax: 0115 946 1183). *Location:* 2 miles from M1 motorway Junction 24 or 25. 23 bay covered, floodlit driving range. 18-hole and 9 hole golf course. *Prices:* information not available. *Eating facilities:* à la carte restaurant, 200 capacity function suite, bar and bar food area. *Opening hours:* 8am until midnight. Professional tuition available, five PGA staff. River trips and walking available. Professional: Mark Taylor (01159 464398; Fax: 01159 461183).

NEWARK. **Rufford Park Golf & Country Club,** Rufford Lane, Rufford, Newark (01623 825253; Fax: 01623 825254). *Location:* situated 400 yards off A614, two miles south of Ollerton Roundabout - map available on request. 16 bay floodlit driving range. 18 hole golf course. Practice greens. *Eating facilities:*

large function suite and clubhouse available for social functions, restaurant with spectacular views offering a warm and genuine welcome to all who enjoy superb food. *Opening hours:* 7.30am to 9.00pm. Tuition available from both professionals. 10 buggies for hire. Corporate hospitality and Society days a speciality. Meeting rooms available. Professionals: James Thompson/John Vaughan. Secretary: Kay Whitehead.
e-mail: enquiries@ruffordpark.co.uk
website: www.ruffordpark.co.uk

NOTTINGHAM. **Cotgrave Place Golf and Country Club,** Cotgrave, Near Stragglethorpe, Radcliffe-on-Trent, Nottingham NG12 3HB (0115 933 3344; Fax: 0115 933 4567). *Location:* two minutes from A52 to Grantham from Nottingham city centre. 10 bay covered, floodlit range. *Prices:* information not available. *Eating facilities:* food available all day in the golf clubhouse. *Opening hours:* 8am to dusk seven days a week. Professional tuition. 36 holes of golf. Ideal for all standards. Buggies available. Golf clinics. Professional: Robert Smith (0115 933 3344; Fax: 0115 933 4567). General Manager: Mike Evans.*
e-mail: cotgrave@americangolf.com

OXFORDSHIRE

DRAYTON. **Drayton Park Golf Course**, Steventon Road, Drayton, near Abingdon OX14 4LA (01235 528989). *Location:* A34 Didcot turn off, through Steventon to Drayton. 21 bay covered floodlit driving range. 18 hole Par 70 Golf Course. 9 hole Par 3 course. *Prices:* information not available. *Eating facilities:* full facilities available. *Opening hours:* 8am to 9pm. Fully qualified PGA Professional. Societies, groups and individual golfers welcome. Professional: Martin Morbey. Secretary: Ian Rhead.

HORTON-CUM-STUDLEY. **Studley Wood Golf Club,** The Straight Mile, Horton-cum-Studley, Oxford OX33 1BF (01865 351122; Fax: 01865 351166). *Location:* 4 miles east of Oxford. 15 bay covered driving range. *Prices:* 25 balls £2.00, 65 balls £3.00. *Eating facilities:* full Clubhouse facilities; bar, restaurant, function room. *Opening hours:* 9am to dusk. Four teaching professionals, short game academy, practice putting green. Eight target greens complete with bunkers, fully irrigated grass practice tee and target greens. Official Callaway Fitting Centre. Professional: Tony Williams. Club Administrator: Annie Anderson. Ladies' Competitions Secretary: Connie Brean.
e-mail: admin@swgc.co.uk
website: www.studleywoodgolf.co.uk

OXFORD. **Oxford Golf Centre,** Binsey Lane, Botley Road, Oxford OX2 0EX (01865 721592). *Location:* just off Botley Road by Halfords. 26 bay covered floodlit driving range. *Prices:* from £4.00. *Eating facilities:* light refreshments. *Opening Hours:* weekdays 10am to 9pm, weekends 10am-8pm. Lessons with Professional from £15.00. Golf superstore, 100s of demonstration clubs, launch monitor, professional club fitting and repairs. Head PGA Professional: Simon Walker.

OXFORD. **Waterstock Golf Club and Driving Range,** Thame Road, Waterstock, Oxford OX33 1HT (01844 338093). *Location:* on Junction 8 M40, one mile from Wheatley, four miles from Oxford, three miles from Thame. 22 bay covered, fully floodlit, open grassed driving range. *Prices:* 50 balls for £3.00, 100 balls for £5.00. Golf prices: 18 holes £23.00 weekdays, £28.00 weekends; 9 holes £12.50 weekdays, £15.00 weekends; day ticket £40.50 weekdays, £48.00 weekends; twilight £16.50 weekdays, £19.00 weekends. *Eating facilities:* full bar and catering facilities. *Opening hours:* weekdays 7.30am to 10pm, Saturdays 7am to 9pm, Sundays 7am to 8pm. Resident Professional offers tuition; large junior and adult golf academy; Pro shop with many demonstration clubs; 18-hole golf course; clubhouse with full facilities (societies and functions catered for).
e-mail: wgc_oxfordgolf@btinternet.com
website: www.waterstockgolf.co.uk

WITNEY. **Witney Lakes Golf Club,** Witney Lakes Resort, Downs Road, Witney OX29 0SY (01993 893011; Fax: 01993 778866). *Location:* two miles west of Witney town centre, turn into Downs Road. from B4095. 22-bay floodlit covered driving range. *Fees:* information not available. *Opening hours:* 7am to 9pm. *Eating facilities:* Greens Sportsbar and Greens Restaurant, Function/ Conference room. Health and fitness club includes swimming pool, gymnasium and sauna. Rawles Hairdresser, Retreat Spa, Beauty Salon, Creche facilities. Large well-stocked golf shop, 3 teaching Professionals. Head Professional: Adam Souter (01993 893011; Fax: 01993 778866). Secretary: (01993 893005; Fax: 01993 778866).
e-mail: golf@witney-lakes.co.uk
website: www.witney-lakes.co.uk

SHROPSHIRE

NEWPORT. **Aqualate Golf Centre,** Stafford Road, Newport TF10 9DB (01952 811699). *Location*: On A518 two miles east of Newport town centre and 400 yards from junction with A41. 20 floodlit bay driving range. *Prices*: £2 for basket of 45 balls. *Opening hours*: weekdays 9.00am to 10.00pm, weekends and Bank Holidays 7.30am to 9.00pm. *Eating facilities*: coffee bar. PGA Professional tuition available by appointment - group and/or personal lessons. Golf Club Memberships available. 9 hole, 18 tee golf course - Pay and Play golf available. Visitors welcome. No handicap restrictions. Professional: Kevin Short. Director: H. Brian Dawes.

OSWESTRY. **Oswestry Golf Driving Range,** Mile End, Oswestry SY11 4JF (01691 671246; Fax: 01691 670580). *Location:* signposted "Mile End Golf Club" off A5, one mile south-east of Oswestry. 11 bay covered, floodlit driving range. *Prices:* £1.00 for 30 balls. *Eating facilities:* bar/catering available to members and green fee paying visitors who adhere to dress code. *Opening hours:* Summer: 8.00am until dusk daily; Winter: 8.00am to 8pm weekdays, 8.00am to 6pm weekends. Group bookings welcome. Many "Try before you buy" demo days. Professional tuition available, fully stocked Pro shop. Par 71 18 hole golf course. Professional: Scott Carpenter (01691 671246). Proprietor: Richard Thompson.
website: www.mileendgolfclub.co.uk

TELFORD. **The Shropshire,** Granville Park, Muxton, Telford TF2 8PQ (01952 677800; Fax: 01952 677622). *Location:* Take B5060 off M54/A5 heading for Donnington. Take third exit at Granville roundabout. *Prices:* information not available. *Eating facilities:* Greenkeeper Bar open from 8am serving food. *Opening hours:* 7am to 10pm. 27 hole golf course, 12 hole Par 3 course, 2 putting greens, retail shop. Entertainment nights, seven function suites, and conference facilities. *Society Meetings:* welcome. Professional: Andrew Holmes (07866 721956).*

SOMERSET

BRISTOL. **Mendip Spring Golf Club,** Honeyhall Lane, Congresbury, Bristol BS49 5JT (01934 852322). *Location:* between A370 and A38. 15 bay covered, floodlit driving range with a grassed area. Practice bunker and putting green. *Prices:* information not available. *Eating facilities:* none at range but restaurant/bar facilities available at the clubhouse. *Opening hours:* 7.30am to 8pm. Tuition available from our team of professionals. Buggies for hire April to September. There is also an active members' social club. Societies welcome by arrangement.

LANGPORT. **Long Sutton Golf Club,** Langport TA10 9JU (01458 241017; Fax: 01458 241022). *Location:* three miles north of A303 from Podimore roundabout on A372 to Langport and Taunton. 18 hole golf course and large practice putting green. 12 bay covered, floodlit, grassed range. *Prices:* information not available. *Eating facilities:* snacks in bar, restaurant. *Opening hours:* 8am till dusk. Tuition from Andrew Hayes by appointment. Secretary: T. Tulk.*

TAUNTON. **Oake Manor Driving Range,** Oake Manor Golf Club and Range, Oake, Taunton TA4 1BA (01823 461993). *Location:* Junction 26 M5, take A38 to Taunton, follow signs to Oake, only seven minutes from motorway. 11 bay covered range. *Prices:* information not available. *Eating facilities:* adjacent bar/lounge, food available seven days all day long. *Opening hours:* 8am to dark. *Visitors:* welcome. 18 hole course, tuition by appointment, new golf academy and 3 practice holes; Pro shop, 4 PGA

Professionals; club fitting centre - free equipment advice service and demo clubs.*
e-mail: golf@oakemanor.com
website: www.oakemanor.com

TICKENHAM. **Tickenham Golf Club,** Clevedon Road, Tickenham BS21 6RY (01275 856626). *Location:* M5 Junction 20, follow Nailsea signs, Centre on left after Tickenham village. 9 hole course, 24 bay covered, floodlit driving range. Power tees. Practice bunkers. *Prices:* 50 balls for £3.00. *Eating facilities:* 19th hole licensed bar, snacks. *Opening hours:* 8.30am to 8.30pm daily. Professionals available for tuition, group lessons, etc.

STAFFORDSHIRE

BURTON-ON-TRENT. **The Craythorne,** Craythorne Road, Rolleston on Dove, Burton-on-Trent DE13 0AZ (01283 564329). *Location:* Rolleston on Dove, one and a half miles north of Burton – A5121/A38 Junction. 14 bay covered floodlit driving range. *Prices:* £1.00 per bucket. *Eating facilities:* 80 cover restaurant open to public every day, two bars. *Opening Hours:* weekdays 7.30am to 10pm. *Society Meetings:* welcome, rates available. Conference and function facilities available; discounts at local hotels. Professional (PGA): Steve Hadfield. Managing Director: A.A. Wright.
website: www.craythorne.co.uk

SUFFOLK

HALESWORTH. **Halesworth Golf Club,** Bramfield Road, Halesworth IP19 9XA (01986 875567; Fax: 01986 874565). *Location:* A12, A144 to and through Bramfield, over crossroads and then first right. 13 bays floodlit (10 covered). *Prices:* information not available. *Opening hours:* dawn until dusk (9pm Winter months). Professional tuition and fully equipped Pro shop; 27-hole golf course, putting and chipping greens. Professional: Simon Harrison. Secretary: D. Cotton.*

IPSWICH. **Fynn Valley Golf Club,** Witnesham, Ipswich IP6 9JA (01473 785463; Fax: 01473 785632). *Location:* two miles due north of Ipswich on B1077. 23 bays floodlit (10 covered). Practice green and bunker. 9 hole par 3 course. 18 hole course. *Prices:* information not available. *Opening hours:* 9am to 9pm Monday to Friday and 8am to 8pm (6pm in winter) Saturday and Sunday. *Eating facilities:* meals available every lunchtime. Evening meals Tuesday to Saturday. *Societies:* welcome. Professional tuition, group lessons, etc. Golf shop. Golf range membership available. Professionals: Danny Barton, Paul Bate, Paul Wilby, Alex Lucas, Simon Dainty. Secretary: A. Tyrrell.*
e-mail: enquiries@fynn-valley.co.uk
website: www.fynn-valley.co.uk

WOODBRIDGE. **Seckford Golf Club,** Seckford Hall Road, Great Bealings, Near Woodbridge IP13 6NT (01394 388000; Fax: 01394 382818). *Location:* signposted from A12 near Woodbridge. 12 bay fixed mats driving range. *Prices:* please phone for details. *Eating facilities:* fully licensed bar and restaurant. Golf lessons available from qualified PGA staff using GASP video analysis system as seen on Sky TV. Hire equipment available. Professional: Simon Jay.

SURREY

CARSHALTON. **Oaks Sports Centre,** Woodmansterne Road, Carshalton SM5 4AN (020 8643 8363; Fax: 020 8770 7303). Covered, grassed and floodlit bays with bunkers. 18 hole and 9 hole courses. *Prices:* £1.50 per bucket of balls. *Opening hours:* 9am to 9.30pm. *Eating facilities:* Cafeteria and bar. Pay and play and membership available. PGA Professional teaching. Professional: Michael Pilkington (020 8643 8363).
e-mail: golf@oaks.sagehost.co.uk
website: www.oaksportscentre.co.uk

CHESSINGTON **Chessington Golf Centre,** Garrison Lane, Chessington KT9 2LW (020 8391 0948). *Location:* off A243, 500 yards from Chessington World of Adventure. Opposite Chessington South Station, Junction 9 M25. Covered, floodlit range, 18 bays. 9 hole course. Private and group tuition available. *Prices:* information not available. *Opening hours:* 8am to 10pm. *Eating facilities:* bar and catering. Tuition, public course.

COBHAM. **Silvermere Driving Range,** Redhill Road, Cobham KT11 1EF (01932 584300; Fax: 01932 584301). *Location:* half-a-mile from Junction 10 on M25 at A3; 30 minutes from central London. Covered, floodlit range, 34 bays. Public golf course. *Prices:* information not available. *Eating facilities:* full service available. *Opening hours:* 8.30am to 9.30pm. Tuition available. Telephone bookings taken. Administrator: Pauline Devereux (01932 584300; Fax: 01932 584301).

CROYDON. **Croydon Driving Range Ltd,** 175 Long Lane, Addiscombe, Croydon CR0 7TE (020 8656 1690; Fax: 020 8654 7859). *Location:* on A222 about two miles east of Croydon. 24 bay covered, floodlit, driving range. *Prices:* £3.75 for 56 balls, £7.00 for 112 balls. *Eating facilities:* snacks/coffee. *Opening hours:* weekdays 9am to 10pm, weekends 9am to 8pm. *Visitors:* very welcome at all times, open to the public. Lessons from 5 PGA qualified instructors, and club repairs available. Professional: Bill Woodman (020 8656 1690; Fax: 020 8654 7859).

ESHER. **Sandown Golf Centre,** More Lane, Esher KT10 8AN (01372 461234). *Location:* signposted from A3, centre of Sandown Park Racecourse. 33 bay covered floodlit driving range, plus grassed area. Three golf courses. *Prices:* information not available. *Eating facilities:* bar and restaurant. *Opening hours:* 8am to 10pm weekdays; 7am to 8pm weekends. Cranfield Golf Acadamy *Visitors:* visitors and societies welcome. General Manager: David Parr (01372 461234; Fax: 01372 461203).*

GODALMING. **Broadwater Park Golf Club,** Guildford Road, Farncombe, Near Godalming GU7 3BU (01483 429955). 16 bay covered, floodlit driving range. *Prices:* information not available. *Eating facilities:* licensed bar. *Opening hours:* 8am to 10pm. Professional, tuition and 9 hole Par 3 course. Professional: Kevin Milton.*

GUILDFORD. **Roker Park Golf Club,** Fairlands Farm, Aldershot Road, Guildford GU3 3PB (01483 236677; Fax: 01483 232324). *Location:* from A3 Guildford take A323 to Aldershot, course two miles on right. Flat parkland course. 9 holes, 3037 yards. S.S.S. 72. *Prices:* information not available. *Eating facilities:* restaurant and bar. *Visitors:* welcome, pay and play course. *Society Meetings:* welcome weekdays only, reductions for parties over 12. Professional: Adrian Carter. Secretary: Mr G. Barnett (Tel & Fax: 01438 232324).*

LEATHERHEAD. **Pachesham Park Golf Centre,** Oaklawn Road, Leatherhead KT22 0BT (01372 843453). *Location:* half-a-mile outside Leatherhead, just off A244. Junction 9 M25. 33 bay covered floodlit range with Power Tees. 9 hole golf course. *Prices:* 30 balls £3.00, 60 balls £5.00, 90 balls £7.00, 120 balls £8.00. Discount range ball cards available. *Eating facilities:* available. *Opening hours:* April to October, weekdays 9am to 9.30pm, weekends 9am to 9pm; November to March 9am to 8pm. PGA teaching professionals. Club membership also available.

NEWDIGATE. **Rusper Golf Club and Driving Range,** Rusper Road, Newdigate RH5 5BX (01293 871871). *Location:* Dorking-Horsham A24, Beare Green roundabout, left to Newdigate, in village turn right to Rusper, club approximately one mile on right hand side. 12 bay covered driving range. 18 hole golf course. *Prices:* please contact the club. *Eating facilities:* fresh food and daily specials available every day; bar. *Opening hours:* dawn till dusk. Qualified professional tuition by arrangement; club hire. Membership available. Professional: Janice Arnold. Secretary: Mrs Jill Thornhill.
e-mail: jill@ruspergolfclub.co.uk
website: www.ruspergolfclub.co.uk

NEW MALDEN. **World of Golf at Beverley Park,** Beverley Way, New Malden KT3 4PH (020 8949 9200; Fax: 020 8336 2856). *Location:* leave the A3 northbound at B282, follow sign to A3 London, entrance on left before rejoining A3. Southbound exit A3 at A298, follow A3 London from roundabout. 60 bay floodlit, covered driving range. Golf School, two coaching studios, floodlit putting green and bunker. *Prices:* information not available. *Eating facilities:* cafe/bar. *Opening hours:* 8am to 11pm daily. JJB Golf Store, club repair service.*
website: www.worldofgolf.biz

OLD WOKING. **Hoebridge Golf Centre,** Woking Road, Old Woking GU22 8JH (01483 722611; Fax: 01483 740369). *Location:* on outskirts of Woking on the Woking to Byfleet Road. 36 bay covered, floodlit range. Two 18 hole courses and 9 hole course. *Prices:* information not available. *Eating facilities:* full catering available. *Opening hours:* 8am to 11pm. Individual and group tuition. Fully equipped video bay available. *Society Meetings:* welcome. Professional: Russell Covey. Centre Manager: Mike O'Connell. Secretary: Mike Waite.*

REDHILL. **Redhill Golf Centre,** Canada Avenue, Redhill RH1 5BF (01737 770204). *Location*: in the grounds of East Surrey Hospital, one-and-a-half miles south of Redhill. 37 bay covered, floodlit driving range. 9-hole golf course (unlimited golf from £9.00). *Prices:* information not available. *Eating facilities:* available at Causeway Pub. *Opening hours*: 8am to 10pm; weekends 9pm. Sponsored by Golf Foundation to give free junior coaching. Lessons available from PGA qualified instructor. Private and group tuition available. Repairs service. Hot and cold drinks available. *Society Meetings:* welcome. Professional: Mike Lovegrove. Secretary: Steven Furlonger.

EAST SUSSEX

HELLINGLY. **Wellshurst Golf and Country Club,** North Street, Hellingly BN27 4EE (01435 813456). *Location:* two miles from the A22 London to Eastbourne Road on A267. 16 bay covered, floodlit range. 18 hole course, two sand bunker bays. *Prices:* £2.00 per large bucket of quality two piece balls. *Eating facilities:* full bar and catering facilities available at all times. *Opening hours:* 7.30am to 9.30pm. Full leisure and conference facilities. Full professional staff for lessons, well stocked pro shop.

HORAM. **Horam Park Golf Course and Floodlit Driving Range,** Chiddingly Road, Horam TN21 0JJ (01435 813477, Fax: 01435 813677). *Location:* 13 miles north of Eastbourne, 7 miles east of Uckfield. Covered floodlit driving range, Astroturf range. 15 bays. Pitch and putt course, floodlit putting green, pitch and putt course. 9-hole golf course, 3092 yards, Par 35. Golf prices from £12.00; call for early bird and twilight rates. *Eating facilities:* restaurant bar and spike bar, seven days, children welcome. PGA golf Professionals, lessons and tuition available. Golf shop. Professional: Giles Velvick.

SEDLESCOMBE. **Sedlescombe Golf Club,** Kent Street, Near Battle, TN33 0SD (01424 871700). Home of The James Andrews School of Golf. *Location:* 1066 Country, five miles north of Hastings on the A21, three miles from Battle. Gently undulating parkland course, 18 holes, 6269 yards. S.S.S. 70. 24 bay floodlit driving range, four practice putting greens, academy hole and bunkers. Residential golf school with 2, 3 and 5 day intensive courses for all ages and abilities. Five PGA Professionals. Facilities include indoor video and computer analysis centre, on-site hotel, golf shop and tennis courts. *Green Fees:* information not available.

Eating facilities: bar and restaurant open seven days. *Visitors:* Course open to public. *Society Meetings:* welcome. Head Professional: James Andrews (01424 871700). Club Secretary (01424 871700). Golf School (01424 871717).*
website: www.golfschool.co.uk

WEST SUSSEX

BURGESS HILL. **The Burgess Hill Golf Academy,** Cuckfield Road, Burgess Hill RH15 8RE (01444 258585; Fax: 01444 247318). *Location:* on the B2036 north of Burgess Hill, on the Burgess Hill to Cuckfield road. 28 bay undercover, grassed, floodlit driving range. 9 hole short course. New practice bunker, synthetic grass tees (first in UK), Augusta style putting green. *Prices:* information not available. *Eating facilities:* Bar and restaurant. Tea and coffee. *Opening Hours:* seven days a week 8am to 9pm. Well stocked golf shop. PGA teaching academy including video tuition. Professional: Mark Collins. Secretary: (01444 258585; Fax: 01444 247318).

CHICHESTER. **Chichester Golf Club,** Hunston Village, Chichester PO20 6AX (01243 528999). *Location:* take B2145 off A27 to Selsey, golf club is on the left after Hunston Village. 27 bay covered, 10 automated Powertee bays, floodlit, grassed driving range. Two 18 hole golf courses, 9 hole Par 3 minigolf. *Prices*: information not available. *Eating facilities:* fully licensed clubhouse. *Opening hours*: 8.30am to 9.30pm, 9.00am to 8.00pm in winter. *Society Meetings:* welcome seven days a week. Video teaching academy. Membership available. Professional: James Willmott.

CRAWLEY. **Gatwick Manor Golf Club,** Gatwick Manor Hotel, London Road, Lowfield Heath, Crawley RH10 2ST (01293 526301 (Hotel); 01293 538587 (Club)). *Location:* A23 Crawley to Gatwick Airport on London Road on right. 9 grassed tees. *Prices:* information not available. *Eating facilities:* hotel facilities at Gatwick Manor. *Opening hours:* 9am to 8.00pm seven days a week.*

CRAWLEY. **Tilgate Forest Golf Centre,** Titmus Drive, Tilgate, Crawley RH10 5EU (01293 530103; Fax: 01293 523478). 35 floodlit bays. *Prices:* £3.00 per bucket of balls. *Opening hours:* 7am to 9.15pm. *Eating facilities:* bar and restaurant. Tuition, practice area, putting green etc. Professional: William Easdale (01293 530103).
e-mail: tilgate@glendale-services.co.uk

THE APPEARANCE OF AN ASTERISK (*) AT THE END OF A CLUB OR COURSE ENTRY INDICATES THAT UP-TO-DATE INFORMATION HAS NOT BEEN SUPPLIED

RUSTINGTON. **Rustington Golf Centre,** Golfers Lane, Angmering, BN16 4NB (01903 850790; Fax: 01903 850982). *Location:* on A259 at Rustington, between Worthing and Littlehampton. 9 holes with 18 tees, 5735 yards. Par 70. 9 hole par 3 course, 3 hole golf academy course, putting green, 30 bay floodlit driving range. Two golf academies work from the facility. *Prices:* information not available. *Opening hours:* 8.30am - 9.00pm, 7 days a week. *Eating facilities:* coffee shop and licensed bar. *Visitors:* welcome at all times. Two golf academies available for tuition of all standards. *Society Meetings:* societies and corporate days welcome. Centre Manager: Gary Salt (01903 850790; Fax: 01903 850982).*

TYNE & WEAR

NEWCASTLE UPON TYNE. **Parklands,** High Gosforth Park, Newcastle upon Tyne NE3 5HQ (0191-236 4480). *Location:* off A1 for Gosforth Park. 45 bay covered, floodlit range. *Prices:* information not provided. *Eating facilities:* bar and restaurant. *Opening hours:* 8am to 10.30pm. Professional tuition, 18 hole golf course, 9 hole pitch and putt. Societies welcome at weekends. Ring for package details.*

WASHINGTON. **George Washington Golf and Country Club,** Stone Cellar Road, High Usworth, District 12, Washington NE37 1PH (0191 4029988; Fax: 0191 4151166). *Location:* just off A1(M), take A194 then exit A195 Washington. 21 bay covered, floodlit, grassed range. 9 hole pitch and putt. *Prices:* information not available. *Eating facilities:* Bunkers Bar – hours vary, serves snacks. Buffets etc by arrangement. Tuition available. Golf buggies. Leisure club with sauna, pool, solarium, multi gym, spa and squash. Professional: Graeme Robinson (0191 417 8346). *

WARWICKSHIRE

COVENTRY. **John Reay Golf Centres,** Sandpits Lane, Keresley, Coventry CV7 8NJ (024 7633 3920). *Location:* three miles from Coventry city centre along A51 Tamworth Road. Covered, floodlit driving range. 60 bays. Golf club repair facility. Teaching professionals using latest video techniques. *Prices:* information not available. *Opening hours:* daily 9am to 10pm. *Eating facilities:* Hogan's Bar & Bistro open every day. *Visitors:* open to the public. Large Golf Shop with all the leading brands of golf equipment. Professional: John Reay (024 7633 3920/3405). website: www.johnreaygolf.com

WARWICK. **Warwick Golf Centre,** The Racecourse, Warwick CV34 6HW (01926 494316). *Location:* A46 off the M40 (middle of Warwick). 25 bay covered, floodlit range. 9 hole golf course (Par 34) open to the public. *Prices:* information not available. *Eating facilities:* bar only. *Opening hours:* driving range 10am to 9pm, 9 hole golf course 8am to 9pm. Professional tuition. Professional: Phil Sharp. Secretary: Roma Dunkley.

WEST MIDLANDS

DUDLEY near. **Swindon Ridge Golf Driving Range, Shop & Golf Club,** Bridgnorth Road, Swindon, Near Dudley DY3 4PU (01902 896191). *Location:* B4176 Bridgnorth/Dudley Road, three miles from Himley A449 Junction. 27 bay floodlit range (22 covered). *Prices:* information not available. *Opening hours:* 9.30am to 8.30pm weekdays, 9.30am to 5.30pm weekends and Bank Holidays. *Eating facilities:* licensed bar and restaurant. 18 hole private golf club on site. Snooker table in bar.*

SUTTON COLDFIELD. **Lea Marston Hotel & Leisure Complex,** Haunch Lane, Lea Marston, Sutton Coldfield B76 0BY (01675 470468; Fax: 01675 470871). *Location:* From Junction 9 of M42, take A4097 towards Kingbury for just over one mile, take second right into Haunch Lane, right after 150 yards approximately. 27 floodlit bays. 9 hole Marston Lakes Par 31 and 9 hole Par 3 pay and play course. *Prices:* information not available. *Eating facilities:* Adderley Restaurant, Sportsman's Lounge Bar and Conservatories. *Visitors:* welcome. Professional tuition available. Golf simulator with 20 courses including Valderrama and the Belfry's Brabazon. Fully stocked golf shop. 83 bedroom hotel, leisure facilities including indoor swimming pool.*

WOLVERHAMPTON. **3 Hammers Golf Complex,** Old Stafford Road, Coven WV10 7PP (01902 790428). *Location:* Junction 2 M54 north on A449, one mile on right. 24 covered floodlit bays. *Prices:* information not available. *Eating facilities:* bookings taken from 10.30am, details on (01902 791917). *Opening hours:* weekdays 9.30am to 10pm, weekends 9.30am to 9pm. 18 hole Par 3 course, two teaching Professionals.

WILTSHIRE

CALNE. **Bowood Golf & Country Club,** Derry Hill, Calne SN11 9PQ (01249 822228; Fax: 01249 822218). *Location:* located off A4 between Calne and Chippenham. Signposted from Junction 17. Part of Bowood Golf & Country Club, a championship course on the beautiful Bowood Estate. 10 covered, floodlit bays. *Prices:* information not available. *Opening hours:* telephone for details. *Eating facilities:* conservatory serving lunches and snacks; bar. Tuition, academy course, putting green. Professional: John Hansel (01249 822228; Fax: 01249 822218).*
e-mail: golfclub@bowood.org
website: www.bowood.org.

www.uk-golfguide.com

SALISBURY: **Hamptworth Academy,** Hamptworth Road, Hamptworth, Near Salisbury SP5 2DU (01794 390155; Fax: 01794 390022). *Location:* halfway between Southampton and Salisbury, one mile off A36. 3 covered bays, 8 grassed bays, bunkers. 18 hole golf course, putting green. *Prices:* information not available. *Opening hours:* 8am till dusk. *Eating facilities:* all-day menu in clubhouse. Tuition, available. Professional: Mark White (01794 390155; Fax: 01794 390022).*
e-mail: info@hamptworthgolf.co.uk
website: www.hamptworthgolf.co.uk

SWINDON. **Broome Manor Golf Complex,** Pipers Way, Swindon SN3 1RG (01793 532403). *Location:* two miles from Junction 15 of M4, follow signs for Golf Complex. 34 bays, 27 covered, seven uncovered, floodlit range (astroturf). *Prices:* information not available. *Eating facilities:* full service available. *Opening hours:* Summer 8am to 10pm, Winter 8am to 9pm. Five PGA professionals - group and individual lessons always available. 18 hole courses, 9 hole course and nearby pitch and putt course. Restaurant available for functions and conferences.*

WESTBURY near. **Thoulstone Park Golf Club and Driving Range,** Chapmanslade, Near Westbury BA13 4AQ (01373 832825; Fax: 01373 832821). *Location:* three miles north-west of Warminster on A36. 20 bay covered, floodlit range. *Prices:* information not available. *Eating facilities:* Clubhouse open 11am to 3.30pm for food and 11.00am to 9.00pm for drinks. *Opening hours:* weekdays and Saturdays 8am to 9pm, Sundays 8am to 6pm. Professional available for lessons, Pro shop (8.00am to 7.30pm weekdays and Saturdays; 7.30am to 6.00pm Sundays). 18 hole course. Professional: T. Isaacs (01373 832808).*

WORCESTERSHIRE

BROMSGROVE. **Bromsgrove Golf Centre,** Stratford Road, Bromsgrove B60 1LD (01527 575886; Fax: 01527 570964; Course Reception: 01527 570505; Conference & Restaurant 01527 579179). *Location:* easily located at the roundabout junction of the A38 and A448, one mile from Bromsgrove town centre, just five minutes' drive from Junctions 4 and 5 of the M5 and Junction 1 of the M42 (exit west bound only). *Facilities include:* 35 bay floodlit driving range, new teaching studio with state-of-the-art computerised video systems. Golf Academy - wide range of tuition available with resident PGA professionals, including on course video tuition etc. Tuition price list available on request. 18 hole "Pay and Play" parkland golf course 5969 yards S.S.S. 68. Large multi level putting green. Conference & function rooms. Large golf shop. *Prices:* available on request. *Eating facilities:* friendly clubhouse with full bar and restaurant facilities. Visitors most welcome. Bar snacks or 'Daily Specials' available in spacious bar/lounge. Sky TV. *Opening hours:* weekdays 8am

to 9pm, Saturdays, 7am to 9pm, Sundays 7am to 5pm (Sunday lunch 12 noon to 4pm). Head Professional: Graeme Long. Assistant Professional: Danny Wall. Secretary: David Went
e-mail: enquiries@bromsgrovegolfcentre.com
website: www.bromsgrovegolfcentre.com

REDDITCH. **The Abbey Hotel, Golf and Country Club,** Hither Green Lane, Dagnell End Road, Redditch B98 9BE (01527 406500; Fax: 01527 406514). *Location*: leave M42 at Junction 2, take A441 towards Redditch, at end of dual carriageway turn left still keeping on the A441, at petrol station turn left into Dagnell End Road (A4101) - hotel and golf club are approximately 600 yards on right. 12 bay range. *Prices*: information not available. *Eating facilities*: extended Bramblings Restaurant and Tawnys Bar. *Opening hours*: 7:00am until 8:30pm in summer, 7:30am until dusk in winter. Fully stocked golf shop. Golf & Leisure Complex . Professional tuition available. Professional: Rob Davies.*

WORCESTER. **Ravenmeadow Golf Club,** Hindlip Lane, Claines, Worcester WR3 8SA (01905 458876; Fax: 01905 458876). *Location*: Junction 6 M5 motorway, take A449 signed Kidderminster, leave at Blackpole exit. At main road turn right, first left into Hindlip Lane, half mile on left. Part of Ravenmeadow Golf Club. 4 grass, 4 outside mats, 10 covered tees. 5 automatic tees. Putting green, chipping green, 9 hole pitch and putt course; finest practice facilities in the country. *Prices:* Driving range £3.00, pitch and putt, £4.00 adults, £3.00 juniors. *Opening hours:* 8am till dusk. *Eating facilities:* bar, snack meals. Professional: Leo Tarrant (01905 756665).

WORCESTER. **Worcester Golf Range,** Weir Lane, Lowerwick WR2 4AY (01905 748788/421213). *Location*: Junction 7 M5 off Malvern Road next to Lowerwick Swimming Pool. 26 bay covered, floodlit, golf range. 9 hole pitch and putt. *Prices*: information not available. *Eating facilities*: cold drinks, free coffee, confectionery and sandwiches. *Opening hours:* 9.30am to 10pm Monday - Friday, 9.30am to 6pm Saturday and Sunday. Three fully qualified PGA professionals always available for teaching. Swimming pool next door. Professional: Mark Dove.*

EAST YORKSHIRE

BEVERLEY. **Cherry Burton Golf Club,** Leconfield Lane, Cherry Burton, Beverley HU17 7RB (Tel & Fax: 01964 550924). *Location*: off the B1248 3 miles north of Beverley. 6 bay covered, grassed, floodlit driving range. One bunker. *Prices:* information not available. *Eating facilities:* licensed bar with snacks. *Opening hours:* dawn to dusk. James Calam Golf Academy. Professional: James Calam (01964 550924 or 07979 596134; Fax: 01964 550924).*
website: www.cherryburtongolfclub.co.uk

SCUNTHORPE. **Grange Park Golf Range,** Butterwick Road, Messingham, Scunthorpe DN17 3PP (01724 764478). *Location:* five miles south of Scunthorpe between Messingham and East Butterwick, four miles south of Junction 3 of M180. 20 bay covered floodlit driving range. 9 hole pay and play course on site. *Prices:* information not available. *Opening hours:* 9am to 9.30pm weekdays, 9am to 8.30pm weekends. Large Pro shop and exclusive golf ladies' wear shop. Smart Golf indoor simulator. Professional available.

NORTH YORKSHIRE

HARROGATE. **Rudding Park Golf,** Rudding Park, Harrogate HG3 1JH (01423 872100; Fax: 01423 873011). *Location:* lies just off the A658 linking the A61 from Leeds to the A59 York Road. Parkland course designed to USGA specifications. 18 holes, 6883 yards. Par 72. and 6 hole Par 3 short course. 18 bay floodlit driving range with four professionals. *Prices:* £1.00 for a basket of 20 balls. *Eating facilities:* Clubhouse open all day everyday, spike bar. *Visitors:* welcome at all times, must have a Handicap Certificate. Shop and buggies available all year round with all year weather buggy tracks, caddies on request. Society and corporate days welcome. Professional: Mark Moore (01423 873400).
e-mail: golf.admin@ruddingpark.com
website: www.ruddingparkgolf.com

NORTHALLERTON. **Romanby Driving Range,** Romanby Golf Course, Yafforth Road, Northallerton DL7 0PE (01609 778855; Fax: 01609 779084). *Location:* on the North West of Northallerton, easy road access. Part of Romanby Golf Course Ltd. 12 covered, grassed, floodlit bays. Practice bunker. Academy Course. *Prices:* enquiries to (01609 778855). *Opening hours:* 8am to 9pm; closes 6pm weekends. *Eating facilities:* Country Club open daily from 8am till 9pm; full bar and restaurant facilities. Lessons available; pro shop. Full disabled facilities. Professional: Richard Wood (01609 760777; Fax: 01609 760660).*
e-mail: richard@romanby.com
marketing: richard.boucher@romanby.com
website: www.romanby.com

SALTBURN. **Hunley Hall Golf Club & Hotel,** Brotton, Saltburn TS12 2QQ (01287 676216; Fax: 01287 678250). *Location:* off A174 at St. Margarets Way in Brotton. Signposted through housing estate, approximately half-a-mile to club. 12 bay floodlit driving range, large practice and chipping area. Picturesque 27 hole coastal courses adjacent to Heritage Coast. *Prices:* £3.50 for 80 balls (members), £4.00 for 80 balls (non members). *Eating facilities:* excellent facilities including restaurant, lounge bar, spike bar, golfers' bar; quality food available all day, every day. *Opening hours:* Summer - 8am to 8pm, 6pm weekends and Bank Holidays. Winter - 8am till dusk, floodlit Wednesday, Thursday and Friday to 7.30pm. Three Star Hotel on site. Club hire, buggy hire and tuition available. *Society Meetings:*

welcome Monday to Saturday, packages available. Golfing Holidays available. Professional: Andrew Brook (Tel & Fax: 01287 677444). Secretary: Liz Lillie (01287 676216; Fax: 01287 678250).
e-mail: enquiries@hunleyhall.co.uk
e-mail: andy@asbrook-golf.co.uk
website: www.hunleyhall.co.uk

SOUTH YORKSHIRE

DONCASTER. **Bawtry Golf Club Driving Range,** Cross Lane, Austerfield, Bawtry, Doncaster DN10 6RF (01302 710841). *Location:* A614 Doncaster to Blyth Roundabout on the A1. Adjacent to the new Robin Hood Doncaster Airport. 10 covered, grassed, floodlit bays. *Prices:* information not available. *Opening hours:* 8am to 8pm. *Eating facilities:* full clubhouse facilities. Tuition available. Professional: Daniel Gregory (01302 710841).
e-mail: enquiries@bawtrygolfclub.co.uk
website: www.bawtrygoldclub.co.uk

SHEFFIELD. **Concord Park Driving Range,** Concord Park Golf Club, Shiregreen, Sheffield S5 6AE (Tel & Fax: 0114 257 7378). *Location:* next to Concord Park Golf Club. 30 covered, floodlit bays; 2 bunkers. Putting green. *Prices:* information not available. *Opening hours:* 7am to 9pm. *Eating facilities:* restaurant in the clubhouse, also fully licensed bar. Tuition available. Professional: Warren Allcroft (07968 618766).

SHEFFIELD. **Rother Valley Golf Centre,** Mansfield Road, Wales Bar, Sheffield S26 5PQ (0114 247 3000; Fax: 0114 247 6000). *Location:* Junction 31 off M1 motorway, follow signs to Rother Valley Country Park. 25 covered, floodlit bays; bunkers. *Prices:* 20 balls for £1. *Opening hours:* 9am to 9pm (10pm in Summer). *Eating facilities:* bar and restaurant. Professional: Jason Ripley.
e-mail: rother-jackbarker@btinternet.com
website: www.jackbarker.com

WEST YORKSHIRE

BRADFORD. **Shay Grange Golf Centre,** Long Lane, off Bingley Road, Bradford BD9 6RX (01274 491945). *Location:* take the A650 Bradford to Bingley road, turn left at Cottingley lights, the Centre will be found on the left after two miles. 32 bay covered, floodlit, grassed range. *Prices:* information not available. *Eating facilities:* fully licensed bar and catering facilities. *Opening hours:* weekdays 9am to 9pm, weekends and Bank Holidays 7am to 9pm. 9 hole (Par 29) course, Golf Academy, all weather putting green, sand bunker, grass short game area. Tuition. Golf clinics - Juniors, Senior Citizens, Ladies. Golf shop staffed by qualified PGA professionals. Manager: T. Grunwell.*

BRIGHOUSE. **Willow Valley Golf,** Highmoor Lane, off Walton Lane, Clifton, Brighouse HD6 4JB (01274 878624; Fax: 01274 852805). *Location:* Junction 25 off M62 to Brighouse A644, right at roundabout A643, 2 miles on right. 24 bay, covered, floodlit, grassed driving range. 18 hole and 9 hole courses. *Prices:* information not available. *Eating facilities:* fully licensed bar and catering. Junior Golf Foundation courses and 3 hole floodlit golf course. Professional: Julian Haworth.
website: www.wvgc.co.uk

HUDDERSFIELD. **Stadium Golf Driving Range,** The Alfred Macalpine Stadium, Stadium Way, Huddersfield HD1 6PG (01484 452564; Fax: 01484 452540). *Location:* off A62 centre of Huddersfield, signposted the Macalpine Stadium. 30 bay covered, floodlit driving range, range grassed. *Prices:* information not available. *Eating facilities:* snack bar serving sandwiches, etc., licensed bar. *Opening hours:* weekdays 9am to 10pm (last balls 9.30pm). weekends 9am to 7pm (last balls 6.30pm). State of the art Panasonic split screen video lessons with PGA qualified instructors. Corporate and group evenings a speciality. Team and video golf fun for juniors to seniors and all in between. Well stocked shop with all major brands. Professional: Simon Roberts.*

LEEDS. **Cookridge Hall Golf Club**, Cookridge Lane, Leeds LS16 7NL (0113 2300641; Fax: 0113 2030198). *Location*: A6120 ring road, 10 minutes Leeds city centre, Bradford city centre, 20 minutes Harrogate centre. 18 hole Championship course. 22-bay driving range with floodlights. *Prices:* £3.50 for 50 balls, £16.00 for range card and 6 baskets. 2 piece golf balls. *Eating facilities*: sports bar, hot and cold sandwiches and drinks available. *Opening hours*: weekdays 8.30am to 9.30pm, weekends 8.30am to 8pm. PGA tuition 7 days a week. Bunker and chipping area, latest in air cushioned mats
e-mail: info@cookridgehall.co.uk
website: www.cookridgehall.co.uk

LEEDS. **Leeds Golf Centre,** Wike Ridge Lane, Shadwell, Leeds LS17 9JW (0113 2886000; Fax: 0113 2886185). *Location:* two miles north of Leeds between A61 and A58 at the village of Wike. 19 bay covered, floodlit range. *Prices:* basket of balls £2.80. *Eating facilities:* bar/brasserie open 8.30am to 10pm. *Opening hours:* 7am to 10pm. Resident teaching professionals, 18 hole championship course, 12 hole Par 3 course. Head Professional: Tony Tomlinson. General Manager: Andrew Levine.
e-mail: info@leedsgolfcentre.com
website: www.leedsgolfcentre.com

THE APPEARANCE OF AN ASTERISK (*) AT THE END OF A CLUB OR COURSE ENTRY INDICATES THAT UP-TO-DATE INFORMATION HAS NOT BEEN SUPPLIED

SCOTLAND

ABERDEEN, BANFF & MORAY

ABERDEEN. **Kings Links Golf Centre,** Golf Road, Aberdeen AB24 1RZ (01224 641577; Fax: 01224 639410). *Location:* in front of Pittodrie football stadium, 56 covered, floodlit bays on two tiers. *Prices:* information not available. *Eating facilities:* vending drinks, vending snacks and sandwiches. *Opening hours*: 9am to 10pm weekdays, 9am to 5.30pm weekends. 5 PGA Professionals available for tuition, club repairs, advise and custom fitting service. Video academy equipped with the latest video analysis equipment. Floodlit outdoor short game area. 3000sq ft golf superstore stocking all the latest golf equipment. Beginners welcome. Director of Golf: Paul Girvan.
e-mail: info@kings-links.com
website: www.kings-links.com

ANGUS & DUNDEE

DUNDEE. **Ballumbie Castle Golf Club,** 3 Old Quarry Road, Off Ballumbie Road, Dundee DD4 0SY (01382 730026; Fax: 01382 730008). *Location:* one and a half miles north of Claypotts Junction, less than 2 miles from Dundee City Centre. 22 bay floodlit driving range, putting green, chipping green. 18 hole course. *Prices:* information not available. *Eating facilities*: clubhouse facilities with menu and full bar. Public house licence. *Opening hours*: 9am to 9pm weekdays, 9am to 7pm weekends. Tuition available. *Society Meetings*: welcome, please telephone for details. Professional: Lee Sutherland (01382 770028).*
e-mail: ballumbie2000@yahoo.com
website: www.ballumbiecastlegolfclub.com

AYRSHIRE & ARRAN

DAILLY. **Brunston Castle Golf Course,** Dailly, Girvan KA26 9GD (01465 811471). *Location:* five miles north of Girvan on B471, five miles from Turnberry. 10-bay floodlit driving range. *Prices*: available on request. *Eating facilities:* full bar and restaurant facilities. *Opening hours:* 8am to 11pm (Summer). 18 hole championship course in most scenic part of Ayrshire. Full PGA tuition by Professional, full practice facilities. 16-seater minibus and trailer available.
e-mail: golf@brunstoncastle.co.uk
website: www.brunstoncastle.co.uk

DUMFRIES & GALLOWAY

GRETNA. **Gretna Golf Course,** Gretna DG16 5HD (01461 337362). *Location:* half-a-mile south west of M74 and A75 junction, half-a-mile on west side of Gretna. 14 bay covered driving range, 7 bays grassed. 9 hole golf course. *Prices:* information not available. *Eating facilities:* available. *Opening Hours:* 10am to dark. *

EDINBURGH & LOTHIANS

EDINBURGH. **Braid Hills Shop & Golf Centre,** 91 Liberton Drive, Edinburgh EH16 6NS (0131-658 1111; Fax: 0131-672 1411). *Location:* leave Edinburgh bypass at Straiton Junction, head towards city centre, take left turn at second set of traffic lights, proceed half-a-mile along Liberton Drive. 32 bay covered, floodlit range. Short game area and 3 putting greens. *Prices:* information not available. *Opening Hours:* 10am to 9pm weekdays, 9am to 6pm weekends. Scotland's top Professionals available for group and individual tuition. S.A.S video tuition. Professionals: Ian Young, Colin Brooks, Sandy Stephen, Mark Berrie, Paul Malone, Craig Waddell.*

EDINBURGH. **Port Royal Golf Driving Range,** Eastfield Road, Ingliston, Edinburgh EH28 8TR (0131-333 4377). *Location:* situated next to Edinburgh Airport. Recently refurbished to cater for golfers of every ability. 25 covered, floodlit practice bays, 17 outside bays, double teaching studio with swing analysis software, 100 square yard Himalayan putting green, 9 hole Par 3 golf course. PGA Professionals and tuition. *Prices:* information not available. *Eating facilities:* licensed cafe/bar area, snacks served all day. *Opening hours:* 10am to 10pm summer, 10am to 9pm winter. Open all year. General Manager/Head Professional: Keith Pickard.*

EDINBURGH near. **Melville Golf Centre, Golf Course, Range & Shop,** Lasswade, Near Edinburgh EH18 1AN (0131-663 8038; Fax: 0131-654 0814). *Location:* south of Edinburgh, three minutes from City Bypass on A7 South (signposted). 22 floodlit, covered bays plus 12 bays. 300 yards long. *Prices:* £3.00 for 50 balls and concessions (subject to review for 2008). *Eating facilities:* hot and cold vended drinks, rolls, etc. *Opening hours:* weekdays 9am to 10pm, weekends 9am to 8pm. Full equipment and shoe hire. Repairs. Golf shop fully stocked, ladies, gents, and juniors. PGA tuition and Swingcam; practice bunker, putting green, 4 hole practice area, pay & play 9-hole golf course. Children under 14 must be accompanied by an adult. A Golf Foundation Starter Initiative Centre. Professional: Gary Carter. Owners Mr and Mrs MacFarlane.
e-mail: golf@melvillegolf.co.uk
website: www.melvillegolf.co.uk

FIFE

ST ANDREWS. **St Andrews Links Golf Practice Centre & Golf Academy,** St Andrews, KY16 9SF (01334 474489; Fax: 01334 479555). *Location:* situated parallel to the Old Course, just 10 minutes' walk from the town centre. *Prices:* 50 balls £3. *Eating facilities:* light refreshments and seated viewing area. *Opening hours:* 7am to 9pm daily. Floodlit driving range with over 60 bays. Short game area with greens and bunkers. Grass tees. Golf club hire available. Locker rooms: (01334 474489).

GLASGOW & DISTRICT

GLASGOW. **Mearns Castle Golf Academy,** Waterfoot Road, Newton Mearns, Glasgow G77 5RR (0141 644 8200; Fax: 0141 644 1133). *Location:* near Newton Mearns. 34 covered, floodlit bays; bunkers. *Prices:* information not available. *Eating facilities:* cafe bar. Tuition available; 9 hole pay and play course, short game facility. Memberships available.* website: www.mcgolfacademy.co.uk

UDDINGSTON. **Clydeway Golf Centre,** Blantyre Farm Road, Uddingston G71 7RR (0141-641 8899). *Location:* near Glasgow Zoo. 25 covered floodlit bays. *Prices:* information not available. Professional tuition. Group rates for parties, schools, colleges, works, offices, etc. Now incorporates Nevada Bob's golf discount superstore, target golf competition. *

HIGHLANDS

INVERNESS. **Fairways Driving Range,** Castle Heather, Inverness IV2 6AA (01463 713335; Fax: 01463 712695). *Location:* on the southern outskirts of Inverness, heading west along the new ring road. 19 bay covered, floodlit driving range. 18 hole golf course and 9-hole course. Practice area. *Prices:* 16 balls £1.00, 50 balls £3.00. *Eating facilities:* restaurant lounge, sports bar. *Opening hours:* Monday to Sunday 8am to 11pm daily. *Visitors:* welcome, buggies, carts available. *Society Meetings:* welcome. Two PGA Professionals, tuition available. Professionals: Martin Piggot, Michael Campbell.
e-mail: info@golflochness.com
website: www.golflochness.com

www.uk-golfguide.com

PERTHSHIRE

WALES

BLAIRGOWRIE. **Strathmore Golf Centre Driving Range.** Leroch, Alyth, Blairgowrie PH11 8NZ (01828 633322; Fax: 01828 633533). *Location:* one mile south of Alyth, (off the A926 Alyth-Kirriemuir Road). 10 bay floodlit driving range. *Prices:* information not available. *Eating facilities:* restaurant and bar at Clubhouse . *Opening hours:* dawn to 10pm. 18 and 9 hole courses available. Golf Operations Manager: Jane Taylor. e-mail: enquiries@strathmoregolf.com website: www.strathmoregolf.com

MIDDLEBANK. **Middlebank Golf Centre,** Middlebank, Errol PH2 7SX (01821 670320). *Location:* midway between Perth and Dundee on the A90. 23 bay floodlit driving range; 7 covered, 16 grassed. *Prices:* £2.70 for 50 balls, £5.00 for 100, 5 credit digicard £11.00. *Eating facilities:* Hot and cold drinks available. *Opening Hours:* Summer 10am to 8pm Monday-Friday, 10am to 5pm Saturday & Sunday, Winter hours may vary. *Visitors:* Open to public. Recently refurbished and under new management. Home of the Andy Lamb Golf Academy. Resident PGA professional Andy Lamb. Extensive golf shop stocks ladies golf clothing, Titleist Custom Fit Centre.

SCONE. **Murrayshall Golf Range,** Murrayshall Hotel & Golf Courses, Scone PH2 7PH (01738 554804; Fax: 01738 552595). *Location:* 3 miles outside Perth (NE) off A94. 18 bay covered, floodlit driving range, 11 grassed, bunkers. Two 18 hole golf courses. *Prices:* information not available. *Eating facilities:* 4 Star Hotel and golf clubhouse on site. *Opening hours:* Daylight until 9:30pm. Video analysis tuition. Professional: Alan Reid.* e-mail: golf@murrayshall.co.uk website: www.murrayshall.co.uk

ANGLESEY & GWYNEDD

ANGLESEY. **Penrhyn Golf Complex,** Llanddaniel - Fâb LL60 6NN (01248 421150). *Location:* A5 turn off at Star Crossroads taking Llanddaniel road. Follow Brown Tourism signs from the village. 14 bay covered and floodlit driving range, 9 hole golf course. *Prices:* 100 balls £4.00, 50 balls £3.00 (2007). *Visitors:* no restrictions. Professional: Paul Lovell (Visiting). Owner: W.R. Carter.

PWLLHELI. **Llyn Golf,** Pen-y-Berth, Penrhos, Pwllheli LL53 7HG (01758 701200). *Location:* Situated off the A499 between Pwllheli and Abersoch. 14 covered floodlit bays and bunker practice area. 9-hole pay and play golf course, 1782 yards, Par 3 and 4. Hire clubs available. *Prices:* information not available. *Eating facilities:* refreshments available. *Opening hours:* open daily.

NORTH WALES

CHESTER near. **Bannel Golf Driving Range,** Mold Road, Penymynydd, Near Chester CH4 0EN (01244 544639). *Location:* A5118 Penymynydd to Mold road, 7 miles from Chester. 10 bay covered floodlit range; three bays open. *Prices:* information not available. *Eating facilities:* light refreshments available. *Opening hours:* 10am to 9pm weekdays, 10am to 6pm weekends. 9 hole putting green, golf shop. Lessons from PGA Professional by appointment. Proprietors: L.J. & J. Povey (01244 544639).*

ST ASAPH. **North Wales Golf Driving Range and 9 hole Course,** Llannerch Park, St Asaph LL17 0BD (01745 730805;). *Location:* on the A525 between St Asaph and Trefnant, one-and-a-quarter miles from St Asaph Cathedral. 14 bay covered, floodlit driving range. New, automatic power-tees. *Prices:* information not available. *Eating facilities:* refreshments, hot and cold drinks, sweets, biscuits, crisps. *Opening hours:* 10am to 9pm seven days a week during Summer, early closing in Winter 5pm Friday to Monday. Lessons with resident Professional by arrangement. 9 hole course also on site - £5.00 pay and play. Non-membership Complex. Secretary: Stephen Mueller (07771 733651 mobile).

THE APPEARANCE OF AN ASTERISK (*) AT THE END OF A CLUB OR COURSE ENTRY INDICATES THAT UP-TO-DATE INFORMATION HAS NOT BEEN SUPPLIED

POWYS

CRADOC. **Cradoc Golf Club,** Penoyre Park, Cradoc, Brecon LD3 9LP (01874 623658; Fax: 01874 611711). *Location*: two miles north of the market town of Brecon (off B4520 Upper Chapel Road (signposted) past Brecon Cathedral). 10-bay undercover floodlit driving range. *Prices*: information not available. *Opening hours*: Monday and Tuesday (1st November to 31st March) 8.30am till 5.00pm and (1st April to 31st October) 8.30am to 8.45pm. Wednesday to Sunday (inclusive) 8.30am to 8.45pm all year. Professional: R.W. Davies (01874 625524). Club Manager Bob Barnes (01874 623658).
e-mail: secretary@cradoc.co.uk
website: www.cradoc.co.uk

SOUTH WALES

ABERGAVENNY. **Wernddu Golf Club,** Old Ross Road, Abergavenny NP7 8NG (01873 856223; Fax: 01873 852177). *Location:* one and a half miles east of Abergavenny on B4521 (off A465). 26 bay floodlit driving range. *Prices:* information not available. *Eating facilities:* lounge bar, bar snacks. *Visitors:* welcome. Professional tuition, 9 hole pitch and putt and 18 hole Par 67 golf course. Contact: Pro Tina Tetley (L.E.T.).*
e-mail: info@wernddu-golf-club.co.uk
website: www.wernddu-golf-club.co.uk

BARRY. **South Wales Golf Range and Course,** Port Road East, Barry (Range: 01446 742434; Mobile: 07986 738744). *Location:* A4050 road Cardiff to Barry. 16 covered floodlit bays. *Prices:* information not available. *Opening hours:* weekdays 9am to 8pm; weekends 9am to 6pm. Professional tuition available from Simon Cox (three times Welsh Champion); 9-hole Par 3 course.

CAERPHILLY. **Virginia Park Golf Club,** Virginia Park, Caerphilly CF8 1LP (029 2086 7891). *Location:* off Pontygwindy Road, next to recreation centre. 20 bay covered, floodlit, grassed driving range. *Prices:* information not available. *Eating facilities:* licensed bar in clubhouse, full catering. Coffee shop in driving range. *Opening hours:* Weekdays 10.30am to 10pm. Weekends 8am to 7pm seven days a week. Professional: Katherine Price. Secretary: Graham Taylor.

CHEPSTOW: **Dewstow Golf Club,** Caerwent, Chepstow NP26 5AH (01291 430444; Fax: 01291 425816). *Location:* Off A48 at Caerwent, between Chepstow and Newport, four miles from Severn Bridge. 26 bay floodlit, covered golf range. Two 18 hole courses. *Prices:* information not available. *Eating facilities:* restaurant, bars. *Opening hours:* on application. *Society Meetings:* welcome weekdays. Limited weekends. Professional: Jonathan Skuse. Golf Secretary:Dave Bradbury (01291 430444; Fax: 01291 425816). Booking Secretary: Hayley Battle.*

COEDKERNEW. **Parc Golf Club,** Church Lane, Coedkernew NP1 9TU (01633 680933). *Location:* Junction 28 M4, then A48 towards Cardiff. 38 bay covered, floodlit driving range. Automatic tee system installed. New 9 hole Par 3 course available. *Prices:* information not available. *Eating facilities:* excellent full facilities. *Opening Hours:* weekdays 7.30am to 10pm, weekends 7.30am to 8.30pm. Three Professionals, individual and group tuition, excellent shop. Function suite, corporate and society days organised. Weddings, seminars, private parties catered for.

CWMBRAN. **Greenmeadow Golf and Country Club,** Treherbert Road, Croesyceiliog, Cwmbran NP44 2BZ (01633 869321; Fax: 01633 868430). *Location:* M4 Junction 26 five miles north on A4042. Turn right at brown tourist sign. Golf Course & Range next to Gwent Crematorium. 26 bay covered floodlit driving range. *Prices:* please phone for details and prices as there are many different packages and options. *Eating facilities:* lounge bar, patio coffee lounge and restaurant, private function room. *Opening hours:* 8am to 10pm all year. *Visitors:* welcome. Professional tuition by appointment. Six floodlit all-weather tennis courts, 18 hole parkland golf course, putting green. Range situated with panoramic views, facing easterly. Professional: Dave Woodman (01633 862626. Fax: 01633 868430). Secretary: P. Richardson (01633 869321).*
e-mail: info@greenmeadowgolf.com
website: www.greenmeadowgolf.com

SWANSEA. **Gowerton Golf Range,** Victoria Road, Gowerton, Swansea, SA4 3AB (01792 875188; Fax: 01792 874288). 20 covered bays, all floodlit. *Prices:* information not available. *Eating facilities:* diner, hot and cold meals available. *Opening hours:* 10am to 9pm, closed at 7pm winter weekends. Tuition available. Putting green, golf course. Professional: Mike Hobbs.
e-mail: waynebattye@yahoo.com
website: www.gowertongolfrange.com

For full details of clubs and courses, plus convenient accommodation
www.uk-golfguide.com

NORTHERN IRELAND

ANTRIM

NEWTOWNABBEY. **Ballyearl Golf and Leisure Centre,** 585 Doagh Road, Newtownabbey BT36 8RZ (028 9084 0899). *Location:* from Belfast take M2 then A8 to Larne, half a mile through second roundabout following exit from motorway turn right to Mossley. Ballyearl one mile on left. 24 bay covered, floodlit range, large grassed area. *Prices:* information not available. *Eating facilities:* squash club with bar facilities. *Opening hours:* 9.30am to 9.30pm. 9 hole Par 3 course, PGA Golf Professional, tuition, fully stocked golf shop, repairs. Squash court, fitness suite, arts theatre.*

ARMAGH

CRAIGAVON. **Craigavon Golf and Ski Club,** Turmoyra Lane, Lurgan, Craigavon (028 3832 6606; Fax: 028 3834 7272). *Location:* half a mile from motorway, one mile from town centre, adjacent to ski slope. Driving range. 18-hole course, 9-hole par 3 course, 12-hole pitch and putt. *Prices:* information not available. *Eating facilities:* full restaurant facilities. *Visitors:* always welcome. Modern clubhouse, showers and lockers. *Society Meetings:* welcome - book beforehand. Professional: D. Paul. *

Co. DOWN

KNOCKBRACKEN. **Mount Ober Golf and Country Club,** 24 Ballymaconaghy Road, Knockbracken, Belfast BT8 6SB (028 9079 5666; Fax: 028 9070 5862). *Location:* outskirts of Belfast, approximately three miles from the centre along Ormeau Road to "Four Winds" public house and restaurant. 36 bays covered, floodlit, and grassed area. *Prices:* £3.00 for 60 balls. Subject to review. *Eating facilities:* bar open seven days a week during normal opening hours, catering available seven days a week 11am to 10pm. *Opening hours:* 10am to 11pm. Tuition available at Golf Academy by PGA professionals. Snooker and pool tables. Professional: (028 9070 1648). Secretary: (028 9079 5666).
e-mail: mt.ober@ukonline.co.uk

WARRENPOINT. **Pat Trainor's Golf Academy,** Milltown Street, Burren, Warrenpoint BT34 3RJ (028 4177 3247). *Location:* six miles south of Newry, at Warrenpoint roundabout turn left for Burren: approximately one mile. Driving range - 10 covered, 20 grassed bays, all floodlit. 9 hole pitch and putt course. *Prices:* information not available. *Opening hours:* weekdays 10am to 10pm; weekends 10am to 8pm. Tuition available at all times for individuals, groups and schools. Indoor video lessons. Owner/Professional: Pat Trainor. Teacher: Paddy Gribben.*

FERMANAGH

ENNISKILLEN. **Ashwoods Golf Centre,** Sligo Road, Enniskillen (028 6632 5321; Fax: 028 6632 5874). *Location:* one and a half miles west of Enniskillen on main Sligo Road. 7 bay covered, floodlit range. *Prices:* information not available. *Eating facilities:* none on site, available 300 yards away. *Opening hours:* 9am to 10pm summer, 9am to 7pm winter. Professional lessons. Professional golf shop stocking full range of clubs, clothes and all golf accessories.*

Co. LONDONDERRY

LIMAVADY. **Roe Park Golf Club,** Radisson SAS Roe Park Resort, Roe Park, Limavady BT49 9LB (028 777 6015; Fax: 028 7772 2313). *Location:* on main A2 Londonderry-Limavady Road, 16 miles from Londonderry and one mile from Limavady. 10 covered, floodlit, astroturfed and 6 uncovered bays. 18 hole parkland course. *Prices:* information not available. *Eating facilities:* Coach Brasserie. *Opening hours:* 8am until 10pm, golf course open from 8am until 8pm. PGA Tuition available. Professional: Shaun Devenney. Golf Manager: Jim Cullen.

LONDONDERRY. **Foyle International Golf Centre,** 12 Alder Road, Londonderry BT48 8DB (028 71 352222; Fax: 028 71 353967). *Location:* one and a half miles from Foyle Bridge towards Moville, Co Donegal. 25 bay covered, floodlit driving range. 18 hole, par 71 course and 9 hole par 3 course. *Prices:* information not available. *Eating facilities:* Pitchers Wine Bar and Restaurant. *Opening hours:* 8.00am to 10.00pm. Tuition available. Professional indoor video analysis. Professionals: Derek Morrison and Sean Young (028 71 352222; Fax: 028 71 353967).
e-mail: mail@foylegolf.club24.co.uk
website: www.foylegolfcentre.co.uk

REPUBLIC OF IRELAND

COUNTY CORK

FOTA ISLAND. **Fota Island Resort,** Cork (021 4883700; Fax: 021 4883713). *Location:* take the N25 east from Cork City, turn off Carrigtwohill/Cobh exit. Follow sign for Fota (100m). Venue for the 2001 and 2002 Murphy's Irish Open. 18 hole championship course. Voted golf course of the year in 2002 by the Irish Golf Tour Operators. *Prices:* information not available. *Eating facilities:* full bar and restaurant. *Opening hours:* daylight only. PGA professional plus assistants available for tuition. Professional: Kevin Morris.
e-mail: reservations@fotaisland.ie
website: www.fotaisland.ie

COUNTY DUBLIN

FOXROCK. **Leopardstown Driving Range,** Foxrock (2895341). *Location:* five miles south of Dublin city centre situated in Leopardstown Race Course. 38 indoor, 38 outdoor floodlit bays. *Opening hours:* 9am to 10pm. *Prices:* information not available. *Eating facilities:* restaurant. Tuition available from three PGA Professionals - practice green. 18 hole golf course. Manager: Michael Hoey.*

ST MARGARET'S. **The Open Golf Centre,** Newtown House, St Margaret's (010 3531 8640324; Fax: 010 3531 8341400). *Location:* 2kms from Dublin Airport, adjacent to N2 (Derry road). 16 bay floodlit, grassed range. *Prices:* information not available. *Eating facilities:* coffee shop. *Opening hours:* 7.30am to dusk. Nine golf professionals on site, groups organised, video, lecture room and club fitting room.*

COUNTY KILDARE

NAAS. **Naas Golf Driving Range,** Kerdiffstown, Sallins, Naas (045 897754 or 045 874489; Fax: 045 871321). *Location:* one mile from N7 and Sallins Village, beside Naas Golf Club. Putting green, pitching area, sand bunker. Covered bays and floodlit outdoor bays. Coin operated automatic dispensing machine. *Visitors:* welcome. *Society Meetings:* welcome any time. Professional: Gerry Egan (085 144 8779), Tommy Halpin (087 987 2682), Gavin Lunny (086 832 6676). Secretary: Gus Fitzpatrick (086 255 6105; Fax: 045 871 321).
e-mail: gusfitzpatrick@eircom.net

COUNTY MONAGHAN

CARRICKMACROSS. **Nuremore Golf Club,** Nuremore Hotel and Country Club, Carrickmacross (042 61438). *Location:* 50 miles from Dublin on N2. *Prices:* information not available. *Eating facilities:* bar and catering facilities in new clubhouse and hotel. *Opening hours:* daylight hours. PGA Professional, all hotel facilities.*

COUNTY WATERFORD

DUNGARVAN. **Gold Coast Golf Club,** Ballinacourty, Dungarvan (058 44055; Fax: 058 43378). *Location:* from Waterford left of N25 two miles before Dungarvan. Parkland bordered by Atlantic. 18 holes, 6788 yards, 6171 metres. S.S.S. 72. *Prices:* information not available. *Eating facilities:* full hotel and leisure facilities. *Visitors:* welcome. *Society Meetings:* welcome, special rates available. Secretary: Tom Considine (Tel & Fax: 058 44055).*
e-mail: info@clonea.com
website: www.clonea.com

CHANNEL ISLANDS

ST OUEN'S. **Les Mielles Golf and Country Club,** St Ouen's Bay, Jersey JE3 7PQ (01534 482787; Fax: 01534 485414). *Location:* centre of St Ouen's Bay. 30 bay covered driving range. *Prices:* information available on line. *Opening hours:* dawn till dusk. *Eating facilities:* restaurant, alfresco eating, kiosk. Public golf facility. Putting green; golf shop. Professional: Wayne Osmand (01534 483699; Fax: 01534 485414). Director of Golf: J.A. Le Brun.*
website: www.lesmielles.com

Index of Clubs & Courses

Aa Saint-Omer Golf Club ST OMER 510

Abbey Hill Golf Centre MILTON KEYNES 72

Abbey Hotel Golf & Country Club REDDITCH 220

Abbey Hotel, Golf and Country Club REDDITCH 574

Abbeydale Golf Club SHEFFIELD 287

Abbeyfeale Golf Club ABBEYFEALE 483

Abbeyleix Golf Club ABBEYLEIX 482

Abbotsley Golf Club & Hotel ST NEOTS 136, 561

Aberdare Golf Club ABERDARE 422

Aberdour Golf Club ABERDOUR 357

Aberdovey Golf Club ABERDOVEY 402

Aberfeldy Golf Club ABERFELDY 382

Aberfoyle Golf Club ABERFOYLE 393

Abergele Golf Club ABERGELE 407

Abernethy Golf Club NETHYBRIDGE 378

Aberystwyth Golf Club ABERYSTWYTH 415

Aboyne Golf Club ABOYNE 311

Aboyne Loch Golf Centre ABOYNE 311

Abridge Golf & Country Club STAPLEFORD TAWNEY 144

Academia de Golf Estoril Sol ESTORIL 528

Accrington and District Golf Club ACCRINGTON 243

Achill Golf Club ACHILL 485

Acre Gate Golf Club FLIXTON 253

Adare Golf Club ADARE 483

Adare Manor Golf Club ADARE 483

Addington Court Golf Ltd CROYDON 102

Addington Golf Club CROYDON 102

Addington Palace Golf Club CROYDON 102

Adlington Golf Centre ADLINGTON 225, 561

Aigas Golf Course BEAULY 375

Airdrie Golf Club AIRDRIE 379

Airlinks Golf Club HOUNSLOW 126

Aix Marseille Golf d' MARSEILLES 518

Albi Lasbordes Golf d' ALBI 515

Alcanada Club de Golf PUERTO DE ALCUDIA 538

Aldeburgh Golf Club ALDEBURGH 158

Aldenham Golf & Country Club WATFORD 150

Alder Root Golf Club WARRINGTON 231

Alderley Edge Golf Club ALDERLEY EDGE 225

Alderney Golf Club ALDERNEY 503

Aldersey Green Golf Club CHESTER 225

Aldwark Manor Golf Club ALDWARK 277

Aldwickbury Park Golf Club HARPENDEN 146

Alexandra Golf Club GLASGOW 365

Alford Golf Club ALFORD 312

Alfreton Golf Club ALFRETON 164

Alice Springs Golf Club USK 435

Allendale Golf Club ALLENDALE 265

Allerton Park Golf Club LIVERPOOL 261

Allestree Park Golf Club DERBY 165

Alloa Golf Club ALLOA 393

Allt-y-Graban Golf Club SWANSEA 432

Almerimar Golf ALMERIA 535

Alness Golf Club ALNESS 373

Alnmouth Golf Club Ltd. ALNMOUTH 265

Alnmouth Village Golf Club ALNMOUTH 265

Alnwick Golf Club ALNWICK 265

Aloha Golf MARBELLA 534

Alresford Golf Club ALRESFORD 74

Alsager Golf and Country Club ALSAGER 225

Alston Moor Golf Club ALSTON 233

Alto Golf & Country Club ALVOR 524

Alton Golf Club ALTON 74

Altrincham Golf Club ALTRINCHAM 250

Alva Golf Club ALVA 393

Alvaston Hall Golf Club NANTWICH 228

Alwoodley Golf Club LEEDS 295

Alyth Golf Club BLAIRGOWRIE 384

Amarante Golf Clube, Quinta da Deveza AMARANTE 530

Amida Golf Course & Teaching Academy TWICKENHAM 128

Ampfield Golf Club AMPFIELD 74

Andover Golf Club ANDOVER 74

Anglesey Golf Club Ltd RHOSNEIGR 406

Anjou Golf and Country Club ANGERS 510

Annanhill Golf Club KILMARNOCK 330

Anoreta Golf RINCON DE LA VICTORIA 535

Anstruther Golf Club ANSTRUTHER 357

Ansty Golf Centre COVENTRY 209

Antrobus Golf Club NORTHWICH 230

Aphrodite Hills Golf Club PAPHOS 539

Appleby Golf Club APPLEBY 233

Aqualate Golf Centre NEWPORT 194

Aqualate Golf Centre NEWPORT 569

Aquarius Golf Club SOUTHWARK 64
Arbroath Golf Course ARBROATH 322
Arcangues Golf d' BIARRITZ 515
Arcot Hall Golf Club Ltd. NEWCASTLE UPON TYNE 268
Ardee Golf Club ARDEE 484
Ardeer Golf Club STEVENSTON 332
Ardglass Golf Club ARDGLASS 451
Arkley Golf Club BARNET 145
Army Golf Club ALDERSHOT 74
Aroeira Golf AROEIRA 527
Arrowe Park Golf Course BIRKENHEAD 259
Arscott Golf Club SHREWSBURY 196
Ashbourne Golf Club ASHBOURNE 486
Ashbourne Golf Club Ltd ASHBOURNE 164
Ashburnham Golf Club LLANELLI 414
Ashbury Hotel OKEHAMPTON 34
Ashby Decoy Golf Club SCUNTHORPE 180
Ashfield Golf Club CULLYHANNA 450
Ashford (Kent) Golf Club ASHFORD 84
Ashford Great Chart Golf & Leisure Complex ASHFORD 84, 565
Ashford Manor Golf Club ASHFORD 124
Ashley Wood Golf Club BLANDFORD 38
Ashridge Golf Club BERKHAMSTED 145
Ashton & Lea Golf Club Ltd. PRESTON 247
Ashton-in-Makerfield Golf Club Ltd ASHTON-IN-MAKERFIELD 250
Ashton-on-Mersey Golf Club SALE 256
Ashton-Under-Lyne Golf Club ASHTON-UNDER-LYNE 250
Ashwoods Golf Centre ENNISKILLEN 580
Askernish Golf Club LOCHBOISDALE 398
Aspley Guise and Woburn Sands Golf Club ASPLEY GUISE 130
Astbury Golf Club CONGLETON 226 - 227
Aston Wood Golf Club SUTTON COLDFIELD 212
Atalaya Golf & Country Club ESTEPONA 534
Athenry Golf Club ATHENRY 473
Atherstone Golf Club ATHERSTONE 203
Athlone Golf Club ATHLONE 489
Auchenblae Golf Course AUCHENBLAE 312
Auchmill Golf Club ABERDEEN 308
Auchterarder Golf Club AUCHTERARDER 384
Auchterderran Golf Club CARDENDEN 357
Austin Lodge Golf Club EYNSFORD 87
Axe Cliff Golf Club AXMOUTH 30
Aylesbury Park Golf Club AYLESBURY 69, 560

Aylesbury Vale Golf Club LEIGHTON BUZZARD 131
Aylesbury Vale Golf Club LEIGHTON BUZZARD 559

Baberton Golf Club EDINBURGH 349
Backworth Golf Club SHIREMOOR 272
Bacup Golf Club BACUP 243
Baden Golf de AURAY 510
Badgemore Park Golf Club HENLEY-ON-THAMES 97
Baildon Golf Club BRADFORD 290
Bakewell Golf Club BAKEWELL 164
Bala Golf Club BALA 404
Balbirnie Park Golf Club MARKINCH 362
Balbriggan Golf Club BALBRIGGAN 468
Balcarrick Golf Club DONABATE 469
Balfron Golf Society BALFRON 393
Balgove Course ST ANDREWS 362
Ballachulish House Golf Course BALLACHULISH 326
Ballards Gore Golf and Country Club ROCHFORD 143
Ballater Golf Club BALLATER 312
Ballina Golf Club BALLINA 485
Ballinamore Golf Club BALLINAMORE 482
Ballinasloe Golf Club BALLINASLOE 473
Ballinrobe Golf Club BALLINROBE 485
Ballochmyle Golf Club MAUCHLINE 331
Ballumbie Castle Golf Club DUNDEE 322, 576
Ballybunion Golf Club BALLYBUNION 475
Ballycastle Golf Club BALLYCASTLE 447
Ballyclare Golf Club BALLYCLARE 447
Ballyearl Golf and Leisure Centre NEWTOWNABBEY 449, 580
Ballykisteen Golf and Country Club MONARD 492
Ballyliffin Golf Club BALLYLIFFIN 466
Ballymena Golf Club BALLYMENA 447
Ballymote Golf Club BALLYMOTE 490
Balmoral Golf Club Ltd BELFAST 451
Balmore Golf Club GLASGOW 365
Balnagask Golf Course ABERDEEN 308
Baltinglass Golf Club BALTINGLASS 496
Bamburgh Castle Golf Club BAMBURGH 265
Banbridge Golf Club BANBRIDGE 451
Banbury Golf Club BANBURY 96
Banchory Golf Club BANCHORY 314
Bandon Golf Club BANDON 462

Bangor Golf Club BANGOR 451

Bangsai Country Club AYUTTHAYA 555

Bannel Golf Driving Range CHESTER 578

Banstead Downs Golf Club SUTTON 108

Bantry Bay Golf Club BANTRY 462

Bargoed Golf Club BARGOED 422

Barkway Park Golf Club BARKWAY 145

Barlaston Golf Club BARLASTON 198

Barnard Castle Golf Club BARNARD CASTLE 239

Barnehurst Public Pay & Play Golf Course BEXLEYHEATH 63

Barnham Broom Hotel & Golf Club NORWICH 154

Barnsley Golf Club BARNSLEY 285

Baron Hill Golf Club ANGLESEY 402

Barrow Golf Club BARROW-IN-FURNESS 233

Barrow Hills Golf Club CHERTSEY 101

Barshaw Golf Club PAISLEY 391

Barton-on-Sea Golf Club BARTON-ON-SEA 75

Basildon Golf Club BASILDON 137

Basingstoke Golf Club BASINGSTOKE 75

Batalha Golf Course SAO MIGUEL 530

Batchwood Golf and Tennis Centre ST. ALBANS 149

Batchworth Park Golf Club RICKMANSWORTH 148

Bath Golf Club BATH 51

Bathgate Golf Club BATHGATE 348

Battle Golf Club BATTLE 111

Baux de Provence Golf des LES BAUX 518

Bawburgh Golf Club NORWICH 154

Bawtry Golf Club DONCASTER 285, 575

Baxenden & District Golf Club BAXENDEN 243

Beacon Park Golf and Country Club UPHOLLAND 248

Beaconsfield Golf Club BEACONSFIELD 69

Beadlow Manor Hotel, Golf & Country Club BEADLOW 130

Beamish Park Golf Club BEAMISH 239

Bearsden Golf Club GLASGOW 365

Bearsted Golf Club MAIDSTONE 89

Bearwood Golf Club SINDLESHAM 68

Bearwood Lakes Golf Club WOKINGHAM 68

Beau Desert Golf Club CANNOCK 198

Beauchief Golf Club SHEFFIELD 287

Beaufort Golf Club KILLARNEY 476

Beauport Park Golf Course Ltd HASTINGS 113

Beaverstown Golf Club DONABATE 469

Beccles Golf Club BECCLES 158

Beckenham Place Park Golf Club BECKENHAM 84

Bedale Golf Club BEDALE 277

Bedford and County Golf Club BEDFORD 130

Bedford Golf Club BEDFORD 130

Bedfordshire Golf Club BEDFORD 130

Bedlingtonshire Golf Club BEDLINGTON 265

Beech Park Golf Club RATHCOOLE 472

Beedles Lake Golf Centre EAST GOSCOTE 170

Beeston Fields Golf Club NOTTINGHAM 190

Beith Golf Club BEITH 329

Belas Clube de Campo BELAS 527

Belfairs Golf Club LEIGH-ON-SEA 141

Belford BELFORD 265

Belfry WISHAW 215

Belhus Park Golf Club OCKENDON 142

Belleisle Golf Course AYR 329

Bellingham Golf Club BELLINGHAM 266

Bellshill Golf Club BELLSHILL 379

Belmont Lodge and Golf BELMONT 168

Belton Park Golf Club GRANTHAM 177

Belturbet Golf Club BELTURBET 458

Belvoir Park Golf Club BELFAST 451

Ben Rhydding Golf Club ILKLEY 294

Benone Golf Course LIMAVADY 455

Bentham Golf Club BENTHAM 277

Bentley Golf Club BRENTWOOD 137

Benton Hall Golf Club WITHAM 144

Berehaven Golf Club and Amenity Park CASTLETOWNBERE 462

Berkhamsted Golf Club BERKHAMSTED 145

Berkshire Golf Club ASCOT 65

Berwick Upon Tweed (Goswick Golf Club) BERWICK-UPON-TWEED 266

Best Western Ufford Park Hotel Golf & Spa WOODBRIDGE 159

Betchworth Park Golf Club DORKING 103

Betws-y-Coed Golf Club BETWS-Y-COED 407

Beverley and East Riding Golf Club BEVERLEY 273

Bexley Heath Golf Club BEXLEYHEATH 84

Biarritz Le Phare Golf de BIARRITZ 515

Bicester Golf & Country Club BICESTER 96

Bidford Grange Golf Club BIDFORD 203

Bidston Golf Club Ltd BIDSTON 259

Bigbury Golf Club Ltd. BIGBURY 30

Biggar Golf Club BIGGAR 379

Billingham Golf Club BILLINGHAM 239

Bingley (St. Ives) Golf Club BINGLEY 290

Birch Grove Golf Club COLCHESTER 139

Birch Hall Golf Club CHESTERFIELD 165

Birchwood Golf Club WARRINGTON 232

Birchwood Park Golf Centre DARTFORD 86, 566

Bird Hills (UK) Ltd MAIDENHEAD 66, 560

Birley Wood Golf Club SHEFFIELD 287

Birr Golf Club BIRR 489

Birtley Golf Club BIRTLEY 270

Bishop Auckland Golf Club BISHOP AUCKLAND 239

Bishopbriggs Golf Club BISHOPBRIGGS 365

Bishop's Stortford Golf Club BISHOP'S STORTFORD 145

Bishopshire Golf Club KINNESSWOOD 388

Bishopswood Golf Club BASINGSTOKE 75

Blaby Golf Centre BLABY 170

Black Bush Golf Club DUNSHAUGHLIN 486

Blackburn Golf Centre and Driving Range BLACKBURN 567

Blackburn Golf Club BLACKBURN 243

Blackley Golf Club MANCHESTER 253

Blacklion Golf Club BLACKLION 458

Blackmoor Golf Club BORDON 76

Blacknest Golf & Country Club ALTON 74

Blackpool North Shore Golf Club BLACKPOOL 244

Blackpool Park Golf Club BLACKPOOL 244

Blackwater Valley Golf Course YATELEY 110

Blackwell Golf Club BLACKWELL 217

Blackwell Grange Golf Club DARLINGTON 240

Blackwood Golf Centre BANGOR 451

Blackwood Golf Club BLACKWOOD 423

Blainroe Golf Club BLAINROE 496

Blair Atholl Golf Club BLAIR ATHOLL 384

Blairbeth Golf Club GLASGOW 365

Blairgowrie Golf Club BLAIRGOWRIE 384

Blairmore and Strone Golf Club DUNOON 326

Blankney Golf Club BLANKNEY 175

Bletchingley Golf Club BLETCHINGLEY 100

Bloxwich Golf Club (1988) Ltd WALSALL 214

Blue Canyon Country Club PHUKET 554

Blue Green Golf d'Ardree TOURS 513

Blue Mountain Golf Centre BINFIELD 65, 559

Blundells Hill Golf Club RAINHILL 262

Blyth Golf Club Ltd. BLYTH 266

Boat of Garten Golf and Tennis Club BOAT OF GARTEN 375

Boavista Golf Resort LAGOS 525

Boca Raton Resort & Club BOCA RATON 544

Bodenstown Golf Club SALLINS 481

Bognor Regis Golf Club BOGNOR REGIS 116

Boldmere Golf Club SUTTON COLDFIELD 212

Boldon Golf Club Ltd. EAST BOLDON 270

Bolton Golf Club Ltd. BOLTON 250

Bolton Old Links Golf Club Ltd BOLTON 250

Bolton Open Golf Course BOLTON 244

Bon Accord Golf Club ABERDEEN 308

Bonar Bridge-Ardgay Golf Club BONAR BRIDGE 370

Bondhay Golf Club WORKSOP 192

Bonnybridge Golf Club FALKIRK 394

Bonnyton Golf Club GLASGOW 365

Boothferry Golf Club HOWDEN 274

Bootle Golf Club BOOTLE 260

Borris Golf Club BORRIS 458

Borth and Ynyslas Golf Club Ltd BORTH 415

Bossey Golf and Country Club de ST JULIEN 514

Boston Golf Club. BOSTON 175

Boston West Golf Club BOSTON 175

Bothwell Castle Golf Club GLASGOW 365

Botley Park Golf Club SOUTHAMPTON 81

Boughton Golf Club FAVERSHAM 87

Bovey Castle MORETONHAMPSTEAD 33

Bowenhurst Golf Centre Ltd CRONDALL 102

Bowood Golf and Country Club CALNE 57, 573

Bowood Park Hotel & Golf Course CAMELFORD 22

Bowring Municipal HUYTON 261

Boxmoor Golf Club HEMEL HEMPSTEAD 147

Boyce Hill Golf Club Ltd SOUTH BENFLEET 143

Bracken Ghyll Golf Club ILKLEY 294

Brackenwood Golf Club WIRRAL 264

Brackley Golf Club SALFORD 257

Bradford Golf Club GUISELEY 292

Bradford Moor Golf Club BRADFORD 290

Bradford-On-Avon Golf Course Ltd TROWBRIDGE 60

Bradley Park Municipal Golf Course HUDDERSFIELD 293

Braehead Golf Club ALLOA 393

Braemar Golf Club BRAEMAR 314

Braeside Golf Club BECKENHAM 84

Braid Hills Golf Centre EDINBURGH 349, 577

Brailes Golf Club Ltd BRAILES 203

Brailsford Golf Centre BRAILSFORD 164, 562

Braintree Golf Club BRAINTREE 137

Bramall Park Golf Club STOCKPORT 257

Bramcote Hills Golf Course BRAMCOTE 188

Bramcote Waters Golf Course NUNEATON 204

Bramhall Golf Club STOCKPORT 257

Bramley Golf Club GUILDFORD 104

Brampton Golf Club BRAMPTON 234, 562

Brampton Heath Golf Centre CHURCH BRAMPTON 568

Brampton Heath Golf Centre NORTHAMPTON 184, 568

Brampton Park Golf Club HUNTINGDON 134

Bramshaw Golf Club LYNDHURST 78

Brancepeth Castle Golf Club BRANCEPETH 239

Brandhall olf Club BIRMINGHAM 207

Bransford Golf Club BRANSFORD 217

Branshaw Golf Club KEIGHLEY 294

Branston Golf & Country Club BURTON-ON-TRENT 198

Braxted Park Golf Club WITHAM 144

Bray Golf Club BRAY 496

Brayton Park Golf Club ASPATRIA 233

Brean Golf Club at Brean Leisure Park BURNHAM-ON-SEA 53

Brechin Golf and Squash Club BRECHIN 322

Brecon Golf Club BRECON 420

Breightmet Golf Club BOLTON 251

Brent Valley Golf Club HANWELL 126

Brest Iroise Golf de BREST 511

Brett Vale Golf Club RAYDON 160

Brickendon Grange Golf Club HERTFORD 147

Brickhampton Court Golf Complex CHURCHDOWN 45, 564

Bridge of Allan Golf Club STIRLING 395

Bridgend & District Golf Club LINLITHGOW 354

Bridgnorth Golf Club BRIDGNORTH 193

Bridlington Golf Club BRIDLINGTON 273

Bridlington Links BRIDLINGTON 273

Bridport & West Dorset Golf Club BRIDPORT 38

Briggens House Golf Club WARE 150

Brighouse Bay Golf Club & Driving Range KIRKCUDBRIGHT 340

Bright Castle Golf Club DOWNPATRICK 452

Brighton and Hove Golf Club BRIGHTON 111

Bristol and Clifton Golf Club BRISTOL 43

Broadstone (Dorset) Golf Club BROADSTONE 38

Broadwater Park Golf Club GODALMING 571

Broadway Golf Club BROADWAY 44

Brocket Hall Golf Club WELWYN GARDEN CITY 150

Brockley Hill Golf Park STANMORE 128

Brockley Hill Golf Park STANMORE 559

Brocton Hall Golf Club STAFFORD 199

Brodick Golf Club BRODICK 334

Broke Hill Golf Club HALSTEAD 88

Brokenhurst Manor Golf Club BROCKENHURST 76

Bromborough Golf Club BROMBOROUGH 260

Bromley Golf Centre BROMLEY 63

Bromsgrove Golf Centre BROMSGROVE 218

Bromsgrove Golf Centre WORCESTER 574

Brookdale Golf Club Ltd. MANCHESTER 253

Brookmans Park Golf Club HATFIELD 147

Broome Manor Golf Complex SWINDON 60, 574

Broome Park Golf club CANTERBURY 85

Broomieknowe Golf Club Ltd BONNYRIGG 348

Brora Golf Club BRORA 370

Brough Golf Club BROUGH 273

Broughty Golf Club MONIFIETH 324

Brown Trout Golf and Country Club COLERAINE 454

Brucefields Family Golf Centre STIRLING 395

Brunston Castle Golf Course DAILLY 329, 576

Bruntsfield Links Golfing Society Ltd EDINBURGH 349

Bryn Meadows Golf Club HENGOED 427

Bryn Morfydd Hotel Golf Club DENBIGH 408

Brynhill (Barry) Golf Club BARRY 422

Buchanan Castle Golf Club GLASGOW 366

Buckingham Golf Club BUCKINGHAM 70

Buckinghamshire Golf Club DENHAM 70

Buckpool Golf Club (Buckie) BUCKIE 315

Bude and North Cornwall Golf Club BUDE 21

Budock Vean Golf and Country House Hotel FALMOUTH 22

Builth Wells Golf Club BUILTH WELLS 420

Bulbury Woods Golf Club POOLE, Near 40

Bull Bay Golf Club Ltd. ANGLESEY 402, 578

Bullpits Golf COurse BOURTON 38

Bulwell Forest Golf Club BULWELL 188

Buncrana Golf Club BUNCRANA 466

Bundoran Golf Club BUNDORAN 466

Bungay and Waveney Valley Golf Club BUNGAY 158

Bunsay Downs Golf Club MALDON 141

Burford Golf Club BURFORD 96

Burgess Hill Golf Academy BURGESS HILL 116, 572

Burgham Park Golf & Leisure Club MORPETH 267

Burghill Valley Golf Club HEREFORD 168
Burghley Park (Stamford) Golf Club STAMFORD 182
Burhill Golf Club WALTON-ON-THAMES 108
Burley Golf Club RINGWOOD 80
Burnham and Berrow Golf Club BURNHAM-ON-SEA 53
Burnham Beeches Golf Club BURNHAM 70
Burnham-on-Crouch Golf Club Ltd BURNHAM-ON-CROUCH 138
Burning Ridge Golf Course MYRTLE BEACH 545
Burnley Golf Club BURNLEY 244
Burntisland Golf House Club BURNTISLAND 357
Burslem Golf Club Ltd. STOKE-ON-TRENT 200
Burstead Golf club LITTLE BURSTEAD 141
Burton-on-Trent Golf Club BURTON-ON-TRENT 164
Bury Golf Club BURY 252
Bury St. Edmunds Golf Club BURY ST. EDMUNDS 158
Bush Hill Park Golf Club WINCHMORE HILL 129
Bushey Country Club BUSHEY 146
Bushey Hall Golf Club BUSHEY 146
Bushfoot Golf Club PORTBALLINTRAE 449
Bute Golf Club ISLE OF BUTE 327
Buxton and High Peak Golf Club BUXTON 164

Caddington Golf Club CADDINGTON 131
Cadmore Lodge Golf & Country Club TENBURY WELLS 220
Caen Golf de CAEN 509
Caerleon Public Golf Course CAERLEON 423
Caerphilly Golf Club CAERPHILLY 423
Cahir Park Golf Club CAHIR 491
Caird Park Golf Club DUNDEE 322
Cairndhu Golf Club Ltd. LARNE 448
Calcot Park Golf Club READING 67
Caldecott Hall Golf Club & Hotel GREAT YARMOUTH 153
Calderbraes Golf Club UDDINGSTON 381
Calderfields Golf Club WALSALL 214
Caldwell Golf Club UPLAWMOOR 391
Caldy Golf Club Ltd CALDY 260
Caledonian Golf Club ABERDEEN 308
Callan Golf Club CALLAN 481
Callander Golf Club CALLANDER 386
Cally Palace Hotel GATEHOUSE OF FLEET 340
Calverley Golf Club LEEDS 295
Camberley Heath Golf Club CAMBERLEY 100

Cambridge Golf Club CAMBRIDGE 133, 560
Cambridge National Golf CAMBRIDGE 133
Cambuslang Golf Club GLASGOW 366
Came Down Golf Club DORCHESTER 39
Camperdown Golf Club DUNDEE 323
Campo De Golf Vilamartin ORIHUELA 538
Campo de Golfe da Madeira MADEIRA 529
Campo Real TORRES VEDRAS 529
Campsie Golf Club LENNOXTOWN 394
Cams Hall Estate Golf Club FAREHAM 77
Canford Magna Golf Club WIMBORNE 42
Canford School Golf Club WIMBORNE 42
Canmore Golf Club DUNFERMLINE 359
Cannes-Mandelieu Golf Club de CANNES 518
Cannes-Mougins Golf Country Club de CANNES 518
Cannington Golf Course BRIDGWATER 52
Cannock Park Golf Club CANNOCK 198
Canons Brook Golf Club HARLOW 140
Canterbury Golf Club CANTERBURY 85
Canwick Park Golf Club LINCOLN 178
Cap d'Agde Golf du AGDE 517
Cape Cornwall Golf and Country Club PENZANCE 26
Caprington Golf Club KILMARNOCK 330
Carden Park Hotel, Golf Resort and Spa CHESTER 226, 561
Cardiff Golf Club CARDIFF 423
Cardigan Golf Club CARDIGAN 415
Cardross Golf Club CARDROSS 347
Carholme Golf Club LINCOLN 178
Carlisle Golf Club CARLISLE 234
Carlow Golf Club CARLOW 458
Carluke Golf Club CARLUKE 379
Carlyon Bay Hotel Golf Course CARLYON BAY 22
Carmarthen Golf Club CARMARTHEN 413
Carnalea Golf Club BANGOR 451
Carne Golf Links BELMULLET 485
Carnegie Golf Club at Skibo Castle DORNOCH 370
Carnoustie Golf Links CARNOUSTIE 322
Carnwath Golf Club CARNWATH 379
Carradale Golf Club CARRADALE 326
Carrbridge Golf Club CARRBRIDGE 376
Carrick Knowe Golf Course EDINBURGH 349
Carrickfergus Golf Club CARRICKFERGUS 448
Carrick-on-Shannon Golf Club CARRICK-ON-SHANNON 489
Carrick-on-Suir Golf Club CARRICK-ON-SUIR 491

Carswell Golf and Country Club FARINGDON 97

Carton House MAYNOOTH 480

Carus Green Golf Club KENDAL 235

Carvynick Golf and Country Club NEWQUAY 26

Casteljaloux Golf de CASTELJALOUX 516

Castell Heights Golf Club CAERPHILLY 423

Casterton Golf Course KIRKBY LONSDALE 236

Castle Barna Golf Club OFFALY 489

Castle Course ST ANDREWS 362

Castle Dargan Estate SLIGO 490

Castle Douglas Golf Club CASTLE DOUGLAS 338

Castle Eden Golf Club HARTLEPOOL 241

Castle Hawk Golf Club ROCHDALE 256, 568

Castle Hume Golf Club ENNISKILLEN 454

Castle Park Golf Club HADDINGTON 353

Castle Point Golf Club CANVEY ISLAND 138

Castle Royle Golf and Country Club READING 67

Castlebar Golf Club CASTLEBAR 485

Castleblayney Golf Club CASTLEBLAYNEY 488

Castlecomer Golf Club CASTLECOMER 481

Castlefields Golf Club BRIGHOUSE 291

Castlegregory Golf Club CASTLEGREGORY 475

Castlereagh Golf Club BELFAST 447

Castlerock Golf Club CASTLEROCK 454

Castletown Golf Links CASTLETOWN 502

Castletroy Golf Club CASTLETROY 483

Castlewarden Golf & Country Club STRAFFAN 481

Cathcart Castle Golf Club GLASGOW 366

Cathkin Braes Golf Club GLASGOW 366

Catterick Golf Club CATTERICK 278

Cave Castle Golf Club BROUGH 273

Cavendish Golf Club Ltd BUXTON 164

Cawder Golf Club GLASGOW 366

Cawdor Castle Golf Course CAWDOR CASTLE 376

Celtic Manor Resort NEWPORT 430

Central London Golf Centre WANDSWORTH 129

Chadwell Springs Golf Club WARE 150

Chalgrave Manor Golf Club TODDINGTON 132

Champ de Bataille Golf Club du NEUBOURG 510

Channels Golf Club CHELMSFORD 138

Chapel-en-le-Frith CHAPEL-EN-LE-FRITH 164

Charlesland Golf Club GREYSTONES 498

Charleton Golf Club COLINSBURGH 358

Charleville Golf Club CHARLEVILLE 462

Charminster Golf Club DORCHESTER 39

Charnock Richard Golf Club CHORLEY 244

Charnwood Forest Golf Club LOUGHBOROUGH 172

Chart Hills Golf Club ASHFORD 84

Chartham Park Golf Club EAST GRINSTEAD 118

Chartridge Park Golf Club CHESHAM 70

Chase Golf Club PENKRIDGE 199

Chateau de Cheverny Golf du CHEVERNY 513

Chateau des Sept Tours Golf du TOURS 513

Chateau des Vigiers Golf & Country Club DORDOGNE 516

Chateau L'Arc Golf International de AIX-EN-PROVENCE 517

Chatham Golf Centre CHATHAM 566

Cheadle Golf Club CHEADLE 225

Chedington Court Golf Club SOUTH PERROTT 41

Chelmsford Golf Club CHELMSFORD 138

Chelsfield Lakes Golf Centre ORPINGTON 90

Cherry Burton Golf Club BEVERLEY 273, 574

Cherry Lodge Golf Club BIGGIN HILL 84

Cherwell Edge Golf club BANBURY 96

Chesfield Downs Golf Club HITCHIN 147

Chesham and Ley Hill Golf Club CHESHAM 70

Cheshunt Golf Club WALTHAM CROSS 149

Chessington Golf Centre CHESSINGTON 101, 571

Chester Golf Club CHESTER 226

Chesterfield Golf Club Ltd. CHESTERFIELD 165

Chester-Le-Street Golf Club CHESTER-LE-STREET 239

Chesterton Valley Golf Club BRIDGNORTH 193

Chestfield (Whitstable) Golf Club WHITSTABLE 95

Chevin Golf Club DUFFIELD 166

Chiangmai Highlands Golf & Spa Resort CHIANGMAI 556

Chiangmai-Lamphun Golf Club CHIANGMAI 556

Chiberta Golf de ANGLET 515

Chichester Golf Club CHICHESTER 116, 572

Chiddingfold Golf Club CHIDDINGFOLD 101

Chigwell Golf Club CHIGWELL 139

Childwall Golf Club Ltd LIVERPOOL 261

Chiltern Forest Golf Club AYLESBURY 69

Chilwell Manor Golf Club NOTTINGHAM 190

Chilworth Golf Club SOUTHAMPTON 81, 564

China Fleet Country Club SALTASH 27, 562

Chingford Golf Club CHINGFORD 124

Chingford Golf Range CHINGFORD 559

Chippenham Golf Club CHIPPENHAM 57

Chipping Norton Golf Club CHIPPING NORTON 96

Chipping Sodbury Golf Club BRISTOL 43

Chipstead Golf Club Ltd CHIPSTEAD 101

Chirk Golf Club CHIRK 407

Chislehurst Golf Club CHISLEHURST 85

Chobham Golf Club WOKING 109

Chorley Golf Club CHORLEY 245

Chorleywood Golf Club Ltd. CHORLEYWOOD 146

Chorlton-cum-Hardy Golf Club MANCHESTER 253

Chulmleigh Golf Course CHULMLEIGH 30

Church Stretton Golf Club CHURCH STRETTON 193

Churchill & Blakedown Golf Club BLAKEDOWN 217

Churston Golf Club Ltd BRIXHAM 30

Cilgwyn Golf Club LAMPETER 416

Cirencester Golf Club CIRENCESTER 46

City of Coventry Brandon Wood Golf Course COVENTRY 203

City of Derry Golf Club PREHEN 455

City of Edinburgh Golf Club EDINBURGH 349

City Of Newcastle Golf Club NEWCASTLE UPON TYNE 271

City of Wakefield Golf Club WAKEFIELD 300

Clacton-on-Sea Golf Club CLACTON-ON-SEA 139

Clandeboye Golf Club NEWTOWNARDS 453

Clandon Regis Golf Club Ltd WEST CLANDON 109

Claremorris Golf Club CLAREMORRIS 485

Clayton Golf Club BRADFORD 290

Cleckheaton and District Golf Club Ltd CLECKHEATON 292

Cleethorpes Golf Club (1894) Ltd CLEETHORPES 176

Cleeve Hill Golf Club CHELTENHAM 45

Cleobury Mortimer Golf Club CLEOBURY MORTIMER 194

Clevedon Golf Club CLEVEDON 53

Cleveland Golf Club REDCAR 280

Cliftonville Golf Club BELFAST 447

Clitheroe Golf Club CLITHEROE 245

Clober Golf Club GLASGOW 366

Clones Golf Club CLONES 488

Clonlara Golf & Leisure CLONLARA 459

Clonmel Golf Club CLONMEL 491

Close House Country Club HEDDON ON THE WALL 270

Clovelly Golf Club FISH HOEK 547

Club at Mapledurham MAPLEDURHAM 98

Club De Golf Novo Sancti Petri CADIZ 535

Clwb Golff Abersoch ABERSOCH 402

Clwb Golff Ffestiniog FFESTINIOG 405

Clydebank & District Golf Club CLYDEBANK 347

Clydebank Municipal Golf Course CLYDEBANK 347

Clydeway Golf Centre UDDINGSTON 577

Clyne Golf Club SWANSEA 433

CMC Golf Club GUZELYURT 539

Co. Tipperary Golf & Country Club DUNDRUM 491

Cobh Golf Club COBH 462

Cobtree Manor Park Golf Club MAIDSTONE 89

Cochrane Castle Golf Club JOHNSTONE 391

Cockermouth Golf Club EMBLETON 234

Cocks Moors Woods Golf Club BIRMINGHAM 207

Coed-Y-Mwstwr Golf Club BRIDGEND 423

Cognac Golf du COGNAC 513

Colchester Golf Club COLCHESTER 139

Colchester Golf Range COLCHESTER 563

Cold Ashby Golf Club NORTHAMPTON 184

College Pines Golf Club WORKSOP 192

Collingtree Park Golf Course Ltd NORTHAMPTON 184 - 185

Colmworth and North Bedfordshire Golf Club COLMWORTH 131

Colnbrook Golf Range COLNBROOK 560

Colne Golf Club COLNE 245

Colne Valley Golf Club COLCHESTER 139

Colonsay Golf Club ISLE OF COLONSAY 396

Colvend Golf Club DALBEATTIE 338

Colville Park Golf Club MOTHERWELL 380

Colworth Golf Club SHARNBROOK 132

Comrie Golf Club CRIEFF 386

Concord Park Driving Range SHEFFIELD 575

Concord Park Municipal Golf Course SHEFFIELD 288

Congleton Golf Club CONGLETON 227

Connemara Golf Club CLIFDEN 474

Connemara Isles Golf Club ANNAGHVANE 473

Consett & District Golf Club Ltd CONSETT 240

Conwy (Caernarvonshire) Golf Club CONWY 408

Cooden Beach Golf Club BEXHILL-ON-SEA 111

Cookridge Hall Golf Club LEEDS 295

Coollattin Golf Club ARKLOW 496

Coombe Hill Golf Club KINGSTON-UPON-THAMES 105

Coombe Wood Golf Club KINGSTON-UPON-THAMES 105

Coosheen Golf CLub SCHULL 465

Copsewood Grange Golf Club COVENTRY 209

Copt Heath Golf Club SOLIHULL 210

Copthorne Golf Club CRAWLEY 117

Corballis Golf Links DONABATE 469

Corhampton Golf Club SOUTHAMPTON 81

Cork Golf Club LITTLE ISLAND 464

Corrie Golf Club CORRIE 334

Corrstown Golf Club KILSALLAGHAN 472

Corus (Port Talbot) PORT TALBOT 432

Cosby Golf Club COSBY 170

Costa Brava Golf Club GIRONA 536

Costessey Park Golf Course NORWICH 156

Cotgrave Place Golf & Country Club NOTTINGHAM 190, 569

Cotswold Edge Golf Club WOTTON-UNDER-EDGE 50

Cotswold Hills Golf Club CHELTENHAM 45

Cottesmore Golf & Country Club CRAWLEY 117

Cottingham Parks Golf and Country Club HULL 274

Cottrell Park Golf Club CARDIFF 423

Coulsdon Manor Hotel & Golf Centre COULSDON 101

Country Club Khao Yai NAKHON RATCHASIMA 557

County Armagh Golf Club ARMAGH 450

County Cavan Golf Club CAVAN 458

County Longford Golf Club LONGFORD 484

County Louth Golf Club DROGHEDA 484

County Sligo Golf Club ROSSES POINT 490

Coventry Golf Club COVENTRY 209

Coventry Hearsall Golf Club COVENTRY 209

Cowal Golf Club DUNOON 326

Cowdenbeath Golf Club COWDENBEATH 358

Cowdray Park Golf Club COWDRAY PARK 117

Cowes Golf Club COWES 83

Cowglen Golf Club GLASGOW 366

Coxmoor Golf Club MANSFIELD 189

Craddockstown Golf Club NAAS 480

Cradoc Golf Club CRADOC 420, 579

Craggan Golf Club GRANTOWN-ON-SPEY 317

Craibstone Golf Centre BUCKSBURN 315

Craigavon Golf and Ski Club CRAIGAVON 450, 580

Craigentinny Golf Course EDINBURGH 349

Craigie Hill Golf Club (1982) Ltd PERTH 389

Craigieknowes Golf Club KIPPFORD 340

Craigielaw Golf Club ABERLADY 348

Craigmillar Park Golf Club EDINBURGH 350

Craignure Golf Club CRAIGNURE 397

Crail Golfing Society CRAIL 358

Crane Valley Golf Club VERWOOD 41

Cranfield Golf at Sandown ESHER 104

Cranford Golf Centre STOCKPORT 561

Cranleigh Golf & Leisure Club CRANLEIGH 101

Cray Valley Golf Club ORPINGTON 90

Craythorne, The BURTON-ON-TRENT 198, 570

Creigiau Golf Club CARDIFF 423

Cretingham Golf Club FRAMLINGHAM 159

Crewe Golf Club Ltd CREWE 227

Crews Hill Golf Club (1920) Ltd ENFIELD 125

Criccieth Golf Club CRICCIETH 404

Crichton Golf Club DUMFRIES 338

Cricklade Hotel & Country Club CRICKLADE 58

Crieff Golf Club CRIEFF 386

Crimple Valley Golf Club HARROGATE 278

Croham Hurst Golf Club CROYDON 102

Crompton and Royton Golf Club Ltd OLDHAM 256

Crondon Park Golf Club STOCK 144

Crook Golf Club CROOK 240

Crookhill Park (Municipal) Golf Club DONCASTER 285

Crosland Heath Golf Club Ltd HUDDERSFIELD 293

Crow Nest Park Golf Club BRIGHOUSE 291

Crow Wood Golf Club GLASGOW 366

Crowborough Beacon Golf Club CROWBOROUGH 112

Croydon Driving Range Ltd CROYDON 571

Cruden Bay Golf Club CRUDEN BAY 315

Cruit Island Golf Club KINCASSLAGH 467

Crystal Bay Golf Club CHONBURI 557

Cuckfield Golf Centre CUCKFIELD 117

Cuddington (Banstead) Golf Club Ltd BANSTEAD 100

Culcrieff Golf Club CRIEFF 386

Cullen Golf Club CULLEN 316

Cumberwell Park Golf Club BRADFORD-ON-AVON 57

Cupar Golf Club CUPAR 358

Curragh Golf Club CURRAGH 480

Cushendall Golf Club CUSHENDALL 448

Cwmrhydneuadd Golf Club LLANDYSUL 416

Dainton Park Golf Club NEWTON ABOTT 34

Dalbeattie Golf Club DALBEATTIE 338

Dale Hill Golf Club WADHURST 115

Dalmally Golf Club DALMALLY 326

Dalmilling Golf Course AYR 329

Dalmunzie Golf Course BLAIRGOWRIE 384

Dalston Hall Golf Club Holiday Park CARLISLE 234

Dalziel Park Golf & Country Club MOTHERWELL 380

Darenth Valley Golf Course Ltd SEVENOAKS 91

Darlington Golf Club (Members) Ltd DARLINGTON 240

Dartford Golf Club Ltd DARTFORD 86

Dartmouth Golf & Country Club DARTMOUTH 31

Dartmouth Golf Club WEST BROMWICH 214

Darwen Golf Club DARWEN 245

Datchet Golf Club SLOUGH 68

Davenport Golf Club POYNTON 230

Daventry and District Golf Club DAVENTRY 184

Davyhulme Park Golf Club DAVYHULME 252

Dawn Till Dusk Golf Club MILFORD HAVEN 417

De Vere Belton Woods Hotel GRANTHAM 177

De Vere Dunston Hall NORWICH 156

De Vere Heron's Reach Golf Club BLACKPOOL 244, 567

De Vere Mottram Hall Golf Course PRESTBURY 230

De Vere Slaley Hall Hotel Golf Resort & Spa NEWCASTLE UPON TYNE 268

Dean Wood Golf Club UPHOLLAND 249

Deane Golf Club BOLTON 251

Deangate Ridge Golf Club DEANGATE 86

Deanwood Park Golf Club NEWBURY 66

Deauville Golf de DEAUVILLE 509

Deer Park Golf & Country Club LIVINGSTON 354

Deer Park Golf Hotel & Spa DUBLIN 470

Deeside Golf Club ABERDEEN 308

Delamere Forest Golf Club NORTHWICH 230

Delapre Golf Centre NORTHAMPTON 185, 568

Delgany Golf Club DELGANY 497

Denbigh Golf Club DENBIGH 408

Denham Golf Club DENHAM 70

Denton Golf Club DENTON 252

Derby Golf Club DERBY 166

Dereham Golf Club DEREHAM 152

Derllys Court Golf Club CARMARTHEN 414

Desert Dunes NORTH PALM SPRINGS 546

Desert Falls Country Club PALM DESERT 546

Dewlands Manor Golf Course ROTHERFIELD 114

Dewsbury District Golf Club MIRFIELD 298

Dewstow Golf Club CHEPSTOW 426, 579

Dibden Golf Centre DIBDEN 77

Didsbury Golf Club Ltd MANCHESTER 253

Dinas Powis Golf Club DINAS POWIS 426

Dingle Golf Links/Ceann Sibeal BALLYFERRITER 475

Dinsdale Spa Golf Club DARLINGTON 240

Discovery Golf & Leisure COALVILLE 567

Disley Golf Club Ltd DISLEY 227

Diss Golf Club DISS 152

Diss Golf Club DISS 158

Dolgellau Golf Club DOLGELLAU 405

Dollar Golf Club DOLLAR 393

Donabate Golf Club BALCARRICK 468

Donaghadee Golf Club DONAGHADEE 452

Doncaster Golf Club DONCASTER 285

Doncaster Town Moor Golf Club DONCASTER 286

Donegal Golf Club DONEGAL 466

Doneraile Golf Club DONERAILE 462

Donnington Grove Country Club NEWBURY 66

Donnington Valley Hotel & Golf Club NEWBURY 67

Dooks Golf Links GLENBEIGH 475

Doon Valley Golf Club PATNA 331

Doonbeg Golf Club DOONBEG 459

Dora Golf Course COWDENBEATH 358

Dore and Totley Golf Club SHEFFIELD 288

Dorking Golf Club DORKING 103

Dorset & Golf Country Club WAREHAM 41

Douglas Golf Club DOUGLAS 462

Douglas Park Golf Club GLASGOW 366

Douglas Valley Golf Club BOLTON 244

Douglas Water Golf Club DOUGLAS WATER 379

Down Royal Park Golf Course MAZE 449

Downes Crediton Golf Club CREDITON 31

Downfield Golf Club DUNDEE 323

Downpatrick Golf Club DOWNPATRICK 452

Downshire Golf Complex WOKINGHAM 560

Drayton Park Golf Club TAMWORTH 201

Drayton Park Golf Course DRAYTON 97, 569

Driffield Golf Club DRIFFIELD 274

Drift Golf Club EAST HORSLEY 103

Droitwich Golf & Country Club Ltd DROITWICH 218

Dromoland Castle Golf & Country Club NEWMARKET-ON-FERGUS 460

Druids Glen Golf club NEWTOWNMOUNTKENNEDY 498

Druids Heath Golf club NEWTOWNMOUNTKENNEDY 498

Druids Heath Golf Club WALSALL 214

Drumoig Hotel & Golf Resort ST ANDREWS 362

Drumpellier Golf Club COATBRIDGE 379

Dubai Creek Golf and Yacht Club DUBAI 549

Dublin City Golf Club DUBLIN 470

Duddingston Golf Club Ltd EDINBURGH 350

Dudley Golf Club LIVERPOOL 262

Dudley Golf Club Ltd DUDLEY 210

Dudmoor Farm Golf Course CHRISTCHURCH 38

Dudsbury Golf Club FERNDOWN 39

Duff House Royal Golf Club BANFF 314

Dufftown Golf Club DUFFTOWN 316

Duke's ST ANDREWS 362

Dukes Meadows Golf Club LONDON 127, 559

Dukinfield Golf Club DUKINFIELD 252

Dullatur Golf Club GLASGOW 367

Dulwich & Sydenham Hill Golf Club DULWICH 63

Dumbarton Golf Club DUMBARTON 347

Dumfries & Galloway Golf Club DUMFRIES 339

Dumfries and County Golf Club DUMFRIES 339

Dummer Golf Club BASINGSTOKE 76

Dun Laoghaire Golf Club DUN LAOGHAIRE 470

Dunaverty Golf Club SOUTHEND 328

Dunbar Golf Club DUNBAR 349

Dunblane New Golf Club DUNBLANE 387

Dundalk Golf Club DUNDALK 484

Dundas Parks Golf Club SOUTH QUEENSFERRY 356

Dunfanaghy Golf Club DUNFANAGHY 466

Dunfermline Golf Club DUNFERMLINE 359

Dungannon Golf Club DUNGANNON 456

Dungarvan Golf Club DUNGARVAN 492

Dunham Forest Golf & Country Club ALTRINCHAM 250

Dunham Golf Club SWAFFHAM 157

Dunkeld & Birnam Golf Club DUNKELD 387

Dunloe Golf Club KILLARNEY 476

Dunmore East Golf Club DUNMORE EAST 492

Dunmurry Golf Club BELFAST 448

Dunnerholme Golf Club ASKAM-IN-FURNESS 233

Dunnikier Park Golf Club KIRKCALDY 360

Dunning Golf Club DUNNING 387

Duns Golf Club DUNS 335

Dunscar Golf Club Ltd. BOLTON 251

Dunstable Downs Golf Club DUNSTABLE 131

Dunstanburgh Castle Golf Club EMBLETON 266

Dunwood Manor Golf Club ROMSEY 81

Durham City Golf Club DURHAM 241

Durness Golf Club DURNESS 370

Duxbury Park Golf Club (Municipal) CHORLEY 245

Dyke Golf Club BRIGHTON 111

Eagles Golf club KING'S LYNN 154

Eaglescliffe Golf Club Ltd EAGLESCLIFFE 241

Ealing Golf Club GREENFORD 125

Ealing Golf Range LONDON 559

Earlsferry Thistle Golf Club ELIE 359

Earlswood Golf Club NEATH 428

Easingwold Golf Club EASINGWOLD 278

East Aberdeenshire Golf Centre BALMEDIE 312

East Berkshire Golf Club CROWTHORNE 66

East Bierley Golf Club BRADFORD 290

East Brighton Golf Club BRIGHTON 111

East Cork Golf Club MIDLETON 465

East Devon Golf Club BUDLEIGH SALTERTON 30

East Herts Golf Club Ltd BUNTINGFORD 146

East Kilbride Golf Club GLASGOW 367

East Renfrewshire Golf Club GLASGOW 367

East Sussex National Golf Club UCKFIELD 115

Eastbourne Downs Golf Club EASTBOURNE 112

Eastbourne Golfing Park EASTBOURNE 112

Easter Moffat Golf Club AIRDRIE 379

Eastern Star Country Club & Resort RAYONG 558

Eastham Lodge Golf Club EASTHAM 260

Eastwood Golf Club GLASGOW 367

Eaton (Norwich) Golf Club NORWICH 156

Eaton Golf Club CHESTER 226

Eccleston Park Golf Club RAINHILL 263

Eden Course ST ANDREWS 364

Eden Golf Course CARLISLE 234, 562

Edenderry Golf Club EDENDERRY 489

Edenmore Golf & Country Club CRAIGAVON 450

Edgbaston Golf Club Ltd BIRMINGHAM 207

Edmondstown Golf Club DUBLIN 470

Edrich Driving Range and Old Nene Golf & Country Club HUNTINGDON 560

Edwalton Golf Courses EDWALTON 188

Edzell Golf Club EDZELL 323
Effingham Golf Club EFFINGHAM 103
Effingham Park Golf Club EFFINGHAM 118
El Bosque Club de Golf CHIVA 537
El Paraiso Golf Club ESTEPONA 534
El Saler Campo de Golf VALENCIA 538
Elderslie Golf Club ELDERSLIE 391
Elemore Golf Course HUTTON-LE-HOLE 270
Elfordleigh Hotel Golf & Leisure PLYMOUTH 34
Elgin Golf Club ELGIN 316
Elland Golf Club ELLAND 292
Ellesborough Golf Club AYLESBURY 69
Ellesmere Golf Club MANCHESTER 254
Ellesmere Port Golf Centre SOUTH WIRRAL 231
Elm Lodge Golf Course LUDLOW 194
Elm Park Golf and Sports Club DUBLIN 470
Elmwood CUPAR 359
Elsenham Golf Centre ELSENHAM 140
Elsham Golf Club BRIGG 176
Elstree Golf and Country Club ELSTREE 146
Eltham Warren Golf Club ELTHAM 63
Elton Furze Golf Club PETERBOROUGH 134
Ely City Golf Course Ltd. ELY 133
Emirates Golf Club DUBAI 549
Emporda Golf Club PALS 537
Enderby Golf Course ENDERBY 170
Enfield Golf Club ENFIELD 125
Enmore Park Golf Club BRIDGWATER 52
Enmore Park Golf Club ENMORE 54
Ennis Golf Club ENNIS 459
Enniscorthy Golf Club ENNISCORTHY 495
Enniscrone Golf Club ENNISCRONE 490
Enniskillen Golf Club ENNISKILLEN 454
Entry Hill Golf Club BATH 51
Enville Golf Club Ltd STOURBRIDGE 201
Epsom Golf Club EPSOM 103
Erewash Valley Golf Club Ltd ILKESTON 166
Erinvale Country Estate & Golf Course
SOMERSET WEST 547
Erlestoke Golf Club DEVIZES 58
Erskine Golf Club BISHOPTON 391
Escorpion Club de Golf BETERA 537
Esker Hills Golf Club TULLAMORE 489
Esporta (Dougalston Golf Club) GLASGOW 367
Essex Golf & Country Club COLCHESTER 140
Essex Golf & Country Club COLCHESTER 563
Estela Golf Club ESTELA 530
Estoril Golf Do ESTORIL 528
Etangs de Fiac Golf des LAVAUR 516

Etchinghill Golf Club ETCHINGHILL 87
European Club BRITTAS BAY 497
Europro Golf Centre BRISTOL 564
Euxton Park Golf Centre CHORLEY 245
Evesham Golf Club EVESHAM 218
Evian Masters Golf Club EVIAN 514
Exeter Golf & Country Club EXETER 32
Eyemouth Golf Club EYEMOUTH 335

Fairfield Golf and Sailing Club MANCHESTER
254
Fairhaven Golf Club LYTHAM ST ANNES 246
Fairlop Waters ILFORD 141
Fairlop Waters ILFORD 563
Fairways Driving Range INVERNESS 577
Fairwood Park Golf Club Ltd. SWANSEA 433
Faithlegg Golf Club WATERFORD 494
Fakenham Golf Club FAKENHAM 152
Falkirk Golf Club FALKIRK 394
Falkirk Tryst Golf Club LARBERT 394
Falkland Golf Club FALKLAND 359
Falmouth Golf Club FALMOUTH 22
Fancourt Golf & Country Club Estate GEORGE
547
Farleigh Court Golf Club WARLINGHAM 108
Farnham Golf Club Ltd FARNHAM 104
Farnham Park Pay and Play Golf Course SLOUGH
73
Farrington Golf & Country Club BATH/BRISTOL 52
Farthingstone Golf Club and Hotel TOWCESTER
186
Faversham Golf Club Ltd FAVERSHAM 87
Fawkham Valley Golf Club DARTFORD 86
Felixstowe Ferry Golf Club FELIXSTOWE 158
Feltwell Golf Club THETFORD 157
Fereneze Golf Club BARRHEAD 391
Fermoy Golf Club FERMOY 464
Ferndown Forest Golf Club FERNDOWN 40
Ferndown Golf Club FERNDOWN 39
Fernhill Golf & Country Club CARRIGALINE 462
Ferrybridge Golf Club KNOTTINGLEY 295
Filey Golf Club FILEY 278
Filton Golf Club BRISTOL 43
Finchley Golf Club. FINCHLEY 125
Fingle Glen Hotel, Golf & Country Club EXETER
32
Fintona Golf Club FINTONA 456
Fishwick Hall Golf Club PRESTON 247
Five Lakes Resort MALDON 142

Five Lakes Resort MALDON 563

Flackwell Heath Golf Club. HIGH WYCOMBE 71

Flamborough Head Golf Club BRIDLINGTON 273

Fleetlands Golf Club GOSPORT 77

Fleetwood Golf Club Ltd FLEETWOOD 246

Fleming Park Golf Course EASTLEIGH 77

Flempton Golf Club BURY ST. EDMUNDS 158

Flint Golf Club FLINT 408

Flixton Golf Club MANCHESTER 254

Fontcaude Golf Hotel de MONTPELLIER 519

Forest Hill Golf Club BOTCHESTON 170, 567

Forest Hills Golf Club Ltd COLEFORD 46

Forest of Dean Golf Club COLEFORD 46

Forest of Galtres Golf Club YORK 282

Forest Park Golf Club YORK 282

Forest Pines Golf Club BRIGG 176

Forfar Golf Club FORFAR 324

Formby Golf Club FORMBY 260

Formby Ladies' Golf Club FORMBY 260

Forres Golf Club FORRES 317

Forrester Park Golf and Tennis Club MALDON 142

Forrester Park Resort DUNFERMLINE 359

Fort Augustus Golf Club FORT AUGUSTUS 376

Fort William Golf Club FORT WILLIAM 376

Fortrose and Rosemarkie Golf Club FORTROSE 373

Fortwilliam Golf Club BELFAST 448

Fosseway Golf Club and Centurion Hotel BATH 51

Fota Island Resort FOTA ISLAND 464, 581

Foulford Inn Golf Course CRIEFF 387

Four Marks Golf Club FOUR MARKS 77

Four Seasons Resort at Terre Blanche VAR 520

Foxbridge Golf Club BILLINGSHURST 116

Foxhills OTTERSHAW 106

Foyle International Golf Centre LONDONDERRY 455, 580

Fraserburgh Golf Club FRASERBURGH 317

Fregate Golf de BANDOL 517

Freshwater Bay Golf Club FRESHWATER 83

Frilford Heath Golf Club ABINGDON 96

Frinton Golf Club FRINTON-ON-SEA 140

Frodsham Golf Club FRODSHAM 227

Fulford (York) Golf Club Ltd. YORK 283

Fulford Heath Golf Club Ltd BIRMINGHAM 207

Fulneck Golf Club Ltd. PUDSEY 298

Fulwell Golf Club HAMPTON HILL 126

Furnas Golf Course SAO MIGUEL 530

Furness Golf Club BARROW-IN-FURNESS 233

Furzeley Golf Club DENMEAD 76

Fynn Valley Golf Club IPSWICH 159, 570

Gainsborough Golf Club GAINSBOROUGH 177

Gairloch Golf Club GAIRLOCH 373

Galashiels Golf Club GALASHIELS 335

Galgorm Castle Golf Club BALLYMENA 447

Galway Bay Golf & Country Club Hotel ORANMORE 474

Galway Golf Club SALTHILL 474

Ganstead Park Golf Club CONISTON 273

Ganton Golf Club Ltd SCARBOROUGH 281

Garesfield Golf Club CHOPWELL 270

Garforth Golf Club Ltd. LEEDS 296

Garmouth & Kingston Golf Club FOCHABERS 316

Gary Player Country Club SUN CITY 548

Gatehouse of Fleet Golf Club GATEHOUSE OF FLEET 340

Gathurst Golf Club WIGAN 258

Gatley Golf Club Ltd. CHEADLE 225

Gatton Manor DORKING 103

Gatwick Manor Golf Club CRAWLEY 572

Gaudet Luce Golf Club DROITWICH SPA 218

Gay Hill Golf Club BIRMINGHAM 207

Gedney Hill Golf Course SPALDING 182

George Washington Golf & Country Club WASHINGTON 272, 573

Gerrards Cross Golf Club GERRARDS CROSS 70

Ghyll Golf Club BARNOLDSWICK 277

Gifford Golf Club HADDINGTON 353

Gillingham Golf Club Ltd GILLINGHAM 88

Girona Club de Golf GIRONA 537

Girton Golf Club CAMBRIDGE 133

Girvan Golf Course GIRVAN 329

Glamorganshire Golf Club PENARTH 430

Glasgow Golf Club GLASGOW 367

Glasgow Golf Club IRVINE 329

Glasson Golf & Country Club ATHLONE 495

Glebe Golf Club TRIM 488

Gleddoch Golf Club LANGBANK 391

Glen Golf Club NORTH BERWICK 355

Glen Gorse Golf Club OADBY 173

Glen of the Downs Golf Club DELGANY 497

Glenbervie Golf Club Ltd LARBERT 394

Glencorse Golf Club PENICUIK 355

Glencruitten Golf Club OBAN 327

Gleneagles Hotel Golf Courses AUCHTERARDER 382

Glengarriff Golf Club GLENGARRIFF 464

Glenisla Golf Centre ALYTH 382

Glenmalure Golf Club RATHDRUM 501

Glenrothes Golf Club GLENROTHES 359

Glossop and District Golf Club GLOSSOP 166

Gloucestershire BRISTOL 43

Glyn Abbey Golf Club KIDWELLY/LLANELLI 414

Glynhir Golf Club AMMANFORD 413

Glynneath Golf Club GLYNNEATH 426

Goal Farm Golf Course PIRBRIGHT 107

Gog Magog Golf Club CAMBRIDGE 133

Gold Coast Golf Club DUNGARVAN 492, 581

Goldenhill Golf Course STOKE-ON-TRENT 200

Golf de Saint Cyprien PERPIGNAN 519

Golf & Country Club De Saint-Julien ST-JULIEN-SUR-CALONNE 510

Golf at Goodwood CHICHESTER 116

Golf Club De Lyon LYON 514

Golf D' Aix-Les-Bains AIX-LES-BAINS 514

Golf De Bondues LILLE 509

Golf De Bordeaux Cameyrac BORDEAUX 515

Golf De Chamonix CHAMONIX 514

Golf De Forges-Les-Bains PARIS 512

Golf De La Grande-Motte MONTPELLIER 518

Golf De L'Ailette LAON 509

Golf De Mazamet La Barouge MAZAMET 516

Golf De Moliets BAYONNE 515

Golf De Poniente MAGALLUF 538

Golf De Sperone CORSICA 518

Golf Du Touquet LE TOUQUET 509

Golf House Club ELIE 359

Golf International Barriere La Baule LA BAULE 511

Golf National PARIS 512

Golf Platja De Pals PALS 537

Golf Pollensa POLLENSA 538

Golf Serres De Pals PALS 537

Golf Spey Bay SPEY BAY 320

Golfe do Morgado PORTIMAO 526

Golfe dos Alamos PORTIMAO 526

Golspie Golf Club GOLSPIE 372

Goring and Streatley Golf Club STREATLEY ON THAMES 68

Gorleston Golf Club GREAT YARMOUTH 153

Gort Golf Club GORT 474

Gosfield Lake Golf Club HALSTEAD 140

Gosforth Golf Club NEWCASTLE UPON TYNE 271

Gosling Golf Range WELWYN GARDEN CITY 565

Gosport & Stokes Golf Club GOSPORT 77

Gotts Park Municipal Golf Club LEEDS 296

Gourock Golf Club GOUROCK 391

Gower Golf Club SWANSEA 433

Gowerton Golf Centre SWANSEA 433, 579

Gowran Park GOWRAN 481

Gracehill Golf Club BALLYMONEY 447

Gramacho Course LAGOA 525

Grande Bastide Golf de la GRASSE 518

Grange Fell Golf Club GRANGE-OVER-SANDS 234

Grange Park Golf Club ROTHERHAM 286

Grange Park Golf Club SCUNTHORPE 180

Grange Park Golf Club SCUNTHORPE 575

Grange Park Golf Club ST HELENS 263

Grangemouth Golf Club POLMONT 395

Grange-over-Sands Golf Club GRANGE-OVER-SANDS 235

Grantown-on-Spey Golf Club GRANTOWN-ON-SPEY 372

Granville-Baie du Mont Saint Michel de Golf GRANVILLE 509

Grassmoor Golf Centre CHESTERFIELD 165, 562

Grassmoor Golf Centre CHESTERFIELD 562

Gravesend Golf Centre GRAVESEND 566

Great Barr Golf Club BIRMINGHAM 207

Great Grimsby Golf Centre (Willow Park Golf Club) GRIMSBY 567

Great Hadham Golf & Country Club BISHOP'S STORTFORD 145

Great Harwood Golf Club BLACKBURN 243

Great Lever and Farnworth Golf Club Ltd BOLTON 251

Great Salterns Golf Course PORTSMOUTH 80

Great Torrington Golf Club TORRINGTON 37

Great Yarmouth & Caister Golf Club GREAT YARMOUTH 153

Greenacres Golf Club BALLYCLARE 447

Greenburn Golf Club FAULDHOUSE 352

Greenisland Golf Club CARRICKFERGUS 448

Greenmeadow Golf and Country Club CWMBRAN 426, 579

Greenmount Golf Club BURY 252

Greenock Golf Club GREENOCK 391

Greenock Whinhill Golf Club GREENOCK 391

Greenore Golf Club GREENORE 484

Greetham Valley Hotel Golf & Conference Centre RUTLAND 174

Grenelefe Golf & Tennis Resort ORLANDO 544

Grenoble Golf International de GRENOBLE 514

Greystones Golf Club GREYSTONES 498

Grim's Dyke Golf Club PINNER 128

Grimsby Golf Club Ltd GRIMSBY 177

Grove Golf Centre LEOMINSTER 169, 565

Grove Golf Club Ltd. PORTHCAWL 431

Guadalhorce Club de Golf MALAGA 534

Guadalmina Club de Golf MARBELLA 534

Guildford Golf Club GUILDFORD 104

Gujan Mestras Golf de ARCACHON 515

Gullane Golf Club GULLANE 353

Habberley Golf Club KIDDERMINSTER 218

Hadden Hill Golf Club DIDCOT 97

Haddington Golf Club HADDINGTON 353

Hadley Wood Golf Club BARNET 145

Haggs Castle Golf Club GLASGOW 367

Hagley Golf and Country Club HAGLEY 218

Haigh Hall Golf lub WIGAN 258

Hainault Forest Golf Club CHIGWELL 139

Hainsworth Park Golf Club HORNSEA 274

Hale Golf Club ALTRINCHAM 250

Halesowen Golf Club HALESOWEN 210

Halesworth Golf Club HALESWORTH 159, 570

Halifax Bradley Hall Golf Club HALIFAX 292

Halifax Golf Club Ltd HALIFAX 292

Hall Garth Golf & Country Club Hotel DARLINGTON 240

Hallamshire Golf Club Ltd SHEFFIELD 288

Hallowes Golf Club SHEFFIELD 288

Halstock Golf Club HALSTOCK 40

Haltwhistle Golf Course CARLISLE 266

Ham Manor Golf Club Ltd ANGMERING 116

Hamilton Golf Club HAMILTON 380

Hampshire Golf Club ANDOVER 75, 564

Hampstead Golf Club HAMPSTEAD 126

Hampton Court Palace Golf Club HAMPTON WICK 63

Hamptworth Academy SALISBURY 574

Hamptworth Golf and Country Club SALISBURY 59, 574

Hanbury Manor Golf & Country Club WARE 150

Handsworth Golf Club BIRMINGHAM 207

Hanging Heaton Golf Club DEWSBURY 292

Hankley Common Golf Club FARNHAM 104

Hanover Golf & Country Club RAYLEIGH 142

Harborne (Church Farm) Golf Club BIRMINGHAM 208

Harborne Golf Club BIRMINGHAM 207

Harbour Point Golf Club LITTLE ISLAND 464

Harbour Town Golf Links HILTON HEAD 545

Harburn Golf Club WEST CALDER 356

Hardelot Les Dunes Golf d' HARDELOT 509

Hardelot Les Pins Golf d' HARDELOT 509

Harewood Downs Golf Club AMERSHAM 69

Harleyford Golf Club MARLOW 71

Harpenden Golf Club HARPENDEN 146

Harris Golf Club SCARISTA 396

Harrogate Golf Club Ltd HARROGATE 278

Hartford Golf Club NORTHWICH 230

Hartford Golf Club NORTHWICH 561

Hartland Forest Golf Club BIDEFORD 30

Hartlepool Golf Club Ltd HARTLEPOOL 241

Hartley Wintney Golf Club HARTLEY WINTNEY 78

Hartsbourne Golf & Country Club BUSHEY HEATH 146

Hartswood Golf Club BRENTWOOD 137

Harwich and Dovercourt Golf Club HARWICH 140

Harwood Golf Club BOLTON 251

Hassocks Golf Club HASSOCKS 118

Hatchford Brook Golf Club BIRMINGHAM 208

Hatfield London Country Club HATFIELD 147

Haut-Poitou Golf du POITIERS 513

Haverfordwest Golf Club HAVERFORDWEST 417

Haverhill Golf Club Ltd HAVERHILL 159

Hawarden Golf Club HAWARDEN 409

Hawick Golf Club HAWICK 336

Hawkhurst Golf Club HAWKHURST 88

Hawkstone Park SHREWSBURY 196

Haydock Park Golf Club NEWTON-LE-WILLOWS 262

Hayling Golf Club HAYLING ISLAND 78

Hayston Golf Club GLASGOW 367

Haywards Heath Golf Club HAYWARDS HEATH 118

Hazel Grove Golf Club STOCKPORT 257

Hazelwood Golf Club Ltd SUNBURY ON THAMES 64

Hazlehead Golf Course ABERDEEN 308

Hazlemere Golf Club HIGH WYCOMBE 71

Headfort Golf Club KELLS 486

Headingley Golf Club LEEDS 296

Headley Golf Club BRADFORD 291

Heath Golf Club PORTLAOISE 482

Heathpark Golf Club WEST DRAYTON 64

Heaton Moor Golf Club STOCKPORT 257

Heaton Park Golf Centre MANCHESTER 254

Hebden Bridge Golf Club HEBDEN BRIDGE 293

Hedsor Golf Course WOOBURN COMMON 73

Hele Park Golf Club NEWTON ABBOT 34

Helen's Bay Golf Club BANGOR 451

Helensburgh Golf Club HELENSBURGH 347

Hellidon Lakes Golf Club HELLIDON 184

Helmsdale Golf Club HELMSDALE 372

Helsby Golf Club HELSBY 227

Helston Golf HELSTON 22

Hemingford Abbots Golf Club HUNTINGDON 134

Hemsted Forest Golf Club CRANBROOK 86

Henbury Golf Club BRISTOL 43

Hendon Golf Club HENDON 126

Henley Golf & Country Club HENLEY-IN-ARDEN 204

Henley Golf Club HENLEY-ON-THAMES 97

Henllys Golf Course BEAUMARIS 404

Hennerton Golf Club WARGRAVE 68, 560

Hereford Municipal Golf Club HEREFORD 168

Herefordshire Golf Club HEREFORD 168

Herne Bay Golf Club HERNE BAY 88

Hertfordshire Golf & Country Club BROXBOURNE 146

Hertfordshire Golf and Country Club BROXBOURNE 565

Hesketh Golf Club SOUTHPORT 263

Hessle Golf Club COTTINGHAM 274

Heswall Golf Club HESWALL 260

Hever Castle Golf Club HEVER 88

Heworth Golf Club GATESHEAD 270

Heworth Golf Club YORK 283

Hexham Golf Club HEXHAM 266

Heydon Grange Golf and Country Club ROYSTON 148

Heyrose Golf Club KNUTSFORD 227

Heysham Golf Club HEYSHAM 246

Hickleton Golf Club DONCASTER 286

High Elms Golf Club FARNBOROUGH 87

High Post Golf Club Ltd SALISBURY 59

High Throston Golf Club HARTLEPOOL 241

Highbullen Hotel Golf & Country Club CHITTLEHAMHOLT 30

Highcliffe Castle Golf Club CHRISTCHURCH 39

Highfield Golf Course CARBURY 480

Highgate Golf Club HIGHGATE 126

Highwoods Golf Club BEXHILL-ON-SEA 111

Highworth Community Golf Centre HIGHWORTH 58

Hilden Golf Centre TONBRIDGE 94

Hilden Golf Centre TONBRIDGE 567

Hill Barn Golf Club WORTHING 119

Hillingdon Golf Club HILLINGDON 126

Hillsborough Golf Club Ltd. SHEFFIELD 288

Hillside Golf Club SOUTHPORT 263

Hilltop Public Golf Course BIRMINGHAM 208

Hilton Park Golf Club GLASGOW 367

Hilton Puckrup Hall TEWKESBURY 50

Hilton Templepatrick Golf CLub TEMPLEPATRICK 449

Himley Hall Golf Centre DUDLEY 210

Hinckley Golf Club HINCKLEY 171

Hindhead Golf Club HINDHEAD 105

Hindley Hall Golf Club WIGAN 258

Hinksey Heights Golf Course OXFORD 98

Hintlesham Golf Club IPSWICH 159

Hirsel Golf Club COLDSTREAM 335

Hobson Golf Club NEWCASTLE UPON TYNE 271

Hockley Golf Club WINCHESTER 82

Hoddom Castle Golf Course LOCKERBIE 342

Hoebridge Golf Centre WOKING 109, 572

Hollandbush Golf Club LESMAHAGOW 380

Hollingbury Park Golf Club BRIGHTON 112

Hollywood Lakes Golf Club BALLYBOUGHAL 468

Holme Hall Golf Club SCUNTHORPE 180

Holsworthy Golf Club HOLSWORTHY 32

Holtye Golf Club EAST GRINSTEAD 118

Holyhead Golf Club TREARDDUR BAY 406

Holywell Bay Golf Club NEWQUAY 26

Holywell Golf Club HOLYWELL 409

Holywood Golf Club HOLYWOOD 452

Homelands Golf Centre ASHFORD 84, 565

Honiton Golf Club HONITON 32

Honourable Company of Edinburgh Golfers GULLANE 353

Hopeman Golf Club ELGIN 316

Horam Park Golf Course HEATHFIELD 114, 572

Horncastle Golf Club HORNCASTLE 178

Hornsea Golf Club HORNSEA 274

Horsenden Hill Golf Club GREENFORD 125

Horsforth Golf Club Ltd. LEEDS 296

Horsham Golf & Fitness HORSHAM 118

Horsley Lodge Golf Club & Hotel HORSLEY 166

Horton Park Golf & Country Club EPSOM 103

Horwich Golf Club HORWICH 253

Hossegor Golf de HOSSEGOR 516

Hotel Quinta da Marinha & Villas Golf Resort ESTORIL 528

Houghton-Le-Spring Golf Club HOUGHTON-LE-SPRING 270

Houghwood ST HELENS 248

Houldsworth Golf Club Ltd. MANCHESTER 254

Hounslow Heath Golf Centre HOUNSLOW 127

Howley Hall Golf Club LEEDS 296

Howth Golf Club SUTTON 473

Hoylake Golf Club WIRRAL 264

Hucknall Golf Cente HUCKNALL 189

Huddersfield Golf Club HUDDERSFIELD 293

Hull Golf Club (1921) Ltd HULL 274

Humberstone Golf Range LEICESTER 567

Humberstone Heights Golf Club LEICESTER 171, 567

Hunley Hall Golf Club & Hotel BROTTON 277

Hunley Hall Golf Club & Hotel SALTBURN 575

Hunstanton Golf Club HUNSTANTON 153

Huntercombe Golf Club HENLEY-ON-THAMES 97

Huntly Golf Club HUNTLY 317

Huntswood Golf Club BURNHAM 65

Hurdwick Golf Club TAVISTOCK 36

Hurlston Hall Golf Club SCARISBRICK 248

Hurst Golf Club READING 67

Hurtmore Golf Club GODALMING 104

Huyton & Prescot Golf Ltd. HUYTON 261

Hylands Golf Complex INGATESTONE 141

Hythe Imperial Golf Club HYTHE 88

Ifield Golf and Country Club CRAWLEY 117

Ilfracombe & Woolacombe Golf Range ILFRACOMBE 33, 563

Ilford Golf Club ILFORD 141

Ilfracombe Golf Club ILFRACOMBE 33

Ilkeston Borough Golf Club ILKESTON 166

Ilkley Golf Club ILKLEY 294

Immingham Golf Club IMMINGHAM 178

Imperial Lake View Hotel & Golf Club CHA-AM 555

Inchmarlo Golf Club BANCHORY 312

Inco Golf Club SWANSEA 434

Indian Wells Golf Resort INDIAN WELLS 546

Ingestre Park Golf Club STAFFORD 199

Ingol Golf Club PRESTON 247

Ingon Manor Hotel & Golf Club STRATFORD-UPON-AVON 205

Innellan Golf Club DUNOON 327

Innerleithen Golf Club INNERLEITHEN 336

Innisbrook Hilton Resort TARPON SPRINGS 544

Insch Golf Club INSCH 317

Inverallochy Golf Club INVERALLOCHY 317

Inveraray Golf Club INVERARAY 327

Invergordon Golf Club INVERGORDON 373

Inverness Golf Club INVERNESS 376

Inverurie Golf Club INVERURIE 317

Ipswich Golf Club IPSWICH 159

Irvine Golf Club IRVINE 329

Irvine Ravenspark Golf Club IRVINE 330

Island Golf Club DONABATE 469

Islay Golf Club PORT ELLEN 396

Isle of Wedmore Golf Club WEDMORE 56

Isle of Gigha Golf Club ISLE OF GIGHA 396

Isle of Purbeck Golf Club STUDLAND 41

Isle Of Seil Golf Club OBAN 327

Isle of Skye Golf Club SCONSER 398

Isles of Scilly Golf Club ST MARY'S 28

Iver Golf Club IVER 71

Ivinghoe Golf Club LEIGHTON BUZZARD 131

Izaak Walton Golf Club STONE 200

Jack Barker's Greenway Hall STOKE-ON-TRENT 200

Jack Barkers Keele Golf Centre NEWCASTLE-UNDER-LYME 199

Jedburgh Golf Club JEDBURGH 336

Jersey Recreation Grounds JERSEY 503

John O'Gaunt Golf Club SANDY 132

John Reay Golf Centres COVENTRY 573

Jubilee Course ST ANDREWS 364

Julianstown Golf Course & Pitch & Putt JULIANSTOWN 486

K Club STRAFFAN 481

Kames Golf Club LANARK 380

Kearsley Golf Driving Range KEARSLEY 568

Kedleston Park Golf Club QUARNDON 167

Keighley Golf Club KEIGHLEY 294

Keith Golf Club KEITH 317

Kelso Golf Club KELSO 336

Kemnay Golf Club KEMNAY 317

Kendal Golf Club KENDAL 236

Kendleshire Golf Club BRISTOL 43

Kenilworth Golf Club Ltd KENILWORTH 204

Kenmare Golf Club KENMARE 475

Kenmore Golf Course KENMORE 388

Kent & Surrey Golf & Country Club EDENBRIDGE 87

Kent National Golf & Country Club BRENCHLEY 85

Kenwick Park Golf Club LOUTH 179

Kerries Golf Club TRALEE 478

Keswick Golf Club KESWICK 236

Kettering Golf Club KETTERING 184

Kibworth Golf Club LEICESTER 171

Kidderminster Golf Club KIDDERMINSTER 219

Kilbirnie Place Golf Club KILBIRNIE 330

Kilcock Golf Club KILCOCK 486

Kilcoole Golf Club KILCOOLE 498

Kilkea Castle Hotel & Golf Club KILKEA 480

Kilkee Golf Club KILKEE 460

Kilkeel Golf Club KILKEEL 453

Kilkenny Golf Club KILKENNY 481

Killarney Golf and Fishing Club KILLARNEY 476

Killeen Golf Club KILL 480

Killeline Golf Club NEWCASTLE WEST 483

Killin Golf Club KILLIN 388

Killin Park Golf & Country Club KILLIN 484

Killiney Golf Club KILLINEY 472

Killiow Golf Club & Driving Range TRURO 28, 562

Killorglin Golf Club KILLORGLIN 476

Killymoon Golf Club COOKSTOWN 456

Kilmacolm Golf Club KILMACOLM 391

Kilmarnock (Barassie) Golf Club TROON 332

Kilnwick Percy Golf Club KILNWICK PERCY 276

Kilrush Golf Club KILRUSH 460

Kilspindie Golf Club ABERLADY 348

Kilsyth Lennox Golf Club KILSYTH 369

Kilton Forest Golf Club WORKSOP 192

Kilworth Springs Golf club NORTH KILWORTH 173

King Edward Bay Golf Club ONCHAN 502

King James VI Golf Club PERTH 389

Kingfisher Country Club MILTON KEYNES 72, 560

Kinghorn Municipal Golf Club KINGHORN 360

Kings Acre Golf Course & Academy LASSWADE 354

King's Hill Golf Club WEST MALLING 95

Kings Links Golf Centre ABERDEEN 576

King's Links Golf Course ABERDEEN 308

King's Lynn Golf Club KING'S LYNN 154

Kings Norton Golf Club Ltd. BIRMINGHAM 208

Kingsbarns Golf Links KINGSBARNS 360

Kingsdown Golf Club CORSHAM 58

Kingsknowe Golf Club EDINBURGH 350

Kingsley Golf Club BORDON 76, 564

Kingsthorpe Golf Club NORTHAMPTON 185

Kingswood Golf & Country Club Ltd KINGSWOOD 105

Kington Golf Club KINGTON 169

Kingussie Golf Club KINGUSSIE 377

Kingweston Golf Club STREET 54

Kinloss Country Golf Course FORRES 317

Kinmel Park Golf Complex BODELWYDDAN 407

Kinross Golf Courses KINROSS 388

Kinsale Golf Club KINSALE 464

Kinsale Golf Course HOLYWELL 409

Kintore Golf Club KINTORE 318

Kirby Muxloe Golf Club KIRKBY MUXLOE 171

Kirkby Lonsdale Golf Club KIRKBY LONSDALE 236

Kirkbymoorside Golf Club KIRKBYMOORSIDE 279

Kirkcaldy Golf Club KIRKCALDY 360

Kirkcudbright Golf Club KIRKCUDBRIGHT 340

Kirkhill Golf Club GLASGOW 368

Kirkintilloch Golf Club KIRKINTILLOCH 347

Kirkistown Castle Golf Club NEWTOWNARDS 453

Kirriemuir Golf Club Ltd. KIRRIEMUIR 324

Kirtlington Golf Club KIRTLINGTON 98

Kirton Holme Golf Club BOSTON 175

Knaresborough Golf Club KNARESBOROUGH 279

Knebworth Golf Club KNEBWORTH 147

Knighton Golf Club KNIGHTON 420

Knighton Heath Golf Club BOURNEMOUTH 38

Knights Grange Sports Complex WINSFORD 232

Knightsbrook Golf Club TRIM 488

Knightswood Golf Club GLASGOW 368

Knock Golf Club BELFAST 451

Knockanally Golf and Country Club DONADEA 480

Knole Park Golf Club SEVENOAKS 91

Knott End Golf Club Ltd BLACKPOOL 244

Knotty Hill Golf Centre SEDGEFIELD 563

Knotty Hill Golf Centre STOCKTON-ON-TEES 242, 563

Knowle Bristol Golf Club BRISTOL 44

Knutsford Golf Club KNUTSFORD 227

Kyles Of Bute Golf Club TIGHNABRUAICH 328

La Bretesche Golf de LA BAULE 511

La Cala Resort MIJAS 535

La Domangere Golf Club de LA ROCHE-SUR-YON 511

La Freslonniere Golf de RENNES 511

La Grande Mare Golf Club GUERNSEY 503

La Manga Club MURCIA 537

La Moye Golf Club JERSEY 504

La Nivelle Golf de SAINT JEAN-DE-LUZ 516

La Quinta Golf and Country Club BENAHAVIS 534

La Quinta Resort & Club (Dunes) LA QUINTA 546

La Quinta Resort & Club (Mountain) LA QUINTA 546

La Vaucouleurs Golf de PARIS 512

Lacanau Ocean Golf Hotel LACANAU-OCEAN 516

Ladbrook Park Golf Club Ltd SOLIHULL 210

Ladybank Golf Club LADYBANK 360

Laem Chabang International Country Club CHONBURI 557

Lagganmore Golf Club & Hotel PORTPATRICK 342

Laguna Golf Course VILAMOURA 526

Laguna Phuket Golf Club LAGUNA PHUKET 554

Lahinch Golf Club LAHINCH 460

Lakeside Golf Club PORT TALBOT 432

Lakeside Golf Club RUGELEY 199

Lakeside Lodge Golf Centre HUNTINGDON 134

Laleham Golf Club CHERTSEY 101

Lamberhurst Golf Club TUNBRIDGE WELLS 94

Lambourne Golf Club BURNHAM 70

Lamerwood Country Club WHEATHAMPSTEAD 151

Lamlash Golf Club LAMLASH 334

Lanark Golf Club LANARK 380

Lancaster Golf Club Ltd LANCASTER 246

Lanes Golfing Academy STOKE POGES 73, 560

Langdon Hills Golf & Country Club BULPHAN 138

Langholm Golf Club LANGHOLM 340

Langland Bay Golf Club SWANSEA 434

Langley Park Golf Club BECKENHAM 84

Lanhydrock Hotel & Golf Club BODMIN 21

Lansdown Golf Club BATH 51

Lansil Golf Club LANCASTER 246

Largs Golf Club LARGS 330

Larkhall Golf Club LARKHALL 380

Larne Golf Club LARNE 448

Lauder Golf Club LAUDER 336

Launceston Golf Club LAUNCESTON 24

Lavender Park Golf Centre ASCOT 65

Laytown & Bettystown Golf Club BETTYSTOWN 486

Lea Marston Hotel & Leisure Complex SUTTON COLDFIELD 573

Leadhills Golf Club LEADHILLS 380

Leamington and County Golf Club LEAMINGTON SPA 204

Leaside Golf Club EDMONTON 124

Leasowe Golf Club MORETON 262

Leatherhead Golf Club LEATHERHEAD 106

Lee Park Golf Club LIVERPOOL 262

Lee Valley Golf & Country Club OVENS 465

Lee Valley Leisure Golf Course EDMONTON 124

Leeds Castle Golf Course MAIDSTONE 89

Leeds Golf Centre LEEDS 297, 576

Leeds Golf Club LEEDS 297

Leek Golf Club LEEK 198

Leek Westwood Golf Club LEEK 198

Lee-on-the-Solent Golf Club LEE-ON-THE-SOLENT 78

Lees Hall Golf Club Ltd. SHEFFIELD 288

Leicestershire Golf Club LEICESTER 171

Leigh Golf Club WARRINGTON 232

Leighton Buzzard Golf Club LEIGHTON BUZZARD 131

Lely Resort NAPLES 544

Lenzie Golf Club LENZIE 347

Leominster Golf Club LEOMINSTER 169

Leopardstown Driving Range FOXROCK 581

Les Bordes Golf International ORLEANS 513

Les Mielles Golf and Country Club JERSEY 503, 581

Les Ormes Golf & Leisure Club JERSEY 503

Leslie Golf Club LESLIE 360

L'Esterel Latitudes Golf de ST RAPHAEL 520

Letchworth Golf Club LETCHWORTH 147

Letham Grange Golf Course ARBROATH 322

Lethamhill Golf Course GLASGOW 368

Letterkenny Golf Club LETTERKENNY 467

Leven Golfing Society LEVEN 360

Leven Thistle Golf Club LEVEN 361

Lewes Golf Club LEWES 114

Lexden Wod Golf Club COLCHESTER 563

Lexden Wood Golf Club COLCHESTER 140

Leyland Golf Club Ltd LEYLAND 246

Libbaton Golf Club Ltd UMBERLEIGH 37

Liberton Golf Club EDINBURGH 350

Lickey Hills Golf Club REDNAL 210

Lightcliffe Golf Club HALIFAX 292
Lilleshall Hall Golf Club NEWPORT 194
Lilley Brook Golf Club CHELTENHAM 45
Lime Trees Park Golf Club NORTHOLT 559
Limerick County Golf & Country Club
BALLYNEETY 483
Limerick Golf Club LIMERICK 483
Limpsfield Chart Golf Club OXTED 107
Lincoln Golf Club LINCOLN 178
Lincolnshire Golf Course SCUNTHORPE 181
Lindfield Golf Club LINDFIELD 119
Lindrick Golf Club WORKSOP 192
Lindrick Golf Club WORKSOP 289
Lingdale Golf Club WOODHOUSE EAVES 174
Lingfield Park Golf Club LINGFIELD 106
Links Country Park Hotel and Golf Club CROMER
152
Links Golf Club NEWMARKET 160
Linlithgow Golf Club LINLITHGOW 354
Linn Park Golf Club GLASGOW 368
Liphook Golf Club LIPHOOK 78
Lisbon Sports Club LISBON 528
Lisburn Golf Club LISBURN 448
Lismore Golf Club LISMORE 492
Litchfield Country Club MYRTLE BEACH 545
Little Aston Golf Club STREETLY 201
Little Chalfont Golf Club LITTLE CHALFONT 71
Little Hay Golf Complex HEMEL HEMPSTEAD
147
Little Lakes Golf Club BEWDLEY 217
Littlehampton Golf Club LITTLEHAMPTON 119
Littlehill Golf Club GLASGOW 368
Littlestone Golf Club NEW ROMNEY 89
Llandrindod Wells Golf Club LLANDRINDOD
WELLS 420
Llandudno Golf Club (Maesdu) Ltd LLANDUDNO
409
Llanfairfechan Golf Club LLANFAIRFECHAN 410
Llangefni Public Golf Course LLANGEFNI 405
Llanishen Golf Club CARDIFF 424
Llantrisant and Pontyclun Golf Club TALBOT
GREEN 435
Llanwern Golf Club LLANWERN 427
Llanymynech Golf Club OSWESTRY 194
Llanyrafon Golf Course CWMBRAN 426
Llyn Centre PWLLHELI 406, 578
Lobden Golf Club ROCHDALE 256
Loch Ness Golf Course INVERNESS 377
Loch Palm Golf Club PHUKET 554

Lochcarron Golf Club LOCHCARRON 373
Lochgelly Golf Club LOCHGELLY 361
Lochgilphead Golf Club LOCHGILPHEAD 327
Lochmaben Golf Club LOCHMABEN 340
Lochranza Golf LOCHRANZA 334
Lochwinnoch Golf Club LOCHWINNOCH 391
Lockerbie Golf Club LOCKERBIE 342
L'Odet Golf de BENODET 511
Lofthouse Hill Golf Club WAKEFIELD 300
London Beach Golf Club TENTERDEN 94
London Golf Centre NORTHOLT 559
London Golf Club ASH 84
London Scottish Golf Club LONDON 63
Long Ashton Golf Club BRISTOL 44
Long Sutton Golf Club LANGPORT 54, 570
Longcliffe Golf Club LOUGHBOROUGH 172
Longhirst Hall Golf Course MORPETH 267
Longley Park Golf Club HUDDERSFIELD 293
Longniddry Golf Club Ltd LONGNIDDRY 354
Longridge Golf Club PRESTON 247
Longside Golf Club PETERHEAD 320
Looe Golf Club LOOE 24
Los Naranjos Golf Club MARBELLA 535
Lostwithiel Hotel Golf & Country Club
LOSTWITHIEL 24
Lothianburn Golf Club EDINBURGH 350
Loudoun Gowf Club GALSTON 329
Loudun-Roiffe Golf de LOUDUN 513
Loughrea Golf Club LOUGHREA 474
Loughton Golf Club LOUGHTON 141
Louth Golf Club LOUTH 180
Low Laithes Golf Club Ltd. WAKEFIELD 300
Lowes Park Golf Club Ltd BURY 252
Lucan Golf Club DUBLIN 470
Ludlow Golf Club LUDLOW 194
Luffenham Heath Golf Club STAMFORD 174
Luffness New Golf Club ABERLADY 348
Lullingstone Park Golf Club ORPINGTON 90
Lumphanan Golf Club BANCHORY 314
Lundin Golf Club LUNDIN LINKS 362
Lundin Ladies Golf Club LUNDIN LINKS 361
Lurgan Golf Club LURGAN 450
Lutterworth Golf Club LUTERWORTH 172
Luttrellstown Castle Golf and Country Club
CASTLEKNOCK 469
Lybster Golf Club LYBSTER 372
Lydd Golf Club & Driving Range LYDD 89
Lydney Golf Club LYDNEY 46
Lyme Regis Golf Club LYME REGIS 40

Lymm Golf Club LYMM 228
Lytham Green Drive Golf Club LYTHAM ST ANNES 246

Macclesfield Golf Club MACCLESFIELD 228
MacDonald Cardrona Hotel, Golf & Country Club PEEBLES 337
MacDonald Hill Valley Hotel, Golf & Country Club WHITCHURCH 197
MacDonald Linden Hall MORPETH 268
Machrie Bay Golf Course MACHRIE 334
Machrie Golf Links PORT ELLEN 397
Machrihanish Golf Club CAMPBELTOWN 326
Machynlleth Golf Club MACHYNLLETH 421
Macroom Golf Club MACROOM 465
Maesteg Golf Club MAESTEG 427
Maeva Latitudes Toulouse Seilh TOULOUSE 517
Magdalene Fields Golf Club BERWICK-UPON-TWEED 266
Magnolia Park Golf & Country Club OXON/BUCKINGHAMSHIRE 99
Magpie Hall Lane Municipal Golf Club BROMLEY 85
Mahee Island Golf Club NEWTOWNARDS 453
Maidenhead Golf Club MAIDENHEAD 66
Maidstone Golf Centre MAIDSTONE 566
Majestic Creek Country Club HUA HIN 555
Malahide Golf Club MALAHIDE 472
Malden Golf Club NEW MALDEN 106
Maldon Golf Club MALDON 142
Malkins Bank Municipal Golf Course SANDBACH 231
Mallow Golf Club MALLOW 465
Malone Golf Club BELFAST 448
Malton and Norton Golf Club MALTON 279
Malton Golf Club ROYSTON 148
Manchester Golf Club Ltd MANCHESTER 254
Mannan Castle Golf Club CARRICKMACROSS 488
Mannings Heath Golf Club HORSHAM 118
Manor Golf Club BRADFORD 291
Manor Golf Club GRIMSBY 177
Manor Golf Club UTTOXETER 202
Manor House Golf Club at Castle Combe CASTLE COMBE 57
Manor of Groves SAWBRIDGEWORTH 149
Mansfield Woodhouse Golf Club MANSFIELD 189
Manston Golf Centre RAMSGATE 90, 566

Mapperley Golf Club MAPPERLEY 190
March Golf Club Ltd MARCH 134
Market Drayton Golf Club MARKET DRAYTON 194
Market Harborough Golf Club MARKET HARBOROUGH 172
Market Rasen and District Golf Club MARKET RASEN 180
Market Rasen Racecourse 9 hole Pay & Play Course MARKET RASEN 180
Marlborough Golf Club MARLBOROUGH 59
Marple Golf Club MARPLE 255
Marriott Breadsall Priory Hotel & Country Club DERBY 166
Marriott Dalmahoy Hotel and Country Club KIRKNEWTON 353
Marriott Forest of Arden Hotel & Country Club COVENTRY 203
Marriott Forest of Arden Hotel & Country Club COVENTRY 209
Marriott Hollins Hall Hotel & Country Club SHIPLEY 300
Marriott Meon Valley Hotel and Country Club SHEDFIELD 81
Marriott Sprowston Manor Hotel & Country Club NORWICH 156
Marriott St Pierre Hotel & Country Club CHEPSTOW 426
Marriott Tudor Park Hotel and Country Club MAIDSTONE 89
Marriott Worsley Park Hotel & Country Club WORSLEY 258
Marriott's Desert Springs Resort & Spa PALM DESERT 546
Marsden Golf Club HUDDERSFIELD 293
Marseille La Salette Golf de MARSEILLES 518
Marston Lakes Golf Club SUTTON COLDFIELD 206
Martin Moor Golf Club LINCOLN 178
Maryport Golf Club Ltd MARYPORT 236
Mas Nou Club de Golf D'aro GIRONA 537
Masham Golf Club RIPON 280
Massane Golf de MONTPELLIER 519
Massereene Golf Club ANTRIM 447
Matfen Hall Golf Club MATFEN 266
Matlock Golf Club MATLOCK 166
Mattishall Golf Club MATTISHALL 154
Maxstoke Park Golf Club BIRMINGHAM 208
Maybole Golf Course MAYBOLE 331

Maylands Golf and Country Club ROMFORD 143

Maywood Golf Club RISLEY 167

McCaulays Fitness & Golf IVYBRIDGE 33

McDonald-Ellon Golf Club ELLON 316

Mearns Castle Golf Academy GLASGOW 577

Medoc Golf du BORDEAUX 515

Mellor and Townscliffe Golf Club STOCKPORT 257

Melrose Golf Club MELROSE 336

Meltham Golf Club HUDDERSFIELD 293

Melville Golf Centre Golf Course Range & Shop EDINBURGH 350, 577

Mendip Golf Club Ltd. SHEPTON MALLET 54

Mendip Spring Golf Club BRISTOL 52, 570

Mentmore Golf and Country Club LEIGHTON BUZZARD 132

Menzies Cambridge Hotel & Golf Club CAMBRIDGE 133

Menzies Welcombe Hotel & Golf Course STRATFORD-UPON-AVON 205

Merchants of Edinburgh Golf Club EDINBURGH 350

Mere Golf and Country Club KNUTSFORD 228

Merlin Golf Course & Driving Range NEWQUAY 561

Merlin Golf Course and Driving Range NEWQUAY 24, 561

Merrist Wood Golf Club GUILDFORD 104

Mersey Valley Golf & Country Club WIDNES 232

Merthyr Tydfil Golf Club MERTHYR TYDFIL 427

Meyrick Park Golf Club BOURNEMOUTH 38

Mickleover Golf Club MICKLEOVER 167

Mid- Kent Golf Club GRAVESEND 88

Mid Yorkshire Golf Club PONTEFRACT 298

Middlebank Golf Centre MIDDLEBANK 578

Middlesborough Golf Club MIDDLESBOROUGH 280

Middlesbrough Municipal Golf Centre MIDDLESBOROUGH 280

Middleton Hall Golf Club KING'S LYNN 154

Middleton Park (Municipal) Golf Club LEEDS 297

Mid-Herts Golf Club ST. ALBANS 149

Mid-Sussex Golf Club DITCHLING 112

Mijas Golf International MIJAS 535

Mile End Golf Club OSWESTRY 194

Milford Golf Club MILFORD 106

Milford Haven Golf Club Ltd MILFORD HAVEN 417

Mill Green Golf Club WELWYN GARDEN CITY 150

Mill Hill Golf Club LONDON 127

Mill Ride Golf Club ASCOT 65

Millbrook Golf Club AMPTHILL 130

Millbrook Golf Course REDCROSS 501

Millennium Course Clube de Golfe Vilamoura VILAMOURA 526

Millicent Golf & Country Club CLANE 480

Millport Golf Club MILLPORT 396

Milnathort Golf Club Ltd MILNATHORT 388

Milnerton Golf Club WOODBRIDGE ISLAND 548

Milngavie Golf Club GLASGOW 368

Minchinhampton Golf Club (New Course) MINCHINHAMPTON 48

Minchinhampton Golf Club (Old Course) MINCHINHAMPTON 46

Minehead & West Somerset Golf Club MINEHEAD 54

Minto Golf Club HAWICK 336

Miramar Clube de Golf de PRAIA DE MIRAMAR 528

Mission Hills Golf Club KANCHANABURI 556

Mission Hills Khao Yai Golf Club NAKHON RATCHASIMA 557

Mission Hills Phuket Golf Resort & Spa PHUKET 554

Mission Inn Golf and Tennis Resort LAKE COUNTY 544

Mitcham Golf Club MITCHAM 106

Mitchelstown Golf Club MITCHELSTOWN 465

Mobberley Golf Club KNUTSFORD 228

Moffat Golf Club MOFFAT 342

Mold Golf Club MOLD 410

Mollington Grange Golf Club CHESTER 226

Monifieth Golf Links MONIFIETH 324

Monkstown Golf Club MONKSTOWN 465

Monkton Park Golf Course CHIPPENHAM 57

Monmouth Golf Club MONMOUTH 428

Monmouthshire Golf Club ABERGAVENNY 422

Monte Carlo Golf Club MONTE CARLO 518

Monte Mayor Golf Club BENAHAVIS 534

Montecastillo Hotel & Golf Resort CADIZ 535

Montrose Golf Links Ltd MONTROSE 325

Moor Allerton Golf Club LEEDS 297

Moor Hall Golf Club Ltd SUTTON COLDFIELD 214

Moor Park Golf Club RICKMANSWORTH 148

Moore Place Golf Club ESHER 104

Moorpark Golf Club STEVENSTON 332

Moors Valley Golf Course RINGWOOD 80

Moortown Golf Club LEEDS 297

Moray Golf Club LOSSIEMOUTH 318

Morecambe Golf Club Ltd. MORECAMBE 247

Moreton Hills Golf Centre MORETON 568

Morlais Castle Golf Club MERTHYR TYDFIL 427

Morley Hayes Golf Club ILKESTON 166

Morpeth Golf Club Ltd MORPETH 268

Morriston Golf Club SWANSEA 434

Mortehoe & Woolacombe Golf Club MORTEHOE 34

Mortonhall Golf Club EDINBURGH 350

Moseley Golf Club BIRMINGHAM 208

Moss Valley Golf Club WREXHAM 412

Mossock Hall Golf Club ORMSKIRK 247

Mount Ellen Golf Club GARTCOSH 379

Mount Juliet Golf Club THOMASTOWN 481

Mount Murray Golf Club SANTON 503

Mount Ober Golf & Country Club KNOCKBRACKEN 453, 580

Mount Oswald Manor and Golf Course DURHAM 241

Mount Pleasant Golf Course HENLOW 131

Mount Temple Golf Club MOATE 495

Mountain Ash Golf Club MOUNTAIN ASH 428

Mountain Lakes Golf Club CAERPHILLY 423

Mountain Shadow Golf Club CHONBURI 557

Mountrath Golf Club MOUNTRATH 482

Mouse Valley Golf Course LANARK 380

Mowbray Golf Club MOWBRAY 547

Mowsbury Golf Club BEDFORD 130

Moyola Park Golf Club MAGHERAFELT 455

Muang Ake Golf BANGKOK 555

Muckhart Golf Club MUCKHART 394

Muir of Ord Golf Club MUIR OF ORD 374

Muirkirk Golf Club MUIRKIRK 331

Mullion Golf Club HELSTON 22

Mundesley Golf Club NORWICH 156

Murcar Links Golf Club ABERDEEN 308

Murrayfield Golf Club Ltd EDINBURGH 351

Murrayshall Golf Course SCONE 390, 578

Muskerry Golf Club MUSKERRY 465

Musselburgh Golf Club MUSSELBURGH 354

Musselburgh Old Course Golf Club MUSSELBURGH 354

Muswell Hill Golf Club MUSWELL HILL 127

Muthill Golf Club CRIEFF 387

Mytton Fold Hotel & Golf Complex BLACKBURN 243

Naas Golf Club NAAS 480, 581

Nad Al Sheba Club DUBAI 549

Nailcote Hall Golf Club BERKSWELL 203

Nairn Dunbar Golf Club NAIRN 378

Nairn Golf Club NAIRN 318

Naples Beach Hotel & Golf Club NAPLES 544

Narin and Portnoo Golf Club PORTNOO 467

National Golf Centre WOODHALL SPA 182, 568

National Training Academy WOODHALL SPA 568

Naunton Downs Golf Club Ltd CHELTENHAM 45

Nazeing Golf Club NAZEING 142

Neath Golf Club NEATH 428

Nefyn and District Golf Club NEFYN 405

Nelson Golf Club NELSON 247

Nevill Golf Club TUNBRIDGE WELLS 94

New Course ST ANDREWS 364

New Cumnock Golf Club NEW CUMNOCK 331

New Forest Golf Club Ltd LYNDHURST 80

New Galloway Golf Club NEW GALLOWAY 342

New Mills Golf Club STOCKPORT 167

New North Manchester Golf Club Ltd MANCHESTER 255

New Zealand Golf Club WEYBRIDGE 109

Newark Golf Club NEWARK 190

Newbattle Golf Club Ltd DALKEITH 349

Newbiggin-by-the-Sea Golf Club NEWBIGGIN-BY-THE-SEA 268

Newbold Comyn Golf Club LEAMINGTON SPA 204

Newburgh-on-Ythan Golf Club NEWBURGH 318

Newbury & Crookham Golf Club NEWBURY 67

Newbury Racecourse Golf Centre NEWBURY 67

Newcastle United Golf Club NEWCASTLE UPON TYNE 271

Newcastle West Golf Club ARDAGH 483

Newcastleton Golf Club NEWCASTLETON 336

Newcastle-under-Lyme Golf Club NEWCASTLE-UNDER-LYME 199

Newmachar Golf Club NEWMACHAR 318

Newport (I.O.W.) Golf Club NEWPORT 83

Newport Golf Club NEWPORT 430

Newport Links Golf Club Ltd NEWPORT 418

Newquay Golf Club NEWQUAY 24

Newton Abbot (Stover) Golf Club NEWTON ABBOT 34

Newton Green Golf Club SUDBURY 161

Newton Stewart Golf Club NEWTON STEWART 342

Newtonmore Golf Club NEWTONMORE 378

Newtownstewart Golf Club NEWTOWNSTEWART 456

Nichigo Resort & Country Club KANCHANABURI 556

Niddry Castle Golf Club WINCHBURGH 356

Nigg Bay Golf Club ABERDEEN 308

Nimes Vacquerolles Golf de NIMES 519

Nimes-Campagne Golf de NIMES 519

Nizels Golf Club TONBRIDGE 94

Noble Place Golf Resort & Country Club CHONBURI 557

Norfolk Golf & Country Club REYMERSTON 157

Normanby Hall Golf Club SCUNTHORPE 181

Normanton Golf Club WAKEFIELD 300

North Berwick Golf Club NORTH BERWICK 355

North Downs Golf Club WOLDINGHAM 110

North Foreland Golf Club BROADSTAIRS 85

North Hants Golf Club FLEET 77

North Inch Golf Course PERTH 389

North Middlesex Golf Club BARNET 124

North Oxford Golf Club OXFORD 98

North Shore Hotel and Golf Club SKEGNESS 181

North Wales Golf Club Ltd LLANDUDNO 409

North Wales Golf Driving Range & 9 Hole Course ST ASAPH 578

North Warwickshire Golf Club Ltd COVENTRY 210

North Weald Golf Club EPPING 140

North West Golf Club BUNCRANA 466

North Wilts Golf Club DEVIZES 58

North Worcestershire Golf Club BIRMINGHAM 208

Northampton Golf Club NORTHAMPTON 185

Northamptonshire County Golf Club NORTHAMPTON 185

Northcliffe Golf Club BRADFORD 291

Northenden Golf Club MANCHESTER 255

Northern Golf Club ABERDEEN 308

Northop Country Park Golf Club CHESTER 407

Northumberland Golf Club Ltd NEWCASTLE UPON TYNE 271

Northwood Golf Club Ltd NORTHWOOD 127

Norton Golf Course STOCKTON-ON-TEES 242

Norwood Park Golf Course Ltd SOUTHWELL 191

Nottingham City Golf Club NOTTINGHAM 190

Notts. Golf Club Ltd. KIRKBY-IN-ASHFIELD 189

Nuneaton Golf Club NUNEATON 204

Nuremore Hotel & Country Club CARRICKMACROSS 488, 581

Oadby Golf Course OADBY 173

Oak Leaf Golf Complex NEWTON AYCLIFFE 242

Oak Park Golfing Complex CRONDALL 76

Oak Park Golfing Complex CRONDALL 102

Oak Tree Driving Range SHAFTESBURY 563

Oakdale Golf Club HARROGATE 278

Oakdale Golf Course OAKDALE 430

Oake Manor Golf Club TAUNTON 54, 570

Oakland Park Golf Club CHALFONT ST GILES 70

Oakmere Park Golf Club NOTTINGHAM 190

Oakridge Golf Club NUNEATON 204

Oaks Golf Club YORK 284

Oaks Sport Centre Ltd CARSHALTON 100, 571

Oast Golf Centre Ltd SITTINGBOURNE 92, 566

Oastpark Golf Course SNODLAND 92

Ogbourne Downs Golf Club SWINDON 60

Okehampton Golf Club OKEHAMPTON 34

Old Colwyn Golf Club COLWYN 407

Old Conna Golf Club BRAY 497

Old Course ST ANDREWS 362

Old Course Clube de Golfe Vilamoura VILAMOURA 526

Old Course Ranfurly Golf Club Ltd BRIDGE OF WEIR 391

Old Fold Manor Golf Club BARNET 124

Old Head Golf Links KINSALE 464

Old Nene Golf Club RAMSEY 135

Old Padeswood Golf Club Ltd PADESWOOD 410

Old Rectory Hotel & Golf Club CRICKHOWELL 420

Old Thorns Golf & Country Estate LIPHOOK 78

Oldham Golf Club OLDHAM 256

Oldmeldrum Golf Club OLD MELDRUM 318

Olton Golf Club Ltd. SOLIHULL 212

Olympic Golf Range SWANLEY 566

Omagh Golf Club OMAGH 456

Omaha Beach Golf d' NORMANDIE 510

Ombersley Golf Club DROITWICH 218

Onneley Golf Club CREWE 227

Open Golf Centre ST MARGARET'S 473, 581

Opio-Valbonne Golf COTE D'AZUR 518

Oporto Golf Club ESPINHO 530

Orchardleigh Golf Club FROME 54

Orkney Golf Club KIRKWALL 397

Ormeau Golf Club BELFAST 452

Ormonde Fields Golf Club CODNOR 165

Ormskirk Golf Club ORMSKIRK 247

Orpington Golf Centre ORPINGTON 90, 566

Orsett Golf Club ORSETT 142

Orton Meadow Golf Course PETERBOROUGH 135

Osborne Golf Club EAST COWES 83

Oswestry Golf Club OSWESTRY 196

Oswestry Golf Driving Range OSWESTRY 570

Otley Golf Club OTLEY 298

Otter Valley Golf Centre HONITON 33

Otterbourne Golf Centre WINCHESTER 82

Otway Golf Club RATHMULLAN 467

Oughterard Golf Club OUGHTERARD 474

Oulton Park LEEDS 297

Oundle Golf Club OUNDLE 186

Outlane Golf Club OUTLANE 298

Overstone Park Golf and Country Club NORTHAMPTON 185

Owston Hall DONCASTER 286

Oxford Golf Centre OXFORD 569

Oxfordshire Golf Club THAME 99

Oxley Park Golf Club Ltd WOLVERHAMPTON 215

Pachesham Park Golf Centre LEATHERHEAD 106, 571

Padbrook Park Golf Club CULLOMPTON 31

Padeswood & Buckley Golf Club MOLD 410

Painswick Golf Club PAINSWICK 48

Paisley Golf Club PAISLEY 391

Palacerigg Golf Club CUMBERNAULD 365

Palheiro Golf Club FUNCHAL 529

Palleg Golf Club SWANSEA 434

Palm Hills Golf Resort & Country Club HUA-HIN 555

Palmares Golf LAGOS 525

Palmetto Dunes Resort HILTON HEAD ISLAND 545

Panmure Golf Club BARRY 322

Pannal Golf Club HARROGATE 278

Panshanger Golf Complex WELWYN GARDEN CITY 151

Parc Golf Club NEWPORT 430, 579

Parcours Formule Golf Ploemeur Ocean LORIENT 511

Park Golf Course WINCHESTER 82

Park Hill Golf Club LOUGHBOROUGH 172

Park Wood Golf Club TATSFIELD 93

Parkhall Golf Course STOKE ON TRENT 200

Parklands Golf Club NEWCASTLE UPON TYNE 271, 573

Parknasilla Golf Club SNEEM 478

Parkstone Golf Club POOLE 40

Parley Court Golf Club CHRISTCHURCH 39

Parque da Floresta Golf and Leisure Resort BUDENS/SALEMA 524

Pastures Golf Club MICKLEOVER 167

Pat Trainor's Golf Academy WARRENPOINT 580

Patshull Park Hotel, Golf and Country Club WOLVERHAMPTON 197

Pau Golf Club 1856 PAU 516

Paultons Golf Centre ROMSEY 81, 564

Pavenham Park Golf Club BEDFORD 130

Peacehaven Golf Club NEWHAVEN 114

Peak Practice Golf BUXTON 562

Pease Pottage Golf Centre CRAWLEY 117

Pedham Place Golf Centre SWANLEY 93

Pedham Place Golf Centre SWANLEY 566

Peebles Golf Club PEEBLES 337

Peel Golf Club PEEL 502

Pelican's Nest Golf Club BONITA SPRINGS 544

Penha Longa Hotel & Golf Resort ESTORIL 528

Penina Golf Club PORTIMAO/PENINA 526

Penmaenmawr Golf Club PENMAENMAWR 405

Penn Golf Club Ltd WOLVERHAMPTON 215

Pennard Golf Club SWANSEA 434

Pennington Golf Club (Municipal) LEIGH 253

Pennyhill Park Country Club BAGSHOT 100

Penrhos Golf and Country Club LLANRHYSTYD 416

Penrhyn Golf Complex ANGLESEY 402, 578

Penrith Golf Club PENRITH 236

Penwortham Golf Club Ltd PRESTON 247

Peover Golf Club KNUTSFORD 228

Percy Wood Golf & Country Retreat SWARLAND 269

Perdiswell Park Golf CLub WORCESTER 220

Perivale Park Golf Club GREENFORD 126

Perranporth Golf Club PERRANPORTH 27

Perton Golf Club WOLVERHAMPTON 216

Pessac Golf de BORDEAUX 516

Peterborough Milton Golf Club PETERBOROUGH 135

Peterculter Golf Club PETERCULTER 318

Peterhead Golf Club PETERHEAD 320

Petersfield Golf Club (New Course) PETERSFIELD 80

Petersfield Golf Club, Pay & Play Course PETERSFIELD 80

Peterstone Lakes Golf Club & Hotel CARDIFF 424

Petworth Golf Course PETWORTH 119

PGA National Golf Club PALM BEACH 544

PGA West Resort Course (Nicklaus) LA QUINTA 546

PGA West Resort Course (TPC Stadium) LA QUINTA 546

Phoenix Golf Club ROTHERHAM 287

Phuket Country Club PHUKET 554

Pike Fold Golf Club BURY 252

Pike Hills Golf Club YORK 284

Piltdown Golf Club UCKFIELD 115

Pincents Manor Golf READING 67

Pine Lakes International Country Club MYRTLE BEACH 545

Pinehurst Resort & Country Club PINEHURST 545

Pines Golf Centre DUMFRIES 339

Pinhal Golf Course VILAMOURA 527

Pinheiros Altos Golf Club QUINTA DO LAGO 526

Pinner Hill Golf Club PINNER 128

Piperdam Golf & Leisure Resort DUNDEE 323

Pitcheroak Golf Course REDDITCH 219

Pitlochry Golf Course PITLOCHRY 389

Pitreavie (Dunfermline) Golf Club DUNFERMLINE 359

Plassey Golf Course WREXHAM 412

Pleasington Golf Club BLACKBURN 243

Plutaluang Navy Golf Course CHONBURI 558

Polkemmet Golf Course WHITBURN 356

Pollok Golf Club GLASGOW 368

Polmont Golf Club FALKIRK 394

Pontardawe Golf Club SWANSEA 435

Ponte de Lima Golfe de PONTE DE LIMA 530

Pontefract & District Golf Club PONTEFRACT 298

Ponteland Golf Club NEWCASTLE UPON TYNE 268

Pontypool Golf Club PONTYPOOL 430

Pontypridd Golf Club PONTYPRIDD 431

Port Bannatyne Golf Club ROTHESAY 328

Port Glasgow Golf Club PORT GLASGOW 391

Port Royal Golf Club HILTON HEAD 545

Port Royal Golf Driving Range EDINBURGH 577

Port St Mary Golf Club PORT ST MARY 502

Portadown Golf Club PORTADOWN 450

Portal Golf and Country Club TARPORLEY 231

Portal, The Premier Course TARPORLEY 231

Portarlington Golf Club PORTARRLINGTON 482

Porters Park Golf Club RADLETT 148

Porthmadog Golf Club MORFA BYCHAN 405

Portlethen Golf Club PORTLETHEN 320

Portmarnock Hotel & Golf Links PORTMARNOCK 472

Portmore Golf Park BARNSTAPLE 30, 562

Porto Santo Golfe PORTO SANTO 529

Portobello Golf Course EDINBURGH 351

Portpatrick Golf Club PORTPATRICK 344

Portsalon Golf Club PORTSALON 467

Portsmouth Golf Club (1926) PORTSMOUTH 80

Portstewart Golf Club PORTSTEWART 455

Pottergate Golf Club LINCOLN 178

Potters Bar Golf Club POTTERS BAR 148

Poult Wood Public Golf Centre TONBRIDGE 94

Poulton Park Golf Club Ltd. WARRINGTON 232

Poulton-le-Fylde Golf Club BLACKPOOL 244

Powerscourt Golf Club ENNISKERRY 497

Powfoot Golf Club ANNAN 338

Praa Sands Golf Club PENZANCE 27

Praia D'el Rey Golf & Country Club OBIDOS 528

Prenton Golf Club BIRKENHEAD 259

Prestatyn Golf Club PRESTATYN 410

Prestbury Golf Club PRESTBURY 230

Preston Golf Club PRESTON 248

Prestonfield Golf Club EDINBURGH 351

Prestwich Golf Club MANCHESTER 255

Prestwick Golf Club PRESTWICK 331

Prestwick St Cuthbert Golf Club PRESTWICK 332

Prestwick St Nicholas Golf Club PRESTWICK 331

Prince's Golf Club SANDWICH BAY 91

Princes Golf Course EDINBURGH 351

Princes Risborough Golf Club PRINCES RISBOROUGH 72

Priors Hall Golf Club CORBY 184

Priskilly Forest Golf Club FISHGUARD/HAVERFORWEST 417

Prudhoe Golf Club PRUDHOE 269

Pryors Hayes Golf Club CHESTER 226

Pulrose Golf Course DOUGLAS 502

Pumpherston Golf Club LIVINGSTON 354

Purley Chase Golf Club NORTH WARWICKSHIRE 204

Purley Downs Golf Club PURLEY 107

Puttenham Golf Club GUILDFORD 105

Pwllheli Golf Club PWLLHELI 578

Pyecombe Golf Club BRIGHTON 116

Pyle & Kenfig Golf Club PORTHCAWL 431

Pype Hayes Golf Club SUTTON COLDFIELD 214

Pyrford Golf Club 1993 WOKING 110

Queens Park (Bournemouth) Golf Club BOURNEMOUTH 38

Queens Park Golf Course CREWE 227

Queensbury Golf Club BRADFORD 291

Quinta da Barca Golfe de ESPOSENDE 530

Quinta da Cima CACELA 525

Quinta da Ria CACELA 525

Quinta do Peru Golf Course AZEITAO 527

R A F Coningsby Golf Club LINCOLN 178

Radcliffe-on-Trent Golf Club RADCLIFFE-ON-TRENT 191

Radnor Golf and Leisure REDRUTH 27, 561

Radyr Golf Club CARDIFF 424

RAF St Athan Golf Club BARRY 422

Raglan Parc Golf Club RAGLAN 432

Ralston Golf Club PAISLEY 391

Ramada Hotel & Golf Resort GLOUCESTER 46, 564

Ramsdale Oark Golf Centre CALVERTON 568

Ramsdale Park Golf Centre CALVERTON 188, 568

Ramsey Golf and Bowls Club HUNTINGDON 134

Ramsey Golf Club RAMSEY 502

Ramside Hall Hotel & Golf Club DURHAM 241

Rancho Las Palmas Country Club RANCHO MIRAGE 546

Ranfurly Castle Golf Club Ltd BRIDGE OF WEIR 391

Rathcore Golf and Country Club ENFIELD 486

Rathdowney Golf Club PORTLAOISE 482

Rathmore Golf Club PORTRUSH 449

Ratho Park Golf Club Ltd EDINBURGH 352

Rathsallagh Golf Club DUNLAVIN 497

Ravelston Golf Club Ltd EDINBURGH 352

Raven Meadow Golf Club WORCESTER 220

Ravenmeadow Golf Club WORCESTER 574

Ravensworth Golf Club Ltd. GATESHEAD 270

Rawdon Golf & Lawn Tennis Club LEEDS 297

Rayong Green Valley Country Club RAYONG 558

Reading Golf Club READING 67

Real Club de Golf Las Brisas MARBELLA 535

Real Club de Golf Sotogrande SAN ROQUE 536

Real Golf de Bendinat PALMA 538

Reaseheath Golf Club NANTWICH 230

Reay Golf Club REAY 372

Redbourn Golf Club REDBOURN 148

Redcastle Golf Club REDCASTLE 467

Reddish Vale Golf Club STOCKPORT 257

Redditch Golf Club REDDITCH 219

Redditch Kingfisher Golf Club REDDITCH 220

Redhill and Reigate Golf Club REDHILL 107

Redhill Golf Centre REDHILL 107, 572

Redlibbets Golf Club ASH 84

Regent Park Golf Club Ltd BOLTON 251

Regiment Way Golf Centre CHELMSFORD 138

Reigate Heath Golf Club REIGATE 107

Reigate Hill Golf Club REIGATE 107

Renfrew Golf Club RENFREW 391

Renishaw Park Golf Club SHEFFIELD 167

Rennes Golf de RENNES 512

Retford Golf Club Ltd. RETFORD 191

Rhondda Golf Club RHONDDA 432

Rhosgoch Golf Club RHOSGOCH 421

Rhos-on-Sea Residential Golf Club LLANDUDNO 410

Rhuddlan Golf Club RHUDDLAN 411

Rhyl Golf Club RHYL 412

Richings Park Golf Club IVER 71

Richmond (Yorkshire) Golf Club RICHMOND 280

Richmond Golf Club RICHMOND 107

Richmond Park Golf Club LONDON 63

Richmond Park Golf Club THETFORD 157

Rickmansworth Public Golf Course RICKMANSWORTH 148

Riddlesden Golf Club KEIGHLEY 294

Ridge Golf Club MAIDSTONE 89

Ridgeway Golf Club CAERPHILLY 423

Ring Of Kerry Golf & Country Club KENMARE 475

Ringdufferin Golf Course KILLYLEAGH 453

Ringway Golf Club Ltd ALTRINCHAM 250

Rio Major Golden Eagle Golf Club RIO MAIOR 528

Rio Real Golf MARBELLA 534

Ripon City Golf Club RIPON 280

Risebridge Golf Centre ROMFORD 143

Rishton Golf Club BLACKBURN 243

Riverside Golf Centre LENTON LANE 189

Riviera Golf Club CANNES 518

RNAS Culdrose Golf Club HELSTON 22

Robin Hood Golf Club SOLIHULL 212

Rochdale Golf Club ROCHDALE 256

Rochester and Cobham Park Golf Club ROCHESTER 91

Rochford Hundred Golf Club ROCHFORD 142

Rodway Hill Golf Course GLOUCESTER 46

Roe Park Golf Club LIMAVADY 455, 580

Roehampton Club Ltd. ROEHAMPTON 64

Roker Park Golf Club GUILDFORD 105, 571

Rolls of Monmouth Golf Club MONMOUTH 428

Romanby Golf Course NORTHALLERTON 280, 575

Romiley Golf Club Ltd STOCKPORT 257

Romney Warren Golf Club NEW ROMNEY 89

Romsey Golf Club Ltd SOUTHAMPTON 81

Rookery Park Golf Club LOWESTOFT 160

Rosapenna Hotel & Golf Links DOWNINGS 466

Roscommon Golf Club ROSCOMMON 489

Rose Garden Aprime Resort NAKORN PATHOM 556

Rose Hill Golf Club BIRMINGHAM 209

Roseberry Grange Golf Club CHESTER-LE-STREET 239

Rosehearty Golf Club ROSEHEARTY 320

Roserrow Golf & Country Club WADEBRIDGE 28

Ross Golf Club KILLARNEY 476

Rossendale Golf Club Ltd. ROSSENDALE 248

Rosslare Golf Club ROSSLARE 495

Rossmore Golf Club MONAGHAN 488

Ross-on-Wye Golf Club ROSS-ON-WYE 169

Rothbury Golf Club ROTHBURY 269

Rother Valley Golf Centre SHEFFIELD 288

Rother Valley Golf Centre SHEFFIELD 575

Rotherham Golf Club Ltd ROTHERHAM 287

Rothes Golf Club ROTHES 320

Rothesay Golf Club ROTHESAY 328

Rothley Park Golf Club ROTHLEY 173

Rouken Glen Golf Centre GLASGOW 368

Roundhay Golf Club LEEDS 297

Roundwood Golf Club NEWTOWNMOUNTKENNEDY 498

Roundwood Golf Club ROTHERHAM 287

Routenburn Golf Club LARGS 330

Rowany Golf Club PORT ERIN 502

Rowlands Castle Golf Club HAVANT 78

Roxburghe Golf Club KELSO 336

Royal Aberdeen Golf Club ABERDEEN 311

Royal Ascot Golf Club ASCOT 65

Royal Ashdown Forest Golf Club (Old Course) FOREST ROW 113

Royal Ashdown Forest Golf Club (West Course) FOREST ROW 113

Royal Belfast Golf Club HOLYWOOD 452

Royal Birkdale Golf Club SOUTHPORT 264

Royal Blackheath Golf Club ELTHAM 63

Royal Burgess Golfing Society of Edinburgh EDINBURGH 352

Royal Cape Golf Club WYNBERG 548

Royal Chiangmai Golf Resort CHIANGMAI 556

Royal Cinque Ports Golf Club DEAL 86

Royal County Down Golf Club NEWCASTLE 453

Royal Cromer Golf Club CROMER 152

Royal Dornoch Golf Club DORNOCH 370

Royal Dublin Golf Club DUBLIN 470

Royal Eastbourne Golf Club EASTBOURNE 112

Royal Epping Forest Golf Club CHINGFORD 124

Royal Guernsey Golf Club GUERNSEY 503

Royal Hua Hin Golf Course HUA HIN 555

Royal Jersey Golf Club JERSEY 504

Royal Livepool Gol Club HOYLAKE 260

Royal Lytham & St Annes Golf Club LYTHAM ST ANNES 246

Royal Mid-Surrey Golf Club RICHMOND 108

Royal Montrose Golf Club MONTROSE 325

Royal Musselburgh Golf Club PRESTONPANS 356

Royal North Devon Golf Club WESTWARD HO 37

Royal Norwich Golf Club NORWICH 156

Royal Porthcawl Golf Club PORTHCAWL 432

Royal Portrush Golf Club PORTRUSH 449

Royal St David's Golf Club HARLECH 405

Royal St. George's Golf Club SANDWICH 91

Royal Tara Golf club NAVAN 488

Royal Tarlair Golf Club MACDUFF 318

Royal Town of Caernarfon Golf Club CAERNARFON 404

Royal Troon Golf Club TROON 333

Royal West Norfolk Golf Club KING'S LYNN 154

Royal Wimbledon Golf Club WIMBLEDON 64

Royal Winchester Golf Club WINCHESTER 82

Royal Worlington and Newmarket Golf Club MILDENHALL 160

Royan Golf de ROYAN 513

Royston Golf Club (Founded 1892) ROYSTON 148

Rudding Park Golf HARROGATE 279, 575

Ruddington Grange Golf Club NOTTINGHAM 191

Rufford Park Golf & Country Club NEWARK 191, 568

Rufford Park Golf & Country Club NEWARK 568

Rugby Golf Club RUGBY 204

Ruislip Golf Club RUISLIP 128

Runcorn Golf Club RUNCORN 231

Rushcliffe Golf Club EAST LEAKE 188

Rushden Golf Club RUSHDEN 186

Rushmere Golf Club IPSWICH 159

Rushmore Golf Club SALISBURY 59

Rusper Golf Club & Driving Range NEWDIGATE 106, 571

Rustington Golf Centre RUSTINGTON 119, 573

Rutherford Castle Golf Club WEST LINTON 337

Ruthin Pwllglas Golf Club RUTHIN 412

Rutland Country Golf Club STAMFORD 567

Rutland County Golf Club STAMFORD 182, 567

Ryburn Golf Club HALIFAX 293

Ryde Golf Club RYDE 83

Rye Golf Club RYE 114

Rye Hill Golf Club BANBURY 96

Ryston Park Golf Club DOWNHAM MARKET 152

Ryton Golf Club RYTON 272

Sable-Solesmes Golf de ANGERS 510

Saddlebrook Resort TAMPA 544

Saddleworth Golf Club OLDHAM 256

Saffron Walden Golf Club SAFFRON WALDEN 143

Saint Laurent Golf de AURAY 511

Saint Malo Golf Club ST MALO 512

Sainte-Baume Golf de la NANS LES PINS 519

St Andrews Links Golf Practice Centre ST ANDREWS 577

St Andrews Major Golf Club BARRY 423

St Augustine's Golf Club RAMSGATE 90

St Austell Golf Club ST. AUSTELL 27

St Bees Golf Club ST BEES 236

St Boswells Golf Club ST BOSWELLS 337

St Cleres Hall Golf Club STANFORD LE HOPE 143

St Davids City Golf Club ST DAVIDS 418

St Deiniol Golf Club BANGOR 404

St Enodoc Golf Club WADEBRIDGE 28

St Fillans Golf Club ST FILLANS 390

St George's Hill Golf Club WEYBRIDGE 109

St Giles Golf Club NEWTOWN 421

St Helen's Bay Golf Resort ROSSLARE HARBOUR 495

St Idloes Golf Club LLANIDLOES 420

St Ives (Hunts) Golf Club ST. IVES 135

St Jean-de-Monts Golf Club de ST JEAN-DE-MONTS 512

St Kew Golf Club WADEBRIDGE 28

St Margaret's Golf & Country Club ST MARGARET'S 472

St Mary's Golf Club PENCOED 430

St Medan Golf Club PORT WILLIAM 344

St Mellion Hotel, Golf & Country Club SALTASH 28

St Mellons Golf Club CARDIFF 424

St Melyd Golf Club PRESTATYN 411

St Michaels Golf Club LEUCHARS 360

St Neots Golf Club ST. NEOTS 136

St Pierre Park Golf Club GUERNSEY 503

St Quentin-en-Yvelines Golf de PARIS 512

St Thomas Priory RUGELEY 199

St. Annes Old Links Golf Club LYTHAM ST ANNES 246

St. Michaels Jubilee Golf Club WIDNES 232

Sale Golf Club SALE 256

Salgados Golfe de ALBUFEIRA 524

Saline Golf Club DUNFERMLINE 359

Salisbury & South Wilts Golf Club SALISBURY 59

Saltburn by the Sea Golf Club Ltd SALTBURN BY THE SEA 281

Saltford Golf Club SALTFORD 54

San Lorenzo Golf Club ALMANCIL 524

San Roque Club SAN ROQUE 536

Sand Martins Golf Club WOKINGHAM 68

Sand Moor Golf Club LEEDS 297

Sandbach Golf Club SANDBACH 231

Sandford Springs Golf Club BASINGSTOKE 75

Sandhill Golf Club BARNSLEY 285

Sandilands Golf Club MABLETHORPE 180

Sandiway Golf Club NORTHWICH 230

Sandown Golf Centre ESHER 571

Sandwell Park Golf Club WEST BROMWICH 215

Sandy Lodge Golf Club NORTHWOOD 127

Sandyhills Golf Club GLASGOW 368

Sanquhar Golf Club SANQUHAR 344

Santa Ponsa Golf Club One SANTA PONSA 539

Santa Ponsa Golf Club Two SANTA PONSA 539

Santiburi Country Club CHIANG RAI 556

Santiburi Samui Country Club SURATHANI 555

Sapey Golf Club BROMYARD 218

Saron Golf Course LLANDYSUL 414

Saunton Golf Club SAUNTON 36

Scarborough North Cliff Golf Club SCARBOROUGH 281

Scarborough South Cliff Golf Club Ltd SCARBOROUGH 281

Scarcroft Golf Club LEEDS 298

Scarthingwell Golf Course TADCASTER 282

Scoonie Golf Club LEVEN 361

Scotscraig Golf Club TAYPORT 364

Scrabo Golf Club NEWTOWNARDS 453

Scraptoft Golf Club LEICESTER 171

Seacroft Golf Club SKEGNESS 181

Seafield Golf & Country Club GOREY 495

Seafield Golf Course AYR 329

Seaford Golf Club SEAFORD 114

Seaford Head Golf Club SEAFORD 114

Seaham Golf Club SEAHAM 242

Seahouses Golf Club SEAHOUSES 269

Seapoint Golf Club DROGHEDA 484

Searles Resort Golf Course HUNSTANTON 154

Seascale Golf Club SEASCALE 237

Seaton Carew Golf Club HARTLEPOOL 242

Seckford Golf Club WOODBRIDGE 161, 571

Secret Valley Golf Club PAPHOS 539

Sedbergh Golf Club SEDBERGH 237

Sedgley Golf Centre DUDLEY 210

Sedlescombe Golf Club SEDLESCOMBE 115, 572

Seedy Mill Golf Club LICHFIELD 199

Seignosse Golf Hotel BAYONNE 515

Selby Golf Club SELBY 281

Selkirk Golf Club SELKIRK 337

Selsdon Park Hotel & Golf Club CROYDON 102

Selsey Golf Club CHICHESTER 117

Sene Valley Golf Club FOLKESTONE 87

Serlby Park Golf Club DONCASTER 286

Servanes Golf de AVIGNON 517

Settle Golf Club SETTLE 281

Severn Meadows Golf Club BRIDGNORTH 193

Shandon Park Golf Club BELFAST 452

Shanklin & Sandown Golf Club SANDOWN 83

Shannon Golf Club SHANNON 460

Shaw Hill Hotel Golf & Country Club CHORLEY 245

Shay Grange Golf Centre BRADFORD 575

Sheerness Golf Club SHEERNESS 92

Shendish Manor Golf Club HEMEL HEMPSTEAD 147

Sheraton Algarve Pine Cliffs Golf & Country Club ALBUFEIRA 524

Sherborne Golf Club SHERBORNE 40

Sherdley Park Municipal Golf Course & Driving Range ST HELENS 263

Sherdons Golf Centre TEWKESBURY 48, 564

Sheringham Golf Club SHERINGHAM 157

Sherry Golf Jerez JEREZ 536

Sherwood Forest Golf Club MANSFIELD 189

Shetland Golf Club SHETLAND 397

Shifnal Golf Club SHIFNAL 196

Shipley Golf Club BRADFORD 291

Shipyard Golf Club HILTON HEAD 545

Shirehampton Park Golf Club BRISTOL 44

Shirland Golf Club SHIRLAND 167

Shirley Golf Club SOLIHULL 212

Shirley Park Golf Club Ltd. CROYDON 103

Shiskine Golf & Tennis Club BLACKWATERFOOT 334

Shooters Hill Golf Club Ltd SHOOTERS HILL 64

Shortlands Golf Club BROMLEY 85

Shortwood Lodge Golf Club BRISTOL 44

Shotts Golf Club SHOTTS 381

Shrewsbury Golf Club SHREWSBURY 196

Shrigley Hall Hotel Golf & Country Club POYNTON 230

Shriveham Park Golf Club SHRIVENHAM 60

Shropshire (The) TELFORD 196, 570

Sickleholme Golf Club SHEFFIELD 167

Sidcup Golf Club SIDCUP 92

Sidmouth Golf Club SIDMOUTH 36

Silecroft Golf Club SILECROFT 237

Silkstone Golf Club BARNSLEY 285

Silloth On Solway Golf Club SILLOTH 237

Silsden Golf Club KEIGHLEY 295

Silverdale Golf Club SILVERDALE 238

Silverdale Golf Club SILVERDALE 248

Silverknowes Golf Course EDINBURGH 352

Silvermere Golf & Leisure Complex COBHAM 101, 571

Silverstone Golf Club STOWE 73, 560

Silves Golf Course SILVES 526

Singing Hills Golf Course Ltd ALBOURNE 116

Sittingbourne and Milton Regis SITTINGBOURNE 92

Sitwell Park Golf Club ROTHERHAM 287

Six Hills Golf Club MELTON MOWBRAY 173

Skeabost Golf Club SKEABOST BRIDGE 398

Skelmorlie Golf Club SKELMORLIE 332

Skerries Golf Club SKERRIES 473

Skipton Golf Club Ltd SKIPTON 281

Slade Valley Golf Club BRITTAS 468

Sleaford Golf Club SLEAFORD 181

Slieve Russell Hotel Golf Club BALLYCONNELL 458

Slinfold Park Golf and Country Club HORSHAM 118

Sociedade do Golfe da Quinta do Lago ALMANCIL 524

Soi Dao Highland Golf Club & Resort CHANTABURI 557

Solent Meads Golf Centre BOURNEMOUTH 38

Solway Links Golf Club SOUTHERNESS 344

Son Servera Golf Club SON SERVERA 539

Son Vida Golf PALMA 538

Sonning Golf Club READING 68

Souillac Country Club SOUILLAC 516

South Beds. Golf Club LUTON 132

South Bradford Golf Club BRADFORD 291

South County Golf Club BRITTAS 468

South Essex Golf & Country Club BRENTWOOD 137

South Herefordshire Golf Club ROSS-ON-WYE 169, 565

South Herts Golf Club TOTTERIDGE 128

South Kyme Golf Club SOUTH KYME 181

South Leeds Golf Club LEEDS 298

South Moor Golf Club STANLEY 242

South Pembrokeshire Golf Club PEMBROKE DOCK 418

South Shields Golf Club Ltd. SOUTH SHIELDS 272

South Staffordshire Golf Club WOLVERHAMPTON 216

South Wales Golf Range and Course BARRY 579

South Winchester Golf Club WINCHESTER 82

Southampton Golf Club SOUTHAMPTON 81

Southend-on-Sea Golf Club SOUTHEND-ON-SEA 143

Southern Valley Golf Course GRAVESEND 88

Southerndown Golf Club SOUTHERNDOWN 432

Southerness Golf Club DUMFRIES 339

Southfield Golf Club OXFORD 98

Southport & Ainsdale Golf Club SOUTHPORT 263

Southport Municipal Golf Club SOUTHPORT 264

Southport Old Links Golf Club SOUTHPORT 264

Southview Golf Club SKEGNESS 181

Southwell Golf Club SOUTHWELL 191

Southwick Park Golf Club FAREHAM 77

Southwold Golf Club SOUTHWOLD 160

Southwood Golf Course FARNBOROUGH 77

Spa Golf Club BALLYNAHINCH 451

Spalding Golf Club SPALDING 181

Spanish Point Golf Club MILTON MALBAY 460

Sparkwell Golf Club PLYMOUTH 34

Spean Bridge Golf Club SPEAN BRIDGE 378

Sportscotland National Centre LARGS 331

Springfield Park Golf Club ROCHDALE 256

Springfield Village Golf & Spa CHA-AM 555

Springhead Park Golf Club HULL 276

Springs Hotel & Golf Club WALLINGFORD 99

Springwater Golf Club CALVERTON 188

Sriracha Golf Club SRIRACHA 558

Stackstown Golf Club RATHFARNHAM 472

Staddon Heights Golf Club PLYMOUTH 34

Stadium Golf Driving Range HUDDERSFIELD 576

Stafford Castle Golf Club STAFFORD 199

Stamford Golf Club STALYBRIDGE 231

Stand Golf Club MANCHESTER 255

Standish Court Golf Club WIGAN 249

Stanedge Golf Club CHESTERFIELD 165

Stanmore Golf Club STANMORE 128

Stanton-on-the-Wolds Golf Club STANTON-ON-THE-WOLDS 191

Stapleford Abbotts Golf Club STAPLEFORD ABBOTTS 143

Staverton Park Golf Club DAVENTRY 184

Stevenage Golf Centre STEVENAGE 149

Stinchcombe Hill Golf Club DURSLEY 46

Stirling Golf Club STIRLING 395

Stock Brook Golf & Country Club BILLERICAY 137

Stockley Park Golf Club UXBRIDGE 129

Stockport Golf Club Ltd STOCKPORT 257

Stocksbridge and District Golf Club Ltd SHEFFIELD 289

Stocksfield Golf Club STOCKSFIELD 269

Stockwood Park Golf Club LUTON 132

Stockwood Vale Golf Club BRISTOL 52

Stoke Albany Golf Club MARKET HARBOROUGH 184

Stoke by Nayland Golf & Spa STOKE BY NAYLAND 144

Stoke Park Club STOKE POGES 73

Stoke Rochford Golf Club GRANTHAM 177

Stone Golf Club STONE 201

Stonebridge MERIDEN 204

Stoneham Golf Club SOUTHAMPTON 82

Stonehaven Golf Club STONEHAVEN 321

Stonelees Golf Centre RAMSGATE 91, 566

Stoneleigh Deer Park Golf Club STONELEIGH 205
Stoney Holme Municipal Golf Course CARLISLE 234
Stornoway Golf Club STORNOWAY 397
Storws Wen Golf Club BRYNTEG 404
Stourbridge Golf Club STOURBRIDGE 212
Stowe Golf Club STOWE 73
Stowmarket Golf Club Ltd STOWMARKET 161
Strabane Golf Club STRABANE 456
Stranraer Golf Club STRANRAER 346
Stratford-on-Avon Golf Club STRATFORD-UPON-AVON 205
Strathaven Golf Club STRATHAVEN 381
Strathclyde Park Golf Club HAMILTON 380
Strathendrick Golf Club DRYMEN 393
Strathlene Golf Club BUCKIE 315
Strathmore Golf Centre BLAIRGOWRIE 386, 578
Strathpeffer Spa Golf Club STRATHPEFFER 374
Strathtay Golf Club STRATHTAY 390
Strathtyrum Course ST ANDREWS 364
Strawberry Hill Golf Club TWICKENHAM 129
Stressholme Golf Club DARLINGTON 240
Stromness Golf Club Ltd STROMNESS 397
Studley Wood Golf Club HORTON-CUM-STUDLEY 98, 569
Sturminster Marshall Golf Club WIMBORNE 42
Styal Golf Club STYAL 231, 561
Sudbrook Moor Golf Club GRANTHAM 177
Sudbury Golf Club Ltd. WEMBLEY 129
Suffolk Hotel Golf & Country Club BURY ST. EDMUNDS 158
Summerhill Golf Course HAY-ON-WYE 168
Sunbury Golf Centre SHEPPERTON 128
Sundridge Park Golf Club BROMLEY 85
Sunningdale Golf Club SUNNINGDALE 108
Sunningdale Ladies' Golf Club SUNNINGDALE 68
Surbiton Golf Club CHESSINGTON 101
Surrey National Golf Club CATERHAM 100
Sutton Bridge Golf Club SPALDING 182
Sutton Coldfield Golf Club SUTTON COLDFIELD 214
Sutton Green Golf Club GUILDFORD 105
Sutton Hall Golf Club SUTTON WEAVER 231
Sutton Park Golf Club HULL 276
Swaffham Golf Club SWAFFHAM 157
Swansea Bay Golf Club NEATH 428

Swanston Golf Course EDINBURGH 352
Sweetwoods Park Golf Club EAST GRINSTEAD 112
Swindon Golf Club DUDLEY 210
Swindon Ridge Golf Driving Range, Shop and Golf Club DUDLEY 573
Swinford Golf Club SWINFORD 485
Swinley Forest Golf Club ASCOT 65
Swinton Park Golf Club MANCHESTER 255
Swords Open Golf Course SWORDS 473

Tadmarton Heath Golf Club BANBURY 96
Tain Golf Club TAIN 374
Tall Pines Golf Club BRISTOL 52
Tamworth Golf Centre Ltd TAMWORTH 202
Tandragee Golf Club TANDRAGEE 450
Tandridge Golf Club OXTED 107
Tankersley Park Golf Club Ltd SHEFFIELD 289
Tapton Park Golf & Leisure Centre CHESTERFIELD 165
Tarbat Golf Club PORTMAHOMACK 374
Tarbert Golf Club TARBERT 328
Tarland Golf Club ABERDEEN 311
Taunton and Pickeridge Golf Club TAUNTON 55
Taunton Vale Golf Club TAUNTON 55
Tavistock Golf Club TAVISTOCK 36
Taymouth Castle Golf Course KENMORE 387
Taynuilt Golf Club TAYNUILT 328
Teesside Golf Club STOCKTON-ON-TEES 242
Teesside Golf Club STOCKTON-ON-TEES 282
Tehidy Park Golf Club CAMBORNE 21
Teign Valley Golf Club EXETER 32
Teignmouth Golf Club TEIGNMOUTH 36
Telford Golf & Spa Hotel TELFORD 196
Temple Golf Club MAIDENHEAD 66
Temple Newsam Golf Club LEEDS 298
Templemore Golf Club TEMPLEMORE 492
Tenby Golf Club TENBY 418
Tenterden Golf Club TENTERDEN 93
Terceira Golf Club TERCEIRA 530
Test Valley Golf Club BASINGSTOKE 75
Tewkesbury Park Hotel Golf & Country Club TEWKESBURY 50
Thai Muang Beach Golf & Marina PHANG-NGA 554
Thames Ditton & Esher Golf Club ESHER 104
Thamesview Golf Centre LONDON 63
Thetford Golf Club THETFORD 157
Theydon Bois Golf Club EPPING 140

Thirsk and Northallerton Golf Club THIRSK 282

Thistle Hotel Roseholm Golf Course IRVINE 330

Thornbury Golf Centre BRISTOL 44

Thorndon Park Golf Club Ltd. BRENTWOOD 137

Thorne Golf Club DONCASTER 286

Thorney Golf Centre PETERBOROUGH 135

Thornhill Golf Club THORNHILL 346

Thornhurst Park Golf Course DONCASTER 286

Thornton Golf Club THORNTON 364

Thorpe Hall Golf Club SOUTHEND-ON-SEA 143

Thorpe Wood Golf Course PETERBOROUGH 135

Thorpeness Golf Club & Hotel THORPENESS 161

Three Hammers Golf Complex WOLVERHAMPTON 573

Three Locks Golf Club MILTON KEYNES 72

Three Rivers Golf & Country Club CHELMSFORD 138

Thurles Golf Club THURLES 492

Thurlestone Golf Club THURLESTON 36

Thurso Golf Club THURSO 372

Tickenham Golf Club TICKENHAM 55, 570

Tidbury Green Golf Club SOLIHULL 212

Tidewater Golf Club MYRTLE BEACH 545

Tidworth Garrison Golf Club TIDWORTH 60

Tilgate Forest Golf Centre CRAWLEY 117, 572

Tillicoultry Golf Club STIRLING 395

Tilsworth Golf Centre DUNSTABLE 131

Tilsworth Golf Centre DUNSTABLE 559

Tinsley Park Golf Club (Municipal) SHEFFIELD 289

Tiverton Golf Club TIVERTON 36

Tobermory Golf Club TOBERMORY 397

Todmorden Golf Club TODMORDEN 300

Toft Hotel Golf Club BOURNE 175

Toot Hill Golf Club ONGAR 142

Top Meadow Golf Club & Hotel UPMINSTER 144

Topgolf Game Centre WATFORD 565

Torphin Hill Golf Club EDINBURGH 352

Torphins Golf Club TORPHINS 321

Torquay Golf Club TORQUAY 37

Torrance House Golf Club EAST KILBRIDE 379

Torrequebrada Golf BENALMADENA 534

Torvean Golf Club INVERNESS 377

Torwoodlee Golf Club GALASHIELS 335

Towerlands Driving Range BRAINTREE 563

Towerlands Golf Clu BRAINTREE 137

Towneley Golf Club BURNLEY 244

Traditions Golf Course 1989 WOKING 109

Traigh Golf Course ARISAIG 375

Tralee Golf Club TRALEE 478

Tramore Golf Club TRAMORE 492

Tredegar & Rhymney Golf Club RHYMNEY 432

Tredegar Park Golf Club Ltd NEWPORT 430

Trefloyne Golf Club TENBY 406

Tregenna Castle Hotel Golf & Country Club ST. IVES 27

Treloy Golf Club NEWQUAY 24

Trent Lock Golf Centre LONG EATON 189, 568

Trent Park Public Golf Course LONDON 127

Trentham Golf Club STOKE-ON-TRENT 200

Trentham Park Golf Club STOKE-ON-TRENT 200

Trethorne Golf Club LAUNCESTON 24

Trevose Golf and Country Club PADSTOW 26

Troia Golf Club TROIA 529

Troon Municipal Golf Courses TROON 332

Truro Golf Club TRURO 28

Tsada Golf Club PAPHOS 539

Tulfarris Golf Club BLESSINGTON 496

Tullamore Golf Club TULLAMORE 489

Tulliallan Golf Club KINCARDINE 360

Tunbridge Wells Golf Club TUNBRIDGE WELLS 95

Tunshill Golf Club Ltd ROCHDALE 248

Turnberry Isle Resort & Club AVENTURA 544

Turnhouse Golf Club EDINBURGH 352

Turriff Golf Club TURRIFF 321

Turton Golf Club BOLTON 251

Tydd St Giles Golf & Country Club WISBECH 136

Tylney Park HOOK 78

Tynedale Golf Club HEXHAM 266

Tynemouth Golf Club Ltd. TYNEMOUTH 272

Tyneside Golf Club Ltd NEWCASTLE UPON TYNE 271

Tyrrells Wood Golf Club Ltd LEATHERHEAD 106

Tytherington Club MACCLESFIELD 228

Ullapool Golf Club ULLAPOOL 374

Ullenwood Manor Golf Course CHELTENHAM 45

Ullesthorpe Court Golf Club LUTTERWORTH 172

Ulverston Golf Club Ltd ULVERSTON 238

Upavon Golf Club UPAVON 60

Upchurch River Valley Golf Courses SITTINGBOURNE 92

Uphall Golf Club UPHALL 356

Upminster Golf Club UPMINSTER 144

Upton-By-Chester Golf Club CHESTER 226

Uttoxeter Golf Club UTTOXETER 202

Uxbridge Golf Course UXBRIDGE 129

Val Queven Golf du LORIENT 511
Valderrama Club de Golf SAN ROQUE 536
Vale de Pinta Course LAGOA 525
Vale do Lobo Golf Club ALMANCIL 524
Vale Golf Club PERSHORE 219
Vale Hotel Golf & Spa Resort HENSOL 427
Vale of Leven Golf Club ALEXANDRIA 347
Vale of Llangollen Golf Club Ltd LLANGOLLEN 410
Vale Royal Abbey Golf Club NORTHWICH 230
Valescure Golf et Tennis Club de ST RAPHAEL 520
Vall D'Or Golf Club CALA D'OR 538
Vaudreuil Golf du ROUEN 510
Vaul Golf Club SCARINISH 398
Ventnor Golf Club UPPER VENTNOR 83
Verulam Golf Club ST ALBANS 149
Vicars Cross Golf Club CHESTER 226
Victoria Clube de Golfe VILAMOURA 527
Vikla Golf & Country Club LIMASSOL 539
Vila Sol Spa & Golf Resort VILAMOURA 527
Villas of Grand Cypress One ORLANDO 544
Villeneuve Sur Lot Golf and Country Club VILLENEUVE-SUR-LOT 517
Vimeiro Golf Club VIMEIRO 529
Virginia Park Golf Club CAERPHILLY 423, 579
Vivary Golf Course TAUNTON 55

Wakefield Golf Club WAKEFIELD 300
Waldringfield Golf Club WOODBRIDGE 161
Wallasey Golf Club WALLASEY 264
Wallsend Golf Club WALLSEND 272
Walmer and Kingsdown Golf Club DEAL 86
Walmersley Golf Club BURY 252
Walmley Golf Club SUTTON COLDFIELD 214
Walsall Golf Club WALSALL 214
Waltham Windmill Golf Club GRIMSBY 178
Walton Hall Golf Club WARRINGTON 232
Walton Heath Golf Club TADWORTH 108
Wanstead Golf Club WANSTEAD 129
Wareham Golf Club WAREHAM 41
Warkworth Golf Club WARKWORTH 269
Warley Park Golf Club BRENTWOOD 137
Warley Woods Golf Club WARLEY 214
Warren Golf Club DAWLISH 32
Warren Golf Club MALDON 142
Warren Golf Club WALLASEY 264
Warren Park Golf Centre CHADWELL HEATH 563
Warrenpoint Golf Club WARRENPOINT 453

Warrington Golf Club APPLETON 225
Warwick Golf Centre WARWICK 573
Warwick Golf Club WARWICK 206
Warwickshire (The) WARWICK 206
Waterbridge Golf Course CREDITON 31
Waterford Castle Golf Club WATERFORD 494
Waterford Valley Chiangrai Golf Course & Resort CHIANG RAI 557
Waterhall Golf Club BRIGHTON 112
Waterlooville Golf Club PORTSMOUTH 80
Waterstock Golf Club & Driving Range OXFORD 99, 569
Waterville House & Golf Links WATERVILLE 478
Wath Golf Club ROTHERHAM 287
Wavendon Golf Centre MILTON KEYNES 72
Weald of Kent Golf Course HEADCORN 88
Weald Park Golf Club BRENTWOOD 138
Wearside Golf Club SUNDERLAND 272
Wellingborough Golf Club WELLINGBOROUGH 186
Wellow Golf Club ROMSEY 81
Wells (Somerset) Golf Club Ltd WELLS 56
Wellshurst Golf and Country Club HAILSHAM 113, 572
Welsh Border Golf CLub WELSHPOOL 421
Welshpool Golf Club WELSHPOOL 421
Welton Manor Golf Centre LINCOLN 179
Welwyn Garden City Golf Club Ltd WELWYN GARDEN CITY 151
Wensum Valley Hotel Golf & Country Club NORWICH 156
Wentworth Club Ltd VIRGINIA WATER 108
Wenvoe Castle Golf Club CARDIFF 424
Wergs Golf Club WOLVERHAMPTON 215
Wernddu Golf Club ABERGAVENNY 422, 579
Werneth Golf Club OLDHAM 256
Werneth Low Golf Club HYDE 253
Wessex Golf Centre WEYMOUTH 41
West Berkshire Golf Course NEWBURY 67
West Bradford Golf Club Ltd BRADFORD 291
West Byfleet Golf Club WEST BYFLEET 108
West Chiltington Golf Club WEST CHILTINGTON 119
West Cornwall Golf Club ST. IVES 27
West Derby Golf Club LIVERPOOL 262
West End Golf Club (Halifax) Ltd HALIFAX 293
West Essex Golf Club CHINGFORD 124
West Herts Golf Club WATFORD 150
West Hill Golf Club WOKING 109

West Hove Golf Club Ltd HOVE 114

West Kent Golf Club ORPINGTON 90

West Kilbride Golf Club WEST KILBRIDE 333

West Lancashire Golf Club BLUNDELLSANDS 260

West Linton Golf Club WEST LINTON 337

West Lothian Golf Club BO'NESS 348

West Malling Golf Club MAIDSTONE 89

West Middlesex Golf Club SOUTHALL 128

West Midlands Golf Club SOLIHULL 212

West Monmouthshire Golf Club NANTYGLO 428

West Surrey Golf Club GODALMING 104

West Sussex Golf Club PULBOROUGH 119

West Waterford Golf & CountryClub DUNGARVAN 492

West Wilts Golf Club WARMINSTER 60

Westerham Golf Club WESTERHAM 95

Westerhope Golf Club NEWCASTLE UPON TYNE 271

Western Gailes Golf Club IRVINE 330

Western Park Golf Club LEICESTER 172

Westerwood Hotel Golf & Country Club CUMBERNAULD 365

Westgate and Birchington Golf Club WESTGATE ON SEA 95

Westhill Golf Club WESTHILL 321

Westhoughton Golf Club WESTHOUGHTON 258

Westin Mission Hills Resort Golf Club RANCHO MIRAGE 546

Westin Turnberry Resort TURNBERRY 333

Weston Park Golf Club NORWICH 156

Weston Turville Golf AYLESBURY 69

Westonbirt Golf Course TETBURY 48

Weston-Super-Mare Golf Club WESTON-SUPER-MARE 56

Westport Golf Club WESTPORT 485

Westray Golf Club WESTRAY 397

Wetherby Golf Club WETHERBY 300

Wexham Park Golf Course WEXHAM 73

Weybrook Park Golf Club BASINGSTOKE 76

Weymouth Golf Club Ltd WEYMOUTH 41

Whaddon Golf Centre ROYSTON 565

Whalley Golf Club CLITHEROE 245

Whalsay Golf Club WHALSAY 397

Wharton Park Golf Club BEWDLEY 217

Wheathill Golf Club SOMERTON 54

Wheatlands Golf Course & Country Hotel JERSEY 504

Wheatley Golf Club DONCASTER 286

Whetstone Golf Club and Driving Range LEICESTER 172

Whickham Golf Club Ltd. NEWCASTLE UPON TYNE 272

Whipsnade Park Golf Club WHIPSNADE 151

Whiston Hall Golf Club & Mansion Court Hotel CHEADLE 198

Whitburn Golf Club Ltd SOUTH SHIELDS 272

Whitby Golf Club WHITBY 282

Whitchurch (Cardiff) Golf Club CARDIFF 424

Whitecraigs Golf Club GLASGOW 368

Whitefield Golf Club WHITEFIELD 258

Whitefields Golf Club & Draycote Hotel RUGBY 205

Whitehall Golf Club NELSON 430

Whitehaven Golf Club WHITEHAVEN 238

Whitehead Golf Club CARRICKFERGUS 448

Whitehill Golf Club WARE 150, 565

Whitehill House Golf Club EDINBURGH (SOUTH) 352

Whitekirk Golf & Country Club WHITEKIRK 356

Whiteleaf Golf Club Ltd PRINCES RISBOROUGH 73

Whitemoss Golf Club DUNNING 387

Whitewebbs Golf Club ENFIELD 125

Whiting Bay Golf Club WHITING BAY 334

Whitley Bay Golf Club WHITLEY BAY 272

Whitsand Bay Hotel Golf Club TORPOINT 28

Whitstable and Seasalter Golf Club WHITSTABLE 95

Whittaker Golf Club LITTLEBOROUGH 253

Whittington Heath Golf Club LICHFIELD 199

Whittlebury Park Golf & Country Club TOWCESTER 186

Wick Golf Club WICK 372

Wickham Park Golf Club FAREHAM 77

Wicklow Golf Club WICKLOW 501

Widnes Golf Club WIDNES 232

Widney Manor Golf Club SOLIHULL 212

Wigan Golf Club WIGAN 249

Wigtown and Bladnoch Golf Club WIGTOWN 346

Wigtownshire County Golf Club NEWTOWN STEWART 342

Wild Wing Plantation MYRTLE BEACH 545

Wildernesse Club SEVENOAKS 92

Wildwood Country Club CRANLEIGH 102

Willesley Park Golf Club ASHBY DE LA ZOUCH 170

William Wroe Municipal Golf Club WIGAN 257

Williamwood Golf Club GLASGOW 369

Willingdon Golf Club EASTBOURNE 112

Willow Valley Golf BRIGHOUSE 576

Willow Valley Golf and Country Club BRIGHOUSE 292

Wilmslow Golf Club KNUTSFORD 228

Wilpshire Golf Club Ltd BLACKBURN 243

Wilton Golf Club REDCAR 280

Wiltshire Golf & Country Club SWINDON 60

Wimbledon Common Golf Club WIMBLEDON 64

Wimbledon Park Golf Club WIMBLEDON 64

Wimereux Golf de BOULOGNE 509

Wincanton Golf Club WINCANTON 56

Windermere Golf Club WINDERMERE 238

Windlemere Golf Club WOKING 110

Windlesham Golf Club BAGSHOT 100

Windmill Hill Golf Club MILTON KEYNES 72, 560

Windmill Village Hotel and Golf Club COVENTRY 210

Windwhistle Golf Club Ltd CHARD 53

Windyhill Golf Club GLASGOW 369

Winter Hill Golf Club MAIDENHEAD 66

Winterfield Golf Club DUNBAR 349

Wirrall Ladies' Golf Club Ltd BIRKENHEAD 259

Wishaw Golf Club WISHAW 381

Witch Golf Club MYRTLE BEACH 545

Withernsea Golf Club WITHERNSEA 276

Withington Golf Club MANCHESTER 255

Witney Lakes Golf Club WITNEY 99, 569

Woburn Golf Club MILTON KEYNES 72

Wokefield Park Golf Club READING 68

Woking Golf Club WOKING 110

Woldingham Golf Club CATERHAM 100

Woll Golf Course ASHKIRK 335

Wollaton Park Golf Club NOTTINGHAM 191

Wolstanton Golf Club WOLSTANTON 202

Woodbridge Golf Club WOODBRIDGE 161

Woodbrook Golf Club BRAY 496

Woodbury Park Golf & Country Club EXETER 32

Woodcote Park Golf Club COULSDON 101

Woodford Golf Club WOODFORD GREEN 144

Woodhall Hills Golf Club Ltd. PUDSEY 300

Woodham Golf and Country Club NEWTOWN AYCLIFFE 242

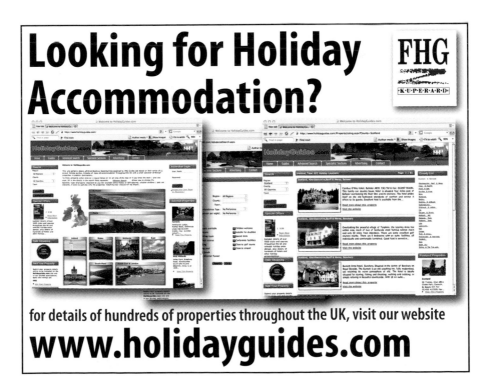

Woodlake Park Golf and Country Club PONTYPOOL 431
Woodlands Golf and Country Club BRISTOL 44
Woodlands Golf Club NAAS 481
Woodlands Manor Golf Club SEVENOAKS 92
Woodsome Hall Golf Club HUDDERSFIELD 294
Woodspring Golf & Country Club BRISTOL 52
Woodstock Golf and Country Club ENNIS 459
Woodthorpe Hall Golf Club ALFORD 175
Wooler Golf Club WOOLER 269
Woolley Park Golf Club WAKEFIELD 300
Woolston Manor Golf Club CHIGWELL 139
Woolton Golf Club LIVERPOOL 262
Worcester Golf and Country Club WORCESTER 220
Worcester Golf Range WORCESTER 574
Worcestershire Golf Club MALVERN WELLS 219
Worfield Golf Club WORFIELD 197
Workington Golf Club Ltd WORKINGTON 238
Worksop Golf Club WORKSOP 192
World of Golf CHISLEHURST 86,
World of Golf at Beverley Park NEW MALDEN 571
Worldham Golf Club ALTON 74

Worlebury Golf Club WESTON-SUPER-MARE 56
Worplesdon Golf Club WOKING 110
Worsley Golf Club ECCLES 253
Worthing Golf Club WORTHING 119
Wortley Golf Club SHEFFIELD 289
Wrag Barn Golf and Country Club HIGHWORTH 58
Wrangaton Golf Club SOUTH BRENT 36
Wrekin Golf Club TELFORD 196
Wrexham Golf Club WREXHAM 412
Wrotham Heath Golf Club SEVENOAKS 92
Wyboston Lakes Golf Course WYBOSTON 132
Wychwood Golf Club CHIPPING NORTON 96
Wychwood Park Golf Club WESTON 232
Wycombe Heights Golf Centre HIGH WYCOMBE 71
Wyke Green Golf Club ISLEWORTH 127
Wyre Forest Golf Club KIDDERMINSTER 219
Yelverton Golf Club YELVERTON 37
Yeovil Golf Club YEOVIL 56
York Golf Club YORK 284
Youghal Golf Club YOUGHAL 465
Yvelines Golf des PARIS 512

Index of Advertisers

Abbey Hotel, Golf & Country Club	220
Aberdeen City Golf	309
Aberdour Golf Club	357
Aberdovey Golf Club	402
Abernethy Golf Club	378
Aberystwyth Golf Club	415
Aboyne Golf Club	311
Academy Plaza Hotel	470
Actons Hotel	464
Aldenham Golf & Country Club	151
Alderney Tourism	503
Alford Golf Club	312
Alice Springs Golf Club	435
Allestree Park	165
Alnwick Golf Club	265
Alresford Golf Club	74
Alsager Golf Club	225
Ampfield Golf Club	75
Anglesey Golf Club Ltd	406
Ansty Golf Centre	209
Ashbourne Golf Club	486
Ashburnham Golf Club	414
Ashton-Under-Lyne Golf Course	250
Ashworth PLC	13
Aston Wood Golf Club	213
Atholl Hotel	310
Auchterarder Golf Club	384
Balbirnie Park Golf Club	362
Ballachulish House & Golf Course	326
Ballumbie Castle Golf Club	323
Ballykisteen Resort	493
Barnham Broom Hotel & Golf Club	155
Bath Public Golf Services	51
Beacon Park Golf & Country Club	249
Beaufort Golf Course	477
Bell Hotel	91
Belmont Lodge Hotel	168
Berwick-Upon-Tweed Goswick Golf Club	267
Bingley St Ives Golf Club	290
Bishop Auckland Golf Club	239
Blackaddie House Hotel	345
Blackwell Golf Club	217
Blainroe Golf Club	496
Blairgowrie Golf Club	385
Blankney Golf Club	175
Blarney Golf Resort	463
Blyth Golf Club	267
Boat of Garten Golf Club	375
Bowood Park Hotel	23
Bradford (Hawksworth) Golf Club	292
Brampton Golf Club	235
Brampton Park Golf Club	134
Bray Golf Club	496
Brean Golf Club	53
Brechin Golf Club	322
Brickhampton Court Golf Complex	45
Brighouse Bay Golf & Leisure Complex	340
Bristol & Clifton Golf Club	43
Brora Golf Club	371
Builth Wells Golf Club	420
Bull Bay Golf Club	402
Burghill Valley Golf Club	168
Burnett Arms Hotel	314
Burnham & Berrow Golf Club	53
Bushmills Inn Hotel	441
Cairndale Hotel & Leisure Club	339
Callander Golf Club	386
Cally Palace	341
Calverley Golf Club	295
Canwick Park Golf Club	179
Cardigan Golf Club	415
Carmarthen Golf Club	413
Castle Park Golf Course & Driving Range	353
Castletown Golf Links	502
Celtic Manor Resort	429
Charleville Golf Club	462
Chester Beatty Inn	499
Church Stretton Golf Club	193
Cleobury Mortimer Golf Club	195
Clyne Golf Club	433
Cockermouth Golf Club	235
Comrie Golf Club	386
Connemara Golf Club	474
Conwy (Caernarvonshire) Golf Club	408
Cookridge Hall Golf & Country Club	294
Coombe Wood Golf Club	105
Cosby Golf Club	170
Cottingham Parks Golf & Country Club	275
Cottrell Park Golf Club	400, 425
Courtyard Cottages	267
Cowal Golf Club	327
Craibstone Golf Centre	315
Craigadam	338
Craigesk Guest House	354
Craythorne	198
Crews Hill Golf Club	125

Croftburn Bed & Breakfast	393
Crusoe Hotel	363
Cullen Golf Club	316
Culloden House Hotel	371
Cutkive Wood Holiday Lodges	29
Dalmunzie Golf Course	384
Darby O'Gill's Country House Hotel	476
Darlington Golf Club	240
Darwen Golf Club	245
Denbigh Golf Club	408
Derrybawn House　Inside Front Cover,	500
Dewstow Golf Club	426
Diss Golf Club	152
Donabate Golf Club	468
Donaghadee Golf Club	452
Draycote Hotel & Whitefields Golf Course	205
Druids Glen Golf Club	499
Druids Glen Golf Resort	499
Duff House Royal Golf Club	314
Dumfries & Galloway Golf Club	339
Dundrum House Hotel	491
Ealing Services	125
East Lothian Golf	348
Eaton Golf Club	226
Eden Golf Club & Driving Range	235
Eden House Hotel	358
Edzell Golf Club	323
Elite Golf Scotland Ltd	12
Ely City Golf Club	133
Enniscrone Golf Club	490
Failte Ireland　Front Cover,	437
Faithlegg House Hotel & Golf Club	494
Falkirk Golf Club	394
Falls Hotel & Spa	460
Farthingstone Hotel & Golf Course	186
Fernhill Hotel	345
Fernie Castle Hotel	358
Filey Golf Club	278
Forest of Galtres Golf Club	283
Forest Pines Golf & Country Club Hotel	176
Forfar Golf Club	324
Fortingall Hotel	382
Fortrose & Rosemarkie Golf Club	373
Foxhunters Inn	36
Fulford Golf Club	283
Garesfield Golf Club	270
Gleneagles Hotel	383
Glenview Hotel & Leisure Club	497
Gloucester Ramada Hotel & Golf Resort	47
Golf Hotel	237
Golf Tee Time Serices	11
Golfbreaks.Com	12
Golfers Scotland Ltd	303
Golspie Golf Club	372
Gowerton Golf Range	433
Grange & Links Hotel	180
Grange Park Golf Club	263
Great Yarmouith & Caister Golf Club	153
Green Acre Public House & Motel	423
Greystones Golf Club	498
Grove Golf Club	431
Hadley Wood Golf Club	145
Hainsworth Park Golf Club	275
Halesowen Golf Club	211
Harleyford Golf Club	71
Haverfordwest Golf Club	417
Heaton Park Golf Centre	254
Henllys Hall Apartments	404
Heritage Golf & Spa Resort	482
Heritage Golf Tours Scotland	11
High Post Golf Club	59
Highbullen Hotel, Golf & Country Club	31
Highgate Golf Club	126
Hilton Puckrup Hall	49
Hinckley Golf Club	171
Hinksey Heights Golf Course	98
Hoebridge Golf	109
Honiton Golf Club	33
Horsforth Golf Club	296
Hull Golf Club	275
Hunley Hall Golf Club	277
Huntercombe Golf Club	97
Hurlston Hall Golf Club	249
Imagine Irelane	443
Imperial Hotel	409
Inchmarlo Golf Club	313
Inchmurrin Island Self-Catering Holidays	347
Inishowen Gateway Hotel	466
Island Golf Club	469
Kenmare Golf Club	475
Kildare Tourism	479
Kilkee Bay Hotel	461
Killarney Golf & Fishing	477
Killiecrankie House Hotel	389
Kilsyth Lennox Golf Club	369
King's Lynn Golf Club	155
Kings Norton Golf Club Ltd	208
Kingsknowe Golf Club	350
Kinloch Hotel	334
Kinsale Golf Club & Driving Range	409
Kirkby Lonsdale Golf Club	236
Kirroughtree Country House Hotel	345
Knightsbrook Hotel & Golf Resort	487
Lagganmore Hotel & Golf Club	343
Lahinch Golf & Leisure	461
Lands of Loyal Hotel	382
Langfield Manor	21
Largs Golf Club	330

Le Strange Arms Hotel	153	Nairn Dunbar Golf Club	378
Lea Gate Inn	179	Newbattle Golf Club	349
Lea Marston Hotel	206	Newmachar Golf Club	319
Leeds Golf Centre	296	Newport Links Golf Club	419
Leven Lnks	361	North Berwick Golf Club	355
Lilleshall Golf Club	195	North West Castle Hotel	345
Lincoln Golf Club	179	Oakmere Park Golf Club	190
Loch Ness Golf Course	377	Oaks Golf Club & Spa	284
Loch Ness House Hotel	377	Old Manor Hotel	363
Loch Tay Lodges	388	Orton Meadows Golf Course	135
Lockerbie Golf Club	342	Overstone Park Golf & Country Club	185
Lodge On The Loch of Aboyne	311	Painswick Golf Club	48
London Beach Country Hotel	94	Palace Hotel	320
Lostwithiel Hotel	25	Park Wood Golf Club	93
Lowes Park Golf Club	252	Parley Court Golf Club	39
Lundin Golf Club	363	Patshull Park Hotel Golf & Country Club	197
Lundin Links Hotel	363	Pedham Place Golf Centre	93
Lyme Regis Golf Club	40	Peover Golf Club	228
Lyndricks House	65	Perton Park Golf Club	216
MacDonald Aviemore Highland Resort	307	Petwood Hotel	183
MacDonald Botley Park Hotel	9	Pine Lodge Hotel	189
MacDonald Cardrona Hotel	307	Pitlochry Golf Course	389
MacDonald Hill Valley Hotel	9	Port Gaverne Hotel	22
MacDonald Hotels & Resorts	9, 307	Porthmadog Golf Club	405
MacDonald Linden Hotel	9, 268	Portpatrick Dunskey Golf Club	344
MacDonald Marine Hotel & Spa	307	Prestatyn Golf Club	410
MacDonald Portal Hotel	9	Prestonfield Golf Club	351
MacDonald Rusacks Hotel	307	Prestwick St Cuthbert Golf Club	332
Machrie Hotel & Golf Links	396	Prestwick St Nicholas Golf Club	331
Machrihanish Golf Club	327	Pumpherston Golf Club	354
Machynlleth Golf Club	421	Pwllheli Golf Club	406
Malahide Golf Club	439, 469	Queenwood Golf Lodge	57
Malton & Norton Golf Club	279	Raglan Parc Golf Club	432
Manor House & Ashbury Hotels	35	Ramsdale Park Golf Centre	188
Marine Hotel	333	Ramside Hall Hotel & Golf Club	241
Marriott Hollins Hall Hotel & Country Club	299	Ravenswood Residential Club	315
Melton Mowbray Golf Club	173	Red House Hotel	384
Mere Golf & Country Club *Inside Back Cover,*	229	Rhuddlan Golf Club	411
Merlin Golf Course	24	Riverdale Hall Hotel	267
Merseyside Golf	259	Rosapenna Hotel & Golf Links	467
Mid Yorkshire Golf Club	299	Rose & Crown	431
Mill at Glynhir	413	Roundwood Golf Club	499
Minehead & West Somerset Golf Club	54	Royal Ashdown Forest Golf Club	113
Moffat Golf Club	343	Royal Clifton Hotel & Spa	264
Monifieth Golf Links	324	Royal Dornoch Golf Club	370
Monmouth Golf Club	428	Royal Dublin Golf Club	471
Montrose Golf Links Ltd	325	Royal Hotel	408
Moray Golf Club	319	Royal Jersey Golf Club	504
Morlais Castle Golf Club	427	Royal Liverpool Golf Club	261
Mortonhall Golf Club	351	Royal Marine Hotel & Leisure Club	371
Moyola Park Golf Club	455	Royal Musselburgh Golf Club	356
Muir of Ord Golf Club	374	Royal North Devon Golf Club	37
Murcar Links Golf Club	309	Rudding Park Golf Club	279
Mycoal Warm Packs	12	St Augustine's Golf Club	90

St Helens Bay Golf Resort	495	Thorpe Wood Golf Course	135
St Margaret's Golf & Country Club	472	Thorpeness Hotel & Golf Club	161
St Mellion Golf Breaks	29	Toft House Hotel & Golf Course	175
St Mellons Golf Club	425	Torwoodlee Golf Club	335
Saltburn-By-The-Sea Golf Club	281	Trefeddian Hotel	403
Sandhill Golf Club	285	Trefloyne Golf Bar & Restaurant	418
Sandilands Golf Club	180	Treglos Hotel	24
Sandwell Park Golf Club	215	Trentham Golf Club	200
Scarthingwell Golf Course	282	Trentham Park Golf Club	201
Scotia Charters	11	Trethorne Golf Club	25
Scotscraig Golf Club	364	Trevornick Holiday Park	26
Seaford Golf Club	115	Trevose Golf & Country Club	26
Seahouses Golf Club	269	Turton Golf Club	251
Seapoint Golf Club	484	Tylney Park Golf Club	79
Searles Leisure Resort	155	Tyndrum	375
Seascale Golf Club	237	Uttoxeter Golf Club	202
Selsdon Park Hotel & Golf Club	102	Village Limits Motel & Restaurant	183
Shannon Development	457	Walmer & Kingsdown Golf Club	87
Sherdons Golf Centre	48	Warren Golf Club	33
Shotts Golf Club	381	Waterford Castle Hotel & Golf Club	494
Silverdale Golf Club	238	Waterfront Hotel & Bistro	344
Sinfin Golf Course	165	Waterville Golf Links	478
Skene House	310	Wavendon Golf Centre	72
Solway Links Golf Club	345	Wellingborough Golf Club	187
South Beach Hotel	332	Wenvoe Castle Golf Club	425
South County Golf Club	468	Wernddu Golf Club	422
South Staffordshire Golf Club	216	West Derby Golf Club	262
Spey Valley At The MacDonald Aviemore	307	West Lancashire Golf Club	261
Spindrift	357	West Midlands Golf Club	213
Springs Hotel	99	Weston Turville Golf Club	69
Standish Court Golf Club	249	Whittlebury Park Golf & Country Club	187
Stinchcombe Hill Golf Club	47	Wicklow Golf Club	501
Stoke-by-Nayland Golf & Spa	160	Windermere Golf Club	238
Stonehaven Golf Club	321	Wishaw Golf Club	381
Storws Wen Golf Club	404	Withington Golf Club	255
Strathpeffer Spa Golf Club	374	Wolfedale Golf Course	39
Sweetwoods Park Golf Club	113	Wolstanton Golf Club	202
Swindon Golf Club	211	Wood Dairy	41
Taunton Vale Golf Club	55	Woodcroft	333
Taymouth Castle Golf Course	387	Woodhall Spa Hotel	182
Taynuilt Golf Club	328	Woodhall Spa National Golf Centre	183
Teign Valley Golf Club	32	Wrag Barn Golf & Country Club	58
Thornbury Golf Centre	44	Wyke Green Golf Club	127
Thornhill Golf Club	346	Ythan Hotel	319
Thornton Golf Club	364		

FHG Guides Ltd have a large range of attractive
holiday accommodation guides for all kinds of holiday opportunities throughout Britain.
They also make useful gifts at any time of year.
Our guides are available in most bookshops and larger newsagents but we will be happy
to post you a copy direct if you have any difficulty. POST FREE for addresses in the UK.
We will also post abroad but have to charge separately for post or freight.

FHG ·K·U·P·E·R·A·R·D·

The original
Farm Holiday Guide to
COAST & COUNTRY HOLIDAYS
in England, Scotland, Wales and
Channel Islands. Board, Self-
catering, Caravans/Camping,
Activity Holidays. ☐

BED AND BREAKFAST STOPS
Over 1000 friendly and
comfortable overnight stops.
Non-smoking, Disabled and
Special Diets Supplements. ☐

BRITAIN'S BEST LEISURE
& RELAXATION GUIDE
A quick-reference general guide
for all kinds of holidays. ☐

Recommended
SHORT BREAK HOLIDAYS
IN BRITAIN & IRELAND
"Approved" accommodation for
quality bargain breaks. ☐

Recommended
INNS & PUBS
of Britain
Including Pubs, Inns and
Small Hotels. ☐

Recommended
COUNTRY HOTELS
of Britain
Including Country Houses
for the discriminating. ☐

CHILDREN WELCOME!
Family Holidays and
Days Out guide.
Family holidays with details of
amenities for children and
babies.

The FHG Guide to
CARAVAN & CAMPING
HOLIDAYS
Caravans for hire, sites and
holiday parks and centres.

SELF-CATERING HOLIDAYS
in Britain
Over 1000 addresses throughout
for self-catering and caravans
in Britain.

The Original!
PETS WELCOME
The bestselling guide to holidays for pet owners
and their pets

Tick your choice above and send your order and payment to

FHG Guides Ltd. Abbey Mill Business Centre
Seedhill, Paisley, Scotland PA1 1TJ
TEL: 0141- 887 0428 • FAX: 0141- 889 7204
e-mail: admin@fhguides.co.uk

Deduct 10% for 2/3 titles or copies; 20% for 4 or more.

Send to: NAME ....

ADDRESS ....

....

....

POST CODE ....

I enclose Cheque/Postal Order for £ ....

SIGNATURE ....DATE ....

Please complete the following to help us improve the service we provide.
How did you find out about our guides?:

☐ Press   ☐ Magazines   ☐ TV/Radio   ☐ Family/Friend   ☐ Other